Gas Pedal to Back-Pedal

The Second Century of Auckland Transport

Keith Mexsom

Copyright © Keith Mexsom

First Published January 2021

ISBN: 978-0-6485129-3-6

Contents

Acknowledgements		1
Introduction		2
Chapter One:	Pre-1940 – The Beginning of a Greater Auckland	3
Chapter Two:	1940 to 1949 – More Cars Cometh	31
Chapter Three:	1950 to 1959 – Let's Debate and Decide	100
Chapter Four:	1960 to 1969 – Let's Debate and Not Decide	220
Chapter Five:	1970 to 1979 – They Will Let You Down	384
Chapter Six:	1980 to 1989 – Congestion Complete	539
Chapter Seven:	1990 to 1999 – Auckland Slows to Gridlock	551
Chapter Eight:	2000 to 2009 – Is There an Exit?	583
Chapter Nine:	2010 to 2019 – A Greater Auckland at Last	641
Chapter Ten:	2020 to Infinity – A Public Transport Victory	709
Afterword		716
Appendices		717
References		719
Index		753

Acknowledgements

First and foremost, my thanks to The Bruce Jesson Foundation which, way back in 2008, thought my ambition to write of the commercial influences on Auckland transport planning worthy of the Bruce Jesson Critical Writing Award for that year. That initial research resulted in the publication of Waka Paddle to Gas Pedal – The First Century of Auckland Transport – the precursor to this volume.

Also, a thank you to the Special Collections Librarians of the Auckland City Library who kindly allowed me to access the papers of the late Sir Dove-Myer Robinson; and to the Interloan and Information Librarians who diligently searched for and provided me with copies of many obscure documents.

Ultimately, both this volume and its predecessor are anthologies; collections of the observations of many learned researchers, journalists, witnesses, and commentators – the voices of both past and presently-living individuals who have either influenced or recorded the events that constitute Auckland's transport history. It is they who deserve the greatest credit for having provided the essence upon which this story is based.

Cover Design: Graham Kennedy

Gas Pedal to Back-Pedal

The Second Century of Auckland Transport – 1940 to 2020

"Is it too much to suggest that the connection of New Zealanders with their land has contributed to the essential liberalism — the placing of individual freedom and material gain over that of the public interest — of New Zealand society?" [1]

Introduction

Gas Pedal to Back-Pedal is the second part of a planned trilogy describing Auckland's transport history from 1940 to 2020.

This part tells a story of countless, costly studies and reports and why most of the advice to create an integrated transportation system was not acted upon. It is a tale of how the parochialism and fragmented vision of city leaders played into the hands of begrudging, purse-string-holding Governments of the day; of Governments all too willing to favour the laissez-faire principles of those tyre-and-tarmac entrepreneurs collectively known as the 'Road Gang' – those descendants of Auckland's 'limited circle' and other 'gentlemen of fortune' who shaped the city's early growth and who continue to dominate its future by way of land speculation and financial control.

The story describes how the motor vehicle evolved from a novelty and a nuisance of the 1920s to an indispensable utility that virtually replaced the city's public transport services with chronic road congestion.

Indeed, it has been a long, overcrowded road since the concept and ambition of an Auckland underground railway was first proposed by a detachment of Royal Engineers surveying Auckland in the 1860s. Then there were the 'Town Hall' and 'Morningside' deviations, planned as early as 1912, but since abandoned many times because of war, shortages of finance or materials, local and central government differences, political machinations, and a distinct lack of speculative daring.

After such a long history of false promise and failure, it was by no means an understatement when the Auckland Council's new Mayor, Len Brown, described the Government's commitment in 2016 to fund half the cost of constructing the City Rail Link (CRL) as 'unprecedented and an historic milestone'.

This is a narrative about those who took many hesitant steps to finally reach that milestone…and those that didn't…

Chapter One

Pre-1940 – The Beginning of a Greater Auckland

Planning and Politics

"In the consideration of the very important question of local self-government, we desire above all things to avoid a contentious and dogmatic spirit…We have fallen upon times when it is imperative that prejudice and partiality should give way before truth." [2]

In 1840, Auckland's first surveyor-general, Felton Mathew, looked from the summit of Mount Wellington and envisaged a network of canals and railway lines linking his chosen site for the new city (now the Auckland suburb of Panmure) with the rest of the country. Unfortunately, Felton Mathew was not in the job for long and most of his plans for the new settlement were subsequently ignored. So were those of another budding town planner of the time and one of the settlement's first land speculators, Bishop Selwyn:

"Bishop Selwyn, notable churchman, statesman, architect, was also a town planner with ideas 100 years ahead of his time. He knew a better site for Auckland. With ideas of providing substantial endowments for his Church he acquired, in the 1840's, considerable areas of land in what are now known as the eastern suburbs — Mission Bay, St. Helier's. He thought that the City of Auckland would probably grow up with its heart in that area.

"To-day, town planners say he had the right idea. Auckland would have been ideally planned with its centre in that area, and with its residential areas spreading out in two wings along the hills overlooking the Waitemata and the Hauraki Gulf on either side. The present city area, centred on Queen Street, would have been a beautifully-situated suburb; the urban area would not now be encroaching on the burnt clay products zone of western Avondale and beyond, and the question of siting for industry and the provision of traffic outlets, north and south, would not be the problem it is now proving to be." [3]

More than a century later, the same problem of *siting for industry and the provision of traffic outlets* remained unresolved when another entrepreneurial visionary, Sir James Fletcher, advocated the redevelopment of the same part of Auckland's eastern suburbs with the reclamation of Hobson's Bay. However, as reported by the August 1955 edition of Comment Magazine, Fletcher's grand plan was sure to follow those of Felton Mathew and Bishop Selwyn to oblivion: "Reclamation and redevelopment of Hobson's Bay, sponsored by Sir James Fletcher, as the biggest scheme ever for Auckland, involving, in effect, transplanting the heart of the city, are proposals which have captured the imagination of citizens with lofty and commendable ideas, but dour people are looking much deeper. And the closer they look the more they get frightened." [4]

Thanks to those *dour people*, the City has remained centred on Queen Street. There are no canals, but there is a railway of sorts and a few roads. And, while many of Auckland's twenty-first century citizens and visitors may not think it, the City's eventual layout and infrastructure has resulted from some planning since its founding. This and later Chapters describe parts of that planning from the early twentieth century, and demonstrates how the layout and progress of any city is ultimately and inexorably defined by its transport systems.

Local Management of Infrastructure

As described in the first volume of this study, *Waka Paddle to Gas Pedal – The First Century of Auckland Transport*, such transport systems have determined the degree of settlement and commercialisation of Auckland city and its environs. As roads and then railways facilitated greater access, the value of the land was improved, generating revenue in the form of rates and taxes. Theoretically, responsible governing bodies then used a large proportion of that revenue to finance improved modes of transport and additional infrastructure, such as bridges and drainage. Although a simplistic overview, its basic premise was nevertheless one that required conscientious management – preferably by a local form of government familiar with local conditions and needs. This ideal of local affairs managed by local people resulted in the creation of New Zealand's hundreds of local bodies and Roads Boards.

The History of Local Government in New Zealand

In its *The History of Local Government In New Zealand*, published in March 1868, The Timaru Herald related how, in 1851, the country's Governor, Sir George Grey, had proposed the division of the English settlements into three classes of municipalities: "Small Municipalities, which are called Hundreds, and which may be regarded as Road districts; Pastoral Districts, extending over the thinly-populated pastoral lands under lease from the Crown; and Large Municipalities, embracing several Hundreds, or Road Districts and possessing largely increased powers. Sir George Grey was not wrong in relying greatly upon municipal institutions as a very important element in the constitution of the country; nor in believing that the inhabitants of New Zealand, generally, would very unwillingly see them swept away to give place to any other system that is as yet to be proposed; the more especially when the system of municipalities provided *that one-third of the gross proceeds realised from the sale of land in their respective districts was to be placed under the control of these municipal bodies.*

Unfortunately for New Zealand, the after legislation which created the Hundreds and Road Districts utterly destroyed the vital elements of the whole system by withholding from those districts a portion of the proceeds arising from the sale of lands within the same." [2]

According to The Timaru Herald's summary, the smaller municipalities could make little progress on their own, or collectively, without adequate reimbursement for their endeavours:

"We have traced the history of local self-government from the day when the Crown administered the revenues of the colony, and appropriated one-third of the gross revenues arising from land for the districts whence they arose to the present moment, when provincial institutions—whatever their other merits, of which we shall write shortly—have manifested beyond dispute their incapacity or unwillingness to deal out an even-handed justice to the weak and the strong, the remote and the near districts alike…The territorial revenue should be kept sacredly distinct from ordinary revenue, and solely applied to its legitimate objects, not to cover the cost of expensive establishments, doubtful guarantees, and unprofitable speculations; and the watchword of every true-hearted colonist should be, *Return to the land the revenue which is derived from it.*" [2]

The Timaru Herald history pointedly singled out Auckland for special comment: "We warn them to beware of the fate of the outlying districts of Auckland. They petitioned and prayed, and while thus engaged the provincial revenues vanished, the provincial debt increased by half a million, and now they have only dry bleached bones to quarrel over, their proportion of the Customs revenue being required to pay the interest and sinking fund of the provincial debts." [2]

Unity Required

Just short of Auckland's 1940 centennial celebrations, its individual *Hundreds* and *Road Districts* had survived their initial financial difficulties. However, the attitude of some citizens toward locally-independent governance changed somewhat over time as they considered the merits of a unified city in the face of rapid growth.

While many local bodies wished to remain independent of any Queen Street interference, there had developed certain reservations about "…a sad lack of unity among the local bodies in whose hands rests the future of Auckland…" as described by an Auckland Star correspondent, R. H., in June 1930:

"It seems but a few years since we spoke of Auckland being sixty years old, a mere babe in swaddling clothes compared with cities in other lands. Time passes all too quickly, however, and soon the tiny settlement founded by Captain Hobson on the banks of the Waitemata in 1840 will achieve the distinction of its hundredth birthday. Then we will refer to things that happened in Auckland 'over a hundred years ago,' with a subtle pride in the knowledge that our city can reach so far back into the past. The dignity of age will fall like a mantle upon the Queen City; a greater civic patriotism will develop; traditions will grow; added lustre and romance will be associated with the names of the men who helped to shape the destiny of Auckland far back in the early days of the city's history.

"In 1840 the population of Auckland was a few hundred; fifty years later it had grown to about 28,000. To-day the number stands at 210,000, and ten years hence, when Auckland reaches its century, the population will probably be round about 350,000. No doubt there will be some sort of celebration to mark the entry of Auckland into the brotherhood of century-old cities. A great Pacific or Empire Exposition, perhaps, with sundry international organisations meeting here during the period — the Press, science, medicine, advertising, Rotary, for instance, to mention just a few.

"But something of much greater permanent value to Auckland would be the steady and systematic development of the city and contiguous districts, according to a comprehensive and unified plan. At present there is a sad lack of unity among the local bodies in whose hands rests the future of Auckland. By Auckland, let me explain, I mean all those districts which come within the metropolitan area.

"When visiting other parts of New Zealand you do not tell people you come from Mount Eden, Mount Albert, One Tree Hill, Onehunga, or even Newmarket: you claim Auckland as your home town. It is of this larger Auckland I write. Development plans are now being prepared by the city and its neighbouring boroughs, but these are independent schemes, and unless they are co-ordinated into one general plan of the whole area they will not achieve their fullest usefulness. Such co-ordination will probably be brought about by regional planning, though this proposal has not yet received the unanimous approval of local bodies. Common sense is more or less an attribute of individual public men, but, as councils and boards, local interests and jealousies all too often over-rule their private views as to what is best for the larger community of which each district is an integral part.

"Let us picture the completed plan of the metropolitan area. It is on a huge scale, all streets, public buildings, railways, wharves, etc., being clearly indicated. It shows the present lay-out and superimposed at various points are various coloured markings which form the key to the Auckland of our dreams. We note, for instance, that it is proposed to form new traffic outlets to give quicker and easier access between the city and certain outlying districts. Further inspection discloses that the designers of the plan have allowed for the Morningside railway deviation, and provided for access to the harbour bridge. Street widening proposals are indicated, and a civic centre is an interesting feature.

"That Auckland's centennial will see air travel and transport between New Zealand and the outside world an accomplished fact is shown by the provision of ample airports for land and sea planes, as well as airships. The Transport Board's co-operation in the plan is evidenced by projected tram and bus routes. As Auckland expands, it is but natural that more parks and playing grounds will be required, and these are also pictured on the plan before us. There must be nothing left to chance; every possible development should be indicated on the plan, each part should fit in with the whole, whether it be a new wharf, a traffic outlet, or tramway line. It is obvious that the closest co-operation between the various public bodies in and around Auckland, as well as Government departments, is essential in its preparation.

"There can be no question that Auckland's development is largely eastward. The new railway deviation and the waterfront road are bringing the beautiful home sites of Orakei, Mission Bay and Tamaki within a few minutes of the city. Orakei, for instance, will be reached in four minutes after leaving Auckland station; Purewa nine minutes, Tamaki 17 minutes. A fast service such as this will do a great deal in making people settle in newly opened areas. Last year the technical group of the Town Planning Association submitted a scheme of new traffic outlets leading east and south-east from Auckland to link up with the Tamaki and Mount Wellington districts. It was stated in their report that there was urgent necessity for some such traffic outlet, as the areas to be served were being rapidly sub-divided. The necessity is even more urgent than it was a year ago, as the railway will be opened in a few months, and home building is bound to receive an impetus. And, of course, all traffic will not go by rail. However urgent this particular case may be, it should be carried out as part of the general scheme of development.

"The Government has had a hand in this eastward expansion. The new railway station and deviation to Westfield which serve the large residential areas of Tamaki and Mount Wellington are estimated to cost £1,000,000. The cost of developing the Orakei block, plus the Government's share in the waterfront boulevard, is about £700,000. The city's share of the waterfront road is £250,000. Not all of this money is being used for the sole purpose of opening up the areas mentioned, but the fact remains that the spending of it is proving an important factor in deciding the trend of Auckland's future population.

"It would appear reasonable to assume, in view of the foregoing, that any undertakings contemplated by local bodies within the metropolitan area will be considered in our relationship to the logical development of the combined districts. Otherwise, trouble is going to occur sooner or later through inexcusable mistakes caused by lack of co-operation and foresight. Auckland in its hundredth year can be a truly great and beautiful city, up-to-date in every sense, if we, its citizens, are prepared to place patriotism before selfish interests and parochial jealousies. Only as our outlook widens can we hope to build a city of which we and those who come after us will be proud." [5]

Transport Plans 1930

As outlined by the Auckland Star correspondent, the settlement of eastern parts of the city was well advanced by June 1930 and these new suburbs were planned to be easily accessed by both road and rail. In a few months, the new railway station at Beach Road would open and trains would run along the new eastern deviation to join the main line at Westfield. Although the station had been sited somewhat remotely from the city centre, this was all part of the grand plan, initially proposed in 1914, for a waterfront railway link, west and north, to join the western line at either New Lynn or Kumeu.

A more direct connection to join the western line at Morningside, by means of a tunnel beneath the city and a station near the Town Hall, became a later priority.

The Waterfront (Tamaki) Drive had been completed by 1930 and the plan then was to augment this with main highways leading east and south-east from the city. Although a Royal Commission had recently decided a harbour crossing was not yet needed to replace the struggling ferry service, a bridge or a tunnel across the harbour was thought to be only a decade away, together with a main highway to the north.

Greater Auckland Plans Fail

Unfortunately, as R. H. feared, *"selfish interests and parochial jealousies"* among Auckland's local bodies, town districts, and Boards continued to frustrate the City's attempts to implement a grand plan *"...of the metropolitan area...on a huge scale...the key to the Auckland of our dreams"*, well into the city's second century. The need to reorganise the country's many local authorities and ad hoc bodies had been called for since at least 1885, particularly when: "Major public works on the scale of water supply and sewerage required finance and technical expertise which was frequently beyond the reach of the numerous small local authorities in the area...Despite several moves by the Auckland City Council for a 'Greater Auckland', although some amalgamation took place, the local government structure remained fragmented. Ad hoc bodies, after the example of the Auckland and Suburban Drainage Board (1908) provided the only means of organising city-wide services." [6]

As observed by planner, Malcolm MacGregor Baxter Latham, in his 1973 study, *'Planning Objectives In Local Government'*: "Small councils, individually as well as collectively, weak in the technical and policy making areas often are not able to direct competent planning resources at the problems they face...So far in New Zealand's history this multifarious collection of local councils has survived 9 attempts on its life since 1889. In the 57 years to 1946 we had no fewer than 5 determined attempts at reorganisation, all abortive. In the 25 years since 1946 we have had no fewer than 4 local Government commissions and still, after 82 years, the universally acceptable answer has not been found." [7]

Local Government Commissions Deferred

What was supposed to be the first of those Local Government Commissions was proposed during the early 1930s, during that period of severe economic downturn when a broad review of both national and local government funding had become increasingly urgent. But, at the same time, there existed an even broader, political ideology that sought to postpone, if not derail altogether, the appointment of such a Commission. This apparent, political agenda was referred to by a Christchurch Press comment published in April 1932:

"The reasons given by the Prime Minister for the Government's decision, announced this morning, to postpone indefinitely the appointment of a Local Government Commission are muddled and unconvincing. Mr Forbes admits that there is a widespread belief that the time is overdue for a complete enquiry into local body finances, but he refuses to institute such an enquiry because the appointment of Commissions is out of favour with the country. Even if his last statement is correct —and if it is the Prime

Minister has been a long time in discovering it—it does not absolve the Government from the duty of instituting an enquiry that is clearly necessary.

"The Coalition (United-Reform Coalition) fought the election on a promise of economy, and until it has done something to reduce the excessive cost of local body administration it will not have fulfilled that promise...The only sure way of easing the burden is to reduce the number of local bodies by concentrating functions and enlarging areas, and that, as all sensible people realise, can be done only after a thorough investigation." [8]

By August 1935, the country's need to reform its system of local government still needed urgent attention, according to the Christchurch Press: "...the system of local government is antiquated, extravagant, and confused. To serve a population of about 1,500,000 there are nearly 700 local authorities. Most of them administer such small areas and have such small staffs that it is becoming increasingly unsafe to entrust them with important functions. It has become necessary, for instance, to superimpose an elaborate system of Main Highways Boards upon the counties because county areas were fixed in the age of horse transport; and there can be little doubt that the roading requirements of New Zealand could be supplied more cheaply if the county councils were abolished." [9]

Long before the 2010 amalgamation of its many local bodies, infrastructure, and services to form the present 'super-city', Auckland consisted of as many as 17 local authorities, each with their own ideas as to how their districts and responsibilities could best be served. But while fragmented governance of the Auckland region too often impeded real progress of the city as a whole, there were exceptions. For instance, the citizens of the borough of Newmarket had good reason to be proud of the accomplishments of its local authority.

Newmarket Borough Council

The borough's Town Clerk, Henry W Wilson, had been sent to America and Canada by the Council in 1937 to study local government methods...paying considerable attention to the question of amalgamation. He returned in October 1937 with the declaration that:

"Local government amalgamation movements are dead in America...The general view there, he said, was that it could only be achieved successfully if supported by public opinion. Bitterness arising from some compulsory annexations in the past was still evident. Annexation or amalgamation was in fact only possible by a vote of the people." [10]

Two months later, obviously keen to demonstrate his Council's right to local body autonomy, Henry Wilson outlined a two-year-plan of progressive development "...which will make Newmarket borough outstanding in the municipal world." The plan called for a loan of £25,000, as detailed by the Auckland Star on 16 December 1937:

"Mr Wilson's proposals, with the estimated cost in parentheses, included the following:—Construction of modern swimming baths in a central location (£4000); replacement of existing public conveniences at the corner of Newmarket Reserve by a modern structure (£3000); an enlarged public library, reading room and ladies' rest room, at the back of the Town Hall Reserve (£5000); beautifying proposals for the Newmarket Reserve (£2000); acquisition and development of areas for the provision of public motor car parking spaces (£3000). Other proposals were: Construction of asphalt tennis courts for the public in Broadway (£250); extension of Outhwaite Park, development of other recreation areas and the provision of children's playing apparatus in parks and reserves

(£7500); purchase of a modern refuse-collecting vehicle (£500); reconstruction of a number of street surfaces (£5000)." [11]

As well as the question of local body amalgamation, Henry Wilson was also commissioned by the Newmarket Council to gather information concerning leading swimming pools in the United States and other countries so it is not surprising that such a facility was proposed for the borough. Newmarket's Olympic Pool, envisaged and financed through the Local Government Loans Board in 1938 and opened on 17 February 1940, was a prime example of just how local body initiative could provide a distinct asset to the greater municipality. As the Auckland Star reported on opening day, "…the new Olympic swimming pool…is considered the finest of its kind in either Australia or New Zealand…the first of its kind in this Dominion." [12]

It is doubtful that a larger authority, and certainly not a national government, would have proceeded at the time with such an amenity. The administrators of the day were too intent on planning roads and motorways that would never fully cope with the inundation of motor vehicles to come. Even the far-sighted Newmarket Borough Council, in line with the national aspirations of the time, borrowed some £3000 to provide municipal parking areas in the borough. Even swimmers had to park somewhere.

Local Government (Amalgamation Schemes) Bill

That's not to say that local body amalgamation was not still a priority during the 1930s. A Local Government (Amalgamation Schemes) Bill was introduced to Parliament by the First Labour Government of Michael Joseph Savage in 1937 and referred to a Parliamentary Select Committee on 28 October of that year. However, the Committee, chaired by W. E. Barnard, reported to Parliament on 11 March 1938 that it "…has been unable, in the time at its disposal, to hear the greater portion of the evidence offering for consideration, or to deliberate on the Bill." [13]

A second Select Committee, this time chaired by D. W. Coleman, was subsequently appointed on 21 July 1938. This Committee did 'report generally upon the provisions of the Bill' in September 1938 and explained in that report: "The proposals as outlined in the draft Bill submitted to the Committee do not provide for the amalgamation of specific local authorities or for any detailed plan as to the reorganization of local government in the Dominion, but are confined to the provision of machinery designed to facilitate local amalgamation schemes." [14]

So the Local Government (Amalgamation Schemes) Bill was only designed to provide a *ways and means* to local government efficiency but not the efficiency itself, despite:

"The desirability of some reduction in the number of local bodies in the Dominion has been recognized by every Government in power for the last fifty years. On numerous occasions in the Governor-General's speeches, in Budget speeches, and in public statements by previous Prime Ministers and other Ministers of the Crown mention has been, made of the intention to proceed with this desirable work, but up to the present time no real progress has been made. It is interesting to notice in passing that every witness examined by the Committee admitted the desirability and necessity of some scheme of amalgamation and some reorganization of local government in the Dominion. The Municipal Association of New Zealand, Incorporated, the New Zealand Counties' Association, and several other local-body associations have all endorsed the principle of amalgamation, subject in some cases to certain preliminary inquiries." [14]

Public Transport

The influence that transport facilities have had on the 'present shape of Auckland' was highlighted by Dr Fred Dahms in his April 1980 New Zealand Geographer article, *Urban Passenger Transport and Population Distribution in Auckland: 1860 – 1961*:

"As long as walking remained the principal mode of travel, cities by necessity were small and densely populated, with little separation between place of work and place of residence…After 1911 it is possible to map population changes precisely, and to relate them to the provision of new modes of intra-urban transport. Although other factors such as land ownership, government policy and entrepreneurial initiative undoubtedly affected population distribution during the period under consideration, improved passenger transport was the key to opening large new areas to settlement both in Auckland and abroad.

"As early as 1861 land speculators were attempting to sell sections far out of town at Waterview. They stressed the new accessibility provided by the omnibus (horse bus) to central Auckland. The north shore of the Waitemata Harbour was served by a sailing ferry which replaced rowing boats, and by 1864 a half-hourly horse bus service plied the route to Onehunga in the Manukau Harbour.

"By 1881, Auckland's passenger transport was still in a primitive state…Auckland could be considered a mature 'pedestrian city' where most journeys to work were of necessity on foot…Although houses had spread along routes across the isthmus, the limit of the compact urban area was still only two miles from the waterfront. The city stretched less than four miles from west to east. Major work-residence separation was not yet possible because passenger transport was either much too expensive or simply not available.

"The provision of electric tram services to previously inaccessible parts of Auckland played a major role in the distribution of its population between 1902 and 1945…While it never carried as many passengers as the electric tram, the suburban railway did provide a convenient and (after 1887) relatively inexpensive mode of travel to work for long distance commuters. It undoubtedly encouraged population growth in places like Henderson, Otahuhu and Papakura long before they became part of Urban Auckland.

"After 1945, the car, the motor bus, and industrial diffusion stimulated residential areas to sprawl far beyond the Urban Area of 1945. They also greatly increased the choice of workplace and residence in Auckland. With the advent of private cars and extensive bus services, workers were no longer tied to a network of fixed transport routes focused on Queen Street. An increasing percentage had become free to live in any part of the Urban Area (or beyond) and work in any other. The great increase in the extent of the Auckland Urban Area after 1945 reflected this new loosening of the traditional workplace-residence ties.

"In spite of the changes that occurred after 1945, one should not lose sight of the importance of the electric tram from 1902 to 1945. During this period it was the dominant mode of intra-urban transport in Auckland…A large proportion of Auckland developed because of the building of houses in areas made accessible by the availability of fast, efficient and relatively inexpensive passenger transport to central workplaces. The character and physical extent of major residential areas on the Tamaki Isthmus continue to reflect the influence of the electric tram. There and almost everywhere in Auckland population growth reflected the passenger transport innovations that gave workers increasing flexibility in their choice of places of work and residence." [15]

The Trams

The years during which Auckland's trams predominated as an efficient and reliable public transport system defined a mass transportation era that was not to be replicated for many decades. In his definitive article, *Urban Tramways in New Zealand, 1862 - 1964*, published in Volume 31 of the 1975 edition of New Zealand Geographer, G T Bloomfield observed:

"Tramways played a dominant role in passenger transport of the larger New Zealand cities from the 1880s to the late 1940s. The earliest phase from inception of horse and steam traction to electrification in the early 1900s had some influence on suburban expansion but with some exceptions did not prove to be very profitable. A second phase began after 1900 with electrification and major expansion of all systems. This phase, which lasted until the mid-1920s, was characterised by growth of traffic, enlargement of route networks and full involvement of tramways in the economic and social life of cities. Tramways became an important municipal symbol of pride and profitability.

"The final phase from 1930 to the closing of most systems in the 1950s was one of gradual decline as buses and private transport successfully competed for passenger traffic. The role of the tramway in shaping the pre-1940 areas of New Zealand metropolitan cities was a significant one. Extensive residential areas with a common style of house, long commercial strips along arterial roads, and many of the features of the central business district bear continued witness to an important mode of public transport." [16]

It was in July 1884 when the first horse-tram, then operated by the St. Heliers and Northcote Land Company Limited, had an experimental run along Auckland's Queen Street. As its title suggests, the St. Heliers and Northcote Land Company was chiefly a speculative real estate concern seeking to encourage potential residents to buy acreage on the periphery of the City by providing easy tramway access. This expansion of city boundaries was an early example of what was to be later described, and condemned by many, as *urban sprawl*.

However, tramway-facilitated urban sprawl was reined in somewhat when real estate sales collapsed across Auckland with the economic depression of the late 1880s. As a result, the St. Heliers and Northcote Land Company Limited (subsequently renamed the City of Auckland Tramways and Suburban Land Company Limited) faced increasing financial pressures.

"In 1893 the Bank of New Zealand Assets Company became the owner of the Auckland City tramways system by being the only bidder at an auction forced by the bank itself. The bank was to run the trams both under its own management and by leasing the management out to private transport operators." [17]

Between 1896 and 1897, Auckland City's tram lines had expanded to a route length of some 11.39 kilometres and its trams carried 1,585,410 passengers. "For about twelve months the tramways were leased to Patterson Brothers, a large horse-bus and carrying firm. Then in 1899 the British Electric Traction Company purchased the undertaking and the Auckland Electric Tramways Company was registered in London." [18]

By 1900, the Auckland Electric Tramways Company had extended its lines "…to Newmarket and Remuera with a branch line down lower Symonds Street and an extension to Epsom." [19]

The horses were replaced by electric power on 24 November 1902 and the service was owned by the shareholders of the Auckland Electric Tramways Company until sold to the Auckland City Council on 1 July 1919.

"The development of Auckland's electric tramways from 1902 also coincided with a long period of economic and population growth in the urban area. The linking of these forces resulted in creation of an arc of 'tramway suburbs' across the isthmus. Mt. Albert and Mt. Eden were amongst the fastest growing New Zealand suburbs between 1906 and 1926 when their combined populations increased from 10,471 to 38,236. Remuera grew from 3,802 in 1906 to 11,821 in 1926 as the earlier large sections were further subdivided. Onehunga and the northern part of One Tree Hill developed extensive residential areas connected with the city.

"Tramways in Auckland aided urban growth and promoted greater urban integration. Local government became less divided in the isthmus as small boroughs and road districts amalgamated with the City. But the rapid growth of suburban population, together with a secure financial basis from increased local rating also allowed the survival of Mt. Albert, Mt. Eden and other Auckland boroughs although largely surrounded by the City." [16]

The Motor-omnibus

However, the tramway system did not have city streets all to itself and had to progressively compete with the private motor car and the motor-omnibus for passengers as the city expanded into areas not sufficiently served by inflexible tram routes. By 1925, it was obvious that tramway operators, such as the Auckland City Council, needed more than just by-laws to reduce the competitive edge of the motor buses. In order to promote their concerns and discuss solutions, the tramway operators organised a conference at Wellington – a forum by which they hoped to convince Parliament that some form of national legislation to regulate motor-omnibus traffic was required to deal with what The New Zealand Herald of 5 August 1925 described as an invasion:

"The motor-omnibus by invading city streets and competing for the patronage of the travelling public has created a problem in which most of New Zealand is interested...The fact is that the motor-omnibus is not only a factor of increasing weight in the transport of passengers; it is a new and often disturbing element in city traffic wherever it has gone beyond the elementary stage of development.

"It has now been established beyond question that municipal authorities throughout New Zealand feel the need for some measure of control over the motor-omnibus. They have decided this in conference and placed their decision before the Prime Minister. The deputation which met Mr Coates brought to him concrete proposals for the licensing and control of motor-omnibus services. Mr Coates remarked at one stage that the core of the problem was to assure the most economical and efficient system of passenger transport. That sums up the whole situation exactly. In places where tramway systems have been long in operation, are owned by the community, and by unprofitable working would cast new burdens upon the citizens, their existence as fixed assets ought to be recognised.

"Some limitation of omnibus competition is not unreasonable in such circumstances. It is all very well to contend, as people have done, that motor transport is the method of the future, that tramways are obsolescent, and that, to put it bluntly, they should be scrapped if they cannot hold their own against unrestricted competition. That contention cannot be allowed quite so lightly as it is advanced, having regard to the amount of public money involved and to the fact that most of it is loan money. What should be determined in such cases is where the greatest good of the public lies then, provided that the right method of determination has been adopted, all parties should be made to accept the decision, even if the result was curtailment of the ambitions and plans of those who operate omnibus services..." [20]

The Motor-omnibus Traffic Act 1926

The Motor-omnibus Traffic Act 1926 certainly curtailed *the ambitions and plans of those who operate omnibus services*. The Act divided the country into 13 Motor-omnibus Districts with each having a licensing Authority. Auckland City was included in No. 1 District, comprising: "All that portion of the North Island situated between the northern boundary of the Waitemata County and the southern boundary of the Franklin County, except the Borough of Takapuna." [21] The Borough of Takapuna had District No. 2 all to itself.

Every person operating a Motor-omnibus service within each District had to be licensed, insured, and:

"With respect to every motor-omnibus service authorized to be carried on pursuant to this Act the licensing authority shall prescribe the routes to be traversed, the time-tables to be observed, the fares to be charged, and such other conditions and matters as may be prescribed by regulations under this Act, or as the licensing authority thinks proper." [21]

Section 15 of the Act also provided for the compulsory acquisition by "the local or public authority" of any "...motor-omnibus service in substantial competition with any tramway service or motor-omnibus service carried on by any local or public authority..." [21]

Not surprisingly, in a city founded on laissez-faire principals, the heavy-handed regulation of public transport was not accepted by all and the Government was soon under pressure to re-visit Auckland's enduring problem.

Auckland Transport Commission

On 4 April 1928, the Government appointed an Auckland Transport Commission to report on certain matters relating to the transport of passengers in the Auckland metropolitan district, including: "(1) The present transport service. (2) The present and future transport requirements. (3) The means by which such requirements may be best provided for." [22]

Auckland Transport Board

The Commissioners, John S Barton S.M., W G T Goodman, and Alfred Edward, reported on 11 June 1928. One of their main recommendations was the creation of an independently-elected Transport Board and such a body was subsequently established by means of the Auckland Transport Board Act 1928 passed on 6 October of that year. Section 58 of the Act defined the Board's responsibilities:

"Subject to the provisions of this Act, the Board, upon taking over the tramway and motor-omnibus undertaking of the City Council, shall, notwithstanding any provision to the contrary contained in any Act, have the sole and exclusive right to own, acquire, construct, maintain, manage, and operate tramways, and shall also have the sole and exclusive right to maintain, manage, and operate motor- and horse-omnibus services and any like public-passenger-conveyance services by any vehicle plying or standing for hire for the conveyance of passengers at separate fares within the district:

"Provided that the Board may from time to time and for such period, not exceeding five years, and subject to such conditions as the Board may impose, grant to any person the right to maintain, manage, and operate motor- or horse-omnibus services or any like public-passenger-conveyance services within the district and require the payment of fees in respect of such right, whether by way of annual fees or otherwise:…" [23]

And Section 3 of the Act defined the Board's initial area of influence:

"The City of Auckland, together with the Boroughs of Mount Eden, Mount Albert, Newmarket, and Onehunga, the Road Districts of One Tree Hill, Mount Roskill, Mount Wellington, and Panmure Township, and the Town District of Ellerslie shall for the purposes of this Act form one district, to be known as the Auckland Transport District." [23]

Section 45 (1) of the Act was of particular relevance to the Board's constituent local authorities because it held them proportionately responsible for the Transport Board's losses:

"In any year in which the amount of the estimated expenditure exceeds the amount of the estimated income the amount of the excess may be raised by a levy upon the local authorities in the district apportioned among them in proportion to the capital value of the rateable property in each constituent district as determined by the Valuer-General under the Valuation of Land Act, 1925, as being approximately correct as on the first day of April in the financial year in which the levy is made." [23]

Section 48 of the Transport Board Act precisely defined rate-paying property owners, many of whom were not necessarily public transport users, as those ultimately responsible for any losses incurred by the Board: "Every contributory local authority liable to pay any contribution under the foregoing provisions of this Act may pay the same out of its ordinary funds, or may if it thinks fit, in addition to its other rating-powers, raise the required amount by a rate to be made and levied for that purpose." [23]

(While any liability for transport services losses would be resisted by many local authorities and their ratepayers, practically forever, transport authorities always maintained that property owners had little to complain about when the provision of transport to their district, whether used or not, could only improve their property values.)

The Auckland Transport Board held its first meeting on 22 December 1928 and full management of the City's tramways and municipal bus services was officially taken over by the Board on 16 January 1929. John Andrew Charles Allum was appointed the Auckland Transport Board's inaugural Chairman, a position he held until 1935. He retained a seat on the Board until 1944 and was the Board's Deputy Chairman during 1940 and 1943.

"On 16th January, 1929, and in terms of Section 57 of the Act, the Board acquired as a going concern the tramway and motor omnibus undertaking of the City Council, with all lands, buildings, plant and other assets used in connection therewith, including all Sinking Funds in respect of Loans relating to the undertaking and with the benefit and subject to the burden of all contracts and obligations, including the loan indebtedness of the City Council in connection therewith." [22]

As of 31 March 1929, the tramway rolling stock consisted of 206 cars, comprising 142 double platform cars with a total carrying capacity (sitting and standing) of 90 passengers each, 15 single platform cars (total of 87 passengers each), 19 open combination cars (total of 69 passengers each), 24 coupled cars (total of 55 passengers each), and 6 converted double-decked cars (total of 63 passengers each). [22]

As a result of the compulsory acquisition provisions of the Motor-omnibus Traffic Act, 1926, the Auckland City Council had acquired some 106 buses from various private companies competing with the City's tramways services. However, by the time the

Transport Board assumed control, "Of the 106 vehicles originally taken over in terms of the 'Motor Omnibus Traffic Act, 30 are still being maintained for service as buses. These 30 vehicles have proved very expensive to maintain, and although the majority of them are in better condition than when taken over some have reached the end of their economic life." [22]

Together with buses otherwise acquired by the Council, the Transport Board started 1929 with 70 operational buses of various makes and passenger-carrying capacities.

Auckland Transport Board Accounts

As might be expected, the Auckland Transport Board's first Annual Report for the financial year ended 31 March 1929 recorded that the fledgling bus network provided little operational value compared to the established tram services. Of the total traffic receipts of £708,397 for that year, the bus services earned just £94,929. No doubt of greater concern was that when working expenses were accounted for, the trams made a profit of £48,004 while the buses made a loss of £46,587. This compared with the 1927-1928 financial year when, under City Council management, trams made a profit of £156,527 and buses a loss of £34,391.

A year later, a downturn in patronage of both trams and buses was reflected in the revenue figures for the financial year ending 31 March 1930: "The traffic receipts totalled £666,252, which is £42,145 less than the previous year...By exercising economy, and by re-adjustment of services, there has been the substantial reduction of £46,051 in expenses, which has more than compensated for the reduced revenue." [24]

By the end of the 1931 financial year, traffic receipts were again down by £16,562 to £649,690. For the first time, tram and bus earnings and expenses were not recorded separately in the main report but the accounts showed a net profit for both of £915. While the bus services continued to operate at a loss, there was little concern expressed in the Board's Annual Report for the year ending 31 March 1931 in which the Chairman, John Allum, projected an optimistic future for the trams as the City's main provider of public transport:

"During the year the Local Government Loans Board approved the Board's proposal to extend the tramway to Avondale, and a subsequent poll of the ratepayers authorised the board to proceed with the work. This completes the board's program of tramway extension, which can be reasonably claimed to adequately serve the metropolitan area.

"With the opening of the various tramway extensions certain omnibus services have been discontinued, and following the approval of the Avondale extension the omnibus service running from the present Mt. Albert terminus to Avondale can be considered as temporary. As the result, it is considered no longer necessary to present separate accounts for the bus operations; to-day, the maximum number of omnibuses in service during the rush hours is 17, and during the slack hours 9. When the Avondale tramway extension is completed the number of omnibuses in service will be still further reduced, and the Board will later on be asked to consider the advisability of itself continuing to operate certain other omnibus services. The ratepayers authorised the purchase of the tramway undertaking, and it is the Board's policy to foster and develop that undertaking, and to operate only such omnibus services as can be considered complementary thereto." [25]

When the tramway extension to Avondale was opened on 30 January 1932, the additional service had little influence on the financial year's traffic figures which recorded a net loss of £18,318. Again, tram and bus services receipts were down at £572,906, which was £76,783 less than the previous year. The Board Chairman, John Allum, explained in his Annual Report for the year ended 31 March 1932: "The traffic receipts were fairly well sustained until the beginning of September, 1931, when a further definite reduction took place to a figure which has held up to the present time. The influence of the economic position is exemplified by the fact that last year nearly 17 million less passengers were carried on the Board's service than in 1928." [26]

The *economic position* referred to was, of course, the Great Depression and its effect on transport patronage continued on into 1933. That financial year, the tramway and bus operations recorded a net deficit of £10,931 despite the Board's belt-tightening: "The year has undoubtedly been the most difficult one in the history of the undertaking, and although the total revenue at £534,263 shows a reduction over the previous year of £44,489, the total expenditure has been reduced to £545,193, showing a total reduction of £51,877." [27]

There was little improvement during the 1933-1934 financial year when the deficit increased to £15,708: "Compared with last year, the total revenue at £518,698 shows a reduction of £15,565, and the total expenses at £534,405, a reduction of £10,788…The Board realises it has a duty to the travelling public, to its staff, and to the ratepayers, and consequently every endeavour to maintain a proper balance between these interests is made. Nothing is to be gained by drastic action, and there is no cause whatever for alarm so long as the cash position remains satisfactory. As previously mentioned, the revenue is holding up, and there is definite indication that bottom was touched some months ago." [28]

Devonport Steam Ferry Company Bus Losses

The Auckland Transport Board was not the only public transport, bus operator experiencing substantial losses from its services. During its annual shareholders' meeting celebrating fifty years of operation by the Devonport Steam Ferry Company, the company's Chairman, the Hon. Ewen William Alison, complained bitterly of the tax imposed on bus proprietors – as reported by The New Zealand Herald on 17 June 1931:

"I regret to have to state that the result of the year's working of the North Shore Transport Company has been so unsatisfactory that no dividend can be paid this year for, after making the insufficient allowance of 13½ per cent, for depreciation on the buses and 10 per cent, on plant, a loss is shown of £53 16s 2d.

"There are two main reasons why the past year's operations have been unsuccessful. The first is that owing to the existing economic conditions, there has been a substantial falling off in general traffic, and secondly, the taxation imposed upon bus proprietors is most oppressive. Referring to the first reason, I may inform you that the residential traffic is fairly well maintained, but owing to the cheapness of the concession tickets issued to residents, the falling-off in general traffic and the excessive taxation, there is great difficulty in carrying out the business successfully.

"I have mentioned that the taxation imposed is oppressive. You often read in the newspapers that the charges placed on bus proprietors are far too light. Those who give expression to such a statement cannot be aware of how much taxation bus proprietors have to pay. Let me tell you the amount of taxation, direct and indirect, paid by the North Shore Transport Company during the past year. The direct taxation paid for licence fees and heavy traffic amounted to £3574 5s 2d and the indirect taxation, including petrol tax of 5d per gallon, to £2869 14s 1d, making the total taxation payments for the year £6443 19s 3d, or a taxation cost for each bus of £140 per annum.

"You can easily realise the enormous mileage the buses have to run and the very large number of fares which have to be collected before these taxation charges are met, but when you add to the taxation payments I have enumerated the cost of petrol (exclusive of tax), payments for wages, repairs and upkeep of buses, overhead, office and general working expenses, the total cost becomes so burdensome that the general traffic requires to be well sustained to enable such heavy expenditure to be earned.

"A shareholder suggested that to enable some dividend to be paid the residential fares should be raised. Well, to do so under existing depressed conditions would, in the opinion of the directors, be ill advised. They would prefer, if possible, to reduce fares. That course, however, is not possible if effective services and well-conditioned buses are to be provided and I feel sure shareholders will agree that to meet the public requirements regular and satisfactory services must be carried out and the buses kept up to a first-class standard of condition end cleanliness. I can assure you the company's business is capably, economically and most attentively managed, and, further, the whole fleet of buses and plant is well maintained and the several services are regularly and efficiently run." [29]

Bus Services Relinquished to Private Contractors

While the Devonport Steam Ferry Company had little option but to make the best of losses incurred by its bus services in order to maintain its objective of complementing its cross-harbour ferries with North Shore buses, the Auckland Transport Board had no such incentive.

By 1934, the losses incurred by the Board's bus services remained unsustainable to the point that their operation was relinquished to private contractors – as explained by Board Chairman, John Allum in his Annual Report for the year ending 31 March 1934:

"During the year the Board gave serious consideration to the loss occasioned by the operation of its bus services, the result being that it entered into a contract for their operation by contractors on the basis of an annual allowance payable according to the bus miles run. Under the arrangement made the Board retains the bus licenses. The contractors commenced operating under this arrangement on the 7th October 1933, and it is estimated the saving to the Board is approximately £4000 per annum." [28]

Auckland Transport Board Empowering Act 1934

The arrangement was validated by means of the Auckland Transport Board Empowering Act 1934 which became law on 13 November 1934. Section 5 of the Act named the parties who had agreed to contract their services to the Board for three years:

"5. (1) The agreement dated the tenth day of October, nineteen hundred and thirty-three, and made between the Board of the one part and Thomas Henry Bonnett, Joseph Bell, and Rupert Leslie Fenton of the other part, a copy of which is set out in the Schedule hereto, is hereby validated, and shall be deemed to have been validly made and entered into by the parties thereto." [30]

Messrs. Bonnett, Bell, and Fenton, referred to in the Act as *motor mechanics* and in the Board's Annual Report as *Transport Bus Services*, would seem to have demonstrated some courage to take on what the Transport Board obviously considered to be very much a lost cause:

"Whereas the Board has for some time past been carrying on the omnibus services enumerated in the Schedule hereto pursuant to licenses issued under the Transport

Licensing Act 1931 And whereas the Board has been making heavy losses on such services but it is considered desirable and in the Board's interests that such services should be continued And whereas the Contractors have offered to provide all labour and materials other than motor-omnibuses for the carrying on of such services on condition that the Board will allow the Contractors to receive and retain the fares paid by passengers on the said services and will also pay to the Contractors a sum of two thousand four hundred and eighty-four pounds (£2,484) per annum and the Board has agreed to accept such offer for the purpose of enabling it to continue such services at a lesser cost than has hitherto been possible Now this agreement witnesseth and it is hereby agreed by and between the parties hereto as follows:-

"1. The Contractors shall during the term of this agreement provide and pay for all labour required in the carrying-on of the omnibus services mentioned in the Schedule hereto including the driving, servicing and repairing of the motor-omnibuses employed therein and also provide all petrol oil tires accessories and supplies required for the said omnibuses, such omnibuses being provided by the Board and to be garaged and kept in the Board's garage at Avondale of which garage the Contractors shall have the exclusive use and control.

"2. The Contractors shall at all times keep and maintain the said omnibuses in good and efficient running-order (fair wear-and-tear excepted) and from time to time as occasion shall require will paint repair and amend the same and supply such new parts and appliances as may be required.

"3. The Contractors will take all necessary steps to ensure that the said services are duly carried out in strict accordance with the terms of the respective licenses therefor held by the Board…" [30]

The bus services operated by the Contractors included:

"…Point Resolution to Commerce Street, Blockhouse Bay to Avondale, Avondale to Point Chevalier Hall Corner, Rosebank Road to Point Chevalier Hall Corner, Waikowhai Park to Greenwoods Corner via Three Kings Tramway Terminus, and Victoria Avenue to Commerce Street." [30]

Section 5(2) of the Empowering Act provided for such future arrangements, as required:

"The Board may subsidize or otherwise assist any motor-omnibus or similar service where the Board is of opinion that such service is beneficial to the undertaking carried on by the Board." [30]

However, in his Annual Report for the year ended 31 March 1935, John Allum was anxious to assure the public and staff that the Board would only outsource its transport services in a responsible manner:

"The Board has on several occasions throughout the year acted as Metropolitan Licensing Authority, and has issued licenses to various omnibus companies operating within its area. The Board realises it has a duty to the travelling public, to its staff, and to the ratepayers, and consequently every endeavour to maintain a proper balance between these interests is made. Nothing is to be gained by drastic action, and there is no cause whatever for alarm so long as the cash position remains satisfactory." [31]

Auckland Transport Board Cash Position

That 1935 Annual Report also recorded a smaller deficit of £8,351 for the financial year with the total transport services revenue higher at £522,685, an increase of £3,988. [31]

Indeed, once the Transport Board had divested itself of its uneconomic bus routes, the financial position of its core tramways services was greatly improved, as recorded by the Board's Annual Reports for the years ending:

31 March 1936: "The total revenue for the year, £544,824, is an increase of £22,139 over the previous year. The year's expenses at £561,010 show an increase of £29,974 – a deficit of £16,187 compared with a deficit of £8,351 last year." [32]

31 March 1937: "…the revenue for the year at £584,860 shows an increase of £40,036 over the previous year. The year's expenses at £448,576 show an increase of £35,517 over those of the previous year…there is a deficit of £12,183 compared with a deficit of £16,187 last year." [33]

31 March 1938: "…the result of the year's working is a surplus of £2,772/13/5, as compared with a deficit of £12,183/9/- last year. The revenue for the year at £632,484 shows an increase of £47,624 over the previous year, while the year's expenses…show an increase of £32,668." [34]

So, by 1938, the Chairman of the Auckland Transport Board, Henry Greathead Rex Mason, (Chairman since 1936) was able to report more optimistically on the financial affairs of the City's public transport operations:

"The accounts are noteworthy in that after long years of difficulty and successive debit balances which have accumulated to a substantial total, and which will require the attention of the Board for some years to come, we have again a credit balance, albeit, a small one.

"An exceptional number of such special events as the visit of the South African Rugby players, and the Roman Catholic Centenary celebrations, as well as the remarkably fine weather conditions of the recent summer and autumn, have combined to sustain our revenue strongly, and largely account of the surplus shown. Changing conditions of transport forbid the hope that the future should hold no difficulties, but there appears ground for the belief that with prudent administration they will be successfully overcome." [34]

That optimism continued into 1939 when Henry Mason had "…pleasure in reporting that the Balance Sheet and Accounts now submitted, which cover the tenth complete year of operation of the services under control of the Auckland Transport Board, show that the result of the year's working is a surplus of £1,821/10/2.

"While this surplus is small, it is arrived at after making all interest and sinking fund payments and providing for all other charges which should properly be met out of the Board's revenue…The revenue for the year at £647017 shows an increase of £14,533 over the previous year, while the year's expenses…at £645,195 show an increase of £15,484." [35]

Auckland Transport Board – Role and Responsibilities

In his Annual Report for the year ended March 1939, the Chairman also took the opportunity to define his Board's role as the operator of Auckland's public transport services:

"I do not think that it is the function or the desire of the Board to make large profits. Its primary object is to render efficient and adequate transport at the lowest possible cost. Such a statement is, however, much more easily made than carried out. It has been pointed out in the past that the Board's responsibility is properly divisible into three parts:

"(a) To the Travelling Public. It is the Board's duty to give the travelling public the most efficient and adequate service possible, after having due regard to the needs of each district and to the necessity of providing for all expenses, including the maintenance of the undertaking, from the revenues available.

"(b) To the Employees. It has always been the desire of the Board to provide its employees with the best of working conditions and with a wage that will provide them with a reasonable standard of living.

"(c) To the Ratepayers. In the last instance the financial responsibility of the undertaking rests upon the ratepayers. It has never yet been necessary for the Auckland Transport Board to collect a rate, and if the undertaking is prudently directed, then I can see no necessity for such an action in the future. I think that the Board can fairly claim to have met all these responsibilities." [35]

The *collection of a rate* obviously referred to the responsibility of constituent local authorities and their ratepayers to contribute to any financial losses incurred by the Transport Board as allowed by Sections 45 and 48 of the Auckland Transport Board Act 1928. So far so good but, as Henry Mason had forewarned in his 1938 Annual Report, *"Changing conditions of transport forbid the hope that the future should hold no difficulties…"* [34]

First Trolley Bus

The first of those *changing conditions of transport* – the advent of Auckland's first trolley bus – occurred in December 1938, as described by the Board Chairman:

"Special Trolley Bus Service From Queen Street To The Farmers' Trading Co., Hobson Street: After unfortunate delay due to fire and to difficulty in obtaining delivery of the chassis from England, this service was commenced on 19th December, 1938. It is without doubt the most popular transport service in Auckland to-day. The vehicles being used are the most modern obtainable and have led to many enquiries as to why the whole transport system in Auckland cannot be operated by trolley bus. While such a course might be thought desirable by the travelling public, it must be borne in mind that the tramway service is modern, efficient and well maintained.

"Further, that there is still outstanding on the tramway service a loan debt of such amount that it would be financially impossible to make any comprehensive change and maintain the present low rates of fare. This is due, of course, to the fact that the new form of transport would have to bear its own capital charges and also meet those of the tramway service – a burden which, as I have said, is impossible at present.

"Nevertheless, one foresees an increasing demand for new forms of transport, and even if this be induced as much by what may be termed mere fashion as by anything else, this demand will give rise to problems which future Boards will constantly have to bear in mind in their administration in defining policy and making their financial commitments." [35]

Transport Board Seeks Petrol Tax Share

While the tramway service certainly had its own financial burden to bear, the *fashionable* new form of transport referred to by Henry Mason – the alarming number of motor vehicles crowding the trams – also cost their operators a good deal to run. Motor vehicles were not cheap to buy and, as well as licensing and repair costs, motorists had been paying a fuel tax since November 1927, following the passage of the Motor-spirits Taxation Act that year. After administration and other costs had been deducted, 92 per cent of the tax collected was deposited into the Main Highways Account and the balance was "…apportioned among those Borough Councils in whose districts there is a population of six thousand or upwards…" to be used for the construction and maintenance of main highways and borough streets, respectively. [36]

The Auckland Transport Board believed that because it was responsible for that part of the roadway along which its tracks ran, it should also receive a fair proportion of the fuel tax, as outlined in its remit to the Conference of the Municipal Association of New Zealand in March 1939:

"The Board submitted the following remit to the Conference of the Municipal Association of New Zealand, held in March last:

"That in each borough where there is a tramway undertaking that maintains a portion of the streets, such tramway undertakings shall receive a share of the petrol tax, provided that the share of such tramway undertakings shall not be allocated from the amount at present allocated to boroughs.

"This remit has been passed at previous Conferences, and representations have been made by the Board to the Government, but so far the Board has been unsuccessful in obtaining a share of the petrol tax.

"When I say that the area occupied by the tram tracks, which are wholly maintained by the Board, comprises 491,848 sq. yds. and extends over a distance of over 44 miles, it will be realised that the Board's claim for a share of this tax is well justified.

"The first cost of laying out bituminous paving on the track reserve was £170,619, disregarding cost of rails or foundations, and to maintain this paving which incidentally occupies over a third of the road surface, cost the Board last year £8,157.

"In these days of greatly increased motor traffic, that portion of the roadway maintained by the Board is carrying more heavy motor traffic than ever before, and the costs to the Board for maintenance are proportionately greater. The Board, therefore, feels that it has an indisputable right to a share of the petrol tax. Although no success has been met so far in obtaining a share of this tax, undoubted justice of the Board's claim well warrants persistence in its prosecution in the future." [35]

Road Transport

"The road is the channel of all trade and commerce; it is fundamental to social existence and its varied effect appears in every department of the state." (Hilaire Belloc – The Old Road)

When Wellington businessman and politician, William McLean, imported the first motor car into New Zealand in 1898, there were few roads upon which such a beast could be suitably conveyed. Road capacity and quality has been trying to cope with vehicle numbers ever since.

The Placement of Streets – A Critical First Step

The planning and growth of any settlement depended very much upon the initial placement of its streets. This basic premise was referred to time and again by speakers who attended the New Zealand Town Planning Conference and Exhibition held at Wellington during May 1919 – a time when the real impact of the motor vehicle on all aspects of planning was still to be realised.

As The Dominion reported on 23 May 1919:

"Messrs. S. A. R. Mair and N. Crofton Staveley presented a paper upon 'City Streets and Country Roads'. The authors were strongly of the opinion that in the past too little attention had been paid to the location of roads which in many instances had become streets. In every case the prime location should be the proper one, regardless of the cost of acquisition or construction. Town-planning should commence with the location of all the roads…The standard of road construction was now being raised so rapidly that the problem of financing the main roads was the principal difficulty to be faced. There was no doubt that when this difficulty was settled developments would follow that would go far to revolutionise the matter of rural transport, and consequently the commercial and domestic life of the country generally.

"Mr H. F. Toogood, engineer to the Featherston City Council…urged that more attention should be given to the provision of adequate arterial roads for the Dominion. It must be realised that the roads leading out of and into a city were as important as the city streets themselves. Mr N. Paterson, of the Wellington City Engineer's department, believed that before one could deal adequately with the planning of roads, one had to possess a vision that could extend twenty-five years ahead, and take into account the tremendous possibilities of the extension of motor traffic." [37]

Main Highways Act 1922

"By 1920, when it became obvious that the motor vehicle was rapidly replacing horse-drawn vehicles as the main form of road transport, roading authorities began to appreciate the need for new standards of roading, particularly for the main arterial roads of the country. Road traffic, which hitherto had been almost local in character, began to assume national significance and the provision of through roads was outgrowing the capacity of local authorities.

"The growing demand from local authorities for some greater measure of national provision, including finance for roading needs, culminated in the passing of the Main Highways Act of 1922. This marked a milestone in the roading history of New Zealand and laid the foundation for an era of great roading expansion. Under this Act provision was made for the declaration of main arterial roads as main highways, and the control of these roads became primarily a national concern…The administration of this Act was entrusted to the Main Highways Board, comprising two members appointed by the Government, an officer of the Ministry of Works, two representatives of county councils, and one representative of motor vehicle owners…" [38]

Naturally, all these new and improved roads attracted folk eager to try them out. As a result:

"The number of automobiles in New Zealand skyrocketed from 37,500 in 1922 to 261,850 in 1938, at that stage the second highest rate of vehicles per capita in the world after the United States. This growing popularity meant that urban development could break free from the constraints of predetermined transit networks and occur anywhere roads were built. Furthermore, commuters were no longer forced to locate close to their place of work or to a streetcar line, leading to a rapid decentralisation of urban growth." [39]

Railways Department Road Motor Services

Roads and the transportation of goods and passengers thereon by motor vehicle naturally piqued the interest of the Railways Department – not just because of the competition it posed directly to its own goods and passenger carrying business, but also as a possible commercial opportunity that could be exploited. This was hinted at by the Minister of Railways, the Hon. W B Taverner, in his Railways Statement for Year Ending 31 March 1929:

"Road Motor Services – Another matter of growing importance, and one which will come more frequently up for decision in connection with the Department's operations in the future, is that of the working of traffic by the Department through the medium of road vehicles.

"My own view is that such operations should be decided upon with very great caution. We are by no means in a position to say that the road-motor operations that are now being carried on in the community are on a sound basis, and I feel that any action on the part of the Department in the direction of embarking on road-motor operations to any great extent requires careful examination as it might have serious results on the Department's financial position.

"I can quite realize, however, that there may well be cases where the Department could, with advantage to itself and for better service to the community, undertake road-motor work; and when a case is clearly established for sound working on these lines then I think there is no good reason why the Department should not undertake the work.

"I am impelled to make these observations, because there have been suggestions that the Department should not carry on road-motor services. I do not think that the matter can be carried to the point of absolute prohibition of any such action on the part of the Department; first and foremost the Department is a transport institution and its duty is clearly to give the transport service for which it is provided by the cheapest and most efficient means. Only when a road proposition is definitely ascertained by examination of all the facts to be the cheapest and most efficient means, and not till then, should the Department turn to that form of transport to enable it to carry on its services." [40]

Traversing the Waitemata

Indeed, many citizens of Auckland chose to decentralise by living on the City's North Shore – not all that far from the CBD, as the crow flies, but on the far side of the world for the motorist prior to the opening of the Harbour Bridge on 30 May 1959.

During the five years to December 1938, the number of motor vehicles plying Auckland's roads had doubled and this growth was soon manifested by a steady increase of cross-harbour traffic that severely tested the carrying capacity of the ferries. This was particularly so at weekends and during holidays when excursionists flocked to the pristine, North Shore beaches.

Harbour Bridge Royal Commission

As the queues for the vehicle ferries grew longer on both sides of the harbour, the construction of more ferry wharves was favoured as the most viable way of improving the service. Indeed, that had been the opinion of the Harbour Bridge Royal Commission as outlined in its April 1930 report:

"For a considerable number of years it will be possible to adequately provide for the requirements of harbour transit at Auckland by a progressive increase, both in size and numbers, in the ferry fleet, plus further landing-stages at each end." [41]

Obviously, "...for a considerable number of years" many cross-harbour travellers disagreed, as per the Letter to the Editor of The New Zealand Herald written by the Secretary of the Waitemata Harbour Bridge Association, R. H. Greville, who asked in 1938:

"Can we therefore anticipate as traffic increases, a string of vehicular wharves on each side of the harbour, and is this a logical solution of the difficulty? There is only one method of solving the problem, that is the immediate erection of the harbour bridge." [42]

While the 1930 Royal Commission had not recommended an immediate start on a bridge to span the Waitemata Harbour, its report did contain precise suggestions as to the positioning of an eventual bridge, its dimensions, construction, and estimated cost. The Commission's report even described various methods by which the project could be financed.

Auckland Town-Planning Association

Of particular importance to later road planning, was the report's inclusion of a technical paper presented by the 'Technical Group of (the) Auckland Town-Planning Association'. The paper analysed the approach routes to the most likely bridge site; describing those that would be required to bypass the congested areas of the city at that time.

But, despite the complexity and detail of the Harbour Bridge Royal Commission's findings and those of the Town-Planning Association's Technical Group, their studies were soon well and truly archived. In fact, only eight years later, as reported by The New Zealand Herald on 15 December 1938, it was as if there had never been a 1930 study when the Labour Government of Michael Joseph Savage required 'fresh' inquiries to be made before the construction of a harbour bridge could be reconsidered:

"In response to representations in regard to the congestion of vehicular traffic across the Auckland Harbour, the Prime Minister, Mr Savage, advised the Automobile Association (Auckland) in a message received at a meeting of the (Auckland City) council…that in his opinion fresh inquiries should be made concerning the proposal to build a harbour bridge before any action was taken. Mr Savage stated that recently the Cabinet had this question under review, but decided to withhold action in the meantime." [43]

The hopelessly-inadequate, trans-harbour service provided by the ferries was described by Auckland's Automobile Association and reported by the Auckland Star on 27 January 1939:

"The harbour bridge controversy was revived last evening, when the Automobile Association submitted figures which, it was claimed, showed the inadequacy of the vehicular ferry service between the city and North Shore. It was suggested that the Auckland city had now reached such a stage in its development, and the density of the traffic was so great, that the present system of trans-harbour transport could not adequately serve the public. The association is of the opinion that the matter is so serious as to demand active steps, firstly to provide adequate service immediately, and secondly, to bring about a permanent solution by the provision of a traffic bridge across the harbour…" [44]

Prime Minister Savage had long since advocated a conference comprising all interested parties to discuss the need for a bridge. However, as indicated by a New Zealand Herald report of 6 July 1939, such a conference was hardly a priority for the Government and became less so as each day of that fateful year passed:

"A letter from the Prime Minister, Mr Savage, advising that, in view of more urgent matters, it was not possible to state definitely when the suggested conference concerning the Waitemata Harbour bridge project would be held, was received at last night's meeting of the Takapuna Borough Council. It was decided to communicate with the Prime Minister, reminding him of his former promises, pointing out that the question of urgency was a matter of opinion, and stating that the council considered the reply most unsatisfactory.

"The Mayor, Mr J. Guiniven, said he considered the Prime Minister was the greatest stumbling block to the construction of the bridge. The scheme was of greater importance to North Auckland than to either Northcote or Takapuna. The Prime Minister had no interest in the development of the North Shore boroughs, and still less in the North. Thousands of acres of land in the North could not be opened because of the lack of the bridge." [45]

As the days of 1939 marched toward Armageddon the ambitions of all bridge supporters were dashed and their appeals to Government rendered pointless…

Suburban Rail

"*If, in a history of railway development in New Zealand, a chapter were devoted to the Auckland suburban area, it could well be entitled A Chapter of Mistakes.*" [46]

Such a chapter could also be described as a *Chapter of Inaction* for it forms a major part of a story almost without end. An incomplete story of unfulfilled ambition to extend the otherwise terminating, southern and eastern railway lines, through the centre of Auckland City, to its western and northern suburbs. It is the story of what was first known as the 'Town Hall Deviation', later, the 'Morningside Deviation', and finally, the 'City Rail Link'. It is the story of the many variations of the Deviation; of how many times they were put forward as the ultimate solution to Auckland's traffic congestion but failed to leave the starting gate. It is a very long story…

…Beginning more than 150 years ago, when a detachment of British Royal Engineers was despatched to New Zealand in 1860 "…upon a surveying expedition to this colony…not only to make an entire survey of the interior of New Zealand, but also to assist in the formation of necessary trunk roads, the erection of bridges, &c." [47]

As The Auckland Star of 4 September 1926 reported:

"In the early days when the Royal Engineers were stationed in Auckland they actually made a rough survey for a railway line north. The idea was to have the central station near where the Town Hall stands, tunnel under the hill to the old cemetery gully, run one line north and put a second tunnel south to Newmarket. Along the Arch Hill gully the land for the railway line of the future was stated to have been reserved." [48]

This original plan was broadened to suit changed conditions when, in 1912, Railways District Engineer, Daniel Thomas McIntosh, selected Beach Road as the new site for Auckland's Railway Station after it was decided to shift the station from Lower Queen Street to make way for the planned General Post Office. While the Beach Road site was notoriously far from the City's centre, it is largely forgotten that Daniel McIntosh's vision, his *great scheme*, also included the Westfield deviation through the eastern suburbs, a connecting tunnel to a second station near Upper Queen Street, and a 'Northern Tunnel outlet to the Kaipara line'.

Following his 1914 comprehensive review of the nation's railway system, the newly-appointed Railways General Manager, Ernest Haviland Hiley, agreed with much of what Daniel McIntosh had suggested for Auckland's suburban railway network, except for the 'Town Hall Deviation'.

Instead of tunnelling beneath the city, Ernest Hiley advocated a more direct extension of the main trunk line to the Kaipara line:

"...at some future period...when the traffic work of Auckland increases sufficiently to justify the expense...straight through the Auckland station [proposed for Beach Road] carrying the line westward over Queen Street and through the suburb of Ponsonby and joining the present railway to Kaipara at either New Lynn or Kumeu." [49]

By July 1924, preliminary work had started on the construction of the Beach Road station, the goods yard, and the deviation via Hobson and the Orakei Bays to Westfield but those intentions of Messrs McIntosh and Hiley to extend the rail network to the west and north of the Beach Road station were otherwise ignored. However, following the Railway Department's own inquiries, the Government did commit to include what had then become known as the 'Morningside Deviation' as part of its Railways programme of works.

Variations of this commitment were also supported that year by a report submitted by British Railway Commissioners, Sir Sam Fay and Sir Vincent Raven, and later, in 1926, by a report from English consulting engineers, Messrs Merz and McLellan.

At this pivotal time, demand for an improved suburban railway service obviously existed and was supported by the Government, its various consultants, the railway leagues, business and, ultimately, thousands of disgruntled, but still potential, commuters. Nevertheless, by 1928, few suburban railway improvements in the Auckland region had been completed while competition from the trams, the buses, and particularly the motorcar, continued to reduce rail passenger numbers.

Railways Department Management Structure Changes

The Railway's traditional monopoly of long-distance, freight transportation was also increasingly threatened by road carriers lacking the commercial overheads of a large, Government entity. As the Evening Post of 3 May 1928 reported, the Government sought to offset that competition by means of changes to its management structure:

"Announcing alterations in the personnel of the Railway management to-day, the Prime Minister and Minister of Railways (the Right Hon. J. G. Coates) indicated very important changes in the system of management which has been in operation since the end of 1922. The system of General Manager administration previously in operation is to be reverted to on the retirement of the present members of the Railway Board at the end of this month, and the position of General Manager is then to be assumed by Mr H. H. Sterling, formerly a member of the board...

"At the same time the Department's operations were placed on a commercial basis, and this also had led to improved efficiency in administration. 'It has been apparent to the Government for some time past,' said the Prime Minister, 'that the commercial aspect of the railways had assumed such importance as to render it exceedingly desirable to secure the services of men with outside commercial training when the time came to make fresh appointments to the management." [50]

Railway's change to its management system had come none too soon, according to one commentator, who observed in an Auckland Star article, published 24 June 1929:

"...motor competition was cutting into the railway traffic to an extent of which probably very few people were aware. Consequently the argument holds good, that the railway system is in serious danger, especially for short distances...That this serious competition is likely to increase in the future, unless drastic means are taken to meet it, seems a logical deduction from the recent statement of the president of the Harbour Bridge Association, that there are now registered in Auckland and suburbs eleven times as many motor cars as there were in 1921…motors were enjoying an utterly unfair advantage, and that this anomaly should be rectified by placing both means of transport on the same footing. Either the motors should pay the whole cost of the roads, as the railways pay for their roadway now, or else the railways should pay towards their permanent way only the same proportion as the motors do now. Competition would then be quite fair, and it would be a case of the survival of the fittest." [51]

As those *motors* continued to threaten the historically-held supremacy of the railway carriage of goods and passengers, many debated the pros and cons of private enterprise seemingly taking unfair advantage of a publicly-owned entity unfit to compete.

Some solutions to what the Evening Post called the *Railway Transport Riddle* were explored by articles it published on 2 October 1929. Those solutions included higher railway freight charges and regulation of the transport industry in favour of the railways in order to deal with:

"…(a) the deficit on the railways caused by developmentalism and road competition, and (b) by the failure of the State to equip the Railways Department for the fight, in that the State has commercialised the Department's working methods but not the policy…" [52]

Railways Annual Report 1929

The Post's article relating to the possible regulation of transport quoted from the 1929 Railways Annual Report and the statement made therein by Railways General Manager, Mr Herbert Harry Sterling:

"As I have already indicated in this report, we find ourselves, in connection with the increasing of our business to make good the present financial deficiencies, faced with serious difficulties, the chief of which is, of course, the unregulated competition of road motor-vehicles. These services start with the great advantage of having a road provided for them, a circumstance which has no counterpart in connection with railways.

"Large sums of money are being spent on the improvement of roads paralleling the railway, thus making increasingly possible the competition of road services with the railways. To the extent that this is being done the country is duplicating, and in some cases (as when sea transport also exists) triplicating, the means of transport.

"More especially in a country such as New Zealand, where the railways are the property of the community, this raises a definite question as to whether it is in the interests of the community that it should continue. If the community by the expenditure of money on a new facility depreciates an existing one, then on any adequate review of the situation such depreciation should be taken into account and provided for. True, the community may prefer road transport to rail transport even at the expense of duplication; but the money invested in the railways has to be provided for, and the two services have inevitably to be paid for though only one is used.

"The difficulty arises largely from the fact that the responsibility is communal, while the advantage is largely individual. Individuals desirous of running or taking advantage of motor services clamour for improved roads to be provided by the community, while the benefit is reaped by comparatively few.

"It must be remembered that the railways are still an indispensable factor in our transport system. It would not only be a physical impossibility for road services to cope with the whole of the traffic, either passenger or goods, but it would be an economic impossibility also." [53]

But, while Herbert Sterling projected a good deal of optimism as to the Railways' place in the scheme of things and the Department's ability to compete with the growing number of trucks and buses, he was certainly under no illusion as to the popularity of the adversary and of how that popularity was achieved. As most clever generals will, when faced with such a massed force, he welcomed the opportunity to parley:

"It was inevitable that the rapid development of road motor traction that has taken place should have a very disturbing effect on the transport industry. As in the case of every new thing of this kind, it was nurtured in its infancy by propaganda. Its principal competitor, the railways, was depreciated to an exaggerated degree, and the 'infant' was just as extravagantly and undeservedly extolled.

"Railways were talked of as a thing of the past, an assertion which even a cursory examination of the facts would have shown to be quite unjustifiable. The result was confusion of thought, and an unfortunate degree of competition where a friendly spirit of 'get together' would have produced benefits to all concerned of a more real and lasting character. There are not wanting signs that improvement is taking place in both these aspects, but the process of stabilization by 'natural forces' is likely to be a long and painful one." [53]

Minister of Railways Statement 1929

In his summing-up of the financial year ending 31 March 1929, the Minister of Railways, the Hon. W B Taverner, expanded upon his General Manager's description of the uniqueness of railway services as an important medium for national development:

"Dealing with the position of the railways from an historical point of view, we start from the point that the railways, in the first place, were undoubtedly constructed as a developmental institution rather than as a profit-making institution.

"Indeed, it is scarcely possible to conceive that much of the mileage of the present railway system, even of the main lines, would have been constructed at all if at the time when their construction was decided upon the question as to whether they should be gone on with or not had been decided on a profit-making basis.

"As the years have gone on this policy has been continued. Nor has it been confined to construction only; it has extended also to operations, and many services and tariff concessions have been given in the past on the basis of the developmental aspect of the railway policy.

"It is, I think, absolutely essential to a proper interpretation of the railway accounts that we should keep these facts clearly in our mind. More especially do I think it timely to emphasize this fact, as there has undoubtedly grown a tendency to regard the deficit as shown in the annual Statement as a 'loss'. In the light of the policy as above enunciated this is quite unjustified. It is beyond the possibility of question that the country has reaped very material indirect return from the existence of the railways.

"This return, however, has not been reflected in the annual Railways Statements. It is none the less real. The whole question resolves itself into one as to whether the time has arrived when the country is paying through the deficit on account of the railway work too much for the indirect returns that it is getting…" [40]

Beach Road Railway Station

Finally, on 24 November 1930, as reported by the Auckland Star:

"Auckland's new railway station was officially opened by the Hon. W A Veitch, Minister of Railways [He had just succeeded William Taverner as Minister], this afternoon, in the presence of a large gathering of people representative of all shades of politics, as well as the business community and railway officials.

"The ceremony commenced at 2 p.m., and after a number of speeches the Minister of Railways opened the station building with a gold key, which was presented to him to commemorate the occasion. In the course of his speech, the Minister mentioned that criticism might be levelled against the location of the station and the relative positions of building and platforms; but these had been enforced by circumstances, which had had the fullest investigation.

"Incidentally, Mr Veitch mentioned that the cost of the Westfield deviation was £790,000. The cost of the complete rearrangement and reconstruction of the Auckland railway station with the yard and all appurtenances had been £1,250,000.

"Some of the leading items in that sum were: Station building (including platforms, verandahs, passenger subways, retaining walls and forecourt), £365,000; new engine depot, £96,000; outward goods shed, £46,000; inwards goods shed, £22,000; signalling, interlocking and flood-lighting, £75,000; new yards, approximately £600,000. A very substantial offset to the cost of the project was the value of the old station site which had been abandoned." [54]

That the Minister chose to mention the criticism of the site of the new railway station as inconvenient during the opening ceremony certainly indicated just how vociferous that criticism had been, and would continue to be, well into the future. During the ceremony, the Leader of the Opposition tried vainly to deflect any criticism that his Government had been responsible for the decision to site the station at Beach Road by blaming the Railway Department's engineers and the 'Government of the day' without elaborating on the decisions that had actually been made some sixteen years previously.

"The Leader of the Opposition, The Rt. Hon. J. G. Coates, spoke of the fixing of the terminal point at the Auckland end. This point was fixed by the Department's engineers and approved by the Government of the day because it was convenient to the city, taking into consideration certain other improvements which would have to be made, such as better access to the North, and the delivery of the suburban passengers from the number of suburbs into the heart of the city.

"It would not be possible at the present time, or in 20 years' time, to handle the whole of the traffic of Auckland by road transport. The congestion would be too great. Electricity and quick services were necessary. Efficient, quick and up-to-date services were essential for users of the railway. They could not carry on their commerce without railways; the railways were not going out. It was essential to the business of the country to maintain rail services." [55]

'*Electricity and quick services*' did not eventuate at Auckland for many decades (while the Wellington suburban railway network was electrified between 1938 and 1940). Nevertheless, "Although Auckland's rail lines were not electrified, and routes there were relatively inconvenient, ticket sales continued to increase in places like Otahuhu, Papakura and Newmarket until the forties. Sales at the Auckland station continued to increase until 1961, despite its somewhat inconvenient location after 1930." [15]

However, as well as the Railway Station's *'inconvenient location'*, "…The economic depression, the development of road transport, both public and private, and the transport difficulties during the war period…" [46] all affected the reduction of suburban, season-ticket journeys:

Year Ended 31 March	Season Ticket Journeys	Journeys Per 1000 Population	Population
1920	3,096,800	20	155,000
1930	5,189,700	26	200,000
1940	2,970,000	12	240,000

Despite a steady increase in the Region's population, season ticket journeys had almost halved between 1920 and 1940 and, while all lines terminated at the Beach Road Station – cut short with the abruptness of a guillotine – the worst was yet to come…

Chapter Two

1940 to 1949 – More Cars Cometh

Planning and Politics
"*At heart, most New Zealanders were liberal individualists who accepted the necessity of a growing, state-erected infrastructure for the continued development and prosperity of a small capitalist economy in a remote and often rugged environment. Generally, government intervention maintained law, order, private property, and social harmony, and revitalized belief in the open-ness of opportunity when individual efforts and laissez faire attitudes failed to sustain it.*" [1]

Benefits of Metropolitan Unity

The Local Government (Amalgamation Schemes) Bills of 1938 did not proceed and the '*preliminary inquiries*' into the principle of amalgamation suggested by The Municipal Association of New Zealand, Incorporated, the New Zealand Counties' Association, and several other local-body associations were soon curtailed by the Second World War. Nevertheless, The New Zealand Herald of October 1943 reminded its readers of the zoning plan then in existence and of the benefits of metropolitan unity as part of a grand development plan for a future Auckland:

"When a city is growing, to make provision for its future so that development may be systematic and orderly, and not haphazard, is sound policy. When anything of this kind is attempted in Auckland the work can never be satisfactorily done for the city alone. What, for want of a better term, is usually called the metropolitan area is essentially an organic whole.

"Though the local government of the area may be in the hands of a number of authorities, though there may be dividing lines between city and neighbouring boroughs, road board districts or town districts, circumstances often compel these divisions to be ignored, the whole territory to be regarded as one. This has had to be done, largely for the provision of drainage, the supply of electricity, and the organisation of passenger transport. When the City Council and the other authorities embarked on town-planning schemes, it must soon have become evident they would have to be co-ordinated if they were to mean anything of value.

"The pity is that it [the zoning plan] cannot include provision for unified administration and local government over approximately the same area—a return to the vision of 1851 with a united City of Auckland occupying largely the territory of the original borough.

"The master plan for zoning, communications and open spaces does not provide for anything of the kind. If, however, as it proceeds, it helps to break down the atmosphere of prejudice, almost of suspicion, which stands in the way of the Greater Auckland ideal, it may achieve something more valuable even than its ostensible purpose." [56]

Auckland City Council Ways and Means Committee

The New Zealand Herald commentary was in response to the publication of a comprehensive report which the city engineer, Mr J. Tyler, had prepared for the (Auckland City Council) Ways and Means Committee. In that report, Mr Tyler observed:

"Considerable progress has been made with the first stage of the movement to co-ordinate the town planning schemes of the local authorities throughout the metropolitan area. Many of these local bodies, notably the City Council, have reached an advanced stage with their individual planning schemes and the Town Planning Board in Wellington has found it necessary to ask that a master scheme for the co-ordination of these projects should be developed. This scheme in effect will provide for the orderly planning and zoning of all the area coming within its scope and when completed will provide for three major issues—zoning, communications and open spaces. The zoning proposals are those now being dealt with.

"The planning unit under review contains an area of 48,174 acres and embraces the whole of the territory in the Auckland Isthmus, from the Waitemata Harbour to the Manukau Harbour, and from the Tamaki River to the Whau River, the four North Shore boroughs, New Lynn, Otahuhu and Mangere East. Of the 17 local authorities in the area, 12 are active participants in the scheme, those not taking part being the authorities responsible for Takapuna, Otahuhu, Panmure and Mangere East. It is stated that New Lynn will be interested only if metropolitan considerations require alterations to its scheme, already approved by the Town Planning Board. The areas under these non-participating bodies amount to 6600 acres, or about 13 per cent of the total. They have, however, been included in the area, as without their inclusion it would not be possible to calculate and plan for a balanced land-use economy.

"In this it is stated that the population of the planning unit is estimated at 217,210. It is estimated that the unit will ultimately be capable of accommodating a population of about two-thirds of a million, but for the purpose of the present planning the Town Planning Board has indicated a figure of 400,000 at the end of 25 years. It is shown that the total area devoted to residential uses is 12,538 acres, occupied by 53,192 residential buildings, averaging just under a quarter of an acre. There are 13,497 vacant building lots, also averaging slightly under a quarter of an acre. The average density of land actually occupied by residential buildings is 16.4 persons an acre, or a gross density of 11.6 persons, if the area occupied by streets, sports areas, etc., is taken into account.

"It is stated that the estimated ultimate densities for the entire metropolitan area is net 18.3 and gross 13 persons, comparable with the densities obtaining to-day in Mount Eden, which is a well-established and an almost fully-developed borough. One of the main objects of the zoning scheme is to provide adequate and suitably-situated areas for future industrial development, adds the report. There is at present within the planning unit an area of 1192 acres devoted to industry, but to provide for a population of 400,000 in 25 years it is estimated that a total of 2312 acres will be required, of which 1068 acres will be needed for heavy industry, 760 acres of light industries and 484 acres for noxious industries, such as those at Westfield devoted to the meat and fertiliser trades. The report also deals at length with the question of the allocation of land for commercial uses.

"Mr Tyler remarks that the Ways and Means Committee has already recommended that the necessary steps be taken to establish a permanent agricultural belt. This and other considerations would necessitate some extensions to the planning unit. The districts of

Glen Eden, Titirangi, the whole of Mangere, the Pakuranga riding, Bucklands and a portion of the Waitemata county north of Northcote and Te Atatu should be absorbed into the area of the scheme to ensure the success of its operation, while the absorption of the Mangere East district into the borough of Otahuhu for administrative purposes seemed desirable. The next major issue to be dealt with was the system of open spaces and recreation facilities, said Mr Tyler, and work on this phase of the scheme was already in hand." [57]

Planning for a Greater Auckland

This planning for a greater Auckland, incorporating the whole region as one, municipal entity continued into 1944. As well as zoning issues, local planners also considered such intangibles as transport and other public services:

"Representatives of Auckland local bodies in the metropolitan area met in conference in the municipal chamber of the Town Hall this afternoon (9 February 1944) to receive and discuss a report from the technical advisor, Mr James Tyler, city engineer, on the Auckland metropolitan co-ordinating scheme, particularly with reference to the progress of the scheme. The conference also discussed steps for the completion of the scheme, particularly with reference to communications and open spaces, and the question of co-opting of transport, harbour and industrial interests." [58]

Two months later, on 4 April 1944, the House of Representatives appointed yet another Local Government Select Committee. Unlike the inquiries set up in 1938, new terms of reference were a lot broader, requiring Committee members "…to inquire into and report upon all phases of the local government system of the Dominion, including questions of finance, elections, and the general structure of the system." [59]

Auckland Regional Planning

But some, such as Auckland's Mayor, John Allum, could not wait for the recommendations of the Parliamentary Select Committee. He, and other proponents of co-operative planning, pressed for an urgent utilisation of resources '…as the most practical means of promoting the economic development of the region', as reported by The New Zealand Herald on 21 March 1945:

"The establishment of a region planning organisation for the Auckland regional area was approved at a conference of members of Parliament and delegates from Government departments, local bodies and other organisations in the Town Hall concert chamber yesterday. Endorsement was also given to the principle of regional planning as the most practical means of promoting the economic development of the region.

"The decisions were made following an address by the Director of Town Planning, Mr J W Mawson. There was a large attendance over whom the Mayor, Mr J. A. C. Allum, presided. Mr Allum said he had called the conference at the request of the Government to discuss the problem of returning to a normal peace-time way of living. We have proved that by the co-operation of all sections of the community we have been able to provide a war machine capable of overcoming the challenges of the tyrant, he added. This conference is an acknowledgment that we expect by that same co-operation to meet and effectively deal with the problems of peace.

"Large shifts of population had taken place, particularly in the Auckland district, and many industries had been completely transformed. A general review of the economic structure of the Dominion was therefore necessary. Taking as an example the projects awaiting the attention of local bodies, Mr Allum said that if this work was not planned and the various authorities competed among themselves for labour and materials there would not only be chaos, but the costs to citizens would rise out of all proportion to the benefits to be obtained. If necessary Government and private works were added, some idea of the immensity of the problem before the Dominion could be obtained.

"The proposals that I desire to bring before you are very simple, he added. It is proposed that we should make provision for the surveying of the resources, both personal, economic and physical, of this Auckland area; that having surveyed them we should in a co-operative way plan for their effective utilisation." [60]

Local Body Suspicion

But before regional and municipal co-operation could produce the economic prosperity and advancement deserved by the citizens of Auckland, inherent suspicion and parochialism had still to be managed:

"So far as I know there is no connection between regional planning and local body reform, said the Director of Town Planning, Mr J. W. Mawson, during his address to the conference in Auckland yesterday (20 March 1945) which considered the establishment of a regional planning organisation. It had been suggested that there was some subtle or sinister connection between the two, he said. One of the arguments that was levelled against regional planning when the legislation was first put on the Statute Book was that it was the thin end of the wedge of amalgamation, Mr Mawson added.

"Regional planning is concerned with the physical and economic development of a region without regard to political subdivisions. Local body reform, as I understand it, is aimed at an adjustment of local body boundaries and functions. A regional planning scheme would still be necessary if there was only one administrative authority for the whole of the region. It had also been suggested that the regional planning committees were to be a kind of super local body which dictate to individual local bodies. Legislation laid it down that they were to be consultative and advisory bodies only and that their schemes were to serve as a guide only. There had been no departure-from that principle.

"It has been said, too, that these conferences and committees are only camouflage and that what is actually contemplated is a high degree of centralisation of these planning functions, said Mr Mawson. If you will reflect on the knowledge of local circumstances, conditions and needs required in the preparation of the schemes and the large number of people who have to be consulted at all stages you will appreciate the absurdity of even attempting to centralise these planning functions in Wellington." [60]

Local Government Select Committee Hearing

While planning of the Auckland region from Wellington may not have been the preferred option in 1945, nor was a single, Auckland-based authority seen as a possible alternative despite the obvious need for just such a centralised and local planning body. While the Auckland City Council saw this need for the whole of the Auckland metropolitan area to be brought under the control of one local authority so that all matters affecting the region could be more efficiently decided, it did not then have the stomach to demand such a move. This was made clear during one of the Select Committee's hearings reported by The New Zealand Herald on 20 April 1945:

"The City Council believes that the community of interest of the people justifies bringing the whole of the Auckland metropolitan area under the control of one local authority, said the Mayor, Mr J. A. C. Allum, when presenting evidence on behalf of the City Council before the Parliamentary Select Committee on local government yesterday.

However, the council was utterly opposed to any compulsory amalgamation as being repugnant to citizens' rights. For the purpose of this submission, Mr Allum continued, I have in mind broadly the area bounded by the Tamaki River, Whau Creek, Manukau and Waitemata Harbours, and including the four North Shore boroughs. Holding this belief, the City Council long ago adopted the policy of accepting amalgamation with any local districts in the area. Over the years Auckland city had thus grown by the addition of ten districts.

"In the past, whenever amalgamation has been discussed in Auckland the matter has proved to be highly controversial, said Mr Allum, and the welter of argument has tended to cloud rather than clarify the issue. In existing conditions, therefore, it is difficult for citizens to get a clear and unbiased lead in the matter of amalgamation. To Mr J. N. Massey, Mr Allum said that as the city was governed at present if a road was needed running right through the area it was necessary to call all the local bodies together and arrive at a settlement. This applied to all major works that might become necessary." [61]

Mount Eden Borough Opposition

The Borough of Mount Eden was certainly opposed to any suggestion of amalgamation, chiefly for financial reasons, reported the Auckland Star on 18 April 1945:

"The residents of Mount Eden had with no uncertain voice on two occasions decided against amalgamation with the Auckland city when polls had been taken on that issue, said the Mayor of Mount Eden, Mr R. J. Mills, when giving evidence before the Parliamentary Committee on Local Government yesterday. 'Amalgamation as it concerns the borough of Mount Eden resolves itself into a question of absorption by Auckland city,' he added. Mr. Mills said the population of the borough was 20,000 and the area 1476 acres. For the year ended March 31, 1932, Mount Eden borough rates were 4/2 [4s 2d] in the pound as compared with Auckland city rates of 3/11 [3s 11d]. The comparison to-day showed Mount Eden rates to be 3/10 [3s 10d] and Auckland city 4/5 [4s 5d]. In 1932 Mount Eden had an overdraft of £45,000. This year the overdraft had been turned into a credit of £8580, in addition to a reserve for works fund which now amounted to £4072.

"It is desired to protest emphatically against two most undesirable features of the Local Government (Amalgamation Schemes) Bill,' he continued. 'No provision is made in it to ascertain the wishes by poll or otherwise of the people of the areas proposed to be absorbed and the onus of proof is based upon the wrong party.' The chairman, Mr R. McKeen, said he believed Auckland had a great future once it could expand. It seemed ridiculous that there should be about 200 representatives running a city the size of Auckland. Perhaps if Mount Eden were not so close to Auckland its rates would not be 3/10 [3s 10d] but 10/3 [10s 3d]." [62]

Auckland's Topsy-Turvy Growth

In an article published 23 July 1945, an Auckland Star correspondent, E. K. Green, also illustrated what he saw as the need for co-ordinated, regional planning with his summation of what he termed Auckland's 'topsy-turvy growth' to that time. His description of the effects of a growing population on the availability of housing, and services such as transport, could have been written for 21st-century readers:

"Auckland, at the moment, is a city of schemes and plans. It is a city with growing pains. It has sprawled out over the isthmus and, unfettered by natural bounds, is continuing to sprawl. Its metropolitan area already covers nearly 50,000 acres; the authorities are already starting to plan for metropolitan area of up to 70,000 acres. The census, when it is held, will tell a striking story of population growth. In 1901 the metropolitan area held a population of 75,065; in 1936 (the last census) it held 203,000. In 1940 it was estimated there were 220,000, and then came a flooding increase, calculated to be between 30,000 and 40,000 people. This growth is from 15,000 to 20,000 above normal—and normal growth was estimated to give Auckland a population of 400,000 by 1965, twenty years hence!

"This figure of 400,000 was that given to the local authorities in 1940 by the Town Planning Board, after consultation with the Government Statistician. Whether it will pan out that way is dependent upon many factors, including Government policy in relation to the dispersal of industry. It may come despite all factors, for a big city is like a rolling snowball; it can't stop growing. Ease of distribution brings industry to a city of big population; industry brings workers, and so it goes on. Modern transport facilities, and projected facilities, lighten the problems of distribution. One city firm has already established an additional factory in a country area, to ease staffing problems. Others may follow the lead. National policy will probably encourage such moves, and electric power problems, housing problems and the like may have a similar tendency, but it is doubtful if they will do more than diminish the rate of growth.

"Whatever happens, Auckland's problem period is no passing phase. Problems will increase with the years. They are here already in plenty, and so are schemes to obviate them. Delving into these problems of growth in the past few days, I have heard so many schemes of development expounded—many of them already in the planning stage — that I find them difficult to digest mentally. If they are not spaced over a period of years, on some basis of planned priority, Auckland may be faced with a dose of financial collywobbles!

"Changing business centres, spreading suburbs, express road outlets, overhead roads, tunnel roads, harbour bridge (or tunnel), harbour developments, underground and other railway extensions, city airports, and replacement of trams by trolley or other buses — all these are in the picture, to say nothing of new civic centres, cultural centres, new Government, local body and business buildings, spreading reserves, and a host of other smaller schemes. All these things are as much an outgrowth of increasing population, industrial expansion, and big city 'growing pains' as they are a development of modern ideas in town planning. The drainage scheme is forced upon us by city growth, and so is the Hunua scheme to provide more water. Coal, gas, electric power, and housing shortages have followed in the wake of population.

"In its efforts to catch up, and maintain its services on a level in keeping with its rapid growth Auckland has a busy time in front of it. A big city outgrows its services as fast as a boy outgrows his pants. London has never caught up; nor has Sydney. In proportion, Auckland's problems are as great. As an advantage, she has their experience to work on. Big cities are costly to administer. Welcome as they have been to a house-hunting populace, the spread of State house suburbs on the outskirts of the city has entailed considerable worry to those who have the task of planning and running the city as an economic unit, with as little cost to the ratepayers as possible. The point is that while the Housing Department, by going out into the open spaces beyond existing city outskirts, reduces its costs by acquiring cheaper sections, the ultimate result may be a heavy burden on city financial resources.

"On existing street frontages in the urban-zoned residential area already fully serviced, there are a total of 10,000 vacant sections. If other land in those same areas were subdivided, with minor extensions to existing services, another 15,000 sections could be provided. Why then, it is asked, is it necessary for the State Housing Department to go to the extreme outskirts of the city? Why, as the most notable example, is it necessary to undertake such a large scale extension to the city limits as is proposed in the Tamaki project, which will house 30,000 people? The land involved is at present zoned as rural land. It contains small farms, mostly producing for city consumption. In the normal way it would probably continue as rural land for up to 15 years. Erecting houses on it will take, ultimately, 2000 acres out of production. In addition to the erection of houses and other structures upon the area the projected Tamaki suburb will require a new main sewerage system, a main water supply extension, a main power extension, a main gas supply extension, a main telephone extension, a main roading and transport extension, and a major development of reserves — all involving a capital outlay running into millions.

"Though it can be argued that the city will reap the benefit in increased resources from the rating of the area, experience has shown that capital costs cannot be recovered while existing services are not being fully utilised. The result, ultimately, would be an increase in rates over the whole city area. That is part of the 'behind-the-scenes' story of city extensions, and has to do, of course, with only the financial side of the question. That is why the city, while agreeing in principle to transfer the area from the rural land to the urban land zone of development, is first demanding that the State should undertake certain capital commitments in the area. Were the housing situation not so desperate there might be stronger opposition to the project, for it can be argued, too, that attempts to solve the housing problem by extending the city limits have a tendency to set back slum clearance, and the rebuilding of decadent areas. It removes some of the pressure on the owners of properties to clear and rebuild." [63]

Obstacles Ahead

In a later article, published by The Auckland Star on 27 July 1945, E K Green warned Aucklanders of the many obstacles ahead on the way to Utopia:

"Lest anyone be too lost in enthusiasm, and forget the constantly recurring cautionary notes, let's point to a few things of the past, and a few things of the present. The harbour bridge was first suggested…100 years ago. The Civic Centre project, an excellent one, was turned down by the ratepayers. The metropolitan drainage scheme? Well, look about and listen, and remember how the North Shore boroughs worst offenders in the disposal of crude sewage into harbour waters, were excluded from the scheme. And, have you ever heard the agitation that arises when a change in a tram stop, or the placement of a telephone box, is suggested?

"On top of all that, remember how matters may be affected by manpower and material shortages by possible booms and slumps, by changes in governmental and municipal policies, and by all the unpredictable things, like the affect that the growth of aviation – passenger, transport and private – may have on the distribution of population. One of the main factors affecting the growth of Auckland will be the realisation of its citizens that they have a magnificent heritage, and a future of great promise – one that demands courageous vision and action." [64]

Arthur James Dickson Rotary Club Address

Arthur James Dickson had been appointed as Auckland's first design engineer in 1936 and City Engineer in 1944, a post he held until his retirement in 1969. He chaired the Technical Advisory Committee of the Auckland Regional Planning Authority for 20 years and was elected president of the New Zealand Institution of Engineers in 1948. [65]

Some of E K Green's frustration at the lack of any co-ordinated town planning and the effects it was having on the city's infrastructure was repeated by Arthur Dickson during an address to the Auckland Rotary Club on 26 November 1945, part of which included:

"In the Auckland Metropolitan area the works of town planners had been difficult and confusing because of the multiplicity of local authorities whose boundaries had little or no relationship to topographical and physical features or to social and economic units, said the city engineer, Mr A. J. Dickson, when addressing the Auckland Rotary Club this afternoon. There had been vexing delays, he added. The city has a provisional town planning scheme which was presented to the Town Planning Board in 1939, but this was held up pending completion of a metropolitan scheme, said Mr. Dickson.

"A metropolitan ways and means committee was set up and a draft metropolitan scheme prepared, but owing to frustrations and difficulties it was necessary to recast the set-up of the organisation. This has been done and it is expected that a staff will be appointed in the near future with the support of all the local authorities, except perhaps one or two. I hope, therefore, that the city will have its scheme approved within a reasonable time provided there are no further complications arising out of the requirements of still wider fields of planning, such as regional and national.

"If only the truth were realised that with town planning better cities could be built at the same cost as were the present ones [then] town planning would have made more progress in the Dominion and in Auckland, continued Mr Dickson. Auckland, he said, is a city endowed by nature, but we have almost caught up with nature's bounty. Our good fortune may have blinded us to what we ourselves can do, for the inevitable decay has set in and we are backward in our planning. We have rapidly filled up our immediate open spaces and polluted our watercourses and harbours and left totally inadequate provision for open spaces and civic amenities.

"Traffic arteries are becoming congested and the car parking problem yearly becomes more acute. There are large residential areas falling into decadence and measures we have introduced for these are ten years too late. Living conditions are congested due to the serious shortage of houses. An electrified suburban railway system would assist in taking traffic off the streets, said Mr Dickson. The need for playing fields is urgent when our people have more time at their disposal than ever before and it is certain that the cultural, educational and recreational side of civic life must receive much more emphasis than in the past.

"We live in an age of perplexity in respect of planning in this country, added Mr Dickson. The reported statement of the Prime Minister last week makes it clear that the Organisation for National Development was a seven days wonder. There is no doubt the Government is faced with difficult circumstances as an aftermath of war. It must make immediate plans to meet any emergency and I cannot see how it can delegate its authority to any other body. Neither am I impressed by any set-up which would further complete an already top-heavy system of local government. What we want is simplification." [66]

Organisation for National Development, Auckland Regional Planning Organisation, and Auckland Metropolitan Planning Committee

As the name implies, the Organisation for National Development was a central planning entity established early in 1944 as a branch of the Prime Minister's Department to "…set in motion machinery to plan and coordinate the economic transition to peacetime conditions and the subsequent development of industrial activity. The Organisation for National Development…sponsored the formation of some twenty-five autonomous bodies, known as Regional Planning Councils, whose functions [were] to examine and advise upon both long-term and immediate projects for the development of their regions and the promotion of full employment therein." [67]

By the end of 1945, the Organisation for National Development would be disbanded but, in the meantime, the Auckland district was left with its surrogates, the 'Auckland Regional Planning Organisation' and the 'Auckland Metropolitan Planning Committee'. Obviously, neither entity could make many decisions that did not affect the territory of the other. Something had to be done, as reported by the Auckland Star on 25 July 1945:

"Confusion as to the respective functions of the Auckland Regional Planning Organisation and the Auckland Metropolitan Planning Committee is expected to be clarified at a conference of representatives of district local authorities in the Town Hall on August 14. Following the recent setting up of the regional and metropolitan organisations, the various committees were convened, said the Mayor, Mr Allum, chairman of the Auckland Regional Planning Council, this morning. It became apparent at the outset that a grave possibility of duplication and conflict existed in the performance of the functions and activities of the organisations and that authoritative advice was needed as to how such functions and activities could be reconciled.

"It was also felt, continued Mr Allum, that as the organisations were of an advisory character and had no statutory authority, legislation should be sought to put them on a sound statutory basis and thus ensure that the results of their work would not prove abortive, as had so often been the case with similar endeavours in the past.

"It had been also pointed out that had it not been for the prior existence and activities of the Auckland Metropolitan Planning Committee the co-ordination of planning activities in the whole region would have been brought under a single organisation, as had been done in the case of other regions in the Dominion, continued Mr Allum. If it were considered desirable it would not be too late to resolve the co-ordination of planning activities into one organisation. This could be achieved by absorbing the metropolitan organisation with proper representation into the regional organisation or by expanding the functions and activities of the metropolitan organisation to embrace the whole region." [68]

Planning Confusion Reigned

But despite the almost a clean slates before them; when the need for clear direction was needed to employ thousands of returning servicemen on worthwhile infrastructure projects, planning confusion reigned. Material for infrastructure and for industries still to be fired up would be short for a while so there was time for planning discussion and the right decisions to be made. If only the planning boffins and politicians could agree on the parameters of their deliberations and just which of their organisations should make those decisions. By September 1945, the debate as to whether or not the Metropolitan Planning Committee should amalgamate with the Regional Planning Organisation continued:

"The desirability of amalgamation with the Auckland Metropolitan Planning Committee was the subject of prolonged discussion at a meeting of the Auckland Regional Planning Organisation this morning (4 September 1945). The meeting, which was presided over by the Mayor, Mr Allum, was addressed on points at issue by Mr J. W. Mawson, Town Planning Officer to the Organisation for National Development. Mr Allum said that the suggestion was that either the Metropolitan Committee or the Regional Committee absorbs the other body. It was also intended that the meeting should discuss the question of seeking legislation to enable the final organisation to put its plans into effect.

"The chairman of the Auckland Local Bodies' Association, Mr I. J. Goldstine, said that the setup in Auckland differed greatly from that in other parts of the Dominion. While the two authorities, Town and Regional, might be suitable for other parts it would seem that they were unnecessary in Auckland. His personal view was that the expansion of the metropolitan organisation would be the most satisfactory solution.

"Mr A. S. Bailey said that the metropolitan committee envisaged the zoning of the whole metropolitan area. The initial work of the original committee had come under the heading of zoning, access, and open spaces. The question of regional development covered a far wider field. He was quite satisfied that under those three headings lay the main work of the metropolitan committee. If they were to spend money and then have the whole scheme capsized by the opposition of one or more local bodies they would, 'like the man with the barrow,' have their work still in front of them.

"Mr Allum said…he would move that the Auckland Metropolitan Committee be requested to carry on work in the metropolitan district, but be invited to join the Regional Planning Organisation, and in any case confer on matter of mutual interest…the motion was carried. After further discussion on the question of seeking legislation making it compulsory for local bodies to comply with the metropolitan plan when completed, it was decided that the matter be deferred." [69]

Local Government (Parliamentary Select) Committee

As long as the two Planning Committees failed to agree on how they could amalgamate, there could be little hope for the integration of regional and town planning and even less chance that Auckland's local bodies would unite under one municipal banner. Meanwhile, on the national front, the Local Government (Parliamentary Select) Committee, appointed in April 1944, tabled its report in September 1945. The report's observations about town planning included:

"We are concerned with the preparation and lack of progress which has been made in the town-planning schemes, and we think a forward policy should be adopted in this regard, particularly in view of the major developments which are expected in post-war years." [59]

The report comprehensively detailed the origins of local body development and the country's need for community government and the development of local responsibility during times of limited communication between those communities. However, it was the view of the Committee that things had long since changed and "…it will be apparent that there is a case for a detailed review of local-body boundaries and functions within the Dominion. We have considered it our function to decide if a case exists for such redrawing of boundaries and redistribution of functions, and we have no hesitation at all in saying that this problem is of extreme urgency if local government is to minister effectively to the development of the Dominion in the future." [59]

Naturally, Auckland received special mention in the Select Committee's report:

"We think it is necessary…to say something specific about the problems of Auckland…In the Auckland metropolitan area, for instance, there are fourteen territorial local authorities. In addition, there are at least six ad hoc bodies dealing with specific problems. At one of our hearings we were informed that there are some 284 members in these local authorities. In addition, there will be twenty separate administrative staffs, twenty offices and necessary appointments, and series of elections. Four of the ad hoc boards have been called into existence solely because of this division of territorial control. These are the Auckland Transport Board, the Auckland Milk Board, the Auckland Metropolitan Drainage Board, and probably the Auckland Power Board.

"We do not think it is a legitimate argument for the continuance of these bodies that their actual administrative costs are lower than those of the Auckland City Council. As we stated right at the beginning of this report, government has no justification as such, and there is no virtue in the multiplicity of governing authorities. If simplicity can be obtained with as close a relationship as possible with the people served then it is better that there should be as few as possible local governing authorities in existence.

"The question of the amenities provided by suburban local authorities in the Auckland area was discussed at some length, and some of these authorities maintained that they did actually provide certain of the amenities necessary for their citizens, but the fact remains that many of these amenities are supplied and paid for by the citizens of the Auckland City territory, and are used generally by the people of the Auckland metropolitan area.

"For instance, Auckland City is responsible for the water supply for the whole area. The fact that the suburban local authorities have at times suggested the setting-up of a Water Board is merely another illustration of the fact that the Auckland metropolitan area is a single economic unit. There would be no value at this stage in reiterating all the evidence which has been adduced. We are, however, firmly of the opinion that the Auckland problem requires immediate attention." [59]

Local Government Committee Opposition

But despite the Select Committee's view that 'immediate attention' was necessary, the effects of peace-time adjustments delayed any local-body, reform initiatives. The delay also allowed those many of a more parochial mind to entrench – particularly those who felt content with their lot, such as the borough of Newmarket's Town Clerk, who expressed his opposition to the Committee's findings in November 1945:

"The findings of the [Parliamentary Select] committee and its expressed views on the question of metropolitan Auckland are definitely opposed to the weight of evidence submitted on the subject, said Mr H. Wilson, town clerk of Newmarket, in a report to a meeting of the Borough Council last night, commenting on the Local Government Committee's report recently submitted to Parliament. No evidence was presented to the committee by any responsible body of citizens, other than the Labour Representation Committee, to indicate that there was any desire for a change in the form of local government on the part of the people of Auckland, said Mr Wilson. From the nature of the committee's report and recommendations it is obvious that it came to Auckland as commissions in the past have done, with preconceived ideas about the solution of what is termed the local body problem in Auckland.

"Mr Wilson said he could visualise the commission recommending the creation of a super-city form of government in Auckland, in which all utilities, essential services and local affairs would be centralised in a central unit with headquarters in Queen Street or thereabouts. That would mean the end of local government as they knew it and there were very definite opinions regarding the wisdom or otherwise of introducing that form of government. The attempt which would be made to take away from the people the right to self-determination should be resisted by the metropolitan local bodies with all the power and force at their disposal, Mr Wilson said.

"The interests of the people and their local government are closely interwoven and we are sure that compulsion applied to the local authorities in the Auckland metropolitan area will be bitterly resented by the electors. In the case of Newmarket, the people are intensely proud of the achievements of their local authority, and 90 per cent would be strongly opposed to any proposal in the direction of amalgamation." [70]

Local Government Commission Finally Established

Nevertheless, as recommended by the Select Committee, "…that a permanent Commission be established, charged with the duty of reviewing in general local-body boundaries and functions in the Dominion," [59 p.157] the Government finally established a Local Government Commission by means of the Local Government Commission Act 1946, enacted on 12 October 1946.

The Commission, consisting of four members chaired by a Supreme Court Judge, was deemed to be a Commission of Inquiry with broad powers to require the attendance of witnesses and the production of documents. The Commission was required to "…review from time to time the functions and districts of local authorities and to inquire into proposals and prepare schemes for the reorganization thereof, and generally to review and to report to the Minister upon such matters relating to local government as may be determined by the Commission or referred to it by the Minister." [71]

Clause 13(1) of the Act explained that "A reorganization scheme under this Act may provide for one or more of the following matters:

a) The union into one district of two or more adjoining districts, whether districts of the same kind or not:

(b) The merger of any district in any other district:

(c) The constitution of a new district or districts:

(d) The abolition of any district or districts:

(e) The transfer of all or any of the functions of any local authority to any other local authority:

(f) Any alteration of the boundaries of adjoining districts:

(g) The conversion of a district into a district of a different kind." [71]

The Shape of Things to Come

In 1946, the Ministry of Works also issued its own regional planning document. Entitled '*The shape of things to come*', "…The plan included completion of the circular rail route on Auckland's central isthmus, plus a roughly four-kilometre long inner-city tunnel that had also been mooted since the 1920s. The Southern and Western radial corridors would cut across the major loop, facilitating transfers." [72]

In his Public Works Statement to Parliament that year, the Minister of Works, Robert Semple, explained his Government's reasons for publishing the long-term plan: "The primary purpose in making known the Government's intentions in regard to developmental works is the realization that, without knowledge of the Government's intentions, it is scarcely possible for local authorities and for private interests to plan safely ahead.

"This is particularly the case in urban areas, and the review of all proposals conducted by the Ministry of Works has shown that it is not possible to regard the works of Government Departments in isolation and that these must be considered jointly with those of local authorities and of private people. It is hoped that, by enlisting the support of local authorities on a regional basis, the Government will have much valuable advice bearing upon its own works, and by this method in time a broad developmental plan for each region will be prepared in which the interests not only of the Government, but of local authorities and of primary and secondary industry, will be fully observed." [73]

Central and Local Government Collaboration

In July 1946, the Commissioner of Works, E R McKillop, also presented a report on the activities of the Ministry of Works covering the period from its establishment in 1943 to 31 March 1946. This report outlined the Ministry's expectations for post-war town and metropolitan planning:

"It is hoped now that with the general supervision of all planning activities by the Ministry of Works, and the attachment of the secretariat of the Town-planning Board to this office, much better progress will be made in the field of town and metropolitan planning. It is of the greatest importance that sporadic and unplanned growth should no longer be allowed to take place.

"The Dominion has reached a stage in its development when proper planning, instead of being regarded as a luxury, has become an absolute necessity. As urban populations expand, an increasing importance must inevitably become attached to the problems of zoning industrial and residential areas; locating of community facilities, schools, and play areas; steering great traffic arteries away from residential and shopping areas; providing suitable transport, services, traffic outlets, water-supply, and similar services and amenities.

"Contiguous both to Wellington and Auckland there are opportunities for planning in areas now being opened up which, if not taken advantage of, will result in unbalanced development and consequently huge economic loss.

"It is an extraordinary fact that expenditure on planning work has in the past often been prevented or even viewed with disfavour. When it is recognized that for many years ahead the Dominion may expect an expansion of urban housing at a rate of some ten thousand houses per annum, involving an investment of considerably more than £20,000,000 per annum in total urban capital, and the work of more than thirty thousand men on the site and in the various supply industries, it will be realized how very important it is to secure the provision at the earliest possible date of town and metropolitan plans to guide the pattern of development, and, on the other hand, what considerable sums can be wasted if this large expenditure is allowed to take place in the absence of co-ordinated plans.

"The greatest problem to be faced in the evolution of these co-ordinated plans, a problem which arises from the multiplicity of local authorities, is the tendency of each local authority to disregard the relation which must exist between its own developments and those of neighbouring local authorities." [74]

In conclusion, Mr McKillop emphasised the importance of collaboration between national and local planning:

"Prior to the establishment of the Ministry of Works there was a tendency to regard Government works, like the functional activity of Government Departments, in isolation. Similarly, local-body works and developments by private enterprise were separately conceived and separately carried out. It should be clear that the operations of these separate agencies have the same basic origin and purpose – namely, to satisfy the needs of the people in any given area or region – the needs of the same people. All works and developments which are initiated by the Government or other interests are therefore complementary and must be fitted into the same economic and social pattern.

"When they are completed all these developments contribute to the creation of the same physical environment, so as to meet the needs of the community in a convenient and orderly way. Even though a development may be conceived on the national scale, at least part of its effect is always local. On the other hand, locally conceived development must conform, where necessary, to national plans. It is essential, therefore, that urban, regional, and nation-wide plans should all be evolved in constant collaboration and with complete mutual understanding.

"Successful co-ordination of the many interests involved in the evolution of any comprehensive plan of physical development is perhaps the most important determinant of its success as a plan. In order that this co-ordination may in fact be achieved it is clear that a co-ordinating authority must exist. By placing the responsibility for physical planning with the Ministry of Works, the Government has made this Ministry responsible for securing that practical co-ordination, without which physical planning work could not be successfully done.

"Town and extra-urban planning are obligatory and are the responsibility of existing local authorities within the boundaries of their own districts. Regional planning as contemplated by the Town-planning Amendment Act, 1929, is based on a voluntary combination of a number of local authorities, and the boundary of the planning area is a matter for determination by the Town-planning Board upon the recommendation of the authorities concerned." [74]

Ministry of Works Statement 1947

During 1947, the Ministry of Works absorbed the Public Works Department and began administering the Town Planning Act 1926 and its 1929 amendments. By way of his 1947 Statement, the Minister, the Hon. Robert Semple, elaborated on his government's intention to advance the country's regional planning with the inclusion of its many local bodies:

"In completing the announcement of the regional schedules of works, popularly, but erroneously, termed 'ten-year plans,' I have faced throughout the country audiences comprising every shade of political thought, and there has been no criticism whatever of the principle of regional planning which, although on the statute-book since 1929, has made little progress. The unusual circumstances following the war required a review of accumulated Government and local-body works, and presented a unique opportunity for the Government in publishing the review to put the principles of regional planning into practical effect.

"Briefly it represented an earnest endeavour on the part of Government to associate local bodies with the forward development of the country by publishing in a comprehensive manner, as a first step only, works currently under consideration. These should now be reviewed by regional authorities in conjunction with the Government

Departments concerned and with all relative information available regarding the natural resources of each particular region.

"This initial step in the planning process should be followed by investigation, planning, and preparation of actual drawings and specifications according to the priority determined from year to year. I hope that plans for the future development of each region will be built up, and when that is done we will have for the first time some conception of what New Zealand can be like in the future.

"I cannot too strongly stress the need to realize that if we are to make advances in this field of development linked with full employment, the Government's policy to associate Central Government with local authorities constituted through regional or metropolitan authorities is of the utmost importance. New Zealand has reached a stage in its progress when the development proposals of Central and local Government, and indeed those of major private interests, must be considered together.

"Improved transport and communications have entirely altered the relations local bodies have to each other, and we cannot wait for local bodies to argue out individual differences whilst rivers, floods, and other natural forces take no notice of administrative boundaries. Land-development, highways, railways, aerodromes, harbours, and similar works can only be decided with due regard to all interests which will use these facilities.

"The Government therefore finds it impossible to plan efficiently ahead on the basis of representations from a very large number of individual local bodies where these are not associated on some basis of community of interest. Nor should it be left to the Government alone—local people know more about their districts than anyone else, and as they have to live amongst and use the works provided they are entitled to some say in the matter." [75]

In order to facilitate this central/local government co-operation, the Ministry of Works undertook to provide trained personnel to local authorities as necessary:

"In one form or another, assistance has been given by the Ministry of Works in regard to the town-planning proposals of most of the local authorities in the Dominion. Having regard to the lack of independent professional advice, town-planning schemes have been prepared for a number of smaller local bodies at their direction and charge, while many more are now in the course of preparation." [76]

Town-planning Division Unable to Cope with Demand

However, by 1949 the Ministry was finding it difficult to cope with the demand to provide the expertise required:

"During the year the staff of the Town-planning Division has been strengthened, but has been unable to cope with the increasing demands for their services. While primarily the responsibility of the Division is the administration of the Town-planning Act 1926, relating to town-planning generally, and the Town-planning Amendment Act, 1929, relating to regional planning, many specific problems of physical development, both within the Ministry and originating from other Departments, are referred to the Division for investigation and report.

"Legally, the responsibility for planning throughout New Zealand falls upon the local bodies concerned, and the Division, in effect, operates both to assist the local bodies with their planning schemes and to ensure that Government development proposals fit in with the local-body plans.

"Pursuant to the requests of the Municipal Association, planning officers have been made available when asked for by individual local bodies to assist with their town-planning schemes. There is a general recognition throughout New Zealand of the need for town planning and the requests for assistance are in excess of the resources of the present staff. In addition to this, a number of local authorities have themselves prepared plans which have been submitted for provisional approval to the Town-planning Board.

"These are referred to the Division for investigation and report back to the Board…The Division has been at a disadvantage in its day-to-day work owing to the absence of up-to-date standards for town-planning practice in New Zealand. Until recently no research has been done on the problems of planning arising in New Zealand, and as conditions here are in very many respects so different from those in other countries it has been necessary to conduct original researches." [77]

Town-planning Amendment Act 1948

In order to enable the Minister of Works to administer the provisions of the principal Town-planning Act, the Town-planning Amendment Act 1948 was enacted on 26 November of that year. The amendment clarified certain provisions of the principal Act and provided the Minister of Works and local authorities with additional powers, such as for the acquisition of land: "In any case where a town-planning scheme or an extra-urban planning scheme has been finally approved by the (Town-planning) Board…" [78]

Local Government Commission Fails

Just as the Ministry of Works failed to adequately provide the planning expertise sought by individual local bodies, the Local Government Commission also failed to provide the way forward to their organised integration. Despite the Local Government Select Committee's call for 'immediate attention', few of its recommendations were proceeded with:

"Despite the intentions of the original parliamentary inquiry, the first Commission was unable to carry out wholesale reorganisation. However it did make some modest changes. It successfully negotiated the amalgamation of six Northland Hospital Boards by 1954. It was able to significantly improve the procedures for boundary changes between authorities and create a body of standard practice. In particular, it aimed to prevent endless tinkering with boundaries by ensuring that any change was sufficient to meet community needs at least 15 years into the future. It also educated local authorities on the need to apply proper town and country planning principles to boundary changes instead of making them at whim, as had been the case." [79]

Local Government Commission Report

According to the Local Government Commission Report for the year ended 31 March 1948, the Commission's lack of progress was due to its concentration on "…the redrawing, where necessary, of the boundaries of local authorities in the Dominion so as to provide a series of administrative areas which will enable the local authorities to give to their inhabitants the maximum service without destroying that important factor of the local self-interest which is the basis of all local government.

"This is obviously a long-term programme. It cannot be proceeded with except after exhaustive investigations, and it is important to remark at this stage that the Commission has not approached its task with any preconceived idea as to the necessity for any specific change. It considers that the interests of the people of New Zealand as a whole should be paramount. While it does not consider that vested interests should stand in the way of necessary changes, it realizes that local government can become too distant from the people it serves and hence become possibly bureaucratic rather than democratic in essence." [80]

In other words, the recommendation of the Parliamentary Select Committee that a consolidation of Auckland's local bodies was urgently needed was determined by the Local Government Commission to be not quite so urgent after all. Like so many costly inquiries, before and since, the findings of yet another were disregarded so as not to upset any parochial interests – at least not until additional *exhaustive investigations* are undertaken – all ostensibly to preserve the democratic rights and interests of individual communities.

Correlation and Integration – A Study in City Building

On 24 February 1949, Arthur James Dickson, addressed a meeting of the influential New Zealand Engineers Institution of which he was then president. His address, entitled *Correlation and Integration – A Study in City Building*, was subsequently published in the May 1949 edition of the Institution's journal, New Zealand Engineering.

Similar to his previous address to the Auckland Rotary Club in 1945, this speech covered a broad range of topics including local and national government town-planning responsibilities, urbanisation, and the transport advancements that had influenced the decentralization of cities such as Auckland since the beginning of the twentieth century. Some parts of Arthur Dickson's speech included:

"It would be admitted…that cities had grown rapidly and haphazardly in recent times. At first centralizing forces held unrivalled sway, but later decentralizing forces altered the situation and added to the confusion. Centralizing influences were industrialization and the mechanical age, steam power, railroads. Electricity had both a centralizing and decentralizing influence. The internal combustion engine and improvement in road design had done more than any other factors to decentralize. Indeed, it was only since the year 1900 that the so-called 'explosion' of cities had taken place.

"This intensive industrialization and urbanization had created many unsolved problems. The outstanding point about urban growth during the last quarter of a century had been the disorderly development of the urban perimeter and the decline of older central districts. Factories shifted from central to marginal sites. There were no adequate plans and control for decentralizing residential and industrial uses; nor did plans exist to fill the central 'vacuum' which consequently degenerated into slums…

"In nearly all growing cities the business centre had not kept pace with growth, with consequent over-concentration of employment and business at the centre. The main traffic arteries leading from the centre to the suburbs were substantially the same roads as existed when the city first began. Large numbers of workers, shoppers and other travellers were destined to spend long intervals of time travelling many miles between their homes and the city centre.

"While populations teemed into cities, rural tracts remained comparatively empty; 63 per cent, of New Zealand's population lived in towns and cities. This trend was made possible by the agricultural surpluses of a scientific and mechanical age. This was an era of production as distinct from any previous era, and the rural population and urban population had become reciprocally dependent. Cities had become a part of a country's basic social and economic framework, and were, therefore, just as much the concern of the National Government as of local government.

"The problems in city building, continued the president, snowballed with the leaping bounds of the Machine Age, and things reached such an impasse that something had to be done. The spark kindled at the turn of the century had grown and grown and burnt its way into the mind of authority to such an extent that it was now recognized in all progressive countries that the planning of new cities and the rehabilitation of old from the ravages of disintegration, urban blight and slums, had become a social and economic problem of the first order.

"It was becoming increasingly recognized that the vast problems could not be solved in a superficial manner without recourse to organic principles. For instance, when traffic congestion became impossible, it was no use merely widening a street to let more flow in. It was no use making matters worse by attempting to maintain land values by intensifying building development. It was no use clearing decadent areas without removing the cause of blight. Putting parking meters in the streets or prohibiting parking did not cure the parking problem.

"In New Zealand few, if any, town planning schemes had exceeded the zoning stage. The planning of the main metropolitan areas was largely uncorrected and haphazard. There existed in a jumbled picture Government planning through various departmental agencies such as the Public Works Department, the Railways Department and the Housing Department, and planning through a number of separate municipal and other local authorities, and, as likely as not, a number of *ad hoc* local authorities for electric power, gas, transport, drainage and hospitals. Was comprehensive and efficient planning possible under such divided control?

"New Zealand town planning legislation did not confer powers to anything like this extent, and judging from recent amendments to the Town Planning Act, it would almost seem that the State was reluctant to give local authorities the powers so obviously needed, but would prefer to do the work itself. In central business district planning special attention must be given to the general accessibility of the central district and ease of traffic movement, to the adequacy and convenience of off-street parking areas, to the convenience and safety of pedestrian traffic, to the provision of ample light and air in all buildings, to the correlation and grouping of land uses to give maximum convenience and efficiency, and to the external appearance and grouping of buildings.

"There should be a minimum of conflict between pedestrian and vehicular traffic. The proposed density of building accommodation was a vital factor. The requirements of a successful shopping centre could not be supplied in streets which were also main traffic routes.

"In his concluding remarks the president touched lightly on a number of facets of his subject. He referred briefly to the Auckland Advisory Committee which, in preparing a master plan for the area, had been faced with very real difficulties owing to the multiplicity of autonomous authorities involved. Furthermore, it had been quite impossible for this organization to bring down a plan until authorities responsible for such vital things as main highways, railways, mass transport, aerodromes and harbour facilities, had made up their minds." [81]

Central Government Change

In December 1949, the First Labour Government was replaced by the First National Government and things changed. Not just a change of policy makers, but an almost complete change of political philosophy, culture, and direction. Labour's socialist principles which, in the broadest of terms, encompassed State development of housing and infrastructure, was quickly replaced by what Christopher Harris referred to in his 2005 paper, 'Slow Train Coming', as 'market liberalism' – specifically, "...the view that land is essentially a commodity to be used privately." [72]

"One could make a case for the proposition that the events following 1949 represented a direct or indirect takeover of the national urban planning agenda by Auckland elites who, in another capacity, and at different times, continued to plead with the central state for transit, provided only that it was not funded out of the profits of speculation or associated with state planning of land development." [72]

Of course, this was nothing short of a continuation of the laissez-faire attitude of the first colonists, and particularly that of Auckland's land speculators...

Public Transport

When the newly-established Auckland Transport Board acquired the tramway and motor-omnibus undertaking of the Auckland City Council as a going concern on 16th January 1929, the acquisition included some 70 operational omnibuses of various makes and passenger-carrying capacities, then mainly used as feeder services to various tramway termini.

Public Demand for Modernity

In the beginning, the integration of bus and tram services proved profitable for the Transport Board, as demonstrated by its accounts for the 1939-1940 financial year showing another "...surplus of £7,142/10/9...The revenue for the year at £678,351 shows an increase of £31,334 over the previous year, while the year's expenses...at £671,208, show an increase of £26,013." [82]

Nevertheless, the Transport Board continued to look to the future; to what its new Chairman, W H Nagle, identified as the *public demand for modernity* in his Annual Report for the year ended 31 March 1940: "If the Board can take some effective steps to assist the remaining sinking funds to meet their loan obligations at due date then successive Boards will be in a better position to consider a change-over to a more modern form of transport at an earlier date than at present seems possible. Whether this trend to modern vehicles is justified or not can certainly be argued on economic grounds, but however much it can be proved that tramways are more suitable and cheaper than an alternative form of transport the Board must in due course be prepared to meet the public demand for modernity. I am sure that members will agree that this position requires full and serious consideration." [82]

Taxi Licensing In Auckland

As well as the increasing use of private motor transport, the Auckland Transport Board also faced some competition from the number of unregulated taxis plying Auckland streets. However, just as the buses had been brought into line in by the Motor Omnibus Traffic Act 1926, by the end of the 1930s, so had the taxi industry, as described by Transport Board Chairman, Henry Mason, in his Annual Report for the Year ending 31 March 1938:

"The question of taxi licensing was the subject of a special enquiry by a Committee appointed by the Government. This Committee recommended that taxis be brought within the provisions of the 'Transport Licensing Act, 1931,' and that the licensing of taxis in Auckland should be conducted by the Auckland Transport Board as Metropolitan Licensing Authority. The Auckland City Council, however, feeling that it should be a licensing authority so far as taxis are concerned, appealed to the Board for its assistance in obtaining legislation accordingly. The Board gave full consideration to the Council's request, but declined it on the grounds that the Board concurred with the recommendation of the Committee of Enquiry above referred to. Legislation will be necessary if effect is to be given to the foregoing recommendation of the Committee of Enquiry." [34]

Transport Licensing Amendment Act, 1939

Licensing of the taxi industry was effected by means of the Transport Licensing Amendment Act 1939 which appointed the Auckland Transport Board as the Metropolitan Licensing Authority. The Board then sought to organise Auckland's taxis as described in the Board's Annual Report for the year ended 31 March 1940: "The Transport Licensing Amendment Act, 1939, required that all Auckland taxis should be licensed by the Auckland Transport Board as Metropolitan Licensing Authority.

After a prolonged public hearing extending over a period of three months, licenses were granted to some 324 operators. At this hearing the Authority received extensive evidence in regard to savings which might possibly be effected by the establishment of one organisation, and when making its decision to grant taxi cab service licenses, it resolved:–

"That all licensees in respect of public taxicabs be informed as follows:

(a) That the evidence submitted shows the Authority that the taxi cab business in Auckland can be and should be organised in a more efficient manner, so as to prevent duplication, waste and dead mileage.

(b) That the authority proposes to give licensees an opportunity to confer and endeavour to agree among themselves upon a plan of re-organisation, and if substantial unanimity can be secured for such a plan, and it appears to be in the public interest, the Authority will adopt and implement it.

(c) That for the purpose of facilitating such conference the Authority will convene a meeting of licensees as early as practicable.

(d) That failing the adoption of a satisfactory scheme by licensees by the 1st May next, and unless altered circumstances have arisen, the Authority will take steps to introduce a scheme and to amend all licenses so as to require licensees to conform to its provisions.

"In pursuance of this resolution a meeting of all licensees concerned was held on the 7th March, when a Committee of Licensees was set up to report on the matter to the Authority. Finality has not yet been reached, but it is hoped that the coming year will see the industry organised in such a way as to best serve the interests of the public and those engaged in the industry." [82]

Now that the Auckland Transport Board had full authority to license and to regulate both its bus and taxi competitors, there was every incentive to sustain the profitability of its own tram services. For the financial year ended 31 March 1941 the Board recorded "…a surplus of £6,953/16/2…The revenue for the year at £746,381 shows an increase of £68,030 over the previous year, while the year's expenses…at £739,427 show an increase of £68,219." [83]

Clunking Tramcars

As can be seen from the results for the 1941 financial year, despite the greater use of the trams by Aucklanders and the resulting increase in revenue, this increase was offset by an almost equal increase in the year's operating expenses. While much of the operational cost was attributable to maintenance costs, wartime shortages of material, such as steel, ensured that tramcars remained somewhat dilapidated. This added to the public's perception that the tramways was fast becoming an antiquated mode of transport; the clunking tramcars seemingly always in the way of more modern alternatives.

Even the free tram service was not immune from the more modern traffic competing for road space, as described by the Auckland Star on 10 February 1941:

"Consideration of a proposal to remove the terminus of the free tram service used by the Farmers' Trading Company to a point off Pitt Street further down Beresford Street was deferred for three months by the Auckland Transport Board to-day. The chairman, Mr W. H. Nagle, said that he and Mr L. C. McClintock had discussed the matter with representatives of the Auckland City Council, who had requested that the tram stop should be moved to the single line further down Beresford Street to permit a free flow of traffic.

"Mr A. S. Bailey said he would like to see the request acceded to, as a difficult problem for car parking had arisen at this point. Something should be done, said Mr J. A. C. Allum. When the trams stopped to disembark or embark passengers, traffic was held up. The stop should be moved to a point where it would not be an interference.

"The manager and engineer, Mr A. E. Ford, said he had watched the traffic at the busiest period and was of opinion that the traffic was not congested at this point to any considerable degree. While there was a measure of obstruction when people were alighting, the position was not serious. A motion by Mr Bailey and Mr Allum that the City Council's request be acceded to was defeated, the amendment by Messrs Anderson and Sayegh deferring decision for three months being carried." [84]

Future Transport Development

The Transport Board was not immune to the need to modernise its fleet, as indicated by its Chairman, William Nagle, in his Annual Report for the financial year ended 31 March 1941:

"As I pointed out in my last year's report, the comparatively short period of ten years was decided upon to enable the Board to consider a change-over to a more modern form of transport as soon as practicable…Although the war makes it impossible for the Board to effect any major alterations or additions to the undertaking, nevertheless a careful watch is being kept on the development, both industrial and residential, which is taking place in Auckland.

"One of the most important aspects of this development is that the suburbs in the last few years have tended to become self-contained shopping areas, with their own places of amusement, etc. The seriousness of this position is that while the morning and evening peak loads are maintained or even increased, the off-peak loading is reduced. In such circumstances, the value of the superior crush-carrying capacity of tramcars over any other road transport is once again demonstrated.

"As I pointed out in my last year's report, however, there is a definite trend throughout the world to replace the tram with a more modern form of transport. Whether this trend can be supported on economic grounds is open to argument, but it undoubtedly exists. The Board realises this and in its consideration of future transport development in Auckland it will give very serious thought to the increasing popularity of alternative forms of transport." [83]

War Rationing

In the meantime, the effects of war rationing resulted in a curtailment of many of the *alternative forms of transport* and a very large increase in tram patronage. This was reflected by the Transport Board accounts for the financial year ended 31 March 1942 which recorded "…a surplus of £20,077/15/11…The revenue for the year at £819,058 shows an increase of £72,677 over the previous year, while the year's expenses…at £798,980 show an increase of £59,553." [85]

In his Annual Report, the new Transport Board Chairman, Joseph (Joe) Callil Sayegh, described the wartime situation and suggested a number of ways in which the traffic problems could be alleviated:

"Due mainly to the benzine restrictions the number of passengers carried during the past year increased to such an extent that many new traffic problems were created. It was immediately noticeable that the morning peak increased substantially and in an effort to meet it the Board made arrangements for many more trams to go into traffic between the hours of 7 and 9 a.m.

"It was not possible to operate more trams during the evening peak as every available tram was already in service. I think it can be fairly claimed that the Board has done its utmost to provide the best possible service to meet a difficult situation. Many of the Board's passengers in 1941 had not been riders on trams for years past and I feel sure that while they found the tramway service was not as fast or comfortable as their own motor-cars, it was, nevertheless, a far more efficient and reliable one than they had imagined.

"While the problems of the past year have been coped with, I foresee many more arising during the coming year. The shortage of rubber is likely to be an even more serious factor than the shortage of benzine, while the two together will almost certainly mean that private cars will be laid up and a further demand will be made on the tramway service. It is, of course, impossible to obtain more rolling stock and the Board must accordingly investigate every method by which its system can increase the number of passengers carried.

"The most frequent suggestion is the staggering of working hours. I realise full well that compulsory staggering of hours will not be universally popular, but overseas experience has, I think, proved beyond doubt that such a scheme can increase the number of passengers which can be carried on a tramway system.

"A further innovation recently introduced overseas is the priority travel badge. These are issued to workers and entitle them to travel during peak hours, persons who are not holders of these badges being debarred from travelling until later in the day. I also noticed in a recent copy of the Transport World, an English journal dealing with passenger transport, that transverse seats in buses are being replaced by longitudinal seats. This alteration has the effect of reducing slightly the seating capacity, and at the same time increasing very considerably the standing capacity over what was previously allowed.

"Another suggestion recently made in England was that shopping hours should be fixed from 10 a.m. to 3 p.m. in order to keep shoppers off passenger service vehicles at peaks, but that suggestion was not brought into effect. The future will call for a thorough investigation by the Board of all methods by which a greater number of passengers can be carried." [85]

Joe Sayegh concluded his report with the observation that the wartime situation was definitely temporary and that the Board had no option but to plan for the future:

"There is no doubt in my mind that the increase in revenue and the consequent increase in surplus shown during the year under review has been mainly due to the benzine restrictions. I feel that while these restrictions are in force and with the further restriction on the use of motor-cars likely to be imposed by the shortage of tyres, the Board can expect its present revenue to continue.

"At the same time, I think it would be very unwise for the Board to expect that these conditions will last more than a limited period, and when conditions return to normal or even, perhaps, before that, the Board can expect a very substantial drop in its revenue. In the circumstances I feel sure the Board will agree that the careful planning and administration which it has exercised in the past must be continued in the future, if it is to carry out its responsibilities to the travelling public, the ratepayers and its employees." [85]

The Transport Board's 1942-1943 financial accounts continued to reflect the effect of wartime shortages on the travelling public – all to the benefit of immediate revenue but at what cost to long term operations?

"The revenue for the year at £950,621 shows an increase of £131,563 over the previous year…A surplus of £25,151 is shown for the year, which means that the balance of the Net Revenue Account is now £14,768 in credit, after having been for many years in debit." [86]

Provision for the Future - The Real Position

Joe Sayegh's Annual Report reminded readers of the realities and the difficulties to come:

"Reference to the Board's accounts shows that the revenue for the year has broken all previous records and also that the Board has made substantial additions to its Depreciation Reserve. To a layman these facts would seem to indicate that the net result of the year's working has been most satisfactory and has resulted in a large surplus. Now let me give the real position.

"It is true that the Board is enjoying a higher revenue, but it is, unfortunately, equally true that in earning the higher revenue the undertaking is being worn out rapidly – so rapidly that when the war ends a very large expenditure will be required to restore the tramway undertaking to its pre-war standard. If, as is more probable, the Board decides not to attempt to fully restore the tramways but instead to install a modern system, the requirements will be the same, namely, the Board should have on hand a very substantial sum as Depreciation Reserve, otherwise the new form of transport will be saddled with two sets of loans.

"The amount of the reserve as at present is barely sufficient to cover the accelerated depreciation and deferred maintenance caused by war conditions. Failure on the Board's part to make proper provision can have only one result – that when the day comes either to restore the tramways to pre-war standard, or to install a new system, further loans will be required to provide substantially the same service as is provided to-day. This, in its turn will mean increased costs which generally can only be met by adjustments either at the expense of the public or of the employees, or perhaps at the expense of both. Thus the Board's policy of building up its reserves is imperative for the protection of the ratepayers and the travelling public on the one hand, and the employees on the other." [86]

By the end of the 1944 financial year, Auckland's tram services continued to trade profitably – at least on paper: "The year's surplus of £26,864 means that the Net Revenue Account is now £41,632 in credit. It will perhaps be news to many that the Net Revenue Account showed a debit balance from the inception of the Board until the year ended 31st March, 1943." [87]

Record Number of Tram Passengers

However, in practical terms, the service was unable to cope with the extremes of demand and failed many commuters, despite the best efforts of the Transport Board: "The number of passengers carried during the year just closed has constituted an all-time record for the Auckland tramway system and the fact that the undertaking was able to cope with the traffic offering, bearing in mind war conditions, is due in no small measure to the excellent work performed by the Management and all employees. The Board is aware that considerable difficulty is experienced by the public in obtaining satisfactory transport during peak hours. This is a condition which unfortunately is likely to exist while petrol restrictions are in force. The Board has done its utmost to introduce schemes to spread the evening peak load, but has been unsuccessful in its endeavours." [87]

Transport Investigation Committee

Those endeavours included "…two attempts…to alleviate the serious position which peak loading has now reached…

"(1) Transport Investigation Committee – On 1st July, 1943, a Conference was called by his worship the Mayor of Auckland, J. A. C. Allum, Esq., to consider peak loading. The Conference was representative of all interests in the City and set up a Transport Investigation Committee to investigate all aspects of the problem…After many lengthy sittings, the Committee reluctantly came to the conclusion that the compulsory staggering of working hours was the most effective method of spreading the peak load, and it reported to His Worship the Mayor accordingly. I am advised that strong representations on these lines were made to the Government, but so far no move has been made to introduce the necessary powers sought by the Committee's recommendation.

"(2) Proposal to Introduce Priority Travel Badges – In view of the apparent failure of the Transport Investigation Committee to obtain the necessary powers for compulsory staggering of hours, I submitted to the Board an alternative proposal designed to ease the evening peak by discouraging as much as possible non-essential travel at that time. Briefly, the scheme was as follows:

(a) That a badge or pass be issued to all regular full-time workers whose finishing hours of work coincide with the evening peak period, viz., 4.15 – 5.30 p.m. Such tokens would preserve the rights of these workers to travel at ordinary fares during these hours;

(b) Non-holders of a token during the above period would be charged a minimum penal fare of 3d. in addition to the ordinary fare, all such penal fares to be paid at regular intervals to the Patriotic Fund…

"This scheme was submitted to the Minister of Transport, the Hon. J O'Brien, who gave his approval of its introduction for a trial period of 3 months. However, when it seemed that at last something would be attempted with the object of assisting the travelling public, the Board learned with disappointment that the Stabilisation Commission would not sanction the proposed penal fare for non-holders of badges. The Board is grateful to the Hon. Minister of Transport for his further efforts in trying to obtain the Commission's approval, but as nothing has been heard for some 2 months, I am afraid the Commission's decision must be taken as final…" [87]

Trolleybuses to Replace the Trams

As the war drew to a close, the Board knew that a great many of its current commuters would not continue to board the trams when the more modern alternatives, such as their motor vehicles, again became available. Therefore, if a viable proportion of the wartime patronage was to be retained, modern alternatives of its own had to be put in place as quickly as possible – as Board Chairman, William Nagle, described in his Annual Report for the year ended 31 March 1944:

"During the year the Board gave serious consideration to its post-war policy of passenger transport development in the metropolitan area. Its decisions were as follows:

"(1) That the trolley bus be approved as the new form of vehicle for the main part of the Auckland transport system;

"(2) That enquiries be made abroad regarding the possibilities of importing a number of completed or partly-completed trolley buses;

Should the result of the enquiries so justify, consideration be given to placing a tentative order for 50 vehicles, subject to confirmation upon, or shortly after, the declaration of peace;

"(3) That the necessary application be made to the Minister of Transport for authority to operate over the following routes: (a) Present tramway routes; (b) Proposed Buckland Road trolley bus route; (c) Proposed Waterview, Avondale trolley bus route; (d) Proposed Glen Innes trolley bus route; (e) Proposed Mt. Roskill trolley bus route; (f) Short sections on City streets to facilitate inter-route and turning movements.

"(4) That when such approval has been obtained, to take up the relevant matters with all civic and town planning authorities concerned.

"These are the essential preliminary steps and the action taken by the Board will ensure at the appropriate time the speedy construction and operation of the new service and the replacement of the present tramway service as quickly as sound finance and other factors incidental to the transition period will permit. It should be noted that the selection of the trolley bus in no way precludes the use of Diesel or any alternative vehicle in any area where their use can be proved to be economic and efficient.

"Further, all routes may be modified or revised in the light of the Government housing location and development, and any future expansion of the suburban railway system must also be taken into account. The steps thus decided upon will save the next Board considerable time and effort and secure early and up-to-date passenger transport for the citizens of Auckland." [87]

New Hospital Service

By 1945, few of the original motor-omnibuses acquired from the Auckland City Council in 1929 were operational and wartime restrictions made newer versions difficult to obtain, as the Transport Board learned on 18 June of that year:

"There doesn't seem to be a body in the country,' said the engineer and manager of the Auckland Transport Board, Mr A. E. Ford, this morning, when reporting to the board on his inquiries regarding the purchase of a bus for the board's new service to the Green Lane and Cornwall Park hospitals. Mr. Ford said the only worthwhile offer which had been made came from a motor company in Wellington, which quoted a chassis at £950 and body at £1950, the total price being £2900. The bus was a 33seater and of good type, and he recommended that the board purchase it, though it was regrettable that delivery could not be made until September or October. On the motion of the chairman, Mr W. H. Nagle, the board empowered Mr Ford to take the necessary steps to institute the service." [88]

Private Bus Acquisitions

As part of its post-war modernisation programme of supplementing and eventually replacing its tramway operation, the Auckland Transport Board acquired fifteen motor-omnibuses from a private company, Transport Bus Services Limited, in 1946. By 1950, the Transport Board was able to report that it then operated "...the largest municipally owned fleet of buses...in the Dominion..." after "...The Penrose service formerly operated by W. J. Wheeler and Sons Ltd., and comprising eight diesel buses was taken over on 29th May, 1949, and on 5th March 1950, the services formerly operated by L. J. Keys Ltd., to Orakei, Mission Bay, Kohimarama, St. Heliers Bay and district, with a fleet of forty diesel and petrol buses, were also added to the Board's undertaking." [89]

The L J Keys operation had originated some forty years previously when: "Leonard John Keys owned a grocer's shop on the corner of Clonbern and Remuera Road. He delivered groceries by horse and cart to customers in Remuera and the waterfront suburbs. He purchased a bus in 1914 to start the first bus service in the area. A garage depot was opened in St Heliers. L. J. Keys buses departed from in front of the CPO until the Britomart Bus terminal was built in the 1930's." [90]

Britomart Bus Terminal

The Britomart Bus terminal referred to was:

"The Auckland Municipal Bus Station opened September 1937 between Commerce Street and Britomart Place. The New Zealand Herald called it *modern and well-planned*." [90] However, "...the Chairman of the Bus Proprietors' Association had a different view. He said, 'The plan and layout have been condemned by every Auckland transport operator'." [91]

Cross-Country Bus Service

As the reach of the City's tram routes and those of its replacement trolleybuses fell increasingly short, the Transport Board was only too glad to implement its modernisation programme with the allocation of its diesel and petrol buses to the newer suburbs:

"To cope with ever-increasing demands for transport by a steadily growing population, services are being extended as circumstances permit. On 20th November, 1949, a Cross-Country Bus Service was instituted from Point Chevalier via Mount Albert, Balmoral Road and Green Lane Road to Cornwall Hospital and Great South Road. This service, which operates during off-peak hours, is becoming increasingly patronised, and is particularly appreciated by visitors to the Green Lane and Cornwall Hospitals. Improvements and extensions to other services in Mount Roskill and Mount Albert new housing areas will be put into effect within a short time." [89]

At the Restart Line

By the time Transport Board Chairman, William Nagle, reported in June 1945, some easing of wartime restrictions was imminent and, as Government and civic leaders approached the restart line, important decisions had to be made:

"It will be seen from the Accounts now submitted that the Board's revenue was £1,091,036. This is £10,562 (.98%) more than in the previous year and constitutes an all-time record. Working expenses at £655,814 increased by £31,559 (5%) over last year.

"Now that war in Europe is ended, it seems likely that the petrol ration will be increased, although perhaps only slightly for some time yet to come. However, even a small increase will undoubtedly have its effect on the number of passengers carried by the tramway system...It must be evident to even the most casual observer that the heavy traffic carried by the tramways during the war years, plus the shortage of manpower and material, has resulted in a general deterioration of equipment and permanent way. While such deterioration has not been allowed to affect the high standard of safety always observed by the Board, it does mean that whereas previously the Board had anticipated a changeover to a more modern form of transport in 1951, it is now faced with either:

"(1) Undertaking substantial work in restoring the tramway system to something like its pre-war standard, or

"(2) Changing over to the new form of transport at a much earlier date than was previously anticipated.

"Alternative No. 1 obviously means the expenditure of a large sum of money on an asset due to be replaced in a comparatively short time. If, as is almost certain, alternative No. 2 is adopted, the Board must have on hand a very substantial Depreciation Reserve, as otherwise the new form of transport will be saddled with two sets of loans – its own and the carry-forward from the tramway system. Thus failure on the Board's part to make adequate provision can have only one result, viz.: increased costs to provide the same service as is provided to-day. [92]

Meeting Increased Costs

"There are only three ways in which such increased costs can be met: (1) By striking a rate; (2) By increasing the fares; (3) By reducing the wages and/or working conditions. Bearing these facts in mind, I think it must be conceded that the policy which the Board is pursuing in relation to its future development is a wise and prudent one in the interests of all concerned." [92]

Any of the three ways by which the tramways operations could be financed, as proposed by William Nagle, would have been difficult to accept by a Board that had, for so long, prided itself on prudent management of the undertaking. While nominal fare increases had occurred during the Transport Board's seventeen-year history, neither a rates demand from its constituent local authorities, as permitted by the Auckland Transport Board Act 1928, nor a reduction of wages or working conditions had ever been necessary. In fact, the reverse had occurred when the Transport Board paid rates to its constituent local authorities for use of the roadways along which the trams ran.

An Expanding City

The ability of the Board to exercise its option to strike a rate, as per the Act, stems from the concept that the trams added value to the land they *opened up*, just as the railways did during the 1800s. However, while the tramways initially promoted urban growth as they extended their tracks to the outer city districts, the rigidity of the straight-line carriageway and its limited reach failed to meet the needs of Auckland's growing population as they settled the more remote suburban areas. The longer tram runs also proved somewhat uneconomical, as described by the Auckland Star's E K Green who, in July 1945, wrote about the large scale extension to city limits that would result from the proposed project to house 30,000 people at Tamaki:

"Increasing transport problems are being encountered as a corollary of this outward thrust of the city. Already the Auckland Transport Board is beginning to look anxiously at what is described as its 'long haul' problem. The further lines have to be extended, and the more the population grows on the outer limits of the city, the more difficult it is to run the tramways service economically. Strange as it may seem, the people who ride short sections pay the highest proportion of tramways revenue. Auckland is a tramway-riding city – apart altogether from the increased pressure on tram services due to petrol rationing and other war circumstances. A total of 96,000,000 tram tickets sold in the course of a year, related to the city population, averages more than one tram ride a day for every person in Auckland – a remarkable total.

"This satisfactory position, from the Transport Board's point of view, is due to the twin circumstances in Auckland of a hilly situation and the humid heat of its summer weather. People tram short distances in the shopping area of the city. The result is that between 60 and 70 per cent of tram passengers are one and two-section riders, and the average fare paid last year was 2.65d.

"This is a fortunate circumstance for those who live at outlying suburbs like Onehunga, and who pay 6d for a five-section ride (or 4/3 for a weekly concession card). If that were considered as a separate service, to be run economically, the fare might have to be as much as 1/6. One of the main factors in this is that the 'turn round' of trams is slow, and the fleet of trams has thus to be much more extensive than would be required to run short sections.

"Another 'strange as it may seem' fact is that the rush hours of crowded trams pays less than the in-between periods of the day. Why? Because tram crews have to be kept 'standing by' on broken shifts for these hours, and the major rush (mainly concession card holders) is to the outer suburbs. Only one rush load can be carried by each tram to suburbs as far out as Onehunga – 80 minutes return – and on the return trip fares are few. I quote these as interesting facts having bearing on the problems of an expanding city." [93]

Trams Worn Out

So, while Auckland's trams had certainly assisted with the city's initial, geographical expansion, by the end of the Second World War, it had become obvious that trams alone would be incapable of playing a major part in the City's future growth. They were simply worn out, as described by the Chairman of the Auckland Transport Board, W H Nagle, during his address to a luncheon gathering of the Y.M.C.A. Optimists' Club on 15 February 1945:

"…At present it [the tramways] had a staff of 1235, operating 231 trams over 85 miles of single track. Fourteen buses were operated under contract. Our capacity is overtaxed, he said. I make no bones about that. We're carrying 2,000,000 passengers a week. The fact that we're carrying 100,000,000 a year shows we're straining every effort to give the service the public wants. The position is, however, that our electric trams have been operating for 42 years and they're facing obsolescence. The board, he continued, intended to replace the tramways with the most up-to-date system procurable.

"Trolley buses were in view, but something even more advanced might be available when the time came. Full account was being taken of future development, and a city of 350,000 was visualised as against 220,000 at present. To avoid past mistakes, the board would closely follow developments in housing, town planning, the provision of industrial, commercial and residential areas, and development so as not to overlap. An important aspect of modern transport was elimination of waste due to overlapping.

"The first elected board inherited a debt of two and a half million pounds, said Mr Nagle. We've paid well over half a million pounds in exchange — a crippling thing to us — and before commencing a new service we intend to see that there's no financial deficit. The war brought us unprecedented revenue, touching the million mark, and by conservation we've set up sinking funds and other vital reserves. Our operating account was in credit for the first time only in 1943 and it has been as low as £120,000 in debt.

"That's now all wiped out. The new system will be installed as soon as conditions permit, but with no antecedent liability. I say that deliberately. It will be more economical and much more comfortable, with an absence of noise and less danger of accident. Mr Nagle said that although the public had suffered discomfort and inconvenience, the war had not necessitated taking tram seats out to increase accommodation, as has happened overseas.

"Auckland's trams were as good as anything in New Zealand or Australia, but many people who had previously used motor cars had been forced to use trams, thus increasing the loads. The board was striving to prepare something that would hold this additional patronage when petrol was no longer rationed — it was seeking a system as good as anything else in the world." [94]

Local Government Select Committee

In September 1945, a Local Government Select Committee produced a wide-ranging report which supported many of William Nagle's comments. The report contained observations relating to New Zealand's tramway operations: "Six of the eight cities and two boroughs operate tramways. Before the war tramway services were, in general, operating at a very considerable economic loss. Temporarily, during the war, they are operating at a profit, but the ultimate future of the tramway services is a matter of considerable debate. At the present time there is a strong tendency to shift to trolley buses." [59]

Tenders for Trolley Buses and Buses Called

Just so, as Wellington's Evening Post of 21 December 1945 confirmed:

"Tenders for 50 large single-dock trolley buses are being invited by the Auckland Transport Board as the first step towards replacing the present tramway system in the city. Although it was difficult to estimate a time for delivery of the new buses, it is expected that it will be 18 months or perhaps longer before the first of them are available, a great deal depending on the supply position of essential parts from overseas. The board is endeavouring to install the new system as soon as possible to relieve the present transport position." [95]

And, in his Annual Report for the year ended 31 March 1946, Auckland Transport Board Chairman, William Nagle, confirmed the Board's *first step towards replacing the present tramway system*: "In pursuance of its comprehensive development scheme, the Board has taken the earliest opportunity to place orders in Great Britain for new equipment.

"Tenders were called for the supply of 50 trolley buses in accordance with specifications drawn up by our Engineering Department. To meet the urgent need, complete vehicles were specified, tenders were duly received, and after full investigation, that of Messrs. Metropolitan-Vickers Electrical Co. Ltd. for the supply of 1 assembled and 49 unassembled vehicles was accepted, the contract price being £173,417 sterling.

"Further tenderers for the supply of 12 bus chassis were called, and that of Messrs. Tappenden Motors Ltd. for 12 Bedford chassis was accepted. Arrangements have been made locally for the construction of the necessary bodies and it is probable that some of these vehicles will be ready for use at the end of 1946. These practical steps should go far to relieve the strain on our present tramway system.

"For a considerable period certain bus services, mainly feeder, have been operated under contract for the Board. A decision has been reached that on the expiry of the present contract in October, 1946, the Board will resume direct operation to these districts, and it is intended when the additional equipment is available to review the routing to give improved service to these areas. In December, 1945, the Board, at the request of the Hospital Board, commenced a bus service to serve the needs of the Greenlane and Cornwall Hospitals." [96]

Record Passenger Numbers Continue

Pending the arrival of the trolley buses, the Auckland Transport Board continued to transport record numbers of passengers both by tram and bus. For the financial year ended 31 March 1946, the Board recorded a surplus of £25,441 after earning £1,085,199 from its transport operations (£5,837 less than the previous year). However, operational expenses continued to increase, amounting to £741,023 for the financial year, an increase of £85,209 (13%) over the previous year.

In his Annual Report for 1945-1946, the Board Chairman, William Nagle, observed:

"I would like to emphasise that over the last few years our operating expenses have seriously increased, while our fares have remained static. Abnormal traffic has assisted us to bear this burden, but the future position in this respect will call for the closest scrutiny...Within recent months the petrol ration has been increased, but in view of the fact that the tyre position continues to be most difficult and few new motor-cars are yet available for private use, we have still to maintain the utmost passenger transport that our equipment and staff can provide, but preserving at the same time the high standard of maintenance the Board has always set in the interests of public safety." [96]

Grand Vision for Public Transport

During his February 1945 speech to the Y.M.C.A. Optimists' Club, William Nagle's assurance that *"Trolley buses were in view, but something even more advanced might be available when the time came..."* indicated that the Auckland Transport Board had a grand vision for the future of public transport – perhaps a transport revolution comparable to petrol rationing that could nullify the private motor car as a serious competitor?

However, such a vision obviously needed a reality check and what better way than by means of an overseas mission to see what was really attainable and, of course, affordable. Accordingly, "After vexatious delays, two of our Executive Officers, Messrs. C. R. Gribble (Secretary and Treasurer) and E. B. Foster (Assistant Manager), left for a visit to the U.S.A., Canada and Great Britain to make a comprehensive study at first hand of modern transport facilities and their operations. Special attention will be given to cities whose topography and development are comparable to our own, and we feel that the results will be invaluable to the Board and its future system and will do much to ensure economic installation and subsequent successful and efficient operation." [96]

Professional Engineers Criticise Trip

But the Transport Board's appointment of just two of its administrators to undertake such an important investigation proved controversial – as reported by The New Zealand Herald on 24 July 1945:

"A further appeal to the Auckland Transport Board to include an engineer in its delegation to go overseas to investigate modern transport has been made by the Auckland branch of the Professional Engineers' Association. The delegation decided upon by the board comprises the secretary-treasurer, Mr C. R. Gribble, and the assistant manager, Mr E. B. Foster.

"'The implementation of the comprehensive transportation plan which will be based on the report following this overseas investigation will necessitate the expenditure of many hundreds of thousands of pounds,' said a statement by the association.

"'Furthermore, the acquisition of not less than 50 trolley buses will cost at least £150,000 almost immediately. This is being proceeded with without any one of the board's competent engineers having seen either what is to be purchased or any comparative transport equipment in America or England. In the case of both Dunedin and Wellington transport, engineers had been consulted. In the interests of the Auckland public, we appeal to the board to reconsider its decision and balance the representation by sending an engineer before this investigation has proceeded far,' the statement concluded. 'A team comprising both engineering and clerical officers, even if it were to find that prices overseas were too high to recommend immediate purchase, would make a report of considerably greater value than any the clerical officers can submit.'" [97]

Gribble and Foster Report

Nevertheless, Messrs. C. R. Gribble and E. B. Foster set off on their trip on 11 April 1946, unaccompanied by an engineer, and returned on 22 October of that year. The content of their report, dated 18 November 1946, was described by the Auckland Transport Board Chairman, W H Nagle, as: "…a comprehensive and diligent investigation. The immediate result is a most valuable report of their findings and recommendations, accompanied by a movie film of over 3000 feet, which shows transport operation in all the cities they visited. Their trip and its result have created a demand to be given the benefit of their research abroad. The experience gained by these Officers will be invaluable in all future stages of development and operation in the Board's area." [98]

But, regardless of the Transport Board's enthusiasm to modernise its fleet, Europe's gradual post-war recovery required some degree of patience from the consumers of its goods and services – particularly those of the Antipodes. While it waited for its trolley buses, the Board could only plan for their arrival, assembly and eventual disposition:

"The Board has made an important decision to operate the first fifty trolley buses in replacement of the present Ponsonby, Herne Bay and Richmond Road trams. The fullest results will be achieved by running in these areas and it will constitute a valuable test of the capacity and suitability of this form of transport for our City's needs. It is difficult to say when delivery will be given of this equipment, but all possible steps are being taken to expedite their construction. The Board has acquired an area of land that will adequately provide for all future garage requirements of a very large fleet of modern vehicles. It is also taking action to secure a suitable building for the assembling of the buses on arrival. The preliminary work in connection with the overhead is well in hand and the necessary material has been received." [98]

Recovery of the Auckland Transport Board's Bus Fleet

However, the Board's modernisation plans included more than just the replacement of its trams by trolley buses. As radical as that was, the Board also decided to reverse its policy of the 1920s and 1930s when it sold its unprofitable bus fleet to private operators. One such operator was Transport Bus Services Limited, to which the Transport Board sold a bus service in 1933 and which, by 1946, it decided to reclaim. This was facilitated by means of Section 34 of the Local Legislation Act 1946:

"Whereas the Auckland Transport Board (in this section referred to as the Board) in the year nineteen hundred and thirty-three transferred to a firm carrying on business under the name of Transport Bus Services certain motor-omnibus services in the city and suburbs of Auckland which the Board had theretofore been carrying on: And whereas the said firm subsequently transferred its business, including the said services, to a company called Transport Bus Services Limited (in this section referred to as the company) ~ and the company continued to carry on such services under and in terms of certain agreements made with the Board and purchased a number of motor-omnibuses for the said services:

"And whereas the term of the last agreement between the Board and the company expired on the first day of October, nineteen hundred and forty-six: And whereas it has been agreed between the Board and the company that the Board shall purchase and acquire from the company fifteen motor-omnibuses acquired by the company as aforesaid at a price which represents, in the opinion of the Board and the company, the market value thereof:

"And whereas, by reason of certain provisions in the said agreements as aforesaid, the Board is in doubt as to whether it can lawfully pay such price: Be it therefore enacted as Follows: The Board is hereby authorized and empowered to purchase and acquire from the company such number of motor-omnibuses as has been or may be agreed on between the Board and the company at such price as has been or may be agreed on between the Board and the company as representing the true market value of the said motor-omnibuses, and to make in connection with such transaction such incidental arrangements as may be agreed on between the Board and the company." [99]

As part of his Annual Report for the Year Ended 31 March 1947, Chairman, William Nagle, reported the Transport Board's acquisition of the bus services operated by Transport Bus Services as well as those previously run by the Hospital Bus Company Limited:

"During the year the service operated by the Hospital Bus Company Limited was acquired by the Board. In addition, the contract under which Transport Bus Services Limited operated on certain routes expired and the Board now operates these services. Both services have been altered to give improved running and further changes are planned to take effect when more buses become available. In this connection, some 10 new buses have been added, while 4 have been withdrawn or sold as uneconomic and unreliable. We trust that soon with our larger and newer fleet of buses we can give improved service to the areas affected and to some extent relieve the present strain on our tramway system." [98]

Tram and Bus Financial Results

Following its re-establishment of bus services, the Transport Board accounts for the financial year ended 31 March 1947 again differentiated between tram and bus results: "…the tramway surplus was £34,138, while bus operation resulted in a deficit of £14,877, making the net surplus for the undertaking £19,261…the Board's tramway revenue for the year was £1,026,249. This is £58,951 (5.4%) less than in the preceding year. Tramway Working Expenses at £719,297 were a decrease by £18,706 (2.5%) over last year.

"In spite of the satisfactory result of the year's working I feel it is my duty to stress that the present day tendency of increasing costs on the one hand and falling revenue on the other, can well create a serious position for the future economic operation of the Board's services. Indeed, at the present time there are definite indications of cost increases that must accentuate the problem. As Members are aware, the travelling public have had the continuous benefit of unaltered pre-war fares, and to maintain that position will be the policy of the Board as long as its financial stability can be maintained at an appropriate level – a factor which is vital to the operation of an efficient and satisfactory service." [98]

Government Ten-Year Plan

As detailed later, the Government had its own plans to relieve Auckland's straining public transport system with the extension and electrification of the suburban railway network. Announced by the Minister of Railways, the Hon. Robert Semple, in September 1944 as part of the post-war rehabilitation programme, the Government's ten-year plan was seen as one of the more positive attempts to accomplish this long-awaited project.

By 1947, little had been accomplished, but the Transport Board nevertheless considered a future suburban railway service to be a possible threat to its own modernisation programme, as the Board's Chairman, William Nagle, outlined in his Annual Report for the year ended 31 March 1947:

"Government Ten-Year Plan – In this connection, the Hon. R. Semple has announced the Government's intention to construct and operate an electrified railway throughout our area. Part of this will be underground and the route proposed will be of a circular nature. The Board has always borne in mind the likelihood of such a scheme, and has intimated its intention to co-operate with the Railway Department to avoid overlapping and wasteful operation between the two Authorities. This has been recognised by the Department. It is obvious that much of the area to be served by this facility will be thickly populated long before the railway will commence to serve. This Board has expressed its willingness to operate suitable services during that period, providing the Department recognises that capital costs incurred may not be liquidated by the time the railway is ready to run, but it is felt that there will be no difficulty in coming to a working agreement satisfactory to all concerned." [98]

The Tramways Carriage Regulations 1947

But while plans were underway to supplement and eventually replace Auckland's trams, some means of controlling the crowds of commuters still battling to board those trams was required. Pending the full introduction of what was then considered the ideal solution to the overcrowding – trolley buses, motor omnibuses, and suburban rail – Parliament passed the Tramways Carriage Regulations 1947 which came into force on 1 December of that year. The Regulations essentially provided for the inspection and licensing of tram carriages with each carriage allocated a suitable, maximum number of seated and standing passengers. The Regulations also stipulated a number of other safety features, including a maximum speed of 30 miles per hour, and the display of head and tail lights at night. [100]

Ministry of Works Statement 1948

That the Tramways Carriage Regulations were not the complete answer to the problem of overcrowding on the trams was acknowledged by the Minister of Works, Robert Semple, in his Ministry of Works Statement for the year ended 31 March 1948:

"The Tramways Carriage Regulations 1947 were enacted for the purpose of securing improvement in facilities and services in this form of public transport. The regulations are not yet fully operative in respect of overcrowding because of the difficulties of providing the additional transport that is necessary." [101]

Order for Trolleybuses Increased

Robert Semple's observation that overcrowding persisted because of *the difficulties of providing the additional transport*, no doubt referred to the delayed arrival of the trolleybuses ordered by the Auckland Transport Board in late 1945. They were then expected to arrive in late 1948, as outlined by the Board Chairman, William Nagle, in his Annual Report for the year ended 31 March of that year:

"Trolley Buses – It has been decided to increase the Board's order for trolleybuses to 55 vehicles, in order that the Farmers' Trading Company's service may be converted at the same time as Herne Bay, Ponsonby and Richmond Road routes. It will then be possible to re-route Pt. Chevalier trams via Queen Street and so permit the elimination of trams entirely from the area west of and including Hobson Street.

"In order to facilitate the early changeover of at least one route, namely Herne Bay, 15 of the trolley buses will be imported completely assembled, except for seats and painting. This work will be carried out in New Zealand, as will the assembly of the remaining 40 vehicles. The English manufacturers expect to be in a position to ship all the vehicles to arrive before the end of 1948, and it is hoped to have the first 15 in operation early in 1949.

"The Assistant Workshop Superintendent, Mr , was sent to England just before the close of the year to study at first-hand at the Works the construction and assembly of the trolley buses on order. The knowledge and experience gained by Mr Everiss will be of considerable value to the Board both in maintenance and assembly of the first 55 trolley buses, and thereafter, in construction of future vehicles." [102]

Pending the commissioning of the trolley buses, omnibus timetables and services were adjusted to cater for the continuing demand for public transport: "Omnibuses – During the year timetables were adjusted to cater for increased traffic and to ensure more economic operation…The Remuera Post Office-Upland Road service formerly operated by Mr Adlam was extended to Tonks Street, and another service now operates from Meadowbank to Remuera Post Office. The continued extension of the Board's bus operations has necessitated the appointment of an Officer to supervise generally the running of the services. Mr H S Wilson of the Traffic Office was accordingly appointed Bus Supervisor." [102]

Bus Operation Deficit

Unfortunately, while the tramway surplus for the financial year ended 31 March 1948 was £30,325, the bus operation resulted in another deficit of £23,991 – some £9,114 more than the previous year – making the net surplus for the undertaking £6,334.

As Board Chairman, William Nagle, observed in his Annual Report:

"It will be noticed that the Board's tramway revenue for the year was £954,900. This is £71,349 (6.9%) less than in the preceding year. Tramway Working Expenses at £767,208 were an increase by £47,911 (6.7%) over last year…Under all the circumstances, I think that the Board will agree that the result of the year's workings has been a satisfactory one. Ever increasing costs of operation, however, render it doubtful whether the Board will be able to carry on much longer without at least a minor adjustment in fares." [102]

The increasing use of buses to supplement the tram service was reflected in the Transport Board's Annual Report for the financial year ended 31 March 1949:

"…the tramway surplus of £16,576 [almost half of the 1947-1948 surplus] while bus operation resulted in a deficit of £19,296, making the net loss for the undertaking £2,719…The tramway revenue for the year was £949,956 while bus revenue was £63,729. These amounts are £4,944 (.52%) less and £17,236 (37.07%) more respectively than in the preceding year. Tramway Working Expenses were £820,659, an increase of 69.7% over the previous year, while Bus Working Expenses were £71,369, an increase of 20.03%." [103]

First Trolleybuses

When the first trolleybuses finally arrived in February 1949, their commissioning was not as straightforward as the Board would have hoped but good progress was nevertheless made, reported new Chairman, Henry Albert Anderson, in his Annual Report for the year ended 31 March of that year:

"Trolley Buses – The first of the 55 trolley buses ordered from English manufacturers arrived in February, others have arrived since, and the remainder are expected by the end of June. Good progress is being made in installing seats and painting enough of the new vehicles for the Herne Bay route, which is the first for conversion. Factors beyond the Board's control caused considerable delay in the erection of a Trolley Bus Assembly Building at the Mt. Roskill Workshops, and anticipations that this building would have been sufficiently advanced for use by the time the cases of trolley bus parts arrived were not realised. The storage of parts and assembly of vehicles is correspondingly hindered.

"Omnibuses – These services are being improved as the opportunity occurs in regard to both timetables and vehicles. 'Through' bus services were commenced to Avondale on 1st August, 1948, and to Blockhouse Bay on 7th November, 1948, replacing feeder services to trams. These are working satisfactorily and have proved very popular." [103]

Dr E P Neale

While the new bus services were proving popular and the commissioning of the first trolleybus was eagerly awaited by the Transport Board, not all sections of the community were convinced that replacing the trams, instead of modernising them, was the complete answer to Auckland's public transport needs. The Secretary of the Auckland Chamber of Commerce, Dr E P Neale, expressed some reservation in a wide-ranging report thought to have been prepared in 1949:

"The Chamber has an open mind on the question of whether or not the Auckland trams should be modernised…or whether they should be wholly replaced by trolley buses. It is aware from inquiries it has made in Australia that the trend in many Australian Cities comparable in size to Auckland is more in favour of modernising trams (and against scrapping them in favour of trolley buses) than some statements that have been made in New Zealand would suggest.

"It has often been stated that the trolley-bus is mechanically less efficient than the modern tram in that instead of working on a smooth rail it works on an uneven road surface and the lower capital cost of the trackless tram (because of the absence of rails) gives no net advantage as compared with the modern P.C.C. tram where the head-way between trips is small, especially when regard is had to the fact that overhead wires for trolley buses need to be double.

"Other advantages of the trolley bus appear to be: -
    (1)   It is silent.
    (2)   There is no waiting at loops (on single track routes).

(3) It picks up its passengers at the side of the road.
(4) It is faster if not fitted for one-man operation.

"Some disadvantages of the trolley-bus appear to be: -
(1) There is more strain on drivers because of the necessity to steer.
(2) In proportion to the road space it occupies, it transports fewer passengers than the tram.
(3) It does not occupy a fixed space on the road like a tram; therefore there is less road available for (and more risks of accidents to) other users of the road than with electric trams.
(4) Its rate of depreciation would appear to be higher than that of a tram because it has more moving parts and does not operate on smooth surfaces." [104]

Nevertheless, Dr Neale observed that the trams were not coping with the demand:

"It is, however, generally admitted that traffic offering for the trams in Auckland is not adequately catered for at peak-times by the present services, complaints being frequent of long waits to catch trams between 4.30 p.m. and 5.45 p.m. by people desirous of joining at other than city termini; encouraging many people to walk in the opposite direction to that of intended travel to the city terminus, where they can be surer of admission to the tram and of a seat. Likewise, there are frequent complaints of inadequacy of the service on certain routes between 7.30 a.m. to 9 a.m. especially from people joining at other than the suburban termini." [104]

His report suggested population increase and poor suburban railway services as the main reasons for overcrowding: "Between 1936 and 1948 the population of Auckland Provincial District increased 28% as against a Dominion average of 17%. The only at all comparable Provincial District figure was Wellington (19%).

"Nearly all the conditions…(population increase and poor suburban railway services) have increased the amount of traffic travelling by the trams, with, however, some diversion of this traffic to private motor-cars since early in the present century and to omnibus services since the early twenties: soon after which however – in 1926 – legislation was passed calculated to limit cut-throat competition between bus and tram along the same route. The omnibuses now for the most part serve the remoter suburbs and country districts beyond the range of the ordinary tram routes." [104]

Suggested Public Transport Improvements

Dr Neale's suggestions as to how the public transport situation could be improved included:

"If the proposed circular electric railway is constructed the tram (or trolley bus as the case may be) system should link up with it (and with ferry services) at all possible points…In the late thirties the City authorities provided an omnibus terminal in the site east of Queen Street released by the transfer of the railway station to Beach Road. This is now entirely inadequate for the demands made on it and already certain omnibus services have their city termini temporarily located in the vicinity of the Civic Square. The Chamber would like to see omnibus services to western suburbs located in a new terminal in the old dock site area or some other part west of and convenient to Queen Street. The trolley bus terminals should be close to other transport routes." [104]

Tram Replacement Overview

In his article, *Urban Tramways in New Zealand 1862-1964*, published in the NZ Geographer in 1975, G. T. Bloomfield provided an overview of why Auckland trams were being replaced by trolley and motor buses:

"The economics of tramway operations, already difficult in the late 1920s, were almost impossible by 1950. Operating costs were high, all the systems were largely obsolete in the equipment and the routes did not reach far enough to the new residential suburbs and employment centres which emerged during and after the war. Capital investment required for a modernised and viable system was too great in comparison with the more flexible bus operations. Even if some cities had decided to continue, the supply of new equipment would have posed major difficulties for the tram and equipment manufacturers of Britain and the United States were diversifying or going out of business." [16]

First Tramway to Trolleybus Conversion

As the decade neared its end, the first Auckland tramway service to yield to the trolleybus was the Herne Bay route. The inaugural trolleybus service began on 24th September, 1949.

Transport Charges Committee/Transport Act 1949

The New Zealand Government also recognised the increasing emergence of road-based vehicles as the prime mode of transportation with the passage of the Transport Act 1949 which came into force on 1 November of that year "…to Consolidate and Amend Certain Enactments Relating to Motor-vehicles, to Road Traffic, and to Commercial Transport Services Carried on by Means of Motor-vehicles or Harbour Ferries." [105]

As referred to in later chapters, this Act was an extensive piece of legislation that provided for the administration, registration, and licensing of motor vehicles and drivers; and the regulation of motor spirits and mileage tax, motor vehicle insurance, and road transport and harbour ferry services – including the fares of trams, buses, and trolleybuses.

The 1949 Act replaced a number of former statutes such as the Motor Vehicles Act 1924, the Transport Licensing Act 1931, the Motor Vehicles Amendment Act 1936, and the Motor Spirits Taxation Act 1927.

As did its predecessor, the Transport Licensing Act 1931, the 1949 Transport Act divided the country into four transport districts, now referred to as Metropolitan Districts: Auckland, Wellington, Christchurch, and Dunedin. Each of these districts had its own Licensing Authority responsible for the regulatory licensing of all public road transport and harbour ferry services. The Auckland Transport Board acted as the Licensing Authority for the Auckland District while the respective City Councils were responsible for the three other Districts.

But while the administration of licensing matters was entrusted to the respective Metropolitan Districts, Section 12 of the Transport Act otherwise centralised control of the newly-created Transport Department (under the control of the Minister of Transport) and a Co-ordination Council of some 16 representatives from all corners of the transport industry:

"(a) To make inquiries into and to report on and make recommendations concerning such matters as may from time to time be referred to it by the Minister:

(b) To institute of its own motion inquiries into any matter affecting public transport of any kind and to make reports and recommendations thereon to the Minister." [105]

Section 120 of the Transport Act 1949 also provided for the establishment of a *Transport Charges Committee* appointed by the Minister of Transport and consisting of:

"*(a)* A Chairman, who shall be appointed as such:

(b) One member, who shall be appointed to represent the owners of transport services:

(c) One member, who shall be appointed to represent the users of transport services." [105]

Section 121(5) also established a *Charges Appeal Authority* [any suitable person appointed by the Governor-General] to which any matter may be referred "If the Committee is unable to reach a decision..." [105] and Section 121(6) stipulated that "All proceedings before the Committee shall be heard in public unless the Committee in any particular case, due regard being had to the interests of the parties and of all other persons concerned, considers that the hearing or any part thereof should take place in private." [105]

Section 122 defined the functions of the Transport Charges Committee as:

"...to fix, review, or alter under the next succeeding section or under section one hundred and twenty-five of this Act the charges for the carriage of passengers or goods or the letting of motor-vehicles on hire by any transport service (including the charges payable under any contract or group of contracts or proposed contract or group of contracts), whether the charges to be reviewed or altered have been fixed before or after the commencement of this Act.

"(2) Where, having regard to all the circumstances in any particular case, the Committee considers it desirable in the public interest so to do, the Committee, instead of prescribing a fixed charge for the carriage of passengers or goods or the letting of motor-vehicles on hire, may fix a maximum charge together with a minimum charge." [105]

Both tram and trackless trolley-omnibus services were specifically referred to in Sections 127 and 128 as being subject to the Transport Act and therefore the regulation of fares by the Transport Charges Committee and any appeal by the Charges Appeal Authority.

No doubt with the social importance of public transport in mind, several other provisions relating to public transport charges were included in the Transport Act, specifically Section 129:

"In any proceedings under this Act to fix, review, or alter any transport charges the Committee or, as the case may be, the Charges Appeal Authority shall have due regard to the necessity of preserving and promoting the social and economic welfare of the people of New Zealand, and in particular to-

(a) The promotion and maintenance of the economic stability of New Zealand:

(b) The desirability of increasing national production by granting concessions on the carriage of producers' goods:

(c) The desirability of providing special fares for all regular users of services for the carriage of passengers:

(d) The desirability of providing that children under the age of four years shall be carried free of charge, and that children who have attained the age of four years but have not attained the age of fifteen years shall be carried at half adult rates:

(e) The desirability of maintaining a reasonable standard of living and satisfactory working conditions in the road-transport and harbour ferry industries:

(f) The maintenance of the efficiency of the transport services to which the proceedings relate." [105]

Over-Regulation?

No doubt legislation such as the 1949 Transport Act went some way toward *'preserving and promoting the social and economic welfare of the people of New Zealand'*. However, what was generally viewed by private transport operators as a commercially unfair Transport Act was also seen by a post-war public, struggling to make ends meet with limited resources, as the necessary regulation of essential services. The latter intention was unashamedly promoted by the Act.

In some cases, the imposition of such regulations and licensing requirements levelled the playing field for many transport industry competitors; but not for all, particularly over time. Nearly thirty years later, the same regulations remained; plus a few more and the result was not entirely favourable – as described by Monte Holcroft in his 1979 book, 'Carapace':

"New Zealanders as individuals are independent to the point of aggression; but they also have strong collective impulses and are ready to impose and accept regulation to an extent not always compatible with democracy. A habit of over-government may be seen as the other side of individualism, as if people who want their own way in certain areas are willing to be regulated in order to constrain their competitors.

"It is now necessary to be licensed for so many reasons that few can know or understand the full range of bureaucratic control. The habit is not new; but motor vehicles gave the system a strong impetus; and in their own field, in private and public transport, the network of supervision has become large and costly…It has led among other things to a perpetual tug-of-war between public and private interests, and to a tenacious defence of territorial rights among transport operators. You can't set yourself up as a carrier by simply buying and registering a truck and opening a depot. The whole country is divided into districts, each with a licensing authority; and anyone who wants to enter the industry must first convince his Authority that room can be found for him." [106]

Road Transport
Tamaki Residential Development

By 1943, the need for new housing space dovetailed neatly with the means of easy access provided by the motor car, as described by the Evening Post on 25 June 1943:

"A roading plan has been prepared for a great residential development covering 3000 acres in the Tamaki district, east of Auckland City. Two thousand acres of the area are involved in a State scheme to build 8000 houses. The total project is by far the most ambitious ever proposed in Auckland. The backbone of the whole scheme is a proposed south-east main highway, to be used exclusively for an arterial traffic route, with no building frontages to it, but linking up at three points with roads to serve the proposed new suburb.

"A comprehensive report on the scheme was presented to the City Council last evening by the engineer, Mr J. Tyler, and deferred for consideration at the next meeting. According to reports, one of the most important business centres of suburban Auckland is expected to grow up at a proposed road junction with the new arterial highway immediately east of Glen Innes station, and the development is planned to link up with this centre…Besides road and street development, drainage, and other services must be provided. The project has been prepared as a result of consultation between the

Department of Housing Construction, the City Council, and the ways and means committee of the Auckland Metropolitan Co-ordinating Town-planning Scheme." [107]

Planning of New Arterial Roads

By late 1943, the planning of new arterial roads was crucial to the connection of a growing city to its outlying districts. Some of that planning was reported by The New Zealand Herald on 25 October 1943:

"Greater attention is now being given to the many projects which will have to be put in hand to make up for the lag in city and suburban development during the war and to provide employment for the large number of servicemen returning to civil life who would not otherwise be absorbed into ordinary trade and industry. The local authorities in the Auckland metropolitan area will have enormous arrears of construction and maintenance work to overtake in their own districts, but many of them, particularly those lying to the south and east of the city, cannot plan for their ultimate development until some finality has been reached on the routes to be followed by the main arterial outlets which are to serve the greatly enlarged city of the future.

"It is certain that sooner or later consideration will have to be given to the construction of a great highway to the north to take the place of the present Great North Road, with its bottle-necks and somewhat circuitous route, but until some decision has been reached on the site for the proposed harbour bridge and the location of the city's airport has been determined, not much progress can be made in that direction. On the other hand, the provision of a new and modern traffic outlet to the south demands much earlier attention. For more than 15 years schemes to carry traffic southward from the city, avoiding the congestion at Newmarket and at various points along the present Great South Road to Otahuhu have been put forward, but none has so far met with general approval.

"In the meantime motor traffic has increased in speed and in density and the need for a bold departure from earlier ideas has become more and more apparent, until to-day, with an eye to the heavy increase in this type of traffic after the war, most road engineers envisage a great highway that will carry fast-moving vehicles, keeping them clear of the existing townships and joining the present south road even as far south as Drury.

"Most of the schemes already put forward favour following the waterfront road to Hobson Bay. One proposal was to branch off where the railway line leaves the road and proceed across Orakei Basin, roughly following the direction of the railway line up the Purewa Creek, and crossing under the St. Heliers Road by a tunnel. This would bring the road out on to the Tamaki flats and give access thence to the concrete Mount Wellington Highway and Otahuhu.

"Another proposal was for the road from Hobson Bay to be continued to the intersection of Orakei and Upland Roads, skirt Orakei Basin to the lower end of Waiatarua Road, pass under the St. Heliers Road by a subway at the Meadowbank corner, and thence pass Lake St. John on the way to Otahuhu. There have been some other proposals which have suggested variations of the route after crossing Hobson Bay, but in nearly all the most suitable junction with the Great South Road has been fixed at a point just past Otahuhu, avoiding congestion in the borough.

"As a result of a preliminary survey an entirely new route beyond the St. Heliers ridge has been proposed by the city engineer, Mr J. Tyler. This route would be along the Tamaki Drive and would follow the railway on its northern side across Hobson Bay, Orakei Basin and up Purewa Creek to St. John's Road, but it would keep to the northern and eastern side and approximately parallel to the railway after passing under St. John's Road until the Tamaki station is reached just eastward of Mount Wellington.

"From this point the new route would depart altogether from the original route and swing eastward, passing under Pilkington Road just south of its junction with Stewart Avenue, from where it would proceed in a south-easterly direction to junction with the Panmure Highway, just north of the Tamaki Bridge approach. It would then proceed across the Tamaki River and continue in a south-easterly direction in easy country, and crossing the Pakuranga Creek would swing south to junction with Preston's Road, following this in a straight line for about three and a-half miles to junction with the Great South Road just north of the Redoubt Road intersection near the Wiri post office.

"Mr Tyler has shown that this new route would be 12¾ miles from the Tamaki Drive junction, and to the same point on the Great South Road would be of equal length to the proposed link with Mount Wellington Highway, and would be only half a mile longer than the old Great South Road." [108]

By July 1945, the urgency for a roading infrastructure remained and there was no shortage of ideas. However, many proposed projects depended on decisions still to be made about others and all were subject to the availability of men and material after a long war. In one of his many articles about the challenges facing a growing Auckland, the award-winning, Auckland Star journalist, E K Green, described the planning and outlay that was then required:

Drastic Remedies Needed

"AUCKLAND, like Topsy, has 'just growed'. Until comparatively recently there was little in the nature of a development plan, and the problems that have grown with the city have now reached the stage where drastic remedies are needed. The result is that Auckland must now plan, and act, on an elaborate scale. It is going to be a costly business. Two of the most urgent problems, because they bear on future development, are the provision of transport facilities for people living and working in the city, and the development of suitable traffic outlets.

"The question of traffic outlets is one that has agitated opinion for a number of years, but it has been possible to do little until now because the position was confused, and trends had to be watched. A number of traffic tallies were taken up to 1939, but none showed congestion had reached a stage that would warrant a large-scale outlet scheme. Now the city is growing so fast that it is imperative that something be done soon. Plans for the extensive State housing suburb at Tamaki make important the provision of a high-speed south-eastern outlet, but that is not the only reason.

"Aerodrome provision, to cater for external and internal air traffic, is another urgent factor. Indications are that the permanent airports of the future will, be in the south-eastern area, and as they must, of necessity, be a fair distance out of the present city limits that distance has to be offset by speed of access. Industrial, commercial and residential building along the present Main South Road is already causing congestion, with resultant slowing down of traffic on that outlet channel.

"Designed to cater for traffic speeds up to 60 m.p.h., the proposed south-eastern outlet—unnamed yet, but generally referred to as the Tamaki highway—is at present planned to follow the railway line from the waterfront road, out past Purewa, Glen Innes and Mount Wellington, swing across the Tamaki River and Pakuranga Creek to open country, joining the main south road about Wiri—though it can be extended indefinitely. It may cost about £1,500,000.

"It is planned as a four-lane concrete highway, with additional cycle tracks and footpaths. There will be no residential, commercial or industrial frontages upon it, and connecting roads will be channelised, or brought into it at roundabouts. All this is designed so that there will be no slowing down factors, no dangerous crossings. Two of the tracks will be for high speed, two for slower traffic. Opposing streams of traffic will be separated by strips, probably planted with hedges or trees, so that at night there will be no need to cut headlights to avoid dazzling approaching traffic.

"The road, at junctions, will be sufficiently wide so that turning or incoming traffic will be able to take refuge until it can easily swing into the stream of traffic. One of the main features of the scheme is that the proposed route will by-pass several suburban townships, where bottlenecks are already causing congestion to through traffic. In this connection there is another problem yet to be decided—whether or not a special stock route should be provided from the Waikato to Westfield. Nearly all this traffic now passes through Otahuhu, where it acts as a troublesome traffic block. Surveys taken indicate, however, that a surprisingly small proportion of stock is driven by road. Future developments may determine that all stock will be brought by rail or truck.

"Not yet determined, but in mind, is the provision of a two-deck highway along Quay Street and part of King's Drive at the city end of the south-eastern outlet. The compelling factor here is the use of Quay Street for rail traffic to the wharves—a traffic that can never be entirely obviated, and a definite block to the outlet. The 'overhead road' would be restricted to vehicular traffic and would run from Hobson Street (with an outlet to Albert Street also) on a bridge type structure, to level out again at Gladstone Road.

"Definite planning for this and some other city projects is dependent upon decision regarding the proposed harbour bridge or tunnel (a vital question in town planning). To cater for the future this cross-harbour outlet to the north will also have to be an express highway by by-passing built-up areas likely to develop bottlenecks and serving the North Shore boroughs through channelised side roads. At the city end it will need to fit into the south-eastern outlet scheme. Before a decision on this question is made, I am told, it will be necessary for some authority to spend anything up to £20,000 on a thorough investigation of possibilities. It cannot be left to guesswork.

"Whenuapai aerodrome, it is announced, will definitely be the interim external and internal airport for the city—a decision which has something to commend it as an initial step, but is definitely not pleasing to aviation authorities as more than a short-term proposal. It raises again the project for a western express highway, via Pollen Island. To cater for a short-term aerodrome it would be a most expensive scheme, though future outlet considerations may require it. Continued across the upper harbour, it might shorten the northern highway by about 10 miles—but would that be needed if a bridge or tunnel scheme were eventually adopted?

"The bridge, or tunnel, is considered an essential to city growth, as the present service or serviceable area on the North Shore would accommodate a potential population of 150,000. The present population is about 25,000. Any structure across, or under the harbour would also carry essential services, such as water and power. [109]

Public Works Statement 1946

Robert Semple, the Minister of Works, provided a definition of what the Government intended to be the blueprint for the planned 'divided highways' in his 1946 Public Works Statement:

"The promotion of every means whereby the safety of highways can be improved for all classes of road-users is one of the most important matters which have received attention. At the outbreak of war, studies were being made of design problems affecting routes in the vicinity of urban areas where conditions were becoming serious because of congestion and the wide variety of traffic involved.

"In approaching this problem it was recognized that what might be termed the traditional roading methods would not offer a satisfactory solution, but that consideration would have to be given to some adaptation of the divided highway which has secured world recognition through the effective results obtained from experience in older and more-developed countries. It is now almost universally recognized that, where traffic densities are not even as great as those of our more important national roads, there must be segregation of motor-vehicles from other forms of traffic, and that, while the all-purpose roads will remain for property access, for pedestrians, cyclists, stock, and for local and inter-village motor traffic, there should, in some cases, be motorways solely for the use of motor-vehicles.

"These would by-pass towns and built-up areas, and would traverse the country without ribbon development. Turn-outs from and entrances to the motorways would be limited to selected points where the layout of the junctions would incorporate the safety principles recognized by highway engineers. The motorways would traverse the country in the manner of a railway with no ribbon development, and with no access except at properly designed junction stations.

"The provision of this type of highway has become a matter of necessity in the interest of safety and economic transport, and to this end motorways are now being surveyed and designed in localities where the demand is most urgent. At the same time, all-purpose and inter-village roads will receive due attention, and the highways farther afield, where traffic densities do not justify motorways, will continue to be developed along lines of safety and economy of transport for both passengers and goods." [73]

Public Works Amendment Act 1947

The Public Works Amendment Act 1947, an Act to amend the Public Works Act 1928, was enacted on 25 November 1947. As explained by the Chairman of the Main Highways Board, F Langbein, in the Ministry of Works Statement for the year ended 31 March 1948:

"Legislation by means of the Public Works Amendment Act, 1947, made provision for the declaration of limited-access highways or, more shortly, motor-ways. It is emphasized that motor-ways are not glorified all-purpose highways. Work is continually in progress to improve the arterial roads of the country, but these improvements will not create the characteristics or allow of the functions of a motor-way. In addition to providing the most efficient and economic transport service, the main distinguishing characteristics of a motor-way are the control of access and the total elimination of ribbon development, both of which will go far to improve road safety and prevent obsolescence.

"Except for North America, the proportion of motor-vehicles to population in New Zealand is greater than in any other country of the world, and since the end of the war there has been a further upward trend of motor-vehicles on the highways. This has been particularly the case with passenger-buses and heavy haulage trucks. It has become apparent that the capacities of the existing main routes adjacent to the chief cities are already being overtaxed, thus leading to much loss in direct transportation costs, and, of even greater importance, the accident potential of these roads is rising at an alarming rate...

"In many respects a motor-way resembles a railway, which provides no property frontage and has access limited to stations located at intervals as will best serve the townships and settlements. Motor-ways will be constructed generally as four-lane routes, with a central hedge or a wide grass plot separating the two up lanes from the two down lanes...

"There will be no need for pedestrians or cyclists on a motor-way any more than they would enter upon a railway, and since between 40 per cent, and 50 per cent, of road accidents involve pedestrians or cyclists, there will be a great saving of life by the building of these special motor roads. Further, with the removal of all but local vehicles from the ordinary streets and roads, pedestrians and cyclists will be able to move about their business in their residential areas and townships without being continually menaced by increasing volumes of fast-moving through traffic.

"Where the density of traffic exceeds 3,000 vehicles per day, the construction of a motor-way will effect tremendous savings in transport costs. If and when, for example, a motor-way can be completed for, say, 30 miles from the centre of Auckland to by-pass and skirt the industrial towns to the south, in travelling time and cost of travel this will be equivalent to only 20 miles of travel along the present Great South Road.

"The equivalent reduction of 10 miles for 5,000 vehicles per day in and out of Auckland represents an annual saving in vehicle-operation costs of nearly £500,000, which means that the 30 miles of motor-way, although expensive in construction, could be paid for from a few years' savings in the cost of haulage. Keeping these facts, together with the safety factor, in mind, it becomes clear that motor-ways adjacent to our chief cities would not be luxuries. It is obvious that they are overdue and urgently necessary.

"Unfortunately, works of even higher priority, such as housing and hydro-electric development, are absorbing most of the materials and man-power at the present time, and it is therefore not possible to push ahead with the construction of motor-ways as the Board would wish. Construction has started to the south from Auckland to by-pass Penrose, and to the north from Wellington between Johnsonville and Porirua, but the chief activity in regard to motor-ways for the moment lies in the carrying-out of surveys and the purchase of the necessary land." [110]

Quality and Cost

However, by 1948, it was not just the preferred routes for these new motorways and highways that had to be decided. The quality of their construction, and therefore their cost, was of prime importance, as referred to by the Minister of Works, Robert Semple, in his Ministry of Works Statement for year ended 31 March 1948:

"With a view to assisting some local authorities and in order to help round off the State highways system, the Main Highways Board, with my approval, classified 1,330 miles of main highways as State highways as from 1st April, 1948. As a result of this further length of State highways the whole of the cost of construction and maintenance, in accordance with the standard prescribed by the Board, will from the date of classification be the sole responsibility of the State…

"The heavier and larger vehicles now being used to transport goods and passengers and the increasing numbers of such vehicles are causing great concern to the Board and the Engineers of my Department. Previously, highways foundations and surfaces were not constructed to cater for such heavy transport, which was generally carried by rail or coastal steamer. Except on the very best of our foundations, this heavy and continuous haulage of goods is severely damaging the surface of our highways, and the cost per mile of new construction to cater for this extra loading will naturally show a substantial increase in future highway costs. There is need for greater co-operation between the roading authorities and the transport-controlling authorities, and it is my intention to foster this co-operation as much as possible in the future. [101]

Ministry of Works Statement 1949

According to Robert Semple's Ministry of Works Statement for the year ended 31 March 1949, little had changed insofar as the maintenance of road surfaces was concerned:

"In common with other roading authorities throughout the world, the Main Highways Board is most concerned at the deterioration of the road surfaces over recent years as a result of the operation of totally different post-war traffic. Long trucks and buses when operated on the many narrow highways of this country are most destructive to the verges of the carriage-way and cause the bituminous pavement on sealed roads to break away badly at the edges. While the longer and wider trucks and buses have involved the Board in more costly construction and greater expenditure on maintenance, it is the increase in numbers and weight that is causing the most serious damage to our roads and bridges. Until the roads can be strengthened to carry this wider and heavier traffic, pot-holing and surface failures must occur despite intensive maintenance.

"The Main Highways Board is fully aware of the importance of road transport to the economy of the country, and will do everything that is humanly possible with the finance available to provide roads that will allow safe and economic transport.

"I mentioned in last year's report that there was need for greater co-operation between the roading authorities and the transport authorities, and I am glad to say that some progress has been made in this direction. It is in the interests of the over-all economy of the country and the preservation of our roads and bridges that the axle-loading issues be determined on a reasonably balanced basis and then strictly enforced." [111]

The Road Problem in Perspective

As part of the Ministry of Works Statement, the Chairman of the Main Highways Board, F Langbein, also observed: "The registration of motor-vehicles showed an increase of 25,809 over the previous year's figures, and the latest figures include 2,984 more heavy trucks – i.e., over 2 tons laden." [112]

The Auckland Harbour Bridge

During the war years, the need for transport infrastructure naturally became less urgent although there were still those with an eye to the future and what would be needed when normality returned. A bridge across the harbour had not been forgotten but its necessity remained debatable, as reported by the Auckland Star on 11 November 1943:

"An Australian company offered to build the bridge some years ago and if the company had been allowed to go on with the work the bridge would have been built by now, said Mr G. Hutchison at the meeting of the Automobile Association (Auckland) last evening. The meeting was considering the Auckland Harbour Board's proposal to build a central wharf at Little Shoal Bay.

"In a letter written to the Northcote Borough Council, of which a copy was before the Automobile Association, Mr Semple, Minister of Works, strongly urged supporting the Harbour Board's proposal for a central wharf to enable the work to be put in hand as soon as possible.

"As far as the harbour bridge is concerned, wrote the Minister, I regret it is not possible to commit the Government in any way. The whole question of transport facilities in the Auckland area will have to be the subject of investigation as soon as possible. Even if the investigation shows the construction of a harbour bridge is justified, under the conditions which will exist after the war, I see no prospect of an immediate start with the construction as soon as the war ends.

"Mr Semple stated that if the bridge was to be built it should form part of the highway system of the Dominion, and not be built as a toll bridge. He intended to arrange that all construction works in the Dominion be carefully reviewed, to form part of a comprehensive national programme, which would be carried out in a definite order of priority. This would apply to all works carried out by the Government and works subsidised by the Government. Even work undertaken without Government assistance would have to be considered as far as its relation to the national plan was concerned, in order to see that it did not conflict with national interests.

"The chairman, Mr F. G. Farrell, said if a central wharf was built it would put the harbour bridge back 20 years. I think the Government wants to side-step the bridge, and the Harbour Bridge Association will have to wake up if it is to have a bridge. It was decided to ask the Harbour Bridge Association to call a conference of all parties interested in improving the harbour vehicular traffic facilities." [113]

Vehicular Ferry Terminal

As might be expected, the Automobile Association maintained its pressure for better vehicular access across the Waitemata, as reported by the Auckland Star on 20 January, 1944: "The proposal to erect a vehicular ferry terminal at Little Shoal Bay, with causeways to Birkenhead and Northcote, was strongly criticised at a meeting last night of the Automobile Association (Auckland). A resolution was carried declaring that the proposal was unsound and should not be proceeded with, and the association announced its intention of objecting strongly to any subsidy being paid from the funds of the Main Highways Board for the project.

"It was pointed out that the proposed terminal would probably involve a sum sufficient to make a substantial contribution toward the construction of a harbour bridge. When petrol restrictions were removed, traffic across the harbour would increase tremendously. Construction of a bridge would become imperative and much of the expenditure on the Shoal Bay terminal would be wasted. The association maintained that the largest city in the Dominion was entitled to better consideration than the proposal indicated." [114]

However, the Government had its own idea of how and when the future of transport in 'the largest city in the Dominion' should be considered and that consideration had to include the needs of the rest of the country as well:

"That there was no prospect of the Auckland harbour bridge project being undertaken in the near future was made clear in a reply by the Minister of Works, Mr Semple, in the House of Representatives to a question by Mr Morton (Nat., Waitemata). Mr Semple said the proposal would require consideration in conjunction with the major question of transport facilities for Auckland. All construction projects, including the harbour bridge proposal, would be carefully reviewed in due course in relation to a comprehensive national programme." [115]

Auckland Harbour Board Support

In the meantime, the Auckland Harbour Board sought to publicly establish its support for a cross-harbour bridge or tunnel, although not all board members were in favour, as reported by The New Zealand Herald of 9 August 1944: "Support for the building of a harbour bridge or tunnel as a national post-war undertaking was pledged in a resolution carried by the Auckland Harbour Board yesterday. The resolution, which was made following a request, from Mr H. Turner that the board define its attitude stated that it was subject to the board's obligation to protect shipping and aircraft facilities.

"A harbour bridge is quite unnecessary, said Mr E. J. Phelan, who opposed the resolution. I can visualise a waterfront road extended west as far as Whenuapai and then a small bridge across the river. That would provide a much better service to the public than a bridge costing £2,000,000. It would make a better gateway to the north. If you were going to cater for the 18,000 people on the North Shore I would say a harbour bridge would be worthwhile, but the idea is not of catering for them.

"Mr Phelan's amendment that the resolution be referred back to the board in committee for further consideration was defeated by eight votes to seven. The motive behind Mr Turner's original resolution requesting the board to define its attitude toward a harbour bridge was that it seemed to be in the minds of the public and some board members that the board was retarding the progress of the city, said the chairman, Mr J. H. Frater. Resolutions and actions of the board on the question between 1928 and 1943, however, had not offered anything to retard the building of a bridge, but had safeguarded the trade and shipping interests of the port." [116]

Waitemata County Council Support

Additional calls for a decision on the construction of a harbour bridge continued with the support of the Waitemata County Council:

"Support for the action of the Northcote and Birkenhead Borough Councils, in urging the Minister of Public Works to come to a decision regarding the proposed harbour bridge, and deploring any delay, was given by the Waitemata County Council at its meeting this morning. The resolution, which was moved by the chairman, Mr H. T. Gibson, and carried unanimously, stated that the excuse of the Minister of Public Works, Mr Semple, that years of preliminary work would be needed before the scheme could be put in hand, was entirely without justification." [117]

A Truly Greater Auckland

By September 1944, many harbour bridge proponents were suspicious of the motives of Mr Semple. As per his Letter to the Editor, published by the Auckland Star on 30 September 1944, at least one commentator also wondered about the apparent lack of planning vision and expertise displayed by those such as Parliament's Public Petition Committee:

"Two men sent a petition to Parliament asking that consideration be given to a proposal for the construction of a traffic tunnel under the harbour. The scheme was referred to the Public Petitions Committee, which reported favourably, and incidentally condemned the harbour bridge project. While this was going on Mr Semple made the statement that the whole question of Auckland transport, including the bridge, would be gone into some time after the war. Now where do we go from here? Mr Semple also stated that for some years after the war there would be neither men nor materials available for the construction of a bridge. How on earth does he arrive at that conclusion?

"The great open spaces at Birkenhead, Northcote and Takapuna are crying out for houses. The harbour on the north side is said to be deeper than on the south, so why should the factories, docks and shipping be confined to one side? In my opinion the Public Petitions Committee is not in its element in tackling the subject of town planning, as it affects the development of a truly greater Auckland. John MacDonald." [118]

Ferry Company Uncertainty

By March 1945, even the principals of the Devonport Steam Ferry Company were anxious for some decision about the harbour bridge to be made so that the company's post-war future could be planned. The ferry company's chairman at the time and prominent businessman, Sir Ernest Davis, favoured another Royal Commission to determine the matter, as reported by the Auckland Star: "Users of the ferry services – both the daily and the occasional users – will see merit in the opinion emphatically expressed by Sir Ernest Davis, on behalf of the Ferry Company, that the time has arrived when the community should make up its mind about the long-projected harbour bridge.

"Is it to be built, and, if so, where and when? The company reasonably says that it is entitled to know this, for as long as the future of the bridge project is uncertain the future of trans-harbour services is unpredictable – and it is difficult to make firm plans when there persists a basic uncertainty. The bridge project remains at the stage it reached long ago – plenty of people want it, but there is no agreement about who should pay for it.

"In recent years, as highway traffic increased (until the war), many have favoured the idea that the bridge should be regarded as part of the highway system, and paid for, in whole or in part, by the State. To these it appears that the problem is to induce the Government, or a Government, to accept the idea, and in election years there are not wanting men willing to suggest, more or less delicately, that a vote for them is a vote for the bridge. Sir Ernest Davis is right in insisting that the question should be re-investigated on its non-political merits, and that a Royal Commission is needed for the purpose.

"As the Harbour Board as well as the Ferry Company is understood to favour an investigation by Royal Commission, the occasion seems opportune for a conference to be held of all organisations that have interested themselves in the project, with the object of making a combined request to the Government. But the Commission, if appointed, should be asked to be precise in its report. If it favoured a bridge, but not its construction immediately, or if it rejected the project, but admitted that conditions later might justify it, the uncertainty would remain." [119]

Request for a Royal Commission

As is usually the case when important decisions are deferred, those affected by a lack of leadership anxiously seek answers. In April 1945, both the Auckland Harbour Board and the Devonport Steam Ferry Company urgently sought some direction so they could plan for the future.

"A joint request for a Royal Commission to investigate and report on harbour transport problems at Auckland has been sent to the Government by the Auckland Harbour Board and the Devonport Steam Ferry Co., Ltd.

"The purport of a long letter sent to the Government by the board and the ferry company was that indecision regarding the possible construction of a harbour bridge or tunnel made them powerless to make the decisions necessary for the orderly improvement of existing harbour transport services. Improvements that the board or company might be prepared to put in hand, regardless of the possibility or other direct access being provided, were opposed by sectional interests on the ground that their prosecution would tend to delay the erection of a bridge.

"Neither the board nor the company, it was stated, had any desire to obstruct the erection of a harbour bridge or any other form of direct access should competent authority, after full investigation, decide that a bridge or tunnel be built. In emphasising the urgency of the request, the letter said that no substantial progress toward the improvement of ferry services and facilities could be made until the matter had again been reviewed by a Royal Commission. It was requested that, before such a commission was gazetted, the proposed order of reference should be submitted to the board and company to ensure that nothing which those organisations require elucidating is overlooked." [120]

Petition for a Royal Commission

But it was not until September 1945 that a petition for a Royal Commission was presented to Parliament. As reported by the Auckland Star, the petition not only emphasised the need for a more efficient system of transport across the harbour but also appealed to the entrepreneurial and charitable hearts of the Government with the prospect of land development and the employment of returning war veterans, respectively:

"A request that a Royal Commission composed of the best engineers available should be set up immediately to make a complete survey and investigation of a harbour bridge at Auckland and to report to the Government is contained in a petition presented to the House of Representatives yesterday by Mr Morton (Nat., Waitemata). The petitioners were the Automobile Association (Auckland) and the Waitemata Harbour Bridge Association. The petition contends that the existing means of transport across the Waitemata Harbour are inadequate and impose extreme inconvenience, delay and economic loss on the public using them.

"The petition lists 27 local bodies which have recommended the building of a harbour bridge and 26 which have requested the Government to set up another commission of inquiry into harbour transport facilities. The petition urges the great improvement a bridge would effect in that great area of land lying to the north of Auckland city and concludes with the expression of opinion that the proposed bridge is of the greatest importance and suitability as a rehabilitation scheme." [121]

Public Frustration and Cost

Meanwhile, the motoring public had plenty of time to ponder the situation as they waited to cross the harbour. Some, like D.R.S., vented their frustration by way of Letters to the Editor, such as that published by the Auckland Star on 5 October 1945:

"With the approach of warmer weather more and more cars will be visiting the North Shore, particularly at the week-ends. For how much longer are visitors and local residents to be subjected to the, long irritating hold-ups in the vehicular traffic such as are occurring every week, when long queues of cars extend along the waterfront and many wait several hours?

"Is the Devonport Ferry Company aware that it has a monopoly of a public utility? Is it conscious of the fact that such a monopoly can be justified only if the service required by the public is being supplied? Is it not high time that the company made a clear statement of its intentions without introducing red herrings such as the harbour bridge, which will take quite a few years to complete? D.R.S." [122]

Cross-Harbour Costs

During its consideration of the harbour crossing petition submitted in September, Parliament's Local Bills Committee provided some detail of how cross-harbour delays cost the travelling public and commercial enterprises, as reported by the Auckland Star on 8 November 1945:

"An indication of the expense incurred by commercial interests and the public generally because of lack of an adequate harbour crossing in Auckland was given in the House of Representatives yesterday by Mr Coleman, chairman of the Local Bills Committee, when the petition relating to trans-harbour transport was being discussed.

"Vehicles using the vehicular ferry numbered 2362 each day, he said, or 862,130 in a year. The evidence showed that vehicles waiting to cross formed long queues, and that it was most unusual if there were not a wait of 20 minutes. It was a waste of time and petrol and a heavy charge on the business community. The cost to-day to users of vehicles was enormous. In 1928 tolls collected by the ferry company and paid to the Auckland Harbour Board amounted to under £4000, but in 1944 the figure was £10,000. The tolls represented only a fraction of the total fares paid by vehicular traffic. The cost for each trip was about 3/ for an ordinary car and up to 10/ and over for a commercial vehicle." [123]

Local Bills Committee's Recommendation

The Local Bills Committee's recommendation was presented to the House of Representatives on 7 November 1945:

"The committee recommends that the petition be referred to the Government for most favourable consideration, and that it be regarded as a matter of extreme urgency. This was the recommendation of the Local Bills Committee of the House of Representatives on the petition of the Automobile Association, the Waitemata Harbour Bridge Association and 12 others praying for the setting up of a select committee of the House and/or a Royal Commission to inquire into and report upon transport conditions across Auckland Harbour with a view to effecting improvements.

"The Prime Minister, Mr Fraser, said that the problem of harbour transport had been recognised by the House for a considerable period, and it would have been investigated before had it not been for the war. The question had arisen, he said, of how best to meet the position – whether by bridge, tunnel or increased ferry services. It might be possible to carry motor transport by a form of floating bridge or something of that nature. There were certain allied problems interlinked to some extent with transport across the harbour.

"Mr Smith (Nat., Bay of Islands) said that the petitioners stressed the point that the Commission should have the advice of expert engineers. He drew attention to the fact that the ferry company, according to a statement made by Sir Ernest Davis, was in an awkward position regarding improvements, because the company did not know what was to be done in future. The Birkenhead and Northcote Borough Councils were in the same position in respect to the Shoal Bay terminal for ferries, which involved an expenditure of something like £50,000.

"Mr Murdoch (Nat., Marsden) said the problem had been before the country for about 20 years. What was wanted now was action. He spoke of the difficulties in regard to delays to motor traffic crossing the harbour. All North Auckland was affected. There would be a considerable amount of support throughout Auckland and North Auckland for the project. He added that there was a certain section in Auckland, not keen on the bridge project, as they were of the opinion that trade might go from the city instead of coming to it. His opinion was that the bridge would have the reverse effect.

"Mr Clyde Carr (Govt., Timaru) said that a bridge was needed in Auckland now. He contended there was no need to have a commission. The urgency was there and should be recognised, and if there had to be an inquiry it should be conducted by a select parliamentary committee, with the experts giving their evidence, but not deciding the matter." [124]

Matter of Extreme Urgency

That urgency had been recognised by the Local Bills Committee when it referred the harbour crossing petition to the Government *for most favourable consideration* to be followed by an addendum that it should be regarded as *a matter of extreme urgency*. An Auckland Star editorial commented further:

"The Auckland Harbour Board and the Devonport Ferry Company have both strongly urged the appointment of a commission, so that the board may come to a definite decision upon its berthage facilities policy and the company may lay down a building programme to cover present and future needs. Neither of these aims can be approached until the questions of whether a bridge or tunnel is to be constructed, and whether either is an economic possibility, have been settled. The issue has been under discussion for over twenty years. It ought to be settled.

"The reception given to the committee's report indicates that the Government will act upon it, and the setting up of a Royal Commission in the near future is certain. It is made the more necessary by Mr Semple's statement concerning the planning of an underground transport system for Auckland at a cost of £5,000,000. Harbour traffic is bound up with this and if a bridge is to be built its site should be determined simultaneously with the planning of the underground." [125]

Underground?

It had been a long time since any type of 'underground' transport system for Auckland had been referred to by the Government. But, sure enough, the Minister of Works, Robert Semple, seemed to think it was needed, as reported by the Auckland Star on 8 November 1945:

"An announcement that the Works Department was preparing plans for improving Auckland's transport system generally at a cost of about £5,000,000 was made in the House of Representatives yesterday by the Minister of Works, Mr Semple…He said that traffic would have to go Underground.

"The Minister said it was realised that Auckland had many bottlenecks in regard to transport, and if the population continued to increase it would be almost impossible to travel by motor car unless something of a radical nature was done. He agreed it was a big engineering problem, perhaps one of the biggest the country had ever been called upon to tackle, and they would have to go underground. If that were done in Auckland it would be the first time underground transport had been provided for in New Zealand. The Auckland job would be a big one, because it would take £5,000,000 to put the city's transport system on a basis to meet future developments, added the Minister.

"It would be a master engineering job. He did not want any wires pulled to go here, there or yonder. They wanted engineering minds to concentrate without interference of any kind, so that the future development of Auckland city and suburbs could be properly planned.

"He suggested that some competent overseas engineer should be called in. He admitted that there were good engineers in New Zealand, but this time it was a question of calling someone in with a wider experience of world jobs of the kind, and while they were here they could look into other projects in addition to that of Auckland. The more examination they gave to any proposed undertaking the better would it be. Hurried jobs did not pay, but brought disaster instead of success. No time would be lost if a commission were to be appointed to inquire into the transport position." [126]

Ministry of Works Plans

"When asked to-day whether details were available of the scheme to solve Auckland's traffic problems, the Minister of Works, Mr Semple, said his Department had been working for a considerable time on the plans, some of which had been completed, and some were still in the course of preparation. He indicated that what was in mind was a new highway out of Auckland to get rid of some of the bottlenecks that at present slowed up the traffic stream, and other necessary reforms that would bring Auckland's traffic system up to a proper standard of safety and efficiency.

"The Minister reiterated the statement he made in the House that, to solve the problem, it would be necessary to take traffic underground, and visualised a tunnel system connecting possibly with the Central Railway Station and touching at other points where there was traffic congestion. He added that the £5,000,000 that he had mentioned as the cost of the work was only a rough estimate which he had formed after discussing the plans already made and those contemplated with the Commissioner of Works, Mr E. R. McKillop." [127]

The Suburban Railway Option

While the plans referred to by Mr Semple seemed to concentrate more on solving Auckland's traffic congestion with the provision of additional roads, albeit underground, there was still those of vision who favoured the suburban railway option that had been proposed for more than thirty years – as described by the Auckland Star on 8 November 1945:

"One of the suggested means of overcoming Auckland's transport difficulties is the provision of an underground, or part-underground, railway system. It has long been recognised that in catering for present and future expansions the railway system in and about the city must have a big share in providing transport facilities.

"Central feature of the whole scheme is the Morningside tunnel project, an underground railway which will run across the city below Albert Park. The main station in this Morningside scheme is to be at Myer's Park, behind the Town Hall. It will have outlets to Karangahape Road and Upper Queen Street. The line will probably join the present northern line on the city side of Morningside station.

"Several years ago, a further step in this development of city-suburban services was under consideration, when a scheme to carry a railway system in a wide circle round the existing outskirts of the city was sketched in broad outline. This circular railway would embrace the Onehunga line, which would be extended through Mount Roskill, with a tunnel in the Hillsboro area and then across the back of Mount Albert to link up with the Morningside scheme near Avondale. The radius would be about six miles from the centre of the city.

"It is believed that both the Morningside scheme and the Mount Roskill plan would involve electrification – a possibility in six or seven years' time – and that the circular route would be a double-track railway. The population of Auckland's outer suburbs would be transported with much greater facility by the provision of these two railways. With electrification, the furthest closely populated point from the city would be 25 to 30 minutes' travel from the heart of Auckland, as compared with Onehunga's 40 minutes by tram to-day.

"Development of State housing throughout the outer suburban areas is likely to be accelerated and, even to-day, is so extensive that existing transport facilities are inadequate. It has already been urged that investigations should be made concerning the projected route of the railway so that necessary land might be reserved. To what extent the Mount Roskill line will be underground has not been revealed, as the plan has never been advanced beyond the elementary stages.

"Engineers are thinking in terms of Auckland with a population of perhaps 400,000. It is estimated that with the present rate of increase there will be at least that number of people in the metropolitan area within 20 to 25 years. The proposed establishment of a central feeder station for the Auckland-suburban railway system in Myers Park, with entrances from Upper Queen Street and Karangahape Road, would be the most revolutionary change made in the city since the Auckland Railway Station with new marshalling yards was established on its present site and the old railway station behind the Post Office abandoned." [128]

Royal Commission

At first, it seemed as though the brief of the proposed, Harbour Bridge Royal Commission would encompass more than just the harbour crossing issue when a question was put to then Minister of Railways, Robert Semple, when departmental estimates were being discussed in the House of Representatives on 20 November 1945:

"Mr R. M. Algie (Opposition Remuera) had asked the Minister where the proposed Morningside tunnel stood on the list of priorities. He emphasised the importance of this work in view of the increase of 50,000 in the population of the Auckland metropolitan area. Replying to this point, Mr Semple said that this was only one portion of the general transport problems of Auckland which would be considered by the commission." [129]

Indeed, by the time this latest of Royal Commissions was officially launched on 22 March 1946, its terms of reference focused mainly on the need for a harbour crossing with the Commissioners required only to be mindful of "…improvements in the railway and roading systems in the area that are contemplated by the Railways Department and the roading authorities respectively". [130]

The appointed Commissioners, Sir Francis Vernon Frazer, William Richard Beaver, and Roland Harry Packwood, were directed "…to inquire into, examine, and report upon the trans-harbour facilities in the Auckland metropolitan area and the approaches thereto, and to report on proposals for the provision of further facilities in the public interest." [130]

The Commission was to inquire into and report upon the following matters:

"(1) What trans-harbour facilities are necessary in the Auckland metropolitan area and the approaches thereto to provide adequately for future traffic requirements of all kinds, both from within and from outside the metropolitan area, including through traffic, having regard to improvements in the railway and roading systems in the area that are contemplated by the Railways Department and the roading authorities respectively;

"(2) Should the facilities include means of direct access between the city and the North Shore suburbs in addition to or instead of the existing ferry services;

"(3) If so, what should be the nature of this direct access, and where should it be located:—

>   (a) If by a bridge, what should be the minimum navigational clearances, and what should be the provisions for traffic on the bridge and its approaches;
>   (b) If by a tunnel or tunnels, what should be the number of such tunnels and what provisions for traffic should be made in each;
>   (c) In either of cases (a) and (b) above, what will be the approximate cost of the proposed access, including the necessary approaches;
>   (d) If any other alternatives are investigated, what are they and what would be the approximate cost of each;

"(4) Upon what basis or bases can such direct access be provided and financed, with special reference to construction, maintenance, and operation;

"(5) If such direct access is not considered necessary at present, within what period of time will the probable growth of population, and the use of motor-vehicles together with other forms of transport, render it necessary;

"(6) If you consider that the existing ferry services should remain in operation, either with or without other means of direct access, what improvements, if any, should be made in the services now provided; and

"(7) Generally, any other matters arising out of the premises that may come under your notice in the course of your inquiries, and which you consider should be investigated therewith." [130]

"Public sittings for taking evidence and hearing submissions were held at Auckland from the 15th May, 1946 to the 12th June, 1946. During that period the Commission sat on 17 days and examined 67 witnesses. It received 85 exhibits and also obtained voluminous data from Government Departments and other sources. The transcript of the proceedings filled 1,271 typewritten foolscap pages.

"The members of the Commission visited those parts of the Auckland metropolitan area in respect of which improved road and rail facilities are planned, and made themselves familiar with the locations of the different works contemplated in the recently announced Auckland Metropolitan Development Plan. They also made detailed inspections of the existing ferry services between the City of Auckland and the North Shore suburbs, and investigated the roading systems of the North Shore and the east coast bays and the means of access to the ferry terminals. Their investigations included an examination of the possible sites for the erection of a bridge across the harbour and for the construction of a tunnel under the harbour, and, in each case, an examination of the location of the necessary connecting roads and causeways." [130]

Report of Royal Commission on Trans-Harbour Facilities

The Royal Commission reported its findings to Parliament on 26 July 1946 – a report that was almost a carbon copy of that provided by the Harbour Bridge Royal Commission of 1930. Just like its predecessor, the 1946 report cited a lack of resources and urgency for an immediate start on a bridge. Once again, the news was not good for those seeking an efficient and enterprising spanning of the Waitemata.

Bridge Not Needed for Ten Years

The 1946 Royal Commission concluded: "A bridge is undoubtedly a desirable traffic facility, and there are sound economic reasons for its inclusion in its due place in the Government's programme of improvements and extensions planned for the metropolitan area of Auckland…Nevertheless, having regard to the greater urgency of other public works, in particular housing, hydro-electric extensions, rural development (including roads, highways, and bridges), and works necessary to relieve congestion of city traffic, we do not regard it as a 'necessary' facility at present, though it will certainly become so at the expiration of the minimum period required for its completion, which we have fixed at ten years, which period, however, may for economical reasons require to be extended to a maximum of fifteen years.

"The construction of a bridge within the next few years would create a competitive demand for materials and labour which would, under present circumstances, seriously hamper the Government and local bodies in overtaking arrears in their respective programmes of urgently necessary works.

"In addition to the large capital sums involved in such works, there is to be considered the further outlay on the large fleet of passenger vehicles (buses and trolley-buses) which, when a bridge is built, will be required to cope with peak loads of passengers, now dealt with by ferries having capacities of upwards of 1,000 passengers. If, as we think, the majority of this traffic should be catered for by trolley-buses (consuming electrical energy instead of imported fuel), the provision of electrical equipment and wiring is also to be considered. These items are likely to be in short supply for some years to come. For these reasons we consider that it would be most inopportune at present to embark on construction work of such magnitude." [130]

Ferries Will Cope

"The existing passenger and vehicular ferry services, augmented and improved in the manner referred to later in our report, will reasonably meet the needs of traffic for the next ten to fifteen years, at the expiration of which time direct access by means of a bridge will undoubtedly have become urgently necessary. When the bridge is in service, scope will still remain for passenger ferry services to a limited number of points, but the vehicular ferry services should then be discontinued." [130]

Five More Years to Prepare

"Having regard to the probable growth of population and the density of the traffic likely to benefit from and make use of a bridge, we consider that a bridge will become a necessary facility, economically justifiable, within a period of time estimated by us at ten to fifteen years, but to be determined more precisely by general economic conditions prevailing five years hence—i.e., in 1951. Within that period of five years, as we have already recommended, the necessary surveys, borings, investigations, designs, economic studies, negotiations, and other steps necessary to establish a reliable estimate of the cost of construction of the bridge and its approaches should be undertaken by the

Government. We discuss the probable growth of population and the resulting increase in traffic in a later part of this report.

"In view of our recommendation that the bridge should be completed between ten and fifteen years hence, we do not recommend that the Auckland Harbour Board proceed with its plans for duplicating the vehicular ferry terminals at Mechanics Bay and Devonport or for providing a new combined passenger and vehicular ferry terminal at Little Shoal Bay. Such improvements as the Auckland Harbour Board deems necessary should be planned and executed on the clear understanding that direct access by means of a bridge will be available within fifteen years, and possibly in ten years. [130]

Commission's General Conclusions

"But for the post-war factors to which we have already referred, we should have had no hesitation in recommending commencement of the construction of the bridge at the earliest possible date, because we consider the provision of direct access to the North Shore area as overdue. We are compelled, however, to take cognizance of the fact that both the Government and the local bodies have six years arrears of public works to overtake, among them literally hundreds of smaller bridges in the Auckland Provincial District alone. All these can be classed as overdue, either in the interests of the safety of the travelling public or as essential aids to rural development and therefore to production; while the principal value of the Auckland Harbour bridge will be the improvement of the internal means of communication of a metropolitan area...

"We cannot overemphasize the need for devoting adequate time to investigations and studies of this project, all directed towards economy. This consideration is of the utmost importance in the planning of a project which is expected to become financially self-supporting from the outset, because any reduction in capital cost will be reflected both in the scale and in the period of application of toll charges. Our recommendation, therefore, is that, as soon as the specialist staff is available, investigations and economic studies should be put in hand, and the actual date of commencement of the work itself should be determined in the light of the economic conditions prevailing when the designs and specifications are completed." [130]

Capital Cost

At the time of their report, the Commissioners estimated the capital cost of the bridge, its approaches, and interest costs to be £3 million. However, they calculated that cost could be reduced to £2.4 million after about five years when world-wide shortages of steel, paint, construction plant, and freight charges would have eased. They also expected that local shortages of cement, timber, electric energy, fuel, and workers would also have improved by then. [130]

Material Shortages

The Royal Commission's concerns of post-war, material shortages were certainly relevant. A March 1948 memorandum from the Public Works Department Engineer-in-Chief, F Langbein, to his Commissioner of Works referred to the Auckland Transport Board having written to the Hon. Minister of Supply. The letter from the Transport Board Manager "...points out that due to inability to obtain steel for essential maintenance works on its vehicles [presumably trams and buses], the time is fast approaching when the vehicles may have to be withdrawn from service." [131]

Mr Langbein comments further in his memorandum: "...it appears to me that merchants should be instructed to give the highest priority to orders from such organisations and to supply their requirements in full before filling orders where the material will be used in new construction." [131]

Public Transport Needs

But while the vision for a bridge across the Waitemata was not yet achievable in the minds of the Royal Commissioners, they did anticipate the need for a future bridge to accommodate pedestrians and cyclists. Not only did they recommend six-foot-wide footpaths on either side of the suggested four-lane carriageway but also cycle-tracks. They were also mindful of the need for a public transport system controlled by a single, city-wide transport body.

"In passing, we express the opinion that a trolley-bus system appears to be well suited to the terrain and transport requirements of the North Shore, and that such a system can easily be incorporated in a unified system for the whole metropolitan area. However, whether a service by trolley-buses or by fuel-driven buses is decided upon, we are convinced that that service can be operated satisfactorily only as an integral part of a single metropolitan system under the control of one central authority…The Auckland Transport Board has indicated its willingness to have its area extended to include the North Shore area if such an extension is desired." [130]

Underestimated Traffic Volumes

But while the Commissioners foresaw the need for a centrally-controlled, public transport system and pedestrian and cycle access across a bridge deemed unnecessary in the short term, their estimation of the number of vehicles that would use this unnecessary bridge was also greatly underrated. This was of course consistent with Auckland's historical and future miscalculation of transport needs.

"Assuming, as for this purpose we do, that the bridge will be opened in 1956, we estimate the total vehicular traffic in 1965 at 8,250 vehicles [per day]. That volume slightly exceeds the practical or working capacity of a two-lane highway. Our estimate of the ultimate volume of traffic is 26,800 vehicles, which is slightly below the rated practical or working capacity of a four-lane highway. We consider that these volumes clearly determine that a four-lane carriageway is appropriate for the bridge, and we have recommended accordingly. It follows, also, that until the traffic volume approaches the ultimate to be expected from the metropolitan area there need be no doubt as to the bridge having reserve capacity to cope with any additional traffic from extra-metropolitan areas—in other words, the bridge alone could meet the requirements of the far North as well as of the North Shore area." [130]

The Commissioners' initial estimation of required bridge capacity wasn't too wide of the mark but their estimation of its future use certainly was. In 1946, they were not to know just how dramatically a Harbour Bridge would facilitate population growth of the North Shore.

The Auckland Harbour Bridge Company

In the meantime, well before the first vehicle crossing, there was some legislative housekeeping to complete. Since the Auckland Harbour Bridge Empowering Act of 1931, private enterprise in the form of the Auckland Harbour Bridge Company Limited had been "…empowered to erect and maintain a bridge across the Auckland Harbour and to impose and collect tolls for the use of the bridge…" [132]

Since its formation, a number of private-enterprise initiatives proposed by the Harbour Bridge Company Limited failed to materialise and the bridge was never started. In line with the findings of the 1946 Royal Commission that a bridge across the Waitemata Harbour would be of 'national value', by 1948, the Government of the day finally decided that the bridge was indeed of such national importance that "...it is expedient that the work should be undertaken as a public work under the Public Works Act 1928." [132]

Following an agreement between the Minister of Works and the Auckland Harbour Bridge Company Limited signed on 28 May 1948, the Auckland Harbour Bridge Empowering Act was accordingly repealed by Parliament on 14 July of that year. [132]

Suburban Rail
Suburban Rail Patronage Declines

By 1940, many Aucklanders were dismayed by the continuing decline of suburban railway patronage. Auckland City's Mayor, Sir Ernest Davis, even suggested a 'half-measure' to improve the suburban railway network. As reported by the Auckland Star on 10 August 1940: "...there should be a re-arrangement in handling the suburban railway traffic, to enable suburban passenger trains to be brought approximately half a mile closer to the centre of the city. Sir Ernest suggests that the vacant railway land at the corner of Britomart Place and Beach Road should be used as the site of a suburban passenger station." [133]

However, such a *half-measure* was just that to those who had retained the vision shared by Daniel Thomas McIntosh and Ernest Haviland Hiley twenty-five years previously. That vision was recalled by H A Robertson in a letter to the Auckland Star, published 14 August 1940:

"I read with keen interest the comments made by Sir Ernest with reference to a railway station closer to the city. Some years ago the Northern Suburban Railway League — a league consisting of all the northern local bodies, the Auckland Chamber of Commerce and the Karangahape Business Men's and Ratepayers' Associations — impressed the then Government with the necessity of providing a new and quicker outlet for passengers and workers, pointing out that traffic congestion would inevitably be the outcome if the matter was left.

"In 1924, the Rt. Hon. J. G. Coates had the whole scheme passed as an Act of Parliament. Included in this scheme of works was the Auckland railway station and the Morningside tunnel, including a double line to New Lynn. The Auckland station was planned and built for this purpose, and had it proceeded according to plan there would not have arrived today any question of congestion. Sir Joseph Ward, who became Prime Minister [10 December 1928 to 28 May 1930], however, stopped this work. Later the world depression made finance difficult and thus the Forbes-Coates Government could not re-instate the scheme.

"The present Government had been waited upon on several occasions, but unfortunately, to date, it has not seen the great benefit that this tunnel would be to the city. I quite agree with Sir Ernest that a station is required nearer the main centre of the city, and as one studies the map of Auckland, a station in Upper Queen Street would seem to be the centre, as it would serve both the city and Karangahape Road. I cannot agree, however, that a station at Britomart Place, as suggested, would be of great benefit. Further, as the Auckland station was built for the purpose of providing a northern outlet on raised land, it would be well-nigh impossible for trains to leave Britomart Place and go north.

"The Railway Department is proceeding with the duplication of the line from Morningside to Swanson, and this work, which will be of great benefit for the quick working of trains, will be almost of no value owing to the bottle-neck at Newmarket. The scheme, therefore, becomes a matter of urgency to the Department as well as the public." [134]

Profound Impatience

As too often occurred during New Zealand's various depressions and the previous war, the funding of the Second World War and the resulting shortages of labour and materials again resulted in the curtailment of many public works. Nevertheless, some with an eye to the future and the engineering projects which might be introduced as part of the post-war rehabilitation scheme expressed their frustration at the prolonged time and indecision that preceded actual construction.

An example of profound impatience was included in a statement issued by the Public Relations Committee of the Auckland branch of the New Zealand Institute of Engineers in April 1944: "…how many long steps, how many halts and how many back-slidings there are between a Cabinet decision to construct an Auckland harbour bridge, a Morningside tunnel or an administrative office block and the day when the engineer advises that labour is wanted?" [135]

Morningside Tunnel Project Revived

However, some hope remained for the construction of the Morningside tunnel as a post-war project that could employ many returning servicemen and get the country moving forward again – as reported by the Auckland Star on 28 September 1944:

"Reference to the future development of the Auckland city and suburban railway facilities is made by the Minister of Railways, Mr Semple, in a letter received by the Mayor, Mr Allum, this morning. I desire to inform you that the Morningside tunnel project is being included in a ten-year plan of railway development, which is being submitted by the Railways Department to the Government as part of the post-war rehabilitation programme, states Mr Semple.

"Regarding the question of electrification, Mr Semple states that any railway development schemes adopted will be carried out in the light of the most modern methods of railway operation known, with regard to the physical difficulties associated with the various works undertaken. The Morningside tunnel scheme was approved by Parliament in 1924, but was removed from the railway works schedule during the depression. It provided for a double-track underground line to avoid the route through Newmarket. Entrance to the main tunnel would be between Beach Road and Anzac Avenue.

"The tunnel would pass below the south-eastern corner of the Supreme Court building, under Government House grounds, and below Albert Park. At Wakefield Street, where the depth would be only 30 feet, an underground station would be provided. From Wakefield Street the tunnel would be on a straight line to its exit just beyond Newton Road. It would be 130 feet below Karangahape Road…The length of the tunnel would be a mile and a half." [136]

Auckland's Suburban Railway Plans

Auckland Star reporter, E K Green, was one of many to show his enthusiasm for what appeared to be a long-awaited commitment to expand Auckland's suburban railway and the subsequent progress that could result:

"In catering for present and future expansions the railways will obviously have a share in providing transport facilities. The Morningside tunnel project, already announced, will be a most important one. As an underground railway, it will run across the city, below Albert Park, with the main station of the suburban railway system at Myers Park, just back of the Town Hall, and with outlets to Karangahape Road and Upper Queen Street. The line will probably join the present northern line on the city side of Morningside station. Mount Albert station would be then only about eight to ten minutes from Queen Street, instead of 24 minutes as at present.

"A further step in this development may see the city-suburban service carried in a wide circle round the present outskirts of the city. It is known in engineering circles that a scheme for such a circle route railway service was envisaged several years ago, the radius being about six miles from the centre of the city. The idea then was to extend the Onehunga line through Mount Roskill, with a tunnel in the Hillsboro' area, and then across the back of Mount Albert to link up with the Morningside scheme near Avondale.

"The Morningside project calls for electrification – a possibility in six or seven years' time – and it is obvious that if the further scheme were undertaken it would also be electrified. A two-track circular route would be a forward step of the greatest importance in providing for the transport of Auckland's outer suburban population. With electrification the furthest point away from the city would be only about 25–30 minutes distant from the centre of the city (as compared with Onehunga's 40 minutes by tram).

"Such a scheme as this seems an obvious future step, but the development of State housing in the outer Mount Roskill and other outer areas at the present time is so extensive that any investigations as to the projected route would need to be made in the near future, so that land can be reserved for the purpose. General electrification of railways on both sides of the city seems another development of the comparatively near future. Henderson and Papakura have been suggested as possible electrification terminals, but it is considered possible that electrification may be carried well beyond these two points." [109]

Mayoral Support

The response of Auckland's Mayor, John Allum, was also supportive of the promised development of the City's suburban rail services, depending on affordability, of course – as reported by the Auckland Star on 31 July 1945:

"Auckland is greatly handicapped by the lack of fast suburban passenger transport which can be provided only by the development of the Morningside tunnel scheme with electrification of the suburban railways. This should not harm the present tramways and omnibus services. In fact, by taking over a great deal of the peak load, a first-class suburban railway system should benefit the present road services.

"In all civic planning regard must be paid not only to what is desirable and, in fact, necessary, but to what the citizens can bear financially. So far as the City Council is concerned, planning for the future is so designed that the work can be spread over a long period and the financial cost kept within reasonable bounds. For my part, said Mr Allum, I am satisfied that citizens are more concerned with wise spending than with the amount which is spent, provided always that the rates do not become unduly burdensome.

"There are many schemes under consideration and these must be developed in a reasonable order of priority and in a manner which will spread both the works themselves and also the financial liability. It is to be hoped that public interest in Auckland's development will be stimulated. Constructive criticism of the proposed works will be welcomed. What is not wanted is mere obstruction which relies upon propaganda and slogans regardless of the facts." [137]

Tunnel to Somewhere

But not all criticism concerned the affordability or otherwise of projects such as the Morningside tunnel scheme. While it had long been agreed that some tunnelling would be necessary to liberate railway traffic from the confines of the Beach Road Station, not all agreed with the direction such tunnelling should take. For instance, those living north of the Waitemata Harbour, awaiting a bridge seemingly forever, saw little benefit in a railway connection to the western suburbs, as explained by NORTHLAND in a letter to the Auckland Star, published 28 July 1945:

"Reading E. K. Green's most interesting articles on the development of Auckland, it struck me that no mention was made as to whether a railway tunnel under the harbour would not greatly exceed any advantage of the Morningside tunnel. I need hardly emphasise the advantages of a quick direct route to the north, beside opening up a large area of land, bringing it in close touch with the city. The present roundabout route, taking an average of an hour by rail to Swanson, and the mere fact of the road to Whangarei being only a little over 100 miles, compared to the railway's 130, show plainly the handicap under which we suffer. And surely the stupid arrangement at Newmarket could be rectified? Northland." [138]

The Shape of Things to Come

Although a harbour tunnel as a more direct railway route to Northland was not yet planned, the Ministry of Work's 1946, ten-year plan, *The Shape of Things to Come*, at least portended some advancement at long last. The Ministry's plan included:

"1. An underground line from Beach Road, adjacent to the Station Hotel, running under Shortland Street, the Civic Centre, and Karangahape Road, with underground stations at these points, and coming out into the open at Newton Valley; a station at Arch Hill, a further short tunnel at Kingsland, and joining the present north line about 10 chains beyond the present Kingsland station.

2. The duplication of the present line from this junction at Kingsland as far as Henderson.

3. A triangular junction at Beach Road to connect the underground line direct with the line to Newmarket via Parnell tunnel.

4. A triangular junction at Southdown-Westfield-Sylvia Park.

5. A new double track line from Avondale to Southdown via Mt. Roskill, Three Kings, Onehunga and Te Papa, with triangular junctions with the main lines at Avondale and Southdown.

6. Marshalling yards between Westfield and Otahuhu.

7. A new double track line from Avondale to proposed Upper Harbour Port area on Rosebank peninsula, with a triangular junction with the main line at Avondale.

8. Multiple-unit depot at Tamaki.

9. Reorganisation of Auckland goods yards with the removal of the present locomotive depot.

10. Electrification of all passenger lines between Papakura and Henderson; i.e. all lines except Kingsland–Mt Eden–Newmarket; Penrose–Te Papa via present line, and Te Papa-Onehunga Wharf.

11. Lifting of present line between Te Papa Fertiliser works and junction with proposed Avondale–Southdown line.

12. Elimination of all level crossings on passenger lines in the suburban area.

13. Modernisation of stations and improvements to station access." [46]

Work Started

According to the Ministry of Works Statement for the year ending 31 March 1947, work had at last started: "Auckland-Morningside Deviation—Survey work is continuing and alternative routes have been examined. Borings have been made to investigate the substrata on the tunnel line." [139]

That work continued, as related by Engineer-In-Chief, F Langbein, in the Ministry of Works' Statement to Parliament for the year ended 31 March 1948:

"Preliminary investigations for the Auckland-Morningside deviation were concluded and preliminary investigations and surveys for a route between Auckland and Kumeu via the waterfront [another proposed rail line from Auckland's Beach Road station to Kumeu] have now been completed." [110]

Further suburban railway surveys continued throughout 1948 and into 1949 as F Langbein outlined in his Annual Report on Public Works for the year ended 31 March 1949: "Investigation into the Auckland Waterfront Railway was continued during the year. The line was amended to suit relocation of the proposed city station and the Auckland Harbour Board's port-development scheme in the upper harbour.

"A permanent survey between the existing Auckland Station and Te Atatu Peninsula has been completed, and the route between the latter point and Kumeu Station has been fixed from several trial lines. This railway, together with Auckland-Morningside, the Avondale-Southdown, and the Penrose-Glen Innes deviations, which have also been the subject of investigations, will be included in the review to be made by the two English authorities who have been invited to report on transportation problems in the Auckland metropolitan area." [112]

Table of Distances

In July 1949, no doubt in anticipation of what now seemed a definite start to the Morningside deviation and other suburban railway improvements included in the Ministry of Works' plan, J R Lee (believed to be an Auckland City Council employee) thoughtfully completed a Table of Distances for existing and proposed city rail routes.

The document included a sketch illustrating the *Overall Pattern of Proposed System* – a pattern not too unlike the route chosen for the City Rail Link eventually started in 2017. A copy is included as (Appendix 1).

Schedule of Land

In the same year, an unknown author (again believed to be an Auckland City Council employee) compiled a *Schedule of Land* through which the proposed Auckland City Railway was expected to pass. The Schedule comprised the legal descriptions of the various properties, the known owners, and the unimproved and capital valuations of most of the properties described. The stated capital valuation of the listed properties totals £559,523 – the minimal, yet relatively substantial, cost of acquiring them from possibly resistant owners.

Divergence of Opinion and Prevarication

Naturally, there was a good deal of opposition voiced against Auckland's planned suburban railway expansion. While the property owners set to be displaced could have expected an adequate measure of compensation, they were hardly likely to recover the additional costs of relocation and business disruption. There were others, like *Northland*, who considered the Morningside deviation, in particular, to be a line to nowhere compared to a harbour crossing to somewhere; there were those set to profit hugely from road building, road-based transportation, and ancillary commodities; and those who resisted any progress until that progress had become the new convention.

Indeed, the *constructive criticism* of plans to improve Auckland's transportation services, welcomed by John Allum in 1945 had, by 1949, developed into a *considerable divergence of opinion* – as described by Robert Semple, in his Ministry of Works Statement for 31 March 1949: "The Government desires to put in hand as soon as possible the provision of additional transport facilities to serve the Auckland metropolitan area, and in an analysis of these considerable divergence of opinion as to the location of these facilities became apparent." [111]

Halcrow and Thomas Appointed

What could the Government do – other than to remain resolute and continue with the railway plan? Why prevaricate, of course, and camouflage its vacillation by availing itself of Auckland's perennial divergence of opinion; postpone by once again seeking advice: "Because of the magnitude of the work envisaged and of the importance of a correct decision to the Auckland area, the Government has considered it advisable again to obtain competent outside advice, and following inquiries made in Great Britain the Government has invited Sir William Halcrow, Past President of the Institute of Civil Engineers, and Mr J. P. Thomas, late Chairman of the Transport Advisory Committee of the London Passenger Transport Board, to come to New Zealand and report on the question. These gentlemen are expected in New Zealand early in September, and it is hoped that as a result of their report an early start can be made upon the actual construction in the city and in the suburban areas." [111]

Overseas Railway Mission

Government inaction was also justified by what was described as a full and thorough investigation of the electrification of suburban railway networks overseas, further delaying the *early start...upon the actual construction in the city and in the suburban areas* suggested by Robert Semple in his 1949 Statement:

"After examining the economics of the system, and the public need for efficient passenger and goods transport, it was clear to the Government that the best means of modernizing the system, paying full regard to our national resources, was to follow a policy of electrification; consequently, a Railway Mission, headed by the General Manager, has been sent overseas to examine electrification problems of other systems. The work of investigation will occupy a number of months, and after a full examination of all the technical and economic considerations involved a report will be submitted to the Government. [111]

Dr E P Neale – Auckland's Transport Problems

While Auckland's commuters awaited the Government's pleasure, the city's suburban railway services remained inadequate, including "...*the stupid arrangement at Newmarket*" referred to by NORTHLAND in his 1945 letter to the Auckland Star.

The *arrangement at Newmarket* was also referred to by the Secretary of the Auckland Chamber of Commerce, Dr E P Neale, in his 1949 report to members, *Auckland's Transport Problems*:

"The circuitous route through Newmarket – with its back shunt dating from the early eighties – has always militated against anything like fullest possible use of our Western suburban railway to Henderson, Swanson and Waitakere. In fact there have in very recent years been very drastic cuts in the Waitakere suburban time-tables, particularly on Saturdays, simply because the trains were not paying for axle grease. With the shifting twenty years ago of the Auckland Railway station from the foot of Queen Street to the present location off Beach Road, rail suburban traffic both North and South has apparently failed to increase in the same proportions as has population. It is rare indeed for an Auckland suburban train to be overcrowded, in sharp contrast to most of the other forms of Auckland urban transportation.

"With the opening of the tram route to Onehunga nearly fifty years ago rail traffic on this route has steadily fallen away, so that this line no longer pays to operate for passenger traffic except at peak-hours; when alone passenger trains are scheduled for this line. That other suburban trains have not been withdrawn since the more recent opening up of the Great South Road, Avondale and Owairaka tram lines is due to the fact that these railway lines (unlike the Onehunga line) have considerable lengths along which they are not subject to tram competition. Much of the…lost traffic, especially the suburban traffic, could be got back to the railways if faster and more direct services were provided with a more central railway station than the present one." [104]

Dr Neale's proposals for railway improvements included:

"Much of the traffic that at present goes by tram to and from Auckland would doubtless go by rail if fast electric trains called at some point (or points) in the heart of the City (say Victoria Street East and/or near the Town Hall). If the saving in speed and strain of driving were sufficient, many businessmen and shoppers who at present motor to the City might even be induced to use the electric trains…the Chamber is strongly in favour of a more centrally situated suburban passenger station than at present exists.

"Capital costs per mile of an electric railway are apt to be higher than for a steam railway (mainly owing to the necessity for overhead wires). Operating costs per train-mile are apt, on the other hand, to be lower for an electric railway than for a steam railway owing to a variety of reasons. Electricity is cheaper than coal; no time is wasted by train crews in coaling or watering; maintenance is cheaper because of simpler construction of electric than of steam locomotives; etc., etc.

"Given sufficient traffic, therefore, the savings in operating costs on an electrified railway more than pay for the interest, sinking fund, etc. charges on the capital cost of electrification. In this connection, Merz and McLellan in 1925 estimated Auckland electrification would return 9.85%, Wellington 8.45% and Christchurch 2.2% on the capital cost of electrification. In a country like New Zealand, where electricity is mainly derived from water power, electric-operation of railways is not wasteful of natural resources as, e.g., steam-operation. (If oil fuel is used on steam locomotives, there is also wastage of dollar resources.)

"The figures of the Merz and McLellan report have never been refuted; and actually the savings on electrification should be substantially higher than in 1925, as coal in New Zealand has increased in price much more rapidly than electricity. Yet Christchurch and Wellington have long enjoyed electric railways, Wellington's last electrification project being already well in hand. Aucklanders can never understand their neglect by the authorities in this matter. Hon. R. Semple when he announced his 10 year plan spoke of stopping short in electrification of the Kaipara Line at Henderson rather than at Swanson, Waitakere or Helensville. Surely electrification to Waitakere would postpone the otherwise urgent need for duplication and grade easement between Henderson and Waitakere." [104]

Transport Licensing

While civic leaders such as Dr Neale expressed their concern and provided various suggestions as to how the Railways could best cope with road-based competition, the Government continued to use regulation as its preferred means of winning the contest – as it had as early as 1926, with the passage that year of the Motor-omnibus Traffic Act to protect the publicly-owned tramways from private bus services.

A brief summary of ensuing legislation that strived to protect the Railways from road-based competition, included:

The Government Railways Amendment Act 1931 – An Act to amend the Government Railways Act, 1926, to make Better Provision for the Control and Management of the Government Railways, and for the Carrying-on of the Business thereof.

– Section 2 allowed for the re-constitution of a Government Railways Board as previously provided for by the Government Railways Amendment Act 1925 and the Government Railways Act 1926 but which was abolished in 1928.

– Section 14. (1) defined the Functions and Powers of the Board: "It is hereby expressly declared that the general functions of the Board shall be to carry on, control, manage, and maintain the Government railways to the end that the railways, while being maintained as a public service in the interests of the people of New Zealand and as an essential factor in the development of trade and industry, shall be so carried on, controlled, managed, and maintained on the most economical basis, having regard to the economic and financial conditions from time to time affecting the public revenues and trade and industry in New Zealand, with a view to obtaining a maximum of efficiency and maintaining a proper standard of safety and a reasonable standard of comfort and convenience for persons using the railways and any other services carried on in connection therewith." [140]

The Transport Licensing Act 1931 – An Act to make Better Provision for the Licensing and Control of Commercial Road Transport Services other than Tramways. [141]

The Act set out the procedures and conditions required for the licensing of road-based passenger and goods vehicles and, for that purpose:

– established a *Central Licensing Authority* and a *District Licensing Authority* for each District.

– appointed the Auckland Transport Board as the District Authority for the Auckland Transport District

– established a *Transport Appeal Board* "…to hear and determine all appeals duly lodged in accordance with this Act against the decisions of Licensing Authorities." [141]

The Transport Law Amendment Act 1933 – An Act to constitute a *Transport Co-ordination Board* and to amend the Transport Licensing Act, 1931.

The Transport Co-ordination Board "…to hold such inquiries, make such investigations as it or the Minister deems necessary or expedient, and to report to the Governor-General through the Minister the result of such inquiries and investigations with such recommendations as it thinks fit for the purpose of securing the improvement co-ordination and development, and better regulation and control of all means of and facilities for transport and all matters incidental thereto:" [142]

The Transport Licensing Amendment Act 1935 – An Act to amend the Transport Licensing Act 1931 – effectively extended the duration of a passenger service licence from 12 months to three years and provided for licences to be revoked if the circumstances under which the licence was granted change materially. [143]

"In 1935 Michael Joseph Savage's first Labour government took power…Savage and his government wasted no time in setting about the instigation of a programme of socialist reform, and it rapidly became clear that the nationalisation of transport was on the agenda." [144]

Nationalisation didn't happen but the provisions of the 1931 Act were later strengthened by means of the Transport Licensing Amendment Act 1936:

The Transport Licensing Amendment Act 1936 – An Act to amend the Transport Licensing Act, 1931, and the Transport Licensing (Commercial Aircraft Services) Act, 1934.

– the Central Licensing Authority established by the Transport Licensing Act 1931 and the Transport Co-ordination Board established by the Transport Law Amendment Act 1933 are both abolished

– the District Licensing Authority established by the Transport Licensing Act 1931 can consist of only one member, appointed by the Minister

– Section 15 of this Act protected the Railways' passenger service by denying licences for any passenger-services having substantially the same terminal points and routes as the railway service:

"Except with the previous written consent of the Minister of Railways, no license shall be granted to any person other than that Minister for a passenger-service having substantially the same terminal points and route as any passenger-service for which the said Minister is for the time being the holder of a license: Provided that nothing in the foregoing provisions of this section shall be deemed to apply with respect to any renewal of a license that does not authorize any extension of the service to which the license relates." [145]

The Government Railways Amendment Act 1936 – An Act to amend the Government Railways Act 1926.

– Section 2 abolished the Government Railways Board which had been established by the Government Railways Amendment Act 1931, and prior Acts and amendments, replacing it with "…a General Manager of Railways…under the control of the Minister."

– Section 8 facilitated the Railways' purchase of private passenger and goods transport services. It is a repeat of the provision previously provided by Section 18 of the Government Railways Act 1926:

"(1) The Minister may undertake the carriage of passengers and of goods otherwise than by railway, and whether by land, water, or air.

"(2) The power conferred by this section shall include power to enter into agreements with other carriers in relation to the carriage of any passengers or goods." [146]

As John McCrystal described in his book, *On the Buses in New Zealand*:

"The government strategy toward private passenger services was far more direct: the Railways Department began purchasing private operators and was not above using its privileged position in licensing hearings to force recalcitrants to sell out…" and [After the Second World War], "New Zealand Railways Road Services stepped up their acquisition of private operators, perhaps in anticipation of a renewed push by the government toward the nationalisation of all long-haul public transport. But the government's attitude after the war was indifferent. It no longer seemed to have the will to take control of the passenger transport sector, and yet it had no thought-out plan for an alternative. The regulation of the bitter rivalry between public and private operators was left to the licensing authorities and was therefore decided on an unplanned, ad hoc basis." [144]

The Transport Law Amendment Act 1939 – An Act to amend the Law relating to Motor-vehicles and Road Transport Services.

– defines certain terms such as goods-services

– Section 17 defines services that conflict with the *carrying of goods more than 30 miles along a rail route*. This Amendment also defined the "…proper Licensing Authority to grant passenger-service licences or exercise jurisdiction in respect thereof." [147]

"To 'protect the public investment' in rail, carriers were prohibited from carrying goods more than 30 miles (50 km) along a rail route. [144]

The Transport Law Amendment Act 1948 – An Act to amend the Law relating to Transport Licensing and Motor-vehicles.

– Section 6 established a *Transport Co-ordination Council*:

"*(a)* To make inquiries into and to report on and make recommendations concerning such matters as may from time to time be referred to it by the Minister:

(b) To institute of its own motion inquiries into any matter affecting public transport of any kind and to make reports and recommendations thereon to the Minister:"

– Section 12 established a *Transport Charges Committee*:

"…to fix, review, or alter the charges for the carriage of passengers or goods (including mails), or the letting of motor-vehicles on hire, by any transport service (including the charges payable under any contract or group of contracts or proposed contract or group of contracts), whether the charges to be reviewed or altered have been fixed before or after the commencement of this Act."

– Section 17 established a *Transport Charges Appeal Authority*:

"20. (1) The functions of the Appeal Authority shall be to sit as a judicial authority for the determination of appeals from any decision of the Committee.

"(2) The Appeal Authority may also from time to time issue directions to the Committee to proceed to fix or review the charges for any service or group of services (including the charges payable under any contract or group of contracts), whether the charges to be reviewed have been fixed before or after the commencement of this Act." [148]

The Transport Licensing Amendment Act 1949 – An Act to amend the Transport Licensing Act 1931.

– Section 2 allows for Tramway fares, tolls, and charges to be fixed by the Transport Charges Committee set up by the Transport Law Amendment Act 1948.

– Section 3 allows for charges for the carriage of passengers or goods by trackless trolley-omnibus to be fixed by the Transport Charges Committee. [149]

The Transport Act 1949 – An Act to Consolidate and Amend Certain Enactments Relating to Motor-vehicles, to Road Traffic, and to Commercial Transport Services Carried on by Means of Motor-vehicles or Harbour Ferries

As referred to earlier, it was not until the passage of this Act that an attempt at an all-inclusive approach to both public and private transport operation finally eventuated. The

Act, which came into force on 1 November 1949, was a comprehensive piece of legislation that provided for the administration, registration, and licensing of motor vehicles and drivers; motor spirits and mileage tax; motor vehicle insurance; and road transport and harbour ferry services, including the fares of trams and trolley buses.

The Act principally required all transport services to be licensed as per:

"95. (1) Except as specially provided in this Part of this Act, it shall not be lawful for any person to carry on any passenger-service or, within a goods-service district, any goods-service or, within a harbour-ferry service district, any harbour-ferry service otherwise than pursuant to the authority and in conformity with the terms of a passenger-service licence or a goods-service licence or a harbour-ferry service licence, as the case may be, granted under this Part of this Act." (1949 Section 95)

In particular, Sections of the Act deterred competition between private transport operators and government entities, such as the Railways Department:

"103. (1) Every application by or on behalf of the Government, or the Minister of Railways, or a local authority or other public body for a passenger-service licence or a goods-service licence shall be given preference over all other applications for such licences if-

(a) There is no existing service for the carriage of passengers or goods, as the case may be, over the route or routes or in the locality or localities mentioned in the application; and

(b) The proposed service is in extension of an existing transport service carried on by the applicant (whether with motor-vehicles or otherwise), or, where the applicant is a local authority or other public body carrying on a transport service, is a new service to be carried on wholly within the district of the applicant; and

(c) The Licensing Authority is satisfied that the proposed service will not unfairly compete with an existing service to the same locality or localities by another route; and

(d) The Licensing Authority is satisfied that the proposed service will be satisfactory, having regard to time-tables, frequency of service, and otherwise." [105]

Section 103 (2) of the 1949 Act continued the Railway's traditional monopoly of freight transportation and, where possible, its passenger services, with a repeat of Section 15 of the Transport Licensing Amendment Act 1936:

"Except with the previous written consent of the Minister of Railways, no licence shall be granted to any person other than the Minister of Railways for a passenger-service or goods-service having substantially the same terminal points and route as any passenger service or goods-service, as the case may be, for which the said Minister is for the time being the holder of a licence:" [105]

The 1949 Transport Act thus shielded the passenger and freight business of the Railways Department from competitive bus and road transport companies.

First Halcrow and Partners Inquiry

The invitation to Sir William Halcrow, Past President of the Institute of Civil Engineers, and Mr J. P. Thomas, late Chairman of the Transport Advisory Committee of the London Passenger Transport Board, referred to by the Minister of Works, Robert Semple, in his 1949 annual report to Parliament, was duly accepted.

The Order of Reference drawn up to guide their inquiry included:

"(a) What improvements to the railway system in the Auckland Metropolitan Area are required and economically justified, having regard to the prospective passenger and goods traffic?

(b) If such improvements are recommended, when should their construction be undertaken?

(c) What would be the estimated cost of the recommended works?" [150]

Halcrow and Thomas provided an interim report to the Minister of Railways on 25 October 1949 and a final report on 14 March 1950 – as detailed in the following chapter.

Chapter Three

1950 to 1959 – Let's Debate and Decide

Planning and Politics
Local Government Commission Investigations

The further *exhaustive investigations* of Auckland's local body problems, referred to in the Local Government Commission's 1948 report, were undertaken during 1949 and 1950 but soon postponed by more pressing matters, as outlined in the Local Government Commission Report for the year ended 31 March 1950:

"The Select Committee which reported to Parliament in 1945 on all phases of the local-government system in the Dominion made special reference to the urgency of the problems of local government in Auckland and the environs. Since it was constituted the Commission has given serious consideration to the approach which should be made to the problems in this particular area…the Commission decided that in reviewing the question of the desirability or otherwise of reorganization of local government in Auckland and the environs it should first investigate the position in the North Shore area. An inquiry was accordingly commenced on the 5th July, 1949.

"The scope of the inquiry included the boroughs of Devonport, Takapuna, Birkenhead, and Northcote, and also areas in the Waitemata County, including the East Coast Bays, extending from Castor Bay to Long Bay, as well as Rangitoto Island and Herald Island, generally known as Pine Island, neither of which islands are within the district of a local authority. The inquiry continued until 22nd July, when it was adjourned until 2nd August. It concluded on the 8th August, 1949.

"As certain aspects of the problem are related to the Auckland metropolitan question, the Commission decided to withhold its report and findings pending an inquiry relating to the latter which was commenced on 7th November, 1949, and adjourned on 14th November. When this inquiry was resumed on the 13th February, 1950, an application was made by counsel for the Auckland Metropolitan Drainage Board for an adjournment, on the grounds that the Board's officers were fully engaged in the preparation of technical and other data relating to legislation of major consequence to the future activities of the Board.

"The future drainage scheme for Auckland was stated to be one of the utmost importance and urgency. Counsel for the majority of the local authorities represented at the inquiry supported the application. The Auckland Chamber of Commerce and the Hon. T. Bloodworth, M.L.C., who had prepared proposals for the reorganization of local government in Auckland and the environs, strenuously opposed the application. Although the Commission desired to proceed with the inquiry as soon as possible, upon consideration of the application, it decided to adjourn the inquiry sine die, and indicated that the progress of the legislation would be watched with a view to resuming the inquiry." [151]

Outline Development Plan

Although *the reorganization of local government in Auckland and the environs* was put on hold for what would become years, some planning co-operation continued with the production, in 1951, of an 'Outline Development Plan' for the Auckland region. The Plan was developed by the Technical Advisory Committee of the Auckland Metropolitan Planning Organisation (later known as the Auckland Metropolitan Planning Authority) which comprised "…technical representatives of local authorities, technical representatives of Government departments concerned in development works, land subdivision, etc., and the technical representatives of such *ad hoc* bodies as the Auckland Harbour Board, the Auckland Transport Board and the Auckland Metropolitan Drainage Board." [152]

New Zealand Institution of Engineers Comments

In its summation of the <u>draft</u> Outline Development Plan, published in its periodical, New Zealand Engineering, on 15 May 1950, the New Zealand Institution of Engineers explained: "The plan is an Outline Development Plan and covers only matters of overall metropolitan significance, although an endeavour has been made to put forward in the scheme suggestions and recommendations as to the form actual development should take in local areas. This procedure was adopted so as to leave the maximum degree of freedom and flexibility within local authority areas for more detailed planning considerations.

"In the light of the information available to-day it appears likely that the next forty to fifty years will see in Auckland:

(a) An addition of some 250,000 to 300,000 people, and the accommodation of a population of up to 650,000 has been allowed for.

(b) The rebuilding of perhaps half the existing urban development.

(c) The construction of a new port and associated industrial areas in the Upper Harbour. This port will be at least equivalent to that existing to-day.

(d) Perhaps three times the amount of road traffic existing to-day.

(e) The construction of some hundreds of miles of new roads.

"The aim of the plan is to guide all this new development in such a way that a satisfactory urban area from all points of view will result. It must be remembered that this development will take place whether there be a plan or not, and the plan should result in a more efficient urban area with better living propensities.

"Auckland is faced with the fact that the area in which this development and redevelopment is to take place is to-day administered by some 20 territorial local authorities each autonomous in respect of the development of the land within its jurisdiction. Twenty independently prepared plans fitting together like a jigsaw puzzle would not suffice to provide a sound integrated basis upon which to guide and consider all future development, and it was for this reason that the Auckland Metropolitan Planning Organization was set up by the local authorities. The Organization comprises representatives of most of the local authorities, although some have not participated." [152]

Auckland Metropolitan Planning Organization

Some eighteen local authorities were represented by the Auckland Metropolitan Planning Organisation and its Technical Advisory Committee included representatives of Auckland City; Waitemata County; Takapuna and Devonport (combined); Henderson, Glen Eden and New Lynn (combined); Mount Albert; Mount Roskill; Mount Eden; One Tree Hill and Newmarket (combined); Onehunga; Ellerslie, Panmure, Mount Wellington and Otahuhu (combined); Manukau County and Howick (combined); Papatoetoe, Papakura, Manurewa, Birkenhead and Northcote (combined); Ministry of Works; Lands and Survey; New Zealand Railways; Auckland Harbour Board; Auckland Transport Board; and the Auckland Metro Drainage Board.

Of the fifteen meetings held by the Technical Advisory Committee between 6 June 1952 and 8 October 1954, the representative of the combined local bodies of Papatoetoe, Papakura, Manurewa, Birkenhead and Northcote attended only one, as did the representative of the combined local bodies of Henderson, Glen Eden and New Lynn. Surprisingly, the representative of the Auckland Transport Board, C. R. Gribble, attended only five of the fifteen meetings held during that time. [153]

Town and Country Planning Act 1953

If post-war, municipal and district planning was to advance in step with the kind of collaborative initiatives encouraged by the Outline Development Plan, the co-ordination and consolidation of political agendas was urgently needed. To that end, some clarification of the bigger planning picture was eventually attempted by means of the provisions of the Town and Country Planning Act 1953 – "an Act to consolidate and amend certain enactments of the General Assembly relating to the making and enforcing of regional planning schemes and district schemes." [154]

The 1953 Act came into force on 1 February 1954 and repealed the Town-planning Act 1926 and amending Acts of 1929 and 1948. However, instead of providing for any consolidation of local government, the Act seemingly encouraged the existence and independence of local authorities:

"Planning control was made mandatory for all local councils in New Zealand…The twenty-three local councils then administering the local areas of Auckland were thus obliged to prepare and operate statutory planning schemes for their areas." [155]

The Act also promoted the resulting regional planning schemes as 'guides' only, and there was ample provision for those local bodies to appeal any decisions made by a higher authority:

"(2) Every regional planning scheme shall be designed as a guide to Councils engaged in the preparation of district schemes, and also as a guide to public authorities and local authorities and all persons in relation to the conservation or development within the region of the public utilities, services, industries, amenities, and other matters dealt with or adverted to in the regional planning scheme.

"4. (1) Every public body and local authority, in the performance of its public duties and functions, shall adhere to the provisions of any regional planning scheme that is operative in its district; but every local authority affected by a regional planning scheme shall have a right of appeal to the Board [Town and Country Planning Appeal Board constituted under this Act] at any time against the regional planning scheme so far as it conflicts with any operative district scheme or any proposed district scheme that has been recommended by the Council for the district to which it relates and publicly notified." [154]

Auckland Regional Planning Authority

At the same time, some semblance of local-body unity was provided with the formation of Regional Planning Authorities which, in the case of Auckland, removed the confusion that had existed since 1945 with the overlapping responsibilities of the Auckland Metropolitan Planning Committee and the Auckland Regional Planning

Organisation. There was now to be only the one planning body, reconstituted by the Town and Country Planning Act as the Auckland Regional Planning Authority:

"8 (1) For the purposes of every regional planning scheme proposed to be prepared as aforesaid there shall be a Regional Planning Authority consisting of the representative or representatives of the several Councils concerned who are appointed to the Authority in accordance with the provisions of this section.

"(2) Each Council whose district is wholly or partly within the region shall be represented on the Regional Planning Authority, either separately or in common with other Councils, by such number of representatives as the Councils may from time to time determine;" [154]

District Planning Schemes

But as well as its encouragement of local-body co-operation, the 1953 Act also primed 'parish pump' culture by requiring each local body to compulsory develop their own district (i.e. local) planning schemes:

"18. Every district scheme shall have for its general purpose the development of the area to which it relates (including, where necessary, the replanning and reconstruction of any area therein that has already been subdivided and built on) in such a way as will most effectively tend to promote and safeguard the health, safety and convenience, and the economic and general welfare of its inhabitants, and the amenities of every part of the area.

"19. (1) Whether or not a regional planning scheme including its district has been prepared or become operative, every Council shall provide and maintain in accordance with this Part of this Act, an operative district scheme in respect of all land within its district:" [154]

Communications and Transport Facilities

The First Schedule of the Act listed the 'Communications and Transport Facilities' to be dealt with by Regional Planning Schemes as:

"*(a)* Railways:

(b) Arterial and regional traffic routes:

(c) Public passenger service routes:

(d) Harbours and navigable waterways:

(e) Airports:

(f) Other communications and transport facilities." [154]

The Act's Second Schedule listed the transport matters to be dealt with by District Planning Schemes:

"5. Public access from place to place, car parks, transport terminals, aerodromes, and public transport systems, including their creation, establishment, closing, removal, alteration, and diversion; traffic routing; the co-ordination of street widths with land uses and population densities; off street provision for vehicles while being loaded or unloaded or standing; the fixing of building lines in relation to highways." [154]

The Municipal Corporations Act 1954 further defined the responsibilities and powers of the country's towns and boroughs when administering such matters.

Town and Country Planning Act Review Committee

But while the Town and Country Planning Act 1953 set some guidelines, the rapid growth of cities such as Auckland soon rendered many of its provisions obsolete. Indeed, a government-appointed, Review Committee was to observe in 1973:

"The committee considers that the regional planning provisions of the [Town and Country Planning] Act have not been successful in achieving their intended purpose. Regional planning authorities have been formed in only a few areas and the schemes that have been produced have often done no more than outline vague policies and the broadest of strategies." [156 p.5]

Poor attendances, such as those previously referred to for meetings of the Auckland Metropolitan Planning Organisation's Technical Advisory Committee, no doubt prompted the Review Committee to comment: "In presenting this report on our review of the Act we must say that neither the present Act, nor any new or amended Act, can of itself guarantee good town planning or provide well-founded solutions to the problems which arise from the physical development of our country. So much depends upon the skill and imagination of the technical officers responsible for the preparation and administration of district planning schemes, the technical resources at their disposal and the local government structure within which they must work. So much also depends on the extent of the commitment of the elected members of local government to the concept of seeking the best environment for all sections of the community which they govern." [156]

In its 1973 report, the Review Committee also observed: "The application of one form of regional planning authority throughout the country as provided under existing legislation is now inappropriate and unacceptable…Within main metropolitan regions the preferred organisation for regional planning is a multi-purpose regional authority…" [156]

The 'Greater Auckland' Concept

As described earlier, the establishment of some form of *"multi-purpose regional authority"* to govern the Auckland region had been attempted by many since the founding of the City. Arthur Myers, after he was elected Auckland Mayor in 1905, tried. However, his concept of a 'Greater Auckland' – "…his scheme for the amalgamation of the multiplicity of local councils and boards on the Tamaki isthmus was killed by their particularity." [157]

"From 1905 to 1928 the Auckland City Council did amalgamate with some suburban borough councils. Parnell and St Heliers had had their own councils but merged with Auckland City. Most suburban boroughs, however, refused to join the scheme." [158]

Long-time Auckland City Councillor, Thomas Bloodworth, (representing Labour and, later, the Auckland Citizens' & Ratepayers' Association 1919-1927 & 1928-1938) "…was a strong advocate of local government reform. In 1919 the Labour Party's municipal policy had included the introduction of proportional representation and the creation of one metropolitan authority in Auckland. During the 1920s he supported reorganisation based on ad hoc boards and in 1928 he unsuccessfully pushed for the establishment of a multi-purpose board of works." [159]

During his single term as Auckland City Mayor between 1953 and 1956, John Luxford remained a staunch supporter of local government, a support he expressed in his *Monthly Letter* published in the August 1955 edition of *Comment Magazine*:

"Good local government is essential to the continuance of our democratic way of life; without good local government there cannot be good general government. Indeed, the system of local government, which has evolved during centuries of trial and error, has become the brightest gem in our constitutional firmament. Its lustre must be maintained and not allowed to dull under the impact of public apathy, or lack of appreciation of the great privilege of exercising the rights of citizenship." [160]

At the same time, John Luxford encouraged co-operation among Auckland's local bodies. He "...convened a conference of regional local bodies to try to develop some system of regional co-operation...The purely advisory Auckland Metropolitan Local Bodies Association that resulted was more anaemic than Luxford had wanted, but it was more than parochialism would concede." [161]

"...there was a cool response to the mayor's idea of a Greater Auckland Authority. He [Luxford] had sought a body that would run all the essential metropolitan functions. The other borough mayors had given him permission to investigate and report on his idea, but their preference for the status quo was clear. Mayor Anderson of Mt Albert offered the opinion that *we have, I think, progressed quite satisfactorily over the years in our present set up. Even if we do no more than stock taking, I think we will have achieved a great deal.* Keith Hay, mayor of Mt Roskill, agreed: *I feel if nothing more comes out of this meeting than the fact that we can meet here, say every six months and discuss our various problems we would still be better off.*" [158]

Auckland Metropolitan Council

"The idea of running a modern metropolis by meeting twice a year is absurd, but that is about all Luxford achieved – a new body called the Auckland Metropolitan Council. It was a discussion forum for local body leaders but had no statutory powers, particularly when it came to financing new metropolitan services and coordinating development. In fact it did not even have limited powers to adjudicate over minor differences of opinion. For instance, a 'no man's land' existed between Devonport and Takapuna because neither would accept responsibility for the maintenance of their boundary road. Closer to the central city, Mt Eden, Mt Albert and Mt Roskill refused to cooperate to improve their drainage systems, which regularly flooded Auckland City properties, including the zoo." [158]

Population Growth

And that sort of disunity could only make things worse for Auckland residents as their numbers grew: "In the ten years between the end of 1935 and the end of 1945 the population increased from 223,200 to 263,370, and that represents a yearly increase of 4,017. In nine years from the end of 1945 to the end of 1954 the population increased from 263,370 to 361,300, which represents an annual increase of approximately 11,000." [160]

Metropolitan Board of Works

In July 1955, the idea of a 'Metropolitan Board of Works' that would incorporate Auckland's many ad hoc boards was also proposed by Auckland City Labour Councillor, Pat [Patrick Thomas] Curran. [162]

At the time, Councillor Curran was "...a director of a city motor firm and a licensed land agent...Because of his particular interest in traffic affairs and road safety, Councillor Curran was council's choice for Chairman of the Public Safety Committee. He is also a member of the Finance, Housing and Property Committees, the International Airport Committee, the Metropolitan Road Safety Council, the executive of the New Zealand Traffic Institute, and the council's representative on the Avondale College Board of Governors." [163]

Curran's proposal, no doubt based on similar boards set up to provide utility infrastructure to cope with the rapid growth of London (1855) and Melbourne (1891), soon failed to attract much local-body support and, of course, plenty of criticism.

Dove-Myer Robinson Opposition

One of the most vociferous critics of both the Curran and Luxford proposals at the time was, in fact, Dove-Myer Robinson (later, Sir Dove-Myer Robinson and long-time Auckland Mayor).

"Dove-Myer Robinson played a leading role in Auckland city politics, beginning with his entry into the Brown's Island Drainage controversy in 1944. He became an Auckland City Councillor in 1952, Chairman of the Auckland and Suburban Drainage Board in 1953 and Mayor of Auckland City in 1959…Robinson was an independent political figure who developed a personal following amongst Aucklanders as well as a strong populist appeal in the working class areas of the city. As such he was unacceptable to the Greater Auckland local body Establishment and particularly to the ruling Citizens' and Ratepayers' Association on the Auckland City Council. His Jewish and working class origins, his wartime activities, his personal life and his personality were also considered dubious by his opponents." [164]

Dove-Myer Robinson was Chairman of the Auckland Metropolitan Drainage Board during John Luxford's term as Mayor – a time when he (Robinson) "…had opposed Luxford's ideas for a central authority. Robinson had written to Luxford while he was still chairman of the Drainage Board insisting it remain autonomous. *It is no use envisaging a new organisation to supersede existing organisations, if those organisations are functioning reasonably satisfactorily. There are so many matters of metropolitan importance which do require coordinating that we should concentrate on them rather than interfere with what is already functioning quite satisfactorily.*" [158]

Dove-Myer Robinson elaborated on his reason for opposing a *central authority* during an address to the Hospital Officers Association on (or about) 17 April 1956:

"He [Dove-Myer Robinson] was convinced that many advocates of amalgamation of local bodies in Auckland were actuated by a desire to use this as a means of weilding (sic) a political stick against the Government said Mr D M Robinson addressing the Auckland branch of the Hospital Officers Association last night. Many people he said were carried away with the idea of amalgamation for amalgamation sake. They appeared to believe that a large organisation would be more efficient and more economic. This would not necessarily be so. If amalgamation destroyed the interest and individual initiative shown by so many of our local body members, amalgamation would be a retrograde step because it would destroy the present very high level of organisation and administration.

"Mr Robinson said that no one could say that the present method of control of local body affairs in Auckland could not be improved. He said the next 10 years is the most crutial (sic) in the development of Auckland. In that time vast new works will be undertaken by territorial and special purpose bodies. The full attention of the elected members and paid specialist officers would be required to complete these important works. Any major alteration in the present form or organisation would create chaos – it would be confusion worse confounded said Mr Robinson.

"He felt that the most valuable feature of local body services was the personal interest and attention to detail of the individual member. This would be destroyed if one organisation had to control the affairs of this vast metropolitan area. Nothing he said could take the place of the individual who is vitally interested in the affairs of his own local or ad hoc body. Mr Robinson said he felt that the road to progress and improvement in local Government in Auckland was the road of co-operation and co-ordination between the various bodies not coersion (sic) by means of amalgamation. A big step in this direction has been taken with the formation of the Metropolitan Local Bodies association which [will] shortly set up an Auckland metropolitan Co-ordination Council. This will prevent overlapping and will ensure better co-operation and co-ordination throughout the metropolitan area. Statutory powers could and would be taken by the Council as a result of experience in the following years." [165]

Response to Lewis Eady

Much the same argument was used by Dove-Myer Robinson in his written response to another proponent of a 'Greater Auckland Authority', prominent businessman, city councillor (1925 to 1929), and Auckland Chamber of Commerce President (1941 & 1942), Lewis Alfred Eady. [166]

When, in 1955, Eady commented that Auckland was then over-governed and needed a single regional authority that could speak with one voice, Robinson responded:

"I cannot agree with Mr L. [Lewis] Alfred Eady that Auckland is over-governed. If Auckland were already fully developed and it was only a matter of administration, this could probably be done by a central authority working through special committee. But the fact is Auckland is the most rapidly developing area in New Zealand, with an anticipated population of about 800,000 by the end of the present century. The complexity, multiplicity and magnitude of the local body works which will have to be undertaken and completed in that time, can easily be understood by the fact that they will cost at least £300,000,000. To suggest that this vast amount of work and concomitant expenditure could be better undertaken and supervised by any other form of authority than by the present local and ad hoc (special purpose) bodies, is to lose touch with reality.

"Although Mr Eady does not say so, I assume that he hopes that greater efficiency, economy and satisfaction to the ratepayers would result from the setting up of a single regional authority. Since he included main drainage as one of the undertakings which could be run by a department instead of an independent Board, may I ask him in what way he thinks drainage affairs could be better administered than by a Board as at present?...The Board's affairs are most capably handled by a competent, highly qualified specialised staff. I can conceive of no other form of authority which would give greater satisfaction, efficiency or economy...

"I do agree with Mr Eady that there are occasions when Auckland should speak with one voice. But this does not require the surrender of present local body authority or powers. Unless convincing evidence is produced that wholesale amalgamation would result in greater efficiency, economy and satisfaction to the people, it is obvious that no amount of coercion will bring about such amalgamation. In my opinion, it is essential to create confidence and community interest as between all the local and ad hoc bodies. This could be achieved through the setting up of a co-ordinating committee...Auckland requires a Co-ordinating Council so as to be able to speak with one voice when required. But this will only succeed if present distrust is succeeded by confidence as a result of regular, friendly discussion and decision on metropolitan problems." [167]

Chaos of Local Government in Auckland

In time, Dove-Myer Robinson would change his mind about the advantages of wholesale amalgamation and, indeed, "...in 1960 he began his struggle for the creation of a *Greater Auckland Authority*, able to coalesce metropolitan opinion and promulgate major metropolitan and regional development." [164 p.iii]

As was observed in 1965 by Noel C Bell, the Secretary of the eventually-formed, Auckland Regional Authority, such a concept of local unity had not been achieved at Auckland since 1851 when: "…Sir George Grey, as Governor, issued a proclamation elevating the town to the status of a borough. A Corporation was set up with powers of self-government on all matters of local interest…Unfortunately, the Borough never became effective…In 1852, with the passing of the Constitution Act, the existence of the Borough was terminated. It is worth noting that the district of the Borough embraced almost the whole of Metropolitan Auckland and today [1965] that same area is governed by some twenty-five territorial and ad hoc authorities…" [168]

As a result: "In the field of local government, Auckland has long been the source of wonderment, concern, frustration and amusement. To the rest of New Zealand, it is a centre of disunity, controversy, procrastination and compromise, where a multitude of opinions are voiced, but a decision seldom reached." [168]

In his lecture to the Auckland Branch of the New Zealand Geographical Society in 1966, John Steel, the first General Manager of the Authority, also referred to:

"The chaos of local government in Auckland [which] led one author to observe that '…the map of Metropolitan Auckland is queerly divided into a pattern reminiscent of feudal times when every baron staked out his claim to a certain area and levied his taxes over it…' Professor K. B. Cumberland referred to the local bodies in Auckland as '…*only a babel of disputing tongues*' and '…*a comic opera of overlapping and ineffectual agencies we miscall authorities.*'" [169]

Central Government Housing Policy

However, Auckland's *comic opera of overlapping and ineffectual agencies* was not entirely the fault of the region's fragmentary local governance. Indeed, as asserted in an unattributed article published in the September 1955 edition of the Auckland City Council's *Comment Magazine*, the housing policy of Central Government contributed to the region's planning disarray, development costs, and disharmony among its citizens:

"Uniformity throws before it the shadow of mediocrity. Psychologically, it is bad. Auckland does not want this thrust upon it in its housing expansion. It wants no segregation in its inter-dependent community. It does not want its streets classified according to the professions in which householders engage, or the size of their bank balances. It wants the spreading influence of soundly-based family life and community interest to pervade residential areas. It wants no 'decaying limbs'. It will no longer accept segregation, by Government compulsion, of housing districts into unbalanced units.

"This city wants less talk of State housing areas and more of community spirit. It does not want one residential area pulling against another. State housing policy to date has done nothing to promote this; a change is overdue. More economic use must be made of our city building sites, which means more blocks of flats must grow upward and not outward. More than that, they must be designed to provide for all home groups, with rentals adjusted according to ability to pay for better accommodation.

"Governed principally by costs of development, Housing Division officials have been taking the easy way out, by selecting good land, easy of subdivision and roading, for housing projects miles from the city centre, instead of redeveloping aging districts where full services exist. This has imposed an intolerable burden on local authorities providing sewerage and water; apart from lengthening miles of dedicated streets for which they must accept maintenance responsibility.

"Criticisms have mainly been restrained, referring to the evils of urban sprawl, but Auckland's Mayor, Mr J. H. Luxford, tackled the matter boldly when he told the Rotary Club that invasion of agricultural land in metropolitan Auckland for housing purposes cannot continue. He referred to low population densities in the inner city area. Regional planners, he said, were aghast at the Government's intentions in the Otara and Mangere areas of Manukau County…

"One of the greatest dangers to the orderly rational development of metropolitan Auckland, said the Mayor, is the Government housing policy. Auckland may have to pay a very great price for the past and present Government policy of trying to put up the greatest number of houses in the quickest time at the cheapest cost on the cheapest land.

"The Auckland Regional Planning Authority is aghast at the Housing Division's intentions with respect to two blocks in Manukau County totalling 8000 acres and known as the Otara and Mangere areas. The stage has passed when agricultural land in metropolitan Auckland can be taken indiscriminately. The extravagances of the past cannot be allowed to continue…The perimeter of Auckland is already stretched too far and the inner areas must be developed so that the present absurd population density can be increased. At present there are only seven people to the acre in the city area and six people to the acre in the whole metropolitan area." [170]

Subdivision of City Land

In the same magazine, Auckland's Mayor, John Luxford, elaborated on just how his Council proposed to develop those inner city areas and called upon property owners for help:

"The Auckland City Council has been seized for a considerable time with the importance of achieving closer subdivision of vacant land in the city to facilitate the building of more homes. The somewhat high standards for subdivision that have obtained for many years have prevented vacant lands in the city, amounting to a large area, from being used for their proper purpose, namely, providing sites for the building of houses. The stage has now been reached where it is not only wasteful but also inimical to the city's interests for these lands to remain vacant because of unreasonably high standards of subdividing them imposed by the City Council. The current costs of essential services – roading, water and drainage – are so high that it is essential from the economic point of view that they supply as many individual units as possible.

"It is of little use to deplore the urban sprawl and ribbon development taking place in Metropolitan Auckland unless we take active measures to ensure that the fully serviced land is economically utilised. When city ratepayers realise they have to pay more than half the cost of extending the main drainage system to areas being developed far outside the city boundaries as well as more than half the losses sustained by the Auckland Transport Board in providing uneconomic services, they will appreciate how important it is to increase the density of population of the city proper.

"One way of helping to achieve this, is by inducing owners of vacant lands or sections too large for single dwellings to cut up their holdings and sell the resultant sections. After a lengthy investigation by the Town Planning Committee, council has adopted certain measures which already have afforded considerable assistance to owners to subdivide surplus land and have been instrumental in providing hundreds of additional building sites throughout the city. These measures include the reduction of required areas for front and back lots, the sharing of physical access to multiple back lots and the grants of financial assistance to form access roads to back lands.

"At the July [1955] meeting of the Council the new subdivisional standards were finally considered and consolidated; and now I am glad to say the whole scheme has been discussed, explained and illustrated in an article published in this issue of Comment. This enables me cordially to invite everybody who has a block of land or large section which he thinks might be subdivided under the new standards, to call at the City Engineer's Department, Town Hall, where officers of the Town Planning section will, I know, be happy to give expert advice as to whether a subdivision of any particular parcel of land into two or more sections is possible." [171]

Parliamentarians' Invitation

As the Auckland region struggled to accommodate its post-war growth, its local politicians sought means to succour central Government support whenever they could, particularly if they could show some unanimity at the same time. As part of his monthly letter, published in the City Council's Comment Magazine in September 1955, John Luxford proclaimed:

"In accordance with a resolution of Council I have extended (through the Prime Minister) an invitation to all members of Parliament to be the City's guests at the time of the unveiling of the stone commemorating the 102nd anniversary of the opening of New Zealand's first Parliament, and to spend three days with us so that they may see at first hand the extent of the problems associated with the rapid growth of the great metropolis. It is to be hoped that other local bodies will be joint hosts with the City Council and that a strong committee will be formed, not only of representatives of all local bodies in the metropolitan area, but of commercial, industrial and financial interests as well. Such a committee will be able to arrange and carry out a programme of inspection, demonstration and illustration which should leave our Parliamentarians in no doubt that the orderly, effective and progressive development of Auckland is essential, not only to the Provincial District of Auckland, but to the whole of New Zealand." [160]

102nd Anniversary of New Zealand's First Parliament

The visit to Auckland of the Members of Parliament, as guests of the Municipalities of Metropolitan Auckland, subsequently took place from 23 May to 25 May 1956. The unveiling of the plaque marking the 102nd anniversary of the opening of New Zealand's first Parliament on its original site (when Auckland had been the capital) was held during an official ceremony on 24 May. As well as Auckland's dignitaries, guests included the House Speaker, Matthew Oram; Prime Minister Sidney Holland and his deputy, Keith Holyoake; and the Leader of the Opposition, Walter Nash. [172]

Programme of Events

An official programme of events compiled by the Auckland Provincial Public Relations Office and published by Whitcombe and Tombs prior to the visit included a number of articles relating to *the problems associated with the rapid growth of the great metropolis*. One such piece, entitled *Plan To Ease Traffic Congestion*, unashamedly emphasised the need for Government support to implement the road-building recommendations of the 1955 Master Transportation Plan for Metropolitan Auckland (detailed in a later chapter):

"More than nine-tenths of Auckland's passenger and goods movement is carried on its road system, on roads spacious by the standards of 100 years ago but now quite inadequate to cope with the motor age. Road congestion, like old age, has crept upon us imperceptibly, but now has the city firmly in its grip. Following upon recent traffic surveys it has been estimated that one million man-hours of paid working time are lost every year within a two-mile radius of the Post Office, a figure which is more than doubled when the whole metropolitan area is considered. Road usage is growing so fast that effective congestion will be doubled within five years, by which time four million man-hours will be lost each year. This, in effect, means that Auckland will be denied the use each year of 2000 of its workmen.

"Losses caused by traffic congestion in five years' time will be about £5,000,000 a year – and there is nothing we can do about it. It will take more than five years to acquire land and to complete the first section of the urban motorways that have been planned. This is not a local disaster – it is a national one. Almost half of New Zealand's overseas trade passes through the Port of Auckland, and the greatest part of this is handled on the roads. More than one-third of the nation's manufacturing is done in Auckland, and it is almost entirely dependent on road transport. The present congestion – to say nothing of what we will be experiencing within five years – leads to increasing inefficiency in trade, industry and commerce. Because congestion is already serious, the rate at which it will increase in future years will be out of all proportion to the city's growth of population or commerce.

"For two reasons, the battle against traffic paralysis must be fought on the roads. Overseas trends indicate greater utilization of roads by transport, and remedial measures there will apply to three-quarters of the urban traffic as against the 5 per cent affected by the proposed rail development. The urban motorways which have been planned for Auckland will cost £15,000,000, but each section will pay its own cost in savings effected in the first five years of its operation. If a start is made immediately, the whole can be completed by 1970 – but it is important that there should be no delay in initiating the project." [173]

While there was no doubt a grand show of complete accord between local body politicians and between local body politicians and those from Wellington during the unveiling of the parliamentary plaque, the political climate was soon back to normal in time to contest the next elections later that year.

Auckland City Council Election

As part of its electioneering for the Auckland City Council election held on 17 November 1956, Dove-Myer Robinson's United Independent Party produced a pamphlet outlining its policies to those voters who it hoped would replace Mayor John Luxford and the predominant Citizens and Ratepayers party. Dove-Myer Robinson's introduction to the pamphlet promotes conciliation in terms of a 'fair deal' for all:

"You must have been alarmed at the great increase in rates during the past three years. And, no doubt, you are disturbed at the reports of squabbles and personal differences in the City Council and other local bodies. The lack of consistent policy, failure to provide essential amenities and indifference to public opinion, must be most disheartening to you. The introduction of personal, political and social ambitions into civic affairs must also be most distressing. All this frustration, mismanagement and disharmony can and must be swept away, if you are to enjoy your democratic rights as a citizen. Greater economy of ratepayers' money *must* be enforced. Ways to reduce the ratepayers staggering burden must be found. Harmony and team work must be restored in the conduct of the city's business. United Independent candidates are pledged to reform civic administration. They are pledged to introduce progressive measures to ensure greater economy, greater progress, greater freedom, greater service and greater harmony." [174]

Election Results

The November 1956 election returned Dove-Myer Robinson to the Auckland City Council but only two of his fellow United Independents were elected: Eric Armishaw and Kenneth Cumberland. The city's former Town Clerk, Thomas W M Ashby, was elected Mayor, as described by Dove-Myer Robinson in his 'President's Report to Members', dated 26 November 1956:

"The new mayor, Mr T W M Ashby, paid us a very gracious, and if I may say so, not unmerited compliment, when he publicly acknowledged (at our election night party) the part United Independents had played in getting him elected. As most of you know Mr Ashby had originally intended to be one of our council candidates. It was on my suggestion that Mr Ashby decided to offer himself for the mayoralty. I think we can take great satisfaction from the fact that his election has again justified our decision to endorse his candidature. For the second time we have been mainly responsible for displacing the sitting mayor and having elected the new mayor. I am sure we all sincerely hope that it will not be necessary to do the same in three years' time. Mr Luxford, unfortunately, proved a bitter disappointment to all of us. He could never forget that he had been a magistrate. He could not tolerate anyone holding a different opinion or opposing him. As mayor, there is no doubt he was responsible for most of the friction which arose at Council meetings...As far as Mr Ashby is concerned, I am sure we have no reason to fear that he will try to weild (sic) the big stick, or run the Council as a 'one man band'...I have determined that I will not allow myself to be drawn into any unpleasant scenes at Council meetings. I am sure Mr Ashby is of the same opinion, and that we will not be subjected to the same attacks, abuse, and exposure to ridicule, such as we have had to suffer during the past three years." [175]

Dove-Myer Robinson Elected Auckland Mayor

By the time Dove-Myer Robinson was, himself, elected Auckland Mayor in 1959 (representing the Civic Reform Party – a coalition of Labour and Independents), he was no longer Chairman of the Auckland Metropolitan Drainage Board and his views as to the inclusion of such ad hoc bodies as part of any 'Greater Auckland Authority' had changed somewhat.

As described by John Edgar in his biography of Robinson, *Urban Legend*, Robinson was now "...a visionary who understood the intimate connection between new power structures and environmental planning, and the quality of life for city dwellers. Just as importantly, he had the personal qualities needed to pursue such a difficult agenda. Campaigning for the mayoralty in 1959 he had been quite clear about his dynamic plans for Auckland. If there were immediate rumblings of discontent, he hit back just as quickly at what he felt were the fractious, visionless laggards standing in the way of reform." [158]

However, John Edgar points out:

"If Robinson were to proceed with urban reform he would have to convince the majority of borough and county council politicians he was right. The fusion of viewpoints depended in part on what they thought of him personally, and the prevailing attitudes did not augur well for his success. Unfortunately, he was regarded in greater Auckland in much the same way he was by his critics on the Auckland City Council.

"A number of boroughs had their own version of Auckland City's Citizens and Ratepayers Association. It was as successful in the boroughs as it was in the central city.

These particular borough politicians viewed Robinson through their own conservative and snobbish prism and did not like what they saw. The new mayor was suspect and not altogether to be trusted. Notwithstanding the conservative alliances in greater Auckland, there was an element of jealousy between Auckland City Council and the smaller councils." [158]

Public Transport
Transport Act 1949

Both tram and trackless trolley-omnibus services were specifically referred to in Sections 127 and 128 as being subject to the Transport Act 1949 and therefore the regulation of fares by the Transport Charges Committee and any appeal by the Charges Appeal Authority. However, the Auckland Transport Board did not altogether agree with this new form of fare regulation, as reported by its Chairman, Henry Albert Anderson, in his Annual Report for the financial year ended 31 March 1950:

"Fixing Of Fares – Legislation passed in November, 1949, brought the control of tram fares under the jurisdiction of the Transport Charges Committee appointed in terms of the Transport Law Amendment Act 1948. Formerly tram fares were subject to control by the Price Tribunal under the Department of Industries and Commerce, while bus fares came within the scope of the Transport Charges Committee, under the Transport Department. There is reason to hope that the position may be simplified further in the near future if proposed legislative authority is given for the Board and similar bodies to fix their own fares, subject to a right of appeal to the Transport Appeal Authority. The enactment of such legislation should speed up decisions – an important factor in transport operation." [89]

Transport Amendment Act 1950

Indeed, hardly more than a year later, *the position* was *simplified* when the public transport, price-fixing structure provided for by the Transport Act 1949 was replaced by provisions of the Transport Amendment Act 1950 which came into force on 23 November 1950. The Amendment Act allowed for a public body, as the owner of a transport service, to fix its own charges instead of the Transport Charges Committee set up by the 1949 Act. The Transport Charges Appeal Authority, also set up under the original Act, remained as the overall arbiter:

"3. (1) Section one hundred and nineteen of the principal Act is hereby repealed, and the following section substituted: - 119. (1) Subject to the provisions of section one hundred and thirty-three of this Act, the charges which may be made in respect of any transport service owned by a public body shall be fixed, reviewed, altered, or revoked by that body or by the Transport Charges Appeal Authority, as the case may be, under the provisions of this Part of this Act, and no Licensing Authority or other authority shall exercise any jurisdiction to fix, review, alter, or revoke any such charges." [176]

The Transport Amendment Act 1950 definition of a *public body* included the Auckland Transport Board: "Public body, for the purposes of Part VI of this Act, means a Borough Council, a County Council, a Town Board, or a Hospital Board; and includes the *Auckland Transport Board*, and any other incorporated body declared by the Governor-General by Order in Council gazetted to be a public body for the purposes of Part VI of this Act." [176]

Fares charged by private owners of transport services, not defined by the Amendment Act as *public bodies*, were now to be regulated by the Commissioner of Transport (the administrative head of the Department of Transport) with a right of appeal to the Transport Charges Appeal Authority.

Herne Bay Trolleybus Service

By the time the Auckland Transport Board Chairman, Henry Anderson, submitted his Annual Report for the year ended 31 March 1950, the City's public transport network had expanded with the introduction of the first trolleybus service:

"Trolley Buses – The Herne Bay Trolley Bus Service, the first to be converted from Tramway operation, was inaugurated on 24th September, 1949. After six months' running the service can be regarded as satisfactory and an amenity to the district served. The conversion involved the removal of some 105 trees from Jervois Road, the provision of a turning circle at Herne Bay terminus, and the erection of a shelter at the City terminus in Albert Street.

"Some controversy still exists regarding the type of shelter and the location of the City terminus. While an entirely free hand in these matters was not open to the Board, it is not unmindful of the problems and consideration is being given to them in an endeavour to effect adjustments which it is hoped will give more general satisfaction. The operation of trolley bus services for the Ponsonby and Richmond Road routes is wrapped up in the problem, as is also the overall plan for conversion of the remaining services, and accordingly, an immediate solution cannot be expected.

"The remaining 40 trolley buses ordered have arrived in a knock-down condition and are in course of assembly at the recently completed Assembly Building at the Workshops. The shortage of labour is causing some delay in this as in other sections of the Board's operations, but all possible action is being taken to have the conversion of the Ponsonby route completed at the earliest possible date." [89]

Motor Bus Expansion

The Board's bus services had also extended their reach during the financial year:

"Motor Buses – Considerable expansion has taken place in the Board's Motor Bus undertaking during the year under review, and the Board now operates the largest municipally owned fleet of buses as well as the largest fleet of tramcars in the Dominion.

"The Penrose service formerly operated by W. J. Wheeler and Sons Ltd., and comprising eight diesel buses was taken over on 29th May, 1949, and on 5th March 1950, the services formerly operated by L. J. Keys Ltd., to Orakei, Mission Bay, Kohimarama, St. Heliers Bay and district, with a fleet of forty diesel and petrol buses were also added to the Board's undertaking.

"To cope with ever-increasing demands for transport by a steadily growing population, services are being extended as circumstances permit. On 20th November, 1949, a Cross-Country Bus Service was instituted from Point Chevalier via Mount Albert, Balmoral Road and Green Lane Road to Cornwall Hospital and Great South Road. This service, which operates during off-peak hours, is becoming increasingly patronised, and is particularly appreciated by visitors to the Green Lane and Cornwall Hospitals. Improvements and extensions to other services in Mount Roskill and Mount Albert new housing areas will be put into effect within a short time." [89]

Gas Pedal to Back-Pedal   Chapter Three

Auckland Transport Board Net Loss
All this expansion of services (and contraction in the case of the trams) naturally influenced the financial outcome for the year ended 31 March 1950:

"…the Tramway deficit was £28,340 while Bus operation resulted in a deficit of £14,167 and Trolley Bus operation in a surplus of £689, making the net loss for the undertaking £41,818…The Tramway revenue for the year was £954,873, while Bus revenue was £116,021. These amounts are £4,917 (.5%) more and £52,292 (82.05%) more respectively than in the previous year. Trolley Bus revenue for the first six months of operation to 31st March, 1950, was £25,813.

"Tramway Working Expenses were £857,118, an increase of 4.44% over the previous year, while Bus Working Expenses were £114,179, an increase of 59.98%. Trolley Bus Working Expenses for the six months were £21,691.

"The year's operations at first sight appear more favourable than was anticipated, but it is to be remembered that due to shortage of labour and inability to secure materials, maintenance has in some respects fallen further into arrears, while, at the same time, for like reasons service to the public has not always been possible to the desired standard. Nor is it to be forgotten that the introduction (since mid-January) of Concession Tickets at the previous cash rate of fares has had the consequential effect of substantial credits to the Board's funds against unused tickets in the hands of the public and unsold tickets in the hands of Agents. This sum is estimated at approaching £40,000. In all these circumstances, it will be agreed the result is reasonably satisfactory, but even with the adjustment of fares the margin of revenue over expenses is very small and the Board must watch carefully its financial position." [89]

Passenger Numbers Decline – Wages and Fares Rise
By March 1951, as the condition of the tramways infrastructure deteriorated and motor vehicle ownership and operation became increasingly easier, the number of public transport passengers had declined significantly. This was reflected in the Transport Board's accounts for the financial year ended 31 March 1951:

"…the Tramway deficit was £8530, while Bus operation resulted in a deficit of £38,908, and Trolleybus operation in a surplus of £864, making a net loss for the undertaking of £46,574…The Tramway revenue for the year was £972,767, while Bus revenue was £211,524. These amounts are £17,894 (1.87%) more and £95,503 (82.31%) more respectively than in the previous year. Trolleybus revenue for the year was £44,502…The large increase in the figures for Bus operation over last year is almost entirely due to the addition to the Board's services of buses formerly operated by L. J. Leys Ltd., which has almost doubled the Board's bus fleet. The fact that fares charged by the Company were not brought into line with those on the rest of the Board's services until November, 1950, accounts for a substantial part of the deficit on Bus operation." [177]

In his Annual Report for the financial year ended 31 March 1951, Board Chairman, Henry Anderson, explained: "A serious decline in the number of passengers carried occurred on the removal of petrol rationing in June, 1950, with a corresponding drop in the Board's revenue, and when no subsequent recovery took place it became evident that the estimated increased revenue from the January, 1950 adjustment of fares would not be realised. To stabilize the Board's finances a further revision of fares became inevitable and while this matter was under consideration a further substantial burden for a wages alone of

£115,000 was added by the Arbitration Court Order of 30th January, 1951, superseding its Interim Order and granting a general wage increase of 15%.

"Acting under authority given by the Transport Amendment Act 1950, the Board in February last adopted new fare schedules which came into effect on 1st April, 1951... It should be remembered, however, that fares did not increase in common with other prices during the war but remained at their pre-war level until January, 1950. The recent increases were decided upon because of our belief in the principle that the transport system should be conducted on a business basis and should be capable of standing on its own feet. The policy of the Board has at all times been against the use of its statutory power of levying a rate to make up a deficiency in operating costs." [177]

Pandemonium of the Gauntlet

Despite what Henry Anderson described as "...*A serious decline in the number of passengers carried...*" a chaotic interaction between private and public transport users and pedestrians increased on Auckland's busy streets during the 1950s. This was graphically described by the late John Hill in his reminiscence of a road journey with his father between Morrinsville and Whangarei about 1955. As they drove through Auckland on their way to the Devonport car ferry, John recalled the pandemonium of the gauntlet they ran:

"Here was a nightmare that I hadn't anticipated. The morning rush-hour, sitting in a very small Bradford with the queues of trams was an enormous shock. There were bells ringing, wheels grinding, sparks flashing off trolley wires, brake compressors cutting in and car horns blowing. There were people running between cars to catch the moving trams, all greeting one another and carrying their newspapers and lunch-bags. When we got to the junction of Manukau Road and Broadway in Newmarket, things seemed to get even worse. People were jumping off the moving trams, and the cars all seemed to be huge American models, perhaps an example of Auckland affluence." [178]

Motor Buses Ordered

An example of Auckland affluence, or not, the increasingly prolific and brasher motor car, trucks, and buses challenged the humble, hard-working tram to yield its centre line. The Auckland Transport Board had little option but to continue with its *Modernisation of the Tramway System*, as Board Chairman, Henry Anderson, reported:

"In anticipation of plans for the modernisation of the tramway services, tenders were called towards the end of the year for the supply of 50 fully assembled motor buses." [177]

"Motor Buses – No further bus services were taken over during the year under review, but improvements and additions were made to the Board's existing services. The Waikowhai and Hillsborough feeder services to Greenwood's Corner, Three Kings and Mt. Roskill trams were reorganised in June, 1950, and an additional feeder service from New North Road, Mt. Albert, via the Stewart Estate to Sandringham Road, Owairaka, was inaugurated, together with a through service from New North Road to Greenwood's Corner, serving the district south of Mt. Albert Road and connecting with the Mt. Roskill, Three Kings and Onehunga tram routes.

"It is recognised that some existing bus services are inadequate, and improvements will be effected as vehicles become available. An order has been placed for 12 diesel bus chassis, the bodies for which will probably have to be built by private contractors as the Board's staff is fully occupied on assembly of trolleybuses and maintenance work. Although these 12 chassis were ordered in July, 1950, present indications are that they are unlikely to arrive in New Zealand for some months yet.

"During the year steady progress has been made with the construction of the new Bus Depot at May Road, Mt. Roskill. It is expected this Depot will be in use at an early date, when the larger portion of the Board's bus fleet will be transferred from Halsey Street. Opportunity will be taken to institute revised timetables to give improved services wherever practicable. Plans are well in hand for extensions to the accommodation and facilities at St Heliers Bay Bus Depot." [177]

"Trolleybuses – The shortage of labour continues to retard the rate of assembly of the 40 trolleybuses which were imported in 1949 in a knocked-down condition. The Herne Bay route consequently remains the only one yet converted from tram to trolleybus operation, but the indications are that provided the present rate of assembly is maintained, sufficient vehicles to operate the Ponsonby service should be completed by approximately the end of 1951. Since December, 1950, Herne Bay residents have had the advantage of the extension of the City Terminal to a point near the intersection of Albert and Fanshawe Streets." [177]

Modernisation Programme

In order to maintain the momentum of its modernisation programme, the Auckland Transport Board sought permission from their constituent local body ratepayers to raise a special loan, as described by Henry Anderson in his Annual Report for the year ended 31 March 1952:

"Modernisation of the Tramway System – Further progress was made in the Board's modernisation scheme during the year. Concurrently with the General Election of Members of the Board held on 17th November, 1951, a proposal to raise a special loan of £2,450,000 for the purpose of modernising and developing the Auckland transport system was submitted to ratepayers for approval. The proposal was carried by a four to one majority and application has been made to the Local Government Loans Board for its recommendation to the issue of the necessary Order-in-Council authorising the raising of the loan moneys.

"It appears that the Board, in common with other Local Authorities, may experience some difficulty in raising its loan requirements at the approved rate of interest of 3¼% under present-day conditions. The orders for a 140 diesel buses and 40 trolley buses mentioned earlier in this report were placed in accordance with the modernisation scheme and involve the expenditure of a sum in excess of £1,300,000." [179]

Net Loss 1952

"…the net loss for the year is £6,934…Total revenue from all services for the year was £1,504,781, which amount is £275,989 (22.46%) more than the previous year. Working expenses amounted to £1,370,389, an increase of 16.84% over the previous year. The percentage of working expenses to total receipts is 91.07% as compared with 95.44% for the previous year. Because of the impossibility of accurately segregating both revenue and working expenses relating to the three types of vehicles operated by the Board, separate Revenue Accounts are not now compiled.

"Revenue receipts for the year were in accord with estimates until August last, when a noticeable diminution in the number of passengers carried became evident. This has continued and is attributed in part to an increase in the number of motor-cars and in part to an increasing tendency on the part of housewives to shop locally instead of travelling to the City.

"When the estimates for the year were adopted in August, 1951, wage payments were included at the then ruling rate and it was pointed out that any variation in wage rates must affect the estimates accordingly. An award was issued in November, 1951, operative as to wages from 8th May, 1951, and the extra wage payment by the Board because of this was £18,915." [179]

Ponsonby Trolleybus Service

While the Transport Board's financial position remained somewhat fluid, so did its transport operations, as described by Henry Anderson:

"Trolleybuses – Conversion of the Ponsonby tram service to trolley bus operation was effected on Saturday, 10th November, 1951. This is the second route converted and is operating as successfully as the Herne Bay service inaugurated in the previous year. As a temporary measure, until such time as further routes are converted and the Ponsonby service is through routed with another service (probably Mt. Roskill), traversing Wellesley Street East, the City terminus of the Ponsonby route is located at the Civic Theatre.

"This means that Ponsonby passengers, who were formerly able to travel to or from the foot of Queen Street by tram, can now only make the full journey by changing vehicles at the Civic Theatre. They are, however, able to do this without extra expense by the use of specially designed 'through' tickets. Good progress has been made with the assembly of further trolley buses and the Richmond Road service will be converted within the next few months…An order has been placed with the Leyland the company for the supply of 40 fully assembled trolleybuses, which, however, are not expected to arrive before the end of 1953." [179]

Motor Bus Services

While the introduction of trolley buses was taking more time than expected, the inclusion of motor buses as a supplementary service was proving to be equally as challenging:

"Motor Buses – No major developments in the Board's motor bus services occurred during the year, but adjustments and additions to existing services were made where practicable. Further improvements are necessary and will be made as vehicles become available. The supply position, however, continues to be most uncertain. Delivery has only just commenced of 12 diesel chassis ordered in July, 1950. Bodies are being constructed for these by New Zealand Motor Bodies Ltd., but it is not expected that the order will be completed before March, 1953. Orders have been placed for 50 Leyland and 90 Daimler diesel buses, all with bodies by the Saunders-Roe Company. Twelve of the Leylands and 87 of the Daimlers are to be imported in the Unit Knocked Down condition and will be assembled at the Board's Workshops. The arrival of these vehicles is expected to commence next September and should be completed by the end of 1953.

"Adjustment Of Bus Fares And Sections – With a view to establishing uniformity of fares and sections over the whole of the Board's transport system, a review was undertaken of the various bus services taken over in recent years. Each route has now been divided into sections, and bus fares are based on the number of sections travelled, as in the case of trams. In some cases the adjustments have resulted in reduced fares, but the ensuing loss of revenue is more than compensated for in the Board's opinion by the simplification of the ticket system arising from the use of cash and concession tickets common to all services.

"The new Bus Depot at May Road, Mount Roskill, was officially opened on the 29th October, 1951. At this stage the Depot comprises a maintenance block with parking areas for motor buses transferred from Halsey Street. An administration block, fuelling station and other facilities are to be added to accommodate an ultimate total of 140 to 150 motor and trolley buses." [179]

Private Motor Vehicles

Although the importation of both trolley and diesel buses was proving to be a laborious process for the Auckland Transport Board, the same could not be said for the public's acquisition and deployment of private motor vehicles. As of 31 March 1950, some 44,622 cars, 219 rental cars, 76 private-hire cars, 454 taxis, and 53 service cars were registered and licensed in the Auckland Postal District. [180]

Two years later, <u>national</u> motor vehicle registrations exceeded all previous records, as reported by the Commissioner of Transport, G L Laurenson, in his Transport Department Report for the year ended 31 March 1953:

"During the calendar year 1952, 36,298 new cars were registered, which is the highest on record, exceeding by 6,354 the previous best in 1937. In addition, 1,960 second-hand cars were imported. During the year, 38,258 additional cars were therefore registered, but the number withdrawn is estimated at only 5,000. The demand for cars is still very great, the vast majority of new vehicles being used to increase the fleet rather than replace obsolescent vehicles." [181]

Net Loss 1953

While the motor car competition assembled, the Transport Board had no option but to bide its time and wait for the full implementation of its modernisation programme to be implemented. In the meantime, the 1952-1953 financial year proved to be another of declining passenger numbers and revenue:

"…the net loss for the year is £70,148…Total revenue from all sources for the year was £1,469,654, which amount is £35,127 (2.33%) less than the previous year…The loss for the year is slightly more than was estimated and is mainly due to a decline in patronage, to which the largest contributory factor is the increased use of private motor-cars. It is evident that until all services are modernised, the Board's undertaking will experience difficult times, especially in view of present heavy maintenance costs on obsolete vehicles, tracks and distribution system. When modernisation is complete, maintenance costs should be substantially less and with the pay-as-you-enter system ensuring the collection of all fares, the Board looks forward to a time when the undertaking will again pay its way.

"The period of transition is, however, a time of high costs, and the Local Government Loans Board in granting approval of the anticipated overdraft at 31 3 53, requested the Board to remedy its financial position. In these circumstances, the Board having already carefully scrutinised all other alternatives, was left with no option but to give serious consideration to the unprecedented course of using its statutory power to make a levy on its constituent Local Authorities." [182]

A First-Time Rates Levy?

The Transport Board's reluctance to defer future operational losses by means of a first-time, rates levy, was to be expected. In the past, modest losses had been offset by equally modest fare adjustments but that was not always the best option, as outlined by Henry Anderson in his Annual Report for the financial year ended 31 March 1953:

"Fares – A special effort has been made to collect revenue which would otherwise be lost by reason of unpaid fares. Conductors were urged to see that every possible fare was collected and at the same time notices were displayed in tramcars reminding passengers that they have a moral as well as a legal obligation to pay their fares. It is difficult to assess the effect of this campaign on the Board's revenue as so many factors such as weather conditions, holiday periods and special events must also be considered, but it was felt that the public generally must approve the Board's efforts to collect all fares and that an improvement in the position would result.

"It has been suggested several times that a reduction in fares would attract more passengers and so increase revenue. Experience in Auckland, and indeed in all parts of the world where a section fare basis is used, shows that normally a simple rule operates in relation to fare adjustments. Increased fares mean fewer passengers but higher revenue. Reduced fares mean more passengers but lower revenue. With costs at their present high level a general reduction in fares is manifestly impossible." [182]

Modernisation Programme Continued

But, regardless of the financial uncertainty occasioned by motor car competition, the Transport Board's modernisation programme continued:

"Trolley Buses – Completion of assembly of trolley buses imported in a knocked-down condition made possible the conversion of two more tram services to trolley bus operation during the year. The new vehicles commenced running on Richmond Road route on 30th August, 1952, and to Westmere on 14th March, 1953. It is expected that trams will be withdrawn from the Three Kings route towards the end of May, 1953, and from other routes at approximately two to three-monthly intervals thereafter. In order to allow for removal of the tram trolley wires and the unhindered erection of the new trolley bus overhead equipment, trams will be replaced in the first stage of conversion by the new Daimler and Leyland diesel buses now arriving from England. When the overhead wiring on one route is completed trolley buses will take over the main part of the service and the diesel buses so released will be transferred to the next route for conversion." [182]

"Maintenance Of Tram Tracks – During the year approximately 2½ miles of double track permanent way has been reconstructed on routes not scheduled for immediate conversion to rubber-tyred vehicles. Payments to the contractors undertaking this work for the Board amounted to no less a sum than £102,583, but with the continued elimination of tram services expenditure in this connection will show a marked decrease in future. Tram tracks on the Herne Bay route have been removed and the roadway restored to a standard suitable for modern requirements." [182]

"Motor Buses – Delivery of the 13 A.E.C., 50 Leyland and 90 Daimler buses on order, some of which are already in service, is expected to be completed within the coming financial year, which will therefore witness a big increase in the Board's motor-bus operations. As previously stated, motor-buses will be used in the early stages of conversion of tram services. Their subsequent use will be in augmenting trolley bus services at peak travelling times, in replacing such of the existing fleet as have reached the end of their economic life and in providing additional services." [182]

City Routing

"City Routing – After discussions between the Board and the Auckland City Council, which necessarily involved considerable time, agreement has been reached as to final routing of modernised services, as to stopping places in the inner City area, and to the interim routing necessary while the change-over is proceeding. The City of Auckland has grown tremendously during recent years and its growth still continues. The day is therefore past when it is practicable for all passenger service vehicles to operate through the lower portion of Queen Street.

"The congestion which in spite of reduction in tram services still occurs at peak periods is clear evidence of this. As a result, future routing aims to reduce the number of vehicles operating in Queen Street and provides for through-routing across Queen Street as far as practicable. This may result in some slight inconvenience to a section of the public which, in the past, has become accustomed to a particular destination in the downtown area.

"However, such a condition of affairs is inevitable when a City grows beyond a certain stage as Auckland has now done, and it is only a matter of time before all the main services will serve Queen Street via Customs Street, Victoria Street or Wellesley Street. For transport up and down Queen Street a frequent shuttle service will be provided." [182]

Roading Investigation Committee

However, where the new rubber met the road, not all was going according to plan. As detailed in the next chapter, in March 1952, a Roading Investigation Committee was appointed by the Minister of Works, William (Stan) Goosman, in order to establish what roads had to be built and upgraded to deal with the motor vehicle phenomenon and what those roads would cost. When the Committee reported in February 1953, it commented on the adverse effects that the relatively new trolleybuses and omnibuses were having on city roads:

"Since the motor vehicle was first introduced there has been a continuous improvement in design, and doubtless this will continue in the future, particularly having regard to those factors which influence economical operation. It is the development of certain of the heavier types of vehicle that has raised special problems of road construction and maintenance.

Trolleybuses

"Trolley-buses – These vehicles have created special major problem of road construction and maintenance for some of our cities. A few vehicles of this class have been in use in New Zealand for approximately twenty years. They are now rapidly gaining popularity, and it seems that in the not-distant future the trolley-bus, in conjunction with the omnibus, will replace the tramcar as the main form of public transport in municipalities. Trolley-buses have advantages over petrol- or Diesel-driven buses, and that they consume electricity rather than imported fuels; they are silent in operation, have smooth and rapid acceleration on hills, and are free from vibration and fumes. Their use, however, involves new problems in road construction and maintenance, besides the substantial capital outlay and maintenance costs associated with the overhead wiring system and substations necessary for the conversion of the alternating current, on which our main electric power reticulation is based, to direct current, on which these units operate.

"Contrary to popular belief, trolley-buses, which appear to be the smoothest of vehicles in operation, are in fact excessively severe on road maintenance. The earlier trolley-buses were 30 ft. in over-all length, but the vehicles now being placed on the roadways are 33 ft. long, excepting in the Auckland Transport Board's area, where 36 ft. has been authorized.

"The design of these buses is such that in some cases the load carried by the front axle is as high as 47 per cent of the total. This means that the tires on the front axle carry a heavier load than those fitted to the back axle, where dual wheels are possible, and that either large tires must be fitted or higher inflation pressures used. The use of heavy vehicles of this type over fixed routes involving frequent stops makes additional demands on roadways, for which very expensive provision will have to be made in the future." [183]

"Recent developments in Auckland afford even more striking evidence of the effects of these vehicles. In one case a length of street which was considered by the District Commissioner of Works 'adequate for residential and commercial purposes' became in urgent need of complete reconstruction after trolley-buses had been running for two months. In all, twelve streets, mostly with considerable thickness of road formation, have been seriously damaged by trolley-bus traffic and now require extensive reconstruction.

"Evidence placed before the Committee revealed a serious lack of co-ordination between roading authorities and public passenger transport authorities with regard to general road maintenance. Even in cases where both are under general administration of the one civic authority the position is far from satisfactory, while in those cases where municipal transport services are operated by a special authority separate from the municipal Council the lack of co-ordination amounts in some cases to a serious clash of policy.

"The policy of some transport authorities appears to be to operate vehicles solely on the basis of their suitability for the transport of a maximum number of passengers without due regard to the general roading conditions in the area. The Committee is of the opinion that the authorities responsible for the decisions to allow trolley-buses in municipal areas did not fully appreciate the seriousness of the problems they were creating." [183]

Omnibuses

While the Roading Investigation Committee blamed trolleybuses for much of the damage to metropolitan roads, the Committee also predicted that the omnibus would eventually become a more widespread destroyer:

"Omnibuses – Apart from the use of trolley-buses in selected localities, it appears likely that the omnibus will in future be the main vehicle used in public transport in New Zealand cities. At the present time large orders have been placed overseas by various public passenger transport authorities for omnibuses of modern types. In its various transition stages the omnibus has passed from the bonneted type to the semi-forward control, to the full-fronted type, and finally to the under-floor engine.

"Each new type has had in view an increased floor area for the carriage of passengers, and the placing of the engine under the floor between the axles has provided a maximum passenger space. The general body design differs little from that of trolley-buses. The under-floored engine vehicle, like its trolley-bus counterpart, has a higher front axle loading than is considered ideal from the tire point of view, but the use of higher tire pressures enables a bigger load to be carried within the limits of present statutory axle loadings.

"These vehicles may carry as much as 43 per cent of the gross load on the front axle, which again is considered higher than ideal. The extended use of this class of vehicle for municipal transport will again make heavier demands on our city roadways than hitherto." [183]

Responsibility for Road Damage

In his Annual Report for the financial year ended 31 March 1953, Henry Anderson commented on the Auckland Transport Board's responsibility for the road damage said to be caused by the Board's trolleybus and omnibus operations:

"Damage To Roads – The question of damage to roads occasioned by the use of heavy diesel and trolley buses is one that remains to be settled between the Board and the Local Authorities responsible for the maintenance of roads. In the meantime, it is fair to say that Auckland's roads were not designed to carry present-day traffic, and that the Board's vehicles are not the only contributors to the deterioration that is occurring. Even if the Board had decided to continue with tram operation, very substantial sums would require to be expended to bring the roads to a standard suitable for modern vehicles.

"Admittedly the weight of the Board's trolley buses exceeds the statutory limit of 12 tons for the short period of the day when they are fully laden, and the Board does not deny that the degree of upgrading necessary on certain main roads will probably be increased by its modernisation plans. The Board has previously announced that it will accept such liabilities as it is legally required to meet in these matters." [182]

Heavy Traffic Licence Fees

One of those legal requirements, heavy traffic licence fees stipulated by Section 59(l) of the Transport Act 1949, fixed those fees at not more than seventy-five pounds per vehicle. [105] However, the Transport Amendment Act (No 2) 1953 amended Section 59(l) by omitting the maximum amount. That meant that, as of 1 April 1954, "…the local authority or other body or person exercising control over any roads…" [184] was no longer limited to a prescribed, maximum, heavy-traffic licence fee.

This legislative effect on the Transport Board's costs was explained Board Chairman, Henry Anderson in his Annual report for the financial year ended 31 March 1954:

"Damage To Roads – While there still remains for settlement between the Board and the Auckland City Council the question of damage to roads used by the Board's heavy passenger vehicles up to 1st April, 1954, the position regarding the Board's contribution to road upkeep from that date has been clarified by recent legislation.

"The Board is now required to pay Heavy Traffic fees much higher than the former maximum of £75 per vehicle per annum and its annual bill for Heavy Traffic fees is likely to increase by some £20,000. For future compensation for road damage the local authorities concerned must look to the National Roads Fund, set up under provisions of the National Roads Act, 1953.

"This Act provides that local authorities responsible for road maintenance are to receive from the National Roads Fund by way of subsidy amounts which it is understood will be substantially in excess of what they formerly received from Heavy Traffic fees, petrol tax allocation and other sources, towards road maintenance." [185]

Net Loss 1954

But an increase in heavy traffic fees in 1954 was the least of the Board's worries, as outlined by Henry Anderson in the same report:

"After making all interest and sinking fund payments and also provision for other items properly chargeable against the year's working, the net loss for the year is £124,336…Total revenue from all sources for the year was £1,553,733, which amount is £84,079 (5.72%) more than the previous year. Working expenses amounted to £1,471,782, an increase of £88,030 (6.36%) over the previous year…The loss for the year is again substantial. This unfortunate result arose from a number of causes of which the most important are:

"(1) The Arbitration Court Order of 19 November, 1953, which increased wages by 10% retrospectively from 15 September, 1953, and added nearly £2000 a week to the Board's wage bill...

"(2) Although excellent progress in the Modernisation programme was made during the year – three heavy main line tram services were converted to buses and two small new services were commenced – it proved to be physically impossible to maintain the rate of modernisation planned when the estimates for the year were under review. This meant that the expected relief in wages costs resulting from one-man operation was not obtained, while on the other hand, the full capital charges on the loan out of which the vehicles were purchased had to be met.

"(3) Shortage of staff continued and necessitated the working of many men on what would be their normal days off duty, at consequential overtime rates.

"(4) Revenue has been lower than expected. During the Royal Visit when record traffic was expected and services were provided in accordance with expectations, the results were most disappointing.

"But for the factors just mentioned a more satisfactory conclusion to the year's workings would have resulted and it appears certain that even when modernisation is completed, the staffing position and stability in wage rates will have an important bearing on the attainment of satisfactory results." [185]

Private Motor Car Competition

"The Board has stated before, and feels it should be repeated, that one of the major reasons for the deterioration in the Board's financial position is the competition of the private motor car. It is an undeniable fact that this deterioration became evident when petrol rationing ceased at the end of May, 1950 (passengers fell almost immediately by 60,000 a week and revenue at the rate of £40,000 per annum) and it has continued since.

"No one can blame motor car owners for making use of their cars and yet the welfare of these same people is very dependent on the operation of an efficient public transport service. They expect it to be there when they need it, it enhances the value of their properties, and above all, it is essential to the good of Metropolitan Auckland. It is equitable that all should contribute towards the cost of the undertaking and although a levy is not perhaps the fairest method of ensuring that this is done, it is the only method open to the Board under the present law.

"It seems to be an unfortunate fact that few, if any, publicly owned transport undertakings in Australia and New Zealand, and also to the best of our information, in England, are making ends meet. All the indications are that transport undertakings are faced with a difficult time in the foreseeable future. Auckland with its low density of population and suburban sprawl, will be no exception. The Board is determined, however, to see that every practicable step is taken to put the undertaking on a self-supporting basis and fully endorses the Manager's view that given stable conditions, the progressive steps being taken in Modernisation result at least in considerable betterment of the position, particularly by reduced expenditure." [185]

Modernization of Municipal Public Transport

In an article entitled *Modernization of Municipal Public Transport*, published in the June edition of the journal, *New Zealand Engineering*, the Transport Board's Chief Engineer, J W F Welch, elaborated on the public transport situation that existed in 1954:

"Before the motor car became an important factor in the problem of street congestion, public transport could proceed through city streets almost without hindrance, and passengers could alight from, or board, public transport almost at their place of business. Today, however, almost half of the travelling time to a distant suburb is occupied in traversing the city section, where congestion and delays at intersections account for the prolonged overall time of the journey.

"Most municipally owned public transport operators in New Zealand are to-day operating at a loss, in some cases the loss being fairly substantial. The main reason for this adverse trading balance lies in the fact that the labour content in a transport industry is extremely high, and the rapid increase in wage rates has far outstripped any consequential increases in the fare structure. It has been calculated that out of every £1 collected from passengers as fares, 15s. is required to pay the wages and salaries of those directly associated with the running and maintenance of the vehicles, and in at least one transport authority, a wage increase of 1d. per hour represents an increase of nearly £20,000 per year in the wages Bill.

"In modernizing their transport systems, operators see some hope in arriving at a more stable financial position, less vulnerable to increases in wage rates because of the reduced staff needed to provide one-man vehicle operation. Another factor which may assist in this direction is that from experience elsewhere the provision of modern vehicles does result in greater patronage.

"What the future holds for those who operate municipal transport it would be most difficult to prophesy. But, given some stability in regard to wage rates and the cost of expendable materials such as tyres, oil, etc., plus the ability of each operator to provide a service which will be more expeditious and more comfortable than the one being replaced, there is a fair chance that deficits in trading operations may be overtaken and converted into a small profit." [186]

Modernisation Programme Continues

Despite the uncertainty of achievable profit margins, there seemed little to deter the Transport Board from proceeding with its modernisation programme; of replacing the trams with road-consuming, public transport. Had the Board then had the gift of prescience; the ability to predict the future of roads so congested that both the bus and the private motor car would eventually run out of space, they might have hesitated. But they did not and went ahead with alacrity, as Henry Anderson described in his 1954 Annual Report:

"Modernisation – Four of the former tram services are now converted to Trolley Buses, viz., Herne Bay, Ponsonby, Richmond Road and Westmere, and three to Diesel Buses, viz., Point Chevalier, Mount Roskill and Three Kings. As soon as sufficient men are trained in the operation of both types of vehicle, Ponsonby, Mount Roskill, Richmond Road and Westmere will be served by what is to be the permanent method of operation, that is, trolley buses for the regular timetable services, augmented by diesel buses at peak travelling times. Herne Bay, Point Chevalier and Three Kings services will be similarly adjusted when more trolley buses arrive from England." [185]

Delivery Delays, Tax and Duty

Despite Henry Anderson's enthusiasm for what was then thought to be progress, it was not all fast-forward:

"Trolley Buses – Delay is being experienced in delivery of the 40 trolley buses ordered in 1952 and the latest information indicates that they will probably be here by the end of 1954. This is at least a year later that they were expected when ordered.

"Motor Buses – Delivery of the 13 A.E.C., 50 Leyland, and 90 Daimler buses ordered in 1951 has been completed, but some of the Daimlers are still in course of assembly before going into service. Also on order since 1952 are 12 Bedford buses and delivery of these too is subject to delay, as they are not now expected to arrive until late in 1954." [185]

Then, when the buses eventually reached the border, the Government showed its support for the need for an efficient public transport system by charging the Transport Board sales tax and customs duty:

"Sales Tax And Customs Duty – The Board's continued efforts to obtain relief from the heavy burden of Sales Tax and Customs Duty on its new passenger vehicles are still without success. No reduction was made in the 1953 Budget, in spite of strong representations to the Minister of Customs, who had previously indicated that the question would be reviewed from time to time and that when it was possible to do so some reduction would be made.

"The amount of Sales Tax and Customs Duty in respect of vehicles in Stage 2 of the Modernisation scheme will exceed a quarter of a million pounds. Faced with this staggering sum and with the knowledge that more vehicles will be required under Stage 3 of Modernisation for further conversions of tram services, the Board must continue to press its claims and this is being done through the Public Passenger Transport Association." [185]

The Public Passenger Transport Association of New Zealand

The Public Passenger Transport Association of New Zealand was formed in 1941, as described by the Auckland Transport Board Chairman, Joseph Sayegh, in his Annual Report for the financial year ended 31 March 1942:

"Formation of The Public Passenger Transport Assn. of N.Z.: As the result of the Board calling a conference of representatives of all public passenger transport systems in N.Z., the above Association has now been set up. Its main object is to hold annual meetings to discuss current transport problems and to make recommendations which will act as a guide to all the bodies which make up its membership. Obviously its decisions cannot be binding on those bodies but it should mean that such decisions, being based on the experience and knowledge of elected representatives and officers from the whole of the Dominion, will prove of undoubted value to the local bodies concerned. The inaugural meeting was held in Wellington in November last and the next meeting will be held in Auckland next November." [85]

Sales Tax and Customs Duty Remains

By mid-1955, and despite what was described as a *substantial national accounts surplus*, the Government-imposed *Sales Tax and Customs Duty on its new passenger vehicles* remained a *heavy burden* for the Auckland Transport Board:

"Sales Tax And Customs Duty: No success has yet attended the repeated efforts of the Board and the Public Passenger Transport Association to obtain relief from the heavy burden of Sales Tax and Customs Duty on passenger transport vehicles, despite an assurance from the Minister of Customs as far back as October 1952, that the question would be reviewed from time to time and that when it was possible to do so some reduction would be made.

"Following the presentation of the 1954 Budget, the Minister informed the Public Passenger Transport Association that the circumstances surrounding Government's requirements for finance were such that relief could not justifiably be given at that stage, but this did not mean, however, that the present rates would never be altered or that the Association's case would be disregarded in the future. The Minister stated further that the case would be examined from time to time with a view to removing or reducing these charges as circumstances in the future permitted.

"This question was again strongly canvassed at the Public Passenger Transport Association conference held in March, when it was decided that urgent representations to Government be renewed. The latest national accounts show a substantial surplus and it is to be hoped, even at this late date, that relief from this burdensome tax will be forthcoming. If no relief is given before completion of the Modernisation scheme, the Board will have paid over half a million pounds in sales tax and customs duty on new vehicles, a sum which fully justifies the Board's action in continuing to press its claims." [187]

A Case Opposing Tax and Duty Remission

However, the Government's imposition of a sales tax and customs duty on imported public transport vehicles was not necessarily just a money-grab. Indeed, the 1953 Report of the Roading Investigation Committee indicated that that the tax and duty could be viewed as the Government's attempt to offset the cost of the damage to the country's roading infrastructure caused by the increasing numbers of these vehicles:

"The Committee was concerned at the evidence placed before it of the strain being placed on some city streets by this new traffic and the great cost of up-grading streets to cater for it. We have noted the strength of the demand now being made for a remission of taxation on these vehicles, but in view of the enormous sums involved in providing adequate roading facilities for their operation, and the fact that some portion of all roading costs will probably become a charge on the national exchequer, the case for special tax concessions may not be so strong as it may appear at first sight." [183]

Sales Tax and Customs Duty Acts

In 1953, the amount of sales tax and customs duty applicable to the importation of motor vehicles was subject to the Sales Tax Act 1932-33 which was administered by the Customs Department. Part III, Section 11(1) of the Act imposed a "…sales tax at the rate of five per centum of the sale value of the goods in respect of which it is payable shall be levied, collected, and paid on all goods (except goods of the classes or kinds for the time being exempted from the operation of this Act)." The only vehicle exemptions, included in the First Schedule of the Act, were those associated with farming, such as tractors, traction-engines, farm-wagons and farm-sleds. [188]

Not long after, a preference for the importation of unassembled vehicles was legislated for with the passage of the Customs Acts Amendment Act 1934, Section 16(1) of which stated: "The Minister shall from time to time, by notice in the *Gazette* determine the goods which may be entered under Tariff item 389(a) as motor-vehicles unassembled or completely knocked down, and may in like manner determine the conditions under which such goods shall be imported into and used in New Zealand and the purposes for which those goods shall be so used." [189]

The Customs Tariff of New Zealand, included in the 1934 Amendment Act, defined Tariff item 389 (a) as:

"Motor-vehicles unassembled or completely knocked down (c.k.d.) – Up to and including 31st December, 1934 – British Preferential Tariff 10 per cent. *ad. val.* [*ad valorem* – in proportion to the value] General Tariff 55 per cent. *ad.val.* On and after 1st January, 1935 – British Preferential Tariff 5 per cent. *ad. val.* General Tariff 50 per cent. *ad. val.*" [189]

First Transport Board Rates Levy

As it had every right to do, in accordance with Sections 45 and 48 of the Auckland Transport Board Act 1928, the Auckland Transport Board levied its constituent Local Authorities for the first time since its inception. The sum levied during 1954 totalled £100,000 but the Board's operating loss was nevertheless considerable, as described by its Chairman, Henry Anderson, in his report for the financial year ended 31 March 1955:

"After making all interest and sinking fund payments and also provision for other items properly chargeable against the year's working, the net loss for the year is £108,698/8/10. Total revenue from all sources for the year, but not including the levy of £100,000, was £1,658,617, which amount is £139,884 (9.21%) more than the previous year. Working expenses amounted to £1,528,513 an increase of £56,731 (3.85%) over the previous year. [187]

Causes of Loss

"The loss for the year is again substantial and I believe is attributable to the following main causes:

(1) An increase in Wages costs arising from an Order of the Court of Arbitration, dated 28th October 1954, involving an extra £10,500 for the period to 31st March 1955.

(2) The cost attributable to the change-over period, when the old and the new systems are working concurrently.

(3) Staff shortage, necessitating the working of employees at overtime rates on their rostered off-duty days.

(4) Increased capital charges on the loans being raised to modernise the services.

(5) Competition of the private motor-car. Only the United States of America is ahead of New Zealand in the proportion of motor-cars to population and transport undertakings in both countries, as in other parts of the world, are continuing to feel the adverse effects.

(6) Development of suburban shopping areas, reducing the necessity for shopping visits to the City.

(7) Reduced attendances at Race Meetings since the provision of off-course betting facilities." [187]

Filling the Roads with Progress

While Henry Anderson viewed the increasing use of the motor car as a substantial threat to the economic viability of public transport, car owners naturally saw themselves as no more than the pioneers of a modern urban society. Regardless of the consequences, both sides continued with their own version of progress, each seemingly anxious to fill the roads with as many motor vehicles as quickly as they could.

According to the 1955 edition of the *Official Civic, Commercial and Industrial Year Book for the City of Auckland*, "…the most recent survey showed that 100 million passengers were carried by trams, buses and trolley buses each year; 3,500,000 by suburban railway services; and 12 million by the harbour ferries. In addition, an estimated 60 million used private cars…" [190]

The Transport Board's Progress

Henry Anderson updated the Transport Board's efforts to modernise Auckland's public transport services in his 1955 Annual Report:

"Modernisation: Steady progress is being maintained with the Modernisation programme and services are being converted as vehicles arrive from England and are made ready for the road. Seven former tram services, viz., Herne Bay, Ponsonby, Richmond Road, Westmere, Point Chevalier, Mount Roskill and Three Kings are now converted to trolleybuses for the regular timetable services, augmented at peak travelling times by petrol and diesel buses.

"Three former tram routes, viz., Owairaka, Great South Road and Victoria Avenue, are now being served by petrol and/or diesel buses and opportunity has been taken to combine the Great South Road service with the former bus service to Penrose. Only three routes, viz., Avondale, Meadowbank and Onehunga remain under tram operation and it should be only a matter of two or three years before trams disappear entirely from the Auckland scene. Tracks are being removed as tram services cease and the used rails and sleepers made available for sale are meeting with a ready demand.

"Trolleybuses: Delivery of the 40 trolleybuses ordered in 1952 is just about completed and they will be placed in service as they are painted and the necessary overhead equipment is erected. On 14th March, 1955, an order was placed for 34 more trolleybuses required under Stage 3 of the Modernisation programme. These will be used to introduce the proposed Railway Station-Queen Street-Karangahape Road Shuttle service and on the remaining tram services. Delivery is not expected until late in 1956.

"Motor Buses: Delivery has been completed of all motor buses ordered prior to the year under review and all are now in service. On 14th February 1955, the Board accepted a tender for the supply of 70 Daimler diesel buses under Stage 3 of the Modernisation programme. Delivery is expected to begin towards the end of 1955." [187]

A New Era in Transport

The Board also promoted its modernisation efforts by means of an article published in August 1955 by the Auckland City Council's Comment Magazine:

"A New Era In Transport – Whilst by far the majority of the millions of passengers carried on the Auckland Transport Board's vehicles make some part of their journey within the Auckland City Council's boundaries, a greater number live outside the boundaries. In fact, although the board's services are confined within an area of but 72 square miles, its passengers are probably drawn from the very limits of Metropolitan Auckland – a much larger area.

"All the adult citizens within the 72 square miles have the right every three years to vote for the election of the ten members of the board and it is the board's duty to determine the overall policy of the undertaking. The fact that only one elector in ten exercises this right may be due to a regrettable apathy or to the fact that the services provided by the board have given general satisfaction. The second alternative is probably the more correct one because the growth of Auckland's transport system has kept pace with that of the city. Unfortunately since the war ended the cost of providing service has increased more rapidly than the revenue.

"The lack of balance between income and expenditure is due to a preponderating degree to the increasing prosperity of people in all walks of life and the availability of private cars for them to buy and use...Whether a man stays at home or moves around by helicopter, he still benefits indirectly from the fact that the city is served by an efficient public transport system.

"The transport system must be maintained in an efficient and solvent state in the interests of the whole city. The full economies to be derived from complete modernisation of the system have not yet been realised. The task of changing over Auckland's transport system from trams to buses is one of great magnitude and although the progress made has been most commendable, another two years will elapse before trams are entirely withdrawn.

"The Board has always endeavoured to produce a 'balanced budget' by reducing expenditure and/or increasing revenue. Neither is a particularly easy task under present-day circumstances. The board nevertheless appreciates that it has a greater duty than ever before to take every step possible to improve its financial position provided it still renders the service to which citizens are entitled.

"As empty sections are swiftly filled with homes, shops and factories, so the public transport system will expand to cope with the added burden. The public, on the other hand, are asked to do their part by supporting the services which are operated for their benefit and which are essential to the well-being of our city." [191]

The article was accompanied by a photograph of a trolleybus, labelled *"The latest and best of its kind!"* Ironically, on the same page, an advertisement, much larger than the photograph, encouraged readers to purchase *American Plymouth Suburban Cars – Now Available* from *Kirk Motors Ltd. – "We Never Close"*. Seven different models of Hillman, Humber, and Sunbeam cars were also promoted as available to *holders of Australian, English or other Overseas Funds*. [191]

A Greater Auckland

The following page in the same magazine also touched on another subject that threatened more than the Transport Board's modernisation programme but its very autonomy:

"Greater Auckland – Soon the Mayor, Mr Luxford, hopes to make another move forward toward the objective for a Greater Auckland, and to call the steering committee together. But, he told local body representatives at the Town Hall, they will have to think up a scheme for themselves...Generally speaking, and with one or two exceptions, he said, there was a recognition among local bodies in the metropolitan area that something had to be done – something logical and to co-ordinate. The master transport plan, due to be brought down soon, would give them something to bite on. He was optimistic that the local bodies would be able to weld some suitable scheme, but it would not be done quickly." [192]

Although achieving the concept of a unified Greater Auckland could eventually result in the replacement of the Auckland Transport Board, the *objective for a Greater Auckland* referred to in the Comment Magazine article was naturally supported by the Board which, in the meantime, needed the collective financial assistance of its constituent Local Authorities:

"Proposed Auckland Central Authority: The Board has supported in principle a proposal by His Worship the Mayor of Auckland, Mr J. H. Luxford, to investigate a plan for the control of metropolitan matters in local government in Greater Auckland by a central Authority…" [187]

Borough Council Rebellion

However, following its inaugural charge of £100,000 levied by the Board on those constituent Local Authorities in May 1954 to offset its projected losses, the Board faced a rebellion. Applications were subsequently made to the Local Government Commission for exclusion from the Auckland Transport District by the Borough Councils of Ellerslie and Mount Wellington, the Panmure Road Board, and the Manukau County Council on behalf of the Mangere Riding of that County. The Commission's decision was described by Henry Anderson in his Transport Board Annual Report for the financial year ended 31 March 1955:

"The present position is that the Local Government Commission, by Order dated 7th February 1955, promulgated a scheme providing for the exclusion of the Mangere Riding, the Borough of Mount Wellington and the Road District of Panmure from the Auckland Transport District but declined the application by the Ellerslie Borough Council. The Board has maintained an attitude of neutrality throughout the discussions, but appeals against the decision have been lodged by all the other local authorities in the Board's district. These have yet to be heard." [187]

The result of those appeals was announced by the new Transport Board Chairman, Norman Berridge Spencer, in his Annual Report for the financial year ended 31 March 1956:

"Alteration of Boundaries: The Local Government Appeal Authority has given a decision amending the Final Scheme, promulgated by the Local Government Commission which provided for the exclusion from the Board's District of the Borough Mount Wellington and the Mangere Riding of Manukau County. The Appeal Authority's decision confirmed the exclusion of Mangere Riding but reversed the Commission's exclusion of Mount Wellington. This Borough, which now includes the former Road District of Panmure, therefore, remains in the District." [193]

Net Loss 1956

While news of an almost intact constituent authority base was comparatively good, the new Board Chairman could hardly say the same about his fiscal report for the financial year ended 31 March 1956:

"After making all interest, sinking fund and debenture loan repayments and also provision for other items properly chargeable against the year's working, the net loss for the year is £214,668/9/4… This accentuates an already serious position and is caused by the fact that the levy collected from the Local Bodies in the Board's area for the past year was actually £69,668 less than the loss for that period.

"This was brought about mainly by the fact that the estimates for the year and consequently the levy collected were based by the previous Board in a hope that the continuing drop in passengers would cease whereas in fact it was increased… Total revenue from all sources for the year, but not including the levy of £145,000 was £1,544,283, which amount is £114,334 (6.89%) less than the previous year. Working expenses amounted to £1,488,379, a decrease of £40,134 (2.62%) compared with the previous year.

"The effect of the energetic steps which have been and are being taken by the new Board to arrest the drift in operating losses has had little bearing on the financial results for the year under review and a heavy loss has again been incurred. In consequence the Board, in its first year of office is faced with the unavoidable necessity of making a substantial levy on its constituent Local Authorities. The chief contributing factor to the loss is the continued decline in patronage resulting in the main from competition of the private motor-car.

"This is a world-wide trend and is likely to continue whilst conditions generally remain prosperous. At the same time costs still remain high. The Board has accordingly adopted a policy of reviewing the whole of its services with the object of adjusting them to the reduced number of passengers who now make use of them." [193]

Few Trams Still Running

Despite the *continued decline in patronage resulting in the main from competition of the private motor-car*, the Transport Board's modernisation programme continued, as affirmed by the Board's 1956 Annual Report:

"Modernisation: The modernisation programme is going steadily ahead and only the two main line tram services to Meadowbank and Onehunga and the Railway Station-Queen Street-Karangahape Road service are still operated by trams. It is expected that these will be converted during the coming year. The absence of trams and the removal of safety-zones will then contribute materially towards the relief of traffic congestion on City streets…The ultimate conversion of the remaining tram services will be to trolleybus operation but this will not be effected until the 34 trolleybuses ordered last year are available. Delivery of these is expected to begin about December, 1956. The interim conversion will be to motor-buses in the same manner as with routes already converted.

"This method permits of dismantling of tramway overhead equipment and substitution of wiring for trolleybuses to proceed without interruption. Delivery of the 70 Daimler diesel buses ordered last year is expected to be completed by August, 1956. These vehicles will be used for the interim conversion of the remaining tram routes as already mentioned, and subsequently for augmentation of trolleybus and motor-bus services at peak hours, for replacement of old vehicles and for extensions of services where warranted. No further vehicles will be necessary to complete the changeover from tram operation." [193]

Visit of Inspection Overseas

In order to expedite the deployment of these *modern* passenger vehicles, a trip to the English manufacturers was necessary with the cost of air travel paid by the Board's New Zealand assemblers:

"Visit of Inspection Overseas: The Board's Chief Engineer, Mr J. W. F. Welch, paid a visit to England from July to October, 1955, in order to confer with the manufacturers of chassis and bus bodies, who are constructing 70 omnibuses and 34 trolleybuses for the Board's services. Incidental visits were made to Australian and American transport undertakings before Mr Welch returned. The modifications arranged as a result of his inspection of vehicles under construction will be of material benefit when the time comes to put the vehicles into service. The experience gained by Mr Welch and the personal contacts made will also be of benefit to the Board and to the manufacturers. The visit was suggested and the cost of air travel borne by the Managing Director of Coutts Transport Vehicles Ltd., who would otherwise have felt obliged to make the trip himself to carry out a factory inspection of the vehicles." [193]

An Improved Net Loss 1957

By the end of its 1956-1957 financial year, the Transport Board's financial situation had improved, as described by Board Chairman, Norman Spencer:

"It affords me very much more pleasure this year to present the Annual Accounts for the year ended 31st March, 1957, than it did twelve months ago. Members will recollect that at that time I had to report a situation which, to say the least, was alarming and very disturbing. The Board finished that year with a deficit far in excess of the estimates and the financial statement of the Board's affairs revealed an astronomical deficit of £341,390. This year Members will note that the Balance Sheet and Accounts covering the 28th complete year of operation under control of the Board, and after making provision for all interest, sinking fund and debenture loan charges and further, making provision for other items properly chargeable against this year's working, show a net loss for the year of only £150,551/13/3.

"The improved financial position of the Board results from several factors, the most important being the introduction on 8th December last year of a higher fare schedule consequent upon the increase in wage rates...On 26th October, 1956, the Court of Arbitration issued a General Order revoking the General Order of 28th October, 1954, which increased Award rates of remuneration by 13%, and replacing it with provision for an increase of 18% as from 19th November, 1956. The Board extended similar benefits to the salaries of Officers not covered by Awards or Agreements. This addition to the Board's wages bill amounts to more than £50,000 per annum."

"Another most satisfactory contributing factor of the reduction in operating costs was the very considerable improvement in maintenance costs which were presented and adopted by the Board last year and were expected to amount to £405,731, but which in fact, through improved efficiency and new methods of control, amounted to only £363,931...A further point which assisted in the satisfactory position disclosed by the Accounts is that revenue, excluding that received from increased fares, was above estimate by approximately £18,000, and finally, a review of the headways on the various services, with a careful check on passenger loading, enabled the Board to reduce the number of trips run on many services with a consequent lower operating cost." [194]

Ratepayers' Levy Increases

However, while the Board's operating loss for the 1956-1957 financial year was greatly reduced, it is notable that its levy of £326,161 on the Board's constituent Local Authorities was more than twice that levied during 1955-1956 (£145,000) and more than three times that levied during 1954-1955 (£100,000). This additional imposition upon ratepayers, whether fare-paying, tram and bus passengers or not, obviously stimulated notions that an improved management system could provide public transport services at less cost.

Auckland Metropolitan Council

As previously mentioned, such an *improved management system* had been suggested by John Luxford, Auckland Mayor from 1953 to 1956, as part of his plan for a *Greater Auckland*. In the first instance, the Mayor established a forum for local body leaders called the *Auckland Metropolitan Council*. The forum was supported by the Auckland Transport Board in 1955 and again in 1957 when Board Chairman, Norman Spencer, wrote in his Annual Report for that financial year:

"Proposed Overall Transport Authority: The Auckland Metropolitan Council, which was formed last year and on which are represented most of the territorial and ad hoc local authorities in and around Auckland, including this Board and all of its constituent local bodies, has formulated a scheme for the establishment of a Metropolitan Transport Authority, to be constituted on a ward basis and to cover an area inclusive of this Board's District and extending from Waiwera in the north to Papakura in the south.

"The main functions of the new authority would be to accept the responsibility for providing reasonable mass passenger transport facilities within the area mentioned, by taking over the present Auckland Transport Board services and having the right, at the request of residents and ratepayers concerned, to take over privately-owned services that may be offered to it. The Board is asked to promote a local Bill to give effect to the suggested scheme and has agreed to do so." [194]

Metropolitan Transport Authority

The Auckland Metropolitan Council's proposal to establish the *Metropolitan Transport Authority*, referred to by Norman Spencer, originated as one of the recommendations made by the Council's *Passenger Transport Committee*. The Committee was constituted by the Council on 25 July 1956 and reported after its final meeting on 10 September of that year. [195]

The *Passenger Transport Committee*, comprised "…the Commissioner of Transport (Chairman) [H B Smith], two members of the Auckland Transport Board [N B Spencer & H G Beechey], one member of the Auckland City Council [Councillor P T Curran], one member of the local authorities within the Board's district [F W L Milne] and two members of the local authorities situated outside the Board's district, one of these to be from the North [R H Greville] and the other from the South of the area concerned [C Mahon]. A request was made that an additional appointment to represent local authorities in the West, be approved, and with the agreement of the majority of the members of the Metropolitan Council, this was arranged [H Brown].

"The instruction to the Committee from the Auckland Metropolitan Council was to enquire into and bring down a report as to the system of operation and co-ordination of passenger transport services best suited in the Metropolitan Area of Auckland." [195]

Passenger Transport Committee Report

However, in keeping with historical, parish-pump attitudes, consensus was not to be easily reached, as the Committee reported:

"Attitude of Outer Areas: (a) North and West: The representatives of the Northern and Western areas indicated quite clearly that their instructions were to oppose any changes in the system in so far as their areas were concerned. In each case, the area is provided with privately operated transport services and the members stated that their information was that the operators had no intention of discontinuing their services.

"(b) South: The representatives of this area stated that some of the local bodies were completely disinterested in the matter and considered that the problem did not concern them, particularly in view of the fact that they were in the main provided with services by the Government, both by road and rail. Another local body considered that if the existing private operator abandoned the services the Government would be forced to provide an alternative whereas a further local body was desirous of forming a separate Transport Board to take over and operate the services at present provided by private enterprise." [195]

In its report, the Passenger Transport Committee summarised the region's public transport services as they then existed:

"...In the Northern area with a population in the vicinity of 50,000, there are four Companies providing extensive services throughout the area with linking or cross routeing services between the spheres of operation of the individual Companies. Some 8,500,000 passengers are carried annually by these Companies using just over 100 vehicles, and the majority of the passengers are carried to and from the ferries. A large proportion of the users will, on completion of the Harbour Bridge, require transport by public vehicles into the heart of the city.

"In the Western area there is a population of just on 25,000 and these people are catered for by four Companies carrying 3,700,000 passengers annually and requiring the use of 68 vehicles. This area is also served by rail and while the actual figure is not available it is established that at least 500,000 passengers use the railway services annually.

"The Southern area has a population in the vicinity of 50,000 and is provided with services by rail, by N.Z.R. [New Zealand Rail] Road Services and by eight Companies, five of which also provide some limited services within the Auckland Transport Board's area. The passengers carried by these Companies and N.Z.R. Road Services total 10,300,000 using up to 148 vehicles.

"In addition, approximately 3,000,000 passengers use the services provided by rail. "The Auckland Transport Board's area has a population of just on 254,000 and apart from the partial services provided by Companies also serving the Southern area, the Board is providing services for some 65,500,000 passengers annually.

"In addition to these mass transportation services, the Metropolitan Area has at the present time some 497 taxicabs licensed for public and private hire, and for the year ended 31st March, 1956, it is estimated that these taxi services carried some 4,700,000 passengers for revenue approaching £1,000,000. In addition to these public services, there are some 72,500 private cars registered in the Metropolitan Area, the total motor vehicle registrations at 31st of March 1956, being 105,000, representing 277 motor vehicles for every 1,000 of the population.

"The Master Transport Plan for Metropolitan Auckland which has been approved in principle makes provision for a road development scheme which it is considered will meet the needs of traffic and transport over the next twenty to twenty-five years. The Committee which drew up that Plan said that there was no evidence before it which would indicate any radical change being necessary in the present system of public passenger transport service control, or which would justify the setting up of any other Authority, although some minor changes may be found beneficial.

"The greatest competitor of the public transportation services is the private car – some 72,500 of them in the area – and this is the root cause of traffic congestion in the inner city area and on the main arterial routes. If possible, travel by mass transportation vehicles must be made so attractive that it will induce car travellers to leave their cars at home and use the public services. It must be demonstrated to the private car owner that the use of public transport vehicles is inherently much more economical than the use of a private car.

"The Committee considers that some changes in the present system are essential and while none of the outer areas has any wish to have any alteration made in its present system of transportation, nevertheless, the representatives appreciate the need for some provision in the event of any one of the operators desiring to discontinue operating.

"In addition to this, the Committee appreciates that the public is entitled to satisfactory mass transportation facilities properly co-ordinated which would give some inducement to users of private cars to use these services. The members are unanimously of the opinion therefore that some changes in the present system are necessary in that some overall body must be entrusted with the responsibility of ensuring that the following basic requirements are met:-

(a) Adequate convenient and attractive mass transportation facilities.

(b) Operating costs plus capital charges should be covered by fare structures and where a levy has to be imposed a more equitable system other than that in use should be evolved. In other words, ownership of property should not be the basis.

(c) Continuous inducements to the public to use mass transportation facilities in preference to private cars.

(d) Establishment of a system of co-operation and co-ordination between the various services, both public and private, (e.g. cross routeing, terminals, time-tables, transfer tickets, etc.).

"In implementing these basic requirements there must be no interference with the ownership of the present system of licensing and control of the services operating in the outer areas." [195]

These basic requirements formed part of the Passenger Transport Committee's final recommendations which also included the establishment of a Metropolitan Transport Authority or Corporation "...To be elected on a ward basis...To take over and operate the services of the Auckland Transport Board..." [195]

As outlined in the next Chapter, the Committee's recommendation to establish a *Metropolitan Transport Authority or Corporation* would find favour as one of the responsibilities of what would eventually become the Auckland Regional Authority but that was not established until 1963. In the meantime, the Auckland Transport Board maintained its oversight of the City's public transport services.

The Last Tram

As outlined by Chairman, Norman Spencer, the Board's 1956-1957 financial year proved to be very significant in terms of its modernisation programme:

"Modernisation: The year under review saw the near completion of the modernisation plan in that on 31st December last [1956] the last tram in the Board's services was taken off the Onehunga run, and all that remains now for the completion of the modernisation plan is the final construction of the remainder of the overhead wires necessary on a few main routes to complete the introduction of trolleybuses. Delivery of the 34 trolleybuses ordered in 1955 is expected to be completed well before the end of the year and they will go into service as they are assembled. This order will satisfy the Board's vehicle requirements under the modernisation programme and no further orders are contemplated." [194]

Investment Needed

After the last tram clanked to oblivion on 29 December 1956, the trolley bus, the motor bus, the motor car, and the truck had more of the road to contest and congest. However, just as the cost of private modes of transport were financed by individual and business owners, the Transport Board's modernisation programme now needed investors – those willing to speculate on the future of the Board's public transport enterprise:

"Loans: At the present time the Board has two issues of the Modernisation and Development Loans open for investment. They are an issue of £700,000 opened on 16th January 1956, and an issue of £400,000 opened on 10th December 1956. At the end of

March investors had taken up £256,780 of the £700,000 issue and only £33,800 of the £400,000 issue. There still remains £809,420 available for investment therefore, and this money is badly needed to enable the Board to meet its contractual commitments. Funds are urgently necessary to pay for trolleybuses now in course of delivery, for the necessary overhead equipment to enable the trolleybuses to be put into service, for the provision of new bus depots at Onehunga and Tamaki, for track-lifting and road restoration, and for various incidental items." [194]

Removal of Remaining Tram Tracks

Of all the infrastructure changes necessary to complete the Transport Board's full modernisation programme, the removal of the remaining tramway tracks was probably the most definitive. When Auckland's last tram route closed in December 1956, some 72 kilometres of tram lines had been laid throughout the city. [16]

Once the tracks were up, there could be no change of mind. A letter from the Ministry of Works, Wellington, to the District Commissioner of Works, Auckland, dated 13 June 1956, signalled the first flame lit beneath that particular bridge:

"Removal Of Remaining Tram Tracks, Auckland – An application has been received from the Auckland Transport Board for an Order in Council authorising the removal of all remaining tram tracks in Auckland. The tracks concerned are those in Queen Street, Wellesley Street East, Symonds Street, Anzac Avenue, Karangahape Road (from Pitt to Symonds Street), Customs Street East, Beach Road, Railway Station loop, Stanley Street, Gittos Street, Parnell Road, Khyber Pass Road, Remuera Road, Broadway, Manukau Road, Trafalgar Street, Queen Street (Onehunga) and Green Lane Road. Please forward a report and recommendation on this proposal as early as possible. F M Hanson, Commissioner of Works" [196]

The Auckland District Commissioner of Works, W L Bell, replied to the Commissioner of Works, Wellington by letter dated 22 June 1956:

"Removal of Further Portions of Tram Tracks Auckland Transport Board – In reply to your memorandum 26/107 of 13 June, 1956 I am able to advise:-

"1. The proposals have received every consideration by the Transport Board, and have already been confirmed in principle by the Loans Board when it approved a loan of approximately £2⅓ million. This work and alternative transport will be provided out of the latest loan of £1⅔ million, for which I have already forwarded a favourable report for loans purposes.

"2. Recommendation: In view of the alternative transport system now proposed by the Auckland Transport Board, it is recommended that the Order in Council authorising the removal be gazetted." [197]

Much to Do

The removal of the tram tracks and the reinstatement of the many miles of road for the *alternative transport system* was not a job to be completed overnight. By 1958, there was still much to be done:

"Modernisation: With modern motor and trolley buses in operation on all routes including all the former tram routes, the modernisation of the Board's services is substantially completed. The erection of necessary overhead equipment for trolleybuses on the Onehunga and Meadowbank routes is proceeding steadily and it is expected that trolleybuses will soon replace the diesel buses at present serving those districts. There yet remains to be done the removal of tram tracks, of which at the present time, a little over half have been taken up, the restoration of road surfaces after removal of tracks and the erection of a new bus depot at Tamaki and a new Head Office building. These projects are, however, unlikely to be undertaken until there is a considerable improvement in the loan investment position." [198]

Net Loss 1958

While many capital works were postponed, awaiting funds, there is little doubt that local body criticism as to the level of recent, public transport levies also contributed to the Transport Board's inability to complete its modernisation programme as quickly as it would have liked. Although transport operations for the 1957-1958 financial year resulted in much the same loss for the Transport Board as it had during the previous year (£147,618 & £150,551, respectively), the subsidy by way of a rates levy on its constituent local bodies was some $100,426 less than that levied the previous year. Nevertheless, as explained by Board Chairman, Norman Spencer, in his Annual Report for the financial year ended 31 March 1958, operating expenses remained high:

"After making all interest, sinking fund, debenture and registered stock loan payments, and also provision for other items properly chargeable against the year's working, the net loss for the year is £147,618/13/8. This figure compares favourably with the loss estimated at the beginning of the year of £225,574...Factors contributing to this improved position were:

1. Revenue was £27,010 in excess of estimates.

2. Running costs were reduced as a result of careful supervision of the services and the elimination of unwarranted trips wherever possible.

3. Capital charges were reduced because of postponement and delays in certain works.

"Total Revenue from all sources for the year, but not including the levy of £225,574 was £1,667,178, which amount is £111,464 (7.12%) more than the previous year's total, due mainly to the fare increase made in December, 1956, having been in operation for a full year. Working expenses amounted to £1,417,734, an increase of £14,642 (1.04%), compared with the previous year's figures." [198]

Thoroughfare or Car Park?

As well as the financial differences of opinion among the Transport Board and its constituent local bodies regarding the levying of rates, the Board's modernisation programme also caused a good deal of operational conflict, particularly with the Auckland City Council, as reported by Norman Spencer in his 1957-1958 and 1958-1959 Annual Reports:

"Queen Street Routing: With the object of providing transport to the central portion of Queen Street, the Board, in May last, approved a tentative scheme for routing eight of its main line services to either run through Queen Street or cross about the centre of Queen Street. A detailed scheme was then prepared by the Board's Officers and submitted to the Auckland City Council as the Authority responsible for traffic control.

"Council did not agree to the scheme and referred the whole matter of transport and traffic in the inner-city area to a Committee representative of Council and the Board. The Committee considered all the difficulties involved in bringing bus routes into Queen Street, where traffic is already congested by the restriction of the available roadway caused by the metered and double parking of other motor vehicles, and produced in December a modified scheme for bringing into Queen Street initially four of the Board's main line services. Although not wholly satisfied with a modified scheme the Board decided to accept the proposals, which were, however, not accepted by the Auckland City Council, which referred the matter back to the Committee referred to earlier." [198]

"Queen Street Routing: The proposal to route eight of the main line services to either run through Queen Street or to cross at about its centre was finally rejected by the Auckland City Council. It is true that difficulty would have been encountered while so much of the kerb-space is taken up by metered car-parking, but it was hoped that Council would have taken the view that its main street should be used as a thoroughfare rather than as a car-park." [199]

First Municipal Parking Meters

While the City's inner streets would serve as car parks ad infinitum, some measure of control had been introduced in June 1953 – as reported by The New Zealand Herald of 2 May 1953:

"More cars are able to park in Auckland city streets now than will be possible when meters are installed next month. In allowing 30 feet for each metered space the City Council is assuming that all the cars using the meters will be large ones and there appears to be no way out of the impasse. Mr R S Harrop, chairman of the council's public safety committee, said yesterday that if the council provided smaller spaces for small cars the larger ones would inevitably try to squeeze in and confusion might result.

"In erecting the meters, standards for which are already being placed in parts of the city, the council hopes to increase its revenue by charging threepence for 30 minutes' parking. A total of 430 meters may be in use by the end of next month, most of them in streets adjacent to Queen Street. There will be no meters in Queen Street, so that 'errand parkers' can make short halts. In spite of the fact that fewer cars than at present will be able to park, the meters are expected to ease mid-city congestion by discouraging motorists from parking too long." [200]

First Municipal Car Park Building

By 1958, most inner-city thoroughfares had become car parks and of course those with metered parking were hardly considered a waste of space by Councils eager to reap the rewards and businesses glad that convenient parking was provided to prospective customers. The concept of off-street parking by means of multi-storey car park buildings served the same purpose in a more condensed form:

"New Zealand's first municipal Carpark which cost £287,000 to build was opened on the Britomart site 11th September 1958. On the first day of business, the 465 carparks were full by 10:30 a.m. and the charges were nine pence an hour." [90]

Net Loss but Some Improvement 1959

Although the Auckland Transport Board Chairman, Norman Spencer, took umbrage at the City Council's preference for motor cars over public transport, his 1959 Annual Report also acknowledged the reality of what he referred to as the *world-wide effect* that such motor cars were having on the fortunes of public transport:

"After making all interest, sinking fund, debenture and registered stock loan payments, and also provision for other items properly chargeable against the year's working, the net loss for the year is £96,214... For reasons which are now well understood and are of world-wide effect, it is not to be expected that this or any other transport undertaking operating under similar conditions will show a financial surplus within the foreseeable future. A levy to cover expected losses will therefore again be necessary, but the improvement in the Board's financial position will ensure a substantial reduction in the amount to be levied, at least for the coming year.

"Contributing factors to the continued improvement were:

(i) The decline in revenue over recent years appears to have been halted, at least for the time being, and the amount received was in fact £529 more than the total for the previous year. Although there is apparently no diminution in the number of vehicles using the roads it seems that the increase of one shilling a gallon in petrol tax made last year has affected the number of passengers carried on the Board's vehicles.

[Nearly 60 years later, an increase in petrol tax was still considered to be the most effective means of encouraging motorists to abandon their cars in favour of public transport.]

(ii) Running costs were reduced by £36,000 from the previous year's figures as a result of revision of the services, particularly those to Eastern districts.

(iii) Further economies were effected in maintenance costs, due in some measure to the closing of St. Heliers Bay Depot.

(iv) Capital charges have been saved because the improved Revenue position has made possible the repayment of temporary loans from Government Departments.

"Total Revenue from all sources for the year, but not including the levy of £196,525, was £1,677,707, which amount is £529 (.0315%) more than the previous year's total.

Working Expenses amounted to £1,364,598, a decrease of £53,136 (3.75%) compared with the previous year's figures." [199]

Sales Tax Repealed

Some working expenses were reduced and would be in future when the Government Budget of 26 June 1958 finally repealed the sales tax on vehicles and spare parts:

"Sales Taxes on Buses: The representations made by the Board itself and by the Public Passenger Transport Association to the Government and to its predecessors over several years past were at last rewarded by a provision in the Budget presented by the Minister of Finance last June. Sales tax of 10% is no longer payable on vehicles or spare parts and although this concession was made too late to be of any benefit in regard to most of the buses and trolleybuses purchased in recent years, some relief was obtained in respect of a small number of buses still in course of construction and the complete remission of sales tax on spare parts will afford further relief in future years." [199]

The Black Budget

The Board and its Chairman could consider itself lucky to have gained any reprieve at all from what was to become known as New Zealand's infamous *black budget*:

"The most famous balance of payments crisis in the second half of the 20th century occurred in late 1957. Arnold Nordmeyer was the minister of finance in the recently elected Labour government. He attempted to deal with the crisis by reducing demand for overseas goods through imposing additional taxes on cars, alcohol and tobacco. In a strict economic sense this was a logical response to the situation, but politically it was a disaster and the Labour Party was saddled with the memory of Nordmeyer's 'black budget' for the next decade…" [201]

Customs Acts Amendment Act 1958

As confirmed by the Second Schedule of the subsequent Customs Acts Amendment Act 1958, passed 25 September 1958, the 'black budget' provided for a "…sales tax at the rate of forty per cent of their sale value (for) motor vehicles, including trailers therefor but excluding motor cycles." However, the Third Schedule of the Act – Goods Exempted From Sales Tax, included "Omnibuses, being passenger service vehicles as defined in Section 2 of the Transport Act 1949, and designed to carry seated passengers exceeding nine in number." [202]

Modernisation Nears Completion

In the meantime, by 1959, the Board's modernisation programme, the replacement of its ageing trams with trolleybuses and, to a lesser extent at first, diesel and petrol buses, first proposed in 1944, was nearing completion:

"Modernisation: A contract for the removal of the remaining tram tracks and the subsequent restoration of road surfaces will shortly be let, and when this work is finished later in the year the Modernisation programme will be virtually completed. When trolleybuses take over the service to Onehunga in a few weeks' time, all former main line tram services will have been converted to trolleybus operation, while diesel and petrol buses serve other suburbs.

"Adjustments and extensions continue to be made to services as the need arises…The rapidly developing district of Mt. Roskill South has been kept constantly in mind for improved services, and extensions of bus and trolleybus services are planned to be put into operation as soon as conditions are suitable, with particular reference to upgrading of road surfaces by the Council concerned to a standard capable of carrying the buses without causing damage either to vehicles or to roads." [199]

Changeover from Trams to Trackless Trolley and Motor Omnibuses

Indeed, with its modernisation just about complete – "By 1959 the Auckland Transport Board were running a fleet of 133 trolley-buses." [144] – the Board appeared to be in full control of Auckland's public transport future.

However, not all was going according to plan. One of the financial benefits arising from the modernisation of its public transport fleet was the employment by the Transport Board of fewer staff to man its driver-only buses. In order to protect its workforce, the Transport Workers' Union naturally resisted this part of the transition both locally and nationally – as outlined by Board Chairman, Norman Spencer, in his report for the year ending 31 March 1959:

"A Committee has been appointed by the Minister of Transport to enquire into matters concerning public passenger transport consequent on the changeover from trams to trolley and motor omnibuses. It appears that the Transport Workers' Union is anxious to have applied to the new transport system certain conditions applicable to tramway operation under the old Tramway Regulations. The Committee, comprised of the Assistant Commissioner of Transport, the National Secretary of the Transport Workers' Union, and the Board's General Manager representing the Public Passenger Transport Association, has heard submissions in the four main centres and will report to the Minister." [199]

Committee of Enquiry

However, when the Committee of Enquiry was appointed in October 1958, its terms of reference included more than an investigation of employment matters arising from the changeover from one form of transport to another – as per the press statement issued by the Committee's Secretary, H C Perry:

"Pursuant to Section 7 of the Transport Act 1949, and having regard to the change over which is taking place or has taken place in many areas from electric trams to trackless trolley omnibuses or motor omnibuses for passenger transport, the Hon. Minister of

Transport has appointed Mr A E Forsyth, Wellington, Mr C R Gribble, Auckland, and Mr P A Hansen, Wellington as a Committee to make such enquiries as may be deemed necessary or expedient and to report upon any alterations to the laws which it considers should be effected in the public interest consequent on such change over." [203]

Mr Perry's subsequent letter to the Permanent Head of the Railways Department inviting his submissions to the Committee also signified the enquiry's broader interest in the effects of the changeover:

"While it is expected that submissions will, in the main, be made by N.Z. Public Passenger Transport Authority's Industrial Union of Employees, and the Tramway Workers' Union, there may be some matters relating to the operation of buses which could affect the control of traffic generally." [204]

Metropolitan Authority

There was also a much greater threat to the Transport Board's fortunes – that of the setting up of a Metropolitan Authority as part of the 'Greater Auckland' concept of amalgamation:

"Metropolitan Authority: The Board has agreed in principle to a proposal by the Auckland Metropolitan Council that the Government be requested to invite the Local Government Commission to consider and report on proposals that a Metropolitan Authority be set up to co-ordinate services which are of a metropolitan character, such as water, drainage, fire-fighting, transport and electric power. When the report is available, the Board will again consider the implications of the proposals." [199]

Such a *Metropolitan Authority*, in the form of an Auckland Regional Authority, would replace the Auckland Transport Board as the operator of the City's public transport systems in the next few years. In the meantime, the Board's fleet of trolleybuses and diesel and petrol buses continued to compete with the private motor car for road space and passengers.

Road Transport
Arthur James Dickson Speech

On 24 February 1949, Arthur James Dickson addressed a meeting of the influential New Zealand Institution of Engineers of which he was then president. His address, entitled *Correlation and Integration – A Study in City Building*, was subsequently published in the May 1949 edition of the Institution's journal, New Zealand Engineering.

Arthur Dickson's address is significant because, only a few years later, as Auckland City Engineer and Chairman of the Auckland Regional Planning Authority's Technical Advisory Committee (previously, the Auckland Metropolitan Planning Authority), he would greatly influence the decision to steer Auckland from its planned public transport system to a predominant, bus and private motor vehicle form of transport and the roads, roads, and more roads that would have to be built to accommodate it.

Although, in his speech, Dickson predicted the Master Transportation Plan that his Technical Advisory Committee would produce in 1955, that Plan's proposals were to differ greatly from those he described in 1949 when he stated: "The master plan should provide for mass transportation as well as for private vehicles, and the consideration required in this regard was difficult because it was hard to forecast the relative importance of mass transport and private transport in the future." [81]

But, despite the uncertainty of forecasting that future *relative importance*, Arthur Dickson's opinion that a future master plan should provide for mass transportation was one he had held for several years. This was apparent from a statement he made in a similar speech to the Auckland Rotary Club in 1945 when he said: "An electrified suburban railway system would assist in taking traffic off the streets…" [66]

Nevertheless, by 1955, Arthur Dickson's views as to the *relative importance of mass transport and private transport* had most certainly changed. Indeed, as Paul Mees describes in his book, *Transport for Suburbia: Beyond the Automobile Age*, "Auckland's City Engineer was a fierce opponent of the plan [Halcrow Thomas 1950], especially the recommendation to restrict spending on roads. He argued that motorways should take priority." [205]

Suburban Railway First

As detailed later, the first Halcrow Thomas inquiry had recommended to the Government that improvements to Auckland's suburban railway transport should be undertaken before the expansion and improvement of the city's roads. However, that advice was subsequently ignored by the Technical Advisory Committee which found in favour of the *impending need for an improved roading infrastructure* as per its 1951 'Outline Development Plan' for the Auckland region.

Outline Development Plan – NZ Institution of Engineers Comments

In its summation of the draft Outline Development Plan, published in its periodical, New Zealand Engineering, on 15 May 1950, the New Zealand Institution of Engineers summarised the Planning Organisation's expectations for transport communications, particularly that *impending need for an improved roading infrastructure*:

"A great deal of study was given to communications, the principal forms of which, concerned with the preparation of the plan, being roads and railways and their relationship with commerce, industry, seaport and airports. Of these, the road communications system undoubtedly exerts the greatest influence upon the life and living habits of the population, and probably no other single factor in a development plan for a large city has so much effect on the efficient and economic functioning of the city as the road communications system.

"Principal arterial roads will enter the Auckland urban area in the future—one from the north via Harbour Bridge, one from the north-west via Te Atatu and Rosebank Peninsula, and one from the south via Otahuhu and Penrose. The plan provides for the linking together of these three arteries and for the linking of each one to an inner ring road around the central business area. It is proposed that this arterial system be constructed to a 'motorway' standard, and the location of these routes provides, in addition, for the linking almost directly of the ports, principal industrial areas and the city centre.

"The remainder of the main metropolitan road network is provided for by the development of a system based generally upon existing main traffic routes. The arterial route connections are practically the only ones involving new route construction. The remainder of the road systems can be developed to a reasonably efficient standard by continual progressive development through the next twenty to thirty years. Standards are given for the various classifications in the road pattern.

"Government proposals with regard to main highway routes, the proposed Harbour Bridge and suburban railway services, are interrelated, and had to be co-ordinated with proposals of the Harbour Board, the Auckland Transport Board, the City Council and other local authorities. To effect this necessary co-ordination the plan for new highways indicated may require some amendment following consideration of the report by recent experts invited to New Zealand to consider aspects of transportation in Auckland." [152]

Road and Rail Co-Ordination

Of course, in order to achieve the Outline Development Plan's *'necessary co-ordination'* of Auckland's transport systems, all modes of transport were essential components of the City's overall planning agenda. As Dr I E Boileau, then Professor of Town Planning, University of Auckland was to point out in 1977:

"There has been a failure adequately to integrate transport planning with town planning, a failure by no means confined to Auckland. The powerful lobbies for the motor vehicle and its users, the separate funding for road development and maintenance and the division of responsibility between traffic controlling authorities and transport providing agencies, whether public or private, all combine to perpetuate a confusion of motives and policies." [155]

But such integration could only be assured as long as the Government remained committed to the Auckland suburban railway system proposed since publication of the Ministry of Works' 1946 ten-year plan, *The Shape of Things to Come*.

First National Government

However, by 1950, the Government's attention had been diverted. The First Labour Government was replaced in December 1949 by the First National Government and William Stanley (Stan) Goosman became its Minister of Transport and Minister of Works (to December 1957) and Minister of Railways and Minister of Marine (to November 1954). Until about August 1954, the Minister was also the Director of a large, road transport business, W S Goosman and Company Limited.

Transport Department's Annual Report

That the Government's management of all transport modes was to change was clearly signalled by William Goosman in his Transport Department's annual report for the year ended 31 March 1950:

"In the first place this Government is firmly opposed to nationalization or socialization of transport. There will be no further purchase of road transport or other services by the State.

"It is proposed to continue the system of regulating road transport as set out in the existing legislation. The present three-year tenure of transport licences will be extended to five years, and the licensing system will be decentralized by replacing the existing full-time Licensing Authorities with more numerous part-time ones. Certain improvements will also be made in the machinery for fixing rates in the road transport industry.

"The growth in the means and equipment of transport in the present generation has raised the question as to where each form of transport fits into the overall transport system and what part it should play…Road transport does not enjoy the same advantages as coastal shipping and the railways in handling large volumes of traffic for long distances, but it has flexibility, speed, and comfort and an ability to do almost anything that is asked of it. It stands high in the public preference, and its rapid development has overshadowed anything else in the transport field in this generation.

"These general comments are sufficient to indicate that there will always be changes going on over the transport field. People buy motor-cars and make themselves independent of the public passenger services, business firms and farmers put on their own trucks and carry their own goods, the railways may attract traffic from the ships, or *vice versa*, and travellers are constantly changing over to air transport. This continual state of flux reflects the play of initiative and enterprise in the different forms of transport and the exercise of a right of choice by their patrons..." [206]

Decentralized Transport Management

However, while there was now to be one Minister in charge of all transport modes, the Transport Co-ordination Council set up by the Transport Law Amendment Act 1948 was to be disbanded in favour of Committees of local men familiar with local conditions:

"Now to deal with the general question of co-ordination of all the forms of transport. It is proposed to change the existing administrative machinery. Instead of the centralized and unwieldy Transport Co-ordination Council, the intention is to have decentralized flexible machinery to deal, in the light of the local conditions, with the transport problems that arise throughout the country. This will mean the appointment, under powers that already exist in the legislation, of Committees comprising men who understand the local conditions to advise on the specific problems as they arise.

"It has always been difficult for centralized machinery to deal with problems of transport which generally affect some particular locality and some particular forms of transport. It is believed that the simple, direct approach by local men experienced in transport and with a full knowledge of local conditions will be more successful than the indirect and distant administration of centralized machinery.

"The Government considers that the time has arrived when all portfolios relating to transport should be administered by the one Minister. This has been done to make it easier for the State in its role of referee as between the claims of the different forms of transport. It will also facilitate the general co-ordination of the transport services.

"Transport is one of those things that touches most businesses, individuals, and families in a very realistic way. No one likes to see the goods he produces held up because of transport difficulties, or be unable to purchase things for the household because of transport shortages, or be unable to get a decent service to and from work. The transport administrative machinery must be decentralized and flexible if we are to deal successfully with the multitude of problems that inevitably arise from day to day." [206]

Expenditure on Infrastructure and Improvement

But while local management of transport issues was favoured, those locals might not get all they wanted as expenditure on infrastructure and improvement was to be *spread as widely as possible*:

"The proper co-ordination of transport must include the sensible direction of the provision of new and additional facilities as well as the operation of existing ones. For example, our expenditure on roads and bridges should be spread as widely as possible throughout the country in making poor roads better, rather than being concentrated on converting a few miles of good roads into 'super' roads. Steps will therefore be taken to see that all expenditure from Government funds on the provision of transport facilities is closely examined from the general transport angle and spent in a way that will enable an improved service to be enjoyed by as many people as possible..." [206]

Confronting Statistics

The Government certainly had some catching up to do as far as expenditure on roading infrastructure and improvement was concerned. The statistics recorded by G L Laurenson, Commissioner of Transport, in his 1950 Annual Report summary were certainly confronting:

"(a) The number of motor-vehicles licensed at 31st March, 1950 (413,363) showed an increase of 26,408, or 6.39 per cent over the figure for the previous year, and is the highest level yet reached.

(b) Petrol consumption by motor-vehicles increased from 102,600,000 gallons in 1948 to 111,500,000 gallons in 1949.

(c) Expenditure on roads in 1947-48 amounted to £10,847,265, an increase of 22 per cent over that for the previous years.

(d) In 1949, 218 persons were killed and 5,317 injured as a result of road accidents.

(j) One thousand two hundred and forty-one new transport licences were granted during the year." [180]

The Roading Investigation Committee

In order to establish what roads had to be built and upgraded to deal with the motor vehicle phenomenon, and at what cost, William Goosman, as Minister of Works, appointed a Roading Investigation Committee in March 1952. The Committee comprised:

"W. A. Sheat M.P. – Parliamentary Under-Secretary to the Minister of Works, as Chairman.

J. L. Burnett – The New Zealand Counties Association (Inc.).

G. W. Knapp – The Ministry of Works.

N. H. Moss – The Municipal Association of New Zealand (Inc.).

T. W. Rait – The Treasury.

H. B. Smith – The Transport Department." [183]

In lieu of direct representation, major interested organizations were allowed to have representatives present as observers during the hearing of evidence. They included:

"W. A. Sutherland – North and South Island Motor Unions.

H. J. Knight – The Industrial Transport Association of New Zealand.

T. M. McKewen – New Zealand Counties Association (Inc.).

A. E. Hurley – Municipal Association of New Zealand (Inc.)." [183]

This Committee's Order of Reference:

"To inquire into and recommend to the Government, what standard of roading in New Zealand is adequate to meet the reasonable requirements of the Dominion, to provide and maintain an efficient road transport system; and to consider and report upon the financial implications necessary to achieve such a standard having particular regard to the following matters: –

(i) What length of construction and reconstruction (as distinct from ordinary maintenance) is necessary to cater adequately for traffic requirements within the next ten years and to estimate what expenditure would be involved.

(ii) What changes, if any, in the present basis of financing roading costs are necessary, and, in particular, to recommend what contributions should be provided by (a) the land owner, (b) the road user, (c) the Central Government and (d) any other interest.

(iii) Whether any alteration in the allocation of petrol tax to cities and boroughs is justified.

(iv) Whether it is sound in principle that heavy traffic should be liable for a special contribution towards roading; and, if so, to what extent and in what manner should such contribution be made and distributed.

(v) Whether the present system of road classification is suitable and to consider what practical steps are necessary to ensure the operation of only those vehicles complying with such classification.

(vi) Whether the existing system of roading administration is capable of improvement; if so, in what respects.

(vii) Generally to consider and report upon any matter, financial or otherwise, considered relevant to the maintenance and improvement of the roading system." [183]

"Following the initial meeting of the Committee held in April 1952, public notice was given inviting interested parties to make written submissions to the Committee before 31 May...Twenty-one organizations, Departments, and individuals presented written submissions and appeared before the Committee. With cross-examination, their evidence totalled upwards of 1,750 pages. In addition, written communications were received from a considerable number of other organizations and individuals. In view of the importance of the issues involved, the Committee gave every opportunity for interested parties to appear and make submissions." [183]

Incomplete Inquiry?

While there seems to be no doubt that interested parties had every opportunity to make their views known to the Roading Investigation Committee, much of the information received must have included a great deal of hearsay. The Minister seems also to have required an inordinately quick result for such an important and wide-ranging inquiry, as indicated by the Committee's almost apologetic admission that their investigation was incomplete:

"To have enabled the Committee to make a complete investigation into the matters referred to it might have required it to travel outside Wellington both to meet interested parties and to inspect actual roading conditions in the different districts of New Zealand. This would have greatly prolonged the inquiry and so have delayed the finalizing of our recommendations. The Committee therefore, in accordance with the indication given by you of your intentions concerning our procedure, confined its sittings to Wellington and relied on evidence brought before it by witnesses, together with the knowledge of its individual members concerning local conditions to provide the basis for its deliberations." [183]

Roading Investigation Committee Report – A Brief History

The recommendations of the Roading Investigation Committee were finalised on 7 February 1953 and its 170-page report presented to Minister Goosman. Before reporting its findings, the Committee outlined the present roading situation along with some relevant background:

"...roading policy has always loomed large in the politics of New Zealand, and particularly in the earlier decades of our development the provision of roads and bridges was a dominant consideration in the public affairs of the country. Considering that the development of New Zealand to its present state has been mainly achieved in the short period of a little over a century, the progress attained in the matter of roading has been considerable.

"The latest statistics disclose that the total length of formed roads and streets in the Dominion at 31 March 1952 was 54,468 miles...For many years now the main roading problem of the country has been the improvement of the existing system rather than its further extension. The scope for further improvement is indicated by the fact that, of the

54,468 miles of formed roads and streets 7,255 miles are still unmetalled 38,781 miles are metal or gravel roads and only 8,432 miles are sealed." [183]

"The growing demand from local authorities for some greater measure of national provision for roading needs culminated in the passing of the Main Highways Act in 1922. This enactment marked an outstanding milestone in the roading history of New Zealand and laid the foundation for an era of great roading expansion throughout the country. Under this Act, provision was made for the declaration of the main arterial roads of the country as main highways and the control of these roads became primarily a national concern.

"The administration of this important Act was entrusted to a body known as the Main Highways Board, comprising two members appointed by the Government, an officer of the Ministry of Works, two representatives of County Councils, and one representative of motor vehicle owners.

"The funds for the Board's operations were provided from the Main Highways Account, a separate account within the Public Account, which was established by authority of the Main Highways Act 1922, and into which was paid at the commencement tire tax, motor vehicle registration and licence fees, and, following the passing of the Motor Spirits Taxation Act 1927, the proceeds of tax on petrol at the rate of 4d. per gallon…

"The next milestone in our roading history was marked by the passing in 1936 of an amendment to the Main Highways Act 1922 which empowered the Main Highways Board to classify any main highway as a State highway, the whole cost of maintenance and construction of these State highways being borne by the State out of the Main Highways Account.

"In 1947 a further change took place when the Main Highways Account was abolished and provision was made that in future maintenance expenditure would be met from a vote in the Consolidated Fund and construction expenditure from one in the Public Works Account.

"In the same year another new feature was added to New Zealand's roading system when the Public Works Amendment Act, as subsequently amended by section 44 of the Public Works Amendment Act 1948, made provision for the declaration of certain highways as motorways. Traffic on these is strictly limited to motor traffic, access is restricted to specially designed junctions, and ribbon development fronting the motorway is totally prohibited." [183]

User Pays

"The inauguration of the Main Highways Board marked the beginning of a new phase in the roading history of New Zealand in that it was based on a recognition of the fact that road traffic had to a large extent ceased to be mainly local in character and that as traffic was now largely national in character the responsibility for financing the road bill should no longer rest mainly upon the local ratepayer.

"A new doctrine began to be preached by roading authorities – namely, the principle that *'the user should pay'*…Motor taxation in various forms became established as an essential source of roading revenue…For many years now the principle that 'the user should pay' has been firmly established as fundamental in our system of roading finance and it has been noticeable during the proceedings of the Committee that no one has challenged the soundness of this principle. On the contrary, all parties have endorsed it at least to the extent of its present application." [183]

Vehicles Registered
The Roading Investigation Committee Report included a note of vehicle growth:
"The increasing number of vehicles registered does not give a complete picture of the growth of motor traffic. Changes in the relative proportions of the various classes of vehicles, and particularly the large increase in commercial and heavy vehicles as compared with private motor cars, have resulted in our roading requirements increasing more than in proportion to the total of vehicles registered. New Zealand is, in proportion to its population, one of the greatest users of motor vehicles in the world.

"At 30 June 1952 the total of all vehicles registered was 529,006...This represents approximately one vehicle for every four of our total population and approximately 8.9 vehicles for every mile of formed road or street.

"From the point of view of road usage the main groups of vehicles involved are:

Passenger Vehicles–	
Cars, private and business	293,236
Public passenger vehicles, taxis, buses, service cars and rental cars	6,561
Passenger trucks	2,151
Goods-carrying vehicles–	
Light trucks	55,421
Heavy trucks	43,247
Government vehicles (all classes)	_12,823_
Total	413,439" [183]

"A comparison of registration figures between those of 1932 and 1952 shows that while the number of cars increased during the twenty-year period from 148,159 to 293,236, the number of trucks increased from 31,319 to 98,668. This means that while the number of cars almost doubled, the number of trucks more than trebled...

"The growing relative importance of trucks to cars in 1952...indicates a fundamental change in the character of motor transport...So far as the purely private use of cars is concerned their use has moved to a major extent from the category of luxury expenditure to the category of essential expenditure. To-day the motor car represents, for a substantial proportion of private users, their essential means of transport, in no sense to be regarded as a luxury.

"So far as the commercial and industrial use of cars and trucks is concerned, it is closely associated with the productive effort of the community. It has become an essential factor in the present-day economy of the country...To-day it can truly be said that good roads are no longer merely a desirable amenity contributing to the fuller enjoyment of the general resources of the country, but are an essential factor in the general economy of the country and of particular importance in any plans for expanding productive and commercial activity." [183]

National Roads Board and National Roads Fund
"In the earlier years of motor transport the capital investment in roads was much greater than that in the vehicles using them and the construction and maintenance of roads was regarded as part of the general works activity of Government and local authorities. When times were favourable, roading expenditure was increased; at other times it was curtailed.

"To-day, however, the situation has changed because the capital investment in vehicles is substantially more than that in the roads, and vehicle owners are constantly demanding improved provision and better standards of roading." [183]

In order to meet the demand for those better standards of roading, the Committee warned: "As the Committee has reached the conclusion that user payments must be increased substantially if the financial requirements of our roading system are to be adequately met, the need for a revision of the basis of distribution becomes even stronger. The Committee believes that a more equitable distribution can best be effected by the pooling of all motor taxation and national roading revenues in a National Roads Fund. We accordingly recommend that such a Fund be established and that it be administered by the proposed National Roads Board.

"It is proposed that the revenue for the National Roads Fund shall comprise–
(1) Motor taxation as follows:–
    (a) Petrol tax (1s. per gallon).
    (b) Mileage tax.
    (c) Tire tax.
    (d) Heavy traffic fees.
    (e) Registration and annual licence fees for motor vehicles.
(2) Such further funds as Parliament may vote annually out of revenue or out of loan moneys, as representing the contribution of the General Government towards roading.

"It is recommended that statutory provision be made for the above items of motor taxation to be paid direct into the National Roads Fund, without the necessity for annual appropriation by Parliament. The Committee heard conflicting opinions on the principle of the earmarking of revenue for roading purposes. The Treasury, in its submissions, strongly opposed the principle, and claimed it had been largely abandoned by countries which had previously applied it. Information available to the Committee from other sources indicates that, particularly in the United States of America, a return to special earmarking of motor taxation for roading purposes has been a notable development in recent years. [183]

Roads of Indirect Value

A substantial Central Government contribution was easily justified by a majority of the Committee: "Roads cannot, except by a tolls system, be made a direct revenue-earning asset of the country, and so cannot directly earn interest on loans spent on their construction. A good roading system, however, contributes substantially to the national revenues by indirect means, both through increased national revenues resulting from the national development involved and through the substantial taxation collected from incomes earned by the operations of commercial transport on the roads. This factor justifies expenditure from national development loans on roading development, and justifies the charging of any interest involved to the general taxpayer through the Consolidated Fund. [183]

Central Government Responsibility

The Committee recommended that the proposed National Roads Fund should receive all road-user taxation as well as a Central Government contribution of approximately 12½ per cent of the nation's road bill. The New Zealand Counties Association representative on the Committee, J L Burnett, also referred to the need for Central Government to contribute to the nation's roads commensurate with the economic importance of the network:

"Before concluding, I would like to make some reference to the responsibility of the Central Government in regard to roading transport. The Committee has arrived at a reasonable assessment for the extra funds required as between the various interested parties concerned, and I am of the opinion that a larger contribution will have to come from the Consolidated Fund in future.

"Judging by the amount of finance made available to the Main Highways Board in the past, and taking into account the heavy cost involved in roading construction and sealing, to say nothing of new bridging to meet the present-day needs of transport, it is difficult to believe that the Government is fully appreciative of the important part road transport plays in the life and economy of the country…

"From statistics available, it seems clear that we shall see a large increase in the volume of traffic on our roads in the near future. Everywhere one hears the clamour for better roads, more sealing, safer and more comfortable travelling; and no Government can afford to ignore this demand. No motorist would object to paying more in taxation, provided he was assured his contribution was devoted towards roading, and not diverted to other purposes. As everyone in this country is vitally affected by road transport in some form or another, it is not unreasonable to expect a contribution from the ordinary taxpayer." [183]

T W Rait Disagrees

While it was clear to the majority of the Roading Investigation Committee just how future roading standards could be achieved with some degree of certainty, those more concerned with maintaining the integrity of the Government's coffers naturally disagreed with the funding proposals. As you would expect, the Committee's Treasury representative, T W Rait, vehemently disagreed with Burnett's call for a greater contribution to roading infrastructure from the taxation received by Government from petrol sales and general taxation:

"I do not consider that there is justification for the permanent setting aside for roading of all taxation levied by the Central Government on petrol. Expenditure on roading is now, by section 7 of the Finance Act 1948, secured to the extent of 6d. per gallon on petrol and registration and licence fees. The balance of the petrol tax (6d. per gallon) is in law and in fact a Customs duty which should remain under the direct control of the Central Government.

"It is clear from perusal of statements of the Governments of the day, made when the tax was imposed, that this is the position, and the taxation was imposed for the purpose of increasing the general revenues of the State. The fact that for many years a sum equivalent to the earmarked revenue has been provided from general revenue for roading does not mean that such a practice should be made obligatory on the Central Government.

"The effect of the Committee's financial proposals is particularly severe on the general taxpayer, as the Consolidated Fund would be permanently deprived of 6d. per gallon on petrol (estimated at £4,250,000 per annum), and, furthermore, an annual payment of £2,500,000 is proposed…The evidence of the Deputy Commissioner of Works indicated that very considerable savings could be derived by road users as a result of further road improvements. For this reason, I consider it equitable that they should provide the major portion of the funds required…Under these circumstances, I am of the opinion that the

existing contribution by the Central Government should not be increased. T. W. Rait."
[183]

Points of Dissension

The foregoing financial debate highlights two, important points of dissension destined to frustrate New Zealand's transport planning (not just roading) for many decades. Probably the most important, as far as its influence on progressive planning is concerned, is the sharing of financial responsibility. Who should pay more? Central Government (and taxpayers collectively) which benefit overall from the operational success of efficient transport services, or the transport users who benefit individually from those services?

The second point of contention is the endless debate as to the governance of infrastructure and services – should central or local government hold the purse strings?

J L Burnett Disagrees

Roading Investigation Committee member, J L Burnett, had that second question in mind when he objected to the Committee's recommendations that road user payments to the proposed National Roads Fund should include heavy traffic fees which, for many years, had been payable to local authorities. The Committee recommended that local authorities should be compensated by way of a subsidy from the Fund but Burnett speculated that larger authorities would unduly benefit from such a scheme:

"The present method of allocating heavy traffic fees is equitable and just, and has given satisfaction over a long period. The Dominion is divided into nineteen heavy traffic districts and the fees collected in each district are pooled and distributed amongst the various local bodies by agreement...The heavy traffic fees are available for immediate expenditure at present where roading costs are high as a result of heavy traffic. An example is the municipalities, which are faced with a heavy expenditure on street reconstruction as a result of the introduction of trolley-buses.

"The evidence states that local authorities would prefer the present method rather than be required to go 'cap in hand' to a central roading authority, with the resultant time lag and the possibility, owing to, say, financial consideration, of the application not receiving favourable consideration. In addition, administration costs are kept at a minimum, and the greatest possible amount is made available for expenditure on the roads and streets...I recommend that the heavy traffic fees be retained by the local authorities and spent on their streets and roads, without any dictation or interference from a central authority."
[183]

Centralisation Opposed

Mr Burnett's preference for retaining local-body control was also expressed in his criticism of the Committee's proposal to set up the National Roads Board:

"The only evidence in support of the setting up of a National Roads Board came from the Ministry of Works. The constitution of such a body would result in *centralization* with its attendant evils, not the least of which would be the lengthy delays in arriving at important decisions.

"The latter is most important from the point of view of road users, when, as so often happens, *time is the essence of the contract*. I maintain that the more remote the control, the greater the delay, and the greater the expense in the execution of road works...with such wide powers vested in the Board, all roads and streets throughout the country would come under complete domination, control, and supervision by a central authority in Wellington.

"This, I consider, would lead to bureaucratic control, which would sound the death-knell of our democratic local government system. Such a retrograde step would not be in the best interests of New Zealand.

"Local body government has functioned well and grown in strength under Government policy, which has been established upwards of seventy-five years. With the exception of arterial roads, which I consider the responsibility of the Main Highways Board, local authorities, especially rural bodies, which are responsible for by far the largest mileage of roads in the Dominion, should be helped to attain complete roading autonomy. This can best be achieved by Government legislation making finance available direct to the local bodies without the cumbersome method of through a second channel as recommended by the Committee." [183]

Motorway Construction

As well as the question of how local roads were to be paid for, the Roading Investigation Committee had to consider the affordability and means of financing motorways, both outside and inside city limits:

"Whilst in the opinion of the Committee traffic developments over the next ten years are likely to be such that only a limited mileage of motorway construction may be justified, the cost of even a small mileage is likely to be substantial. This is due firstly to the almost certain need to adopt entirely new alignments or routes involving the purchase of land, and secondly, to the cost of constructing a new roadway up to four-lane standard.

"It appears to the Committee that the time may not be far distant when, owing to traffic congestion, in addition to the provision of motorways approaching metropolitan areas, the national interests will require the extension of such motorways for some distance into a city area to provide facilities for inwards and outwards traffic. In this event the liability for constructing and maintaining these motorways should fall upon national roading funds in the same manner as now applies to motorways outside city areas." [183]

Roading Investigation Committee Report Conclusion

As part of its conclusion, the Roading Investigation Committee Report emphasised:

"…the importance of an adequate roading system to the whole economic and social life of New Zealand. Road transport…plays such a vital part in the general economic activity of the community, and private motoring is such a strongly established feature of modern life, that the provision of good roads is of first-rank importance to every citizen." [183]

While acknowledging that: "The deficiencies in our roading provision are evident to all who travel on our roads…" the Committee was mindful, at the same time, of how its proposed changes could affect the existing status quo:

"While we realize that our proposals involve some drastic encroachments upon the established powers and prerogatives of existing roading authorities, we trust that they will be considered by those concerned not solely from the viewpoint of their effect upon particular interests or privileges, but by the general advantage they offer to the roading system as a whole. If judged on this basis we feel confident our proposals, based as they are upon representations from a wide range of interested parties, will be recognized as a genuine effort to reconcile conflicting interests and divergent viewpoints in a plan which endeavours to make adequate provision, to the limit of resources likely to be available, for all phases of our national roading needs." [183]

Goosman's Enthusiasm for Motorways

Despite those *conflicting interests and divergent viewpoints*, and unlike its correlative, the Railways Commission, the Roading Investigation Committee at least managed to promote the growth of road construction and management as a viable way forward. Not at all surprising given Transport Minister Goosman's new enthusiasm for motorways, as previously noted. That official enthusiasm, obviously lacking for suburban railway services, would naturally lead to roads, roads, and still more roads – the management and funding of which, was facilitated by the passage of the National Roads Act 1953 and the establishment of the National Roads Board.

National Roads Act 1953

The National Roads Act 1953 – "An ACT to consolidate and amend the law relating to the construction, maintenance, and control of main highways, roads, and streets" [207] – came into force on 1 April 1954, repealing the Main Highways Act 1922 and its amendments.

National Roads Board

The new Act also replaced the Main Highways Board with the National Roads Board, as earlier recommended by the Roading Investigation Committee:

"3. (1) There is hereby established for the purposes of this Act a Board, to be known as the National Roads Board.

(2) The Board shall consist of –

(a) An officer of the Ministry of Works, who shall be appointed as the Chairman of the Board:

(b) An engineer of the Ministry of Works, who shall be appointed as the Deputy Chairman of the Board:

(c) An officer of the Ministry of Works who is competent to advise the Board on administration:

(d) An officer of the Transport Department, to be nominated by the Minister of Transport:

(e) Two members, to be nominated by the New Zealand Counties Association Incorporated:

(f) One member, to be nominated by the Municipal Association of New Zealand Incorporated

(g) One member, to represent the interests of persons being owners of commercial motor vehicles:

(h) One member, to represent the interests of persons being owners of private motor vehicles.

"5. The Board shall have the following functions –

(a) To administer the National Roads Fund in accordance with the provisions of this Act and of any other Act relating to the receipt and expenditure of public moneys:

(b) To provide an advisory service in respect of the whole roading system of counties, boroughs, and town districts throughout New Zealand, and to report to the Government from time to time on the progress being made in providing a roading system adequate for the needs arising from current developments in motor traffic:

(c) To advise the Government of any changes deemed necessary in the legislation and regulations relating to the usage of roads:

(d) To act as the final authority in dealing with disputes relating to the class or classes of traffic that may use any road:

(e) To advise the Government of any changes deemed advisable in the provision of finance necessary for road construction and maintenance, and particularly of any changes considered advisable in the levying and collection of motor taxation, including the granting or withdrawing of exemption or partial exemption from any form of motor taxation:

(f) To assist and advise local authorities generally on roading matters, and in particular on any special roading problems that may arise from the development of industries or from any other circumstance creating special roading problems in any area:

(g) To undertake, at intervals of not more than five years nor less than three years, a comprehensive survey of the roading position in New Zealand, including standards of construction and maintenance and the progress achieved in improving those standards, the growth of traffic and developments relating thereto, the adequacy or otherwise of financial provision for roading requirements of New Zealand, and to publish a report of that survey for the information of roading authorities and of the general public:

(h) To give effect to any special matter of roading policy communicated to it by the Government:

(i) To initiate and conduct research into roading problems in New Zealand:

(j) To collect information relative to roading developments in other countries and to make that information available to roading authorities in New Zealand:

(k) To undertake any other activity deemed necessary for the provision of a roading system adequate both for the needs of an efficient road transport system and for the benefit generally of motor vehicle operators and the safety of the public in relation to motor traffic.

"*District Roads Councils*

"7. (1) For the purposes of this Act the Board shall by resolution published in the *Gazette*, constitute such number of Roads Council districts as it thinks fit, and define the boundaries thereof, and the boundaries of any such district may from time to time be in like manner altered.

(2) In defining the boundaries of any district regard shall be had by the Board to geographical situation and to community of interest, and to such other considerations as the Board deems to be relevant.

(3) For each district the Board shall appoint a District Roads Council (hereinafter referred to as a District Council)

"*Financial Provisions*

"22. (1) There shall be an account within the Public Account to be called the National Roads Fund. All moneys in the Fund shall be kept available at all times for immediate expenditure by the Board.

(2) For the purposes of this Act there shall be credited to the National Roads Fund without further authority than this section all moneys received in respect of every financial year commencing after the thirty-first day of March, nineteen hundred and fifty-four, from the following sources:

(a) All moneys payable into the Fund under subsection one of section thirty-four of the Transport Act 1949 (being fees and charges received on behalf of the Crown in respect of the registration and licensing of motor vehicles):

(b) All licence fees paid in respect of heavy traffic licences under regulations made pursuant to section fifty-nine of the Transport Act 1949:

(c) All moneys payable into the Fund under Part IV of the Transport Act 1949 (being moneys received in respect of motor spirits tax and mileage tax):

(d) All moneys received under Tariff item numbered 205 (6) appearing in the First Schedule to the Customs Acts Amendment Act 1934 (being Customs duties in respect of pneumatic rubber tires, solid rubber tires, inner tubes, and tiring material):

(e) All moneys paid to the Board from any source in respect of the construction, maintenance, or control of any main highway:

(f) All moneys received from transfers, sales, or hire of materials or plant or property of any kind or from the execution of works for other organizations:

(g) All other moneys lawfully credited to the Fund.

"25. (1) All moneys received by any local authority by way of subsidy under this Act shall be kept in a separate account by the local authority, and shall be expended on the construction and maintenance of roads…

"30. (1) In respect of the construction and maintenance of main highways under this Act (whether the work of construction or maintenance is undertaken by the Board or by a local authority) the Board shall, save as may be otherwise determined in accordance with the provisions of this Act, provide out of the Fund not less than three-fourths of the cost of construction and maintenance of the carriageway, and the residue of the total cost of construction and maintenance shall be payable by the several local authorities within whose districts any part of the highway is situated, in such proportions as may be fixed by the Board.

"*Motorways*

"39. (1) Except as provided in this section motorways shall, for the purposes of the provisions of this Act relating to the cost of constructing and maintaining main highways, be deemed to be State highways, and no local authority shall be required to contribute to the cost of any motorway.

"43. (3) Every reference to the Main Highways Board in any Act, regulation, order, or by-law, or in any agreement, deed, instrument, application, notice, or document whatsoever shall, unless inconsistent with the context, be hereafter read as references to the National Roads Board.

(4) All obligations, liabilities, contracts, and engagements of the Main Highways Board subsisting at the commencement of this Act shall, as from the commencement of this Act, be obligations, liabilities, contracts, and engagements of the Crown, and shall be enforceable by or against the National Roads Board on behalf of the Crown under the provisions of this Act.

(5) Every highway district constituted at the commencement of this Act shall be deemed for the purposes of this Act to be a Roads Council district constituted under this Act." [207]

Roads – Policy Statement by William Goosman

In his capacity as Minister of Works, and following the implementation of the National Roads Act 1953, Stan Goosman tabled in the House of Representatives a *Statement of Policy* that he described as: "A new and progressive policy…to provide New Zealand with a roading system conforming fully to standards of durability, economy, and safety demanded in this modern transport age. It has its foundations in the changes made in the methods of roading finance and administration which came into force on 1 April this year." [208]

His introduction to the policy statement continued: "On that date the National Roads Board, appointed under the National Roads Act 1953, took office as successors to the Main Highways Board, which had been the administrative authority on roading since its formation in 1922. The change was made of necessity – a necessity arising directly from the march of the years. The thirty-year-old financial and administrative system previously in use had been outpaced by the times.

"The position briefly was this: The country was investing large sums of money in equipping itself with modern motor vehicles of size, weight, and loading capacity unthought of before the last war, and was also paying proportionately large sums for the petrol it used, but it had no adequate means of putting the necessary amount of money into a parallel effort to provide itself with the type of roads needed in the new transport age in which it found itself after the war.

"The damaging effect of the war on the country's roads is too well known to be reviewed here in detail. Shortages of man-power and materials seriously restricted the amount of maintenance that could be carried on, and at the war's end there was the inevitable result that a mountain of deferred works had built itself up. A big effort was called for to retrieve this position, this effort being made all the more complicated and difficult because post-war traffic began to expand at a pace easily outstripping that which the roadmakers of that period could maintain.

"The Government, after an intensive examination of all aspects of the roading situation, concluded that a new authority with a fresh outlook and with wider jurisdiction than the old Board was needed. There was an urgent need to come more firmly to grips with roading problems generally, and there was also the necessity of devising a method of coping quickly and adequately with the big changes in roading and transport which, though they had their beginning long ago, are continuing throughout the country with gathering force. The total of motor vehicles licensed to operate on the roads was climbing rapidly, until today there is a proportion of 1 of these vehicles to every 3½ persons living in the Dominion.

"More and more vehicles of heavier and still heavier classification are making their appearance, and there is no evidence that saturation point has been reached in the importation of these machines. Rather is it to be expected that the future will bring an even greater number of vehicles on to the roads through the increase in population.

"This can only mean a heavier demand on the carrying capacity of the road foundations. That is only part of the situation that must be faced, but the Government believes that the legislation passed last session has opened the way to the achievement of early and practical results in modern roading within this country, and also in halting deterioration that is mainly attributable to the obsolete financial and administrative system of the past.

"Through the passing of the National Roads Act 1953 the new Board has been able to approach its task – one of the most difficult of the day – with advantages that its predecessor lacked. These are:

(1) Wider representation of local authorities and road users.
(2) More money to spend, especially for local authorities.
(3) Greater jurisdiction over all classes of roads and streets.

"Out-moded ideas which restricted the activities of the old organization have been eliminated and the way has been cleared for the new Board to operate a policy designed to provide New Zealand with a roading system in keeping with its expanding economy. It is the purpose of this paper to show what has been done and is being done through the new administration towards achieving this goal." [208]

Road Management History

The Minister's Statement of Policy continued with a brief history of the financial and administrative machinery that had existed prior to the passage of the 1953 National Roads Act: "In the middle 1920's many changes were made in both the financial and administrative machinery necessary for roading purposes. This period saw the introduction of motor taxation to provide roading funds and the application of the principles of earmarking finance and user payment. A modification of local-body control was also introduced with the formation of the Main Highways Board. Broadly speaking, the position that obtained in the twenties was in existence some thirty years later in spite of the fact that the whole character of motor transport and engineering techniques had undergone many changes.

"Before the introduction of the roading legislation last year control of roads and the responsibility for their maintenance was divided by three main administrative groups.

"The first of these was the Main Highways Board. This body was comprised of three Government representatives, two county representatives, and one of the private motorists. It was formed in 1922. Its formation resulted from the realization that certain roads were becoming more and more part of a growing national system, which increased their importance beyond that of purely local interests.

"The Main Highways Board, with the object of providing good connections between centres of population and one district and another, declared certain routes to be main highways. Local bodies were then entitled to a measure of financial assistance from the Board, and this body laid down the standards for any work undertaken.

"The original proposals were progressively altered until 1936, when State highways were declared, with the Board providing the full cost of construction and maintenance. The Board also found at least three-quarters of the cost of main highways. The Board's sole concern and responsibility was the State and main highway system, totalling 12,789 miles. It had no jurisdiction over, or any interest in, anything other than the highway system.

"The other two main controlling groups were the county councils and the municipalities. These local authorities were concerned only with their own roading requirements, No co-ordinating authority or organization with a wide enough charter to guide or assist the various authorities in establishing a satisfactory overall roading system was in existence." [208]

Minister Goosman's Statement continued:

"It can be seen that unwieldly, inadequate, and complicated arrangements had been put together, somewhat haphazardly, to provide the country with much-needed roading funds. Summed up, these included:

"(a) A subsidy on rates to local bodies which had been in existence since 1877. This was payable from the 'Highways Maintenance' vote in the Consolidated Fund.

(b) Payment to boroughs over 6,000 of a share of the petrol tax. This was chargeable against vote 'Transport'.

(c) The sharing by local bodies of heavy traffic fees (a national charge) which had been paid into a district pool for distribution.

(d) Two parliamentary votes for expenditure incurred by the Main Highways Board.

"Apart from the complex system that applied to the use of national moneys, the Roading Investigation Committee showed conclusively that the proportion of motor taxation used by local bodies for roading purposes was most inconsistent. Some authorities, for instance, were spending motor taxation exclusively on their roads and streets without any local contribution, whilst in other cases motor taxation represented a minor share of expenditure. It is obvious that there was need for a change which would do away with the out-dated subsidies and ensure a more equitable distribution of moneys paid by the motorist." [208]

Growth of Motor Traffic

"It is not necessary to go too far into the past to get the picture of the spectacular and rapid increase in the use of motor transport in New Zealand. This is the case, particularly in the post-war years. In 1940 registration totalled 317,527, but during the war registrations dropped by 25,389 to 292,137 in 1944. In the short period of ten years, however, this figure has doubled itself, and on 30 June 1954 the total registrations in New Zealand had grown to 587,751, and what is of more importance is the rapid increase in the number of heavy motor vehicles now using the roads.

"The industrial use of motor transport has expanded rapidly in recent years and now must be treated as an essential part of New Zealand's economy. Since its introduction to rural areas its progress has exceeded all bounds of expectation. In a matter of a few years the droving of stock has almost disappeared and its place has been taken by fast and heavy motor trucks used to transport sheep and cattle. Increased use is being made of fertilizer, which is transported by road, and regular road services to outlying districts have been introduced. These are factors of vital concern to the primary industries for whom a breakdown in the roading system, from any cause, would be disastrous.

"The secondary industries, too, are now relying heavily on road transport for the movement of raw materials and for the distribution of finished products.

"Public passenger services also are making more and more use of the roads. Once looked upon as a luxury, road transport is now essential to the whole economic well-being of the country, and it is obvious that its efficiency must be protected as well as improved. With a capital investment of over £300,000,000 in vehicles, roads, and services, the industry is worth protecting. We thus have a valuable and essential industry dependent upon an efficient roading system. To meet its demands and requirements there existed prior to April this year an obsolete administrative and financial system which the Government felt it was in duty bound to change." [208]

A Tax or User Payment?

The Minister was anxious to allay the fears of those who objected to increased taxation as a means of paying for the construction of the nation's roads, as his Statement demonstrates:

"The levying of a special payment upon the motoring community for roading is not so much a tax as a user payment for a service sought and given. The motorist in New Zealand (and this term applies to every user of any sort of motor vehicle using the roads) is willing to pay a reasonable sum in order that he may be assured of a roading system in keeping with the needs of present-day motor vehicle traffic. As long as the payment imposed upon him is judiciously used and is expended through an authority thoroughly seized with its responsibilities and conscious of New Zealand's roading needs he has expressed himself willing to make a user payment on condition that he is given good roading in return for his money.

"The motorist has been promised a new deal, and the Government, through the National Roads Board, is setting out to see that he gets it. Revenue collected through the charge made on the petrol consumed while the motorist is using the roads now goes back directly into roading along with other income derived by the Board. The old system of finance has been abandoned. The country cannot go back to it and at the same time hope to provide itself with the type and class of roads it needs." [208]

"It should always be borne in mind that by virtue of increased operating costs on inadequate roads we pay for good roads whether we have them or not. The Government is determined to leave no stone unturned to the end that the towns, the rural areas, and the backblocks have the good roads for which they must pay by one means or another, and accordingly the National Roads Fund has been established and the National Roads Board set up to give New Zealand the roads which it deserves." [208]

Road Haulage Industry

Perhaps predictably, given his personal, road transport interests, the greater part of William Goosman's *Statement of Policy* continued to accentuate the need for better roads to accommodate the road haulage industry, particularly in the more rural areas:

"The Government fully realizes the importance of road communications. The standard of living, the requirements of defence, and the national economy of the Dominion depend to a major extent on our road transport. For large volumes of goods to be hauled over long distances across the land the railways have unrivalled advantages, but road transport has flexibility, speed, and comfort and the ability to provide a personal and door-to-door service. Road transport stands high in the public preference, and its rapid development has overshadowed anything else in the transport field in this generation. The extent to which we have come to rely on road transport, and particularly on the motor truck, is not always appreciated.

"If all motor transport came to a stop overnight the New Zealand way of life would cease abruptly, and the larger cities would face a grave food shortage. Trucks carry vegetables, milk, meat, and other fresh foods from farm to market, and practically all foodstuffs are trucked from wholesaler to retailer. It is by motor transport that essential and critical materials are delivered to farms and factories, and without this delivery the wheels of industry would stop; widespread unemployment, distress, and an economic crippling would result. The motor vehicle is dependent upon roads, and the better the roads the cheaper and the more efficient is motor vehicle haulage." [208]

Motorways

By comparison, the growing problem of city-traffic congestion received little mention in the Minister's Statement, other than reference to motorway construction *needed for the elimination of serious traffic bottlenecks*: "On the construction of motorways adjacent to the large centres expenditure has been mounting up to considerable proportions year by year with the completion of only very limited sections. Too much money has been lying idle for too long on partly completed motorways. Even though it may mean some postponement of the commencement of other desirable construction works, the finance will be allocated and the motorways pushed to completion in suitable sections.

"Motorways leading to and from the main centres are not luxuries, but are needed for the elimination of serious traffic bottlenecks and in the interest of safety and economy of vehicle operation. It is aimed to complete the Auckland Southern Motorway to Redoubt Road by the end of the coming summer. This may be a little ambitious, but with suitable weather conditions and with materials coming to hand it can be done. Auckland will then have some 8 miles of well worthwhile motorway." [208]

Motorway Progress

Stan Goosman's reasons for the slow progress of motorway construction were much the same as those that had been provided by the Chairman of the Main Highways Board, F Langbein, in his 1948 Ministry of Works Statement:

"It is obvious that they [motorways] are overdue and urgently necessary. Unfortunately, works of even higher priority, such as housing and hydro-electric development, are absorbing most of the materials and man-power at the present time, and it is therefore not possible to push ahead with the construction of motor-ways as the Board would wish." [110]

Nevertheless, that urgent need for better and faster highways and motorways prevailed as described by Rosslyn J Noonan in her *A brief history of the Public Works Department*:

"In spite of the problems some very significant developments occurred in roading in the early fifties. The most spectacular was undoubtedly the opening of New Zealand's first section of motorway in December 1950. It ran for 3 miles between Takapu Road and Johnsonville, part of the main approach to Wellington City. The decision to construct motorways in areas of high density traffic had been made in the early forties, but it was the same old story of necessary restrictions and delays." [209]

"In 1950 the first construction began on the Southern Motorway which was planned to eventually reach Drury. Progress in the early stages was restricted by the available finance. The first 29 miles of motorway between Penrose and Mt Wellington Highway were opened to traffic in 1953. At the beginning of 1954 the National Roads Board was constituted and more funds were available." [210]

National Roads Board Chairman

Not only were there now more road funds available to accommodate the increasing number of vehicles clogging Auckland's roads, there was also a go-getter on the ground to help the city spend that funding in the most appropriate manner, as reported by The Auckland Star on 24 November 1954:

"For the first time for years a decision of vital importance to Auckland has been reached without the usual accompaniment of controversy. This situation is as surprising as it is encouraging. The announcement yesterday by the chairman of the National Roads Board, Mr F M H Hanson, that top priority would be given to completion of the southern motorway from Auckland to Hamilton represented a complete reversal of policy. No one expected anything of the kind. The best that seemed in prospect was completion of the motorway as far as Papakura. Carrying the job on to Hamilton was something for future generations.

"Now the future suddenly looks very much brighter. It looks brighter because Mr Hanson is not only the top policy maker as far as the main highways are concerned, but he also holds the purse strings. Yesterday he promised the necessary money would be made available. The National Roads Board, he said, would plan its work throughout the

Dominion so that money was available for urgent jobs – 'and the southern motorway is urgent.'

"Aucklanders, of course, have been stressing the inadequacies of the present highway for years. They have long claimed that it should be treated as an urgent job. They have had no success and had almost given up hope. Yet personal observation of the density of traffic on the Great South Road on Sunday was all that was needed to convince Mr Hanson that if a motorway was needed anywhere in the world, it was needed here.

"As he watched the snail-like progress on Sunday afternoon, Mr Hanson (a soldier with a most distinguished record in the last war) may well have recalled the old Army adage that time spent on reconnaissance is seldom wasted. It has been one of Auckland's chief criticisms that those with the power to influence policy have spent far too little time on reconnaissance in these parts. Although the rest of New Zealand may be reluctant to concede it, the plain fact is that the Auckland province is going ahead faster than any other part of the country.

"When the Government decided to replace the old Main Highways Board with the National Roads Board it was pointed out that performance was what counted. Merely changing the name would accomplish nothing. In the comparatively short time that the new board has been in existence it has achieved a good deal. To be fair to its predecessor, it must be admitted that the National Roads Board has been given much wider powers, but what is so encouraging is that it is prepared to use them. There is a sense of urgency about the new board's approach to the roading problem which was not evident in the past.

"Auckland can do with much more of this 'let's get on with the job' approach. The construction of the motorway will solve the problem of travel to the south, and the northern outlet and harbour bridge will ease congestion on the way north.

"But the problem of transport within the city is still unsolved and it is a problem that cannot be solved by the city alone. If it is considered that instead of railway electrification and a tunnel under the city a system of expressways would be best suited to the city's needs, the National Roads Board may have to come into the picture. For this reason the investigating committee might well seek Mr Hanson's advice at this stage. His opinion would not necessarily be conclusive, but if the decisiveness with which he reacted in the case of the southern motorway is any guide, it would be an opinion well worth having."
[211]

Call for a Comprehensive Transport and Traffic Plan

It would be a great many years before it was realised that motorways alone would not be enough to alleviate the *serious traffic bottlenecks* that were to be experienced by cities such as Auckland. By 1954, Auckland's traffic congestion had become so severe that (then) City Councillor Dove-Myer Robinson was prompted to call for more overseas experts to prepare a transport and traffic plan:

"What I am concerned with is that there seems to be no properly co-ordinated master plan which deals with the whole problem and provides a sound economic solution, to the problem as a whole. There is no doubt that the situation is very serious and unless a sound solution can be found and remedial measures applied within a very short time, as Dr Cumberland [fellow-Councillor, Kenneth Cumberland] has said, the arteries of Auckland will become so clogged that they cannot function and '*confusion will become worse confused*'.

"Transport problems become more complicated day by day, whilst traffic conditions have become almost chaotic. Unless we can find a solution to these problems within the next few years, our public transport system may become a very heavy burden on the ratepayers (even if not bankrupt); our roads may be pounded to dust by unsuitable loads; the time and cost of travelling within the Metropolitan area may be doubled or trebled; trade and commerce may be strangled and, as has happened overseas, the ultimate ruination of the city will be only a matter of time.

"Serious though the decadence of buildings in the heart of the City may be, the solution to the traffic problem, only next to Drainage, is of highest priority. The solution to the traffic problem is not merely a question of providing a Harbour Bridge, or an Underground Railway, nor is it merely a question of widening roads, provision of one or two Free-ways or a few (possibly wrongly sited) Parking buildings. It is all these things combined.

"In some respects it is the most involved problem we have to deal with because it involves other territorial authorities and ad hoc bodies. It involves also the question of making our public transport system pay its own way so as not to become a permanent burden on the ratepayers and a host of other associated problems.

"To deal with any of these things as separate and apart from an overall consideration of the whole problem, may only create more confusion than we already have. For instance, though the Harbour Bridge may solve the trans-harbour transport problem, it is going to accentuate the City traffic congestion problem. So far as I am aware, no plans have yet been made as to how we are to cope with the additional traffic which will be thrown on to the City streets. No provision has been made for a Bus-terminal, nor for the up-grading of roads, nor for the apportionment of the cost of this up-grading." [212]

Notice of Motion to Auckland City Council – Notes

On 2 September 1954, only a few days after the recommendation by the New Zealand Railways Commission that the proposed upgrade of Auckland's railway system be cancelled, and obviously before that recommendation had become firm Government policy, Councillor Robinson submitted a notice of motion to the Auckland City Council. Notes that he had prepared to accompany that Motion included:

"Regarding the Underground Railway, it appears that this may cost the Government something like £12,000,000 and that there may be an operating loss that may run into well over £350,000 yearly. We already have a public transport service which is losing money heavily. The Transport Board hopes that in about 4 years, when their modernisation programme has been completed, the Board's services may again be on a payable basis. I wonder what the position would be if a new public transport facility such as the Underground Railway comes into operation in competition with our present Transport Board's facilities or the Transport Board merely operates feeder services for the Underground Railway.

"It seems to be quite certain that instead of having one public facility losing money, we will have two public facilities losing very large sums of money every year. It is no use saying that the Underground Railway is the Government's responsibility. Every public facility should be economically sound – if they lose money we all contribute towards the loss, either directly as ratepayers or indirectly as Tax-payers.

"We have no more right to use political pressure to force the Government to undertake economic projects, than we as Councillors have to waste ratepayers' money ourselves. I know it will be said that Auckland badly needs many new public services of all kinds. But we must be careful that we don't behave as greedy children and look upon these projects as just so many glittering expensive new toys. We must be certain that whatever we do serves a necessary purpose and is economically justified.

"I would not like it to be thought that I am opposing the proposed Underground Railway, or any other project for that matter. What I am concerned with is to ensure that competent, fully qualified experienced people survey the whole situation and bring down a report, recommending the immediate and long term solution of the transport and traffic problem as a whole, which we can adopt and implement in the knowledge that it is the best that the world's leading authorities can devise for us…

"Councillors will note, my motion proposes that this Council take the lead in calling in a Panel of world experts, free from any local political ties, to examine the whole traffic and transport problem, and give us their proposals for its solution. We cannot deal with this problem piece-meal, every part must fit into the picture as a whole. I am satisfied that the report of such a panel of world experts would be so valid that its very validity would ensure the adoption of their recommendations by the Government and all other authorities concerned." [212]

Original Notice of Motion to Auckland City Council

Councillor Dove-Myer Robinson's original Motion to the Auckland City Council read: "THAT in view of the urgency of preparing and putting into operation a co-ordinated plan to ensure the smooth flow of traffic in the Auckland metropolitan area; involving as this does, consideration of problems relating to Town Planning, Public Transport, the proposed Underground Railway, integration of traffic from the proposed Harbour Bridge, the provision of free-ways, parking facilities, widening of roads, traffic control and related problems; the Auckland City Council initiate immediate steps to obtain the co-operation of such other interested and affected Governmental, Local Body and ad hoc authorities as are willing to co-operate in engaging the services of a Panel of overseas experts, of world reputation, to survey the present Auckland situation and prepare a plan for the early solution of present traffic problems and the future transport and traffic development of the Auckland Metropolitan area." [213]

Special Committee Amendment

For reasons not immediately apparent, but more likely in keeping with most Auckland affairs requiring quick and decisive action, vacillation in the form of yet another *special committee* was first required. Accordingly, Robinson's Motion was amended to:

"That in view of the urgency of preparing and putting into operation a co-ordinated plan to ensure the smooth flow of traffic in the Auckland Metropolitan Area involving as this does consideration of problems relating to town planning, public transport, the proposed underground railway, integration of traffic from the proposed harbour bridge, the provision of freeways, parking facilities, widening of roads, traffic control and related problems, the Auckland City Council set up a special committee to report to the next meeting of Council on the possibility of taking steps to obtain the co-operation of such other interested and affected governmental local body and ad hoc authorities as are willing to co-operate in engaging the services of a Panel of overseas experts of world reputation to survey the present Auckland situation and prepare a plan for the early solution of present traffic problems and the future transport and traffic development of the Auckland Metropolitan Area." [213]

Notice of Motion Further Amendments

In order to extend the vacillation, Councillors K. N. Buttle and P. T. Curran proposed another amendment: "That the following words be deleted '*engaging the services of a Panel of overseas experts of world reputation to survey the present Auckland situation*' and the altering of the word '*prepare*' to '*preparing*'."

Fortunately, that amendment was lost and a third, appointing the special committee, was carried. The special committee comprised Dove-Myer Robinson, K. B. Cumberland, K. N. Buttle, P. T. Curran, and A. J. R. Dreaver. [213]

A First Step Toward A Metropolitan Authority

In a bit of an about-turn from his earlier objection to the loss of autonomy by public bodies such as the Drainage Board, Dove-Myer Robinson now envisaged the whole of the Auckland district, and its many local bodies and Boards, amalgamated and managed by a single, all-encompassing Metropolitan Authority. He saw the whole process of central and local Government involvement in another transport inquiry as a preliminary means to an end; the kind of co-operation that he hoped might lead to the formation of that Greater Auckland – as he concluded in his motion to the City Council:

"Finally, may I say a word regarding the time of such an investigation? I doubt very much whether a team of experts could complete such a task in under 6 months, because they would be required not only to resolve questions of traffic congestion, but they would have to consider the economics of our public and private transport system. To me this is immediately essential. It cannot wait until we have succeeded in setting up a new Metropolitan Authority. Indeed the setting up of such a Panel; the consideration and co-ordinated implementation of its recommendations; will perform one of the essential functions of the Metropolitan Authority which we hope will eventuate at a later date. In the meantime, the very operation of this investigation is the first step in Metropolitan organization." [212]

Cost of Transport Inquiry

That *Metropolitan organisation* was not to eventuate until very much later – not until the Auckland Regional Authority was formed in 1963. In the meantime, there was the cost of the expert inquiry to consider, and how that cost might be shared among a number of disparate public bodies, boroughs, and ad hoc entities, as contemplated by Dove-Myer Robinson:

"I feel that as the Government is so heavily involved in Auckland's transport problem, that they would be prepared to share the cost of such an investigation. We could also approach the Transport Board, the Harbour Bridge Authority and the other local bodies and authorities likely to benefit from such an investigation and report – this is a matter which could be dealt with subsequently. In the meantime, the matter is of such great importance to this Council that I think we should decide to proceed on our own and pay the whole cost ourselves, if other authorities are not prepared to co-operate in the first instance. We cannot allow any question of parochialism or local self-interest to prevent us getting on with this matter at the earliest possible moment. I am sure that the proposal I have made will give us a plan that will solve our traffic and transport problems satisfactorily and economically for many years to come. Whatever its cost it will be more than amply justified by the saving of time and money which must result from the operation of a co-ordinated plan for transport and traffic in the Metropolitan area." [212]

Central Government Changes Its Mind

As Christopher Harris points out in his paper, *Slow Train Coming: The New Zealand State Changes its Mind about Auckland Transit, 1949-1956*:

"Until mid-1954 both Labour and National maintained a formal public commitment to the Auckland rail upgrade announced in 1946…" [72 p.12]

However, as the November 1954 general election approached, the Government wanted to present itself as a modern, and therefore motor car-perceptive, administrator for the next three years and, as recorded by Christopher Harris, this was reflected by an Auckland Star report published on 21 October of that year:

"*If Auckland is to forget about the underground – at least for the time being – the Government is believed to be prepared to offer some financial help with an alternative – express roadways…But the Government does not want the underground to become an election issue, on the ground that this would lead to confusion over what is essentially a technical problem.*" [72]

Christopher Harris continued…"The government seems to have been anxious to have rail removed from the campaign lest it be forced, under pressure from the Labour opposition, to reaffirm the commitment from which it was trying to resile.

"On 23 October, the Star editorialised that: "*With the Labour Party committed to the underground it is unlikely, at election time, that the National Party would oppose it. What is to be hoped is that it will not be tempted, for reasons of political expediency, to bind itself irrevocably to it. In this matter great responsibility rests on the City Council. If the Council were to recommend at its meeting next week that there be an immediate re-examination of the present underground project in relation to metropolitan Auckland's whole transport problem, the Government would lose nothing by agreeing.*" [72]

Roads or Railways – Which?

While the City Council's Special Committee considered how it might best obtain Government and local support to commission a team of overseas experts to begin its enquiry, there remained many differences of opinion about the financing of Auckland's transport systems and whether or not the construction of roads was a better option than an upgrade of suburban rail.

While there was agreement that an all-encompassing transport plan was desperately needed, some in Government and a few Auckland City Councillors had already decided that the plan should favour a roads-based system and not rail. Indeed, private vehicles and public-transport buses were seen by those advocating motorways and improved city streets as the preferred replacement for Auckland's trams and an unimproved suburban railway service.

A J Dickson Report

"On 20 October (1954), the City Engineer (A J Dickson) prepared a report for the Council's Special Committee advising that the construction of motorways could 'kill two birds with one stone,' in the sense of catering for both cars and bus transit…" [72]

Iron Horse Letter

However, the arms-open-wide acceptance of the motor vehicle as a more convenient and cost-effective means of transport could only prevail if suburban rail services were relegated to the status of the horse and cart and, although increasing motor vehicle traffic inexorably demanded more and faster roads, not everybody was in favour of an option that could cost far more than the suburban railway improvements that had once seemed the ideal answer. One such concerned citizen expressed his opinions by way of a Letter to the Editor of The New Zealand Herald. Entitled *Auckland Obeys 'No-Men* and signed *Iron Horse of Frankton*, the letter was published on 3 November 1954:

"Sir, – Your leading article last Monday should make Auckland citizens sit up and take notice. Or will it? One can be forgiven if one questions the decision to 'examine the possibility of arterial roads' and if one wonders what influence is at work to check a vitally necessary railway link in the Auckland transport system. Elsewhere, it was reported that the City Council had lodged a claim against the Crown for land depreciated in value by a motorway. This will be the order of the day if the proposed 'express roads' are constructed; the taxpayers will have to foot the bill for sums that will make the cost of the undoubtedly more efficient electric railway look paltry by comparison. The Government has held the gun at Auckland's head and has said: 'Roads or railways, which? You cannot have both'. Wellington has both, and promises of more. So what are you citizens of Auckland going to do about it?" [214]

Dove-Myer Robinson Response

As might be expected, this comment from *Iron Horse* elicited a response from Dove-Myer Robinson, who promptly wrote to the Herald's editor:

"The letter, *Auckland Obeys No-Men* in this morning's Herald indicates that some members of the public misunderstand the reason why the City Council decided to seek a full enquiry into Auckland's traffic problems, and a master plan for their long-term solution…Nothing could be further from the truth than to say 'The Government has held the gun at Auckland's head…' The Government had nothing whatever to do with it.

"What actually happened was this, Dr. K. B. Cumberland a member of the 'United Independents' group, made a careful study of Auckland's transport problems and particularly of the proposed railway tunnel and electrification of suburban railways. As a result of Dr. Cumberland's investigations, I became convinced that the railway proposals, if implemented, would not solve more than a fraction of our transport and traffic difficulties. It was understood that the railway proposals would involve the expenditure of something like twelve million pounds (£12,000,000) of public money.

"As, in my opinion, the expenditure of this large sum of money would solve only a small part of the problem, it would be very wrong to allow the Government to commit itself to this huge expenditure, unless we were certain that it would be an economic proposal; and one which would fit in with a master transportation plan for the whole of the Metropolitan area. For this reason, I moved that an investigation of the whole problem (including the railway proposals) be undertaken by technically experienced people.

"I am not opposed to the railway proposals. Nor do I support any alternative solution such as high speed motor-ways. I have refused to make up my mind as to what is the best solution so as to prevent myself becoming an advocate of this or that solution. I am sure the whole council shares my view that we should not pre-judge the question. We have agreed that the whole matter should be impartially investigated by technical experts…We, as the elected representatives of the public, will have the opportunity of deciding whether we think they provide for the proper solution of the problem or not. At that stage Council could decide whether we should call in overseas experts to further advise us…

"I think the Council's viewpoint is indicated by the Mayor's (John Luxford) attitude. It is well known that His Worship is of the opinion that the underground railway and electrification proposals are the right solution. Yet, in spite of this, he has shown breadth of mind in agreeing to support a completely impartial examination of the whole question;

at the same time reserving his own opinions until the report has been studied. May I commend this open-minded attitude to 'Iron Horse' and all others who wish us to get on with a tremendous undertaking without an adequate examination of all relevant factors. Yours faithfully, D. M. Robinson" [215]

Technical Advisory Committee to Undertake Transport Study

Despite the City Council's initial intention and many calls for Auckland's transport study to be *impartially investigated by technical experts* (ideally from overseas), the Technical Advisory Committee of the Auckland Regional Planning Authority (ARPA), led by the City Engineer, Arthur Dickson, put themselves forward as the ideal experts to consider the matter:

"At its meeting on 28 October 1954, the Auckland City Council endorsed *without a dissenting voice* (Auckland Star 1 November 1954) the recommendation of its special transport committee that a Master Transportation Plan to decide the rail-versus-motorways issue be requested of the Auckland Regional Planning Authority (ARPA), an appointed board known prior to the Town and Country Planning Act 1953 as the Auckland Metropolitan Planning Organisation (AMPO). Although Cumberland and Robinson had previously sought to have the Plan prepared by overseas experts, it was assigned to the technical committee of ARPA: the latter body agreed to this request on 29 October 1954. The technical committee of ARPA was headed by the Auckland City Engineer, who had not only introduced the 'two birds with one stone' argument on 20 October, but also co-authored a disparaging review of the Halcrow rail plan three years earlier." [72]

The New Zealand Herald Editorial

In *Slow Train Coming*, referred to earlier, Christopher Harris refers to The New Zealand Herald editorial of 1 November 1954 which describes the political machinations and bias that (in the editorial writer's opinion) influenced the Auckland Council's decision to let the Technical Advisory Committee of the Auckland Regional Planning Authority to produce a Master Transportation Plan. The editorial, in part, observes:

"The [Auckland] city council has walked blithely into the trap prepared by the 'no-men' of Wellington [in that city's capacity as the seat of national government]…The position up to the end of last week was that the present Government had approved in principle the building of the city underground railway and the electrification of suburban lines…Now the whole affair has been shifted from the level of a State undertaking to the plane of local body politics….[Councillors] apparently accept the city engineer as an authority on rail transport and they will accept the 'master transportation plan' from a group of individuals largely preoccupied already with elaborate schemes for arterial highways." [72]

John Luxford's Version of the Origin of the Transport Study

In his introduction to the 1956 publication of what was to become the Master Transportation Plan for Metropolitan Auckland and Survey of Basic Information, Auckland Mayor and Chairman of the Auckland Regional Planning Authority, John Luxford, explained his version of the Plan's origins: "The decision to prepare an overall transportation plan for the metropolitan area arose out of a proposal by the Hon. W. S. Goosman, Minister of Works, that Auckland consider the advisability of giving preference to a system of express motorways into and through the city area, instead of the underground railway project, to which the government was committed. It was during the discussions on this proposal that Mr A. J. Dickson, the Auckland City Council Engineer, suggested that an overall Master Transportation Plan be prepared, with a view to ascertaining which proposal – express motorways or underground railway – should be given priority." [150]

Auckland Harbour Bridge Contract Signed

"On the day following the Council resolution to commission the Master Transportation Plan, the New Zealand government signed a contract to build the Auckland Harbour Bridge. The bridge would eventually be opened in 1959 with pedestrian and cycle access prohibited between the city proper and the North Shore... It is difficult to avoid the impression that central government assent to spending on the Bridge was contingent upon Auckland City Council sending the railway proposals off to a committee chaired by Dickson, with the fact that this had been done before the November 13 general election perhaps an added bonus." [72]

Transport Study Begins

Despite the suspicion of a biased approach and a predetermined outcome in favour a roading solution that would fit nicely with the construction of a harbour bridge, on 28 October 1954, the Auckland City Council formally requested the Technical Advisory Committee to "...undertake a complete survey of all the Metropolitan Area's transport and traffic problems and prepare a detailed report and a master transportation plan for the area." [150]

Technical Advisory Committee Members

As it had during the production of its *Outline Development Plan* in 1951, the Technical Advisory Committee comprised various representatives of Auckland City, including its Director of Planning, F W O Jones; its still-numerous Boroughs (18); Manukau County; Auckland Transport Board; Auckland Harbour Board; Auckland Metropolitan Drainage Board; Ministry of Works; New Zealand Railways; and the Lands and Survey Department. The Committee Chairman and *ex officio* member of all its Working Committees was the City Engineer, Arthur James Dickson.

"Four committees manned by 30 authorities on transport, engineering and town planning, were involved in the preparation of the technical advisory committee's master transport plan.

They were:

"Executive committee –

Mr A J Dickson (Auckland city engineer) chairman;

Messrs N L Vickerman, chief engineer, Auckland Harbour Board;

C Bland, Auckland city traffic superintendent;

W L Bell, district Commissioner of Works, Auckland;

O G Thornton, engineer, Ministry of Works, Auckland;

Professor C R Knight, Dean of the Faculty of Architecture, Auckland University College and member of the City Council town planning committee.

"General Information Committee –

Professor [Cyril] Knight (chairman), and Messrs:

C W Firth, city waterworks engineer;

W E Begbie, resident engineer, Mt Albert Borough;

C E H Putt, city town planning officer;

P S Roe, chief surveyor, Lands and Survey   Department;

A Greville Walker, consulting engineer;

H H Thomson, borough engineer, Mt Roskill;
R P Worley, consulting engineer; and
J Hall, borough engineer, New Lynn.
"Traffic Committee –
Mr Bland, chairman; and Messrs
W G Macky, Manukau County Council engineer;
C H McCormick, borough engineer, Mt Eden;
C R Gribble, general manager, Auckland Transport Board;
(C E H) Putt;
A T Griffiths, borough engineer, Devonport; and
(co-opted) L B Boyce, city traffic engineer.
"Transport Committee –
Mr Vickerman (chairman), and Messrs
(W L) Bell;
(C R) Gribble;
E G McLeod, (district railways engineer);
W I Gardiner, (borough engineer, Onehunga);
C C Collom, (chief engineer, Auckland Drainage Board);
(O G) Thornton; and
(co-opted) L E A Turrell (assistant district traffic manager, NZR) and
J I Moir, (assistant manager, Auckland Transport Board).
"The metropolitan town planning officer, Mr F W O Jones, was director of planning.
Local body representatives not on the various committees were:-
Mr J E Fitzgerald, Mount Wellington;
H A Truman, One Tree Hill; and
P E Fraser, Papatoetoe." [216]

At the time of the transport study, almost all Technical Advisory Committee members were Registered Municipal Engineers; Associate Members of the Institution of Civil Engineers and/or Members of what was then the New Zealand Institution of Engineers. There was only <u>one</u> representative from the Railways Department – District Railways Engineer, E G McLeod.

Why did the Committee comprise so many engineers? By this time, Arthur Dickson may have lost some confidence in the ability of a suburban railway system to provide Auckland's transportation needs, but he had not changed his mind about who should take charge of town planning, as he so forthrightly declared in his 1949 address to the New Zealand Institution of Engineers of which he was then president:

"The president commented on the dearth of trained planners in New Zealand. He said there was little doubt that the engineering profession must remain the backbone of planning in New Zealand." [81]

1954 General Election Result

As expected, the 1954 General Election resulted in Sidney Holland's National Party retaining its majority, albeit with five fewer seats in Parliament. Following the election, an Auckland Star editorial of 16 November 1954 called on the Prime Minister to appoint an Auckland Member of Parliament as Minister of Transport:

"…the three most important questions vitally affected by Government policy are those of transport, electricity and housing. Of these the major issue is transport because

Auckland's shortcomings and troubles in this field are much more grave than anywhere else in the country. The Government can make, if it will, an enormously helpful contribution to the solution of this problem, or, if it fails to take a keen and active interest, and gives the appearance of being not genuinely interested to the point of doing something positive, it can allow a frustrating situation of stalemate and inaction to develop...

"He [the Prime Minister] could, for instance, appoint one of the Auckland Government members Minister of Transport. Were he to do this it seems almost inconceivable that the new Minister would not engage himself in a special study of Auckland's progressively deteriorating transport situation. He would certainly find plenty of work ready to his hand...All is at sixes and sevens in suburban railway transport. Instead of playing a major part in the daily travelling of the public, the suburban railways, for a variety of reasons, are of third-class status...

"The statistics speak for themselves – trams, trolley buses and buses carry 100 million passengers annually, trans-harbour ferries 12 million, railways only 3½ million. That so insignificant a proportion of the load is taken by the State-owned railways reveals the degree to which the Government is, or should be, committed to the inauguration of a scheme to improve the transport system...

"Added to this is the fact that there is not now any certainty that the 'underground' project will be undertaken. Indeed, it begins to look less and less likely that anything will come of it. What then? Abandonment of the 'underground,' even for the best of reasons, factually-based as the result of a thorough investigation, would of itself be no advance. It is action that is necessary. Public transport must not, on any account, be permitted at this late and urgent stage to become a mere political battlecock.

"No real progress can be made without an active Government policy, motivated by the will to make a beginning in the constructional field as soon as possible...Whatever else an Aucklander might do, if entrusted with the portfolio of Transport, he could confer no greater benefit on the metropolitan area than in making everything appertaining to the suburban transport system, and major transport outlets, his first and continuing interest..." [217]

William Goosman Remains Minister of Transport

Despite the entreaties of the Auckland Star, the Member for Piako, William Stanley Goosman, remained the Transport Minister after the 1954 election. He also remained the Minister of Works, but forfeited the Railways portfolio to John Kenneth McAlpine. William Goosman thereby relinquished his total authority over all modes of transport – on paper, at least.

Auckland's Highway Planning

However, in Auckland's case, William Goosman's loss of the Railways portfolio was no loss at all and highway planning continued – as described by the 1955 edition of the Official Civic, Commercial and Industrial Year Book for the City of Auckland:

"Working in conjunction with the Government, the city is planning or actually building express roads which will funnel traffic out of the immediate city area at the maximum rate. The city has the whole responsibility for some of these, but the new main highway outlets to the north and south will remain within the purview of the Main Highways Board, while yielding their benefits directly to the city.

"To the south a motorway planned on the lines of overseas main highways is by-passing the industrial areas of Penrose and Otahuhu, slicing directly through to Drury, some 15 miles out of the city. Every effort is to be made to speed its completion and to push on south, to Hamilton.

"From Avondale, which will be brought nearer to the city when urban express roads are completed, another new highway is nearing completion. It will allow northbound traffic to clear the city on a fast, direct road into the country instead of having to make a tortuous way through the traffic snarls of built-up areas.

"Some idea of the cost of this roading development may be gained from the fact that an engineer's assessment of the South motorway's price was in the neighbourhood of £200,000 a mile…

"Realising a dream of many years past, building of the Auckland Harbour Bridge across the Waitemata Harbour will commence this year. The provision of a direct link to join the suburbs on the North Shore with the City of Auckland has been the subject of much discussion and activity, both local and governmental, since the turn of the century…The population of metropolitan Auckland at the present time, is 361,000, 47,100 of whom live on the North Shore. Access across the harbour is provided by means of passenger and vehicular ferries, which carried 10,500,000 passengers and 1,500,000 vehicles respectively for the year ended April, 1954. The only alternative for North Shore residents is a road journey of some 45 miles to reach the City of Auckland…Provision of this direct link will open up for development large areas of some of the most desirable residential land in New Zealand. The road distance from Northcote to the Chief Post Office will be reduced from nearly 40 to three miles.

"At the present time in Auckland, there is an increasing sprawl of the urban area southwards. This sprawl is absorbing rural land in its path which has been used for dairying and market gardening purposes. It is hoped that the opening of large areas on the North Shore will arrest the sprawl southwards, when people realise that to the north, within six or seven miles of the Chief Post Office, there are at present thousands of acres of land suitable for residential use." [190]

Suburban Rail Underused

In the meantime, the Auckland Star had a right to be concerned that Auckland's public transport services, and suburban rail in particular, was of *third-class status* and not *playing a major part in the daily travelling of the public*. Despite the huge cost and chaos of too many trucks, buses, and private cars jostling for supremacy on what seemed to be too few roads in 1954, Aucklanders commuting on the city's fewer suburban trains were having a comparatively hassle-free ride at little cost to the taxpayer.

This information was divulged, by someone who should have known, to the Transport Committee of the Technical Advisory Committee (one of four committees then preparing the Master Transportation Plan for Metropolitan Auckland) at a meeting held in the Regional Planning Offices on Friday 4 March 1955:

"Present: N L Vickerman (Chairman) W L Bell, C R Gribble, M Moir, E G McLeod, L E A Turrell, W I Gardiner, C C Collom, O G Thornton. Apologies: A J Dickson.

"The Chairman welcomed Mr K Frogatt, Accountant, New Zealand Railways, Head Office, to the meeting, who attended to assist in supplying information with regard to railway development and costs. He [Mr Frogatt] pointed out that in the existing Auckland suburban train services, the cost per passenger mile was approximately 2½d when the overall loss of £202,000 per annum was taken into account, but he pointed out that this figure must be used with the utmost caution because it could be completely misleading if applied to other suburban systems. The annual loss took into account cost of operation of suburban trains and the capital charges involved in the provision of rolling stock (both locomotives and cars) and only a share of the depreciation of the track structure.

"In response to a question from the Chairman, Mr Frogatt stated that accommodation for passenger traffic on existing lines and existing rolling stock is not fully taxed, and the expense of strengthening these trains to carry additional traffic on existing lines is comparatively small. Traffic on these existing lines and services could be increased by 100% at relatively small additional cost, even allowing for peak hours, but were the whole area to be electrified and run truly as a suburban service, the Department would be faced with very heavy expenditure for plant and construction. It was pointed out by Railway Department Officers that freight traffic is meeting, in practice, the passenger losses in the Auckland area." [218]

Car Parks at Suburban Railway Stations

As an aside, it is interesting to note that during his interview with the Technical Advisory Committee's Transport Committee, Mr Frogatt suggested the concept of road and rail co-ordination which most certainly went over the heads of the Committee at that time (or, more probably, was ignored by those unwilling to credit the potential of suburban rail):

"Mr Frogatt suggested that a number of factors have to be taken into account in regard to bus feeder services to rail. The Hutt Valley services gave some indication of the difficulties, but he suggested that there might be changing circumstances in that area which would not, necessarily, be a true indication [of] conditions that might operate in other places. He suggested, also, that adequate parking spaces at suburban railway stations could influence travel habits." [219]

Master Transportation Plan Produced

Following what John Luxford described as *eight months' intensive work*, the Technical Advisory Committee produced its *Master Transportation Plan For Metropolitan Auckland* on 8 July 1955. The Master Plan included a *Survey of Basic Information*, described as "…an objective survey and appraisal of existing and probable future urban development in the area as a whole, and of local government structure and functions, as well as of existing transport and traffic problems." [150] The Plan and Survey were reprinted as a single volume for general distribution to the public in September 1956.

Arthur Dickson Foreword to the Master Transportation Plan

In his *Foreword to the Master Transportation Plan*, Arthur Dickson described the need for such a plan and some of the reasoning involved in forming the Committee's recommendations:

"It is universally acknowledged that transportation is the cornerstone of existence in large cities and that modern roadways and other facilities in keeping with constantly improved vehicles are essential to every urban dweller.

"The form and structure of Metropolitan Auckland through the years has been largely determined by development in urban and suburban transportation. During the last 25 years, the overall effect of motor transportation has so radically changed the pattern that Auckland is now one of the most dispersed cities in the World. The individual has been freed from absolute dependence on tramways and railways with their fixed inflexible routes. Local transport of goods has become fast, cheap, and flexible.

"A common motor transportation system has integrated outer areas and extended the radius of influence of Auckland. The pattern of travel has become more diffused and traffic cannot now be channelled along a few fixed routes with the same destination. There is a rising curve of motor car usage and a decline in the use of public transportation. The swelling tide of motor vehicle use has produced a similar result and problems in cities throughout the World…If creeping paralysis is not to choke Auckland's transportation arteries, immediate action on the recommendations is necessary." [220]

A summary of those recommendations included:

"(i) Road Development:

(a) That a system of urban motorways be constructed from the city centre to provide main traffic routes over the Metropolitan Area:

(b) That an inner ring road be constructed as far as practicable to a motorway standard, around the central business area linking together the urban motorway routes:

(c) That existing main traffic routes, both radial and cross roads, should be improved progressively and integrated with the proposed urban motorways to form a Metropolitan Main Road system:

(d) That the urban motorway development work should be commenced immediately and carried out in the order set out in this Report to provide 'stages' which can be fully used as completed.

"(ii) Road Traffic Terminal Facilities:

(a) That the present bus terminal be developed further as necessary; that a further terminal be provided on the western side of the central city area readily accessible to the business and commercial areas; that provision be made for a further bus terminal in the future on the eastern side of the city; and that one of these terminals provide for long-distance road transport:

(b) That provision be made for a trucking terminal, or terminals, adjacent to or readily accessible to the inner ring road system:

(c) That provision be made for long-period car parking facilities generally adjacent to and inside the ring road system; that provision be made for increased shorter period parking as near as possible to the main shopping and business premises and that this work should be commenced immediately, as the provision of these facilities is complementary to road development.

"(iii) Railway Development:

(a) That immediate investigation be made with a view to – extending a line from the present railway station to a new station in Victoria Street East to enable diesel-driven passenger trains to be brought into the centre of the city; OR – re-arranging the present station and yard layout to allow vehicles nearer to the platforms of suburban passenger trains and thus providing for more rapid and more convenient transfer of passengers:

(b) That the Morningside Deviation would not carry enough passengers to allow deferring road construction, and should not be embarked upon:

(c) That the Avondale-Southdown railway connection would not, either alone, or in conjunction with the Morningside Deviation, have any appreciable effect on the daily urban transportation, but is most desirable from the point of view of main line railway operation and should be constructed as a part of the main line development.

"(iv) Public Passenger Transport:

(a) That provision should be made on all motorway routes for a limited number of properly designed bus pick-up and set-down stations on special loop lanes free of the motorway wherever these routes pass through areas which could be served in this way; and that public passenger road transport services should be developed as far as possible for express services by the use of the urban motorway routes:

(b) That bus terminals, the railway station, major car parks, and the main parts of the central business area should be linked together by public passenger services either by shuttle services, by cross or through routing of services, or by a combination of these methods:

(c) That once bus routes have been consolidated in normal streets carrying considerable traffic, bus loading bays should be provided, where practicable, off the normal roadway." [150]

"(v) Finance:

(a) That the proposed Metropolitan Main Road system (which is estimated to cost £12,000,000) should be financed by

– a considerably increased annual contribution from the National Roads Fund;

– a substantial contribution from the Government towards the cost of arterial routes (where these routes would fulfil functions which the railway development was originally intended to perform):

(b) That works ancillary to the Main Road system construction should be financed from local body sources with resource, in some cases, to finance provided from National Roads Fund contributions:

(c) That the construction programme and the financial provision should ensure the carrying out of the plan by 1965, or at the very latest, 1970:

(d) That transport terminals should be financed, in the first instance, by local body finance, but should be self-supporting through charges on the transport using them (although some special consideration may have to be given to bus terminal facilities):

(e) That car parking facilities in the central area should be financed, in the first instance, by local body finance, but should be self-supporting through charges on the vehicles using such facilities.

"(vi) Administration:

(a) That the only really effective method for carrying out the construction and development of the proposed Metropolitan Main Road system would be by means of a small Commission, Metropolitan Board of Works or similar Authority having the necessary legal, financial, and administrative powers:

(b) That such a Commission or Authority should be established:

(c) That, as the construction of the urban motorway system is a matter of urgency and as there would be some considerable delay in the setting up of any Metropolitan Main Road Authority, construction work in respect of arterial routes should be undertaken immediately by the Ministry of Works in conjunction with the City Council; and that the City Council and other local authorities undertake the remainder until a properly constituted Metropolitan Commission, or Authority, is established; and that in all cases, the work be carried out in collaboration with the Regional Planning Authority:

(d) That while some minor changes might be found beneficial, there is no evidence before the Committee which would indicate any radical change being necessary in the present system of public passenger transport service control, or which would justify the setting up of any other authority." [150]

Plan Recommendations Summarised by The New Zealand Herald

On 21 September 1955, The New Zealand Herald reported its interpretation and assessment of certain aspects of the Master Transportation Plan and its accompanying Survey:

"Auckland's traffic problems and congestion, says the survey with the master plan, are due to:

–The growth of the metropolitan area from 270,000 population in 1945 to 370,000 in 1955.

–A steadily increasing ratio of motor vehicles to population, from about 170 per 1000 to about 260 per 1000 over the same 10 years.

–Increasing use of private cars.

–Great industrialisation and use of trucks.

–Insufficient provision of new or better roads and of car parks and terminals.

–The general national roading policy which has concentrated expenditure from national roads funds on main highway development outside main urban areas." [221]

Traffic Statistics

The Herald article observed that the Survey reinforced the Plan's recommendations with seemingly solid statistics:

"At least 40 per cent of passenger trips made each year in the Auckland metropolitan area are made by motorcar, and 40 per cent of the road space is taken up by truck traffic.

"These figures are given in the survey with the master transport plan. It analyses passenger trips as follows:

Transport Board – 90 million annual trips – 50 per cent

Private Bus Companies – 10 million annual trips – 5.5 per cent

Railways Department Buses – 1 million annual trips – 0.5 per cent

Railways Department Trains – 4 million annual trips – 2.0 per cent

Private Cars and Taxis – 75 million annual trips – 42.0 per cent

The survey says that trucks make up about 25 per cent of the total traffic, but allowing for their greater size they use about 40 per cent of the road space." [222]

Cost of Traffic Congestion

The Survey's estimation of the enormous costs of traffic congestion only added to the urgency of the situation:

"Congestion in the Auckland metropolitan area already costs between £4 million and £5million a year – plus the effect of accidents and other cumulative effects. If the city traffic expands according to present trends and is confined to the existing street system, congestion in the decade 1960-1970 will cost between £50 million and £100 million.

"The transport survey says that traffic congestion in Auckland has not yet reached the acute stage that it has in many large overseas cities, but conditions are such that small increases in traffic will cause relatively large increases in congestion.

"Already losses of time within a radius of two miles of the chief post office, excluding increased time of travel to and from work, are estimated to amount to a minimum of one million man-hours a year. At minimum wages rates this is worth £250,000 annually. The loss of earning time of buses and commercial vehicles (or increased capital charges) in the same area totals a further £500,000 a year. Increased operational costs on all vehicles probably amount to £1 million annually.

"These figures, totalling £1.75 million to £2 million a year, exclude the cost of accidents and the effects on leisure time and working efficiency of a further loss of one million man-hours a year in travelling to and from work. They are, therefore, considered generally conservative. Investigations suggest that the losses over the rest of the metropolitan area are probably of the same order, giving £4 million to £5million as the present annual cost of congestion." [223]

Relief of Traffic Congestion

However, full and early implementation of the Master Transportation Plan was expected to greatly reduce commuter travelling times and costs, according to The New Zealand Herald's interpretation of the Technical Advisory Committee's report:

"Public passenger transport will be assisted by the general relief of congestion which can be expected with the motorways and inner ring road, the committee which prepared the master plan believes. This transport should then be developed for express services as far as possible, using the motorways. All the motorways should have a limited number of properly designed bus stops on loop lanes, says the report. This would enable the maximum use to be made of motorways and express transport services. It would retain some of the advantages of the rail system, while retaining the flexibility of road transport - which can 'peel off' and continue on the ordinary road system.

"The report says that passenger bus terminals, the railway station and the main part of the central business area should be linked together by public passenger services. This may be achieved either by shuttle services, by cross or through routing of main services, or by a combination of these. Once bus routes have been consolidated in normal streets carrying considerable traffic, loading bays should, where practicable, be provided off the normal roadway at all stops." [224]

Parking and Terminals Needed

But if, by default, buses were to become the principal public transport conveyances, and if trucks were to jam the new roads, more and improved facilities, would be needed. Both private and public transport must also have somewhere to park, according to the Master Transportation Plan quoted by The New Zealand Herald on 21 September 1955:

"The present city bus terminal should be further developed as necessary says the report and another terminal provided on the western side of the city, readily accessible to the business and commercial areas. One of these terminals should provide for a long-distance road transport. They should, as far as possible, have ready access to the urban motorway system. A trucking terminal (or terminals) is also proposed for the central business district. Access to both the ring road system and the general business area will be important.

"Long-period (four-hour and over) car parks should be provided near and immediately inside the ring road system. As far as possible they should be near streets and passenger services leading to the central business area. Facilities for shorter parking will be required as near as possible to shops and businesses. These are needed as urgently as road development, and should be started immediately. The arrangements made in the city for public transport vehicles, trucks and cars are 'just as important as improved traffic ways', says the report. Much of the benefit that would result from motorway and street construction would be nullified without properly designed and adequate off-street facilities." [225]

And there was a warning for those who would be encouraged to drive along the planned freer-flowing motorways to work and shop in the city:

"Needing 6000 parking spaces, the central area of Auckland now has 4402. By 1963 the demand will have gone up to 13,000 spaces, computed at half short-term and half long-term, on the current trend. Present plans for parking buildings provide for 1456 more parking spaces – 452 at the bus terminal and 504 in Sturdee Street (both municipal) and 500 in the Farmers' Trading Company's new building. Of the spaces already available in the central business area 2489 are on the street, and about half of these are 'all-day' areas. More than half (1125) of the 1913 off-street parking spaces are privately owned." [226]

John Luxford's Introduction to the Master Plan

As well as explaining how the formulation of the Master Transportation Plan originated, John Luxford's introduction to the version of the Plan and accompanying Survey, subsequently released for general publication in September 1956, also described "The epoch making plan..." as having been "...enthusiastically hailed as the most realistic and practical approach to the solution of the metropolitan transport problems that had ever been made." [227]

Practical Detail Again Omitted

Not only did John Luxford's description ignore the many variations of suburban railway plans proposed since at least 1914, it also glossed over the fact that the final Master Transportation Plan actually lacked the detail required to implement *the most realistic and practical approach to the solution* of Auckland's *metropolitan transport problems*. As the Master Plan's *Scope Of Plan* explained:

"This Master Plan does not, in fact cannot, attempt to deal with matters of detail. It aims at defining the principles and setting the pattern or the framework within which more detailed planning can be carried out and within which actual work can be programmed." [150]

In that respect, the Technical Advisory Committee had again produced a blueprint that was much like the Committee's 1951 *Outline Development Plan for the Auckland Region*. The latter plan was also described by the Committee as one designed "...*to leave the maximum degree of freedom and flexibility within local authority areas for more detailed planning considerations.*" [152]

Broad Outline

In other words, the members of the Technical Advisory Committee had again delivered just a broad outline of the challenges to be met and not the practical detail required to meet those challenges. Worse still, the Committee's solutions, suggested as being realistic and actionable, targeted only certain aspects of the overall traffic congestion problem that was to plague the streets of Auckland well into the twenty-first century. This was despite the advice of many overseas experts, past and future, that the *overall problem* of urban transportation required a comprehensive solution consisting of a viable public transport service (suburban railway and buses) *as well as* modern roadways to accommodate the increasing numbers of private motor cars and commercial vehicles.

Indeed, in as little as fourteen years, in early 1969, a report presented at the fourth International Congress on Urban Transport in the United States by Mr W H Liskmann, a leading Californian town planner and architect, advised: "Faced with the problem of strangling vehicular circulation, most of the world's major cities seem to have decided that relief lies in the construction of rapid transit systems or the improvement of existing ones." [228]

The Predominance of Technical Material Favouring Roads

Regrettably for Auckland commuters, those who struggled to traverse their city in 1955, and who were to continue to struggle to 1969 and far beyond, the Technical Advisory Committee found overwhelmingly in favour of road construction as the *predominant* solution to their transportation problems. This solution managed to sidetrack, by various means, alternatives such as public transport – as described by Paul Mees and Jago Dodson in their *Urban Research Program, Issues Paper 5, Backtracking Auckland: Bureaucratic rationality and public preferences in transport planning*. In that Paper, published April 2006, Paul Mees and Jago Dodson described how the predominance of technical material favouring roads, contained in the Master Transportation Plan for Metropolitan Auckland and its accompanying Survey of Basic Information, purposely obscured what was then believed to be the public's preference for public transport, particularly suburban rail:

"The committee's report…derisorily dismissed the rail proposal as unsuited to a dispersed city and adopted the motorway plan. Gunder [229] and Mees and Dodson [Mees & 230] attribute the outcome change in planning emphasis primarily to regional actors – politicians and officials of the ARPA [Auckland Regional Planning Authority] and local councils – but Harris [72] demonstrates that central government also played an important role. What these authors also highlight is the extent to which the outcome differed from the preferences of the region's citizens, who have been more supportive of public transport. The technical preferences of the officials had prevailed over those of the public." [231]

Instances of Strategic Misrepresentation

Technical Preferences

Not only did the roading lobby try to confuse the public with a good deal of what Mees and Dodson described as *technical preferences*, the compilers of the Master Transportation Plan engaged in a little misrepresentation as well – as Paul Mees described in his book, *Transport for Suburbia: Beyond the Automobile Age*:

"Although the ruse of declaring the rail-motorway issue a 'technical problem' had prevented it becoming an issue at the 1954 election, motorway supporters remained concerned about public opposition. After all, the great majority of Auckland's population were public transport users, while motorists remained in the minority. The Master Plan was published in 1956 as a glossy public relations document, replete with breathless endorsements and high-quality photography.

"Five full-page photos of traffic congestion in Auckland contrasted with eight of free-flowing American roadways, such as the Arroyo Seco and Santa Ana Freeways in Los Angeles. The contrast is accentuated by the fact that the Auckland photos appear to have been taken during overcast weather, while the Los Angeles freeways are bathed in Californian sunlight.

"Given the low rate of car use in Auckland at the time, the report's authors struggled to find convincing examples of congestion…The most convincing photo shows another arterial road in peak hour. The roadway is jammed, but mainly with public transport vehicles: there are six trams, seven buses, nine cars and a taxi. Assuming that the trams and buses were full but not overcrowded, they would have carried 300–400 passengers compared with fewer than 20 in the cars.

"Streets jammed with full trams and buses might have led readers of the report to wonder why the option of an underground railway had been rejected, so what were the technical arguments on which the decision was based?

"They were those Cumberland [Kenneth Cumberland, Chairman of the Auckland City Council Town Planning Committee] had offered in his op-ed piece [published by The New Zealand Herald on 26 August 1954], the same reasons that had been used in 1937 by the Automobile Club of Southern California: *The form and structure of Metropolitan Auckland through the years has been largely determined by developments in…transportation. During the last 25 years, the overall effect of motor transportation has so radically changed the pattern that Auckland is now one of the most dispersed cities in the World. The individual has been freed from absolute dependence on tramways and railways with their inflexible fixed routes…The pattern of travel has become more diffused and traffic cannot now be channelled along a few fixed routes with the same destination.*" [205]

Population Density

Under the heading of *The Low Population Density of Auckland*, the Master Transportation Plan stated: "Auckland, when compared with similar to larger cities, has one of the lowest gross population densities in the World. This low density and 'urban sprawl' adds to the cost and difficulties of public transport. The population living within reasonable walking distance of an inflexible transport service such as railways is very limited. This means that feeder bus services have to be used over extensive areas if the potential carrying capacity of a rail service is to be anywhere near as fully used." [150]

The compilers of the Plan then provided a table of figures representing the approximate population densities (persons per acre) of various cities ranging from Paris (150) and County of London (54) to Los Angeles(5) and Brisbane (5) up to 1946. The population density for Auckland is given as 4 persons per acre and mention is made that "The foregoing figures with the exception of those for Auckland, are quoted from *X-Ray the City!*, by Dr. E Fooks, 1946." [150]

As Paul Mees pointed out in *Transport for Suburbia: Beyond the Automobile Age*:

"Nobody apparently noticed at the time, but the use of these figures was a complete misrepresentation of the point Fooks was making in his book, and apparently a deliberate one…The Technical Committee knew what it was doing: Professor Knight, who was a town planner as well as an architect, chaired the sub-committee responsible for the 'general information' in the Master Plan. The Committee carefully sifted the Fooks table, deleting all the anomalous cities…The Committee then added its own density estimate for Auckland, calculated using the very methodology Fooks wrote his book to debunk, namely dividing the population of the region by the gross area under the jurisdiction of the Auckland Regional Planning Authority. This was not an inadvertent error either, as the same Technical Committee (with much the same membership) had only four years earlier estimated the urbanized area of the region at 30,000 acres, instead of the 113,000 used for the Master Plan's calculations. This gave a density of 15 residents per acre not 4,…double the figures for Australian cities cited in the Master Plan and triple the figure given for Los Angeles." [205]

Inflated Cost Estimates

Paul Mees also commented on the Master Plan's cost estimates which compared the expected cost of suburban railway development with that of constructing the proposed motorways and connecting roading systems:

"The Auckland Technical Committee's cost estimates proved to be no more robust than its density calculations. It had claimed that the rail scheme would cost £11 million, almost as much as the £15 million price tag for the motorways. In 1962, an engineer named Joseph Wright claimed that both figures had been distorted to favour motorways.

"Motorway costs had been underestimated, with the true figure close to £40 million, while rail costs had been inexplicably inflated from the Halcrow estimate of £7.25 million. 'Where did the figure of £11 million come from?' he asked. 'I understand that the committee which produced the Master Transportation Plan had 26 members, only three of whom had any experience of handling public transport…The whole Master Transport Plan has a motor car complex'.

"The Halcrow report had been correct: the new rail system should have been built before the motorways, and a central authority was needed to coordinate all forms of public transport. Wright was no car-hating train-spotter: he was the Ministry of Works engineer in charge of the Auckland motorway project." [205]

As a result, wrote Paul Mees:

"Public transport collapsed in Auckland because the city transport planners made a conscious decision to abandon it and make roads the priority, even though this was the more expensive alternative. Los Angeles opted for freeways only after attempts to rescue public transport foundered; Auckland made the choice at a time when upgrading public transport was the more practical option. The city's transport planners deliberately adopted a transport policy that only evolved by historical accident in Los Angeles. Because this policy was unpopular with the public, the planners and their allies conspired to prevent the community having a say…" [205]

Master Transportation Plan Proposals Not All That Surprising

Of course, anyone who had paid attention to the various statements made by Auckland City Engineer and Chairman of the Technical Advisory Committee, Arthur Dickson, during the previous decade or so, would not have been all that surprised by the overall transport policy proposed by the Master Transportation Plan.

As previously referred to, in an address he gave, as president, to the New Zealand Institution of Engineers on 24 February 1949, and subsequently published in the May edition of the New Zealand Engineering Journal, Arthur Dickson predicted one of the Plan's main proposals for an inner city motorway system:

"In Britain strong support had been given to the idea of having an inner ring road (traffic route) around the central business area to act as a traffic collector and distributor. The main traffic radials and interconnecting rings needed special consideration and should be limited access routes… It was generally agreed, he said, that the remedy for present-day traffic problems lay in planning new thoroughfares rather than widening, extending and improving existing streets. In most cities where the latter had been done in the past, usually at high cost, the results, from the point of view of traffic relief, had been disappointing." [81]

But Who's Paying?

So there it was…as with the suburban railway system…*widening, extending and improving existing streets*…at *high cost*…wouldn't cut it…only *new thoroughfares* would do.

But who was to pay for these new thoroughfares? Surely not the City and its associated local bodies?

Outside Finance Sought

"Up to £1,250,000 will have to be spent yearly if the proposed motorway system is to be built to the standards and in the time advocated by the technical advisory committee…But the committee believes sources outside the city – the National Roads Fund and the Government - should foot the bill for the roads. Urban road users' taxes to the fund (paid mostly in petrol tax) are far greater than the amount spent from the fund in urban areas, says the report in justification for its claim for a bigger fund contribution.

"Last financial year road users in the Auckland urban area contributed an estimated £3,000,000 to the fund. But only £1,000,000 from the fund was spent in the area. The committee quotes the 1953 Roading Investigation Committee report:

"'The existing allocation of petrol tax to cities and boroughs is seriously inadequate to compensate them for the lack of State and main highways in their areas'…Parking facilities, passengers and freight terminals, and some road junctions should be financed from local body funds and their cost is not included in the 15 million estimate for the roading system. The ancillary facilities would be paid for by users – bus terminals through charges on the services using them and car parks through parking meters." [232]

Transport Plan Discussions in Wellington

Obviously, Government assistance was required, as reported by The New Zealand Herald on 16 November 1955:

"The Mayor of Auckland, Mr J H Luxford, and members of the Auckland Regional [Planning] Authority's special committee are expected to discuss the master transport plan with the Government in Wellington next week. They hope to get approval for the Ministry of Works to construct the network of new urban highways recommended in the plan.

"After safely negotiating two hurdles, the plan has still to carry the fences of local government in the metropolitan area. The first hurdle was the City Council and the second the regional planning authority, both of which endorsed the plan in no uncertain manner. Now all the outer constituent local bodies of the planning authority have been asked if they will approve the plan.

"They have also been asked whether they are willing to let the authority act on their behalf; whether they agree to the Ministry of Works constructing the roads; and whether financial aid should be sought from the National Roads Fund or other public moneys. Mt Wellington and Ellerslie have already approved the plan in principle. The planning authority's committee which is to confer with the Ministry of Works is willing to answer any questions which local bodies want answered before they give their approval." [233]

Government Non-Committal

However, any Government approval and financial assistance could not be taken for granted and nor, in line with the normal decision-making practice, could any commitment be given without first appointing a committee to study the matter further – as reported by The New Zealand Herald on 25 November 1955:

"The Government was 'all for' the development of Auckland, but it had to be always remembered that there were other places as well. This was stated by the Prime Minister, Mr Holland, yesterday after meeting a delegation of Auckland local body representatives to discuss their major works programme.

"Mr Holland said the meeting explored ways of reaching the greatest agreement on important matters over which there might be some difference of opinion because of the structure of local body government in Auckland. The delegation will report back to its local authorities on a proposal that a joint committee of local body and Government representatives be set up in Auckland to bring down a scheme for the orderly carrying out of Government and local body capital works.

"While the meeting in the morning was a success, an afternoon session in which a committee appointed by the Auckland Regional Planning Authority met the Minister of Works and chairman of the National Roads Board, Mr Goosman, to discuss the master transport plan is believed to have been less successful. After the meeting, Mr Luxford said that no final decision had been reached, but arrangements had been made for a further meeting in Wellington next month. The committee discussed with Mr Goosman the question of the Ministry of Works carrying out the transport plan and the possibility of the Roads Board contributing to the cost. Mr Goosman would make no comment on the meeting." [234]

As Time Goes By

As 1955, the year of the Master Transportation Plan, drew to a close and 1956 rolled on, the debate between Government and Auckland's local bodies continued, and the Auckland Regional Planning Authority grew more concerned for the future of the City's transport services – as reported by The New Zealand Herald on 1 March 1956:

"Everything possible should be done to hasten the carrying out of works proposed in the £15 million Auckland master transport plan, said the Mayor, Mr J H Luxford, yesterday. The technical advisory committee of the Auckland Regional Planning Authority, which prepared the plan last year, said work on motorways and main traffic routes should be finished by 1965, or at the very latest, 1970. Mr Luxford said yesterday he would do all he could to see the works were completed by the earlier date.

"Set up to speed negotiations on financial and constructional aspects of the plan, a committee of the planning authority has sought an early meeting with the Prime Minister, Mr Holland. It is expected that this meeting will be held soon after Mr Holland's return from Australia on March 6.

"The proposed joint committee on Auckland works priorities, said the Mayor, would decide just how the scheme could be hastened. This was vital. New arterial roads would be necessary to cope with greatly increased vehicular traffic, which would be further swollen once the Auckland harbour bridge was finished in July, 1958. Even then, two elevated roads serving the St Mary's Bay bridge approach would not – according to the scheme – be ready until 1965.

"Once an announcement on National Roads Board subsidies for the plan had been made, priorities could be decided. The master transport plan was announced five months ago. Since then it has been referred to the Government and back to local bodies for approval." [235]

Urgent Start Needed

Meanwhile, Auckland's streets became increasingly congested, John Luxford's concern was certainly warranted, as explained in the September 1955 edition of the City Council's magazine, Comment:

"It is expected within the next 12 months that the number of vehicles registered in the Auckland urban area will reach 100,000, thus giving an approximate ratio of one vehicle to every 3½ persons. There is no sign that the rate of increase is slowing down but there are indications that unless there is improvement in the street system, and our roads are brought up to standard to cope with modern traffic, the margin between traffic movement and stoppage will rapidly shrink…Citizens of the largest and most rapidly growing urban centre in the Dominion cannot be satisfied with a piece-meal policy of minor improvements and making do. All must join together to see that our roading system is adequate safely to take the traffic of this great metropolis." [236]

Motoring Cost

Seemingly *joined together*, the steadily-increasing number of Auckland motorists continued along whatever roads were available, bumper-to-bumper, but still confident that their chosen mode of travel was the future. This was despite the cost of motoring that also rose steadily with the number of motorists, apparently regardless of the normal rules of supply and demand.

Reference has already been made to New Zealand's infamous *black budget* brought down as a result of the balance of payments crisis of 1957. The Minister of Finance, Arnold Nordmeyer, attempted to deal with the crisis by reducing demand for overseas goods. To do this, he imposed additional customs duties on cars and petrol as described by Rob Vosslamber in his 2010 paper, *Tax history and tax policy: New Zealand's 1958 black budget*:

"How much did the budget affect prices? In the case of motor vehicles it is difficult to make a general assessment, as the duty only applied to imported components, and differed depending on whether imperial preference applied [A scale of tariffs that favoured British imports]. However, the [Christchurch] Press suggested that the price of a new car or truck would rise from £100 to nearly £500 depending on the model, and indicated that the £1,090 price of an ordinary family sized Standard Vanguard car included sales tax of £145 before the increase; with a doubling of the sales tax the price would thus increase by around 13 percent.

"Second hand car prices were also expected to increase, except for cars with higher fuel consumption. The main effect of this increase would be on those hoping to purchase their first car; those who already owned a car would feel the increase less given the increased value of their trade-in." [237]

The Highway and Byway Plan

However, such price rises did little to restrict demand for motor vehicles and the roads along which they must travel. Accordingly, there was a lot to do to meet that demand and to complete the arterial roads recommended by the Master Transportation Plan in the minimum time required. The Plan had recommended:

"…five new roads, built to motorway standards, and a ring road around the perimeter of the central business area linking the five. For part of its length, the ring road would be elevated, above Quay Street. These motorways, with twin carriageways, without intersections on the same level and without access from the frontages along them, would radiate from the central business area to:

"Dominion Road, via route beginning in Nelson Street. (To be finished by 1960)

"The Southern Area, to join the existing southern motorway at Penrose, via a route bypassing Newmarket. (By 1963)

"The Eastern Area, joining the Mount Wellington Highway and (via Tamaki) the southern motorway at Mount Wellington. (By 1966)

"The Western Area, via Arch Hill Gully, joining the already-built north-west State highway. (By 1967)

"The North Shore, as far north as Albany, via the Harbour Bridge. (By 1968)

"Existing main roads would, under the master plan, be improved and integrated with the new motorways. Such a network of roads, says the report, would link via congestion-free routes the business area, the port, the Auckland railway station, the Penrose industrial area, the future Upper Harbour development and the major suburban districts." [238]

Existing Main Roads

Those *existing main roads to be improved and integrated with the new motorways* were not inconsiderable, as described by John Roughan in his New Zealand Herald article, *Auckland: The bridge builders*, published 27 August 2010:

"Auckland's first stretch of motorway was a four-lane strip between Penrose and Mt Wellington, built in 1953. Next to be built was the causeway from Pt Chevalier to Te Atatu as far as Lincoln Rd, finished in 1955, which shortened the journey to the airport, then at Whenuapai. That same year the southern motorway was extended from Mt Wellington to Wiri and the approaches to the Harbour Bridge were built, from Fanshawe St in the city and northward to Northcote Rd… Auckland's Harbour Bridge would be more than a crossing to the North Shore, it would be part of a new mode of roading, a motorway." [239]

Master Transportation Plan Published

As previously noted, The New Zealand Herald and The Auckland Star reported extensively on the recommendations contained in the Master Transportation Plan when it was first completed in July 1955. However, it was more than a year later, September 1956, before the Plan and its accompanying Survey was printed for widespread public consumption. By then, the question of who was to pay for the proposed roading and the ancillary infrastructure, such as the necessary bus depots and car parking facilities, had generated more public exposure to the overall plan. This additional publicity naturally invited a greater public participation of Auckland's civic leaders in the debate about how the proposed roading projects could be financed.

Who's Paying? (Still Undecided)

Dove-Myer Robinson was in favour of the recommendation of the Master Transportation Plan that suggested the *whole* of the scheme should be paid by the National Roads Fund, together with a contribution from the Government. Unfortunately, this view was not shared by everybody on the Auckland City Council, including the Mayor, John Luxford. The difference of opinion came to a head during the Council meeting held on 26 April 1956, as described by Councillor Robinson:

"Standing Orders do not require me to apologise to the Council said D M Robinson…in commenting on his walk-out from a recent City Council meeting…Mr Robinson explained that the walk-out arose from the fact that the Mayor (John Luxford), who had previously agreed that the Government should pay 100% of the cost of Auckland's urgently needed Master Transportation Plan, was now prepared to accept a subsidy of £3 for £1.

"When I moved the original motion in the City Council which initiated the investigation into the question of Auckland's transport chaos, and which resulted in the production of the Master Transportation Plan, the Government was committed to an expenditure of approximately £12,000,000 for the electrification of Auckland's suburban railways and the Morningside Underground deviation.

"The report of the Technical Advisory Committee recommending the adoption of the Master Transportation Plan showed that the £12,000,000 spent on the Railway plan would have served only 5% of Auckland's population and would have involved a loss of £7,000,000 for operation costs over the next 20 years. Therefore the City Council's action has saved the Government the unwise spending of £19,000,000.

"It seems only fair therefore that the Government should pay the whole £12,000,000 cost of the Master Transportation Plan said Mr Robinson. Assuming that it would take 10 years to complete the work, this would mean that the National Roads Board would have to contribute £1,200,000 p.a. – this is only a little over a quarter of the £4,000,000 yearly which motorists in the Auckland metropolitan area pay to the National Roads Board by way of petrol tax yearly. The report of the Technical Advisory Committee recommends the financing of the scheme in these words:-

"<u>Financing of Road Development Scheme</u>: It is proposed that the Road Development Scheme of urban motorways and main road routes should be financed by:

(a) increased contributions from the National Roads Fund;

(b) a contribution from the Government to the cost of arterial routes where these routes would fulfil the functions which the Morningside Deviation Railway Development Scheme was intended to perform;

"This report and the recommendations contained in it were unanimously adopted by the City Council on the motion of the Mayor himself. Therefore the Mayor is committed to the demand that the Government pay 100% of the cost of the scheme. I understand that the Mayor persuaded the Council to postpone further consideration of my motion, that the Government should pay the whole cost of the scheme, on the grounds that negotiations for the construction of a Spur Line Underground Railway from the present Railway Station to a site near Albert Park are under consideration.

"If this means that the Mayor is prepared to sacrifice quarter of the cost of the Master Transportation Plan (£3,000,000) in order to persuade the Railways Department to put in a Spur Line Railway at a cost of £2,000,000, it simply means that the ratepayers of Auckland will be paying £3,000,000 for a £2,000,000 Railway Department project.

"I strongly resented the Mayor's statement that I was trying to prevent commencement on this urgent project until we have received an assurance that the Government will pay the whole cost of it. In my notice of motion which was printed on the Order Paper, and in moving my motion, I emphasized that negotiations for an increased subsidy or any other steps taken must not be allowed to delay commencement of the work for one moment.

"It was because the Mayor said that I had demanded that it be a condition precedent that the Government give the Council the additional subsidy before starting on the plan, and other similar misrepresentations by the Mayor, that I decided to walk out as a protest.

"The position now is that unless steps are taken to persuade the Government to increase the subsidy from 75% to 100% the ratepayers of Auckland will have to find the difference which is £3,000,000 – this will increase city rates by about 8d in the £1 within the next 10 years and will mean that by the time the loans are paid off, city ratepayers alone will have had to find between £3½ and £4 million which should properly be paid by the National Roads Board." [240]

Full Subsidy Called For

Despite his best efforts and to his chagrin, Dove-Myer Robinson and the few United Independents on the City Council were unable to persuade Mayor Luxford and the majority of the Councillors (Citizens and Ratepayers) to back his call for the full subsidy.

"It seems that there is now little hope of persuading the Government to pay the whole of the cost of the Metropolitan part of the Master Transport Plan. It is no good crying over what might have been. What we have to do now is to get right in behind the plan and get agreement amongst the local bodies on ways and means of finding our £3,000,000 share of the cost. If we don't, Auckland's traffic congestion will cripple the city's transport and impose a financial burden on everybody, much greater than the portion of the cost we will now have to share.

"Mr Luxford has never done anything to get the full subsidy, in fact he has always opposed any attempt to get it. Even when sent by the Metropolitan Council to see the Prime Minister, he left it to someone else to make the case on Auckland's behalf. I think Mr Luxford should now turn his energies towards getting the support of all the other local bodies for the plan and towards finding our part of the finance, rather than attacking his councillors and blaming them for initiating these important moves." [241]

Master Transportation Plan Approved

By September 1956, John Luxford was able to announce, by way of his introduction to the published version of the Master Transportation Plan:

"The recommendation that the motorways specified in the plan should be constructed in priority to the underground suburban railway project, has now been approved by the Government and by nearly all the metropolitan local bodies. The National Roads Board has agreed to pay 75 per cent of the cost of construction of the roadworks, and the Ministry of Works has agreed to carry out the work. All that remains to be done before the work can be started is the apportionment of the 25 per cent of the cost among the metropolitan local bodies." [150]

United Independent Party Pamphlet

As recounted earlier, Dove-Myer Robinson's United Independent Party produced a pamphlet outlining its policies to those voters who it hoped would replace the City Council's Mayor and the predominant party, the Citizens and Ratepayers, at the Auckland City Council elections to be held on 17 November 1956. Part of the pamphlet was set out as a leading question and answer sequence – such as question 21:

"And why are citizens so surprised at Mr Luxford's 'about face' over the Master Transport Plan? Because, they recall his recent public statement, 'All the talk in the world will not alter my confirmed view that the underground railway project is ESSENTIAL. The tube would provide what can properly be called Auckland's basic transport system…The topography of Auckland limited the use that could be made of the express road system.'

They also realise Mr Luxford's difficulty in approving an idea brought forward by United Independents." [174]

The pamphlet clearly indicated that Dove-Myer Robinson and his United Independent Party had fully accepted, and were keen to promote as their own idea, the recommendations put forward by the Master Transportation Plan – as the pamphlet's authors assert:

"Master Transportation Plan – The Labour Party is still opposed to the Master Transport Plan. It wants the Morningside underground. But the Citizens and Ratepayers already claim credit for the system of urban motorways. They say they have had it in mind for years. If so, why have they not done something about it? They've been in absolute power long enough. But they've little to show for it. But rather than argue, let's see what an impartial observer of the local body scene has to say about the Master Transport Plan and who prepared the way for it. This quotation is from the Auckland Star editorial of September 21st, 1955.

"Little more than a year ago Auckland was to have an 'underground railway' as the scheme was…misleadingly called. But doubts had begun to form…[they] were crystallized by Dr Cumberland, chairman of the City Council's town planning committee, in an article published in the Auckland Star 12 months ago. The United Independents group subsequently raised the matter with the City Council, and at length there was undertaken the searching investigation which has produced the master plan…[This] may prove to have saved both the Government and the people of Auckland millions of pounds.

"The plan has indeed saved the Government £12,000,000 on the construction of the 'underground'. And it has saved [an] estimated annual loss on £500,000 on uneconomic suburban railways for the next 20 years. It will save Auckland £5,000,000 a year. This is the estimated cost to Aucklanders of the time they waste, the petrol they use, the wear and tear on their vehicles, the accidents and mental worry they suffer as a result of the congestion on a road system designed, not for today or tomorrow but, for 80 years ago. United Independents don't have to argue their part in this. Others shout their praises. The Auckland Star doesn't seem to have much to say about the Citizens and Ratepayers' part in the Master Transport Plan. Everyone with any first-hand acquaintance with the city's affairs knows they had NO part in originating it. But they've naturally jumped on the band wagon." [174]

Slow Payers

Unfortunately, not all were quite so eager to *jump on the bandwagon* when it came to paying for the roads and infrastructure recommended by the Master Transportation Plan. This was despite the estimated savings quoted for foregoing the *uneconomic suburban railways* as well as reducing the indirect cost of traffic congestion, as quoted by the originators of the Plan: "The Technical Advisory Committee recommended an immediate start on the construction of the roading plan with a target date for completion in 1970. The Committee also pointed out that unless congestion was speedily overcome the indirect loss to the community resulting from congestion would be of the order of $100 to $200 million in the decade 1960–1970." [242]

National Roads Board Subsidy

Indeed, little was accomplished until March 1963, some <u>eight</u> years after the completion of the Master Transportation Plan, when a National Roads Board subsidy was then authorised to enable the Technical Advisory Committee to commit to a much-needed Comprehensive Transportation Survey needed to facilitate the design of the proposed citywide roading system. It was the type of Survey that should have been included as part of the Master Transportation Plan instead of the one formulated by the Committee solely as a marketing tool to sell its road transport proposals. As described later, the Survey was eventually undertaken by the American engineering consultancy, De Leuw, Cather and Company, following its appointment by the newly-formed Auckland Regional Authority on 14 May 1963.

The Auckland Harbour Bridge

The repeal of the Auckland Harbour Bridge Empowering Act on 14 July 1948 was followed by the passing of The Auckland Harbour Bridge Act 1950 which subsequently came into force on 1 January 1951 "…to Provide for the Constitution of the Auckland Harbour Bridge Authority, to Define Its Powers and Functions, and to Provide for the Construction, Maintenance, and Control of a Bridge Across the Waitemata Harbour." [243]

Auckland Harbour Bridge Authority

The Auckland Harbour Bridge Authority comprised seven members representing the Minister of Works (two), the Auckland City Council (two), the other city-side councils and boards (one), and the North Shore Councils (two). The Authority was chaired by Auckland's Mayor, Sir John Allum. As the bridge would span the jurisdictions of the Auckland City and Northcote Borough Councils, not to mention their provision of approach roads, it was prudent that those Councils were each represented as members of the Authority's board.

As if in anticipation of the future amalgamation of Auckland's many local bodies and boards, one Bridge Authority member was to represent the city-side bodies which included "…the Borough Councils of Mount Eden, Mount Albert, Newmarket, One Tree Hill, Onehunga, Otahuhu, Ellerslie, Mount Roskill, Papatoetoe, New Lynn, Henderson, Manurewa, and Papakura, the Town Boards of Glen Eden and Howick, the Road Board of Mount Wellington, and the County Council of Manukau." [243]

Representation by the Harbour Board was of course a special case in that the construction of a bridge impinged upon its prime responsibilities "…in so far as safeguarding the Waitemata Harbour for shipping and navigation generally is concerned." [243]

Commercial shipping frequently navigated the Waitemata up-harbour from where the proposed span was to be constructed. As Auckland Harbourmaster, Captain H. H. Sargeant, explained to the 1929 Waitemata Bridge Commission, "…There was at present, and had been for many years, a considerable amount of large shipping to the Chelsea Sugar Works, averaging about 40 large steamers annually, whose masts varied in height from 90ft to 121ft above waterline." [244]

The Auckland Harbour Board had considered further wharf construction at Chelsea since at least 1929 and, according to Captain Sargeant during his testimony to the Waitemata Bridge Commission, "…it might be necessary at some future date to make use of the valuable foreshore…between Northcote and Kauri Point for port expansion…" and "…It must be remembered that there was a splendid waterway extending from Kauri Point to Hobsonville…an area which with some dredging could be utilised for future port expansion." [244]

Ferry Operation Compensation

Indeed, in anticipation of some ingress upon the interests of the Harbour Board during the construction of the bridge but, more particularly, to ensure the continuation of harbour ferry services during that time, the Auckland Harbour Bridge Act 1950 provided for compensation to be paid "…in respect of loss incurred by the Board on account of expenditure incurred by it, during the period between the date of commencement of this Act and the date when the bridge is first open for public transport, in the provision, during that period, all vehicular and passenger landing facilities necessary for the carrying on by the company (the Devonport Steam Ferry Company Limited) of an adequate harbour ferry service…" [243]

The Act also provided for, by way of a Commission of Inquiry, the examination of any compensation claimed by the Devonport Steam Ferry Company or its employees "…which it finds payable to the company in respect of loss incurred through the operation of the bridge."

Again, this part of the Act was designed to ensure an uninterrupted ferry service during construction of the bridge and included compensation for "The amount of capital expenditure incurred by the company with the approval of the Authority…in maintaining or augmenting its fleet of vessels…The right of the company to receive compensation…shall be conditional upon the company maintaining, at all times during the period between the passing of this Act and the date when the bridge first becomes open for public traffic, an adequate harbour ferry service serving the same localities and traversing the same routes as are served and traversed, at the passing of this Act by the harbour ferry service owned by the company." [243]

Auckland Harbour Bridge Amendment Acts

A subsequent amendment to the Act in 1956 allowed for the appointing of a Commission of Inquiry to inquire into and determine what compensation might be due to members of the Devonport Ferry Company's Employees' Industrial Union of Workers. [245]

Another amendment in 1957 provided for the determination of compensation that might be payable to the ferry company for losses incurred due to the depreciation of its vessels while the bridge was being built. [246]

A third amendment to the 1950 Act, enacted in September 1958, changed the definition of *tolls* to be collected by the Bridge Authority to apply to the passage of any *authorised* traffic over the bridge – previously defined as "…persons, animals, or vehicles…" – but now, *vehicles* only. [247]

Bridge Finally a Possibility

Of course, "After three Commissions of inquiry and 99 years of opposition from the more myopic sections of the community…" [248], the bridge had first to be built and the Act certainly intended to make that possible:

"The Authority shall, as soon as practicable after the commencement of this Act, cause to be prepared complete plans and specifications of the bridge, and conditions of contract in respect of the construction of the bridge and its approaches." [243]

Public Works Annual Report

In his Public Works Annual Report for the year ended 31 March 1950, Engineer-in-Chief, F Langbein, provided a progress report as to the work then completed:

"The precise engineering survey of the bridge-site, the preparation of plans, and the collecting of tidal data, &c, were completed early in the year. The plans have been taken to the United Kingdom by a departmental representative (Mr. Packwood), whose mission is to collaborate with Messrs. Freeman, Fox, and Partners. This firm of consultants has practically finalized a preliminary bridge design. Field-work during the year consisted of foundation investigations required by the designers. A total of twenty-five bores has been put down." [249]

Bridge Design Complete

Indeed, by 1952, all this planning advanced the spanning of the Waitemata as an inevitable reality at last. The reclamation of some 14 acres to provide a contractors' working site at the southern end of the proposed bridge had started and the design of the bridge and its approach roads had been completed. [248]

The plans and specifications for the bridge and its approaches were subject to the unanimous approval of the Minister of Works, the Minister of Marine, the Auckland Harbour Board, the Auckland City Council, and the Northcote Borough Council and were generally the same as those recommended by the 1946 Royal Commission.

The Commission had recommended the bridge span the Waitemata between Point Erin and Stokes Point with a width capable of supporting four road lanes flanked by two, six-foot-wide footpaths to facilitate pedestrian and cycle traffic in both directions. This configuration was based on the need to accommodate the Commission's estimate of an ultimate volume of some 26,800 vehicle crossings per day by 1965, originating from both suburban and regional areas. Other than that estimation, "…The Bridge Authority had nothing to guide them. However, they decided to double the traffic that was being carried by the ferries, and they fixed on an average of 9,000 vehicles per day for the first 12 months." [250]

Compromises

"But further investigations raised fears the commission had underestimated population growth, and six traffic lanes might be needed, prompting the Ministry of Works to opt for a five-lane compromise." [251] It was intended that the central (fifth) road lane be used as an overflow lane to take either north- or south-bound traffic as required.

Unfortunately for the future of public transport, the Commission's previously-reported observation "…that a trolly-bus system appears to be well suited to the terrain and transport requirements of the North Shore, and that such a system can easily be incorporated in a unified system for the whole metropolitan area," [130] was ignored.

Also ignored was the suggestion that the bridge should carry a railway:

"Controversy was continuous. Critics variously questioned the lack of a railway; condemned the proposed bridge as 'ugly'; argued for greater North Shore representation on the authority; renewed the case for a tunnel instead of a bridge – the list was almost endless. The Authority heard every argument but allowed none to hold up the job in hand. While lamenting the lack of a railway, one newspaper admitted that in getting on with its job, the Harbour Bridge Authority has set a standard that might well be copied by other local authorities." [252]

Consulting Engineers Appointed

Freeman Fox & Partners of London were appointed consulting engineers for the Auckland Harbour Bridge project and "…confirmed in the task of undertaking engineering surveys, preparing detailed plans and estimates, and supervising construction of the bridge, the southern approaches and the northern approaches from the bridge head to Onepoto Stream. By July of 1951, a survey party from London had arrived to conduct the engineering survey of both shores…And by January of 1952 the authority was ready to call tenders throughout the world for the construction of the bridge proper.

Tenders Received

"Tenders closed in June (1952) and those received included:
Cleveland Bridge-Dorman Long (Britain) £4,236,036

Pacific Bridge Corporation (United States) £7,015,000 (target price).
(Alternative price for a suspension bridge: £6,970,000)
Cable Price Corporation (New Zealand) £5,607,564
(Alternative prices for different methods of construction: £5,430,849 and £5,583,044)
Entreprises Métropolitaines et Coloniales (France) £4,445,720
(fabricated steel work only)." [252]

The lowest tender, submitted by the two British companies, was eventually accepted. The Cleveland Bridge and Engineering Company of Darlington and Dorman Long & Company of Middlesbrough (which had built the Sydney Harbour Bridge) were normally competitive companies but they joined forces on this occasion. [253]

"An American firm had put forward a target price of £6,970,000 for a suspension bridge of 1,820-ft span and quoted a still higher price for the official cantilever design. However, they gave no details at all with their tender, and would have been disqualified for that reason, even if their price had been competitive, which it was not. In fact it was £2,000,000 higher than the successful tender." [250]

By this time, even the lowest tender well exceeded the 1946 Royal Commission's estimate of a capital cost of £3 million. This had been anticipated by the Bridge Authority which "…had lodged in May an application to the Local Government Loans Board for permission to raise £8,122,000. This was estimated to cover the cost of the bridge (£3,500,000), approach roads (£2,123,000), engineering fees, and interest payments to be paid during construction." [252]

Waiting for the Money

"Then trouble started. The Local Government Loans Board took an interminably – and to North Shore people, suspiciously – long time in making up its mind. The tunnel advocates had a final fling. The then Prime Minister, Mr S. G. Holland, (Sidney Holland – National Party) turned down an Authority proposal to borrow £4,500,000 in London for four years at 4%.

"MPs, local authority members, newspapers urged that housing, airports, electric power schemes, electric railways, a new university – anything, apparently, except a bridge – be given priority. 'I have not yet heard one reputable and unbiased citizen,' wrote one public accountant to a newspaper, 'do other than unhesitatingly condemn the bridge as completely unsound and uneconomic.'

"In November 1952, six months after the Authority's loan application had been filed, the Local Government Loans Board referred it back – a tacit refusal of the Authority's proposals. Mr Holland, seeing Auckland divided against itself, refused to intervene. In February (1953), he ruled that funds for the overseas content of the bridge must be raised overseas before any contract were let and in March the British Government refused the Authority permission to borrow £4,500,000 in London, at the time the most likely source of overseas funds." [252]

Bridge Must Wait

"So negotiations had dragged on for 10 months before the Prime Minister, in March 1953, felt compelled to declare his hand. The bridge, he said, must wait. Other works were more urgent." [252]

"Prime Minister Syd Holland published a list of public works priorities that ranked houses, schools and an underground electric railway in Auckland ahead of the harbour bridge. Sir John Allum, chairman of the bridge authority, spoke out against 'croakers' and called on the people of Auckland to 'stick together' against two Government departments that he did not name. Over the next few months he strenuously lobbied Holland and Deputy Prime Minister Keith Holyoake. They agreed to let the authority go to the London market for £4,500,000 (about $10 million), considerably less that the almost £8 million it wanted.

"The bridge plans had to be pared back, losing footpaths, a cycling lane and approach roads on the western side of both shores. Then the British Government weighed in, refusing to give its consent to a loan from the London market. Chancellor of the Exchequer R. A. Butler cabled Holland that he could not agree to 'money being raised for this project in New Zealand when I can certainly not agree to money being raised for a similar purpose in the United Kingdom'. Holland accepted that, Allum did not. Auckland must have the bridge,' he said. 'It is unthinkable that two growing communities should be denied permanent access.'" [239]

"Thwarted in its attempt to carry out the only task it was empowered to do, the 'Auckland Harbour No-Bridge Authority' (as a newspaper wit dubbed it) might in March 1953, have thrown in its hand. Instead, it kept pressing the Government to change its mind. The Authority was fortified by the knowledge that the Westhaven reclamation, at least, had gone too far to be stopped and that the North Shore was solidly behind it." [252]

"A crowd of 10,000 gathered at Windsor Reserve, Devonport in the evening of March 25, 1953, to demand that a loan be permitted." [239]

Approval at Last

"By September 1953, the time allowed for confirming the Cleveland Bridge-Dorman Long tender had twice been extended, and the Authority owed £500,000 – most of it for work on the Westhaven reclamation. Mr Holland, (when) asked what the Authority should do about the £321,190 it was committed to spend during the 1953-54 financial year, suggested a conference to discuss the future of the Authority. Mr B. C. Ashwin, Secretary of the Treasury, attended the conference on the Government's behalf. After some plain speaking from both sides, he was convinced that the Authority's bridge proposals were financially sound – and from that point, opposition from Government quarters melted." [252]

"At the 1953 mayoral election, Allum was defeated by J. H. Luxford who claimed the bridge would place untold costs on ratepayers for upgrading roads. But Allum, still chairman of the bridge authority, got Government approval in December for a four-lane bridge that could be financed within the country." [239]

An 'Austerity' Bridge

"In December 1953, 17 months after the first application to the Loans Board, Mr Holland was able to make the announcement: Provided the bridge, approaches and all other expenses did not exceed £5,000,000, the Authority could go ahead. In London, Freeman Fox and Partners began their design work over again. At high speed, they produced plans for an 'austerity' bridge. It was cut to four traffic lanes and no footways (saving £771,000), and the major approach roads were deleted for a further saving of £2,500,000. Only the simplest of access roads, to Curran Street on the city side and to Queen Street on the Northcote side, were provided for." [252]

"February 1956, the northern approach to the bridge was changed to Shoal Bay thus saving Northcote's Queen Street." [254]

"Later, but before the bridge was completed, all the major access roads were reinstated as finance became available. Only the fifth traffic lane on the bridge itself, which could not be reinstated once construction began, was finally omitted. Auckland may yet regret its absence, when this is measured against a comparatively small saving of £771,000. But in 1953 the choice was simple: no fifth lane, or no bridge." [252]

Less obvious cost-cutting measures were also incorporated during construction, as described in a discussion paper published by the Institution of Civil Engineers (ICE) in its journal of 18 April 1961:

"…one-half-in. thick asphalt surfacing was adopted on the bridge mainly for reasons of economy…during the tendering stage the cost of the project had to be drastically reduced and the use of thin asphalt carpet was one of the means of doing this. However, this thickness was not unusual in New Zealand where the technique of mixing and laying was perhaps in advance of British practice. The asphalt adhered to the concrete very well and as far as they knew the deck was waterproof at the moment. The concrete used in the slab was excellent, and they did not really know whether it was the asphalt or the concrete that kept the water out, but they would back the concrete." [250]

Bridge Contract Signed

"Contract documents for the construction of the four-lane Auckland Harbour Bridge were signed on October 29, 1954…The price, £3,465,000, was negotiated between the consulting engineers and the Dorman Long-Cleveland Bridge partnership, as the lowest tenderers on the earlier scheme; it covered the bridge only, and not the approach roads or viaducts. With the approval of the Local Government Loans Board, the Authority immediately set about raising the necessary £5,000,000. Under an agreement with the Prudential Assurance Co. Ltd; it arranged to borrow £1,265,100 progressively over five years, repayable over 50 years. The balance was raised in 10 public loan issues, the first of which – for £375,000 – was floated in December 1954. Like all later issues, it was quickly subscribed. Later, as the approach road system was expanded to its original size, further loans totalling £1,700,000 were raised." [252]

User Pays

"Sir John Allum (Chairman, Auckland Harbour Bridge Authority) said that…When it came to deciding the finances, they determined on a policy which shook some of the people in the United Kingdom. They were making future generations pay their share. They had borrowed £2 million for 50 years, and that would be repaid in the early years of the next century. They had another £5 million on the basis of a 39-year loan. The money had been taken up for varying periods, and they were already repaying the loan. The amounts of their repayments would grow as the years went by and their revenue increased.

"That seemed to shock some of the financial experts, but in his judgment it was sound. Their principles were, first of all, to let the people who used the facility pay, and, secondly, not to throw too much of the burden on the present generation when dealing with capital works of that nature. He thought that there was a good reason for doing such works – bridges, tunnels, and highways in big countries on the basis of toll facilities so that the user paid. This took many of those projects out of the realms of politics and they were done and not indefinitely delayed." [250]

The 'user-pay' (in this case, by means of a toll) concept of financing the harbour bridge had of course been mooted for many years but, by 1954, the difference was that the project now had the backing of the Government as a national endeavour. Even so, the structure then planned and financed remained very much an 'austerity' bridge, described in May 2009 by Auckland Regional Council chairman, Mike Lee, as:

"...a sad indictment of short-sighted planning which continues to hamper Auckland. The fact it didn't cater for all forms of transport is a product of a lack of vision and the people who built the bridge sold Auckland short...the bridge's inadequacy for even the growth of local traffic was compounded when the Holland Government yielded to lobbying by Sir John Allum to make it part of SH 1, instead of developing the western ring route for that role. That led to the destruction of Auckland suburbs such as Grafton and Freemans Bay and now we're trying to put back the ring road at enormous cost." [255]

Better Than No Bridge

However, the realization of a bridge, no matter how minimal in size, was considered by many to be better than no bridge at all after such a long time without one. That was certainly the view of Harry Julian (former Chairman of the Auckland Harbour Board) who responded in a subsequent letter to The New Zealand Herald: "Auckland Regional Council chairman Mike Lee criticises by implication the foresight of Sir John Allum, father of the Auckland Harbour Bridge. Sir John knew well 50 years ago that Auckland should have a larger bridge with more lanes but wisely cut his cloth to meet the financial restrictions of the time. Many times in my professional life I have had to restrict ambition to achieve the first step on a project, leaving the way open to take further steps at a later date...We have so many flat earth society people dead set on trying to stop progress. To achieve anything at all, smaller steps than desirable are sometimes forced on to us..." [256]

Construction Begins

Those 'smaller steps' to span the Waitemata finally began in late 1955, as described by John Roughan in his New Zealand Herald article, *The bridge builders*, published 27 August 2010:

"...the bridge began to take shape on the harbour. First, Aucklanders noticed a reclamation at Westhaven that was completed in September, then pontoons were anchored a little way out in the harbour where the first bridge pier would rise. It would be built using 'caissons', big steel boxes open at the top and bottom with two compartments. Concrete walls were built within the upper compartment, their weight pushing the caisson lower in the water while the rising walls remained above sea level. When the weight of concrete caused the descending caisson to meet the harbour bed, its grounding had to be precise within a tolerance of 23cm.

"Twice a caisson had to be refloated for a second attempt. Once in the correct position its metal edges went into the harbour floor and the water in its lower compartment was replaced with compressed air. Workers then went into the lower compartment to excavate mud until the caisson was down to bedrock. Several times the work was held up by boulders in the sediment that had to be blasted. Once a caisson struck a layer of uneven strength and the pier tilted to an angle of 24 degrees. Fortunately nobody was working under it at the time, but it took a fortnight of work to right it. When each caisson was on its base rock, its bottom chamber was filled with concrete. The piers may look slender above the water but they are massive below.

"Those working down in the compressed air were liable to suffer the 'bends' as divers do, if they returned to the surface too quickly. Aucklanders were asked to be patient with men who might appear inebriated – they might be building the harbour bridge.

"One by one, the piers rose, each higher than the one before. By December 1956, the piers were ready to receive the steel superstructure. It was prefabricated in six spans of different lengths, some of which were cantilevered from one pier to land on the next. The longest spans are those forming the navigation arch and the span immediately to its south, which is over the deepest water. The placement of that span involved a remarkable act of engineering, witnessed by many Aucklanders.

"The long span was first built on top of a much shorter span at the city end of the bridge. Then, using pontoons on a rising tide, the whole structure was floated off the piers and taken to midstream. There the monster was moored until calm weather and a falling tide might permit the long span to be lowered into position. The weather was not that calm on November 29, 1958, but the 'pick-a-back' operation went ahead to avoid holding up the construction programme.

"Retired engineer Ken Grant of Castor Bay, a student painting bridge trusses at the time, remembers 'the control under the wind and tide was incredible'. Fifty-five years later, he met the meteorological officer who was stationed at Mechanics Bay that day, and whose job it had been to forecast the weather and wind for the operation. 'He said the maximum wind they could handle was 15 knots. He forecast 25 and they still went ahead. The actual speed was 18 and all went well'." [239]

The 'Pick-a-Back' Operation

Harry L Julian, as marine adviser and contractor to Cleveland Bridge and Dorman Long during construction of the Harbour Bridge, was in charge of the tugs towing and overnight securing of the barge-supported, 600-foot top span during the 'pick-a-back' operation.

In his autobiography, *Sea in my blood*, he describes the initial floating of the structure when "Every headland and vantage point overlooking the harbour bridge site was thronged with thousands of spectators. The harbour was alive with hundreds of spectator craft, positioned as close as our guard boats would allow.

"When the full weight of the piggyback was transferred from the piers to the barges, the complete structure was winched to the west, clear of numbers one and two piers, ready for the tow. By this time I had a tug on each corner with myself on *Mona's Isle* on the northeast corner, *Barbara W* on the southeast corner, *Romo* on the southwest and *Te Kopuru* on the northwest corner.

"The plan was to unload the 600-foot top span the next morning at high water, then return the small lower span to its original position to the south. Although there was a 10-25 knot southwester blowing by mid-morning, no concern was felt or expressed as the rig was well secured with the moorings holding nicely without excessive strain." [257]

But the weather was soon to change: "By 10 pm we were in serious trouble. As each squall struck us the moorings, even though we were towing on full power, would come home a little. We were getting closer and closer to the piers we were supposed to unload on to the next day…I knew that if we could hang on until about 1 am, the wind would drop and we could re-group for the following day before the next southwesterly onslaught that usually commences about 11 am. We did hang on and daylight saw us still in one piece…

"The third morning dawned fine, calm and clear. The southwest fronts had disappeared to the east of Auckland. The rig was winched into position at high water, and with immaculate precision, the span was positioned on its piers." [257]

During a discussion about the harbour bridge design in 1961, the Institution of Civil Engineers, described the landing of the final span:

"Landing on was due to be completed at 14.00 hours on the 30th, which meant that the critical period for weather was 30-36 hours after the final forecast. In practice, the weather began to deteriorate early in the afternoon on the 29th. The eccentricity of the lateral wind load caused the whole assembly to yaw in the rising wind and put an uneven load on the anchors and temporary wind bracing. The south-west stream anchors, which had not been checked by divers owing to the hurried preparations, dragged suddenly. The whole assembly had to be precariously maintained in position by tugs, and it was 02.40 on the 30th before those anchors were re-laid.

"By 04.30 on the 30th the wind was gusting up to 30 m.p.h. and a request was made to the Auckland Harbour Board for a tug to relieve the south-west anchors. It was the admirable handling of that tug (William C. Daldy) over the next 24 hours which probably saved the day.

"During the afternoon of the 30th the wind was gusting up to 36 m.p.h., but it gradually abated, and on 1 December conditions for landing on were perfect. The only serious hitch in landing on occurred when the rocker arms were floated over Pier 2, and a check measurement showed that the gap between them was too much. Trial lowering and checking of the rocker structure was another operation omitted because of lack of time." [250]

Harbour Bridge Opens

"Before the bridge was opened, more than 100,000 people walked over it, marvelling at the new addition to the city." [258]

The bridge opened for traffic at 3pm on 30 May 1959 when a car carrying New Zealand's Governor General, Viscount Cobham, was the first to cross.

"On that first day, the 1000 invited guests at the buffet luncheon for the grand opening required 3600 oysters, 25 large hams and 100 crayfish to feed them. By the end of that first day, over 34,000 vehicles had crossed the bridge, in spite of congestion and breakdowns that caused traffic jams stretching back to King's Wharf on the city side and Hall's Corner in Takapuna. The bridge had its first accident that day – a nose-to-tail – and its first jam. A pattern had been set." [258]

Bridge Paying for Itself

"Cars and taxis were tolled 25¢, motorcycles 15¢, buses 50¢ and 40¢ for commercial vehicles. Motorists could pay their toll at any one of the 14 toll booths on the northern approach to the bridge." [259]

"By August 17 [1959], when Geoffrey Robbins stopped at the toll booth and received a silver tray from Lady Allum for making the millionth crossing, there was no doubt the bridge would pay for itself – there was only regret that short-sighted national financial controllers had not allowed Auckland to build a bigger one." [239]

Despite that short-sightedness which would soon result in additional expense to meet demand, Auckland's Waitemata was spanned – at last!

Suburban Rail
First Halcrow and Partners Inquiry

As referred to earlier, Sir William Halcrow, Past President of the Institute of Civil Engineers, and Mr J. P. Thomas, late Chairman of the Transport Advisory Committee of the London Passenger Transport Board, provided an interim report to the Minister of Railways on 25 October 1949 and a final report on 14 March 1950.

Some of the more important recommendations contained in that final Report included:

"(a) That the suburban railways of Auckland be rehabilitated and electrified as soon as possible between the limits of the City, Henderson and Papatoetoe or Papakura.

(b) That the Morningside Deviation commencing at the present Auckland Station (Beach Road) and proceeding underground and joining the existing North Auckland Main Line at Kingsland, be constructed with sub surface stations in the City at Shortland Street, New Civic Centre (and at Victoria Park if found necessary later), also a new station at Arch Hill.

(c) That the underground running tunnels be arranged at the Karangahape Road Station site so that the station can be provided later on if required…

(i) That connection be provided at Auckland Station to allow of trains from Newmarket running on to the new line to the City. The total capital cost of the recommended scheme is £5,456,500. The operating account would show a gain of £13,000. The total miles of railway to be electrified is 40 and the number of passengers 25,000,000 to be carried annually, rising to 33,000,000 ultimately.

(j) That expenditure upon arterial streets in Auckland Metropolitan Area be restricted until results of the recommended schemes are seen.

(k) That new marshalling yards be provided at Westfield at a cost of £150,000 and that improvements in the Auckland yard to relieve congestion be given immediate consideration…

(l) The reconstruction of the Auckland Transport Board or the creation of a new traffic authority to administer all forms of public service transport in Auckland, including suburban railways, the electrification of which should be conditional upon this.

(q) That particular attention be given to the amenities and appearance of existing new stations.

(r) That a special study be made of the car parking problem and its relation to the rehabilitation of the railways.

(s) That consideration be given to developing the forecourt of the present Auckland station as a central bus terminus." [150]

The Halcrow and Partners Report outlined what remained a prime condition for the overall improvement of Auckland's entire transportation network when it called for the integration and co-ordination of the City's transport systems wherever possible. For instance, recommendations (r) and (s) specifically encouraged the integration of the suburban rail network with that of existing public bus services and the private motor car. However, the Report's recommendation (j) warned *that expenditure upon arterial streets in Auckland Metropolitan Area be restricted until results of the recommended schemes are seen.*

Recommendation (l) suggested an efficient means by which the *necessary co-ordination* of the City's transport systems could best be managed:

"The consultants recommended that the rail scheme be supported by integrating rail and bus services to form a multi-modal transport system. They proposed the establishment of a single public authority to plan and co-ordinate all forms of public transport in the metropolitan area." [230]

Government's Response

Not surprisingly, the Government's official response to the Halcrow and Partners recommendations was somewhat reserved. In the Ministry of Works Statement for the year ended 1950, the Commissioner of Works, E R McKillop, confirmed that the report had been received and that it "...contains a number of far-reaching recommendations involving considerable expenditure, and is still under review by the Ministry of Works and the Railways Department. To some extent the report must be related to proposals being put forward by the General Manager of the Railways for electrification of the railway system in that area. As soon as the joint review is completed recommendations will be made to the Government." [260]

Criticism of the Halcrow and Partners Report by Dove-Myer Robinson

Perhaps, because they were *overseas experts*, many were disappointed by the Halcrow and Partners recommendations – recommendations that, more or less, repeated those that had been ignored since 1914. Indeed, the Halcrow and Partners recommendations, calling for the construction of the Morningside Deviation and electrification of the suburban rail network, differed little from those of the Ministry of Work's 1946 proposals, the planning and surveying of which had been undertaken during the preceding four years. This similarity was later criticised by Dove-Myer Robinson (later Sir Dove-Myer Robinson, Auckland City Councillor, and long-time Mayor):

"At this stage, it is most important that the circumstances of this investigation and report should be clearly understood. The general public has the impression that the experts made an investigation of the problem in Auckland, and themselves, formulated the scheme recommended in their report. This is not correct. As they were in Auckland for barely six weeks and in fact produced a preliminary report in less than four weeks after their arrival they obviously did not have time to study the whole problem in the way that it has been assumed. What they did do was to examine the two schemes already mentioned [the Morningside tunnel (as proposed by the Railways Department in 1946 and earlier), and the line to Kumeu via Freemans Bay, Point Chevalier, Te Atatu Peninsula, and Whenuapai (a version of which was first proposed in the Hiley Report of 1914)] and, with certain reservations said that they considered the Railway Department's scheme would serve Auckland's needs better than the other. In other words, they judged the merits of two already prepared schemes on the basis of evidence placed before them. They did not consider any other scheme nor state in any way that some other scheme would not be a still better one. It is no criticism of these experts to say that while they judged the matter on the basis of their knowledge of conditions existing in England and some other countries, they could not possibly have gained during their short visit, a full appreciation of all the local conditions nor of the special factors having a bearing on the matter. They were provided with necessary statistics, but these would not make up for a lack of local knowledge as to localities, industry, transport problems and difficulties and our mode of life. While therefore, the opinions of such men are to be respected, it is considered that there are sound grounds for differing from them in some respects." [46]

Government Committee of Enquiry

There is no evidence to suggest that the Government was listening to Dove-Myer Robinson but it nevertheless determined that additional investigation of the Halcrow and

Partners recommendations was necessary and appointed yet another Committee of Enquiry in 1951: "…under the Transport Act 1949 to consider questions relating to the electrification of suburban services and the construction of the Morningside Deviation.

"The Committee comprised:
Messrs. H. B. Smith (Chairman), Transport Department
C. R. Gribble, Auckland Transport Board
A. T. Gandell, Railways Department
C. A. Linehan, Railways Department
N. B. Spencer, Auckland Omnibus Proprietors"

However, unlike the more basic inquiries undertaken by Halcrow and Thomas, the questions to be considered by this Committee of Enquiry were more concerned with the protection of capital outlay and how an improved suburban railway might affect competing public transport and the general public:

This Committee's "…Order of Reference was: to make such enquiries as may be necessary and to report to the Minister on any action the Committee may consider should be taken to ensure that the public capital to be invested in the electric railways will be adequately protected and that the public will receive an efficient and satisfactory service. In making such report the Committee shall have regard to the existing public passenger transport services in the area and the general public interest." [150]

In other words, the Committee was to focus on the financial implications of the proposed suburban railway service improvements, apparently ignoring any public service benefits that could be achieved. Accordingly, the Committee's Summary of Recommendations included suggested legislation that would "…provide the maximum protection possible to the Auckland Electric Railway having due regard to the public interest…" and "…the best means of protecting the public capital to be invested and minimising any losses." [150]

Concern for Bus Operators

As well as the Committee's concern for the protection of the public interest, the majority (not the two Railways Department Committee members) also expressed its concern for the affect that any suburban rail expansion might have on rival bus services:

"That, in order to ensure that the bus services are continued on a satisfactory basis, between the time the Railway proposals are commenced and their completion, legislation be promulgated at the appropriate time setting up an independent Judicial Tribunal to consider applications for payment of compensation, excluding any allowance for goodwill and solely in respect of any capital loss, from bus operators who continue to provide a satisfactory and adequate service up to the time the Railway proposals are completed." [150]

As did Halcrow and Thomas, the Committee also recommended:

"That a special Authority with responsibility for the control and operation of passenger transport throughout the whole Auckland Metropolitan Area be set up by Statute…" and, in the meantime, that an advisory body consisting of one representative from the "…Auckland Transport Board, the Railways Department, the Bus Operators, the Auckland City Council, and the Suburban Local Authorities…to report on any matters relating to transport development and co-ordination as they arise…" [150]

New Zealand Railways Problems

In the meantime, New Zealand's railway operations had more pressing, country-wide problems to deal with, as reported by the Launceston Examiner on 28 February 1952:

"New Zealand's State owned railways soon will go under the eye of a Royal Commission to prescribe a cure-all to put this country's biggest transport organisation in shape to meet its mounting obligations. One present drawback is lack of modern equipment. The other is a critical staff shortage. These problems are known to the Government. But to solve them at a time of persistent labour shortage throughout industry, at a time when steel supplies are limited and costs continue to soar, has been a continuing worry through the post-war years.

"Since 1939, with insufficient replacements to rolling stock, when the gross ton mileage was swelling more than 40 per cent to a record 3791 million last year, the railway staffs have been heavily depleted. This lack of men to drive the trains, service the tracks, and overhaul the locomotives, is putting trains off the schedules and laying them up in crowded railway workshops. The Minister for Railways (Mr Goosman) said. 'Soon the railways will not be able to handle all the traffic offering.'

"Part of the Royal Commission's job, he said, would be to study whether it was desirable to abandon any of the less lucrative services. One solution the Royal Commission may offer for the staff shortage may be to endeavour to recruit over the next few years from Great Britain a substantial number of youths of 16 to 18 years and indenture them to the department in the required callings." [261]

Auckland Suburban Railway Services

Of course, one of those *less lucrative services* had to be Auckland's suburban rail transport, the patronage of which had steadily and substantially declined between 1930 and 1953. This decline was graphically illustrated by a *Table of Season Ticket Journeys* believed to have been recorded by Dove-Myer Robinson, who commented:

"Even the present traffic is being maintained only because such low fares are being charged. The loss on the suburban service was officially stated in 1949 as being about £130,000 per annum. It is probably greater today, and it appears that suburban passengers are now [sometime after 1953] being carried at somewhat less than half the actual cost. Other factors have influenced the trend following the shifting of the station site in 1930. The economic depression, the development of road transport, both public and private, and the transport difficulties during the war period, all have affected the situation." [46]

Year Ended 31 March	Season Ticket Journeys	Journeys Per 1000 Population	Population
1920	3,096,800	20	155,000
1930	5,189,700	26	200,000
1940	2,970,000	12	240,000
1950	2,595,700	9	300,000
1953	1,964,400	6	325,000

But while 1953 season ticket journeys were only about 38 per cent of those taken in 1930, not all suburban passenger routes had followed the downward trend to the same extent. As Fred Dahms pointed out in his April 1980 New Zealand Geographer article, *Urban Passenger Transport and Population Distribution in Auckland: 1860-1961*:

"Although Auckland's rail lines were not electrified, and routes there were relatively inconvenient, ticket sales continued to increase in places like Otahuhu, Papakura and Newmarket until the forties. Sales at the Auckland station continued to increase until 1961, despite its somewhat inconvenient location after 1930." [15]

New Zealand Railways Royal Commission

In the meantime, the Royal Commission referred to by the Launceston Examiner article, was appointed on 3 March 1952 and commenced sitting on 24 March of that year. The Commissioners appointed included: Auckland Mayor, Sir John Andrew Charles Allum (Chairman); Walter Oswald Gibb, Company Director and Manager of Wellington; and Carl Victor Smith, Company Director of Dunedin. [262]

The Commission was appointed "…to inquire into and report upon all aspects of the New Zealand Government Railways, their future development and sphere of operations, and, in particular, but without in any way limiting the scope of the inquiry and your powers relating thereto, to inquire into and report upon the following matters:

"1. The adequacy and efficiency of all services operated by the New Zealand Railways Department, and of its motive power, rolling-stock, road service vehicles, stations, sheds, workshops, yards, and similar establishments.

"2. The adequacy in numbers, experience, efficiency, and mobility of the existing staff and steps, if any, necessary, to conserve and augment the staff or improve its location by means of housing, hostels, and the like.

"3. The incidence of competition by other transport operations, the effect of subsidies on services, and the desirability of delineating a sphere of operations for railway services and other transport operations.

"4. The desirability or otherwise of the abandonment of working (either wholly or partly or temporarily or permanently) of any portion or portions of the railway system or of any stations thereon having regard to the present and prospective resources of the railways in staff and facilities, the financial results of operating such lines or stations, and the extent to which they are used, and the alternative transport arrangements (if any) which should be made available in the event of such abandonment.

"5. The adequacy and suitability of the scale of goods rates, passenger fares, and all other charges for railway services having regard to the proper sphere of railway operations, the costs of operation, the competitive situation, and the capacity of the railways to handle existing and prospective traffic. And generally to inquire into and report upon such other matters as may come to your notice in the course of your inquiries and which you consider should be investigated in connection therewith, and upon any matters affecting the premises which you consider should be brought to the attention of the Government." [262]

The Railways Royal Commission Report

As always seems to have been the case when such an important, far-ranging, Government inquiry was needed, time was of the essence but limited. This Commission was no exception with a reporting date required "…not later than the 30th day of June 1952." While their final report was tabled in Parliament in plenty of time, on 20 June 1952, the Commissioners had no option but to limit their inquiries to major problems and possible solutions, as they explained at the beginning of their report:

"We commenced our duties immediately after our appointment, and in dealing with the various topics contained in the order of reference we have given careful consideration to the points raised and have endeavoured to answer all matters contained therein. The order of reference is wide and overlaps in parts; because of this a certain amount of repetition has been unavoidable. As the completion of this report was regarded as urgent, we decided to direct our attention more to the major facts creating the present position of the railways and endeavoured to find a solution, rather than investigate a wide range of details which should be the responsibility of management." [262]

Railways Financial Position

Indeed, in order to adequately investigate the financial position of the Railways, as required by Order of Reference 5, the Commissioners needed some help and "…arranged to engage the services of Mr L C Nisbet F.P.A.N.Z., who has in recent years had extensive experience in investigating and reviewing the financial returns and costs of several large industrial organizations, including transport…" [262]

The financial aspects of the Railways' operations were certainly in need of such extensive investigative experience, as illustrated by the Commissioners' 'brief outline of the present position':

"(1) The gross earnings for the year ending 31st March 1952 increased by £1,907,695, but the gross expenditure increased by £3,115,973.

(2) As a result, the operational earnings fell from a profit of £5,790 in 1951 to a loss of £1,202,488 without provision for any interest.

(3) With interest charges added the total loss amounted to £4,199,005."

(4) The operating earnings increased by 76.18d per revenue train-mile, but the operating expenses increased by 99.87d.

(5) Largely owing to the dislocation caused by the [waterfront] strike, necessitating a serious curtailment of passenger services, the number of passenger journeys decreased by 3,531,519.

(6) The tonnage carried increased by 212,914 tons…

(10) The New Zealand Railway Road Services show a loss of £28,200 in 1952, compared with a loss of £52,504 in 1951.

(11) The staff shortages as submitted by the Department amount to 4,920…

(13) At 31st March 1952 over 280,000 private motor-cars were registered, an increase of 30,000 over 1951. At the same date, 95,181 commercial vehicles were registered, being an increase of 10,260 over 1951.

(14) There is increasing competition from road transport, brought about mainly through a substantial increase in the number of licences (temporary or otherwise) granted by the Licensing Authorities for the carriage of goods and comparatively little policing of the Transport Regulations. (The number of temporary licences now being granted a month averages 1,644)." [262]

Decline of Rail Passenger Services

"The following table shows the progressive decline in rail passenger services:

	Before 1951	May 1952	Number Not Now Running Owing to Crew Shortages
Auckland Suburban			
North Line	117	48	69

| South Line | 338 | 257 | 81 |

"We consider that these services [nationwide] are inadequate and the infrequency is having the effect of forcing an increasing number of people to other forms of transport. Although very little can be done in the immediate future, it is the aim of the railways to provide by smaller units, faster and more frequent services, and we agree that through this policy passenger traffic should increase…there has been a very definite lowering of the standard of service to the public. Railways are no longer a monopoly, but have to face the competition of road and air services and the private motor-car.

"Price is not the only factor in securing business, and any disadvantages such as high charges and lack of flexibility that the railways may suffer compared with road or other transport can in some measure be offset by service and goodwill…We do not subscribe to the view held by many people that rail passenger traffic is dying and that the whole future of the railways lies in goods haulage. On the contrary, with the prospective development of railcars, diesel electric, and also electric traction, bringing faster and more frequent services, passenger traffic should increase. It is all the more important, therefore, that a high standard of service be established." [262]

Incidence of Competition

With regard to their investigation of Reference No. 3 (*the incidence of competition by other transport operations…*), the Commissioners provided a broad outline of the competition then faced by the Railways:

"The railways have always been faced with the competition of coastal shipping, but in recent years there has been acute competition from road services and more recently from air transport. It was in 1926 that the competition of road transport first became sufficiently serious to require legislative action with the object of giving a measure of protection to publicly-owned transport undertakings. Since that time attempts have been made by further legislation so to regulate road transport as to prevent its operations unduly adversely affecting the publicly-owned services. Goods and passenger services have been licensed, and in an endeavour to ensure the fullest protection the railways purchased a number of the licensed services, some of which have been abandoned and some of which are still operating.

"In theory, the provisions of the Transport Licensing legislation should give a very substantial measure of protection to the railways, but in practice this has not always proved to be the case. Private operators have discovered loopholes, the use of which has resulted in substantial road operations which it appears clear were never contemplated when the legislation was enacted, and, in the case of goods transport, an extraordinarily large number of temporary licences is issued authorising the carriage of goods over routes.

"As regards passenger transport, at present there is legislative provision (Transport Licensing Regulations 1950, Amendment No.3) for the running of contract road passenger services for traffic which properly comes within this category…We are informed, however, that there are a number of contract licences in existence which contain no proper contracting conditions, and these are used often in conjunction with subordinate booking agencies to cover services which are wastefully competitive with the regular passenger services by rail and road. It seems to us that all such licences should be reviewed, and that contract trips should be run only as authorized by the legislation." [262]

Providing a Reasonable Service

Despite what the Commissioners viewed as *wastefully competitive* practices [nationwide], they did concede that providing the public with a reasonable service was the first priority, regardless of whether or not the provider was a public or private entity:

"We must, however, make the comment that we consider it the clear duty of the railways to give the public reasonable service and not to rest on any protection which is afforded. If it can be established that a service is necessary, it is our opinion that it is the duty of the railways to supply the service or not to oppose the application of a private operator.

"We desire here to draw attention to what is to us the surprising recommendation of the Commissioner of Transport: 'That the Railways Department be relieved of responsibility for running non-paying passenger trains, and that any necessary services be provided by private enterprise road services. We can see no justification for this negative attitude, which assumes that the railways passenger service will always run at a loss and ignores the possibility of their providing more frequent and more profitable services by the use of railcars, &c. It further ignores the large volume of indirect expenses at present borne by the passenger services, which would be a very severe penalty on the freight rates if the passenger services were discontinued." [262]

Royal Commission Supports Halcrow Thomas Proposals

The main purpose of the *New Zealand Royal Commission to Inquire Into and Report Upon the New Zealand Government Railways* had been to provide a national perspective of Railways operations. Nevertheless, no doubt because of what they saw as the future importance of Auckland passenger services, the Halcrow and Partners report received particular support from the Royal Commissioners:

"We have perused the report on Auckland transport submitted on the 14th March 1950 by Sir William Halcrow, M.I.C.E. and Mr J. P. Thomas, M.I.E.E. both of London, and we recommend an early decision on their recommendations. Sir William Halcrow and Mr J. P. Thomas deal extensively with the suburban railways of Auckland, and it appears that until the recommendations of these gentlemen, who are eminent in their respective spheres, are substantially adopted the railways cannot successfully operate a suburban railway passenger service in Auckland." [262]

William Goosman Announcement

The Government appeared to agree with the Royal Commissioners when the Minister of Railways, Stan Goosman, announced on 4 October 1952 that improvements to Auckland's suburban transport facilities *were being put in hand*. As reported by The New Zealand Railway Observer in its January-March 1953 edition, these improvements were to include:

"...construction of the Morningside deviation and underground stations, with electrification between Henderson and Papakura; extension of electrification from Papakura to Frankton Junction; construction of a new marshalling yard at Westfield; rearrangement of Auckland yard; improved freight facilities at Newmarket and Penrose; and reconstruction of Frankton Junction yard and station. The Morningside deviation will give a more direct link between Kingsland, on the main line from the north, and Auckland station. On leaving Kingsland station, the new line will enter a tunnel eight chains long, and will then run through an open cut for 70 chains in Newton Gully before entering the main two-mile tunnel.

"On leaving the tunnel the line will fork, one branch running into Auckland station and the other making a junction with the existing main line to Newmarket and the south. The first work to be undertaken will be construction of the two bridges across Beach Road near Auckland station. Initial earthworks and tunnelling will also be begun at the Kingsland end of the line and construction should be under way by the end of 1953.

"Although no estimated dates of completion were announced, the Auckland papers hailed the news with delight, which was heightened by the sight within a week of a drilling rig doing test drills for the Beach Road bridges. At present (February), the survey team is busy above the line of the tunnel." [263]

Railways Management

But, while the Royal Commissioners considered the improvement of Auckland suburban railway services to be important, the national management of such a huge entity as the Railways, with the many challenges to be met, was of even greater concern to them:

"The railways and ancillary services, with assets valued at £88,070,000, an income for the last financial year of nearly £24,000,000, and a staff of approximately 25,000 persons, constitute the largest commercial undertaking in New Zealand. Notwithstanding its vitally important position in the national economy the railways have only restricted monopoly of transport and must face the growing competition of other forms of transport. Indeed, during the past twenty-five years the competition of road transport in particular has been and remains severe, and now there is the developing competition of the air services. However much protection may be granted to the railways, it is not probable that they will ever enjoy a complete monopoly, and great skill and judgment will be necessary wisely to manage and to meet the inevitable competition.

"As regards management, we find that since 1st June 1928, a period of twenty-four years, seven gentlemen have occupied the position of General Manager, the term of six of them averaging less than four years. The present General Manager took office on the 1st August 1951. The unwisdom of these relatively rapid changes has just been well demonstrated in the matter of the proposal to electrify the North Island Main Trunk. The last General Manager recommended Government to adopt his proposal and to make an immediate start with it, and Government accepted the scheme in principle.

"The present General Manager holds a different view; he believes that electrification can wait and he desires to develop an alternative proposal for consideration…no business of this magnitude has any hope of being successful if changes in major policy can occur every few years with a change of managership…Furthermore, we do not believe that in these days of constantly changing economic conditions it is possible for one man to run successfully a trading concern with a turnover of £24,000,000 annually." [262]

New Zealand Railways Corporation

The solution seemed obvious to the Commissioners: "In the best interests of the railway we believe that (a) steps must be taken to relieve the Minister of the continual demands on his time and energy in dealing with day-by-day matters and (b) the actual management should be shared by more than one man…accordingly we recommend:—

1. That there shall be established a Corporation, to be called the New Zealand Railways Corporation, and that the Corporation shall take over, manage, and develop the railways system and its ancillary services.

2. That the Corporation shall consist of five (5) Directors to be appointed by the Governor-General…" [262]

The Commissioners explained their preference for a Corporation:

"In the past Boards or Commissions that have been set up to run the railways have met with limited success. We think one of the main reasons for this has been that railways require such specialization that men trained in the railways are necessary on such managing bodies...We consider that such management would also be greatly assisted by someone with financial ability." [262]

However, their preference for such a governing body was tempered somewhat by reality: "We do not see how the railways can be completely divorced from political control, no matter how desirable that may be. The Government is responsible to the people for the money it has expended and will expend in the future. Although the final control must be in the hands of the Government, it is desirable that those composing the management be given as free a hand as possible and that, after policy has been decided upon by Government, full responsibility for carrying out that policy be left with them." [262]

New Zealand Railways Commission

However, as the Commissioners suspected, the Government was not quite ready to cut the apron strings and they did not get the semi-independent Corporation asked for. Instead, the Railways had to settle for what the Commissioners considered to be a second-rate alternative – a Commission – established by the Government Railways Amendment Act 1952, passed in October of that year:

"2. (1) There is hereby established a management commission in respect of the railways and services lawfully carried on by the New Zealand Government Railways Department, which Commission shall be called the New Zealand Railways Commission.

"(2) The Commission shall consist of five Directors to be appointed from time to time by the Governor-General, of whom three shall be appointed from the members of the Department or full time employees of any service organization, and two shall be appointed from persons outside the Government service.

"5. (1) There shall from time to time be appointed a General Manager of Railways, who, under the control of the Commission, shall be the Chief Executive Officer of the Commission, and the Permanent Head of the Department.

"11. (1) The general functions and duties of the Commission shall be to do all things which, in its opinion, are necessary for the efficient management, operation, and development of the Government railways and every service lawfully carried on by the Commission, within the limits of the moneys appropriated by Parliament for expenditure out of the Working Railways Account.

"12. In the exercise of its functions and powers the Commission shall-

(a) Have regard to any representations that may be made by the Minister in respect of any functions or powers of the Commission; and

(b) Give effect to any decision of the Government in relation thereto conveyed to the Commission in writing by the Minister.

"14. (1) The Commission shall from time to time determine the capital works which it considers necessary in order to provide an adequate service to meet public requirements.

(2) The Commission shall prepare and present reports on all such proposed works to the Minister; and, in notifying the Commission of the decision of the Government on any such matter, the Minister, after consultation with the Minister of Finance, shall advise the Commission when the necessary capital moneys will be made available for the works.

(3) On being advised of the Government's decision on the proposed capital works, the Commission shall take such steps as may be necessary to ensure that the works shall, to the extent to which they have been approved, be carried out in an orderly and progressive manner." [264]

New Zealand Railway Commissioners Appointed

"On January 7 [1953] the Minister of Railways announced that the Governor-General (Sir Willoughby Norrie) had approved the appointment of Messrs. W. E. Hodges, C. H. Bray, A. T. Gandell, R. Martin and W. L. Wyber as the New Zealand Railways Commission. Their warrants were to be effective for three years as from January 12. Business to be dealt with at the first meeting, which was held on January 21, was expected to be mainly concerned with organisation and the delegation of authority. Later the problems of finance, the working of wharves at railway ports, branch lines, and other important matters would come up for consideration." [263]

Second Halcrow and Partners Inquiry

For much the same reasons as its aversion to the establishment of a Railways Corporation, the Government did not share the Royal Commission's enthusiasm for the Halcrow and Thomas recommendations. Because of its ongoing concerns for *protecting the public capital to be invested and minimising any losses*, which had been the focus of the previous Government Committee of Enquiry set up in 1951, the Government decided to commission yet another inquiry into the viability of improving Auckland's suburban railway services.

Accordingly, "In April, 1953, the Government engaged Sir William Halcrow and Partners as Consultants to advise further with regard to the Auckland Morningside Deviation.

The Order of Reference was: – 'To undertake a preliminary investigation and submit a report with sketch plans and rough estimate of the probable cost of the Auckland Morningside Deviation.'

"Sir William Halcrow and Partners reported in April, 1954. This Report dealt mainly with civil engineering aspects of design and construction, and provided an estimate of £4,250,000 for the civil engineering works involved, with the provision for a further £200,000 to complete the Karangahape Road Station." [150 p.130]

Merz and McLellan Report

Also in April 1953, the Government again engaged the English consulting engineers, Messrs. Merz and McLellan to examine the logistics and cost of the electrification of the Auckland Suburban Railway System. As detailed in the first part of this study, *Waka Paddle to Gas Pedal – The First Century of Auckland Transport*, the same engineers had been engaged in 1924 to survey the same system, including the proposed Morningside Deviation. When Merz and McLellan favourably reported in 1926, then Minister of Railways, Joseph Gordon Coates, commented "…other countries were moving fast in the direction of electrification of railways, as it was realised that quick services were a big inducement for people to travel by train." [265]

"Messrs. Merz and McLellan reported in May, 1954. This Report dealt mainly with the technical aspects of electrification, but it also provided the basis of the cost of electrification between Henderson and Papakura." [150]

In hindsight, it is known that none of the recommendations of Halcrow and Partners (two reports), Messrs. Merz and McLellan, or the Government's Committee of Enquiry were expedited.

This is despite the observation of Halcrow and Partners in 1950 that Auckland was running out of time to implement a co-ordinated public transport network: "Our study of transport arrangements in Auckland leaves no doubt in our minds that the inquiry was most necessary, and it is in our opinion very desirable that a comprehensive scheme for the suburban railways should be decided upon at an early date." [150]

Railways Commission Memorandum

However, an early decision in favour of suburban railway transport was not to be. All the time and resources already expended by the Railways Department surveying and planning Auckland's suburban railway upgrade, as per its 1946 ten-year plan, *the shape of things to come*; the cost of the Halcrow and Partners and Merz and McLellan reports; and the Government Committee of Enquiry – not to mention the countless pre-war inquiries and reports – were seemingly forgotten when:

"On 27 August [1954] the Chairman of the New Zealand Railways Commission, an entity set up to restructure rail, submitted a memorandum to Cabinet, with the concurrence of the Railways Minister, W. S. Goosman, recommending that Auckland's rail upgrade be cancelled." [72]

Railways Commission Findings

The New Zealand Herald of 21 September 1955 summed up the findings of the Railways Commission as follows:

"The Morningside deviation with electrification of the suburban railway system between Henderson and Papakura was estimated to cost £10,876,000 said the commission. This was on the basis of recommendations made in April and May, 1954, by Messrs Merz and McLellan and Sir William Halcrow and Partners, who had been engaged as consultants. The project was estimated to take five and a half years to complete from the time instructions were given to proceed.

"The memorandum to the Minister continued:—To ensure a reasonable financial return on the high capital cost involved it is essential that this modern form of rail transport receive the maximum possible public patronage, having full regard to the necessity for other forms of public transport in the City of Auckland. For this reason the commission is of the opinion that the carrying out of this work should be conditional on:-

"(a) The establishment of an overall public transport co-ordinating authority for the Auckland metropolitan area, invested with power to control and so ensure the orderly co-ordination of all means of public transport.

"(b) The adoption of the best possible route for the Morningside deviation from a railway operating viewpoint, especially in respect of the siting of adequate and convenient underground city railway stations, three of which, in the Karangahape Road, Civic Square and Lower Queen Street localities, are considered desirable.

"If these conditions can be fulfilled it is considered that 25 million passenger journeys per annum will accrue to rail in the early years of operation (say 1960-1963), increasing to 35 million passenger journeys by 1980.

"With this patronage it is estimated that during the first years of electric operation the existing steam operating loss of £189,000 (excluding interest charges) will be reduced to £97,000. In other words, the railways will earn an additional operating profit of £92,000 per annum, which represents a return of 0.85 per cent on the net capital investment of £10,876,000. If interest at 3½ per cent on a reducing balance is taken into account, the capital expenditure involves an increase of £297,000 in interest charges, and the present aggregate annual loss of £202,000 is increased to £407,000 – an increase of £205,000.

"By 1980 it is estimated that the operating annual loss (excluding interest charges) will be reduced to £25,000, as compared with £189,000 at present and £97,000 in 1960. The improved operating position will then represent a return of 1.4 per cent on the capital investment. Taking interest at 3½ per cent into account, the aggregate annual loss will be £353,000 in 1980 as compared with £202,000 at present and £407,000 in 1960.

"The adoption of suitably sited, convenient and attractive underground city stations for the Morningside deviation is one factor vital to the above financial returns. The commission has closely examined the consultants' recommendations for the Queen Street and Civic Square stations and considers that these stations as planned do not ensure the maximum possible patronage.

"The extent to which the desirable improvements could be effected and the additional cost of making such improvements is a matter requiring further discussions with the consultant civil engineering firm. These discussions may indicate that reasonable and satisfactory improvements cannot be achieved except at greatly increased costs because of physical difficulties associated with major drainage systems and building foundations. In that case further protracted and detailed engineering investigations will be necessary to ensure that a more satisfactory route is adopted.

"The topography of Auckland allows of considerable flexibility in selecting a route for the Morningside deviation but it is clear from the investigations to date that under the most favourable alignment the cost of the suburban project will not be less than £10 million." [266]

Railways Commission Conclusion

Clause 9 of the Railways Commission memorandum to Cabinet concluded:

"The Commission is not satisfied that an effective co-ordinating transport authority for the Auckland Metropolitan Area can be readily established. Without essential control and co-ordination of public transport there can be no assurance that an electrified suburban rail system will attract adequate patronage, and for this reason the project cannot be considered as other than a doubtful proposition at the present time. In these circumstances the Commission is unable to recommend that the project be proceeded with. W E Hodges, Chairman, New Zealand Railways Commission." [150]

Public Transport Management

It is now only of paradoxical significance to ponder that *an effective co-ordinating transport authority for the Auckland Metropolitan Area* could not, in the Commission's opinion, *be readily established* – particularly when any *lack of administrative capacity to implement bus-rail coordination* was then the direct result of earlier disregard of the Halcrow and Partners and Committee of Enquiry recommendations for *the creation of a multi-modal transport system managed by a single Authority*.

For instance, the first Halcrow and Partners Report had specifically urged:

"*The reconstruction of the Auckland Transport Board or the creation of a new traffic authority to administer all forms of public service transport in Auckland, including suburban railways, the electrification of which should be conditional upon this.*" [150]

Like so many others, this recommendation was ignored and there seems to have been little further discussion by any transport planners or administrators as to how such an authority could be established or, indeed, why the Auckland Transport Board could not have taken on the added responsibility.

Auckland Transport Board

It would seem that the New Zealand Railways Commission (and the Railways Minister, William Goosman) chose to ignore the existence of the Auckland Transport Board which had been operating Auckland's trams since 1928 and was managing a growing fleet of replacement, electric trolley buses by 1955.

In fact, the Auckland Transport Board had a long history of competent public transport management, often during years of war shortages and recessions, and it had definite plans in place to meet Auckland's future public transport needs.

While some administrative re-organisation of the Board would have been necessary, the already tram-and-bus-tested Board was otherwise more than capable of managing any additional bus-rail coordination required. As early as 1945, the Board had been planning its own transport evolution with its proposal to acquire 50 trolley buses, at a cost of some £150,000, to supplement and ultimately replace its expiring trams. [267]

Auckland's first trolley buses had been running since December 1938, as a free service courtesy of the Farmers Trading Company but trolley buses did not seriously replace any of the city's tram services until September 1949. By 1955, the Auckland Transport Board was attempting to raise £300,000 to increase its fleet. According to an advertisement on page eight of the September 1955 Comment Magazine, (a communications facilitator for the Auckland City Council), the Transport Board was then offering debentures in units of £50 at 4 per cent "…to complete another stage of the modernisation programme – Modern transport for a modern city" [268]

However, despite its long history of financial sustainability, the Transport Board's losses, resulting from decreasing passenger numbers and the rising cost of wages and maintenance, had meant that the Board had had to levy its constituent local bodies for the first time in 1954. The need for this subsidy of £100,000 with more to come, ultimately paid by the City's ratepayers, many of whom no longer availed themselves of the Board's services, provided the New Zealand Railways Commission with a ready excuse not to consider the Transport Board as the authority to manage the needed *essential control and co-ordination of public transport.*

And, as Paul Mees points out in *Transport for Suburbia: Beyond the Automobile Age*, "Goosman may have also been influenced by opposition from public and private bus interests, who opposed the establishment of a new public transport authority and demanded compensation if one was established." [205]

Profit or Public Service

For whatever reason, the necessity for financial profit to be gained from the provision of a public service had influenced the establishment of a suburban railway system. In most cities, rate- and tax-payer subsidies are essential to ensure the continuation of their public transport systems. The burden is considered to be a justifiable means of providing an essential social service or, alternatively, as an unnecessary imposition by those souls who insist that all enterprises should make a profit or go out of business.

Obviously, the Minister of Railways had assumed the latter persuasion when: "During August and September (1954), Goosman floated concerns about increasing subsidies…in the media." [72]

Government Priorities

Although Minister Goosman and others of the Cabinet were soon persuaded by the Railways Commission to defer Auckland's proposed electrified suburban railway system, Goosman, in particular, may have been influenced somewhat by his additional responsibilities as Minister of Transport and Minister of Works. Indeed, it is likely that, as with so many Government decisions that seemingly ignored social benefits and, instead, fixated solely on cost, the decision to shelve Auckland's suburban railway proved an easy way out of a major Government commitment. Indeed, the prioritisation of many such projects was foreshadowed by William Goosman during his delivery of the Ministry of Works Statement for the year ending 31 March 1950:

"It is evident that the Government is faced with a formidable task in endeavouring to overcome arrears of construction and to satisfy the demands being placed upon it from all quarters for works and buildings of every description. Unfortunately, many are prone to believe that these demands can be satisfied at once, but each year's programme must be related to the physical resources available and, further, must take cognizance of the funds available to the Government for capital construction work.

"These factors prevent decisions being given which would be pleasing and acceptable to all sections of the community. However, I have been careful to point out the limitations, financial and otherwise, which must be placed upon the construction programme if this is to maintain a reasonable balance with other expenditure to which the Government is committed." [269]

William Goosman Change of Mind

Nevertheless, the 1954 dismissal of Auckland's railway project was quite an about-turn for Minister Goosman who had, in his Railways Statement for the year ending 31 March 1950, stated: "There can be no doubt that the railways are the backbone of the Dominion's transport industry. For many years now there has been a continued, steady increase in tonnage and as the average length of haul per ton has also extended over the years the pressure on the railways has become such that measures must now be taken to ensure that they will possess the physical capacity to enable them to cope with the traffic of the future…

"By reason of the view which I hold of the importance of the railways I am of the opinion that their stability and progress must not be impaired by unnecessary and wasteful competition. The Dominion is dependent upon the railways for services which cannot, or would not, for various reasons, be performed by any other form of transport, but the ability of the railways to perform the over-all services that are required in the public interest depends upon the retention by the railways of the more lucrative lines of traffic which are those generally sought by competitors. This statement involves the principle that where the railways are able to provide such service as may reasonably be required then they should not, in the public interest, be subjected to uneconomic competition." [270]

That statement of confidence in the future role of the railways, was followed by his October 1952 assurance that the Government would "…proceed with a programme of improvements to Auckland's suburban railway transport facilities." [271]

But, what a difference a year can make…

"Enthusiasm for motorways increased in 1953 when the National Roads Board, responsible for rural roads, opened New Zealand's first section of motorway in Auckland's outer suburbs.

"At the ceremony, the national Transport Minister, W S Goosman – responsible for both road and rail – told a journalist who had the temerity to ask about rail: 'my boy, the future of Auckland is with the motor car'." [205]

Dove-Myer Robinson Uncertainty

But Stan Goosman was not the only politician to have hesitated on the station platform. Contrary to the modern-day view that Dove-Myer Robinson had always been an avid crusader for a suburban railway system for Auckland, that was not, in fact, the case. During his early tenure as a city councillor, Dove-Myer Robinson had warned of too readily accepting the suburban railway proposals as a solution to the city's transport problems:

"Any scheme of such scope would have considerable merit; as this one has. To the people of Auckland, so long denied modern railway facilities, there is a great temptation to accept it without question. Yet haste at the last minute after so many years, is surely neither logical nor wise." [46]

Although Dove-Myer Robinson would eventually come to regret his hesitation, he needn't have worried about any haste, *illogical or otherwise*, for it would be a very long time before such an extensive suburban railway plan would again be considered. In the meantime, his misgivings seemed to be based, rightly or wrongly, on the perceived construction difficulties of tunnelling beneath the city and the revenue shortfall (and therefore the cost to ratepayers) that an improved suburban railway could ultimately incur:

"In a recent press report, the Minister of Railways mentioned that the cost would be a good deal more than what was estimated in 1949. This probably left the impression that any increase is due to general cost increases since then, but it is much more likely that the detailed investigation which has been carried out in the meantime has revealed the difficulties of construction to be such that it will cost very much more than originally estimated. If this is so, it is certainly not surprising.

"The tunnel section under Shortland Street – Queen Street intersection, for instance, will be at a level of at least 30 feet below street level. This brings it below sea level in reclaimed ground immediately adjacent to multi-storeyed buildings. A worse combination it is difficult to imagine. If construction is undertaken from the surface by cut-and-cover method, pumping would be necessary. What effect this would have on the foundations of the adjacent buildings is anyone's guess. As the present value of these buildings must be upwards of £2,000,000, no chances can be taken…" [46]

By September 1954, Dove-Myer Robinson had, more or less, made up his mind:

"Regarding the Underground Railway, it appears that this may cost the Government something like £12,000,000 and that there may be an operating loss that may run into well over £350,000 yearly. When we realise that it is reported that the Hutt Railway is losing about £100,000 yearly, we can easily see that the loss on an electrified underground Railway in Auckland could assume very great proportions. Besides which, I do not think that the Underground Railway will solve Auckland's transport problems." [212]

Kenneth Brailey Cumberland Uncertainty

Robinson's uncertainty as to the viability of the suburban railway proposals could also have been influenced by the opinion of his friend and fellow-Auckland City Councillor, Kenneth Brailey Cumberland:

"The first open opposition [to the Halcrow Thomas report 1950] came from Professor Kenneth Cumberland, head of Geography at Auckland University from 1946 to 1980, and the Chairman of the Auckland City Council's Town Planning Committee. In an op-ed piece for the Star, Cumberland called the railway scheme a 'white elephant' that 'may well prejudice any chance of getting any material improvement of our highway system'. Those pointing to successful rail systems overseas 'must remember that Auckland, with its low population densities and sprawling area, is not to be compared with a city of 1,000,000 people and more in a smaller area'. Cumberland concluded: 'A full-scale expert inquiry seems to be the first necessity'." [205]

It seems that, regardless of any impartiality that should perhaps have been expected from a Planning Committee Chairman, Kenneth Cumberland saw fit to publish his preference for road transport as widely as possible:

"On 26 August [1954], the *New Zealand Herald* had also published an article by the Chairman of the Auckland City Council Town Planning Committee K. B. Cumberland, which called for transfer of the cost of the railway upgrade to the building of motorways..." [72]

Master Transportation Plan for Metropolitan Auckland

Dove-Myer Robinson, Kenneth Cumberland and others of political influence were persuaded to support the eventual, *full-scale expert inquiry* set up to resolve Auckland's transport dilemma once and for all. The choice between road and rail was finally decided by the Auckland Regional Planning Authority's Technical Advisory Committee and its Master Transportation Plan for Metropolitan Auckland published July 1955.

With one possible exception, "A practical spur line...from the existing Auckland Railway Station to a passenger terminal station located in Victoria Street East..." [150], the Plan unceremoniously dumped suburban rail in favour of motorways and road-based public transport.

Technical Advisory Committee's Findings

A New Zealand Herald article summed up some of the Technical Advisory Committee's findings:

"Auckland, with only four people to the acre (compared with New York's 40, Greater London's 20 and Sydney's 8½), is one of the most dispersed cities in the world. That is the main reason why the technical advisory committee favours, in its master transport plan, a roading system rather than suburban railways for Auckland. The population living within reasonable walking distance of an inflexible system such as railways is very limited, the report says. This means that an extensive feeder bus service would have to be used if the potential carrying capacity of trains was to be anywhere near fully used.

"New Zealand with the highest ratio of vehicles to population, after the United States, is following the United States in traffic and transport trends. In the whole of the United States there is not one city of a size similar to Auckland's which has mass rail transport facilities the report says. Over 90 per cent of Auckland's passenger and goods traffic travels on the road today, and there is every indication that the total traffic movement will be doubled, even trebled, within 25 years. Public transport uses road space much more efficiently than private cars – only a tenth as much per passenger carried in present peak-hour traffic. But the trend away from public transport to private cars must be faced, the report adds." [272]

Spur Line Compromise

An Auckland Star editorial, published 21 September 1955, agreed:

"…a 'dead-end' spur line from the Auckland station to Victoria Street East seems to be a compromise. It warrants investigation, as the committee recommends, but at first glance it is hard to see justification for spending £2 million on a project which would serve such a comparatively small section of the travelling public. There would appear to be greater merit in the alternative suggestion that the layout of the Auckland station should be rearranged to provide more convenient means of transferring to buses or trams. The crux of the committee's case is that an underground railway would not avoid the immediate necessity to undertake extensive highway development. To seek both would be patently unrealistic…One of the advantages of the motorway project is that, unlike the railway scheme, it would be carried out in stages, with each coming into use on completion." [273]

Some Doubt Because of Questions Insufficiently Answered

Nevertheless, The New Zealand Herald of 21 September 1955 did not agree fully with the proposals of the Master Transportation Plan and expressed some doubt because of questions insufficiently answered:

"ROADS, not railways, in the opinion of a committee of engineers, offer the best solution to the transport problem in metropolitan Auckland. The recommendation is for a system of urban motorways to be completed 'by 1965 or, at the very latest, 1970', at a cost of about £12 million to £15 million. All earlier plans for a modernised, electrified system of suburban railways, with some underground transport, go into the discard. The engineers pin their faith to bus services, trucks and vans for commercial purposes, and an ever-increasing use of the private motor car. New bus terminals and parking stations are accepted as part of the price that Auckland will have to pay for reliance on road transport.

"This 'master plan' emanates from a technical advisory committee of 26 members, with a few seconded and co-opted assistants. By and large, it is the product of local body engineers who, naturally enough, take a lively personal interest in roading. On the main advisory committee and on the various working committees, experts in the handling of bulk passenger traffic have been in a minority, although not, as far as one can gather, a dissenting minority.

"The report of the committee and the very exhaustive survey of physical and other factors on which the report is based, have been extraordinarily well prepared, and present a cogent case for the development of road transport. The City Council, which originally asked for the report in October of last year, has already given sufficient evidence of its sympathies to suggest that recommendations so firmly made will be enthusiastically adopted.

"In the lay mind, however, some doubts may remain. How is it, for instance, that a committee largely composed of local body engineers has been able to dismiss the studied recommendations of two such eminent overseas authorities as Sir William Halcrow and Mr Thomas? Has rail transport been pushed too rudely into the background? Does not the unusual proposal for a spur underground line from the Auckland railway station to Victoria Street, near Albert Park, suggest that railways still have a place in the scheme of things? Can the flexibility of motor transport be guaranteed under an open invitation for more and more traffic, public and private, to crowd the proposed new urban motorways?

"The engineers have doubtless considered these matters from their own individual viewpoints. The City Council has still to consider them from the viewpoint of elected representatives of the travelling public. In a large and rapidly growing metropolitan area like Auckland, transport concerns everyone, not least the workers, the shoppers and the business community in general. All these people may feel disposed to judge a public transport system by its cheapness, its speed and its convenience. They will expect their elected representatives to watch their interests, especially as a concentration on urban motorways may make the bus uneconomic in competition with the private car. [274]

Will the Roads Cope?

"The advisory committee seems satisfied that its proposed system of motorways will be able to cope with all predictable increases in motor traffic. That remains to be seen. Over the past 20 or 30 years, the registration of motor vehicles has exceeded all estimates, and nobody can say when saturation point will be reached. Nevertheless – and these reservations not withstanding – metropolitan Auckland urgently needs a new roading system. With the changeover from trams to buses nearing completion, most road users will support the committee's recommendations. And, with local professional advisers opting so firmly for road transport, the Government will naturally regard itself as being relieved from any responsibility for improving the suburban rail services.

"The important thing, therefore, is that the City Council should consider the latest transport plan as a matter of urgency and seek to provide the new motorways with the least possible delay. They will be needed, and badly needed, long before they are completed, even if they do not provide the final answer. Matters of finance, of course, will loom large in all discussions of the 'master plan'…Much hard bargaining is thus in prospect. Admittedly the Government will escape from its acceptance in principle of railway development costing about £11.7 million, but it is hardly likely to transfer that sum to the cost of a roading programme over which it has little or no control.

"And Auckland, if it is wise, will not reject railway development completely. By 1970 the new motorways may be crowded and the need for fast suburban rail services acute. The plan is before the people. In spite of its limitations in certain directions, it is bound to command considerable public support. Whether the recommendations offer a partial or complete answer to the transport problem, they are, broadly speaking, necessary. The City Council must now determine whether the professional advice it has received meets all the needs of the community. Then, with any necessary reservations for the future, it must endeavour to make the best financial arrangements it can while pushing forward vigorously with all the work required to save a city dependent entirely on road transport from becoming a city of traffic jams." [274]

Auckland, If It Is Wise

Obviously, The New Zealand Herald's advice that railway development should not be completely rejected was the very antithesis of that propounded by the Technical Advisory Committee and the supporters of its recommendations for an extensive road-building programme. As a result, any proposal for caution went mostly unheeded, particularly by those enticed by the promise of the increased mobility and independence provided by the motor vehicle and, of course, those who stood to profit from the increased use of motor vehicles and road construction. Nevertheless, there were still some who were not persuaded that *the needs of the community* would best be served by more and bigger roads.

The Henderson Borough Ratepayers' and Citizens' Association

In October, and again in December, 1955, the Henderson Borough Ratepayers' and Citizens' Association wrote to the Minister of Railways:

"…the Henderson Borough Ratepayers' and Citizens' Association views with grave concern the report of the special investigating committee of local bodies with regard to general road development as proposed for Auckland, and feels that the outer suburbs will not be adequately served by this means and also that further development of the roads to the detriment of the suburban railways should be strenuously opposed and that railways should be developed as set out in the Halcrow-Thomas report or any other practical schemes." [275]

After a subsequent meeting with the Chairman of the Henderson Borough Ratepayers' and Citizens' Association, Mr Gregory, the Auckland Railways District Engineer, replied to the Railways Manager, Wellington on 3 February 1956:

"As instructed, I have had a discussion with Mr Gregory, Chairman of the Henderson Borough Ratepayers' and Citizens' Assn., regarding the decision reached by the Committee which made the investigations and prepared the Master Transportation Plan for Metropolitan Auckland. Mr Gregory stated that the Association's main concern was on account of a current rumour that reductions were to be made in the existing North suburban train services, as a result of the decision made by the Committee. He said that his Association did not support the proposal to construct roads and expressways, in place of railways, and that it intended taking action to oppose the roading scheme.

"Regarding the rumour of cuts in train services, the Transport Officer, District Traffic Manager's Office, advised Mr Gregory that no consideration had been given to such a suggestion, but he did draw attention to the fact that several of the trains from Henderson were poorly patronised, and were being run uneconomically. He suggested to Mr Gregory that better patronage of these services would protect them against any future possibility of reduction.

"Regarding the Committee's decision for roading, Mr Gregory appeared satisfied that the Department's interests had been protected by its representatives on the Committee, but in his opinion, the Committee should have been comprised of some members representing those sections of the community affected by the decision, and not by professional men and Local Body Engineers, who, on account of their occupations, were mainly interested in roads." [276]

Borough of Papakura to the District Engineer

Similar opposition to any reduction of suburban railway services attributable to the Master Transportation Plan recommendations were also expressed in a letter from A L Cooper, Town Clerk, Borough of Papakura, to The District Engineer, New Zealand Railways, dated 16 March 1956:

"Passenger Transport – This Council has been much concerned respecting future development in relation to transport and having studied the Auckland Transportation Scheme feels it is entirely outside the scope of the City Schemes. Papakura has grown up centred on the Railway and having observed the problems arising from motor traffic and having noted in the report submitted some time since by the Railway Department in which the railways are shown still to have the potential to provide cheap transit for large numbers of people, Council feels it must plan for co-ordinated action in the future to adequately meet the needs of its people. With this end in view I have been directed to inquire if you could make available a member of your staff qualified to speak on these matters and who could meet the Road Safety Committee of this Council at an evening meeting to discuss the matter." [277]

Lack of Public Consultation

While, in both instances, the correspondents sought reassurance from Railways management that *the needs of the community* and *needs of its people*, respectively, would be catered for, the first response, at least, indicates that those in charge of railway transport were all too ready to fall on their swords in deference to their road rivals. If the railways could surrender so readily to the recommendations of the Master Transportation Plan and its supporters, what hope was there for the defenders of public transport to voice their opposition?

Some, like J Rose, chose one of the few avenues of dissent then available – a letter to the newspaper. The response to his criticism of Dove-Myer Robinson's support for the Master Transportation Plan was swift and to the point:

"Sir, Your correspondent J Rose asks on what high authority I claimed that the Master Transportation Plan will save the Government £12,000,000 as compared with the underground railway scheme. The report of the Technical Advisory Committee of the Regional Planning Authority showed that the Morningside deviation and electrification of suburban railways would have cost nearly £12,000,000, would have served only 5% of the total urban traffic, and would have shown an operating loss of £350,000 to £400,000 annually for at least 20 years:- a minimum loss of £7,000,000.

"Mr Rose also asks why, after my drainage experience, I am willing to accept the opinion of 'local' experts. The original motion which I moved in the Council, which initiated the Master Transportation Plan investigation, called for the engagement of 'overseas experts' to conduct the investigation. This was amended by the City Council and all reference to 'overseas experts' was deleted from the final motion which was adopted. I am quite satisfied with the results of the 'local' experts report because:–

1. The investigation and report were prepared by 26 leading engineers, Transport Board and Railway Department experts.

2. Because the recommendations were unanimously approved by the whole 26 of them.

3. Because the report appealed to me as being the logical solution of Auckland's present transport problems.

"The Master Transportation Plan is altogether different (from the original Brown's Island drainage reports), because every one of the 26 persons concerned with its preparation have knowledge of local conditions, and are experts on the particular part of the problem they were dealing with…" [278]

Sir John Allum Stresses Value of Rail Transport

Sir John Allum, Auckland Mayor from 1941 to 1952 and a veteran proponent of public transport, also remained sceptical of the proposals included in the Master Transportation Plan, as reported by The New Zealand Herald on 27 March 1956:

"Newmarket business men should press for an early start on the master transport plan for Auckland, Sir John Allum told members of the Newmarket Business Association at a luncheon yesterday. He also urged them to press for the electrification of the suburban railways. Sir John said he believed that more stations would also be necessary. There would be a problem inducing people to take the trains, but he thought that if 20 per cent of the people coming into the city to work could be persuaded to come by train, and not by car, there would be immeasurable relief to traffic congestion.

"The average number of cars a head of population in New Zealand was one car to every four people, whereas the world average was one car to 15 people. We are desperately in need of better facilities for getting the motorist into the heart of the city, said Sir John. He did not want to lose sight of the possibility of taking transport underground. When things are too crowded on the ground, we should go underground. When they are too crowded there, we shall have to take to the air.

"Apart from all the worry about the transport difficulties, Sir John said he thought it was still the tram that got the passengers where they wanted to go and in the shortest possible time. You can talk about your trolley and diesel buses, he said, but you can't beat the tram for speed, cost and reliability." [279]

Sir John Allum's suggestion that *"When things are too crowded on the ground, we should go underground"* was not some ephemeral concept of little practical value. Indeed, the September 1955 edition of the City Council's Comment Magazine included a plan by which the City's buses could avoid the chronic traffic congestion of the Khyber Pass/Symonds Street/Karangahape Road/New North Road intersection by means of a labyrinth of tunnels. [280]

Needless to say, the bus tunnels were never built and Auckland's last tram route closed in December 1956 leaving the City's under-funded, suburban railway service, operating from a remote main station, as a very poor substitute for the mass transportation of its commuters. As the voices of pragmatic critics such as Sir John Allum and J Rose were ignored, the way was clear for those all too willing to provide their motor vehicles with pathways to the future.

Chapter Four

1960 to 1969 – Let's Debate and Not Decide

Planning and Politics
Auckland Regional Planning Authority

By 1960, Auckland had only the one planning body, the Auckland Regional Planning Authority. As noted in the previous chapter, this Authority had been formed from what had once been the overlapping responsibilities of the Auckland Metropolitan Planning Committee and the Auckland Regional Planning Organisation. This important step of planning amalgamation, provided for by the Town and Country Planning Act 1953, encouraged some semblance of local-body unity, in line with Mayor John Luxford's plan for a *Greater Auckland*.

Lack of Central and Local Government Planning Leadership

Unfortunately, by the time Dove-Myer Robinson became Auckland City Mayor in 1959, that vision of a united Auckland remained elusive. Disunity between City Council, borough, and county council politicians continued, compounded by a lack of Central Government-sponsored, consistent and reliable, regional and town planning leadership.

The co-ordination that should have promoted such leadership was to have been provided by the Local Government Commission, supported by the 1946 Local Government Commission Act. However, this had not materialised – as described in a report prepared by the Local Bills Committee of the House of Representatives.

Entitled *The Structure of Local Government in New Zealand*, the Bills Committee report included the view that the Commission's leadership failure had been exacerbated by central government's lack of support for its decisions. In his 1967 article, *The Role of Local Government in Expanding Auckland*, this perspective was explained by John Steel, the first General Manager of the Auckland Regional Authority:

"…the Local Bills Committee in reviewing the ineffective work of the Local Government Commission referred to '…the failure of Government to support the Commission's proposals…' and later to '…the inability of the Commission to get to grips with the Auckland problem…'

"The Committee noted that '…once again reform has been stifled and the pressure brought to bear by local political interests had been sufficient to render ineffectual a procedure which had been considered by the Parliamentary Select Committee of 1945 to be the most logical for bringing about local government reform. It again demonstrates quite clearly that the possibility of achieving any major reform must depend on resolute action by Parliament and Government." [169]

In his article, John Steel also observed:

"The picture presented by the Local Bills Committee is accurate and clear. The 'local political interests' are stronger than Government, and will continue to be so until Government adopts its rightful responsibility. The attitude of most local bodies is one of entrenched opposition, reinforced over the years by the power of inertia. The whole history of local government reform in New Zealand merely illustrates the power and strength of the local political jurisdictions, and it must be manifest that no substantial reform can be obtained by consent between local bodies.

"The public remains largely disinterested, local political parochialists regard themselves as the sole indispensable defenders of the rate, and Government, as ever, avows impotent concern. Notwithstanding such a formidable array of failure and defeat, the press, many enlightened and courageous citizens, and many Members of Parliament, continually engender rays of hope by a sober and intelligent appraisal of the subject which illumines the dark jungle of local body bias and prejudice." [169]

Administrative Confusion and Procrastination

As that *dark jungle* sought to house and otherwise nurture increasing numbers of people and their chattels, the expansion of the metropolis to predefined boundaries and beyond only added to what G T Bloomfield described in a lecture delivered to the Auckland Branch of the New Zealand Geographical Society in 1966 as *administrative confusion*:

"Public control, especially local authority control, has been characterised by much administrative confusion. The large number of Highway Districts constituted in the 1860s have remained until the 1960s as independent boroughs. The formation of *ad hoc* boards was often the only way to provide the facilities required – whether a harbour bridge, airport or even milk supply, but an excessive number of these *ad hoc* authorities had been established by the 1960s. Boundaries of the local authorities established in the mid-19th century when the area was rural now have little relevance when the city sprawls over such a large area." [6]

Sprawl

John Steel also blamed the growing process of *sprawl* for many of the problems experienced by cities such as Auckland:

"Basically and initially, the problems and shortcomings arise from the impact and various repercussions, resulting from rapid urbanisation. Urbanism, as an instrument for orderly, intelligent and coherent development, has been much neglected. City and regional planning is only now being recognised, somewhat belatedly, as the only means to meet, control and guide the rising tide of urbanisation.

"In retrospect, the entire political history of the need for local government reform in New Zealand has been one of conscious procrastination. As early as 1885, the Hon. R. Stout addressed the House of Representatives on the need for administrative reform. The matter was before Parliament from time to time, Bill after Bill was introduced and allowed to lapse, committees were formed, governments were changed, and nothing was done." [169]

Imagine There's No Government

Nevertheless, such a sad lack of Central Government support for local government reform and the resulting *administrative confusion* was by no means a barrier to Auckland's *rising tide of urbanisation*. As the then Chairman of the New Zealand Business Roundtable, Rob McLeod, pointed out in his address to the Howick Rotary Club in June 2004, entitled *Imagine There's No Government*:

"Great cities like London, Paris and Rome were built without anything like our modern planning laws. Much of the early design of New Zealand cities was done by the New Zealand Land Company. The first town and country planning statute in New Zealand dates only from 1926. There was fierce debate for many years before it was enacted, with many voices raised in opposition." [281]

Auckland's Population Growth

By 1961, the population of the Auckland urban area was estimated to have exceeded 448,000, an increase of some 17.7 per cent since the 1956 census. By 1963, the City's population had increased again to more than 550,000 souls. [282]

Not quite London, Paris, or Rome, but Auckland's new citizens had to live and work somewhere and, if their wants were to be efficiently provided for, some urban reform and planning was urgently needed.

Urban Reform and Planning Urgently Needed

This need was graphically described by R T Kennedy, Professor of Town Planning, University of Auckland, in his contribution to the series of lectures organised by, and delivered to, the New Zealand Geographical Society in 1966:

"The typical urban scene or townscape has become too varied, full and restless for visual comfort. The great majority of the city's inhabitants are distracted, confused and disturbed by it whether it be in Queen Street, Karangahape Road or in Broadway, Newmarket where, in the last place, it seems to have reached the limit of sheer ugliness. What might have continued to be acceptable visually is now made completely unacceptable and to many quite unendurable by the fumes, noise and bewildering movement of traffic.

"The state of visual confusion and traffic chaos in the principal commercial areas is also to be found in varying degree throughout the whole built-up area, in the heterogeneous mass of mixed industrial, commercial and residential areas and even in some of the most recent areas of suburban expansion. The streets may be swept and well lit, the sewerage and refuse collection a great improvement on the standards of a generation ago, but by themselves these things are not all that could be asked for in a tolerable urban environment.

"It is known that this state of affairs is avoidable and that town planning is expected to put matters right but town planning, either in the making of plans or in the exercise of planning control, has so far not affected any marked improvements in New Zealand. Much of what has been done in efforts to improve city conditions has been done not without planning thought, but not through the kind of planning for which the Town and Country planning legislation was provided." [283]

Auckland Regional Authority

By early 1960, the new Auckland Mayor, Dove-Myer Robinson, had managed to convince his Council and a majority of borough and county councils to form an establishment committee to advance his vision for an Auckland Regional Authority:

"…almost all the borough and county councils had agreed in principle to the creation of a regional authority and with this agreement Robinson was able to have an ARA Establishment Committee set up and empowered by statute." [158]

Auckland Regional Authority Establishment Act

That statute, the Auckland Regional Authority Establishment Act, enacted on 30 September 1960, provided "…for the establishment of a Committee to promote legislation in the form of a Local Bill to constitute a regional authority for the Auckland Regional Area." [284]

The Committee was to comprise:

"(a) The Mayor for the time being of the City of Auckland:

(b) The Mayors for the time being of the Boroughs of Helensville, East Coast Bays, Birkenhead, Northcote, Takapuna, Devonport, Henderson, New Lynn, Glen Eden, Mount Albert, Mount Roskill, Mount Eden, Newmarket, One Tree Hill, Onehunga, Ellerslie, Howick, Mount Wellington, Otahuhu, Papatoetoe, Manurewa, Papakura, Pukekohe, Tuakau, and Waiuku:

(c) The Chairmen for the time being of the Counties of Rodney, Waitemata, Manukau, and Franklin:

(d) The Chairman for the time being of the Town District of Warkworth:

(e) The Chairmen for the time being of the Auckland Transport Board, the Auckland Metropolitan Drainage Board, the North Shore Drainage Board, and the Auckland Regional Planning Authority:" [284]

Really in Business Now

As the Auckland Star described it on 3 November 1960, the Establishment Committee administration was in place:

"A missing nameplate on a door in the Town Hall and a new type of letter paper on the Mayor's desk were small signs today of one of the biggest moves in Auckland's history. The plate carried the name of Mr Noel Bell, senior committee clerk of the City Council. A new plate soon to go up will add the title, 'Secretary, Auckland Regional Authority Establishment Committee'. The new letter paper carries the committee's title, too, along with a drawing of the North Island, prepared by Town Hall officer Mr R Murphy, showing the area which the proposed authority will cover. 'You see? We're really in business now, said the Mayor, Mr D M Robinson, today.

"As secretary, Mr Bell is serving the sub-committees, appointed last week, which will have a variety of tasks designed to bring the authority into being with legislation to be introduced into Parliament next year. He is already busy arranging meeting dates and paving the way for negotiations with the ad hoc bodies, some of which would be merged in the proposed authority. The toughest tasks are expected to fall on the shoulders of the representation sub-committee, which will recommend the way in which authority members should be elected or appointed, and on the finance committee. Negotiations are to take place not only with ad hoc bodies willing to take part in the scheme at the start, but also with bodies which may be prepared to come within the authority's orbit after it is operating." [285]

The Planning of the Auckland Regional Authority

"The easy part was over. The Establishment Committee now had to draft a bill detailing a future ARA in specific terms – who would run it, how its members would be elected, what functions it would perform and how it would be funded. The committee had a statutory life of a year to do this…But Robinson's supporters were in the minority. Other mayors showed their tacit opposition by attending few of the meetings. From October 1960 until September 1961 the ARA Establishment Committee met 13 times.

"Ten mayors – almost a third of the membership – were present at less than half of the meetings, some attending only once or twice…It was, however, a smaller group of mayors who caused Robinson the most trouble. From the outset of the committee deliberations this group actively opposed parts of the reforms they believed threatened their own councils' powers and rating autonomy." [158]

As a result, the Establishment Committee failed to agree, a majority voting on 29 September 1961 to withdraw the draft ARA (1961) Bill from the consideration of

Parliament. According to Robinson, "One third of the opposition was against the chairman of the establishment committee (him), a third was due to parochial interest and a third arose from ignorance." [158]

An Extension of Time

Fortunately, the Auckland Regional Authority Establishment Act provided for an extension of time and this was duly granted. Dove-Myer Robinson now had another year to convince borough and county councils to agree to the composition and responsibilities of a regional authority. Convincing special purposes organizations such as the Auckland Harbour Board, Auckland Harbour Bridge Authority, Auckland Regional Planning Authority, Auckland Transport Board, the Auckland, Waitemata, and Franklin Power Boards, two Auckland Fire Boards, the Auckland and North Shore Drainage Boards that they should relinquish authority over their realms of influence was to prove even more difficult.

"Most heads of these boards had never considered compulsory incorporation a serious threat. Spencer (Norman Spencer, Auckland Transport Board Chairman) spoke for them when he said they all had a right and a duty to refuse to join the ARA if they considered it ran contrary to their duty to carry out their functions efficiently and economically. He refused to attend any more ARA Establishment Committee meetings." [158]

An Incomplete ARA

"Robinson realised there was only one way through the difficulty – he would have to give way on the inclusion of some of the special purpose boards. The ARA Establishment Committee had agreements with the planning, water supply, sewerage, airport, parks, pest control and civil defence agencies to join…Robinson wrote to the prime minister (Keith Holyoake) to tell him: *If Parliament does nothing but validate the agreement that has been made, we will have a strong and effective authority. You may be sure that we will not make the task of the Local Bills Committee of Parliament more difficult than it need be by making the approval of the bill contingent upon bringing into the authority bodies which have refused to join voluntarily.*" [158]

The Local Bills Committee

The Local Bills Committee considers, clause by clause, new private and local Bills introduced to Parliament as well as representations submitted to it from interested persons or organizations. At this particular time, the Committee included William John (Jack) Scott, Acting Chairman of the Committee and National Party Member of Parliament for Rodney, and Alfred Ernest Allen. Allen was the normal Committee Chairman but, because he also sat on the Board of the Auckland Electric Power Board, he stepped aside in favour of Scott during the ARA hearings.

Both were extremely critical of the regional authority concept with Allen quoted by The New Zealand Herald on 28 May 1963:

"Mr A.E. Allen, MP, chairman of the Local Bills Committee, declares the bill presented to Parliament by the Auckland Regional Authority Establishment Committee is *conflicting, confusing and contentious* in a speech to the Auckland Electric Power Board. *By failing to achieve agreement among the local bodies in Auckland, the establishment committee has shown itself incompetent to do the job.*" [286]

Super Cities Alternative

It came as no surprise to the likes of Dove-Myer Robinson and his supporters that both important and not-so-important politicians, and others, failed to understand that the

Bill's conciliatory provisions were needed to advance their objective of ultimately establishing a regional authority. What did surprise was that:

"Scott and Allen decided there would be other preconditions before the bill could proceed and unveiled what they believed was the real solution to Auckland's fragmented local government structure – compulsory amalgamation of the boroughs and counties into four or five large cities.

"They said they would dispatch the Local Government Commission to Auckland in the New Year to prepare plans for their multi-city vision...The other mayors were horrified that their jobs were in Scott and Allen's firing line...There was considerable newspaper coverage of the ambitious scheme the commission had for Auckland. No borough was to be spared in the creation of four super cities...By comparison, Robinson and his ARA were no longer deemed such a bad thing." [158]

Auckland Regional Authority Act 1963

Consequently, but only after some intervention by a sympathetic Prime Minister, Keith Holyoake, and other National and Opposition Labour MPs, the ARA Bill was eventually put to a Parliamentary vote. The legislation was finally passed as the Auckland Regional Authority Act 1963 on 25 October of that year.

The Authority's boundaries encompassed: "...the cities of Auckland and Takapuna; the Boroughs of Helensville, East Coast Bays, Birkenhead, Northcote, Devonport, Henderson, New Lynn, Glen Eden, Mount Albert, Mount Roskill, Mount Eden, Newmarket, One Tree Hill, Onehunga, Ellerslie, Howick, Mount Wellington, Otahuhu, Papatoetoe, Manurewa, Papakura, Pukekohe, Tuakau, and Waiuku; the Counties of Rodney, Waitemata, Manukau, and Franklin; the town district of Warkworth; and the road district of Waiheke." [287]

Also included as part of the ARA's responsibilities to be co-ordinated region-wide was a whole range of regional services and functions previously administered by the Auckland City Council and ad hoc boards, including bulk water supply, main sewerage (Auckland Metropolitan Drainage Board), the airport, regional roads and reserves (Auckland Centennial Memorial Park Board), and civil defence.

The ARA's responsibilities, also comprised the functions of the Auckland Regional Planning Authority which, at the same time, was constituted by the Auckland Regional Planning Authority Act 1963 as "...a body corporate with power to acquire lands for regional reserves in the greater Auckland area...(with) proper provision...(for)the bearing of the costs of acquiring and administering such lands." [288]

At last, on paper at least, some centralised planning of the whole Auckland region seemed possible. Section 45 of the Auckland Regional Authority Act 1963 also allowed the Authority to "...take over as going concerns and assume the functions, assets, and liabilities of..." both the Auckland Metropolitan Milk Board and the Auckland Transport Board. [287]

Auckland Transport Board Assimilated

"The Auckland Regional Authority was an elective body, elected triennially, which was funded by direct levy on the 30 territorial councils in the region and revenues from services and amenities, government grants and subsidies. It had four standing committees: Auckland Regional Board of Works; Auckland Regional Passenger Services Board; Planning Committee and a Policy and Finance Committee." [289]

The Auckland Transport Board was assimilated as the Auckland Regional Authority Transport Committee, responsible for main public transport arrangements and chaired by former Auckland Transport Board member, John Allsopp-Smith.

Political Compromise

But the ARA was not able to wrest from its powerful administrators the 'functions, assets, and liabilities' of the North Shore Drainage Board; the Auckland Metropolitan and North Shore Fire Boards; the Auckland, Waitemata, and Franklin Electric Power Boards; the Auckland Harbour Board; or the Auckland Harbour Bridge Authority. Those profitable entities remained the singular domains of some of the most prominent of Auckland's citizens.

As a result, the creation of the ARA was viewed by many as merely a political compromise that failed to fully accomplish the administrative ideal of a unified Greater Auckland.

This view was explained by John Edgar in his 1987, University of Waikato thesis, *Metropolitan Reform And Decision Making: Dove-Myer Robinson's Challenge To Local Body Morphological Fundamentalism*.

[Morphological Fundamentalism is defined by John Edgar in his thesis as: "…self-protective guardianship…The capacity of New Zealand local bodies to perceive their geographical identities and political autonomy as enduringly useful and to jealously protect these against proposals for structural change…" [164]

According to John Edgar, "The Auckland local bodies had accepted the Auckland Regional Authority not in ardour but as an act of political compromise to save their geographical identities from the threats of the Local Bills Committee and the Local Government Commission." [164]

"[Dove-Myer Robinson] had been quite explicit about the autonomy vested in the ARA. During the reform process he had maintained for instance:

"No machinery or organisation exists whereby this essential regional co-operation and action can be taken. The old wearisome process of negotiating, duckshoving, buckpassing and procrastination has to be gone through every time. [The ARA will be] an organisation powerful enough and farsighted enough to plan the future development of Auckland…an organisation that at long last can and will speak with one voice for Auckland.

"But there were people who had opposing viewpoints. They were prepared to question the Auckland Regional Authority's policies and in doing so they were endeavouring to preserve their political autonomy within the new two tier style of local government." [164]

"After the establishment of the Auckland Regional Authority, it was only a matter of time before morphological fundamentalism was again taken up by the municipal local bodies to protect the political authority and pre-eminence they had enjoyed in the preceding local government structure. In deference to the attitudes associated with the preceding Auckland local government – parochial jealousies and rivalries, consultation between municipalities and inter-municipal agreement on large works, resentment of the central city and timidity in relations with central government – succeeding Auckland Regional Authority chairmen, H D Lambie and T H Pearce had developed a benign regionalism for the Auckland Regional Authority.

"Its limited objectives were designed to pre-empt any challenge to the body and let the municipal bodies see the body as an extension of their own authority, successfully implementing objectives they had wanted but had not been able to agree on funding. In effect, morphological fundamentalism was being allowed to win by default." [164]

Benign Regionalism

This *benign regionalism* was

"…aptly summarised by a statement by Lambie to the Auckland Regional Authority Policy and Finance Committee in August 1967:

"Parliament set up the Auckland Regional Authority to do things which no other Authority was capable of doing. In other words Parliament infused into the structure of Government something between central government and local government…I have felt it imperative that the Auckland Regional Authority should create an image of co-operation and tolerance with an overriding willingness to serve rather than to control. If there was any suspicion that central government or local government would suffer as a result of Parliament creating this new creature, it could well be prevented from performing satisfactorily." [164]

Selective Governance

"Lambie had also believed that the special purpose bodies were doing an efficient job on their own. F W O Jones, Lambie's close friend who served as Director of Planning for the Auckland Regional Authority (1963-1974), recalled that Lambie felt the regional authority should emerge with the following 'Lincolnian' philosophy:

"We developed a theme on Abraham Lincoln's definition of government. The function of government is to do those things that need to be done and cannot be done at all or as well by the individual acting alone. We applied that to what was being done not by individuals but by individual local authorities. There were individual local authorities dealing with water, sewerage, transport and such things like that, but there were no authorities dealing with regional parks or co-ordinating regional roading. Looking back and following this through the right form of the authority was not a multi-purpose authority, but one that would handle functions not already performed and could have other functions added rather than taking them all in." [164]

"Lambie did consider public transportation to be a function existing local bodies could not administer by themselves and he supported the rapid rail scheme, as it emerged from the de Leuw Cather consultants commissioned by Robinson's Auckland Regional Authority in 1964.

"However, there was a pervading belief that the ARA performed separate and particular functions for the lower tier local bodies in Lambie's philosophy, rather than a conception of the authority as a leader organisation, which espoused an integrated plan for metropolitan development. This belief may well have militated against the sort of integrated planning and administrative approach that Robinson wanted of the authority and that was essential for an integrated transportation solution." [164]

Morphological Fundamentalism by Default

"The Auckland Regional Authority leadership worked then, to reassure the membership and the lower tier local bodies that there would be no great departure from the metropolitan programme like providing regional roading, better sewerage and regional reserves which the pre-metropolitan structure had agreed upon and had struggled to achieve in its clumsy fashion before the inception of the Auckland Regional Authority.

"At the same time, this emphasis upon basic functions did not engender parochial jealousy among the municipalities. The ARA was likely to be seen as implementing the policies of the lower tier municipalities. The latter were being encouraged to see the ARA as an extension of their own political authority, rather than as a separate, paramount body accountable only to itself and its levied ratepayers. While the Lambie/Pearce programme continued, the ARA's role and political position were unresolved. More importantly, local body councils' political autonomy was not challenged and morphological fundamentalism was allowed to win by default. The ARA was being accommodated by those within it into the former local government system." [164]

ARA Inaugural Report

In his report to the Auckland Regional Authority of 19 June 1964, its Chairman, Dove-Myer Robinson, presented his view of what he hoped a successful Authority would accomplish by way of improved passenger transport services:

"If this Authority is to be an effective, smooth working organisation, it must ensure the equitable distribution of costs over the whole area of benefit. But the determination of such area of benefit will require time and resolution on the part of all members to appraise carefully every aspect of the matter. Without a spirit of give and take, this Authority could be involved in a series of arguments over matters of only local or sectional interest. As such it could never function effectively, and would almost certainly fail to survive.

"We must therefore examine the situation very carefully because unless tolerance and reasonableness are shown in the present situation there is every possibility of weakening or destroying the Authority. More importantly, perhaps, we might defer indefinitely any possibility of inaugurating the public passenger transport system which is required by the travelling public, and which will be an essential factor in preventing catastrophic traffic congestion, and crippling roading costs…

"What are we trying to accomplish? The Authority has already approved in principle the production of a comprehensive public passenger transport plan. This will provide for the inauguration of a fully integrated passenger service to, from, and through every district in the region. When the plan is approved and implemented, every area will be assured of fast, cheap, comfortable, convenient and safe public passenger services. This should help to reduce the pressure on available road space resulting from the ever-mounting volume of motor vehicles. It should also greatly reduce the amount of capital required for, and the annual costs of, roading throughout the region.

"There can be no doubt that Auckland will be facing a crisis in traffic congestion and roading costs within a few years, unless action is taken immediately to avoid it. The Authority has recognised this by improving in principle the Passenger Transport survey. Such a survey, and the preparation of the resultant plan, including as it does integration of services, routes, timetables and fare schedules, will take some time – possibly twelve months. But even this delay will be worthwhile because the benefits to the citizens of the region, resulting from the adoption of such a plan, will be so great that nothing whatsoever should be allowed to jeopardize it."

"At all costs the Authority must press on with its plan for a fully coordinated public passenger transport service. The economic prosperity of the region – especially the industrial areas – may depend on it. Nothing, not even the temporary continuation of inequitable legislative provisions, must be allowed to delay the steps the Authority is taking to bring such a plan into being.

"It is clear that the sweeping changes resulting from the adoption of a new passenger transport plan cannot be effected under existing legislation. Before the approved scheme could be brought into action, new legislation would be required. Provision would have to be made to ensure coordination of publicly and privately owned bus services. Means of integrating buses with suburban railway services, ferries, and all other present and future services (including underground) will have to be given statutory authority. Altogether a whole host of new matters will have to be provided for in a new Bill to allow the Authority to bring such a plan to fruition.

"The boroughs concerned must be assured of the goodwill of the members of this Authority, and that members wish to remove all unfairness and at the same time provide them with the best possible passenger transport services as soon as possible." [290]

John Steel Observations

In his contribution to the series of lectures organised by, and delivered to, the New Zealand Geographical Society in 1966, Auckland Regional Authority General Manager, John Steel, observed:

"The creation of the Auckland Regional Authority to administer several services was a positive and courageous step in recognising that the existing local bodies were structurally inadequate to meet the regional needs of a fast-growing population. However, it is now apparent, after three years' operations, that the Auckland Regional Authority Act attained political feasibility essentially as a document of compromise, and eventually emerged from Parliament as another local body empowered to cope with only a few of the regional problems. Commendable as it is, and despite the fact that the Auckland Regional Authority has 'impressed everybody with its competence', it should be considerably more vigorous and aggressive, and, therefore, should be viewed as merely a first step towards sane local authority reform in the area. The *next step* should be equally positive and courageous, and deal with the excessive political jurisdiction in the area." [169]

John Steel continued: "The various investigations carried out by the author lead firmly and conclusively to the view that the present basis of representation of local authorities on the Auckland Regional Authority is deleterious to balanced political accountability and is not sound in democratic equity, and is conducive to dissension and dissatisfaction…on the present basis of representation, having regard to the multiplicity of local authorities, there is ample opportunity for considerable improvements on a more equitable basis.

"This can only be done by a reduction of the contributing local authorities and, in turn, such a logical change in territorial boundaries would have the eventual benefit of securing a much greater degree of mutual acquiescence and unanimity. At present, it can be reasonably argued that Auckland City is not under-represented, but that the balance of the region is over-represented. A reduction in the number of local bodies in the area is the simple and effective procedure to achieve a proper balance in representation." [169]

Furthermore, it was John Steel's view that such a *balance in representation* and thus the *future progress of the region* would not be achieved until the "…Government, the Local Government Commission, and all local authorities in the area…face the question boldly and openly…what is the 'role of local government in expanding Auckland'?

"If reasonable efficiency and economy in government is to be achieved, the existing governmental boundaries must be eliminated. They presently provide only a deterrent to efficient and logical services, and fail to recognise that Auckland is one metropolitan community, regardless of political boundaries…Few cities in the world have discussed the problems of local government fragmentation as much as Auckland during the last 60 years. Few cities have achieved less than Auckland." [169]

Population Growth

The lack of representative balance caused by Auckland's perpetual, *local government fragmentation*, as defined by John Steel, was of course only exacerbated as the City's population increased – the effects of which were described by an Auckland Star article published on 5 April 1967:

"The pattern has become familiar now. Every time statisticians and the planners make predictions about Auckland's growth they are forced within a few years to revise their estimates upwards. It was inevitable that the development boom throughout the country during the past five years would be reflected in an unexpectedly rapid increase in Auckland's population.

"Even so it is astonishing that the results of the 1966 census should cause such a drastic revision of the date by which the city population can expect to reach one million. Instead of 1986 the latest prediction is 1982-4. On the past record there is every chance that this estimate also will turn out to have been too conservative. In the five years between the 1961 and the 1966 census, Auckland's population growth was 20.6% – nearly double the national average...

"Much of the forward planning done in Auckland during the past few years has been based on estimates of growth now shown to be too timid. The need to meet the deadlines laid down in these plans therefore becomes doubly urgent. There seems to be a feeling in Wellington that some of the city's proposals, particularly in the field of transport and roading, are too ambitious. The opposite may be true...Why, for instance, should the Auckland Regional Authority be denied funds to protect the routes of future regional roads? And why should the Government withhold for a year a decision in principle on the De Leuw, Cather rail-bus proposals?

"An earlier decision on the city's major public transport system would involve no outlay of scarce capital. It would, however, enable the city to get ahead with an inner city plan that needs to be integrated not only with the Harbour Board's downtown scheme but also with the development of the outer suburbs.

"As the Regional Authority's figures show, the growth rate of some outer areas is spectacular. In the five years that preceded last year's census, Manukau grew by no less than 86.6%. Population explosions of this sort raise serious problems for the metropolis of the future. Motorways leading out of the city could stimulate ribbon housing and shopping development that would make Auckland one of the world's best (or worst) examples of urban sprawl.

"Does Auckland really want such a distinction? If not, more thought will have to be given to ways in which population growth can be absorbed within the metropolitan area already provided with roads, drains and other services.

"This will involve far-sighted action not only on transport but also on housing and urban redevelopment and town planning. As things stand the Regional Authority seems to lack the power to carry a comprehensive regional plan into effect. Is the Town and Country Planning Act, framed in 1953, adequate to meet the problems of a city growing far faster than envisaged then? In this, and other fields, the time may be coming when Auckland's size will warrant planning legislation and financial provisions different from those applicable to the rest of the country." [291]

Absolute Madness

During his visit to Auckland as part of a world-wide study trip, the President of the Town Planning Institute of Great Britain, Professor Arthur Ling, observed in an August 1969 edition of The Architects' Journal:

"Auckland's 600,000 population spreads over an area of 160 sq miles. The city once boasted a much greater size than the old London County, but only one-sixth its population. It is still spreading. The quarter-acre section status symbol is responsible, but how much longer can New Zealand afford this waste of land?

"As we passed through a typical suburb of bungalows, I asked our taxi driver. He had no doubts. 'Absolute madness.' Milk and meat production was being pushed further out. More land had to be claimed from the bush to make good the loss, and capital had already been spent on doing this. Services were longer and more expensive, so much so that Auckland could not afford to put the telephone and power lines underground.

"People had to travel further to work, but they were so scattered that transport services were uneconomic and more and more motorcars congested the centre. Few wanted so much lawn to mow, and at least they should build two-storey houses on half the land. He would make a good planning officer.

"But pioneer methods of subdividing land and freedom of ownership are the starting points for development which make town planning a 'follow the trend' activity. This in fact seemed to be the philosophy of the Auckland School of Planning, from whose chair Professor Kennedy retires at the end of this month.

"Since the low density suburb served by the motorcar was what the people wanted, that should be the starting point for planning. Mayor 'Robbie' however – the representative of the people and the only independent politician in New Zealand – cannot understand this (to him) negative attitude and has been battling for a rapid transit system to relieve the city of an impossible future burden of motorcars…" [292]

A Summary: Development in the Auckland Region

*The problems of a city growing far faster than envisaged…burdened by an impossible future of motorcars…*were certainly the predominant concerns of the Planning Division of the Auckland Regional Authority – as outlined in its May 1968 report, *A Summary: Development in the Auckland Region*. The summary comprised Regional Master Plan Survey Data and Preliminary Report series published during 1967 and formed the basic survey material from which regional planning proposals would be evolved.

In his forward to the Summary, the Chairman of the Authority's Planning & Reserves Committee, A R Turner, described the scope of the study:

"This publication is a summary of the principal information contained in, and conclusions drawn by, a series of comprehensive surveys and reports recently prepared by the staff of the Planning Division of the Auckland Regional Authority. The surveys were in the nature of a stocktaking of 'Auckland 1967' and the reports draw attention to current development trends and the wide range of problems found to be associated with rapid metropolitan growth. Also, they suggest some worthwhile regional planning objectives which will ensure the evolution of a more attractive and more efficient community.

"More than 90% of the region's land area is devoted to rural pursuits and will remain so for a considerable time. But approximately 90% of the population in the region live and work on the remaining 10% of the land. Auckland then is clearly a metropolitan-dominated region. In the past this metropolitan area has tended to develop in a fragmented and therefore uncoordinated way, largely because of artificial local body boundaries.

"If worthwhile regional planning goals are to be achieved, this tendency must be firmly resisted, for it has been aptly said by the late President John F Kennedy: '*The city and its suburbs are inter-dependent parts of a single community bound together by a web of transportation and other public facilities and by common economic interests. Bold programmes in individual jurisdictions are no longer enough. Increasingly, community development must be a co-operative venture towards the common goals of the metropolitan region as a whole.'*

"The purpose of this booklet is to provide a background against which the public of Auckland, led by the Authority and other local bodies, can evolve and adopt positive and acceptable statements of regional planning policy and programmes of action directed towards those common goals." [293]

The Planning Summary included:

"Existing Developed Areas

"Within the older parts of the metropolitan area, a stable or slowly changing pattern of trade catchments has developed. In the future, extension of the motorways network and the development of a system of regional roads could have an effect on this trading pattern, which could in turn have some influence in bringing about a gradual redistribution of commercial development.

"It is likely, however, that the inadequacy of parking space and the increasing conflict of pedestrians and vehicular traffic in older commercial centres, are the two factors most likely to stimulate the development of new shopping centres in competition with the old. Inadequately controlled development of this sort could lead to accelerated deterioration of older centres. The best defence against such competition would be to improve the older centres, but because of the multiplicity of ownerships and the capital costs involved, redevelopment of this magnitude presents considerable problems.

"The initiative for such work should come from the private developer. Local bodies could act as co-ordinating and planning agencies. The nature of the improvements which could be carried out vary from centre to centre, but the aim should generally be to improve the availability of parking, and to reduce the conflicts between the pedestrian and vehicular traffic.

"New Suburban Areas

"It is in the new suburban areas which will develop on the periphery of the present urban area over the next twenty years, that the greatest opportunity lies to bring about a pattern and form of commercial development which recognises the changing living patterns of today's urban society. The concept of planning units suggested in the new suburban areas should aim at the provision of a suburban type shopping for each population group of 15,000 or more. [294]

"Associated Uses

The Summary continued:

"While retail uses constitute the basic content of suburban commercial centres, associated office and service functions normally occupy a proportion of the space in each centre. Furthermore, if regional and suburban centres are to become truly a focus for the communities they serve, cultural and recreational facilities should be integrated with the commercial centres. All of these uses have similar requirements in regard to accessibility, and are generally compatible. In particular, integration of these uses would enable the one parking area to cater for all, because the peak demand in respect of each would occur at different times." [294]

"Passenger Transport

"Transportation in the Auckland Region is a major undertaking in terms of capital invested, employment, and the diversity of equipment needed:

- each day an average of nearly 1,000 people pass through Auckland international ports.
- each day approximately 20,000 people move in and out of the Region.
- over 1,000,000 personal trips are made daily in vehicles within the urban area.

This mass movement is increasing at the rate of about 6% per annum and it is obvious that careful planning and co-ordination of transport services is essential on both regional and national levels to ensure maximum efficiency and economic operation.

"**Regional**

"With 25% of New Zealand's population living in the Auckland Region the trip interchange with other parts of the country is high. While about 90% of all trips are made by road transport, the major highways outside the urban area are free of congestion at present except during holidays and weekends.

"Provision of additional capacity to cope with this congestion should be balanced against the needs of urban roads where weekday peaks occur causing delays to commercial and business traffic – delays which can be measured in increased transport costs. However, some expansion of travel in the main corridors will take place with increased urbanisation, and the gradual upgrading of all major roads in the region will be necessary to cater for this.

"In contrast to air and road transport, rail passenger transport within and beyond the region is declining due to a preference for more convenient door-to-door service provided by road transport; a faster, more comfortable and personal service provided by air; and a lessening of amenities provided by the Railways Department. Some rail services have been withdrawn and facilities have become unattractive and inconvenient to passengers. While the travelling public is obviously expressing a preference for other modes, the present situation of increasing capital expenditure on some modes, with under-utilization of capital investment in other, can be questioned in the light of overall transportation economics." [294]

"**Urban**

"A fresh approach to the urban transportation problem is required which will recognise the need to provide for the basic function of moving people in a manner most acceptable to the community both economically and socially. Transportation is too important and too costly a part of urban development to be left uncoordinated under the control of a group of public authorities and private companies. A single authority must be responsible for a comprehensive transportation plan which would provide for:

- an urban-wide implementation programme for major works, based on priorities determined by cost/benefit studies related to the entire urban area.
- co-ordinated collection and expenditure of transportation funds from which money would be allocated according to the above priorities.

"This co-ordinated planning and financing assumes greater significance now with reduced roading finance, a faster growing population and motor vehicle ownership than forecast, and possible delays in the implementation of the rail rapid transit proposals. [294]

"**The Road Network**

"The 1965 De Leuw, Cather Transportation Plan sets out broad proposals only for motorways, expressways, and urban arterial roads. It is now necessary to prepare a detailed plan. For efficiency the net-work requires classification by function and type into a hierarchy of roads from motorways down to local street level. At present, insufficient physical distinction between different road types leads to the indiscriminate use of roads with congestion of major arterials and wastage of space in residential streets.

"Planning standards must ensure satisfactory integration of roads with surrounding land uses, with particular attention given to the aesthetics of road design. Geometric standards must relate to the function and future needs of the road while some standardisation of cross-sectional elements of minor roads is desirable. An assessment of priorities for an urban road implementation plan must include needs studies, capacity analysis, cost/benefit studies. Consideration of operational improvements should be included in the implementation plan, there being many such inexpensive improvements which could achieve greater efficiency of the existing road net-work in Auckland.

"Public Transport

"An extensive and efficient public transport system is essential in a city of Auckland's size and growth potential and any investment in transportation must consider the economic benefits of public transport particularly in the major travel corridors. In order to be effective as an integral part of a transportation network, public transport must compete favourably with private transport in terms of door-to-door travel time, comfort and cost.

"In many respects the existing public transport system in Auckland fails to do this. While the central business district generates more than 50% of all public transport trips in Auckland the area is not well served since most bus routes skirt the major generating area and terminate on the fringe, as do the ferry and rail services.

"There are other deterrents to the use of public transport:

- little co-ordination of scheduling and fare systems
- few facilities for easy transfer from one system to another
- infrequent services in off-peak
- use of old equipment with little passenger appeal.

"De Leuw, Cather recommended spending about $40 million (based on 1964 costs) on a comprehensive transport system to meet the 1986 requirements. Not to introduce such a scheme could be more costly when the alternatives of additional motorway lanes, parking facilities, surface street improvements, motor vehicles, traffic engineering and control, and the cost of congestion are considered..." [294]

Ministry of Transport Act 1968

On the national front, the Government introduced the Ministry of Transport Act 1968 which was duly passed by Parliament on 25 November of that year. Described as "An Act to establish the Ministry of Transport to provide for the development and administration of an efficient and economical transport policy for New Zealand, and to provide for matters incidental thereto". [295]

The new Ministry was assigned the functions of:

"(a) It shall be responsible for advising the Minister on the development of an efficient transport policy for New Zealand:

"(b) It shall undertake research into all aspects of transportation, including the economics of the various forms of transport, whether by road, rail, sea, or air:

"(c) It shall be responsible for advising the Minister on investment in transport, whether by road, rail, sea, or air, with particular reference to priorities for Government or other expenditure:

"(d) It shall maintain close liaison with the New Zealand Government Railways Department, the Marine Department, the New Zealand National Airways Corporation, Air New Zealand Limited, and other Departments of State and public corporations which are concerned with transport." [295]

Transport Advisory Council

The Ministry of Transport Act also established a Transport Advisory Council comprising:

"(a) The Minister of Transport [as Chairman] (b) The Minister of Marine [as Deputy Chairman] (c) The Secretary for Transport (d) One member, to represent the National Roads Board (e) One member, to represent the road transport industry (f) One member, to represent the aviation industry (g) One member, to represent the shipping industry (h) One member, to represent the Transport Commission (i) One member, to represent the farming industry (j) One member, to represent commerce and industry other than farming (k) One member, to represent the New Zealand Federation of Labour (1) One member, to represent local government (m) One officer of the New Zealand Government Railways Department…(n) One officer of the Treasury…" [295]

Transport Advisory Council Abolished

While many of its responsibilities were varied and superseded over the years, the Transport Advisory Council continued as an advisory body until September 1990 when it was abolished by the Ministry of Transport Act Repeal Act 1990 and replaced by a Road Traffic Safety Research Council.

The Practical Politics of Achieving Success in Planning and Implementation

In the meantime, the practical politics of local body planning continued. In his address entitled *The Practical Politics of Achieving Success in Planning and Implementation*, presented to the Australian Institute of Urban Studies Conference in Canberra on 10 July 1969, Dove-Myer Robinson, as Mayor of Auckland and a former Chairman of the Auckland Regional Authority, included the following advice about urban and regional planning:

"In planning the development of urban areas we are interfering with the right of the individual to do as he pleases. No longer can he be sure that he will be allowed to build a house, a shop or a factory anywhere he chooses. Soon, because of the confusion and congestion caused by the unregulated use of private motor cars, he will not be allowed the free use of his car on public roads.

"Undesirable as is regulation of the lives of others; because of the rapid population expansion, planning and its implementation is absolutely essential, if people are to live, work and play without anarchical and ruthless infringement on the rights of other members of his community. It is only natural that many people will not understand the need for planning and that they will resist it, and where their interests are directly and detrimentally affected, the resistance will be very strong indeed. If my conception of the need for and objectives of planning is correct, then we must be conscious of what we are doing, why we are doing it, and how to achieve it…" [296]

"Planning in the sense in which I am speaking today means, of course, provision for the physical, social and economic development of a country, a region, or a city and its people.

"But speaking as a local authority member, responsible for planning an inner city and also a region of some 2,000 square miles, of which the city is the heart, I am conscious that planning involves social and economic factors that require deep understanding in order to plan the future physical environment in the best interests of the people. To do this effectively it is necessary to understand the historical role of the part played by central cities in the development of metropolitan areas.

"Questions such as avoidance of fragmentation of local government and the prevention of urban sprawl, the conflict of interest of parochial local bodies, spreading the financial burdens of development equitably, and a host of other purely political considerations, have to be taken into account by the local body politician who wishes to turn his untrained hand to wisely and effectively planning the future…Here indeed is need for broad-based strategy with almost visionary conceptions of desirable objectives; planning for residential, commercial, retailing and industrial developments; transportation systems designed to encourage desirable forms of development or restrain undesirable.

"So that our amateur untrained politician must be a dreamer imbued with a very wide outlook, but possessing also a realistic appreciation of his limitations. Unfortunately, local body members with these attributes are all too rare, yet on the other hand, when found, even one individual occupying a strategically important position can influence dramatically not only the planning, but also the economic and social development of the area within his domain.

"He must be possessed of almost clairvoyant foresight, and a Messianic dedication, yet with a clear eyed appreciation of the limitations of the financial and political possibilities. He must be prepared to spend long hours on his 'homework', studying both the theoretical and practical aspects of the subject. At one moment he must be able to rise above the clouds and inspire his colleagues and their officers with his dreams, yet he must be capable of cool appraisal of the realities of the situation. Such men are rare – but on finding, keeping and using such people to maximum advantage depends the future successful planning of our cities, towns and countries of the future, and avoidance of social upheavals…" [296]

"Politics is called 'the art of the possible' or 'the art of compromise', and planning may be referred to as 'the art of the impossible'. But these negative potentialities must be vigorously repressed. Compromise on major principles must never be accepted, and the politician must be prepared occasionally to propose the seeming impossible, whilst joining the professional planner in keeping his eyes on the objective, and his feet on the ground. As in military campaigns, the greatest single asset is judgment based on experience, so it is in planning…

"In New Zealand we have difficulties peculiar to a small country with a basically agricultural economy. We often exercise the best and the most skilful judgment, think we know exactly the plan which will fit the particular circumstance and which will be the most satisfactory. We often have all the information and 'know-how' necessary to implement the plan, but even if the plan is the best, the most exciting, the least costly, and the most economical, we often lack the funds to bring it to fruition.

"Particularly in Auckland we have many large development plans such as a transportation plan, motorways plan, rapid rail transit plan, urban renewal plan (both residential and commercial), civic projects, marinas, and many others, all adding up to hundreds of millions of dollars. It is so easy to dream – and of course these plans <u>are</u> essential and they must sometime be implemented – but, and it is always this same 'but' – what about finance?

"Once again I revert to my theme that planning for development and redevelopment can be carried out in the way of a military campaign. Money is always, somehow, found for war; is finance, to create the kind of environment we want to live in, any way less essential?

"In New Zealand and in Auckland in particular, where the regional population will soon reach the million mark, we need a lot of finance to enable us to bring to completion the many development plans we have. But of even greater importance we need enlightened understanding, humane leadership initiative, drive, tenacity and the ability to seek, evaluate and accept advice from trained planners, and the capacity to use this advice to make the right decisions. Conditions are rapidly changing, and the measure of our success will, to a large extent, depend on how well we are served with information on which to base our decisions. This can, at times, be our biggest problem..." [296]

Urban Renewal

The *many large development plans* for Auckland referred to by Dove-Myer Robinson were contained in the Auckland City Council's District Scheme which became operative in June 1961. The Scheme included the long overdue renewal of the City's older suburbs such as the Freemans Bay Reclamation Area. However, by 1969, the much-needed renewal of Freemans Bay and other redevelopment had been delayed by transport-related indecision – as explained by Mayor Robinson in a statement dated 30 July 1969:

"For over 20 years, the City Council has been struggling to get a firm permanent policy agreed by Government, and it is only because successive Governments have refused to face up to the issue that so little progress has been made. Even the recently announced decision to redevelop a 3¼ acre block in Hobson Street and provide car parking, bus terminal and rapid rail station, with the approval of the Local Authorities Loans Board, is entirely dependent upon early agreement with the Government on financing and target dates for completion of the rapid rail proposals.

"Coincidentally, we have been informed that the Minister of Housing, the Honourable John Rae, is to meet representatives of Council tomorrow, Friday, to discuss the question of Government subsidies for urban renewal which of course, in particular, affects the Freemans Bay redevelopment proposals.

"Members of Council concerned with redevelopment spent 2½ hours with seven senior members of Council's staff on Tuesday afternoon of this week, discussing proposals for the reorganisation of Council's internal administration, so as to better equip Council and its staff to cope more expeditiously with all the development and redevelopment proposals before us, immediately we get the green light from the Government regarding subsidies for redevelopment of decadent areas and final decisions on the bus-rail rapid rail transit proposals which are of crucial importance before a real start can be made.

"Auckland is on the threshold of the greatest leap forward in the development of the city and the metropolitan area, and all that is necessary to trigger off this ever-widening developmental activity is agreement with the Government. The whole question of Auckland's future is fairly and squarely in the lap of the Government, and neither the City Council nor the Regional Authority can make much progress in these matters until the Government has decided to give Auckland its fair share of the country's economic resources." [297]

Redevelopment on Hold

On the same day, Mayor Robinson wrote to the Editor of The New Zealand Herald, Mr O S Hintz, expressing his gratitude for the recent publication of various articles about the deferred Freemans Bay project and the Policy of the Civic Action Party on City Transport:

"As a matter of interest, I had a letter only this morning from the Fletcher organisation, regarding the proposed Auckland City Council redevelopment in Hobson Street and the Freemans Bay area. They inform me that they are well ahead with their feasibility studies, and there is no doubt that within a very short time we will receive a proposal from them to undertake this large redevelopment project.

"Unfortunately, however, we will not be able to take this any further from then until we have a definite undertaking from the Government regarding the financing and, even more important, the target dates for the coming into operation of the rapid rail transit scheme. This is the reason why we are compelled at this awkward time, just before a General Election, to press the Government for an early answer. Otherwise, the whole of the City Council's and the Regional Authority's planning for development and redevelopment will grind to a halt." [298]

ARA Constrictions & Achievements

The very real constrictions imposed on the Auckland Regional Authority by the Government were explained in a brief extract from the report of the Local Government Commission to Parliament in July 1969. The extract was provided in a letter from Dove-Myer Robinson to a critic of the Authority's role, Mr L K Brown:

"The regional authority is not a form of two-tier local government. Like territorial local authorities, the regional authority is a 'creature of statute'. It may do only those things which Parliament has given it authority to do. It is subject to very much the same rules, checks and restraints and subject to very much the same requirements as they are – on the raising and expenditure of money, on banking and investment, the raising of loans, the annual preparation and audit of accounts, disclosure of records and the rest. It certainly has no mandate to spend what it likes and demand that the local authorities foot the bill.

"In fact evidence was presented to us [the Commission] that the Auckland Regional Authority has in its comparatively brief term achieved impressive savings. In three of its four budgets it has reduced its levies. Its levy was stated to be less than the aggregate of the levies of the several ad hoc bodies it took over and its administrative staff fewer by 50 than the total administrative staff employed by those bodies. These economies have been effected despite the carrying out of a wider range of functions than previously performed by the ad hoc bodies." [299]

Core City or Satellites?

While the redevelopment of Auckland's older suburbs remained in limbo, the steady expansion of the City's infrastructure continued to its suburbs and beyond. The correlation of this expansion with the need for a form of public passenger transport was the theme of a number of submissions made to the Committee of Inquiry into Urban Passenger Transport (Carter Inquiry) (as described in the next chapter) which sat in Auckland during March and June 1969:

Civic Action Party Inc. – Michael Alan Charles Hart, President

"This submission is particularly directed at Item 3 of the Committee's terms of reference, that is, the relative levels of services of public and private transport and the integration of public passenger transport and town planning.

"It is common sense as well as a recognized planning principle to acknowledge that transport needs arise in response to the demands of a land uses. Without land uses there would be no need for transport. As land uses exhibit certain characteristics of type, intensity and location, transport must respond to these characteristics. In general terms as land uses intensify, their demands, or traffic generation characteristics, similarly intensify. As land uses diversify their generation is similarly diversified. As they locate in certain patterns the demand is for a system of connections which reflects these patterns. Transport is not entirely subservient to land use to the extent that patterns of transport may influence the location of certain land uses. However while transport is one of many factors affecting land use location, the transport system exists solely to serve those land uses and for its efficiency must ultimately rely on the manner in which it connects the various parts of the system.

"It should be obvious that any development of urban passenger transport must take account of the likely future distribution of land use. It is my submission that to date insufficient attention has been paid to this question of future land use patterns in Auckland. Those predictions that have been made appear to rely heavily on an intuitive approach and consequently do not provide sufficiently certain data on which major investments on transport should be committed…

"I consider it important to emphasise this trend in land use for all the recent work on transport in Auckland has in my opinion been based on the unverified traditional hypothesis that the C.B.D. will continue to expand and dominate the metropolitan region in employment and that although the population increases are peripherally located the predominant transport demand will be for C.B.D. orientated trips.

"The Auckland Regional Authority planning data used as a basis for the De Leuw Cather transportation study reflects this traditional hypothesis and as I understand it was derived in an intuitive manner and not by the systematic evaluation of the factors influencing the patterns of urban growth.

"Had the Regional Authority adopted the hypothesis of decentralisation rather than that of continued C.B.D. growth, the findings of the De Leuw Cather study could have been quite different from those which were actually presented and upon which much of the current promotion of a rapid rail transit scheme is based. All this should emphasise the necessity to establish empirically the form of the urban system in Auckland as the fundamental basis for transport decision-making…

"In determining the most appropriate form of transport to suit the predicted pattern of urban growth the evaluation should be based on cost benefit analysis. Before the alternatives are evaluated standards of environment and standards of travel should be determined. The alternatives can then be tested against these standards. Depending on whether the cost limit is stated the choice can be made on what mode or combination of modes provides the greatest benefits for the stated cost, or alternatively the choice can be made on the basis of which proposals allow the attainment of the desire of environmental and travel standards at the lowest cost." [300]

David Adrian Clarkson Dodds – Chairman, Policy Committee, Civic Action Party Inc. and Auckland City Council staff member

"…it is my contention that land use planning…has not kept pace with transport planning…in considering transport in Auckland it is essential at all times to regard this as a metropolitan facility, that the basis for planning, the basis for study of this must be the metropolitan area. Any other division occurring to statutory boundaries is just quite ludicrous. The other point I would like to make is that it is in my opinion extremely dangerous to directly compare the Auckland situation with overseas cities. I think this needs to be emphasised because there has been quite an amount of this done before to justify one point of view or another. I think there are valid lessons we can learn from overseas but I do say it is very dangerous to compare overseas cities with Auckland. This is a very different area from areas overseas." [301]

City Central v Satellite Cities

The latter submission to the Urban Passenger Transport Committee drew a response from the City Council's Acting Director of Works & City Engineer, B D Duffield, who immediately wrote to the Town Clerk on 12 June 1969:

"My attention has been drawn by His Worship the Mayor to a report in this morning's 'Herald' on submissions made by a member of Council's staff to the Commission of Enquiry on Urban Transport. From enquiries made I have ascertained that Mr Dodd (sic) made his submissions in a private capacity and with the personal knowledge of His Worship the Mayor even to the extent of having given a copy of his submissions to His Worship some months ago.

"In his submissions Mr Dodd (sic) criticises the basic data on which De Leuw Cather's forecasts on future growth in the City are made. These limitations were fully appreciated by De Leuw Cather and by Regional Authority officers who supplied the basic land use and other data, as were the limitations inherent in any forecasts made from this data. In this regard I would quote from the report on the Comprehensive Transportation Plan prepared by De Leuw Cather: 'In preparing the trip forecast it was assumed that aggressive policies on the part of the central area commercial establishments and governmental agencies would be maintained, to enhance and preserve the inherent strength and advantages of central location.'

"In his submissions as reported it appears Mr Dodd (sic) is relying on past trends to dictate a form of city where the central city's role is of lesser importance with the formation of a number of smaller outlying city centres.

"Council's policy is to arrest and modify this trend to ensure that the Central Area is not only a commercial and employment centre of some strength but also a social and cultural centre of a stature which is worthy of the Region as a whole. In accordance with and to further this policy, the Council adopted the Transportation proposals of De Leuw Cather because it is evident from experience in larger cities throughout the world that there are many disadvantages in attempting to rely solely on automotive transportation to handle massive peak-hour traffic loads.

"Such a policy would result in enormous financial burdens involved in acquiring rights-of-way and constructing motorways, in addition to the costly parking structures required for day storage in the central city, and would deprive the city of the benefits referred to above." [302]

'Core City' Principle

This argument for the principle of the 'core city' to remain the predominant focus of all future infrastructure planning continued to divide Auckland's many local and regional bodies. This was illustrated by a Dove-Myer Robinson comment published by The New Zealand Herald on 3 September 1969:

"Satellite cities around Auckland would be much more expensive than the present course of development, and would not solve the basic transport problems, says the Mayor of Auckland, Mr D M Robinson, who is chairman of the rapid transit committee of the Auckland Regional Authority.

"In a letter to the editor of the Herald, replying to comments published yesterday morning by the Mayor of Takapuna, Mr A F Thomas, Mr Robinson says:

"It is understandable that Mr Thomas, Mayor of Takapuna – a satellite city itself – should favour the 'satellite city' principle of urban development. This might have been practicable if we were planning an entirely new city, but Auckland is already committed to what is called the 'core city' principle by 130 years of development. To contemplate the promotion of decentralised satellite cities now, would be vastly more costly than the further development and rationalisation of the present form.

"The provision to satellite 'cities' of essential services such as water, sewerage, roading, power, transport and other services, would be enormously more expensive than the present proposals for the development of the urban area based on a rapid transit transportation system.

"The central business district of the city is the hub of the region, into and through which flows a vast volume of traffic from outer areas. The more widespread these outer areas (satellite cities) become, the more transportation, both public and private, will be required; increasing the numbers of cars, trucks and buses which will have to use the street system of the city and surrounding boroughs, even when the rapid transit system is in operation...

"Mr Thomas' suggestion that the transportation needs of Auckland could be met by upgrading, extending and perpetuating the all-bus system, is completely impracticable. Mr Thomas is himself the main opponent of the extension of Regional Authority services to the North Shore. His scheme requires priority for buses on express routes and access to the central city on reserved rights-of-way. It is notable that the Takapuna City Council shows no sign of doing this in or around the congested areas of Takapuna, the obvious reason being that Takapuna is in the same situation as the city – a deficiency of street space. There simply is not enough room to provide for separate bus routes or to provide more roading for private motorcars than has already been planned.

"The answer to the problem is maximum accessibility for all vehicles to the central business district, which will be considerably helped by taking a major proportion of movement on to separate rights-of-way underground. To leave all public transport above ground and exclude private vehicles is negative thinking. What is needed is improvements, not restrictions. Mr Thomas' support for the satellite city principle appears to be based on a misconception of the place of the central business district.

"The former chairman of the Auckland Regional Authority, Mr Hugh Lambie, who was himself at that time Mayor of Manukau City, in an ARA leaflet, said –

"The place of the central business district: Whatever decentralisation takes place as the city grows the central business district of the largest city in New Zealand must remain an all-important focal point of business and commercial activity. Provided its accessibility can be maintained, it must remain the most valuable, the most sought-after and perhaps in certain respects, the most important land in New Zealand. As a city such as Auckland grows, some degree of decentralisation is not only inevitable but desirable in the interests of efficiency. But in some respects decentralisation may be more apparent than real. As suburban areas grow, so a larger proportion of the total retail function is located outside of the central business district – employment and industry become more dispersed. All of these things are natural and indisputable, but the real business and commerce of the city continues – the port, the Government, local government, civic

functions, the university, technical institute, hotels, Customs, banking, insurance, export-import activities - all of these things must grow to serve not only an expanding region but a strongly growing province.'

"The fact is that the North Shore and southern areas of Auckland are integral parts of the urban area of Auckland – not separate cities – nor can they ever be turned into satellites of Auckland, whatever decentralisation might take place. The concept of development in Auckland is a controlled growth of the main urban area in certain directions, served by main corridors of movement with a growth of residential and employment opportunities in centres such as Waiuku and Pukekohe (which is taking place today). It is the main urban areas of Auckland which will need an effective public passenger transport system, come what may.

"The alternative – if it is an alternative – would be to draw a tight and rigid line or fence around the existing urban development boundary, prohibit any further growth and then possibly create new towns some distance away. This is impracticable – it is not what people want – it would be most costly with the creation of new drainage systems and water supply systems, new civic amenities and other services. Above all, it would not prevent the need for a public passenger transport system in Auckland…

"Mr Thomas is quite right in saying that there are many alternatives to the present rapid transit proposals. But all known alternatives have been scientifically examined and rejected by such authorities as Halcrow-Thomas, De Leuw, Cather, Professor Buchanan, Professor Ling [President of the Town Planning Institute of Great Britain], the Auckland Regional Authority, the Auckland City Council, and the Government's own 'Officials Committee'.

"As Mr Lambie said two years ago – *'Any scheme or plan involving the expenditure of public funds needs fair and careful examination on its merits – and at all times we must welcome, as a public authority, any examination of any plan we are concerned with on its merits. Putting forward an alternative scheme is not necessarily examining the original scheme on its merits – an alternative must arise out of a logical process of economic and physical analysis; put forward purely as an alternative, it is the surest way of 'killing' any scheme.'*

"It is recognised that the roading, railway, buses and other facilities required to provide Auckland with the public transportation system which is necessary within the next 20 years, will be very costly. Present figures indicate that roading alone, without rapid transit, would cost $600 million. With rapid transit, the cost will be between $430 million and $450 million; a saving of at least $150 million against an all-bus system, suggested by Mr Thomas.

"If the satellite city proposals advocated by Mr Thomas were ever adopted, it would be necessary to add to this minimum of $450 million several hundred millions of dollars for additional roading, sewerage, water supply and other services. There is no doubt that the present scheme is not only by far the least costly, but is the only one which will guarantee the maximum prevention of urban sprawl and traffic congestion but which will at the same time provide Auckland with a satisfactory public transportation system." [303]

Social Planning Responsibilities

As a final conclusion to a decade of little progress toward needed urban renewal and a satisfactory public transportation system, Councillor E P Salmon of the Auckland City Council's Urban Renewal Committee reminded the Council of its social planning responsibilities in a report presented on 10 December 1969:

"Social planning it is now a catch phrase covering an important area which must be the concern of any enlightened community. It isn't an end in itself, but must be recognised as part – an important part – of planning in general: physical planning of a city, economic planning and all those other facets which are part of planning in general. It is too serious a matter to be left only to specialists and social planners; it involves everybody and certainly members of this Council should know the basic factors of social planning. I do hope Councillors will not fight shy of their responsibility to learn and to understand what is involved.

"New Zealand, with the utmost goodwill, has produced houses – but not homes. It has tended towards places to live in, but not towns; environments but not communities. When town planning is discussed the needs and desires of people are often overlooked.

"The two items on the report of the Urban Renewal Committee underline a recognition by this City Council of its moral obligation to provide for the welfare of its citizens – of all its citizens…Auckland is fortunate in the calibre of the men – and women – working on town planning in general, and in specialised fields. The Central Area Study has been a big task extending over some years. Survey work as part of the study has involved data collection covering some 6,000 establishments with a total floor area of nearly 30,000 million square feet in the Central Area. This information is stored on magnetic tape. Staff resources have limited the progress on basic mapping and preparation of reports on use of floor space.

"Employment within the Area has been surveyed, as well as the distribution, age and condition of buildings. This information is on punched cards which must be constantly updated.

"A model of the Central Area has been on exhibition a number of times and has proved useful and of considerable interest. Monographs have been prepared on such subjects as the influences which have affected the growth of the Central Area, the visual character of the area, pedestrian movement in the city, possible growth points and, not least of all, transportation and traffic flow.

"I have asked for the preparation of a plan and proposals covering the inner city so that the Town Planning Committee can recommend to Council the adoption of a Statement of Intention. The statement would guide Council and Council Officers, developers and investors, commerce and industry – and home seekers. The Statement of Intention would remain flexible but would provide a blueprint for the city of the future.

"In this study people must not be overlooked: their desires and needs for living and working, play and education, general welfare. The people of this City must be the prime concern of any sort of planning. In this context then…a joint committee of Council and social workers…has set up a sub-committee to bring down proposals covering the social aspects of planning and, more particularly, the welfare of residents in Ponsonby and Freemans Bay. Ponsonby area is in a transitional stage; Freemans Bay is an area to be planned as a 'new town' within the City limits. We welcome the co-operation of the social workers of this City.

"I asked for a report on the sort of social work now being carried out. This report lists some 60 organisations concerned, but the total number probably runs to nearer 100. I feel that Council has a duty to give a lead in co-ordinating these activities. Some overlap, but there are obvious gaps which should be filled. A primary function of the working committee must be to schedule the City's objectives. Obvious ones are the provision of better housing and a more pleasant environment, social and welfare centres, recreation and education facilities…" [304]

Gas Pedal to Back-Pedal　　　　　　　　　　　　　　　　　　　Chapter Four

Public Transport
Auckland Metropolitan Council
One of the more predominant issues dividing the City's local body leaders was the question of subsidising the public transport losses incurred by the Transport Board. These losses had resulted in the Board having to levy its constituent local bodies for the first time in 1954 – an imposition viewed as an additional tax on ratepayers, whether fare-paying, tram and bus passengers, or not.

As a means of reaching some agreement on a plan to provide public transport services at less cost, Mayor John Luxford established a forum for local body leaders called the *Auckland Metropolitan Council*. This forum subsequently appointed a *Passenger Transport Committee* which, in due course, proposed the establishment of a *Metropolitan Transport Authority* to:

"…enquire into and bring down a report as to the system of operation and co-ordination of passenger transport services best suited in the Metropolitan Area of Auckland." [195]

Metropolitan Transport Authority
Part of the Passenger Transport Committee's final recommendations when delivered in September 1956, included the establishment of a Metropolitan Transport Authority or Corporation "…To be elected on a ward basis…To take over and operate the services of the Auckland Transport Board…" [195]

This recommendation to establish a *Metropolitan Transport Authority or Corporation* would find favour as one of the responsibilities of what would eventually become the *Auckland Regional Authority* but that was not established until 1963. In the meantime, the Auckland Transport Board maintained its oversight of the City's public transport services.

Auckland Regional Authority Establishment Committee
It was not until August 1960 that the original Passenger Transport Committee's report was referred to an *Auckland Regional Authority Establishment Committee* by the Minister of Transport. The report was subsequently referred to the Establishment Committee's *Passenger Transport Sub-Committee*, chaired by Transport Board Chairman, Norman Berridge Spencer. The sub-committee amended the original recommendations to include:

"(a) That the Auckland Regional Authority control all public transport in the Auckland Region, with the exception of the Counties of Rodney and Franklin and the Borough of Helensville and the Town District of Warkworth in conformity with the policy of the Establishment Committee, hereafter called the Auckland Regional Transport Area.

(b) The operative area to mean that portion of the Regional Area over which the Regional Transport Authority for the time being is itself operating mass transportation services.

"For these purposes the Authority shall:
(i) Take over and operate the services of the Auckland Transport Board.
(ii) Keep in close touch with the passenger transport needs of the regional area and ensure that these are met.
(iii) Have the right at the request of the local authority controlling any portion of the Auckland Regional Transport area not included in the operative area, to take over and provide services in any such portion of the area as and when the existing private operators

wish to discontinue operations or dispose of their services other than to another private operator.

(iv) Co-ordinate all services within the operative area.

(v) License all bus and taxi services operating solely within the regional area except that no licence should be required for services operated by the Regional Authority, except when any change in service affects a private operator there should be the right of appeal to the Transport Appeal Authority.

(vi) Fix fares on its own services.

(vii) Maintain a close liaison with the traffic control authorities for the purpose of ensuring maximum efficiency in street utilisation.

(viii) Have all such additional powers as may be necessary to enable the Authority to fulfil the basic requirement of providing reasonable mass passenger transportation facilities within the whole or any portion of the area." [305]

Financing the Cost of Transport

As Chairman of the Passenger Transport Sub-Committee, Norman Spencer obviously supported the establishment of a Regional Authority. He no doubt saw such an Authority as a means to establishing a financial arrangement that did not rely on the levying of constituent local bodies and their ratepayers, many of whom were now motor vehicle owners and no longer public transport users:

"The Committee feels that with the rising costs of transport everywhere, the public could be served better if the Regional Authority could find some method of financing the cost of transport other than a levy on ratepayers or increased fares." [305]

Conflict of Interest

Nevertheless, as Auckland Transport Board Chairman, Norman Spencer also remained dedicated to the continuance of the Board's responsibilities independent of the establishment of any such Authority. This was made clear in his Annual Report for the financial year ended 31 March 1960:

"Auckland Regional Authority: The Board has given its support to a Bill for the purpose of setting up a statutory committee of representatives of all the local authorities concerned to prepare a further Bill for the subsequent constitution of an Auckland Regional Authority to coordinate services of a metropolitan character, such as water, drainage, fire-fighting, transport and electric power. This action does not at this stage commit the Board to participation in the Regional Authority and the matter will be considered again when the proposals of the statutory committee become available." [306]

User Should Pay

Pending the realisation of such an Authority, the Transport Board sought alternative methods of financing the Board's losses – as was made clear in the same Annual Report:

"Net loss £69,039 (previous year £96,214)…This favourable situation is in the main resultant on the Board's prompt action in passing on to those who use its services the extra wage cost imposed firstly by the General Order of the Court of Arbitration issued in September, and secondly by other increases in the wages bill…The Board has only two sources of revenue from which to recover increased costs, either an increase in fares or an increased levy on ratepayers and in accordance with its policy of steadily reducing the levy, it decided that the user should pay.

"Total revenue from all sources for the year, but not including the levy of £106,505 was £1,686,719, which amount is £9012 (.54%) more than the previous year's total.

Working expenses amounted to £1,386,956, an increase of £22,358 (1.64%) compared with the previous year's figures." [306]

Path to Modernisation

In the meantime, the Transport Board continued on its own path to modernisation, including the construction of a new headquarters which could only cement its position as the sole entity suited to the management of Auckland's public transport. If only the City Council could keep up…

"Conversion to trolleybus operation of all former main line tram services is now completed and work is in progress on removal of the last remaining tram tracks. There remains only the erection of a new head office building to complete the entire Modernisation of the Board's undertaking. Construction of the new building has begun and it is hoped that the staff will be in occupation before the end of 1961.

"Development of the services is in no sense at a standstill with the completion of modernisation, and services will continue to be extended where such action is warranted and the condition of the road surface concerned will permit. In July last the Benson Road bus service was extended during off-peak hours to Lucerne Road and a cross-country bus service was instituted also during off-peak hours between Point Chevalier and Glen Innes, serving en route the hospitals in Green Lane.

"In November the May Road portion of the Mount Roskill trolleybus service was extended along White Swan Road to a new terminus at Griffen Road. A proposed extension of the Owairaka service along Richardson Road to New Windsor Road is held up until such time as the Auckland City Council improves the road surface to a standard suitable for modern buses." [306]

City Council Rejects Bus Shelters and Seats

The Transport Board's complaint about the City Council's apparent slowness to improve road surfaces was not the only dissatisfaction expressed by Norman Spencer in his 1959-1960 Annual Report:

"Advertising On Seats And In Shelters: The Board has received an offer from its Advertising Agent Company to provide seats at bus stops at its own cost in return for the right to advertise on those seats. The Company also seeks the right to provide advertisements in shelters, thereby providing revenue for the Board to supply more of this amenity.

"I would like to make it clear that the Board is not responsible for its inability to accept this offer. On two occasions the Board has requested the Auckland City Council's approval of the provision of seats similar to those in other parts of Auckland and also of advertising in shelters, but on each occasion Council has declined the request. The Board is aware of the value of seats and shelters to the public and deeply regrets Council's attitude in the matter." [306]

Queen Street Buses

In his Annual Report for the financial year ended 31 March 1961, Norman Spencer also revisited the issue of buses running up and down a Queen Street clogged by motor cars:

"Bus Services In Queen Street: Although the existing system of operating services in the inner city area is by now well established the question of buses traversing Queen Street instead of crossing at intersections as at present has again been before the Board on several occasions. The matter has also been very thoroughly considered by an Inner City

Transport Committee, comprising representatives of the Auckland City Council and of the Board.

"This Committee informed the City Council that in its opinion no good purpose would be served by further considering the matter until such time as Council had decided that the prohibition of parking of private cars in Queen Street has become possible as the result of the provision of adequate off-street parking buildings. Council resolved accordingly to re-affirm its present policy, that is, apart from the shuttle bus services, no further main line services be permitted into Queen Street. It is not practicable to operate services in Queen Street without the co-operation of the Auckland City Council and the matter must therefore rest until the time arrives when congestion of other motor traffic has forced the elimination of parking privileges in Queen Street." [307]

Transport Board's Case for Survival

Pending a Regional Authority with the foresight and knowledge of what was best for the city as a whole and which could, in theory, eliminate disagreements such as those that existed between the Transport Board and the City Council, ad hoc bodies such as the Board had their own opinion of how best to secure their futures:

"Regional Authority: Little progress has been made towards the preparation by an Establishment Committee representing all the Local Authorities concerned, of a Bill for the constitution of an Auckland Regional Authority to co-ordinate services of a metropolitan character, including the transport undertaking administered by this Board. Before any decision can be reached by this Board regarding participation in the proposed Regional Authority it is essential that a definite scheme must be submitted by the Establishment Committee for the Board's consideration.

"As I understand it the three main objects of forming a Regional Authority are first, to provide for the orderly development of the City, secondly, to provide for a central body to speak for Metropolitan Auckland in all metropolitan matters and thirdly to reduce taxes. The first two of these objects could be achieved better by leaving the Transport Board as it is and providing for strict co-operation by the Board with the Regional Authority. This necessary liaison could be affected by one of the members of the Transport Board being co-opted as a member of the Regional Authority.

"With regard to the saving of the ratepayers' money, I think more could be saved by leaving the Transport Board as it is. In all the other cities which I know of that have Regional Systems such as is envisaged for Auckland, the Transport Authorities are independent but co-operate with the central system. This is necessary because the Transport Board is really a commercial body and will not benefit by being joined with other ad hoc bodies such as those for Drainage or Water. The main thing is to ensure close co-operation with the Regional Authority in overall transport policy." [307]

Transport Board Losses 1961

However, the success of the Transport Board as a *commercial body* was again put to the test with the presentation of its accounts for the financial year ended 31 March 1961:

"The Annual Accounts now presented, after making all interest and sinking fund payments and matured debenture and registered stock redemptions, and also provision for all other items properly chargeable against the year's working, show a net loss for the year of £53,599. This amount is an improvement on the previous year's loss of £69,039, and is considerably less than the estimated loss for the year of £159,863. The position would have shown even greater improvement had it not been for the new Industrial Awards in respect of members of the Engineers' Union and the Transport Employees' Union…Total Revenue from all sources for the year, other than the levy of £97,403, was £1,694,737, which amount is £8018 (.48%) more than the previous year's total… Working expenses amounted to £1,411,806 an increase of £24,850 (1.79%) compared with the previous year's figures." [307]

Transport Board Losses 1962

The following financial year's operations again resulted in a comparatively large loss, as described by Transport Board Chairman, Norman Spencer, in his Annual Report for the year ended 31 March 1962:

"The Annual Accounts now presented show a net loss for the year of £83,094 compared with last year's loss of £53,599…Total revenue for the year other than the levy of £88,717, was £1,676,760, which amount is £17,977 (1.06%) less than the previous year's total. Working expenses amounted to £1,409,650, a decrease of £2,156 on the previous year's figure. This reduction was achieved despite the increases in wage rates payable to both Traffic and Maintenance staff, referred to in my last year's report." [308]

Cuts to Services

While working expenses were recorded as somewhat less than for the previous year, it would seem that a lot of this saving was achieved by way of cuts to services, as explained by Norman Spencer:

"…in July and August last [1961], after the fullest investigation, adjustments were made to frequency of service on a number of routes during evenings and weekends and this gave substantial savings in operating costs." [308]

Reduced Bus Patronage

With the reluctance of many ratepayers to subsidise the public transport service, and the disinclination of the Transport Board to increase fares, the Board had little choice but to tailor its trolleybus and bus services to routes and timetables that provided the greatest return at least cost. But, like the proverbial vicious circle, this reduction of public transport services naturally encouraged the greater use of more convenient, private transport.

As a result, by 1962, many of the City's public transport services were not attracting sufficient patronage. In his article, *Drastic Measures Are Called For To Woo Passengers Back To Travel-By-Bus*, included in the 1962 publication, *Auckland Expanding To Greatness*, John Lyne warned not to expect too much from the newer suburbs:

"Not all the bus companies in metropolitan Auckland are feeling the pinch in dropping patronage. Those servicing new areas, with the exception of Mangere where few people are going by choice, are finding that new housing means increased loading. But their present experiences were shared long ago by other old-established concerns which covered State housing areas. Loading in these rose steadily as more and more houses went up. Then the pattern changed as tenants went in for cars and bus users fell rapidly. Family cars are killing weekend and night loading, so much so that transport concerns are now slashing services at these times.

"The transport board has its fleet of 368 buses – 133 trolley, 223 diesel and 12 petrol – in good condition. The buses are clean, well-kept and are pleasant to travel in. The fleet is ahead of its nearest competitor and streets ahead of other companies." [309]

Historical Public Transport Usage

"Passenger services using Auckland Transport Board services have dropped from the peak in 1945 of 99½ million to last year (1960-61) 50 million. In 1949, four years after the peak, passengers had dropped to 89 million – without any fare alteration. These figures tell the story of the decline in public transport during the 16 years in which metropolitan Auckland has increased its population beyond all expectations. While the affairs of the Transport Board are in the hands of a capable team of members, the limits to which they can go are determined on the extent of public use of the transport system.

"The ATB's last profit was made in 1948, since then losses have been up and down despite stringent economies, cuts in services and rises in fares. The first levy to meet losses amounted to £35,000 for the year 1953-54. The next year it had to be increased to £100,000. This was still not enough to meet accumulating deficits, so the peak levy of £326,161 had to be put on in the year 1956-1957. That was a rise of £181,161 on the £145,000 the year before. By prudent management and close direction the board was able to reduce the levy to £88,717 last year. But with passengers dropping fast for the last three months of the year the chances are that the levy will start rising again, despite the possible use of some reserves to help offset it. [309]

Slow Strangulation

Unlike the trams, with their dedicated piece of roadway, the buses and trolleybuses now had to fight the motorcar for every inch of space and the picture, as described by John Lyne, wasn't pretty:

"Auckland's public transport system, already paralyzed by the private car, is doomed to slow strangulation unless some positive and urgent action is taken to clear streets so that buses can move freely. People are turning away from public transport because of slow travel, brought about through buses being bogged down in streets choked by vehicles of all kinds with interminable delays at traffic lights and traffic bottlenecks.

"Better services, arising from a freer flow of bus traffic could well lead to a change in travelling habits, herald the turning of present losses into profits and even the return to cheaper fares. The city has been nurtured on a good and efficient public transport system run by both municipal and private concerns. The system cannot be abandoned lightly. It is too valuable and has cost too much. Values of city properties would not have reached present levels without efficient mass transport." [309]

Worth the Fight

It was John Lyne's view that public transport was worth fighting for and the march into battle should be led from the top:

"Transport concerns can do a lot right now to encourage people back to using public transport. A first-class public relations organization should be appointed and charged with the responsibility of stimulating interest in mass transport. But such a staff would need to be backed by positive action by executives of transport concerns working as a group.

"Some points worthy of consideration are: Quicker running time by using less congested routes, more express buses at peak hours by direct routes, simplification of the fare systems, lighter loading so that strap hanging is not necessary, more attention to passengers' comfort and to their complaints and less of the attitude that the staff is always right.

"Executives and others at the top would be wise to use their buses frequently to see for themselves some of the shortcomings of services and staff and what can be done to improve travelling. Too often people are forced away from public transport by small incidents which they have magnified in their minds." [309]

Strain on Space

John Lyne was of the opinion that more had to be done to reduce the number of vehicles clogging the City's main thoroughfares:

"Public transport here has its problems with steadily-declining patronage but it is not being given a fair chance to carry people were they want to go. A bus with 70 people takes no more road space than three cars – surely an economical way to move numbers of people!

"The inner city is being choked by various forms of transport – stationary and moving. But bus users and car owners seem content to allow chaotic traffic conditions to continue as more and more cars, scooters, motor cycles and trucks are imported. Obviously there is not space for everybody to do as they please, even if paying for the privilege of kerbside parking.

"The car population has grown so much in the last five years that New Zealand has moved up from fourth largest car-owning country per head of population to second – that is, second to the United States, the home of the automobile. Cars are increasing by the importation of 40,000 new models yearly.

"The strain on space cannot continue much longer; something must give way. And that something is the private car squatting on the kerb, whether all day or for a few minutes. Roads were made to be used by traffic and not for leaving standing vehicles, even if the space is being paid for by meter charges.

"Bus users complain about the inconvenient location of public transport, of time wasted in walking up and down the city to connect with buses, and compare the days when most mainline tram services ran through Queen Street. Many wish for the return of those days by the routeing of buses through Queen Street. But until the kerbs are cleared of parked cars and meters and the city council has a change of heart public transport had no chance of meeting people's wishes.

"The solution to the whole problem of unpopular public transport and its steady decline in recent years lies in the hands of the council. It can allow the rot to continue or, by sacrificing that money-spinner (the parking meter) in the centre of the city it can give public transport the chance to make good." [309]

Auckland City Council Remains Unsupportive

Instead of giving *public transport the chance to make good*, as advocated by John Lyne, the Auckland City Council continued with the ideology promoted by the Master Transportation Plan for Metropolitan Auckland, produced in 1955 by the Technical Advisory Committee of the Auckland Regional Planning Authority. As detailed earlier, the Advisory Committee, chaired by City Engineer, Arthur James Dickson, had advocated roads, roads, and more roads but little in the way of improvements to public transport infrastructure apart from an almost casual reference to "…improvements to bus transport and the construction of a spur railway line (capable of extension) from the present railway station [then at Beach Road] to Victoria Street…a matter for the Railway Department which had already had previous reports from British Consultants." [310]

Road Traffic Regulation

In fact, it would be many decades before a *spur railway line* of any sort would be constructed and *bus transport* was forever committed to sharing the yet-to-be-completed motorways and city roads with increasing numbers of private motor vehicles and goods traffic. The Government's solution to the problem of road congestion was, of course, to regulate and this it did with the Transport Act 1962 which came into force on 1 May 1963.

Transport Act 1962

The Transport Act 1962 – "An Act to consolidate and amend certain enactments of the General Assembly relating to motor vehicles, to road traffic, and to commercial transport services carried on by means of motor vehicles or harbour ferries." [311]

The 1962 Act repealed the Transport Act 1949 and all subsequent Amendments – in effect, it updated all foregoing legislation to reflect the more intense public and private transport conditions of the 1960s; consolidating the procedures and regulations for the registration and licensing of motor vehicles and drivers; the regulation of motor vehicle movement and third party risks; the licensing of public transport, including taxis and harbour ferry services; and the taxation of motor spirits and mileage.

Licence Application Considerations

Section 119 of the Act listed the: "Matters to be considered before determining applications for passenger-service or harbour-ferry service licences-

"(1) In considering any application for a passenger-service licence (not being a taxicab-service licence) or for a harbour ferry service licence, the Licensing Authority shall generally have regard to-

    (a) The extent to which the proposed service is necessary or desirable in the public interest;

    (b) The extent to which an improved standard of transport service in the district is necessary or desirable in the public interest; and

    (c) The needs of the district or districts or any parts thereof in relation to passenger transport or harbour-ferry transport, as the case may be; and

    (d) The necessity in the public interest of protecting the public funds involved when the application is for a licence in respect of a passenger service having substantially the same terminal points and routes as any passenger service which has been purchased by the Minister of Railways and for which that Minister is for the time being the holder of a licence - and, if it is then of opinion that the proposed service is unnecessary or undesirable, it shall refuse to grant a licence.

"(2) If after having regard to the matters mentioned in subsection (1) of this section the Licensing Authority proposes to give further consideration to the application, it shall take into account-

    (a) The transport services of any kind, whether by air, land, or water, already provided in respect of the proposed routes or the localities to be served:

    (b) The financial ability of the applicant to carry on the proposed service:

    (c) The desirability of providing and maintaining a reasonable standard of living and satisfactory working conditions in the transport industry:

    (d) The likelihood of the applicant's carrying on the proposed service satisfactorily and, in the case of an existing licensee or a person who has previously held a licence of the kind to which the application relates, the manner in which the service has been carried on:

    (e) The timetables or frequency of the proposed service, if it is intended to be of a regular nature:

    (f) The vehicles or harbour ferries proposed to be used in connection with the service:

(g) In the case of an application for a passenger-service licence, the condition of the roads to be traversed on the route or routes, and any restrictions of load or speed or other lawful restrictions affecting vehicles of the class proposed to be used, including restrictions arising out of any classification of roads under regulations made pursuant to section 77 of this Act:

(h) Any evidence and representations received by it at the public sitting on behalf of the Minister of Railways, local authorities or other public bodies, or any persons carrying on transport services of any kind (whether by air, land, or water) likely to be affected, and any representations contained in any petition presented to it at a public sitting signed by at least twenty-five adult residents of any locality proposed to be served." [311]

Auckland Transport Board

Defined as a 'Public Body' by Section 91 of the new Transport Act, the Auckland Transport Board retained its right to operate public transport services within the Auckland Transport District as constituted by the Auckland Transport Board Act 1928.

Auckland Regional Authority Opposed

Not surprisingly, despite its many difficulties, the Auckland Transport Board maintained its belief that only it could efficiently manage the City's public transport services and therefore could not support the proposed Auckland Regional Authority:

"The Auckland Transport Board, in common with all other ad hoc authorities in Regional Auckland, realises the need for some kind of Regional Authority to ensure the orderly development of Auckland and its surrounding districts.

"During the past year the Regional Authority Establishment Committee, as well as many local authority members, have spent a great deal of time and energy in an endeavour to evolve a Regional Authority satisfactory to both territorial and ad hoc authorities. The first Bill drawn up got as far as Parliament but was withdrawn owing to the opposition of some of the territorial authorities.

"A new Bill has now been drawn up embodying a complete amalgamation of all fifteen ad hoc authorities in the Auckland Regional District. It is felt by this Board, in common with most of the other ad hoc authorities that such a body could only result in largely increased rates and a general lowering of efficiency. The only benefit which could accrue from such an amalgamation would be in planning – a benefit which could be gained without the complete amalgamation and transfer of assets provided in the proposed amalgamation.

"Consequently, this Board, in conjunction with most of the other ad hoc authorities, has decided to oppose the Bill before the Local Bills Committee, should it be presented to Parliament." [308]

Alternative Regional Authority Rejected

The following year, Transport Board Chairman, Norman Spencer, provided an update to the Auckland Regional Authority proposal, and the Board's opposition to it, by way of his Annual Report for the year ended 31 March 1963:

"Auckland Regional Authority: Last year I referred to the Regional Authority Bill promoted by the Regional Authority Establishment Committee and to the opposition of most of the ad hoc authorities which were to be fused into the body of the proposed new Authority. This Board, with the support of other ad hoc authorities, sponsored an alternative Bill in the House of Representatives, with emphasis on regional planning with powers of enforcement, and the carrying out of certain purely regional functions.

"Following recommendations of the Local Bills Committee, Parliament rejected this latter Bill and the first Bill is to receive further consideration in this year's Session. It is not clear at the present juncture what amendments will be proposed by the sponsors of the Bill, but it is essential that this Board should take all possible steps to protect the interests of the ratepayers of its district and of its passengers, by ensuring that its functions are excluded from the proposed new Authority." [312]

Public Transport Losses Increase

But, while the Transport Board fought to retain responsibility for the City's public transport services and, of course, *to protect the interests of the ratepayers of its district and of its passengers*, operational losses continued to increase during 1963 and 1964 – as reported by Norman Spencer in his Annual Reports for the financial years ended 31 March of those years:

1963 – "Financial Results: The Annual Accounts now presented show a net loss for the year of £128,182 compared with last year's loss of £83,094…Total revenue for the year other than the levy of £99,136 was £1,643,047, which is £33,713 (2.01%) less than the previous year's total. Working expenses totalled £1,425,487, an increase of £15,837 (1.12%) on the previous year's figures – a very small increase after taking into account the cost increases being borne by the Board in both wages and in the cost of parts and stores used in maintenance of our transport fleet." [312]

1964 – "Financial Results: The Annual Accounts now presented show a net loss for the year of £152,355, compared with the last year's figure of £128,182…An analysis of ticket sales shows a continuation of the loss of passenger journeys within the one to five-section area, and an increase in journeys to the outer areas from six to nine sections, indicative, of course, of the gradual transfer of families from the older and nearer suburbs to the new State and group housing areas…On the expenditure side, close attention to the running and maintenance costs has produced savings, but some comparatively minor wage movements and an increase in rates payable on the Board's properties have offset part of the gains…Working expenses at £1,442,781 show an increase of £17,294 (1.2%) on the previous year's total." [313]

Property Speculation Alternative

As a result of its inability to make its modernised public transport services pay, the Transport Board sought to earn additional income from an alternative source familiar to many Auckland speculators of the past, present, and future:

"Alteration To Board's Act: During the 1962 Session of Parliament, the Board sought an Amendment to its statutory powers to enable it to invest part of its reserve funds in the acquisition and development of land and buildings where it was considered advantageous to the Board and its finances so to invest. It was the Board's opinion that by providing services to developing areas it created an immediate increase in property values to the benefit both of owners and territorial authorities, but was denied the means of participating itself in the increase as a partial offset to the seemingly inevitable losses incurred in present day transport operation.

"The Local Bills Committee, after several hearings, decided that the Bill should not proceed, but it is understood they were not unsympathetic to the Board developing any properties acquired under its present powers and which later prove surplus to the Board's requirements. A further attempt will therefore be made in the coming year to obtain an Amendment to the Act giving the Board such restricted powers." [312]

Auckland Transport Board Amendment Act

Indeed, a further attempt to obtain such an Amendment proved successful. However, the measure restricted the Board's property speculation to property it already owned:

"Alteration To The Board's Act: During the 1963 session of Parliament the Board was successful in obtaining an amendment to its Act enabling the investment of part of its reserve funds in the development or improvement of any of its property. This should prove to the financial benefit of the Board." [313]

Auckland Transport Board's Demise

Unfortunately for the Auckland Transport Board, its attempt to generate a second income stream, one that would almost certainly have proved successful, came too late. With what seems to have been a good deal of consensus, the Board had successfully transitioned Auckland's public transport services from the perceived obsolescence of the trams to the uncertain future of trolleybuses and motor buses. Now, it was to be swallowed by an equally uncertain organisation of local government and ad hoc authorities with little history of consensus of any sort:

"Auckland Regional Authority: Despite our strenuous efforts to ensure the exclusion of this Board from the proposed Authority at the present time, Parliament saw fit to include the undertaking among the various Authorities and functions to be merged with the Regional Authority in the initial stages of its existence. Unfortunately the Authority's Act did not include many provisions which will be essential to the continued successful operation of the Board's services and its financial affairs.

"Some of these omissions have been the subject of considerable negotiation since the close of the year under review, and the position at the time of writing this report is that at the request of the Authority, the Board has agreed to extend its control of the undertaking from the previously agreed date of take-over (1st June, 1964) to the 1st October, 1964, to enable amending legislation to be passed by Parliament dealing with some of the more urgent requirements to facilitate operation under the Authority." [313]

Takeover Delays

Indeed, an amendment to the Auckland Regional Authority Act 1963 was quickly required if the Auckland Transport Board's public transport services were to continue uninterrupted under the management of the new Authority. The situation was outlined by the Regional Authority's Chairman, Dove-Myer Robinson, in his report to the Authority, dated 19 June 1964:

"The main purpose of the Transport Board section of the Bill is to maintain the status quo until the Authority is in a position to promote new legislation to overcome what are claimed to be anomalies and provide better passenger transport services.

"In his covering report, which you have just read, our Treasurer has explained why it is impossible to implement our Act as it affects public transport. He has pointed out that until the areas (benefiting from the service) have been clearly defined, it is impossible to assess the contributions which would be payable by them. Furthermore it is extremely doubtful whether the Government Departments concerned could provide in time the basic population and valuation figures which would be required before any assessment could be made. For these reasons, irrespective of the opposition of certain boroughs, amending legislation is necessary in any case.

"Even if we decided not to proceed with this section of the Bill, and every effort were made to operate the Act in its present form, it would be almost inevitable that the Authority's decisions on 'areas of benefit' would be open to argument. It would need only one local authority to exercise its right of appeal (against the levy) to the Supreme Court, to hold up all assessments (except drainage) until the Court gave its decision; and that decision may be subject to further appeal.

"So that whilst the matter was being finally decided, all the Authority's levies (apart from the Drainage levy) could be held up to the assessment year 1966/67. This could mean that in that period payment of the levies could be seriously delayed and this could so cripple the Authority that it may not be able to function.

"Lest it might be thought that the Establishment Committee had been remiss in framing the relevant clauses of the Regional Authority Bill, it should be pointed out that *there were no clauses in that Bill containing specific details of arrangements for taking over the Transport Board.*

"The Establishment Committee's Bill did include detailed clauses covering all arrangements for the absorption of the Drainage Board, the Airport Committee, the City Council's Bulk Water Supply and other functions, *because those bodies had agreed to amalgamate in the Regional Authority. It was therefore possible to include in the Bill detailed arrangements covering the special circumstances in each case*. But in the case of the three Power Boards, Milk Boards, Transport Board, Harbour Board, Harbour Bridge Authority and others *this was not possible because, having refused to join the Regional Authority, these bodies would not negotiate detailed arrangements for the taking over and carrying on of their functions…*

"The fact of the matter is that whilst the Establishment Committee was firmly of the opinion that the Transport Board should come in to the Regional Authority, the Committee had no indication that Parliament intended to include the Board. As a result, *the Committee had no discussions with the Board, and therefore there was no need to study the Transport Board's legislation, or how it would affect the Authority if the Board was included.*

"It was only when the Authority came to negotiate the take-over date with the Board that the difficulties in applying section 61 (4) of the Act became apparent. For this reason the date of take-over was advanced to enable the Board itself to strike the levy for 1964-65." [290]

Assessment of Levies

Section 61 of the Auckland Regional Authority Act 1963 stipulated how contributing authority levies were to be assessed by the Authority for

"(2) (a) Any service or activity conducted or carried on for the benefit of some portion or portions only of the district…

(4) The amounts payable…shall be assessed and charged to the respective local authorities of the respective portions of the district for whose benefit the respective service or activity is being carried on, in proportion to the mean percentage of rateable capital value and population of the respective local districts or of the portions thereof so benefitted, as the case may be." [287]

The Auckland Regional Authority Amendment Act 1964, subsequently passed by Parliament on 13 October of that year, updated a number of provisions in the original Act that hadn't fully addressed the practicalities of taking over entities such as the Auckland Transport Board. For instance, Section 7 of the Amending Act clarified the provisions of the original Section 61 while Section 12 allowed for the local authority levies, originally payable to the Transport Board during the period of transition, to be collected by the Regional Authority "...in like manner as the same could have been recovered by the said Board had the principal Act not been passed." [314]

Auckland Transport Board Signs Off

Once the anomalies inherent in such a takeover had been recognised and legislated for, there was little else for long-time Auckland Transport Board Chairman, Norman Spencer, to do but to reluctantly sign off with a final piece of advice:

"Conclusion: This will be the last report I will make to the Board, and from all indications it will also be the final Annual Report made to the Auckland Transport Board as such. I think we all regret that the undertaking will shortly lose its identity as an independent ad hoc Authority, and it must be our sincere wish that its present high state of operational efficiency is not lost in its future control by the new Authority. Transport is an industry with peculiar and ever occurring problems. Successful operation calls for a high degree of technical skill plus an appreciation of the users' views on both the adequacy and overall cost of the service given.

"The obvious is not always the correct answer to the problems of the industry, and I trust that our successors in control of the undertaking will appreciate to the full the assistance and advice which will be readily forthcoming from the General Manager and his Executive Officers who have taken such a leading part in building the present efficient organisation – one which is held in the highest regard in the field of passenger transport in Australasia. To those officers and all members of the Board's staff I extend thanks for their support and good work not only in the past year, but in the difficult years which have faced this and earlier Boards since the early 1950's." [313]

Providing a Regional Public Transport Service

Norman Spencer's reservations as to the Auckland Regional Authority's ability to successfully manage the Transport Board's responsibilities were shared by many, particularly by distrusting borough councils anxious to avoid higher transport levies. It was therefore important that any such dissension was actively defended against, as illustrated by Dove-Myer Robinson's press statement of 6 February 1964:

"I am sure that every member of the Regional Authority will carefully consider the opinions expressed by Mr N B Spencer, Chairman of the Auckland Transport Board, when he says that if the Regional Authority takes over a privately owned transport companies it may increase the transport levy by a quarter of a million pounds. However, Mr Spencer is under a misapprehension. As far as I am aware there has been no serious suggestion that the Regional Authority take over privately owned transport companies; in fact the Regional Authority act does not give the Authority power to take over private transport companies.

"However, in order to provide the public, for the first time in Auckland's history, with what the public so obviously requires – a fully co-ordinated and integrated <u>regional</u> public transport system, it is necessary that the Regional Authority or the No. 2 Licensing Authority have the necessary power to bring about this co-ordination without which it is impossible to provide a regional public transport service. I am sure that there will be no difficulty in obtaining the necessary statutory authority to bring this about, without the Regional Authority having to take over privately owned transport companies.

"Provided that the Authority has the necessary powers its policy of providing an adequate overall regional transport service will result in greater use being made of publicly and privately owned public transport services. In which case the result may well be an ultimate reduction of the transport levy, rather than the increase predicted by Mr Spencer.

"I would like to assure the public that the Regional Authority will carefully consider every move in its endeavours to provide the public with the transport service it requires without unnecessarily increasing the transport levy." [315]

Ministerial Assistance Sought

However, if he was to achieve *a fully co-ordinated and integrated regional public transport system*, Dove-Myer Robinson would need a lot more than just a press statement to outflank naysayers as influential as Norman Spencer. The backing of the Minister of Transport would be a start and that is no doubt why Dove-Myer Robinson wrote a personal letter to the Honourable John Kenneth McAlpine on 13 March 1964:

"… As I told you when I spoke to you over the telephone the Regional Authority has adopted as one of its first objectives the implementation of a fully integrated regional public passenger transport system. In considering a plan to give effect to this policy, the possibilities of integrating suburban railways, ferries and buses will be considered, together with the question of at least one spur line underground railway from the present railway terminus to somewhere in the heart of the city.

"Naturally, the integration of operation of publicly owned and privately owned bus services will be a major consideration, because without the closest co-ordination of these services such a plan would be unworkable. Another point of crucial importance is the matter of the licensing authority. Unless the Regional Authority itself is a Licensing Authority, or, alternatively, the No.2a Licensing Authority is instructed (which may be inadvisable) to implement the decisions of the Regional Authority, the whole scheme would be impracticable.

"As you will see, therefore, it is essential that we should fully inform you as soon as possible of what we have in mind in order to learn from you the extent to which you are prepared to assist us so that this re-organisation and improvement to public passenger transport in the Auckland region can be brought about.

"If I remember rightly, on the occasion of your first public address in Auckland, shortly after your appointment as Minister of Transport four years ago, you said that you hoped to bring about a co-ordinated public passenger transit system very much in line with what we have in mind. If my recollection is correct, then I am sure you will be very happy to know that we have adopted this policy and that Parliament has set up an Authority capable of undertaking a project of this magnitude. I am writing this letter to you personally so that you will know my own thoughts in this matter which I am sure are shared by the majority, if not all, of the members of the Regional Authority…

"Mr Passmore [C S Passmore, Chairman of the Auckland Regional Authority Transport Committee] and I have been asked by the Transport Committee to endeavour to ascertain your attitude on certain points which are an essential prerequisite before the Authority can take the next step to have the matter fully investigated and reported on.

"We realise that such an investigation will take a minimum of six months and may extend possibly to 12 or 18 months. It will, of course, be essential that the Railway Department co-operate with us and our consultants from the outset. The advisability of such co-operation will be for you to decide, as also will be the question of licensing. Other matters of importance will be the legislative authority to ensure co-ordination of services involving consideration of legislation to compel this co-ordination, and if necessary authority to buy out willing sellers or services operated by companies unwilling to accept complete integration.

"We realise that we are embarking on unchartered [sic] seas, but we are firmly of the opinion that with your moral support and practical assistance, we will be able to bring into being a service which will give the public of Auckland the transportation system which they desire at an overall economic cost." [316]

Tentative Support

The Minister's reply in a letter to the Chairman of the Auckland Regional Authority's Transport Committee, C S Passmore, dated 7 August 1964, was as supportive as any Auckland local government entity could expect from Wellington:

"This is to confirm my earlier verbal advice that the Railways Department will be pleased to co-operate with the consultants engaged to the extent specified in the terms of the agreement between the consultants and the Authority. In offering this full and positive co-operation I must at the same time make it clear that the Department's concurrence in any of the recommendations made by the consultants will be without prejudice to Government's consideration of the final report and such recommendations as may be submitted to the Government by the Authority.

"Your request for financial assistance towards the cost of the investigation has been given full consideration and it is regretted that Government cannot contribute other than by meeting the cost of the technical services the Department will offer in making professional officers available to the consultants." [317]

De Leuw, Cather and Company

The consultants referred to by Dove-Myer Robinson and John McAlpine represented the American engineering firm of De Leuw, Cather and Company, appointed on 14 May 1963 by the Auckland Regional Planning Authority – known later as the Planning Division of the newly-established Auckland Regional Authority. The firm was "…commissioned to prepare a detailed plan for a comprehensive transportation strategy for Auckland, including a separate report on a rapid transit system." [158]

Half Million Speech

As the Transport Survey continued throughout 1963 and 1964, Dove-Myer Robinson sought at every opportunity to reassure the public that such a survey was necessary and that the newly-formed Regional Authority was the body to implement the findings of the De Leuw, Cather investigations. Such an opportunity occurred on 2 June 1964, during his speech to celebrate the arrival of the Auckland Region's half millionth citizen:

"The Transport Problem – Surveys have shown that the average car carries less than two persons per trip. A bus can carry up to 52 persons. So that one bus can carry as many passengers as about 42 cars, but the bus occupies only 40 ft. of road space. If a fast, cheap, comfortable, convenient and safe public passenger transport system were provided, it may be possible to persuade a large percentage of motorists to leave their cars at home and use public transport for their daily journeys to and from their place of work or business…

"There is in the region a Metropolitan Transport Board (soon to be taken over by the Regional Authority), at least 14 privately owned bus companies, the suburban railway services, a small number of ferries, and a fleet of taxis. There is little if any coordination between all these services. Travel by public conveyance is not always fast, cheap, comfortable or convenient.

Gas Pedal to Back-Pedal   Chapter Four

"There is a very great amount of wasteful overlapping and dead mileage. During peak hours buses are often overcrowded and intending passengers have to wait for long periods to catch one. What is worse, many buses part-empty pass intending passengers because the operators are not licensed to pick up or set down passengers on certain routes.

"Yet in off-peak hours, buses often run at a great loss, less than half full. All this is frustrating and results in higher fares than would otherwise be necessary. It results in driving more and more people to buy a motor car and abandon altogether the use of public transport. The effect is to increase the loss on public transport, and increase the cost of private transport.

"Already 28% of the National income is spent on transport. The cumulative effect is that congestion is already costing ratepayers in the region about £8 million yearly, which, together with the increased cost of private transport and losses on public transport, represents an annual expense to each ratepayer far greater than the cost of rates. *The Regional Authority is hoping to change all this.*

"A Regional Transport Plan – The authority is taking steps to have the consultants, who are carrying out the Transport Survey, investigate the whole question of public passenger transport in the region, and bring down a plan for a fully integrated public passenger transport system. The consultants will be asked to devise a scheme which will make the best coordinated use of publicly and privately owned buses, suburban railway services, and harbour ferries. They will also be asked to consider the economics and advisability of an underground spur-line railway from the present railway station to the heart of the city, as well as investigating all other forms of public passenger transport. This survey will include the economic feasibility of an underground railway system, cross routing and circular routing of buses.

"When all this has been done, the consultants will prepare a scheme which will coordinate all services, routes, timetables, and fare schedules. This plan would provide citizens with a public transport service that would carry them – wherever practicable – from any point in the region to any other point. Where not practicable to provide direct services, it is envisaged that transfer tickets and alternative means of public transport would be available.

"Because of the complex nature of existing public passenger transport, a great deal of time will be required to prepare such a scheme. However, if we are to prevent our roads from being clogged with almost immovable masses of private cars and other vehicles, causing accidents, wastage of time, the destruction of property values and causing huge annual losses, it is essential that a plan of this kind be adopted and made to work.

"Greater utilization of public transport is essential to the solution of the congestion problem. If we fail to find a satisfactory solution, the consequences would be complete blockage of our traffic arteries within a few years, and a very considerable increase in the cost of living through unnecessarily high transport costs.

"Planning Provides The Answers – Experience overseas shows that such a plan is feasible. Assuming that it is equally successful in Auckland, what can we expect from it? It would reduce the pressure on available road space and would prevent or at least reduce losses due to congestion. It would help to avoid the need to provide many expensive new roads, and would reduce the amount which would have to be spent on upgrading, widening, and straightening existing roads.

"This could reduce the amount which might otherwise have to be spent on roading within the region, in the next ten years, by as much as £10,000,000, with a saving of capital and maintenance costs of one, to one and a half, million pounds yearly.

"It would also provide the public with a regional passenger transport service which could not otherwise have been hoped for. By preventing congestion it would save the region the £8 million now being wasted yearly. It would save motorists and the public generally a very considerable part of their travelling expenses in the region. And – as far as our old friend the ratepayer is concerned – it should save him many pounds yearly by holding his rates down to a far lower level than otherwise." [318]

Transport Summary

Of course, before the Auckland Regional Authority could implement changes to the City's public transport system, and try to reverse the losses incurred during the Transport Board's management, the Authority's members had best learn how the system operated.

The Passenger Transport Committee of the Authority took over the Board's responsibilities on 1 October 1964. A week later, the Authority's General Manager (and former Transport Board General Manager from 1947), C R Gribble, provided a summary of the transport undertaking to the Authority's Chairman and Board:

"The Division operates some 29 services…and for this purpose has a fleet of 368 passenger vehicles comprising 133 trolley buses, 223 diesel buses and 12 petrol buses. (The latter are necessary to operate a service across Grafton Bridge, which has a weight restriction of 10 tons).

"The estimated loss for the year amounts to £286,163, which is £96,466 above the assessed loss for the year ending 31. 3. 65. The reasons for the increase in loss are apparent…In the first place there is the ever-increasing cost of operation – both in wages and materials. The impact of wage increases is particularly severe in the transport industry because this item makes up approximately 60% of our working costs.

"Secondly, there is the steady decrease in revenue. With some 60,000 new motor-cars coming into New Zealand each year it is obvious that public transport must be affected. In the Division's case the effect is the more severe because most of its routes are through developed areas where there is little hope of obtaining additional passengers to offset the loss to motor-cars.

"A further factor, the importance of which should not be overlooked, is the increasing number of new shopping centres in the suburbs. These are designed to cater for the motorist and it cannot be denied that in these days when goods deliveries by shops are not common, the motor-car offers a most attractive means of carrying the family shopping. There are other factors which could be mentioned but the foregoing are probably the most important ones.

"I make these points not as excuses but as facts which cannot be ignored. It is, of course, a comparatively simple matter to improve the financial position of the undertaking. First, there would be an increase in fares and then when patronage fell, as it always does when fares are increased, the services would be decreased. Cuts in service often bring a further reduction in passengers, but overall there would be an improvement in finances, and perhaps, if the changes were drastic enough, even a profit.

"The other side of the picture is easy to forecast. There would be increased use made of motor-cars, increased congestion, and increased demand for parking areas. The cost of these would, I am certain, add up to considerably more than the amount by which the Division's undertaking had benefited.

"I am aware that in making these comments I am touching on what is undoubtedly a policy matter which the Authority itself must decide. However, I introduce the subject deliberately because of its importance, particularly at a time when the undertaking's estimated loss shows a substantial increase and when all the indications are that this trend will continue – at least while the present era of prosperity lasts." [319]

De Leuw, Cather Plans

De Leuw, Cather and Company produced its *Regional Transit Plan* in July 1965 and its *Comprehensive Transportation Plan* in October of that year. The Consultants also provided a *User Benefit Analysis* and a *Priority Programme for Motorway Construction* on 21 October and 12 November 1965, respectively. [310]

The Regional Transit Plan considered the merits of 'An All-Bus System' and a 'Coordinated Bus and Rail Rapid Transit System'. A summary of the two systems, in the form of a four-page brochure, signed by Charles E De Leuw and dated 15 July 1965, was provided to the Chairman and Members of the Auckland Regional Authority:

"An All-Bus System – This plan envisioned an improved bus system generally similar to existing services except that routes would be coordinated and duplication of service eliminated through control of operations by a single agency. Bus lines would be extended to serve newly-developed areas where needed and express bus operation on motorways would be introduced to expedite the movement of passengers during peak periods where practicable.

"Downtown Auckland constitutes the largest employment center in the region and, therefore, affords the best opportunity for planning improvements in bus services. Present routing of many buses to a terminal in the downtown district at the extreme south end of the area imposes unnecessary walking on crowded downtown sidewalks, and adds to the travel time to reach downtown destinations of the great majority of bus patrons. Since most transit passengers have destinations in the vicinity of Queen Street, it is apparent that direct delivery of passengers to Queen Street sidewalk stops would accomplish the greatest possible improvement in bus service to the downtown area.

"The existing four lanes in Queen Street do not have sufficient capacity for two-way operation of all of the buses, even though parking were to be strictly prohibited during rush periods. We have, therefore, planned two downtown delivery loops with each bus routed along Queen Street only once, either on the inbound or on the outbound trip. Buses arriving from the south and the east use Symonds and Customs Streets and then south along Queen Street on their outbound journey. Buses arriving from the west and the north would deliver passengers northbound on Queen Street and then travel outbound via Customs and Albert Streets. Curb loading space on Queen Street is thus used to greatest advantage.

"Although this operating plan would function with existing passenger volumes, it would substantially reduce other traffic movements along Queen Street during peak periods. Also, it would be necessary to construct a new bus terminal near Queen Street, in addition to the existing bus terminal...

"Auckland has and will continue to experience vigorous growth. The all-bus transportation plan can be developed and will function reasonably well for a limited time.

However, in a few years, congestion on Queen Street would require prohibition of motor cars from using that street during peak periods.

"Analysis of the operating results of an all-bus system indicates that the annual operating revenues, based on present conditions, would be sufficient to cover the annual operating expenses. However, fixed charges on the capital investment required for modernization estimated at more than £9,000,000 require substantial annual subsidies.

"On the basis of the foregoing analysis, together with a comparison to the alternative coordinated bus and rail system, we find that the all-bus system would not fulfil the transit requirements of the area. We recommend against an all-bus system in the Auckland Metropolitan Region." [320]

Central Business District Concerns

While this aspect of bus services, the *direct delivery of passengers to Queen Street sidewalk stops*, would seem to be of little significance today, the matter was of considerable concern to Queen Street traders of the early 1960s. Those concerns were outlined by Dove-Myer Robinson, then Mayor of Auckland City and Chairman of the Auckland Regional Authority, in his opening address at the *Conference on Problems of Central Business District* held on 7 May 1964:

"This Conference has been convened at the request of the Auckland City Development Association and other City commercial and business associations. Representations were made to me that because of certain trends and developments in the central business district, those concerned should have the opportunity of placing their views before me – as Mayor of the City – in order that I may help to find ways in which the City Council might assist this extremely important section of City ratepayers…

"Whilst opinions may differ on the validity of the complaints frequently heard, that trade in the central business district is not keeping pace with the development of the metropolitan area, there is no doubt that this meeting would not have been requested if a large section of the business community was not seriously concerned about the present situation…

"As Mayor of the City, and also as Chairman of the Regional Authority (because these problems directly and indirectly affect the Authority), I feel it to be my duty to listen sympathetically to any representations affecting the welfare of the City, the Region, or any section of it. As an elected representative of the people, I feel that I have a duty to lead, to advise, to assist, and you try to explain to all interested persons, the reasons for Council's policies and decisions. I also have the duty to listen to all complaints, criticism, or advice which may be helpful in considering modifications to or confirmation of Council's policies and decisions…

"May I now outline the situation as I see it, against the back-cloth of world developments. Today we are in the era of population explosion. Economic and sociological changes, too powerful to be controlled by any group of men, or even by individual governments, are at work changing our habitual patterns of life and thinking. No longer can we afford to think of the problems of today or even the immediate future. We must think 25 to 50 years ahead. Long before any short term solutions could be implemented, the problems these solutions were designed to overcome would already be upon us and in many cases would have passed us by, and left us lagging far behind.

"Here is the position as I see it. Today we have approximately 200,000 motor vehicles in the Auckland Region, and already we experience periods of traffic congestion. The

Council's officers think that by the application of stricter traffic control where necessary, and other methods which are available to us, we can prevent this congestion from becoming too serious for the next few years. However, the Regional Planning Authority states that within ten years it is expected that there will be approximately 400,000 more vehicles in the Region – double the number of motor vehicles but only the same – or very few more – roads to accommodate them. Unless steps are taken immediately to avoid it, we could be faced with ever-recurring traffic jams that could paralyse the traffic arteries of the central business district for long periods, during peak hours.

"The solution which is being applied in many cities in a similar position in other parts of the world, is to attempt to persuade the motorist to leave his car at home for what is called 'commuter services' (the daily trip to and from his place of work), and to use public passenger transport services. This will not be easy, but when it is realised that one bus can carry the equivalent of the average number of passengers carried by 25 to 50 motor cars, whilst occupying only 40 feet of road space, it can be seen how essential it is that we should use every endeavour to persuade the public to use public passenger transport to the maximum possible extent, and so lessen the demand on the available road space.

"I am convinced that if we can show the motorist that by leaving his car at home for his regular commuter journeys he will save time and have less frustration by using public transport, and we will be able to make worthwhile savings in roading costs, and at the same time help to prevent or relieve congestion. This may be accomplished if a fast, cheap, comfortable and convenient fully coordinated public transport system is provided throughout the region...

"You will be aware that Council has had in mind for many years the provision of a Western bus terminal and a large-sized parking building incorporated in it. Preliminary steps are being taken to implement Council's policy in this regard. However, I want to make it quite clear that Council cannot make a final decision in this connection until the comprehensive transport survey, which is at present under way, is available. It may be that when that report is completed we may be advised to consider another location or modify our plans in other ways, and Council must reserve the right to make its final decision based on the evidence contained in a report.

"On the assumption, however, that the report will confirm the desirability of a Western (and possibly a South-Eastern) bus terminal, with an associated car parking building, Council is of the opinion that traffic congestion could be still further reduced by the provision of a free, frequent, fast, and convenient shuttle service throughout the central business district. This would most likely entail a special rate in the areas receiving benefit from this service, and that is a matter, of course, in which Council would be unlikely to proceed without firm support from the business community.

"Personally, I am convinced that a free shuttle service in the central business district would encourage those motorists, who for one reason or another must bring their cars into the City, to leave their cars at the proposed car parks at the bus terminals and use the free shuttle service for their errands in the City...

"I recognise, of course, that many of you are concerned over the question of more buses and parking in Queen Street. I can assure you that this matter, as well as the question of bus cross-routing of Queen Street and the City, and all other aspects of bus routing, will be considered by the consultants and will be dealt with in full in their report…But I think we must not try to anticipate what recommendations will result from this full scale independent investigation by an organisation of world repute.

"What I have said will, I think, indicate to you how I look at your problems. It also indicates some of the projects on which the City Council and the Regional Authority are working. We must remember, however, that the interests of the Region must be considered as a whole, and that regional considerations are of more importance than any special interests of the City, or any other part of the Region.

"On the other hand, I am utterly convinced that sound Regional planning, the closely coordinated provision of Regional services, the economies which can be effected as a result of centralised control, and the application of the whole concept of the Regional principle, will not only benefit all the Region but must in even greater measure be a benefit to the Central Business District of the City.

"I can assure you that my Council is anxious and willing to do everything practicable to assist you, commensurate with our other responsibilities. Within the next six to twelve months, plans and proposals of great potential benefit to the central business district will be announced. I ask you to bear with us a little longer until our plans are completed and we are ready to apply some of these remedial measures." [321]

De Leuw, Cather Plans (Continued)

The *plans and proposals* referred to by Dove-Myer Robinson were of course those then expected from the 1965 De Leuw, Cather report, Charles E De Leuw's summary of which continued:

"Coordinated Bus And Rail Rapid Transit System – A coordinated bus and rail rapid transit system was analyzed in considerable detail and was found feasible both operationally and economically. We recommend that this system be adopted for transit service in the Auckland Metropolitan Region.

"It would consist of a modern rail rapid transit facility, utilizing multiple-unit cars, each individually powered by electric motors operating along trunk lines in the several principal corridors where railway facilities are now located. The bus lines tributary to the rapid transit corridors will provide feeder services to the rail stations, thus spreading the benefits of faster service and a vastly improved delivery to downtown Auckland over a much larger section of the urban area.

"Initially, the rail rapid transit operation would be along the existing rail lines from both Puhinui and New Lynn via Newmarket to the vicinity of the present Auckland railway station and thence to downtown Auckland by a new extension alongside Beach Road to a subway under Customs Street and Queen Street. Two new subway stations are planned in the Central Business District; one at Customs and Queen Streets and the other, the terminal Civic Centre station, at Wellesley and Queen Streets. These routes total 18 miles of surface lines and 1.2 miles of underground, all of which would be electrified. Rehabilitation of the existing 24 outlying stations is contemplated, together with provision for parking and rubber-to-rail transfer facilities.

"The second stage of rapid transit development would be the extension of the initial transit operations to Henderson and Papakura. Additional coverage would be provided through a connection from Westfield to the Auckland railway station via Tamaki. An extension of the rapid transit operation from the Civic Centre station southerly to connect with the existing railway line in the vicinity of the Mount Eden station may be found feasible in the next generation.

"High-speed rapid transit cars are proposed – of modern design and capable of speeds up to 60 m.p.h. One-way travel time from Puhinui and from New Lynn to the Civic Centre is estimated at 21 minutes and 19 minutes respectively. During peak periods, trains would operate on 5 minute headways on each line, increasing to 10 to 15 minute headways at other times. We have estimated the capital outlay required to put the recommended transit system in operation at £21,000,000 on the basis of present day costs. Approximately £15,000,000 would be required for the rail rapid transit system including the downtown subway extension, the improvements to existing railway facilities and the purchase of 114 new cars. The remaining £6,000,000 would cover the investment over a period of years in 545 new buses and new bus depots.

"Considering the time required for organization, legislation, negotiations, financing and acquiring and constructing the necessary facilities, we have assumed 1970 as the earliest year of initial rapid transit operation. Therefore, estimates of financial results of operation were prepared for that year. For the purpose of computing revenues, we assumed that the transit system would continue to operate on a zone-fare basis. The present weighted-average fare per passenger was established at 11d. as the basis for estimating revenues. The gross annual revenues were computed on the basis of this average fare and an estimated 87,000,000 passengers, producing a total of £3,990,000 in the year 1970.

"Operating expenses for the bus portion of the transit system were based on present experience on bus operations throughout the region. The average of £1 16s. per bus hour applied to the estimated hours to be operated in 1970 produced annual operating expenses of £2,380,000. Annual operating expenses on the rail rapid transit system were estimated with the assistance of the New Zealand Government Railways at £1,240,000 – a grand total for the system of £3,620,000.

"The financial results of the initial year of operation, 1970, I summarized as follows: Operating Revenues £3,990,000; Operating Expenses, £3,620,000; Operating Income £370,000.

"Based on experience on similar transit systems, operating income may be expected to increase in future years by from 1 to 2 per cent per annum. Based on present day levels of costs, wages and fares, our studies show that the proposed transit system would produce an operating income and, therefore, would be self-supporting except for fixed charges. Annual fixed charges on the capital investment would range from £1,000,000 in 1970 to approximately £1,400,000 in 1982, based on an interest cost of 5½ per cent per annum. The operating income of some £370,000 could be used to defray a portion of the annual charges.

"Benefits Of A Modern Coordinated Transit System – Major improvements in convenience to the public will develop from the coordinated bus and rapid transit operation. Major benefits to patrons of the combined transit operations will result through time savings, clocklike regularity of service and vastly improved delivery throughout the central area. Benefits would flow to all motorists through a reduction in the number of buses and automobiles on the surface streets.

"Increases in land values and construction of new housing and commercial buildings would add substantially to the development of the entire region. Experience elsewhere indicates that increases in tax values in the areas directly involved, attributable solely to construction of the recommended rail rapid transit, might well be sufficient to repay the entire cost of the project in a period of 15 to 20 years.

"Rail rapid transit is competitive to the private automobile because it provides faster, safer, less expensive, more dependable and almost as convenient service, especially during peak periods of travel to and from the downtown area. The comparatively small central business district contains a concentration of daytime population and activities which require maximum access facilities during peak periods. Most of the persons who work in the downtown area do not require an automobile during the day. It is more economical to provide attractive rapid transit facilities to serve this major business and commercial center than to provide the additional highway and parking facilities otherwise required.

"While it is difficult to estimate the cost of such additional facilities, preliminary estimates indicate the added cost would be substantially greater than the cost of the recommended rail rapid transit system. A consideration of the many anticipated direct and indirect benefits to the various groups and to the community as a whole, leads to the conclusion that there is full economic justification for this important project.

"Management And Control Of Regional Transit – We recommend that the Auckland Regional Authority be responsible for the management and control of all operations of the recommended regional transit system. The Authority should be empowered to determine routes, service standards, type of equipment and the fare schedules for all transit services. It should, moreover, have the right to contract for any of the services, bus, rail or water, with other public agencies or with private operators. It is logical that the New Zealand Government Railways operate the proposed rapid transit system under contract, and that certain private bus operations be continued, also under contract with the Auckland Regional Authority." [320]

ARA Supports De Leuw, Cather Plans

The response to the De Leuw, Cather reports were favourably received by the Auckland Regional Authority, as reported by The New Zealand Herald:

"Mr Lambie reported last night that the meeting of the combined committees, which was attended by 24 of the 33 members of the authority, had approved its recommendations unanimously. At the end of a two-hour discussion the meeting also voted unanimously to adopt the recommendations." [322]

Although lacking the support of nine members, the Authority was confident of a successful approach to the Government for financial assistance. After all, it did have majority agreement and purpose, normally so lacking in Auckland local body politics, and now so necessary:

"In making the decisions the authority adopted recommendations by an earlier combined meeting of four authority committees – planning, roads, transport and policy and finance. The recommendations largely followed those put forward by the general manager of the authority, Mr J Steel, in a comprehensive report on the de Leuw, Cather proposals.

"Only one major change was made from Mr Steel's recommendations. Specific recommendations by Mr Steel on sharing of rail costs (based on estimates for the de Leuw, Cather proposal) were not proceeded with. Mr Steel had suggested that the Government should pay £650,000 and the authority £450,000 of the annual running costs and charges of the system. He also considered the authority should be responsible for annual charges on the rapid rail system rolling stock.

"A recommendation that the authority indemnify the Government for any running losses was also abandoned. The authority agreed that unified control of passenger transport in the region under the authority was a prerequisite for the rail-bus scheme.

"The authority appointed a committee to open immediate negotiations with the Government on financial participation and to report back each month on progress. Members of the committee include the chairman, Mr H D Lambie; the deputy-chairman, Mr L A Manning; the planning committee chairman, Mr A R Turner; the transport committee chairman, Mr J Allsopp-Smith; and the roads committee chairman, Mr T H Pearce. Mr Steel was given authority to obtain professional and technical advice for further investigation of the schemes and the costs involved. He is to report back within three months.

"As soon as the authority reaches agreement with the Government on a financial formula, Mr Steel will report on how the authority can appoint consultants to implement the various parts of the rapid transit scheme. The authority will ask the Government to bring down empowering legislation, including legislation, giving the authority full control of the recommended regional transport system and the power to decide routes, service standards and fares." [322]

John Steel's Report

Some reservations as to the implementation of the De Leuw, Cather recommendations were expressed by the Authority's General Manager, John Steel:

"The reports and recommendations of the two de Leuw, Cather investigations could not be ignored, the general manager of the Auckland Regional Authority, Mr J Steel, said in a report to the authority last night. But he emphasised that there must be no thought of such expenditure without a master plan for downtown Auckland. He was also not prepared to recommend the implementation of the rail-bus scheme without government participation.

"He felt that as the government had from time to time considered plans for providing better Auckland suburban rail services, it was now opportune for Auckland to press its claims for a new rail service. Mr Steel said that in his opinion the traffic problem would assume such proportions in the future that an expenditure of £21 million on the rail scheme was justified now.

"To build motorways only, he said, is to faithfully copy the mistake of the American city. The estimated cost £15 million to provide 20 miles of rail transit – about £750,000 a mile – compared favourably with the £1 million to £2 million cost a mile of motorway construction.

"Also it had been calculated that a single rail track could accommodate up to 20 times as many people as a single lane of express highway. If no action was taken on the rail proposals, it was clear a policy of decentralisation for Auckland would be necessary. Reports by the director of planning, Mr F W O Jones, and by the manager of the transport division, Mr C R Gribble, supported adoption of the schemes." [323]

Government Financial Participation Sought

The Regional Authority members agreed with their General Manager that Government assistance would be essential to progress the De Leuw, Cather proposals:

"The Auckland Regional Authority will open immediate negotiations in an attempt to obtain Government financial participation in the de Leuw, Cather bus-rail and highways schemes. At a special meeting last night the authority gave 'general approval in principle' to the schemes. It has been estimated that the projects will cost at least £160 million over the next 20 years. "The authority, in a series of major policy decisions on the proposals, also decided to: Request investigations by the authority general manager, Mr J Steel, into extending the suggested underground railway line through the central city to join up with the North Auckland line as part of the initial development of the rapid rail system. The de Leuw, Cather proposal would end the line initially at the Town Hall.

"Ask the Government to assume responsibility for building the downtown subway extension, improving existing railway facilities, supplying rolling stock and running the rail services to schedules laid down by the authority.

"Leave the authority responsible for providing and running the whole bus system and bus feeder services to the rail system, either directly or under contract to private companies.

"Negotiate with the Government on sharing the running costs and charges – estimated at £1.1 million annually for the scheme using a Town Hall rail terminus." [322]

Opportunity for Railways

The Auckland Regional Authority had every reason to believe that the Government, through its Railways Department, would have what a New Zealand Herald editorial, published on 19 August 1965, described as:

"...the best of reasons to favour the new proposals for public transport in Auckland. The suggested extensions of city and suburban railway services presents the Railways Department with the opportunity to turn a wasting asset into a vigorous, profit-earning enterprise. Ten years ago, when suburban railway electrification and an underground rail link through the heart of the city were traded for a network of motorways, the Government agreed that the project was deferred, not abandoned. To that extent it remains committed in principle to the proposition revived in the de Leuw, Cather report.

"The Minister of railways thinks it is too soon to consider a sharing of the costs of the bus-rail transport plan. But it must be obvious in Wellington that long before the 1980s, when Auckland will attain a population of one million, the railways can reap a rich harvest from metropolitan transport at the price of a relatively small investment.

"Fully 75 per cent of the needed facilities are already in existence. The State, through the National Roads Board, would also be saved its share of a good deal of additional motorway construction at a cost of at least £1 million a mile. When the waste and extravagance of traffic congestion are likewise taken into account, prompt railway development in Auckland clearly offers advantage to the State as well as benefit to the regional community." [324]

The Best Way Forward

Indeed, there was a great deal of optimism that the Government could be persuaded the best way forward for Auckland was De Leuw, Cather's bus-rail scheme:

"Plans for road and rail transport in Auckland based on the de Leuw, Cather reports could determine the shape and economy of Auckland, Mr H D Lambie, chairman of the Auckland Regional Authority, said last night...Each department of the authority, he said, had tried to determine the problem facing the community. Implementation of the reports was technically and economically feasible. The traffic situation would become more critical in the next 20 years. The reports showed that daily movements of people would rise from one million to three million and vehicle movements from 600,000 to 1.6 million in 20 years.

"It did not make sense to rely on motorways alone. To do that would be to copy mistakes made overseas. Public transport in Auckland had been losing money. The railways were running at a loss. Mr Lambie said the rail system could be transformed into an electrified facility with nine or ten times the capacity of motor vehicles and cheaper than a motorway. Mr J Allsopp-Smith, chairman of the passenger transport division, said the North Shore was not receiving the consideration it merited. He called for a closer look at the proposed underground route from the Town Hall to the northern rail link.

"Mr T H Pearce, chairman of the roads committee, said the aim must be to implement the report or a better one if it became available. Mr A R Turner, chairman of the planning and reserves committee, said by adopting the plan the authority set itself against a policy of decentralisation. It would inhibit the march into valuable rural land and make for greater economic use of metropolitan area assets." [325]

Disunity as Usual

As was to be expected, the Auckland Regional Authority was unable to command complete consensus, particularly from those who saw no immediate benefits from the De Leuw, Cather proposals – as reported by the Auckland Star on 18 August 1965:

"It would be 'gross injustice' if the North Shore had to pay a share towards the proposed £21 million bus-rail transit scheme for Auckland, the Takapuna City Council considers. The council has instructed its town clerk, Mr B L Byrne, to arrange a meeting of all North Shore local bodies with the idea of presenting united opposition to North Shore contribution to the scheme. It rejects statements by the chairman of the Auckland Regional Authority, Mr D M Robinson, and other members that such services would benefit the North Shore.

"The only areas it assists are the inner city area and the western and southern areas, said Mr A F Thomas at a meeting of the council last night. Some member of the council spoke of trying to form a North Shore Regional Authority...Mr S L Corbett said the city solicitors should see if they were finally committed to the Auckland Regional Authority.

"Councillors agreed that the North Shore was already paying for the cost of its own passenger transport service to Auckland, bridge tolls and petrol and tyre tax, estimated at £100,000 from vehicles travelling over the Harbour Bridge. This sum was contributed through the National Roads Fund towards the cost of roads other than the Harbour Bridge. To pay for the latest transport scheme on top of this would be 'gross injustice.'

"The chairman of the Auckland Regional Authority, Mr D M Robinson, said today he could not agree with the Takapuna City Council when it said the bus-rail transit scheme would not benefit the North Shore. We cannot consider Takapuna apart from the Auckland region. What benefits the region will also benefit Takapuna, he commented. Some will not benefit to the same extent, but when the scheme is analysed they will recognise that they do benefit.

"The co-ordination of bus services provides for a rapid service to the North Shore. Also, North Shore people working in Auckland will make use of the increased facilities in Auckland the same way as people from all over Auckland use Takapuna beach. He said there must be a readiness to share collective responsibility for collective benefit." [326]

Progress Too Soon

Unfortunately, such readiness was not always forthcoming – as reported by The New Zealand Herald on 19 August 1965:

"An Auckland City Councillor, Mr E C Armishaw, said last night that the de Leuw, Cather plan for a £21 million co-ordinated rail and bus rapid-transit system was 30 to 40 years ahead of its time. Auckland could not afford it, and if it were built it would be for many years a 'white elephant' and a 'dead loss.' No city in the world has yet adopted such a rail-bus scheme unless its population has been greater than one million, said Mr Armishaw. We should forget it now until about the year 2000, when our population is expected to hit a million. On a population basis, we can't make it pay yet. We're asking for a system we cannot afford at the moment.

"Where is the money coming from? Their computers didn't give the answer to that one. The answer to the transport problem in the meantime, said Mr Armishaw, was a modernised, revitalised bus system controlled by the Auckland Regional Authority and similar to the improved system the consultants had recommended for the North Shore. Mr Armishaw said he intended to put his views to the City Council. I'll certainly be watching the interests of the ratepayers in the grandiose scheme, he said. I'm picking it to be a white elephant.

"North Shore Mayors yesterday had mixed feelings on the Takapuna City Council move to seek the help of other North Shore councils in objecting to paying for a share of the scheme…The chairman of the Regional Authority, Mr D M Robinson, commenting on the Takapuna decision, said it was premature to discuss sharing the cost for the scheme until it had been adopted in principle and negotiations on cost made with the Railways Department, the National Roads Board, the Auckland Harbour Board and other interested parties. The Auckland region, he said, must be regarded as one economic and social unit. No one area can arbitrarily divide itself from the rest as is proposed by the Takapuna City Council." [327]

The Road Gang

However, it was a more subtle opposition to the bus-rail proposals of the De Leuw, Cather reports that would stifle those proposals and ensure that there was little advancement toward a viable public transport system for at least the next fifty years. While many civic leaders, such as the Chairman of the Auckland Regional Authority, Hugh Lambie, and of course Dove-Myer Robinson, believed that: *"It did not make sense to rely on motorways alone. To do that would be to copy mistakes made overseas,"* [325] that was not the view of Auckland's 'Road Gang' – those in favour of roads, roads, and more roads.

Arthur James Dickson

Arthur James Dickson, Auckland City Engineer from 1944 until his retirement as City Engineer and Director of Works in 1969, was always a supporter of motorways as the main means of conveying Aucklanders into and out of their city. Indeed, he

"…was a fierce opponent of the [1950 Halcrow Thomas] plan, especially the recommendation to restrict spending on roads. He argued that motorways should take priority." [205]

For twenty years, Arthur Dickson chaired the Technical Advisory Committee of the Auckland Regional Planning Authority which, in 1955, produced the Master Transportation Plan for Metropolitan Auckland – the plan that advocated the construction of roads and motorways and ignored the Halcrow Thomas advice that the development of the suburban railway service should be undertaken first.

By 1965, and despite the problem of Auckland's growing traffic congestion, the findings and proposals of the De Leuw, Cather and Company studies had not undermined

Arthur Dickson's preference for road-based transport. This was clear from a report on the De Leuw, Cather findings, dated 7 March 1966, prepared by Arthur Dickson at the request of Roy McElroy, Auckland's Mayor from 1965 to 1968.

Arthur Dickson Report

While supposedly explaining some of the more technical aspects of the De Leuw, Cather recommendations to the City's Mayor and Councillors, Arthur Dickson took every opportunity in his report to justify the proposals of the 1955 Master Transportation Plan, particularly where they conflicted with those of De Leuw, Cather. While Arthur Dickson acknowledged that some priorities had changed between 1955 and 1966, he nevertheless stressed that the road-based transport system remained the most viable option:

"Particularly in respect of motorways, the [De Leuw, Cather] recommendations follow the 1955 Master Transportation Plan *but with important modifications in the light of improved knowledge now available*. In 1955 when the population was 370,000, emphasis was placed on motorways because such construction promised the greatest benefit for the carriage of passengers and goods *with the money available*. A ten year staged programme was recommended, but it has not been possible to keep to this…It is important to remember that the 1955 Report recommended more than motorways. Not only did it recommend the upgrading of main traffic routes, the provision of terminal facilities for road vehicles and car parking, but it also envisaged improvements to bus transport and the construction of a spur railway line (capable of extension) from the present railway station to Victoria Street. *This was a matter for the Railway Department* which had already had previous reports from British Consultants." [310]

Public Transport Downplayed

While the 1955 Master Transportation Plan did indeed include bus and suburban rail services, the inclusion was perfunctory, to say the least. In his report to the City Council, Arthur Dickson continued to downplay the public transport alternatives of bus and suburban rail recommended by De Leuw, Cather, particularly with regard to the future need for those alternatives:

"As has been indicated, the [De Leuw, Cather] report is not really a technical document and very little of the basic information used in the study is given. Plan A [the all-bus system] is dismissed with relatively little explanation. The Consultants say Plan A would function reasonably well for a limited time. However, they state that in a few years congestion on Queen Street would require prohibition of motor cars from using that street during peak periods. The report does not indicate the total kerb space and street lanes needed for bus operation, but it is evident that it is the changed routeing rather than the increased total number of buses that will cause the congestion. Furthermore, the increase in passengers in 20 years is estimated to be only 13%, notwithstanding the concentration in routeing and new facilities." [310]

Cost Benefit Questioned

Arthur Dickson's summation of the De Leuw, Cather reports also questioned the projected cost-benefit of their recommendations:

"It is to be noted that in the all bus Plan A, it is assumed for 1964 that after a capital expenditure of £9,000,000 the system would carry no more passengers than at present. With Plan B [the preferred bus-rail system] for 1964 it is estimated, after an expenditure of £21,000,000, to carry 82,000,000 passengers or 5,000,000 more. It is estimated that 26,000,000, or 32%, would use the rapid rail facility. Presumably the majority of this 32%

would enjoy improved service although some would not. It would appear, therefore, that it is proposed that the co-ordinated bus and rapid rail system, at an extra cost of £12,000,000 more than the all bus system, would induce an extra 7% more riders and provide an improved service for say 25% to 30% of all transit users.

"What is termed the modal split between different kinds of transport is a matter which is open to question between experts and in view of this it cannot be said how realistic that meagre 7% increase is. There does not appear to be a fully reliable analytical method of making a modal split prediction. As the Consultants claim, bus patronage overseas has declined but it is equally true that rail patronage has also a fallen off overseas. The fact is that all public transportation in cities has been falling off in motorised western countries until the hard core of riders is made up of those without an alternative." [310]

Guidance Limited

Arthur Dickson also referred to the De Leuw, Cather reports as providing only general guidance insofar as bus transport was concerned:

"Bus routeings in the down-town area are said [by the De Leuw, Cather report] to be designed in accordance with the Comprehensive Transportation Survey recommendations that several streets be converted to one-way operation when the motorway is extended to serve the central business district. During detailed planning for the changeover, however, serious consideration should be given to maintaining two-way bus operation on these streets, utilising special bus lanes. The report does not give the full detail for bus routeing, but emphasizes that the report provides general guidance only. There is thus much detailed planning to be done, calling for co-operation between the transit authority (A.R.A.) and the traffic authority (A.C.C.)." [310]

Too Small…Too Poor

As well as promoting the recommendations of the 1955 Master Transportation Plan as still relevant to the needs of Auckland's transportation system, Arthur Dickson's review of the De Leuw, Cather reports also implied that the City was then too small and too poor to consider the type of public transport system proposed:

"This position is not stated with the intention of belittling the value of rapid transport in large, fully motorised cities where, with reasonable standards of environment, it is not possible to provide for all travel on roads. But it does indicate that there is a timing and cost factor which could be related to the size and the resources in a city at any particular time…On the question of finance it is stated that the proposals would be self-supporting in as far as operations are concerned. However, other sources would be required to meet a substantial portion of the fixed charges on the capital outlay. Here is the rub, for it raises the question of State aid or some special method of taxation. No doubt the Auckland City Council will want to know what extra cost, if any, is to be imposed on its ratepayers and citizens." [310]

De Leuw, Cather Inquiries Cost

Arthur Dickson's reference to the possibility that De Leuw, Cather's rapid transport recommendations could impose *extra cost, if any, on its ratepayers and citizens* for a benefit, at best uncertain, was a very effective, if unsubtle way to influence any civic leader wary of upsetting his electorate. After all, the De Leuw, Cather inquiries had already come at a cost, as Mayor McElroy informed his Councillors in his own report "…offered to Councillors as an aid to their consideration of the report of the Director of Works and City Engineer…The cost of the two [De Leuw, Cather] Reports was £155,000 of which the City Council's share was £32,000 approximately, but the City Council is paying an additional £15,000 being the share of 4 local bodies which declined to contribute…" [328]

Mayor Praises Dickson Report

The Mayor praised Arthur Dickson's review of the De Leuw, Cather reports as a "…penetrating analysis and constructive examination…of great assistance to Council." [328] He also pointed out to Councillors that their Director of Works and City Engineer set out "…a number of reasons for doubting that the recommendation of a combined bus/rail rapid transit system affecting '*only two transportation corridors*' within the total area of greater Auckland, will not at this stage achieve benefits commensurate with the estimates of cost given by de Leuw Cather." [328]

Indeed, Roy McElroy quoted, and obviously agreed with, Arthur Dickson's assertion that "*The new* [De Leuw, Cather] *Comprehensive Transportation Plan report vindicates the 1955 report (i.e. The Master Transport Plan) prepared by the technical advisory committee of the Regional Planning Authority some 10 years ago.*" [328] The Mayor assured Councillors that:

"The City Engineer's comments on this matter are entitled to great respect by reason of his own extensive experience and his deep study of this problem both here and overseas." [328]

Difference of Opinion

Whatever Arthur Dickson's *deep study* of local and overseas transport systems may have been, his conclusions of the De Leuw, Cather proposals very definitely conflicted with those of the Americans who clearly stated in their report:

"Experience in larger cities in Western Europe and America has proven the many disadvantages of attempting to rely solely on automotive transportation to handle massive rush hour traffic loads. Such policies result in enormous financial burdens involved in acquiring rights-of-way and constructing motorways in addition to the costly parking structures required for day storage in the large focal centers." [320]

Recommendations Ignored

By supporting Arthur Dickson's depreciation of the De Leuw, Cather proposals for a public transport system and his promotion of the 1955 Master Transportation Plan, Mayor McElroy continued the Auckland tradition of ignoring the recommendations of well-paid planners and consultants.

Just as that of Halcrow Thomas and many others before them had been, the ambition and vision of De Leuw, Cather was to be overlooked by civic leaders in favour of Arthur Dickson's preference for a road-based transport system – and for much the same reasons – the avoidance of cost and responsibility.

This avoidance was evident from the Auckland City Council resolutions subsequently passed on 6 April 1966:

"1. Council places on record its appreciation of the constructive examination and analysis of the two Reports of Messrs. de Leuw Cather & Company carried out by the Director of Works and City Engineer and notes with approval his comments in respect of both Reports.

"2. That with regard to the de Leuw Cather Report dated October 1965 entitled 'Comprehensive Transportation Plan', Council notes the City Engineer's comment that 'The new Comprehensive Transportation Plan' report vindicates the 1955 Report (The Master Transport Plan) (with some amendments and additions). The Council therefore approves the system of motorways outlined in the de Leuw Cather Report of October

1965 to the degree of finality and detail set out therein, and records that the City Council is continuing to co-operate with the Ministry of Works in respect of the design of inner city motorways and the street connections thereto in order that there should be no delay on these urgent works.

"3. Any works which the City Council is obliged to carry out consequent on the motorways, shall be the subject of applications to the National Roads Board for grants.

"4. Council affirms the principle that the whole cost of motorways and regional roads should be borne out of the National Roads Fund and that no part of such cost should be a charge on ratepayers.

"5. In order to aid Council and its technical advisers in the determination of the best possible street connections to the inner city motorways, Council empowers the Finance Committee to engage in a consultant capacity, the services of Professor C. Buchanan of London, Consultant Engineer and town planner and author of the Buchanan Report to the United Kingdom Ministry of Transport and, subject to his acceptance of the appointment, that Professor Buchanan be invited to visit Auckland at an appropriate time.

"6. With regard to the de Leuw Cather Report of July 1965 entitled 'A Regional Transit Plan' recommending what it calls a 'rail-bus rapid transit system' Council affirms the principle stated by the Director of Works in his report (at p.11A, para 5) 'the City must know what it will be required to pay and weigh such costs against the benefits gained.'

"7. Applying the foregoing principle, and for the reasons set out by the Director of Works on page 10 of his Report of 7/3/66 Council is not satisfied that the present proposals of the Consultants, de Leuw Cather, will achieve commensurate benefits to justify the costs to be incurred.

"8. Council is satisfied that the future development of greater Auckland will require the construction of a modernised system of rail transport for its urban and suburban population and with that end in view strongly supports representations to the Government to re-examine forthwith the Halcrow-Thomas Report of 1953, and earlier Reports, in the light of conditions now existing, and of all information now available, so that the best route or routes for the most efficient system of rail passenger transport to serve greater Auckland may be determined, and having been determined, that such route or routes shall be acquired by purchase or otherwise so that the 'right of way' may be protected and there may be no delay or hindrance to construction from this cause.

"9. That this Council request the Auckland Regional Authority to supply the evidence which would warrant the suggested change in ownership and operation of the bus passenger services within greater Auckland in order that Council can give full and proper consideration to this matter." [329]

Responsibility (and Cost) Deferred

By means of Resolutions 3 and 4, the City Council was able to defend the motorway connections proposed by the De Leuw, Cather reports by assigning the expected cost to National Roads Fund subsidies and the National Roads Board.

The Council's immediate responsibility for the motorway work was diverted, by means of Resolutions 2 and 5 which split the responsibility for *the design of inner city motorways and the street connections* between Council planners, the Ministry of Works, and yet another consultant to be hired, Colin Buchanan and Partners of London.

Resolutions 8 and 9, deferred any City Council responsibility to the Government for the development of the proposed suburban railway and to the Auckland Regional

Authority to justify *the suggested change in ownership and operation of the bus passenger services within greater Auckland.*

After that Council meeting, the Mayor and his Councillors might have left the building feeling that they had done a fine job. They may then have found themselves in very long queues of traffic and wondered why it was taking so long to reach home.

Auckland Regional Authority Resolutions

The day before, on 5 April 1966, the Auckland Regional Authority had also passed a number of resolutions relating to the De Leuw, Cather proposals. However, unlike the City Council, the Authority's preference was the same as De Leuw, Cather's – the bus/rapid rail system.

Accordingly, the Authority's resolutions included:

"(a) the authorisation of negotiations with Government relative to financial participation.

(b) that Government assume responsibility for the downtown subway extension and the improvements to existing railway facilities necessary to the operation of a modern rail rapid transport system and for the supply of rolling stock and operation of the rail services.

(c) that the ARA assume responsibility for the provision and operation of the whole of the bus system and bus feeder services to rail and for the annual charges in respect of the rapid rail transport stock." [330]

Colin Buchanan and Partners

While the Regional Authority chased Government interest and money for suburban rail services, the Auckland City Council proceeded with the appointment of the British transport planning and urban design company, Colin Buchanan and Partners.

The Council's 'invitation' was forwarded "…in a letter dated 7 April 1966 from the Mayor 'to advise upon the re-arrangement of the inner city street system consequent upon the motorways'. But we have also borne in mind the Mayor's subsequent wish, as expressed personally to us, that we should feel ourselves free to comment on any aspects of the planning of the City which appear to us to be relevant to the first invitation. In the event our assignment has resolved itself into a commentary on the future planning of the central area of the City." [331]

Entitled *City of Auckland – Planning in the Central Area – An Assessment*, the ensuing report was produced by Colin Buchanan and Partners in July 1966. As requested, the report commented on the re-arrangement of the inner city street system and on a number of planning aspects relevant to public transport, including the mass transport systems recently proposed by De Leuw, Cather.

The Buchanan Report

The Buchanan report began with an overview of the region and the plans and conditions then in place:

"The area which can be regarded as looking to Auckland as its 'centre city' appears to extend from Rodney County in the north to Franklin County in the south, a distance of some 90 miles. Within this area of about 2,000 square miles, there are four county authorities, and twenty-eight urban or borough authorities. The total population of this area at 1965 was estimated to be about 584,000, including Auckland City with 149,400.

"Each local authority within this area is under obligation to prepare a district planning scheme for its own area. These schemes, which are due for review at five yearly intervals, appear to consist essentially of zoning plans indicating, when read in conjunction with supporting written material, the precise use or uses to which any parcel of land may be put." [331]

"City of Auckland District Scheme – The District Planning Scheme for the City of Auckland became operative on 12 June 1961. It consists of the Scheme Statement, Code of Ordinances, detailed Land Use Zoning Maps, and maps showing Development Works. These last maps show reservations for civic and cultural purposes, schools, hospitals, open spaces, etc. (i.e. in general, works to be undertaken by statutory authorities). They also indicate the existing main traffic routing system, the proposed urban main street system, proposed motorways, etc." [331]

"Traffic in the Central Streets – …there is…cause for concern of over-riding importance. This relates to the proposed retention of most of the central business and shopping streets of the City as traffic distributors. In our opinion, to come quickly to the point, this is a completely unacceptable design concept for the future of the City.

"We have closely observed the present conditions in the main streets, especially in Queen Street on a Friday afternoon and evening, and we regard them as unpleasant almost to the point of being uncivilised. The heavy traffic, the noise, the continuous random cross-movement of pedestrians through the traffic, and the damming up of pedestrians at the four corners of the main intersections in anticipation of the so-called 'Barnes Dance' crossing seem to us a far cry from the kind of conditions that should be in anticipation for an important city.

"We realise that this is an expression of personal opinion in relation to Auckland, but we rely on the evidence which is now accumulating from all over the world of the value of shopping streets and areas which are substantially free from the danger and nuisances of traffic. This evidence cannot be overlooked…

"We think this is really the nub of the matter. The City centre is in process of being rebuilt, Queen Street in particular is being redeveloped from end to end, and we suggest with great respect that it is for the City Council to ask themselves whether they have set their sights high enough as regards the standards of the environment that should be sought. It is not only a question of traffic in shopping streets of course, it is the intrinsic convenience, pleasantness, variety and architectural character that are involved.

"Increase of Traffic in the Central Streets – Present plans, far from easing the position in the central streets, would make them worse…In our opinion, these increases in the traffic volumes in the central streets are quite unacceptable. They are, in a sense, the more unacceptable because they arise in spite of massive expenditure for the solution of traffic problems. The central area, for example, is planned to be ringed round by a motorway of formidable dimensions.

"We do not question the need for it, but there is no doubt that to insert a motorway on this scale into standing development is an expensive and painful operation. One would expect the benefits from this expenditure of public funds to be very substantial indeed and to include at the least a high degree of withdrawal of traffic from the central streets and the University area. Instead, as already mentioned, there is to be an increase of traffic in the shopping streets, and the University, instead of being endowed with a precinctual character, remains divided into four by traffic routes.

"Intensive Development in the Centre – There are other related matters regarding the central area about which we feel some concern. It seems to us, for example, that large new buildings of considerable height are being erected at the play of the property market but with very little regard to the overall appearance of the City or to the problems of traffic and concentration of people to which they give rise...if this policy is continued for the whole redevelopment of the central area there is bound to be a considerable increase of central area activity and employment." [331]

Environmental Impact

As well as practical and aesthetic considerations, the Buchanan report continued with its emphasis on the environmental impact that the projected traffic influx would have on the City's development:

"Overloading of the Central Streets – In general terms it seems to us that the motorways as planned and the other roads feeding into the centre could eventually bring in more traffic than the central streets can accommodate, even if no regard is paid to environmental questions. If regard is paid to the environment then there will be serious overloading.

"It is not difficult to see how this situation has arisen – it could have been avoided if the motorway system had been planned as part of a combined operation with the planning of the central area, so that the capacity of the motorways (and other approach roads to the central area) to discharge traffic was kept in balance with the capacity of the central area itself to receive and circulate traffic with due regard to environmental conditions...recent experience has shown the absolute necessity for linking transportation studies very much more closely to urban redevelopment studies, especially where important centres are concerned, and to ensure that full regard is paid to environmental standards which are ever in danger of being eroded by traffic.

"Need for a Comprehensive Study of the Central Area – ...The central point is that if the question of traffic in the main streets is to be taken seriously then there is no avoiding a complex design study to see how the traffic can be dealt with. This involves the whole of the central circulation problem, the amount of traffic that is acceptable in the streets has to be decided, the location of car parks must be considered, questions of servicing buildings must be investigated, bus routes must be considered, the form and design of buildings and the amount of traffic they will 'generate' must be studied, and so on. It is in fact a comprehensive civic design study that is required to reveal the possibilities for future development." [331]

Queen Street Bus Services

With its coverage of public transport planning, the Buchanan report also commented on the routing of bus services in and around Queen Street:

"Buses in Queen Street – The routing of bus services would be a very important part of the study we have described – meanwhile we ourselves would hesitate to permit a greater number of buses in Queen Street unless some corresponding reduction of other traffic could be achieved at the same time. There is quite enough traffic in the street as it is...

"We would, however, go so far as to suggest that one of the associated objectives of this study should be that of devising ways and means of ensuring that the majority of buses destined for the Central Business District were able to penetrate and distribute passengers into the heart of the main commercial and shopping area. This would be one way of maintaining an element of attractiveness for the public transport vis-à-vis the use of private transport. As we have stated before, the ideal situation as far as the general conditions for shopping in Queen Street are concerned would be one in which all traffic is excluded, at least during shopping hours.

"This would mean that all bus services would have to be routed along the nearest adjacent streets. But in Auckland, the rather unique combination of inter-related circumstances – the topography, the present form of the development (and its future potential) and the open spaces, together with the discontinuity of the streets on the east side – all point towards the desirability of maintaining services in Queen Street.

"This is not to say that an attempt must be made to route all services up and down the whole length of the street. We can, for instance, see distinct possibilities in the idea of arranging a number of looped routes in combination with the one-way working of Wellesley Street and Victoria Street, with some routes entering on these streets and others entering via other streets to the north and south and then continuing along only part of the street before turning off again.

"Another idea which we put forward (merely as a possibility which could be considered while more positive plans for the centre are being made) is that of designating part of Queen Street for buses only, say that section between Wellesley Street and Victoria Street. This section could, in effect, become a minor bus station, through which it is obvious that normal traffic would not be permitted (with the possible exception of vehicles required for the essential servicing of frontage premises). Undoubtedly, there would be many problems of design and management associated with such a project, but this again is one of the many reasons why a comprehensive study of the development possibilities of the centre is required." [331]

Further Study Required

"The Proposed Mass Transit System – It was recommended by Messrs De Leuw, Cather that existing railway lines extending to the eastern suburbs be upgraded and extended for a short distance in tunnel into the central business area. Prima facie this is an attractive proposition. But we share the doubts of the City Engineer whether, in the circumstances of Auckland with its very low residential densities, this could possibly be a viable economic concept.

"Yet, on the other hand, the result of the central area study which we have recommended would undoubtedly be to reveal a limit to the amount of traffic that the centre could accommodate, and from this it would follow that there was a residual commuter load which would have to be carried by some form of public transport.

"Precisely what form or combination of forms of public transport would be most appropriate seems to us still to require more consideration. The De Leuw Cather Report dismissed somewhat summarily the possibilities of bus services of various kinds (feeder and express services) operating on the improved highway network.

"Our experience suggests that it will not be possible to make either bus or rail services pay in the conventional sense; but we think improved bus services might be more flexible, cheaper in capital outlay, and generally less of a liability than a rail service. But, as mentioned, we regard the matter as requiring a great deal of further study." [331]

Planning Disparity

During the course of their observations, the compilers of the Colin Buchanan and Partners Report soon recognised a disparity between the infrastructural results of local and national planning. The report's authors were bemused by the apparent discordance between the financial sustainability of Auckland's central city construction and the approaching motorway system at a time when the building of the latter could not be afforded by many British cities.

"To summarise, the impression we are endeavouring to convey is of a quantitative and qualitative study of the central area which is developed on the basis of a number of alternatives from which in all probability one will eventually emerge as the 'best' or 'preferred' design. Whether or not such a design would be capable of being implemented within <u>present</u> legal and financial systems seems to us to be largely irrelevant. It is the long term future of the City that is at stake and there surely can and must be some anticipation of both a strengthening of powers in the future and of a more favourable financial climate.

"With regard to the latter, however, the position somewhat puzzles us. We have not attempted to study the matter in detail but we do observe a considerable building programme in course of execution in the central area, and we also observe a massive urban motorway system in course of execution. This last is something which most cities in Britain are finding it very difficult to initiate for financial reasons. To this extent Auckland seems a good deal better off than many cities we know. But in a sense this increases the dangers.

"If the buildings in the centre are to be renewed and if the encircling motorway is to be driven ahead, both without benefit of or relationship to a central area plan, then there are very serious risks that the centre of the City will degenerate into confusion as regards traffic circulation and architectural form. It will be asked how such a plan could be prepared. We can appreciate there are staffing difficulties at present – there is only one member of the City Engineer's staff allocated to central area work at present and he is not yet in port…The emphasis would need to be on a <u>team</u>.

"We think the normal town planning, architectural and engineering skills would be needed, but it is essential that there should also be continuous access to sound urban-economics advice…As to the time that the study would take, we consider that a balanced team of 8–10 staff under vigorous leadership would cover the ground in a year to eighteen months. [331]

Buchanan Report Conclusion

The Buchanan Report went on to outline specific proposals in line with its primary brief *to advise upon the re-arrangement of the inner city street system consequent upon the motorways*. But while the approaching motorways and the increased traffic they would bring compelled a re-arrangement of the flow patterns of inner city streets, there were also bus routes, the proposed mass transit (rail) system, and environmental standards to be considered as part of any redevelopment of the city centre. The importance of a team effort to quickly develop a comprehensive, central city plan was again emphasised in the Buchanan Report's conclusion:

"Our main submission is that a central area study should be undertaken to reveal the possibilities for the future development of the area and to ensure the traffic needs and environmental standards are suitably reconciled. We have indicated the principles which we consider should be applied in the planning of the centre, and we have discussed some of the results that might follow. We have suggested that a special effort should be made to muster a team to undertake the study, and we have said that we think the resources of skill could be found within New Zealand for what is probably the most important planning task in the country.

"It only remains to emphasise the urgency of the position. Plans for improving the accessibility for motor traffic to the central area have been driven ahead, but the complementary planning task to reorganise the centre to deal with the traffic has lagged seriously behind. The urgency arises from the fact that the centre of the City is actually in process of being redeveloped, and if major improvements for the public good are to be achieved, it is essential to take advantage of this process of redevelopment. Opportunities lost now may never be recovered." [331]

Regional Master Plan

However, the urgent need for a team to develop a comprehensive, central-city plan was not the only priority. As part of its introduction, the Colin Buchanan and Partners Report described the Auckland region as consisting of four county, and twenty-eight urban or borough authorities each looking to Auckland as its 'city centre'. For the region to succeed as a whole, it was obvious to the consultants that a great deal of harmonisation of the various district plans of these counties and local bodies would be necessary.

But, after more than a century of parochial governance that was easier said than done. Although a Regional Master Plan was eventually prepared by the fledgling Auckland Regional Authority in 1967, each local authority retained its right to ignore or vary any proposals it might disagree with or which conflicted with its own – as John Steel, General Manager of the Auckland Regional Authority, described:

"Despite the preparation of a Regional Master Plan, which will endeavour to co-ordinate the district plans to produce a coherent pattern of development, the fact remains that each local body is the planning authority for its own area, and the necessary acquiescence to a Regional Master Plan can give rise to serious disputes and appeals.

"As already stated, Auckland is faced with increasing urbanisation, and it is becoming increasingly urgent that piece-meal and timid approaches, usually dictated by financial considerations, should give way to bolder conceptions which will benefit the larger community as a whole. Undoubtedly, the peripheral areas, with their sprawling developments, can continue with each growing conurbation requesting political status, but such drifting developments will only perpetuate the present pattern of fragmented government and compound the present difficulties.

"One of the most important aspects of modern local government is, of course, that of finance. Smaller local authorities are continually faced with limited resources and are therefore hindered in their performance by inadequate finance. Here again, it is obvious that the creation of larger units of government will not only enable such units to be stronger politically, but will enable them to draw upon greater financial resources, establish better capabilities relative to loan monies, and, most important, determine priorities in major projects. In addition to all of the foregoing, many other matters, such as uniformity in zoning by-laws and building by-laws would be capable of achievement.

"This would be of tremendous value to the various developers who operate throughout the metropolitan area and who are aggrieved that the lack of uniformity within, what even they recognise as, a single metropolitan area." [169]

Officials Committee

This lack of local government consensus had often been criticised by central government and the situation would remain one of the main reasons given by it for not contributing financially well into the future. It was also good reason for the Government to undertake its own inquiry into the De Leuw, Cather proposals for the Auckland region's urban transportation needs. Accordingly, on 30 May 1966, Cabinet directed the formation of an Officials Committee comprising the Commissioner of Works: P L Laing, Deputy Secretary of Treasury: J D Lang, General Manager of Railways: I Thomas, & Commissioner of Transport: R J Polaschek (Chairman).

The Committee's brief: "...to discuss and make recommendations on the financial implications of the Auckland Transport scheme.

"The Committee considered information available at the time of the preparation of the Auckland Regional Authority proposals together with that which has become available since. The Committee carried out an independent analysis of the proposal and this has been compared with the consultant's findings. A visit was paid to Auckland at the invitation of the Auckland Regional Authority to enable members and officers of the Authority to express their views. A similar meeting was also held with members and officers of the Auckland City Council." [332]

Decision Wanted

But, while the *financial implications of the Auckland Transport scheme* were the subject of yet another inquiry, a new year which many frustrated Aucklanders hoped would herald less talk and more action had commenced. The Auckland Star editorial of 2 January 1967 reflected that frustration when it included as one of the newspaper's seasonal resolutions:

"...On the regional level, Auckland...wants a decision on the railroad rapid transit system which experts have recommended for this city. It does not expect it to be operating tomorrow (long ago it learnt that little gets done here without great argument). But it wants in 1967 at least a decision that this is the shape of things to come and plans to realize it in the foreseeable future." [333]

Holiday Mode Consideration

As one might expect from a Government in holiday mode, the Star's wish for a speedy decision would not be granted – as the newspaper reported on 13 January 1967:

"The Minister of Works, Mr Allen, today revealed that Cabinet had not considered the special report it ordered on the Auckland rapid transit scheme. The report and recommendations, prepared by a three-man officials committee headed by the Commissioner of Transport, Mr R J Polaschek, was given to the Government on October 28. 'I'll be taking the report to Cabinet early in the new year on resuming duties, said Mr Allen from his Whakatane home today. I'm not going to say anything further at this stage.'

"He said the new Minister of Transport, Mr Gordon, had taken the report to study it over the holiday break. Mr Allen, who has spent the Christmas and New Year period at his home – 'I've been doing nothing: just having a quiet time' – said he expected to be back in Wellington next week. He would not say at which Cabinet meeting he would present the report.

"There was no comment today from the Auckland Regional Authority officials on the Government's delay in studying the report on the transit scheme...The chairman of the authority, Mr H D Lambie, is holidaying in Noumea. But he was quoted as saying late last year that it was 'the right decision that we (the authority) want rather than a hurried one.' The Government has had the rapid transit plan 'under consideration' for more than nine months. The authority unanimously adopted the recommendations for a rail-bus rapid transit system, plus a network of motorways, expressways and street improvements, on April 5 last year. Then it asked the Government for financial help. The report on

Auckland's transport needs was commissioned from the De Leuw, Cather and Co. in May 1963. They presented their final plan to the authority in November 1965." [334]

New Minister of Transport

Any decision was further delayed by the appointment of a new minister:

"The appointment of a new Minister of Transport is causing a further delay in consideration by the Cabinet of the rapid transit road and rail scheme proposals for Auckland. The Minister of Works, Mr Allen, said yesterday that he was not prepared to submit the report and recommendations on the De Leuw, Cather road and rail proposals to the Cabinet until the new Minister, Mr Gordon, had studied them…Mr Allen said he could not say on what date he anticipated placing the report before the Cabinet. 'It will be when Mr Gordon has studied the report and is quite happy about it – not before.' The consultants' recommendations…were adopted by the Auckland Regional Authority on April 5 last year. Since then Mr H D Lambie, chairman of the authority, has said that delays in acting on the proposals will adversely affect the development of Auckland." [335]

Unacceptable Delay

A delay, for whatever reason, was unacceptable to the Auckland Regional Authority as well and its chairman sought to provoke a faster response, as reported by The New Zealand Herald on 2 February 1967:

"A plan for implementing de Leuw, Cather recommendations which give priority to fast bus and rail services instead of to roads is being prepared by the chairman of the Auckland Regional Authority, Mr H D Lambie. Mr Lambie said yesterday he was confident that the Government, local authorities and the business community would find his suggestions economically acceptable. He said it was obvious that the Government was having misgivings over the economic implications of the de Leuw, Cather plans. 'I am sure that what I have in mind will be good economics,' he said. 'The idea is to concentrate on the mass transport of people rather than spend large sums of money on roads and parking buildings.'

"Mr Lambie will give details of his plan at a conference he intends calling…It is understood that Mr Lambie's plan has been prompted by indications that the Cabinet is unlikely to give approval to the recommendations in the de Leuw, Cather report in their present form…Other factors which are believed to have influenced the authority in preferring emphasis on mass transport are reports before the Cabinet from Government officers favouring fast commuter services." [336]

Another Red Herring

News of Mr Lambie's plan drew an immediate response, as reported by The New Zealand Herald the following day:

"The Auckland Chamber of Commerce will ask the chairman of the Auckland Regional Authority, Mr H D Lambie, for full details of his plan to implement de Leuw, Cather recommendations which give priority to fast bus and rail services instead of to roads. Mr J E Beachen drew members' attention to the announcement of Mr Lambie's plan. 'It looks as though he intends to introduce a scheme that will be just another red herring,' said Mr Beachen. Mr D A Highet said: 'I think Mr Lambie feels that the economic situation being what it is the Government might not be prepared to implement the plan in full and he is seeking a compromise…" [337]

Government Assurance

While no doubt still in holiday mode, the Minister nevertheless responded to Auckland's uncertainties as positively as he could, promising a future rapid transit solution despite the country's 'financial difficulties':

"The Minister of Works, Mr Allen, has given an assurance that the Government is not neglecting the idea of an underground link for downtown Auckland as proposed in the De Leuw, Cather report. Writing to the Mayor of Auckland, Dr McElroy, he said no one in the Government had denied that in the very near future the surface transport system of streets and motorways would have to be supplemented by some form of rapid transit – probably rail.

"However, the financial problems were difficult to resolve, Mr Allen said. Dr McElroy had written to the Prime Minister, Mr Holyoake, seeking an assurance that the government was still interested in the proposed underground. He pointed out that last year the City Council had adopted the recommendation of Professor Colin Buchanan, a transportation expert, to prepare a comprehensive scheme for the future development of the downtown city area. The council had organized a specially qualified section to develop such a city scheme, he said. But for the purposes of the plan it was necessary to know the route of the proposed underground rail link.

"Dr McElroy said that having regard to the country's economic problems he did not say that such a system should be built at once. Indeed, advantage could be taken of a delay by studying underground systems being built overseas. But he hoped that in four or five years it would be possible to get on with the job." [338]

City Council Undecided

The idea expressed by the Mayor that Auckland could wait another four or five years before implementing a plan that not even been fully accepted by the City Council drew an immediate response from councillors:

"The position of the Auckland City Council on the de Leuw, Cather rapid-rail system was described as 'airy fairy' by Mr T H Pearce at a council meeting last night. Mr Pearce was supporting Mr T R Sussex and Mr I W McKinnon who criticised the Mayor, Dr R G McElroy, for remarks made in a letter to the Minister of Works, Mr Allen.

"Mr Pearce said the council appeared to be asking the Government to implement a report on which the council had made no decisions. Mr McKinnon said Dr McElroy had given the Government an excuse for a further delay.

"Mr Sussex said he was also confused by the council attitude. The consultants' report had never been fully debated. 'I think we were side-tracked by Professor Buchanan's visit,' he said. 'Our engineers could have covered everything he told us. We paid £5000 to be told to get on with the job.' Mr Sussex said it was wrong for the Mayor to say the de Leuw, Cather recommendations should be implemented sometime in the nebulous future.

"Dr McElroy: 'Within five years – there's nothing nebulous about that!'

"Mr Sussex: 'Why put five years on it? Whose opinion is that? Yours or the council's?'

"Dr McElroy: 'My personal opinion.'

"Mr Pearson asked if it was the definite policy of the council to support and press for an underground railway in the city. 'I'm not being difficult,' he told the Mayor, 'but I would like to know what our policy is on this matter.'" [339]

City Council Dissent

The Auckland Star of 9 February 1967 reported further dissent among City Councillors:

"A lack of co-operation between the Auckland City Council and the Auckland Regional Authority on implementing the De Leuw, Cather transport report was claimed by Mr T R Sussex at the city council meeting last night. 'The De Leuw, Cather report is an important document which has not received attention from the city council it deserves,' he said. 'There has not been a full debate on it, though we may have adopted it in very broad and vague terms. I don't think this council has had the liaison and co-operation with the Regional Authority which is necessary for the progress of Auckland. How long is it since we had any discussions with the Regional Authority about the report – or the Government's delay in implementing it?' he asked." [340]

Call for Local Unity

Published in the same edition, the Star followed up with a comment from the Minister of Works and a call for a greater show of local unity:

"The Government, according to the Minister of Works, 'is not neglecting the idea of an underground link for downtown Auckland.' Mr Allen may be right, all appearances notwithstanding. Nevertheless, the Minister and his department will be bound to take some notice of reports of the discussion at last night's meeting of the Auckland City Council. Whatever the council has or has not approved in the past, it is clear that the Auckland region is still far from united in its attitude to the De Leuw, Cather rapid railroad transit plan. So long as this continues, what is the use of expecting the Government to commit itself to it?

"Ten months ago, the Auckland Regional Authority approved the £21 million scheme in principle. It asked the Government to accept responsibility for building the subway, improving existing railway facilities and running the rail services to schedules fixed by it. The authority has spent most of the 10 months, first in getting the plan considered by the Government's officers, and then in trying to obtain the Government's decision. It has still not had a decision. In November the Prime Minister promised action at the earliest opportunity. Three months later his Minister of Works is saying that the financial problems are difficult to resolve…

"Auckland city is the largest local body in the Regional Authority. It is essential that the scheme have its backing. There is no point in badgering the Government for action until Auckland is united on this issue and clearly seen to be in Wellington. Surely the time has come for closer liaison between the Regional Authority and the Auckland City Council? "Some of the questions asked earlier should be easier to answer now. The authority's hand would be greatly strengthened if it became clear that the plan has the council's blessing. Any doubt on that point should be resolved. It will remain so long as it can be alleged that the Mayor appears to be asking the Government to implement a report on which the council has made no decision.

"If there are any differences between the Mayor of Auckland and the Regional Authority chairman, they could be discussed informally. The authority should welcome the Mayor's support and do what it can to assist the City Council to a similar decision…This question is too important for the development of the Auckland region to be allowed to develop into a dispute between its two largest local government bodies. If Auckland is at cross-purposes, where is the obligation on the Government to show more interest in meeting regional problems? Whether this is a pretext for delay or not, it will be entitled to say that it cannot commit itself till Auckland has made up its mind what it wants.

"The Mayor has come to take a larger view where initially he was mainly concerned with the benefits, or lack of them, to people in Auckland city itself. He now sees, as surely the council must, that the planning of the city itself is wrapped up in the fate of this transport plan for the wider region. First, let Dr McElroy and Mr Lambie confer, and then the members of the authority with the city councillors to see whether or not cross-purposes can be transformed into a common purpose." [341]

City Council Delay

Auckland City Mayor, Roy McElroy, was quick to respond to the suggestion that his council did not support the rapid rail proposals, albeit with some reservations: "Any suggestion that the Auckland City Council was seeking to delay by one day the introduction of an effective rapid rail transit system for Auckland was completely unfounded, the Mayor, Dr R G McElroy, said yesterday. Dr McElroy was asked to comment on repeated statements that the council was 'dragging its feet' over the de Leuw, Cather proposals. He was also asked to clarify council policy on the consultants' recommendations in view of doubts expressed by council members at a meeting on Monday.

"Dr McElroy said the council position over the rail system was made clear in one of nine resolutions passed at a meeting in April last year and has not changed since then. The resolution was: Council is satisfied that the future development of greater Auckland will require the construction of a modernised system of rail support for its urban and suburban population and with that end in view strongly supports representations to the Government…Dr McElroy said that the council was still of the opinion, as expressed in a second motion at the April meeting, that the system outlined by the consultants would not achieve benefits to justify costs." [342]

Ramifications of Inaction

But while the Government and the City Council continued to talk of only *future development* and the *benefits and costs* associated with the construction of a rapid transit service, the ramifications of inaction had begun and were gaining momentum:

"The chairman of the authority's planning committee, Mr Arnold R Turner, said that unless the rail plan was adopted promptly, the present trend towards decentralization from Auckland's central business district would be accelerated. This would weaken the importance of downtown Auckland. The rapid rail system would be a big influence against urban sprawl and would encourage redevelopment in central Auckland. The cost of the rail system should be judged against the cost of decentralization and urban sprawl. If the Government decision were against the scheme because of cost, the Government should assure Auckland that alternatives would not cost more, said Mr Turner." [343]

Decentralisation Trend

"Mr Turner said that the Government decision on the proposals would be one of the most important town-planning decisions in the history of the city. The authority's move to ask the Government to adopt the rail system, he said, highlighted the need to consolidate and strengthen the central business district – the chief commercial centre of the region. 'The rail system is essential to save the city from being strangled by the motor car,' he said.

"Mr Turner said that in Melbourne, 72 per cent of people going into the centre of the city used public transport but in Auckland the figure was only 34 per cent. 'Unless the rail plan is adopted,' he said, 'the present trend toward decentralisation will be accelerated, weakening the relative importance of downtown Auckland. 'The cost of the rail system,' he said, 'should be judged against the cost of decentralisation and urban sprawl.'" [344]

CBD Exodus

Former Auckland Mayor, Dove-Myer Robinson, agreed:

"Auckland's central business district was being 'slowly bankrupted' through business houses being driven out by traffic congestion, the former Mayor, Mr D M Robinson, said today. The only solution was to build the rapid rail transit system planned by De Leuw, Cather and Company and adopted and wanted by the Auckland Regional Authority, he said. 'We can't afford to wait any longer for a decision on when we are going ahead with this scheme,' continued Mr Robinson. We certainly can't afford to wait five years, for in the meantime, the situation in the city becomes worse every day.'

"Many thousands of square feet of office space in central Auckland was going unused because of traffic congestion. This represented a big economic loss, particularly when coupled with the extra expense faced by companies which were rebuilding in outer suburbs to beat traffic chaos. This exodus from the city centre could prove costly to the Auckland City Council and ratepayers, said Mr Robinson." [345]

Conference Sought

Prompted by Dove-Myer Robinson, the Auckland Regional Authority sought to promote an active, local front by way of a conference with the City Council:

"The Auckland Regional Authority last night decided to call an urgent conference with the Auckland City Council with a view to co-operating in the implementation of the de Leuw, Cather proposals. The motion was first put by Mr D M Robinson, who proposed an urgent meeting to secure a speedy beginning of the de Leuw, Cather proposals. It was later amended by Mr T H Pearce and passed in a form mentioning the co-operative aspect of the conference…Mr Robinson said…'If we could get together at a meeting we could tell each other what we were thinking, and between us make rapid progress instead of acting as ad hoc bodies.'

"Mr Pearce supported the proposal and cautioned against the current defeatist talk that because of the present economic situation 'we have no money. The continuation of this talk will lead to recession,' he said. 'It's no use finding money is going to be available and we aren't ready. We must plan well ahead and this meeting should be a step in the right direction.'" [346]

What Economic Situation?

While the country's poor economic situation had always been given as a valid excuse by Governments unwilling to commit to capital expenditure, it was seen as an unnecessary distraction in this instance – as reported by The Auckland Star on 14 February 1967:

"The economic situation does not in any way detract from the need for a Government decision on the De Leuw, Cather rapid transit plan for Auckland, the chairman of the Regional Authority, Mr H D Lambie, said today. Such a decision would allow planning to proceed and priorities and programming to be laid down. Mr Lambie made his comments after the authority spent most of yesterday afternoon in committee discussing the frustrations it had encountered so far in getting on with its job… In his statement, Mr Lambie said the Government had had sufficient time to examine the full implications of the De Leuw, Cather proposals…The authority had received no decisions, though it was known that departmental officials [the Officials Committee] had finished a report on the scheme for Cabinet." [347]

Private Bus Operators Desperate

But it may as well have been one of New Zealand's regular recessions as far as Auckland's private bus operators, the alternative to a rapid transit scheme, were concerned – as per the letter from K Nilsson, Chairman, Omnibus Proprietors' Association to The Hon. J B Gordon, Minister of Transport, dated 21 February 1967:

"Your Commissioner will have made you aware of the progressive deterioration in the financial position of the private bus operators in Auckland over a considerable period but particularly during the past two years to the point where at this time very few companies are earning even a reasonable profit and many are operating at a loss. This situation has been further aggravated by the increase in costs consequent upon the recent General Wage Order and the further increase which will result from the current negotiations with the Union concerning a new award.

"It has become abundantly clear to Operators, individually, and to the Omnibus Proprietors' Association, as a Group, that something must be done as a matter of extreme urgency if many Proprietors are to remain in business. It is generally accepted that the answer to the problem does not lie in simply further increasing fare levels or reducing services, as the point has been reached where the principle of diminishing returns may well apply. After several discussions, our Association invited the Institute of Economic Research to investigate the problem in Auckland… the Institute Report deals at length with the problem from the aspect of 'Public Interest' presents a clear and logical appraisal of the factors involved, and reaches a definite and clear-cut conclusion…" [348]

K Nilsson's letter continued…

"Private Operators are controlled by the Transport Licensing Authority whose approval is required for fare structures, routes and timetables, and by your Department in several other respects. This means that it is not possible for any operator to make an undue profit and, indeed, profit margins have been so rigidly controlled in past years that many companies have not been permitted to accumulate the necessary reasonable reserves for application to future vehicle replacement programmes. Although it is by no means the only factor, the point is made at the outset, as being one substantial contributor to the unsatisfactory state of many of the vehicles now operating in the Auckland area and to the lack of accumulated funds in the hands of operating companies.

"The operation of public passenger transport by private companies and individuals is an enterprise conducted for profit. This point is emphasised because there has been a growing tendency for the private operator to be regarded as a quasi-Government or Civic Agency. A reasonable return on his invested capital is the very last consideration taken into account by Municipal Authorities, Trade Unions and the general public, nor do they appreciate that if all private operators were taken over by the Regional Authority the cost to the ratepayers of Metropolitan Auckland would be enormous.

"Public passenger transport is an international problem of particular concern to this Country since we probably spend more per head of population on transport than any Country on Earth due to the high cost of vehicles, running costs, and the ever increasing low utilisation of vehicles. Every year the Country spends more and more on magnificent highways right into the heart of the Cities to enable the private car operator easier access and on parking buildings and parking facilities to accommodate this ever increasing volume of private traffic. Every million spent to assist the private car owner is another nail in the coffin of public passenger transport.

"We do not propose to go into detail on the question of the structure of our drivers' award other than to draw attention to the fact that it results in large numbers of drivers being idle for several hours each day for which they must be paid. We believe that such restrictive practices are not in the interests of anyone, including the men themselves, but we do not envisage any change as likely. The point is made as the drivers' wages bill is the largest single item of cost of all operators.

"Another factor which contributes greatly to increased operating costs is traffic congestion, particularly at peak hours, resulting in a much longer elapsed time for round trips. This means increased staff for no additional revenue and additional strain on vehicle parts resulting in higher maintenance costs. There does not appear in sight any likely alleviation of this problem and, indeed, it seems likely to increase and, of itself created as it is by Government planning, demands a short term revenue solution. This same congestion, created by the private car, is driving industry away from the Cities to the outer suburbs, making it almost impossible for regular services to suit their needs which again reduces loadings during the worker periods.

"We submit that if present operators are to continue they must have some form of financial assistance to enable them to do so. The day is long past when bus operation can be regarded as a profitable form of private investment and it would be perhaps the very last type of business which could attract equity or even loan capital. The present situation for most of our members is desperate. Unless they receive some definite assurance that they can look forward to an improvement in their revenue position in the very near future many of them must seriously contemplate either terminating their services or so drastically reduce them as to make them quite unacceptable to the travelling public.

"Operators do not want a subsidy. What they do want is relief from certain present forms of indirect taxation which should not be applied to this industry and which of themselves contribute to a situation which aggravates their problem. What they seek can be summarised as follows:-

1. Relief from payment of fuel taxes, both petrol and diesel.
2. Abolition of heavy traffic licences on buses.
3. Access to Government Agency loan finance at reasonable interest rates to encourage and assist in fleet replacement and modernisation.
4. Freedom of duties on suitable imported vehicles and parts.
5. A co-ordinated national campaign to give publicity to public passenger transport and to make people aware of what it costs them to run their own motor cars and the vital part the service plays in the community.
6. A detailed appraisal of all the manifold issues involved in the industry by a qualified Committee set up for this specific purpose. It may well be that a Commission should be considered as appropriate having regard to the major issues involved.

"The present situation has widespread political implications and overtones, the least of which is the financial welfare of the private operator whom we represent. We believe that unless Government is prepared to grasp and to deal with this problem along the lines which have been suggested it will have to accept the responsibility for a situation which, when it inevitably develops, can be held to be one which could have been avoided." [348]

Institute of Economic Research Report

As referred to by K Nilsson, the findings of the Contract Research Unit of the New Zealand Institute of Economic Research did indeed support his plea for the financial support of public transport when it reported in 1966:

"Urban passenger transport in New Zealand is evidently in financial difficulty to-day. Most publicly-owned services are losing money heavily and the relatively few private operators, mainly in the Auckland area, are barely breaking even. This situation is relatively new but it is deteriorating rapidly…It is generally agreed that the widespread use of the private car is the main reason for the serious financial position of public transport to-day.

"This report examines some of the immediate issues involved but the subject merits a much fuller appraisal. Only bus services are dealt with here and attention is focused on Auckland where the problem appears most acute…

"It is not easy to estimate the extent to which costs could be reduced, if at all. It is, however, instructive to examine the cost structure of private firms for they have most to lose by inefficient operation and have no access to public funds to make good their losses.

"Cost Structure of a Typical Urban Bus Service: % of total costs

Drivers' wages, etc.	45
Servicing and maintenance	26
Licence Fees	4
Taxes on Fuel	6
Fuel (excluding taxes)	9
Overhead Expenses	10

"We may therefore tentatively conclude that the raising of fares within 'acceptable' limits will not make urban bus services financially viable and neither will cost-cutting or amalgamation. If bus services are to be kept going in the case of private operators and if losses on local authority services are to be kept within bounds, some form of financial assistance is necessary unless radically different terms of employment can be negotiated.

"Subsidies are not only justifiable but also desirable where the benefits of an operation accrue not only to the direct users but also to a wider section of the community. In the case of urban bus services, benefit obviously accrues to passengers who pay fares for the privilege, but nearly all sections of the community benefit from the existence of an efficient public passenger transport system.

"Motorists benefit in having less congested roads than would otherwise be the case; employers benefit from being able to recruit labour from further afield and Government and local authorities benefit through not having to provide as many roads, parking buildings and other facilities as they would if all commuters came by car. There is thus a strong case for holding that the 'user-pays' principle is unjust because a small section of the community is paying for benefits enjoyed by society as a whole. Accordingly, fare revenue may properly be augmented by some form of subsidy…

"A large part of the Auckland metropolitan area is served by the Auckland Regional Authority, and the remainder by 15 private companies. The Auckland Regional Authority operates about 340 buses and the private companies about 360. Last year [1965] the Regional Authority suffered a trading loss of £237,000 and the private companies were also in financial difficulties: no company made substantial profits, some made small profits, and many made no profits.

"Furthermore, the situation is deteriorating. The private companies are faced with wage claims which, if granted, would put them out of business unless the wage increase was offset by increased revenue from fares. Present indications are that such fare increases would have to be very large, and there is no means of telling whether the effect would be to raise revenue sufficiently, but there is a presumption to the contrary. In any case past experience shows that there would be a large switch to the use of private cars.

"The private companies operate buses that are in many cases sub-standard and which do not provide the private car with strong competition. Because of their low profitability the bus companies are unable to raise loan finance for better fleets, and even if they could, they would not readily commit themselves to large capital expenditure because of uncertainty about their financial viability in the future.

"If the private companies do cease to operate because of financial losses, they will have to be taken over by the Regional Authority, or else no service will be provided at all. If the Regional Authority were to take over existing companies and operate them at a loss, those services would in effect be subsidised by Auckland ratepayers...

"The De Leuw Cather screen line counts of bus transport show that about 22,000 passengers travelled into or out of the central business district at peak times...in 1963. The figure is probably about the same to-day. If all publicly-and-privately-owned bus services were to be discontinued, therefore, about 22,000 people would have to find alternative means of transport into the city in the morning and out again in the evening. In the short run at least most of these people would presumably have to come by car, because their residential areas would not be conveniently served by ferries or trains.

"These cars would all have to come into the central business district, where parking space is already at a premium. Hence 10,000 to 13,000 additional parking spaces would have to be provided, which, at the De Leuw Cather estimate of £1,000 per space, would cost £10m - £13m. This expenditure is over and above that which already has to be incurred to cope with natural increase, and does not provide any parking space whatever for casual parkers.

"Clearly, if the number of vehicles using the roads at peak times is increased, better roads are needed if congestion is not to become intolerably worse. It is not easy to estimate the amount that would have to be spent on roads but an estimate can be made within very broad limits to obtain an order of magnitude. The De Leuw Cather report considers that to meet the natural increase in the volume of traffic, £3.5m will have to be spent each year for the next 10 years. This is the figure reached even when the greatest possible use is made of public transport.

"...the fact remains that discontinuing all bus services would cause, at a conservative estimate, at least a 33% increase in peak traffic, and possibly quite a substantial amount more. Clearly this would require considerable roading expenditure...A conservative lower limit would be £25 million.

"Subsidies would appear the only practicable short-run a means of ensuring the continuing operation of private bus companies, and the cost of adequate subsidies would clearly be much less than the cost of replacing buses with private cars.

"A subsidy is readily variable, so that if bus companies earned unduly high profits with subsidies, the subsidies could be cut. Subsidies might take the form of fixed cash payments, the covering of trading losses, or the remission of taxes.

"The second, that of covering losses, is unattractive as it provides no incentive to an operator to work efficiently. The other two methods would both be readily workable, although the latter, the remission of taxes proposal, would seem to be the more sensible: it would avoid taxes being collected and then reimbursed. The level of the subsidy payment should be just sufficient to enable the most efficient operators to earn modest profits.

"If all licence fees, petrol tax and mileage tax were remitted, operators' costs would be lowered by about 10%. This would enable the private companies to continue to operate and would be a major incentive for them to modernise their fleets…

"The cost of so remitting all taxes paid by bus operators, both public and private, in the Auckland Metropolitan area, would be well under £250,000. The 15 private companies now pay a total of about £115,000 a year in fuel taxes and licence dues. A payment of £250,000 is about eight times cheaper than the estimated cost of all commuters coming into the city by car." [349]

Additional Approaches to Government

There was certainly no shortage of approaches to the Government by concerned Auckland leaders during early 1967. For instance, Auckland's Mayor, Roy McElroy, wrote to the Minister of Works, Mr Allen, on 20 January in which he referred to a 17 November 1966 report to the National Roads Board by the Director of Roading, J H Macky, and a later report by the Commissioner of Transport, Mr R J Polaschek, following their study tours abroad:

"Mr Macky made in that report some very penetrating observations on the urban population 'base' for a rapid transit rail system or 'subway'. He first noted that whereas United States experts tended to think of a million as a minimum urban population for a subway, in Europe half a million was usually adopted as a minimum urban population. He further noted that 16 European countries were building rapid urban subways, and one had a population of only 320,000. The most significant observation he made was that: '…subways tend to dictate the development of a city. The sooner you put one in the sooner you can determine which way your city will develop.' The application of this principle is a matter vital to the future development of Auckland City…it is quite vital to know the route of the projected subway for the City of Auckland, especially that portion of the route to be followed in the 'down town' area of the city…

"In only 10 years Greater Auckland will have a population of nearly three-quarters of a million and in only 16 or 17 years it will have reached a population of one million. Nothing can stop this growth, but unless it can be properly planned now the city is unlikely to be a pleasant place in which to live and work. Instead it will become as some overseas cities already are – a vast sprawling metropolis without character and bedevilled with traffic problems. It is not sufficient to rely on motorways for carrying 'commuters' from their homes to their places of work. Mr Macky made this plain when he said, speaking of subways and motorways: '…when you get to a certain size you have to have both.'

"The unmistakable evidence is that Auckland is fast approaching the 'certain size' to which Mr Macky refers. The views of Mr Macky are underlined by observations of the Commissioner of Transport, Mr R J Polaschek, who said, only four weeks after Mr Macky's report: 'Main New Zealand cities would be completely choked by cars within 15 years if no action was taken to improve their internal road systems. He also said: 'Motorways alone are not the answer' and he added: 'There is a limit to the extent to which you can disrupt and destroy the city to accommodate the private car.'

"Mr Polaschek, like Mr J. H Macky, made his observations just after returning from a study tour of the United States, England and Europe. It is significant that Mr Polaschek's tour, which led to his remarks, has taken place since a report to Cabinet of himself, Mr Laing and Mr Gandell on the de Leuw, Cather recommendations. Mr Polaschek makes the point that New Zealand is approaching the car population ratio that now exists in the United States, and in 15 years would have overtaken that figure. These observations of Mr Macky and Mr Polaschek have tremendous relevance to the City of Auckland and its future…" [342]

Government Reply

Mr Allen replied to the Mayor:

"May I say right away that no one in Government has ever denied that at some time, and not a very distant time, the surface transport system on roads, streets and motorways must be supplemented by some form of rapid transit, probably rail. The officials committee report delivered to Government late last year accepted this and made recommendations which line up very well with your own views as expressed in your letter. The financial problem posed is more than difficult to resolve and any failure of Government to publicise the report or to announce decisions is due entirely to the need to consider very carefully all the implications.

"It would be most unfortunate if decisions in principle were adopted now only to find that these could not be followed up successfully by executive and financial action. It is certainly the desire of my engineers that planning and design action should be taken to define the route and I hope that decisions will be possible to enable this to proceed. As you say, very important studies are proceeding overseas and it is hoped New Zealand will be able to take advantage of these when the time comes to move on transport works in our cities…" [342]

Public Transport Decision Delayed

Alas, despite what appeared to be wise advice, all correspondence to the Government was to no avail – as reported by The Auckland Star on 1 March 1967:

"Auckland can expect no government approval of the De Leuw, Cather transport plan for at least 12 months. The Minister of Transport, Mr Gordon, told the committee chairmen of the Auckland Regional Authority of this yesterday. 'I have given the authority an undertaking that by the end of 12 months the Government will have come down with some answer to the report,' said Mr Gordon after the meeting. In the meantime, an official Government committee and he would consider this and other reports. 'But there will not be any action from the Government before 12 months,' he added.

"The minister told the meeting he would confer with the authority on matters which needed to be 'cleared up' in the proposals during the 12 months. The chairman of the authority, Mr H D Lambie, said after the meeting the 12 month delay was 'not too bad.'

"'At least Mr Gordon has given us a definite date - before now we have had nothing to go on at all. 'Though there will be no action for 12 months, I think it will be a time for decision-making – I think the period will be quite profitable,' Mr Lambie added. The Mayor, Dr McElroy, said the interval of 12 months would not be disappointing if it was 'well spent in active examination' of the rapid rail transit project by the Government…" [350]

Delay Unacceptable

But while both Hugh Lambie and Roy McElroy saw the Government announcement as some form of progress, The Auckland Star did not:

"As motorways reach into the city motorists travelling on them are beginning to realize how vital it is that the central business area should be carefully planned. Otherwise, Auckland might find itself with a highly efficient road system outside the city and massive congestion inside it. The danger becomes all the more real with yesterday's announcement by the Minister of Transport, Mr Gordon, that it will be 12 months before the Government is ready to make any decision on the De Leuw, Cather rapid rail transport plan.

"Where does this leave the City Council team which is trying to draw up a comprehensive plan for streets, buildings and traffic within the central area? It can hardly be expected to reach any very firm conclusions before it knows whether Auckland will even have an underground railway, let alone the route of it. Public transport cannot be ignored as an essential factor in inner-city planning. The De Leuw, Cather team considered it so important that they made it the subject of a special interim report.

"That was more than 18 months ago. Since last October the Government has had available to it a report on the proposals by an inter-departmental committee drawn up after wide-ranging technical discussions. Yet Mr Gordon now proposes a delay of another full year. The one sop he offers is a firm promise that 'some answer' will be ready by then.

"Both the Mayor and the chairman of the Regional Authority have jumped at this consolation. But this is not a matter which should be affected in the slightest by the country's current economic difficulties. Nobody is asking the Government to begin spending money on an underground system for Auckland – or even to commit itself to a starting date. What is wanted, and urgently, is a decision that will allow the city, in its overall planning, to take account of a future rail-bus system or of some alternative if the Government turns it down. Auckland is developing too fast, both inside the city and on its fringes, for such a fundamental decision to be delayed a day longer than is necessary.

"To some extent, Auckland has itself to blame for the delay. The Regional Authority and the City Council are not as united as they should be on the scheme they want. They should now determine to press on with technical discussions. The sooner they are agreed on exactly what Auckland wants the sooner they can urge the Government to hasten its approval in principle. A rail-bus scheme deserves exhaustive study. But it should not need a further year for a decision." [351]

Local Co-Operation Called For

The Mayor of Mount Albert also called for unity:

"The Auckland Regional Authority should be helping territorial local bodies, including the Auckland City Council, to overcome problems of road and rail service said Mr F G Turner, mayor of Mt Albert, at the monthly meeting of the Authority. The Authority has approved the proposals of the de Leuw Cather report but the Auckland City Council has not yet declared its policy. 'We don't want to give the Government the opportunity of saying that Auckland local bodies, as usual, are all going in different directions with each pushing its own affairs, said Mr Turner. 'We have a golden opportunity of offering co-operation in this matter and in the redevelopment of the central area.'" [352]

City Council Too Nebulous

As usual, both the writer of the Auckland Star editorial and the Mount Albert Mayor were ignored by the City Council's finance committee which craved a piece of the action and actually received it – as The Auckland Star subsequently reported on 9 March 1967:

"The Mayor of Auckland, Dr McElroy, last night gave an assurance that the Auckland City Council was wholeheartedly behind the Auckland Regional Authority in pressing for an underground railway for the city. He was replying to a question at a council meeting from Mr T H Pearce, who is also chairman of the Regional Authority's roads committee. Mr Pearce asserted the council was 'in one hell of a mess' because it was 'too nebulous' in its thinking.

"Mr T R Sussex opposed a finance committee recommendation that the committee be empowered to negotiate with the Government over the underground. 'This is the most important item to come before the council in its present term of office,' he said. 'It is a question in which we should at all times seek the active co-operation of the Regional Authority. I do not agree that the finance committee should be empowered to negotiate on its own.'

"Mr I W McKinnon said that the De Leuw, Cather report had been called for by the Regional Authority, on which the City Council area had six members. He said the correct channel of approach to the Government would be through the council's six representatives on the authority. 'If one party tries to have separate and parallel negotiations with the Government it would be most disadvantageous,' he said.

"Dr McElroy said the council had the right to approach the Government on matters which affected its ratepayers. The committee's recommendation was carried. A further recommendation that the finance committee of the City Council and the Regional Authority confer so that the 'utmost progress may be made in securing for Auckland the most efficient system of rapid rail transit' was also carried." [353]

No Positive Planning

However, all negotiations with the Government, *separate and parallel*, or not, were to prove fruitless – as reported by The New Zealand Herald on 13 April 1967:

"Mounting concern that no positive steps are being taken to plan for the proposed rapid rail transit system is expected to come to a head at a meeting of the Auckland Regional Authority on Monday. The Minister of Transport, Mr Gordon, told the authority early last month that a Government decision on the de Leuw, Cather plan, which includes an underground railway, could not be expected for at least a year. A few days later the Minister of Works, Mr Allen, said he would send the authority a letter confirming what had been discussed at meetings between the two Ministers and authority representatives. The authority expected an indication from Mr Allen on the form joint planning on the transport system would take.

"It is understood that concern within the authority arises from the fact that, more than a month after the visit to Auckland by the two Ministers, no indication of the Government's intention has been received. The authority is anxious that discussions begin urgently between the authority, the Auckland City Council and the Government so that planning is at an advanced stage when the Government makes its final decision which, according to Mr Gordon's estimate, will be early next year.

"The main points at issue are differences of opinion between the authority and the council over the route of the underground link in Queen St and the reluctance of the

Gas Pedal to Back-Pedal   Chapter Four

Government to disclose details of a report on the transit system made by senior Government officials late last year. The council, which has a team of planners preparing an inner city development plan, has asked that the route of the underground and the position of terminals be determined urgently so that it may proceed with its development." [354]

Decision to Defer

Finally, at long last, the Government did make a decision but not the one Auckland politicians and planners were expecting – as reported by The Auckland Star on 18 April 1967:

"The Minister of Works, Mr Allen, said today the Government had decided that 'not one penny piece' should be spent on the Auckland rapid transit system in the next 12 months, because of the economic situation. 'It is no good the members of the Auckland Regional Authority saying they are confused,' he said. 'I told them face to face in discussions on February 28, and later confirmed in a letter, that Cabinet had deferred for 12 months a decision on recommendations made by a committee of senior departmental officials. If they want to discuss anything, I am willing to discuss it, but no work on anything connected with the project can be done until after next February.' This applied to the proposed survey work on the underground railway route.

"Asked what the departmental officials had recommended to Cabinet, Mr Allen said he could not disclose this. 'The recommendations will not be known until after Cabinet has considered the matter again 12 months from the deferment.' Mr Allen said that to clear up confusion he would like the Star to publish in full the letter he had sent to the Regional Authority.

"His letter to Mr Lambie early last month read:

"'This will confirm the information which I gave to you and a committee of the Auckland Regional Authority during my recent visit to Auckland, regarding the Auckland transportation plan. You will remember that the Government appointed a committee of senior departmental officials to meet with you and then to report on the De Leuw, Cather Report.

"'The inter-departmental committee reported to me on the weekend that the General Election commenced and, as you will readily agree, this was not the best time for the Government to consider such a report. I accordingly held any action on this until mid-February, when I referred the report to Cabinet. Cabinet's decision was to defer for 12 months a decision on the recommendations, but a sub-committee of Cabinet was appointed to continue discussions with the departmental officers.

"'This sub-committee of ministers will be meeting the officials in the very near future. I did mention to you that it would be my desire to set up a survey team to determine and survey routes both for Auckland and Wellington for underground railways, and I hope that this will be one of the matters dealt with in 12 months when I report back to the Government.'

"Mr Allen confirmed a meeting of the Cabinet sub-committee met this morning on the Auckland scheme. He would not say what had been discussed. Last night the Regional Authority resolved to ask the government for an assurance that it will fix and survey the route for the planned Auckland rapid rail transit scheme within 12 months. The move followed receipt of Mr Allen's letter. The authority chairman, Mr Hugh D Lambie, said he was sure Mr Allen was setting up a survey team to determine and survey routes for the Auckland railway within the 12 months.

"Mr F S Stevens labelled the Minister's statement 'ambiguous'. Which 12 months was the Minister talking about he asked. Mr I W McKinnon said what was wanted was a firm undertaking to do specific things at a specific time and in full consultation with the authority. A delay of 12 months was quite unacceptable, and the authority should tell the government so. Mr T H Pearce said the authority should insist on knowing what the committee recommended. It should also refuse to be bluffed by talk about economic stringency." [355]

Government Decision Criticised

Criticism of the Government's reluctance to show some leadership and vision continued with another Auckland Star editorial published on 19 April 1967:

"Nearly two months ago Auckland was told that it could not expect Government approval of the rapid rail transit plan for the city for at least 12 months. It accepted that decision, even if it could not see any compelling reason for it. But now it is disclosed that the decision went further than that. The Minister of Works says that no work on anything connected with the project can be done until after next February...

"This is a decision that cannot be accepted in Auckland without protest. It means that for at least 12 months longer, and probably more, the Government is committed to nothing. Auckland has not asked for large sums of money to be voted for the scheme this year. Indeed, if by some happy chance they were, they could not be spent. They could not be spent because the Government, it is quite clear, has not authorized and is not going to authorize essential surveys and planning. This is what Auckland is entitled to complain about.

"From now on many acts of omission by the Government are going to be excused by economic circumstances. How good is the excuse in this case? How much money, in overseas or local currency, would it cost the Government to make up its mind on this scheme now rather than at some shadowy future date? Would an insupportable strain be imposed on the coming Budget if a few thousand pounds was voted in the estimates for route planning and surveys and protecting the proposed right of way? The questions have only to be posed to suggest the kernel of the problem is the Government's reluctance to commit itself to the scheme.

"The interdepartmental committee which examined the plan reported to the Government more than five months ago. It has made certain recommendations. What these are the public does not know. The Minister declines to reveal them and says they will not be revealed for 12 months. Why? Auckland is more vitally concerned in this issue than the Government and the Minister. If it cannot get any action from the Government, it would at least like to know what action, if any, the Government's expert advisers suggest.

"Auckland has reason to fear the consequences of delay. It suffered the process in the case of the Harbour Bridge and was forced to accept an inadequate bridge or do without. Now it is incurring the expense of making good the inadequacy. Is the sorry story to be repeated in the case of the proposed underground and regional rapid rail transit system?

"It must be realized that the Government is not being asked to carry the whole cost. The Regional Authority, and the local bodies represented in it, are prepared to meet their share. They are not dogmatically tied to any scheme in all its details. The City Council has asked that all reports be considered in planning the best system for the region's circumstances.

"The only activity Mr Allen can promise this year is that a sub-committee of Cabinet will continue discussions with departmental officers. What this may lead to is anybody's guess. The country's economic difficulties, according to the Government, are temporary. Why, then, should it be unable to make up its mind now about the scheme, authorize route surveys at trifling cost, protect the route that is decided upon, and say that it hopes a start can be made on building the system in five years, or after whatever other interval it thinks must elapse?" [356]

Local Disagreement Continues

Of course, the Government could always rely on continuing Auckland disagreement – the same old arguments as to what type of transport system the City really needed:

"De Leuw Cather's rejected all-bus system is more likely to give Aucklanders a good public transport system – and more quickly – than the proposed rapid rail transit scheme, says the head of Auckland University's town planning faculty, Professor R T Kennedy. He said that as a town planner, motorist and citizen he found the proposed rail system quite unconvincing…Professor Kennedy said the case for the rapid transit scheme, which was wanted by the Regional Authority, was based on two very big assumptions. That a large number of people in an unspecified area would prefer it to bus and car. [and] Population density in the area would be enough by 1986 to justify adoption of the plan.

"Professor Kennedy said Auckland needed a comprehensive transport system for both public and private road transport, and rail transport. However, the De Leuw, Cather rapid-rail proposals did not convince him. He questioned the 26 million passenger loading on the proposed rail scheme and asked how many Aucklanders could be induced to use it…Professor Kennedy questioned how people of Hillsborough and St Heliers, for example, could be persuaded to travel four miles to the nearest rail station. Howick people (included in the urban area) were seven miles from a station.

"He doubted that people in these areas would take a bus or drive a car to a rail station to catch a train into the central business district. Professor Kennedy pointed out that overseas cities with similar schemes had a much higher population density. The expected deficit for Auckland on 26 million passengers a year was £810,000, he said. How much greater would it be if that 26 million was not realized." [357]

Dove-Myer Robinson Replies

As usual, Dove-Myer Robinson's reply was quick and to the point:

"Auckland's ex-Mayor, Mr D M Robinson, today labelled as 'superficial' Professor R T Kennedy's view on the De Leuw, Cather recommendations on transport. In backing an all-bus system instead of the rapid rail transit scheme, Professor Kennedy had completely ignored the fact that the transport report had to be considered in conjunction with De Leuw, Cather's report on roading, plus development of the region as a whole…Under the rapid rail scheme, the cost of all roading in the region in 20 years was put at £140 million.

"But if the all-bus plan was used, roading costs would probably exceed £200 million. Mr Robinson pointed out that the suburban rail system already existed, a fact ignored by Professor Kennedy. All that was needed was to modernize and extend the system to get an efficient service. Mr Robinson said that as an Auckland city representative on the Regional Authority he was very concerned that traffic congestion may strangle the city as the economic and social centre of the region. The rapid rail scheme would provide people with a fast transport service and ease pressure on the roads; the all-bus system could only add to traffic congestion and make it even more difficult for people to use their own cars." [358]

Some Political Support

Dove-Myer Robinson did have some Government support for his stance on public transport, albeit in the form of a newly-elected, Auckland Parliamentarian (who much later would become a Cabinet Minister):

"Traffic chaos in Auckland was predicted in Parliament last night by Mr Highet (Govt. – Remuera) unless people were encouraged to use public transport and leave their cars at home or at suburban railway stations. He said in his maiden speech that the answer to traffic chaos in Auckland was the establishment of a rapid rail system along the lines – but not necessarily the route – recommended in the Halcrow Thomas and De Leuw, Cather reports.

"He urged the Minister of Works, Mr Allen, the urgency of the rapid rail system. The report of the Government officials committee was being studied by a Cabinet Committee, he said. 'I firmly believe that the motorway system, supported by a modern rapid rail system carrying passengers from suburban stations into the very heart of the city, is the solution to the traffic and transport problem,' said Mr Highet.

"'I appeal to the members of the Cabinet committee to give urgency to the study and implementation of these reports so that an early decision can be reached to proceed as soon as the economic situation has improved. Once this decision is reached in principle, and the sharing of capital and running costs are settled between the Government, the Auckland Regional Authority and the Auckland City Council, studies can be undertaken to define the route. The land required for the rail system must be protected from further encroachments. I cannot emphasize too strongly the necessity for the Government to make an early decision on this matter." [359]

Fragmentation Alert

The Chairman of the Auckland Regional Authority, Hugh Lambie, also forecast a less than dignified future for Auckland if transport planning was delayed any longer – as reported by the Auckland Star on 13 May 1967:

"Auckland must do something about its transport system if it is to survive the next 20 years with any dignity or character, the chairman of the Auckland Regional Authority, Mr H D Lambie, said today. He was addressing the Northern Regional Jaycee conference. Mr Lambie said a rapid comfortable rail system was a 'must' not only to keep older business areas from being choked to death but also provide transport for the workers so desperately needed in industry, and whose numbers will grow to around 400,000 in the next 20-year planning period. Neither the individual nor the nation could afford the daily use of cars with a 1.5-person occupancy using a million-pound-a-mile highway.

"'Somehow we have got to get people out of their cars, and to do that we have to face something much better than we have at present. New Zealand has got to get into dealing with its transport as an urban problem, and to do this it will have to integrate bus, rail and road transport,' he said. Mr Lambie said that unless Auckland got this form of transport in the next five years it would fragment itself, and the South Auckland area would develop into a city of its own." [360]

More Discussion Planned

All this 'local' talk of *chaos* and *loss of dignity* elicited a Government response of sorts:

"The Minister of Works, Mr Allen, does not want to see complete inactivity on Auckland's rapid rail transit plan despite the fact that the Government has deferred for 12 months the implementation of the De Leuw, Cather recommendations. He wants to discuss the plan jointly with the Auckland Regional Authority and the Auckland City Council after he returns from the United States, he said today.

"He was pleased to see the regional authority and the city council getting together on the plan recently and he hoped this spirit of unity would be maintained so that he could meet both bodies after his overseas trip. Mr Allen said he must have discussion on certain aspects of the plan with both bodies. The city council would have to be consulted on the underground railway through the city and there would have to be discussions with the regional authority on the overall plan, he said." [361]

Divide and Rule

However, for once the ARA and the City Council showed some unity by rejecting the Minister's offer to meet separately with their transport sub-committees – as reported by The Auckland Star on 1 May 1967:

"Executives of the Auckland Regional Authority have told the Minister of Works, Mr Allen, they believe an authority-Auckland City Council sub-committee on the De Leuw, Cather transportation plan is unacceptable at this stage. Mr Allen suggested such a sub-committee meet the Cabinet sub-committee appointed to consider the De Leuw, Cather plan. The Minister's move was an attempt to apply the Wellington City Council-Government arrangement on works to Auckland (Wellington is also seeking an underground railway)…It is understood that the Minister has been reminded that only the authority is in a position to speak and negotiate for the whole of the region. It has been pointed out that Auckland city has six representatives on the authority (two of them are city councillors) and the authority unanimously approved the De Leuw, Cather scheme. The suggested authority-council sub-committee would have bypassed other local bodies in Auckland involved in the transportation plan…" [362]

Joint Approach

The joint approach to the Minister of Works, Mr Allen, was soon announced – as reported by The New Zealand Herald on 9 May 1967:

"The Auckland Regional Authority and the Auckland City Council are to make a joint approach to the Government seeking an early decision on the route of the proposed rapid rail transit system. The two bodies feel that although a Government decision on the proposals cannot be expected until early next year, because of the financial climate, survey and planning work can go ahead without special financial provision being made for it.

"The decision to make a joint approach to the Government was announced yesterday afternoon after a meeting between the Mayor of Auckland, Dr R G McElroy, the deputy-Mayor, Mr A O Glasse, and members of the policy and finance committee of the authority. Mr H D Lambie, chairman of the authority, and Dr McElroy said in a statement of joint policy, agreed at the meeting, that the council and the authority realised the current financial restrictions made it difficult for the Government to commit itself to constructing the rapid rail system. The two bodies were, however, most anxious that a year should not elapse without action at the planning stage. Representations were to be made as soon as possible to the Minister of Works, Mr Allen." [363]

Technical or Policy Talks?

Those representations to the Minister of Works proved successful – as reported by The New Zealand Herald on 18 July 1967:

"The Auckland Regional Authority last night accepted an offer from the Minister of Works, Mr Allen, for the Government officials committee to visit Auckland to discuss the rapid-rail plan for the city. The discussion would centre on a tunnel route through the central business area and would be held with the authority technical officers. A sentence in the authority resolution put by the chairman, Mr H D Lambie, thanking Mr Allen for his courtesy drew opposition from Mr T H Pearce, Mr I W McKinnon and Mr A R Turner. The point at issue was whether technical staff should have discussions before or after members meet the Minister...

"Mr Pearce said the authority and the people of Auckland were entitled to a statement from the Government whether or not it was prepared to proceed with planning the route. 'The minister is not facing up to his responsibilities on this matter,' he said. 'We never asked him to go into the technical details. He should either say he is prepared to meet us or say he is not.'

"The question, he said, was one of policy and nothing to do with technical staff. 'The Minister has no right,' he declared, 'to ride over a request from the City Council and the authority, the elected representatives of 500,000 people.'

"Mr McKinnon said the consultants' report had been before the Government for years. Any meeting other than a face-to-face meeting at the highest Government level would amount to a delaying tactic. 'The authority has waited far too long for a Government statement on this on this issue,' he said.

"Mr Turner said it was still not clear whether the Government intended to authorise planning to proceed. 'We are not gaining the co-operation we could expect from the Minister,' he said. 'Either we are permitted to proceed with planning or not.'

"Mr D M Robinson said the authority should not antagonise Mr Allen. 'If you want to get the honey,' he said, 'don't kick over the hives.'

"A motion by Mr Pearce that, irrespective of the technical discussions, the Minister be asked to indicate whether he intended to meet the authority and the council to determine the route was defeated by 16 votes to 14. Mr Lambie said Mr Allen had been most co-operative. It could be inferred from the letter, he said, that the Minister intended meeting the authority and the council at the appropriate time." [364]

Officials Committee Report

The report of the Officials Committee was finally published during the second week of August 1967. The first part of the report outlined the anticipated financial viability and patronage of De Leuw, Cather's alternatives of the proposed all-bus and bus/rail public transport services:

"The consultant Company recommended against the all bus system which they estimated would cost £9,400,000 and, after allowing for interest on and amortisation of capital, run at an annual loss of £630,000. Instead they endorsed the co-ordinated bus/rapid rail system at an estimated capital cost of £20,400,000 and an estimated annual loss of £1,100,000.

"The consultant Company allotted 76,800,000 passengers to the all bus system in 1964 and estimated that the total would increase to 85,000,000 in 1986...the 1970 passenger total would be 79,000,000. For the bus/rapid rail system the Company estimated 82,000,000 passengers in 1964, 87,000,000 in 1970 and 100,000,000 in 1986...based on the assumption that the improved service offered by the rail system would attract an increase of 25% in public transit patronage in the rail corridors. We consider this to be a high allowance for induced traffic. [332]

The Officials Committee then compared De Leuw, Cather's findings with the results of its own studies: "As far as we can ascertain from studies made for the Committee, including a study of trends since the de Leuw Cather report was prepared, patronage of the co-ordinated bus/rapid rail system in 1970 is likely to be in the vicinity of 78,000,000.

"The patronage on the all bus system is also likely to be lower than that estimated by the consultant. It is difficult to estimate with reasonable certainty the patronage for either system in the 1980s. Our investigations could not substantiate the projected 100,000,000 bus/rapid rail passengers for 1986 and in our view this estimate is optimistic…The effect of a reduced annual patronage would be reflected in increased annual losses.

"Because we believe that patronage would be lower and capital costs higher than the consultant estimated, we believe that annual losses on the co-ordinated bus/rapid rail system would be likely to be of the order of £2,000,000… [332]

The Officials Committee then went on to substantiate its preference for an all-bus, roads-based transportation system as the better option, at least for the *immediate future*:

"Since the de Leuw Cather Report the Auckland Regional Authority has effected moderate fare increases. However, a 56 per cent increase on the average fare assessed by de Leuw Cather would be required for the service to cover all costs, and it is clear that a price rise of this order would lead to a substantial drop in patronage and thus would contribute to, rather than reduce, traffic congestion. It is likely that further fare increases would be possible, but the percentage which could be added without substantially reducing the number of people travelling cannot be estimated at the present time…It seems to us that even under conditions of increasing street congestion, an all bus system could cope for a number of years ahead with the volume of patronage likely to be available.

"The patronage forecasts relied upon by the consultant company indicated 100,000,000 passengers on the bus/rapid rail system in 1986. Passenger figures on Auckland's bus services show that the bus services together with existing rail services were carrying this number of passengers in 1955. While road traffic densities have increased in the ensuing 12 years, the completed sections of motorways and those under construction or planned for the region should take care of much of this increased traffic.

"With reasonable planning and control, congestion may well be kept to an acceptable level for a number of years, although there may be difficult short-term problems during the period when necessary roading adjustments are taking place. [332]

Indeed, the future remained uncertain so the Officials Committee hedged its bets just a little:

"If buses were used indefinitely, traffic congestion would increase to the stage where very heavy additional expenditure on roading would be required to enable road traffic to move with a reasonable degree of freedom. It could well be that such additional expenditure would exceed that necessary to introduce a bus/rapid rail service; on the other hand the rate of growth of the private car is such that additional expenditure on roading would be needed to relieve congestion in the 1980s in any case.

"The extent to which a bus/rapid rail system would relieve congestion is uncertain. The consultant Company estimates that the bus/rapid rail system would have carried 5,200,000 more passengers than the all bus system in 1964, but this we believe would not have offered substantial relief to the congested street system. However, it could be that in 15 to 20 years' time the co-ordinated bus/rapid rail system would provide the only feasible method of moving large numbers of passengers to and from work at peak hours in a congested city.

"Because of the uncertainty of future development in either the Auckland region or the Auckland central city area; because probable patronage of the proposed co-ordinated bus/rapid rail system would be less than would be the case in some cities overseas where there are higher population densities in the urban areas; and because an all bus system provides greater flexibility than a system centred upon a railway, it is our view that the Auckland region can continue to be served by an all bus system supplemented by the existing rail suburban services and trans-harbour ferries for the immediate future. However it is our belief that a firm decision should be taken now to ensure that a bus/rapid rail transit system could come into operation during the 1980s. [332]

Cost Remains the Greatest Concern

But regardless of the future, immediate costs and who was to pay remained the greatest concern, as always, particularly to the Government and its Officials Committee:

"Largely because of the growing popularity of private cars, municipally owned urban passenger transport is now running at a loss…Traditionally, the cost of passenger transport has been met from fares paid by passengers. Where this has proved to be inadequate, the loss has been met by the operating agency – in the case of the railways from profits on freight haulage or from national taxation, and in the case of a local authority from property rates and other revenue. At the present time, it seems clear that heavy capital expenditure and considerable and growing operating losses are an inescapable part of the provision of adequate urban passenger services…[332]

Decisions Deferred Again

Accordingly, the Committee's recommendations deferred the decisions then necessary – a hiatus that would, of course, allow for ever more customary discussion and inquiry:

"We recommend that plans should be made for the introduction of a co-ordinated bus/rapid rail system in the Auckland region to commence operations in the 1980s; the system to be operated by the Regional Authority, either directly or through contractors. The Authority should now plan for the assumption of the necessary financial responsibility;

"That an essential pre-requisite to the introduction of the bus/rapid rail system is the preparation of a development plan for the Auckland region;

"That a group representative of New Zealand central and Auckland local and regional government officers be appointed to determine the precise rail route in the light of this plan; That a special investigating team be appointed to consult with Auckland local authorities and passenger bus operators on ways of maintaining adequate public passenger services in the Auckland region in the interim period to the 1980s…" [332]

Recommendations Endorsed by Government

A copy of the Officials Committee Report was forwarded to Auckland's Mayor, Roy McElroy, by the Prime Minister, Keith Holyoake.

The report was accompanied by a letter, dated 9 August 1967, in which the Prime Minister informed the Mayor:

"Government has endorsed the recommendations in the Committee's report but wishes to stress that the annual charges to be met by the Regional Authority will include the cost of servicing the capital expenditure of the development of the rapid rail system including the purchase of land and buildings and the provision of rolling stock." [365]

Critical Reactions

Reaction to the publication of the Officials Committee Report, such as that published by The New Zealand Herald on 13 August 1967, was to the point:

"Approval in the form announced yesterday has already taken more than two years to obtain since the presentation of the De Leuw, Cather report. The doubts expressed by the committee of departmental officials on forecasts for the rail scheme suggest that they still cling to hopes that the city's transport problems can be solved by buses alone. In view of the regularity with which rates of growth in Auckland exceed the estimates, their forecasts of traffic for the rail system seem excessively cautious.

"Certainly calculations are made more difficult because the existing Auckland suburban rail service is so antiquated as to be an almost negligible factor in regional transport. But experience in big cities elsewhere indicates that efficient rail systems tend to become of prime significance in rapid transit and a major influence in determining patterns of growth.

"Consignment of the service to an exceedingly indefinite date 'in the 1980s' makes further inflation of costs inevitable. The interim measures needed to prevent traffic paralysis on the roads could also become prohibitively expensive." [366]

The Auckland Star

The Auckland Star also criticised what its editorial writer described as a timing delay of historical precedent:

"Aucklanders who leapt up and down this week at the talk of a city bus-rail scheme 'sometime in the 1980s did so for varying reasons. Some screamed: 'At last - a decision.' Others looked at the time lag – and the small print in the Government announcement – and simply screamed...

"Which brings the issue back to Wellington, to planners, policy-makers, economists and controllers. Perhaps they have beaten us to the precedents of history. If they have, then it makes the issue all the more worrying - and there will be plenty of spare time for thought as we sit in the fuming traffic pile-ups of the seventies.

"How horrifying if that glossy, thoroughly modern, 20th-century and already two-year-old De Leuw, Cather report has been considered in Wellington against a background of 'Rome wasn't built in a day.'

"If that was the philosophy, then Auckland might be wise to agree quickly, throw in a classical reference or two to the Vandals - no names, no pack-drill - and point out that whatever the construction schedule might have been, it didn't take too long for strong-minded critics of the Roman administration to take that city to pieces either - officials, decision-makers and all." [367]

House of Representatives Opposition

The Government's reluctance to fully commit itself to the De Leuw, Cather proposals also elicited a response from the Opposition in the House of Representatives, including the deputy-Leader of the Opposition, Hugh Watt:

"The Government had had the consultants' report for two years before it gave Auckland an answer on the scheme this month. The first responsibility was on the Government to provide the necessary capital. 'I have never heard anything so ridiculous,' he declared. 'All reports so far produced indicate that even by 1970 road traffic congestion in Auckland will be such that some other transport system will have to be provided. Yet the Government says it will not contribute a penny and that the transit system cannot begin until the 1980's. By 1980, more than one million people will be living in Auckland.'

"The statement by the Prime Minister and his colleagues, added Mr Watt, had merely been a method of putting the transit scheme proposals aside. No financial aid had been offered to get the scheme under way...Mr N V Douglas (Oppn-Auckland Central): 'If ever the kiss of death was given to any one project, the Government gave the kiss of death to the de Leuw Cather report.'" [368]

Arthur Dickson Summary

No doubt to counter such opposition, the City Council's Director of Works and City Engineer, Arthur Dickson, compiled his own summary of the Officials Committee's findings.

Dated 16 August 1967, but not presented publicly to the City Council until 20 September of that year, Arthur Dickson's summary was very much an '*I told you so*' statement that illustrated, in whatever way he could, how the Officials Committee Report agreed with his earlier (March 1966) review of the De Leuw, Cather Reports.

As he did with his 1966 review, Arthur Dickson took every opportunity to promote the roads-based proposals of the 1955 Master Transportation Plan and to emphasise the cost of any suburban rail scheme, repeating the Prime Minister's advice that, should the rapid rail system be proceeded with, the Auckland Regional Authority would be responsible for "...total annual losses, including all capital servicing costs..." [369]

Arthur Dickson's summary of the Officials Committee Report added: "We have no additional information since first receiving the De Leuw Cather Report and the discussion and information in the Officials Committee Report must be taken in good faith...By way of comment, it should be noted that the Council approved in principle the system of motorways outlined in the De Leuw Cather Report to the degree of finality and detail set out therein...

"It will be recalled that I pointed out that the original De Leuw, Cather] reports were not detailed technical reports and that it was difficult to express opinions without more information. It would now appear that the civil engineering and railway aspects have been examined. The result appears to confirm important doubts which I raised.

"I also said that the major decisions to be made would be political, financial and legislative, and this is confirmed by the Committee's report. Furthermore, I pointed out that there remained a great deal of work to be done before the matter could be finally determined.

"The Committee questions the allowance made by the Consultants for induced traffic. In addition, the Committee is of the opinion that, while it is difficult to estimate with reasonable certainty in the 1980s, the Consultants have been over optimistic in their estimate for both the all bus and the bus/rapid rail in respect of the number of passengers to be carried at that time.

"I also questioned these estimates. Since the Consultants made their report decentralisation in respect of Auckland for living space, factories and shops seems to have accelerated. The technical press indicates that this is also the pattern in overseas countries with highly motorised populations, and it would seem that there is little difference between cities with and without rapid rail transit." [369]

"The average population density in the Auckland Region is considerably lower than in Los Angeles, which is one of the most decentralised cities in the world. Some city authorities, with a good deal of propriety as a result of experience, do say that their cities are compelled to do what the people want...The Regional Authority is preparing a

Regional Plan and the City has set up a City Development Section. The work of the two organisations must be complementary, and the existence of a large number of District Planning schemes for the many local authorities in the region cannot in themselves guarantee the ultimate form of regional development. Unfortunately it must be admitted that there is much uncertainty about the future development of the region except to say that it is certain to be of low density in character." [369]

Arthur Dickson concluded:

"The aim of the recommendations of the Officials Committee appears to be for the purpose of planning for a [rapid/rail] service to begin in the 1980s, and this is dependent upon the prior preparation of a Regional development plan. There appears to be no imminent prospect of a rapid/rail service…

"I have already referred to the excessive costs if Auckland tried to carry this scheme alone. The Officials Committee indicate that the overall benefits (if any) are marginal…When possible escalation of costs is taken into account the financial implications are even worse, and if modern experience and research is of value in regard to the place and effect of rapid/rail transit in modern motorised cities, there appears to be little prospect of the rapid/rail transit proposals materialising in the foreseeable future.

"Having regard to the moderate size of Auckland and the low density development of the region, the report of the Officials Committee, our own departmental examination, the cost burden, the view of Professor Buchanan, the need to introduce an all-bus system for say 20 years in any case, and the prospective rapid growth and development of Auckland in that 20 year period, it seems inescapable that the City Development Section should preferably prepare a central area plan predicated on an all-bus transportation system.

"Unless some firm decision is made in the near future it would seem that the situation is likely to remain vague, unresolved and not conducive to further progress in the planned development of Auckland, and the City Development Section cannot be expected to plan effectively in such an atmosphere." [369]

Arthur Dickson Rejects Rail System

"Without debating it, the council last night referred Mr Dickson's report to its town planning and finance committees…After the meeting Mr Dickson was asked whether in fact he was recommending that the council reject the rail system. 'In the meantime, yes,' he replied. 'I think it would be irresponsible for any Government or local authority to proceed with a scheme knowing that it will result in annual losses of $4 million for many years. We could put an underground railway in now,' he added, 'but what is the use of it if we cannot pay for it?'

"He said it was very unlikely that ratepayers in areas of the city such as the North Shore, St Heliers and Mt Roskill, who would not receive benefit from the rail system, would agree to bear a share of the large costs. 'I would say that we would do well to go ahead with the bus system and take another look at the question in say 15 years' time.'" [370]

(Although, in hindsight, the opinion of Arthur Dickson proved somewhat short-sighted, it should be remembered that, as commented upon by a contemporary town planner, Mr I B Reynolds:

"By dint of his considerable experience Mr Dickson commands much respect in the City Council administration and his views and judgments will be a strong influence when any firm decisions are made.") [371]

Professor Buchanan Views

Although Arthur Dickson could rely on his long-standing reputation as City Engineer, and the supporting views provided by the Officials Committee and Professor Buchanan, the ideas of the latter may not have been an ideal choice – as reported by The Auckland Star on 22 September 1967:

"It seems that Colin Buchanan, the English town planner whose visit here last year cost the city $14,390, is being listened to after all. He was the one who knocked the rapid rail transit system advocated in the De Leuw, Cather report and supported the report's alternative, improved bus services. The city engineer, Arthur Dickson, is of the same opinion in a report he has brought down this week, a report which is upsetting the rail supporters. But even though his ideas are supported here, the professor is having trouble, it seems, back home.

His move out of plush offices in Kensington to 'something smaller' is because his ideas are too radical, say transport people in London. The move follows rumours that Professor Buchanan was planning to close down altogether because of the lack of work. 'He tells people plainly that if they want to live with the motor car they must plan their cities for it, and spend enormous amounts of money on the job. His idea is to wipe out everything that has gone before and start again from scratch,' says a civil servant." [372]

Distinct Lack of Planning Co-Operation

Following the formal submission of Arthur Dickson's report to the City Council, the Auckland Star revealed a distinct lack of planning co-operation between the Council and the Auckland Regional Authority, when it reported on 21 September 1967:

"A report on the De Leuw, Cather rapid rail transport proposals, compiled by the city engineer, Mr A J Dickson, and presented to Auckland City Council last night was today described as a 'bombshell.' The comment was made by Mr D M Robinson, who was chairman of the Auckland Regional Authority when the De Leuw, Cather report was made. The present chairman, Mr Hugh D Lambie, said he was 'somewhat surprised' that the costs and benefits of the system had been considered only from the City Council district position.

"Mr Robinson said: 'It is unfortunate that this note of disharmony should come at this juncture. It's very disturbing that Mr Dickson had not had any discussions with the authority's planning officers.' He said it would have been better for the future of Auckland had discussions taken place and urged that the officers of the council and the authority meet to 'iron out any difficulties.'" [373]

Transport Unity Needed

Indeed, The New Zealand Herald had the same advice – as reported on 22 September 1967:

"The essential point about Auckland transport is that before much longer something must be done. The urban population is expected to reach a million in the early 1980s, and a continued growth of private motoring could throttle movement in the city. Over more than 40 years successive reports by overseas experts have urged the city to improve and make use of its sadly neglected suburban railways.

"Most recently the city was advised to adopt a fast electric train service extended into Queen St and fed by buses at suburban stations. The Auckland Regional Authority has given the proposal general approval. The City Council has supported a rapid rail transit system, with reservations about details. The Government, though uncommitted, has not rejected the idea. But just as Auckland appears set to plan bus-rail services, City Council planners say they believe that the system should be based entirely on buses.

"The professional views of the planners and of the city engineer naturally warrant study. But their pronouncement places Auckland right back in the position of speaking with two or more voices. It takes little effort to imagine the reaction in Wellington as politicians and officials happily realise that they can forget the whole thing until Auckland decides what it wants. On past form, the situation is set for years of delay. The Regional Authority was supposed to help Auckland to speak with one voice. In the interests of the city, divided counsels cannot be allowed to continue. The authority and the council should get together urgently and thrash out a common approach." [374]

Buchanan Report Criticism

Indeed, it had been one of the Buchanan Report's more noteworthy criticisms that there had been very little dialogue, let alone co-operation, between the City Council and the Auckland Regional Authority:

"We could perhaps at this stage mention the question of the relationships between the City Council and the Regional Authority. The simple point we wish to make is that the central area of the City serves the whole region. The kind and quantity of the activities in the central area are, to a large extent, dependent upon the functions which the centre performs for the region. Of necessity, therefore, the planning of the central area must be to some extent a combined operation between the City Council and the Regional Authority.

"It appears to us that there is every readiness to co-operate between the two authorities at staff levels, but we are less sure about the position at the political level. If complete readiness to co-operate had existed, we do not think the present position would have arisen in which the motorway network has been driven forward to the point of construction whilst the planning of the central area is still in an embryo stage.

"We hope we will not be regarded as impertinent if we stress the need for these two bodies to work together. The Regional Authority's functions are of crucial importance at the present stage of the region's growth, and it is indeed one of the most interesting and advanced administrative concepts we have come across." [331]

[An unknown author, but believed to have been Dove-Myer Robinson, has written on a page extract copy of the above:

"By July 1966 the harmonious relationships between the C.C. [Auckland City Council] & A.R.A. [Auckland Regional Authority] had already deteriorated almost to a point of non-cooperation at the political level. In the whole three years of his office the present Mayor [R G McElroy] has not once called together the city's representatives on the A.R.A. to discuss the city's affairs." [375]

CBD Bankruptcy

The Auckland Star's commentary of 21 September 1967 continued:

"Responding to Arthur Dickson's report to the City Council about the costs to implement the various transport systems, Dove-Myer Robinson said:

"'…it was also premature at this stage to talk of costs to ratepayers of the rail system. 'Talks have not even started with the Government about finance – and it must be remembered that when the system is introduced Auckland will probably have a population of 750,000.' He added on the face of it he thought it would be 'impossible' for an all-bus system, as recommended in Mr Dickson's report, to be the answer to Auckland's transport problems. 'The roads are already overcrowded – this proposal would only lead to the bankruptcy of the central business district.'

"Mr Lambie said the rapid transit plan dealt with a large area and a large population and was related to the economy of the whole of the Auckland area, not just one part of it. On a percentage basis the financial liability of Auckland City under the scheme would be far less than the present percentage paid on the transport division's existing bus deficit. Mr Lambie pointed out that Mr Dickson's report was one of a number of technical reports which had yet to be considered in relation to an overall policy on transportation. An investment of the kind Auckland was considering to provide a rapid rail-bus system was extremely small in the overall economy of the area and this needed to be kept in perspective, continued Mr Lambie." [373]

All-Bus Support

However, Arthur Dickson was not without some support for his advocacy of an all-bus public transport system. One such supporter was Kenneth Brailey Cumberland, professor of geography at Auckland University and a former city councillor.

Professor Cumberland had also been the Chairman of the Auckland Regional Planning Authority when the Authority's Technical Advisory Committee formulated the 1955 Master Transportation Plan advocating motorways as the main solution to Auckland's traffic problems.

In a previously-referred-to Auckland Star editorial, Kenneth Cumberland described the suburban railway system recommended by the 1950 Halcrow Thomas Report as "...*a 'white elephant' that 'may well prejudice any chance of getting any material improvement of our highway system'.*" [205]

In a similar article published by the Auckland Star on 22 September 1967, Professor Cumberland maintained this point of view:

"The support for an all-bus transport system by the Auckland city engineer, Mr A J Dickson, was 'the first sober, down-to-earth, yet authoritative comment on the rather fanciful De Leuw Cather proposals,' Professor K B Cumberland said today.

"Professor Cumberland...said Auckland had grown up as a decentralized, wide-spread, low-density metropolitan area. It had no dense and congested residential areas like older cities. 'As a result, flexible bus transport rather than one fixed under-used rail artery will be socially and economically desirable for many years to come,' he said.

"No rapid rail transport will ever take a man from Devonport to Te Atatu or from Mangere to Takapuna. But a well-organized metropolitan bus service could well do this – and it would not cost the ratepayers $4 million a year.' Professor Cumberland said an all-bus system was broadly the conclusion reached 12 years ago when the urban motorways plan was first adopted. It was apparent then that for a city like Auckland with such low residential population densities, rapid rail transit would be wasteful, if not economically impossible for many years – until Auckland developed areas of high residential densities and had a population nearer two million." [376]

Social Benefit Analysis

It is interesting to note that in the foregoing article, Kenneth Cumberland referred to: "...*flexible bus transport rather than one fixed under-used rail artery will be <u>socially</u> and economically desirable for many years to come...*"

He was probably echoing Arthur Dickson's reference to the *social benefits of the two De Leuw Cather proposals* in the conclusions to his summation of the Officials Committee Report when he (Dickson) wrote:

"The Council's Planning Division has carefully examined the *social benefits* of the two De Leuw Cather proposals, and the result was in favour of the All-bus Scheme. This analysis was submitted to a well-known public accountant who clearly confirmed the result. This analysis was conducted using the De Leuw Cather data. This exercise was done because so much is now being stated in favour of the more flexible bus transit in decentralised cities by investigators and authorities and published by the technical press, and it was desired to verify this in the context of the Auckland proposals." [369]

While their definition of *social benefits* was not fully explained by either Arthur Dickson or Kenneth Cumberland in the literature examined, their reference to the concept may have been a reaction to earlier comments made by an Auckland town planning consultant, Mr I B Reynolds. He had been quoted in a New Zealand Herald article, published on 5 September 1967, in which he referred to the social benefits of commuter interaction during train travel in Wellington:

"Another significant result is the warmth of social spirit that followed daily community contacts made on the station platform and trains. By contrast the motor car and even the bus appear to foster aggressiveness and isolation in neighbours travelling to and from Auckland districts…" [371]

Neither Arthur Dickson nor Kenneth Cumberland would have welcomed any publicity about the perceived anti-social effects of private motor vehicle use.

The *social benefit analysis of the two De Leuw Cather proposals* stated by Arthur Dickson to have been examined by the City Council's Planning Division had actually been produced by a Mr W Bell who submitted his analysis to the City Council on 29 June 1967. Two weeks later, Arthur Dickson passed Mr Bell's analysis to the public accountant referred to, Ernest D Wilkinson of Wilkinson, Christmas, Steen & Co., Auckland.

The accountant subsequently replied to Arthur Dickson on 31 July 1967:

"I refer to the telephone conversation which I had with you on Friday, 14th instant, when you asked me whether I would examine the social benefits of two alternative transport plans, as computed by Mr. W. Bell, with the object of advising you whether or not the basis on which the social benefits as computed in his confidential memorandum of 29th June last, have been computed on a generally accepted basis…

"It is, I feel, unnecessary for the purpose of this brief report – in which I am able to deal with general principles only – to recapitulate the relevant factors of each of the…transport plans, except to draw attention to the fact that in computing the social benefits arising from each Mr Bell has included the cost of the motorway and expressway systems.

"…Mr Bell assessed the social benefit rate of return for scheme (a) – i.e. the bus transit plan – at 18.4% and for the rapid rail transit plan 16.7%…If the present day value of the capital cost of the motorways and expressways are excluded…the social benefits rate of return becomes 105.6% [bus plan] and 56.1% [rapid rail transit plan].

"Finally, it must be apparent that an assessment of social benefits on the basis generally adopted is a highly academic exercise because the benefits are those which could be expected to accrue to the public en masse and do not take account of personal preferences. The standard of living in the country for which the assessment is made is an important factor: where that standard is high, convenience and comfort will generally be evaluated more highly than mere cost alone. In this context nothing can match the use of a private car, more especially when the cost of operation, excluding depreciation, compares reasonably favourably with that of public transport...

"These and many others are factors which are not taken into account in social benefits studies because it is so difficult to make an assessment of them, but they are questions which are important in the public mind. Never in our history has travel by private motor car been so highly valued as it is today. With the advent of the mini car to the standard of efficiency and comfort which has been attained with this type of car and which is likely to be raised even higher in the future, this trend seems almost certain to continue.

"In conclusion, I would mention that time has not been available to me to study as carefully as I believe to be necessary the reports of Messrs. De Leuw Cather and Company...Neither have I had the opportunity of checking the calculations made by Mr Bell in his assessment of social benefits but, as already pointed out, I confirm that the methods employed in making these calculations are in accordance with generally recognised principles." [377]

Dickson Desperate to Convince

This final paragraph of Ernest Wilkinson's letter to Arthur Dickson would seem to conflict with the latter's statement contained in his summary of the Officials Committee Report and which was also published by the Auckland Star on 21 September 1967:

"This analysis was submitted to a well-known public accountant who clearly confirmed the result." [373]

Indeed, in seeking to obtain such expert verification, or otherwise, of Mr Bell's assessment of the *social benefits* of the De Leuw, Cather recommendations, Arthur Dickson seemed particularly desperate to convince the City Council, the Auckland Regional Authority, the Government, and the public that the roads-based transportation system was not only best for Auckland in terms of dollars and cents but also *socially* beneficial as well.

Ultimate Benefits of Public Transport

However, not everyone agreed that any advantages derived from the provision of public transport could be measured both in financially profitable and socially beneficial terms. The two were diametrically opposite. By way of illustration, an unknown author, but probably Dove-Myer Robinson (as the document was found with his papers), prepared a document, entitled *Benefits Of Rapid Transit That Cannot Be Evaluated In Terms Of Cost In Dollars And Cents*, which listed those benefits as:

"1. Rapid Transit provides transport for the young, the old, the infirm, the sick and lower income groups who cannot afford to provide their own private transport, and therefore must have satisfactory public transport available for their use.

2. Rapid Transit prevents the development of slums, ghettoes and increased anti-social and criminal activities.

3. It allows free access to all parts of the region served, and thus permits residents in the overcrowded parts of the region to move freely to beaches, parks and other parts of the region.

4. It helps to prevent motor congestion on the limited amount of roading available and allows motorists who have to use private transport freer and better use of the roading.

5. All consultants who have studied cost benefit schemes of this kind are agreed that the intangible social benefits to the citizens of the area are of far greater value to them than any benefits that can be evaluated merely on the basis of dollars and cents.

6. Expenditure by local bodies in providing satisfactory public transport for all sections of the community is of far greater value than can be estimated on the basis of costs in dollars and cents.

7. To attempt to estimate the value of satisfactory transport merely on the basis of dollars and cents is to ignore the very much greater intangible values.

8. It must also be remembered that any alternative scheme for public transport depending on an all roading system, will cost the local bodies and their ratepayers considerably more for provision, upgrading and maintenance of roads and other facilities than the cost of an exclusive right-of-way rapid transit system." [378]

Social Benefits

While the list certainly includes the social needs that could be met by a reliable public transport service, the environmental benefits of such a service are implied but not stated as objectively as in the Buchanan Report:

"…recent experience has shown the absolute necessity for linking transportation studies very much more closely to urban redevelopment studies, especially where important centres are concerned, and to ensure that full regard is paid to environmental standards which are ever in danger of being eroded by traffic." [331]

Environmental Damage

While Colin Buchanan's reference to *environmental standards* were interpreted by most readers of his report as relating to the concept of *social benefits*, his prescient interpretation meant far more than that. Although he was principally concerned about the adverse interaction then occurring between the pedestrian and the motor vehicle, Colin Buchanan also appreciated the damage that could be caused to a city's physical environment by too many motor vehicles – decades of exhaust pollution that would contribute to the future phenomenon of climate change – a result not appreciated in 1967 – as reported by The Auckland Star 21 September 1967:

"The increase in exhaust fumes from an all-bus transport system would not necessarily cause any problem, the chairman of the Air Pollution Research Committee, Dr O H Keys, said today. He was commenting on the report by the Auckland city engineer, Mr A J Dickson, favouring an all-bus system for Auckland as opposed to the proposed bus-rapid rail plan.

"'Obviously some increase in fumes would be inevitable, but there's room for a bit more in the atmosphere without causing any alarm,' Dr Keys said. 'It would take a very great increase to cause concern.' He said cities like New York had overcome the problem by installing 'after-burners' on their buses – a device that converted carbon monoxide into the relatively harmless carbon dioxide and also burnt off any unburnt fuel. The committee would make a detailed investigation into the matter only if the all-bus plan was eventually adopted, Dr Keys said." [379]

Cascading Mass of Private Vehicles

In the meantime, what of the social and environmental impact of all motor vehicles and trucks? – described by Dr Graham W A Bush, of the political studies department of Auckland University, in his letter to the Editor of The New Zealand Herald, published 27 September 1967, as the *cascading mass of private vehicles*:

"Reliance on bus transport in Auckland ignores overseas trends – and perpetuates half a century of shortsightedness, says Dr G W A Bush…Dr Bush writes: Recently the Auckland Regional Authority stated that rapid rail transit was basic to its regional development plan. Two days later the other local planning experts, those of the Auckland City Council, came out in favour of an all-bus system. The latest episode in the endless unedifying history of Auckland transport problems must induce despair among citizens who cling desperately to the hope that one day the city will be blessed with local authorities and a Government with the vision and resolution to recognise the central needs of the problem, and then act.

"Look at Cost – Auckland has repeatedly been sold short by Governments of all political persuasions. Newspaper reports of 40 years ago suggest that the promised electrification of an expanded Auckland rail system was 'just around the corner.' Government after Government has seemed to act on the convenient principle of avoiding expenditure on the city's transport requirements.

"The criterion is apparently not 'What are Auckland's needs?' but 'Look at the cost – it can't be afforded.' How the Government must applaud the spectacle of local authorities strengthening its excuse to procrastinate and temporise. It would be manifestly unfair to level all the blame on the two contending local authorities. They assert that they are at the mercy of the Government, which exercises a financial veto. The latter in turn ripostes by claiming that it would be irresponsible to spend millions when the authorities concerned cannot agree among themselves on how best to meet Auckland's needs.

"Issues Obscured – The net result of this 'don't blame us' ritual is inaction. Yet another plan is amended, mutilated or scrapped. Plans may not be as costly as an actual transport system, but you cannot ride to work on a plan. Leaving aside the question of whether the stated 'social benefits' of an all-bus system are not, in plain fact, anything more than financial economies, the City Council planners in their report have succeeded in once again obscuring the central issues.

"Buses can travel only as fast as other traffic using the road. They are trapped among the cascading mass of private vehicles now clogging up the central area. For example, in the last hour, it takes up to 15 minutes to reach the top of Symonds St (one and a half miles) from the bus station, half an hour to get to Green Lane (five miles) and a full hour to arrive at Howick (14 miles).

"Can the City Council planners be serious in offering this sort of answer to the city's transport needs? It is a mere masquerade of progress. The irony of the present predicament is that one of the arguments most often advanced for getting rid of trams was that, in monopolising the centre of the road, they were reducing its availability for other traffic. Far from easing the problem of inner city congestion, buses aggravate it.

"Distant Prospect – One wonders how much longer the citizens can reasonably be expected to show any confidence in their local authorities over this matter. It is incredible that the city engineer's 'solution' should be to take another look at the problem in 15 years' time. In the interim, the problem becomes increasingly acute, the cost of repairing half a century's short-sightedness spirals and – happy thought – further surveys can be commissioned. But the prospect of the only right solution being implemented remains as distant as ever." [380]

Regional Development Plan

The Auckland Regional Authority's *Regional Development Plan* referred to by Dr Bush was being prepared on the basis of incorporating a rapid rail transit system – as reported by The Auckland Star on 19 September 1967:

"The Auckland Regional Authority is to tell the Government that Auckland's regional development plan is being prepared on the basis of incorporating a rapid rail transit system. The authority's transit plan sub-committee was last night authorized to negotiate with the Government.

"The authority had before it a joint report from its transport manager, Mr C R Gribble, and director of planning, Mr F W O Jones on the De Leuw, Cather rapid transit scheme and the Government's reaction. The recommendations in the joint report were adopted.

"It should be made clear that the transportation plan was part of a general development plan for the urban area. It had always been understood that a transport plan could not be considered without this general plan.

"The Gribble-Jones report said that delaying the introduction of the rapid rail scheme until the 1980s (as suggested by the Government officials) would seriously reduce the projected number of passengers to the point where the service might be ineffective at that date. The point was made that the De Leuw, Cather proposals were designed to meet the needs of a million people in urban Auckland by 1986. This figure, on present trends, was now likely to be reached about 1982. At the same time, the current reduction in road spending indicated that the recommended highway network would not to be in use before 1986. Thus the introduction of the rapid rail system assumed a greater degree of urgency than predicted by De Leuw, Cather." [381]

Dove-Myer Robinson Opposes Deferment

Dove-Myer Robinson also declared his opposition to any deferment of De Leuw, Cather's bus-rail proposal, as reported under the headline, *Go Rail Or Decay*, published by the Auckland Star on 30 September 1967:

"Either we get traffic off the roads and back onto the rails or the heart of Auckland City – the hub of the region – is doomed to rapid decay, Mr D M Robinson, City representative on the Auckland Regional Authority and former Mayor, said today. Mr Robinson questioned whether the city engineer, Mr A J Dickson, in his report, which opposed the bus-rail scheme mainly on the grounds of capital and annual costs, had taken all the factors, both physical and financial, into consideration.

"'If he had, I am sure he could not have come to the conclusion he did,' Mr Robinson said. 'The Regional Authority's consultants pointed out that if an all-bus system was adopted, at least $16 million extra would have to be spent on new roads over and above what would be required for the bus-rail plan,' said Mr Robinson.

"'On top of this it would be necessary to provide an additional 10,000 car parking spaces at a cost of $20 million. Then we would have to add on the cost of petrol and fuel for the extra buses and cars which would have to be used. This fuel has to be paid for with scarce overseas exchange. Electricity for the proposed electrified suburban rail system is generated locally and, apart from capital costs, will cost practically nothing annually in overseas exchange.'

"Even more important is that to plump for an all-bus scheme is to ignore the fact that it won't work, for the simple reason that it won't overcome or prevent traffic congestion. It will increase it to the stage where congestion will paralyse the traffic arteries of the city.

In other words, no matter how cheap or expensive an all-bus scheme would be, it would not achieve the main object of overcoming congestion and allowing traffic to move freely through the traffic arteries of the city and the region. Auckland would be paying for something and getting worse than nothing in return...'

"When all factors are taken into consideration, the bus-rail scheme is cheaper and is the only practical solution to Auckland's traffic problems because it is the only physically practicable scheme. It is no good saying Auckland can't afford the bus-rail scheme. If the city is going to survive as the commercial heart of the region we can't afford not to do it." [382]

All-Bus Service Struggles

But even while the bus-rail scheme remained in abeyance, seemingly forever, the alternative all-bus system was faring no better as it struggled to provide a viable public transport service to Aucklanders. Again, Government indecision proved difficult to explain – as reported by The Auckland Star on 12 September 1967:

"The Government is studying the passenger transport position in Auckland with a view to improving the service to several areas served by private bus operators. This is revealed in a letter from the Minister of Transport, Mr Gordon, to the Glen Eden Progressive Ratepayers' Association. The association had asked Mr Gordon to hold a public inquiry into the operation of the Auckland Bus Company's services. The company had recently taken off more than 50 buses, the association said.

"Mr Gordon replied that the Licensing Authority and Transport Department officers were aware of the deficiencies in the Auckland Bus Company's services, but there was little that could be done to improve them. The company has been operating at a substantial loss and its financial position, like that of many other transport operators in the Auckland area, is not good,' he said.

"'If it was forced to operate extra unprofitable services, it is possible that the firm would be unable to continue its transport operations at all. And it would seem unlikely that other privately-owned companies in the areas would be able to provide an adequate alternative service. The Government is at present studying the whole position of passenger transport in the Auckland area. It is hoped as a result to effect some improvement in the bus services provided by the private companies to several areas, including your own." [383]

Letters to the Editor

While the Government's study of *the whole position of passenger transport in the Auckland area* continued, seemingly forever, those travelling aboard the City's buses were having their say by means of Letters to the Editor:

"Public Transport – The city engineer, Mr A J Dickson, in commenting on Auckland's future public transport system, agrees that an all-bus system is preferable to a rapid rail scheme. We have had an all-bus system for the past 10 years. In that time patronage has steadily declined and losses mounted. To extend this unpopular system would be throwing good money after bad. A transport system that must share the road with heavy motor traffic can only be described as makeshift.

"As buses are inefficient, and rapid rail system is apparently not warranted for many years, the only possible form of transport remaining is a tramway. The authorities are not, however, likely to consider re-installing the trams as this would be an admission of past blunders. One may assume that Auckland will have a very poor transport system for many years to come. Discouraged, One Tree Hill." [384]

"Transport System – What transport system does Auckland want? Your editorial (21-9-67) asks. The answer would appear to be that our citizens just don't care. They are prepared to travel by the most comfortable form of modern transport, the bus, which replaced a much more convenient system, the trams. They also don't object to paying taxes for expensive overseas consultants of world renown who invariably advise electric trains only to have their reports vetoed and shelved.

"When will this farce end? The bus has now proved that in shifting large numbers of passengers in metropolitan areas, it is as obsolete as the horse and buggy. It is time the citizens of Auckland stirred themselves and called a halt to this obstruction by those whose vision sees only miles of concrete and clover-leaves. Percy V Bunting, Mangere." [385]

"Motorways – In view of the almost total destruction of Grafton Gully, as well as the authorizing of too many turnoffs from the new motorway right into the heart of the city, to say nothing of leading the traffic right through the university complex, should not the public of Auckland hear something in justification for this sort of pandering to the motor car from the City Council's chief engineers and its motorway engineers? Graduate, City." [386]

"City Transport – The recent objection of the De Leuw, Cather rapid-rail transit plan by the city engineer, Mr Dickson, does not seem in accordance with the views of many Auckland planners. De Leuw, Cather recommended against an all-bus system because of its prohibitive long-term cost. The rapid-rail recommendation came after intensive study of Auckland and the lessons learned from the growth of cities in the United States with similar low population densities. Roads will inevitably become more clogged with traffic in the future and bus trips are going to become slower than ever. Mr Dickson always seems to have had a bias against electrified railway proposals.

"He helped to kill the 1950 Halcrow-Thomas report; he advised against rail transit in the 1955 master transport plan; and now comes the most recent episode. Perhaps Mr Dickson is still trying to shape Auckland development even though the Auckland Regional Authority has now been formed. Bus User, Mt Eden." [387]

Bus Delays

A report provided to the Auckland Regional Authority by its traffic manager confirmed what its public transport travellers already knew – as reported by The New Zealand Herald on 10 October 1967:

"Heavy traffic was delaying more and more buses and the situation was likely to get worse before it got better, the Auckland Regional Authority transport division traffic manager, Mr H S Wilson, said yesterday. Mr Wilson said the effects of congestion were becoming far more noticeable, especially at peak periods in such places as Symonds St, with traffic from the motorway and Pitt St. He told the passenger transport committee of the authority that there had been 123 delays, missed trips or uncompleted trips in August, compared with 76 for the previous month.

"About half of them, 63 compared with 37 the previous month, were caused by defective buses, but 17 resulted from traffic congestion compared with only three in July. The number of complaints received was 62, against 48 for the previous month." [388]

All-Bus or Bust

However, despite the obvious shortcomings of an all-bus public transport system, support for the concept, and its main advocate, Arthur Dickson, was nevertheless maintained by the Mayor of Auckland, Dr Roy McElroy – as reported by The Auckland Star on 12 October 1967:

"Auckland must plan now for an all-bus transport system to cover the 12 to 15 years before the bus-rapid rail transit system could be built, the Mayor of Auckland, Dr McElroy said yesterday…in a statement to the finance committee yesterday Dr McElroy pointed out that in 1966 the council had 'affirmed positive support of the principle of a rapid rail transit system.' But the report of the Government-appointed officials committee…had said that a regional plan was a key requirement before the feasibility of the bus-rapid rail scheme could be judged, he said. It was therefore the job of the Auckland Regional Authority to complete its regional plan.

"Meanwhile it is crystal clear from the officials' committee report that because of the sheer magnitude of the expenditure involved in the current rail-bus proposals there is little prospect of its coming into effective operation in less than 12 to 15 years,' Dr McElroy said. 'This time corresponds approximately to the effective usable life span of the average bus. It becomes clear then that the advice of the city engineer that Auckland must plan now for an all-bus system for this interim period must be given attention. Auckland city planning for the next 15 years cannot operate in a vacuum…'" [389]

Joseph Wright

Joseph Wright, MICE, FNZIE had been in charge of the construction of the Auckland urban motorways from their inception until his retirement from the Ministry of Works in 1962. By that time, he'd had more than 50 years' civil engineering experience. His opinion therefore mattered and was readily published by The New Zealand Herald on 14 October 1967:

"Another tragic chapter of errors will be added to the transport history of Auckland if City Council planners are allowed to impose their concept of an all-bus system on the region. It will be in keeping with the blunder in 1955 when Auckland looked a gift horse in the mouth by rejecting the idea of building the Auckland-Morningside underground railway.

"At that time the Government was ready to start construction – at its own expense. The trains could have been running five years ago had the local bodies not opted for urban motorways instead. On the occasion of my retirement from the Ministry of Works in 1962, I stated that preference should have been given to an electric suburban railway system as recommended by the English consultants, Sir William Halcrow and Mr J P Thomas. Now, five years later, I am more than ever convinced of the need for the railway…

"City planners have used the comparatively low population density as an argument in favour of an all-bus system for Auckland. In fact, such an argument supports the need for a railway. A railway would not be necessary if 300,000 people were concentrated in the centre of the city; but it is the best means of transport for long trips when the population is spread over a radius of 20 miles or more…The railway has been described as costly and remote. No doubt it will be costly, but it will only be remote if lack of vision makes it so." [390]

Passenger Transport Review

The cost of a railway solution to Auckland's transport problems had to be worth it, according to the Chairman of the Auckland Regional Authority, Hugh Lambie, during his review of Auckland's passenger transport system in October 1967:

"This review of Auckland's passenger transport system was originally published in 1957. Time has not varied the essential facts nor has it lessened the importance of the problem…

"<u>The need for decision making</u>: I do not mean to over-dramatise the situation. But there is a need in Auckland to emphasize the situation we appear to be facing – a wariness in the face of a real need for decision making on matters which are vital to the future – a hesitation to accept the responsibility for decision making on matters which will be more vital to the people of the future than to us.

"There comes a time – in business, in industry, in private affairs and in public affairs – when having examined a situation, a decision has to be made – a decision demanding some degree of courage as well as judgment. It is inconceivable that we should sit back recognising that growth will take place, that public passenger transport services will be essential and, at same time, allow the existing services to run down, deteriorate and lose passengers against an estimated increasing deficit.

"<u>The basic facts of transport and transit</u>: In Auckland we have an urban area already worth some thousands of millions of dollars. We have a central business district worth some hundreds of millions of dollars. We are spending, as a community, some hundreds of millions of dollars each year in operating our transport system as a whole.

"There will be more people, more traffic, more movements were person in the future – the particular detailed arithmetic does not matter – the main fact here is that we have to contemplate spending possibly some tens of millions of dollars as a capital investment at this stage on a rail supplemented passenger transport system – that is spending, perhaps, $20 million more than we would have to spend in any case on a minimal all-bus system – a system which would be likely to become progressively less effective not only in terms of our total transportation system, but in terms of the absolute number of people carried.

"The 'saving' of this $20 million by not investing in a rapid rail scheme implies, of course, a spending much more than this in terms of both capital investment and annual operating expenses on other forms of transportation; more highways, more parking, more congestion, more traffic restrictions. There is no more vital element in the city of today and tomorrow than its transportation system. Accessibility is the primary pre-requisite to the value of any property. And transportation is one matter on which we dare not take a short term day-to-day view.

"In this rapid rail transit scheme we seek to make use of the railway right-of-way which is already in existence and which is capable of being used much more intensively – we seek a short extension of about one mile of the permanent way of this railway into the centre of the city – and as this becomes a part of the permanent way and the permanent assets of the government's railway, we feel it is not unreasonable that the government should accept the cost of this extension and associated cost of capital improvements to its railway system – which, while run down from a passenger point of view, is operating in this part of the country at a substantial profit.

"We seek the assistance of the government as the authority responsible for running the railway trains on the rail right-of-way – for these services we suggest we meet the operating losses which might arise from the provision of the purely commuter services.

"At the same time, we expect as a local responsibility, to provide the bus services to feed the railway and to provide the bus service which would have to come directly to the central business district from areas not served by rail. To do this, I think we all agree that the Regional Authority would need to co-ordinate schedules so that a fully comprehensive and integrated transportation system would operate.

"Such a system would operate to serve the whole of the urban area, not just the central business district – it would serve every major employment centre – it is one element, one essential element, of the large city as against a collection of suburbs or a collection of contiguous small towns. A rail based system provides the simplicity in concept that is essential to an easy understanding and an effective working of transport in a large and complex area.

"General conclusion: I feel there is a great deal of loose talk concerning costs, concerning escalation, concerning uncertainties and difficulties. There has appeared to be a certain amount of fear of this project engendered by lack of knowledge or confidence. But when all the facts are presented, I come to the conclusion that this scheme is merely good business – that it would be bad business indeed to defer decisions and micawber-like wait for something to turn up. It is for these reasons that we have to make the decisions we are concerned with ourselves, that we have to get the decisions other people are concerned with and then we have to get the job done." [391]

Feasibility Study

Hugh Lambie's attempts *to get the job done* finally showed some sign of progress – as reported by The New Zealand Herald on 14 November 1967:

"Every hour of every day was being used to advance the De Leuw, Cather combined bus and rail plan for Auckland a stage further, said the chairman of the Auckland Regional Authority, Mr H D Lambie, last night. Mr Lambie told members of the authority that a preliminary step toward a feasibility study would be taken within the next few weeks…'As you know we have had a setback,' he said. 'But things are moving now.'

"The authority had been concerned that at the present rate of development it seemed unlikely that the $52 million system would be in use by 1986. 'If we do not get it going before then,' he said, 'we will be in trouble.'" [392]

The Working Party on Rapid Transit

That 'feasibility study' eventually took the form of a *Working Party on Rapid Transit* set up: "At a meeting of representatives of the Auckland Regional Authority, the Auckland City Council and Central Government, held in Auckland on 23rd February, 1968…

"It was decided that the Working Party should comprise one representative from the Auckland Regional Authority [E A Flynn], the Auckland City Council [A J Dickson – replaced by B D Duffield after Dickson retired on 7 April 1969], the Ministry of Works [F F Abey] and the New Zealand Railways Department [R H Newton], the Auckland Regional Authority's representative being the Chairman.

"It was further decided that the Working Party should report simultaneously to the Minister of Works, the Chairman of the Auckland Regional Authority and the Mayor of Auckland.

"The order of reference of the Working Party was to investigate and make recommendations on the most desirable route for a rapid rail transit system in the Auckland Region, having regard to:

(a) The costs of construction of the rapid transit system;
(b) The operating costs of alternative routes and their supporting systems;
(c) Service to the public; and
(d) The planning requirements of the Region." [393]

Committee of Inquiry into Urban Passenger Transport

However, almost as a reminder to Aucklanders that theirs was not the only New Zealand city to experience transport problems; that their need for a rapid transit system was not unique, the Government appointed a Committee of Inquiry into Urban Passenger Transport (more commonly known as the Carter Committee) on 12 December 1968:

"…to examine and advise on urban passenger transport in New Zealand."

The Committee comprised:

D J Carter, M.P. (Chairman) - Parliamentary Under-Secretary for Agriculture
D W A Barker, C.M.G. (Deputy Chairman)
M W Croy
C R Gribble
Horace S J Tilly (of Dunedin)

"The Committee shall inquire into and recommended to Government what standard of public transport is necessary to meet the reasonable needs of balanced and efficient passenger transport systems by all forms of transport for urban communities in New Zealand; and shall consider and report upon the financial and organisational arrangements necessary to achieve such standards, having particular regard to the following matters:

(i) What steps should be taken to ensure sufficient patronage of private and publicly-owned passenger services to promote an economical means of public transport in urban communities?

(ii) As part of such steps, what special financial measures may be necessary to assist public and private operators of urban passenger services to adequately meet their reasonable capital requirements and to operate economically?

(iii) What levels of service are required to ensure a reasonable balance between public and private transport in large, medium, and small communities; and what further provision should be made for the proper integration of public passenger transport with town planning in New Zealand?

(iv) What changes, if any, are necessary in present methods of organisation and operation of urban public passenger services to secure, *inter alia*, their future sound management and better co-ordination; and what scope there is for the operation of these services by or under contract to a territorial local authority or authorities, or any other public body?

(v) Any other matters considered relevant to this enquiry…

"While being careful to keep within the bounds of the terms of reference, the Committee has found it more satisfactory to report on the problems of urban passenger transport generally, rather than to confine itself to specific answers to each question as set out above. This procedure also follows the way in which much of the evidence was presented to the Committee…

"Public hearings for those who wished to present evidence in person commenced in Wellington on 18-20 March 1969. Further hearings were held in Wellington on 15-16 April and 20-22 May; in Auckland on 24-26 March and 11-12 June; in Christchurch on 21-22 April; in Dunedin on 23 April; and in New Plymouth on 13 June." [394]

Report of the Working Party on Rapid Transit

While the national (Carter) inquiry continued, the Working Party on Rapid Transit (Flynn) reported on 30 May 1969.

A summary of its conclusions and recommendations included:

"Conclusions:

"1. That the form of transit be a duorail rail system, i.e. steel wheeled vehicles on twin steel rails;

"2. That the question of a separate right-of-way requires considerable investigation;

"3. That the speed and rate of acceleration and weight of rolling stock upon which calculations by the consultants were based, are not realistic and are unlikely to be attained on a 3'6" gauge;

"4. That stabling sidings are required as close as possible to the city for use during the day;

"5. That a service on 3'6" gauge track is unlikely to attract people from other forms of transport;

"6. That land purchase for station car parks be commenced as soon as financial agreement has been reached;

"7. That the system be as fully automated as possible.

"Recommendations:

"(a) That the outer terminals be initially at Manurewa and Henderson (Sturges Road) and extended to Papakura as and when required (We anticipate that an extension to Papakura will be necessary by the early 1980s);

"(b) That…the stations which are proposed are sited at approximately one mile intervals in accordance with (a) Proximity to trip generation; (b) Car access and parking facilities; (c) Bus access and terminal facilities; and (d) Pedestrian access.);

"(c) That provision be made for an extension to the International Airport (The Working Party thought it advisable to consider a future extension of rapid transit to the International Airport as a facility which mounting road congestion will make increasingly desirable…);

"(d) That the route within the central area and the siting of stations therein [Town Hall, Hobson Street, & Shortland Street] be as shown (The Working Party reviewed all previously suggested routes in the inner city area and did detailed studies on six alternatives. We are unanimous in our recommendation that the route selected…would best serve the needs of the inner-city.);

"(e) That all level crossings on the line of route be eliminated (The Working Party considers that it will be necessary to eliminate all level crossings within the length used by rapid transit irrespective of any engineering problems that may be encountered.);

"(f) That the route in the central area should not preclude future extensions (It is possible to bring additional lines into the loop system at a later date. This would require the completion of the Princes Street connection and after this lines could be brought into and out from the loop to enable connection to the North Shore or for more direct connections to the line to Henderson to be implemented if and when these can be justified…);

"(g) That provision be made for a link between the inward and outward lines beneath Princes Street (Adequate provision should be made while tunnelling is in progress for the link between the inner and outer lines beneath Princes Street to be constructed.);

"(h) That a team be established to investigate and report upon the implications of alternative track gauges and carry out cost/benefit studies (paragraph 18 - We were expected to take into account four factors in deciding upon the route of the rapid transit line which we would recommend...To comply even in a general way regarding the first two factors was beyond the Working Party's resources.

"We recommend that a freshly constituted Working Party with membership drawn from the Auckland Regional Authority, the Ministry of Works, the Auckland City Council and the New Zealand Railways Department be established to examine the possibility of upgrading the 3'6" gauge track to meet rapid transit standards, to carry out the comprehensive survey and design work necessary to establish the feasibility and probable cost of a wider gauge system and to update and extend the cost/benefit studies. (Requisite financial resources must be provided on some shared basis.)" [393]

Preliminary Assessment of Cost

The Working Party did provide a "Preliminary Assessment of Cost of the Recommended Route in the Central Area of the City [based on 1968 figures] of $9,640,000 plus contingencies at 25% - $12,000,000." [393]

Report to Railways' General Manager

After taking more than a year to investigate and recommend the most desirable route for a rapid rail transit system, costs, and other matters, the Working Party decided that much of what was required of them was beyond its resources and recommended that *a freshly constituted Working Party...be established*. The reasons for the Working Party's failure to achieve little more than a brief overview of the proposed transit system were best summed up by the Working Party's Railways representative, R H Newton, in his report to the Railways' General Manager, Ivan Thomas, dated 8 July 1969:

"As requested by you the following report sets out my personal comments on the Conclusions and Recommendations in the Working Party's report to which I was a signatory.

"General - The working party met at irregular intervals over a period of some 12 months. I made it clear from the outset that my presence on the working party did not commit the N.Z.R. in any way to agreeing with or contributing towards any proposed recommendation.

"It soon became clear that to implement fully the order of reference was beyond the resources of the Working Party and we concentrated generally on the broad issues of establishing a route.

"There was much discussion as to whether Auckland needed or could sustain a rapid rail transit system. Apart from the de Leuw Cather report (which the Working Party considers to be somewhat superficial) no objective analysis was made to support the contention that Auckland must have a Rapid Rail system. Various statements were made that the present motorway system as planned could cope with a bus transport system up to the 1980's beyond which additional motorways would be needed to the extent that the C.B.D. would be eroded.

"My personal opinion is that because of its geography, low density of population and the hold that the private motor car has, Auckland cannot afford or sustain the luxury of an expensive Rapid Rail system. However the order of reference assumes that a rapid transit system of some type is needed and it is on the general basis that the report was prepared.

"Comments & Conclusions

"(a) Route in the central city area - There was unanimous agreement that the de Leuw Cather route involving cut and cover up Queen Street and a dead end station at the Town Hall was undesirable for the following reasons.

1. Construction would create chaotic condition in Queen Street.
2. Dead end operation would restrict capacity on line.
3. Cost of property acquisition between Customs Street East and Queen Street.

"The circular route recommended by the Working Party apart from being cheaper to construct has considerable operating advantages and is capable of extension in almost any direction in the future. It also permits a better coverage of the city area. A preliminary survey indicates that the tunnel would be drilled largely in Waitemata series sandstone.

"(b) Route - Suburbs

"The location of the intermediate stations and the terminals was fixed on information supplied by the Planning Division of the Auckland Regional Authority. The basis of fixing the location of the station was:
1. Population concentration – present and planned.
2. Proximity of major feeder roads.
3. Availability of land (not necessarily railway land) for provision of car parks.

"Station Car Parks (paragraph 10)

"The figures in this paragraph were supplied by Auckland Regional Authority I have some reservations as to their validity. Although parking might be available for 16,000 cars, it has still to be shown that this will be used. If it is a fact the $30,000,000 could be saved on road construction, there could be a good case for at least a portion of the finance coming from National Roads Board funds.

"Gauge & Speed

"The Working Party is aware that I don't fully subscribe to the idea that a wider gauge is either necessary or desirable. It was put forward mainly by the Auckland Regional Authority representative who considered that:

"1. Light weight rolling stock needed for economical operation was not stable in high winds on 3'6" gauge.

"2. The standard of accommodation, speed and acceleration of the units should be of a very high standard and could not be provided on a 3'6" gauge. The very high standard would be needed to attract patronage.

"A preliminary survey was made by a member of my staff and member of the D.C.O.W.'s staff which indicated that a separate 5'6" route was possible but there would be many problems to be overcome, especially in the avoiding of interference to existing railway facilities. No attempt was made to assess the cost of such a route.

"I do not subscribe to the premise that a really 'swept up' service is needed. I am sure that a good suburban service on the lines of an updated Wellington service but with similar maximum speeds and accelerations and serving the C.D.B. (sic) would attract very little less patronage than a 'super' service on 5'6" gauge. I feel that further investigations will show that the extra capital cost needed for a separate R.O.W. and 5'6" gauge will be out of all proportion to the benefits gained. The one main benefit to N.Z.R. would be that the whole of the operations of a service with its own right of way could be divorced entirely from N.Z.R. operations.

"Level Crossings

"I fully agree that all 'at grade' level crossings should be eliminated. This is basically a roading problem and will have to be faced up to by the Roading Authorities sooner or later whether a Rapid Transit system is provided or not.

"Automation

"Although I agree with the principle that any service provided should be as fully automated as possible, I pointed out it would be difficult under our existing Railway practices to provide the degree of automation some members envisaged. For example it is difficult to see Union agreement to one man operation for a whole train (including guard) and for stations to be completely unattended and all ticket selling and collection automated.

"<u>Conclusion</u>

"Although the Working Party has made a number of recommendations concerning route, station location etc., the validity of the premise that Auckland needs or can afford a Rapid Transit system still requires testing. Until <u>detailed</u> costing of various alternatives (gauge, separate R.O.W. combined R.O.W. with N.Z.R. etc.) is carried out followed by a full cost benefit analysis (which should include hidden social benefits) it will not be possible for any party be it Local Body or Government, to assess whether the anticipated patronage and other benefits make a rapid rail system an economic proposition for Auckland. This costing is going to require far greater engineering investigations than was done for the de Leuw Cather report and was well beyond the resources of the Working Party." [395]

Rapid Transit Bias

It would seem from his report to the Railways General Manager that R H Newton had been a reluctant participant in the Working Party from the start. His admitted *personal* opinion that Auckland was not ready for a modern suburban rail service would certainly not have encouraged a more positive report.

Of course, he may very well have been more concerned about his career prospects and simply conformed to the (unofficial) Railways Department and/or Government policy of non-committal to the rapid transit concept. Whatever Mr Newton's rationale may have been, his negative influence could only have been enhanced by the equally negative presence of the City's Director of Works and City Engineer, A J Dickson, as part of the Working Party.

Although Arthur Dickson retired on 7 April 1969, that was only a month before the Working Party published its report. Certainly, some of the phrasing used by R H Newton in his report to Ivan Thomas about the 'hidden <u>social</u> benefits' which should be investigated as part of a full cost benefit analysis of the proposed Rapid Transit system was reminiscent of that used by Arthur Dickson during his criticism of the De Leuw, Cather Reports.

Changes Needed

For quite different reasons, many Aucklanders also doubted the adequacy of the recommendations and plans proposed by the Working Party on Rapid Transit – as reported by The New Zealand Herald published on 11 June 1969:

"Some of the leading business men and engineers in Auckland would like to see changes made to the newly announced plans to route a bus-rail, rapid transit scheme from the south and west through the inner city. The general feeling among those questioned yesterday was that the plans do not go far enough and that the system will not serve the maximum number of people.

"However, they do see the scheme, estimated to cost about $61 million, as a starting point. Their main criticism was levelled at the one-way, single-line underground rail loop through the central business district, which could cost $12 million. Most of the engineers would prefer the system to be a two-way track and linked in some way through Karangahape Rd to the main north line at Morningside...

"The president of the Queen St Business Association, Mr F A Carter, said the scheme could 'not come soon enough.' The association, he said, agreed with the scheme in principle and recognised the fact that if there was not some relief from the growing traffic congestion, real problems would arise. However, said Mr Carter, he was surprised that the underground system, through the one-way track, lacked potential for growth.

"Mr J Wright, a long-serving Auckland engineer, formerly with the Ministry of Works, said the scheme was 'disappointing' and not one of which he would be proud. 'I would have preferred to see the underground section carried on to link up with Avondale, Mt Roskill, Onehunga and Mt Wellington,' said Mr Wright. 'With its single track and small inner loop the proposed system does not appear to have enough scope.'" [396]

Politically and Financially Impracticable

Joseph Wright continued his criticism of the Working Party's recommendations in a subsequent article published by The New Zealand Herald on 16 September 1969. The following day, Dove-Myer Robinson, as Chairman of the Auckland Regional Authority's Rapid Transit Committee, rejected what he viewed as Joseph Wright's outdated opinion:

"Don't Confuse The Transport Issue – Everybody seems to think he knows best what kind of transport scheme Auckland should have. In his article on the city transport system in yesterday's 'Herald', Mr Joseph Wright criticizes the modified scheme recommended by the Working Party recently. It rather appears that Mr Wright is living in the past and has a nostalgic yearning for the old Halcrow-Thomas scheme. This ignores the enormous changes and developments which have taken place in Auckland in the last twenty years...

"One can sympathise with Mr Wright in wishing for wider coverage by rail than is provided for in the first stages of the scheme. However, the key to the whole problem is the provision and servicing of the capital costs...As it is, it is going to be very difficult to persuade the Government to accept Auckland's point of view regarding the financing of the railway part of the scheme...

"If Auckland were to demand the fully developed and extended railways plan suggested by Mr Wright, it would put up the cost colossally and this of course would help the Government to justify the delay in coming to agreement on the financing of the railways part of the scheme. Because a modern, balanced rapid transit scheme is going to be of such great benefit to everybody in every area of the Region, it is essential that it be provided as soon as possible. For this reason, Auckland initially should be satisfied with the minimum required to provide this service as adopted by the Auckland Regional Authority. To demand at this stage the ideal, fully developed scheme, envisaged by Mr Wright, could make the whole proposal politically and financially impracticable..." [397]

Acceptance of Second-Best

In other words, even Dove-Myer Robinson had accepted that if Auckland was to receive Government financial support for any form of rapid-rail public transport, he and the ARA would have to settle for far less than the ideal recommended by the De Leuw, Cather reports and lobbied for by Joseph Wright. Of course, with the acceptance of second-best as an expedient measure, Dove-Myer Robinson was simply replaying that part of Auckland's transport history that, for decades, had resulted in a dead-end suburban railway line, an incomplete motorway system, and a Harbour Bridge much smaller than needed. This was just another instance of what The New Zealand Herald referred to in

October 1967 as "False Transport Economy…official acceptance of the notion that an inedible crust may be better than no bread." [398]

Yet Another Inquiry

Also in keeping with past transport history, just how much, or how little, Government money might be forthcoming to fund Auckland's transport needs naturally depended on the findings of yet another Committee – a Steering Committee recommended by the Working Party to *'investigate and report upon the implications of alternative track gauges and carry out cost/benefit studies'*.

As reported by The New Zealand Herald on 11 June 1969, who would pay for this further study and how long it might take had first to be determined:

"The Minister of Works, Mr Allen, said yesterday that the cost-benefit studies probably would represent some two years of work. 'I will push on as much as I can to get this consulting team set up,' said Mr Allen. 'The Government is sincere in doing all it can to push ahead with planning.

"The Minister said that representatives of the Government and of the Auckland Regional Authority would shortly get together – and he would be consulting the chairman of the ARA, Mr T H Pearce – on the question of how to apportion the cost of some $200,000 for the work of the consulting team. But those will be cost-sharing negotiations for an aspect of further planning – not for the capital or running costs of the transport system itself.

"Mr Allen said he could not be at all definite but it could be three years and possibly much longer yet before ground was broken for the subway segment of the scheme. It would be doubtful, said the Minister, whether the Railways Department could or would want even to start improving the north and south suburban lines until such a vital matter as track gauges to be used had been settled on the advice of the consulting group.

"Mr Allen declined to discuss a prediction by the Mayor of Auckland, Mr D M Robinson, that the Government would be anxious to agree on financing before November [National Election due then]. Mr Robinson said that within a very short time it should be possible to bring down final estimates of capital costs and start negotiations on financing. But the Government is understood already to have made it clear that it will not be prepared to negotiate on the basis of cost assessments compiled in Auckland by Auckland…" [399]

'Talk Money' Called For

As reported by The Auckland Star on 10 June 1969, it was time to discuss more than just the cost of the second inquiry:

"The Government must now be prepared to 'talk money' for the Auckland rail-bus rapid transit scheme, the chairman of the regional authority, Mr T H Pearce, said today. It was no use going ahead with costly engineering investigations unless there was 'an earnest desire on the part of the Government to make known at the earliest possible date' its finance contribution, he said.

"Mr Pearce said he was very pleased with yesterday's technical committee report which recommended a $12 million inner-city underground loop rail line and terminals at Manurewa and Henderson. But the report recommended the establishment of another technical team to investigate the implications of using a wider rail gauge and to carry out cost-benefit studies. This second technical report could cost at least $200,000, said Mr

Pearce. 'This means it is now more important to discuss the financial aspects of the scheme with the Government.'

"He was backed up by the regional authority's general manager, Mr E A Flynn, who also chaired the technical committee which reported yesterday. 'Until now we have been able to share the costs (the authority, City Council, Ministry of Works and Railways Department) because they have not been very much. But from now on the cost could be high. We can no longer get by with men on part-time. We will need full-time staff on the second investigation', said Mr Flynn...

"The Prime Minister, Mr Holyoake, said in a statement yesterday following a Cabinet discussion on the report, that the Minister of Works, Mr Allen, had already instructed his inter-departmental officials committee to report as quickly as possible on the possibility of a New Zealand working party being set up to carry out the additional technical and economic studies that had been recommended." [400]

Telegraphic Pressure

Not one to miss an opportunity to apply pressure to the Government at any time but particularly on budget day, Dove-Myer Robinson sent a telegram on 26 June 1969 to both Keith Holyoake and his Minister of Finance, Robert Muldoon, reminding them of Auckland's needs:

"Last night's meeting Auckland City Council unanimously resolved to draw Government's attention to rapidly deteriorating public transport services in Auckland and request Government to provide up to date electrified suburban railway passenger service by 1975 at latest. Respectfully suggest some reference to this matter which is of vital importance to Auckland be made during budget statement tonight." [401]

No Commitment

Needless to say, the 1969 budget statement made no reference to Auckland's public passenger transport needs and nor did the Government's written reply to Dove-Myer Robinson provide any definite commitment – as per the letter from J B Gordon, Minister of Transport, dated 1 July 1969:

"The Prime Minister has discussed with me your telegram to him about public passenger transport in Auckland, and has asked me to reply. Government shares your concern about the problems confronted by public passenger transport services. These are by no means confined to Auckland alone, but are being encountered to varying degrees by all large cities in New Zealand. It was because of the gravity of the issues involved that the Government set up the Carter Committee of Enquiry to bring down recommendations directed at effecting improvements...

"As far as the rapid rail proposals are concerned you will be aware that a working party on which your Council was represented and which was chaired by Mr Flynn, General Manager of the Auckland Regional Authority, has recommended that 'a team be established to investigate and report upon the implication of alternative track gauges and carry out cost/benefit studies'. Government has accepted this recommendation and if you have not already heard from my colleague the Minister of Works, no doubt he will get in touch with you shortly.

"The studies recommended by Mr Flynn's Committee...are a pre-requisite to the detailed design work that must be undertaken before construction can begin. I do not think that it is possible at this stage, until more work has been done, to set a firm target for the opening date of the line, but Government is anxious that each step forward should be undertaken as expeditiously as possible.

"At this point in time, we do not know of the total capital cost of the system or its probable annual operating loss or profit. Again, an accurate assessment of these figures is dependent to some extent on the completion of the studies…recommended by Mr Flynn's Committee. I do not see how Government can enter into a financial agreement at this stage without knowing how much it will be called upon to pay." [402]

Steering Committee

That *team*, later named as a Steering Committee was eventually proposed by the Minister of Works, Percy B Allen, in a letter to Dove-Myer Robinson, also dated 1 July 1969:

"Cabinet has again considered the report of the Working Party on the Auckland bus, rapid-rail transit system. Recommendation (h) of the report suggested 'that a team be established to investigate and report upon the implications of alternative track gauges and carry out cost/benefit studies'.

"Government feels that a Steering Committee should be set up to direct this work and is of the view that it should be located in Auckland and consist of representatives of the Auckland Regional Authority (Chairman), Auckland City Council, the Ministry of Works and the New Zealand Railways. No doubt the Steering Committee would set up technical sub-committees to assist it in some facets of the work.

"The Government considers that a suitable order of reference for the Steering Committee would be – to control and co-ordinate the second-stage investigations into the recommendations of the Working Party on the proposed bus, rapid-rail transit system for the Auckland Region, and in particular to:

(a) investigate alternative track gauges;
(b) investigate possible extensions and additional rail routes not covered in the report;
(c) carry out cost/benefit studies of the complete bus/rapid-rail system;
(d) examine the town planning implications of the recommendations;
(e) undertake such other studies as may be necessary for a complete evaluation of the recommendations.

"In as far as the payment of any necessary expenditure is concerned Government holds the view that each contributing organisation (e.g. A.R.A., City Council, Ministry of Works and Railways Department) should pay the salaries and related expenses (such as travelling expenses) of such of its staff as are seconded to the studies, and that other costs of the second-stage investigations should be met by the Auckland Regional Authority, with Government subsidising on a 2 for 1 basis any such costs incurred up to $100,000, and thereafter on a 1 for 1 basis up to a maximum of $200,000. Money will be made available for this purpose in the Vote – Transport administered by the Ministry of Transport in the Supplementary Estimates. If this proposal is acceptable to you I should be glad if you would let me know as soon as possible so that the Steering Committee can get under way." [403]

Dove-Myer Robinson Response

Dove-Myer Robinson's reply to the Minister was swift – dated 3 July 1969:

"Following a discussion with Mr T H Pearce, Chairman of the Auckland Regional Authority, and subject to agreement by the members of my Rapid Transit Committee, Mr Pearce will probably be informing you sometime today of our acceptance of the

Government's terms for this further preliminary study… I do thank you for your prompt action in this matter, and hope that it will be very soon possible for us all to meet in Wellington to discuss agreement on principles and target dates…" [404]

A Rebuff

Just in case Dove-Myer Robinson thought he had an inside line to the Prime Minister, that idea was soon rebuffed in a letter from Keith Holyoake to him, dated 9 July 1969:

"Further to my letter of 1 July, I have been advised by my colleague, the Minister of Works, that he has already informed you of Government's views on the report of the Working Party on its investigations into the Auckland Rapid-Rail Transit proposal. His letter has apparently crossed yours to me in the mail.

"In the meantime, I am not setting a date for the discussions which you requested as you will no doubt wish to consider, before any visit to Wellington, the Government's views stated in Mr Allen's letter… May I suggest that if you have any further comments to make to my colleagues or me, you address your letter to the Hon. P.B. Allen, Minister of Works, who at the present stage has responsibility for the subject in which you are so interested." [405]

Minister's Assurance

The Prime Minister's letter to Dove-Myer Robinson was promptly followed by an assurance from the Minister of Transport, J B Gordon, that the Government was keen to continue talking about and studying Auckland's transport problems, but without committing to any financial responsibility at this time:

"Thank you for your letter of 3 July about public passenger transport in Auckland. I would like once again to reiterate Government's desire for continued progress in the resolution of Auckland's transport problems. This is illustrated by our prompt agreement to further studies being undertaken immediately and by our willingness to participate in and share the cost of these studies.

"As far as the question of Government meeting the cost of the railway facilities is concerned, I think you will agree from your own experience with financial budgeting that Government cannot commit itself until it knows with reasonable certainty how much it is committing itself for. The cost of the facilities could vary significantly depending on the size of the gauge chosen. In our view, we cannot reasonably be expected to agree to provide an unspecified sum of money.

"It is important that the work necessary to provide an underground railway proceed as quickly as possible. If this is done there will be no unnecessary delay. Government would like to see this happen. If it does happen, then the question of setting a target date for opening the rapid transit system seems to be of little significance at the present time." [402]

More Discussions and Inquiries

According to the Minister Gordon's letter, the choice of railway gauge had seemingly assumed more of a financial significance than the previously-debated issues of rapid transit routes and who was to pay the capital cost. By focusing on the relatively important but less contentious subject of gauge, the Government was able to gain some relief from the capital cost argument. In the meantime, costly decisions could be delayed by ever more discussions and inquiries undertaken by the national Committee of Enquiry into Urban Passenger Transport (the Carter Enquiry) and the proposed Steering Committee.

Steering Committee Set Up

The Steering Committee recommended by the (Flynn) Working Party was eventually set up in July 1969 "...to investigate and report upon the implications of alternative track gauges and carry out cost/benefit studies..." [393]

As well as the retired Arthur Dickson, the Steering Committee essentially comprised those who had been part of the original Working Party – B D Duffield, Director of Works & City Engineer, Auckland City Council; R H Newton, District Engineer, New Zealand Railways; R R Parsons, District Commissioner of Works, Auckland.

"Mr. F F Abey, late District Commissioner of Works, Auckland was an original member of the Committee and served until his untimely death in April 1970... Mr. E A Flynn, General Manager, Auckland Regional Authority was Chairman of the Committee from the time it was set up in July 1969 until his resignation in July 1972. Although the constitution of the Committee called for the appointment of a representative from the Authority, Mr Flynn was not replaced." [406]

Cause for Delay Denied

As reported by The New Zealand Herald on 8 July 1969, the Minister of Works was conscious of the criticism that the setting up of yet another enquiry was an excuse to delay the start of actual construction of a rapid transit system:

"A steering committee is being established to direct further investigations into the proposal for an Auckland rapid transit scheme, including an underground railway... Announcing Government approval for the investigations, the Minister of Works, Mr Allen, said yesterday that he had been criticised for saying that the surveys – which had been sought by all bodies concerned – could take up to two years. 'The two years,' he said, 'was mentioned by an executive of the ARA when I met the authority and the City Council in Wellington recently. I was only requoting what I considered to be a fairly honest opinion. As soon as these surveys have been completed, we will be ready to discuss finance with the Auckland Regional Authority and the Auckland City Council.'

"The Minister said that while professional men and, if necessary, consultants were evaluating the track gauge and other aspects of the proposed new rail services, engineering feasibility studies of the underground segment would have to be completed and assessed. The proposed cost-benefit studies would be a major undertaking and provision would have to be made for redevelopment with high-density accommodation at or near all suburban stations.

"Until these things are done or near-enough complete for me to get a full picture,' added the Minister, 'I shall not be in a position to make a recommendation to the Government. But I give an assurance that I shall do everything in my power to expedite these studies.

"Asked whether the question of additional or extended rail routes did not reopen all previous planning, Mr Allen said he believed that a full study – such as the one about to be undertaken – had to bear in mind the possibility of some western rail link to the existing northern line. 'It could vitally affect the economics of the whole thing,' said the Minister, 'but it is certainly not intended to cause delay.'" [407]

Delay intended or not, for reasons described in the following chapter, the report of the Steering Committee was not published until August 1972...

Carter Enquiry Submissions

In the meantime, the national Committee of Inquiry into Urban Passenger Transport (the Carter Inquiry) continued its hearings up and down the country. Most of the submissions received from both public and private transport operators illustrated the failure of bus services to compete with private transport using increasingly congested roads. A precis of some of those submissions include:

Auckland Regional Authority Submission

"1. Auckland is now at a stage where a significant change is taking place and will accelerate. Development will move out into larger tracts of land previously the preserves of the pastoral farmer – into areas of both flat and hill country land served by a relatively sparse initial pattern of roading. Regional or local planning cannot stop this process, it can merely guide it.

"Urban renewal or redevelopment will be inevitably a slow process and will not have a significant effect from the public passenger transport point of view. Higher density housing, while it may increase to meet a certain demand, will amount to a very limited proportion of the total accommodation.

"2. The regional planning objective is to guide this new development in certain directions – basically along main lines of communication or transportation routes rather than along a general outward growth on the whole periphery by suburban accretion.

"3. From certain points of view the motorcar will remain the supreme and most convenient form of transport no matter what is done in the field of public passenger transport – nothing can replace it as the most convenient means for the housewife in her daily or weekly shopping trips or in her general movement activities – nothing can replace it for the purpose of family recreational trips – nothing can replace it for numerous other activities.

"Any steps to reverse these advantages by artificial means would be negative, of very limited effectiveness and of very doubtful validity from the social point of view. The one trip in which public passenger transport services can be effective is the trip to work and from work – the trip is made regularly as a matter of getting from one fixed point to another fixed point every working day.

"4. This means two peak loading periods daily. If these trips are provided for only by bus on the ordinary right-of-way used by every other motor vehicle the situation will be self-defeating no matter how good or attractive the bus vehicles themselves.

"5. There is one answer only to this situation – rapid mass transit routes on main corridors of movement. Whether on rubber or rail, rapid mass transit can be achieved only by the use of exclusive rights-of-way – not necessarily for the whole length of the trip but definitely on the main corridors.

"6. This can be done in Auckland if firm steps are taken to a comprehensive plan today. Railway rights-of-way exist – a system of planned motorways is to be developed and a supporting system of major arterials are an integral part of the transportation plan which exists. On the rail and motorway routes exclusive public transport rights-of-way can be provided and some preferential treatment for public passenger transport services is feasible on some arterial routes. Immediate steps to provide these rights-of-way would be a positive step and the most logical basic plan on which to build.

"7. Two main points or conclusions arise:

(a) The position in Auckland needs to be considered in the light of the particular circumstances existing in this City and if Auckland's requirements are going to be assessed on the basis of a very general case applicable to any other city, effective decisions are unlikely to be made.

(b) After a plan is firmly adopted for implementation the questions of sources of finance and other matters can be dealt with.

"8. Concern is felt that investigation after investigation goes by without an answer. Soon it may be too late." [408]

"Summary of Proposals:

"1. The Auckland urban area will not be able to function effectively without solutions to its transport problems emanating from the recommendations of the Committee of Inquiry.

"2. Competition between the private motor car and public transport for the patronage of the urban population must be weighted in favour of public transport by the passing of legislation to implement the following:

(a) fares based on operating expenditure only and capital or capital costs provided by the community.

(b) improved forms of public transport of which mass transit on separate rights-of-way is the only proven technology.

(c) priority in traffic movement for surface public transport.

(d) pricing penalties on peak hour motor car traffic.

(e) physical restrictions on peak hour parking.

(f) subsidies for concessions given to any special class of passengers.

"3. An organisational change must be made to place the control of all matters connected with the items listed in 2 in the hands of one overall planning and controlling authority.

"4. The controlling authority referred to in (3) must be given preferably Government finance or, if not, access to finance from its own taxes for its work to be done competently. Such taxes to be broadly based…" [408]

Auckland City Council Written Submissions

"We believe that now is the time for bold far sighted decisions. We ask your Committee to join with us & the ARA in impressing on the Government the essentiality of such decisions this year. Council's conclusions and recommendations are summarised as follows:

"(1) That unless urgent remedial measures are taken, escalating congestion on roadways in urban areas will produce the same disastrous consequences in New Zealand cities as has already occurred in other cities of the world.

"(2) That control of all passenger transport and licencing thereof in Auckland be under single control, and that the logical body to discharge this function is the Auckland Regional Authority which is the largest passenger transport operator in the metropolitan area as well as being the regional planning authority. Thus providing for closest and most effective coordination of regional and transportation planning.

"(3) That complete reorganisation and consolidation by the Auckland Regional Authority of operations, routing, timetables, fare structures and allied matters is urgent and crucial.

"(4) That the passenger transport structure in Auckland must be a balanced system of roading, bus and rapid rail components.

"(5) That construction of the rail component of the de Leuw Cather Bus-Rail Rapid Transit System (with such technical modifications as may be necessary) commence at the earliest possible date, and that Government accept responsibility for the provision and servicing of the capital for the railway part of the scheme.

"(6) That Government recognise the principle that urban passenger transport is an integral part of the national transport system and that Government adopt a policy of paying subsidies, equivalent to annual deficits, to public authorities operating urban transport systems." [409]

Prior to the City Council's submission, its Mayor, Dove-Myer Robinson, provided the Council with an overview of the transport situation as he saw it:

"The issue before Council today is probably the most important we have had to decide for many years. Auckland's public transport system is visibly collapsing about our ears. The situation is very serious. Regional Authority losses on transport this year could run into $750,000 of which this Council would have to meet nearly $500,000.

"Two of the largest private operators are now in difficulties, Auckland Transport Holdings has offered its undertaking to the Auckland Regional Authority and the Passenger Transport Company is now negotiating with four of the South Auckland Local Authorities for subsidies.

"Desperate attempts are being made by all the North Shore local bodies to prevent the sale of Transport Holdings to the Auckland Regional Authority so as to avoid spreading the levies on to them; and the same is happening in South Auckland.

"If these moves succeed an opportunity of relief of this Council's levies by wider spread will be lost. Also the opportunity for the Auckland Regional Authority to take a positive step towards coordination and reorganization of services through single control will be lost.

"Public transport passengers in Auckland are falling by nearly two millions yearly leaving fewer passengers to carry the heavy overheads, increasing congestion and resulting in heavy losses of business in the central business district. Costs are rising and revenues are falling every year resulting in poorer services, higher fares and heavier levies. Within a few years losses on all forms of public transport in Auckland will exceed $1,500,000 yearly…" [410]

Auckland City Council Oral Submissions – 12 June 1969

In answer to a question from Committee member, Horace Tilly:

"You feel if a private operator gets to the stage where he is making losses he should sell out to the government or council?"

Dove-Myer Robinson replied:

"Yes. This is a situation you will have seen reported in the morning paper where two largest companies endeavouring to sell to the Regional Authority. This is a situation we have seen coming, within a few years there will be no private operators. And I think at that stage rather than subsidising them to enable them to carry on, they should come over and be operated by a public organisation such as the Regional Authority and we take it for granted we will get the normal satisfactory service that we expect from such an organisation.

"The Chairman – You wouldn't agree with the charge that has been put before this Committee on several occasions that private transport is much more efficient than the public transport?

"D M Robinson – I don't believe that is true. If the private operators provided the standard of service and the unprofitable service, service which is obviously unprofitable but which is provided to enable people requiring public transport to use it, if the private operators had to do that I believe they would be less efficient than the public operator...

"When it comes to the subsidies for private operators I would prefer to leave that to the Government to decide, but when we talk about efficiency, if we put them on a comparable basis, private operators are no more efficient or even as efficient as the local authority. They get by what I call a form of sweated labour – father, mother and the whole family join in, helping to run the service, they don't pay normal award wages, they don't have to put up with the restrictions the A.R.A. have to, the trade union, award conditions. If they had to operate under the same conditions as the A.R.A. I doubt whether they would be as efficient." [411]

Separate Petrol Tax Sought

As reported by The New Zealand Herald on 13 June 1969, Dove-Myer Robinson also suggested a public-transport funding solution to the Committee of Inquiry during his oral submission:

"The Mayor of Auckland, Mr D M Robinson, yesterday proposed a separate tax on petrol to subsidise urban public transport. Mr Robinson put the suggestion to the committee of inquiry into urban passenger transport which sat for the last time in Auckland yesterday…Mr Robinson said the Auckland City Council advocated that a special petrol tax be imposed. The tax would be paid to a fund 'for the sole purpose of subsidising by way of capital grants public passenger transport.' He further submitted that all present motor taxation should go to the National Roads Board to enable the board to accelerate its roading programme.

"We recognise that this will involve political considerations,' he said. 'We feel that increasing petrol tax to subsidise urban transport can be easily justified because of the enormous amounts contributed for many, many years by taxpayers and ratepayers in subsidising roading and other facilities for motorists. 'Therefore the time has now arrived for the motorist in turn to make a reasonable contribution toward the restoration of satisfactory public transport which has been adversely affected through the competition of the private motorcar.

"The council believed that motorists would accept the view that it was in their own interests to improve public transport. The move would reduce road congestion, enabling motorists using cars in peak hours easier access to available roading space. We also believe that any reasonable increase in petrol taxation to subsidise public transport would be absorbed and accepted by motorists within a very short time of its imposition…" [412]

Letter of Dissent

However, not every motorist accepted the idea, as illustrated by the letter to his Worship the Mayor from Miss Honor J Morton (on behalf of a group of disabled people):

"Dear Mr Robinson – We are disabled, and we are appalled by your suggestion to increase petrol tax to subsidize the Public Transport. The badly designed buses, the inconsiderate bus stops and bus routes, and the rough driving of these vehicles make it impossible for most of us who are disabled to use these facilities. So we are forced to provide our own transport, or taxi, or rely on others, so that we may try and earn our own living.

"We do not have cars for status symbols but as necessities to take us to our places of employment. Our cars must replace our legs, but at what a price! Not only do we struggle to buy a car with no sales-tax deductions, but also we are faced with high maintenance and the crippling, and ever-increasing, taxes on petrol. Other bodies besides yourself threaten to add to our burden with petrol-tax increases.

"For most of us, our disability restricts our earnings capacity, therefore the majority are in the low-income bracket. We try to lessen the burden on the community by trying to support ourselves, yet we have little encouragement. Instead of suggesting that we, the disabled, help subsidize a public transport we cannot use, could you not suggest a little relief – perhaps a small discount on petrol.

"Until the public transport is able to cater for the disabled, we really cannot be expected to support it. We have sufficient hardships – we have parking difficulties, we are unable to climb the steps of the buses (because they are too high and awkward), we are prevented the use of public conveniences (again the steps), we cannot enter many public buildings (again the stairs), we cannot operate some elevators (because the buttons are placed out of reach – especially for wheelchair people, and we have difficulties with the doors), we cannot even enter the churches!

"Although we are in the minority, one person in seven is disabled, may we ask for a little thought before such a cruel decision, such as the one you suggest, is made to increase our difficulties. We do hope that you will see our plight, and may your way clear to help us become a little more independent on society." [413]

As usual, Dove-Myer Robinson's reply was to the point:

"Dear Miss Morton – …I can well appreciate your apprehension at the possibility of any large increase in the price of petrol. However, the suggestion was for only a small increase of about 3 cents per gallon, which should not bear very heavily on anyone, particularly as most pensions have recently been increased by $1.00 a week. In any case, as you are probably aware, anyone suffering from a handicap is entitled to make application to the Social Security Department for special assistance, and if the proposed tax were adopted by the Government, I am quite sure that satisfactory arrangements would be made to assist people in similar circumstances to your own.

"As you will appreciate, the Government will have to find some additional source of income if it is to meet the demand for assistance for public transport services, and it occurred to me that as motorists are already very heavily subsidised by both ratepayers and taxpayers, it was not asking too much that motorists generally make a small contribution towards the cost of providing public passenger transport services. I do hope the above will help to reassure you." [414]

New Zealand Railways Department Submissions

"(a) In Auckland for 1967/68, rail services carried 2,900,000 passengers at a cost of $731,000, giving a loss of $535,000 after deducting revenue of $196,000. The loss is 18c per passenger.

For the same year Auckland Railways Road Services carried 1,720,000 passengers at a cost of $320,000, giving a loss of $58,000 after deducting revenue of $262,000…

"(b) Both fares and losses are extremely reasonable when viewed in the overall context of urban transport. Reasonable though they may be in this context, however, it is submitted that the losses are proving extremely detrimental to the New Zealand Railways as a business.

"(c) Freight increases on goods traffic have had to be at a higher level than would have otherwise been the case in order to endeavour to recoup the passenger losses on suburban activities. This has, of course, worsened the railways activities in competition with other forms of transport and has lost valuable goodwill.

It is imperative both for the financial viability of the Railways and for the benefit of the country as a whole that profit derived from freight be no longer used to defray expenses incurred in the provision of suburban passenger transport.

"(d) The profits on freight and on long distance road passenger services could be used to provide capital development funds.

"(e) If nothing is done about the present passenger transport situation then the services will be gradually eliminated if for no other reason than simply because of lack of funds for replacement equipment..." [415]

Ministry of Transport Submissions

"(a) Because of their value to the urban community it is considered that urban public passenger services deserve greater financial assistance than they have enjoyed in the past.

"(b) 'Urban Transport Authorities' are proposed to, control, co-ordinate, fix fares for, operate or contract out urban passenger transport services. Present transport licensing would cease for urban mass transit. Fares fixed would be subject to appeal to the Charges Appeal Authority.

"(c) The Auckland Regional Authority as an Urban Transport Authority should in time include all cities and boroughs within the region and the Harbour-ferry Services District...

"(e) After a stated period, all scheduled public passenger services within the region should be operated by or under contract to the Authority, and the cost of providing these services be shared on a wider base accordingly...

"(h) Where an Authority assumes the cost of maintaining railway urban passenger services, Government assistance be given on a reducing scale over the first three years.

"(i) Does not recommend exemption for buses from petrol or mileage tax paid to the National Roads Board.

"(j) Consideration should be given to a reduction in registration and licensing fees for buses.

"(k) Operating losses should not be directly subsidised by the Government.

"(l) Authority should have power to raise rates or make levies on constituent local bodies on a proportionate basis.

"(m) It is recommended that government subsidies, or in some cases loans at medium or low rates of interest, be made for approved capital projects up to one half of the cost...

"(n) Government capital assistance to be provided from an 'Urban Transport Fund' administered by the Ministry of Transport and made up of firstly, part of receipts from registration and licensing of cars, and secondly, one cent per gallon of the 3.3 cents duty on petrol levied since 5. 5. 67. Both these receipts are now paid to the Consolidated Revenue Account...

"(p) The Ministry considers that it is appropriate to use part of the monies already raised by motor vehicle taxation to assist urban passenger transport because the use of private cars has adversely affected urban passenger services and contributed greatly to the heavy financial losses on the services operated by local authorities and to the poor returns to private operators.

"(q) Proposed projects and investment should be considered in the light of gain in revenue and patronage, reduction in road congestion, value of savings in travelling time and other relevant factors. Importance should be placed on maintaining fares at levels which would encourage the use of public transport and so reduce the need for additional road and parking space for private cars and for greater investment in private cars." [415]

National Roads Board Submissions

"(a) Suggests that further surveys and research are necessary in regard to the following possibilities: –

(i) change in public transport systems:

(ii) increased parking charges and zones of scaled charges for motor cars in central city areas:

(iii) suburban parking areas close to public transport facilities:

(iv) transport to be provided as a community service financed entirely from rates.

"(b) There is clear recognition of the fact that public transport systems which will attract and retain public support and patronage will defer the construction of urban motorways and expensive street works. For this reason the Board is keen to assist in measures designed to promote greater efficiency and increased popularity of public transport.

"(c) The Board is opposed to subsidising losses on public transport and is firmly convinced that a positive approach is required.

"(d) Examples where Board could assist: –

(i) incentives to provide clearways:

(ii) incentives to accord priority for buses on selected routes at peak hours:

(iii) by subsidising fringe parking at suburban railway stations and outlying bus terminals." [415]

Ministry of Works Submissions

P L Laing, Commissioner of Works

"The Ministry of Works is not directly experienced in either the economics or operational problems of urban transport and does not wish to pretend to any specialised expertise. On the other hand it is concerned with town and country planning and through its service to the National Roads Board and the design and layout of highways, it is brought face to face with many of the problems arising from urbanisation…There may therefore be areas of fact-finding in which the department could help the Committee. If this is the case, the officers of the department are very anxious to be of assistance. Such matters as estimated capital costs of road works, rail works, parking buildings and the like may be required. Traffic capacities and traffic modal splits and other criteria used in design of works could be of interest. Town and country planning data is almost certain to be required.

"Other officers of my department, after reading this submission, have criticised it for too willingly accepting the motor car. It is true that I argue against positive discouragement of the car and look entirely to ways and means of improving public transport as a method of adjusting the balance between private and public transport. This I regard as no more than practical realism and some of my officers think more direct pressure on private motoring could be justified. I don't.

"(a) Does not consider private car usage should be restricted by pricing or other restrictions. It is desirable to discourage private cars by good public transport but considers proportionate effect is not great.

"(b) Large cities based predominantly on private transport are unpleasant, inefficient and because of decentralisation, expensive.

"(c) Form of public transport and form of property development ought to be connected.

"(d) Costs of public transport should be shared between beneficiaries –

(i) user, should pay a substantial share as a fare or a combination fare and tax:

(ii) urban property, by rates with a zoning of rating for public transport:

(iii) local and national community, from general or special taxation. Possible allocation – 60% fares by user, 20% zoned rating, 20% subsidy from taxation…

"(g) Subsidies should be related to operating loss, severity of problem, capital expenditure for new or improved facilities. Discretionary authority vested in a National Transport Board. Subsidy levels should leave a sufficiently large responsibility with the owners of the transport system to ensure efficiency…" [415]

T F S Johnson, Chief Town Planner submission:

"(a) Town planning needs to be inter-related to and modified by transportation surveys and planning.

"(b) Financial position of transport operations improved as follows:

(i) by land use planning for – higher densities – two way peak movement by location of employment – operational needs of buses in developing suburbs:

(ii) if the community decides that public transport is worth retaining all transport facilities must be controlled in a way that assists public transport. For example – exclusive bus lanes – strict control of kerbside parking in city centre to encourage buses rather than cars for shopping – preference for buses at controlled intersections – parking buildings and sites selected where they can be served by public transport:

(iii) reduce diseconomy of peaks by – greater patronage off peak – staggering working hours to spread peaks – introducing shift work – employment location planning for two way peak movement.

"(c) The administrative arrangements for private and public transport – Roads Board funds as against public transport fares – militates against balanced investment in the two parts. Investigations are needed to suggest ways of rectifying the present imbalance.

"(d) There is a good case for one regional authority controlling land use at a generalised level, planning of network of principal streets, the provision of all public transport and the subsidising of its losses.

"(e) the community must accept the financial loss on transport operations and tolerate increasing losses: –

(i) as a social service which provides mobility for those who, for a variety of reasons, cannot use private transport, and

(ii) because the losses are made up in other spheres, notably through promotion of economic growth and through savings on private transport facilities in vehicles and highway network." [415]

J H Macky, Assistant Commissioner of Works – Notes of Overseas Trip – submission:

"In Europe I was told that rapid transit systems become necessary when the population reaches half million or even less. Thirteen cities in Europe were building undergrounds and some had populations as low as 350,000. They realise that an underground cannot pay at this population level but claim that other factors justify early construction of subways – e.g.

savings by deferment of construction of motorways, loss of property etc. but <u>most important it shapes the development of the city and therefore the sooner it is built the better</u>. Losses incurred in early years are offset by gains in other directions. The gains may be difficult to measure…

"In all the cities with rapid transit systems which I visited in North America and Europe there has been recognition that an underground does not have to pay. In all cases a substantial part of the capital cost has been met by the city or government or both…" [415]

Department of Internal Affairs Submissions
Mr P J O'Dea, Secretary for Internal Affairs

"(a) Basically, efficient public transport must be undertaken as a public service, as the most economical way of moving large numbers of people. To achieve this, and to ensure higher patronage of both private and public services, regional environmental planning and the provision of these services should be under the same control. More attention should be given on a regional basis to the proper location of residential areas in relation to city centres, and the density of population in these areas.

"(b) If transport services are to remain a local responsibility whether under present arrangements or on a regional basis, some new sources of finance for local government should be further investigated. If this is not done, the only alternative appears to be some greater degree of subsidisation of transport services by central government, and this is not considered desirable.

"(c) The future levels of service to be provided by public passenger transport cannot be considered apart from questions of urban planning and urban renewal. The basic problems of traffic and transport will not be solved until the future pattern of environmental planning is determined. Better planning in future, coupled with the renewal of inner-city areas, could help to resolve many of the existing problems of transport.

[Page 2 of the Department of Internal Affairs submission also included the observation:

"… It could be a matter for investigation by this committee, how far fragmented control of planning, lack of co-ordination, or lack of effective action by those responsible for the planning within the wider metropolitan area, have contributed to the present unsatisfactory state of urban passenger transport."]

"(d) The Department would be in favour of control of urban passenger transport by general purpose regional authorities administering regional services, but not by special regional transport authorities. It would favour control of all urban passenger transport services under the one regional authority, with provision for the operation of services by or under contract to a territorial local authority or authorities, private contractors or any other public body including the New Zealand Railways." [415]

Auckland Transport Holdings Limited Submissions – Rolf Porter, Managing Director

"Possibly, nowhere else in the World, in a City of this size, is there a situation comparable to that which now exists in Auckland: –

"16 individual Bus Operators –
- some with profitable routes;
- some with marginal routes;
- some with almost impossible routes as regards profit making;

- with the Auckland Regional Authority operating over half the Service;
- with all Companies operating some restricted services;
- with two Licensing Authorities, i.e., the Auckland Regional Authority as regards its own services and the No. 2 Licensing Authority as regards all Private Operators;
- with two Awards – one a relic of the old Tramway Award, and the Private Operators under a 25-mile radius award which is, again, different from the National Award;
- with all Private Operators trying to make a profit by increasing fares and restricting services;
- and with the loss on the Auckland Regional Authority's operations being borne by a relatively few Boroughs.

"Although it is recognised that Public Passenger Transport is an essential service, it is similar to any other business venture; that is, it must give a service acceptable to the people otherwise the people will not use it. Therefore, with this thought in mind, which I feel must be the predominant thought in the operation of any business, the first essential is to proceed further with the Investigating Committee's transport scheme drawn up last year but so design the Service as if one Company or Authority owned and controlled all the vehicles…

"It is apparent to me, although I have been a strong advocate of private enterprise, that there is no alternative to the Auckland Regional Authority being the owner and operator of all the bus services in Metropolitan Auckland. There will be strong opposition by many Local Bodies to the above suggestions but I feel it is time we all realised that Public Passenger Transport is an essential service like water, sewerage or power, and that although the user will bear the major portion of the cost, all citizens must contribute their share, as without a Public Passenger Transport System their properties could be almost valueless, industry could not function and the whole City would come to a standstill.

"In our earlier submissions to the Minister of Transport we drew attention to the assistance the Government must give in subsidising Public Passenger Transport…I would like to point out the ridiculous situation of Public Passenger Transport contributing to the building of freeways, etc., in a City which enables the private car to slowly drive the bus off the road.

"No City can possibly operate without an efficient Public Passenger Transport System as the cost of providing parking if everyone used motor-cars would be astronomical, therefore it is of the greatest urgency, if the Auckland City does not wish to die, that Public Passenger Transport is substantially upgraded, a perfect service is provided, and the Government gives relief either by remission of duties or subsidies to an Industry controlled and administered by an Authority.

"It has been recommended by several Experts on Transport that as a Public Passenger Transport System is so vital to the life of the Community and as it is in the Public Interests for as many as possible of its citizens to use that Service, then it should be provided free. On the face of it this sounds a ridiculous proposition, but is it so ridiculous?

"On the Auckland Harbour Bridge alone statistics will prove that one bus carries approximately the same number of people as forty cars to and from work; that that one bus requires virtually no space for parking in the City, whereas the forty cars must be stored almost stationary throughout the day; that one diesel bus uses little more fuel than the average car; therefore, when the possible savings in freeways, parking buildings, freeing of kerb space, total expenditure on motor cars in general, petrol, oil, etc., is added it may prove to be greater than the loss in fares.

"In this connection, a thorough investigation should be made into the suggestion of free transport and I would recommend that the New Zealand Institute of Economic Research be asked to accept this task on a contract basis." [416]

Auckland Boilermakers' Union – F Harris, Vice-President

"Auckland, the largest City in New Zealand, is a city almost devoid of any sense of community responsibility. A city where a person with a pair of shoes becomes a second-class citizen and is not catered for. Large banners proclaim on bridges and motorways 'No Pedestrians'. If one needs more proof, count the number of drinking fountains – I know of one.

"What has happened to our city? We have succumbed to a new religion - 'the cult of own your own car'. Large concrete temples are being constructed to this new God; vast motorways are leading to these temples. Not content with this, kerb-side shrines have been erected which tick greedily while they digest their not too meagre offerings. The high priests of this new cult roar in amongst their flock on motorcycles making sure they obey their road code commandments.

"Where else in the world can you get such splendid organised madness. The concept that everyone should own his or her own car is a ridiculous concept. The average worker is forced to buy a car in order to get to work. The employers today are demanding their employees have their own transport as can be seen in the advertisements for labour. This means the people are forced to spend a large percentage of their earnings to provide their own transport, thus limiting their purchasing power for other commodities, which must effect (sic) all sections of the community.

"Obviously the solution to the greater number of problems connected with transport would be the rapid rail. Wellington has a fast and efficient rapid rail operating on three lines with a total of 2213 trips a week, including 212 trips on Saturday and 126 trips on Sunday. Poor Auckland has a vintage rail system with no trains whatsoever on the weekends, the rail in Auckland being reserved for pigs, sheep, horses and bags of cement. The stations have been allowed to run down and the Railway Department seems to want to concern themselves with just freight cartage…

"Fumes are choking the city along with the congestion. The rise in cancer has risen over the years in proportion with the number of cars on the road. Cigarettes are not the only cause. It has been estimated that in Auckland alone 33,000 tons of fumes are generated per year, most of it from engine exhausts. One only has to visit Queen Street during rush hour and the fumes are overpowering. It certainly is not a healthy area for office and shop assistants to be working in…

"…let's look at this concept that the Railways should pay? Have you ever heard of a motorway paying? Do the Armed Forces pay? To be consistent, the Government should send the Navy out fishing, and the Air Force top-dressing. No, I'm afraid that argument won't hold water. A rapid rail would save millions in overseas funds relaxing the purchase of tyres, petrol, oil, spare parts, as well as cars. Halt the need for motorways and the large sums spent on the purchase of land and construction of same. Hospital bills would be lighter and the stresses and strains involved in people driving in traffic would be eased.

Who is to say that driving stresses do not cause nervous breakdowns and mental disorders. The savings would be astronomical in human lives, money and HAPPINESS…

"It must be pointed out that the Boilermakers, and indeed the Trade Union movement as a whole, is concerned for the welfare of the people and we feel that a mass transport system would make life more pleasant, enjoyable and less hazardous, not only for the workers but also for the old people, children, and others caught in the scheme of things, and it is to this end that we feel a greater sense of community responsibility, instead of rugged individualism is needed in transport if this city is not going to be choked to death with parking lots and traffic, and we hope the day will come when a citizen will once again be able to find a drinking fountain." [417]

The Municipal Association of New Zealand (Inc.)
"The Association's views may be briefly summarised as follows: –
(a) The major problem facing urban transport operators is the losses being incurred on these services.
(b) As an essential community service, losses should be spread over the community generally and should not fall on one section of the community alone, such as the ratepayer.
(c) The only practicable way, so far as the Association can see, by which these losses can be met on a community basis is by way of direct financial assistance from the State.
(d) Any changes in present methods of organisation of urban passenger transport services should be determined on an individual basis in relation to the problems of each particular area." [418]

J R Dart, Department of Town Planning, Auckland University
"In providing a public transport service, the goals, I suggest, are not to make a profit. Public transport service is not there to make a profit, is not there to extract a revenue from the community but to provide a service which can be measured, and I suggest should be measured on quite different bases, those of convenience, comfort and speed, and the measure of the degree of efficiency of a public transport service is not the measure of the profit made or the reduction of losses received but the measure of patronage attracted to that service. This is the proper way, I suggest, for the community to measure, the one, the efficiency of the service, and two, to acknowledge the aims of that service.

"Captive patronage of the service is that part of the population which is the most vulnerable. At the present time it includes those who cannot afford motorcars but I think in New Zealand as in comparable societies that is a declining percentage. In other words, the price of cars remains more or less constant in real money terms. Income from households increase to the point where all those who wish to own a motorcar will be able to do so.

"The section that cannot is the most vulnerable. This is the percentage that public transport must recognise, the weakest section of the community. It is quite wrong to try to provide a service for that vulnerable section, to seek in terms of profit or minimising of loss." [419]

Further Approaches to Government
Pending the findings of the Carter Enquiry and the formation of the Steering Committee, Auckland's Mayor, Dove-Myer Robinson, continued to press the Government to meet with the City Council and the Regional Authority as per his report to the Council's Finance Committee on 14 July 1969:

"...it is essential that this Council and the A.R.A. know Government's decisions as soon as possible, otherwise constructive planning and implementation will be completely frustrated. It is therefore recommended:

"1. That the Government again be requested to meet representatives of the A.R.A. and Council as soon as convenient, to discuss, as a matter of urgency, the financing of the rail portion of the rapid transit plan and the setting of target dates for starting work on and coming into operation of the scheme.

"2. That His Worship the Mayor be authorised, if necessary, to convene separate meetings of Auckland members of both political parties to inform them of the situation and seek their advice and assistance." [420]

Rival Approaches to Government

However, while the City Council and the Regional Authority attempted to convey a unified front to the Government, political opponents sought to undermine them with their alternative public transport system.

Further to their submissions to the Carter Inquiry, Michael Hart and David Dodds of the Civic Action Party met with the Minister of Transport and Minister of Railways, John Gordon and Minister of Finance, Robert Muldoon, on 24 July 1969. This meeting was followed by a letter from Michael Hart to Peter Gordon, dated 31 July 1969:

"We have now had an opportunity to obtain the cost benefit comparative analysis of the all bus and bus/rail systems carried out by the Auckland City Council in June, 1967. The analysis, which was modelled on a similar study for the London Victoria Line underground railway extension, is quite detailed although its areas of consideration are limited.

"However, it does indicate the valuable contribution that this type of comparative analysis could make toward arriving at a decision which will be in the best interests of all concerned. It may be useful for the Steering Committee in organising their studies to inspect this analysis. On a number of occasions we have discussed the Auckland transportation studies with well qualified Auckland transportation engineers and planners, and a considerable number of them are inclined to the view that an updated transportation study should be commenced immediately in view of the following factors:

"1. It is five years since the De Leuw Cather study was commenced and six to seven years since the data was collected.

"2. The urban motorway programme for Auckland is a number of years behind schedule.

"3. The rate of private car usage has considerably exceeded estimated quantities.

"4. The recent growth in land use has been unevenly distributed within the urban region and has led to unanticipated traffic generation in certain areas.

"5. Public transport patronage has further declined.

"6. Various economic changes have occurred, e.g. devaluation and wage increases.

"In view of these opinions, we are convinced of the necessity for steps to be taken along the lines proposed in our submissions of 21st July.

"Aside from any action which you could initiate on the above points, we consider it imperative that a comparative cost benefit analysis of the two transit proposals be undertaken by the Steering Committee. Unless this is done, the Government could conceivably face criticism for expending large sums of public money without carrying out adequate evaluation of alternatives. We are hopeful that your administration is conscious of the necessity to evaluate thoroughly alternative proposals before an irrevocable decision is made.

"It should be obvious to anyone who examines the history of the De Leuw Cather transportation study and subsequent studies that at no stage have the two alternative transit systems been compared other than on a value judgement basis. This is evidenced by the findings of the Officials Committee in 1967 that the Bus/Rail system 'could' be required in the 1980s and that the Bus system would be likely to cope with the demands, at least up to that time, if not beyond. Our reading of the Officials Committee report is that it shows remarkable similarity to our submissions in respect of the areas of doubt that are attached to the De Leuw Cather & Co. studies and recommendations.

"We trust that our request will receive your serious considerations for we are very concerned at the possibility of the wrong decision being made on this major undertaking, when an opportunity exists for this to be avoided to some extent at least.

"To summarise our stand on this issue, I would emphasise three points:

"1. The deeper we look into recent transportation planning in Auckland, the more convinced we are of the considerable areas of doubt that exist.

"2. We are pressing the Mayor, the Regional Authority and the Government to take steps to reduce these elements of doubt as urgently as possible so that the citizens of Auckland can feel more confident that the final plans adopted will be in their best interests, both economically and socially.

"3. Without wishing to prejudice in any way the final decisions on the transport system to be adopted for the Auckland Region, we urge that immediate attention is paid to maintaining and improving existing bus services in the interim period. If further study should show conclusively in favour of the Bus/Rail scheme, it is vital that existing public transport patronage be maintained at as high a level as possible if this plan is to have any chance of success." [421]

Minister's Response

Peter Gordon responded with the Government's usual lack of financial commitment:

"Thank you for your letter of 31 July about the Auckland passenger transit proposals. It is intended that a new comparative cost/benefit analysis be undertaken of the alternatives available and this will include a study of the all-bus system. This is being done for much the same reason as those outlined in your letter.

"You talk in your letter of the Government spending large sums of money, but I must point out at this stage that the Government has not decided the extent, if any, of its contribution to what is essentially an Auckland metropolitan area facility. We will need to know with greater precision than at present the probable capital and operating costs and revenue before Government could arrive at its decision." [422]

Fiscal Responsibility

This attitude that the proposed Auckland passenger transit system was "...*essentially an Auckland metropolitan area facility*..." was interpreted by many Aucklanders as somewhat discriminatory; a demonstration of National Party obedience to its rural support base taking priority over the fiscal and social needs of the country's largest city. However, such a political motive was insufficient reason to withhold taxpayer funding so the Government had to establish a more convincing policy of fiscal responsibility.

This concept was promoted by Finance Minister, Robert Muldoon, during his opening address to the Auckland Rapid Rail Symposium held on 15 and 16 August 1969. The

Minister then "…stipulated…that a prior condition for Government financial assistance in respect to the capital cost of a transit system was that a cost-benefit analysis should be undertaken in conjunction with the technical and planning investigations." [423]

Auckland Rapid Rail Symposium

The Symposium, sponsored by the Auckland Branch of the New Zealand Institution of Engineers, included presentations from many engineers, planners, academics, public and private transport operators, and local body politicians. During his long address to the Symposium, Dove-Myer Robinson referred to the Government financing of the Wellington railway network:

"This Government proposal, that Auckland provide the capital for the railway part of the scheme, is in sharp contrast to its action in accepting full financial responsibility for the electrification of Wellington's suburban railway services some years ago…Auckland is simply asking the Government to provide Auckland's citizens with a service (which it is the Government's responsibility to provide) through a Government Department established for this purpose.

"The Government joined with Auckland in calling for and paying for the De Leuw Cather investigations and reports, and therefore has a joint interest and responsibility in the matter. But the Government, having accepted and endorsed the De Leuw Cather reports and recommendations, then added an entirely new condition which it must have known would be entirely unacceptable to the people of Auckland.

"Auckland is asking no special favours. As <u>taxpayers</u> (but not as <u>ratepayers</u>), Aucklanders will have to meet their share of capital costs as they did some years ago for improved suburban railway services in Wellington. [The Wellington suburban rail network was electrified between 1938 and 1940.]

"As taxpayers they will have to pay their share of the cost of providing similar services in any other city or town where the need is proved, and accepted by the Government. Delay in reaching agreement is totally unnecessary, no alternative can be as effective or as cheap. Once the principle of government responsibility is accepted, and the sooner final agreement on financing and on target dates for starting and completion can be reached, the less it will cost the Government and the greater the financial and social benefits to Auckland." [424]

Briefly, the Situation

Dove –Myer Robinson continued his argument in a letter to Mr J Hauge, the Director of De Leuw, Cather of Australia dated 14 October 1969:

"…Briefly the situation, as I see it, is as follows:

"1. The arguments which we have produced and the evidence and submissions in support of the scheme have put the Government in the position where it has no adequate reason for not agreeing to go ahead with the project.

"2. The Government is playing for time by advancing the argument that until it has a much firmer estimate of the capital and annual costs, it is not prepared to negotiate on the question of provision and servicing of capital costs. The further investigations recently approved will probably take an additional 8 - 12 months.

"3. The Government takes the attitude that the ratepayers of Auckland should meet these capital charges. This, the Auckland City Council and the Auckland Regional Authority, representing the ratepayers, are firmly opposed to, on the grounds that as the

Railways Department is a Government-owned Department, it is the Government's responsibility to provide and service the capital cost of the railway part of the scheme.

"These submissions have been made at length to the Government, and we are awaiting Government's reply to our submissions with very little expectation that Government will agree to them, or even go far along the road to meet them.

"However, unless we receive this reply within the next week or two, there is very little more we can do. But I can assure you that if the Government is not prepared to accept these costs as the responsibility of the <u>taxpayers</u> of the country as a whole, and not just the responsibility of the <u>ratepayers</u> of Auckland, all hell will be let loose in Auckland, even though it is on the eve of the Parliamentary Elections, due to take place on the 24 November. You will see from the above that it is not technical information which we require at this point, but rather political agreement..." [425]

Interim Report of the Committee of Inquiry into Urban Passenger Transport

By September 1969, the Committee of Inquiry into Urban Passenger Transport (Carter Inquiry) had found itself unable to report by the end of that month, as originally planned. However, many urban passenger bus operators were by then experiencing such dire economic problems that the Committee felt compelled to issue an interim report, which it did on 15 September 1969:

"...during its hearings and discussions, the committee has received the strongest representations on the need for immediate relief for operators of urban passenger services. The committee recognises this urgent need and also that it is in the public interest to arrest further reduction of timetables, increases in passenger fares, and the abandonment of urban passenger bus services by some private bus operators.

"I therefore have the honour to submit an interim report from the committee...In making such recommendations, I would emphasise that these are intended merely as urgent temporary measures for the immediate relief of urban passenger bus operators. I would, therefore, on behalf of the committee, formally ask for an extension of time until 31 December 1969 for the presentation of a final report. Yours sincerely, D J Carter, M.P., Chairman.

"Briefly, the committee recommends as a temporary measure:

(a) That grants be made to operators of scheduled urban passenger bus services (including trolley buses) based on the amount paid in heavy-traffic fees for buses use solely or predominantly for these services. This scheme should apply to all operators of urban passenger bus services, including those operated by New Zealand Railways Road Services.

(b) These grants be at the rate of 200 per cent of heavy-traffic licence fees paid for urban passenger buses in the previous quarter. (Proportionate grants would be necessary in some cases.)

(c) The grants be paid quarterly from the Consolidated Revenue Account through the Ministry of Transport's Vote.

(d) The first grant to be payable in December 1969 related to the heavy-traffic fees paid in the quarter commencing 1 September 1969.

The committee further recommends that Government should at this stage accept this responsibility for the next two quarters. It is estimated that the two payments that would be made in the financial year ending 31 March 1970 would amount to approximately $415,000.

"The committee is strongly of the opinion that the Consolidated Revenue Account, i.e. general Government revenue, is the logical source of such interim assistance. No actual remission of motor vehicle taxes is intended at this stage. The committee recognises there is a national interest in maintaining this important community service until other more appropriate measures can be introduced." [426]

[As described later, a further extension was granted and the final Report of the Committee of Inquiry was eventually presented on 27 February 1970.]

Holding the Government to Ransom

While the Committee of Inquiry into Urban Passenger Transport sought urgent help for Auckland's urban passenger bus services, the Mayor of Takapuna, Mr A F (Fred) Thomas, expressed a view published in a lengthy article in The New Zealand Herald on 2 September 1969, namely, that: *"There is a deliberate policy of running the present passenger fleet into the ground in an attempt to hold the Government to ransom."* [427]

This statement had followed some concern referred to weeks earlier by Dove-Myer Robinson in a letter to the Manager of the Auckland Regional Authority's Transport Division, Trevor Long. In that letter, Dove-Myer Robinson wrote:

"Questions have been asked publicly why the Transport Division of the A.R.A. cannot take interim steps to improve public passenger transport in the Metropolitan area, pending the inauguration of the bus-rail rapid transit plan." [428]

Following Fred Thomas' allegation, Dove-Myer Robinson wrote to the Takapuna City Council on 4 September 1969:

"As a member of the Committee, I was distressed to read Mr Thomas' statement because, to the best of my knowledge, it was quite incorrect. My understanding of the situation was confirmed during discussions at the meeting of the [Auckland Regional Authority Transport] Committee yesterday, and the Chairman of the Committee, Mr J Allsopp-Smith made a public statement repudiating Mr Thomas' allegation…" [427]

Fred Thomas responded by letter to Dove-Myer Robinson on 15 September 1969:

"I have had referred to me your letter of the 4th instant, objecting to my statement that there is a <u>deliberate</u> policy of running the Auckland passenger bus service into the ground in an attempt to hold the Government up to ransom. My comment was in fact derived from various statements you have made in recent times…

"Dealing specifically with my statement, I refer you to your address earlier this year to the Chartered Institute of Secretaries where you said '<u>at the present rate of loss of passengers and growing dissatisfaction, the public transport system in Auckland will be non-existent by 1975. The position will grow worse until it reaches crisis proportions within the next five or six years.</u>' I take this to mean that the bus services in Auckland are already pretty run down and a crisis is fast approaching.

"Again on the 12th August last you were reported in the Herald as saying: '<u>It is absolutely impossible for the Auckland Regional Authority and the Auckland City Council to take any effective steps towards even an interim improvement of bus transport until finance and target dates [for implementing the de Leuw Cather proposal] are resolved with the Government.</u>'

"I deduce from this that there is absolutely nothing you can do to avert the crisis which is fast approaching. This is an admission of great weakness in handling an important public problem, and, if I may be pardoned for saying so, I think you have adopted a most 'un-Robinson-like-attitude' to this question! It is fact, that even with the rail scheme, the vast majority of people will still travel by bus, and no valid reason has been given for deferring action on replacing the ageing bus fleet.

"Finally both the Herald and Star printed your demands to the Government that, as far as you were concerned '<u>November was the deadline for reaching agreement with the Government.</u>' I interpret this as an attempt to hold the Government up to ransom. If I am wrong in coming to this conclusion then perhaps you will explain what your statement meant.

"In conclusion may I point out that there is so much that could be done to upgrade the existing service if the same effort, energy and enthusiasm which you have devoted to your rail scheme, had been applied to getting a better bus service. Unfortunately a large majority of those making decisions are predominantly private car users and give little real consideration to those dependent on public passenger transport.

"Like many thousands of Aucklanders, I still nurture the hope that some positive steps will be taken, by both the Auckland Regional Authority and the Auckland City Council, to improve the present bus service, because whatever happens it will be several years before the rail system can be upgraded. I support 100% the upgrading of the existing rail system and believe this to be a Government responsibility. However, the more grandiose scheme needs further careful study to clear up many questions which still remain unanswered?" [429]

Dove-Myer Robinson responded by letter on 16 September 1969:

"…I feel you should know why your statement caused some consternation in the minds of the members of the Transport Committee. What worried us was your use of the word 'deliberate', which of course means that the Authority is intentionally creating a situation for the purpose of politically blackmailing the Government. Of course this is not correct and, as a member of that Committee, I felt very hurt at such a suggestion from you…

"…any reference I have made to a November deadline for reaching agreement with the Government obviously means that if agreement is to be reached with the present Government, it must be before the November elections, because there is no certainty that the present Government will still be in office after the elections or, if it is still in office, the new Government's policy may not be identical with the present members' policy.

"Again I repeat that through no fault of its own, the Regional Authority is placed in such a position that it is vital, in the interests of continuity of adequate transportation services and the day to day planning decisions which have to be made by all local bodies in the Metropolitan Area, that finality with the Government should be reached as soon as possible." [430]

Conspiring With the Opposition

While any *deliberate* degradation of the City's bus services may not have been planned, achieving *that finality with the Government* to finance the proposed, public transit service was certainly open to whatever means Dove-Myer Robinson could otherwise employ. That included conspiring with the Opposition, as per a letter he wrote to the Hon. Hugh Watt, Deputy Leader of the Opposition, on 15 September 1969:

"I am enclosing three suggested questions which it would be very helpful if you could ask the Minister of Works and obtain replies to… As you will see the questions are designed to get the Minister to commit the Government to acceptance of the present scheme – as modified by the recent report of the Working Party, and also to agreeing that all steps possible should be taken to reach agreement before the General Elections.

"If the Minister is prepared to go as far as this, any argument that final agreement should be delayed until as nearly as possible exact costs have been determined, purely for the sake of satisfying the Government what it is going to cost, is just sheer waste of time and money ($2 1/2m to $3m per year) as well as to continue wastage through traffic congestion, enforced usage of private cars because of lack of adequate public transport in Auckland amounting to at least an additional $50m a year cost to the people of Auckland.

"If we can get answers to these questions there are several others which I think could advantageously follow. The main thing is that having taken the initiative we must keep it in our hands and not let the present opportunity slip through our fingers.

"<u>Suggested Questions to be asked of Minister of Works</u>

"1. Are the present engineering and cost benefit studies being undertaken for the purpose of deciding if the present rapid-transit scheme is the best for Auckland, or for the purpose of determining accurately the estimated cost of the railway part of the scheme.

"2. Has the Govt agreed that the present scheme is the only economically practicable scheme for Akd.

"3. In view of the detrimental effect that delay in reaching finality on costs & timing is having on day to day planning decisions of the A.R.A., A.C.C. and other local bodies in Akd, will the Govt give an assurance that every effort will be made to reach agreement before the general elections?" [431]

Confidential and Anonymous

Nor was Dove-Myer Robinson averse to sharing confidential information with the press, as per a letter to him from the Editor of The New Zealand Herald, O S Hintz, written on 9 October 1969:

"Thank you very much for sending me the confidential copy of the City Council's submissions to the Local Government Commission. You had sent me an earlier copy and I can assure you it has been most useful for background in support of changes for which we have long campaigned. We shall certainly not disclose the source of information." [432]

Rapid Transit not Rapid Rail

Special criticism was reserved for those who appeared to be ignorant of the complete, regional transport proposals, as per the press statement issued on 9 October 1969 by Dove-Myer Robinson, as Chairman of the ARA Rapid Transit Committee:

"I was quite perturbed to hear of the statements made in Parliament yesterday by Mr George Gair, Member for North Shore. As reported, Mr Gair's statements show the same superficial and uninformed misunderstanding of the situation so prevalent amongst those who have made no special study of the question. I hope Mr Gair's statement does not reflect the Government's attitude. Mr Gair says that the estimated cost has risen in a short time from $40 million to more than $70 million. He probably does not know that this included about $15 million rise in costs through delay in starting construction, and a <u>maximum</u> estimate of $25 million which I made to allow for the modifications and extensions recommended by the Working Party in June of this year…

"It should be clearly stated that Auckland's scheme should not be described as a rapid rail scheme. It is a rapid transit scheme, the major factor in which is $375 million worth of motorways. The rail component of the scheme is only a small, relatively costly, but absolutely vital link in the chain. By far the greatest percentage of the scheme provides for the use of cars, commercial vehicles and buses on the roading system, the railway part of the scheme providing the essential steel backbone which will link together all the public transport system.

"This will ensure greatly improved public transport for the whole of the Region, whether directly served by the railway or not. It cannot be dissected and considered part by part in isolation; the scheme must be considered in whole. I would suggest to Mr Gair that when he has finished with electioneering in the next two months, he come and spend a few hours with me, and gain a full understanding of the urgency and importance of this scheme to the whole of Auckland." [433]

Government Concedes

Whether prompted by the urgency imparted by the Interim Carter Report, the pressure exerted by Dove-Myer Robinson, or the pending election, the Government finally conceded to a *political agreement*. A letter to the Chairman of the Auckland Regional Authority, Tom Pearce, from the Minister of Works, Percy Allen, dated 15 October 1969, certainly seemed to be such a concession, albeit with several conditions attached:

"You will recall our most recent discussions and correspondence about the method that should be adopted for sharing the cost of the railway portion of the proposed Auckland rapid transit system. This issue has been the subject of extensive investigation, but there still remain problems in arriving at a final decision until capital costs and operating profits or losses are known with greater precision. Nevertheless, in the light of the known facts, Government is willing to share costs with your Authority on the basis set out below:

"(a) Government will provide the capital and construct the facilities for the rail component of the scheme. The Railways Department would operate the rail service for the Regional Authority on a contract basis, the contract price being calculated to include:

(i) full normal operating costs plus overhead and management fees,

(ii) depreciation based on normal railway practices.

"These two items would be different depending on the rail gauge finally chosen, but the principles on which they would be based are set out in schedules attached to this letter.

(iii) interest on all new capital investment.

"However, if as a result of the adoption of any findings of the Carter Committee, capital subsidies are paid for transport to local bodies, a corresponding subsidy should be applicable to the rapid rail system, and interest paid by the Regional Authority reduced accordingly.

"(b) The rapid rail system should be distinct and separate from an accounting and financial point of view from all other activities of the Railways Department. The Regional Authority would have the power to fix fares and determine train timetables and frequencies. All fare revenue should be paid to the Regional Authority.

"Parking facilities are an integral part of the system and should be provided on this basis. Space for other revenue-earning assets (e.g. advertising space, shops let on concession, etc.) would be provided as part of the scheme, and any revenue derived from the use of this space would accrue to the Regional Authority.

"(c) It is agreed that to avoid undue delay, the present investigating work should continue through to the planning and construction stages without interruption, subject to the Regional Authority advising Government that it and its constituent local authorities accept these financial proposals.

"(d) An early construction date would reduce cost escalation to a minimum, and would reduce the adverse effects of the continuing decline in patronage on the existing bus system. However, full information which will indicate the most desirable target dates for commencing and completing construction, will not be available until the Steering Committee has completed its cost/benefit study next year. Provided investigating and planning work proceeds as recommended, this deferment in fixing target dates will not delay progress, and decisions will be more soundly based than is the case at the present time.

"(e) The Regional Authority in respect of its bus operations should receive the same treatment as other public bodies if the findings of the Carter Committee of Inquiry result in financial assistance to public transport authorities, and appropriate legislative changes should probably be made to enable it to play a somewhat wider role in transport in Auckland. However, decisions on these matters should be deferred until the Carter Committee has reported.

"I would like once again to emphasise the difficulties associated with the fact that the gauge width has not yet been determined, and that as a consequence precise financial estimates are not yet available.

"No doubt your Authority will wish to have discussions with its constituent local authorities in line with paragraph (c) of the Government's proposals. When these discussions have been completed, I and my colleagues would be happy to have a further meeting with you to discuss what additional progress can be made." [434]

U.S.S.R. Proposal

There were also others eager to discuss what *additional progress could be made* – namely, the Russians – as outlined in a letter to Dove-Myer Robinson from Andrew Reid, Managing Director, General Equipment Co. Limited, Auckland, dated 20 November 1969:

"I would like to confirm in detail, some of the matters discussed during a general exploratory conversation…on Tuesday 18th November, and also at a further meeting on Thursday, 22nd [20th?] November. On the latter occasion Mr A Ivanzov, Minister for the U.S.S.R. in New Zealand and his Secretary Mr Druzhin were also present.

"My company represents several of the larger Export Organisations of the U.S.S.R. in New Zealand and the Pacific, and because of this, as you will recall, I approached yourself as Chairman of the Transport Committee concerned with the Rapid-Rail Project, with a suggestion for the construction and financing of this scheme through these Organisations.

"It is obvious that Auckland must have this transport system operational in the early 70's if serious traffic problems and large financial losses to the business community and the travelling public are to be avoided. I think it is also very obvious, that any attempt to implement this scheme by sectionalizing it, and allotting various portions to different contracting countries for the supply of the components required, can only end in such chaotic conditions, that the resultant delays must considerably increase the final cost.

"We suggest therefore that a much more satisfactory result would be achieved if the whole of the Rapid-Rail System was negotiated as a packaged deal. This would entail all excavation work, rail laying etc., and the completion of such a scheme inclusive of all ancillary work and installations, together with the necessary rolling stock etc., completed to the finished stage ready for operation.

"However, whatever economies may be effected by careful design and operational planning, it still leaves a major question unanswered. How the scheme is to be financed.

We are dealing with a sum of 60 million dollars plus, and this is a considerable amount of money for a country like New Zealand to raise, in addition to its other commitments.

"With this problem in mind, I made an approach to the Commercial Counsellor of the U.S.S.R. Legation, Mr A I Naumov, and the Minister for the U.S.S.R. in New Zealand, Mr A Ivanzov, with the suggestion that it may be possible to negotiate a contract for the supply by the U.S.S.R. of all equipment, etc., required, using wool and other New Zealand products, as part payment. This idea was very favourably received by both of the above gentlemen and resulted in the discussion which took place in your office when Mr Ivanzov and his Secretary were present.

"I must point out that the final decision on this matter, as far as the U.S.S.R. Commitment is concerned, must of course be confirmed by the Government of that country, but I would emphasise that a precedent has already been set on this, on a previous occasion, when the Government of the U.S.S.R. agreed to buy four million dollars' worth of wool, if New Zealand would accept four hundred thousand dollars' worth of Machinery in exchange.

"Finally Mr Chairman, if you feel this matter is worthy of further consideration by your committee, I would be happy to assist in supplying any further information you may require." [435]

Dove-Myer Robinson Response

It was not an opportunity to be missed and Dove-Myer Robinson responded straight away:

"Thank you for your letter of the 20 November 1969. In view of the importance of this matter, and many different aspects which should be considered, I think it would be helpful if you could attend the next meeting of the Rapid Transit Committee of the Regional Authority, to discuss this matter with members. The meeting commences with lunch for members at 12 noon, and the actual meeting starts at 12:30 p.m. We would be very pleased if you could join us for lunch on the first floor of Regional House at 12 noon on Wednesday, 26 November, and thereafter take part in the discussion as the first item on the agenda, at 12:30 p.m." [436]

Andrew Reid

As a Takapuna City Councillor and advocate for the Rosedale Sewerage facility (as opposed to the Wairau Valley), Andrew Reid was well known to Dove-Myer Robinson. At the time of the Russian approach, his company, General Equipment Co. Limited, was supplying spare parts and other material to the Russian fishing fleet which then had quite a presence in NZ coastal waters. At the time, New Zealand was having some trouble selling all of its wool and Russia did not have the U.S. dollars to buy it - hence the barter proposal. Russia was apparently quite experienced by then in the construction of underground transportation systems having opened its first rapid transit line in Moscow in 1935.

However, the United States, as a world market leader, apparently frowned on the practice of barter, particularly with Russia, and dissuaded countries such as New Zealand from entering into such agreements.

This was not the first time that Andrew Reid had proposed such a 'reciprocal' trade arrangement between the U.S.S.R. and New Zealand. In 1967, he approached the Government through his local Member of Parliament and received the following reply, dated 31 May 1967, from the Minister of Overseas Trade at the time, John R Marshall:

"Mr N J King, M.P. has approached me concerning your proposal for a reciprocal trade arrangement with the U.S.S.R. as a result of which the District Officer of the Department of Industries and Commerce in Auckland sought further details from you.

"It is apparent that your proposal is identical, except for the amount of trade involved and the type of goods to be imported, with one which the Commercial Counsellor of the Soviet Legation made to my Department a short time ago. After consideration by Cabinet it was decided that the proposal could not be approved, and the Legation was advised of this decision on 14 April [1967]. The principal reason for the decision is that reciprocal trade arrangements involving the granting of special import licences are in contravention of our obligations under the General Agreement on Tariffs and Trade.

"Even if a breach of our international commitments could be successfully defended, agreement to one proposal would give rise to requests from other countries for reciprocity which might have to be accepted with a resulting breakdown of our normal trading patterns. The subject of reciprocal trade has been raised in Parliament, and the Government has explained fully why it cannot accept these proposals. Since your proposal introduces no new elements which would justify a change in the Government's decision, I can see no advantage in your coming to Wellington to discuss the matter further." [437]

Heavy Stocks of Wool

By early 1970, New Zealand was finding it difficult to sell all of its wool overseas – as reported by The New Zealand Herald:

"The Wool Commission's total purchases of 706,437 bales since the 1966-67 season have been reduced by 48 per cent, the chairman of the New Zealand Wool Commission, Mr E L Greensmith, said yesterday. In a report to the mid-year meeting of the electoral committee of the New Zealand Wool Board, Mr Greensmith said the residue of the stockpile, comprising 368,819 bales, had cost the commission $36,200,000. Sales of this wool at present prices would involve losses of about $3,750,000…Mr Greensmith said storage and insurance costs on the stockpile amounted to $1,036,000 in the 1968-69 season. Estimated cost for the two items in the present year was $500,000. Mr Greensmith said that while total stocks had diminished by 48 per cent, relatively heavy stocks were still held at several selling centres, notably Auckland, Dunedin, Invercargill and London." [438]

Wool for Rapid Rail Doubtful

Nevertheless, not only was a barter system with U.S.S.R. – wool for a rapid-rail transport system – doubtful but, according to the Minister of Overseas Trade, John Marshall, so was the need for a rapid rail system – as per his letter to Andrew Reid on 13 March 1970:

"I have been giving some thought to the matter you raised when you called on me on 17 February in the company of Mr King, M.P. and Mr A I Naumov, Commercial Counsellor at the Soviet Legation.

"I understand that the proponents of a rapid-rail transport system have only reached a preliminary stage in their formulation of a scheme. Their main efforts are directed at present at establishing the need for a rapid-rail system, and its economic benefit and viability. As planning proceeds, consideration will necessarily have to be given to the method [of] financing the system and the manner in which it will be constructed and operated.

"Dealing particularly with the problem of financing the scheme, I have noted the suggestion that organisations in the U.S.S.R. might be interested in undertaking some of the work and that payment could possibly be arranged on a barter basis.

"You will appreciate, however, that it is usual for contracts of this size to be let on the basis of competitive public tendering. In these circumstances any Soviet organisations that are interested in the contracts would need to tender, and all tenders will be considered on a non-discriminatory basis. In the event of a Soviet tender being accepted, arrangements could then be made for the payments made under the contract or part of them to be used for the purchase of New Zealand wool, dairy produce or other products. Arrangements of this kind have been made on previous occasions with Yugoslavia and India.

"However, I should like to emphasise again, that it is too soon to consider particular aspects of the proposed scheme at this stage. You will be aware that the Government has recently held an enquiry on the subject of urban transport, chaired by the Hon. D J Carter. The Committee's report is now being studied by the Government and it could well give rise to decisions affecting the Government's attitude to the proposed Auckland rapid-rail transport system." [439]

Summary of Various Public Transport Inquiries Undertaken During the 1960s

The myriad of public transport inquiries and other talkfests that had dominated the 1960s included:

Passenger Transport Committee of the Auckland Metropolitan Council – reported November 1960;

The De Leuw, Cather Inquiries – appointed May 1963 and reported July, October and November 1965;

The Buchanan Inquiry – appointed April 1966 and reported July 1966;

Institute of Economic Research – reported 1966;

The Officials Committee – appointed May 1966 and reported August 1967;

The Working Party on Rapid Transit (Flynn) – appointed February 1968 and reported May 1969;

The Committee of Inquiry into Urban Passenger Transport (Carter Inquiry) – appointed 12 December 1968 – interim report September 1969 and final report February 1970;

Steering Committee (proposed by the Flynn Working Party) – appointed July 1969 and report published August 1972.

Despite all these inquiries and reports, by 1970, any hope for a rapid-rail transit system for Auckland remained as out of reach as ever. And the National Party won the 1969 election as well...

Road Transport

National Roads Board Subsidy

It was not until 1960 that the National Roads Board offered grants to local bodies so they could start contributing to Auckland's road-building program. However, little was accomplished until March 1963, some <u>eight</u> years after the completion of the Master Transportation Plan, when a National Roads Board subsidy was then authorised to enable the Auckland Regional Planning Authority's Technical Advisory Committee to commit to a much-needed Comprehensive Transportation Survey needed to facilitate the design of the proposed citywide roading system.

The Committee was informed of the granting of the subsidy and its conditions by way of a letter from C N Johnson, Secretary, National Roads Board, Wellington, to The Director of Planning (F W O Jones), Auckland Regional Planning Authority, dated 4 March 1963:

"Dear Sir, Your Authority's application for subsidy on the cost of your Master Transportation Plan was considered by the National Roads Board on 19 February. The Board has decided that a contribution of 30% will be paid to your Authority on the actual cost of Master Transportation Plans up to the stage of outline geometrics only and estimated to cost £120,000. It considers that the work involved beyond the preliminary design stage should be the responsibility of the engineering authority undertaking the construction work and for which the Board allows a percentage on-cost for subsidy purposes. An extension of Master Transportation Surveys beyond the outline survey stage, therefore, will not be eligible for subsidy. Progress payments will be made by the District Commissioner of Works, with whom arrangements should be made." [440]

Comprehensive Transportation Survey

Following receipt of the National Roads Board letter, F W O Jones reported to the Chairman and Members of the Technical Advisory Committee, Auckland Regional Planning Authority, on 12 March 1963.

Parts of his report included:

"National Roads Board:

"1. The National Roads Board has approved a contribution of 30% of the actual cost of the proposed Comprehensive Transportation Survey.

"Local Authorities:

"2. Practically all the local authorities in the Region have now agreed to the financing of the proposed Comprehensive Transportation Survey on an allocation which has been circulated.

"3. This allocation assumed a contribution of 30% from the National Roads Board.

"4. One or two local authorities have expressed their agreement in qualified terms, and two relatively small local authorities have not so far agreed.

"5. The total estimated annual allocation to all local authorities (for a period of each of three financial years) is £28,000. The total annual allocation which is in doubt as a result of any reservations or non-agreement by local authorities is approximately £1,400.

"Decisions Of The Executive Committee:

"6. The Executive Committee of the Authority at its last meeting, held on 7 March, 1963, decided to recommend to the Authority:

(1) That the Authority proceed with the Survey.

(2) That the Auckland City Council, as the 'principal' Council in terms of the Act, should be asked to guarantee the additional amount remaining outstanding from full agreement, pending completion of further negotiations with the local authorities concerned (which could proceed while the Survey is in progress).

(3) That the Director of Planning be authorised to proceed with the necessary staffing for the work of the Survey.

"Future Work:

"12. The reliability and value of the results of the survey will depend, to a considerable extent, on the reliability of the basic planning data provided. The population and land use projections to be considered in relation to the Regional Development Plan in a subsequent item on the Agenda are the first steps in this direction." [441]

As described in previous chapters, the *Comprehensive Transportation Survey* referred to by F W O Jones was that undertaken by the American engineering consultancy, De Leuw, Cather and Company, appointed by the new Auckland Regional Authority on 14 May 1963.

Motorway Construction Slows

By 1963, the Southern Motorway had been extended from Wiri to Takanini but little motorway construction had been completed at the city end. Indeed, almost all main road construction was stopped pending the results of the De Leuw, Cather survey – as per the letter written to the Chief Civil Engineer from the District Engineer, Auckland, on 7 July 1964:

"…I have received the following reply from District Commissioner of Works, Ministry of Works, Auckland:- "The matter of final location of motorways etc. cannot be determined until after the report on the traffic survey at present being carried out for the regional Planning Authority is available. This is not expected before the end of this year. Further discussion on the matter should therefore be postponed until definite information is available."

"There is merit in holding this matter in abeyance until the Traffic Survey Report is completed provided that in the meantime the Ministry of Works refrain from further motorway construction in the Symonds Street to Newton Gully area. If they do not the result could be that motorways construction and commitments will force the adoption of current roading proposals and their future amendment to suit the Traffic Survey recommendations for road rather than rail. I suggest a suitable tie up be arranged at Head Office level for the proper consideration of road and rail interests in Newton Gully relative to the Traffic Survey Report. Will you kindly instruct." [442]

To Control and Live With the Motor Car

When Auckland celebrated the arrival of its half millionth citizen in June 1964, Mayor, Dove-Myer Robinson, reflected upon the City's growth and the effect it was to have on its transport infrastructure:

"It is estimated that within 10 short years the region's present 200,000 motor vehicles will double to 400,000. To provide an adequate and safe roading system will cost local bodies and the Regional Authority an enormous amount of money. New roads will have to be built in accordance with the findings of the transport survey already ordered by the Regional Planning Authority. Existing main roads will have to be up-graded, widened, re-aligned and straightened.

"Properties will have to be acquired and demolished and occupants removed and rehoused. Approximately 410 miles of roads of regional importance have been listed under three categories. Including the cost of property acquisition and compensation, road construction and other expenses, it is estimated that road works in the next decade may cost territorial bodies and the Regional Authority up to £40,000,000. This is exclusive of State highways and motorways which are the responsibility of the National Roads Board.

"It may be thought that the spending of forty million pounds on roading in ten years would be too great a financial burden for the region to bear. But there is no practicable alternative. Experience in New Zealand and overseas has shown that it is impossible to legislate against the use of the motor car; we have to learn how to control and live with it.

Assuming, as we must, the doubling of motor traffic in ten years, the region's roading system must be able to cope with it. If we can't or won't regulate the ever increasing flood of motor traffic, it will strangle the life of the city.

"This would mean wiping out untold millions in property values, and possible ruination of well-established residential, retail, commercial, and industrial areas. "Whatever ingenious traffic control techniques are adopted, it is inevitable that the region must face up to enormous roading costs in the next few years. Fortunately, however, there are ways of minimising these costs. The most important steps we can take being to reduce the number of vehicles using the roads during morning and evening peak hours. This is an integral part of the Authority's Public Passenger Transport proposals." [318]

De Leuw, Cather Plans

As detailed in an earlier chapter, De Leuw, Cather and Company provided the Auckland Regional Authority with a *Regional Transit Plan* in July 1965 and its *Comprehensive Transportation Plan* in October of that year.

The Consultants also provided a *User Benefit Analysis* and a *Priority Programme for Motorway Construction* on 21 October and 12 November 1965, respectively. While the Regional Transit Plan recommended the steps to be taken by the City to develop a viable public transport system, De Leuw, Cather's Transportation Plans set out broad proposals for motorways, expressways, and urban arterial roads.

Need for Revision

However, by this time, the southern motorway had "...advanced from Penrose to Ellerslie, cutting that borough in two, then to Green Lane. It reached Market Rd, Remuera, in 1965." [239]

Because of the progress already completed, there was therefore a need for a revised Motorway Plan, as explained by B Duder, Planning Officer, Auckland City Council, in his contribution to the 1967 publication, Auckland In Ferment:

"The interim motorways proposals of the De Leuw Cather Company were significant in that they were not acceptable to the Ministry of Works, the agency responsible for carrying out motorways development in Auckland. Due to the commitments already made in land purchase under the earlier Master Transportation Plan, together with the colossal expenditure that would be required for the implementation of the interim proposals, the consultants were requested to revise their scheme more in terms of the Master Transportation Plan.

"Consequently, the De Leuw Cather Company finally produced a plan which they describe as 'minimal' in its capacity to deal with Auckland's future transport requirements. Due to the restricted capacity, of the revised motorways proposal, it was considered that an all-bus system of public transport would ultimately place an unacceptable burden upon the inner motorways system around the Central Business District and that a combined bus-rail solution would be more appropriate. This decision was reached even though it was estimated that a completely new bus fleet would be £12 million cheaper to bring into operation than a combined bus-rail system." [443]

De Leuw, Cather for Manukau

As much an indication of the growth of the Auckland metropolitan region as the scope of the original De Leuw, Cather studies, the Manukau City Council had decided, by May 1967, that it also needed to commission a detailed traffic plan:

"The Manukau City Council will engage the De Leuw, Cather Company – which prepared Auckland's transport report – for a South Auckland traffic study. The council's officers will gather the information and send it to the De Leuw, Cather Company in America to be processed. The council will spend about £2500 on the study. The Auckland Regional Authority will contribute £1000. The council says De Leuw, Cather's Auckland report outlined broadly South Auckland's traffic problems. This study will give a detailed traffic plan for the area." [444]

Colin Buchanan and Partners

In April 1966, another consultant was hired by the Auckland City Council – the British transport planning and urban design company, Colin Buchanan and Partners – to comment on the re-arrangement of the inner city street system and on a number of planning aspects relevant to public transport, including the mass transport systems recently proposed by De Leuw, Cather. The Buchanan Report, entitled *City of Auckland – Planning in the Central Area – An Assessment*, was produced in July 1966.

Stumbling Block

However, despite the myriad of recommendations produced by the 1950s Master Transportation Plan, the 1960s De Leuw, Cather Plans, and the Buchanan Report, none were immediately implemented. Although there continued a great deal of disagreement as to which mode of transport should dominate, the overall stumbling block to any progress remained, as always, capital investment – as reported by The Auckland Star on 10 February 1967:

"A four-man Auckland Regional Authority deputation will go to Wellington to discuss the provision of regional roads with the National Roads Board…The decision to send a deputation was made yesterday by the authority's roads committee after they had discussed the failure of the National Roads Board to make any money available for regional roads or the protection of regional road routes. Committee members attacked the attitude of the National Roads Board, pointing out that the authority had been given a specific job of work to do by Parliament, but was not being allowed to get on with it." [445]

Transport Costs

That's not to say that money wasn't being spent on roads and road transport nationally – as reported by The New Zealand Herald on 20 March 1967:

"More than four out of every five pounds spent on transport in New Zealand is for roads and road transport. The Minister of Labour, Mr Shand, drew attention to the cost of transport last week when he quoted an annual transport bill of more than £600 million - about a third of the total national income…Comparable figures for the year ended March 31, 1965, were:-

Road transport, roads…Running expenses £316.3 million and Capital spending £124.7 million…Railways…Running expenses £40.6 million and Capital spending £5.0 million…" [446]

Vehicle Numbers

Of course, the construction and maintenance of roads was costing more because there was more demand for them – as indicated by the City of Auckland Traffic Department Report for 1967 which recorded the number of vehicles of all types registered within the Auckland postal district for the previous three years, including:

"Cars: 1965 - 165,336; 1966 - 181,162; 1967 - 189,378

"Goods Vehicles 1965 - 31,250; 1966 - 30,087; 1967 - 31,729" [447]

A Small Miracle

But, while not quite enough was apparently being spent on Auckland roads, the City's drivers seemed to be coping well, thank you very much – at least according to the same City of Auckland Traffic Department Report which reproduced the part of an Auckland Star 'Leader' published on 11 April 1967:

"Not many Auckland drivers fretting in a five o'clock road jam will be willing to admit it, but during the past 10 years a small miracle has been achieved in the control of city traffic.

"In 1954 when studies were made for the Master Transport Plan, there were about 92,000 vehicles in the metropolitan area. Today there are more than 200,000 - a figure not expected before 1975. Not only that, more people are bringing their cars to work instead of travelling in buses or trams and there are far more commercial vehicles on the roads.

"And yet traffic congestion has not increased to anything like the extent that might have been predicted. The motorways cannot be thanked for this - they have hardly yet reached the inner city.

"Congestion has been forestalled by better traffic control and engineering - by lights, lanes and stop signs, by restrictions on parking and turning and by rerouting. In other words, Auckland is getting more use out of roughly the same street system." [448]

More Cash Needed

This reference to the *small miracle*, like all miracles, could perhaps be believed with a grain of salt when it is realised that the Traffic Department Report was produced by the Auckland City Council and that Dr. Roy McElroy, an avid proponent of a road-based transportation system, was then the City's Mayor.

But, making do, or not, the City needed more roads and, to construct them, more cash – as reported by The Auckland Star on 29 April 1967:

"The mammoth £1.5 million Dominion Rd motorway interchange is now forging ahead. The next portion of the complex – ramp B, carrying traffic from Dominion Rd citywards into New North Road – is expected to be open by May 11, and the complete interchange is due to be finished by February-March next year.

"But things were not always running so smoothly. In December last year the Auckland City Council threatened to stop work on the interchange and cancel all contracts because it was not getting sufficient grants for the project from the National Roads Board. The story of the threatened stopwork has only recently come to light in correspondence released by the City Council.

"The interchange – a top priority in the Auckland Master Transport Plan – is being constructed by the city council on behalf of the Mt Albert and Mt Eden Borough Councils, in whose territories it is situated. It is being financed by grants from the National Roads Board. The agreement was signed by the Crown, the Roads Board, the City Council and the two borough councils in 1960 and work began…The interchange was originally designed to link up with the Newton Gully motorway complex and was estimated to cost £1.25 million.

"But in 1965, following the investigations of the De Leuw, Cather transport consultants, the Ministry of Works ordered a change in the design so that the interchange would now join Upper Queen St. The additional cost of this was then not known. Work on the revised design continued until by mid-1966, the Roads Board had paid out the full grant of £1.25 million as provided in the original agreement. The grants then suddenly stopped.

"While the City Council hurriedly prepared estimates of the increased costs resulting from the change in design, it found itself facing a rapidly mounting overdraft in its accounts for the interchange. By August 1966 the overdraft amounted to £64,000...But, unaccountably, the Roads Board in Wellington deferred consideration of the sum.

"On December 16 the city engineer, Mr A J Dickson, wrote to the District Commissioner of Works, Mr E A Flynn. Mr Dickson mentioned the deferment...and went on: 'It is evident that the Auckland City Council appears to have no option but to terminate all contracts and refer all claims resulting therefrom to the National Roads Board, including its own over-commitment.'

"The threat had its desired effect. A progress grant of £50,000 was promptly forthcoming from the Roads Board...Today the council is still carrying an overdraft of £36,000, but in the interests of continuity of work has indicated that it is prepared to bear this..." [449]

Motorway Work Delayed

But, while one road project forged ahead, others were delayed – as reported by The New Zealand Herald on 9 May 1967:

"The Grafton Gully motorway outlet into Wellesley St is not expected to be open until 1969 the No. 2A District Roads Council was told yesterday. The chairman of the board, Mr E A Flynn, told the meeting that unless the National Roads Board would allocate more funds, the delay was inevitable. He said it was extremely unlikely that more funds would be available with the...reduction caused by the Government's latest economic measures. A ramp for the Symonds St entrance to the Southern Motorway is not expected to be opened until 1970 and the extension of the Southern Motorway from Runciman southward is not expected to begin for another 10 years." [450]

Robert Muldoon's Mini-Budget

The Government's latest economic measures, referred to by the Herald article, was the 1967 mini-budget introduced by Finance Minister, Robert Muldoon, – the reasons for which were explained by Keith Rankin in his paper, *New Zealand's Income Tax in the Rollercoaster Muldoon Years: 1967-84*, presented to the Asia Pacific Economic and Business History Conference held at Hamilton, 13 to 15 February 2014:

"The period from 1967 to 1984 represented easily the most difficult external economic conditions faced by New Zealand since the Great Depression of the 1930s. New Zealand's terms of trade fell precipitously at the end of 1966, and generally declined for two decades...For the most part, New Zealand's financial story was one of government deficits funded by overseas borrowing.

"In addition to the more general need to reform the tax structure in light of substantial economic growth and creeping inflation, Muldoon inherited what had the potential to become a major balance of payments crisis, instigated by a big fall in world wool prices.

More than any other commodity, it had been wool that had made New Zealand one of the richest nations in the world, *per capita*, in the previous 100 years. The roller-coaster ride had begun... Muldoon had to act, principally to forestall IMF (International Monetary Fund) intervention..." [451]

Reasons for the Delay

Just how the Finance Minister's mini-budget had delayed the country's road-building and maintenance programme was explained by The Auckland Star on 17 May 1967:

"The National Roads Board has cut its spending by 10% to cover a £3.1 million drop in its estimated revenue. The result will be a slowdown in road works by counties and municipalities and a sharp cut in State highway construction. The Auckland motorway is expected to be among the many victims.

"After the board met in committee this morning the chairman and Minister of Works, Mr Allen, emerged to announce a 'minimum 10% cut all over New Zealand.' In some areas the cut would be slightly more…One of the major reasons for the cut has been the Government's recent 'mini-budget,' which diverted vehicle registration and licence fees into the Consolidated Revenue Account.

"But even without this measure, said Mr Allen, the board would have had to recast the primary allocations made last December because of a decline in the board's expected revenue. He pointed out the board had been watching petrol sales since December. That month sales were static, in January they were slightly up, only very slightly up in February, static in March and down in April…" [452]

Auckland's Allocation Cut

"A cut of almost £3 million in the Roads Board allocation for Auckland State highways over the next three years has set the city's motorway programme back at least two years, the Works Ministry's Auckland district highways engineer, Mr R R Parsons, said yesterday…" [453]

National Roads Board

As detailed previously, the National Roads Act 1953 created the National Roads Board and a National Roads Fund into which was credited fees and charges received on behalf of the Crown in respect of the registration and licensing of motor vehicles; licence fees paid in respect of heavy traffic licences; moneys received in respect of motor spirits tax and mileage tax; customs duties in respect of pneumatic rubber tires, solid rubber tires, inner tubes, and tiring material. From that Fund, the Roads Board paid for the construction, maintenance, and control of main highways, roads, and streets.

Diversion of Funds

The intended diversion of vehicle registration and licence fees to the Government's Consolidated Revenue Account caused a great deal of concern – as reported by The Auckland Star on 17 May 1967:

"The New Zealand Road Federation is gravely concerned at the Government's diversion of funds from the National Roads Board to the Consolidated Fund for general purposes, the federation's president, Mr S E Anderson, said yesterday…Mr Anderson said it was obvious the diversion would lead to a serious reduction in what the National Roads Board and local authorities could do. This meant funds would have to be used to the greatest possible advantage. There would be no room for 'wasteful' expenditure…" [454]

National Roads Board Independence Threatened

Despite the concern, the Government proceeded to formalise its fees appropriation by means of legislation – as reported by The Auckland Star on 22 May 1967:

"One of the bills the Government hopes to push through the House before the June recess will deprive the National Roads Board of revenue from motor vehicle registration and licence fees.

"Neither the Opposition nor the motoring public should allow this amendment to pass without protest. Motorists did not escape lightly from Mr Muldoon's mini-Budget. In addition to the increase of 4d in petrol tax, registration, change of ownership and annual licence fees are all going up and sales taxes is to rise from 33⅓ to 40%.

"Under the economic circumstances it would have been too much to expect the Government to resist such a convenient target for indirect taxation as motoring has now become in this country. As a means of cutting consumer spending, including demand for overseas funds, the increases will be swift and effective. But why has the Government chosen to interfere with the financial basis on which the National Roads Board has operated so well almost since the day it was established?

"By switching motor vehicle licence and registration fees to its own pocket, the Government will cut the board's revenue by nearly £4 million. In return, it will make a contribution this year of £1.5 million from the Consolidated Revenue Account. But this sum is variable and may be increased or decreased next year at the whim of the Government. The Roads Board thus becomes dependent for a small but significant portion of its income on political factors.

"It is hard to understand why the Government has decided to assert its authority over the board so soon after it agreed (in 1965) to give the board full financial independence by stopping the £1 million contribution which the board used to receive annually from the Consolidated Fund. With its income from motor vehicle fees, together with petrol tax at 1s 5 3/4d a gallon the board was in a position to meet the country's increasingly costly roading needs without running to the Government for funds.

"If the Government was seeking extra revenue for general purposes it should have been content with a petrol tax surcharge. If it wanted to reduce roading expenditure at the same time it could have required the Roads Board to freeze a proportion of its income. Instead it is threatening the future independence of the board. Why?" [455]

Transport Amendment Bill

Apparently regardless of the criticism, the Government's Transport Amendment Bill was introduced to Parliament – as reported by The New Zealand Herald on 25 May 1967:

"Spending on roading in New Zealand had been outrunning the growth of national output and would have had to be checked, quite apart from the present economic crisis, which was the worst in 30 years, the Minister of Finance, Mr Muldoon, declared in the House of Representatives last night. He was speaking during the second reading debate on the Transport Amendment Bill.

The bill imposes higher fees on vehicle registration, switches fees worth £3.8 million a year from the National Roads Fund to general Government revenue and provides for a 4d a gallon fiscal surtax on petrol. Mr Muldoon said that in the 11 years since 1955, the gross national product had risen by almost 100 per cent but the spending of the National Roads Board had soared by 150 per cent.

"Even in good times,' he said, 'we could not justify spending a greater and greater proportion of our national resources on roading just because of the formula which had been fixed previously. By changing that formula, under the provisions of this bill, we propose to bring the two into line. The Government will take no measures beyond the minimum necessary to carry us through this difficult period and provide us with a firm base from which to move on.'

The proportion of our national resources being spent on road had got too high and was growing at a much faster rate than other aspects of the national economy. But even without the adjustments in this bill, even without the emergency budget, events had shown that estimates adopted by the National Roads Board in December were too optimistic and that there would have had to be some cut, in any event.

"Mr Watt, the deputy-Leader of the Opposition, moved to deny the bill a second reading… Mr Watt said people resented having to pay for the product of Government ineptitude and muddlement. The bill dishonoured the 1953 agreement between a National Government and roading authorities and motorists' organisations. The transfer of fees to general Government revenue was 'a complete breach of faith' and was helping to shrink the Roads Board budget by 14 per cent from £39.2 million to £33.6 million.

"Mr Gordon, Minister of Transport, moving the second reading, said the motoring measures contained in the emergency budget had increased the cost of running an average family car by only 0.235d a mile. The annual cost of running a medium-sized car 6000 miles a year was now £58.15s. 'This is still cheap monitoring,' he said. 'In the Netherlands the cost would be £78 and in Britain £85.'" [456]

Motoring Costs Challenged

As the Parliamentary debate of the Government's Transport Amendment Bill continued during an all-night sitting, those motoring costs were challenged by the Opposition:

"Mr Tizard (Lab-Pakuranga) said New Zealand had to repay loans totalling £100 million in the next five years and the Government had introduced a series of short-term, stop-gap measures to cope with these loan repayments. The Government had relied on short-term borrowing and it could not plead that it did not know what the consequences would be, Mr Tizard said.

"There was nothing in the Bill to show that any of the money would be spent on motoring or road safety. 'All it does is take money from the motorists and kicks the transport industry,' he said. He challenged the Minister's figures comparing the costs of motoring in New Zealand with some other Western countries. The extra sales tax charged in New Zealand would more than offset any lower motoring costs, Mr Tizard claimed." [457]

Facing the Problems of Future Planning

The collection of petrol tax solely for road construction and maintenance also came in for some criticism from a British architect – as reported by The Auckland Star on 18 April 1967:

"The financing of the National Roads Board by petrol tax could create a built-in distortion in New Zealand's pattern of capital investment and the development of our cities, the secretary of the Royal Institute of British Architects, Mr Malcolm McEwen, said here today.

"Mr McEwen said New Zealand's petrol tax made money available for freeways, but not for other forms of comprehensive planning and development - including other forms of communication, land use and the way buildings were to be built. But freeways created problems as well as solving them, and there might not be money available to solve the problems the freeways created.

"The ultimate effect of motorway development and present land use, which meant that one could not exist without a car, might be a generation of traffic volumes too heavy for the city centre to cope with without costly redevelopment. The economic recession could increase this distortion and create a further imbalance of investment, since a rising petrol tax could continue to make money available for roads while building development was curtailed. A recession was all the more reason why the Government, cities and local bodies should face the problems of future planning." [458]

Transport Amendment Act 1967

The Transport Amendment Bill eventually became the Transport Amendment Act 1967 which came into force on 1 July of that year, allowing the Government's diversion of vehicle registration and licence fees to the Consolidated Revenue Account.

Roading Symposium 1967

However, a lack of funding was not the only impediment to the provision and maintenance of the country's roads – as was discussed at a Roading Symposium held at Wellington on 29 August 1967 for three days:

"Present and future roading problems will be critically examined by 350 experts at the New Zealand Roading Symposium which begins in Wellington today and continues tomorrow and on Thursday. Organised by the road research unit of the National Roads Board, the symposium is the first to be held on a national scale for six years…Those taking part include county, municipal, departmental and consulting engineers, economists, geologists, town planners, contractors, university staff and suppliers of road materials and equipment…

"Maintenance, reconstruction and sealing of roads and streets and new motorways are financed by the National Roads Fund, an independent fund at the board's disposal into which all road-user tax is paid. Revenue comes mainly (about 70 per cent) from petrol tax and mileage tax (diesel). Petrol tax is now 18 cents a gallon in an average retail price of 38 cents. Of this tax, 3 cents - an emergency tax - goes into the general funds of the Government and the balance to the roads fund. Taxation on 'the user pays' principle assures continuing income and facilitates long-term planning…The board must, under the National Roads Act, allocate not less than 26 per cent of motor taxation revenue to county roads, not less than 49 per cent to State highways, including motorways, and not less than 14 per cent to municipal streets. Eleven per cent is reserved for special allocations at the discretion of the board." [459]

Cost of Road Building and Maintenance

Covering the Roading Symposium, The New Zealand Herald published comments made by D W Beatty, Programming Engineer for the Ministry of Works, when he outlined the actual cost of road building and maintenance, and the damage caused by heavy traffic:

"Over the past five years $159 million has been spent on the 7189 miles of State highways, $43 million on the 5794 miles of municipal streets, and $82 million on the 45,096 miles of county roads. In addition the local authorities have spent $148 million from their own income. This may seem a large expenditure but roads are built to be used and the investment represents only one and a half cents for each mile travelled by a motor vehicle.

"The motor vehicles themselves cost a good deal more. An ordinary family car costs at least 8 cents a mile to run and an 8-ton truck approximately 15 cents. Bad roads mean higher costs of operation and maintenance so that investment in roads, by helping to reduce operating and maintenance costs, can result in considerable economic savings to both the individual and to the country as a whole.

"In the 10 years between 1954 and 1964 the numbers of motor vehicles rose 77.2 per cent to 902,054 and in the next 10 years the number is expected to rise to 1,340,000. This means that the roading network will have heavy demands made upon it. In the urban areas it will become increasingly urgent to relieve congestion, and in rural areas to develop a balanced and fully effective inter-regional system of State highways and feeder roads...

"It is not so very long ago when the catch-word from rural communities was 'get us out of the mud'. Today our roads are built for all-weather access but in some localities the position is far from satisfactory. Admittedly most roads are metalled and some sealed but now, with the advent of milk-tankers, stock and fertiliser transporters and logging trucks, roads built in comparatively recent times are deteriorating under the impact of heavy traffic.

"It is little wonder that one finds sessions in this symposium devoted to planning road system development, pavement construction, roading aggregates and rural maintenance. It is of paramount importance that primary production, the basis of wealth and the main source of overseas funds, has ready access to markets and ports." [460]

Road Surface Failures

Unfortunately, despite the importance to the nation of plentiful, robust roads, the cheaper option had again been taken and a number of road surfaces failed during the 1960s. In his address to the Pacific Regional Conference of the International Road Foundation held in Sydney in March 1961, the Minister of Works, William Goosman, explained the role played by the National Roads Board to remedy the breaking up of New Zealand's early road surfaces:

"To meet the situation the Board gave, along with general maintenance, the rebuilding of sealed surfaces and bridge replacements first call on funds. At the same time greater drive and new techniques were brought to bear on extending road sealing to eliminate the dust nuisance and to reduce the cost of vehicle operation. The Board continues to grant a high priority to these particular fields of roading.

"In pursuing this policy the Board was not unaware of traffic and transport problems both within and on the outskirts of urban areas. On the approaches to cities the value of high-standard State highways and motorways was being threatened by traffic channelling into low-capacity and congested streets, and beyond those limits the capacity of the State highways themselves was being overtaxed...Frustrating delays and costly holdups are the common experience in urban travel and, after allowing for any progress that has been made with mass transportation of people, the fact remains that the steady increase in congestion on urban and near urban thoroughfares goes on uninterruptedly..." [461]

Less is More

One such road surface failure was discussed by the National Roads Board in 1967 – as reported by The New Zealand Herald on 15 December 1967:

"By using only a 1½-inch thickness of asphaltic concrete New Zealand has been getting its roads on the cheap, the director of roading, Mr J H Macky, said at a National Roads Board meeting yesterday. 'But we run the risk of failures such as have occurred on the Auckland Southern Motorway,' he added. Mr Macky defended use of thin paving because he said it had allowed the board to get a majority of the roads in New Zealand paved within the limits of its economic resources.

"The board was discussing failure of the Green Lane-Ellerslie section of the motorway, which Mr Macky in a report tabled on Wednesday attributed to a departmental error of judgment on foundation material. Mr Macky said Auckland was pressing strongly for a three-inch asphalt cover. 'But experience overseas shows that with thicknesses up to five inches you get cracks,' he said. 'Britain uses seven inches on her motorways and Germany about eight but they are built for a far greater strength than we require.'

"The chief highways engineer, Mr F A Langbein, said that rather than rushing in and thickening the surface, the board should concentrate on adequate sealing and drainage to prevent water seepage. Cracks had occurred even on the newest sections of the Auckland motorways but they were inevitable in the conditions prevailing." [462]

Poor Drainage

"Mr Hugh Watt, MP for Onehunga, said yesterday [15 December 1967] he was pleased the Ministry of Works had carried out a full investigation into the failure of a section of Auckland Southern motorway. 'I am certain all will expect that in future this mistake will not be repeated,' he said.

"Mr Watt, speaking as a former Minister of Works and Roads Board chairman, said he made no apologies for raising the question of the failure of the motorway section in Parliament. 'I would have been failing in my duty if I had not done so.'

"Replying to criticism by the present chairman of the board and Minister of Works, Mr Allen, that the basic decisions on the motorway were taken during his (Mr Watt's) term of office, Mr Watt said the decision to move from a flexible base course to a semi-rigid base course was right as this had been used successfully in many parts of the country. The failure on the Ellerslie-Greenlane section was due to poor drainage." [463]

Economic Uncertainty

As 1967 drew to a close, economic uncertainty continued resulting in further cuts to State highway construction – as reported by The New Zealand Herald on 14 December 1967:

"The National Roads Board yesterday approved a $1,100,000 cut in spending on State highways for 1968-69 and issued a warning that because of economic uncertainty and the impending rise in the price of petrol, a further review will be made before the annual estimates are prepared in April.

"Faced with a projected $2,880,000 drop in revenue the board has also trimmed primary allocations to counties and municipalities and reduced its reserves to what it describes as a dangerously small figure. Motorways, particularly in Auckland, are hard hit and the board concedes that the amount granted is insufficient to maintain reasonable progress, even on current commitments.

"The Auckland No. 2A road district will receive a State highway allocation of $4,920,000, $3,908,000 of which will be required for motorways. For 1967-68 the allocation was $5,001,900, with $4,079,300 for motorways.

"In his introduction to the report on allocations the assistant-director of roading, Mr P F Reynolds, said the uncertain economic climate, the advent of devaluation and the impending increase in the price of petrol all combined to make an accurate prediction of future revenue very difficult." [464]

Feeling the Pinch

"Roading, like other sectors of the economy, is feeling the pinch. After substantially cutting back expenditure during the present year, the National Roads Board has provided even less in 1968-69 for State highways and motorways, counties and municipalities. The board has sensibly insisted that maintenance and bridging must have first call on funds, leaving the reduction in State highway expenditure to be borne by new construction.

"But Auckland, in particular, must wonder whether economy has to be so enforced as to cut the recommended rate of progress on local motorways to less than 56 per cent. The cuts, inevitable though they may be, appear all the more serious in the light of traffic growth since highway needs were assessed. Failure to keep ahead of expansion today could bring chaotic problems tomorrow. General economies by the Roads Board could also affect employment throughout the country. That alone presents an anxious consideration for the Government, on both a national and a regional basis." [465]

Patched Maintenance

"Extra lanes for the Green Lane-Ellerslie section of the Southern Motorway will not be provided before 1969. But the chief highways engineer of the Ministry of Works, Mr F A Langbein, said last night that traffic growth would probably force the National Roads Board to provide money for the new lanes soon after that. Mr Langbein had earlier told a meeting of the board that there was no provision for the work in the 1968-69 allocations.

"The Ministry intends to delay full reconstruction of the one and a half miles of cracked pavement on the motorway until the extra lanes are built. Meanwhile the surface will be patched in an attempt to maintain it. 'With the buildup of traffic on the motorway,' said Mr Langbein, 'it would be impossible for us to lift the carriageway now without causing tremendous congestion. When we did 40 chains in March there were big holdups at peak times.'" [466]

Auckland v Wellington

With money so tight, there was naturally some curiosity as to who was getting what – as reported by The Auckland Star on 16 December 1967:

"The National Roads Board decision this week to allocate $4.8 million for motorways in Wellington and only $3.9 million in Auckland on the face of it could provoke claims of preference for Wellington. On a population basis, Auckland, it might be said, should get twice as much. This argument can be supported by Auckland's contribution to petrol tax revenues.

"In reality, of course, Auckland has had a fair crack of the whip. In the five years from 1962-63 through to 1966-67, it received $20.6 million from the National Roads Board in direct expenditures on new motorway construction. By comparison, Wellington received $10.7 million. The proportion is changing at present because a major construction contract is underway in Wellington.

"Auckland motorway construction had a peak of $4.96 million in 1965-66 when the Newmarket viaduct was nearing completion. The National Roads Board, in reducing expenditure on motorways, is well aware that it is falling short of targets laid down in the De Leuw, Cather reports for both Auckland and Wellington. And is not happy about it.

"In Auckland's case, present allocations are only about 60 per cent of the rate of progress recommended by De Leuw, Cather. And in Wellington the rate is not much better. Because of the cut in allocation no new motorway works will begin in Auckland in the coming year. The bulk of the money is required for commitments already begun…" [467]

The Newmarket Viaduct

The Newmarket Viaduct was completed in December 1965, some seven months ahead of schedule. However, "In its first year of operation, it showed an opening of construction joints which should have not occurred. It took a great deal of work to establish the cause – the temperature gradient from upper to lower surfaces of the box girders was much higher than had been expected…" [209]

"The Newmarket Viaduct contract is the largest ever let for a bridge structure by the New Zealand Ministry of Works for the National Roads Board. The design was prepared by the Ministry of Works and a contract was awarded in September 1963, to Wilkins and Davies Construction Co. Ltd. and Taylor Woodrow (Overseas) Ltd. at a contract price of $1,038,792. The Viaduct is an integral part of the Auckland Urban Motorway system and is wholly financed by the National Roads Board.

"It crosses over two suburban railway tracks and several city streets, including the densely trafficked Newmarket Broadway and has a total length of 2,259 feet. Its purpose is to keep the motorway clear of the heavily congested areas of Newmarket Borough. Over most of its length it is about 70 feet above ground level, the peak height of 74 feet being at a point about half way between Broadway and Gillies Avenue…The superstructure has an overall width of 80 feet and will carry three lanes of traffic in each direction, accommodated on two 37ft wide carriageways, separated by an 8ft wide median strip." [468]

Motorway Route Undecided

While some Auckland suburbs such as Newmarket were by-passed by the new motorways, others were not so fortunate. In keeping with the historical norms of parish pump politics or, as John Edgar called it in his previously-referred-to thesis, *Local Body Morphological Fundamentalism*, Mount Wellington resisted bisection – as reported by The Auckland Star on 15 December 1967:

"After more than a year of negotiations the Auckland Regional Authority still has not sited the south-eastern motorway. The authority has met stiff opposition from the Mt Wellington Borough Council, which last week decided to reject the two proposed routes. The council said it would not agree to site a motorway on its town plan.

"Earlier the council had agreed to site a motorway on its plan subject to certain conditions, which were unacceptable to the authority. The council's new decision appears to be an effort to free the 'freeze' on Mt Wellington properties in recent months. The town clerk, Mr L A Young, advised residents they could now develop the land as they wish.

"But a motorway through the borough is inevitable - at one end the Manukau City Council has included it on its plan and at the other end the Auckland City Council has it on its plan. In the latest edition…of the New Zealand Gazette, the construction of the south-eastern motorway and the Pakuranga motorway - which it links - has been authorized. So the freeze is likely to remain on the borough's properties until the route has been announced. And because the siting of the route is urgent (it is needed before planning can begin on the Pakuranga route) the authority is likely to take action early next year…

"Two routes are favoured - route 'C' which goes right through the centre of the Mt Wellington shopping centre, and 'D' which cuts the eastern end of the centre. It is understood the authority favours route D. The Pakuranga motorway is considered urgent because of the congestion already occurring. Construction is expected to start in 1970." [469]

No Complaint

There was at least one section of the community that did not complain about making way for a motorway – as reported by The New Zealand Herald on 27 October 1967:

"Three perches of land in the closed Symonds St cemetery is to be declared a public street under the Reserves and Other Lands Disposal Bill which came before Parliament yesterday. The land will be used to widen the Symonds St-Karangahape Rd intersection and will enable a free left-hand turn to relieve congestion of traffic leaving the motorway." [470]

As pointed out by John Roughan in his 2010 New Zealand Herald article, *Auckland: The bridge builders*:

"Governor Hobson's grave in the Symonds St cemetery looked to be in the path of a ramp but it avoided him by a few metres. Many other colonial graves were not so fortunate. They have been memorialised on a wall." [239]

In the same article, John Roughan also recorded:

"Late in 1968 contracts were let for the first of the Karangahape Rd underpasses that were to become 'spaghetti junction' and work resumed on the northwestern motorway from the city to Western Springs." [239]

Regional Roads Report

"At its July meeting the [Auckland Regional] Authority adopted a report on Regional Roads (dated 16th June 1969) from the Roads Engineer. Among other things, the report recommended that an immediate start be made on operational improvements to Regional roads as soon as the Authority is permitted to do so by legislation. Operational improvements (e.g. channelisation at intersections, medians, lane markings, signs, etc.) will increase the capacity of existing streets besides effecting safer motoring.

"Concurrent with the enactment of the steps dictated by legislation to enable the routes defined in the aforementioned report to become regional roads, it will be necessary to determine the improvements required for each route so that they can be implemented as soon as each route legally becomes a regional road.

"Rather than engage consulting engineers for this purpose, it is proposed to set up a technical working committee which will recommend operational improvements along each route for the Authority's consideration. The Committee would comprise members representing or with access to the disciplines of civil and traffic engineering, town planning, and traffic control.

"The primary function of an arterial is to cater for through traffic but its efficient movement depends on the control of land use adjacent to the roadway and its access, and the traffic regulations & bylaws imposed along the route and their enforcement. It is suggested that the Committee contain two representatives from the A.R.A. and one each from the Auckland City Council, the Ministry of Transport, and the City or Borough in which the regional road under consideration at any particular time, passes…" [471]

The Auckland Harbour Bridge
Momentous Event

As previously described, the four-lane Auckland Harbour Bridge opened for traffic at 3pm on 30 May 1959. The day after the bridge was officially opened, The New Zealand Herald commented:

"The bridge is in use and Auckland will never be the same again. The city has still not fully grasped the extent of the changes arising from this momentous event in its history." [472]

The New Zealand Herald's John Roughan later recorded:

"In its first year the bridge carried an average of 13,300 vehicles a day, compared to the 3800 daily average of vehicle ferries the year before. In its second year the bridge averaged 15,200 vehicles a day. At that rate of increase the four lanes would reach capacity by 1969." [239]

The *momentous event* was further described by Gordon McLauchlan in the 1989 edition of *The Illustrated Encyclopedia of New Zealand*:

"...its effects were immediate...The rate of traffic vastly exceeded forecasts. In the first ten months, 4,092,307 vehicles used the bridge. The total was 5,543,973 in the year to 31 March 1961, 15,153,659 in the year to 31 March 1970 and exceeded 32 million by the mid-1980s..." [473]

Bridge Operation

When discussing the harbour bridge with the Institution of Civil Engineers (ICE) in 1961, the Chairman of the Auckland Harbour Bridge Authority, Sir John Allum, commented:

"They [the members of the Auckland Harbour Bridge Authority] had not worried themselves about the construction or the maintenance. The construction was left to the consulting engineers and the contractors whom they supervised, and the technical people would look after the maintenance.

"But operation of the bridge was something quite different, because there was no other toll facility in New Zealand. In fact, as those present would know, there were very few in the British Commonwealth. Consequently, they had no experience in New Zealand to guide them. Therefore, they sent an officer round the world to see what was being done elsewhere.

"They very soon realized that if they were to run the bridge efficiently they would have to have quick collection and automatic recording of the tolls to ensure that the traffic flowed freely. They also wanted to ensure that there was courtesy on the part of their staff. By the co-operation of the Automatic Telephone & Electric Co. (Auckland), they had installed satisfactory recording and accounting equipment.

"The driver passed through the toll lane and saw the amount of the toll which he had paid, and the supervisor saw that the correct toll had been charged, and the whole transaction was automatically recorded in the equipment in the administration building. Consequently, the staff of the Authority was very small indeed. Two or three clerks in the morning could extract the classes of vehicle which had passed through and determine the total amount of toll which should have been paid and check it with the money handed in.

"The Authority had special vehicles to ensure the free flow of traffic. It was surprising how many people ran out of petrol on the bridge and had other little troubles. He sometimes thought that they did it because of the very special treatment they received. All their officers were asked to pass the time of day with the motorist and to say 'Thank you'. That was also common practice in the U.S.A. The Aucklanders thought that it would not last long, but it had lasted well. The men liked doing it.

"The next problem was to determine the amount of traffic. One tried to determine how much traffic would use a special facility. Some of those present no doubt had to do so in order to advise their clients whether a project would succeed. The Bridge Authority had nothing to guide them. However, they decided to double the traffic that was being carried by the ferries, and they fixed on an average of 9,000 vehicles per day for the first 12 months. In fact, they had over 13,000. They thought that for the second year they would follow the experience of other toll facilities elsewhere, and the experience there had been that in the second year the traffic was substantially the same as for the first year, because the curiosity traffic would have been lost and the natural increase, which was usually 5%, would have been gained.

"Again they were wrong. He had not got the figures for the second year because it had ended only two days previously, but from a cablegram which he had received he knew that in the first 2 years a total of 10½ million vehicles had crossed the Auckland Harbour bridge.

"He had a figure also for 5 days when 90,033 vehicles crossed the bridge. Those were very large figures when one considered the relatively small population involved. Auckland had only 430,000 people – 375,000 living on the south side and 55,000 on the north side. As a result of that big increase in their revenue, they reduced the tolls by 20 to 50%, and he believed that the previous day a further reduction had been decided upon." [250]

Long-Term Prospects

"As the Auckland Harbour Bridge Authority celebrated its tenth anniversary in March 1961, the success of the bridge from an operating standpoint seemed assured. Income in the financial year ended March 1961 was £262,000 ahead of current expenditure (though £245,000 of this surplus had been needed for capital works); receipts from tolls and tickets, at £716,000, were ahead of last year's estimates…The long-term prospects were no less reassuring. Auckland's population is still growing rapidly; so is traffic on the bridge. In 20 years from opening day, according to town planners…given reasonable prosperity in New Zealand as a whole, the total number of motor vehicles in use is expected to double.

"However accurate these forecasts turn out, one hard fact remains: Traffic on the Auckland Harbour Bridge was 16.3% higher in the second year of operation than in the first. And even at an average annual increase of 10%, traffic will by 1972 reach the point where a second trans-harbour crossing will need to be in use. Preliminary steps in this direction have already been taken." [252]

Auckland Regional Authority Objection

Those *preliminary steps* taken by the Harbour Bridge Authority were not welcomed by some members of the Auckland Regional Authority – as per the report to the Regional Authority by its Chairman, Dove-Myer Robinson, on 15 May 1964:

"No doubt you read the statement by the Chairman of the Harbour Bridge Authority in the 'Auckland Star' last Wednesday. This indicates that in the opinion of that Authority, with present methods of traffic control, the Harbour Bridge will reach saturation point before 1971. Therefore, the Authority says, it is necessary to prepare immediately for a second Harbour Bridge, alongside the present one, without waiting for the report and recommendations following the transportation survey which is at present under way [De Leuw, Cather & Company appointed by the ARA on 14 May 1963].

"It appears that an unnecessary and hysterical note of urgency is being introduced into these discussions. Unless common sense and prudence are exercised at this stage, Auckland could be stampeded into agreeing to hasty action which may result in the erection of a new harbour bridge which may not be needed; or erecting a bridge at an unsuitable place.

"This would result in a great loss of public money and disruption of orderly planning of the regional road system. If alternative, suitable, but less costly trans-harbour facilities can be provided by way of, say, a motorway via Hobsonville and Greenhithe, it may save the heedless expenditure of £10 - £20 million of public money.

"It has been stated that 'the congestion on the Bridge will reach frustrating and even dangerous proportions before 1971, the earliest date by which a parallel crossing could probably be built if planning began now.' This argument is now being used to justify immediate panic action, without awaiting the report of the transportation survey which is to be ready in December of this year, and in disregard of the legality of such actions.

"If money is spent on preliminary investigations, or if any other commitment is entered into before that report is available, Auckland could find itself faced with a 'fait accompli' and committed to the construction of a bridge which the report may show is either not needed, or in the wrong place.

"The current [Harbour Bridge Authority] survey is, inter alia, concerned with investigations involving the question of suitable foundations for a bridge structure in order that the feasibility aspects may be fully taken into account. The current investigations being undertaken by the Harbour Bridge Authority appear to be based on the assumption that any duplication of a bridge crossing will be immediately adjacent to the existing bridge. If the results of the survey indicate that a further crossing would be located in this position, then the current work would not be wasted.

"However, if the assumption that a second crossing will parallel the bridge is not substantiated by the results of the survey, then either the current work would be wasted or, alternatively, there would be a danger of it being used as an argument against any other proposition which may be recommended as a result of the Comprehensive Transportation Survey.

"Apart from the cost involved in the current investigations being carried out by the Harbour Bridge Authority, the obvious danger lies in the distinct possibility that decisions based on this work could run contrary to the recommendations arising from the Comprehensive Transportation Survey which by its very nature, will be treating a further trans-harbour crossing as being part only of an integrated highway network serving the region as a whole.

"The argument which is being advanced is that time is so pressing that the Bridge Authority cannot afford to await the report of the traffic survey and that it must commence planning immediately. No other reason is advanced why the Bridge Authority should not await the report before taking further action. It therefore boils down to a question of how urgent is it that planning should begin immediately? To be convincing, any argument that is advanced must be of overriding validity…

"There are further very serious implications in this precipitate action by the Harbour Bridge Authority. If it goes ahead with its present plans for a second bridge alongside the present Bridge, it would prejudice the transport survey report before it is even completed. If it is shown that a motorway route, or a bridge in another location, would be a more practicable solution than a twin bridge, the whole of the road pattern of the central business area of the City and of the North Shore would be irrevocably fixed without consideration of other factors, and could not be altered except at enormous cost.

"This would be the negation of proper planning, and we should not allow this or anything else to happen that might prejudicially affect recommendations which may be contained in the transport report. We must regard this precipitate action as being contrary to orderly and coordinated planning procedures. It would be a very bad beginning for this

Regional Authority if the recommendations of a transport survey costing ratepayers £120,000 were to be largely wasted, because of undue haste by the Harbour Bridge Authority.

"There is another vital principle concerned. The Regional Authority was created to coordinate planning and the provision of capital finance in the region. The proposed action of the Bridge Authority would drive a bulldozer clean through these principles. What hope would there be of ensuring compliance with planning decisions, if the Bridge Authority is allowed to take unilateral action that will materially affect regional planning, without consulting the planning authority or awaiting a vitally important report which had that Authority's support?" [474]

Population Explosion

"The bridge triggered an explosion of development on the North Shore and the early traffic growth at more than 13 per cent a year led to the decision in 1964 to add two more lanes on each side of the bridge. A map of the Proposed Auckland Harbour Bridge, produced in the late 1940s or early 1950s, shows a combined 'North Side' population at that time of 26,820. "By 2006, the population of North Shore City alone had reached 217,000, and the combined population of North Shore City and Rodney District (further north but also connected to Auckland CBD by the bridge) was 309,000. The population of areas serviced by the bridge therefore increased approximately tenfold over 60 years. This compared with a 2.4-fold increase in New Zealand's population over the same time." [473]

The Nippon Clip-Ons

"In 1964 the Bridge Authority announced an extra four lanes would be added, two on each side of the bridge. Freeman Fox had devised a method of supporting the additions on the existing piers. The cost could be easily covered by existing tolls and this time there was no objection from Wellington to the raising of loan finance." [239]

Auckland Harbour Bridge Amendment Act 1965

The enactment of an amendment to the original Auckland Harbour Bridge Act of 1950, the Auckland Harbour Bridge Amendment Act 1965, was required in order to extend the legislative powers of the Bridge Authority to the new lanes created by the proposed bridge clip-ons. The amendment was passed on 24 September 1965. [475]

Design and Construction

The design and construction of the harbour bridge extensions was described by B G Smith, resident engineer for Freeman Fox and Partners, in his paper published by the journal of New Zealand Engineering on 15 March 1974:

"Foreseeing intolerable peak-hour congestion by about 1970, the bridge authority in 1964 commissioned its consulting engineers, Freeman Fox and Partners of London, 'to report without delay on the engineering feasibility and the material cost of duplicating the present facility on its existing general alignment . . .'.

"Approximately two years later a contract was let to the Tokyo firm, Ishikawajima-Harima Heavy Industries (I.H.I.), for the construction of extensions to the main bridge. Other contracts for extensions to the approaches followed about a year later and the first extension, comprising two additional traffic lanes on the east side, was opened on 25 January 1969. Both extensions, providing a total of eight lanes, were open by 29 January 1970.

"In the light of subsequent traffic increases, it appears that the provision of additional capacity was well timed. The average daily traffic during the year ended 31 March 1970 was

41,516 — more than three times the 13,000 count taken immediately after opening the bridge in 1959...

"The extensions consist of two additional traffic lanes on each side of the original four-lane deck...They are carried on all-welded continuous steel box girders which are anchored to new foundations alongside the original bridge anchorage at Northcote Point and supported through rockers on brackets attached to the original bridge piers. Above the pier bracket level the extensions are structurally independent of the original bridge.

"The concept of widening the existing structure aroused much curiosity when the proposal first became widely known. How was it that the superstructure of a bridge, designed and built within the previous decade, could be doubled in width while still being carried on the same piers and foundations?

"A number of fortuitous circumstances contributed to the answer to this question. The scantlings of the lower parts of the piers were governed mainly by construction requirements during caisson sinking and those of the upper parts by minimum wall thicknesses and other dimensions to suit the superstructure. Thus, the piers themselves possessed considerable strength reserves above their original service requirements. The original bridge superstructure rests on rockers carried on bearings within the piers, the upper walls of which, varying in height between 13 ft and 25 ft among the six piers, were non-structural, serving merely to surround the rockers. These upper parts of the pier walls could therefore be modified as required without affecting the supports of the original superstructure.

"It was estimated that a new four-lane bridge alongside the original one and standing on separate piers would have cost some N.Z. $4 million more than the extensions and it would undoubtedly have taken considerably longer to build. In addition, much saving was made on property purchase, land reclamation and construction works for the approaches by adoption of the bridge widening concept.

"The method of erection chosen by the contractor was imaginative, bold, and essentially simple...The two 250-ton capacity floating cranes were specially constructed by the contractor for the bridge extensions. They were towed to Auckland in echelon from Japan, a voyage of 5,000 miles lasting 40 days, and they were delivered ready for use just over a year after the commencement of the contract...Within one year of their arrival at site they had erected all 9,000 tons of steelwork and started their return journey to Japan.

"For transport of the girder sections to Auckland, the contractor modified a tanker of 23,000 deadweight tons, the *Daikyo Maru*, which could carry up to four girder sections in the inverted position on deck. The normal round trip, including loading, unloading, and the double journey, took approximately six weeks, and seven trips were made. The hull of a second old tanker, of 38,000 deadweight tonnage, was modified and used as a storage barge, moored in the Waitemata Harbour." [476]

Tolls Reduced

Prior to the opening of the first bridge extension, the Harbour Bridge Authority reduced the tolls paid by a number of vehicles crossing the bridge – as reported by The New Zealand Herald on 29 July 1969:

"The Minister of Finance, Mr Muldoon has approved the decision of the Auckland Harbour Bridge Authority to lower the toll for private cars from 12c to 10c. The authority yesterday received a letter giving the Minister's approval and passed a formal resolution to reduce the toll. The toll of 15c on caravans and trailers is also to be reduced to 10c. The resolution is to be confirmed at another meeting of the authority on August 23 when a date will be set for the introduction of the new toll.

"The chairman of the authority, sir John Allum, said after yesterday's meeting that if possible the new toll would be brought in on September 25, the day the bridge extensions are to be opened. 'But we have to go through several statutory requirements first,' he said. 'There's always the chance of hitches.'

"The authority also received a letter from Mr P W Grayburn, secretary of Auckland Transport Holdings, Ltd. He said: 'We feel that in view of the struggle the passenger transport industry is having, serious consideration should now be given to the complete elimination of bridge tolls for buses.'" [477]

The Motorway North

Of course, with the completion of eight lanes across the bridge, the increasing volume of bridge traffic ideally needed open highway along which it could continue its flow north. Unfortunately, it would be some time before various sections of an enabling motorway would be finished – as reported by The New Zealand Herald on 19 December 1969:

"At 4.15 p.m. yesterday the Northern Motorway extension on the North Shore was opened for traffic and made an impressive sight looking north from the Northcote Rd overbridge. It was quickly apparent from the limited use of the extension by motorists and the large number who continued to use the old route via Taharoto Rd to the East Coast Bays and elsewhere that the new extension will not be used to anything like its full potential until the turnoff at Tristram Avenue is finished next year. This will give access to the east and to the East Coast Bays Borough.

"Traffic to these areas still poured along Northcote Rd and Taharoto Rd, bypassing the extension as it must do temporarily. In the meantime traffic to and from the north and holiday and tourist traffic will benefit immensely from the extension. There will be less congestion in Northcote Rd and Taharoto Rd and the number of accidents there at peak periods should be reduced.

"Using the extended motorway a car can reach Wairau Rd at the junction of Hillside Rd, where the extended motorway ends, in about two minutes. The old circuitous route, Northcote Rd - Taharoto Rd - Wairau Rd, at the worst peak periods could take 10 minutes because of congestion at red lights. There are danger spots for speedsters on the extension where the road narrows near Rangitoto College and the bend at the end of the extension but the Ministry of Works has clearly signposted the areas where speed must be reduced. For the rest of the extension the 60 miles an hour limit is permitted." [478]

The Greenhithe Bridge

Perhaps because of its remoteness from the central city and lack of grandeur, the Greenhithe Bridge has always received less publicity than that accorded the Auckland Harbour Bridge throughout their respective histories. However, as noted by historian, David Verran, in his article, *The History of the Greenhithe Bridge*, the Upper Harbour crossing between Hobsonville and Greenhithe had once been put forward as an alternative to the main span eventually erected between Westhaven and Northcote.

But, by the early 1960s, when the four lanes of the Auckland Harbour Bridge could no longer cope with the traffic, the upper harbour was no longer considered an alternative when the position of a second harbour crossing was discussed. It wasn't until 29 May 1968 that:

"...the Waitemata County Council approved the construction of a bridge...encouraged by plans to develop nearby Albany into a large residential area. The bridge was to be two lanes, less than half a kilometre in length and the approach roads and a causeway would link Hobsonville Road and View Road in Greenhithe. Tenders were called in April 1972. The bridge itself was to be on a 1 in 20.5 incline, with seven spans of pre-stressed concrete and six piers driven into the harbour bedrock.

"Tenders were accepted in September 1972, with Downer and Company Ltd to do the bridge construction, Beca Carter Hollings and Ferner to be the designers and consulting engineers. The Greenhithe approach road was to be constructed by McBreen Jenkins, while the Hobsonville earthworks were to be done by Dryden Construction Company. It was the largest single engineering project for the County ever and ultimately won the first Auckland environmental award for an engineering structure in 1976. The first sod was dug on 7 November 1972.

"The local body reorganisation of 1974 meant that Greenhithe became part of the new Takapuna City while Hobsonville became part of the new Waitemata City and Rodney County also became involved in the area. The Waitemata County Council went out of existence and loan repayments to the National Roads Board were now re-allocated to those three Councils. The total cost of the project was almost $24 million in today's currency. The very much upgraded bridge and motorway are now funded by central government, as part of State Highway 18.

"The new bridge opened ahead of schedule on 1 November 1975 and was designed for 15,000 vehicles a day. However, for some months part of View Road remained unsealed and required widening and footpaths to be provided.

"Vehicles were also restricted to 70 kilometres an hour along View and Hobsonville Roads and down to 50 kilometres an hour on the approaches and the bridge itself.

"By June 1977 the bridge was reaching 5,500 vehicles a day, but there was little effect noticed on the traffic flows across the Auckland Harbour Bridge. However, shop owners in Browns and Mairangi Bays, offering Saturday shopping, did notice an increase in trade from West Aucklanders. By 2003, there were 27,400 vehicles a day coming across the bridge. The formerly rural areas of Greenhithe and Hobsonville were now on the 'main road', literally." [479]

Suburban Rail
Social and Political Dimensions
As part of an article written by Dove-Myer Robinson for the July 1969 journal of the New Zealand Railway Tradesmen's Association, the author included a quote said to have been recently uttered by the (unnamed) Secretary of the U.S. Department of Housing and Urban Development:

"A transit system has to be more than vehicles and tracks. There are also social dimensions and political dimensions. A forward-looking transportation system can inject new economic vitality into a failing and deteriorating isolated area. It can be the means of directing and encouraging new and untapped areas of metropolitan growth. In short, it can give the city a new image for urban design." [480]
Suburban Rail Services
As previously described, Dove-Myer Robinson had, for some years, been advocating a combined bus/rail transit system as the most suitable transport arrangement for Auckland.

He and his supporters argued that the existing suburban rail services could be improved along established corridors far more cheaply than the building of intrusive motorways.

While it could hardly be described as *a forward-looking transportation system*, the suburban rail services operating during the early 1960s already provided many commuters with a reasonably satisfactory service – as described by the 1962 publication, *Auckland Expanding to Greatness*:

"…in 1961 26 passenger trains ran into Auckland daily from Papatoetoe, including 17 from Papakura…the Auckland-Waitakere area is served by about 14 passenger trains or railcars on weekdays, on much faster schedules than formerly, despite a large increase in the number of stopping places on the line. In the year ended 31st March, 1961, the number of tickets issued for passenger journeys by rail in the Auckland suburban area covered approximately 3,860,000 journeys, or some 77,000 in a normal week." [481 p.144]

Dr Fred Dahms also described Auckland's suburban rail services in his article, Urban Passenger Transport and Population Distribution in Auckland: 1860 -1961, published in the New Zealand Geographer in 1980:

"Even in 1963, the railway retained some importance for long-distance commuters in Auckland. The largest number travelled from places like Henderson, Papakura, Manurewa, Avondale and Otahuhu, which are on the main lines to downtown Auckland and Newmarket. On the other hand, the central part of the Isthmus has never been served by the railway. Locations close to downtown Auckland have always had either bus or tram service that was less expensive and more convenient than the railway. Thus, these modes of transport had a greater influence on population growth and distribution on the Tamaki isthmus than their rival the train." [15]

Railways Department Co-Operation

As observed previously, the newly-established Auckland Regional Authority appointed the American engineering firm of De Leuw, Cather and Company in May 1963 "…to prepare a detailed plan for a comprehensive transportation strategy for Auckland, including a separate report on a rapid transit system." [158]

Such a study naturally required the co-operation of all those responsible for the various transportation services then operating, including the Government's Railways Department. In a memo addressed principally to the Railway's Transportation Superintendent, Chief Civil Engineer, Chief Mechanical Engineer, Chief Accountant, and Chief Commercial Officer, the Railway's General Manager, Alan Gandell, advised:

"As discussed…the essential thing is to offer full cooperation in advising as requested by the consultants, while at the same time leaving the consultants to put up the proposals – it is not for us to attempt to unduly influence the proposals. Generally I intend that the Projects Committee have the overall responsibility for the advice tendered. In this way it will be easier for the Projects Committee to advise Management from the Railway viewpoint on the recommendations as contained in the final report." [482]

Scope of Railway's Co-Operation

The General Manager also outlined in his memo the scope of the Railways Department's co-operation with the De Leuw, Cather inquiry:

"On 17 September 1964, in company with Mr R H Newton, District Engineer, Auckland, I spent two hours with Mr Jones (Auckland Regional Authority) and Messrs De Leuw, Gilboa and Northcutt (De Leuw, Cather and Company) discussing the extent to which Railways might co-operate in the transit survey. I stressed that generally Railways would co-operate to the full in advising on the rail component of any overall transport proposals, but without prejudice to Government as covered in a memorandum from Minister to Chairman of Authority.

"Later I paid courtesy calls on Mr Robinson with Mr Passmore [Chairman of the Auckland Regional Authority Transport Committee] present, and also on Mr Gribble [General Manager, Auckland Transport Board]. I told Mr Robinson that earlier investigations showed that a rail component could not pay as a Railways Department project, but as a component of an overall urban transport system it might have merit and be attractive to an authority controlling all forms of urban transport. He said that from talks with Mr D Leuw he gathered this was also the viewpoint of the consultants. I promised full co-operation and assured him I would take a personal interest in following the investigations and having discussions as necessary from time to time." [482]

De Leuw, Cather Transport Survey Progress Report

On 8 December 1964, a Railways Department Assistant Engineer, D T G Bolz, provided his District Engineer with a progress report on the De Leuw, Cather survey:

"About eight different rail routes into the C.B.D. have received close study as regards the various engineering problems, convenience to commuters and allowance for ultimate development for through routing to Mt Eden. The nature of the various materials to be encountered in tunnelling or cut and cover has been investigated.

"As is generally known the City is built for most part on the banded Waitemata mudstones and sandstones; north of Fort Street and west of Britomart Place these are covered with reclaim and marine muds at depths of 40 to 70 feet. A line under Queen Street would tunnel through thick basalt between Vulcan Lane and Victoria Street; and south of this it would lie in organic clays, running into the Waitemata south of the Town Hall.

"Near Kitchener Street, a line to Victoria Street would run out of sandstone into the loose volcanic debris and lava associated with Albert Park. A study of the rock conditions is also important in indicating the probable founding levels of buildings near any of the routes so that interference with foundations will be minimized. Local consultants have been approached to obtain soil and foundation information for the more recent construction projects in the City.

"On the 5th November a rail passenger count was organised with the co-operation of the Traffic Branch. Counters travelled on the afternoon suburban passenger service between 3 p.m. and 7 p.m. and noted the number of passengers boarding and alighting at each station. The information has been drawn up in map form…Tentative bus routes have been worked out and bus and rail passengers for 1966 are being assigned. This assignment of passengers will determine the frequency of services.

"Outbound running times for rapid rail transit have been calculated for 1966 and 1986 services…The effects of grades and curves were considered. The running times obtained on this basis are highly competitive with other forms of transport, but with rail vehicles of lower performance than that assumed, the times would no doubt be somewhat longer. A plan showing the entire suburban system on one sheet has been prepared for use in the study, and a copy of this is being forwarded to you…

"In the event of plan B (rail and bus) various modifications to existing stations will be necessary. To date, most of the stations have been inspected with this in view and some rough drafts of station rearrangements have been prepared… Generally speaking feeder bus facilities will be required at stations near the C.B.D., and large parking areas at some of the present stopping places, where land is readily and economically available.

"Ticket collection facilities will probably be provided at stations, and raising of all platforms to high level might be necessary. Some stations would have to be moved closer to overbridges to improve the access. It would be desirable for stabling facilities to be provided at outlying termini, and on this account and also because of car parking, it would be more desirable to have the 1966 terminus at Puhinui rather than Papatoetoe.

"On the 19th November I was present at a meeting between Messrs. Newton, Muir, Holst, and Redway of the N.Z.R [New Zealand Railways] and Mr Northcutt of De Leuw Cather and Company, the consultants. The main purpose of the meeting was to discuss interference to a rapid suburban service, from freight trains, long distance passengers and local shunting services. It was agreed that it would be sufficient to determine the workability of the scheme by considering only that part of the line between Newmarket and Papakura. Because of double track, outward bound trains only were considered.

"A train timetable diagram had been prepared showing the freight and long distance passenger. From this it was decided that neither of these services should be a problem, although it could be advantageous to have a long layby loop near Homai. Shunting services however, caused some concern at this meeting and Mr Muir promised to prepare a diagram showing a fortnight's shunting movements during the passenger peaks. This has since been received and studied, and it now appears that shunting interference would be insignificant. It would however, be beneficial to provide an extra track between Penrose and Southdown.

"It may be of interest to note that an interim report on the Comprehensive Transportation Study is now to hand. Work on the Public Transport Study, being done at present, is the assigning of passengers to the various services and the rearrangement of station yards…" [483]

Suburban Railway Speculation

As the De Leuw, Cather survey continued, The Auckland Star reported on speculation as to whether the Railways Department or the Auckland Regional Authority would run suburban railway services if recommended and, more importantly, who would pay the inevitable losses incurred:

"It is believed the Railways Department has given some consideration to a suggestion that the Auckland Regional Authority be asked to finance and run extensions to the suburban rail system, together with an underground link. No suggestions have been made to the Government, but it is believed consideration would be given such a proposal.

"If the Railways Department were relieved of suburban services, it could concentrate on long-distance freight haulage, at which it cannot be beaten economically. The possibility that Auckland may be asked to take responsibility for suburban rail services stems from the fact that the De Leuw, Cather transportation survey report will probably make a strong recommendation for an expanded rail service for the city.

"On a recent visit to Auckland, Mr Charles De Leuw admitted that extension of the suburban rail system, and an underground link, were being closely examined…Some sources in Auckland believe the Government might be reluctant to move on rail services because of the large sums already being spent on the motorway systems. The way round would be a suggestion that the Regional Authority build the rail extensions and run the system, integrated with both public and private bus services.

"This, however, would raise the very real problem of who would foot the loss which the suburban rail system would inevitably incur. Some years ago when an underground was mooted for Auckland it was estimated that the loss would be about £500,000 a year. On present-day costs this could be closer to £1 million. Could Aucklanders be expected to find the money for such a loss and continue to pay their general taxes, some of which go towards the loss on other New Zealand suburban rail systems, notably Wellington's? The answer at this stage is no…" [484]

Public Image Concern

However, of more immediate concern for Railways management was their public image once the De Leuw, Cather recommendations were released – as per the internal memo from Railways' General Manager, Alan Gandell, to his senior departmental officers, dated 24 June 1965:

"It is possible when this report is first made public that press and radio agencies will immediately seek a re-action of all interested parties to the report. Approaches may well be made separately to Auckland District Controlling Officers, to Branch Heads, and to Management. Since the Department's co-operation in the survey was conditional on any Departmental views being without prejudice to Government, it is essential that senior Departmental officers avoid being drawn into any unofficial discussion over the pros and cons of the proposal. In the special circumstances I desire that any comment made be confined to the following aspects: –

"1. The Authority engaged the consultants and the Railway Department was not a party to the survey. However, the Department did co-operate with the Consultants to the extent of advising on local train running aspects, likely Departmental operating costs, and the general practicability of their proposals from a purely operating viewpoint.

"2. The rail components proposals originated with the Consultants and since these concern top level Railway policy any Departmental comment must appropriately come from Management.

"3. From a personal viewpoint the report presents an interesting and fresh approach to a very complex matter.

"In anticipation of Management being approached I am preparing a personal statement, which I propose to discuss with the Minister, and will read at Conference shortly for general information…" [485]

Procrastination Continues

As previously detailed, the publication of the De Leuw, Cather Regional Transit Plan in July 1965 resulted in little progress being made toward the improvement of Auckland's suburban railway services. That was in keeping with previous years of neglect – as described by a New Zealand Herald article published on 10 October 1967:

"Regional Authority planners find the general atmosphere in the Auckland railway station rather bleak and forbidding and the standard of some of the services which it provides to be less than desirable. Thousands of people who regularly use the building will agree. But much of the criticism which can be levelled at the present station is, perhaps, a little pointless.

"The station has never fully served the purpose for which it was planned, and the prospect of its ever doing so seems to be growing more remote. The station, which was opened in 1930, was planned to suit the projected Auckland-Morningside tunnel line.

Later, it was proposed that Avondale and Southdown stations be linked to complete a ring railway system for the city.

"But the underground proposal was shelved when Auckland opted for urban motorways in 1955. Although the station may have languished a little over the years, a decision to proceed with an adequate metropolitan railway system would quickly enable it to fulfil the function for which it was designed. In such circumstances, much of the criticism of the station could be directed with more justification toward the procrastination which has hindered metropolitan transport for half a century." [486]

Rail to the North Shore

A chance to end such procrastination by means of a second chance to extend suburban railway services across the harbour to Auckland's North Shore, was suggested by the North Shore Chamber of Commerce in a letter from the Chamber's Secretary-Manager, Derek I Lamb, to the Minister of Railways, J B Gordon, written on 1 July 1968. The proposed *Upper Harbour link* was eventually to become the Greenhithe Bridge.

"This Chamber has for many years urged the Department to provide railway facilities on the North Shore, and has always received replies declining to take action due to the absence of heavy industry and the cost of establishing the connection. The first objection is rather a chicken and the egg question but action at this stage could clear the second objection. The Waitemata County Council has proposed an Upper Harbour link which would develop the Albany area and if a railway line can be incorporated in these plans further extension of the North Shore Industrial Areas would be eventually possible. We would appreciate your consideration of the opportunities opened up by the Waitemata County Council's far sighted approach." [487]

Rail Not Warranted

In keeping with *the procrastination which has hindered metropolitan transport for half a century*, the Minister passed the Chamber of Commerce letter to the Railways' Chief Civil Engineer, G F Bridges, who subsequently sent it to Auckland's District Engineer, R H Newton, for a report of the County Council's proposed link.

Auckland's District Engineer responded on 15 July 1968:

"I have had discussions with Mr F W O Jones, Director of Planning, Auckland Regional Authority on the ultimate development of the North Shore. He is firmly of the opinion, that although there will be some industrial development, it will not be of such significance as to warrant direct rail service. The North Shore will continue to be essentially a dormitory area. Indications are that most industrial expansion will continue to take place to the South of Auckland. There has been little industrial growth in the Henderson area where suitable land handy to rail is still available. Mr Jones confirms my opinion that a rail linked to the North Shore would generate little industrial development.

"The proposed road link will enable goods to be transported readily to existing rail facilities either at Henderson or later, if required, to new facilities in the Kumeu area. However, in my opinion, goods will continue to come by road over the Harbour Bridge to the Auckland goods yard, especially with better road access being provided by way of the Northern Motorway.

"The Working Committee on the Auckland Rapid Transit Rail Scheme (of which I am a member) is taking the population growth on the North Shore into consideration in its investigation into the best route for such a scheme, but it is most unlikely that a passenger rail link to the North Shore will be recommended. I do not consider any further investigation into a rail link as suggested by the North Shore Chamber of Commerce is warranted." [488]

Election Uncertainty

As well as a general procrastination forestalling progress, there was always a general election to add to uncertainty and indecision. And there was nothing like political party loyalty to further obscure the greater good – as illustrated by the Labour candidate for the Parliamentary seat of Remuera, Hamish Henry Cordy Keith, during a speech he gave at the Newmarket Community Hall just before the November 1969 election:

"There is an issue in this election which is, perhaps, the most vital to every citizen of Auckland, regardless of their political point of view. It is an issue on which the future of every one of us, and thousands not yet born, depends. It is an issue which can ensure that Auckland remains a place worth living in, or that it becomes a New York or Los Angeles in miniature with every bit as much deprivation, physical discomfort, violence and riot. If nothing is done to immediately begin work on the rapid transit system, by the end of the decade Auckland will be a dead city – strangled by motorways, parking buildings and freeways, clogged with cars, choked with fumes and facing violent social problems undreamed of in this country.

"Last night, the National candidate for Remuera, repeated the claim he made earlier in the week, that Labour's proposal to let this scheme go ahead immediately was 'foolhardy'. He even went further and said it was irresponsible. Mr Highet knows better than that. He has been an enthusiastic advocate of the scheme and has gone on record in support of its urgency. But he is sacrificing the interests of his electorate, the people of this city and Auckland itself, to play party politics. This is supporting the worst kind of political parochialism. The most short sighted, even irresponsible, decision the National Government has made about the nation's largest city. To keep National support in the South and in the countryside, they are prepared to put the future of this city in jeopardy.

"Auckland is the pulse of this nation. Its growth and health is in the national interest. If Auckland dies as a city – and make no mistake without rapid transit now it will – then the whole country will suffer. We will experience crimes of violence and social unrest unparalleled in our history. And this is being ensured just to secure votes…

"…Already we have more cars per capita than Los Angeles, second only to Detroit, we already have more miles of roads and motorways per capita than Los Angeles. And that city is the world's greatest carbungle.

"Do we want it? Will our children thank us for the distinction, when they spend hours, even days, jammed in traffic clog-ups. When more of the city is for cars than people. When deaths from respiratory disease and lung cancer become this city's most common killer. When the economically deprived are trapped in ghettos, like Los Angeles' Watts district. When their only recourse to claim justice is to riot. If we start immediately we can avert this situation. Must we wait for another report on a report, as Mr Highet suggests, before we save the future health of this city?

"I would like to ask Mr Highet who he really represents – the people of this electorate and city or his party alone? If it is the former, then I beg him to take an independent stand on the matter. Assert his humanity and his real supporters. <u>Defy the Spoiler, Speak for the people, not the National Party</u>. This is too vital an issue to be fobbed off for party platforms. Our future depends on it…

"The New Zealand Herald has covered Mr Highet's claims not once, but twice in the same week, word for word. They have not given an inch to our side of the story. Tonight I am giving them another opportunity to prove their impartiality and to demonstrate the sincerity of the claim they made in an Editorial on 11 September that Labour brought this up politically 'as a perfectly legitimate issue'.

"There is a lot of justice in the claim of the newspapers of this city to cover political meetings in terms of their 'news value'. They cannot cover everything, but is it news to repeat word for word only three days apart a statement by one candidate on an issue vital to our future in this city and to ignore a challenge to that statement made by his opponent. They may dispute the substance of what I have said, but the proper place to dispute it is in the editorial columns they write for this very purpose, not objection by omission from news coverage." [489]

Slow Train to Auckland

However, some newspaper columnists, such as Noel Holmes, another unsuccessful 1969 electoral candidate and a popular writer for the Auckland Star during the 1950s and 1960s, chose to also present their views privately – as he did on 27 November 1969 in a letter to Neville G Walker, the principal of Auckland's Modern Bags Limited:

"I have seen rapid rail in operation in many cities and concede its advantages readily. But I'm not at all convinced that Auckland's plan will produce anything like rapid rail transport for the bulk of its citizens. Basically, all that is proposed is to put a city loop on an existing highly-inefficient, slow, rail service coping with only a fraction of Auckland passengers.

"As for Queen Street falling away in popularity as a shopping centre, to deny this is to deny something that has already happened. Down-town Auckland is about halfway towards the stage reached by down-town Sydney, which is now a dead area for retail trade with the exception of specialty shops. I know mine is not a popular view, but it is my honest opinion. I might point out my remarks were made to a Howick audience who were singularly unenthusiastic about the prospect of taking a bus to Panmure and then waiting for a slow train to Auckland." [490]

Constructive Remarks Needed

Neville Walker responded in a letter to Noel Holmes dated 4 December 1969:

"Thank you for your letter of 27th November 1969. I have read this with great interest, and I cannot help feeling that a person in such a position as yours with a leading New Zealand newspaper, is doing a disservice to our city with these negative remarks. I can only hope that you will study more closely the envisaged modern electric rapid rail plan which would be actually servicing the most densely populated areas in New Zealand. I refer to the South Auckland line to Papakura, and in the North the line to Henderson.

"The remarks in your letter are so astounding to me, I am passing them on to the Queen Street Business Association and to our Mayor, Robbie. It may be that you are purposely exaggerating to wake us up. I do hope that this is your purpose, but I do sincerely ask you Mr Holmes, if you would kindly do your level best to help, by constructive remarks, this wonderful city of ours and its outstanding Mayor." [491]

Up the Chute

Outstanding Mayor, Dove-Myer Robinson, naturally responded to Neville Walker's call to arms in his letter to Noel Holmes on 9 December 1969:

"…Noel, your comments on the rapid transit scheme, as published in the newspapers before the election, and your letter to Neville Walker, convince me that in this instance you are right up the chute. For one in a prominent and popular position such as yourself, this is a deplorable situation, and I feel that it is my moral duty to educate you. However, I don't propose to go into the whole scheme at length here, and suggest that at a time convenient to both of us, you give me say an hour or two to enable me to next explain the whole scheme in detail.

"This is a <u>regional</u> plan, designed to benefit firstly the metropolitan or urban area, and secondly the whole of the region of Auckland. In fact, it is the opinion of all but one or two members of the Regional Authority that its early implementation is the most vital issue concerning Auckland today, and that unless it is operating by 1975 or 1976, there will be so much traffic congestion in many parts of the metropolitan area, as well as the Central Business District, that the whole development of Auckland will be frustrated, and the whole economy of the urban area will be seriously and adversely affected.

"Might I just comment on one point you made in your letter to Neville Walker. You say 'Basically, all that is now proposed is to put a city loop on an existing highly inefficient, slow, rail service coping with only a fraction of Auckland passengers'. Noel, this is just 'hooey'.

"What is proposed is to lay a separate track alongside the present tracks on the present foundations, with a wider gauge, to allow the new electric trains to travel at a maximum speed of up to 60 m.p.h. on the bends. Initially the new track will be electrified as far south as Manurewa, and as far north as Henderson. The average speed planned is 34-36 m.p.h., <u>including stops</u>. All railway stations will be completely remodelled up to 1975 standards, with escalators, and three modern underground railway stations in the city.

"As a comparison between the speed and time of buses on increasingly crowded motorways, the time scheduled for rapid rail between the city and Papatoetoe is 20 minutes, as opposed to up to 75 minutes, which I understand is the time taken by buses at peak hours for the same journey. 'WOW'

"Sorry you did not do better in the elections, but maybe when I have finished your education you will do better next time! Come in and see me soon." [492]

Chapter Five

1970 to 1979 – They Will Let You Down

Planning and Politics
"The present shape of Auckland can be explained in terms of the aims of those who built it and of the powers and resources devoted to the management of its physical equipment, its streets and buildings, its parks and gardens, its transport facilities and public utility services." [155]
What Town Planning?
In his report to the Auckland City Council in December 1969, Councillor E P Salmon, Chairman of the Council's Urban Renewal Committee, summed up a decade of little progress toward needed urban renewal and a satisfactory public transportation system. In February 1970, The Auckland Star summed up this lack of progress by asking, "What's wrong with our town planning?"

"Town planning is a matter of vital concern to every citizen. It has a direct bearing on the environment and circumstances in which he lives, works and seeks his recreation. There is a growing concern that town planning procedures in this country are not operating as well as they should. Various reports and suggestions have been made on how the system should be amended…What is needed is a wholesale overhaul of town planning legislation to replace the present legal contest between opposing parties with a more informal approach which private citizens can understand and in which they can participate.

"The chairman of the Auckland City Council's town planning committee, Mr E P Salmon, says that citizens should not have to go to the expense of engaging legal counsel to defend their property rights. At the same time an applicant should be assured that his application will not spend many months circulating through the hands of several officials and tribunals. Mr Salmon also commented: 'There is a lot of evidence to show that planning is at its best when the public is able to participate in the process at the earliest opportunity and to discuss proposals before they become too firmly fixed in people's minds…'

"Ultimately it must be asked whether town planning in New Zealand is achieving its original objectives. Is it working effectively if, in spite of zoning and other planning controls, housing areas such as Otara can still be created? There are many questions and no easy answers. A thorough investigation needs to be made into not only the administration of town planning but also its fundamental conceptions, ideals and order of priorities. The Auckland City Council is asking the Minister of Works, Mr Allen, to initiate such a full study. It is urgently needed." [493]
Town and Country Planning Acts Review
In 1970, a Town and Country Planning Review Committee was appointed by the Government to review the Town and Country Planning Acts of 1953 and 1957. The Committee published its report during 1973:

"The Town and Country Review Committee concluded that the basic system of local planning was sound and well suited to New Zealand conditions. It was flexible and

adaptable and had been progressively amended to increase the rights of the public to participate in planning. It found however that some important changes were long overdue:
- The Act needed simplifying and arranging in a more logical form;
- Third party rights to participate should be further extended;
- Environmental considerations should be brought directly into the planning process;
- More effective links should be created between planning at all levels – national, regional, and local." [494 pp.8 & 9]

Town and Country Planning Act 1977

The Committee's review led to the enactment of the Town and Country Planning Act 1977.

"In introducing the Bill into the House, the Minister of Works and Development said that the Bill promoted a closer relationship and communication between national, regional, and local planning and provided wide ranging opportunities for the public to take part in the planning process. He also acknowledged 'present concern for the protection of the environment', and noted that the Bill gave more emphasis to environmental considerations.

"The zoning system was criticised at the time for imposing an overly rigid development pattern. To ameliorate some of these concerns the 1977 Act consolidated previous amendments and introduced new provisions aimed at providing more flexibility. They included, for example:
- Giving councils the power to issue discretionary ordinances which dispensed with or waived certain requirements as to the design and external appearance of buildings, landscaping, and amenity protection;
- Consolidation of councils' powers to permit an exemption from the scheme…" [494]

Central Government Influence

"In 1973, an amendment to the 1957 [Town and Country Planning Amendment] Act introduced central government policy directives in the form of 'matters of national importance'. These were matters which had to be recognised in all schemes, and focused on the avoidance of encroachment of urban development on land having a high, actual, or potential value for production of food, and the prevention of sporadic urban subdivision." [494]

Central Government Carrot & Stick

However, that local flexibility could be limited when it encroached upon central government interests – as illustrated by a letter to the Auckland City Council from the Minister of Works and Development, Hugh Watt, dated 30 January 1975:

"I refer to the series of proposed changes relating to the central area of your council's district scheme and in respect of which I requested a deferment of the hearing of objections whilst the changes were being considered by Government. This examination took longer than expected and I regret any inconvenience the delay may have caused to the council.

"I would like to commend the spirit of the changes insofar as they are intended to improve the environment of the central city area and welcome the emphasis on providing for the pedestrian. Even so, I think the changes could go further in some respects.

However, rather than lodge formal objections, I have arranged for the district commissioner of works, Auckland, to forward some practical suggestions to the council for discussion. I trust that the council will find these suggestions useful.

"From the public works viewpoint, Railways Department has expressed concern over the council intention to realign Britomart Place across the railway station yard and also over the proposed rezoning of railway land fronting Beach Road. Further discussion seems desirable, particularly in regard to the Britomart Place proposal as there is no way by which this could be implemented other than by mutual agreement." [495]

[The district scheme referred to by the Minister was the Council's First Review of its 1961 District Scheme, subsequently proposed in 1968 and operative on 21 December 1970.]

"Whilst I will not be lodging any objections to the present changes it is apparent that major changes to the Central Area Plan naturally raise questions relating to the City's changing function within the region, the effect of the proposed rapid transit system, the revision of motorway programmes and the whole problem of transport to and across the Isthmus. These are issues on which the Crown and the City should now be in close consultation and the forthcoming review of the whole district scheme provides an ideal opportunity." [495]

The City's Changing Function

The Minister's reference to the *City's changing function within the region…*was subsequently elaborated on in a Letter to the Editor of The Auckland Star by Dr M J Taylor, Senior Lecturer in Geography, Auckland University – published 9 August 1975:

"No one would dispute that Auckland as a whole is growing very rapidly, particularly in its manufacturing and commercial functions. Indeed, during the 1970s, manufacturing employment in Auckland has increased at a rate of 3.43% a year, compared with a national rate of 2.51%. Office employment has grown even more rapidly, with employment in the finance and insurance activities, for example, having increased at a rate of 8.03% a year in contrast with the national rate of 4.03%.

"But the centre of Auckland has not shared in this growth and has lost to the rest of the urban area in both absolute and relative terms. This loss can be demonstrated for the period 1962 to 1973 for the downtown area. In absolute terms, employment in central Auckland has declined by some 4000 jobs, with growth having been accommodated in the suburbs. Manufacturing has lost more than 6000 jobs, and the only growth has been in transport activities and services which have added an extra 5204 jobs in the centre of the city.

"It must be admitted that the data possess some limitations which may somewhat exaggerate the absolute loss of jobs in central Auckland, but it must be remembered that Auckland as a whole has been growing very rapidly in the 1960s and 1970s, growth which the central area has not shared…

"Three maps, in which the Auckland urban area is divided into 50 districts, show the areas that have experienced more than average growth in employment in the 1962 to 1973 period – the positive shifts. The map for engineering and metal working shows the growth that has occurred in South Auckland and the decline of manufacturing in the central city and its adjacent districts. Positive employment shifts also demonstrate the suburbanization of distribution and finance activities resulting from the growth of suburban shopping complexes and the growth of suburban office centres, particularly Takapuna.

"This same pattern is evident in the map of employment in domestic and personal services and administrative and professional services in which there has been a notable loss of employment to the North Shore…" [496]

District & Regional Planning Schemes

However, despite any central government interference:

"In the late 1960s and 1970s there was a shift in planning practice. Local governments began to intervene through the planning process to voice and resolve community conflicts and to promote local community interests. Councils moved away from administering zoning that controlled the built environment towards a broader strategic and policy-focused function…

"The stated purposes of district and regional schemes were potentially far-reaching, concerning not just the essential amenities and services and physical environment of urban areas, but also the welfare of their inhabitants…One analysis of the [1957 Town and Country Planning] Act argues that its ideology and impact was materially shaped by an underlying and dominant ideological position privileging individual property rights…

"The Appeal Board reinforced this ideological approach by encouraging an adversarial approach to disputes, and favouring conservative outcomes in which the rights of landowners and developers predominated…The Act's formal structure did, however, impose some control and scrutiny over private developers and helped prevent gross violations by unscrupulous property developers." [494]

Fundamental Conceptions, Ideals and Order of Priorities

That legislation such as the Town and Country Planning Acts could be viewed as having incorporated *an underlying and dominant ideological position privileging individual property rights* should not have surprised. A preoccupation with the enhancement of (and, of course, profit from) property values – the laissez faire attitude that had so influenced Auckland affairs since the City's founding – was normal operating procedure.

And, as also illustrated by past and future events, Auckland's failure to define and then decide *its fundamental conceptions, ideals and order of priorities*, as described by the Auckland Star, was not just a planning failure but one of consensus – a failure by the City's many local bodies to agree on just what those *fundamental conceptions, ideals and order of priorities* were and how best to implement them.

Their collective disagreement about so many civic issues and failure to communicate unity to the Government in Wellington continued even after the formation of the Auckland Regional Authority in 1963 – the organisation that was supposed to represent all 'greater Auckland' interests and decide the way forward by majority decision.

Cost Responsibility

As usual, there was always the question of what *fundamental conceptions, ideals and order of priorities* would cost and how and by whom that cost was to be funded. In the case of those services provided by the Auckland Regional Authority, its first Chairman, Sir Dove-Myer Robinson, was in no doubt as to the best funding arrangement:

"…The disadvantages of the levying system are that it constitutes every contributing local authority as a watchdog able to hold a big stick over the Regional Authority, and thus weaken its independence… It must be remembered that Parliament itself and the great majority of local bodies in Auckland, favoured direct rating because it would make the members of the Regional Authority directly responsible to the ratepayers who would know exactly what the provision of Regional services are costing them, and would therefore be able to judge whether the services provided by the Authority warrant the rate.

"The only reason it was later decided to continue the levy system was because it would save a relatively little cost. I personally have always favoured direct rating because it would mean that the Regional Authority is a completely independent body directly responsible to the ratepayers.

"If the levy system is to continue and the local bodies are to continue to be responsible for collecting the levy from their ratepayers and getting the criticism that results from that, then the local bodies should have the right to appoint the members of the Authority, which would turn it into a cockpit of parochialism. If – as I think they should be – the members of the A.R.A. are to continue to be directly elected, then the Authority should be directly responsible to those who elect them." [497]

Auckland City Council Centenary

A consolidation of funding arrangements for the services provided by the Regional Authority would, of course, have been a major step toward the absorption of the region's local bodies into a Greater Auckland – an eventuality that would certainly not have been before time after more than a century of the City's existence.

Indeed, 1971 marked the centenary of the Auckland City Council and to mark its establishment in April 1871, the Council organised a series of lectures presented at the Auckland War Memorial Museum by various notaries. One such address, given by the City's Mayor, Sir Dove-Myer Robinson, entitled *The Development and Future of the City*, referred to the need for that *Greater Auckland*:

"For many years it has been recognised on almost every side that Auckland – and the rest of New Zealand – is over governed, and that we have too many local and ad hoc authorities for efficient co-operation, financial strength and effective administration. Yet any suggestion of change is strongly opposed by some local bodies, especially if change means amalgamation involving loss of identity of particular areas...

"What is proposed for Auckland is that the present 27 local authorities in the metropolitan area be reduced to four or five large towns (or small cities) with ultimate maximum populations of about 300,000 to 400,000 each, a total for the whole metropolitan area of 1¼ to 1½ million people.

"Because of the spasmodic and uncoordinated settlement of the isthmus, there has been no isthmus-wide plan of development. Every local authority has had sovereign rights of planning and zoning within its own boundaries. Several local authorities which include areas suitable for industry have zoned disproportionately large percentages of their areas for industrial use.

"From these rapidly growing industries they are receiving such a large proportion of their total rates that they can keep their residential rates at a lower level than surrounding districts which have a better balance of residential and industrial zoning.

"On the other hand the central city includes the port (from which the city receives hardly any rateable income) and the headquarters of many social, religious, sports, cultural and educational organisations. The city receives little or no rate revenue from such organisations because they are either legally or morally entitled to a remission of rates.

"This means that the ratepayers of the city are subsidising other surrounding bodies in the metropolitan area which use amenities provided by the city. In addition, the city receives little or no revenue from the port, the university and the technical institute. Thus

Auckland city ratepayers are subsidising importers and exporters throughout the province, as well as the central government's Department of Education.

"So long as such anomalies exist, it is going to be a mammoth task to convince those financially benefiting from the present situation to agree to amalgamate or accept a levelling of financial responsibility commensurate with the benefits available to and used by all...

"In the absence of any physical or other natural boundaries on the isthmus, is there any need for the artificial boundaries that divide into nine virtually autonomous districts an area which is physically one area, and should be one area politically?

"In such circumstances, for Aucklanders of the future the present political picture is disheartening, unless local body administrators and other citizens adopt a more enlightened outlook and think in terms of the welfare and progress of a Greater Auckland." [498]

'Core City' Control

However, a unified jurisdiction over the greater geographical area was increasingly complicated by the City's rapid expansion, particularly to the south and north. This expansion also frustrated Dove-Myer Robinson's preference for the central city area, particularly its business district, to remain the predominant focus of all future infrastructure planning.

As described in a previous chapter, it was Dove-Myer Robinson's opinion, expressed in September 1969, that the urban development of outlying and decentralised, satellite cities "...would be vastly more costly than the further development and rationalisation of the present form..." [303] – what he referred to as the *core city principle*.

Rapid Rail Criticised

The longstanding proposal to link Auckland's suburban railway system to the central business district by way of an underground loop – a perennial dream of many – had, by the early 1970s, attracted vehement criticism from those who viewed the rapid-rail project as just another example of Dove-Myer Robinson's *core city principle* at work. When commenting on the rail project in 1973, J R Dart of the Department of Town Planning, Auckland University, observed:

"The benefits of the investment may be seen to be the maintenance of the present dominance of Auckland's CBD and especially the enhancement of its property values...The present proposals pre-suppose an agreement upon Auckland's future which has not been aired, let alone agreed upon, and are built upon highly suspect assumptions concerning such as the future role of the CBD, the nature of suburban growth, and the degree of public acceptability of an urban rail system of passenger transport." [499]

Auckland Public Transport Action Committee

Acceptance of the rapid-rail concept promised by the incoming Labour Government in 1972 was based on the ARA's insistence that the project would eventually benefit the whole of the Auckland region. To have what it thought to be *agreement upon Auckland's future* subverted by such criticism was also a threat to the ARA's fundamental reason to exist. To its great consternation, opposition to the project grew, fast becoming what John Edgar was to describe in his 1987 thesis as:

"...a watershed for morphological fundamentalists in Auckland local government. The municipalities were acting to protect their own political autonomy by openly disputing

Auckland Regional Authority policy…local bodies became increasingly successful in the defence of their political autonomy.

"Some local body members, for instance, joined a private lobby group which promoted an all bus solution to the metropolis' transportation needs. Co-chair was [Takapuna Mayor] Thomas, and other members were Councillor Witten of Manukau, Onehunga's Mayor T V G Beeson, New Lynn's Deputy Mayor V Watson, and E A Flynn, lately General Manager of the Auckland Regional Authority, who addressed some of their meetings.

"Part of their aims were: To ensure that all local authorities are consulted in relation to planning matters affecting their areas in any public transport scheme adopted for Auckland and that due note is taken of their opinions. At one public meeting where the lobby group and the Auckland Regional Authority were represented, J N Kirk, a Waitemata County Councillor and member of the Auckland Harbour Bridge Authority, argued for limiting rapid rail to the inner city and spending the rest of the money on roading/bus/ferry proposals for the rest of the metropolis…

"The integrated nature of rapid rail was being undermined. Kirk's Harbour Bridge Authority had begun a study on the feasibility of a second harbour bridge to solve transport problems. This body was a remnant from the special purpose bodies who had fought to be excluded from the Auckland Regional Authority Bill. Its autonomous existence was an anomalous legacy of morphological fundamentalism – the bridge was an intimate part of the regional roading network that the Auckland Regional Authority was in charge of. The body was now trying to ensure its longevity by promoting a second bridge that it wanted to run. Its study was in direct contradiction to Robinson's rapid rail that depended on a tunnel crossing for transit traffic to the City and the Shore…

"The dissent continued in a persistent fashion. Ralph Witten in Manukau began a series of articles criticising the rapid rail in the South Auckland Courier. Fred Thomas remained intransigent and his Auckland Public Transportation Action Committee held meetings against the proposal and gained an audience with the Prime Minister.

"The New Lynn Mayor, C J R McCorquindale left on an overseas trip determined to bring back information that cast doubt on the cost effectiveness of rapid transit; the East Coast Bays Borough Council called for a further cost/benefit study of rapid rail by the Auckland Regional Authority and the Government; and the Harbour Bridge Authority continued its investigations into a second harbour bridge crossing, the member for Waitemata, J N Kirk now giving it publicity…

"If the Auckland Regional Authority could not demonstrate that it was the superior Auckland local body agency, then it could not effectively lobby the government. Unchecked dissent in the lower tier together with an ineffectual regional authority, invited governments to exploit the divisiveness…" [164]

A Godfather Offer

And exploit the divisiveness they did – such as when the Labour Government offered a scaled-down version of the originally-promised rapid transit plan – as reported by The Auckland Star on 18 July 1973:

"The Government's offer of an underground city rail loop and a narrow-gauge electric train service to Papakura is like an offer from the Godfather – it's one we can't refuse, Auckland Regional Authority chairman Mr T H Pearce said today. Mr Pearce said the choice facing the regional authority was simple – either it accepts the offer, or it doesn't get a bus-rail scheme. The Government has rejected the ARA's request for a wide-gauge rapid-rail system running on its own right of way…

"Sir Dove-Myer…said today that hopes for a rapid transit scheme as the ARA had envisaged were 'down the drain'. 'But I am going to stay and fight,' he said. 'I don't run away from my responsibilities.' He was prepared to accept the scheme offered by the Government provided Auckland local bodies did not pay anything towards losses on a 'Government department service'. 'This is not a rapid transit scheme, and it is not what the Government solemnly pledged before and after the election,' he said. He will recommend to the rapid transit committee that the ARA refuse to make any contribution to the scheme…" [500]

Offer Accepted

"[ARA Chairman] Pearce asked for and got a unanimous vote in favour of [Minister of Works and Development] Watt's scheme. Robinson had his reservations recorded, but the bulk of the membership were comfortable with the pallid government offer. Even [Robinson] supporters, like Brian Berg, voted for the proposal, arguing that after such a long time it was better to get some gain rather than hold out for more…" [164]

Rapid Transit Committee Disbanded

With acceptance of the Government's version of a suburban railway system, some in the ARA felt there was no longer a need for a Rapid Transit Committee and its dissatisfied Chairman, Dove-Myer Robinson:

"Allsopp-Smith's [ARA] Transport Committee recommended to the Policy and Finance Committee that the Rapid Transit Committee be disbanded and the latter committee adopted the recommendation. Pearce then put the recommendation to a full Auckland Regional Authority meeting on August 20, 1973…Robinson's Committee could potentially raise his version of rapid rail again and so it was to be silenced…Pearce's recommendation was accepted by the Auckland Regional Authority and the Rapid Transit Committee was disbanded. Only Robinson and his deputy chairman, Brian Berg, voted against the motion." [164]

Dove-Myer Robinson Objects

As you would expect, Dove-Myer Robinson had a few things to say at that August 1973 meeting:

"I want to sincerely express my appreciation of the recognition, expressed in the second recommendation, of the thousands of hours of study, writing reports, addressing over 100 meetings, several overseas investigations trips, and thousands of dollars of my own money that has gone into this work.

"My appointment as Chairman of the Committee was implied agreement by the Authority that because of my continued interest in this project for over 10 years since its inception in 1963, I was the one who should lead the negotiations with the Government. However, the preamble to tonight's recommendations makes it clear that if they are approved tonight, the Committee is dissolved and the leadership of negotiations is taken over by the Chairman of the Authority, who to say the least of it, has made so many statements varying from lack of enthusiasm to fullest support, that no-one knows exactly where he stands on the matter.

"I intend to move the following amendment: – *'That the Rapid Transit Committee go out of existence when it has achieved an agreement with the Government, satisfactory to the Authority, in accordance with the purpose for which the Committee was established.'*

"Let me recount briefly a series of events. In September 1969, a deputation representing the Authority met representatives of the Government in Wellington to discuss the then recently produced report of the Working Party. However, instead of discussing the report, the Government representatives produced a copy of a garbled report in a suburban newspaper of what I was supposed to have said at a meeting of the Orewa Rotary Club. (This report was subsequently proved, and accepted by the Government, as totally incorrect).

"However, at the time the Government representatives used it as an excuse to ostracise me, and for nearly three years, I was ignored by the Government. It was only early last year when Mr Marshall became Prime Minister, that I again was recognised as Chairman of the negotiating committee. This, no doubt, is the reason that the report of the Steering Committee…which was promised to be ready in about 10 months, did not become available until September last year, three years later.

"I now have documentary proof that in July 1969, before representatives of this Authority were allowed to meet representatives of the Government, a dissident group of local body aspirants whom I had criticised at the Orewa Rotary Club meeting, had been down to Wellington and had presented submissions to the Government mainly advocating an all-bus system based on a policy of decentralisation. This was in direct opposition to this Authority's policy of a bus/rail system, and the 'core city' basis of our regional plan.

"The correspondence shows that the then Government gave that deputation a sympathetic hearing. Subsequent events indicate that both the previous and the present Governments were influenced more by this group's views than those of this Authority…

" …I have in my possession, documentary evidence that the dissident group…again met representatives of the present Government on June 1 of this year, and again put forward arguments against this Authority's approved scheme and favouring the decentralisation which is opposed to the Authority's 'core-city' regional plan.

"It is clear that before the Government was prepared to meet the elected representatives of the people of Auckland, it dickered with an unrepresentative group whose aims were entirely antagonistic to this Authority's key policies, and latest developments indicate that the Government was more influenced by them than by us.

"But even worse has now developed. Transport is the most important tool in the hands of planners for the proper co-ordinated planning of the region, yet in last Saturday's Star, the Minister of Works is quoted as saying: *'A comprehensive study of Auckland's traffic needs, with a special emphasis on a possible alternative to a second harbour bridge, will be started within a few months.'* and further:– *'We are going to investigate the whole of Auckland's transport system.'*

"This is clearly a case of the Government usurping the prerogative of this Authority which, under its Act, has sole responsibility for deciding on the most suitable form of passenger transport for Auckland.

"On the one hand we have the Minister for Local Government saying that local authorities are running away from their responsibilities and throwing them into the lap of central government, and on the other hand, the Minister of Works calmly announces that the Government is going to take over two of this Authority's most important functions – transport and its overriding effect on planning. If this Authority accepts this situation without effective protest, Aucklanders of the future may well say we 'sold out' without a fight…" [501]

Political Autonomy Protected

"Robinson's rapid rail campaign showed that the lower tier's morphological fundamentalism, in this case protection of its political autonomy, had seriously influenced ARA decision making. Lambie and then Pearce's leadership has facilitated this. They encouraged a bland 'benign' regionalism that allowed the lower tier (and its sympathisers on the ARA) to view the authority as an instrument of their own policy rather than a threat to their political authority...The demise of rapid rail invited Auckland municipal councils to seek further influence in ARA decision making...His [Robinson's] vision of the ARA as an agency politically independent from and dominant of the other Auckland local bodies had not been realised. The outcome of his rapid rail campaign was an important step in the municipalities' efforts to preserve their own political authority and contain that of the ARA." [164]

Help Sought from Business Community

While Dove-Myer Robinson was no longer Chairman of the ARA Rapid Transit Committee, he was still the long-serving Mayor of Auckland City and it was from this position that he continued his campaign to promote the City's need for a viable public transport system. Only a week after the dissolution of the Rapid Transit Committee, Dove-Myer Robinson wrote to the President and Members of the Executive, Auckland Chamber of Commerce:

"Gentlemen:-At a time when Auckland needs unity as never before, it is being rent by personal and political animosities that threaten to wreck its future. Insidiously – either by design or chance – forces, inimical to the future growth and welfare of Auckland, are conspiring to deprive our city of the material, financial and moral support it requires.

"In pursuance of its basically sound philosophy of regional development, the Government is often, unconsciously, slowing down the 'natural' development of Auckland. I say 'natural' development to differentiate between the development which (unless impeded by political expediency) would, in any case, occur here, as against 'artificially' stimulated development which must, almost inevitably, fail when the politically expedient supports are withdrawn.

"Because of its natural advantages of topography, geography and climate, Auckland would be destined (unless impeded) to be one of the great cities of the world, enjoying material prosperity and social and cultural conditions matched by very few other cities in the world.

"Despite certain difficulties resulting from our multi-racial population, which can be overcome by wise, far-sighted integrating policies, the greatest danger to the achievement which I foresee for the Auckland of the future, is the lack of unity resulting from the personal and political animosities that are demonstrably encouraging the political and other moves which will slow down and inhibit the natural development of the City. The end result will certainly be the deferment, if not the complete frustration of the attainment of the commercial, social and cultural development that should be Auckland's ultimate noble destiny.

"Relating the above to a specific example is the foreseeable disaster resulting from the Government's decision to provide (not until 1982) Auckland with an up-dated Wellington kind of electrified rail service to Papakura; and the Auckland Regional Authority decision to accept it 'in principle' without objection and indeed before the Authority knew the physical and financial implications of the Government's decision.

"…the present decision…falls far short of what Auckland will need by 1982. At the same time, the Government has made it a condition that Auckland bear the almost inevitable operating losses on both buses and rail passenger services. What the Government is offering is only an up-dated extension of the national railway system; it is not a modern, commuter system and therefore will not provide growing Auckland's needs from 1976 (the year in which congestion in parts of the metropolitan area is expected to reach paralysis during the morning and evening peak traffic hours) until the end of the century and onwards.

"As it will be part of the national railway system, it will be only an extension of a Government department service. To expect Auckland to meet operating losses on a departmental function is introducing a new principle into the financing of Government works – the principle that the people, in the area in which the service is located, should pay for it. This may be a convenient way to shift the Government's financial burdens from itself to the citizens – from taxpayers of the whole country, to the ratepayers in specific areas.

"Politically this may be good for the Government of the day, but for ratepayers, it is a potentially dangerous and disastrous change in the tax and rate burdens. It is for these reasons that I felt it necessary to bring these matters to the attention of the Chamber of Commerce, as the one body in Auckland which combines in itself, concern for the future development of the city and its social, cultural and financial future…" [502]

The Reorganisation of Local Government

As well as the possible transfer of financial burdens referred to by Dove-Myer Robinson, the Government also sought to reorganise local government by means of the Local Government Act 1974, most of which came into force on 1 December 1974 to: "…consolidate and amend the law relating to the reorganisation of the districts and functions of local authorities, to make better provision for the administration of those functions which can most effectively be carried out on a regional basis, and to make provision for the establishment of united councils, regional councils, district councils, district community councils, and community councils…" [503]

With its repeal of the Local Government Commission Act 1967 and its Amendment of 1969, the 1974 Act established a new Local Government Commission:

"To prepare schemes for the creation of regions, united councils, and regional councils, so as to ensure that every part of New Zealand is, by not later than the 31st day of December 1979, or as soon thereafter as may be, included in a region…

"To review and report and make such recommendations as it thinks fit to the Minister upon such matters relating to local government as may be determined by the Commission, or be referred to the Commission by the Minister…" [503]

While the 1974 Local Government Act allowed for the Commission to prepare 'schemes', as required, for the constitution or abolition of new districts or regional and local authorities and the setting of boundaries – all subject to appeal – no such schemes were so designated by the Act. For instance, the status of the Auckland Regional District and the Auckland Regional Authority, as constituted under its 1963 Act, remained "…as if that district were a region, and each local district thereof were a constituent district, and the Authority were a regional council…" [503]

Central City Benefit

By August 1975, *the future development of the city and its social, cultural and financial future* awaited a start to be made on any form of suburban railway improvements. And while decisions remained pending, as they always seemed to be, criticism that rapid transit would overwhelmingly benefit the central city remained – as per a letter to the Auckland Star from Dr M J Taylor:

"It can be contended…that a rapid transit plan, as is favoured by Sir Dove-Myer Robinson, is simply a prop to support the flagging central city and a system that is being outmoded by the gradual change that is occurring in the economic structure of the urban area. Effectively, the proposed rapid transit system is spitting against the wind, with Sir Dove-Myer's stand being the truly 'blatant parochialism', as is to be expected from the mayor of those areas that are experiencing the least employment growth and even decline – the only areas that can benefit from making journeys to the centre of the urban area less arduous." [496]

Dove-Myer Robinson Properties

There was even a suspicion that Sir Dove-Myer Robinson could personally benefit from the plan he favoured – as reported by The New Zealand Herald on 1 July 1975:

"The Mayor of Auckland, Sir Dove-Myer Robinson, says he has nothing to hide over his property interests in the inner city. Last week the council voted against receiving a question from Mr J P Anderton which asked the mayor to make public any financial interest he had in land or buildings in the inner city. Mr Anderton said that in view of the articles Sir Dove-Myer had written in a Sunday newspaper, alleging that opponents of the Auckland rapid transit scheme were doing so for personal gain, the mayor should make public his own property interests.

"In reply to questions from the Herald yesterday, Sir Dove-Myer said that he did have interests in two buildings in Fort Street, neither of which were freehold. One property was bought in February, 1963, and the other in December, 1963 – before there was any suggestion of a rapid transit scheme for Auckland. An agreement for the sale of one of the properties was entered into in August last year and it was expected to be completed in the coming weeks. Sir Dove-Myer said the other leasehold property, Patterson Building, in which he had a half share, was let on a long-term lease.

"'In neither case do I own the freehold,' he said. 'They are both leasehold properties and apart from my own house they are my only property interests in the city. My major investment is in property in Onehunga.' He said the question from Mr Anderton, which the City Council decided not to accept, implied that he was supporting the rapid transit scheme because of his property interests in the city. This was a preposterous allegation and clearly not so…" [504]

The Big Sell

That's not to say that Dove-Myer Robinson was not capable of a bit of property speculation. Such speculation had featured as the main commercial activity of fellow Aucklanders since 1840. Of course, not every speculator had the benefit of a little inside knowledge of the type the Mayor described to his Wall Street broker friend and possible investor, John Hood. In his letter of 22 November 1963, Dove-Myer Robinson first set the stage for his investment proposal by lauding Auckland's progress. Then came the big sell:

"Well, things are really booming here. We have managed to arrange the finance for our civic administration building, which together with modifications is now expected to cost about £1,850,000. Quite apart from this building, other buildings costing about £15,000,000 are at present being erected within about one mile radius of our Town Hall.

"Parliament enacted our Regional Authority Bill a month ago and within a few months we will have a Regional Authority…This will be the first time in Auckland's history that we have managed to unify local government. I am enclosing a brochure covering this…As you can see within 23 years we expect to double our present population and reach the one million mark. The total amount of capital which will have to be invested in that time by central government, local government, industry, commerce and private people will be not less than £2,000,000,000 (big money, even for a Wall Street Broker!).

"At the moment I am considering the formation of a private company to invest in city properties. Because of my position and my close connection with the commercial community, I frequently hear of properties which can be bought below Government valuation. These properties in no way concern the City Council, and there would be no legal or moral conflict between my civic and private interests if I invested in them. Already I own three fine city commercial buildings valued at approximately £300,000. Do you think there would be any possibility of getting some of your clients interested in a proposal to back me if I should decide to go into this in a bigger way? Briefly, my proposal would be as follows:

(a) That the investor or investors, should appoint a reliable solicitor or accountant in Auckland to act on their behalf.

(b) Any proposed purchase would be submitted by me to their legal representative for approval before purchase.

(c) On receiving approval the Title Deeds would be held in the name of the investor. This would ensure the fullest security for the capital.

(d) I would pay 8% interest annually, and this would be backed by my own personal collateral security.

(e) The properties would be rented to reliable tenants.

(f) If and when a satisfactory and profitable sale could be negotiated, the investor would be entitled to 50% of the nett profit.

"This could be a very sound and a profitable investment in one of the most suitable and rapidly growing cities within the British Commonwealth, and may be of interest to some of your clients. Would you be good enough to let me have your comment on the above…" [505]

Where is the Master Plan?

But whether transport planning was unduly influenced by parochialism or property speculation seemed irrelevant to Mission Bay ratepayer, Noel Gardiner. In his Letter to the Editor of the Auckland Star, published 18 August 1975, Mr Gardiner asked, 'Where is the master plan?'

"In his letter on the rapid transit plan Dr Taylor poses the rhetorical question, 'Who is blatantly parochial?' What he should have asked was, 'Why is parochialism so much in evidence?' and 'Is it because Auckland has been allowed to grow like Topsy?'

"The answer is yes and the reason is that the regional master plan, completed after many years of effort and research and at considerable cost to the ratepayers, was never given any legislative teeth, nor did the Auckland Regional Authority, which sprang from the planning section, ever make a concerted effort to implement it. How can any large metropolitan area with a multiplicity of local authorities and ad hoc organizations like

Auckland maintain balanced and orderly growth without a comprehensive plan which has been mutually agreed upon?

"Parochialism admittedly has been a militating factor against implementation but by no means the sole one. Such things as the inability of those chosen to do the job, to make up their collective minds, and the action of all kinds of other organizations and authorities, long-standing and recently conjured up, toting their own pet theories have been more effective in its relegation.

"Some in authority are even now drawing up newer and better (?) plans to control our growth and get us out of the chaos that precipitate independent action by some of the larger local authorities continues to get us into. This is why we see Auckland's mayor tilting at the chairman of the harbour board for wanting to enlarge his container wharf with all its repercussions, instead of getting on with his upper harbour as already planned.

"And why we see a team of backroom boys charged with the duty of asking the motorists at the Whau where they are off to each morning and night and why they continue to choke the motorway, when the answer is as clear as a pikestaff: 'No work out our away; we're off to the industrialized south.'

"The current procrastinator is the newly arrived holier-than-thou environmental man; he fears all growth and progress, fails to get his priorities right and cannot or will not appreciate that most thinking people are lovers of nature and adhere to its laws. If the Auckland Regional Authority cannot or will not implement its regional master plan, it is high time the central Government directed that it do so and at the same time provided legislation to ensure that other large local authorities do not prejudicially jump the gun. What is required is balance within the region. Meanwhile the poor, impotent ratepayer can do nothing but accept the ensuing chaos and pay again and again for work already done." [506]

Auckland Comprehensive Transportation Study Review

While, in Noel Gardiner's opinion, the Auckland Regional Authority had not actively implemented its regional master plan, or any plan for that matter, it had not entirely sat on its hands. In fact, behind the scenes, yet another investigation – the Auckland Comprehensive Transportation Study Review – had been undertaken since its authorisation by the ARA in April 1970.

"A Technical Advisory Committee was established in December 1971 to advise on content and methods to be used in this Study, and approval for subsidy was given by the National Roads Board in September 1972. The Study was commenced in March 1973, and was conducted by the staff of the Authority's Planning Division with assistance from the Ministry of Works and Development. The Technical Advisory Committee was under the chairmanship of the Authority's Director of Planning and comprised representatives of the National Roads Board, Ministry of Works and Development, Ministry of Transport, Auckland Regional Authority and the territorial local authorities of the region…

"The overall objective was to enable a land use/transportation planning process to be established which will be capable of continuing operation for the testing and review of alternative forms of urban growth, and the establishment and review of transportation works programmes…" [507]

Alternative Growth Strategies

Four alternative growth strategies were developed by the ARA Study Review, to be evaluated in terms of objectives on housing, employment, recreation, transport and public utilities. These were included in the Review's interim report published 23 March 1976:

"<u>Alternative 1</u>… Growth and change in Auckland continues with little interruption to present trends. There is a rapid population increase to 1.5 million in the urban area by the year 2001. Existing physical life styles remain basically unchanged with low density, suburban living, high mobility and outdoor leisure activities predominant…The development strategy calls for some shift in peripheral growth from the south to the north and to a lesser extent to the west…

"<u>Alternative 2</u>…This is essentially a scaled down version of Alternative 1. Growth continues at a somewhat slower rate, due to factors such as declining birth rates and national migration controls and the urban area population reaches 1.1 million by 2001. Existing life styles remain basically unchanged, but choices are restricted, first by scarcity of resources, but in the longer term by a positive approach of balancing population and economic growth with available resources…

"<u>Alternative 3</u>… Auckland continues to grow and major changes are made in development patterns, life styles and institutional arrangements. Rapid population growth continues to 1.5 million by 2001. More people live in town houses and flats both in inner and outer suburbs and public transport is efficient and widely patronised. Strong regional and central government policy direction is aimed at urban renewal of existing communities and the provision of expanded public facilities including an intensely used Central Area…

"<u>Alternative 4</u>… Auckland's population growth slows down as in Alternative 2, affected by a declining birth rate, restrictions on overseas migration, and regional development programmes favouring growth in other areas of New Zealand…" [508]

Summary of Conclusions

The interim report's Summary of Conclusions listed:

"<u>Land Use Implications</u>

"1. An optimum land use form, from a transportation point of view, might be seen as one which minimises the need for travel by localising travel desires. Although there will be an increasing proportion of local travel due to decentralisation within the Auckland urban area, travel in the major radial corridors linking the outer sectors to the isthmus will continue to increase regardless of the form of future development.

"2. An optimum transportation system is one which minimises both investment costs in the system and travel costs of the user; has the least social and environmental cost; and maximises benefits to the whole community…

"3. Differences between a low density, peripheral form of development and a higher density, concentrated form will be less significant in their impact on travel patterns than the degree of decentralisation…

"4. The degree of decentralisation can be expressed in terms of the ratio of jobs to resident labour force in the outer sectors compared with that on the isthmus. Past trends would suggest that the highest ratio will be attained in South Auckland, followed by the west and the north…

"5. A preferred land use strategy, from a transportation point of view, will therefore: –

    (i) promote a high level of self-sufficiency in the outer sectors, especially in the north and west;

(ii) limit the growth of the CBD and other isthmus employment centres;

(iii) develop the outer sectors in such a way as to promote greater use of the non-radial transport corridors.

"Transport Implications

"6. A substantially increased investment in public transport is required to produce marginally increased modal split ratios over the transportation system as a whole. As most travel will still be made by private transport, any reduction in road capacity which is not compensated by an equivalent shift of demand to public transport will result in a reduction in the level of service to the majority of users.

"7. There is, however, a demand for public transport in some corridors and for some purposes which is sensitive to the quality of service provided...

"8. Thus there is scope for optimising travel costs and benefits on a corridor or local area basis rather than on an urban-wide basis...

"9. There will be an optimum ratio of public transport to private transport investment in these corridors up to which major capital expenditure on roading can be avoided or at least delayed. Beyond this ratio, increased public transport investment and operating costs will exceed any additional benefits.

"10. Travel costs and benefits in most other areas will be optimised by investment in private transport. While public transport will still be required to meet a fixed, captive demand in these areas, greater benefits will accrue from investment in roading...

"Preferred Land Use/Transportation Policies

"11. Decentralisation of jobs and other major trip attractors away from the isthmus is essential for optimisation of the transportation system and to restrain the growth of travel in the major radial corridors.

"12. Existing capacity of the major radial corridors should be increased by greater investment in public transport where this can defer the need for large capital investment in new roading facilities.

"13. There should be a shift in emphasis in roading investment away from the traditional radial corridors to areas where such investment would be consistent with promoting a policy of decentralisation.

"14. The next stage of the Study should evaluate the application of these policies to a 1986 land use/transportation plan. Following this, a return should be made to the longer term evaluation to more clearly define a preferred land use/transportation plan.

"15. Policies to restrain the use of motor vehicles, such as road pricing, high parking costs and incentives for carpooling have not been investigated in this stage of the Study. Such policies will need to be investigated in relation to the most restrained parts of the transportation system as part of the continuing evaluation.

"The Corridor Options - Southern Corridor

"30. Job self-sufficiency in South Auckland has traditionally been high and is anticipated to remain so. However, there is a strong interdependence between South Auckland and the eastern isthmus, and this creates a high demand along the central part of the radial corridor between Newmarket and Wiri. The Southern Motorway lies along this principle desire line and additional roading capacity along this alignment will be difficult to provide.

"31. There is thus scope for investment in public transport to provide increased capacity in this critical part of the radial corridor. While express bus operation in exclusive or contra-flow lanes on the Southern Motorway would be difficult due to the balanced peak flows, spare capacity is available in the rail right-of-way.

"32. The Study results show that investment in an upgraded rail service between Wiri and the Auckland Railway Station, preferably extended to the Downtown bus terminal and supported by improved bus service in the south-eastern and south-western corridors, would produce similar benefits to the full Stage 1 Auckland Rapid Transit proposals for only a small part of the capital investment.

"33. In the southern corridor therefore, following the completion of the Mangere Bridge and the widening of the Southern Motorway, further additional radial capacity can be provided between the isthmus and South Auckland by improved public transport. At the same time, investment in roading facilities in the non-radial corridors should assist decentralisation policies and delay the need for additional radial capacity."

"A.3 Trip Characteristics - Total Trips

"1. Of more than 2 million trips generated daily in Auckland, 98% have origins and destinations within the Study Area.

"2. About 70% of all travel is by private car, 13% by trucks and 11% by bus passengers. Motor cycles, taxis, trains and ferries combined account for only 6% of the total.

"3. In the case of CBD based travel, about 49% is by private car, 16% by trucks and 28% by bus." [508]

Reaction to the ARA's Transportation Study Interim Report

Following publication of the Interim Report, The New Zealand Herald responded:

"The Auckland rapid-transit proposals are less efficient and more costly than an all-bus alternative. That is the conclusion reached in the interim report of the Auckland comprehensive transport study review released yesterday. The report incorporates the first cost-benefit and comparative study of the ART proposals and finds that an all-bus system would have lower capital and running costs and carry more passengers.

"A spokesman for the technical advisory committee which was set up by the ARA to prepare the review, said whether the findings would mean an end of ART would be a political decision. 'But what we have established is that there is really a much cheaper alternative that will be just as good,' he said. 'From the technical point of view the sensible thing will be to investigate this cheaper alternative and work something out in more detail.' Such a decision seems likely to be made at a special meeting of the full ARA on Monday night…The report did not take social and environmental impacts into account as these will be considered when the preferred plan co-ordinating land use and transport is chosen." [509]

And The Auckland Star commented:

"In its study of alternative transport ideas for the next 25 years, the ARA found that running trains on the existing line between Wiri and Auckland with shuttle buses from the central station to the downtown bus terminal, and supported by improved bus links with the south-west and south-east, would be $175 million dollars cheaper than ART. Yet it would provide much the same sort of service and would achieve similar savings in roading costs.

"The report, part of a three-year $200,000 study, doesn't provide a plan for the future of Auckland's transport network – that will come in the final report in a few months. But it gives plenty of clues. It makes it quite clear that the car will be our major form of transport in the foreseeable future. In most areas, it says, while public transport will still be required to meet a fixed, captive demand, greater benefits will accrue from investment in roading..." [510]

Transport Investment Needed

During his address to the National Roads Board on 21 April 1976, the Board's senior design engineer, Mr J Foster, expressed some concern that some of the interim findings of the Transportation Study were inconclusive. While he acknowledged some need for greater investment in public transport, he urged that a number of critical decisions be made first – as reported by The New Zealand Herald:

"Investment on transport in Auckland must increase during the next 20 years if citizens were to retain their present mobility, the senior design engineer for the National Roads Board, Mr J Foster, said yesterday. Mr Foster told the monthly meeting of the board that the projected growth of Auckland would not allow it to get by with its present levels of investment on transport...Mr Foster described the proposed rapid-transit rail scheme as 'rank stupidity,' unless the city had much greater sums to spend on transport...

"In his submission to the board, Mr Foster said a comprehensive review of transport planning within the Auckland metropolitan area had been underway since early in 1973. The board was a full partner to the study and provided 30 per cent of the finance. The results of the investigations were described in an interim report recently released by the Auckland Regional Authority for public comment.

"'Although the study has attempted a neutral analysis of two growth forms and alternative transport policies involving a greater or lesser emphasis on public transport, the report displays a rather inconclusive stance to these main issues,' Mr Foster said. 'This is because the staff of the authority and some local body officers were initially convinced that many, if not all, of the region's transport problems could be solved by firm controls on development form and emphatic change of emphasis from private to public transport.

"Analysis has failed to confirm these convictions. On the contrary,' said Mr Foster, 'it is apparent that the growth form has only a minor influence on the overall demand for movement in the main travel corridors and in spite of large investments in public transport, critical demands will still remain for private transport facilities.

"'The huge investment involved in the rapid-rail proposal to serve the central area has been shown to be clearly inappropriate. Nevertheless, study has shown that a judicious mix of such solutions has some chance of matching the problems.' Mr Foster said an assured method of finance for investment in public transport was urgently required to provide the necessary basis for detailed planning. The existing arrangements for the management and co-ordination of a subtle mix of planning controls, transport investment in appropriate forms and private transport restraint measures were inadequate. It was, therefore, apparent that a number of critical decisions would have to be taken before transport investments could be decided with confidence, Mr Foster said. The board agreed to pay $18,000 of the additional $60,000 needed to complete the Auckland transport study review." [511]

Desirable Priorities

In his 'Politics and Planning' column for the City News, published 6 April 1976, John Morton lamented the Interim Report's lack of transport planning goals:

"First, the ARA's interim transport study disposes – finally it may be – of Rapid Rail. This scheme had never before been subjected to a planners' report (the odd way we do things in Auckland); and if it cannot stand up to planning and cost scrutiny, it need not be lamented by too many. But the report is chill and disappointing in offering nothing worthwhile in Rapid Rail's place. It's not that planners did not do a good job. But their political masters had little to tell them of what ought to be desirable priorities, social and financial. And without such goals, planning can't properly begin.

"The Plan is unrealistic in claiming that jobs ought to be distributed to minimise transport problems. Transport is just one of the problems coming in the tail of growth; and won't be able to wag the whole dog. And if Auckland Region has no better powers or determination than today, to plan its regional growth, it is unlikely that distribution of employment patterns will really help transport. The central business district must always be important, with people wanting to get to it.

"Auckland isthmus must be the hardest city in the world to transport-plan. Its great aggregation of people and building is on the same sinew that goes right through it from north to south. The through motorways are encouraged to bring traffic into Auckland, that is swelling – and poisoning – the centre like a thrombosis...

"The Report makes clear its belief that the private car will be our major form of transport in the foreseeable future. Greater benefits – in consequence – will accrue from investment in roading. Public transport will still be needed to meet a 'fixed, captive demand' presumably those prepared or economically constrained to take second best...

"New Zealand is the second highest motorised country today, after the United States. The private car is today a selfish and un-rational instrument, with massive disadvantages to the environment, economy and lifestyle...I have written and talked constantly – it seems – about the case for good public transport; for providing a service people will want to use, <u>before</u> making private car use more difficult. We shall have to look at the whole operation of moving people to and fro, as it affects the total economy.

"Whether by penal charges on entering the bus, or by spread-out citizens' tax, we shall all of us be paying for passenger transport. But today we happen to be doing it the dirty and expensive way: whenever we come to the city, bringing half a ton of cast iron and pressed steel with us, paying for the fuel used and the space to leave it immobile all day.

The interim transport study probably gives an accurate enough reflection of the outlook and assumptions of today's Aucklanders on passenger transport. The only thing wrong is with the Aucklanders and those of us who share these assumptions. We are collectively crazy." [512]

Auckland Comprehensive Transportation Study Review – Final Report

In hindsight, that concept of *collective craziness* was seemingly perpetuated by the final report of the Auckland Comprehensive Transportation Study Review, completed in September 1976, and presented to members of the Auckland Regional Authority by Study Director, W D Pringle:

"...The report has been prepared by Auckland Regional Authority staff under the guidance of a Technical Advisory Committee. This was set up by the Auckland Regional Authority in consultation with the National Roads Board which has subsidised the Study. Members of the Technical Advisory Committee are officer representatives of the territorial local authorities and Government Departments...

"Work on the Study has now been completed to the stage where recommendations can be made on a preferred land use/transportation strategy and a 10 year implementation plan. However there is flexibility in these recommendations, and the transportation planning process will continue beyond the publication of this Final Report for the continuing review of alternative proposals to meet changing needs.

"Foreword

"1. …The conclusions and recommendations in this report differ from those in previous transport reports on the Auckland Region in several ways.

"2. The de Leuw Cather report of 1965, and the various and rapid transit reports since, have all promoted actions which require a high public investment to achieve. Resources at the required rates have never been available to implement these reports. Even fewer resources for transport are likely in the future. Therefore, this report stages its recommendations so that high cost capital works are put off as long as possible, and none is to be committed until the need has been clearly demonstrated.

"3. Whereas the previous reports referred to have all taken a confident line towards future transport needs, this report is more cautious in its assessment. It is beyond the power of anyone to accurately predict the next 10 years of transport requirements for the Auckland region in the detail necessary to implement precise recommendations. This report concentrates on moving one step at a time within a general strategy. There are frequent opportunities, built into the sequence of recommendations, for review and for alternative actions.

"4. Another characteristic of the previous reports is their reliance upon a limited mix of transport modes in isolation from land use development plans. While this report does not overcome those deficiencies it does try to blend transport and land development policies in a subtle mix and avoid too heavy a reliance upon single, high cost solutions.

"5. There is one more matter that needs to be raised at the outset. If adopted, the recommendations in this report will not succeed unless they are accompanied by the setting up of some form of urban transport authority within the region. The form of such an organisation, and its powers are not matters for this report but the need for it cannot be ignored.

"6. The recommendations in this report will need to be considered by several bodies within and outside the Auckland region…

"Resources Strategy

"A conservative view of transport resources has been taken. There are several reasons for this attitude. Firstly, the current and future levels of expenditure on urban transport over the next 10 years are likely to remain well below that required to achieve previous plans…Secondly, there is a high overseas funds cost to New Zealand of liquid fuels which, through price changes, has forced some changes in attitude towards transport behaviour.

"The increasing cost of motoring to the individual is now a major economic problem for the country…Thirdly, there is widespread public feeling against the social and physical impacts of major road works within urban parts of the region, where those works are likely to disrupt people and their homes.

"The immediate response to these factors must be to make better use of existing resources. The biggest available transport resource is the road space and vehicle fleet capacity already in existence. There will be a need to increase total person carrying capacities within existing rights of way and especially in the major radial corridors where a large capital investment would be required to extend vehicle capacity beyond that currently committed.

"The study has shown that better utilisation of existing arterial roads can be achieved with techniques such as peak period clearways, tidal flow operation and intersection improvements which can provide additional capacity over most of the network at a comparatively low cost. Also, improvements to peak period public transport can be made by re-organising services to more closely suit travel patterns; extending the use of express services; and by improving bus flows in congested areas with techniques such as kerb lanes reserved for buses and priority at intersections.

"In some areas, such as the central isthmus, these measures should meet most travel needs for the next 10 years. It is the intention of the Resources Strategy that where these low cost measures can prolong the life of existing facilities then they should be given a high priority…

"Incentives to increase private vehicle occupancies by voluntary car-pooling schemes, and the carriage of fare paying passengers in private cars, should have a high potential in corridors serving areas of concentrated trip generation such as the CBD. A further opportunity for getting more out of the available transport resource is direct intervention in the pricing mechanism. The effect this may have on reducing the overall level of demand is not known, but pricing policies can be applied selectively to divert demand from one part of the network to another, and from one mode to another…

"A further potential means of achieving a selective reduction in demand for road space is the application of parking policies within the main areas of traffic generation such as shopping centres, employment areas and the CBD. This Study has shown that the availability and cost of parking will influence the choice of travel mode to the CBD in peak periods.

"More efficient use of existing transport resources will be unable to supply all the additional capacity needed over the next 10 years. Extensions to the motorway and major road networks, as well as additional public transport vehicles, will be required to meet the increased travel resulting from urban growth. The Study has shown that a policy of no further capital investment would result in a drop in the efficiency of the transport system, and a substantial rise in user costs.

"<u>Investment Strategy - Concentrated or Dispersed</u>

"Out of a total annual expenditure of about $30 million on roading in the Auckland region, it is estimated that about $12 million is spent on major road works within the urban area. Most of this is spent on State Highways, and over the last 5 years expenditure has been concentrated mainly into the central motorway system in an effort to complete that project. An undesirable but unavoidable result has been lack of funds for other main roads throughout the urban area.

"Had inflation not happened to the extent it has, a strategy of concentration of roading finance might not have had such widespread effects in reducing funds available elsewhere in Auckland. It would be prudent to assume that funds for roading in Auckland will show no large increases over the next 10 years and that there will be an increasing gap between the budget for roading and the demands for capital works.

"<u>Investment Strategy - Public and Private Transport</u>

"One of the principal objectives of this Study has been to evaluate alternative public transport systems for Auckland. There has been much discussion on 'modal split' – the proportion of total trips made by public transport. Aucklanders have enjoyed an increasingly high level of personal mobility and the outcome of this has been that all forms of public transport combined carried, in 1973, only 12.5% of the total people travelling each day and 20% of those travelling in the peak periods.

"A series of alternative public transport systems has been evaluated in the Study in an attempt to determine what effect innovation in these systems might have on modal split ratios, and what level of investment in public transport can be sustained as a substitute for investment in roading. "The results of these analyses suggest that over the transport system as a whole, the additional capital investment and operating costs required to expand public transport services are not offset by savings in capital expenditure on roading and private transport operating costs.

"However in some corridors, especially the major radial routes serving the CBD, it has been shown that expanded services would result in an increase in the proportion of trips by public transport in those corridors and would increase their total person carrying capacity at a lower cost than by other means. It could also defer the need for some capital intensive road works.

"The theme of this final report is that urban transport is now mainly a management problem. New capital works will continue in Auckland and large sums of public money will be invested each year in transport in the region. But the problem has changed from one of building a transport system to one of getting the best out of what we have. If the Auckland community really wants to do that, then Auckland must grapple with the problem of managing the urban transport system.

"The process of bringing disparate transport interests together for the benefit of the region cannot be achieved without also confronting the question of whether executive authority remains principally in Wellington or alternatively is to be progressively decentralised to the region. It is clear from this study that the integration of regional transport management is crying out for attention.

"The consequence of failing to face up to this issue is simple; more money will have to be spent (or standards will suffer, or both) merely because we will have failed to re-organise the decision making machinery so that the existing resources are better used. The recommendations of this report will not succeed unless they are accompanied by the setting [up] of some form of urban transport authority within the region." [507]

A Confession of Failure

That concept of *collective craziness*, symbolized by the findings of the Auckland Comprehensive Transportation Study Review, was summed up by the New Zealand Tribune, published 29 November 1976:

"The $200,000 Auckland transport report will raise cheers in the ranks of the oil companies and the property speculators – to whom most of the benefits will go. As Auckland's Mayor Robbie says, the report is 'motor car and motorway madness.' The report's emphasis on low-cost solutions, including preference for bus over rail and extended use of the motor car, amounts to a further encouragement of the urban sprawl.

"ARA deputy chairman, Mr Holdaway, said 'the transport facility which clearly has the greatest unused capacity and the most obvious need for immediate improvement, is the suburban railway.' He was a lone voice among those concerned with the report.

"This transport study shows that Auckland's transport problems are not technical but financial. So, for this reason, the report concentrates on 'low-cost' projects in an abortive attempt to settle the transport crisis within the framework of permanent economic crisis. The report is quite specific when it says, 'It is unrealistic to accept that investment in real terms in the next 10 years will match levels called for in the de Leuw Cather report of 1965...'

"That is a confession of failure by big business interests to get their priorities right and cater for the needs of the travelling public. This transport blue-print is tailored to suit the requirements and interests of the oil barons, the tyre-makers (like Firestone who upped profits 120.9 per cent over last year) the road makers and the property speculator developers, while practically leaving the rail to rot. The report is an admission of the monumental incapacity of capitalism to meet one of Auckland's principal requirements – an adequate attractive and efficient public transport system." [513]

Auckland City Council Accounts

Just what Auckland City ratepayers actually paid by way of transport levies to the Auckland Regional Authority and for additional transport-related services was recorded by the City's accounts for the 1976-77 financial year. The following year's estimates were also recorded in the Mayor's Annual Report for 1977-1978:

Payments	Actual 1976-77	Estimate 1977-78
Levies - A.R.A.	4,272,188	5,599,893
Roads, Streets, Bridges	3,558,752	4,076,900
Traffic Control & Parking Buildings	3,323,439	4,079,805
Receipts		
Rates	21,392,911	26,585,398
Traffic Control & Parking Buildings	2,882,056	3,455,000
Petrol Tax	969,037	925,000

In his report, Sir Dove-Myer Robinson emphasised his Council's provision of services "...at the lowest commensurate cost...Council finished the year with a small credit balance of $67,506... Despite rising costs resulting from inflation, such as wages and salary increases of $1,200,000, and increased costs of materials...the 31% increase in the Auckland Regional Authority levy, over which your council has no control..." [514]

Success, Failure, Frustration

The Mayor's reference to a lack of control over the levy increase was but one instance of the ill feeling engendered between the ARA and Auckland's many local and ad hoc bodies by the end of the 1970s. A few reasons were suggested by D G Rankin, Department of Geography, University of Auckland, in his article, *Auckland Regional Authority 1963-1978*, published by the New Zealand Geographer, April 1979:

"The problems arising from an admixture of territorial and ad hoc local government authorities and the tensions that exist between local and central government have provided a difficult environment within which to establish and develop a multifunctional regional authority...The history of local politics is a narrative of parochialism and friction. The present structure may once have served identifiable local communities, but the land use configuration in the region and the daily household activity patterns generated by it, show a metropolitan region which is at least functionally integrated.

"The ebb and flow of commuters binds together the extensive low density suburbs, made possible by the high level of car ownership in the post-war period, and the relatively localised employment areas of the region...The history of the ARA is a mixture of success, failure and frustration. Some of the problems encountered by the Authority were exogenous to the region and latterly its financial position reflects economic circumstances, common to the whole country…" [515]

Public Transport
A Garden City
In his article, *The Essential Nature of Auckland*, published in *Auckland At Full Stretch - Issues Of The Seventies*, Professor Kenneth Cumberland explained his views on urban sprawl and the proposed rapid rail system:

"Auckland is a liberally expansive city, a spacious city, a green and open city, a garden city. It is a far-spreading, far-reaching metropolitan complex. The interloping estuaries, inlets, harbours and arms of the sea, and again the generous setting-aside of reserves and domains, the green sward of horse-racing courses and sports grounds, and the intrusion of volcanic cones and of lofty and broken water catchment areas to northwest and southeast, all require the built-up area to spread and reach further than would be the case in a city where people huddle in multi-storied apartment buildings or are bereft of open spaces…

"Such dispersion renders the centre difficult and expensive to reach, and makes the downtown area a human desert at the weekend. It makes the provision of public transport expensive: it makes even a rapid rail system difficult to justify, and the journey to work time-consuming and expensive." [516]

A Difficult Decade
By the 1970s, that journey to work was also proving expensive for the private motor car driver, as described by Vince Dravitzki & Tiffany Lester, in their Opus International Consultants (circa 2005) paper, *Economics drove our first sustainable urban transport system*:

"The 1970s was a difficult decade for New Zealand as the economy had to adjust to restricted access to its main export market for farm products following the United Kingdom's entry into the European Economic Community.

"This setback was compounded by the steep rise in international oil prices following the oil export embargoes/price increases by OPEC of 1973 to 1975 and then further price rises at the end of the decade surrounding the Iranian Revolution. These resulted in first a threefold increase in fuel prices followed then by a further doubling of prices. The Government introduced a number of fuel restriction measures, mainly focused around the 'Oil Shock' events (but some imposed for longer periods) including:

- Reduction of open road speed limit from 90 or 100 km/h to 80 km/h;
- Graduated vehicle sales taxes and licensing costs that favoured smaller engine sizes;
- Banning of petrol sales on the weekend;
- Carless days, where for each household vehicle one day per week was nominated when that vehicle would not be used (imposed from July 1979 to May 1980);
- Rules on the extent of hire purchase arrangements for car purchase.
- Allowing Government workers flexible start times so as to spread congestion (late 1970s); and
- Establishing agencies to identify alternate energy sources, including as CNG, LPG, and biofuels.

"Most of these measures were focused on discouraging travel that used more fuel but several measures sought to alter vehicle-purchasing behaviour. Although vehicle numbers continued to rise over the decade, and travel restriction measures were resented and often circumvented, those measures targeting purchasing behaviour were more successful…

"The Government's measures were notable for there being almost no encouragement to shift travel to public transport. Even without this encouragement, given that petroleum fuels rose steadily in price (600 %) over the period 1973 to 1979, and there were also restrictions on its use, an increase in public transport use would have been expected. However, concurrently bus fares rose steeply, and this may have weight in explaining the decline in patronage.

"The *Urban Public Passenger Transport Council* noted in its reports of the period that the effects of the rapidly rising operating costs were worsened by the age of their bus fleet. For the Local Authorities' fleet of about 1,200 buses, 50 % were over 15 years old and 30 % more than 20 years old. In short, the buses that had been bought in the 1950s to replace the trams and expand the service in that period, needed in the 1970s to be replaced, but the justification and finance to do so were becoming increasingly difficult.

"Faced with ongoing budget deficits and sliding currency devaluations the Government first had little money for, and second even less commitment for public transport expenditure. Government focus was on liquid fuel self-sufficiency to insulate New Zealand against overseas trends, and the 'Think Big' expenditure that followed in the early 1980s was to further this goal…

"The 1970s were a stark contrast. The public transport system had been converted over to be a largely diesel-based system in the 1950s. Fuel costs rose steeply in the 1970s period and these rising operating costs were translated to the public transport system as rising fares. The fuel price rise also triggered wage and price inflation also compounding the rise in public transport operating costs.

"The *Urban Public Passenger Transport Council* reports service impacts from an ageing fleet. Fares rose steeply to attempt to cover these rapidly rising expenditures. Though public transport patronage was already falling prior to the oil shocks, patronage started falling at an even greater rate. The result was patronage declined by more than 25 % over the period." [517]

Carter Inquiry Final Report

That decline in public transport patronage had resulted in such dire financial problems for private bus operators by late 1969 that the Committee of Inquiry into Urban Passenger Transport (Carter Inquiry) then sitting felt compelled to issue an interim report, which it did on 15 September of that year. The final Report of the Committee, eventually presented on 27 February 1970, provided some obvious conclusions:

"12. The Committee is of the opinion that urban passenger transport is basically a community service vital to the future welfare of urban areas. In this regard the Committee acknowledges the part played by both publicly and privately owned passenger services and recognises that there is a place for both in our urban transport system. It is hoped that, in the future, public transport will cease to be judged on its profit or loss result, and instead will be judged on the contribution it is making to the welfare generally of the city it serves.

"13. The principal reasons for maintaining urban passenger transport services, even if they no longer pay, are that they provide an alternative to the use of the private car, and that they are inherently the most efficient and economical means of moving large numbers of people, especially at peak periods of travel.

"Also, the provision of reasonably cheap and convenient transport services for the young, the old, and the handicapped is a desirable community objective in itself, quite apart from the value of these services for workers, shoppers, and others. The private motorist himself expects a service to be available when for any reason he cannot use his car.

"14. The Committee is firmly of the opinion that the situation in which public transport passenger transport is almost totally eliminated in favour of the private motorcar should be resisted for social and economic reasons. From a purely economic standpoint, losses on urban passenger services are likely to be much less of a burden (as a national cost) than attempting to provide an increased amount of road space and other facilities for all who wish to use their private motorcar in preference to public transport.

"An orderly growth of both forms should be aimed at. Without urban passenger transport, traffic congestion in our larger cities would lead to their degeneration and to an even greater flight from the central business area.

"15. The Committee feels that the primary responsibility for the provision and financing of urban passenger services rests with areas receiving the benefit of these services. The main beneficiaries are, of course, the users, but since direct and indirect benefits are conferred on the area as a whole (and in this context the Committee is thinking particularly of urban regions), the responsibility is not the users alone. The Committee also believes that the present burden on ratepayers for local authority services could well be spread over a broader base.

"16. In order to discharge this responsibility, and in the long-term interests of the areas served, regional control of the principal urban passenger services should be established in all four main centres as soon as possible. This control could be extended to other areas later, if found desirable.

"17. There is some national interest in the continuation and improvement of urban passenger transport – as there is in the provision of other important community services. This is in recognition of the overall savings possible to the nation through reducing pressures on roading expenditure, and of the general benefit to the life of cities and towns.

"18. The Committee regards it as important that as soon as possible town planning, the planning of the roading network, and the operation of public passenger transport should be more closely associated and eventually be fully integrated within regional organisations. This offers the best hope of reconciling divergent policies in these interrelated fields." [518]

A Summary of the Report's Major Recommendations included:

"Organisation and Services

"(1) That an Urban Passenger Transport Council be set up to administer national aspects of urban passenger transport. This council would have six members comprising three Government representatives and three other persons.

"(2) (a) That in Auckland, Wellington, Christchurch, and Dunedin, urban passenger transport authorities be established...

(b) That the Auckland Regional Authority...be designated [an Auckland] urban passenger transport [authority].

"(5) That the primary function of such an authority would be to control and co-ordinate all scheduled urban passenger services within its area, viz:
   (a) Scheduled urban bus services where individual fares are charged:
   (b) Licensed harbour ferry services:
   (c) Urban rail services.

"(8) That financial responsibility for urban rail and bus services operated by the New Zealand Railways Department be assumed by urban passenger transport authorities over a period of 8 years.

"Finance

"(10) That the primary responsibility for the provision and financing of urban public passenger services should rest with the areas, and particularly the urban regions, receiving the benefit of these services.

"(11) (a) That the system of grants to urban passenger transport authorities, based on payments of heavy-traffic licence fees, be continued at the rate of 200 per cent of the licence fees paid each quarter.
   (b) That the existing partial exemption from motor fuel taxation be continued for operators of passenger bus services. (This amounts to 3.3 cents per gallon of petrol and equivalent mileage tax.)
   (c) That the Urban Passenger Transport Council have the power to make grants or loans for new expenditure of a capital nature on urban public passenger services.
   (d) That where frequent and extensive rail services exist, or are constructed for urban passenger transport, assistance should be given to these services from the National Roads Fund…"

"(12) That power to raise a regional petrol tax, in addition to levies on constituent local authorities, should be given to urban transport authorities.

"(13) That the functions of town planning, the planning of the roading network, and the operation of urban passenger transport be brought under the control of one authority, wherever possible.

"(14) That a formal programme of research into urban transport and related matters be instituted."

"Background to the Problem

"20. …some of the factors which are causing difficulty in urban passenger transport…
   (a) Declining patronage, especially so in the case of local authority services…
   (b) Rising costs of operation. On average, expenditure for local authority services over this 10-year period has risen by 17 per cent, but again this is not uniform…
   (c) Increasing losses. The greatest loss on urban passenger transport operations was incurred by suburban rail services.

"21. A high standard of living has brought a 67 per cent increase in the number of private cars in New Zealand between 1959 and 1968…

"22. This concentration of passenger travel into the peak hours, and the imbalance between peak and off-peak loading, is a major factor in the financial difficulties facing urban passenger transport generally.

"23. Roading expenditure in the four metropolitan areas for the year ended 31 March 1969 was $15.8 million, a large part of this being expended in the Auckland metropolitan area…

"24. Anything that can be done to improve public passenger transport services in a manner which would improve operating conditions for commercial vehicles could achieve a significant saving in commercial and industrial costs…

"Traffic Factors

"6…The figures show that traffic densities, or more particularly, vehicles per mile of road have increased at rapid rates. This is particularly pronounced in the Auckland urban region where the increase in both vehicles per mile of road and motorcars per mile of road are significantly higher than other urban areas…Urban roading and motorway expenditure have undoubtedly increased in recent years, but the growth in motor vehicles is outpacing roading developments. It is probable also that where improved access has been made to central urban areas to relieve traffic congestion problems, a certain amount of additional traffic has been generated.

"There can be little doubt that the declining patronage of public passenger transport can be chiefly attributed to increased competition from the private motorcar, and a decline in terms of speed and convenience of urban bus services." [518]

Carter Inquiry Responses

Following the release of the final Carter Inquiry Report, The New Zealand Herald commented on some of the Committee's findings and recommendations:

"Urban passenger transport undertakings, most of which are in serious financial straits, have marked time for a year or more while the Government-sponsored Carter Committee investigated their difficulties. The committee's report as finally presented suffers chiefly from lack of precision, especially in its arithmetic…

"Objections are bound to be raised against the area of allowing regional bodies, some of which are not constituted on an elective basis, to impose petrol tax. Parliament has shown no inclination to relinquish its exclusive right to exercise fiscal powers. In any case, a local tax would almost certainly create administrative difficulties…The committee makes a valid point when it says that the city motorist may have to pay more for the privilege of using his car; the private vehicle has been a major cause of public transport difficulties.

"The inadequacies of the report could create further delay in the rehabilitation of urban services. Such a hold-up would be especially serious in Auckland where the bus-rail rapid transit plan has long since become an urgent necessity. It is difficult to see how the report will assist the Auckland Regional Authority in its present cost-benefit studies. The Minister of Transport should ask the committee to do some more homework as fast as it can." [519]

Subsidy Scheme Extended

"Releasing the report, Mr Gordon [Minister of Transport] acknowledged the complex political implications of some of the recommendations and said the report was being carefully studied by the Cabinet transport committee. In the meantime, he said, the temporary subsidy scheme for bus operators, which expired on March 31, has been extended for three months." [520]

Wellington Before Auckland

The New Zealand Herald continued its commentary:

"The Auckland bus-rail rapid transit scheme, involving the construction of a subway system, goes unmentioned in the 45-page report from the Carter committee. There are no specific recommendations for separate or special forms of subsidy for it. New petrol tax provisions proposed by the committee would apply generally within urban areas. By contrast, existing Wellington rail services are singled out for special treatment. The committee urges payment of an annual lump sum, initially $250,000, toward Wellington suburban train losses – in addition to other forms of assistance proposed generally." [521]

Areas of Benefit

"The primary responsibility for providing and paying for town bus and rail services rests with the areas receiving the benefit of them, declares the Carter Committee in its report…The main beneficiaries, it says, are the users. But since direct and indirect benefits are conferred on an area as a whole, the responsibility is not only that of users. Committee members believe that the present burden on ratepayers for local body services could well be spread over a broader base…

"Hopes that public transport will cease in future to be judged on profits or losses, instead of on the contribution it is making to the general welfare of the region it serves. Even if they no longer pay, the main reasons for maintaining such services are that they provide an alternative to the car.

"They are inherently the most efficient and economical means of moving large numbers of people, especially at peak periods…As soon as possible, town planning, roads planning and the running of public passenger transport should be more closely associated and eventually should be fully integrated within regional bodies." [522]

Only a Temporary Scheme

"Just how losses on Auckland Regional Authority buses would be made good under the latest proposals for financing public passenger transport had yet to be determined, said the Minister of Agriculture, Mr Carter, yesterday…'The committee has outlined the means for making up losses,' said Mr Carter, 'but it has left it to others to decide just how this should be done in any particular case or in any particular year…Our scheme is a temporary one and is intended to prevail until some new form of comprehensive regional authorities and new methods of financing various regional services can be devised and agreed upon.'

"The first form of support for ARA bus deficits would come from the continuing State-paid subsidy, at the present rate of $186,000 yearly, he confirmed. The regional authority would then have to determine how much of the remaining deficit could be financed locally – from levies reaching ratepayers, from the proposed new regional petrol tax or from a proportion of both…He doubted whether ratepayers would ever completely 'get out from under' the burden of helping to meet such losses. If they did demands for bus services might become unrealistic…" [523]

Transport Industry Reactions

The New Zealand Herald also published various reactions to the findings and recommendations of the Carter Report:

Private Motorists

"Private motorists will be 'stung again' if the recommendations of the Carter Report are adopted, says the acting-president of the New Zealand Automobile Association, Mr T M Rodger. 'I consider the committee's proposals so serious that I immediately called an emergency meeting of our executive,' he said. 'The report seems to have adopted a completely defeatist attitude to the plight of urban passenger transport.

"As far as we can see, it makes no practical suggestions to attract greater patronage or reduce losses. Rather it presents a completely unsupported visionary hope that an increased tax on petrol in the metropolitan areas would divert car users to the public system. It has adopted the easy way of meeting losses by making car owners pay and suggests no method or incentive to make the public services themselves pay. This decision is most disturbing, particularly as the one group not represented on the committee was the private motorists who would be called upon to meet the present and escalating burden…'

"'The National Roads Board was established to provide and maintain a modern roads system for the whole country. The basis of its revenue was a definite agreement between the users and the Government that all road taxes should be used on the roads. The committee has conveniently ignored this agreement…The road user in New Zealand is already paying more than $142 million a year in taxes, of which more than half goes to the Consolidated Fund. Should financial assistance be required for urban passenger transport, this should not be a further call on the motorist.'" [524]

Private Bus Operators

"Recommendations in the Carter committee report on urban passenger transport were likely to find favour among private bus owners, Mr Rolf Porter, chairman and managing director of Auckland Transport Holdings, the largest private bus company in the country, said yesterday.

"It was pleasing, he said, to see that the report appreciated the value and essential nature of public passenger transport and that the giving of a first-class service was the first essential in persuading the consumer to use it. 'We mustn't look upon a bus service merely as a profit-making thing. Rather it should be viewed as an essential service.'

"Mr Porter said one of the main points in the report, the suggested petrol tax of up to 2 cents a gallon, would mean that everyone would contribute to the cost of providing services, instead of just the ratepayer…" [525]

Road Carriers

"Adverse comments on aspects of the urban passenger transport inquiry report were voiced by the New Zealand Road Carriers Association and the New Zealand Road Federation – a body representing all sections of the transport industry interested in roading standards.

"The president of the New Zealand Road Carriers Association, Mr W W Knox, condemned the proposal to transfer petrol tax to urban transport, and Mr C G Costello, president of the New Zealand Road Federation, said the proposed regional tax appeared to be impractical to implement.

"Mr Knox said…his industry was deeply concerned that some of the recommendations were diametrically opposed to long-established and well-founded taxation philosophy.

"Mr Costello…said the $4 million of present petrol taxation, which should properly be available for road construction and maintenance, was proposed as a subsidy for inefficient public passenger transport, both road and rail. 'This $4 million, the present road-user contribution to the consolidated fund as a remnant of an emergency economic situation three years ago, is desperately needed to maintain our roads.'

"Mr Costello said his federation agreed that public passenger transport must be developed properly as part of the over-all transport of the community. 'But we submit,' he said, 'this should be on the user-pay system, the only known way of providing a viable transport system.'" [526]

Municipal Association

Not long after the final Carter Report was released, the Municipal Association appointed a sub-committee to analyse it and that sub-committee reported to the Association's President, Sir Francis Kitts, and Members on 21 May 1970:

"2.1 In general terms the recommendations of the Committee of Inquiry are unacceptable. They leave a great deal of uncertainty, and in many instances are considered impracticable. The committee appears to have been unduly preoccupied with losses on the urban passenger services of the New Zealand Railways, and its recommendations on the future of these services seem to have been made without due regard to their practicability.

"2.2.1 (a) The subcommittee considers that the operations of the New Zealand Railways must be regarded as a single national transport system. As local rail passenger services could not be operated separately from the other national services we consider that financial responsibility for local services should not be removed from the Railways...

"After a careful study of the report the subcommittee has been unable to find any concrete reasons advanced as to why the losses being sustained by the New Zealand Railways urban transport systems should be off-loaded onto the ratepayers in the areas concerned.

"(b) The subcommittee considers that the cost of the provision of urban public passenger transport by local authorities is a community responsibility and should not rest only on the ratepayers of the locality concerned.

"2.2.2 We firmly believe that the question of financial assistance to local government must be approached on the basis of some alternative source of revenue which will be available to territorial local authorities generally, and not by way of additional sources of revenue for particular functions. For this reason we are opposed the proposed petrol tax being levied on an area basis for urban public passenger transport services alone.

"2.3 The subcommittee does not agree that there should be any diversion of the revenue available to the National Roads Board under existing statutory arrangements to expenditure other than roading. All of the present revenue of the Board is essential to meet roading needs.

"3 (1) The subcommittee…considers an Urban Passenger Transport Council to be unnecessary and can see no reason why another government-dominated statutory board should be set up to exercise further control over local government…" [527]

New Zealand Urban Public Passenger Transport Council

The formation of an Urban Passenger Transport Council, as recommended by the Carter Report and considered unnecessary by the Municipal Association's subcommittee, was eventually established as the New Zealand Urban Public Passenger Transport Council with the passage of the Ministry of Transport Amendment Act 1971 on 27 November of that year.

The 1971 Act amended the Ministry of Transport Act 1968 to include a Section 13A that listed the prospective members of the Council to include the Secretary for Transport (Chairman), the Secretary to the Treasury, the Secretary for Internal Affairs, and three members (not having any pecuniary interest…in any urban public passenger transport undertaking) to be appointed on the recommendation of the Minister of Transport. [528]

A 1975 amendment to the Act subsequently increased the number of Council Members recommended by the Minister from three to five.

"Functions and powers of the Council-

"(1) The Council shall have and undertake such functions as are necessary for the administration of Government assistance to urban public passenger transport operators in New Zealand (other than the operators of taxicab services), and such other functions as the Minister may direct…

"(2) Without limiting the general functions specified in subsection (1) of this section, the Council shall have the following functions:
(a) To advise the Minister on any matters concerning urban public passenger transport:
(b) To determine priorities for Government assistance to the capital expenditure of urban public passenger transport operators (other than the operators of taxicab services), having regard to the extent of other assistance available, and national, regional, and other factors:
(c) To receive applications for assistance with capital expenditure from any Regional Transport Authority and from any persons or bodies which provide urban public passenger transport services (other than taxicab services), whether by road, water, or by rail, and to allocate finance by way of loans or grants in accordance with the priorities determined pursuant to paragraph (b) of this subsection:
(d) To encourage and conduct research into urban passenger transport and associated matters:
(e) To maintain such liaison with other national organisations as the Council considers beneficial:
(f) To make proposals to the Local Government Commission pursuant to the Local Government Commission Act 1967 for the preparation of local schemes relating to Regional Transport Districts and Regional Transport Authorities, including…the transfer of any urban passenger service from any public body (whether a territorial local authority or not) to any Regional Transport Authority, and any such local scheme may provide accordingly." [528]

The New Zealand Urban Public Passenger Transport Council was eventually abolished with the passage of the Urban Transport Act 1980.

Transport Advisory Council

What the Municipal Association subcommittee referred to as "…*another government-dominated statutory board…to exercise further control over local government…*" was probably what it saw as the duplication of the proposed New Zealand Urban Public Passenger Transport Council with the previously referred to Transport Advisory Council, established by the Ministry of Transport Act 1968. The latter Council continued, at least in name, until abolished by the Ministry of Transport Act Repeal Act 1990.

New Zealand Transport Policy Study

The role of the Transport Advisory Council was questioned during a Parliamentary debate that took place on 15 September 1972. The existence of yet another transport study by overseas consultants was also revealed during that debate on Ministry of Transport Appropriation Bill Estimates when Mr Isbey (Opposition Labour Party, Grey Lynn) questioned the Minister of Transport, the Hon. John Gordon, about an expenditure entry that read:

"The economics division is engaged in long-term and short-term studies into various aspects of transportation and is assisting consultants who are making a comprehensive study of New Zealand transport policy." [529]

Mr Isbey continued: "The fact that the economics division of the ministry was assisting overseas consultants linked up with the information given at page 9 of the ministry's report. Among the organisations mentioned in the report were Wilbur Smith and Associates of the United States, the New Zealand firm of Beca, Carter, Hollings, and Ferner, the academic staff of Victoria University of Wellington, the New Zealand branch of the P. E. Consulting Group, Louis T. Klauder and Associates, Consad Research

Corporation, R. L. Banks and Associates of the United States, and officers of the applied mathematics division of the Department of Scientific and Industrial Research.

"How many members of the staff of Wilbur Smith and Associates would be employed on the survey? What number of New Zealand personnel would be employed? How much had been spent to date on the services of Wilbur Smith and Associates? What was the final estimated cost? What had happened to the Transport Advisory Council appointed by the Minister 4 years ago?

"Mr Isbey said that the fact that the National Government, having appointed the council, had needed to employ overseas experts proved that the council had been a failure. Why was the Minister lunging wildly into more surveys? When would the Minister himself accept the responsibilities of his ministry and clear up the mismanagement instead of trying to get those most costly experts to do the job for him?" [529]

"Hon. J B Gordon: Perhaps the member for Grey Lynn, who thought the Wilbur Smith study was unnecessary, could state what was the wear on an ordinary motor vehicle in relation to an 8-ton axle, one of the thousand questions that required answering in order to rationalise the transport system. That was part of the information Wilbur Smith had been trying to ascertain.

"The total task force included Wilbur Smith and Associates' management team of six, who visited New Zealand from time to time; Beca Carter's two full-time personnel plus 14 New Zealanders in a support role; the universities' three part-time personnel; the DSIR's two full time; the National Roads Board's representatives part time; and the Ministry of Transport's three full time and two part time." [529]

World Bank Loan

As the Ministry of Transport Estimates debate continued, the reason for another transport study was explained:

"Sir Basil Arthur [Timaru]: Would the Minister confirm that the transport study being carried out by Wilbur Smith and Associates was at the direction of the World Bank and was tied up with loans from that bank for railways expenditure?

"The New Zealand Railway Review of 25 September 1971 had published a reprint of an article by Mr Oswin of the World Bank railways division to the effect that the function of the World Bank was not simply to provide capital but also to impose a financial discipline which forced governments to take a fresh look at their overall transport policies.

"The Minister had said that although most of the people involved in the transport study were New Zealanders, six people from the staff of Wilbur Smith and Associates would be visiting New Zealand from time to time. Were they in fact World Bank personnel charged with ensuring that the instructions of the bank as laid down in the conditions to the loan to the Railways Department were being followed? If the survey was really justified, why was it not being carried out by personnel of the Ministry of Transport and the specialist staff within the universities?" [529]

"Mr Wilkinson (Rodney) said that the Government had been criticised by the member for Grey Lynn for retaining the services of Wilbur Smith and Associates on the grounds of expense. Did the Labour Party suggest that the Government should engage any firm but the best to conduct one of the most comprehensive national transport reviews ever undertaken?"

"Hon. J. B. Gordon: The member for Timaru had cast an aspersion on the Wilbur Smith report. He had read from a railway magazine of September 1971 and claimed that the Wilbur Smith report had been demanded, or at least influenced, by the World Bank. The World Bank deal for the railway loan had been signed on 1 March 1971, 8 months before the reference he had read.

"The easiest way for the Government to cover the overseas allocation of the funds needed had been to put in for a World Bank loan, and in the proposition made by the Railways in its application it had stated that, to be the commercial viable operation that the World Bank required and to enable it to repay the interest and the principal, the department was prepared to borrow the money and take part in the Wilbur Smith study, although at that stage it had not been a rail study alone, but a total transport study.

"Sir Basil Arthur—That was part of the conditions of the loan?

"Hon. J. B. Gordon said it had been, in just the same way as there would be conditions if the member applied to his bank for a loan. Conditions set out the way it was intended to repay the loan and operate the trains. It had been stated in the application to the World Bank that a study would be made to ensure that the railways ran as a commercial viable operation so that the money borrowed could be repaid." [529]

"Mr Faulkner (Roskill) said that for some reason or other the Minister had preferred either to delay or to dodge answering some of the questions asked by Opposition members. First, there was the question of the World Bank survey. He was always suspicious of overseas experts telling New Zealanders how to run things, because normally New Zealanders knew more about their own country than experts who were brought here at great cost. The staff engaged on the study would be mostly expert New Zealanders, and the computer study of the future of transport in New Zealand would be determined by their input of expert advice. Not one Minister had yet justified a cost of $850,000 for the study and the intervention of the World Bank...

"Hon. J. B. Gordon (Minister of Transport said that the member for Roskill could not have been listening to his previous statements regarding the transport study. The Railways Department had applied to the World Bank in 1970 for a loan, which was agreed to, and a contract was signed on 1 March 1971.

"A perfectly legitimate condition...had already been included in the offer made by the Railways Department when it applied to the World Bank. As the supplicant, the Railways Department had to tell the World Bank what it proposed to do to make its operations viable. For instance, there was the vexed question of road versus rail transport, and information was needed to ascertain whether it would be cheaper to transport goods by road, railways, or coastal shipping, so that a study was required of the whole ambit of transport operations...

"Hon. J. B. Gordon said that both the member for Timaru and the member for Roskill had overlooked the fact that the transportation study by Wilbur Smith and Associates was setting a pattern. That firm had as New Zealand associates 14 members of the staff of Beca Carter Hollings and Ferner, two of whom were working full-time, two members of the Victoria University of Wellington staff, two members of the staff of the Department of Scientific and Industrial Research, working full-time, part-time assistance from National Roads Board staff, and three full-time staff members and two part-time from the Ministry of Transport. The study had originally been asked for by the National Development Council and later by the Transport Advisory Council.

"He did not think Opposition members could take any exception to the supervision by overseas consultants of such a massive transport study...It was totally incorrect for a member to state that the World Bank had dictated to New Zealand about the loan to the Railways Department. Any Applicant wanting a bank loan, whether in New Zealand or anywhere else, had to state why he wanted the money and how he would repay it, and that was exactly what the department had done in the case of the World Bank loan…The World Bank expected New Zealand to carry out a transport survey because that was part of the deal." [529]

Wilbur Smith & Associates – Transport Policy Study

That *transport study*, the Transport Policy Study undertaken by Wilbur Smith & Associates, with the assistance of others, began on 1 February 1972 and the final report was published in two large volumes on 31 October 1973.

The report introduced the Study as:

"In one of the most comprehensive reviews of its type ever to be undertaken on a nation-wide basis, the New Zealand Government authorised this Transport Policy Study be undertaken under the direction of the Ministry of Transport to provide Government with:

'…*an appropriately phased series of measures to coordinate the use and development of the various modes of transport in the country, so that resources devoted to transport are used in the most efficient manner.*'

"The scope of the Study extended to all internal long-distance transport and transport facilities of significance to the national economy, namely railways, roads and road transport, ports and coastal shipping, airports and civil aviation. Suburban passenger train services were also required to be considered, owing to their financial impact on the New Zealand Railways Department, however, urban transport matters were specifically excluded from the Study's objectives, as were policies regarding international transport. The time frame for the Study extended up to 1985.

"…this Study excludes Urban, local and short distance movements of less than 40 miles…the Study is a policy study and not a planning study. A sound set of policies governing transport decision-making is the framework within which correct investment decisions will be made. Investment decisions depend on accurate forecasts of the level of transport demand, whereas transport policies need not (and desirably should not) vary within a reasonably broad range of possible future demands.

"Accordingly, this Study does not make recommendations on specific projects, or on specific future technologies. Rather, it recommends a set of Government policies and actions which will promote responses at the enterprise level which are effective in promoting the public interest.

"Overview – The implementation of the recommendations of this report are expected to realise savings of about $38 million per annum based on present traffic volumes. These savings are principally dependent on the implementation of the recommendations concerning pricing, taxation and the restrictions on competition with rail…

"Uncertainties in Transport – Perhaps there has never been a time when transportation faced so many changing demands and as many economic uncertainties. Typical of these are the requirements related to environmental impacts, social impacts, and energy crises…

"Transport Co-ordination in New Zealand – Traditionally, in New Zealand, each mode has been treated as a separate entity and administered accordingly. Emphasis was placed on the efficient operation and development of the individual modes and problems which were not specifically within the domain of any one department were dealt with on an ad hoc basis. Royal Commissions, Commissions of Inquiry and Indepartmental Committees were constituted to deal with particular problems as they arose. This procedure had one major deficiency. It failed to promote the development of a comprehensive national transport policy and failed to co-ordinate pricing, fiscal and investment planning in recognition that the transport sector is a single entity…" [530]

ARA To-Do List

Without the guidelines that a *comprehensive national transport policy* could have provided, and pending any Government decision on the funding of the rail/bus rapid transit scheme, the Transport Division of the Auckland Regional Authority reflected on what upgrades to the City's suburban transport system were needed in 1970:

"1. A programme for the replacement of an aging bus fleet (some units are now 20 years old) must be decided upon as early as possible but until a firm date for the introduction of rapid transit is known, it is impossible to recommend to the Authority the number and type of buses that will be required.

"2. A revision of inner city bus routes is necessary, but any permanent arrangement is dependent upon the rail element.

"3. The installation of ticket machines on buses is dependent upon an inter-relationship with rail requirements.

"4. Development is going on around suburban railway stations where rail/bus interchange facilities should be provided for now.

"5. If the Government adopts recommendations from the Carter Committee to provide assistance for improved bus service, the Authority would want to act on this, but if no target date for rapid transit is available, the status quo will inevitably be preserved within the area of influence of the railway.

"6. If the Authority has to act on the basis of an all-bus system –
(a) Special bus ways to motorways now under construction should be provided.
(b) Bus depot sites must be planned at an early date.
(c) Additional off-street bus terminals will be required.
(d) Exclusive bus rights-of-way over certain roads at peak periods will be needed." [531]

Expansion to the North Shore

However, by early 1971, the Transport Division had also to consider the expansion of its services as some of the City's privately-owned bus operators continued to experience financial difficulties. It was therefore left to the ARA to consider the acquisition of those services so the buses could keep running:

"The Authority at a special meeting on 1st March 1971 agreed in principle to the acquisition of the services operated by Passenger Transport Co. Ltd, Suburban Buses Ltd, and North Shore Transport Co. Ltd [a subsidiary of Auckland Transport Holdings Limited], and appointed a special committee to continue financial negotiations and details of settlement.

"Any commitment by the Authority was first to be subject to scrutiny by the Authority solicitors. In the case of the North Shore Transport Co. Ltd the Authority also resolved that negotiations be continued to arrive at a firm price but no action was to be taken for up to six weeks to enable the North Shore local bodies to make their own investigations." [532]

North Shore Transport Company
Those investigations were undertaken by Anderson and Partners, Chartered Accountants, and an explanation of their report was subsequently passed to Sir Dove-Myer Robinson by way of a memorandum from the Auckland City Treasurer, R D Coates, on 14 April 1971:

"In the brief issued by the four North Shore local bodies, Anderson and Partners were asked to report on the cost, by way of levy to the four local bodies, of the North Shore Transport Company's service being operated by the Auckland Regional Authority:

(a) As an extension of the present A.R.A. transport district or

(b) As a separate transport district.

"In addition, the Accountants were asked to consider proposals for chartering buses, for subsidising private operators and the operation of a North Shore Transport Authority and finally to make any other suggestions for the provision of public passenger transport on the North Shore to the benefit of the area as a whole...

"...the Accountants report on the proposal to pay an incentive subsidy. They deal with this under two headings:

(a) Subsidies of Inefficiency

(b) Incentive Subsidies

"Under (a) they cover subsidies which include all re-imbursements of costs, payment towards cost increase, any type of profit guarantee, guaranteed return on capital and/or guaranteed minimum dividends.

"This is, in effect, is a cost plus scheme with all its inherent disadvantages. These are pointed out by the Accountants and they justifiably recommend against this type of subsidy. They then deal with incentives subsidies and suggest that a subsidy based on one cent per passenger carried which would cost about $54,000 per annum. This figure could be increased, of course, if as suggested by the Accountants, new routes are developed which previously would have been marginally unprofitable.

"Reference is made to the refusal of the Directors of the North Shore Transport Co. Ltd to consider any form of subsidy and it is the Accountants' opinion that this attitude of the Directors is influenced by what the Accountants consider the high price at which the sale is being negotiated. They believe that if the sale negotiations were substantially lower (and they think that the price should be substantially lower) then there is a possibility of negotiating an incentive subsidy scheme...

"A study of the report and the various alternatives leads to the view that the maximum advantage to the North Shore boroughs would be gained by the A.R.A. controlling the bus operations under a single area of benefit. The report covers another possibility of a separate transport district (ward system) with the transport operations on the North Shore being kept physically separate from the A.R.A. services.

"The annual deficiency calculated by the A.R.A. to be $245,900 would be increased by the extra costs of operating separately. These are estimated by the Accountants to be $95,000 per annum. Their report points out the obvious disadvantage of this system that the new North Shore Authority would lack the experience of the A.R.A. in the transport field...

"Ultimately, the maximum advantage would be gained by the A.R.A. being responsible for all transport operations on the North Shore and no doubt in time this will come about. It would certainly lead to rationalising the bus operations in that area, and remove the present situation where the residents are frequently required to change from one bus to another within the North Shore area..." [533]

Jurisdictional Issues

The possibility of the ARA operating the North Shore buses as a separate service from the rest of the City would have been an illogical arrangement and a contradiction to the unifying principle responsible for the Regional Authority's existence. Nevertheless, a doubt as to the legality of the ARA to charge the North Shore local bodies with a transport levy following the acquisition of the Shore bus services was raised with the ARA by the Town Clerk, Takapuna City Council, on 14 April 1971:

"re...the proposed purchase [by the ARA] of the buses and other physical assets of North Shore Transport Holdings Limited. Whilst this must necessarily be a matter to be resolved only between the Authority and the Company, my Council remains vitally interested in the outcome because of its obvious obligation, along with that of the Authority, to ensure that the best possible service is provided for its citizens, and at a reasonable cost. Recognising this obligation, my Council offers the following comments which are intended to be purely constructive in their effect.

"My Council has been advised that the Authority, whilst acting as the successor of the Auckland Transport Board, does not have power to operate public bus services on the North Shore without having first enlarged the Auckland Transport district, with the consent of the North Shore local authorities concerned, in the manner provided in Section 3 of the Auckland Transport Board Act 1928. I understand that other legal advice, given quite independently of my Council, is to precisely the same effect. If these opinions are correct, then it follows that the Authority cannot arbitrarily impose levies outside the present Transport District in respect of services run wholly or partly within that District...

"You will appreciate that it would be my Council's duty to oppose any levy upon its ratepayers if it considered that the Authority had acted in excess of its jurisdiction to impose it. If the Authority does not take cognisance of the above matters, then my Council will have no option but to make application to the Supreme Court for a Declaratory Judgment in order to settle the legal position." [534]

Auckland Transport District

The Section 3 of the Auckland Transport Board Act 1928 referred to by the Town Clerk, in particular, Section 3(1), named the suburbs included as the Auckland Transport District which was subsequently overseen by the ARA when it took over the Transport Board's responsibilities in 1964.

Although that Transport District did not then include the suburbs of the North Shore, Section 3 (2) of the Transport Board Act did provide for the alteration of the Transport District's boundaries "...with the approval of the Minister and of the local authority of the area concerned...by including therein any local district or part thereof not now included therein, or by excluding therefrom any local district or part thereof now included therein;" [23]

A Legal Opinion

No doubt, it was that latter provision to which the Minister of Transport, Peter Gordon, referred in his letter to the ARA of 18 March 1971:

"Further to discussions between the Auckland Regional Authority, North Shore Local bodies, local Members of Parliament, and myself on the possible re-organisation of North

Shore passenger transport, Government has now obtained a legal opinion. Its three principal points have been summarised...

"1) Under the Auckland Regional Authority Act 1963, it appears that the Auckland Regional Authority does have power to assume control of passenger services in the region comprising the City of Takapuna and the Boroughs of Helensville, East Coast Bays, Birkenhead, Northcote and Devonport. This power covers both existing and new services in these districts.

"2) The Auckland Regional Authority has the power to impose a transport levy on the local authorities in the areas mentioned above.

3) Both the Auckland Regional Authority and the North Shore local authorities have the power to acquire and hold shares in a private transport company." [535]

Transport Services Levies

But, as well as the issue of what suburbs could be included in the ARA's Transport District, the method of calculating the levy due to the ARA for the provision of transport services and, of course, for the losses incurred, had been subject to debate since the early days of the Transport Board – as described by John Allsopp-Smith, a former Transport Board member and Chairman of the ARA's Passenger Transport Committee:

"This obligation to pay a full levy to the Board, irrespective of the level of service received from the Board, was a very contentious issue amongst the local authorities receiving limited or no service. I recall that representations were from time to time made by some of these local authorities, seeking their exclusion from the Auckland Transport District...

"I recall representations being made to have the basis of levying for passenger transport losses altered. Some local authorities favoured an 'area of benefit basis'. Some also favoured population, as the apportionment factor while others favoured rateable capital value...

"The A.R.A. Act formula required the Authority's levies to be calculated upon the basis of the mean of rateable capital value and population of the respective local districts or parts thereof which were benefited by the services. This relieved the areas, like Mt Wellington, which receive no service from any obligation to pay a levy for transport purposes...This new basis of levying was to continue in force only for the Authority's first few years, until the direct rating system then provided for in the A.R.A. Act could come into force in 1967...

"That proposal was included in an Amendment Bill in 1964 and was rejected by Parliament...Once the amendment had been rejected, the Authority proceeded on the basis of the A.R.A. Act [area of benefit] formula...This involved consultation with the local authorities and a basis was determined on which levies were paid from then on.

"From time to time in the years since then, the principles decided upon for determining the area of benefit have been modified to take account of changing conditions. So far as I am aware, there has always been consultation with the local bodies...and, down to 1971, this was never challenged by any local authority." [536]

Bus Company Acquisitions

"In 1971, something of a crisis arose in the passenger transport industry in Greater Auckland. The Passenger Transport Company Limited and Suburban Buses Limited, running independent services in parts of Central and South Auckland, and North Shore Buses Limited, running services to the North Shore, all private companies, found themselves facing increasing financial difficulties. The companies were offered to the Authority, which agreed to acquire the shares in the companies and, through the company structure, to continue their services itself. While the Passenger Transport Company Limited and Suburban Buses Limited operated services substantially within the Auckland transport district, North Shore Buses Limited ran in areas outside that district, on Auckland's North Shore.

"In 1971, the Authority's levy was struck in the usual manner and challenged by appeal under Section 62 of the A.R.A. Act and by declaratory proceedings in the High Court. These challenges were made by Takapuna City Council, Northcote Borough Council and the then Waitemata County Council and others. The proceedings were successful in that parts of the transport levy for that year were declared invalid. By agreement between the local authorities involved, validated by special legislation, (the Auckland Regional Authority Empowering Act 1972), the resulting difficulties were resolved…" [536]

Levy Refunds

That resolution resulted in refunds to a number of contributing authorities including $18,269 to the Takapuna City Council, $11,713 to the East Coast Bays Borough Council, and $828 to the Northcote Borough Council.

"Part of the agreement was that the local authorities concerned would all have their districts included in the Auckland transport district and that was duly done. In most cases, the whole territorial district was included. This gave the Authority some flexibility to extend the area of benefit as its services were extended, without having to enlarge the Auckland transport district on each occasion…" [536]

Extension to West Auckland

"Then, in late 1973, a similar situation arose with the Auckland Bus Company Limited providing services to parts of West Auckland, some of which were outside the Auckland transport district. The Company gave notice of its intention to cease providing transport services and offered its assets and transport licences to the Authority.

"On 5 December 1973, the Authority convened a meeting of representatives of the Western area local authorities affected by the Auckland Bus Company Limited services…The purpose of that meeting was to explain to the Western area representatives the offer, which had been made to the Authority by the Auckland Bus Company Limited, and its implications.

"…I [John Allsopp-Smith] explained how the company's services would be integrated into the Authority's public passenger transport system if taken over by the Authority. I made clear the following points: –

"(a) The areas outside the Auckland transport district and served by the company's services would have to be included in the Auckland transport district;

"(b) The Authority would then extend its passenger transport area of benefit to include the areas served by those services, using the then currently accepted principles for determining the areas of benefit;

"(c) The Authority's passenger transport levies would then be calculated on the formula in the A.R.A. Act to which I have referred and in respect of the whole of the extended area of benefit.

"In the ensuing months, all the local authorities concerned did agree to this. Henderson Borough Council gave unqualified consent. Some of the others imposed conditions, similar to those applied by some of the local authorities in 1971 and 1972, to the effect that the levies should be on the area of benefit basis.

"In March 1974, the Auckland Transport District was enlarged accordingly...The Authority then acquired the company's services and extended the area of benefit...

"In its first levy over the extended area of benefit, the Authority included a substantial deficit carried forward from the previous two or three years when attempts had been made to keep the levies fairly consistent by accumulating deficits and carrying them forward.

"Glen Eden Borough Council appealed against this aspect of the levy and was supported by Henderson Borough Council. In the event, the appeal was determined in favour of Glen Eden Borough and the deficit was re-allocated to the local authorities comprising the area of benefit before it was extended in 1974.

"From then until I retired from local authority affairs in 1977, I remained Chairman of the Authority's Passenger Transport Committee. In each year, the passenger transport levy was made on the basis I have outlined and paid by each local authority without challenge." [536]

Unprofitable Bus Services

While the term, *area of benefit*, might well have defined the parameters of the bus services provided, it certainly did not describe the profit to be made from such services – as reported by The New Zealand Herald on 5 June 1975:

"The Auckland Regional Authority has taken a long, hard look at its bus running methods and has found where it is losing the most money. The authority, which had to subsidise bus losses to the tune of $3.8 million by a levy on ratepayers in 1974-75, has found it takes 32.7 per cent of this subsidy – $1.2 million – to keep its fleet rolling in Auckland city.

"A cost study by the ARA transport controller, Mr J V Brown, which was received by the transport committee yesterday, found that Auckland city services were losing $2734 a day. And after questioning by the Mayor of Auckland, Sir Dove-Myer Robinson, Mr Brown said it cost the authority between 9c and 10c a passenger mile to run its fleet. Average trip length was 3 1/2 miles and average cost a passenger 27.75c. The cost of running a bus for a mile was 92c...The study put labour costs as a big part of prime operating costs for buses – 19.9c per bus kilometre, with running costs only 5c.

"Sir Dove-Myer said people did not realise what a 'terrific percentage' of costs went in wages and he launched a verbal blast at uninformed critics of the bus service. 'We are constantly under attack for running a rotten bus service,' he said. 'I don't agree. We have no magic wand to wave to transform what people consider is a bad service overnight. You would think we were damned obstinate if you listened to them. You would think we didn't want to give good service. But this can only come through trial and error over a long period. We are doing our best under adverse circumstances.'

"The committee chairman, Mr J Allsopp-Smith, said the ARA had to get through to the Government that regional transport in all major cities in New Zealand was necessarily the charge of central government. 'If we had the 250 buses we want from Hungary we could do something about bus services and unless we get Government capital assistance as in all other Commonwealth countries – New Zealand is the only exception – we can't get the buses to provide the service,' he said. (Mr Allsopp-Smith and Mr Brown will go to Hungary on a bus-buying mission later this month, returning on July 8.)" [537]

The Apcon Plan

In the meantime, there was Apcon, a group of Auckland consultants of various occupations who suggested 'an alternative rapid transport system for Auckland':

"Introduction - This dynamic transport system, which aims to serve all sections of the population at all times, and give unlimited flexibility and adaptability, is based on the principle of short-route high-frequency shuttle bus services. The system, which can be implemented on the busiest sectors of our city almost immediately, utilizes present rolling stock without any need for expansion in the short term.

"It will offer present car commuters benefits which will make it not only more economical but also more convenient to use the shuttle services rather than take the car into the city. Two of the more obvious benefits are the saving of 10 to 20 miles/day mileage, all day parking at extremely low rates of, say, 20 to 30 cents/day. The stage by stage approach of implementation allows development to be effected out of revenue in many instances...

"Express System - The ultimate system would comprise about 5 nodes or terminals connected by express or shuttle bus to the city and cross linked. Each terminal draws its passengers from outer carpark facilities designed to absorb the majority of car users, who would normally attempt to park in the city all day. The ordinary suburban buses would range into these terminals at high frequency. In the city, loop line bus services would drop passengers essentially just off Queen Street and the inner city.

"Capital Cost - Construction of suitable terminals would be very simple and compared to an underground rail, extremely cheap...

"Battery Electric - Clearly the opportunity exists to use battery-electric buses...In one stroke, a large percentage of petrol and diesel fumes is removed from the high density centre area of Auckland. Another significant fuel saving is introduced...

"Parking tolls can be placed on all roads leading into the inner city, and cars driving into the city will collect a time-stamped ticket, which they have to present when leaving the inner city and pay parking fees according to the time spent there. This will obviate the need for parking meters...Eventually the system may become so efficient and convenient that the only vehicle traffic in the inner city will be service vehicles and non-pollution buses." [538]

Crackpot Scheme

The Apcon plan may well have been a concept ahead of its time but it was not likely to find much favour with the proponents of the bus/rail rapid transit scheme as they awaited a decision from the Government – as reported by The New Zealand Herald on 24 September 1975:

"It [the Apcon plan] has not won favour with the Mayor of Auckland, Sir Dove-Myer Robinson. 'It's a crackpot scheme,' he said yesterday...Sir Dove-Myer said...that an acknowledgment by the authors that the report was somewhat shallow was the understatement of the year." [539]

Institute of Economic Research Study

However, a not-so-shallow report was soon to inflict more damage to the suburban bus/rail ambitions of Dove-Myer Robinson and fellow supporters – as reported by The Auckland Star on 9 September 1975:

"An all-bus system for Auckland rather than a rapid rail-bus scheme appears to have everything going for it, according to an Institute of Economic Research study. The author, economist Mr T K McDonald, has taken figures published by the Auckland Rapid Transit directorate in its latest massive study. He has also used findings of the latest Auckland Regional Authority surveys of travel patterns.

"The new information 'significantly increases the cost margin in favour of buses,' he says. Bus costs are shown to be lower even if one takes the directorate's patronage estimates which most favour the rapid rail scheme. 'Under 'average' conditions, bus travel costs are only 30% to 40% of rapid rail travel costs.' He has predicted that a rapid transit scheme will lose $19 million a year – 'heavy losses for the limited results envisaged from it.'

"The new data on which his study is based, he says, bears out his former estimates that only 5 million passengers would be carried annually by the rail-bus system. (The ART directorate estimated 21 million.) But, by the directorate's own admission, that figure was an 'arbitrary subjective judgment,' he argues. It assumed that a passenger bound for the central business district would change from car to bus to rail or various combinations up to five times in the course of one trip. But for a public transport user to make more than two changes 'is unrealistic in New Zealand.'

"It is the order of magnitude of this range between bus and rail costs that suggest a rapid rail system might not be the best solution in Auckland. The first comparison shows bus costs at 40% of bus-rail costs. In the second comparison bus costs shrink to 27%.

"The economist emphasizes that he has used the directorate's own figures, including the most recent cost estimates. 'I have also carried out a full, discounted cash flow appraisal exactly as the scheme is specified in the ART directorate report. My results are not definitive or as comprehensive as might be liked. Nor are they as detailed or as soundly based in some aspects as might be wished.'

"Nevertheless, he says, the study is the only one of its kind so far produced on Auckland's rapid transit scheme. Its findings 'should raise sufficient doubts about the ARA scheme for an appraisal of alternatives without a rapid rail component to be undertaken…'

"In this study, Mr McDonald again calls for a detailed comparison before any new commitments to rapid transit are made. 'There are good grounds for considering that an all-bus public transport system for Auckland would be preferable,' he says. 'Both should be fairly appraised before a decision is made.'" [540]

Wellington-based Conspiracy?

As usual, Dove-Myer Robinson's response was immediate:

"Auckland's Mayor, Sir Dove-Myer Robinson, today attacked 'a Wellington-based conspiracy to deprive the city of a modern transport system.' He was commenting on yesterday's Auckland Star report by Institute of Economic Research economist Mr T K McDonald. The report came down heavily on the side of an all-bus system rather than the proposed rapid-rail-bus system.

"The Mayor ('I'm in a boom-lowering mood') said that as the institute was a semi-Government body, he wanted to ask the Government these pointed questions.

1. Who asked Mr McDonald to produce this report?

2. What is the connexion between the Secretary of Transport, Mr R J Polaschek, and Mr McDonald?

3. Did the Secretary of Transport engage Mr McDonald to prepare the report on the rapid-rail system?

4. Why was the report released at the same time as negotiations between the Auckland Regional Authority and the Government were taking place – a timing that could be 'most embarrassing'?

5. What was the factual basis and accuracy of the figures in the report?

"Sir Dove-Myer said: 'I believe that this is a Wellington-based conspiracy to deprive Auckland of a modern transport system. If it succeeds, this will condemn Auckland to depend on an all-bus system that cannot be much improved without a utilization of rail facilities. The final result would be a colossal set-back to the orderly planning and development of Auckland.' And project manager at the Auckland Rapid Transit office, Mr I A Mead, said: 'Mr McDonald is wrong. Using the ART Directorate estimates…the economic cost of rail travel is shown to be less than bus…Growth and expansion of the ART system will increase utilization of capital facilities and decrease rail costs considerably.'" [541]

Conspiracy Charge Rebutted

"The accusation by the Mayor of Auckland, Sir Dove-Myer Robinson, that there was a 'Wellington-based conspiracy' to deprive Auckland of its proposed rapid-rail transport scheme was totally unfounded, the deputy secretary of the Ministry of Transport, Mr A J Edwards, said yesterday.

"'Mr McDonald of the Institute of Economic Research prepared an independent report on this matter which was certainly not requested by the Government, the secretary for transport (Mr R J Polaschek) nor the Urban Public Passenger Transport Council, said Mr Edwards. The suggestion of some connection between the secretary of transport and Mr McDonald over this matter is totally without foundation,' he added.

"The only supposed 'connection' between Mr McDonald and Mr Polaschek was in relation to a research project on 'Urban Transport and Land Use' in New Zealand carried out for the Urban Public Passenger Transport Council (of which Mr Polaschek is chairman) by the Institute of Economic Research in 1972, said Mr Edwards." [542]

Suspicions Remain

In a draft article sent to The New Zealand Herald on 12 September 1975, Dove-Myer Robinson elaborated on his conspiracy suspicions:

"I can't accept the assurance by the Deputy Secretary of the Ministry of Transport, Mr A J Edwards, that neither the Ministry nor its Secretary, Mr R J Polaschek, were unaware of T W (sic) McDonald's report until two days ago. Mr Polaschek is Chairman of the Urban Passenger Transport Council which commissioned the 360 page McDonald report: it has been on sale for months. I was informed over 3 months ago by a very high government official that Mr Polaschek had engaged Mr McDonald to report adversely on the Auckland plan and thereby deprive Auckland of a very modernised version of the bus-rail system which Wellington has had since about 1927 and which carried over 14 million passengers in 1974.

"I am prepared to disclose the name of my informant and the circumstances to the police on two conditions (a) that the name of the government informant is kept strictly confidential and (b) an assurance by the Government that all the circumstances of this report, such as who ordered it, when and for what purpose, will be investigated and made public.

"In the meantime, I repeat that all the circumstances point to it being a Wellington based conspiracy to deprive Auckland of a badly needed modern transport system." [543]

Looking to the Future

Looking to the future and recalling past mistakes, The New Zealand Herald summed up the case for the bus/rail plan with its editorial of 15 September 1975:

"Have those who advocate an all-bus system to cope with the passenger transport needs of present and future Aucklanders given sufficient thought to the dramatic rate of population growth in the region? Have they paused to consider that their case may be based on the same sort of cost accountancy and parochialism that led to the Holland Government's grave error of judgment in pruning the original plans of the harbour bridge?

"While guesstimates are used to compare the rapid-rail scheme unfavourably with the use of buses, the population of the region increases by more than 100,000 in four years. Such a dramatic rate of growth strengthens the railway concept; it could mean that twice as many people will live within Auckland's narrow confines in about 20 years' time.

"Traffic congestion can be expected to increase in something like the same proportion. Just as the bridge authority was compelled, within a short time, to resort to clip-on extensions to overcome the short-sightedness of transport experts and politicians, so the bus advocates, if allowed their way, will eventually be obliged to demand additional road works.

"For, if an ever-expanding fleet of buses is to provide fast and efficient services, such conveyances will need their own rights of way to avoid being marooned in traffic jams. How much more rateable land can this beautiful city afford to sacrifice, especially on the crowded isthmus, to road construction?

"A rapid-rail system as the main artery of the future transport network represents the only real hope of escaping future motorway and street congestion and, by encouraging higher-density living along its accesses, of countering urban sprawl. Future growth will necessarily need to adapt itself to the transport system, not the other way round. Nor should it be overlooked that railway routes are, to a large extent, already available without the need to disturb private land. Compared with urban roads, the permanent ways are at present grossly under-used. Would Aucklanders tolerate further acquisitions of land and improvements to enable the face of the city to be disfigured with express busways?

"If account is taken of the massive cost of building, maintaining and lighting urban roads, to say nothing of the loss of land and the accident toll, the proposed outlay on the rapid-rail system is seen in proper perspective.

"Arguments that the railways will mainly benefit Queen St, or Manukau City or some other sector are parochialism at its worst. The scheme can only be undertaken in stages and should eventually become a lifeline for the whole metropolitan area. Auckland, it should not be forgotten, is laying plans for passenger transport to meet the needs not just of the present but of future generations, for whom private motoring may become impossible. It could be disastrous if, at this stage, narrow economic considerations and petty parochialism encouraged the Government and the Regional Authority to back-track on their commitments." [544]

Cost of Urban Roads

Not only was the cost of urban road construction and maintenance an issue but also who would be liable for that cost. This was discussed by Dove-Myer Robinson in his article published by the Auckland Star on 7 October 1975:

"There is one important aspect which appears to have been overlooked by the all-bus advocates – the losses of an all-bus system together with otherwise unnecessary additional roading would have to be paid entirely by the ratepayers of Auckland, without any Government assistance whatsoever…The National Roads Board subsidy on regional roads is 3:1, which means that the ratepayers pay one quarter of the cost of regional roads through their local body levies to the Regional Authority. Money spent on local body roads is subsidised by the N.R.B. at the rate of 3:4 – which means, the ratepayers pay four sevenths of the cost of upgrading existing, and providing additional, roading.

"In 1974, $26,812,000 was spent on roading in the Auckland region; of this $21,141,000 was paid by the N.R.B., and $5,671,000 by Auckland local authorities. This means that an undefined but sizeable part of the cost of providing roading used by buses must be added to the losses on buses operated by the A.R.A. (about $6 million), so that the actual cost to the ratepayers is much more than the rates directly paid to make up the deficit on bus operations. Probably a total of $8-$10 million…About two thirds of all money spent on roading is for maintenance only.

"If all traffic is to be carried by roads, by 1981-2 the annual cost of providing additional roads and maintaining existing roads, could well exceed the $5.6 million spent by local authorities in 1974. This must be added to the estimated loss on buses of $6.4 million, which would mean that ratepayers would have to meet a bill of about $12 million annually, directly and indirectly attributable to an all bus system with none of the benefits and savings which could be anticipated from a combined bus and rail service.

"Not only would rates increase at a very much greater pace than otherwise, but Auckland would be stuck for the foreseeable future with an all bus system that has already proved quite inadequate for the requirements of this growing city. Only when it is possible to orient the re-organised bus services around, and spreading out from, the 14 stations on the railway that will serve them, will it be possible to provide the improved public transport service Auckland needs." [545]

The Energy Crisis

The use of roads by fuel-burning vehicles of all types was also a cost that could not be afforded by a country suffering from the rapid rise of imported fuel prices. But, it was hardly an expense that could be reduced by motor vehicle-dependent commuters with few viable, public transport alternatives – as described by The New Zealand Herald on 10 October 1975:

"The energy crisis has brought a new dimension to the case for improving public transport and persuading people to use it. The Minister of Energy Resources, Mr Freer, has presented the Cabinet with 32 proposals for reducing the total use of oil and says that the main emphasis will be on expediting a change from oil to other fuels and on encouraging the use of public transport.

"In the midst of this situation, the Auckland Regional Authority proposes to introduce a new system of zonal bus fares which will reduce prices for some travellers but may make journeys dearer for many more. The move looks like being a calculated gamble. Whether it will attract people away from their cars, or whether it will cause a decline in bus travel, is anyone's guess. Regarded logically, travel by bus is still probably cheaper for most people than travel by car; but tremendous numbers of people seem willing to pay a stiff premium for the convenience, real or imagined, of driving to work and elsewhere.

"Perhaps, when the authority is levying $6.4 million to cover the cost of passenger transport, anything with half a chance of offering either relief to ratepayers or advantages to travellers is worth trying. If the system increases the deficit or proves markedly unpopular, it can be revised or abandoned…" [546]

Zonal Fares

Indeed, the ARA's new system of zonal bus fares and 'honesty box' payment system was announced in November 1975:

"The ARA…has just announced that the 18 fare sections of its bus system will be rationalised to four zones as from January 25th next. A fare of 25 cents will be payable for each zone travelled, with passengers putting their money into an honesty box. No change will be given. Concession tickets will provide a much reduced cost of travel – in many cases, passengers buying concession cards will pay less to ride than they do at present…

"Transit believes that this will be the first time that a zonal fare system, accompanied by an honesty box collection of cash fares with the driver handling no money at all, has been selected for use in New Zealand or Australia, although it is the norm in Europe and North America. Other transport operators will be watching the outcome with interest…The inner city shuttle trolley bus route, from the Railway Station to Karangahape Road, will be free, and transfers from one route to another within a specified time limit will be permitted." [547]

Trolleybuses

It was a wonder that trolleybuses were still operating along some city routes by 1975 as a phasing out of the service had been planned some three years earlier – as outlined in a December 1972 letter to Auckland's Mayor, Sir Dove-Myer Robinson from the Business Manager of the ARA's Passenger Transport Department, L J Fry:

"Because most of Auckland's trolleybus fleet of 126 vehicles are over 20 years old and production of this model ceased several years ago spare parts are almost unprocurable and must be specially made at extremely high cost. Most of the vehicles have now travelled in excess of half a million miles each and consequently breakdowns occur much more frequently. The Authority faced with these facts, had to consider the future of trolleybus operation in Auckland. The following factors were taken into account in arriving at the eventual decision to phase trolleybuses out:

"1. <u>Cost of replacement trolleybuses</u> – Most of the world's cities who have used trolleybuses have taken the decision to phase them out. Accordingly they are manufactured in very limited numbers and in limited countries. The Authority's investigations reveal that replacement trolleybuses would cost in excess of $100,000 per vehicle. New diesel buses cost $40,000 apiece.

"2. <u>Overhead equipment and underground cables</u> – The present wiring system has had over 20 years wear and tear. The underground cables being used were original tram cables and many of these exceed 50 years of age. Most of the poles supporting the wiring were also original tramway system poles and are of similar age. For a new system much of this would have needed a complete replacement at extremely high capital cost and would perpetrate the unsightly wiring complex of the city's environment.

"3. <u>Operating costs of trolleybuses against diesel buses</u> – Experience over the life of the present fleet has disclosed that the present day costs of operating trolleybuses exceed the comparable cost of diesel buses. It is becoming increasingly difficult for the Authority to recruit, train, and retain the technical staff necessary to maintain the overhead lines as this work is becoming more difficult and dangerous in the heavily traffic congested streets.

"4. <u>Inflexibility of trolleybus operation</u> – Auckland is a rapidly expanding city. Modern traffic demands a vehicle which is highly manoeuvrable and versatile, which can be easily diverted when necessary and is unaffected by the problems of overhead wiring. The trolleybus does not meet these criteria.

"5. <u>Atmospheric pollution</u> – Trolleybuses up to date have had a considerable advantage over diesel buses insofar as they are pollution free. However, overseas diesel bus manufacturers are required to meet extremely rigid requirements to ensure that the modern diesel vehicle is as pollution free as possible. Auckland's new Mercedes-Benz buses exceed the requirement of the world standards in this respect and their other many advantages over the trolleybuses made the diesel bus the only logical choice for Auckland at this time." [548]

Is There a Future?

Not surprisingly, by November 1975, the trolleybus was following the tram – as reported by Transit Magazine which asked, "Is There a Future?"

"Despite the many pro-trolley bus opinions voiced in Auckland at the height of the oil crisis in late 1973, the future of electric street transport in the city now hangs by very insecure threads, with the recent announcement by the Auckland Regional Authority Transport Committee that two more trolley routes, to Point Chevalier and Avondale, are to give way to diesel buses. In May 1973, when events looked like they were moving to produce a major oil shortage in New Zealand, the Chairman of the Transport Committee, Mr John Allsopp-Smith, stated that trolley buses would continue to run in Auckland almost indefinitely – this against all previous ARA statements that the system was to be replaced with the new Mercedes Benz diesels, of which today nearly 100 are in service.

"Mr Allsopp-Smith told the news-media that trolley buses used no oil, caused no pollution and were extremely light on electricity. 'The Transport Committee will be giving early consideration to the possibility of making greater use of trolley buses in order to save fuel,' he said. 'But I think it should be emphasised that trolley buses will be part of the city scene for a very long time to come, regardless of the oil situation. I would still expect them to be running through the central city long after I have gone – and I intend to be around for at least 25 years longer.'

"The announcement, then, that another two trolley bus routes were to be abandoned has come as somewhat [of] a blow in light of the previous praise given the vehicles by the Chairman. The official reason for closing the routes is cited as being the need to scrap 25 of the oldest trolley buses, and to relieve the pressure on the electricity substations and feeder system, some components of which date back to the turn of the century and were used originally to supply the tramway system, which the trolleys displaced between 1949 and 1956.

"Transit was told by a member of the ARA Transport Department that no attempt has been made to procure new trolley buses or equipment. It is understood that the Authority has not even considered buying new trolleys, and all the present arguments at Committee meetings revolve around whether to purchase more Mercedes buses or Leyland Nationals.

"An Authority spokesman, who wished to remain anonymous, told Transit that it was impossible to obtain spare parts for the buses and overhead at reasonable cost, and that staff could not be hired that were prepared to work on the overhead wires in busy streets. 'The trolley bus is finished.' He said bluntly. The cost of upgrading and overhauling the electrical distribution system would be prohibitive, and in any case, the Department did not want a vehicle that was tied to overhead wires. The spokesman said that the ARA was not prepared to spend valuable overseas funds to upgrade a system that had had its day.

"Transit did not put forward the leading question that the purchase of diesel buses also involves spending overseas funds, and that fuel oil is purchased entirely outside New Zealand. The Authority also stated that new trolley buses could not be bought at reasonable cost, because they would have to be converted to running on the left hand side of the road. It is worth noting that if this is the case, why is Auckland getting German buses that also have to be altered to run on the left?

"Trolley bus motors and equipment have an indefinite lifespan, and as coach bodies are already manufactured in New Zealand, it seems reasonable to surmise that the chassis of the existing fleet could be overhauled and installed in a new, modern body, as has been done with great success by the Toronto Transit Commission – at a cost well below buying either new diesel or trolley buses.

"This course of action would mean that the spending of overseas reserves would be kept to a minimum, and because most of New Zealand's electricity needs are generated from hydro stations, continued operation of trolley buses would place no strain on the balance of payments. However, Transit understands that the ARA has not considered such action, and is unlikely to in the short or long term...

"Many trolley buses in the Auckland fleet, especially the old, BUT vehicles built from 1949 onwards, are in a sorry state, with battered panels sporting several shades of shabby green paint, seats slashed by vandals and dirty interiors, whining differentials and noisy compressors. However, large numbers of the Leyland trolleys, numbered from 60-133, have received the new yellow livery and show some evidence of panel repairs. All of the Queen Street shuttle buses have been so treated and the change in appearance is quite remarkable.

"When asked by Transit if the trolley bus had a future in Auckland, Mr Allsopp-Smith said that in the short term; the next decade perhaps, the answer was 'yes'. 'But in the long term – no. First of all, let me say that the cost of a trolley is immaterial. It is the cost of feeder lines, converter stations and underground cabling that weighs against the trolley. It is far cheaper to burn diesel in a diesel bus than in a power station from where it is transferred to the trolley bus lines. In this way, I say that the trolley bus is a hopelessly uneconomic user of fuel.'

"When asked to comment on the fact that the Government was insisting that the use of oil-fired power stations be kept to a minimum, and the ultimate aim was to phase them out completely, Mr Allsopp-Smith said that only when every oil fired power station was gone, would he agree that power costs of a trolley bus would be more economic.

"This constitutes somewhat an about face on the part of Mr Allsopp-Smith, because as recently as May 25, he was reported in the Wellington 'Sunday Times' as saying that it was worth keeping trolley buses on the road. 'You could call it a suspended sentence. We are not taking back all the things we said about them – they are still condemned but for the moment have become a viable proposition again.'

"One Aucklander who is emphatic that the trolleys should be retained is Mr J W F Welch, who in his time as Engineer for the Auckland Regional Authority and its predecessor, the Auckland Transport Board, was responsible for much of the installation of the network.

"According to Mr Welch, an independent report should be prepared to determine the real economics of trolley bus operation. He is certain that this could only favour the electric vehicle. 'Some people might say that I've been out of the business for a long time, since my retirement. But I've kept in touch with things. There would always be a way to keep trolleys on the road if the administration wanted to. I would be very sad if they were all taken off.'

"Transit supports the idea of an independent engineer making a cost-benefit study of trolley bus operation. In a hilly city such as Auckland, the high tractive effort of trolley bus motors is ideally suited to its transport needs. The travelling public needs an assurance that a cheap, pollution-free transport vehicle will not be discarded without any real effort being made to find out the facts in their fullest perspective." [549]

(The last trolleybus service "…to operate in Auckland [a Queen Street to Karangahape Road shuttle service] closed on 28 September 1980." [144]

Marginal Recognition

When considering the increasingly unaffordable cost of motor fuel, even the most ardent supporter of road-based transport had a tough time downplaying the role played by the saintly motor vehicle and could only extend 'marginal' recognition of the part that public transport could play to alleviate the situation – as reported by The Auckland Star and The New Zealand Herald on 15 and 16 October 1975, respectively:

"Director of Roading Mr F A Langbein…just back from a tour of England, Austria, Switzerland, Sweden, France, Germany, Belgium, the United States and Canada said: 'The emphasis is on improved management techniques and on making best possible use of what already exists.' He was speaking to a meeting of the National Roads Board…

"Referring to the road-motor vehicle system, Mr Langbein said: 'Everything points to the fact that motorized, rubber-tyred vehicles travelling on roads are best able to provide the required level of mobility to meet the needs of society at the present time and for many years to come.'

"The car was essential for many journeys that could not be undertaken in any other way. But there was recognition that it was undesirable and unrealistic to try to cater for unrestricted use of the private car in the larger cities at all times. There was a recognized need to make conditions marginally more attractive for public transport and less attractive for the private car." [550]

"The director of roading, Mr F A Langbein, yesterday advocated more active involvement of the National Roads Board in public transport. In a report to board members, he said the board was vulnerable to criticism as long as it confined its attention to the construction and maintenance of roads. Nowhere was this more apparent than in the case of urban motorways. 'There could well be advantage in the board's becoming more deeply involved with public transport with a view to promoting the reorganisation of local government on a regional basis and to making more efficient use of roads and road space,' he said. 'Consideration could well be given to expanding the scope of works eligible for subsidy from the board.'

"Commenting on a recent overseas trip, Mr Langbein said the emphasis overseas was on increasing the use of public transport and decreasing the use of private cars, often by parking restraints." [551]

A Mixed Message

Nevertheless, Mr Langbein's report contained observations detrimental to the rapid rail system proposed as a public transport solution for Auckland:

"There has been a very marked swing away from building underground rapid rail systems in Europe and North America because of the huge costs involved...Symptomatic of the current emphasis there on low cost solutions to transport problems was the so-called light rail transit, Mr Langbein said. This was, in effect, the re-birth of the tramcar with its own right of way...

"In Auckland today the Mayor, Sir Dove-Myer Robinson, reacted: 'What else can you expect from a roads man?' He said: 'Over 80 cities in the world are building rapid rail systems or extending existing ones...The light rail transit cited by Mr Langbein as a solution to rising costs was exactly what Auckland was getting. It will be light rail serving a reorganized bus service, giving the buses much wider distribution and destination points,' he said." [550]

General Election Looms

By the end of October 1975, the General Election loomed and the Labour Government had still not committed itself to funding the capital cost of its July 1973 proposals to upgrade the existing suburban rail services in South Auckland by extending the line to Papakura and underground into downtown Auckland City. In a statement provided to The Auckland Star, Dove-Myer Robinson speculated as to the outcome:

"The excuse that has been advanced by the Government for not committing itself at this time is obviously designed so as not to risk offending voters in any part of the country, on the eve of a general election. It is obviously the fore-runner to the alternative repudiation of the Government's solemn last election promises to provide Auckland with a satisfactory public transport service.

"A few weeks ago, I publicly charged that there is a Wellington-based conspiracy for this end and my charge has not been answered or repudiated. I am satisfied that the timing of the recent overseas visit and negative report of the Director of Roading was 'rigged' in order to give the Government an excuse for again postponing a decision until after the election.

"The obviously inevitable intention to ultimately reject the rapid transit plan will delight Auckland's enemies in other parts of the country and the local quislings within Auckland itself. When this happens it will be the greatest blow to the orderly, controlled development of Auckland it has ever suffered. The annual cost to Auckland ratepayers will constitute the largest single burden they will have to bear, and the continued inconvenience of an unsatisfactory transport system will bring up the annual losses on transport to as much as nineteen million dollars a year.

"Though the Government may hope that this is the beginning of the end of Auckland's transit scheme, as far as I am concerned, it is only the beginning of the fight to get for Auckland the kind of transport system it needs, and must have for its economic survival." [552]

Statements of Intent

Dove-Myer Robinson left on his own trip of inquiry to the United States on 30 October 1975 but not before seeking statements of intent regarding their Auckland transport policies from the Prime Minister, Bill Rowling, and the leader of the Opposition,

Robert Muldoon. The main points of his letters and additional comments were published by The Auckland Star:
"Assuming you are the Government after next month…will you agree that:
- As the Government has a monopoly of railway services in New Zealand, it has a duty to provide long distance and suburban services wherever a need is demonstrated.
- As the Railways Act confers a monopoly on the Railways Department, the department must accept responsibility for all capital and operating costs of any service wherever provided.
- The minimal suburban railway service as recommended by the Auckland rapid transit directorate is essential for the orderly control and the effective economic life of greater Auckland.
- The Railways Department be responsible for meeting all capital and operating costs of the railway part of the Auckland scheme provided Auckland accepts all costs of the bus part of the plan.
- Because of the urgency of a final decision and the mounting costs of inflation a start on actual work be made in 1976 at the latest.

"'National put a decision off before the last election, now Labour has learnt the same tricks,' said Sir Dove-Myer. 'By the time I get back on November 16 I expect to have the answers to these questions.' In spite of the Government's refusal this week to share the operating costs of the scheme and yet another postponement of the final decision, Sir Dove-Myer still plans to collect films, pictures, brochures and tapes on rapid rail during his two weeks in the US… 'I will have a factual evidence, not just my own theories,' he said.

"The mayor said indecision on rapid rail was holding up city planning. 'An Auckland Regional Authority deputation told the Government six years ago, in August, 1969, that the rapid transit delay was having disastrous effects on planning,' he said. 'Now the Auckland City Council has to promote a local Bill to allow it to defer the statutory revision of its district scheme by 12 months. The main reason holding up the review,' he said, 'is the uncertainty of transport services, particularly the siting of railway stations. We have thousands of town planning applications we cannot answer until the scheme is reviewed. The ARA can't go further ahead with its growth alternatives study until it knows what's happening. That's how serious the Government's indecision is.'" [553]

National Party Response
Robert Muldoon was the first to reply to Dove-Myer Robinson, by letter dated 17 November 1975:
"The New Zealand Railways have this year reached a crisis point due to the Government's decision to hold railway charges for three years. The estimated operating deficit for the year ended 31 March, 1976 is $72 million compared with $45 million for the year ended 31 March, 1975.

"With a problem of this magnitude, any Government's first priority as far as the New Zealand Railways is concerned, is to conduct a comprehensive audit of its operations and carry out appropriate rescue operations. This must be done as a matter of priority, before any other commitments are made.

"My answers to your questions are as follows:

"1. 'The Government has a duty to provide suburban services wherever a need is demonstrated.'

"With costs escalating as they are at present it would be imprudent of me to commit the incoming National Government without updated costing or alternatively studying other services which could better serve the needs of Auckland. I understand that initially it was proposed that Auckland would bear all the operating costs. Would the people of Auckland still agree to this? I am sure you will understand information available to the Government is not available to the Opposition and I would be less than honest if I was to give an unequivocal assurance that the Rapid Rail would proceed until all relevant information had been received and studied in depth.

"2. 'That because of the railways monopoly the department must accept responsibility for all capital and operating costs of whatever service is provided.'

"I do not agree that the Railway Act confers a monopoly except in the 40-mile transport limit regulations and its many variations. The Rapid Rail proposal called for the operation to be carried out by the railways on behalf of the Auckland Regional Authority with the ARA accepting the financial running costs.

"3. 'A minimum suburban rail service as recommended by the Auckland Rapid Transport Directorate is essential for the orderly control and the effective economic life of Auckland.'

"The New Zealand Institute of Economic Research has expressed a contrary view, but as I do not have access to all the relevant information of the Directorate or the Institute, it is difficult until we take office after 29 November 1975 to know the correct information.

"4. 'The Railways must be responsible for meeting the capital and operating costs of the railway part of the Auckland scheme provided Auckland accepts all costs of the bus part of the plans.'

"National renews its pledge to find the capital cost provided the ARA guarantees to meet the operating costs including interest, but in light of today's disastrous economic situation, I can give no assurance that we can commence Stage 1 of the project with a commitment of probably $300 million in the immediate future.

"5. 'Because of the urgency of a final decision and the mounting cost of inflation, a start on actual work should be made in 1976 at the latest.'

"The National Government will make no commitment until such time as all Auckland Local Bodies concerned acknowledge to it their acceptance of and support for the scheme." [554]

Labour Party Response

Bill Rowling did not respond until 1 December 1975, by which time he was no longer Prime Minister, Labour having lost the election. Not surprisingly, his reply was somewhat bland – suggesting that waiting for the results of yet another inquiry accounted for his Government's lack of action:

"I must first assure you that Government is very much aware of difficulties being experienced not only by Auckland City but indeed by the whole Auckland region, in the efforts being made to control future growth and development of the area. I also appreciate the fact that your own Central Area Plan provides for an integrated bus and rail public passenger transport system, and that public transport facilities are one of the essential guidelines to be decided upon in planning for future development.

"It was partly for this reason that Cabinet decided that consideration should be given to information on public transport which may become available from the Comprehensive Transportation Study being carried out by the Auckland Regional Authority as an integral part of their alternative growth study. It will be remembered that the Auckland Rapid Transit Project Report deals only with the Southern Corridor, East Loop and Central Business District. It is hoped that the Transportation Study, when it is released, I believe early in 1976, will provide information that will assist in resolving the public passenger transport problem for the whole region…" [555]

Beginning of the End

In his reply to Bill Rowling, Dove-Myer Robinson expressed little hope for the future of the transport solution that had once been so close. Nevertheless, the fight was to continue:

"I was very interested to read your comments, which certainly indicate that had the Labour Party continued as the Government, we would have been able to have continued discussions with every possibility of reaching a solution satisfactory to Auckland.

"Of course, now that the Labour Government is going out of office, whatever progress has been made to date, will almost certainly be nullified by the change of Government, and especially the National Party's pre-election statement that action by the National Government would depend upon Auckland local bodies being unanimous on any proposed agreement.

"As far as I am aware, Auckland has never been unanimous on any subject and this is one of the tragedies of our too fragmented local government system. Therefore, the demand that Auckland be unanimous is tantamount to saying that the National Party government is not prepared to continue negotiations on any basis.

"Of course, such a proposal is completely untenable and it seems that Auckland will just have to amass what pressure it can to persuade the new Government to revise its pre-election policy and help Auckland to get a satisfactory transport system at a price that Auckland can afford.

"To paraphrase the late Sir Winston Churchill – 'This is the end of the beginning and the beginning of the end'. The Chairman of the Auckland Regional Authority, Mr Tom Pearce and I are both agreed that we will have to fight even harder to achieve our objective and that irrespective of the National Party's obvious desire to abandon the whole project, we must continue the fight until Auckland gets the system on a satisfactory sharing of the cost basis that it requires." [556]

Disgusted Aucklander

While no doubt as a show of municipal unity, Dove-Myer Robinson had to mention the support of Tom Pearce in the ongoing battle, not everyone believed that he, the ARA, or the media had provided the enthusiasm needed – as per *Disgusted Aucklander's* letter to the Editor of The Auckland Star, published 19 November 1975:

"…I am fed up reading…uninformed comment and your staff reporting which, coupled with the cynical Bromhead cartoons seeking to deride the [rapid transit] scheme at every opportunity, has almost kicked it to death. This, in my opinion, has done more than anything else to bring the scheme to its present sorry position during the negotiating stages and has enabled the powers that be in Wellington all but to repudiate their earlier promises.

"It has been left mainly to two persons to battle away on their own in defence of the scheme – the Mayor of Auckland, Sir Dove-Myer Robinson, and Mr Ian Mead, the project manager of ART, with the chairman of the ARA, Mr Tom Pearce, chiming in (albeit too rarely) from time to time. Apart from these three, little else has been heard from officials refuting these ill-informed statements…Where, however, are the ARA voices raised in support of their own scheme and why has the ART directorate not spoken out from time to time?

"It is high time that all supporters of the scheme realised that unless they make their voices heard now and let the Government of the day know loudly and clearly that Auckland wants and deserves the same treatment as Wellington gets with its public transport system, then a very fine opportunity may be lost forever. Disgusted Aucklander, Mount Eden" [557]

Socialist Unity

There remained political support as well. Although not exactly mainstream, the opinion of the Socialist Unity Party, published by the South Auckland Courier on 11 December 1975, at least expressed the views of the many commuters affected by inefficient public transport services:

"While others seem content to adopt a 'wait and see' attitude to Auckland's public transport problems, there is no doubt that the catalyst to activate the rapid transit (rail plus bus) system is the Mayor, Sir Dove-Myer Robinson. In the opinion of the New Zealand Socialist Unity Party he is completely right in his intention to call a series of public meetings on the public transport question. The greater the involvement of ordinary people, the more likely is success to be achieved.

"Too many of the 'experts' concerned seem to be speaking with one eye on vested interests, such as the oil and motor car monopolists who have a stake in selling cars, petrol and tyres to the private motorists. The more cars the greater the profit – it is as simple as that.

"With a further substantial petrol price rise coming up and car, repair and maintenance costs also going the same way, the car is becoming a financial burden on most families, with the consequent lowering of general living standards. This, plus other detrimental effects on the community, pollution, destruction of homes for motorways etc., makes it essential to get at least a large proportion of commuters' cars off the roads and substitute public transport. 'Authorities' and 'experts' of all kinds are reluctant to do the correct thing in this regard…

"The Socialist Unity Party is strongly in favour of the proposed rapid transit system and points out that any further delay in getting it started and into operation could be financially and environmentally disastrous. We believe the public will support such a system, provided it is financially attractive enough, i.e. cheap fares, has frequent and punctual services throughout the day, seven days a week, and is comfortable.

"It is for these reasons we endorse the attitude of Auckland's Mayor and support his decision to involve the people in the area in decision making to get the rapid transit system underway. G Roberts, Sth Akld Branch, NZ Socialist Unity Party" [558]

Reaction Negative

Unfortunately for motor vehicle owners struggling with increased fuel and maintenance costs and seeking public transport alternatives, competing with existing bus and railway commuters was not the easiest of options – as reported by The New Zealand Herald on 10 October 1975:

"One problem is that the authority does not have as many buses as it might wish. With some idea, perhaps, of easing the situation, the authority will ask the Railways Department if it can improve suburban services, especially on the line through the western suburbs.

"The initial reaction of the Railways Department is the dishearteningly negative. No one is asking at this stage for the electrified lines it talks about; the point, as one member of the authority said, is that 'we have a perfectly good railway which is not really being used.' The Minister of Railways, Mr Bailey, should tell his department to stop thinking of reasons why it cannot do things and to think of a few why it can.

"New Zealand has a compelling need to save and to make the very best use of imported fuel. Here is yet another telling argument for a proper rail-bus system – and for even a modest start in that direction to be made as soon as possible." [546]

Stopgap for Rapid-rail

By March 1976, that *modest start* to a *proper rail-bus system* had not eventuated and nor had the funds for second best:

"The Auckland Regional Authority may ask the Government for a cash grant as high as $13 million for the replacement of buses. The move would be part of a widespread feeling that the Government has been ignoring public transport for too long…While the [rapid-transit negotiating] committee did not feel it was practicable to push ahead with the Auckland rapid-transit scheme immediately because of the economic climate, there was support for a government grant to keep the buses running until rapid-rail began. The ARA carries 200,000 passengers a day and some of its fleet replacement plans have been hampered by the government freeze on local body loans until September. The first order for 100…Mercedes-Benz buses was to have gone to tender earlier this year.

"The Mayor of Auckland, Sir Dove-Myer Robinson…said last night that the ARA was still committed to the rapid-transit scheme, but the committee thought a postponement until the economy improved was the best course…'It would be stupid of me to continue to demand that the Government go ahead with rapid-rail immediately in view of the country's economic position and the Prime Minister's known opposition to it,' said Sir Dove-Myer. 'I want a proper transport system for the people of Auckland and if in the meantime new buses will alleviate the position, we must have new buses.'

"The deputy-chairman of the ARA, Mr L I Murdoch, who is also on the committee, said the ARA could not afford to get the huge loans needed for bus replacements and a grant was the answer. However, he thought it unwise to put a figure on the grant for bus replacements in the light of the troubled economy. He added: 'Perhaps the authority will delay a grant application and make buses last that much longer until things improve.'" [559]

Government Neglect

The country's economy had not improved much by September 1976, when Dove-Myer Robinson addressed the Auckland Conference of the Public Passenger Transport Association, parts of which included:

"What I am concerned about is the present state of public passenger transport in urban areas right throughout New Zealand and I think that nobody could deny that it is a very severe criticism of past and present Governments that they have not appreciated or at least demonstrated the appreciation of the importance to the social and economic life of the country of public passenger transport.

"Whether it is because the government is getting $140 million a year out of customs duty and sales tax on the sale of motorcars and whereas governments obviously know that it is necessary in the public interest that they should subsidise public passenger transport, but if you were a Minister of Finance you would look at it this way: 'the more we encourage private motoring the more duty and sales tax we are going to get but the more we encourage public transport the more it is going to cost us.' So they have a very good motive for not subsidising public transport…

"…by neglecting public transport and leaving it to the ratepayers to subsidise suburban roading, which has to be done by the local bodies of the area on a basis of a 3 to 1 subsidy…the ratepayers are making a very large contribution to providing roading for private motorists and to a very small extent buses. However on top of all this, in the case of Auckland…through the Regional Authority, the deficit on the public transport operations is a direct levy on the ratepayers of metropolitan Auckland, which means the ratepayers are paying what should rightly be borne by the taxpayer…

"This continued neglect by the government of public passenger transport is a very good way of reducing taxation and increasing rates, it is a very good way of making the ratepayer make up what the government would otherwise get out of the taxpayer and thereby relieves the government of a certain amount of opprobrium…

"An efficient public transport system is just as much a social service as anything else I can conceive. It is absolutely essential for the social and economic well-being of any community. Governments seem to have completely neglected this aspect of the matter altogether. They [are] compartmentalised in their thinking and they are concerned with what seems on the surface, to be the immediate problem of restoring the economy to a sounder basis.

"But an examination of transport problems, the savings that could be effected in our overseas funds, the improvement of service, the lessening of the cost of service, the greater satisfaction that could result, seem to be entirely beyond their comprehension or at least beyond their sphere of interest…" [560]

Budget Speech

As if to contradict Dove-Myer Robinson's opinion of Government's *comprehension* and *interest* in such matters, the 1977 Budget included the mention of a number of measures designed to reform the organisation and financing of urban transport. In his Budget Speech to Parliament on 21 July, Finance Minister, Robert Muldoon, outlined his Government's intentions:

"Urban transport is an area of great social and economic importance which has become a matter of widespread concern. The Government recognises the need for reform of the organisation and financing of urban transport. Our approach builds on the report of the Carter Committee, published in 1970, which identified three basic principles.

"First, public transport should be evaluated in terms of its contribution to the welfare of the urban community. Secondly, the primary responsibility for the provision and financing of urban passenger services should rest with the area receiving the benefit. Thirdly, all aspects of the urban transport system should be planned and managed on a co-ordinated basis and should be integrated with land use planning for each urban region.

"After wide-ranging discussions with local authorities and transport operators in the main centres, the Government has decided to introduce substantial reforms in the urban transport field. In order to overcome the fragmentation of responsibility for different aspects of the urban transport system, it has been decided that one organisation in each major urban area should be designated the urban transport authority. It will have responsibility for overall planning and programming, for designated regional roads and for all public transport services in its area except railways. It is proposed to use existing organisations for this purpose wherever possible...

"In line with this new approach, which places emphasis on co-ordination, the Government has decided that changes are also needed at the national level. The Urban Public Passenger Transport Council will be reformed to create an institution with a wider view of the urban transport system which will provide the Government with advice on national policies for the development of urban transport.

"The new body will be named the Urban Transport Council. It will be given responsibility for co-ordinating central Government involvement in urban transport and for central Government assistance, both financial and advisory, to urban public transport other than railways. It will report to the Government annually, in conjunction with the National Roads Board and Railways, on the co-ordination of national programmes for urban transport...It is hoped that, with this new structure, the Government can encourage urban transport authorities to initiate and implement their own schemes for improved urban transport...

"Concurrently with the deterioration in urban transport, investment in new buses and railway carriages has been delayed with the result that a large percentage of the fleet is aged and costly to maintain. Accordingly, we are bringing in a programme designed to replace buses over 15 years old in the four main centres. This programme is estimated to cost $50 million over 5 years. The funds will be distributed by way of grant, and $6.8 million is being made available for this purpose in the current year. In later years it is expected that the bus replacement programme will be merged with the new arrangements for urban transport, whereby all Government financial assistance will be disbursed on the basis of comprehensive and co-ordinated urban transport plans...

"The Government is conscious that the Railways' suburban passenger rolling stock is in poor condition and that repairs are increasingly uneconomic. Accordingly, the Government has decided on a replacement programme. The cost of Stage I of this programme is assessed at $44 million which will be spread over the next 4 years. This will cover replacement of the carriages used on the major suburban rail routes which are the Wellington commuter lines and the Auckland—Papakura line.

"Taken together, the Government's decisions to replace the suburban rail carriages, to institute a bus replacement programme and to introduce reform in the organisation and finance of urban transport in this country, make up a determined effort to revitalise a sector which has lagged behind. From now on, urban transport should make its proper contribution to the social and economic welfare of our cities." [561]

Urban Transport in New Zealand

Following the overview introduced in the Budget Speech, the Minister of Transport, the Hon. Colin McLachlan, presented a comprehensive white paper, *Urban Transport in New Zealand*, in which he explained the decisions made:

"<u>Background</u> – A community's urban transport system is the means by which the citizens' needs for mobility are satisfied. Its components are road and rail networks, pedestrian facilities, harbour ferries, and vehicles in private, public, and commercial transport...Rising costs, the greater use of cars, low-density residential development, and other factors have, however, seriously impaired the ability of operators to finance adequate passenger transport services...

"In 1976 the regional land use and transportation studies undertaken in Auckland by the Auckland Regional Authority showed that continuation of the existing degree of reliance on the private car to satisfy urban transport needs was not feasible because the costs of providing the necessary roading system greatly exceed the resources likely to be available. The Auckland study, and a similar one in Wellington, showed that greater investment in public transport, particularly in the major urban corridors, was justified to meet future requirements...

"<u>Developments Since the Carter Report</u> – One result of the Carter Report was the establishment of the Urban Public Passenger Transport Council, whose activities have been largely confined to dispersing Central Government finance in the form of loans and grants mainly for the purchase of buses, and supporting a modest programme of research...While the council has served as a national focus for the discussion of urban transport issues, it has been unable to make any significant impact due in part to the limited funds available...

"Problems have been encountered in maintaining present services and in providing additional public transport to new residential areas...Increasing use of the private car has intensified traffic congestion (although some of the worst effects of congestion have been avoided by the introduction of new traffic management systems).

"<u>The Urban Transport Problem</u> – Although public awareness of increasing traffic congestion, pollution, and public transport losses is extremely high, there has been little agreement until recently on appropriate solutions. For most of the post-war period, the universal strategy has been to meet the problem by creating more road space. However, this has proved to be a most expensive approach which overseas experience has shown must, in the long term, fail because land and other resources are limited. Public transport has suffered meanwhile from a scarcity of investment capital and a declining image because of equipment and financial problems...

"<u>Organisation</u> – Urban public transport services throughout the country are marked by a variety of organisational structures leading to inconsistencies in service levels, varying fare schedules, inequitable subsidies, and different financial bases...Existing organisations do not have the powers needed to achieve a solution to urban transport problems, which must be considered as a whole. Under the current organisational structure responsibility is fragmented. Roads, buses, trains, ferries, car parks, traffic management, bridges, and tunnels in each of the five main centres are not under unified control and management. In addition the financial arrangements for the different components are inequitable...

"<u>Finance</u> – ...Capital and operating costs are rising at an increasing rate while patronage generally has fallen. Under pressure to hold expenditure, many public transport operators have been obliged to reduce, and sometimes abandon, weekday evening and weekend services. For financial reasons a majority of operators have been unable to adhere to regular bus replacement programmes and are now burdened with a high proportion of vehicles approaching or past the end of their economic lives. This results in high maintenance and repair costs and disruptions to services through breakdowns...

"<u>Operations</u> – ...If there is to be any long-term improvement, the approach to urban transport must change and the image of public transport as an acceptable alternative to the private car must be improved. To achieve this, service levels and the efficiency of operations have to be raised; this will require new equipment.

"Equipment Replacement – From evidence supplied it is clear that a programme of bus replacement over the next 5 years is essential. Some local authorities have already produced such programmes and are now exploring ways to finance them. It is apparent that the $1.2 million per annum made available to the Urban Public Passenger Transport Council is inadequate for this purpose. It is estimated that if all buses 15 years and over were to be replaced it would cost the industry approximately $56 million…

"Organisational Requirements – To achieve efficiency in planning, investment, and operations it is necessary for all features of urban transport to be considered as a whole. This should be the essential aim of any reorganisation at both the local and national level. National, regional, and local responsibilities and powers must be defined so that they are in balance and allow all aspects of urban transport to be planned and operated on a consistent basis…

"The Government adheres to the view that urban transport is basically the responsibility of the region and that the organisation which deals with it should therefore be regional. An existing example of this type of organisation is the Auckland Regional Authority. An organisation at this level can best give effect to the interests and needs of the population served by urban transport. However, there is also a considerable degree of national interest in the effective and equitable provision of urban transport…

"Government Proposals – The situation has been studied closely by the Government, and a number of proposals have been announced. Broadly, the proposals have the objective of ensuring that all sections of the urban community, including the commercial sector, have an acceptable degree of mobility. This must not, however, be gained at the expense of the urban environment, which urban transport systems can assist in creating and preserving. Urban mobility must be achieved in the most efficient and economical manner, taking into account the complexities and inter-related costs and benefits within the urban transport system. Financial and organisational changes are necessary at both the national and the regional level to meet these objectives.

"Organisation at the Local Level: Urban Transport Authorities – The major change at the local level will be in the emphasis on planning and co-ordination in urban transport. In each major urban area, the planning, implementation and provision of all components of the urban transport system, including roading and NZR suburban passenger services, will be undertaken on a more effectively co-ordinated basis. The planning and implementation of the urban transport system will be integrated with land use planning for the urban region and it will be developed on the basis of a comprehensive rolling programme.

"To carry out these principles, provision will be made for the establishment of Urban Transport Authorities (UTAs)…responsible for preparing overall transport plans for their areas…prepared in consultation with the proposed Urban Transport Council, the National Roads Board, and, where appropriate, Railways…

"Organisation at the National Level: The Urban Transport Council – Again, at the national level, the emphasis will be on planning and co-ordination of urban transport and the Urban Public Passenger Transport Council will be recast as the Urban Transport Council (UTC)…The Urban Transport Council will be responsible for co-ordinating Central Government involvement in urban transport, and for advising the Government on national objectives for urban transport. The Urban Transport Council will have an advisory and supportive role in relation to the Urban Transport Authorities...

"The membership of the Urban Transport Council will consist of representatives from Government departments, local authorities, and independent bodies. As the Urban Transport Council will be required to discharge its responsibilities for the urban transport system in conjunction with the National Roads Board and the Railways Department, these two bodies will be represented on the council.

"<u>Local Finance</u> – Each Urban Transport Authority will have rating powers and the usual borrowing powers. In addition, the Urban Transport Authorities will receive revenue from their transport activities.

"<u>National Finance</u> – At the national level, financial programmes will be presented to the Government each year by the Urban Transport Council, the National Roads Board, and Railways, based on the plans submitted by the Urban Transport Authorities. The three programmes will have been co-ordinated at both local and national level so that the Government will only be resolving outstanding issues and determining the overall level of funding...

"Because of the serious economic difficulties facing urban public passenger transport, the Government has recognised the need to provide additional finance in the early years, and it considers that the most appropriate way to do this is to grant finance for the replacement of older buses, as this is one of the most pressing problems facing operators...In the first year (1977-78) this assistance will amount to $6.8 million mainly for the replacement of buses in Auckland and Wellington as these centres have already placed orders for new buses..." [562]

Central Transport Control

As described in the next chapter, despite the urgency communicated by the Transport Minister's Urban Transport Statement, its content was not incorporated as actual legislation until passage of the Urban Transport Act 1980.

In the meantime, the overall impression gained from the National Government's 1977 urban transport policy was that the Government sought to limit its own costs by consolidating its control of all modes of transport and transport planning in each of the main centres in such a way that the local populace would pay a greater proportion of those costs instead of the general taxpayer.

To that end, the proposed Urban Transport Authorities (such as the Auckland Regional Authority) would provide the local management, overseen by a national Urban Transport Council. This arrangement would certainly avoid any future disputes such as when the Government had been pressed to fund Auckland's Rapid Transit scheme – a cost it had been fortunate to avoid thanks to Auckland's disunity, not to mention the economic conditions then prevailing – inflation, high oil prices, and a lack of overseas funds.

Urban Transport Bill

When the Urban Transport Bill was eventually introduced in late 1979, commentators such as Dove-Myer Robinson saw the Government's intentions as a major threat to local body autonomy:

"Governments with a propensity to shift taxation onto ratepayers' shoulders have worried local bodies for years. This trend has accelerated recently and now the increased contribution made by ratepayers to meeting government department costs is verging on a national scandal. Ratepayers grumbling at sharp rate rises blame these on the local bodies without realizing that much of the increase results from new responsibilities imposed by government, with no provision for meeting these costs except from ratepayers' pockets.

"Whilst local bodies have taken these new imposts lying down, the latest proposals in a draft Urban Transport Bill have aroused bitter hostility. These proposals are opposed by the National Roads Board, the Executive of the N.Z. Municipal Association, the Auckland Local Bodies Association, and by many members of the Auckland Regional Authority…

"Whilst the five local Urban Transport Authorities will, theoretically, be autonomous as proposed, they will be subservient to the Urban Transport Council which must act as directed by the Minister of Transport, so that in the final analysis the whole control finally rests in the hands of the government through the Minister…

"The four principles in the proposed legislation which have aroused great indignation in local government circles are –

- Sweeping planning powers overriding the 'Town and Country Planning Act' and all other acts, will be vested in the Urban Transport Authorities, and through them, the Urban Transport Council.
- Urban Transport Authorities will be required to take over the control of the Railways Department passenger services and accept responsibility for present and future operating losses. There is no assurance of commensurate maintenance and/or improvement of railways passenger services.
- The draft bill makes no provision for alternative and additional sources of income for the Urban Transport Authorities and it seems clear that the ratepayers in each Urban Transport Authority area will have to foot the bill. In the Greater Auckland area this could run to $1.5 to $3M yearly.
- It will not be necessary for a Urban Transport Authority to obtain the approval of the affected territorial local bodies in plans which affect that local body's street system, its parking meters and parking buildings, or its own traffic control. These are roughly twenty to seventy-five per cent of the major functions of any local authority…

"The Prime Minister and the Minister of Transport have stated that any consideration of maintaining, upgrading and extending railway passenger services in Auckland must be dependent on the enactment of the new Urban Transport legislation. This appears to be a subterfuge to persuade us to accept heavy additional charges without any prospects of getting the improved railway services which alone would justify consideration and acceptance of the government's bait. As such it must and will be strongly resisted by everyone concerned for Auckland's future economic viability and continued social welfare. Auckland is entitled to the same treatment as Wellington." [563]

Gigantic Fraud

Sir Dove-Myer Robinson's criticism of the Transport Bill was also published by The Auckland Star on 8 September 1979:

"The Government's new plan for urban transport is a gigantic fraud, says Auckland's Mayor Sir Dove-Myer Robinson. He claims the Bill to be introduced into Parliament to set up urban transport authorities to oversee road and rail cannot work. Robbie added: 'It's a bluff, to make us think the Government is going to do something when all the time it is going to do nothing.

"Mr McLachlan (Minister of Railways) talks about calling for more reports into the railways. These facts have been known for years and it is just another delaying tactic. The Government has decided to blackmail Auckland into finding millions of dollars extra to maintain a railway service which has no prospect of being improved. It expects us to take over its losses.'

"Sir Dove-Myer said there is no support for the urban transport authorities and he doesn't think the Bill stands much success in getting through Parliament. But Mr McLachlan sees the urban transport authorities as the key to future commuter transport in this country…he said the Government hopes to have the Bill in Parliament in about a month. It will set up new urban transport authorities which will be responsible for overall transport, road and rail. Where rail is involved, it is likely that the urban authorities will be able to 'contract' services from the Railways Department…" [564]

Passenger Transport Summary

As the 1970s drew to a close, the New Zealand Geographer published an article by D G Rankin of the University of Auckland Geography Department. Entitled *Auckland Regional Authority 1963-1978*, parts of the article summed up the struggles of passenger transport to that time:

"Transportation Planning - The problems of timing, finance, co-ordination between government departments of all types, and the lack of a sense of urgency and vision which have typified the period of Auckland's rapid growth coalesce in the area of transportation planning…

"It became evident in the early 1970s that careful consideration had to be given to the possible directions for Auckland's future. In 1973 a Comprehensive Transportation Study Review was started, primarily to update the 1963 data base as a means of evaluating alternative growth strategies and public transport systems….

"Coupled with transportation planning are the difficulties faced by the ARA in discharging responsibilities in the public transport sector that were acquired from the Auckland Transport Board in 1964. In 1965, carrying 47 million passengers, the service incurred a deficit of $397,000 but by 1972 patronage had declined to 38 million and the deficit increased to $864,000.

"The private sector were in the same predicament and in 1968 two of the largest private operators approached the Authority with a view to being taken over…Further takeovers occurred in 1971, 1974 and 1977 and in 1973 the Authority began the renewal of its fleet with Mercedes Benz buses. By 1977 the deficit of expenditure over revenue was over six million dollars and productivity, as measured in terms of passengers carried per employee, had declined markedly from 48,203 in 1965 to 34,575.

"Since the ARA assumed responsibility for the greater proportion of passenger services operating in the region it has been innovative in its attempts to increase patronage. There have been experiments with zonal fare systems, loop routes, incentives for concession card purchases, and incentives for off-peak travel.

"However it has been fighting a losing battle against the flexibility afforded by the private car. The extensions to the motorway system have only enhanced the benefit of private travel. The limited success of the car pool system on the North Shore as a means of alleviating peak hour congestion on the harbour bridge suggests that the delay levels are still below the intolerance barrier of the average commuter. When the efficient use of energy is of national concern and all public-owned transport systems are losing money, the debate on the future of public-private transport alternatives is beginning to take form." [515]

Road Transport
"Since World War 1, the form, the growth and the physical expansion of the metropolis have been tied ever more tightly to the development of transport technology. The electric tramways, the suburban railways and – the later advent of the motor vehicle and the provisions subsequently made to accommodate its mounting numbers – these have powerfully shaped the size and rate of growth of the urban area. With perhaps an excessive degree and rate of urbanisation, transport technology – the private car in particular – has come also to provide the urban region's major problems and most frightening costs." [516]

Roads to Resources

Just how some of the *frightening costs* of the motor vehicle were accommodated was explained by the Minister of Works and Chairman of the National Roads Board, Percy B Allen, during his presentation of a paper to the Sixth World Meeting of the International Road Federation at Montreal during October 1970:

"New Zealand is a small country with a population of just under three million people. No one would suggest that New Zealand is a wealthy nation, but such wealth as we have is due in large measure to improvements in our roading system…New Zealand's roading system has been developed as the result of a partnership between central government and local government i.e. since 1954 between the National Roads Board and the local authorities. The latter are road controlling authorities in their own right and in respect of expenditure on roads are eligible for subsidy payments from the board to supplement their own revenues derived principally from rates (taxes on land).

"In the main, roading is financed from the National Roads Fund which is administered by the National Roads Board. This fund which is derived largely from petrol tax is used for the maintenance and improvement of existing roads. The board's income is currently of the order of $80 million per annum, and is apportioned according to fixed percentages with 50 per cent allocated to state highways, 23 per cent to counties and 16 per cent to municipalities. These sector percentages have been varied twice in the last 10 years in the light of changing needs.

"In addition, funds are provided each year from the Roads Vote of the Consolidated Revenue Account under the direct control of the Minister of Works. This vote of $2 million per annum provides for the construction of new roads for development purposes and back blocks access. It is a separate vote, independent of the National Roads Board.

"Motor revenue is paid into the National Roads Fund, a separate account within the Public Account and the following illustrates the various sources of revenue and shows the amounts so received during the year ending 31 March 1970:-

	$ Million
Petrol tax	64.93
Mileage tax	3.88
Heavy traffic licence fees	9.52
Miscellaneous credits	0.75
Contribution by central government	0.01

"(a) Petrol tax – Rate is 17.1 cents per gallon and is collected by Customs Department when released from bond. Owners of non-road-using vehicles may claim a rebate.

"(b) Mileage tax – Paid by owners of non-petrol-powered road using vehicles mainly diesel vehicles. Tax varies from 59.83 cents per 100 miles for vehicles not exceeding 2 tons laden weight to $2.73 per 100 miles for vehicles of 30 tons laden weight.

"(c) Heavy traffic licence fees – Fees are payable quarterly and rates vary from $2.66 for farmers trucks to $259.00 for commercial vehicles operating at the legal maximum of 86,000 lbs gross." [565]

Steering Committee Report

The Steering Committee set up in July 1969 '…to investigate and report upon the implications of alternative [rapid transit] track gauges and carry out cost/benefit studies…' reported to Robert Muldoon, Minister of Finance; Tom Pearce, ARA Chairman; and Dove-Myer Robinson on 31 August 1972.

Part of the Committee's report <u>relating to road-based transport</u> included a good deal of pessimism as to the future:

"1.1 …The preparation of a meaningful cost/benefit analysis as required by the Committee's terms of reference gave rise to unforeseen difficulties chiefly because of the absence of up-to-date figures on which to base estimated future travel by private and public transport and the anticipated diversion from private car to a new form of rapid transit.

"1.2 The difficulties have been aggravated by two main factors, viz. motorway construction falling seriously behind its planned programme and the increase in the number of motor vehicle trips in many areas being considerably in excess of earlier estimates. The Committee was therefore denied the facility of being able to predict future travel by the projection of known trends.

"1.3 De Leuw Cather & Company's first report recommended that the rapid rail system should be operating by 1970; the second one recommended a roading programme in three sections – 1966/1976, 1976/1986 and post/1986 – on the assumption that the 'Regional Transit Plan' would be adopted and implemented.

"1.5 Between 1965 and 1972 the increase in motor vehicle trips into and out of the isthmus area has been some 60 to 75% greater than the consultants forecast when the transportation proposals to cope with this traffic were put forward.

"1.6 The authorities concerned thus find themselves in 1972, as the result of a decision made in 1956, committed to a program of road building on which the progress is such that there appears to be little hope of achieving the target; in fact, having dropped so far behind schedule, it is extremely unlikely that the programme can do anything but drop further behind as the years pass unless firm governmental action is taken.

"The Committee is firmly of the opinion that it would be unwise to suggest at this time that there should be any change in what is in effect an integral pattern of motorways for Auckland, the result of intensive planning and research.

"Being committed to a policy of building these motorways, a railway system should not be built in substitution for any part of the motorway network. Our recommendations regarding rail transit are therefore made on the understanding that their implementation shall be in addition to, and not in substitution for motorway construction.

"1.7 Although unable to quote an authoritative public statement to this effect, the Committee understands that the likelihood of the programme being completed before the end of the century is remote. The Committee is deeply concerned at the deleterious effects this fourteen years' delay would inevitably have on the social, economic and transportation pattern of the city and recommends that without departing from the principle set out in paragraph 1.6 above, urgent steps be taken to accelerate the work of road construction that still remains to be done.

"The means by which to achieve such a speeding up and the time at which sections should be brought into operation require a firm programme of roading works in terms of physical rather than financial units. This 'firm programme' should be based on the needs of the situation rather than the availability of finance through customary channels.

"1.9 If, as mentioned in paragraph 1.5, motorcar usage has in eight years exceeded the estimated rate of increase by as much as 75%, it is highly probable that the rate of increase will tend to accelerate rather than decline and thus bring the date by which congestion on any main corridor will have reached an unacceptable level so much nearer." [406]

Road Expenditure Insufficient

The General Manager of the Auckland Regional Authority, E A Flynn, had been a member of the Working Party on Rapid Transit set up in February 1968 and then Chairman of the subsequent Steering Committee established in July 1969. However, because he did not agree with some aspects of the Committee's final report, Mr Flynn resigned his position in July 1972, shortly before the report was published.

In September 1972, E A Flynn reported, as General Manager of the ARA, to the Authority's Rapid Transit Committee revealing his frustration as to the lack of funding for the roading programme planned from 1965:

"The report of the Steering Committee clearly shows the dilemma the Committee found itself enmeshed in…it is clearly stated that from 1965 to 1972 there has been insufficient money available to provide for the programme of motorways which, itself…is not geared to the actual growth of traffic. So…the Committee desires to see a speeding up of expenditure on roading.

"On 1st April 1971, the needed expenditure to cope with traffic growth, with some congestion up to 1987, was estimated as follows:-

N.R.B. [National Roads Board] Sector	123,960,000
A.R.A. [Auckland Regional Authority] Sector	65,958,000
Second Harbour Crossing	47,290,000
Total	$237,208,000

"There was doubt whether the Second Harbour Crossing was feasible from the view point of finance but no doubt as to its need from the view point of traffic…The Committee was is in no doubt as to the desire of the average inhabitant of the Region in regard to transport. By far, the greatest majority of the inhabitants of the Region desire to travel by means of their own motor vehicles.

"The records of public passenger transport since the last World War has been one of steadily decreasing patronage which inevitably, on any form of statistical forecast, must show a steady reduction in the number of passengers to be carried by the buses in the future. The factor which will change this trend is increasing congestion on the roads. It is, however, exceedingly difficult to forecast just exactly how much congestion would be required before a particular number of travellers were prepared to leave their motor vehicles and to travel by public passenger transport of any particular form…

"In particular, before the degree of congestion can be ascertained, it is necessary to know what roads will have been built and will be operating at that particular time under study. With the desire of the Steering Committee to increase the expenditure on roads, obviously more work will be achieved and the lesser number of passengers on public passenger transport must result.

"It must be clearly stated, once and for all, that the more money that is spent on roading the less effective public passenger transport will be in obtaining patronage. People prefer to use their own motor vehicles, and if roads are provided it is exceedingly probable that people will travel, for the most part, in their own motor vehicles by those roads." [566]

Integrated Transport or Chaos?

In a paper produced by the Auckland Regional Authority's Rapid Transit Committee, dated 5 March 1973, the Committee attempted to convince readers that the establishment of the proposed bus/rail public transport system was vital to the future prosperity of the region; that the alternative of a road-based system would not be enough:

"The number of modern vehicles registered in Auckland at June 30, 1972 was 369,201 and these have been increasing at the rate of about 8% per year. If that rate of increase continues, Auckland will have at least 553,801 motor vehicles (i.e. over 50% more than today) by 1978/80. Imagine the congestion that will result, not only on the isthmus, but also in the surrounding areas if all this traffic has to depend on the use of the limited amount of road space that will then and in the future be available for the continued increase in road traffic.

"Already we are seeing congestion on the existing motorways and roading network increasing almost daily. As the motorway system which is under construction is not likely to be completed until somewhere about the year 2020 (if not abandoned before then) the question that must be answered is: 'What is going to happen to the metropolitan area between say, 1980 (when traffic congestion will become critical) and the year 2020 even if the motorway system is completed and in use?' Because, even if it is completed, the planned motorway and roading system of Auckland will be totally inadequate to meet the requirements of a city of more than 1 million people..." [567]

The Motorway Network

An information 'leaflet' explaining just how much of the motorway network had been completed and what was planned was published by the National Roads Board in March 1973:

"Approximately 32 miles of motorway in various sections have been opened since 1953. Construction is at present proceeding at many points throughout the motorway system. The following table shows the progress which has been made on the Southern Motorway.

"**Southern Motorway**

	Miles	Opened
Ellerslie-Mount Wellington	2.0	July 1953
Mount Wellington - Wiri	5.9	Dec 1955
Wiri - Takanini	3.4	May 1963
Greenlane - Ellerslie	1.3	Dec 1963
Market Road - Greenlane	0.8	April 1965
St Marks Road - Market Road	0.5	June 1965
Takanini - Runciman	5.4	Dec 1965
Khyber Pass - St Marks Road (incl. Newmarket Viaduct)	1.1	Sept 1966
Symonds Street - Khyber Pass	0.4	Dec 1966

(Off ramp, on ramp opened Dec 1971)

"The existing four-lane Southern motorway has been widened to six lanes between Market Road and Ellerslie and this work is expected to continue south along the motorway for a number of years to provide capacity for the rapidly growing traffic flows using this route.

"In conjunction with this work, Mount Wellington Interchange will be extensively modernised and two ramps will be added to Papatoetoe Interchange to convert it to a full diamond. One of these ramps was opened recently.

"Increases in the numbers and weight of heavy vehicles using the Southern motorway have also required a major programme of pavement strengthening. The Southern motorway is being extended south from Drury to ultimately connect with the existing State Highways 1 and 2 at Pokeno.

"At present vehicle flows on the existing highway are, on the average, as high as 9500 per day, with holiday peaks as high as 22,000 per day. Work is currently proceeding on a 5.5 mile length which will join the existing State Highway near St. Stephens College at the foot of the Bombay Hills. A further 6.5 miles of motorway over the hills will then be needed to complete this length at Pokeno.

"South Western Motorway

"The first section of South-Western motorway to be constructed will be Mangere Bridge including its immediate approaches. It is scheduled for completion by the National Roads Board in 1978. The motorway approaches will then be extended north to near Dominion Road, and south to the Airport Motorway junction, from which point the Auckland Regional Authority will construct a motorway to Mangere International Airport.

"Ultimately, when motorway connections from the South-Western motorway to Newton and Wiri are completed, the route as a whole is expected to become the major southern outlet for Auckland. This major route has been designated State Highway 20. This motorway is being designed for expansion to 8 lanes, whereas the existing Southern motorway is not capable of expansion beyond 6. Just north of Mangere Bridge, State Highway 20 may for a short stretch carry as many as 10 lanes of traffic to cater for weaving manoeuvres between interchanges.

"From Mt. Roskill to Point Chevalier the South-Western motorway is the responsibility of the Auckland Regional Authority, as is the Henderson-Avondale section which leads off it. Stage I of the Henderson-Avondale section will form a by-pass route from Avondale to New Lynn and is expected to be under construction by 1974. Extension westward and connection to the South-Western motorway at the Avondale Interchange will follow later.

"South Eastern Motorway

This motorway together with the Pakuranga loop is also the responsibility of the Auckland Regional Authority. Work is at present underway on a new bridge across the Tamaki River between the suburbs of Pakuranga and Mount Wellington. This will relieve congestion at the present Panmure Bridge and will ultimately be incorporated in the motorway. Further construction on these routes is not scheduled within the current period.

"North-Western Motorway
  1. Pt Chevalier-Lincoln Bridge (2 lane) – 4.9km opened   Dec. 1955
  2. Lincoln Bridge-Lincoln Avenue (2 lane) – 0.6km

3. Widening of 1 and 2 to 4 lane – 1960-1963
4. Lincoln Avenue-Hobsonville Road – 1.7km – Sept 1961

"The existing 4-lane Newton-Pt chevalier route is at present one of the most congested routes in Auckland. It is planned to complete 6 motorway lanes from Newton to Western Springs first, followed by the link to Point Chevalier (Waterview Interchange).

"In Point Chevalier, presently the most congested traffic area in Auckland, traffic from the North-West, the city, and Henderson/New Lynn meets. When the proposed motorway interchange is completed, three major routes will be joined. In addition, Point Chevalier is the most likely spot for a second harbour crossing, which would considerably increase traffic volumes. From Point Chevalier to Te Atatu, the 4-lane North-Western motorway is being widened to 6 lanes, for which earthworks have been completed. Te Atatu Interchange will be extended to a full diamond, and the present overbridge will be duplicated. This work is expected to be completed within the next five years.

"**Northern Motorway**

Sections already constructed:	Miles	Opened
Tristram Avenue-Northcote Road	1.2	Dec. 1969
Toll Plaza-Northcote Road	2.2	May 1959
Victoria Park Viaduct	0.5	April 1962

"In addition the Auckland Harbour Bridge and approaches constructed and operated by the Auckland Harbour Bridge Authority totalling 2.4 miles was opened in 1959. The bridge and approaches have been widened to eight lanes and the Northern motorway north of the bridge has been widened to six lanes from Takapuna to Northcote Road to cater for the additional bridge traffic.

"Work will now progress steadily northwards except that a 4 lane section between Silverdale and Orewa may be built ahead of sections further south to relieve congestion in the area. Between Tristram Avenue and Silverdale the up-graded East Coast road will provide a secondary route to State Highway 1 so the motorway need is not so urgent. Between Silverdale and Orewa the new motorway section will effectively by-pass Silverdale, the Whangaparaoa Peninsula and Orewa thus relieving major sources of congestion. Motorway construction will be preceded by an up-grading of State Highway 1 to give temporary relief in the next year or two.

"**Central Interchange**

"In the centre of Auckland work is in progress on the central city interchange complex. Construction is concentrated at present on the connection of the Northern and Southern motorways through the central city area including the provision of access to the central business district. At the top end of Grafton Gully three bridges have been recently completed and the new on ramp from Symonds Street brought into operation. Construction has been completed on the bridge which will carry Karangahape Road over the future North to South connection and work is now underway on three other bridges over this route. They are the Hopetoun Street Viaduct and the Upper Queen Street and Symonds Street bridges.

"Work is now also underway on the connection from Newton Interchange to the North-Western motorway, to be completed by 1980. A temporary two-way connection from the Southern motorway to Wellesley Street in the heart of the central business district was opened in 1969. This route will revert to one-way northbound lanes in a few years as further extensions are made to the motorway system.

"The Auckland City Council have also designed and constructed for the National Roads Board the Dominion Road Interchange as an adjunct to the Newton Interchange in the centre of the city." [568]

Concrete Jungles

However, not everyone was happy with the concrete jungles created by motorway construction – as reported by The Auckland Star on 19 May 1973:

"About 400 Mt Eden homes will be taken to make way for the Newton-Mt Roskill motorway if it follows the Auckland Ministry of Works recommended route to the east of Dominion Road, the Mayor of Mt Eden, Mr Bob Mills, said today. 'It will cut the borough in two, and take some of the best houses in Mt Eden,' he said. 'It would be far cheaper to put the motorway on the Sandringham side of Dominion Rd, where the houses are not so good and would be cheaper,' he said.

"But when he meets visiting National Roads Board members next week, Mr Mills will tell them the motorway is not necessary at all. 'If Mt Eden and Dominion Rds were each widened 14ft that would cope with traffic for 20 or 30 years. There are enough concrete jungles in the city now without turning Mt Eden into another one...'

"The Newton-Mt Roskill motorway was added to the De Leuw, Cather report recommendations in September 1965, and was scheduled for start in 1976. But the Ministry of Works yesterday told the National Roads Board that the programme had fallen so far behind that the motorway could not be started until after 1987. Mr Mills said that the motorway was not necessary at all, but if it had to be built it should be on the western side of Dominion Rd." [569]

Congestion Cost

While the Ministry of Works struggled to complete its workload, the struggle by road users to travel through and across the City became ever more time consuming and expensive. An estimate of that cost in time and money was outlined in a 1975 report prepared for the Auckland City Council by employee, J. Wilson:

"It was estimated in 1955, in the 'Master Transportation Plan for Metropolitan Auckland' that the losses due to traffic congestion that can be assessed in terms of money would be in the order of $100 million to $200 million in the decade 1960-1970. This includes time and petrol wastage and other transport operating costs but excludes factors for which no scientific basis of assessment exists such as traffic accidents arising from congestion, loss of man-hours due to mental stress, etc…

"The Motorway system has, of course, siphoned off some of the traffic which would otherwise have contributed to congestion on streets in the City but the growth rate of population and vehicle registrations has more than compensated for the relief thus obtained…To attempt a prediction of the costs of congestion five years from now is virtually impossible but if we are permitted some licence with past estimates it is possible to arrive at some conclusions which are staggering…

"As I have already stated, the 1955 estimate for the decade 1960-1970 was between $100 million and $200 million. Let us assume that this was based on no inflation, a zero population growth and no increase in operating costs for a motor vehicle. We can then evenly distribute the estimated cost over the period and say that congestion would cost something between $10 million and $20 million each year.

"We all know that this would not have been the basis of the estimate but consider for a moment what would have happened during the past five years to that $10 million to $20 million that it cost in 1970 – Have wages remained the same? Does it cost the same today as it did in 1970 for a man to sit in his vehicle in stationary or snail's-pace traffic? Is the price of petrol the same? Only recently, as we know, the price of petrol went up 25%, tyres 15% and in January there was a Cost of Living order of 3%. All of these add to the cost of traffic congestion.

"We can say then that…costs will have escalated by at least an amount equal to the inflation rate in the past five years. Take for example the operating cost of a Goods Service Vehicle in Auckland in 1971. These were calculated by the Economics Division of the Ministry of Transport as being 31.5 cents per mile compared with the Rural cost of 27.4 cents per mile.

"Why should the operating cost per mile be greater in the urban area than in the rural area? The answer lies to a great extent in the delays caused by traffic congestion. So, in this one sector, we can see a differential of approximately 14% between the Urban and Rural operation of a Goods Service Vehicle. The cost, of course, is passed on to the Urban Consumer.

"Consider now the increase in operating costs for that same Goods Service Vehicle in Auckland in the period between 1971 and 1974. It cost 31.5 cents per mile in 1971 and 91 cents for the Average Goods Service Vehicle in 1974. In three years, then, operating costs have almost tripled. Dare we project this for another five years at the same rate of increase? Dare we assume that the costs of congestion almost tripled between 1971 and 1974 as have operating costs?

"…We now have a figure of between $30 million and $60 million as the cost of congestion this year. Project this over the next five-year period at the same rate of increase and we have the cost at between $90 million and $180 million in 1981…" [570]

Car Parks Needed

The deferred public transport system also meant that the ever-increasing number of cars had to be accommodated within the City boundaries – as reported by The Auckland Star on 1 August 1975:

"The Auckland City Council may be forced to provide two more carparks, costing $5 million because of delays in getting a decision on the rapid transit scheme, says the Mayor, Sir Dove-Myer Robinson. The traffic committee yesterday recommended that the two proposed buildings, one in Albert St and the other in Kitchener St, be included in the five-year works programme. The Albert St building will have space for between 300 and 400 cars and the Kitchener St building for up to 500. Both are expected to be finished by 1980.

"It was first thought that the Albert St building could be started and finished in 1978. The committee chairman, Mr W J Strevens, said this was 'optimistic' after the council's experience with the civic underground building which is 18 months behind schedule.

"Sir Dove-Myer…said two years ago, when the council adopted in principle a policy of erecting another 15 parking buildings, he had stated strongly that they should be designed so they could be converted easily and cheaply to other uses if they were made obsolete by the rapid transit scheme…

"The city's seven parking buildings (two of them privately owned) provide about 2000 spaces. The new civic underground building will provide another 1400 when it is completed at the end of next year. Sir Dove-Myer said this was 'nowhere near sufficient' for the demand, though he expected this would reduce with the introduction of rapid transport." [571]

Car Park Alternative

An alternative to the construction of car parks, proposed by Auckland City Councillor, Jim Anderton, was not well received by Dove-Myer Robinson who sought advice from John Allsopp-Smith by way of a note dated 15 August 1975:

"...Below is the text of a notice of motion which I have received from Councillor Anderton advocating the encouragement of the use of privately owned mini buses. I think I know most of the answers to this stupid suggestion, but you are the expert and I would appreciate it if you would let me have (in confidence) some notes that I could use at the Council meeting this coming Thursday, 21st August.

"That this Council recommends to the Traffic Committee that it reconsider its priorities for capital expenditure over the next five years and replace its proposed two new car park buildings with the purchase of a fleet of mini-buses to serve the city area either as part of the A.R.A. bus fleet or run by private operators." [572]

Environmental Impact

Dr I E Boileau, Professor of Town Planning, University of Auckland, agreed that inner city car parks were unnecessary but for reasons other than just cost:

"A major responsibility of the Auckland City Council has been the provision for traffic circulation, the control of motor traffic and arrangements for parking. It is now clear that too much has been done for the motor vehicle. Extensive devastation has been caused by the motorway programme. Motor traffic tends to expand to fill the space provided for it, and hence the motorways serve to channel more traffic into streets that are already over-trafficked from the point of view of environmental quality.

"The policy of the City Council in requiring private developers to provide off-street parking and itself providing capacious parking stations in the centre of the city, whilst it gets some parked vehicles off the streets, attracts more vehicular traffic to an area that can well do without it. The irony of the situation lies in the fact that the parking policy is designed to maintain the primacy of the central business area whereas it may have exactly the opposite result if shopping becomes so apparently dangerous and uncomfortable due to vehicular traffic that shoppers go elsewhere." [155]

Second Harbour Bridge?

One of those motorway channels disgorging motor vehicles into the City was, of course, the Harbour Bridge. By May 1975, the need for a second crossing was considered but ultimately discounted by a Waitemata Harbour Crossing Study Committee – as reported by The Auckland Star on 26 May 1975:

"If industrial and commercial activities were established on the North Shore there would be no need for a second harbour bridge, the secretary of the Waitemata Harbour Crossing Study Committee, Mr Barry Donovan, said today. 'The present bridge only approaches capacity very briefly at peak times,' he said. 'By overseas standards it is still under-used.'

"He told the Auckland Star that the peaks were produced by people going to the city and Southern suburbs for work. 'There are 125,000 people on the North Shore but almost no places where they can be employed,' Mr Donovan said. 'If industrial and commercial areas were established, these people could work closer to their homes. The saving of the cost of the second bridge, and savings in fuel and time spent in travelling to the south shore, would benefit the economy,' he added.

[Some old-fashioned parochialism or at least a conflict of interest is revealed by Mr Donovan's next statement.] "Mr Donovan, who is also chairman of the Pt Chevalier Community Committee, said it was unfair to destroy one suburb and change the lifestyle of its inhabitants so that people who live in another could travel through it more easily on their way to work. This is what would happen to Pt Chevalier if a second bridge from Kauri Point landed on Meola Reef and an approach road were cut through to the Newton-North Western motorway.

"Mr Donovan estimated that to achieve this, 150 houses in Pt Chevalier would have to be pulled down and another 150 would be affected. He pointed out that people from Massey and Te Atatu already travelled through Pt Chevalier and considered it a bottleneck. 'But we live there,' said Mr Donovan."

"[Auckland Harbour Bridge Authority Chairman, Mr B P Stevenson] said heavy industry could not be established on the North Shore because there was no railway serving the area. 'Anyhow, it is an ideal residential area and I feel that's the way its development should continue,' he said. Mr Stevenson pointed out that the final decision about a second harbour crossing would rest with the Government." [573]

Cross-Harbour Resolutions

The New Zealand Herald also reported on the subsequent public meeting held on 26 May 1975:

"The Government, the Auckland City Council and the Auckland Regional Authority are to be told that there has been no need for a third Waitemata Harbour crossing yet demonstrated, a public meeting in Auckland decided last night. The meeting, under the chairmanship of the Mayor of Auckland, Sir Dove-Myer Robinson, was held by the Waitemata Harbour Crossing Study Committee to discuss whether or not Auckland needs a second major crossing. About 70 people attended.

"The meeting decided on the action as a result of a motion by Mr C B Mead, a member of the Grey Lynn-Westmere Community Committee. The resolution also decided that investigations be made into alternatives of easing the transport flow across the harbour, such as exclusive bus lanes on the present bridge, promotion of ferry transport, the erection of car park buildings and more flexible working hours.

"A third part of the resolution, passed unanimously, stated: That, if and when another crossing of the harbour is required, it be a railway tunnel to connect the North Shore with the proposed Auckland rapid transit scheme and the main North Island Main Trunk railway system…" [574]

Railway Losses

Even though the road-building programme struggled to keep pace with demand, the railways found it increasingly difficult to compete with road-based passenger and freight services. This was despite the railways' long-held, competitive advantage of the 40-mile restriction - as described by M H Holcroft in his book, Carapace - The Motor Car in New Zealand: A Roadside View:

"This licensing system [for road freight] was introduced in 1931 to protect the railways from competition which was diverting too much freight to the roads; but it has also been used by transport operators to repel intruders…The major enemy, with whom peace can never be reached, is of course the Railways Department, in whose interest carriers were forbidden to operate longer distances beyond forty miles if the area was already served by government rail…

"In 1977 the trucking companies succeeded at last in convincing Government that the road-limit should be extended [to 150 km]. The Railways Department protested vigorously, and with good reason, since it was suffering enormous losses as passenger traffic declined...

[At a time of economic difficulty] "Road transport drew more heavily on overseas funds than any other sector of the economy. Money for the maintenance of roads was hard to get, and was being spent carefully; and yet the trucks and road-trains, including many-wheeled monsters, were now free to use more petrol and extend their grip on the pulverised highways..." [106]

Mileage Restriction Relaxed

The Government's decision to relax the Railway's mileage restriction was announced by the Minister of Transport, Colin McLachlan, during a Parliamentary Debate on 21 July 1977:

"First, the present restriction on the transport of goods by road in competition with the railways is to be relaxed. Exemptions from the existing 40 mile restriction have been available but the effect on road haulage remains severe. It is apparent that overall transport costs are higher than necessary because for some transport tasks rail is a less suitable and more costly mode than road transport. This was a major conclusion of the transport study commissioned by the Government from the consultants, Wilbur Smith and Company...

"After considering various alternatives, the Government has decided that at this stage the most appropriate step is to extend the limit on road transport from 40 miles to 93.5 miles. In metric terms, the limit will increase from 64 kilometres to 150 kilometres.

"The Government recognises that not all road transport users will benefit from this extension. However, it does mean that for shorter trips the transport user will have a free choice between the two transport modes. In particular, two major transport corridors, Auckland-Hamilton and Wellington-Palmerston North, will be open to road haulage. The new limit will come into effect on 1 October 1977." [575]

Tax and Distance Charges

At the same time, the Minister announced a new 'distance charge' for heavy vehicles as well as a few tax changes anticipated to improve the funding of road construction and maintenance:

"While studying the extension of competition between road and rail, the Government considered the structure of taxation of heavy road transport vehicles. The present structure of road taxation developed over the years in a haphazard fashion. While the total taxation revenue accruing to the National Roads Board and the Consolidated Revenue Account from commercial vehicles is sufficient to cover the roading and other community costs which can be attributed to them, there are some basic anomalies from an economic point of view.

"The wear and tear on the roads and the strength which must be built into new roading structures increases exponentially with laden axle weights. It is apparent that very heavy vehicles are not, at the present time, paying their due proportion of road costs, while lighter trucks are paying too much.

"With the extension of competition between road and rail, it is clearly important to ensure that the heavier trucks, which are most competitive with rail, are paying their share of roading costs. The Government therefore proposes to introduce a new distance charge for all heavy road transport vehicles, which will increase in relation to the laden axle weight of the vehicle.

"This charge will be levied on all heavy vehicles, including trailer units which are not at present subject to road taxation. It is not, however, the intention of the Government to increase the tax burden on the industry as a whole and, accordingly, other taxes on heavy vehicles, such as petrol tax, mileage tax, heavy traffic fees, and sales tax, will be either abolished or phased down.

"The reduction of sales tax will take place in a series of steps. Sales tax on all vehicles other than motor cars and motor cycles will be reduced from 40 per cent to 30 per cent on 1 April 1978. Sales tax on vehicles with a gross vehicle weight exceeding 3½ tonnes will then be reduced from 30 to 20 per cent on 1 April 1979 and further reduced to 10 per cent on 1 April 1980.

"In order to remove anomalies within the road transport industry, trailers with a gross laden weight exceeding 3½ tonnes will be charged 10 per cent sales tax with effect from tonight. The proceeds of the proposed distance charge will be paid into the National Roads Fund, the magnitude of the charge being set by agreement between the Government and the National Roads Board in relation to a forward roading programme.

"This arrangement will ensure that the National Roads Board receives the appropriate amount of revenue from the road transport industry and will have the financial resources needed to enable the Board to perform adequately its vital function.

"As an interim measure, the Government has provided an additional 1 cent per litre on petrol tax as from 1 April of this year in recognition of the impact of inflation on the Roads Board's programme of works. This will increase the Board's income this year by a further $20 million. However, the Government believes that a major readjustment of funding arrangements for the board is required.

"The introduction of a forward roads programme and the new distance charge will represent a considerable improvement on past procedures and will provide a better framework for the discussion and planning of future roading improvements." [575]

Summary

From a roading point of view, the 1970s can best be summarised by a passage from M H Holcroft's book, *Carapace - The Motor Car in New Zealand: A Roadside View*:

"Motorways were expected to celebrate the triumph of the motor car as the supreme form of land transport in this country. But they have taken too long to build and changes in economic and social thinking were beginning to overtake them before they were finished. They are earth-gobblers in a thin-waisted and mountainous country which has already lost too much first-class land.

"New Zealand is a small country, not wealthy, and with a living standard more likely to move downwards than upwards in the remaining years of this century. It cannot afford to allow a few multi-million dollar strips of concrete to grow into roads that would resemble race-tracks up and down our islands. They may look promising on maps for district schemes, and motorists may like to dream of a time when they could travel as if almost on wings, above the countryside or walled in from it, in a straight line from north to south. But this ultimate freedom may already be slipping beyond their reach. There are, I suspect, a growing number of people who hope, as I do, that motorways remain unfinished, marking the limits of an invasion that nearly succeeded." [106]

Suburban Rail
Unfortunately for all commuters, by 1970, the planned roads were years behind schedule, the bus service was unreliable and uneconomic, and a start had yet to be made on any improvement to the suburban railway service.

Political Machinations
In his 1987 thesis, *Metropolitan Reform and Decision Making: Dove-Myer Robinson's Challenge to Local Body Morphological Fundamentalism*, John Edgar described the political machinations that, by the end of the 1960s, had derailed the ambition for a rapid rail scheme for Auckland:

"In 1969, Robinson was informed by Finance Minister, Robert Muldoon, that the government would not be prepared to service the interest on the capital costs of the rapid rail scheme and that the Auckland local bodies would have to do so. Robinson was angered. He made a speech at a Rotary Club function criticising the Auckland politicians whom he believed had refused to give sufficient support to the rapid rail project.

"Afterwards Robinson maintained that he was criticising Auckland local body politicians which was partly true. He was impeded by the Auckland Regional Authority's inability to take a decisive course on his bold plan and its inability to lobby the government for funds as he had hoped it would. But he also meant Auckland M.P.s because he had made the remark that the only man to enter Parliament with honest intentions was Guy Fawkes.

"Robinson's speech drew an angry response from parliamentarians. A group of them wrote a letter threatening legal action while there was talk of bringing him before the bar of the House to apologise for his remarks.

"Robinson gained a retraction from the editor of the paper that had printed the statements he had made, but as suitable punishment the three Ministers associated with the rapid rail negotiations – Muldoon, P B Allen, the Minister of Works and P Gordon, the Minister of Transport, refused to have any more dealings with Robinson or his project. 'Robinson's remarks were so extravagant and insulting that it was no wonder the Cabinet Ministers took the action they did,' Muldoon maintains." [164]

Returned to Favour
"Given this rebuff, Pearce and Allsopp-Smith assumed responsibility for the negotiations. They took this opportunity – that Robinson's tactlessness had offered – to consolidate their deviation of Robinson's rapid rail advocacy. Nothing of substance transpired between April 1970 and March 1972 when Robinson wrote to the new Prime Minister, John Marshall, who made a conciliatory gesture and Robinson was returned to favour..." [164]

George Gair Criticism
But not all was forgiven, particularly between Dove-Myer Robinson and the National Party Member of Parliament for the North Shore, George Gair – as described by the Mayor in a statement dated 4 October 1971:

"Mr George Gair again exhibits the intense parochialism which always prevents Auckland uniting behind any project, no matter how vital or urgent it may be to the Auckland Region. He is in fact incorrect in accusing Mr Hugh Watt of electioneering at this time in repeating the Labour Party's two years old pledge that if Mr Watt's party becomes the Government, it will provide Auckland with a modernised, electrified suburban railway passenger system. Mr Watt has always supported the bus/rail plan since 1965, but Mr Gair has always found reasons for opposing it.

"Mr Gair's argument that the Railway part of the scheme should be deferred until the motorway plan is completed, demonstrates his lack of knowledge of the timing of the plan. The De Leuw Cather report, which is still the basis of our planning, states clearly that the motorway plan they recommend would be adequate for Auckland's requirements until 1986 ONLY if the railway part of the bus/rail scheme was completed by 1970.

"Present estimates and delays show that the motorway plan cannot be completed until some time after the end of this century. If we wait until then before starting on the railway part of the scheme, we would not get it until about the year 2025, by which time the City and the Government would probably be bankrupt.

"Mr Gair's statement that electrified railways are only found overseas in cities with populations much larger than Auckland's is contrary to fact; he should know that it is now generally recognised, as stated by the present Commissioner of Works, Mr Jim Macky, that any city of over 350,000 needs electrified suburban railway services. By the earliest time we could possibly complete our rapid rail system in Auckland (about 1976) Auckland's population will be over 750,000 people.

"Mr Gair forgets that the Government provided Wellington with an electrified suburban railway system long before Wellington's population was anything like as large as Auckland's, and the Government is at present planning to extend Wellington's suburban railway services. Why the discrimination against Auckland, and why does Mr Gair so actively oppose something so obviously vital to the Auckland electorate which he represents?" [576]

Balanced Transportation

It was criticism such as that from George Gair that prompted Dove-Myer Robinson and his rapid transit supporters to more vociferously include the roading component as part of a 'balanced' public transport solution for the City, as originally advocated by the de Leuw Cather study. At the same time, no opportunity was lost to emphasise the additional cost of adopting a bus-roads-only policy instead of a balanced transportation system - as per the statement issued by Dove-Myer Robinson on 2 February 1972:

"The rapid transit proposals have been described as a rapid rail scheme or an underground railway scheme. It is neither of these. It is a balanced transportation scheme, utilising the roading system – motorways, expressways, and the ordinary urban roading system providing for motor cars and other motor vehicles – together with the electrification and extension of our existing railway system, as well as a short, 2 mile underground extension under the heart of the central business district.

"By far the largest and most expensive part of this program is the upgrading of the existing street system, and the provision of more expressways and motorways. The railway part of the program is only a small, relatively expensive but vitally important link in the whole transportation chain…"

"It is estimated that by 1982 to 1986, Auckland will have a population of 1 million people. At that time, we will probably have well over half a million motor vehicles. As the central part of the metropolitan area is situated on an isthmus bounded on the north by the Waitemata Harbour, on the south by the Manukau Harbour, to the west by the Whau River and to the east by the Tamaki River, it is obvious that we cannot increase the amount of roading available for motor traffic to any extent larger than that already planned by the present motor way scheme.

"In other words, because of the physical limitations of the isthmus, we cannot indefinitely extend the roading system to accommodate, and especially at peak hours, the roading that will be available for the tremendous volume of motor vehicles wishing to use it. Some alternative means of off-loading the tremendous volume of passenger traffic will have to be provided if we are to avoid strangling congestion and the resultant delays and frustrations."

"Although I have no inside information as to what is likely to be contained in the [Steering Committee] report, I assume that as the 1965 estimate of the cost of the modernisation of the railway system was about $40 million, the latest estimate will be somewhere in the region of $100 million; an escalation of $60 million due entirely to procrastination. Yet even if the latest estimate should be in the region of $100 million, the question should not be can Auckland afford this, but can Auckland afford not to do this.

"It has been estimated that without an efficient suburban railway system, it would be necessary to spend about $1000 million on roading, but we would still be left with the problem of congestion and possible ruinous traffic jams during peak hours. On the other hand, it has been estimated that with an efficient suburban railway system, whilst it would still be necessary to spend somewhere about $600 million in the next 20 years on roading plus about $100 million for upgrading the railway system, the total cost of $700 million will show a saving of about $300 million." [577]

All Overdue

Dove-Myer Robinson's statement was followed by a letter to the Editor of The Auckland Star, part of which included:

"...Let me reiterate that de Leuw Cather & Co. reported that if all the motorways now planned were completed by 1970, they would be sufficient for Auckland's traffic requirements up to the year 1986 <u>only if the rapid rail part of the whole scheme were completed and available by 1970</u>.

"So far we have not even reached agreement on responsibility for paying for the upgrading of the railway scheme, much less having made a start on construction. The earliest date on which we can now possibly hope to have the railway part of the scheme completed and in operation is 1975/76.

"In the meantime, because of shortage of National Roads Boards' funds and other circumstances, the motorway system which should have been completed by 1970 will not now be completed until sometime after the year 2000, i.e. at least 30 years later than required. The sum total of all this means that the Auckland central area and the isthmus will almost certainly be faced with crippling traffic congestion by 1975." [578]

Window of Opportunity

Dove-Myer Robinson's frustration was supported by an Auckland Star article written by Paul Bradwell, (journalist, editor and publisher) – published by the Star on 31 August 1972:

"Only one thing is really certain about Auckland's rapid-transit report, due to be made public soon - it is the city's last chance to avoid slipping into an irrecoverable condition of clogged arteries. For if the issue is pigeon-holed again, Auckland will have done far worse than just dodge a contentious and difficult issue: It will have committed succeeding generations to the traffic blight that is choking nearly every other modern city in the world.

"There certainly isn't one city in Britain – or in Europe, for that matter – that wouldn't envy the opportunities that Auckland still has to plan the movement of large numbers of people with the hindsight of experience. 'In the next two or three decades, cars will virtually destroy many towns and cities throughout the world. They will kill and maim millions. Their place in the world economy will become too heavy to bear.'

"The words are those of Alisdair Air, author of the recently published *Automotive Nightmare*. Few people would seek to challenge them. For the car is now king – choking inadequate road systems, filling the air with the noxious fumes, bringing cities to a standstill because no workable alternative transport system exists.

"In other words, the modern world has worshipped the vehicle and the principle of freedom of movement without ever designing a system to contain it. Public transport has a poor image – it is expected to pay its way, but with facilities created in Victorian times. So services are reduced to a minimum and fares set at a maximum. Because an alternative system isn't there, people use their cars and add to the congestion. More cars – more roads. But always too many cars and never enough roads…

"In terms of area, Auckland ranks among the world's biggest cities. Its urban sprawl is in many ways its charm – to every man his detached house, his garden and his non-polluted country or suburban air. But that also means that Auckland city workers are commuting 20, 30, or even 40 miles each day by car – from Orewa and from Waiwera, from Papakura, and from points beyond.

"It means too, that as the car population grows – as it inevitably must, in a prosperous society – Auckland will have to build more and faster roads, and provide more and bigger city centre car parks…till the city ultimately reaches saturation point, where the buses can't run because there are so many cars, and the cars can't move either because there's nowhere to go…

"Auckland's suburban sprawl and its high proportion of long-distance car commuters, already present the ideal conditions for chaos. The commissioning of a rapid transit report shows that the awareness is there. The means are also probably still just attainable. Against all this background, disputes like those surrounding the size of railway gauge in Auckland become less than academic. They become pathetic – if sight is ever lost of the main objective." [579]

Report of the Steering Committee

The rapid-transit report referred to by Paul Bradwell was that of the Steering Committee established in July 1969. The report was also published on 31 August 1972.

The Steering Committee's specific Order of Reference included:

"To control and co-ordinate the second stage investigations into the recommendations of the Working Party on the proposed bus, rapid rail transit system for the Auckland Region and in particular to:-

(a) Investigate alternative track gauges.
(b) Investigate possible extensions and additional rail routes not covered in the report.
(c) Carry out cost/benefit studies of the complete bus rapid rail system.
(d) Examine the town planning implications of the recommendations.
(e) Undertake such other studies as may be necessary for a complete evaluationof the recommendations." [406]

Steering Committee members included:

Edward A Flynn - General Manager, Auckland Regional Authority - Chairman
until his resignation in July 1972
B D Duffield, Director of Works & City Engineer, Auckland City Council
R H Newton, District Engineer, NZ Railways
R R Parsons, District Commissioner of Works, Auckland (replaced F F Abey who died in April 1970) [406]

Steering Committee Conclusions

"(i) The present motorway network as planned for Auckland cannot be extended or enlarged without such detriment to the land use in the Auckland metropolitan area as to be completely unacceptable.

"(ii) The growth of motor traffic is such that congestion of the motorway system (even when completed) is inevitable and will occur progressively from approximately 1980 onwards.

"(iii) Unless alternative means of moving people are found by that time, the planned development of the Region, including the CBD, will suffer. The ultimate cost both in money and resources would far exceed the cost of the alternative transport system.

"(iv) Although some alternative form of public transport is needed, its provision should not be at the expense of completing as quickly as possible the motorway system as planned.

"(v) Congestion on motorways will throw further traffic on to the general road system and this congestion will in turn prevent a bus system from providing an acceptable alternative to the motor car for moving people because it will be similarly afflicted.

"(vi) The only proven form of public transport which will meet the requirement of being able to shift large numbers of people quickly, is that of rail.

"(vii) The previous reports both by De Leuw Cather and Company and by the Working Party were restricted to the city section and lines south and west only. Subsequent investigation has shown that because of ultimate road congestion, other corridors of travel will need relief, some ahead of the West Line.

"(viii) To meet the public transport needs of the Region into the twenty-first century a rail transit system may ultimately be required to serve the following areas, each route commencing from a central city loop: South to Papakura, North to Whangaparaoa, South to Onehunga and the Airport, West to Henderson and Hobsonville, South-east to Howick

"(ix) The order in which these lines will be constructed and the time will be dictated largely by road congestion. Other conditions not now apparent could influence the date of commencement and order of construction. These might be environmental factors, a shortage of fossil fuels or a change in the economic climate or of the public attitude towards public transport.

"(x) Although a true rapid transit system on its own right of way is capable of giving higher speeds, greater frequency of service, slightly improved comfort and, because there is no possibility of interference by goods traffic, a higher degree of reliability, the higher capital costs as compared with a rail service using existing tracks cannot be economically justified in present conditions.

"(xi) Estimates of capital costs show that the major savings to be derived from using a 3'6" gauge occur on the South and West Lines where existing tracks can be utilised.

"(xii) All railway working in N.Z. is on 3'6" track. To obtain the benefits of standardisation any further extensions or additions to the system should be on the same gauge track…" [406]

Edward Flynn

In his thesis, John Edgar described the part played by Edward Flynn prior to his resignation from the Steering Committee:

"The steering committee took from 1969 to 1972 to bring down its report. Flynn was having real difficulties with his brief. He believed that because of Aucklanders' preferences to move by car, the [rail] scheme was not feasible. He admits he 'chain-dragged' because he could not resolve his position with the majority on the Steering Committee. Finally he submitted his own confidential minority report.

"In an interview with the author [Edgar] he spoke of the reservations he described in his report – rapid rail would not be economically viable until the roads were sufficiently congested to attract people into public transport. The more money that was spent on roading the less likely this was. He also considered public transport in a decentralised metropolis of Auckland's population size 'a money loser', and until patronage was increasing on buses (and it had been shrinking since the last war) then it was not an appropriate time to invest heavily in public transport extension…

"Flynn resigned as Chairman of the Steering Committee and brought down his minority report against the Committee's findings. At that time he also retired from the Auckland Regional Authority. He later joined a private lobby group which…canvassed local body opinion on the merits of an all road/bus system for Greater Auckland." [164]

Flynn's Minority Report

Part of Edward Flynn's minority report, presented to the ARA's Rapid Transit Committee on 7 September 1972, included:

"It is possible to predict the results of a policy of inaction. Any transport service faced with rising costs and falling patronage can only exist if the ratepayers (or the taxpayers) are prepared to meet the ever increasing deficits. As more and more users of public passenger transport abandon it for the private car, then the pressure for more and yet more expenditure on roading will increase.

"It has not been possible to provide sufficient finance in the past and there is no reason to forecast any change in that position in the future. In this case congestion is inevitable resulting in further cost increase and further less patronage until inevitably the day must come when the number of passengers ceases to constitute an adequate benefit to those who are paying and the public passenger service will cease.

"If the Authorities who control the roads are prepared to take strong and resolute action to prohibit the use of certain lanes on specified streets to all motor vehicles except public passenger and emergency vehicles…then a bus service can be kept operating indefinitely. "Action on these lines has been taken in many places overseas and has produced some dramatic improvements. One moving lane as well as the stopped lane has been found necessary at all bus stops and special phases at some traffic lights may be necessary.

"Action on these lines will not be popular with the motorists and may not be politically acceptable. It is undoubtedly the cheapest solution but increases the problems for those who from either necessity or desire would use motor vehicles. It also affects all commercial vehicles caught in the congestion at peak periods." [580]

Dove-Myer Robinson Reaction

Dove-Myer Robinson also provided his reaction to the Steering Committee's Report. His presentation to ARA Members on 21 September 1972 included a comprehensive history of studies undertaken by national and international parties culminating in that of the Steering Committee:

"The Steering Committee was to have completed its report in about ten months, at a cost of $200,000 shared two-thirds by the Government, and one third by the Authority…The report generally – with two or three exceptions – is most favourable and it can fairly be said that it confirms the urgent need for a suburban railway system, complementary to a re-organised bus system if the whole planned future development of Auckland is not going to be hopelessly disrupted…" [581]

Dove-Myer Robinson's summary of recommendations included:

"It is recommended that the Authority be requested to authorise this [Rapid Transit] Committee to negotiate an agreement with the Government for the earliest possible start on the construction of the route from Auckland to Manurewa and the 'City Loop' referred to as Stage I in the Steering Committee's report on the following terms: –

"1 (a) That the rapid transit service shall run on a separate right of way on standard (4'8½") gauge track.

(b) That the Authority shall fix fares and timetables.

(c) That the N. Z. Railways Department shall operate the service.

(d) That the Authority shall receive all revenue from fares, advertising, rents, etc. and shall use such revenue to meet the cost of its agreed responsibilities.

"2 (a) That the Authority accepts responsibility for any operating deficit.

(b) That the Authority accept responsibility for depreciation charges.

(c) That the servicing of all capital costs shall be the responsibility of the Government.

"3 That the Chairman of the Authority be requested to call a special meeting of the Authority to approve the terms and conditions set out in 1 and 2 above or as modified.

"4 That immediately the Authority has defined its policy the Chairman of the Authority be requested to call a meeting of representatives of all local authorities, to inform them of the Authority's intentions." [581]

A Fair Deal and a Rapid Start

The New Zealand Herald of 21 September 1972 obviously agreed with Dove-Myer's assessment of what now had to be done and called for 'a fair deal and a rapid start':

"Finance for the Auckland rail transit plan looks like continuing to be a matter of major dispute between the region and the Government. The Auckland Regional Authority was told this week that the Government would meet capital costs of the scheme but that operating costs, depreciation and capital charges would have to be met by Auckland.

"Auckland should smartly and decisively say 'Thanks – but no thanks.' The provision and servicing of the capital charges of the railway system should be a national responsibility. Operating costs may be a responsibility for Auckland if the area accepts the proposal for the Railways Department to run the service under contract to the regional authority, but the deal must be much better than 'heads I win, tails you lose.'

"Those who say that the matter should be kept out of politics are unrealistic; the matter is already political. The 1969 Labour policy said: 'Labour will accept the full responsibility for the capital cost and charges of the rail system providing the Auckland Regional

Authority accepts full responsibility for the bus feeder service and the land purchase for parking associated with this service...'

"According to some civic strategists, Auckland's fundamental mistake was to opt for motorways in the mid-1950s. Had the city persisted in demanding rail services, so the argument goes, the Government would have been forced by events to build motorways (as happened in Wellington) and then Auckland would have had both.

"Auckland now desperately needs the railway it should have received many years ago. Anything short of unified pressure for well-defined goals would be a plain invitation to the Government to sit tight until Auckland made up its mind. No one should doubt that traffic chaos will result if the system is not built urgently. Auckland should take a firm stand on finance and show real determination to get a fair deal and a rapid start on the job." [582]

Auckland City Council Support

In a report to the Auckland City Council's Policy & Finance Committee on 11 October 1972, its Chairman, Dove-Myer Robinson, continued to rally support for the ARA's stand on Government finance for the proposed rapid transit scheme:

"Members of the committee will no doubt be aware of the reports of impending traffic congestion in the central business district reaching acute proportions within 3 to 5 years. Members will also no doubt have already experienced the onset of increasing congestion and the delays and frustrations resulting therefrom. The latest report of the Steering Committee on the Auckland Regional Authority's rapid transit scheme, gives even greater cause for apprehension of the threat to the prosperity, development and progress of the central business district.

"As the elected representatives of the City of Auckland responsible to ensure the welfare of the central business district, it appears that this Council should take some positive action to assist the Auckland Regional Authority in its endeavours to persuade the Government to accept the responsibility for providing and paying for a rapid transit scheme that will enable traffic and citizens free access to the central business district. Failure by the city council to take such action would be a dereliction of duty.

"I therefore recommend that it be a recommendation to the next meeting of the City Council that the following resolution re-affirming its policy be forwarded to the Minister of Transport immediately, and a copy be sent to the Minister of Finance and the Auckland Regional Authority.

"1) That the Auckland City Council is gravely concerned at the dislocation of the free flow of traffic within the central business district within the next few years, and the detrimental effect on the planning of the C.B.D. and the region which would result from the increasing traffic congestion predicted from 1978 onwards.

"2) The Auckland City Council therefore strongly supports the Auckland Regional Authority in its efforts to ensure satisfactory agreement with the Government in order to get a very early start on the provision of essential rapid rail passenger services within the Auckland metropolitan area." (Robinson)

Auckland Chamber of Commerce

The Auckland Chamber of Commerce also supported the ARA's stance that the Government should meet all capital costs of the proposed rapid transit system – as per its Executive's views of 27 October 1972:

"4. a) Auckland is entitled, along with any other major city in New Zealand, to have the benefit of a modern passenger rail system capable of moving large numbers of people both quickly and comfortably.

"b) Such a rail system should be provided by the Government as a basic element of service to the region.

"c) Construction of the new system would merely re-instate the rail service which Auckland had up until the time when the city railway station was moved from Queen Street to Beach Road. Patronage fell sharply from that time and when the Government failed to restore the service to the foot of Queen Street, Aucklanders began to make increasing use of road transport, in particular private cars.

"d) The Auckland Regional Authority's decision that it would meet operating losses, if any, is a realistic attitude. Auckland should insist that the Government meet all capital costs involved.

"e) The rail portion of the scheme provides the basic network but it is important to realise that the trains would be fed by a comprehensive network of bus feeder services provided by the Auckland Regional Authority at no cost to the Government.

"In particular, it was agreed that a decision on the rapid transit system was required urgently because there were already signs that road congestion in the region was increasing alarmingly. In this regard, the view was expressed that steps would have to be taken to strongly discourage the private use of motor vehicles. An increase in petrol tax could achieve this and at the same time, produce additional revenue which could help meet losses in running the rapid transit system." [583]

In a memorandum to Members of its Executive, the Auckland Chamber of Commerce had previously outlined the history of Auckland's rapid transit proposals and the recommendations re finance and gauge included in the Steering Committee's Report. The memorandum also included a summary of the ARA's meeting of 2 October 1972 at which the ARA:

"a. rejected the Steering Committee's finding that the gauge be 3'6" and approved the adoption of the 4'8-1/2" gauge;

"b. re-affirmed its insistence that the Government pay capital charges for the system (the Government previously promised to find capital but refused to pay loan charges)…

"The Authority believes that Government should be told Auckland expects it to provide and pay for what it considers to be a normal Government service even though in this case because of its size and the population of the area covered, this scheme will be very costly…" [584]

Normal Government Service

Costly or not, not everyone agreed that the Government should fund the proposed railway system without also having some say as to how it was to be constructed – as per the letter from B H Picot, Chairman, Progressive Enterprises Limited (Foodtown Supermarkets), to Mr A T Mortiboy, Secretary of the Auckland Chamber of Commerce, dated 12 October 1972:

"…you state that the Authority believes the Government should be told that Auckland expects it to provide and pay for what it considers to be a normal Government service.

"The writer feels that if this is a normal Government service, then the Government should surely have the right to determine the form, the schedules, the equipment, the routing and all the other planning decisions that must be made by a Government in providing a normal Government service. Whereas, in this instance, it appears that Auckland is saying 'We want this system to our specifications' and the ARA has gone even further by saying 'Not only do we want this system to our specifications, but we are not prepared to accept the Steering Committee's finding in respect of gauge'.

"The writer would feel that it is perfectly in order to expect the Government to foot the bill for a requisite rapid rail transport system, but if the Government is expected to foot the bill, then surely it is the Government's prerogative to decide what form of rapid rail system will be instituted. Again, it will be for the Government to determine the possible economic viability of the scheme that it (the Government) finally decides is appropriate for the Auckland situation.

"In conclusion, it would be fair to ask the writer what alternative there is to a direct Government subsidy in the form of interest-free money, and in this regard I would think that the whole of the Auckland Metropolitan Area will be beneficiaries to an effective rapid rail transport system and is this one instance where a citizens' tax as against property rating may be justified? Or, conversely, is there a case for increasing the cost of motoring in some manner in the Auckland Metropolitan Area, because private motoring is clearly too cheap in comparison with public transport to allow the economic viability of public transport to date." [585]

Seeking Consensus

As usual, the Government was in no great hurry to make any decisions on the questions proffered by Mr Picot and naturally needed more information – as per a letter from the Minister of Transport, John Gordon, to ARA Chairman, Tom Pearce, dated 27 October 1972:

"In my letter of 9 October I advised you that the Officials considering the Auckland rapid transit proposals were preparing a report for the Cabinet Economic Committee, and that I would write again when a Cabinet Committee had finished its deliberations. The questions you raise in your letter and the views of the Officials Committee have been considered by the Cabinet Committee.

"As you will appreciate, the benefits of any rail transit system constructed in the Auckland area would accrue primarily to the local community and the views of those charged with local administration are, therefore, particularly relevant. The Cabinet Committee felt that perhaps the most important requirement at present was to know what support your Authority and the constituent local authorities would be prepared to give to the scheme.

"It was considered therefore that the local authorities should be asked, through your Authority, what degree of financial involvement they would be prepared to accept for the continued operation of the total scheme and also of the rail component.

"Government would also like your Authority and the local bodies to give an indication of whether this involvement would vary depending on whether an 'improved Wellington' type system on a 3'6" gauge, or a separate rapid transit system on a 4' 8½" gauge, were constructed. Meanwhile, Government officials are working with priority on the issues raised by the Steering Committee's Report…" [586]

A General Election Issue

The Government also had an election to face in November, an event that Dove-Myer Robinson sought every opportunity to remind it of – as per his memorandum to all local bodies in the Auckland region:

"All of the evidence and reports of consultants, government officials and Auckland Regional Authority officers confirm that the whole future of every part of the greater Auckland area will be seriously affected if Auckland fails to persuade the Government of the imperative necessity to provide a truly rapid bus/rail system starting to operate by 1978 – only a little over five years from now.

"The Authority has agreed to continue to meet operating costs on its bus services and also on the rapid rail part of the plan; but it is insistent that as the railways are a government responsibility the Government must meet the capital costs of the railway. The Prime Minister has said that this is not an election issue and the Deputy Prime Minister has said that the Government is adamant that if Auckland wants this essential facility Auckland (that is, Auckland ratepayers) must pay for it…

"If this is not an Auckland election issue, it is difficult to know what is. I therefore suggest that all members of local bodies in Auckland publicly ask – particularly at election meetings – that candidates pledge themselves, if elected, to press the government to undertake to meet the capital cost of and the capital charges on the railway part of the plan and to see that work starts on Stage 1 at the latest by 1973. (Stage 1 is the City Loop and a rapid transit service to Manurewa.) Can Auckland depend on you to do your part during the next few weeks to get the necessary assurances from candidates and the Government that Auckland will get this vital facility at the earliest date possible?" [587]

An ARA Rebuff

At the time, Dove-Myer Robinson may well have been Chairman of the ARA's Rapid Transit Committee and the Mayor of Auckland City but that did not give him the right to politicise the City's need for a passenger transport system – according to the ARA Chairman, Tom Pearce, who promptly countermanded Dove-Myer Robinson's missive with one of his own sent to the region's Town and County Clerks:

"My attention has just been drawn to a recent Circular sent out to all members of Territorial Local Authorities in the Auckland Region, under the signature of the Chairman of the Rapid Transit Committee. I wish to make it quite clear that this statement does not completely reflect the considered opinion of the Auckland Regional Authority and is in no way be construed as an expression of policy. On the contrary, much is quite repugnant to the Auckland Regional Authority as it has expressed itself firmly not to request candidates of any party to pledge themselves in any way towards the Rapid Rail or to make a direct political issue of the matter.

"In view of the tremendous financial implications involved this is a matter which must be negotiated with any Government which is in power, in a reasonable and temperate manner. Sir Dove-Myer Robinson's Circular, while it may express his personal viewpoint or that of the City Council, is in no way be construed as Authority policy…" [588]

A Personal Viewpoint

That personal viewpoint had been held by Dove-Myer Robinson for some considerable time – as stated in his response:

"Any thinking person would realise that after only a few minutes consideration that the provision of suburban passenger railway services anywhere in New Zealand is the responsibility of the Government Department which runs those services, and that it is wholly unrealistic for the Government to expect Auckland ratepayers to pay for what is a normal Government service.

"In any case – as taxpayers - Aucklanders pay their share of Government taxation. It is disappointing that the Auckland Regional Authority has decided that it will not officially make this an election issue, but it has left it to the individual to decide for himself.

"As far as I am concerned, this is the most important issue of the election affecting Auckland. The whole future of this great City of ours is dependent upon our having an efficient, comprehensive public transport system covering the whole of the metropolitan area. It is a recognised practise that electors ask questions of candidates at elections and even bring pressure to bear on them to declare where they stand in important issues affecting the electorate.

"Well, in the Auckland area, there are 18 parliamentary seats. Is there anything wrong in asking all candidates to pledge themselves that if elected, after the election they will support Auckland's claim that the Government should provide and meet the capital charges on a modern, 4'8-1/2" gauge rapid transit suburban railway system?

"To me it appears the most legitimate question to ask of candidates, and I hope that those who agree with my point of view will not hesitate during the next two weeks to ask candidates of all parties to pledge themselves to support this vitally important Auckland project.

"I don't think Auckland is being parochial or selfish in expecting the Government to provide and pay the capital cost and interest on the railway part of the great scheme. After all, the A.R.A. is paying all the costs of running its bus services, and has agreed to meet the deficit (if any) on the operation of the railway part of the plan. This is more than Wellington is doing for its suburban railway services, because in Wellington, the Government pays for the lot.

"At the same time, whilst Auckland taxpayers have for about 30 years helped to pay for Wellington's railways, we Auckland taxpayers accept it as only reasonable that we pay our share (as taxpayers – not as ratepayers) of the capital cost of our suburban railway services, and similar facilities anywhere else in New Zealand where the need is proven.

"Remembering the great share of the Government's income that comes from the Auckland Region, surely it is in the national interest that the Government ensure the continued progress and welfare of Auckland by providing the modern, high speed, suburban railway system essential to its continued social welfare and economic security." [589]

ARA in Charge?

Despite his political disagreement with the ARA Chairman, Dove-Myer Robinson maintained his belief that the ARA had, since its establishment, the absolute right to speak for all Auckland regional local bodies on transport issues. He therefore viewed the Minister's proposal *to consult those charged with local administration* as nothing more than another delaying tactic – as he noted on a 'Notice of Meeting of the ARA Rapid Transit Committee' called to discuss the matter:

"Ministers letter is opening the door for disention (sic) & disunity & to give the Govt a good reason for doing nothing." [590]

This reaction was in line with his Steering Committee's Report comments to the ARA on 21 September 1972, when Dove-Myer Robinson had informed members:

"It must be remembered that this [Rapid Transit] is an A.R.A. project, and the Authority is under no legal obligation to discuss it with, or receive the approval of, the local bodies within the region although there is obviously no harm in obtaining an expression of opinion from them on a project which will affect the entire region." [581]

Devonport Borough Council Support

One such local body opinion – that of the Devonport Borough Council – not only supported the ARA's stance but also highlighted the passenger service unusually forgotten for a city surrounded by so much water:

"So far as the financial aspects are concerned the Council supports moves to ensure that the Government finances the rapid transit scheme as to the initial capital cost, the loan servicing payments and net operating cost but in the event of the Auckland local authorities having to meet any of these costs these be apportioned on an area of benefit basis as is the present case with the Passenger Transport Division costs of your Authority.

"On the technical aspects of the [Steering Committee] report the Council feel that they are unable to comment to any great extent on the matters contained therein as it appears from the report that the proposals have little direct effect on Devonport. The Council does, however, express surprise as to why water transport which would be complementary to other forms of rapid transport, is not covered in the report as a suggested feeder service to work in conjunction with the rapid rail, in the same way as is suggested for feeder bus services.

"Patronage on the existing ferry service can be increased without additional capital costs and their use together with possible extended use of ferry services from Birkenhead and Northcote areas with buses feeding to the loading points on the North Shore would reduce the need for buses to use the Harbour Bridge and accordingly the need to provide for stopping places for these buses on the southern side of the harbour or for the buses to use the roads on this side of the harbour at all.

"As a continuation of this theme the Council is a little perturbed that a station is not provided in the rapid transit scheme close to, or in, Quay Street so as to make use of the ferry potential and to the potential of the development of the downtown area." [591]

ARA and Local Bodies Meet

In order to establish what, if anything, Auckland's Local Bodies were prepared to contribute to the capital funding of the proposed rapid transit scheme, and their preferred track gauge, a meeting of Auckland Regional Authority and local body representatives was held on 13 November 1972. At that meeting, Dove-Myer Robinson, as Chairman of the ARA's Rapid Transit Committee, provided the following report:

"This meeting has been convened by the Auckland Regional Authority to ascertain whether the contributing local authorities are prepared to make contributions towards the capital charges of the proposed railway part of the bus/rail rapid transit scheme, and also their views on the gauge of the line which would be the best from a revenue and patronage point of view for the future requirements of the Auckland region…It is obvious from the Minister's letter that the Government is hoping that the local bodies in Auckland will be prepared to make a contribution towards the capital charges for the railway part of the rapid transit scheme.

"However, three resolutions carried unanimously by the Rapid Transit Committee – last Monday, November 6 – make it quite clear that the Rapid Transit Committee (and I am quite sure that the Authority itself will endorse the Committee's decision) would not be prepared to recommend that the local bodies in Auckland make any contribution towards the capital charges for a service that is definitely a Government responsibility to provide, wherever required in the country...

"The Steering Committee in its report recommended, purely on the grounds of cost, the use of the existing 3'6" gauge line. This would mean that high speed rapid transit passenger trains would have to use the same lines as slow speed goods trains, and this would inevitably mean each type of transport would interfere with the other to the detriment of one or both.

"The relatively small additional cost and annual charges of providing the separate wider gauge lines would be more than offset by the increased revenue from the larger number of passengers who would be attracted to use them and therefore, from an overall point of view, the wider gauge coaches would be a much more economic proposition...

"Because of the wider gauge, these 4'8½" coaches would be less liable to lateral sway on bends and at high speeds, they would be more comfortable, faster and cheaper to operate than the narrower gauge coaches. Because of their greater weight, the narrow gauge coaches would not be able to accelerate as rapidly as the 4'8½" gauge, and in every way, the 4'8½" gauge would be very much more satisfactory and attract more patronage than the narrower 3'6" gauge coaches...

"At this stage, it is not necessary to emphasise the importance to Auckland of having the first stage of the railway part of the rapid transit scheme available for use by 1978, nor should it be necessary to emphasise that the provision of railway services anywhere where proven necessary in New Zealand, is the responsibility of the Government.

"Sufficient to say, that unless this essential first link in the bus/rail transport plan for Auckland is available by 1978 – 1980, the whole of the planning, progress and economic welfare of the region will suffer to an extent from which it may never recover...

"For the reasons stated above, I recommend that this report and summary be adopted as the views of the local bodies represented at tonight's meeting, and that this report be forwarded to the Minister of Transport in reply to the request contained in his letter." [592]

Apparent Consensus

Dove-Myer Robinson's report and summary was indeed adopted by the meeting – as stated in a subsequent memorandum from the ARA Secretary, Noel Bell, to the Town and County clerks of the local bodies concerned:

"At a meeting of Mayors and County Chairmen convened by the Authority Chairman on 13th November, 1972 it was resolved that a report from the Chairman of the Rapid Transit Committee of that date be adopted...The Authority resolved that the [ARA] Chairman and the Rapid Transit Committee Chairman call on the Prime Minister as soon as possible with a view to ascertaining the Government's attitude towards - (a) Government meeting capital charges (b) The points raised in the report of the Rapid Transit Committee. The Authority also resolved at the meeting that the Chairman convene a meeting early in the new year of Mayors and County Chairmen concerned in the region for further discussion on the rapid transit proposals..." [593]

Dissent Revealed

However, by December 1972, the Government had changed; the Third Labour Government assumed power and, of course, a new attitude to Auckland's public transport needs. It was a time for the various proponents and opponents of the rapid transit scheme to exert what influence they could on the new Government and the scheme's opponents acted first – as described by ARA Chairman, Tom Pearce, on 11 December 1972:

"I think it is time that the Authority made its position clear concerning the Rapid Transit Scheme. By a series of resolutions, the Authority adopted its attitude towards Rapid Rail. Certain attitudes were made known to Mr P Gordon, the ex-Minister of Transport, after he requested that the Authority confer with all local bodies within the area to ascertain their views over payment of the scheme and width of gauge etc.

"A meeting of Mayors was duly called at which the Authority's attitude was made known. Several Mayors advocated an immediate start on the Rapid Rail and there were no dissentients. The questions asked by the ex-Minister regarding payment and gauge were overwhelmingly endorsed in accordance with Authority policy, and the only dissentients were in favour of the Government paying for the capital and operating costs as well.

"Although invited to do so, no further comments were made and in addition Mr Thomas, Mayor of Takapuna, thanked the Authority for calling the meeting and for being so frank with the facts. I remarked that it was refreshing at this stage to hear Mr Thomas praising the Authority for a change and everyone laughed. It should be mentioned at this time that as soon as the Steering Committee's report was received some three weeks earlier, I had forwarded copies to all local bodies in the Region, so they were fully apprised of the position.

"The meeting concluded in a good spirit of mutual understanding and co-operation, which was subsequently commented upon favourably by the Press. I might mention that it was not the policy of the Authority to pressurize either political party, but to deal with the matter quite factually and logically.

"Subsequently, unknown to the Authority, certain Mayors held a meeting expressing feelings (see telegram next page). I repeat emphatically, that no attempt was made by me, as Chairman of the Mayors' meeting, to stifle discussion and I could not assume that such an experienced body of Mayors, well versed in meeting procedure, could have been effectively silenced.

"This is the history of events that have transpired. The Authority has always bent over backwards to co-operate with local authorities, but it cannot remain a 'shuttlecock' to be manipulated between them. I realise that without the goodwill of the local authorities the Transit Scheme can never come to fruition, because in the long run any deficit must be met by ratepayers. For this reason, I recommend that I call a further meeting of Mayors within the Region early in the New Year, and in the meantime all reports, additional to the Steering Committee's Report, be sent to them." [594]

Dissent by Telegram

The telegram sent by the Mayors to the new Government read:

"We are gravely concerned at press reports that rapid transit plans will proceed next year before the inner city motorway links are completed. We request that no Government decision to be made until local authorities have the opportunity to discuss the report of the Steering Committee in detail in accordance with the undertaking given by the Auckland Regional Authority. We are requesting Mr Pearce to convene a further meeting for this purpose."

"For the Mayors of Takapuna, Devonport, Birkenhead, Northcote, Mt Albert, Mt Eden, Mt Wellington, One Tree Hill, Onehunga, Newmarket, Howick, Otahuhu, Papakura – M C Ensor, Town Clerk, Mt Albert" [595]

Gas Pedal to Back-Pedal   Chapter Five

The Disunity Story Again
In a subsequent report to ARA members, Dove-Myer Robinson expressed his regret that the dissenting Mayors had apparently reneged on past undertakings and had refused to attend an ARA meeting to be held on 11 December 1972:

"On April 5, 1966, the Authority passed a number of resolutions authorising negotiations with the Government regarding financial participation, Government responsibility for meeting capital service charges, and other details of the Railway part of the Bus/Rail Rapid Transit Plan. Wide publicity was given to the Consultant's recommendations and the Authority's decision regarding them, and copies were forwarded to all local bodies in Auckland.

"As far as is known, objections were received from only one body, the Auckland City Council, which subsequently reversed its decision in February 1969 and now strongly supports the Authority's decisions regarding financial responsibilities, routes, order of priorities and gauge. The Auckland City Council is quite content to leave this highly technical and financial matter in the hands of the Auckland Regional Authority.

"In the intervening period, right up to the presentation of the Steering Committee's report in September of this year, (as far as is known) no objections, representations, opposition or assistance were forthcoming from the local bodies in Auckland. Copies of the Steering Committee's Report were sent to all local authorities early in September 1972.

"A special meeting of the Authority and representatives of all the local bodies in Auckland was held in the Board Room on November 13, at which representatives of the local bodies were asked to express their opinions on two questions asked by the Hon. P Gordon, then Minister of Transport, who had requested that the Authority ascertain the attitude of local bodies...

"That meeting unanimously decided:-
a. That the local bodies in Auckland were not agreeable to making any contribution towards the capital charges;
b. That the local bodies and the Authority would not be prepared to accept less than a 4'8½" gauge line;
c. By a 19-3 majority, the representatives of the local bodies agreed that the Authority should meet operating costs. The three who voted against the resolution did so because they were of the opinion that the Government should be responsible for capital and operating charges, but the overwhelming majority of those present, agreed that this would be an unfair proposition that would have no chance of being acceptable by Government...

"As a result of a public statement by the new Deputy Prime Minister, the Hon. Hugh Watt, that he hoped to have discussions with representatives of the Authority before the end of this year, a meeting of the Rapid Transit Committee of the Authority was called for last Tuesday to consider and make recommendations on other details of the scheme on which the Authority has not yet decided its policy. The Rapid Transit Committee's report and recommendations are on the agenda for tonight's meeting for adoption or modification as determined by the Authority.

"However, without any notification to the Chairman of the Rapid Transit Committee or the Chairman of the Authority, (or as far as is known, to any other member or official of the Authority), a number of Mayors gathered together in the Mt Albert Borough Council Chambers last Wednesday night and decided to send a telegram to the Prime Minister asking that further progress on the rapid rail scheme be held up until the local bodies had had an opportunity of discussing the details. This caused a lot of indignation because those details are only tonight coming before the Authority for its approval or otherwise…

"It is therefore surprising that at this late hour when it appears that the Authority has every possibility of reaching agreement with the Government, particularly on the capital charges which is the most important of all, that we should now receive a demand for what is virtually a re-opening of the whole scheme, and in fact, querying the necessity for a rapid rail scheme at all.

"It must be pointed out that the Regional Authority is the only body charged with the responsibility of inaugurating a new bus/rail rapid transit plan for Auckland, and whilst the Authority has shown the local bodies every courtesy in keeping them informed of developments, it must be remembered that the Authority is under no obligation to do so.

It is statutorily empowered to make its decision without consulting any local body, unless, as a matter of courtesy, it wishes to do so.

"It should also be pointed out, that if at this late stage, the Authority is prepared to throw the whole matter back into the melting pot, it would not only be abrogating its statutory responsibilities, but it would almost inevitably set back progress for a considerable time – possibly years – which would have a most seriously injurious effect on the future development of the Auckland metropolitan area." [596]

Hope of Rapid Rail Start

Despite the lack of local government unity, the new Labour Government seemed intent on solving Auckland's transport problems – as reported by The New Zealand Herald on 20 December 1972:

"The Government agreed that a start on the Auckland rapid-rail transit scheme should be made next year, Sir Dove-Myer Robinson said after talks in Wellington yesterday. A meeting of Auckland local bodies would be called early in February to discuss the proposals.

"Sir Dove-Myer, chairman of the Auckland Regional Authority rapid transit committee and Mayor of Auckland, was a member of an ARA deputation which called on the Government yesterday…The other deputation members were the ARA chairman, Mr T H Pearce, and the authority general manager, Mr E A Flynn.

"They met the Prime Minister, Mr Kirk, the Deputy Prime Minister, Mr Watt, and the Minister of Transport, Sir Basil Arthur. Sir Dove-Myer said after the meeting: 'The Prime Minister firmly reiterated the Government's undertaking to finance the capital construction and the service charges of the scheme, with the regional authority accepting responsibility for the operating costs.' The question of the gauge of the scheme and other details would be discussed by the authority and the Government in February, once the Government had received a report on the scheme from its own officials…" [597]

Motorways Not Forgotten

While the rapid transit system seemed to have finally been endorsed, the Government nevertheless appeased the 'road gang' by announcing in the same breath:

"…any Government spending on the rapid rail system would not be done at the expense of the motorway programme. 'The Auckland steering committee's recommendation that the motorway construction programme should continue was accepted by the Government,' they said. 'At the same time, further measures to improve the city's transport problems must be found and the Government is anxious to play its part in providing a solution to the problem as soon as possible.'" [598]

Bogey of Local Body Disunity

The news reports reflected the content of a letter of 20 December 1972 from the Deputy Prime Minister, Hugh Watt, to the ARA Chairman, Tom Pearce, in which the Government confirmed it would: "…certainly honour its promise given, both prior to and following the election, that it will make the capital available and meet the capital service charges on any [rapid transit] scheme that is ultimately agreed between Government and the Regional Authority…" [599]

However, there remained the bogey of local body disunity – referred to by Hugh Watt:

"We can confirm that any expenditure by Government on the provision of a rapid rail system would not be undertaken at the expense of a curtailment of the motorway programme. This was made clear at our meeting and should help to allay some of the fears that have been expressed by other local body representatives in your area…It is expected that the Regional Authority will be responsible for getting some unanimity from its own members regarding the proposal and that this will not be a responsibility of the Government…" [599]

Combined Meeting

So, as 1972 drew to a close, the new Labour Government had granted Auckland its Christmas wish, as announced by an ARA statement to all representatives of local bodies and members of the Authority invited to a meeting on 5 February 1973:

"Copies of the letter from the Deputy Prime Minister dated December 20, 1972 which have been sent to all local bodies, confirm that the government has accepted responsibility for the major costs (capital and service charges) and this, for a separate 4' 8-1/2" gauge track represents a government investment over the whole scheme of $273,000,000 (at 1970 costs) in the Auckland region.

"Such an offer must be regarded as most satisfactory and Auckland should not allow arguments regarding routes, gauge, order of priority of the various stages, or other reasons to jeopardise what must be regarded as the most beneficial offer Auckland has ever had from any government to ensure further progress in the economic and social development of the Auckland region…" [600]

Dissidents Beware

The ARA had good reason to fear that possible local body arguments about comparatively minor aspects of the project could make it easy for the Government to hesitate – just as such disunity had provided an excuse for previous Governments:

"…On rapid rail, the Labour government proved no exception to its predecessors. This consequence had been feared as soon as the local bodies began to question the project. Robinson, for instance, had said the divisive action of the municipalities: 'would give the Government a glorious opportunity, if it wished, to take advantage of it and say: 'If Auckland can't make up its mind what it wants, the Government can't take any further action until it is presented with a united policy.'

"The New Zealand Herald editor echoed this, writing [18 December 1972]: 'The dissident voices now heard in Auckland would give any government the chance to save its money – to shrug its shoulders and say it would listen when Auckland made its mind up, knowing full well that it would be almost permanently immune from any need to act.'" [164]

Benefits for All

It was therefore imperative that a full agreement was reached at the combined meeting of all representatives of local bodies and members of the Authority that took place on 5 February 1973. For its part, the ARA did as much as it could to convince the local bodies of the benefits that would accrue to the whole Auckland region as well as to the individual areas they represented:

"1. All the evidence points to the fact that by 1978 – only 5 years from now – traffic congestion in many parts of the metropolitan area will have crippling results not only in the areas directly affected, but that congestion in one part will adversely affect all other parts of the region.

"2. <u>There is, physically, nor more land available in the isthmus for more motorways when the present motorway plan is completed</u>. The only practical way to prevent disastrous congestion is to ensure that an alternative (railway) system is progressively available from 1978 onwards.

"3. It will be remembered that the De Leuw Cather Comprehensive Transport report made it clear that the motorway system they recommended should be completed by 1970 and would only then be sufficient for estimated requirements to 1986 <u>provided the first part of the railway plan was available by 1970</u>.

"4. Unless the railway part of the plan is progressively available from 1975 onwards, the cost, in terms of wastage of valuable land, disruption of orderly planned development of the region, and detrimental effect on the economic and social life of citizens and other factors would far outweigh the total capital and annual costs of the railway part of the plan.

"5. The fact that <u>the government has accepted responsibility for the major item of cost – capital service charges</u> – means that the local bodies, through their levies to the A.R.A., will have to meet small, if any, part of the annual <u>operating</u> costs; out of all proportion to the benefits the scheme will confer on their residents and ratepayers.

"6. If for any reason the railway part of the bus/rail plan is deferred or not proceeded with immediately, local body shares of costs of providing new roads and upgrading and maintaining existing main and secondary roading in their areas to carry ever increasing motor traffic, will be greatly in excess of their share of any operating deficit on the railway part of the plan.

"7. If the benefits of this railway scheme are to become fully available, it is necessary that Stage 1 (Manurewa to, and through, the City) and desirably Stage 2 also, (City to Wairau Valley on the North Shore) be commenced this year, 1973, and be completed by 1978.

"8. As stated in the Steering Committee's report, <u>there is no practicable alternative</u> – we either get on with the railway scheme, or condemn the metropolitan area to stagnation within a few years.

"9. The most costly part of any roading or railway scheme is the acquisition of already developed land for the right-of-way. The government already owns most of the right-of-way for the railway part of the bus/rail scheme, therefore the capital and operating costs will be considerably lower than for a scheme involving expensive acquisition of land for rights-of-way.

"10. The railway part of the bus/rail plan is the vital link that will connect together the reorganised bus services throughout the region. <u>Therefore every local body area, whether</u>

directly served by the railway or even remote from it, will greatly benefit from improved bus/rail facilities anywhere in the region.

"11. Congestion in any area could and does affect all other local body areas and therefore as improved bus services, which will result from co-ordination with the railway system, will benefit all parts of the region, it is essential to the region that the vital rail links be available as soon as possible.

"12. At the present and foreseeable rate of motorway construction, the roading recommended in the Comprehensive Transport report, which should have been completed together with the rail plan by 1980 (to avoid otherwise crippling congestion by 1986) will not now be completed until about 2020, i.e. 40 years behind target. The paralysis that will be inevitable if neither the planned roading nor the railway is available by 1980 can therefore be realised.

"13. It is therefore essential that at least Stages 1 and 2 of the rail plan be available for 1978/80 to avoid the additional congestion resulting from the present estimated 40 year delay in completion of the roading plan.

"14. The total cost of the whole railway part of the plan was estimated by the Steering Committee at \$273,335,000 on 1970 costs for a 4' 8-1/2" gauge system. Stages 1 and 2 were estimated by them at \$85,273,000. Allowing for escalation of costs to 1980 this figure would then become \$129,180,000 for stages 1 and 2. Stage 2 alone was estimated on 1978 cost at \$43,000,000.

"The Steering Committee also reported that by 1980 the Harbour Bridge would be running at maximum capacity and that additional means of access to the North Shore would have to be available by then.

"The two alternatives were: (1) a new Harbour Bridge (2) Railway access (by tunnel under the harbour). The estimated cost of a new harbour bridge together with access roads and ancillary costs would be, at 1980 costs, \$76,000,000.

"15. If the railway plan is not implemented, a new harbour bridge will be essential. This would only increase the congestion on the isthmus roads and would not relieve congestion on either the north or south sides of the harbour.

"Stage 2 of the rail plan – estimated at 1978-80 costs – will be \$43,000,000 and will provide better service to the residents of the North Shore and at the same time become an integral link in the regional bus/rail plan serving the whole urban area, at a saving of \$33,000,000 as compared with the otherwise essential new harbour bridge. It seems clear that from every point of view (saving of capital costs, better service and prevention of additional congestion) the railway extensions to the North Shore is by far the better proposition." [600]

A Majority in Favour

In a subsequent memorandum to the Chairman and Members of the ARA, Acting Secretary, J H Coulam, was happy to announce:

"After full discussion the meeting resolved by 22 local authorities to four – 'That this meeting of Auckland local authorities representatives agree that the establishment of a rapid rail system is the responsibility of the Auckland Regional Authority and that the Authority be asked to commence negotiations with the Government to implement a system as soon as possible.' The four authorities voting against the resolution indicated that they did so because they considered more details were needed before they could make a decision." [601]

Those Opposed

Those civic leaders still opposed to the proposed rapid rail system included:

"The Mayor of Ellerslie, A T Bell, feared operating losses if there was no 'firm promise' on the gauge, that is, a proper wide gauge for speedy transit traffic. L Witten, a Manukau City Councillor, was probably the most outspoken rapid rail critic in south Auckland. He was concerned that the gains that Auckland City would make out of rapid rail. He maintained: 'by expending this very large sum of money to take people to the Auckland Central Business District, we are going to have a lot of private capital and public investment and further employment concentrated in the Central Business District, forcing more and more people to travel long distances. While his council colleague, Pearl Baker argued 'the main purpose of rapid rail is to take people out of the suburbs and bring them for shopping, into Auckland City.'

"The South Auckland critics of rapid rail were joined by a New Lynn borough councillor, G A Hill, who maintained that 'it is obvious that the Mayor of Auckland, Sir Dove-Myer Robinson, wants to bring shopping traffic into downtown Auckland.' The Mayor of Mount Eden, R C Mills, also said rapid rail was designed 'to send everything into Queen Street, this is the area of benefit – it should pay…'

"Fred Thomas, Mayor of Takapuna, was the most vocal critic of rapid rail…Thomas believed that an express bus system which had right of way lanes on regional roads, was a cheaper alternative and more applicable to the sprawling Auckland metropolis. Most of all he maintained heavy investment in public transport was not wise." [164]

What Should Be Done?

Fred Thomas outlined his views in a lengthy article published in March 1973 and which was subsequently circulated at the Municipal Conference in Rotorua:

"No one will deny the need for Auckland to plan now, a comprehensive public passenger transport system, to cope with the increasing congestion which will occur in the early 1980s, if nothing is done. The argument is about what should be done. An absurd situation has arisen, whereby the wrong public passenger transport system may be chosen for Auckland solely because of a policy which states that rail is a Government responsibility, and buses a local body responsibility…

"It may be a much better investment if the cost of Auckland's Rapid Rail was used to improve public transportation throughout the whole country. Auckland has been pressing its case vigorously, and if it is successful in getting $300,000,000 from Government, what will be left for other centres, which are in far greater need of help than Auckland. It seems that Auckland is prepared to take advantage of all the benefits of being big, without assuming responsibility for the problems that go with size…

"Funds allocated to one sector of public spending obviously are not available for another. To get maximum benefit for the whole community from $300 million, a reallocation on a functional as well as a territorial basis may be necessary…The inner city motorway links, if given priority, will rid Central Auckland of much of the existing congestion and pollution created by 'through traffic' which at present is forced into the Central business district from all directions.

"Auckland's mayors have been assured by the Chairman of Auckland's Rapid Transit Committee that Government will provide the $300,000,000 required for the Auckland scheme. Although this is a compelling argument in favour of Auckland Local Bodies supporting the proposal, it is only one of the many factors which should be considered when deciding what system will be best for Auckland.

"There must remain doubts as to whether Government is in fact committed to the A.R.A. Rapid Rail Scheme. Nowhere can we find support for this. Mr Watt has given an assurance that Government will contribute the capital cost of 'any scheme that is ultimately agreed upon'. At best this is a qualified commitment.

"Those who have studied the problem confronting large cities must conclude that the ultimate goal must be – not to eliminate congestion, or maintain investments in real estate, or transport facilities, but to 'improve urban living'. Traffic congestion is but one aspect of 'urban living', one which cannot be considered in isolation from other equally important aspects; social, technical, economic, environmental and political...

"Clearly, the A.R.A. Rapid Rail proposals are designed to alleviate the problem of moving people into and out of the C.B.D. at peak hours. The system appears to have become a goal in itself, taking no account of people, and of the broader social and planning considerations, which contribute to 'urban living'.

"During peak hours the capacity of a single express bus corridor would be more than sufficient to cope with the estimated needs from any outlying area, to and from the Auckland C.B.D. The same applies to a rail system. The busiest line will be the Southern corridor, the estimated patronage of which will be well below the capacity of a single express bus lane...

"A comparison of the advantages and disadvantages of both a rapid rail and the alternative express bus systems proves overwhelmingly that an express bus system is best suited for Auckland's special circumstances. In fact there is little argument left to justify a rapid rail scheme...

"Opinion is swinging away from rail to an express bus system. Many who previously supported rapid rail, now firmly believe that the advantages of an express bus system are irrefutable. Many others believe that a thorough cost benefit investigation of the alternative bus and rail proposals should be carried out before a final decision is made.

"If Government is forced to make an early decision then it is unlikely to approve the A.R.A. proposals; more probably it will suggest the upgrading and electrification of the existing rail system. This could be carried out on the Southern line. Meantime, an express bus service could be operated for the rest of the region, or at least those areas where congestion may become serious. This is in fact recommended by the Steering Committee for the North Shore, pending the building of a tunnel...

"It is necessary to expose the weaknesses in the rapid rail proposals, to ensure that a decision, when made is made in the knowledge of all the facts and in the best interests of the people of the Auckland region and the whole country; not just because of the whims and fancies of any one Mayor at any particular time. Auckland public transport has been plagued by local politicians for too long..." [602]

A Private Comment

B H Dudson, was another rapid rail critic who published views similar to Fred Thomas – as per his letter to the Auckland District Engineer, New Zealand Railways, on 10 February 1973:

"I have enclosed a copy of a report I have written concerning Auckland's rail transport proposals. I am currently employed as an Assistant Chief Town Planner by the Auckland City Council, leading a team responsible for the planning of the centre of the city.

However I have been so disturbed by the report of the Steering Committee, and the subsequent political play, that I have felt obliged to comment in a private capacity.

"Most Aucklanders seem to be blissfully unconcerned at the magnitude of the cost of the proposals. The annual subsidy required for the south line alone of the rapid rail proposal, without allowing for escalation, is likely to be over $5,000,000. On this basis, the cost of the complete 5 line rapid rail scheme is likely to be over $25,000,000 A YEAR - repeatedly: YEAR AFTER YEAR.

"Even if the Government was to make a substantial contribution towards the subsidy required, the cost to the city could still be great. But the real issue should not be whose money is spent, but could this money be spent to greater social advantage within the city, or the country as a whole? I believe that it could, and that it can be shown that the rail transit proposals are an extravagant and inefficient means of solving imaginary problems...

"It is possible that some compromise solution would be contemplated, such as a subsidy for a start on the southern line. But the southern line would serve only about 1/5th of the city, and the cost would still be considerable. Very likely, the same money would buy a modern bus system serving the whole region, which would be both faster and more convenient than a combined bus rail operation..." [603]

Critics Answered

Naturally, the ARA's Rapid Transit Committee was always ready to reply to the critics of the rapid transit proposals – as per its report, 'Integrated Transport Or Chaos?' published 5 March 1973:

"Opponents of the proposed bus/rail scheme overlook the fact that the railway part of the total scheme is only a very small, but vitally important link that will join together most bus routes and so give Auckland, for the first time, a fully integrated transport system covering all parts of the metropolitan area. When completed, the railway part of the scheme will represent only about 10% of the whole public transport network, and about 90% of the traffic will still be carried by bus...

"Whilst orthodox cost/benefit studies usually concentrate on the financial aspects of providing these [public transport] facilities – (whether they will show a profit or a deficit) – the intangible benefits of better living standards so far outweigh any possible financial costs as to render cost/benefit studies based only on an analysis of probable financial results worthless. All the present arguments for a financial cost/benefit study are, in reality, red herrings to further frustrate the efforts being made to give our city the most suitable kind of public transport system designed to meet our existing and future conditions..."

"We don't think it is necessary or advisable to answer in detail all the objections which have again been raised lately, but we would like to point out that every objection that has been made and played up recently has been the subject of argument over many years. Every one of these factors, – planning, costs, effect on the rates, effect on the environment and the quality of life, and the shape and development of the City and surrounding areas, – all have been considered at length, debated at great length at symposiums, and at public and private meetings, and some have been adopted; those which have been rejected have been rejected for sound reasons...

"We are satisfied that the combination of buses and railways will speed up public transport to such an extent that we will find the patronage of the buses increasing again, possibly to the stage where the revenues from passengers will equal the cost of running the buses, which will cut out some of the big losses that we are incurring today.

"We can't see any future for private or public road transport if we are going to depend wholly on the roading system. We must have some means of off-loading a very large percentage of the passengers from private cars on to a railway system, particularly at peak hours. So that whatever it costs the ratepayers of Auckland to subsidize a satisfactory transport system, we are satisfied it won't cost them very much, if anything like the loss on an all roading system..." [567]

Studies Overseas

Both Dove-Myer Robinson and the Deputy Prime Minister, Hugh Watt, spent some time overseas during April 1973 – Dove-Myer Robinson in North America, and Hugh Watt in Britain and Europe – as per The New Zealand Herald article of 31 March 1973:

"British and European rapid rail systems will be studied by the Deputy Prime Minister, Mr Watt, during his month long visit overseas. Mr Watt, who leaves for London tonight, said yesterday that he would be holding discussions with at least one British firm on the construction of rapid rail stations and ticketing systems. His interest in the subject was related to the proposed Auckland rapid rail system, he said, but his discussion would, of course, only be consultative at this stage. Mr Watt will also study rapid rail developments in France." [604]

Hugh Watt provided home with a number of despatches during his trip:

"London: Wednesday – Deputy Prime Minister Watt said after a meeting with British Environment Minister Geoffrey Rippon here today he was convinced proposals to install a rapid rail system in Auckland were 'absolutely right'. 'My discussions with Mr Rippon over transport systems in Britain made it clear that we must encourage people not to use the motor car in big cities,' he said. 'The things I learnt today convince me that Auckland's rapid rail proposals are absolutely right.'" [605]

"Watt: Rapid-bus plan is 'not on' – Deputy Prime Minister Mr Watt says, 'It's just not on. It's out as far as I am concerned as a rapid-bus system would only create more problems than we have now,' he said. Mr Watt also had a word to say to those who have called for a cost-benefit analysis of a rapid transit scheme. 'I just don't think we can do it,' he said.

"Mr Watt said that most experts he had spoken to during his recent overseas trip had told him that Auckland should go ahead with its rapid transit scheme. 'I have seen rapid rail in cities with more topographical problems than Auckland,' he said. Mr Watt said there should be no hesitation in starting on the scheme. 'The experts say that it is most important for the future of Auckland,' he said." [606]

Local Conspiracy

Shortly after his return from North America, Dove-Myer Robinson submitted a report to the Rapid Transit Committee. During his presentation, he referred to the papers critical of the proposed rapid transit project published by Fred Thomas and B H Dudson:

"Study of these two documents indicates that an organised attempt is being made to inflame local bodies, Members of Parliament, and other people in other parts of New Zealand to bring pressure to bear on the Government not to proceed with its intention to conclude an agreement to provide the capital charges of our proposed rapid transit scheme. At today's meeting, copies will be made available to members of the Committee of a circular showing that a local committee has been established for the same purpose.

"Whilst I have every confidence in the Government's intention to honour its promise, I am apprehensive of the effect that this organised opposition may have on the Government and the delays which could result…As I have stated, although I have confidence in the Government, no-one can tell what effect these attempts will have, and I think members of the Committee will agree that we should have all the information to answer the charges that are being made, only if and when necessary." [607]

Auckland Public Transport Action Committee

The committee referred to by Dove-Myer Robinson, the *organised opposition* of which he was so apprehensive, was the Auckland Public Transport Action Committee established at a public meeting in February 1973. The Committee included:

"Chairman: Mr M A C [Michael Alan Charles] Hart – [President, Civic Action Party Inc.]
Deputy Chairman: Mr A F Thomas – Mayor of Takapuna
Secretary: Mr S E K Reeves – Barrister and Solicitor
Treasurer: Mr B Mason – Management Consultant
Mrs Pearl Baker – Member, Manukau City Council
Mr T V G Beeson – Mayor of Onehunga
Members: Mr J R Dart – Town Planner
Mr D A C Dodds – Town Planner
Mr J N Kirk – Member, Waitemata County Council and Auckland Harbour Bridge Authority
Mr Hugh Meharry – Broadcasting Technician
Mr Ivan Mercep – President, Auckland Architectural Assn.
Mr Owen McShane – Policy Analyst
Mr V Watson – Deputy-Mayor, New Lynn
Mr David Willmott – Transportation Engineer
Mr R J F Witten – Member, Manukau City Council" [608]

Minister Meets the Action Committee

Despite Hugh Watt's earlier proclamations from Europe that: *proposals to install a rapid rail system in Auckland were 'absolutely right'* and *a word to say to those who have called for a cost-benefit analysis of a rapid transit scheme. 'I just don't think we can do it,'* he nevertheless agreed to meet a delegation from the Auckland Public Transport Action Committee at Wellington on 1 June 1973 when he was presented with the following statement:

"Mr Minister - the Auckland Public Transport Action Committee is grateful for the opportunity to present its submissions to you in person in addition to our submissions to the Prime Minister in letters dated 4/5/73 and 24/5/73...We appreciate the opportunity for this meeting because we realize our Committee has no statutory status and we clearly understand that Government is dealing directly with the Auckland Regional Authority in this matter.

"We respectfully suggest that the Auckland Regional Authority has not carried out its responsibilities in the matter of Public Passenger Transport otherwise there would have been no need for the formation of our committee and to have made submissions and representations in the manner we are doing.

"Let me [Michael Hart] say from the outset that our Committee…is well-balanced politically, geographically and technically and our primary objective is to assist the Government with our expertise and knowledge, in ensuring that 'any scheme finally accepted provides a fast, convenient, flexible public transport service of benefit to the largest number of Aucklanders (particularly those with the greatest need) and at a reasonable cost'. We appreciate that there may be some urgency in taking action now but we submit with respect, that while some decisions on Auckland's Rapid Transit Proposals can be made immediately many should and must be deferred until all relevant data has been assessed.

"It is important to note that our committee is not 'anti' anything and is certainly not seeking to delay or frustrate for the sake of it but are strongly in favour of urgent and positive action for a short term solution while further 'in-depth' studies are carried out…We respectfully submit that the Steering Committee totally ignored its terms of reference when it failed to give more than fleeting reference to not only cost-benefit analysis but also the Town Planning implications of its report.

"As you will be aware the Prime Minister has stipulated that Auckland must resolve their differences and there must be substantial unanimity in Auckland before the Government would agree to discuss final proposals with the Auckland Regional Authority. To most people the decisions made at the meeting of Mayors and local authority representatives on February 5th indicated that agreement had finally been reached.

"No doubt the ARA forwarded the resolution passed (22-4) at the meeting. On close examination and in discussion with several of those who voted at the meeting it appears that the wording of the resolution (in fact thanking the Government for their very generous offer) made it very difficult to vote against and also that the report presented to the meeting for discussion was only made available that evening.

"We have information (which can be verified) that over 10 local authorities, representing over 350,000 people in Auckland are very dissatisfied with the Auckland Regional Authority's attitude over the whole matter. These authorities do not support the proposals adopted and have in fact called for further information and greater detail on the whole proposal…

"We respectfully suggest that the following action be taken:
(a) The motorway network for Auckland be completed as soon as possible
(b) The Bus System be improved now. (The bus component of any Bus-Rail system will constitute approximately 90% of the system and only 10% of the cost)
(c) Land (rights of way) be acquired as soon as possible
(d) An express bus-lane be incorporated on the Auckland Harbour Bridge
(e) Buses travelling across the Harbour Bridge be toll-free
(f) An inner-city bus terminal be built immediately (for northern and western traffic)
(g) A serious look at Harbour Services be undertaken – an improved ferry service could run to Devonport and Waiheke and a new service should be looked at for East Coast Bays, Northcote, Birkenhead and other harbour suburbs and a cost/benefit analysis of these improvements against bridge duplication or rail extensions should be made.
(h) The bus service to South Auckland and the North West could be substantially improved
(i) The Government charge the Auckland Regional Authority to appoint a widely representative committee (with expert facilities available to it) to consider evidence and submissions from all interested parties on Rapid Transit proposals - to prepare an interim report which should be circulated widely and to bring down a final report for the Authority and Government which can then be implemented without further delay – Such report must place considerably less emphasis on technical and engineering matters and give substantial consideration to environmental, sociological and planning matters." [608]

Delegation Progress

The Auckland Passenger Transport Action Committee must have made an impression with its approaches to the Government because The New Zealand Herald reported on 29 June 1973:

"A deputation from an Auckland group is to ask the Cabinet subcommittee for further investigations into the need for a rapid rail system in the city. The deputation, from the Auckland Passenger Transport Action Committee, is to meet the committee – consisting of the Deputy Prime Minister, Mr Watt, the Minister of Finance, Mr Rowling, and the Associate Minister of Finance, Mr Connelly, on a date to be decided. It will suggest that the Auckland Regional Authority be asked to form a committee to hear submissions from interested groups on the proposed rapid rail scheme…" [609]

Government Offer of Suburban Rail to Auckland

As Governments do, particularly when a decision is to be made in the face of divided opinion, this Government offered the consolation prize of a cheaper option – designed to appease both the rail- and road-biased sides at the same time – as reported by The New Zealand Herald of 18 July 1973:

"An electric train service from Papakura leading into an underground rail loop beneath the central city has been offered to Auckland by the Government. The offer was made to the Auckland Regional Authority last night by the Deputy Prime Minister and Minister of Works and Development, Mr Watt, in giving the Government's decision on plans for a rapid transit system. In effect, the Government has offered Auckland the first stage of the system – including the underground railway – proposed last year by the Rapid Transit Steering Committee, with an extension from Manurewa to Papakura…

"The Government has decided, as the committee proposed, that existing 3-foot 6-inch lines to South Auckland should be used so the cost can be kept down. At the same time it has rejected a self-contained system on a 4-foot 8-1/2-inch track as sought by the ARA and other Auckland local bodies.

"The Government's decision carefully refers to an Auckland rail transit scheme, with no mention of the word 'rapid', but Mr Watt said last night that it was intended to be a fast, modern rail service…Total cost was estimated at $60.8 million against $273 million for the ARA scheme. The Government's approval is subject to two provisions:

- That before construction begins, firm estimates of cost and   details of proposals are submitted to the Government for approval after discussion with the regional authority;
- That the new service be regarded only as a trial system.

"Part of this second provision was that no further extensions of the rail system would be agreed to until the extensions and alternative passenger transport systems for Auckland had been fully evaluated and compared by means of a systematic and comprehensive analysis of their service characteristics, their financial and economic consequences, and social implications…

"Other points made by Mr Watt: The Government will accept responsibility only for the first stage to Papakura and the city loop. Only the southern route is regarded as urgent for a high-capacity public transport facility. Some new lines will be built near existing tracks so that freight and long-distance passenger services are adequately catered for. The idea of a lane exclusively for buses on the Harbour Bridge is supported." [610]

Terrible Disappointment

Reaction to the Government announcement was mixed, depending on which side of the fence critics sat (or no side at all in the case of the ARA Chairman):

"The Government proposal was immediately attacked by Mr Sir Dove-Myer Robinson…Emphasising that he was speaking personally, Sir Dove-Myer said he was terribly disappointed because the Government had solemnly promised Auckland, both before and after the election, a rapid-rail service. 'But what they have offered us is an improved Wellington suburban type service. I am satisfied this will not attract anything like the number of passengers that would be required to make it an economic service. And if Auckland accepts financial responsibility for operating losses which would be inevitable, it would impose an intolerable burden on ratepayers.

"The chairman of the ARA, Mr T H Pearce, was less critical. He said the offer was quite a generous one. It was the first time a tangible offer had come from any Government. He would not say whether he thought the authority would agree to the proposal." [610]

Expensive Experiment

Despite the fact that the Government had obviously taken their views into account, members of the Auckland Public Transport Action Committee were not entirely satisfied – as reported by The Auckland Star:

"The Government proposal on the rapid rail scheme is 'a very expensive experiment to upgrade the southern line to see if people would use it,' the acting head of the town planning department at Auckland University, Mr J R Dart, said today. It would affect only a small minority, and he expected it would show that a rail system was not appropriate to Auckland's needs. He hoped that now the rail system had been outlined, something would be done about the public transport system as Auckland already knew it. This urgently needed upgrading, with more frequent buses, improved designs and adequate shelter at bus stops.

"Mr Dart said the assumption that an upgraded bus service would create traffic congestion was superficial. It assumed nothing could be done to discourage peak-hour car use through stricter control of entry of cars into the city, increased parking fees, and licensing parking areas. No one move, including the rail proposal, would solve the traffic problem on its own. The test of the rail system would be its ability to attract passengers to drive to suburban stations rather than its use by those within walking distance, Mr Dart said.

"The chairman of the Auckland Harbour Bridge Authority, Mr B P Stevenson, said the authority could put exclusive bus lanes on the bridge 'tomorrow' – but they would be of no real value until a freeway was created to eliminate the Fanshawe St bottleneck. A new road would have to be built from Fanshawe St to the bridge. Mr Stevenson said a second road bridge would be needed whether the rail system was extended to the North Shore or not. Now that the rail link was not planned in the foreseeable future, a second road crossing was essential. A new bridge linking with the proposed Pt Chevalier motorway would help avoid inner city congestion.

"The Mayor of Takapuna, Mr A F Thomas, said the Government had shown commendable restraint when more essential needs were struggling for limited finance, labour and materials – including hospital services, garbage disposal and the completion of inner city motorways. 'Exclusive bus lanes on the harbour bridge would boost the

Auckland public transport system,' he said. 'Bus services could be much improved, and express services at peak hours would help the North Shore and improve patronage.'" [611]

Breach of Promise

Dove-Myer Robinson's criticism of the Government's 'rapid rail' proposals continued with his report to the ARA's Rapid Transit Committee on 20 July 1973:

"The Government's offer to provide Auckland with an electrified 'suburban' railway between Papakura and the City, is merely an extension and upgrading of normal railway department facilities which should be available to any area in New Zealand requiring suburban passenger railway services, and is a breach of the Government's solemn election promise to provide Auckland with a Rapid Rail service.

"It was because the Government promised a 'rapid rail' service that the A.R.A. agreed to meet operating deficits (if any). For this reason there should be no thought of agreeing that, as the Minister stated last Tuesday, the ratepayers of Auckland should be responsible for operating costs of the greatly inferior upgraded Wellington type of suburban rail service which the Government is offering. If Auckland did agree to accept this responsibility, it could be quite as logically argued that Auckland should be responsible for meeting the costs of the University or any other government service simply because they are situated within the City of Auckland…" [612]

ARA Accepts Government Offer

On July 30, the Auckland Regional Authority accepted the Government's offer 'in principle' as stated in the resolution: *"That this meeting accepts Government's decision on a bus/rail transit system in principle, subject to further discussions on parking lots, stations and operating costs in view of the proposed adoption of a 3'6" gauge on the existing lines to make an exclusive right of way."* [613]

As a result, Dove-Myer Robinson's criticism of the Government's offer extended to his concern for what the less-than-hoped-for scheme would cost the Auckland City Council's ratepayers – as per his report, as Mayor, to Members of the Auckland City Council's Policy and Finance Committee on 9 August 1973:

"In essence, The Government is offering to provide, on a trial basis, an electrified suburban railway service, between the City and Papakura, to come into operation about 1982, and it is a condition that the ARA meet operating losses. Although this is far less than was asked for by the ARA, because it is a Railway Department project and will be operated by the Department – not by the ARA – neither the ARA nor the local authorities have the right or the power to refuse it.

"On the other hand, the agreement by the ARA to meet operating costs was for a true 'rapid rail' system on exclusive lines and using the latest automatic controls. It is therefore clear that neither the ARA nor the contributing local authorities should have any moral or legal obligation to meet operating losses on a scheme so different to that which the ARA had in mind when it made the offer to meet operating costs.

"This is of considerable importance to the City Council because if the same 'area of benefit' provisions apply to this new rail project as with the ARA bus services, the City could find itself saddled with the same 66% of losses – which, in this case, could be of the order of $2 million or more annually…

"It must also be remembered that the overwhelming number of the members of the Authority are not in the 'area of benefit' and if they finally vote for acceptance of the Government's proposals, including agreement to meet operating losses, these non-affected members will be committing the City to a large, but unknown increase in ARA levies. It is for this reason that the City Council must view with concern the action of the ARA...

"The implications are now: –

1. The Authority has accepted 'in principle' indefinite proposals for a scheme completely different from its previously adopted policies.

2. That Auckland, especially the City, could be committed, in the same ill-considered manner, to meeting large, but unknown, operating costs.

"May I again repeat that Auckland has no right or power to reject the Government's proposals, but we have every right – provided the members of the ARA have the courage to do so – to refuse to meet any of the capital or operating costs. I would therefore suggest that Council inform the ARA that until all the matters in doubt have been clarified, and Council is satisfied with all the details of the scheme as finally agreed between the Government and the ARA, Council will not be agreeable to meeting any part of the operating costs." [613]

Defeat of Rapid Rail and Dove-Myer Robinson

However, the provisional acceptance of the Government's version of a rapid rail service by the ARA was of far greater significance to Dove-Myer Robinson than just the acceptance of a cheap, ineffectual, and perhaps costlier alternative – as described by John Edgar:

"Robinson's challenge to the local bodies' jealous defence of their political autonomy and prerogative had failed. They had not been silenced and had now given the government a way out of an expensive scheme. The government and lower tier local bodies had been aided by those on the authority who had undermined Robinson's initial challenge to the conception of the ARA. His rapid rail project, all along, had been the only serious contradiction of that conception."

"In Watt's proposal, [ARA Chairman] Pearce saw a way of quietening the dissenting elements of the lower tier and bringing the ARA back into a safer role. If he advocated that the ARA accept Watt's proposals then there would be improvements in public transportation but more importantly the scheme would fit into the authority's philosophy and direction – it was being offered by government and did not involve aggressive lobbying, it was compatible with road transportation objectives currently undertaken by the Auckland Regional Authority and by local bodies before it; it did not call for switches in funding priority or set the authority on an innovative urban transportation course; it did not advantage certain municipalities to any great extent; it would be palatable to the Auckland Regional Authority membership who shared Pearce's philosophy of 'benign' and bland regionalism and it would be acceptable to the lower tier municipalities. Pearce pursued the Watt scheme with vigour, calling it 'an offer from the Godfather. It is one we can't refuse.'" [164]

Dismay and Indignation

Obviously, Dove-Myer Robinson disagreed with Tom Pearce and vented his dismay and indignation by means of an article published by The New Zealand Herald on 8 August 1973:

"My dismay and indignation on hearing of the Government's decision arises from the fact that not only will this proposal be ineffective and have a disastrous effect on the future properly controlled growth and prosperity of Auckland, but from the way in which up to the last minute we were led to believe we were to get a 'rapid rail' or 'rapid transit' system.

"In all its statements on this matter, before and since the last elections, the Government promised a 'rapid rail' system. What we are now offered is a 'suburban' system using a hotch-potch of the 1927 type of Wellington system, with late model coaches on the same narrow gauge lines, and using most of the outdated methods already abandoned almost everywhere else in the world." [614]

Auckland Rapid Transit Directorate

A hotch-potch system or not, a start had at least been made on its planning by November 1973. A rapid transit project office, estimated to cost $20,000, had been approved and would subsequently be operating from 149-155 Parnell Road, Auckland. [615]

An Auckland Rapid Transit Directorate had also been appointed – "…a three-man managerial team consisting of the ARA general manager, Mr J F Y Schischka, the Railways Department chief engineer, Mr G F Bridges, and the Ministry of Works chief civil engineer, Mr A G Stirrat, who is the chairman." [616]

In a memo to the District Commissioner of Works, Auckland on 4 December 1973, the Commissioner of Works, Wellington, N C McLeod, confirmed that an Auckland Rapid Transit Directorate had been established to:

"…control the planning, design, and eventual construction of the system..." and also "…two departmental project teams are becoming established…

"We see the Directorate as being primarily responsible for ensuring that the scope and timing of investigations, designs and plans undertaken by each of the departments and the Authority are such as to adequately cover the requirements of the whole project. Much of the necessary co-ordination will be achieved by officers working together on related tasks.

"The question of chairmanship of the Directorate has now been resolved. Mr Stirrat is to carry out this responsibility. It will be his duty to supply regular progress reports for the information of the Minister. Your office will be required to undertake any secretarial work for the Directorate.

"Even though at Government level, co-ordination of the work is a responsibility of the Minister of Works and Development, at officer level, it is appropriate that we should adopt the normal client department relationship. This is a railway project, and we are servicing N.Z. Railways as a client. This is the relationship on similar work currently in hand, e.g. Kaimai Deviation, and will continue to be so on future works.

"I believe that good progress is being made in the establishment of the two project teams. While each team will retain its own departmental identity from an administrative point of view, the two will be working very closely together on all aspects of the work. This will be helped considerably by the fact that they will be sharing the new project office, which has been arranged by N.Z.R.

"The division of responsibilities between the two teams should be defined as carefully as possible, but will in any case need review from time to time. It will tend to follow the areas of expertise in each department. I see no need to be too specific on this point, but generally speaking, while N.Z.R. will have an important role on overall management of the transit system, location and frequency of stations (in conjunction with the A.R.A.), design standards, rail duplication, rolling stock, signalling and electrification, Ministry of Works will be primarily responsible for site investigations, most of the civil and structural engineering and station design. Inter disciplinary aspects such as town planning, environmental assessments, aesthetics, legal and land purchase, will of course receive attention from both departments, depending on availability of expertise.

"Financial authority for this project and similar future works, is being transferred from Vote Works to Vote Railways from 1 April 1974. Expenditure incurred until 1.4.74 is to be met by N.Z.R…All land purchase and compensation associated with new work on the underground city section will be handled by M.O.W. N.Z.R. will be responsible for purchase and compensation on the existing southern corridor, and for the use and exploitation of all land purchased.

"The department's staff resources will not allow the project team to be of such a size that it will be able to handle all the design work. It is envisaged that design briefs will be prepared by the Project Engineer, and the detailed work will be undertaken by District Office and Head Office. Normal policy on the approval of designs and the engagement of consultants will be followed." [617]

Rapid Transit Plans Extended

It would seem that the team that made up the Auckland Rapid Transit Directorate had the ambition and foresight to create something more than just *a hotch-potch of the 1927 type of Wellington system* originally proposed by the Government as the solution to Auckland's transport problems – as reported by The New Zealand Herald on 20 March 1974:

"Plans for the Auckland city underground rail loop have been changed drastically to provide for a double track and a greatly extended system taking in Karangahape Rd and the Upper Symonds St and Newmarket areas.

"Details of the changes in the originally proposed rail transport scheme were announced yesterday by the Minister of Works and Development, Mr Watt. In Auckland last night the changes, and the very fact that Mr Watt had announced them, were being hailed as 'the end of reports, committees and inquiries and a start to the finished product.'

"The two major changes indicated by Mr Watt's announcement are: The underground city loop has been lengthened to run through or near Customs St, from the central railway station, Karangahape Rd, Khyber Pass Rd, Newmarket and Parnell; it will be a double track with trains running in both directions.

"In addition, it is possible that an eastern loop, along the route of existing railway tracks, will run to and from the city to Orakei, Glenn Innes, Mt Wellington and Westfield. The original rail scheme offered by the Government to the Auckland Regional Authority in July – involving as a first stage an electrified route branching from a city loop to Papakura – appears otherwise unaltered.

"Mr Watt said yesterday that the realigned and extended city underground loop gave 'more value for money.' He emphasised that much detailed planning was still needed for both the city loop and the electrification of the train service from Papakura. It is understood that the details Mr Watt gave were recommended by the Auckland Rapid Transit directorate…

"Mr Watt said that although the new scheme had not been costed it might be 'a little dearer' than the plan proposed last year. (The cost of the rail system from Papakura to the city, including an underground city loop, was put then at $60.8 million.) Mr Watt said preliminary investigations indicated that Auckland would get a better transport system than was first planned." [616]

The ART Investment

In its summary of the new Auckland Rapid Transit (ART) proposal presented to the Auckland Regional Authority, the Directorate described the City's current problem as:

"The transport straitjacket of cars, traffic congestion, noise and pollution…" and went on to outline the rapid transit scheme the Directorate saw as the solution:

"The ART Investment - The emphasis must now be placed on people instead of on vehicles. Public money is better spent on transport systems which serve the public as a whole rather than as individuals because of the high cost of maintaining a personal transport system. The proposals for the ART scheme are designed to reshape the priorities of investment in transport in Auckland. They are based on social as well as economic considerations. Social objectives are implicit in the Cabinet's decision that planning and design of the first stage of a rapid transit scheme be put in hand…

"A prime social asset of ART is that rail rights of way already exist for its construction and that the city loop passes underground through the heavily built-up inner city area. ART thus avoids any need for large-scale disruption of housing and the urban landscape in general. Such disruption is today much less acceptable to the public than formerly.

"The southern corridor and inner city area of Auckland have been chosen for the first stage of the ART scheme, together with the East Loop through Orakei because of the Directorate's opinion that, through the addition of a further, well-developed passenger catchment directly served by rail, it has undoubted advantages for Stage 1.

"The southern corridor is an area of high growth for housing and industry. Its population is now approximately 200,000 and while its pattern of development has been basically linear it has room for a considerable degree of lateral expansion. These factors make the southern corridor a logical choice for the first stage of a rapid transit system. The high-capacity rail service would provide the spine of the system, while the bus component, for both ART rail interconnection and separate local services, results in a comprehensive, flexible and modern solution to cater for present and future transport needs in this area.

"ART is a comprehensive and ambitious project. It provides for rail and bus services to be operated on a fully integrated basis, with buses over a widespread network, feeding the rail system and vice versa. This will provide flexibility which will maximise patronage by efficiently serving both the intensive catchments most immediate to the railway and the less developed outer areas while preserving options for the service of future requirements.

"High Standards - ART will provide a high level of service. Its operational aims are speed, reliability and frequency. Its aesthetic and psychological aims are attractive design, comfort, convenience of access and transfer and completely modern design and staffing attitudes. Caution has no place in the design of a scheme intended to attract a population which for the last decade has been mainly concerned with finding alternatives to public transport.

"The scheme must be innovative and attractive to experience. It must generate a feeling of providing a real public transport service and be psychologically dependable to a population accustomed to frustration and delays in using existing public transport. It must set a new standard if it is to accomplish a major modification of Aucklanders' travel habits.

"Should these objectives not be attained, ART will fail because the public will have no stake in its survival. Therefore a high investment in modern facilities is required. The boldness of the investment must anticipate the boldness of ART's public appeal. ART will need to convince the public of its worth if other methods to reduce dependence on the private car are to be credible." [618]

Costs

The initial bold investment was outlined, in dollar terms, by the Rapid Transit project office to the Chief Civil Engineer on 1 October 1974:

"Expenditure On ART: Stage 1 – The estimated cost up to completion of the Project Report Stage - now the end of October - is $440,000 total. The estimate to 31.3.75 remains at $634,000…" [619]

Any budget shortfall was covered, according to a letter from the Finance and Accounts Branch, New Zealand Railways, to the Chief Accountant, Ministry of Works and Development, dated 6 November 1974:

"…on 21 October Cabinet: agreed to over-expenditure of up to $300,000…to permit the Auckland Rapid Transit project planning team to operate up to 31 March 1975…noted that any such over-expenditure will be no more than is necessary to continue planning and design for stage 1 only this financial year…The approval above means that subject to the restraints stated, expenditure authorised for the 1974/1975 financial year is now $500,000.

"It is now apparent that at this early stage Government intends to authorise expenditure on a year to year basis with the annual sum to be provided in the Capital Estimates…" [620]

ART Cost Estimates 1975 – 1976

The following year's estimates were naturally to increase – as outlined in a letter from the Rapid Transit project office to the Chief Civil Engineer, dated 12 December 1974:

"Estimates of next year's expenditure…Costs are based on present wage levels – the most recent 4% increase is not included. Summarising:

"A. Investigation and design only – No monies voted for actual construction but investigation and design activities being pursued on the assumption that the scheme will proceed – $800,000.

"Estimates of Project Office Expenditure for Y.E. 31.3.76

"A. Investigation and design only
1. Salaries…$558,000
2. Local Authority charges for design work on services relocation…$49,000
3. Investigation…$75,000
4. Consultants and outside services…$35,000
5. Project Office costs…$24,000
6. Vehicles…$14,000
7. Miscellaneous - Tunnel Test - Survey Equipment…$40,000

"B. Investigation, Design and Construction
Stage 1: Construction - Civil…$1,700,000 Land…$1,400,000 – Total $3,900,000
"East Loop: Construction - Civil…$400,000 Land…$800,000 – Total: $1,200,000" [621]

Financial Estimates Hushed-up

As the rapid transit design work progressed, and costs naturally increased, those escalating costs were a natural target for those opposed to the scheme – as demonstrated at an Institute of Engineers panel discussion in February 1975:

"An economist yesterday clashed with the Mayor of Auckland, Sir Dove-Myer Robinson, over the cost of the proposed Auckland rapid transit scheme. Mr T K

McDonald, an economist with the Institute of Economic Research, claimed that the cost of the scheme had risen dramatically in the past 18 months and that revised financial estimates have been hushed-up at Government level. He said that the last public estimate, based on mid-1973 figures, put the entire capital cost of the rapid transit scheme at $75 million. Now, he claimed, new estimates showed that stage one of the scheme alone would cost between $100 million and $200 million.

"Mr McDonald, who was speaking during a panel discussion organised by the New Zealand Institute of Engineers, said it was impossible for him to be more precise because the new estimates were a closely guarded Government secret. Accusing some experts who backed the scheme of 'fiddling figures,' he said $100 million to $200 million would be enough to overcome most of the difficulties afflicting public transport systems in most other urban areas in New Zealand.

"'Instead, all this money is to be spent on one rail corridor catering for only 2 per cent of the passenger trips in Auckland – and catering for the sector that is growing most slowly,' he said. 'That seems to be a pretty expensive trial system.'

"Sir Dove-Myer, who was in the audience, replied that the rapid transit scheme was not just a rail extension. It was a comprehensive regional transport system which would be 90 per cent dependent on a co-ordinating bus system. The extension of the railway to the centre of the city would simply restore the situation of 30 or 40 years ago when the Auckland railway station was right behind the central post office. Sir Dove-Myer said he was fed up with erroneous criticisms of the rapid transit scheme. The time had come for action, not further debate…

"Mr McDonald added: 'If the mayor is correct and the system will be 90 per cent buses, then why are we paying between $100 million and $200 million for the 10 per cent?'" [622]

Automated Ants in Concrete Canyons

But more debate was still sought by rapid transit opponents – as reported by the South Auckland Courier on 19 February 1975:

"Mr Ralph Witten, Auckland Regional Authority member, Manukau City Council member and chairman of the council's Town Planning Committee, is critical of the Press and the Auckland Rapid Rail Scheme…In a prepared statement submitted to the Courier he says:

"The recent announcement by the Minister, Mr Watt that he will make a recommendation to Cabinet this month on the Auckland Rapid Rail Scheme may raise aspects of public interest on this matter which have not been adequately debated in public. Decisions involving hundreds of millions of dollars of taxpayers' money have yet to be resolved…

"Insurance companies and Building Societies figure largely in the downtown Auckland where the new Central Area Plan proposes 25 million square feet of new development and some 30,000 new jobs during the next 20 year planning period. The need to cart people into the central area to fill these buildings is the primary justification for the massive investment into the Rapid Rail scheme…is this city serving the needs of people or people being reduced to automated ants in concrete canyons to serve a few downtown property owners?

"It appears that with such large sums of public money at stake and the quality of life of so many people involved the foregoing points are legitimate items for public debate by responsible authorities and the metropolitan media, for debate is an essential ingredient in both arriving at the solution and in informing the public who pay for and are affected by these proposals." [623]

Far From a Done Deal

Despite the time and cost of the design work expended since the rapid transit office was established more than a year before, rapid transit opponents such as T K McDonald and Ralph Witten need not have worried. The scheme was far from a done deal and the Government's leading supporter was about to be lost to the cause. Nevertheless, some optimism for the scheme's future was expressed by The New Zealand Herald on 19 February 1975:

"The departure of the Minister of Works, Mr Watt, for his new post as High Commissioner in London, need not, and should not, be a cause of further delay in implementing the Auckland rapid transit system. A paper on the revised plan for the scheme's first stage is due to be placed by Mr Watt before Cabinet near the end of this month. Will the minister have time to achieve a decision within the following two or three weeks? Is it possible, or necessary, that a replacement minister should wish to recommit the issues, ostensibly until he has had time to familiarise himself with details?

"In his enthusiasm for the rapid transit scheme, Mr Watt has had the advantage of being an Auckland minister with a knowledge of Auckland's needs. However, the commitments to go ahead with the project have not been made just by Mr Watt in his own name. They have been party commitments, and firm ones at that…" [624]

Oh So Slow

That final Government commitment which could finally lead to a start on actual construction was still to be confirmed as Hugh Watt's departure neared – as reported by The Auckland Star on 5 March 1975:

"There appears to be nothing rapid about the preparation of submissions for Auckland's rapid-transit scheme. The Minister of Works, Mr Watt, stated in January this year he intended to present a submission based on the project report to the Cabinet Works Committee early in February. A submission was drafted and sent back to the departments concerned – Works, Railways and the Auckland Regional Authority – for comment. The Minister's office is still waiting for all the comment to arrive.

"But even if it does there is doubt that the Minister of Works, Mr Watt, will be in a position to take a submission to Cabinet. He leaves for London and his High Commissioner's posting soon. It appears likely that his as yet unnamed successor will be left with the task of pressing ahead with the scheme – or holding back…

"Mr Watt said earlier that when the Cabinet Works Committee had considered his submissions and departmental comments, he would be in a position to discuss the report fully with the Auckland Regional Authority…It now seems likely that the Auckland Regional Authority will have to discuss the report with a new Minister of Works. The question left unanswered is: Will this Minister support the scheme as much as Mr Watt?" [625]

An Embarrassing Wait

While Hugh Watt remained an influence, Dove-Myer Robinson threw him a last roll of the dice by means of a letter, dated 5 March 1975:

"My purpose in writing you, is to draw your attention to the fact that my Council recently adopted – after 10 years study – a Central Area Plan which is based on the assumption that the central business district of the city will be directly connected with the main trunk line via several strategically located stations within the city. Objections to this Plan are to be heard within the next few weeks, and I feel it is essential to my Council to know if and when the Government is to implement its pre- and post-election pledges to provide the city with this vital railway connection which would become the key factor in the reorganisation of all other public transport facilities within the Auckland regional area.

"Almost every day, important town planning decisions have to be made, and it is increasingly embarrassing, both to my Council and to the private developer, that we cannot say with certainty if and when the rail connection will be made. Our city streets almost daily are becoming more and more congested with vehicular traffic; pollution of the atmosphere on occasions reaches almost dangerous levels, and the whole of our planning for the future is stultified because this vital statement by the Government has not yet been made…" [626]

ARA Restive

Much less insistent than Dove-Myer Robinson, the ARA Chairman, Tom Pearce, felt he had motive enough to approach the new Minister of Works, Michael Connelly, sometime soon…

"The Auckland Regional Authority is getting a little restive about the length of time the Government is taking in stating what it proposes to do about the Auckland rapid transit system. At a meeting last night the chairman of the ARA, Mr T H Pearce, said that in two weeks he would get in touch with the Minister of Works, Mr Connelly, and asked him what the Government proposals were. He said he had a 'vested' reason for wanting to know what the Government decision was, for he had been castigated by the late Prime Minister, Mr Kirk, for doubting his (Mr Kirk's) word that the rapid transit system would be built…Sir Dove-Myer Robinson said he understood the Government would be making an announcement shortly – possibly within a week or so – on its proposals." [627]

Auckland Rapid Transit Directorate Report

As usual, that *week or so* lengthened to a month or so and it wasn't until 15 May that the three-volume, 625-page project report was finally presented to the ARA and then publicly released. Representing a year's work for the 30-member Auckland Rapid Transit Directorate set up in July 1973, the report more or less recommended the rapid transit concept earlier proposed by Hugh Watt – as reported by the Auckland Star:

"A fast suburban rail system, fed by a big bus fleet and operating into an inner city underground loop – that's the way you'll travel to work and the city within 11 years, according to a rapid transit scheme the Government has approved. Planners have told Cabinet that the combined rail-bus link is better than an all-bus system. This advice is behind the Cabinet support for the rapid transit project for Auckland…

Mr Connelly also revealed that the cost of stage one of the project has risen from the 1973 estimate of $45 million to $154.5 million for a replanned stage. He said a rapid transit system based on trains and feeder buses was the best that could be evolved. He also said that if the final decision to go ahead with the project is taken, the first year it could be in service would be 1986…

"Mr Connelly sounded warnings when he said that the Cabinet was most concerned at the rise in costs. 'At the same time, we are aware that there is not unanimous support for the concepts as proposed in the report. It has been suggested that insufficient thought has been given to an all-bus system which is the only alternative.

"I must point out that the decision to proceed with rail-bus was made only after much deliberation on all available forms of public transport. We must ensure that comparisons made with any other alternatives are on the basis of an equivalent level of service.' Mr Connelly said that although design work was far from complete, it had reached the stage where realistic cost estimates could be determined." [628]

Doors Left Open

However, well before the determination of those cost estimates, the Government was again leaving several doors open as possible escape routes. As well as the inescapable and escalating costs of a rapid transit scheme that could prove unaffordable for the Government, Michael Connelly also suggested that the bus fleet needed could prove unaffordable for the ARA as well. Also, despite the previously-held view of the ARA and Dove-Myer Robinson that the Government should be responsible for all railway operating costs, this point seems to have been blurred by Mr Connelly – as reported by The Auckland Star on 16 May 1975:

"If the proposed Auckland Rapid Transit is to proceed, the next move is up to the Auckland Regional Authority, the Minister of Works, Mr Connelly, told a Press conference yesterday.

"'The Government has made no new commitment to the scheme. In fact it is 'greatly concerned' at the escalation in the estimated cost, the minister said…'The next step is an initiative by the ARA. We must be guided by the authority. Everything depends on what the authority decides. If it decides it doesn't want to proceed there will be no further discussion…We cannot say the Government is committed to anything until the Government and the ARA can reach agreement. If the authority decides it wants the scheme or any part of it, it will be up to it to seek further discussions about cost sharing,' he said.

"Under the original Government commitment, the authority would be required to pay the capital cost of 224 rail feeder buses, about $9.2 million worth, and fund all operating, maintenance and depreciation costs of both rail and bus parts of the system. 'What's best for Auckland is best decided by those who speak for Auckland,' the Minister said." [629]

Time for a Decision

The Auckland Star felt it knew what was best for Auckland and said so in its editorial for 16 May 1975:

"Is Auckland ever to have a modern rapid public transit system? After more than a decade of argument during which report has been piled upon report the question is still unanswered. The time for an answer surely has come with the release of the report of the Auckland Rapid Transit directorate yesterday. Mr Pearce, chairman of the regional authority, acknowledges this in saying: 'It is time for finality…' The region should not be allowed to live in the twilight world of indecision any longer.

"The scheme would be expensive and the cost is bound to escalate the longer the delay. But against the cost must be offset the substantial expenditure on roads, motorways and so on that would have to be incurred if the scheme were rejected…The case for accepting the net cost of an integrated rapid rail and bus system rests on the proposition that there is no alternative that would be so efficient and convenient…The plan may be criticized in detail but at least in stages it would provide the rapid rail spines on which a new system of public transport could be based…

"The question of where the money comes from will have to be settled before the authority makes a final decision on the directorate's report. Also involved is the wider issue of finance for regional authorities generally on which the ARA is again about to make representations to the Government.

"That another report recommends a rapid transit system may prompt the cynical retort that 'we've heard all that before.' On this occasion, however, the exercise has been a joint Government - ARA one. Both seem to accept that they must now move beyond their earlier acceptance of rapid transit in principle. The hard negotiating over the fine print should begin without delay. Or else hopes that something may eventually come of it all should be abandoned and fresh stock taken of the Auckland region's public transport needs." [630]

And The New Zealand Herald agreed – as per an editorial of its own at the time:

"It has become almost a matter of routine that fresh proposals for a rapid-rail system from Auckland should pre-date each general election. It is a matter of history that none of the proposals has been carried out. Inevitably, the need of New Zealand's largest metropolitan area for an adequate rail system has grown more acute, and the cost of providing it has gone higher and higher...

"The lesson of the [Auckland Rapid Transit Directorate] report is not that it will cost too much to make a start on building the rapid rail, but that it is too costly to accept further delay. The weight of road transport is already starting to choke the metropolitan area. If that is not enough, the high price of imported oil makes further growth of car and bus traffic uneconomic." [631]

Building Uncertainty

As usual, there were still many dissenters who felt left out of the decision-making process with good reason to complain – such as Auckland City Councillor, Jim Anderton:

"The people of Auckland have recently learned that a report on the city's rapid rail scheme has been prepared at a cost over $800,000. Although the scheme is supposedly to benefit them – or rather some of them – they have not been asked whether they want it. Nor have they been generally consulted or asked for their opinions during the report's preparation.

"What worries me is that the general public and the business community along the proposed rail route have not the faintest idea what is in store for them if this grandiose and outdated scheme goes ahead...In a classical statement of professional uncertainty, the design and construction section of the report states that buildings along the route may have to be underpinned, repaired after the rail construction or even demolished. The engineers are not sure which...

"Although the rapid rail engineers plan to dig up the city streets and either shore up or demolish some of its buildings, they did not seem to think it was necessary to issue a copy of the report to the city council or to the councillors who are the elected representatives of the people of Auckland. It is true that every member of the Auckland Regional Authority – all 34 of them – have rightly been given a copy of the report. The Mayor has a copy by virtue of his membership of that body. But the city council, like the people of Auckland, has been left in ignorance of what is to happen to their city..." [632]

Jim Anderton's criticism that there had been a lack of consultation about the proposed rapid transit scheme was quickly answered by ARA Chairman, Tom Pearce, who pointed out that:

"…a special meeting of local body representatives in 1972 agreed by 19 votes to three to leave negotiations with the Government to the ARA. This was subsequently confirmed in 1973 by a vote of 24 to four. On both occasions the city council representative voted for this line of action…" [633]

Demolition Shock

However, it was the possible demolition of some of the City's buildings referred to by Jim Anderton, and subsequently reported by The Auckland Star on 30 May 1975, that drew the biggest reaction:

"Demolition of 13 inner city buildings is involved in the planned first stage of the Auckland Rapid Transit system. And most owners did not know their buildings were earmarked for destruction until told by the Star today. This information is contained in the massive, limited-circulation report of the rapid-transit directorate. Even Auckland City councillors have been unable to get copies. Earmarked for possible demolition are four more buildings whose foundations could be so badly affected by tunnelling as to be uneconomic to repair…

"The buildings all lie on the route most favoured by the rapid transit directorate. Their owners were deliberately not informed of the possibility of demolition because, says project engineer Mr Mike Lancaster, planners wanted to prevent 'any unnecessary alarm'. Investigators discovered as much about the buildings as they could without actually approaching the owners…

"The required properties will probably be taken under the controversial Public Works Act (1912) compulsory purchase provisions. Mr Lancaster confirmed that the rapid transit project would be treated as a normal Government project and therefore, not be subject to the normal Town and Country Planning Act objection procedures…" [634]

Needless Apprehension

Always one to quickly react to criticism of the proposed rapid transit scheme, Dove-Myer Robinson wasted no time this time either:

"Auckland Mayor Sir Dove-Myer Robinson attacked the Star today for publishing yesterday that 13 inner city buildings would be demolished to make way for the rapid rail scheme. He said the Star had been 'almost irresponsible' and 'needlessly caused apprehension. My real comments are unprintable,' Sir Dove-Myer said. 'My telephone was going like mad for about an hour after the Star came out. And when I went into the matter with the people responsible for the report, they said that the buildings were not likely to be affected at all.

"'It was premature and it is likely to do more harm to rapid transit than anything else. Until the route is defined and many other factors have been established, until we know exactly where we are going, we cannot say who is going to be affected. I don't believe in concealing facts from the public where there are facts – anybody knows that. But there is still a great deal to be considered,' he said." [635]

It was all a big furore for nothing, reported The New Zealand Herald:

"None of the 13 city buildings marked for demolition to make way for the Auckland rapid transit scheme is on New Zealand Historic Places Trust preservation lists. Most of the buildings are described as 'ancient' and some were destined for demolition anyway. Only one of the buildings, the Civic Theatre in Queen St, has been suggested as worth saving for its historical, cultural and architectural value. The theatre, built in 1929, is being restored." [636]

A Leisurely Pace

Pending cost-sharing negotiations between the Government and the ARA, the rapid transit scheme, like many before it, waited patiently at the station:

"An air of waiting pervades Transvision House in Parnell where the Auckland Rapid Transit project team occupies two floors. The pace is nearly leisurely. At the end of last year outside consultants plus 32 staff members – most of them engineers – were going at frantic pace trying to meet a Government deadline for producing a detailed cost and engineering report on the first stage of the proposed rapid transit scheme. They were also trying to answer criticisms, including some on broad planning grounds, voiced in a Commission for the Environment audit. It was this report which shocked city property owners this week with planning which involves demolition of at least 13 inner city buildings…

"The Government asked us to keep the project team together and has given us the finance to do it. But work is at a very much lower key now, explains Mr Ian Mead, who shares responsibility for the office's smooth running with Mr Mike Lancaster, project engineer for the Ministry of Works…

"It has cost the Government $820,000 so far, a factor that has caused critics to warn that the scheme whose future is still not settled, could be pushed through as a fait accompli…The rapid transit proposal has changed shape many times since it was first suggested 12 years ago. Whether it will be built appears no more certain today than two years ago, when both the Government and the ARA approved a scheme in principle. Criticism hasn't abated. Many planners have insisted that changing travel patterns now make it unnecessary…" [637]

Dove-Myer Robinson Articles

While Dove-Myer Robinson was no longer so closely involved with rapid transit plan negotiations between the ARA and the Government, this did not diminish his attempts to influence the Government and the public whenever and wherever he could. Newspapers were always a favourite medium – that is, when editors could be persuaded that publishing his opinions were in the public interest and could engender further debate (and sell more papers).

The New Zealand Herald obviously thought that to be the case when it published six consecutive articles by Dove-Myer Robinson between 23 and 28 June 1975. While these articles described the need for suburban rail as a means of reducing road congestion and rejuvenating inner city development, resulting in social benefits, their overall argument was one of finance – of how the bus-rail service was to be paid for and of how much would be saved from not building the roads (and a second harbour bridge) that would otherwise be required. These articles were subsequently reprinted as a booklet and widely distributed by the Mayor – particularly to critics of the proposed rail scheme.

City Council Dithers

Auckland City Councillor, Jim Anderton, was one of the most vociferous of those critics – as reported by City News on 4 June 1975:

"There was more soul searching at last week's council meeting on whether or not councillors should be banned from smoking during meetings than on the two hundred million dollar question of rapid rail. A notice of motion from Jim Anderton asking that the council express to the ARA and the Minister of Works its strongest opposition to the scheme, provoked little more than a reactionary bite from the council's C & R [Citizens & Ratepayers] faction…

"The grounds for Mr Anderton's notice of motion were that:

- The people of Auckland had never been consulted on whether they wanted the kind of system outlined in the report;
- no cost/benefit analysis of alternatives such as an all bus service containing rapid buses, mini buses and dial a bus services had ever been carried out and therefore no rational decision could be made in favour of rapid rail;
- the full social, environmental and economic consequences of the scheme had never been conveyed adequately to people in the area, and reports which had been made public had been severely criticised;
- large amounts of capital investment were needed now from Central Government not only for public transport but for urgent needs such as sewerage and stormwater separation;
- immediate finance should be made available by the Government to assist the ARA to develop an all bus system with the advantages of immediate availability, flexibility and service to the whole region.

"Speaking to the motion, Mr Anderton said he had been accused by the Mayor in the press of being disloyal to Auckland in his obstruction of the scheme. 'If trying to prevent social, environmental and economic chaos overtake the city is being disloyal then so be it. But let me warn the Mayor if he is looking for a future monument then the epitaph could read, to the Mayor who thought of the scheme that sent Auckland bankrupt…'

"The motion, seconded by Councillor Ken Dobson was lost but a consequential motion by Councillor Kath Tizard, which will at least put a brake on the proceedings, was passed. This was that the ARA be asked to delay any final commitment to the scheme until it has met with the City Council to discuss its impact on the city…" [638]

ARA and Government to Meet

A meeting between the ARA (including Dove-Myer Robinson as Chairman of the Rapid Transit Committee) and the Government was eventually arranged for the 20th of June – as reported by The New Zealand Herald:

"The Auckland Regional Authority will meet two Cabinet ministers on Friday in Wellington for talks which could decide the future of the Auckland rapid transit scheme. The ARA has decided just how much of the capital and other costs it wants the Government to pay for the stage one central city loop and east loop through Panmure.

"The Minister of Works, Mr Connelly, and the Minister of Railways, Mr Bailey, will represent the Government in the negotiations on the terms of the agreement for the first stage, which will probably cost about $200 million. The Government has pledged to support by paying capital costs and service charges but was surprised by the rapid increase in costs.

"The ARA is also worried about $8.8 million it will need for new buses for the rapid-rail-bus scheme and is hoping for relief. The chairman of the authority, Mr T H Pearce, who will lead the ARA group in the talks, reaffirmed last night that he hoped the negotiations could be completed one way or another before the general election…" [639]

New Formula Denied

The Wellington meeting did not result in much consensus apparently because of the ARA's insistence that, as well as the rail component of the rapid transit scheme, the Government also pay the capital cost and servicing charges of the buses that would be needed – as reported by The Auckland Star:

"The chairman of the Auckland Regional Authority today denied that the ARA is trying to change a cost-sharing agreement with the Government on the Auckland rapid transit scheme. 'On every occasion, the authority has made it clear that it reserved the right to open negotiations on the question of operating costs,' said Mr Tom Pearce. 'We're not asking for any changes at all.' The chairman's remarks followed a report from Minister of Works Mr Connelly, who said an ARA deputation last week sought a new formula, but it was late in the issue for any changes…The Minister said he invited the ARA to submit a report on its new formula and told the deputation that any change would require a Cabinet decision…" [640]

New Formula or Not?

That *report on its new formula* took the form of a letter of explanation written to Michael Connelly by Tom Pearce on 27 June 1975:

"It has been accepted from the outset that we wish to negotiate the financial aspects with Government, and to enable these negotiations to commence it was necessary to determine the costs involved. To provide this information Government set up the A.R.T. Directorate to investigate and report. Our meeting with you on 20th June was simply the first possible negotiating meeting with Government after the release of the Report. It in no way involved a new proposal. Government's proposal has clearly been accepted by the Authority subject to the negotiations mentioned above…

"As explained at the meeting, the Authority is this year levying its ratepayers for existing transport losses alone, the sum of \$6.4 M. If the Authority were to accept Government's proposition they would have to meet operating losses of the A.R.T. project of \$6.4 M, plus the capital servicing costs for buses of a further \$1.5 M making a total of \$7.9 M. If transport levies remained the same there would therefore be a grand total of \$14.3 M to be met by the ratepayers of Auckland. This is clearly not acceptable.

"The 231 buses directly connected with A.R.T. is not the full quantity of buses required by the Authority to service the area, for which an additional 151 will be required. This is in addition to its existing fleet of 600 buses for which progressive replacements will be required without providing for increased services. These burdens are emphasized as being beyond the capacity of the ratepayers to handle, but not beyond the reach of the taxpayer.

"The Authority would contend that it is entitled to a bus/rail service at least equivalent to a modernized Wellington/Hutt Service for which the Government meets the total cost of rail and buses. Further this is within the Government's responsibility as the statutory rail authority for passenger services within New Zealand. On this basis, the Government would meet all capital and operating costs of A.R.T.

"As a minimum the Authority would contend that the Government share of A.R.T. should be the capital and servicing costs of both rail and buses and to provide for replacements when required. This would remove the question of any depreciation from the costings of the project.

"The question of any losses to be met by the Auckland Regional Authority should be subject to further negotiation…This proposal, that Government should pay the capital cost and servicing charges of buses, is well within the established practice in practically every country other than New Zealand where governments provide the capital cost of public transport and many also make substantial contributions to operating expenses..." [641]

Government Doubt

When it came down to it, all argument as to the future economic, social, and environmental benefits of an Auckland rapid transit system – a system that could reduce the City's severe motor vehicle congestion – was reduced to what the Government and the ARA and ratepayers were willing to spend on it. Neither was prepared to ease the other's burden – as reported by The New Zealand Herald on 7 July 1975:

"The Deputy Prime Minister, Mr Tizard, yesterday expressed doubts about the Auckland rapid rail scheme getting off the ground. Making it clear that the Government would not be spending any more than what had been promised, he questioned whether, in the circumstances, Auckland would be prepared to go ahead with the scheme.

"Mr Tizard, who is Minister of Finance, made his thoughts known at the Auckland regional conference of the Labour Party. A member of the Auckland City Council, Mr J P Anderton, raised the subject of finance for the rapid rail scheme after Mr Tizard had spoken of the need for priorities in Government financing.

"Suggesting that the priority for the scheme was very low and something the Government could ill afford, Mr Anderton asked the minister where it was on the Government list for finance. Without answering directly, Mr Tizard said the Government had made a promise of finance, but there were certain conditions. 'The Government will provide the capital for the rail system,' he said, 'but the local bodies will have to pay for the operating expenses.'

"The Auckland Regional Authority was trying to move away from that situation, but the Government would stay firm, he said. 'The Labour Government is not going to go beyond the promise it made,' he said. 'But if the ARA decides to meet the operating expenses we will keep our promise.

"Looking at it realistically,' he told Mr Anderton, 'the promise still stands. But I don't know if the ARA will want to afford to operate the system.' And to cries of support from people at the conference, he added: 'I don't think the city is prepared to pay to make it work.'" [642]

Don't Delay

"The cost of Auckland's proposed rapid transit scheme should not be the major factor, according to the Mayor, Sir Dove-Myer Robinson. 'The main thing to consider is not how much it's going to cost, but how much more it's going to cost the people of Auckland if they don't go ahead with it,' he said yesterday, commenting on reports that the scheme might be shelved. 'It's going to mean bankruptcy for Auckland City and the region as a whole if they don't go ahead with it. It's vital to the central area of Auckland that the project should go ahead. The alternative is that all the traffic from all directions will be going right through the centre of Auckland City. Our city streets would have to be sacrificed to the demands of the motorcars and buses and trucks.'" [643]

Rapid Rail Roundabout

Just history repeating itself, according to The New Zealand Herald:

"The Deputy Prime Minister, Mr Tizard, appears to have embarked on a process with which Aucklanders are only too familiar – encouraging rifts over rapid transit. These are standard tactics for all governments when it seems that something might actually have to be spent on the scheme – other than calling for more reports.

"Mr Tizard is not breaking any promises. Before the last election Labour undertook to meet capital costs and loan charges and has held to this undertaking. Responsibility for operational costs has not been resolved, but hitherto there has remained some prospect of a compromise.

"By insisting that the Government will contribute nothing to this purpose, Mr Tizard makes progress unlikely. With the existing system of local body finance already imposing crippling burdens on ratepayers, the possibility of their undertaking fresh liability for rapid transit deficits on the transport of the community as a whole is negligible.

"Wariness of governments about becoming involved in such costs is based on fears that a precedent would lead to all cities and towns demanding similar help with their transport. But this reasoning is faulty on two grounds. One is that the precedent has been set already. The Wellington suburban railway system has long been subsidised by taxpayers throughout the country. The second point is that no other New Zealand city will attain anywhere near the population of Auckland for very many years. Accordingly the need for a transport system to ease traffic and commuter problems is very much more acute in Auckland than elsewhere in the country.

"The fatal weakness in Auckland's perennial quest for an adequate suburban rail system has been disunity. Politicians who win support by undertaking to back the scheme can find it is absurdly easy later to sow doubts among the multiplicity of local bodies or among groups in the major councils before it becomes necessary to find the money. Then it simply becomes a matter of standing back while Auckland itself frustrates further action. Arguments develop on whether the scheme can be afforded, alternative plans are advanced and the interminable roundabout continues. As with all roundabouts it gets nowhere. The result is that Auckland gets the worst of both worlds – neither rapid transit nor any adequate alternative. The process can plainly be seen starting all over again." [644]

Inflation and Devaluation

And with each repeat of history, the cost naturally increases – as reported by The New Zealand Herald on 14 August 1975:

"Rapid inflation and its new mate, devaluation, have caught up with the Auckland rapid transit project. While the scheme has been waiting since May last year for a green light from the Government and the Auckland Regional Authority, costs have gone merrily ahead. Inflation and devaluation have escalated costs overall by about 15 per cent.

"While the situation could have been much worse but for some estimates in June, 1974, which were made on the 'high side,' the cost of stage one – the city loop and expanded southern corridor – has jumped by about $30 million in a year. The rapid transit project team report presented to the ARA last May put the cost of stage one at $170 million, but now it would top $200 million. This is a rise of more than $500,000 a week since the estimate…

"Devaluation will chiefly hit the purchase of rolling stock overseas for the rapid rail. The June, 1974 estimate of $28 million for rolling stock, however, might not be too far from the mark if the scheme goes ahead this year. The rapid transit project manager, Mr I A Mead, said yesterday competition for rolling stock contracts was keen and this would tend to keep prices down in spite of devaluation…But the message of inflation and devaluation is clear. If the rapid transit scheme is to go ahead procrastination over agreeing on the final cost-sharing terms between the Government and the ARA is costing many thousands of dollars a week." [645]

Passed By?

Not for the first time, Dove-Myer Robinson could see the rapid transit scheme slipping away and his confidence would not have been bolstered by a letter he received from Mrs P M Hoyle Bennett, dated 16 August 1975:

"That was a worthwhile and worthy dream of yours to have a Rapid Rail System for Auckland but aren't you now rather inclined to think that Time has passed it by? By the time it could now be built perhaps the need for it will have receded: suburbs are growing in importance and self-sufficiency; computers will have lessened the need for large office space for files and offices may be nearer home; and I am quite sure the Down Town area will lessen in importance by the end of the Century. It may become increasingly important to have a flexible rapid system that can be changed with changing needs…" [646]

Compromise Sought

Of course, Dove-Myer Robinson could never accept that time had overtaken the rapid transit dream. There was always the chance that compromise could save the day – as he suggested to the Prime Minister, Bill Rowling, by letter dated 1 August 1975:

"I am writing to you again because of my concern about rumours which are current that certain opponents of the proposed bus and rail rapid transit plan for Auckland are stirring up opposition to the plan from Labour Party Members of Parliament and that as a result of this pressure, the Government may delay final agreement or even abandon the whole proposal…

"As it seems likely that the revenue from the railway part of the scheme should show a surplus over operating costs, and the bus part of the operation will show heavy annual losses (but much less than an all bus and roading system), a proposal from the Government along the following lines should be acceptable.

"1. That the Government offer to accept financial responsibility for every aspect of the railway part of the scheme and

"2. That the Auckland Regional Authority similarly agree to meet all costs for the bus part of the scheme.

"The advantage of simplifying the matter in this way is that each authority (the Government and the Auckland Regional Authority) would accept their normal share of providing operating and financial responsibility for their particular function. It is obvious that an all bus and roading scheme would be very much more costly to the Auckland Regional Authority, in capital and operating costs, than the cost of providing the bus service for a combined bus and rail scheme, and therefore, this proposal should be acceptable to the Auckland Regional Authority and the ratepayers of Auckland..." [647]

Sustain the Dream

Unfortunately, the country was broke and so, to sustain the dream, Dove-Myer Robinson suggested another compromise – as per his second letter to the Prime Minister, dated 15 August 1975:

"…it has occurred to me that the situation is rather different from what it was when I wrote you on August 1st. Since then the dollar has been devalued by 15% and it is obvious that in spite of all the Government has been able to do, the finances of the country are for the time being under great strain. I would assume under those circumstances that there would be some, or a great deal of opposition to the Government committing itself to starting on a big project, such as this, immediately.

"I would therefore add a further suggestion if the Government is prepared to go on with the scheme; that it should give instructions for commencement of preparation of working drawings, tender documents and any other preliminary work that would be necessary. The date for actually calling tenders to be deferred until the country's economic position is showing positive signs of improvement. The date for calling tenders to be reviewed within 12 months of the announcement.

"This would avoid the possibility of the Government being charged with making a large financial commitment to Auckland at a time of great national economic difficulties. At the same time the firm assurance by the Government, backed by evidence of its good faith by giving instructions for preparation of working drawings, tender documents etc., would assure Auckland that the government is merely deferring the start of the project until the economy of the country is in better shape than it is at present. I feel sure that such a proposal and assurance from the Government would be acceptable to the Auckland Regional Authority and the people of Auckland." [648]

A Delicate Situation

Apparently, the Government had more to do than respond to the needs of its largest city and this prompted another letter from Dove-Myer Robinson – this time to the Minister of Development, Michael Connelly, dated 22 August 1975:

"…it is now nearly 2 months since Mr Pearce, the Chairman of the Auckland Regional Authority, wrote to you replacing our letter of June 27th with a simplified proposal for Government consideration. To date, I am not aware that any reply has been received from you on the Government's behalf and I am naturally becoming concerned at the delay. I do feel that the situation is very delicate.

"I, and my Council, are in an invidious position because we have accepted the assurances given by the Labour Party before the last Elections and confirmed since the Election by the present Government and I do hope that this delay in receiving a reply to Mr Pearce's last letter, does not indicate that the opponents are influencing the Government to repudiate what I consider to be a binding commitment by the Government providing Auckland with a satisfactory suburban railway service. I would appreciate anything you could let me know, in confidence, regarding the Government's probable reaction to the proposals contained in Mr Pearce's letter." [649]

Auckland's Evil Genius

Dove-Myer Robinson also pressed the Government for a decision through the media and he was not reluctant to imply that such a decision was imminent even when he knew it was not – as per The New Zealand Herald article of 28 August 1975:

"After a decade of countless investigations, arguments and reports, and the expenditure of over $2 million, a final decision on the Auckland bus-rail transport plan may be only a few days away, said the Mayor, Sir Dove-Myer Robinson, yesterday.

"Discussions between the Government and the Auckland Regional Authority on routes and the allocation of financial responsibility for the bus and rail components of the plan were described by the mayor as being at a delicate stage. 'This is a time when Auckland should be united in demanding that the Government provide Auckland with the first stages of a modern suburban railway system to serve the reorganised comprehensive bus service now being planned by the regional authority,' he said. 'But, as usual, Auckland's evil genius – disunity – is at work again. Bedevilled by opposition from outside, and hindered by sectional influences from within, Auckland could find itself left holding the responsibility to pay for an outmoded surface-roading-bus service with no financial or other help from the Government…'" [650]

Experts Disagree

Pending some form of agreement, or not, between the ARA and the Government, a disagreement between two urban transport experts at a New Zealand Roading Symposium certainly defined the ideology that had divided Aucklanders for decades – as reported by The Auckland Star on 21 August 1975:

"Rapid rail transit for Auckland received a boost and a knock from experts yesterday. The differing views were expressed at the NZ Roading Symposium.

"The director of the economic planning and research division of the NZ Railways, Dr C Vautier spoke of rapid rail being a main transport artery capable of handling peak traffic well into the future at a relatively low cost. Dr Vautier said the concept that private cars or personal transport would continue to dominate the future was a fallacy.

"Professor A G R Bullen, director of environmental systems engineering at the University of Pittsburgh, disagreed. He is a former New Zealander who used to be a traffic engineer with the Ministry of Transport. Professor Bullen maintained the bus would continue to be the backbone of urban public transport services in New Zealand and, by default, there was no alternative to the motor car. Heavy capital requirements and the ability of much cheaper alternatives to provide equivalent or superior services cast doubt on expansion of urban rail transport, he said…" [651]

Speaking Up – No

But it was not just the so-called experts who argued the pros and cons of rail- and road-based transportation systems. There were also those considering the personal cost of the proposed rapid transit scheme – as revealed in a letter to Dove-Myer Robinson from Auckland resident, S W Cope:

"A few days ago you asked through the paper for people to 'speak up' regarding the Rapid Rail proposals. After much deliberation we must say that both myself and my wife are <u>against</u> the Rapid Rail system because of its <u>cost</u> to build. Even if Government does foot some of the initial cost we realise that ratepayers will foot the balance plus running costs. We feel a preferential system using buses would be easier and immediate in its effect." [652]

Speaking Up – Yes

And then there were organisations, such as the Auckland Chamber of Commerce, whose investigators had contemplated the City's future needs and arrived at a more positive decision – as reported by The New Zealand Herald on 5 September 1975:

"Proponents of the Auckland rapid transit scheme were given a big boost yesterday when the Auckland Chamber of Commerce backed the rapid rail system. The chamber, which set up its own two-man committee to study the ART scheme, gave it unanimous approval to the project at its monthly meeting. Both members of the committee, the chamber president, Mr B H Picot, who is chairman of Progressive Enterprises Ltd (the Foodtown supermarket company), and Mr W Wilson, a city chartered accountant, told the meeting that before the study they had opposed the scheme. 'If you want to see development for Auckland city, you must have this ART system,' Mr Wilson said…" [653]

The Costly Alternative

There was also both the financial and social cost of the motorways under construction and those that would be needed if a rail solution was not implemented soon – as Dr Graham Bush observed in his letter to the Editor of The Auckland Star, published 6 September 1975:

"On the front page of a recent issue of the Auckland Star were two headings: 'Cost the Killer: Dead Stop May Be Rapid Rail's Fate' and 'Bush Won't Grow in Ghastly Gully'. Their juxtaposition was ironic, because the latter article dealt with the inner-city desert which motorway development has produced in Grafton Gully. When one thinks of the similar devastation wreaked on Newton and Arch Hill, the two articles seem to be pointing to a classic case of cause and effect.

"Although the cost of rapid rail seems to have been laboured almost to death, the real costs of perpetuating the current, virtually all-road system are conveniently glossed over. Exactly how much has been spent on the Auckland motorway system to date, and what is the ultimate expected cost?

"Is there any real assurance that it will 'solve' the problem of urban transport in Auckland? What are the social costs and those of congestion, pollution, accidents, the drain on overseas funds, devastation of suburbs, dislocation and the like? As the motorways impose their rigid grip on the city, these questions are never answered...

"Before our decision-makers reject once again a considered recommendation that Auckland puts some 'steel' into its transport network, they should really confront the true, total costs of a monopolizing all-road system." [654]

Decision Still Pending

Unfortunately, the Government had still not confronted anything – and certainly not a decision – as per the reply from Deputy Prime Minister, Warren Freer, on behalf of the Prime Minister (presently out of Wellington) to Dove-Myer Robinson, dated 3 September 1975:

"Although it is now some weeks since the Ministry of Works and Development received the views of the Auckland Regional Authority on acceptance of the project and the method of sharing costs, I can assure you that while there has been no finality reached, the whole scheme and the results of the negotiations, have been given serious consideration.

"The Minister of Works and Development is studying the project in the light of Auckland's public passenger transport needs and added problems such as the increasing cost of imported fuels. I understand that Mr Connelly will be reporting to Cabinet on the project in the near future. Government's views will be conveyed to the Auckland Regional Authority without delay, as soon as discussions are completed." [655]

Recruiting the Cabinet

Always ready to recruit to the rapid transit cause, Dove-Myer Robinson was quick to reply to Warren Freer's letter:

"My purpose in writing this very short note to you is because we have known each other for so many years and knowing my general political outlook, it would possibly be helpful to all parties if you would convey to your colleagues in the Cabinet, your personal knowledge of me and the extent to which the Government can trust me in these matters." [656]

General Election Restart

Unfortunately, trusting Dove-Myer Robinson and his assurances as to the viability of the rapid transit scheme was hardly a priority for the Labour Government slogging its way through a severe financial crisis of rampant inflation and a balance of payments deficit.

As the November 1975 general election approached, it was also not a good time for the Government to offend financially-struggling voters by making any rash big-ticket decisions. Not that it mattered – the National Party won with a sizeable majority and all bets were off as far as Auckland's public transport plans were concerned. It was time for a new three-year cycle of talking, planning, and more talking and planning to begin…

Much Alive

The talking with the new Government was to start early in the New Year – as reported by The New Zealand Herald on 13 February 1976:

"The Mayor of Auckland, Sir Dove-Myer Robinson, said last night that the Prime Minister, Mr Muldoon, wanted to discuss with him the issue of transport for Auckland. 'I told him I was delighted the door was still open (on a rapid transit scheme),' Sir Dove-Myer said. 'In my opinion the matter is still very much alive…'

"Meanwhile, the Minister of Works and Development, Mr W L Young, said in Wellington yesterday the scheme would not be considered until an approach to the Government was received from the authority…The minister repeated Mr Muldoon's November statement that no commitment would be given until Auckland local authorities had indicated support…

"Sir Dove-Myer said: 'It is obvious as time goes on that the Government will have to electrify the (North Island) main trunk railway system to save fuel and overseas funds. Once they do that we will have our rapid transit system…'" [657]

Finance Available

While Dove-Myer Robinson may have retained some hope that the Government would eventually find a financial need for some semblance of a rapid transit scheme, there remained the perennial question of affordability – the dollar-sign camouflage of many past Governments. The present Government had recently borrowed $200 million for its Maui oil project so it had a willingness to invest in certain infrastructure and there seemed to be plenty of finance on offer – as reported by The New Zealand Herald on 5 March 1976:

"Bankers from seven countries and the World Bank have approached the Mayor of Auckland, Sir Dove-Myer Robinson, with offers of a $126 million loan for stage one of the Auckland rapid transit scheme. The latest offer came earlier this week from one of the top five banks in the United States, when representatives called on the mayor in his council office. Sir Dove-Myer said yesterday that he had also had offers from banking organisations or groups in France, Italy, West Germany, Japan, Britain and Canada.

"He has forwarded all offers to the Government, including some to the former Labour Government. The Canadians also offered the services of five engineers to help launch stage one of the rapid rail project, but it took the Labour Government four months to write and decline the offer, Sir Dove-Myer said.

"'There is a world-wide interest in financing the project. The recent claim by the Prime Minister, Mr Muldoon, that the Government has no money for rapid-rail doesn't really cut much ice,' he said. The Americans could not understand why a start had not been made with stage one, he added. When told the Government had no money, they said they would make a loan. There was also a keen interest in financing the total project at an estimated cost of $300 million plus inflation…" [658]

Of Greater Value

Dove-Myer Robinson also commented:

"Government policy, not a lack of finance, was responsible for the rundown of railway passenger services, the Mayor of Auckland, Sir Dove-Myer Robinson, said last night. He said that since the Labour Government had stated it would provide Auckland with the 'relatively small railways part' of a bus-rail transport scheme, he had received numerous offers from overseas banks for all the money required to finance the project. All offers, said Sir Dove-Myer, had been referred to the Government. 'Of course, capital repayments, plus interest, would not be light, but savings in other directions resulting from providing satisfactory railway services would show, overall, a very large net saving of government funds,' he said.

"The mayor said that the Government had taken a 'cold accountant's' view that because passenger rail services did not show a balance-sheet profit, it was not interested in accepting offers of overseas loans for railway passenger purposes. Governments, said Sir Dove-Myer, got so much money in taxation from motor vehicles that they were not going to discourage the use of vehicles and encourage the use of public transport, which, prima facie, would have to be subsidised.

"Sir Dove-Myer said that from the limited view of profit and loss on railway services, passenger services lost money. But from the wide view of the national economy they showed great savings. These, he said, were savings on overseas funds in the importation of motor vehicles and the importation of petrol and diesel fuel, savings on motorways and ancillary roading services, operating costs, repairs and parking of motor vehicles, deaths and pollution caused by motor vehicles, and savings in time, overheads and wages lost from traffic congestion. Sir Dove-Myer said there were also other social benefits to all sections of the public which could not be assessed in money terms but which were of even greater value." [659]

Railways Embarrassment

Whatever access to finance may have been available during the early part of 1976, it could not be counted on to pay for Auckland's public transport needs and the ARA was resigned to fending for itself – as reported by The New Zealand Herald on 4 March:

"There seemed little hope of an integrated bus-rail service in Auckland and this was 'appalling' a member of the Auckland Regional Authority transport committee, Mr B K Berg, said yesterday. Mr Berg made his comments during a visit to the committee of a two-man Railways deputation yesterday led by the assistant district traffic manager for Auckland, Mr J McAleese.

"Mr McAleese could give no assurances that there were any plans to upgrade the 1940s fleet of suburban trains now running in Auckland and this disappointed the transport committee. In fact, a letter from the general manager, Mr T M Small, told the committee that a substantial increase in rail patronage in the suburbs would embarrass the Railways.

"With big question marks hovering over the future of rapid rail, the transport committee was hoping to integrate bus and rail services for more efficiency and to cut down the number of buses coming to the city centre from outlying suburbs.

"After listening to the deputation, Mr Berg said the ARA should not accept a stock phrase that had been fed out since the 1940s that when rolling stock was available the service would be upgraded. 'We want to run a total transport system in Auckland and it should be in cooperation and with the assistance of the Railways,' he said.

"The chairman of the transport committee, Mr J. Allsopp-Smith, said the ARA would have to continue to re-organise its services without the Railways because, 'frankly they have nothing for us to co-ordinate with…'" [660]

The Chicken and Egg Argument

In its editorial published 27 March 1976, The New Zealand Herald suggested an even better way the Railways could attract more patrons than just modernising its carriages was to locate a station closer to the main thoroughfare of Queen Street at Britomart Place.

A station would eventually be situated there but not for some thirty years. In the meantime:

"The latest suggestion in the saga of Auckland transport is that the regional authority may ask the Government for $13 million to replace some buses. No doubt the expenditure is necessary. But there is room to wonder whether millions might just as usefully be spent on an existing and largely wasted asset, namely the railways.

"The poor patronage of suburban lines opens the way to a 'chicken and egg' argument. Is patronage low because of poor service and aged carriages? Or are the service and rolling stock inadequate because of poor patronage? When did anyone last see or hear a campaign to attract Auckland commuters to the trains?

"Until 1909 the Auckland rail traveller had access to Queen St. Then the station was altered to allow for the Chief Post Office; and in the late 1920s the station was pushed back to its present disastrous site on the promise, never kept, of a tube line linking the city with the northern line at Morningside. There would have been a station near the Town Hall.

"Even if an underground system may be temporarily out of reach, perhaps a start could be made on bringing people nearer where they want to go by putting a simple terminal at Britomart Place, to which railway land extends. If politicians, civic leaders and assorted experts would put as much effort into concrete action as they have into drawing plans and finding reasons for inertia, Auckland might soon get an improved transport system." [661]

Immediate Renovation Needed

A month later, The New Zealand Herald again criticised the suburban passenger services provided by the Railways Department and suggested some improvements that could be made:

"For an agency whose functions are founded in motion, the Railways Department shows a disturbing degree of paralysis in its management of Auckland suburban passenger services. Indeed, service is probably too generous an expression for the primitive conditions and pathetic timetables offered.

"Aged, dirty rolling stock and stations, some apparently receiving more regular attention from vandals than from authorities, represent a policy of neglect. Well may Aucklanders wonder at a public passenger transport carrier which cites its own potential embarrassment at any significant rise in commuter patronage. Nor can plans for a vast future investment in a rapid-transit system, with a new subway loop and, perhaps, its own wider gauge, convincingly excuse present inaction. Such are present and prospective economic conditions that the hope of several generations has, in any event, again receded.

"For a fraction of the costs contemplated in the rapid-transit proposals, better use could, in the meantime, be extracted relatively readily from the existing assets of permanent way and track. That more modern equipment cannot be found within the national system strains credulity. But a commuter service for the largest city in the country should surely at some stage even warrant the extreme of new equipment.

"To be sure, the site of the Auckland central station – precisely because it is not central – contributes to the unpopularity of suburban trains. Their decline dates from the removal of the station from behind the Chief Post Office to its present Parnell isolation. It may be argued, therefore, that suburban services will remain unappealing and uneconomic until they reach closer to the heart of the city.

"Yet compromise can be accepted. Immediate renovation need not await expensive electrification or subway extensions. On the face of it there do not seem to be daunting physical obstructions to a suburban terminal on the goods sheds site in Britomart Place – several steps nearer Queen St. The cost of relatively modest improvements can be justified, even if services remain uneconomic. After all, no rail passenger services in New Zealand, least of all suburban lines in Wellington, make money. That Auckland suburban train patronage is rising in spite of so many deterrents, discomforts and inconveniences makes departmental indifference harder than ever to sustain." [662]

Railway Management Response

A response to the criticism was published by The New Zealand Herald on 21 April 1976:

"The deputy general manager of railways, Mr T M Hayward, said yesterday that he shared the disappointment that the department was not able to offer a large number of high standard rail passenger services. In a letter to the editor of the Herald in response to an article on April 15…Mr Hayward said many thousands of loyal, long-serving railwaymen also shared his disappointment, as well as many other New Zealanders.

"Mr Hayward's letter read: 'The plain facts are, however, that passenger trains and railcars do not pay, and they cannot reasonably be made to pay. For this reason the department is not able to finance new or replacement services out of earnings and must look to the Government (and the taxpayer) for the necessary funds…Successive governments have declared that the country cannot, because of the state of the economy, afford expensive replacements, and that is where the position must lie for the time being, with buses being introduced where necessary.'

"'Turning to the local scene, Aucklanders will be well aware of the succession of reports and prolonged public debate on the future of Auckland's urban passenger transport services. The department has actively contributed towards the investigations and has anxiously awaited a decision for a comprehensive scheme. Nothing has materialised, and now that there is no agreed scheme it has become convenient for some people to turn to the Railways and try to make them the scapegoat.

"'But what is the position? The department has only old pre-war suburban rolling stock and a limited workshop staff with which to maintain it. The service is popular up to a point – all credit to the staff who have gained the well-deserved praise in the transport reporter's article but it is impossible to make a silk purse out of a sow's ear.

"'The only real answer is new, high-capacity rolling stock providing the degree of timing and comfort which will attract people to the service. 'This is the department's aim, but it must await the availability of finance and at present this is just not obtainable, either locally or nationally. In the meantime, I am naturally sorry that the suburban rail services do not match passengers' expectations, but we are doing everything possible within the resources available.'" [663]

Rapid Transit on Ice

Unfortunately, the inertia continued, with the ARA and even Dove-Myer Robinson deciding to tread water pending a more opportune time to resurrect rapid transit. There was even a Government freeze on local body loans preventing the ARA from replacing some of its bus fleet – as reported by The Auckland Star on 30 March 1976:

"Economic ills and Government coolness toward spending – these were the official reasons why the Auckland Regional Authority voted to put the proposed Auckland rapid-transit system temporarily on ice last night. A minority of members tried to have the $200 million-plus scheme shelved permanently but failed. The resolution says immediate pursuit of the scheme is 'impracticable'...

"The chairman, Mr T H Pearce, who headed an ARA team which tried to negotiate a cost-sharing deal with the former Government, said the team could have opened talks with the new Government. But it is believed the Prime Minister, Mr Muldoon, would merely restate his opinions about the poor economic climate and the need for belt-tightening. The team wanted to establish 'some rapport,' with the Government, he said...the chairman said the ARA should leave its options open with the Government. 'Who's to say rapid transit won't be suitable in 10 years?'

"Sir Dove-Myer Robinson, said the ARA would be burying its head in the sand if it pursued rapid rail now. 'For the time being, we're letting the Government off the hook.'

"The bus fleet, whose replacement has been halted by a Government freeze on local body loans, was the most immediate need, said the resolution supporters. 'It's falling apart around our ears,' said Mt Eden member Mr B N Mason. Passenger transport committee chairman, Mr John Allsopp-Smith, said that without new buses the ARA's 200,000 daily passengers would soon be walking." [664]

Down but Not Out

The New Zealand Herald also had plenty to say about the postponement of the rapid transit scheme:

"It is tempting to say that Auckland's rapid-transit scheme has been derailed. But in fact it has never really been on the rails; it has been the victim for half a century of too many lukewarm, short-sighted political and civic leaders who have preferred to encourage an eminently wasteful form of transport, the motorcar, at the expense of what could be a fast, efficient and (mark the word) comfortable system of knitting Auckland together and shifting large numbers of people to where they want to go.

"The country has now fallen upon times in which the decision by the Auckland Regional Authority to postpone the rapid-transit system indefinitely could not, perhaps, have been avoided. The Government looks in no mood to consider such an expenditure in the next year or two. As the probable result will be increasing traffic congestion (and anyone who can think back for 30 years or more will know what can happen), the reported attitude of some members of the authority appears singularly fatuous.

"The authority has at least avoided the foolishness of accepting an abandonment. Even if members had tried to pronounce the scheme dead, they would have found it would not lie down. From the standpoints of rapidly rising costs and developing traffic chaos, the sooner Auckland comes back to rapid transit the better." [665]

Rapid Transit Killed

However, the Muldoon Government wasn't listening – as reported by The Auckland Star on 20 May 1976:

"The Government today killed Auckland's plans for a rapid-transit scheme. It will not provide the finance necessary. Announcing this afternoon, the Prime Minister, Mr Muldoon, said Auckland had other ways of providing satisfactory transport at a lower cost. Mr Muldoon said the rapid transit scheme would cost an additional $125 million, made no additional savings in road costs and did not offer additional overall benefits. He said the comprehensive transport study review would consider ways of improving transport services in the region, including a better rail service on the southern corridor…" [666]

[As detailed earlier in this chapter, the (Auckland) *comprehensive transport study review* referred to by the Prime Minister had published an interim report on 23 March 1976 and would present its final report in September 1976.]

Yet Another Transport Study

In the meantime, what better way to avoid spending money on actually constructing something than to spend it on another committee to study urban transport? This time, in order to avoid any inter-city jealousy and pacify the National Party's more rural supporters, the study was to include the four main centres:

"Mr Muldoon also announced the setting up of a special committee of departmental officials to study urban transport in the four main centres. The Government recognized the need for improved urban passenger transport services in the main centres, Mr Muldoon said. It also recognizes that there is an immediate problem over the provision of finance for the replacement of buses in Auckland and other main centres. The new study committee will have representatives of the Ministry of Transport, the Treasury and Internal Affairs and other departments. It will study and report on the financial and organizational requirements in the main centres.

"Serious planning of rapid rail began in 1968, when the Government set up a working party to study the De Leuw Cather report. This had been interpreted as recommending a rapid underground and above-ground rail transit system. In 1973, the Cabinet agreed to set up a three-man Auckland Rapid Transit directorate composed of representatives of the Ministries of Works and Railways and the Auckland Regional Authority. The committee staff, installed in two floors of a Parnell office, has been preparing detailed plans ever since. Their studies were reported to have cost the Government $820,000 up to last May." [666]

Nothing Is New

Learning that rapid transit was not to proceed was nothing new to Dove-Myer Robinson – as reported by The New Zealand Herald on 21 May 1976:

"As long as there was a breath left in his body the Auckland rapid transit scheme would not die, the Mayor of Auckland, Sir Dove-Myer Robinson, said last night. Sir Dove-Myer made the comment on his return to Auckland from Wellington where the Prime Minister, Mr Muldoon, said yesterday that the Government would provide no cash for the rapid transit scheme. 'So long as I am alive rapid transit is alive and I will keep it alive until I'm no longer able to sustain life myself,' said the mayor, who insisted that he was not disappointed with the Government decision. 'The National Party had never promised anything,' he said. 'Nothing is new. It is just another deferment.'" [667]

The Second-Best Option

Even Government finance to purchase urgently-needed buses for Auckland's second-best public transport option was not to be provided without some delay:

"A deputation led by the chairman of the authority, Mr T H Pearce, and including the Mayor of Auckland, Sir Dove-Myer Robinson, yesterday asked Mr Muldoon for financial aid with replacing ageing buses in Auckland…'Mr Muldoon gave us a fair hearing. We are quite satisfied,' Mr Pearce said. He said he had asked the Government to pay $2.5 million a year for five years. This, and the annual $1.5 million from the authority, would pay for 38 new buses a year. By 1981 the authority would be able to carry on by itself, Mr Pearce said. Mr Pearce said the issue had already been discussed at caucus level and the Government would make a decision in three months." [668]

One Report After Another

While yet another decision was patiently awaited, The New Zealand Herald summed up the reality of the situation in an editorial published 22 May 1976:

"In the present straitened economic circumstances the Prime Minister's blunt indication that the Government will never put money into the Auckland rapid transit scheme is likely to be accepted without much question. His attitude is strengthened by the decision of the Regional Authority some weeks ago to shelve the plan indefinitely. Mr Muldoon, of course, speaks only for the present Government. Economic circumstances have a habit of changing rapidly.

"It may well be that some future Administration may be impelled for cogent political reasons to support the rapid transit scheme, or some modification of it, in order to rescue congested streets from complete chaos. If the density of population continues to increase, it is hard to imagine that more and more buses would be poured into existing corridors while the railways were allowed to go to waste.

"To try to kill the rapid transit idea, much use has been made in various quarters of an interim report, known – with characteristic official tautology – as 'the comprehensive transportation study review.' This document attempts to analyse alternative transport policies. Its prognostications on whether there will be a greater or lesser emphasis on public transport in the future are by no means conclusive. The authors were probably deliberately cautious because the future growth of private motoring has become problematical.

"Investigations by the Herald a few weeks ago confirmed that the rundown suburban rail system is attracting increasing patronage, even though the Railways Department is making little or no effort to promote such travel. Steep increases in the cost of commuting by private car may yet send people in droves back to public transport. Upgraded railways will then have an invaluable place in the scheme of things.

"In the meantime, Auckland, along with other cities, must wait to see whether the Government is prepared to help to finance bus replacements. If experience is any kind of guide, Auckland commuters would be foolish to pin high hopes on a departmental committee which the Government has considered necessary to set up to report on the financial and organisational requirement of public transport in Auckland and the other main centres. Wellington-based committees have rarely shown a great deal of sympathy for Auckland's growth-created problems. One report has led to another report, and that, sad to relate, has been largely the story of attempts to improve the transport system for the past 50 or more years." [669]

Gas Pedal to Back-Pedal Chapter Five

A Clownish Attitude

As the *story of attempts* continued, many expressed their discontent about the deterioration of the legacy railway services – as reported by the NZ Tribune on 4 October 1976:

"If Muldoon thought that 'New Zealand the way you want it' was a signal for all hands to take everything lying down, he had better have another think. It is hard to recall anybody or any organisation during the Government's short life who has raised no sort of protest at the ineptitude of our rulers...

"Not the least vocal are various bodies and the Auckland Chamber of Commerce, over the Auckland rail commuter service. Already local bodies on the southern line, plus the Auckland Suburban Rail Improvement Committee (ASRIC) have put the case for a better service to the Government Caucus Committee on Transport.

"Unless they do something quickly, Muldoon and his misnamed Minister of Railways will be blasted with a broadside from the Auckland Regional Authority and the Chamber of Commerce, plus the local bodies on both the northern and southern lines. ASRIC won't be idle either, in organising present and potential rail travellers for action.

"Brian Berg, Mayor of Glen Eden (on the northern line), says that 'residents of west Auckland are no longer prepared to remain silent while an existing transport facility (i.e. rail) was allowed to rot and disintegrate.' Mr Berg pointed out that an up-graded rail service was needed to cope with the population growth in his area. The population in western Auckland had increased from 55,200 in 1961 to 109,750 in 1975, and forecasts for the same region are for an increase to 150,000 by 1984 and to a possible 300,000 in 25 years.

"The Railway Department is still moaning that it can't up-grade the existing rolling stock and put on more trains because it would cause it to wear out more quickly! This clownish attitude must surely qualify as one of the silliest of this century.

"Tribune has drawn attention before to transport conditions just across the Tasman, in New South Wales, and is doing so again. The Public Transport Commission of NSW says 'we all know the need to modernise our transport system...This can only be done by spending vast amounts of money on updating our buses, trains and facilities. For 1976/77, the Commission will have available a total of more than $160 million for this purpose.'

"This is progressive thinking in the transport world, quite unlike the bone-headed muddle we have here. The point is, the Aussies see public transport as a service, while our Muldoon-McLachlan crowd see only profits – particularly for the multinational oil monopolies. It would not surprise us if an argument were advanced for the closing down of the whole commuter rail system, which would leave the people at the mercy of an inefficient bus service. After all, successive NZ Railway General Managers have said again and again that passengers are an embarrassment. Therefore, what government would be more likely to close down the rail than the present one?" [670]

Beyond Comprehension

The fear that existing railway passengers could be abandoned altogether was also expressed by Deryk Yates in his article published by City News on 12 October 1976:

"Auckland's Rapid Rail programme, having once more been shelved, is in great danger of being abandoned completely at a time when overseas balance of payments are greatly endangered by the amount of oil this country is buying for frivolous needs. That this government should decide Rapid Transit is no more than an expensive plaything when they are also telling the public to travel by public transport is almost beyond comprehension.

"True, the last administration also suffered from a short sighted approach towards this excellent concept in long term transportation planning, but that fact or the present economic climate is little excuse for abandoning something that will solve not only commuting ills but many other problems brought about by excessive use of the private automobile.

"Nowadays anyone travelling into Auckland becomes aware of the dilapidated conditions of many ARA buses. Veritable bone-shakers with the exception of a few Mercedes or other buses of recent vintage that one may be lucky to find using their route. And, because of traffic build-up, buses become later and later.

"Building more motorways is definitely not the answer to our travel problems as many overseas countries have tried this approach only to realize that traffic problems increase with the number of motorways built. The rapid transit steering committee concluded that motorways by themselves will not solve Auckland's rapidly increasing commuter traffic problems and from approximately 1980 onwards we can expect congestion that will occur progressively until they no longer provide speedy traffic movement.

"This is already evident with the Harbour Bridge. The report states that by 1978 and no later than 1980 the bridge will reach its capacity, yet anyone using it on week days between 8-9am and 5-6pm already find it a stop-go situation.

"With the Southern motorway also approaching clogging point, Auckland faces a traffic bound future that no one appears willing to solve even though they have had the answer to such a dilemma since the publishing of the rapid transit steering committee report some four years ago…

"In Auckland, city hall, together with the ARA and NZR, hired a group of outside experts to come up with the answer to Auckland's future transportation needs. Not content with that, they carried out further investigations that showed other areas of need and possible extension of this service to other communities later.

"Instead of being greeted with open arms, the report has been treated almost with contempt. Both the National and Labour Governments have failed to understand its comprehensive approach to integrated transportation and the ramifications of ignoring such far reaching proposals to combat creeping paralysis of city life…As more people take to their cars the more delayed buses become and this in turn makes them more unreliable, more crowded and less attractive to commuters. Which of course leads more commuters on to the roads. Can we afford not to have Rapid Transit?" [671]

A Four-Year Ambition

While the Rapid Transit system recommended by so many past reports might remain *no more than an expensive plaything* to the Government, the Railways Department's new general manager expressed an inclination to improve the current system in an ambitious four years – as reported by The New Zealand Herald on 21 October 1976:

"The new chief of the New Zealand Railways has his heart set on a multi-million dollar new deal for suburban rail passengers in Auckland and Wellington. Mr T M Hayward, who took over as general manager of the Railways this week, said yesterday that he aimed to bring about widespread improvements in suburban rail in the four years he had left with the department before retirement.

"He said it would cost about $40 million to buy new rolling stock for the Auckland and Wellington suburban services, but it would take a political decision before things could start to move. A Railways report on future suburban needs was with the Minister of Railways, Mr McLachlan. 'This is big money and will no doubt be given close Treasury scrutiny, but we have told the Government what we think is needed,' Mr Hayward said. 'We see an initial increase of rolling stock of 25 per cent with the major expenditure not coming for two to three years.'

"Mr Hayward scotched persistent rumours that the Railways was intent on getting out of the passenger business and concentrating on freight haulage. 'I believe we will remain in passenger transport, especially in commuter services,' he said." [672]

Not That Simple

However, the measure of Government enthusiasm that Mr Hayward could expect for any improvements to the suburban rail service was illustrated by the Minister's response in November 1976 to a plea from a De La Salle College student, Martin Devoy:

"Thank you for your letter of 5 October 1976 about the extension of the 3.15 p.m. train from Auckland to serve Papakura...I have now had the opportunity to fully investigate your proposal and I can clearly see the advantages to the school pupils you represent of extending the train service to Papakura. Unfortunately the situation is not as simple as your representations imply. My Department must have regard for the wishes of all its clients.

"There are two ways in which your needs could be met. These are to run the train earlier so that it arrived back in Auckland at the same time, or to maintain the present departure time with the result that the train would arrive back in Auckland somewhat later than at present. Earlier running of the train would mean that many people who have been patronising it for many years would no longer be able to do so. They would be faced with a wait of up to 50 minutes for another train. The alternative would require eight other commuter services to be rescheduled, disrupting very many regular passengers in the process.

"I am very sorry but the only options open at this stage to the pupils you represent are to use the later train which goes to Papakura, or to connect with a bus at Manurewa and travel on to Papakura." [673]

Minister's Papatoetoe Meeting

However, there was more than just *schoolboy* pressure for the Minister of Railways, Colin McLachlan, to reply to when he met with Auckland representatives in the Papatoetoe City Council Chambers on Saturday, 20 November 1976:

"There was a fairly full representation of South Auckland authorities, and Western areas were represented by His Worship the Mayor of Glen Eden. Mr Lee Murdoch represented the Auckland Regional Authority, and I [Dove-Myer Robinson] represented the Auckland City Council. The Minister was accompanied by the General Manager Railways, Mr T M Hayward, and members of the Government caucus railways committee." [674]

Coronary Coming

Submissions to the Papatoetoe meeting by the Auckland Suburban Rail Improvement Committee (Asric), said to represent 'the opinions of ordinary New Zealanders', were reported by the South Auckland Courier on 2 December 1976:

"Asric supports the efforts of the local bodies to improve the suburban rail services and we reaffirm our policy that public transport must be seen as a service before it is a profit maker...The movement of people, in an area such as Auckland, cannot be left to the private motor car... Most other countries are accepting the fact that tough economic circumstances are a good reason to take action to develop public rail transport and not turn it down as has been done here in the past.

"We are concerned that the Government so far has not taken any action to revise policies which encourage private motor vehicles, rather than public, particularly rail, transport, which imposes an enormous burden on the balance of payments because of the cost of imported fuel. Some scientists predict a run-down of the world oil supply by the year 2000, with staggering price rises for fuel beginning in the late 1980s.

"If the private car continues to be the major form of commuter transport then road congestion will be as big a headache as the price of fuel. Apart from the costs, both visible and invisible, will the Auckland isthmus be able to cope with such a car population? Reliable forecasts of the car population in the Auckland area are enough to bring on a coronary!

"By 1981, we are told, there will be 400,000 motor vehicles winding, grinding and weaving their way back and forth across the isthmus. And we are finding to our cost and consternation, that contrary to popular opinion, our wind-blown country is subject to severe air pollution, and the private car, with its average of 1.3 persons occupancy, is responsible for two thirds of the 60 per cent of the pollution emitted from all motor vehicles...

"We know from contacts in the railways in Auckland that because of staffing problems the rail is suffering particularly on the passenger side. We have been informed by reliable and responsible members of the staff that serious shortages of tradesmen are complicating and delaying repairs to rolling stock. We understand that railway pay rates today are based on those in private industry in 1974 and tradesmen's rates are in fact 25 cents per hour behind the private sector. According to the latest issue of the RTA 'Journal' morale, too, is at a low ebb." [675]

ARA Resolutions

Six months later, little had been done to improve Auckland's suburban railway services and the Government's negativity continued – as illustrated by a letter from the Office of the Minister of Railways to the Secretary of the Auckland Regional Authority, J H Coulam, on 17 June 1977:

"My Private Secretary has referred to me your two letters...of 24 May conveying resolutions by the Authority following its deliberations on a report on the Auckland Comprehensive Transportation Study.

"The possibility of a rail passenger terminal in the vicinity of Britomart Place has been suggested on a number of occasions over the years but the routing of train services through the goods yard would interfere considerably with the shunting and discharge of goods wagons. It was also concluded that because the terminal would only be within walking distance of lower Queen Street, commuters proceeding beyond the Town Hall area would still need to use buses. In the circumstances the Authority might consider that there is little point in pursuing the matter.

"It is acknowledged that the rolling stock used on the suburban trains at Auckland requires replacement. A similar position obtains at Wellington and a proposal for new rolling stock for both centres is at present being carefully evaluated in the light of the considerable amount of expenditure involved." [676]

A Skyline Aspiration

Always eager to stimulate some degree of interest in Auckland's suburban railway needs, Dove-Myer Robinson was quick to respond to the Minister's letter – particularly if renewed interest could be generated from a new official – Allan McCready, then Acting Minister of Railways:

"The Secretary of the Auckland Regional Authority has forwarded to me a copy of your letter to him of June 17th. As the mover of the motion adopted by the Auckland Regional Authority, which was referred to you, I think I should explain, possibly more fully, what I had in mind when I moved the motion.

"The lower end of Queen Street is still the most important point of origin and destination of people wishing to enter or leave the Central Business District of the city. Knowing that people are not prepared to walk more than about one hundred yards or so, it occurred to me and members of the Council's Planning and Traffic Engineering staff that to be effective in increasing patronage on the suburban railway, the main station must be located as close as possible to Queen Street – preferably where the old station was located, right behind the C.P.O. As you know this area is now occupied by our principal bus terminal.

"We believe that the possibilities, and cost, of an overhead railway connection from a point in the vicinity of the present railway station to a station above our bus terminal, should be thoroughly investigated. The advantages would be: –

"(1) There would be no interference with the present Goods Yard or any ground level facilities.

"(2) The City Council's Britomart Place parking building was constructed to take an additional floor if necessary. Therefore that building would be strong enough to carry railway traffic.

"(3) The location of a railway station above the bus terminal would allow almost instant transfer of railway passengers to buses and vice versa.

"(4) The distances from the proposed new railway station to Queen Street would be so short that it would not deter people from using it and the suburban railways served by it.

"The above briefly outlines my proposal. If you are prepared to have the practicability of it investigated, Council's officers (and I am sure also Auckland Regional Authority officers) would be pleased to co-operate in what could be a major breakthrough in providing suburban railway service access right to the heart of the city. I would be pleased to have your comments at your very earliest convenience." [677]

New Railway Coaches for Wellington

Unfortunately for the aspirations of Dove-Myer Robinson and the improvement of Auckland's transport systems, the National Government remained in power after the November 1978 elections. To rub salt into the wound of Government intransigence, it was announced that Wellington was to be supplied with the railway coaches so desperately needed by Auckland – as per the statement released by Prime Minister Muldoon on 16 March 1979:

"The Prime Minister, the Rt. Hon. R D Muldoon, announced today that a Hungarian firm – Ganz-Mavag – has been awarded the contract to supply forty-four two-coach electric passenger units for use by New Zealand Railways in its Wellington commuter services. The award had been made after a protracted technical, financial and economic evaluation extending over several months. The evaluation process involved a visit by New Zealand Railways engineers to Hungary to evaluate technical and production factors and elsewhere to evaluate the operational performance of Hungarian railway rolling stock.

"The order for the new electric units at approximately $33M is the biggest single contract for new rolling stock ever placed by New Zealand Railways. The new units which will replace carriage trains in the Wellington suburban area will be of the most modern type,' said the Prime Minister. The first of the new units is expected to arrive from Hungary about December next year, with delivery being completed six months later.

"Ganz-Mavag is associated in the tender with General Electric Company of the United Kingdom which will provide the traction motors and other major electrical components. Railways have had long experience with this company formerly known as English Electric… "The process of evaluating the tenders and the overall projects of which they form a part, was complicated not only by the extremely wide range of technical considerations which necessarily arise in a project of this nature, but also by the factors which have to be considered in evaluating the various credit arrangements offered by tenderers and the value to New Zealand of the various proposals for offset purchases of New Zealand products,' said Mr Muldoon.

"There was fierce competition for the tender and the field was narrowed eventually to tenders from Japanese and Hungarian sources. The Japanese suppliers have an established place in the New Zealand market and the quality of the products they were offering is well known and respected. As against this, the credit terms they were offering were less attractive, especially when viewed against the complex of economic and financial considerations relating to the possible future of the exchange parity of the yen...

"On the other hand, the Hungarian tenderer offered a credit denominated in sterling on very favourable terms and agreed to supply (also backed with sterling credit) traction motors and related equipment manufactured in Britain.

"It is hoped, continued Mr Muldoon, that this substantial contract in favour of a Hungarian supplier which has not previously been established in the New Zealand market will lead to a significant expansion of trade between Hungary and New Zealand. The Hungarian Government has in fact indicated to the New Zealand Government its desire to open up opportunities for substantial trade between our two countries. The present level of trade between us is quite small, and the contract arrangements I am announcing will present an opportunity for both countries to develop markets which are new to them.

"This is of considerable importance to New Zealand at a time when we are confronted with severe balance of payments problems and are denied the opportunity of trading freely with our traditional trading partners, because of the quantitative restrictions and other restrictive regimes imposed by them on international trade in the temperate zone agricultural products, in which New Zealand enjoys such a marked comparative cost advantage." [678]

Auckland Not Forgotten

Auckland was not forgotten altogether – the City was to get just what it had always needed – yet another investigation of the overall transport requirements of the area:

"In awarding the contract for the Wellington trains to Hungary, the Government decided to defer a decision on the purchase of new carriage stock for the South Auckland suburban services. This has been decided in order to facilitate a further investigation of the overall transport requirements of the area by officials from Treasury, the Ministry of Transport, Ministry of Works and Development, and Railways in conjunction with the Auckland Regional Authority and other affected local authorities.

"The capital cost of providing a new suburban service between Auckland and Papakura would be to the order of $16M and the projected annual loss of the service would increase to over $2M. Clearly in the context of these figures the Government must re-assess the position in South Auckland to determine the most effective and economic method of meeting the area's urban transport needs…" [678]

What Loss?

In his report to the Auckland City Council on 23 March 1979, Dove-Myer Robinson was quick to criticise the Prime Minister's calculations:

"Councillors will note the Prime Minister estimates that if new railway coaches were provided for the Southern railway line at a cost of $16M the projected annual losses on the service would increase to over $2M; an increase over present losses of only about $500,000 annually.

"But this does not take into account the increased number of passengers which would be likely to be carried as a result of integrating Auckland Regional Authority bus services, fare schedules and time tables with the railways. The benefits of such integration could easily cancel the anticipated increased deficit of $500,000 or even entirely eliminate the whole of the anticipated losses on the railway part of the system.

"…It is clear that at this stage the final decision is entirely at the political level. It is my firm conviction that provided sufficient pressure on the government could be generated in Auckland at this crucial juncture, the government could be persuaded to take the plunge, make the investment and provide Auckland with the only major opportunity available to integrate Auckland Regional Authority bus services with railway passenger services and give Auckland a very considerably improved bus/rail passenger transport system…" [679]

Personal Pressure

Pressure of any kind was not appreciated by the Prime Minister who decided to take it personally and responded accordingly – as reported by The New Zealand Herald on 23 and 24 March 1979:

"The Prime Minister, Mr Muldoon, has accused the Mayor of Auckland, Sir Dove-Myer Robinson, of making 'insulting personal remarks.' The accusation is contained in a telegram to Sir Dove-Myer sent in response to a call by the mayor for Mr Muldoon to make an unequivocal statement on the Government's policy concerning the future of Auckland rail services. Mr Muldoon told Sir Dove-Myer in the telegram: 'I suggest you might reconsider your insulting personal remarks as reported in the press before approaching me for further comments.' Sir Dove-Myer said later he was not certain what remarks Mr Muldoon might be referring to…" [680]

"The argument between the Prime Minister, Mr Muldoon, and the Mayor of Auckland, Sir Dove-Myer Robinson, has reached a stalemate. Mr Muldoon is waiting for a reply to his telegram accusing Sir Dove-Myer of 'insulting personal remarks' and the mayor does not see any need to reply.

"The Prime Minister explained yesterday that the mayor had been reported in the press referring to the controversy about Auckland trains saying: 'He (Mr Muldoon) has never been an Auckland MP. He has never worried about Auckland or lifted a finger to help Auckland as far as I am aware.'

"Sir Dove-Myer said last night: 'It was a fair comment for a mayor of Auckland to make regarding local members of Parliament who he thinks have let his city down.' He did not think Mr Muldoon's telegram referring to 'insulting personal remarks' called for a reply. However, Sir Dove-Myer said: 'I would be very happy to resume and continue my normally friendly relationship with Mr Muldoon.'" [681]

"…Criticism is inescapable in public life, and public men need to develop a philosophy about what is virtually a condition of the job. It seems that the mayor, at least, can dismiss the memory of what has been said. He replies that he is not certain to which remarks the Prime Minister refers.

"When the orderly running of Auckland requires good communication between the city and the Government, any breakdown in dialogue, no matter how it originates, is dismaying. The affairs of the city (and of the country) are bigger than the feelings of individuals, and public leaders should be able to put aside personalities and approach dispassionately the matters at hand. Antagonism and hurt feelings, if sustained, could eventually harm the public interest. Whether they like it or not, in some matters local and national leaders must have official dealings with one another. For the sake of sensible administration, the public would surely like to see the mayor and the Prime Minister bury the hatchet." [682]

A Problem of Vision – Again

In the meantime, rumours abounded that Auckland's already limited suburban railway services could be cut altogether. The City's leaders needed to show some solidarity if they were to save their railway – as reported by The Auckland Star on 27 March 1979:

"Auckland mayors, MPs and others interested who met at Papatoetoe yesterday, want the Government to give satisfactory assurances within three weeks, on the suburban railways it plans to abandon. Many brave words have been spoken since the Government announced that $33m would be spent on the Wellington service, and nothing on Auckland's.

"While ARA members dither, 16 Auckland mayors have rallied to defend the railway. And if the Government's intention to impose more Auckland urban transport costs on the Auckland ratepayer is not thwarted by public outcry, it is obvious Opposition MPs are ready to make it a powerful political issue. Yet the reaction has been less than strident, and if Wellington fatalism is not to spread north, it is obvious that local campaigners are going to have to offer the Government more attractive alternatives than have been found up to now. It is time for a good idea – for sound proposals involving the full use of existing assets.

"The problem seems one of vision, in which people see only a rundown system and talk about the $470-a-head cost of carrying 2300 passengers a day, rather than of revitalizing an integral part of urban transport. This very fatalism was evident in the fact that with no apparent thought for the symbolic opportunities, hardly anyone attending yesterday's meeting thought to go by train.

"There is no doubt that the affair of the Auckland suburban trains is a serious affront to the country's main centre of population, and a matter of deep-seated anger in Auckland. This must be made clear to Minister of Transport Mr McLachlan when he meets South Auckland mayors on Thursday morning. He should also be presented with some evidence that Auckland is making better progress towards a rational system using all its resources than has been apparent in the past." [683]

Execution Day Deferred

That meeting between the mayors and the Minister of Transport (and Railways), Colin McLachlan, took place on 29 March 1979 – as reported by The Auckland Star:

"An axe still hangs over Auckland's suburban railways – but execution day has been put off. Today the Minister of Transport, Mr McLachlan, promised a fresh look at the decision not to re-equip the city's railways with new rolling stock. He met mayors from South Auckland and Auckland City Mayor Sir Dove-Myer Robinson in Papatoetoe council chambers this morning. "After the meeting he announced: 'We are sending officials here to reappraise it.' He said they would look at the economic, social effects and overall future of transport in Auckland when making their decision. He added: 'The Government has been big enough to reappraise and we shall do the job as fast we can.' Mr McLachlan would not be drawn into making a comment about what would replace the trains if the railways were run down.

"Sir Dove-Myer said he was happy that the Minister was going to have another look at its decision. He added: 'We have got our foot in the door and so long as Auckland remains united in this fight we shall win through in the end.'

"The Minister also promised he would look at Sir Dove-Myer's suggestion of a meeting with elected representatives of local bodies to discuss the whole question of planning in Auckland and the transport system. The mayors were also promised that the reappraisal would be dealt with as quickly as possible." [684]

Hopes Dashed

Unfortunately, Colin McLachlan was not really in charge of such matters – as reported by The New Zealand Herald on 31 March 1979:

"Briefly raised hopes that the Government might reconsider its decision not to upgrade Auckland railways appear dashed. The Prime Minister, Mr Muldoon, last night once again made it clear he would not countenance new trains being bought for the rundown services. 'We are not prepared to buy new rolling stock for a commuter service which costs $1.6 million in direct costs and takes only $440,000 in fares,' Mr Muldoon said.

"His statement counters one from the Minister of Railways, Mr McLachlan, who said on Thursday the Government was 'big enough to take a second look' at its decision.

"Ominous signs that the West Auckland line to Waitakere could close soon also emerged yesterday. This service carries far fewer passengers than the South Auckland routes to Papakura. A Railways survey of West Auckland travel habits is almost complete and should be made public by May. A Railways official asked yesterday why nothing was being said about the Waitakere line when so much fuss was centering on South Auckland services, said 'Put two and two together.'

"No Railways official seems prepared to deny the Waitakere line will close when the survey is finished. Rumours that it will close have abounded for a year. Closing the Waitakere line would release extra carriages to keep the South Auckland service going a while longer.

"Suburban lines in both Auckland and Wellington are chronically short of rolling stock because old carriages have had to be scrapped. The capital is getting relief in the form of $33 million worth of Hungarian electric trains, announced by Mr Muldoon the same day he said Auckland would not get new trains. Government officials were this week studying South Auckland travel needs to determine a 'suitable' form of transport for the area. Mr McLachlan said their report would be finished as soon as possible…" [685]

Public Transport Crisis

While Government officials continued their study of South Auckland travel needs, ad nauseam, the rest of the region struggled to maintain some semblance of a public transport service – as reported by The Auckland Star on 31 March 1979:

"The fate of Auckland's public transport system is in the balance – and the region's leaders are heading for a showdown with the Government. A review of today's transport situation shows a city in siege with:

- The Prime Minister dashing hopes that the Government might upgrade South Auckland rail services after all
- Widespread rumour that the west Auckland rail line will close soon
- A call for a referendum to decide the future of the region's public bus system
- A 28% jump in the ARA bus deficit (to $10.9 million) that will probably mean cutbacks in services or boosted rate demands
- Moves to wrest all North Shore bus services from the ARA
- A Government refusal to fund the extension of the carpool scheme through the region

"It's a situation that has prompted the Regional Authority to seek an urgent meeting with the Prime Minister and Minister of Transport for an explanation of the Government's stand on transport. News of the final veto on new South Auckland trains is 'typical of the Prime Minister's negative thinking,' said Sir Dove-Myer Robinson today. 'He is, and always has been the rock on which all of Auckland's fondest hopes have been wrecked,' he said. 'This has called for a showdown.'

"Chairman of the Regional Authority Mr Lee Murdoch said it confirmed his opinion that the further investigation promised by the Government was to 'find a better way of justifying the closing down of suburban rail. I tried to keep an open mind on this because I thought it was unthinkable…'

"At a special meeting of the Regional Transport Committee yesterday, the deputy chairman, Mr Jim Anderton, called for a referendum on buses. 'I'm looking for a decision in principle from the Government,' he said. 'They have told us what they are not going to do – but what are they going to do? If they tell us they will not pay for public transport we will have no false expectations,' he said.

"The meeting was also told by a transport controller Mr John Brown that to cut $1 million of the bus levy would involve a 25% cut in peak hour services.

"Meanwhile, East Coast Bays Mayor Mr Alan McCulloch is leading a move to turn North Shore bus routes over to private enterprises. 'I've had talks with private bus operators, and it's a real possibility. By this time next year I think we will be out of ARA transport.' A meeting of all North Shore local bodies has been called to discuss the plan, which may include leasing buses from the Authority.

"The carpooling horizon looks bleak. The scheme has received only $8000 from its request to Government for $56,000. 'It's so ridiculous,' says chairman, Mr Ralph Witten. 'Just how real is the fuel crisis?'" [686]

Mayors' Resolutions

In a letter to the Minister of Railways, Colin McLachlan, and the Railways General Manager, Tom Hayward, dated 4 April 1979, the Papatoetoe Acting Town Clerk, M J

Turley, set out the resolutions adopted by the Auckland Mayors at their recent Papatoetoe meeting:

"1. That in view of the Prime Minister's statement of March 16, 1979, the Government has deferred its decision on providing new Railway coaches for Auckland Suburban Rail Services and

"2. It is estimated that the present losses on existing Rail Services of $1.5 Million would increase by $0.5 Million to $2 Million.

"3. As there is the probability that improved Railway coaches and services would reduce or eliminate the expected losses, the final decision is entirely at the political level.

"4. Therefore, this meeting requests that the Government decides within a reasonably short time to provide the new coaches and improved services promised in the present Government's 1978 Election Manifesto.

"5. We request that this assurance be available for a further meeting of Mayors and other interested parties to be held three weeks from this date." [687]

An Accountant's Response

The Prime Minister, Robert Muldoon, obviously thought the matter warranted an accountant's response – as per his reply to M J Turley, dated 10 April 1979:

"I acknowledge your letter of 4 April. It is not the view of myself, my Ministers or our advisers that improved railway coaches and services would reduce or eliminate the expected losses on the South Auckland service. Indeed, our advisers tell us that the loss is likely to escalate beyond $2 million. Merely stating that the meeting of Mayor does not agree with this estimate is not an argument that disproves it. It might be appropriate for the meeting of Mayors to consider whether Auckland local bodies or the Auckland Regional Authority are prepared to make some contribution towards this loss.

"I noted the comment of the Mayor of Auckland that if the commuter service ceases the Regional Authority will incur additional bus losses of $5 million within a few years. I do not know the basis for this allegation but if it is correct a contribution towards the Railways loss of $2 million would be a preferable option." [688]

A Political Decision

By August 1979, the Prime Minister's *political* decision to buy railway carriages for Wellington and not for Auckland continued to generate criticism – as reported by The New Zealand Herald:

"A political decision and a disaster for Auckland was the reaction of Auckland Labour MPs to the Government decision not to buy new railway carriages. The deputy Leader of the Opposition, the Hon. R J Tizard (Otahuhu), said the Government had taken the attitude that the passengers did not vote National and so was not bothering about them. Most sections of the two lines passed through solid Labour territory, Mr Tizard said, but it was an appallingly short-sighted decision. 'What are the passengers going to do?' he asked. 'Walk?' 'Diesel fuel is short and if the trains are replaced by buses where are they going to get the diesel to run the buses?'

"Mr E E Isbey (Papatoetoe) said the decision was sheer lunacy, especially in view of the fuel crisis. 'They are not only proposing to slash the trains, they are also getting at people both ways with carless days,' he said. 'This is a devastating blow for the people of Auckland…'" [689]

Gas Pedal to Back-Pedal   Chapter Five

More Study Required
During a Parliamentary debate on 4 September 1979, Pakuranga MP, T de V Hunt, supported his Government's decision to ignore the needs of commuters travelling on the southern line:

"In Auckland, only 1 per cent of commuters used rail transport, while in Wellington 20 per cent used rail transport. Only 2300 people travelled between Auckland and Papakura, and most of them got on and off at intermediate stations. Six hundred of them were school children. If freezing works at Westfield and Otahuhu moved to other areas, a large number of passengers would stop using the Auckland-Papakura line.

"Even if the number of passengers doubled to 5000 the annual subsidy for each passenger would be $435. It would be cheaper to pay each passenger a taxi fare each day. Unless the people of Auckland were prepared to use the service, there could be no justification for spending $16 million on it. A survey of commuters in the Auckland area should be carried out before further capital investment was made." [690]

Surprise…Surprise
The Herald also revealed that the cancellation of new carriages for Auckland had also surprised the Railways Department and that Wellington suburban railway losses during the previous financial year were nearly four times that of Auckland – as reported on 1 September 1979:

"The Railways Department spent $25,000 rebuilding and relocating Westfield station on the southern line in the expectation of getting new rolling stock. The work was part of a general programme to upgrade southern stations started last February. The programme came to an abrupt halt in March with the Government's unexpected decision not to uphold its earlier promise to spend $13 million on 50 replacement carriages.

"The Railways Department's local district engineer Mr I A Mead insisted yesterday that the new Westfield station was no 'white elephant' as it was being used by existing passenger services. But he conceded that some of the work at Westfield would not have been done had the department thought the new stock was not to be bought. Westfield was the only station to be upgraded and no work was undertaken on any other, he added.

"Meanwhile, sources revealed yesterday that Wellington suburban rail services are running at three times the loss of similar services in Auckland – yet the Government is to spend 33 million on new stock for the capital. They point out that services to the two centres are hard to compare, but say the losses are significant in terms of the Government's refusal to upgrade rail at Auckland.

"In the year to March 31, Wellington suburban rail services lost $5,997,500 compared with $1,600,500 in Auckland for the same period. The sources say the Wellington loss will rise by at least $3 million annually as a result of depreciation alone on the new trains." [691]

Penny Wise – Pound Foolish
The New Zealand Herald also commented:

"The Government's decision to allow the South Auckland suburban passenger rail service to wither and, doubtless, die makes no sense to the ordinary person being asked to leave the private car at home in the interests of energy conservation…It is no more rational than running dilapidated carriages through the rebuilt and relocated Westfield railway station.

"That the South Auckland service is under-patronised is due in considerable measure to the state of the carriages and to an increasing air of neglect. Such is also the case in West

Auckland where services seem to face the same negative fate. Yet new rolling stock and an imaginative approach to suburban passenger rail could provide Auckland with an economic, energy-efficient system. Auckland railway services have, since the turn of the century, been a sorry tale of, 'If only we had…' The present penny wise-pound foolish policy is one which will, almost certainly, be regretted." [692]

Gone Too Far?

Dove-Myer Robinson continued the criticism of the Government's decision with an article published by the Auckland Star on 5 September 1979:

"If we can't trust a government to honour a pre-election and post-election pledge to maintain Auckland's suburban railway passenger services, is it going too far to believe that the same government would discriminate against Auckland in order to win political support in other parts of the country?

"Auckland's railway passenger services have been under intensive study since 1928. They have been the subject of dozens of reports – one, a few years ago, cost $800,000. The government can't plead that it was unaware of the position when it made those pledges. They knew what they intended to do, but cynically made election promises they hadn't the slightest intention of keeping.

"Once more a government has shown its contempt for Auckland but this time they may have gone too far. Never before has Auckland been so united in demanding fair treatment, and if Auckland maintains its present unity and uses its political clout those who have so badly let us down may regret it in 1981. The consequences to all Auckland, if the government's latest decision is not reversed, will be nothing short of disastrous. Maybe this is what some members of the government want?

"Here are some facts. Auckland's main public passenger bus service run by the Auckland Regional Authority will lose $10,000,000 this year, next year it will be $13,000,000 or more, and within a few years it will be $20,000,000. The losses have to be paid by Auckland's ratepayers. At the same time, depending on buses alone, the Auckland Regional Authority knows it can never provide the satisfactory services demanded by present and potential passengers unless its buses are integrated with the railways so that each contributes the service it can do best.

"The Auckland Region Authority losses on its buses occurs mainly at peak hours when nearly 300 extra buses have to be put on for a short time to carry the large number of extra passengers. Each bus has to have a driver paid for a full eight hour shift. This means that each working day the Authority has to pay about 300 drivers wages for two full shifts (16 hours) for only two to four hours work. This is where the big losses occur. It is no criticism of the union or the drivers.

"These conditions are usual in this kind of broken-time work. But with the trains the position is different. During slack hours a train may have only one or two carriages with one driver. As traffic builds up to a peak, extra carriages can be hooked on, so that a train of say ten carriages can carry a thousand passengers, <u>but still with only the one driver</u>, and that driver's wages.

"By relieving the buses of the need for so many extra drivers at peak hours, the losses on the buses will be cut down enormously, and because of the large loads on the trains (at practically no extra cost) the trains would operate more economically…

"It is no exaggeration to say that, at a time when the Auckland Regional Authority is desperately fighting to improve transport services and cut down the ratepayer's losses on the buses, the government's latest decision will deal Auckland such a staggering blow that it may never recover from it. Auckland must be united in its determination to maintain the present inadequate railway services and then upgrade and extend them so that a fully integrated time-table and fare system with the Auckland Regional Authority buses will give us the kind of service we need and deserve.

"If Auckland fails to secure this we must prepare ourselves for rising costs and declining transport services and at the same time, a falling ability to compete with other industrialised cities. Our whole way of life and our economic standard is dependent on our winning this battle for survival." [693]

Prime Minister's Response

As you might expect from both an accountant and a politician, Prime Minister Muldoon's response to Auckland's criticism was first to target the profit and loss aspect of the railway improvements called for and then the political motives of his critics – Dove-Myer Robinson, in particular – as published by The Auckland Star on 11 September 1979:

"Auckland's urban sprawl lends itself to flexible bus services rather than a single-track railway corridor, the Prime Minister, Mr Muldoon, said today. Mr Muldoon told the Star today: 'The Auckland commuter train service has never been adequately patronized and the revenue is so much out of proportion to its running costs that there is no justification for replacement of the rolling stock. In its motorway system, funded by general road taxation, Auckland has fared better than any other metropolitan area. There is strong criticism of this from other parts of the country, particularly from counties in respect of rural roading,' he said.

'When the Auckland Regional Authority becomes the urban transport authority, it will have the opportunity of co-ordinating urban transport and deciding what kind of commuter system it wants, limited only by willingness to pay,' he said.

"The Prime Minister said the current criticism from Auckland was not unconnected with the fact that the local body elections would be held next year. Mr Muldoon also charged Auckland local body members – including the mayor, Sir Dove-Myer Robinson, with electioneering by criticizing the Government. 'I am sure that the Mayor of Auckland is now starting his campaign for re-election, using the tactics that have served him well in the past, namely continued abuse of central government,' Mr Muldoon said.

"Asked to comment on the promises by the Leader of the Opposition, Mr Rowling, last night on the Auckland rail service, he said: 'As usual, the Labour Party is going to promise everything that anyone asks for.' He said he believed the public had had enough of that kind of election bribery.

"The urban sprawl of Auckland being better suited to buses than trains, has been one reason for the lack of patronage of the rail service. 'The strong feeling I get is that individual citizens would much prefer an efficient bus service to the present rail service. Doubtless, those who are politically motivated will back any kind of anti-Government campaign that is whipped up by candidates for local government office,' he said. 'I believe that our proposed urban passenger transport legislation will provide the opportunity for transport co-ordination and a fair sharing of the burden of costs in accordance with the views of the public.'" [694]

Urban Transport Bill

As detailed in an earlier chapter, the *proposed urban passenger transport legislation* referred to by Robert Muldoon had been foreshadowed in his 1977 budget speech and the Colin

McLachlan white paper. The legislation would allow for the establishment of urban transport authorities to be enabled *to control, co-ordinate, fix fares for, operate or contract out urban passenger transport services* in the main centres.

When the proposals were eventually introduced as the Urban Transport Bill in October 1979, civic leaders such as Dove-Myer Robinson saw the Government's intentions as a major threat to local body autonomy and a means by which the Government could eventually transfer the cost of providing suburban railway services to the Auckland Regional Authority which would become a transport authority under the proposed legislation.

Fight and Survive

What Robert Muldoon described as an *anti-Government campaign* but what was nevertheless considered by Dove-Myer Robinson as a *battle for survival*, gathered pace – as reported by The New Zealand Herald on 11 September 1979:

"The struggle to save Auckland suburban rail services was boosted last night by fighting talk from political, civic and union leaders. Amid talk of the future of Auckland being threatened by the rundown of the rail system, about 70 people demanded that the Government change its decision not to buy new carriages for Auckland rail services. The demand followed two and a half hours' discussion about the future of the region's suburban rail passenger services.

"Many mayors, MPs, union representatives and interested groups attended the meeting called by the chairman of the Auckland Regional Authority, Mr L I Murdoch. He warned that if the rail services were allowed to go Auckland would never get them back. Aucklanders could not sit idly by over the treatment they had received from the Government, especially when Wellington services were being upgraded. 'This decision is a disservice to Auckland and in fact, an insult to the people of Auckland,' said Mr Murdoch…

"The Mayor of Papatoetoe, Mr R H White, said 36,000 people had signed petitions supporting the southern Auckland rail services and there would be 100,000 signatures by the time the petition closed. 'I do not really think that Wellington is aware Auckland is in unison over the issue,' he said…

"…the Mayor of Auckland, Sir Dove-Myer Robinson…said Auckland was now in a crisis situation. 'It is either fight and survive, or give way and die quietly without a whimper,' he said. 'This is a fight for survival for Auckland.'

"The meeting decided to demand that the Government take steps to ensure the present suburban rail service was maintained and developed. It also called on the Government to endorse the principle of an integrated public passenger transport system. A motion was passed saying that the fuel crisis had emphasised the need to modernise public transport, and it urged the electrification of the railway system. The meeting also decided to organise a full public meeting in the Auckland Town Hall to discuss the issue. A committee was formed to push the resolutions passed during the meeting." [695]

Now Highly Political

In its editorial published 3 October 1979, The New Zealand Herald lent its support to the *fight for survival*:

"The big need for the Railways seems to be less cost accountancy and more vision. Auckland in particular has suffered from a history of bad decisions, long neglect, broken political promises and sheer short-sightedness. The decision of seven months ago, which may amount to a final blow for Auckland suburban services if it is not reversed, was clear political back-tracking – and not four months after an election. The 1977 budget promised a $44 million programme spread over four years to 'cover replacement of the carriages used on the major suburban rail routes, which are the Wellington commuter lines and the Auckland-Papakura line.'

"Having promised Auckland bread, the Government proffered a stone. It decided that Wellington would receive $33 million worth of electric trains and Auckland would receive nothing. The latest cheerless bulletin from the Government is that no decision has been made to phase out Auckland suburban trains but that a report will be made on the feasibility of continuing rail services with the present type of rolling stock. It seems at least a possibility that, if deferment can be spun out for a little while, the services may conveniently fade away as the carriages crumble.

"In recent years, perhaps because of the attitude of its political masters, the Railways Department seems to have shown little real fighting spirit. Services have been allowed to run down, and when, unsurprisingly, customers stay away, the reaction tends to favour abandoning the services instead of campaigning to improve and fill them…

"Auckland's claims are not to be brushed away lightly. The matter has become highly political with Labour's promise last month to upgrade the South and West Auckland rail lines and to investigate a third line linking Avondale with Southdown, a route for which the department bought land years ago. Aucklanders have reason to be sceptical of political promises about railways, but Labour's pledge is nailed to the mast. Governments come and go. Auckland's railway hopes are not dead, and the present Government still has time to show that it appreciates the situation." [696]

An Olive Branch

To provide the Government with an opportunity to *appreciate the situation*, an olive branch of sorts was offered to the Prime Minister – as per a letter from the Mayor of Papatoetoe, Robert (Bob) H White, to Robert Muldoon, dated 15 October 1979:

"You may or may not be aware that the Mayors and County Chairmen of Auckland formed a Metropolitan Association of Mayors and Chairmen and have a luncheon meeting at approximately two-monthly intervals, meeting at each Municipality's headquarters in turn.

"At the last meeting held on Tuesday 9 October 1979 at the Howick Borough Council, it was unanimously resolved that I be requested to invite you to a meeting to be held in the Papatoetoe City Council Chambers, at a time and date convenient to your good self, with a view to discussing with you public transport in Auckland. Trusting you will be able to accede to our request…" [697]

Unfortunately, the invitation was declined:

"I acknowledge your letter of 15 October 1979. You will doubtless be aware that I read the contents of it in the press some days before it reached me. The continual personal insults directed towards me by certain Auckland Mayors, led by the Mayor of the City of Auckland, do not pre-dispose me towards giving your colleagues a further opportunity to publicise themselves at my expense.

"The Urban Passenger Transport Bill will be introduced into the House within a few weeks and will be available to local bodies for study and the presentation of submissions to the Parliamentary Select Committee to which it will be referred during the coming recess.

"Until such time as the Bill is introduced, there is little point in my discussing public transport with you and your colleagues and, having had one experience this year of the atmosphere generated in Auckland local body meetings, I see no good purpose that would be served by agreeing to your request." [698]

Bob White was quick to point out the irony of the Prime Minister's refusal to meet Auckland's civic leaders:

"Thank you for your letter of 30 October 1979 and in reply, I would express disappointment on behalf of my colleagues that you can see no good purpose in meeting with us. You have, I understand, suggested in the past that Auckland Municipalities are fragmented and not willing to act as a whole for the benefit of Auckland, yet – when invited to a meeting of the heads of Local Government in Auckland, both Municipal and County – you do not see any good purpose in agreeing to our request.

"I can assure you that the Metropolitan Association of Mayors and Chairmen of Auckland do not desire to further publicise themselves at your or any other person's expense, as we do not admit the media to our meetings and only make Press statements when necessary. May I suggest that you confer with the Hon D A Highet, Minister of Local Government, who was our guest at the last meeting of our Association held at the Howick Borough Council Chambers, and I feel sure he will confirm my comments.

"With regard to the Urban Passenger Transport Bill, the draft discussion documents have been well studied by all sections of Local Government in Auckland and though an Urban Transport Authority to co-ordinate all Transport could be of benefit to the region, there does not appear to be - to the writer – any suggestion as to how it is to be financed.

"At a Railway protest meeting held in Avondale, Mr D Jones, MP, stated that if Auckland wishes to have a railway passenger system, then Auckland will have to pay for this privilege as would other Municipalities.

"I have, therefore, referred this statement to His Worship the Mayor of Wellington for obviously, if Auckland has to add the $1.6M railway loss to the present $11M A.R.A. Transport loss, then Wellington will have to take over the $5.9M loss they now incur.

"These are only some of the questions that it would have been of advantage to have discussed with you and I can only request that you reconsider your decision and accept our invitation to a meeting to be held in Papatoetoe where you will be received with the courtesy due to your Office." [699]

Save Our Trains

By November 1979, with little response from the Government, the struggle to save Auckland suburban rail services continued. In his call for railway supporters to attend an Auckland Town Hall meeting, the Auckland Regional Authority Chairman, Lee Murdoch, also referred to the Government's proposed urban transport reorganisation as just an accounting exercise – as per his Sunday News article published on 2 November 1979:

"If all the reports on improving Auckland's suburban passenger train services were laid end to end they would go further than the railway lines themselves. Enormous energy and manpower has been spent on thinking about improving the services, while the lines have been deteriorating. Now the very existence of suburban passenger rail services is under threat by a government which seems to have little appreciation of their value to thousands of Aucklanders. That's why concerned groups will be in the Auckland Town Hall tomorrow night to make it plain to the government that we want to keep our trains…

"The Government has talked of scrapping the trains and having buses do the job, but buses would lose more money than the extra $500,000 a year which the Government says would be the cost of introducing better carriages. Of course, the Government would like to see buses take over because that would make it easier for it to hand the cost of urban passenger services to local or regional government, making the ratepayer, instead of the taxpayer, liable.

"That is certainly implicit in the Government's proposed urban transport reorganisation. What we don't seem to be able to drum into the Government is that we do not want a grandiose, new and costly train system. All we want is better carriages – which can be built here – increased train frequencies and some enthusiastic promotion of services.

"It's now widely accepted that New Zealand has to make much better use of present resources, particularly in transport. We have the resources in the southern and western rail lines and we must preserve them. We can't easily increase road capacity, but we can easily put more and longer trains on the lines. If we let the Government take the trains away, we'll never get them back. So, let's see a great turnout at the Town Hall tomorrow night to demand that our trains be saved." [700]

Last Opportunity

A month later, yet another public meeting at the Town Hall was organised – as reported by The Auckland Star on 3 December 1979:

"The main absurdity in the Government's plan to run down Auckland suburban train services is that it comes during an energy crisis. Future Aucklanders will find it hard to believe that such a move could have been contemplated at the very time when all the emphasis should have been on the potential advantages of rail travel.

"Many of today's Aucklanders, of course, have seen the absurdity of it all. More than 30,000 of them have signed a petition calling for the suburban system to continue. The region's Mayors have discussed tactics for saving the passenger trains. And tonight there'll be another public meeting in the Town Hall to discuss the issue.

"Auckland Regional Authority chairman Mr Lee Murdoch sees this as the last opportunity for Aucklanders to convince the Government that the services should stay. Maybe it is. Certainly the Government, since it broke its promise to upgrade the services, has given no indication of any change of heart.

"It has called for various reports, but Aucklanders are well accustomed by now to the lack of action resulting from such stalling devices. Only a determined show of pro-rail feeling by Aucklanders, it seems, is likely to convince this Government that its short-sighted policy must be revised.

"Essentially, too, Auckland has to demonstrate how integrated bus and rail services can provide the sort of public transport system the region needs. Sensibly, the ARA is pushing ahead with plans to integrate bus services with South Auckland trains.

"It intends from next June to run buses to four South Auckland rail stations to encourage commuters to take the train to work. It's a step in the right direction. But further steps can only be taken if the Government agrees to upgrade the rail service. Auckland, at any rate, must persuade the Government that a fully integrated public transport system could be good value. It won't be an easy job. Future Aucklanders, though, will have reason to respect us if we make the effort." [701]

Fight or Forfeit

The Auckland Star subsequently described the 'Save the trains' Town Hall rally in its report of 4 December 1979:

"Fight for Auckland's suburban rail or forfeit your future: That's the warning Sir Dove-Myer Robinson has for local Members of Parliament. More than 1000 people at last night's 'Save the trains' rally applauded when Sir Dove-Myer called them to judge their MPs on their commitment to suburban rail.

"The mayor warned MPs that if they were 'not prepared to give us the rail system we shall raise heaven and hell to keep you out of Parliament.' He told the enthusiastic crowd to start a pressure campaign: 'You've got to write to the MPs. You've got to tell them that you are demanding the present system be continued, maintained and upgraded as usage demands.'

"He said votes were the only language politicians understood. In front of a platform loaded with Labour MPs – including deputy leader Mr David Lange – Sir Dove-Myer said neither political party had lived up to its obligations to Auckland and neither had his support.

"The meeting passed unanimously resolutions…passed without a hitch – provoking the ARA's chairman, Mr Lee Murdoch to praise: 'That's really something for Auckland to do something unanimously. I congratulate you…'

"The meeting also passed resolutions from the floor. These included a motion from Mt Albert's mayor, Mr Frank Ryan, that 'in the long term the Auckland railway station be situated as near as possible to Queen St.' Further motions that the ARA stop building new roads, divert roading money into public transport and consider a rail link between Sylvia Park and Southdown were passed." [702]

An Irregularity?

As the 1970s drew to a close, Dove-Myer Robinson had good reason to distrust those Auckland politicians who had not more actively represented the apparent unity of the region's civic leaders and supported the public transport needs of their city and region.

Also, at least where matters of transport were concerned, Auckland's Mayor had reason to doubt the probity of Robert Muldoon's National Government – informed as he was by certain suspicions contained in a letter written to him by John Malcolm Bottomley, dated 12 September 1979:

"I am writing to confirm my telephone call of this morning to provide you with information which may be of use to you in furthering the cause of improving suburban railway services in Auckland.

"For a period of two years and until the end of June 1979, I was associated with the Italian firm of Ansaldo in submitting tenders for the supply of electrical equipment for the new suburban rolling stock being purchased for the Wellington region…Along with a number of other suppliers, my principals submitted a tender in conjunction with an overseas firm which was not competitive.

"I understand that a gross irregularity occurred in handling the whole tender in that a firm, namely Public Transport Ltd, 16 Tuhimata Street, St Heliers, Auckland, Managing Director Mr Hilton Lowndes, acting on behalf of Messrs. Ganz of Hungary, which was allegedly not on the short list of tenderers when prices were initially considered by the N. Z. Railways, was permitted to provide an amended price, whereas none of the other tenderers were given the opportunity to do so.

"I also understand that the Prime Minister's Department intervened in the matter, an act which may or not have been justified, but the point is that proper tendering procedures were not followed if the above-mentioned information is correct.

"I have felt that this matter requires ventilation in public and in doing so it may assist the cause of Auckland's railway services in an indirect manner if it can be shown that the whole package of decision making on providing improved services in both cities is highly suspect.

"I have not wished to take the matter up personally since it may have prejudiced the interests of my former principals, Ansaldo S.p.a. in future dealings with the Railways, and they are of course also tendering for the Auckland bus requirements!! I therefore ask that the above information be used in the manner you consider most appropriate with the exclusion of my name and that of Ansaldo S.p.a…" [703]

Dove-Myer Robinson promptly replied:

"Thank you for your letter of the 12th re tendering for railway coaches. I have decided that the best way to deal with this matter is to refer it to Richard Prebble, MP, with the condition that he keep your name and your former company strictly confidential. Also I have asked him to communicate direct with you should he feel it advisable to do so." [704]

What Irregularity?

The suggestion of any irregularity that resulted in the choice of the Hungarian trains for Wellington was soon obscured by what was portrayed as a much needed deal at a time of severe economic difficulty – as described by Adrienna Ember in her 2008 thesis, "*Enlarged Europe, Shrinking Relations? The Impacts of Hungary's EU Membership On The Development of Bilateral Relations Between New Zealand and Hungary*":

"As this was the biggest single contract for new rolling stock ever placed by the New Zealand Railways and the winner was a communist country, Prime Minister Muldoon was forced to justify the decision to the public on a number of occasions, particularly since Japan had also made a very competitive bid. The Hungarian Government had also agreed to buy reciprocal New Zealand exports to the value of the purchase. Japanese credit terms could not be accepted because of the uncertainty around the appreciation of the yen at that time, and Prime Minister Muldoon considered not just the cost advantages of a single order, but rather hoped for further "opportunities for substantial trade" between the two countries…

[Muldoon]: "This is of considerable importance to New Zealand at a time when we are confronted with severe balance of payments problems and are denied the opportunity of trading freely with our traditional trading partners because of the quantitative restrictions imposed by them on international trade in temperate-zone agricultural products, in which New Zealand enjoys such a marked comparative cost advantage." [705]

Questions Asked

One of the few times the Prime Minister was seriously questioned about the choice of Hungary as the supplier of railway coaches for Wellington occurred on 14 August 1980 – during an In Committee, Appropriations Bill, Estimates debate as to the vote of monies to be apportioned to the Prime Minister's Department:

"Rt. Hon. W. E. Rowling (Leader of the Opposition) said that the amount of $670,000 voted for personnel included the payment of the advisory groups to the Prime Minister…Until February 1980 the department's energy and transport expert had been Dr

Allan. Had the Government acted on his advice in deciding to accept the Hungarian tender—which was not the cheapest—for rail units?

"Had he prepared the press statement in March 1979 relating to the decision to buy Hungarian rail units costing $33 million, because of the good credit terms and the fact that the Japanese would be taught a lesson and trade with Eastern Europe would be encouraged? It had been rumoured that the Railways Department, the Ministry of Transport, and Treasury had preferred the cheaper but superior Japanese model, because the Hungarian units would deteriorate in Wellington's weather, would be subject to rust, and were of doubtful technical worth when compared with other units that had been offered.

"In March 1980 Dr Allan had commenced employment with Mr Lowndes—an Auckland entrepreneur who held the agency for the Hungarian rail units. How much had the Lowndes organisation received in commission for the sale of the Hungarian units to the New Zealand Government? What had prompted the Government to prefer the Hungarian rail units to the Japanese?

"Rt. Hon. R. D. Muldoon (Prime Minister) said that the decision to buy the Hungarian equipment had been made by the Cabinet on the advice of the Cabinet economic committee. Ministers of the Crown had made the decision in the normal manner. Dr Allan had had no role other than that of a member of the Prime Minister's Department, and a member of an officials committee that had analysed the various tenders to be placed before the Cabinet economic committee. He was not aware which department, if any, had recommended one tender or the other, but that would not be difficult to find out.

"He had made a detailed press statement at the time stating that the award had been made after protracted technical, financial and economic evaluation extending over several months. The evaluation process had involved a visit by New Zealand Railways engineers to Hungary to evaluate technical and production practice, and to evaluate the operational performance of Hungarian railway rolling stock. The Japanese suppliers had an established place in the New Zealand market, and the quality of their products was well known and respected, but their credit terms had been less attractive, especially when viewed against the complex of economic and financial considerations relating to the possible future of the exchange parity of the yen – and against sterling.

"The Hungarian tenderer had offered a credit-denominated sterling on favourable terms, and had agreed to supply traction motors and related equipment manufactured in Britain. It had been hoped that the substantial contract in favour of a Hungarian supplier, which had not previously been established in the New Zealand market, would lead to an expansion of trade between Hungary and New Zealand.

"The Hungarian Government had indicated to New Zealand its desire to open up opportunities for substantial trade between the two countries. Counter-purchase offers had been attached to the deal, and in the last month or two it had been reported that the counter-purchase opportunity with Hungary was working out extremely well.

"Some months after the deal had been completed, the agent for the Hungarian Government had approached Dr Allan, who had been seconded to the Prime Minister's Department for a period of about 2 years, and had asked him whether, when his term with the Prime Minister was finished, he would be interested in going in with him. The Hungarian agent had apparently admired Dr Allan's ability.

"The decision to purchase the Hungarian rolling stock had been made by the Ministers in the Cabinet economic committee – it had had nothing to do with Dr Allan. The Cabinet had accepted the responsibility for the decision, and was prepared to justify it, as it had justified the decision when it was made – on its merits, which had been proved in practice. New Zealand was trading with Hungary. The currencies had moved in the expected manner. The deal had been the best deal offered; it had been accepted on that basis, and that was what it had proved to be.

"Mr Caygill (St Albans) said that Dr Allan had been a transport specialist in the Prime Minister's advisory group. The decision to buy the units had been an amazing one, because they were not the cheapest, they would not go through the Johnsonville tunnels, and they were not rust-proofed.

"When the decision had been announced the Prime Minister and emphasised that the deal would lead to opportunities for substantial trade between New Zealand and Hungary. It was a fact that Dr Allan had left the Prime Minister's Department to work with the person who was the agent for the Hungarian trains. The partnership was the New Zealand firm that would benefit more than any other by way of commission from the trade the Prime Minister had said would flow from the decision.

"What was at issue was how the decisions had been made in the Prime Minister's Department. How had the decision been arrived at? Would the man and his partner benefit financially from the decisions that had been arrived at? What part had Dr Allan taken in the decision? Who had drafted the press statement? Was it correct that the press statement had been drafted by Dr Allan? In protest at the circumstances that had been disclosed, he moved, *That the vote to be reduced by $5.*

"Rt. Hon. R. D. Muldoon said that it was impossible to take the amendment seriously, because it was based on unsubstantiated rumours. Dr Allan had not drafted the press statement. Dr Allan's part in the whole matter had been a minor one; he had been one official on a very large committee. He had come into the department from the private sector and, after finishing his contract, had gone to another job in the private sector with the man who had been involved in the deal, which was the best deal for the country.

"If Labour members wanted to make scandalous assertions…If Labour members made a case based on incorrect information, he would tell the truth about them. The fact that they were prepared to attack an honourable citizen, a very able man, to try to score a cheap political point indicated the poverty of their argument. There was no truth whatsoever in the suggestion that Dr Allan had been responsible for the Government's decision; it had been made by Ministers, the Cabinet economic committee, and the Cabinet.

"He invited Labour members to make that allegation outside the Committee, so that they could be appropriately dealt with by Dr Allan. If they were not prepared outside the privilege of Parliament, to make the allegation that Dr Allan had improperly influenced the Government in deciding on the Hungarian purchase in order to get a job, they should shut up.

"Hon. J. A. Walding (Palmerston North) said it was necessary for the Prime Minister to explain why it had been decided to buy trains from the Hungarian Government. In the press statement the reason given had been currency adjustments, and that explanation had been repeated during the debate. The New Zealand dollar had appreciated by 3 per cent since March 1979, and sterling had appreciated by 17 per cent in that period, which made nonsense of the explanation given.

"What advice had been given by the Railways Department? Had it been to accept the Japanese or the Hungarian tender? What recommendations had been made by the Ministry of Transport? Dr Allan had worked in the Prime Minister's Department, and must have had some say – rightly or otherwise – in the decision-making process…

"Mr O'Flynn (Island Bay) asked what advice the Prime Minister had received from Treasury and other departments on the Hungarian trains? Why had he bought the trains…? Were members to believe that the Government had intended to buy trains for about $30 million for only part of the Wellington suburban service? In Britain a decent interval had to elapse before a civil servant involved in a certain type of work left to take up similar employment elsewhere.

"Rt. Hon. R. D. Muldoon said…Dr Allan had not been a civil servant. He had come in on contract from the private sector. It would have been unconscionable to put a restraint on a man who had come in from the private sector on contract for 2 years, and not to permit him to go back to the private sector…The whole matter was just a nonsense…he deplored the unsubstantiated attack by several Labour members on a former member of the Prime Minister's Department.

"During the tea adjournment he had examined the papers for the Hungarian tender for Railways rolling stock. Several departments had contributed, the Prime Minister's Department had not. The Department of Trade and Industry had advocated that the Cabinet economic committee and Cabinet, accept the Hungarian tender; and the tender had been accepted because of the opportunities that would be opened up. The tenders had been very close.

"The Hungarian tender had been in sterling, and the Japanese tender in yen. The inference had been that the yen would appreciate more rapidly than sterling, and that had been another factor that had been built into the long-term payment, other things being equal. The final paper prepared for the Cabinet economic committee had been prepared by two departments – the Railways and Treasury.

"The paper had recommended that the Cabinet economic committee should make the decision. The Department of Trade and Industry had felt that the trade advantage favoured the Hungarian tender; the Cabinet economic committee had agreed, and Cabinet had finally accepted the tender. The units had not been intended to go through the tunnels on the Johnsonville line.

"Mr Prebble (Auckland Central)…According to an article in the *New Zealand Herald*, the Prime Minister had said his department had not been involved in buying the Hungarian passenger carriages. Mr Lowndes, who had organised the deal, had said that he had met Dr Allan when he had been a member of the officials committee that had studied and negotiated the details of the train purchase.

"Dr Allan had said he had not wanted to be associated with a company with which he had contact, so a new company had been formed. Mr Lowndes completely owned the first company, Public Transportation Ltd. The only difference between the two companies had been a legal one, and Dr Allan could not pretend that his contact had become good when he had formed a new company with a person who owned all but one of the shares in the other company. Had Dr Allan discussed the matter before he went into business with Mr Lowndes?

"Rt. Hon. R. D. Muldoon said that Dr Allan had been a member of the officials committee. The final report that had been presented to the Cabinet economic committee had been provided by the Railways and Treasury, and had had nothing to do with the Prime Minister's Department. That report had stated that the committee should make the decision. In an earlier report, the Department of Trade and Industry had advocated the acceptance of the Hungarian proposal on trade grounds.

"The Prime Minister's department had made no recommendation at any stage, and Dr Allan's involvement, as far as the Ministers had known, had been zero. In the light of the scurrilous and totally unwarranted attack by the Parliamentary Labour Party, what would be the position of any public servant who went into private industry…?

"The very able man who had been attacked had not been a public servant, but had come in from the private sector and gone back into the private sector. The decision to accept the Hungarian proposal had been made in the way that Government decisions were normally made." [706]

Defending Dr Allan

It is notable from the foregoing that the Labour spokesmen failed to mention John Bottomley's suspicions that the Prime Minister's department had directly interfered in the tendering process for the supply of railway carriages for Wellington. No doubt, wishing to protect the identity of their possible whistle-blower, they chose instead to concentrate on the involvement of one of Robert Muldoon's advisors, Dr Allan, with Hungary's agent, Hilton Lowndes.

As a result, Robert Muldoon did not have to publicly answer any allegations that he may have personally influenced the tendering process. Nor was the Prime Minister questioned about his personal association with Mr Lowndes who was then a prominent constituent in his electorate of Tamaki. Instead, he had only to defend Dr Allan's reputation.

The Ganz Mavag Run

The first two-car Ganz Mavag unit ran on Wellington's commuter train lines in June 1982 and, by March 1983, all 44 units were in service. By the time the last Ganz Mavag ran on 27 May 2006, it is estimated that the trains carried some 67 million Wellington region passengers. [707]

Chapter Six

1980 to 1989 – Congestion Complete

Planning and Politics
Comprehensive Transportation Study Review
As previously described, a number of studies of Auckland's transportation needs were undertaken by numerous government, local government, and consultants over many long years. One such study, the Auckland Comprehensive Transportation Study Review, was commenced by the Auckland Regional Authority in 1970 and its final report was released in September 1976.

"In 1984 the Regional Authority gave consideration to updating the CTS [Comprehensive Transportation Study] Review, and was then approached by the National Roads Board with a request to set up a joint ARA/NRB study team to review the transportation needs of the Region. The brief suggested by the NRB for this joint study was:

"1. To update the master transportation plan through to the year 2000 with a view to recommending a programme of capital works (in priority order) which has full regard to expected financial attainment.

"2. To integrate within the master transportation plan the necessary public transport systems and any associated capital requirement...

"At its meeting in March 1985 the Authority's Urban Transport Committee resolved that a review of the CTS should be carried out and that the appropriate planning teams should be established. Work commenced on the review but the new study, known as the 'Comprehensive Transportation Study Update' was not formalised until April 1986 when a Technical Liaison Committee (comprised of representatives of Local Authorities, Government Departments and public transport operators) was established and a Brief adopted...

"The purpose of the CTS Update...to identify future travel demand that can be expected in the short and medium term if established development patterns continue, and to investigate ways of dealing with these demands. It does not look at long term needs or at the consequences of significantly different patterns of distribution of employment and population, major changes to the regional economy, or major changes in the way that work and travel are carried out...

"The C.T.S. Update is a strategic study covering the whole of the Auckland Urban Area, and is not designed to examine in detail the requirements of particular local areas..."

The Stage 1 report, released in October 1987, concluded:

"1. The predicted growth in travel demand in the major travel corridors by the year 2001 will require major investment decisions to be made within the next 5 years.

"2. Additional capacity will be required on the Waitemata Harbour Crossing and in the Northern, Western and Southern Corridors in order to avoid unacceptable levels of congestion on existing facilities.

"3. Additional capacity may also be required in the South-Eastern and South-Western corridors, and across the Tamaki River, to provide for growth and to alleviate congestion in other corridors.

"4. The scope for new roading is generally limited to the Waitemata Harbour Crossing, South-Eastern and South-Western corridors and the Tamaki River Crossing. There is limited scope for widening existing motorways and arterial roads in other corridors.

"5. Choices exist between investment in roading and investment in public transport. The implications of investment in roading are a continuation of present employment and travel patterns with pressure on access to the CBD, and a continuation of present lifestyles with the private car as the dominant mode. Investment in public transport will require a dramatic change in attitude to the use of this mode and a change in lifestyles, and carries with it a risk of failure as a 'solution' if these changes do not occur." [708]

The Hearn Review

"In November 1986, the Government appointed A Hearn QC to review New Zealand's town and country planning legislation. The need for such a review arose for a number of reasons, including:

- The unclear position which State Owned Enterprises appeared to occupy in respect of town and country planning regulation;
- The general move to review all regulatory regimes as part of government policy;
- The desire to create "more room" for " the more market approach" in the planning system, including giving more thought to the object, need for, and cost of intervention;
- The need for greater co-ordination between planning legislation and other resource management regimes;
- The creation of the Department of Conservation and the Ministry of Environment which raised important questions about the regulation of resource exploitation; and
- The persistent perception that town and country planning regulation acted as a deterrent to development because of a lack of flexibility, slow decision making, and a lack of integration in resource management statutes.

"Hearn noted that many of the criticisms that were levelled at the 1953 Act were repeated in respect of the 1977 Act. Hearn's review of the 1977 Act recommended many changes to existing legislation to address the identified issues. It sparked the genesis of the Resource Management Law Reform process which resulted in the passing of the Resource Management Act 1993." [494]

A Decade for Change

"In the late 1980s the Fourth Labour Government, consistent with its policy of corporatising and privatising government-owned entities, looked to other quasi-commercial entities to apply the same process to…In 1989 the local government Minister Michael Bassett concluded a reform of all local government in New Zealand. This greatly reduced the number of territorial councils in Auckland but did not materially alter the ARA, which essentially retained its previous functions under the new name of Auckland Regional Council (ARC)…

"The power to corporatise local government operations as local-authority trading enterprises (LATEs) modelled on state-owned enterprises, was created. However this was voluntary, with the exception of transport, where council road design and delivery operations were required to be corporatised. Council bus operations were likewise required to be corporatised, with the ARC bus operation emerging in 1991 as Transport Auckland Ltd, trading as the Yellow Bus Company." [709]

Local Government Amendment Act (No. 2) 1989

In 1989, the Labour Government set out on an overhaul of local government legislation, the biggest in more than a century. Counties and boroughs were scrapped, replaced by district and city councils. This was achieved by means of the Local Government Amendment Act (No. 2) 1989 which amended the Local Government Act 1974.

Most of the new Act's provisions came into force on 1 November 1989 and Part IA included definitions of local government and its purposes under the new structure:

"37K The purposes of local government in New Zealand are to provide, at the appropriate levels of local government, –

"(a) Recognition of the existence of different communities in New Zealand:

"(b) Recognition of the identities and values of those communities:

"(c) Definition and enforcement of appropriate rights within those communities:

"(d) Scope for communities to make choices between different kinds of local public facilities and services:

"(e) For the operation of trading undertakings of local authorities on a competitively neutral basis:

"(f) For the delivery of appropriate facilities and services on behalf of central government:

"(g) Recognition of communities of interest:

"(h) For the efficient and effective exercise of the functions, duties, and powers of the components of local government:

"(i) For the effective participation of local persons in local government.

"37L – Structure of local government – …every part of New Zealand…that is within the district of a territorial authority shall also be within the region of one or more regional councils.

"(2) Every territorial authority shall be either a city council…or a district council…

"(4) Every regional council and every territorial authority shall be a body corporate with perpetual succession and a common seal, and, subject to this and any other Act, shall be capable of acquiring, holding, and disposing of real and personal property, of entering into contracts, of suing and being sued, and of doing and suffering all such other acts and things as bodies corporate may do and suffer." [710]

Local Government Commission Remains

Part IIA of the 1989 Act allowed for the continuation of the Local Government Commission and stipulated that the next general election for Auckland Regional Authority members was to be held on 10 October 1992 and on the 2nd Saturday in October in every three years after that. The election was to be conducted by postal vote. [710]

Public Transport
The Last Trolleybus
As previously noted, Auckland's first trolleybus service was a free service operated from Queen Street to the Farmers Trading Company department store in Hobson Street from December 1938. The City's first replacement of the trams by trolleybuses was on the Herne Bay route in September 1949. "By 1959 the Auckland Transport Board were running a fleet of 133 trolley-buses." [144]

However, as early as 1962, in his article about bus transportation published in *Auckland Expanding To Greatness*, John Lyne questioned the future of the trolleybus and, indeed that of the diesel bus:

"The trolley-bus, a splendid vehicle and pleasant to ride in, is on the way out overseas. It will go from busy streets here also because of its being tied to overhead wires and not being able to follow crowds. It is merely a trackless tram. The efficient diesel bus is also doomed to a short life in the inner city because of fumes. Numbers could certainly not be used in Queen Street, with its increasing tall buildings. The inner city transport must surely be something on the lines of a gas-turbo engine bus." [309]

John Lyne was at least right about the trolleybus. With the final, ceremonial run on 28 September 1980, the question about the future of Auckland's trolleybus service, asked by Transit Magazine in November 1975, '*Is There a Future?*' could be answered, and the answer was no. With the passing of the cheap, pollution-free trolleybus, the travelling public now had no option but to take the befouling bus, ferry, or motor car.

Urban Transport Act 1980
As previously referred to, the Ministry of Transport Amendment Act 1971 had established the New Zealand Urban Public Passenger Transport Council to administer Government assistance to urban public passenger transport operators (other than the operators of taxicab services). The amendment stipulated that the Council was to consist of the Secretaries for Transport, Treasury, and Internal Affairs, together with three members recommended by the Minister who could not have a pecuniary interest in any urban public passenger transport undertaking.

With the passage of the Urban Transport Act 1980 which came into force on 1 April 1981, the New Zealand Urban Public Passenger Transport Council was replaced by an Urban Transport Council of 12 members from a much broader spectrum of urban transport interests, representing: the Minister, each of the four regional authorities, the Municipal Association of New Zealand Incorporated and the New Zealand Counties Association Incorporated jointly, the Federation of Labour, the National Roads Board, Government Railways, the Ministry of Transport, and the Treasury. [711]

The responsibilities of the Urban Transport Council included: advising the Minister, regional and territorial authorities on matters related to urban transport; to advise and otherwise assist regional authorities in the preparation of their urban transport schemes and regional implementation programmes; give financial assistance to regional authorities and other bodies or persons for urban transport purposes; to conduct, or engage persons to conduct, research and demonstration projects concerning urban transport and associated matters…" [711]

Urban Transport Schemes
The 1980 Act stipulated that Urban Transport Schemes were to be prepared by regional authorities for its urban transport area and that such schemes were to include an

Operational Plan specifying "…administrative and operational matters relating to the existing or proposed urban transport system in the area, including matters relating to public transport, traffic management, parking, and policies relating to fares and charges…" [711]

Regional Authorities were also required to prepare Annual Regional Implementation Programmes that were to be prepared "…in consultation with the Urban Transport Council, the National Roads Board, the Government Railways, and all local authorities and operators of urban transport services that, in the opinion of the regional authority, are likely to be affected…" [711]

Financial Assistance

"A regional authority may, in its regional implementation programme or at any other time, apply to the Council for financial assistance for urban transport purposes…All financial assistance given by the Urban Transport Council…shall be payable out of money to be appropriated by Parliament for the purpose." [711]

Transport Licences

"It shall be a condition of every passenger-service licence, harbour-ferry service licence, and taxicab-service licence granted under this Act…that the service to which the licence relates shall be carried on in conformity with the provisions of any approved urban transport scheme relating to the area in which the service is carried on." [711]

The Auckland Curse

Despite the overhaul of the nationwide system of urban transport management and planning, there remained perennial disagreement among Auckland's local bodies as to the apportionment of transport levies to be paid to the Regional Authority to cover public transport losses. The 'area of benefit' principle had operated for many years but, by the early 1980s, some local bodies sought change – as reported by The Auckland Star on 7 March 1983:

"The curse of Auckland has struck again, says former Auckland Mayor Sir Dove-Myer Robinson of a decision by local bodies to support a sector approach to the urban transport levy. The local bodies met the Auckland Region Authority and voted 10 to 6 to support a sector basis for dividing the transport levy. The sector basis means the four main sectors of Auckland will be billed for the transport levy and then decide among themselves how to divide it up. The vote was despite the advice of the ARA's solicitor and an outside opinion sought by the authority that said such an approach might not be legal.

"The authorities which voted against the sector approach had earlier in the meeting tried to retain the existing transport levy which is paid by local bodies receiving ARA bus services with voluntary contributions from those with private services. Sir Dove-Myer said the sector approach would perpetuate and intensify the parochialism responsible for Auckland's local body fragmentation. 'That lack of unity since Auckland was founded has damned most of the progressive moves towards unity of local government and co-ordination and cost savings for local body works.'

"The ARA chairman Mr Hugh Aimer presented a paper suggesting a uniform levy, reflecting the level of service in different districts. But the local bodies felt they had not had enough time to study this proposal and objected to the high costing given rail services – the same as that for high frequency ARA bus services. He said if the decision of the local bodies could be legally implemented, it would put sector against sector and aggravate the efforts of each sector to get the biggest slice of the cake. 'We, who were responsible for the formation of the ARA in 1963, hoped it would obviate the curse of fragmentation in Auckland,' he said. 'It now appears the formation of the ARA has intensified it.' Sir Dove-Myer said the ideal spread of the transport levy would be an equitable one across the whole region because everyone living in the region directly or indirectly benefited from the transport system." [712]

Deregulation of Public Transport

While local government entities continued to disagree about 'who should pay what' for their underfunded public transport services, the Government negated the argument by opening everything up to competition. As described by Anatole Sergejew, Principal Advisor, Ministry of Transport, in his 2007 *Review of Regulation of Commercial Urban Bus and Ferry Services in New Zealand*:

"To promote the efficiency of the public transport system, a package of legislation was passed, taking effect from 1 July 1991, based on the principles that:

- government policy should be clearly separated from regulatory and service delivery functions;
- the ownership and operation of service delivery is best carried out in a corporate form, preferably by the private sector, on a commercial, competitive basis; and
- there should be competition within and between transport modes with minimal central and local government involvement and influence in the commercial environment.

"Local government transport operations were required to be divested to commercial entities operated on a commercial basis at arm's length from the council that owned them. Regional councils were prohibited from having an ownership interest in public transport operations. "All publicly funded public transport was required to be contracted through competitive tendering, with a view to maximising competition by giving all operators the opportunity to tender for services." [713]

Transit New Zealand

To achieve its objectives, the Government established a Crown entity, Transit New Zealand, created by means of the Transit New Zealand Act 1989. As with most deregulation exercises, the principle objective was to save the Government money or, in terms of the Act: "…to promote policies and allocate resources to achieve a safe and efficient land transport system that maximises national economic and social benefits." [714]

To achieve this rationalisation of transport services, the functions of Transit New Zealand (the Authority) included:

"(a) To prepare an annual national land transport programme…

"(b) To manage the implementation of the following classes of outputs in approved national land transport programmes: (i) Local roading: (ii) Safety (construction and maintenance):

(iii) Passenger transport: (iv) State highways: (v) Administration:"

"(f) To control the State highway system, including planning, design, supervision, construction and maintenance…

"(g) To assist and advise local authorities in relation to their functions, duties, and powers under this Act, and to audit the performance of every local authority as compared with the statement of intent of the local authority contained in the relevant land transport programme..." [714]

The new Authority was not to be an autonomous body, separated from Government influence, as Section 7 of the Act revealed:

"In the exercise of its functions, duties, and powers under this Act the Authority shall have regard to the policy of the Government in relation to land transport, and shall comply with any general directions relating to that policy given to it in writing signed by the Minister..." [714]

And, of course, the Government held the purse strings:

"There shall be paid into the Crown Bank Account and separately accounted for-

(a) All excise duty determined and collected pursuant to section 100 of this Act:

(b) All fees and charges collected under the Road User Charges Act 1977:

(c) All fees and charges collected under Part I of the Transport (Vehicle and Driver Registration and Licensing) Act 1986..." [714]

Local regional and territorial bodies were required by the Act to:

"...not later than the 1st day of February 1990, establish a regional land transport committee for its region... Each year, by a date set by the regional land transport committee of the region or regions of which it is part, every territorial authority shall submit to that committee or committees, and make available to the public, a district land transport programme for the next year which shall comprise the territorial authority's recommendations concerning the land transport needs of its district... Each year, by a date set by the regional council, each regional land transport committee shall submit to that council a regional land transport programme for the next year, which shall comprise the committee's recommendations concerning the land transport needs of its region for that year..." [714]

With so much oversight legislated by the Transit New Zealand Act, the unique services provided by the National Roads Board and the Urban Transport Council were no longer required and those bodies were abolished. [714]

Transport Services Licensing

The Transport Services Licensing Act 1989 – *an Act to reform the law relating to land transport licensing* – and which came into force on 1 October 1989, defined the classes of transport licences required for providing a goods, passenger, rental, and vehicle recovery services. [715]

"The Transport Services Licensing Act 1989...gave public transport service operators the right to register and operate commercial services – for instance, where they believed the services could be fully funded through farebox revenue – and to deregister such services if, for instance, they were no longer profitable...

"Regional councils can only decline to register such commercial services if they are likely to have a material adverse effect on the financial viability, or increase the net cost, of any existing contracted services, or if the service 'is contrary to sound traffic management or any other environmental factor identified as being of importance to the region.'" [713]

The Act also required transport operators to provide detailed accounts of their operations: "...every holder of a passenger service licence who proposes to operate a passenger service on or after the 1st day of July 1991 shall, not later than 21 days before the service is to be commenced, and earlier if possible, notify details of the service, including routes or areas of operation, timetables or operating hours, fares, and such other matters as may be required by the Secretary or the regional council, to every regional council in whose region the service is to operate." [715]

Regional Control Lost

Further deregulation of the transport industry was achieved by stripping all regional and territorial authorities of their ownership and management of all passenger transport operations by stipulating that: "…no <u>local authority</u> shall conduct a passenger transport operation after the 30th day of June 1991, or after such later date as the Minister in any particular case may allow…" [716]

Nor could <u>regional councils</u>:

"(a) Hold any equity securities or debt securities in any passenger transport company formed pursuant to this Part of this Act; or

"(b) Hold any equity securities or debt securities or have any interest whatsoever in any body corporate or unincorporate which engages, directly or indirectly, in any passenger transport operation or includes in its assets any passenger transport undertaking; or

"(c) Conduct any passenger transport operation, whether or not on its own behalf; or

"(d) Include in its assets any passenger transport undertaking – whether or not any local authority has or has had any interest in the passenger transport operation or passenger transport undertaking." [716]

The Act required those passenger transport interests, undertakings, and operations of each regional council to be disposed of or sold and did not allow a regional council to:

"(a) Administer competitive process in respect of a contract or agreement for the provision of a passenger service in its region; or

"(b) Negotiate any contract or agreement for the provision of a passenger service in its region; or

"(c) Enter into any contract or agreement for the provision of a passenger service in its region." [716]

Public Transport Services Divided

As explained by Andrew Heal in his Metro Magazine article, *Road Rage*, published May 1997: "From the late 80s onward, public transport was deregulated, with services being divided into unsubsidised commercial services and contracted services awarded by tender. Regional councils had the job of tendering out the latter but, in the interests of market purity, were banned from having any direct interest in passenger transport operations." [717]

Auckland Regional Land Transport Committee

With the prospect of a completely-changed, public transport playing field, there came the opportunity to better plan for the future. To that end, an Auckland Regional Land Transport Committee was formed in 1989 – "…a statutory body made up of the ARC, city and district councils, Transit New Zealand, the Land Transport Safety Authority and the Ministry of Transport, charged with setting out the vision for Auckland's transport future. The committee has the job of producing a regional land transport strategy. The brief: to provide an investment framework for the coming five years and to set a longer-term strategic direction.

"The committee's objectives include limiting the growth of vehicle travel demand; reducing the proportion of trips made by single-occupant cars; increasing the proportion of trips made as car passengers by passenger transport and by cycling and walking; improving accessibility by increasing residential densities within the major passenger transport corridors; and reducing the adverse effects of transport on the natural and physical environment.

"According to its brief, such a system must contribute to the sustainable management of the region's natural and physical resources, reduce the adverse effects of transport on the natural and physical environment, meet the accessibility needs of all groups in the community and enable the efficient movement of people, goods, services and resources.

"When it arrived, the strategy seemed a step forward, spurning short-term, reactive planning and admitting that the costs of relying on the car – environmental, economic and social – were too great to concentrate on building more motorways. It emphasised the need for land-use planning and transport planning to be integrated and for the need for public transport to be seen as a serious alternative to the car…" [717]

But the same had been said for decades…

Road Transport
The Planning of Roads
On 14 March 1989 – the eve of "…major reforms…being proposed for Local Government and for Central Government's Roading, Road Safety and Urban Transport programmes…" the Audit Office published *The Planning of Roads* which focused "…on the manner in which overall national roading objectives are formulated and met." [718]

Parts of that report included:
"Executive Summary - New Zealand has about 51,300 km of paved roads and 41,800 km of unsealed roads. In the current year, about $800 million (or 1.5% of GNP) is planned to be spent on those roads. Their planning affects the social and economic well-being of everyone. The benefit that the country obtains from road planning is dependent on the extent to which that planning meets the needs of road users and the community.

"There have been limited funds available for new roads. During the last 30 years, the volume of traffic has continued to grow at a relatively constant rate, while the amount of money that is spent on the roads has declined as a proportion of national income. Because of the need to keep the existing roads in a serviceable condition, an increasing share of spending has had to go into maintenance. In recent years, spending on State Highways maintenance has taken over 70% of the funds that are available in that sector.

"There is no integrated transport decision-making framework. This can mean, for example, that decisions about closing rail services are taken without consideration necessarily being given to the effects on the congestion or condition of the roads. Decisions relating to building and maintaining roads have been kept separate from road safety enforcement.

"Proposals are at present under consideration to bring urban transport (buses, passenger trains, ferries, etc.) and road building and maintenance together under a single authority, and to bring the administration of those areas closer to road safety and traffic enforcement. This offers the opportunity for decisions affecting any one of these areas to be made taking into account the costs and consequences in the other areas. This has often not been the case in the past.

"It is not possible for Parliament or the public to easily ascertain whether the National Roads Board (NRB) is doing a good job. The NRB does not declare its strategic aims or report publicly on the overall condition of the roads. Any changes in the administration of roads should require greater accountability from the agencies that may succeed the NRB.

"Relatively few members of the NRB or its District Roads Councils directly represent the road users who pay for the roads. Most Board and Council members are appointed by local authorities. In any restructuring of roading administration, a greater voice should be given to the user representatives. In future, roading administration should also have stronger financial and management skills.

"Present legislation requires the NRB to deal with many minor issues that would be more effectively dealt with at a local level. In any new structure, such issues should, wherever possible, be dealt with locally, where they are most likely to be well understood...

"Road funds are distributed in a generally effective manner. However, some changes are required. There is, in our review, no justification for the present system that allocates at least 39% of revenue to local authority roads and a minimum of 47% to State Highways. The NRB should allocate funds on the basis of need..."

"The Condition of the Roads – Towards the end of the 1940s, New Zealand adopted the flexible road pavement in preference to the more permanent asphalted concrete or Portland Cement surfaces. That decision was largely because of plant limitations and the high cost of the more permanent materials.

"The flexible pavement is a low capital/high maintenance cost design whereas the permanent pavements are generally higher capital/lower maintenance costs. The flexible pavement allows for different surfaces to suit local conditions. The regular addition of tar/chip seal increases the strength of the road, reducing the risk of damage from heavier traffic.

"There is a general view that the use of flexible pavements had been an effective way of developing the country's roads. However there is some evidence that, while our light tar seal roads are good for light traffic, they are less cost effective for heavy vehicles. With the deregulation of heavy traffic and greater volumes of freight carried by road, it is essential that road designers keep their planning assumptions under review...

"In recent years, maintenance and basic reconstruction work has formed a growing proportion of the roading workload. Today, approximately 70% of all funds are spent on keeping existing roads in an acceptable condition. The availability of funds for new road works is therefore limited.

"Accountability - It is essential that road-users are able to judge how effectively the funds collected from them for roading purposes have been used. The roading authorities, both national and local, must be held to account by Parliament, Ministers and rate- and taxpayers (as the ultimate owners of the roads) for their use of public funds and resources." [718]

Auckland Harbour Bridge

Following the passing of the Auckland Harbour Bridge Authority Dissolution Act 1983, the Auckland Harbour Bridge Authority was dissolved and bridge tolls abolished from 1 April 1984. With the dissolution of the Authority, all the property for which it was responsible, including the bridge, passed to the Crown and the bridge was declared to be a motorway subject to the jurisdiction of the National Roads Board and the National Roads Act 1953. [719]

Before the Waitemata was finally bridged in 1959, the population of Auckland's North Shore was about 27,000. Suddenly, after decades of slow growth, came the bridge and the population increased tenfold to some 309,000 by 2006. As a result, traffic flows across the bridge vastly exceeded forecasts: 5 million vehicles in 1961 - 15 million in 1970 - 32 million by 1985. [720]

This additional load was bound to result in damage. In 1985, "Inspections revealed cracking of the box girder clip-ons. A two-year programme of works ensued with bans on heavy vehicles [using the clip-ons] and a review of the concrete asphalt used on the bridge." [259]

Suburban Rail
The Prime Minister's View
A new decade…and the Prime Minister's umbrage at Dove-Myer Robinson's criticism had mellowed somewhat. That's if his letter to the Mayor of 9 April 1980 is anything to go by. Robert Muldoon is responding to a third party letter, forwarded to him by Dove-Myer Robinson, which compares New Zealand's railway system with that of Ireland (Coras Iompair Eireann (C.I.E.). Robert Muldoon's response, only a part of which is included here, is conciliatory; an almost too friendly chance to make a point about his view of public transport:

"…New Zealand Railways has only a limited passenger carrying fleet and the remaining passenger trains in New Zealand reflect social conditions, especially the dominance of the private motor car for private travel. In fact in the New Zealand situation it has been shown that modern road coaches are a more economical solution to inter-urban transport needs than the purchase of new railcars or diesel-hauled trains.

"It is the relative dominance of the private motor car in New Zealand which forms the basis of so much of the difference in passenger transport between C.I.E. and New Zealand Railways. From the early 1950's the growth of private motor car ownership and its use for commuter and inter-urban transport has had an effect on investment in rail passenger services in New Zealand. Except in the Wellington area, where the demand for commuter rail services has been maintained resulting in the recent decision to buy new electric rolling stock, the public has demanded facilities for, and increased its use of, private motor vehicles, to the detriment of rail passenger services.

"Such has not been the case in Ireland, where traditionally there has been a much lower level of private ownership of motor vehicles and the use made of rail passenger services reflects a continuing need for public transport. Had the demand for rail passenger services in New Zealand been similarly maintained it is fair to say that the Wellington situation would have been repeated in other areas of the country; but this has not happened.

"The rapidly increasing cost of commuter transport in particular dictates that decisions must be made on the extent and modal split of urban transport. It is Government's view that the people who will be directly affected by the decisions on these important matters should themselves direct the course of action to be taken. This is of course the intent of the current Urban Transport Bill, which is designed to involve local communities in determining the nature and extent of the services they are prepared to support." [721]
Financial Support
"…prepared to support *financially*…" is what Robert Muldoon could have written because, as Graham Bush observed in his book, *Local Government and Politics in New Zealand*,

"…a principle objective [of the urban transport legislation] was progressively to shift the burden of subsidy from the taxpayer to the regional ratepayer…" [722]

Regional Responsibility for Losses

This *principle of financial support* had been referred to in the New Zealand Transport Policy Study undertaken by Wilbur Smith & Associates between February 1972 and October 1973. With regard to Railway Suburban Passenger Services, the Wilbur Smith report noted:

"Urban passenger transport services are provided on a non-profit basis throughout most of the world on the principle that social benefits exceed the losses incurred. New Zealand Railways provides suburban rail passenger services in Auckland, Wellington and Dunedin.

"Estimates of costs per passenger mile determined by this Study indicated that rail services are as efficient as bus transport alternatives, with the Wellington operation comparing favourably with other major services, suggesting that economies of scale were being achieved. However, the amount by which avoidable costs, which would not be incurred if these services were abandoned, were in excess of revenues received was $1,852,000 in 1971, representing a shortfall in revenue of 10 cents per passenger journey.

"Financial considerations assume particular importance when a public service is provided at a loss. This has led to a reluctance to invest in new equipment or to encourage new traffic. The continuance of the services relies on the fact that there are a number of beneficiaries of public transport services within the community in addition to the users themselves. These include landowners, residents, employers and commercial establishments.

"There are both equity and economic efficiency warrants for requiring that these beneficiaries should contribute to suburban rail costs. NZR should not be required to subsidise either the capital or operating costs of suburban rail services. Passenger charges should be calculated on the basis of long-run marginal costs determined on the assumption that passenger vehicles are 'optimally' used.

"Operating deficits should be paid by the community, while subsidies for capital should be provided in terms of a 'package' involving all forms of transport, public and private, so that investment and disinvestment decisions are made on a uniform inter-modal basis.

"Suburban rail services should be provided as part of the regional transport system and within the framework of a comprehensive regional plan. The region should, in consultation with NZR, determine the standard of service and take responsibility for operating losses." [530]

Chapter Seven

1990 to 1999 – Auckland Slows to Gridlock

Planning and Politics
Reform and More Reform
As detailed earlier, the Labour Government began an extensive overhaul of local government in 1989 - some of the biggest changes in more than a century. Counties and boroughs were scrapped and consolidated into the city councils of Auckland, Manukau, Waitakere, and North Shore, and the district councils of Papakura, Rodney and most of Franklin. The Auckland Regional Authority became the Auckland Regional Council.

Resource Management Act 1991
With the inclusion of the Resource Management Act 1991, greater planning consideration was to be given to the natural and physical environment of regions - as explained by Nicola Legat in her article, *City Limits*, published in the September 1995 edition of Metro Magazine:

"It's fair to say that in the past there was little management: the urban forms of the various boroughs and cities which existed before local government reform in 1989 developed in an unstructured and uncoordinated way. It didn't seem to matter: there was plenty of space, and we were not as concerned about the greenhouse emissions of thousands and thousands of car journeys along the roads or the run-off of heavy metals from exhaust emissions into our streams and rivers…

"The Resource Management Act 1991 stipulated the creation of documents known as regional policy statements, drawn up by regional councils, which would, through arcane and slow-moving statutory processes (proposals, submissions, hearings, a rewrite, republication, more submissions and hearings), eventually transmogrify into regional development plans, a kind of regional planning bible with which local authorities (the city and district councils) must comply." [723]

Specific Requirements
More specifically, the Resource Management Act 1991 and the Resource Management Amendment Act 1993 required:

"Every regional council shall have the following functions for the purpose of giving effect to this Act in its region:

(a) The establishment, implementation, and review of objectives, policies, and methods to achieve integrated management of the natural and physical resources of the region:

(b) The preparation of objectives and policies in relation to any actual or potential effects of the use, development, or protection of land which are of regional significance:" [724]

The individual was affected by means of the provisions stipulating that:

"No person may use any land in a manner that contravenes a rule in a district [or regional] plan…unless the activity is -

(a) Expressly allowed by a resource consent granted by the territorial [or regional] authority responsible for the plan…" [724]

Radical Shift in Planning Ideology

In what it described as a *radical shift in planning ideology*, a New Zealand Productivity Commission Research Note of June 2015 described how the Resource Management Act affected New Zealand's development planning (with reference to a 2001 publication by Harvey C Perkins and David C Thorns: *A decade on: reflections on the Resource Management Act 1991 and the practice of urban planning in New Zealand*):

"The Resource Management Act (RMA) radically restructured New Zealand's planning system. The British-style town and country planning scheme was repealed and replaced with a very different form of statutory environmental planning and management. The Act attempted to do away with zoning. It established in its place an effects-based system, elaborated locally in a District Plan.

"Any land use or activity could be permitted so long as it did not undermine the sustainable management of natural and physical resources The Act was part of the third Labour government's broad reforms of the state sector which were based on increasing the role of the private market, extending choice, and privileging the individual consumer. Planning under the existing legislation was seen to be a bureaucratic process which intruded too much into the market place and increased the cost of development through delays as applications went through the local government system (Perkins and Thorns, 2001, p.641)…

"One empirical study in the late 1990s concluded that the new legislative environment of the RMA and the amended Local Government Act 1974 displaced city-planning from the central role it had previously occupied in local government activities (Perkins and Thorns, 2001, p.648-9). It noted that some councils had difficulty dealing with the shift from zoning to effects-based management under the RMA as it has reshaped, and effectively restricted, their ability to control activities." [494]

Reaching Capacity

And those activities were becoming more complex as Auckland's population increased considerably – as described by *A brief history of Auckland's urban form*, published by the Auckland Regional Council in December 2019:

"Tāmaki Makaurau/Auckland experienced considerable population increase during the 1990s, driven in large part by a change in national immigration policy that allowed new migrants to enter New Zealand based on skills. Three quarters (76 per cent) of the nation's growth between 1991 and 2001 occurred in the Auckland region, which had reached one million residents by the 1996 census.

"As the region's population and economy continued to increase, pressures intensified on transport, housing and infrastructure. The removal of tariffs on imported vehicles in the early 1990s resulted in a flood of cheap imported cars on the market, which were eagerly snapped up and contributed further to the traffic dilemma. Public transport patronage was decreasing and traffic congestion was increasing. Much of the region's infrastructure (water supply, wastewater treatment, stormwater systems, refuse disposal, transport, power, gas and telecommunication networks) was already reaching design capacity and needed upgrading to meet higher environmental standards as well as increasing demand. In 1995 and 1998, Auckland experienced water and power supply crises." [725]

Population One Million

Auckland continued to grow, as outlined by Nicola Legat in her September 1995 Metro Magazine article, *City Limits*:

"The population of the Auckland region reached one million in March 1994...The Auckland region has 28 per cent of the nation's population; 32 per cent of the nation's workforce; 38 per cent of the nation's business enterprises...70 per cent of the region's population growth has been through natural increase.

"Auckland attracts 80 per cent of new permanent migrants to new Zealand...The region has been growing by 15,000 people per annum since 1986 but now, given natural increase and migration, Auckland faces population growth more like 34,000 per annum...

"Aucklanders own almost one vehicle for every two people...Aucklanders make on average 2.1 trips a day; 72 per cent of these are by car. The average distance travelled to work has increased 17 per cent between 1981 and 1991.

"Using Transit New Zealand estimates, which include an estimate of the value of time spent travelling, the operating cost of Auckland's transport system is $5 billion per annum. 1.9 million tons of CO_2 is produced each year by Auckland's transport system...

"The concern that population growth is placing undesirable pressure on the region's environment, and eroding the natural values which attract people to it, has been expressed throughout the region as each of its seven cities and districts (Auckland, Manukau, Waitakere, North Shore, Rodney, Franklin and Papakura) moves towards completing the district plans which will set town-planning criteria for the next decade..." [723]

A Century of Sprawl

The population growth referred to by Nicola Legat obviously had to fit somewhere – but not everywhere – as described by *Auckland Today* in its December 2004/January 2005 edition:

"To many people the term 'urban sprawl' may seem to have sprung to the fore in recent years as new developments rise across Auckland at an apparently escalating rate. However, sprawl is nothing new. Even back in the 1930s, Auckland residents witnessed the 'sprawling' suburbs of Mission Bay, Kohimarama and St Heliers take shape as Tamaki Drive opened up access to new areas for development. Like the slow but determined creep of 'middle-aged spread', for several decades urban sprawl has been pushing Auckland's metaphorical waistline further and further out as we grapple with growth...

"By 1991 the region's population reached 954,000 and it was absorbing 57% of the nation's growth. With the benefit of hindsight and experience, Auckland's planners determined during the 1990s that decisive action was required to curb endless sprawl and to manage the Auckland region's growth responsibly...before we succumb to further ill effects of what was starting to look like 'urban obesity'." [726]

Auckland Regional Services Trust

It soon became obvious that, despite the best intentions of the Resource Management legislation to govern the natural and physical environment – *to curb endless sprawl* – a more concentrated management of the Auckland region's assets was also needed if the region was to cope with its exponential growth.

One of the main architects of local government reform, Labour's Michael Bassett, was deposed by the election of the National Government in November 1990. In line with its ideals, the new Government continued to promote the diversification and privatisation of local body businesses including those presided over by the Auckland Regional Council.

By means of the Local Government Amendment Act 1992, which came into force on 1 July of that year, the Auckland Regional Services Trust was created to "...assume ownership of the specified assets and responsibility for the specified liabilities..." [727]

The assets transferred included the Regional Council's shareholding in Ports of Auckland and the Yellow Bus Company.

Auckland Community Trust

The Local Government Amendment Act required a trust deed to be prepared, the Auckland Community Trust – "...all property vested in, or belonging to, the Community Trust shall be held in trust to be applied for purposes beneficial to the community principally in the Auckland Region, including charitable, cultural, philanthropic, recreational, heritage, and other purposes." [727]

Asset Sales

In a later submission, *Concerning the Future of the Auckland Regional Services Trust*, the New Zealand Business Roundtable (an organisation of chief executives of major New Zealand business firms) commented:

"...the [Auckland Regional Services] Trust...arose from a reform of the Auckland Regional Authority, which at the time had accumulated debt with a market value of $224 million. With the reform, the Auckland Regional Council retained regulatory functions while the Trust was given the responsibility to manage and ultimately eliminate its debt through a programme of asset sales." [728]

Left Wing Control

However, as explained by political commentator, Keith Rankin, when discussing the future of the Auckland Regional Services Trust:

"The Auckland Regional Services Trust is an organ of local Government, convened in 1992 as a vehicle to repay the city's debts through the privatisation of its assets. The central government plan came unstuck when Auckland voters gave the 'left-wing' Alliance Party control over the trust in 1992, and proceeded to repay all of the debts out of revenue, thus removing the need to sell the city's assets." [729]

The Future of the Auckland Regional Services Trust

Naturally, during an era of privatisation, the efficient success of the Auckland Regional Services Trust could not be tolerated for long. By 1997, the future of the Trust was being questioned by the New Zealand Business Roundtable in its submission on a Discussion Document, *Pathways for Auckland*:

"The Auckland Regional Services Trust was established as a temporary structure and is an anomaly in local government. No comparable structures exist elsewhere in the country. The net assets of the Trust as at 31 December 1996 were $1,249 million – or $1,160 for each resident (about $3,500 for each household) in the Auckland region. The Trust is New Zealand's fifth largest business.

"The fundamental issue in the review should be whether the Trust is undertaking activities which are a proper role for local government. Local government is part of the public sector and its role is to ensure the provision of local public goods, including necessary local regulation. The Trust is essentially engaged in commercial activities which are the proper role of the private sector. Accordingly they should be transferred to the private sector as rapidly as possible. The Trust was established by parliament essentially as a transitional vehicle for this purpose, and it has no ongoing rationale..." [728]

Infrastructure Auckland
The demise of the Auckland Regional Services Trust and its financial arm, the Auckland Community Trust, was eventually legislated for with the passage of the Local Government Amendment Act 1998. This amendment was enacted "…for the purpose of making better provision in relation to the infrastructure of the Auckland Region by –

"(a) Dissolving the Auckland Regional Services Trust "…as from the commencement of 1 October 1998…" and establishing, on that date, a body called *Infrastructure Auckland* [as a body corporate] which took on all assets and liabilities of the Auckland Regional Services Trust…

"The principal function of Infrastructure Auckland is to contribute funds, by way of grants, in respect of projects, or parts of projects, undertaken in the Auckland Region for the purpose of providing –
(a) Land transport; or
(b) Any passenger service; or
(c) Any passenger transport operation; or
(d) Stormwater infrastructure,- where the projects or parts of projects   generate benefits to the community generally in addition to any   benefits that accrue to any identifiable persons or groups of   persons." [730]

The 1998 Act called for the preparation by the Auckland Regional Council of a *regional growth strategy* (Section 37SE) and the establishment of a *regional growth forum* to be appointed by the Auckland Regional Council (Section 37SG)

"The function of the regional growth forum is to advise on and approve the regional growth strategy prepared under section 37SE and any amendment to that strategy before any such strategy or amendment is adopted by the Auckland Regional Council." [730]

The Auckland Regional Growth Forum
The Auckland Regional Council described the Auckland Regional Growth Forum in its pamphlet, *A brief history of Auckland's urban form*, published December 2019:

"In 1998 the Auckland Regional Growth Forum was established, following population growth and capacity concerns, as well as a number of inter-council Environment Court cases.

"The Forum's objective was to develop a Regional Growth Strategy, which was released in 1999. It provided a vision for what Auckland could be like in 50 years with a population of two million. The purpose of the Regional Growth Strategy was to ensure growth is accommodated in a way that meets the best interests of the inhabitants of the Auckland region. Key principles of the strategy included:

- A compact urban form, with most growth within existing metropolitan area focused around town centres and major transport routes to create higher density communities;
- Focus on a variety of housing and mixed use activities to provide for employment, services and recreation;
- Limited managed expansion into greenfield areas outside of   current Metropolitan Urban Limits (MUL) where   environmental quality, accessibility and infrastructure development criteria can be met;
- Protection of the coast and surrounding natural environment." [725]

A Place Sought by Many

The roles of the Regional Growth Forum and Infrastructure Auckland were described in a pamphlet subsequently published by the Auckland Regional Council, *A Place Sought by Many: a brief history of regional planning for Auckland's growth*:

"The Growth Forum's role is to develop a Growth Strategy to accommodate growth in a manner that best meets the interests of the regional community. Infrastructure Auckland's role is to make grants to projects that help address the region's land and passenger transport, and stormwater problems. These grants cannot be inconsistent with the Growth Strategy or the regional transport and stormwater strategies.

"The Regional Growth Forum has delegated powers to:

1. Address growth issues in the Auckland region by ensuring co-ordination and liaison on a regional basis, to facilitate the production of a Regional Growth Strategy.

2. Give effect to a Regional Growth Strategy by developing and approving a regional plan under the Resource Management Act 1991 and by such other means as are considered appropriate.

3. Make recommendations to Auckland's local authorities and other key parties on appropriate growth strategies for the integrated and sustainable management of the Auckland region.

"The Regional Growth Forum is funded by the Auckland Regional Council through the regional rate. The other participating councils also fund the time of their elected representatives and staff to support the Growth Forum." [731]

Almost a Greater Auckland

During the 1990s there was first established the Auckland Regional Council and the condensing of the region's many local bodies to just seven city and district councils. Then came the Regional Growth Forum which provided for the co-ordinated planning of the whole Auckland region.

When Auckland's trams were struggling in 1928 to provide an adequate public transport service to an expanding city, and finding it difficult to compete with increasing motor-omnibus use, the Government set up the Auckland Transport Commission to find a solution. After many days of hearings, the Commission found in favour of the establishment of the Auckland Transport Board to manage public transport operations as the best compromise in the face of much disunity. However, the Transport Board was not its preferred choice, as it reported on 27 July 1928:

"To our minds the solution of this difficulty is a simple one. It lies in the voluntary abandonment of the parochial and arbitrary boundary-lines and the amalgamation of all the contiguous local authorities with the city. We can find no other opinion expressed by any outside and impartial observer…" [732]

Such sentiments were echoed at various times for more than a century by many civic leaders, including Arthur Myers, John Allum, and Dove-Myer Robinson – their vision of a Greater Auckland was now much closer to being realised...

Public Transport
Improved Bus Services

Despite the demise of the trolleybus a decade earlier, public transport services had improved by the 1990s – as John McCrystal describes in his book *On the Buses in New Zealand*:

"...urban services were in the best shape they had been in since the 1950s. New services, some of them intelligently designed to maximise commuter convenience, had been created, such as...Auckland's Link bus service – one which ran a circuit around the CBD and the inner city suburban shopping precincts of Parnell, Newmarket and Ponsonby and another which mimicked the job once performed by Birkenhead Transport and the North Shore Bus Company in feeding North Shore ferry services..." [144]

"In one of those strange circularities of history, by the mid-1990s bus services were beginning to be established to feed ferry services in Auckland, exactly as they used to do before the Harbour Bridge was opened in 1959. So congested had the bridge become that it was far faster to catch a bus to the ferry and cruise across underneath it rather than try to battle the traffic across by car or bus." [144]

"The regions – even Auckland – were investing not only in the buses but also in the infrastructure that helps to make bus services run smoothly, such as bus-only 'green lanes', bus-priority traffic signals, real-time timetable information, integrated ticketing and top-grade facilities such as North Shore City's park-and-ride terminals...and, of course, after several drafts and much argument, the spectacular new Britomart transport terminal, which improved the integration of Auckland's various public transport modes." [144]

Effects of the 1989 Public Transport Reforms

In his later *Review of Regulation of Commercial Urban Bus and Ferry Services in New Zealand*, Principal Advisor to the Ministry of Transport, Anatole Sergejew, commented:

"Effects of the 1989 public transport reforms – It is generally agreed that an immediate effect of the public transport reforms in New Zealand was to reduce the cost of public transport. A study of three large local government owned operators showed a 35% reduction in real terms in the average operating cost per bus-kilometre between 1989/90 and 1993/94. [Ref: Travers Morgan (NZ) Ltd. (1994). *Passenger Transport Trends and Transport Law Reform*. Draft report prepared for Transit New Zealand, Wellington p.2].

"This saving was achieved mainly through staff cuts – the local government owned operators cut staffing levels by at least 40%. While driver wages remained largely unchanged, driver productivity was improved through requiring drivers to drive longer hours, and through improved scheduling. The operating costs of privately owned operators did not change in real terms over the same period. Local government owned operators had to reduce costs to the more efficient level of private operators to survive competition or the threat of competition [ibid., pp.3-4].

"Maximum fare levels were controlled by regional councils. Between 1989/90 and 1993/94, fares increased only modestly. The total bus-kilometres of public transport services provided in the urban areas changed very little in that time [ibid., p.9-10].

"Overall, public funding from regional councils and central government was reduced by 20% in real terms between 1989/90 and 1991/92, while fares and service levels were little affected [ibid., p.25].

"There was a short-term adverse effect on patronage. And while in 1994 it was claimed that there was no evidence of a persisting adverse effect on patronage in the longer term [ibid.,p.15], it took eleven years for bus patronage in the major centres to recover to 1990 levels [Auckland Sustainable Cities Programme, 2006a, pp.37]." [713]

Public Transport Patronage

Indeed, as published in the August/September 1992 Passenger Transport Magazine, and as reprinted by the Greater Auckland blog on 22 April 2017, a survey of peak-hour commuters travelling to central Auckland by bus, train and ferry, undertaken by the Auckland Regional Council during April 1992:

"...revealed a 14.5 per cent drop in patronage compared with 1991. The survey has been carried out annually since 1986, (except 1989 when there was an ARC bus strike).

"In 1986, 24,430 people travelled into central Auckland by public transport, this figure remaining stable for the next two years, then plummeting abruptly from 1988. Between 1988 and 1990 patronage dropped by 22 per cent, a further 15.4 per cent between 1990 and 1991 and 14.5 per cent in the last year [to 1992]. The total decline between 1988 and 1992 is 42 per cent.

"Reasons attributed by regional council staff for the precipitous drop in patronage include the hardy perennials of reduced city centre employment, increased unemployment generally, availability of cheap car parking and second-hand Japanese imports.

"Buses carry 89.3 per cent of the passengers entering the Central Business District and bus patronage declined by 14 per cent. The slight slow-down in the rate of decline was treated as a hopeful omen by the eternal optimists at the ARC. Train patronage dropped by just under 10 per cent and carry 2.4 per cent of the passenger load into the Central Business District (at over 10 per cent of the total subsidy cost). Ferries carry 8.3 per cent of city-bound commuters and their patronage has remained stable...

"City rail trains only carry an average of 35 passengers each although their peak load point is outside central Auckland. Overall City rail patronage is rising: [Ed: In 1992, trains carried 1.019m passengers in the entire year].

"Birkenhead transport has the highest occupancy of any bus operator with 33 passengers per trip, down from 38 in 1991. Yellow Bus Company flyer buses coming off the Southern Motorway carry an average of 59 passengers and City Line express buses [from Papakura] carry an average of 39 passengers. Yellow Bus Company services from the North Shore have their highest average occupancy with 37 passengers per bus. This should improve further with the development of the revised North Shore busway proposal.

"Whenuapai buses are now only carrying an average of 26 passengers per bus and Whenuapai is now able to use minibuses to run its peak hour services. This is partly due to more Whenuapai passengers working and shopping in New Lynn, where no direct service is available...

"Current Auckland isthmus contracts expire in 1996 and Auckland City is concerned that there may not be many public transport passengers left by then. However, the Auckland Regional Council considers that 'it is debatable whether the Council can take immediate action that will be effective in reversing patronage trends.' The Council has taken a stance that a comprehensive review process provides the best opportunity for the long-term survival of passenger transport in the region. This leaves operators scrapping over a declining market and leaves all the initiative for service improvements with the operators.

"One bright note in this sorry saga is that the current Auckland City review of Central Business District routes and terminals may alleviate some of the anomalies where the terminals are located nowhere near where passengers want to go and buses take circuitous routes to leave the Central Business District." [733]

Problems and Conflicts

In his 1996 presentation to the Australasian Transport Research Forum, held at Auckland in 1996, the then Manager of Auckland City Council Transportation Planning, Ross Rutherford, observed:

"Some of the problems and conflicts inherent in the existing legislation are illustrated by the difficulties in implementing the Waitakere & Auckland Isthmus Passenger Transport Strategy (WAIPTS). The WAIPTS study was initiated by the Auckland City Council and undertaken jointly by the Auckland City, Waitakere City and Auckland Regional Councils plus Transit New Zealand.

"The primary objective was to design a public transport system for the two cities better meeting the needs of existing and potential users within current funding constraints. "The study was undertaken by consultants at a cost of $300,000 over a 2 year period from 1993 to 1995. It involved extensive surveys and detailed computer analysis supplemented by good knowledge of the existing system. There was a strong emphasis on consultation throughout. The recommended strategy included better cross city routes, a simplification of the current complex route system, higher frequencies in some areas, and more use of the rail system.

"The current system in Waitakere City and the eastern suburbs of Auckland City is to be converted to a line haul feeder system focusing on appropriate local centres. Such a concept is consistent with the development of mixed use, medium density, public transport oriented development along the existing rail corridors being strongly promoted by Waitakere City Council. The new service contracts for the two cities are to commence in January 1997…

"The bus operators, however, have shown little enthusiasm for the line hall feeder system, and have yet to fully accept an integrated ticketing system. They have registered a relatively large number of commercial services based very largely on the status quo.

"The Regional Council's reaction has been that it feels it has little choice but to accept this situation and to design contract services to 'fill the gaps' in service provision. The overall service network offered in January 1997 is, therefore, likely to be very similar to that available today.

"This appears to leave the local authorities in a position of being unable to ensure that the public transport system will support strategic land use policies, particularly the introduction of higher density development at selected rail stations. It bodes ill for future major investment in passenger rail requiring an integrated, complementary public transport system to be fully effective." [734]

Competitive Pricing of Public Passenger Transport

The effects of the 1989 public transport reforms were also of interest to the Audit Office which produced a study of the matter by its Deputy Controller and Auditor-General, J W Cameron, on 14 August 1992:

"More than $100 million is spent every year to subsidise the operation of public passenger transport services. However, the way in which those services are provided changed from 1 July 1991, as part of the Government's reform of the transport sector. It is therefore timely to review how the new policy was applied and whether value for money was obtained from this substantial investment of public money. I hope that the comments in this report will make a contribution to future management of the public passenger transport sector and that the lessons learned from this, the first round, will be heeded..." [735]

"The audit was carried out under a section 25(3) of the Public Finance Act 1977. It assessed the effectiveness and efficiency with which the new Competitive Pricing Procedures (CPPs) for public passenger transport were developed and subsequently implemented in July 1991.

"Passenger Transport Reforms – The reforms were designed to address shortcomings in the previous regime. There was no requirement for competition in the supply of services, and costs were not transparent. The reforms are incorporated in three main features of legislation; the Transport Services Licensing Act 1989, the Transit New Zealand Act 1989 and a 1989 amendment to the Local Government Act 1974." [735]

"Funding Of Public Passenger Transport – Transit was set up in 1989 to plan and manage all central government expenditure on roads and passenger transport out of a Land Transport Fund which was set up for that purpose. Allocating funds to different land transport activities requires Transit to make explicit trade-offs between investment in roading and passenger transport, subject always to current government policy.

"Arguments in favour of road users contributing to funding public passenger transport rests on assumptions about transfers of costs and benefits between private motorists and users of public transport.

"CPP Development – Section 20 of the Transit New Zealand Act 1989 states that after 30 June 1991 neither Transit nor any local authority may make any payment in respect of a passenger transport service unless the amount of that payment is determined by a competitive pricing procedure.

"The responsibility for approving competitive pricing procedures lay with Transit. Transit issued a Manual of Competitive Pricing Procedures which all councils were required to follow in purchasing passenger transport services. Individual councils were free to develop their own detailed procedures within the broad requirements laid down in Transit's manual." [735]

"Funding Of Public Passenger Transport – In drafting the manual, Transit recognised the need to keep the CCPs flexible for operators and regional councils without compromising its provisions for encouraging competition...The CPPs are an important mechanism for ensuring that public money used to fund transport services is spent in the most cost-effective manner. They are designed to ensure that services are obtained at the best possible price. They do not ensure that this is the best use of that money.

"What is also required are objectives setting out what these subsidies are designed to achieve. Thus, where public money is used to fund public passenger transport, we expected to find sound reasons justifying any such expenditure...Transit has committed $44.3 million to passenger transport services from the Land Transport Fund for 1991-92. Transit is accountable for this expenditure to the Government and to road users from whom taxes are collected to meet the costs of land transport related activities." [735]

"Accountability also requires Transit to be able to justify to the Government and road users how public money is spent; that is, what services the money is supporting, and to what extent regions, communities, transport users or others benefit from that money.

"A subsidisation policy therefore serves two purposes. It provides a means of deciding how much money is to be spent on public passenger transport. It also enables the

Government to justify its decisions about the nature and extent of the services it subsidises in each region...

"Regional councils are responsible for planning and implementing passenger transport policies in their regions. They make the decisions about what services should be supported from rates. However, central government also contributes to these regional transport services...

"Regional councils have wide discretion as to the amount of money they spend on passenger transport, and how that money is spent. Regional goals include reducing costs for all users of public transport, addressing social needs by subsidising special groups in the community, providing mobility for people with no private means of transport, improving road safety, and reducing traffic congestion.

"Conclusions – Our analysis of Transit's subsidisation policy and funding mechanisms revealed shortcomings in its ability to account for the road user funds which it spends on passenger transport. While we recognise that there are difficulties in establishing a subsidy justification policy, the absence of a sound rationale has implications for the involvement of central government in public passenger transport.

"At the present time, it is not possible to establish whether public passenger transport is over-funded or under-funded. This has consequences for the funding of passenger transport in the future...

"Future Funding of Passenger Transport – Without a coherent subsidisation policy, Transit was unable to respond effectively to a recent move by the Government to cut funding to passenger transport. Transit's targeted funding of $44.3 million for passenger transport in 1991-2 was based on regional council expenditure for 1990-91.

"In July 1991, however, the Minister of Transport announced a reduction in passenger transport subsidies to $32.2 million. There was no clearly stated and researched funding policy which the Government could have used to identify the consequences of this cut; nor, once its funding was reduced, was Transit in a position to know how that new reduced level of funding should be allocated.

"The Government recently gave regional councils the power to supplement funding for passenger transport by levying a petrol tax on motorists. Taken together with the decision to reduce central government funding, this and other proposals such as road tolls indicate a move on the part of the Government to transfer the responsibility for funding passenger transport to the regions." [735]

Regional Petrol Tax

The regional petrol tax, introduced in 1992 to compensate for reductions in the level of direct government spending on public transport was legislated for by the Local Government Amendment Act (No. 2) 1992 – Section 200c (1) of which stated:

"For the purpose of funding any passenger service in their respective regions (and only for that purpose), the Auckland Regional Council, the Waikato Regional Council, the Wellington Regional Council, the Canterbury Regional Council, and the Otago Regional Council are, subject to this section, each hereby authorised to levy a tax, to be called the regional petrol tax, on all leaded and unleaded petrol...

"200F. Application of proceeds of tax – All revenue raised by a regional council under this Part of this Act shall be credited to the Land Transport Disbursement Account established under section 18 (1) of the Transit New Zealand Act 1989 and applied only for passenger transport..." [736]

Resistance to Reforms

The Audit Office Report continued with an analysis of the preparedness of the Auckland Regional Council for the Government reforms of the early 1990s:

"Network Planning – Auckland Regional Council delayed preparation for deregulation on 1 July in the belief that its resistance to the reforms would lead to a change in government policy. This stance left the council without time to do any service planning. In addition, the council had not previously undertaken the detailed service-level planning necessary for ongoing management of the network, and therefore had no researched information about the suitability of existing services. It proposes to carry out this work over the next few years.

"The council also did not have current information on future transport needs. The last transportation planning model for the region was developed in 1972-76, with some additional work in 1986. The council was aware that the region had changed substantially since that time, making the existing models obsolete.

"The council's 1991-92 Annual Plan identified both service-level planning and longer-term regional planning as major transportation activities for the year. We found that no work had been started on the first of these. The council had, however, begun work on a new computer model to assist in medium-term to long-term planning. This is scheduled for completion in 1993.

"The council developed a Regional Passenger Transport Plan and consulted with local territorial authorities and passenger transport operators. This plan was published in October 1990. It contained a schedule of specified services which was based on the routes and timetables of the existing operators.

"However, because the council had no information about the levels of patronage on those services, there was no assurance that the services it elected to provide after 1 July were either necessary or appropriate to meet the demands of users.

"On the contrary, the council's own Regional Passenger Transport Plan indicated that these were far from ideal. The schedule of specified services included public input through the submissions of the area's community boards. They had sought new local services and these were included in the schedule." [735]

"Commercial Services – The [1989] reforms anticipated that only some services would need to be subsidised. Other services would be commercially viable, and so could be provided without public money. For this reason, the first step in the new process called for transport operators to register with the councils' services which they would be prepared to run without subsidy. The operators were free to apply for registration of any services they wished, whether these were specified in the councils' plans or not.

"The legislation allowed councils to decline registrations only in certain limited circumstances. These were where:

- There was already an existing registered service; and
- There were adverse environmental or traffic management effects.

"In Auckland, commercial registrations constituted 8% of total service kilometres in the region. The council had declared its intention to tender for services which were essentially the same as the services being run by the existing operators, and in their traditional operating areas. This made it easier to subsequently integrate subsidised services with commercial services in the tendering process. Since operators registered selected services which matched their existing networks, there was no conflict with the council's own service requirements, and the council had only to tender out the services remaining." [735]

"Developing Service Specifications – Service Features – From a passenger's point of view, the ideal transport system is cheap, handy, frequent, fast and comfortable – and always has seating available. Councils have to try to accommodate these expectations within the limited available funds. They must weigh up the benefits of providing anything more than a basic service against the costs which will be incurred by doing so.

"Auckland Regional Council sought to preserve the quality of transport services by specifying standards for buses, trains and ferries. It did not assess whether these criteria imposed costs or offered tangible benefits for users. The council decided to base its service specifications on existing routes and timetables, and so avoid any disruption to passengers.

"However, these services had developed under a regime which protected incumbent operators from competition. There was no pressure from competing operators to run services more efficiently; for example, by using different vehicles, timetables or routes. In adopting existing service features, the council missed an opportunity to make its services more attractive.

"Service Capacity – A council's choice of vehicle capacity in its service specifications can also have an important impact on costs and patronage. Large-capacity vehicles may be required at peak times, since travellers prefer not to travel standing or squashed in. Certainly, they do not want to be left behind because there is no room on board, and may abandon public transport if this happens.

"On the other hand, investing in large-capacity vehicles is expensive and they may be unnecessary during off-peak periods. Mini-buses may accommodate the smaller numbers of passengers travelling at those times. They may also provide services for a lower subsidy than conventional buses because of their lower capital costs. Thus, designing services to accurately match passenger numbers creates opportunities for operators of smaller vehicles.

"We therefore expected councils, in designing their service specifications, to determine the appropriate capacity for every service. They must balance the costs of supplying such a service with users' needs, operational requirements, and the need to promote competition amongst operators. The vehicles used by existing operators formed the basis of Auckland's specifications. It did not obtain current patronage information to determine whether these were appropriate. The council risked paying for buses which were either under-utilised or overcrowded.

"The CPP manual required councils to set fares for services they were funding. Fare levels are vital in the trade-offs which councils must make when weighing up the service they want against the cost of providing it. Fares help offset the subsidy costs incurred by councils. If fares paid cover a high proportion of the cost of services, then operators are more likely to register them commercially. Even where this does not lead to commercial registrations, the level of subsidy that operators require to provide such services will be reduced.

"However, the level of fares also influences the behaviour of travellers. An increase in fares can drive people away from public passenger transport. The subsequent decline in patronage then offsets the anticipated gains in revenue. Thus, councils must balance the objective of minimising subsidy costs with that of making public passenger transport sufficiently attractive to maintain or enhance patronage.

"The fare schedules specified in Auckland were based on those of the Yellow Bus Company, which was carrying the majority of passengers in Auckland. Seeking to limit adverse effects on the travelling public, and on subsidy costs, Auckland Regional Council adopted fares designed to disrupt the fewest people.

"Auckland placed considerable importance on avoiding any changes to the system. This was to avoid disruption to travellers and the consequent loss of patronage this could cause. In doing so, it adopted the existing system. However…the council was aware that this system was inappropriate and that…patronage was declining.

"Consequently, the council missed the opportunity to introduce, through the service specifications, any of the necessary changes which it had identified as desirable. This may have been successful in addressing the immediate impact on passengers, but does nothing to address the continuing long-term problem of declining patronage." [735]

"Auckland Regional Council had the responsibility for tendering transport services. At the same time, it owned Transportation Auckland Corporation Ltd, which in turn owned the Yellow Bus Company, the major operator in the Auckland area. To avoid a conflict of interest, the council set up the Competitive Pricing Special Review Committee to deal exclusively with matters relating to the tender process.

"Auckland elected to use the ministerial directive allowing it to give a price reference to incumbent operators. It also made use of the provision which allowed councils to extend the contract periods for up to five years. However… incumbent operators faced few competing bids. This meant that there were few cases where the directive was relevant…Consequently, in practice, the directive had no bearing on the process of evaluating bids.

"In using historic subsidy levels as a benchmark, the council was accepting them as appropriate. In our view, they were unlikely to be satisfactory, having been developed under a protected environment where operators had escaped any competitive pressure to restrain prices.

"In the case of the Yellow Bus Company, at least, the council had information which showed that that operator's costs reflected a high level of inefficiency. The use of existing contract prices as benchmark made it possible for any operator inefficiencies from the previous system to flow through into the new contracts. This was particularly so where the incumbent operator was the only bidder, and so not subject to challenge." [735]

The Yellow Bus Company

"…the Yellow Bus Company…Its fleet of more than 500 buses dominates the market. The fleets of all other operators combined equal fewer than 170 buses, with the largest having only some 40 vehicles…

"Negotiations with the Yellow Bus Company – Having selected the successful bidders, the council found that it faced a potential shortfall in funding. It had a policy of maintaining the existing levels of service, but did not want to impose a higher rate burden to do so. Accordingly, councillors instructed officers to enter into negotiations with the Yellow Bus Company to seek a reduction in costs. The value of the work won by that company exceeded $34 million, representing 78% of all contracts by value. Thus, reductions on these contracts had the greatest potential to redress the council's budget imbalance.

"On 1 May 1991, officers wrote to the company informing it of its success in winning the contracts and advising that further negotiations would be pursued. We question how such negotiations could have been effective when the council had already formally awarded the company the contracts. The company clearly had no incentive to change its position. Councillors and council staff did, however, hold further discussions with the company. These led to concessions, but not in favour of the council.

"The council had already determined the duration of its contracts. However, as a result of the negotiations, it not only agreed to the company retaining its contracts at the original price but also extended the term of some contracts. These extensions applied to two geographical areas. Contracts for services in the west of the region were extended from three to four years, and those for services on the isthmus from four to five years.

"Documents held by the council show that the Yellow Bus Company's viability was sensitive to the length of its contracts. Accordingly, the company sought and obtained these extensions from the council. Contracts worth $4.7 million annually were extended to four years, and others worth $12.5 million were extended to five years. Three other operators working in the same areas were also beneficiaries of this policy, but the total annual value of their contracts was small – less than $1 million in total.

"...as a consequence of the council's decision to accommodate the Yellow Bus Company:
- That company, and three other operators, will avoid the competitive pressure of the tendering process until 1995 or 1996;
- An additional $17 million of public money has been committed for 1995, and $12.5 million for 1996;
- Any cost savings which might have been achieved through tendering these services earlier have been deferred; and
- Reviews of services in those areas will occur later than originally planned.

"Its concern to ensure that the Yellow Bus Company secured work on the operator's own terms over-rode the council's responsibility to promote competition and minimise subsidy costs. There may be valid reasons for supporting the company through ratepayer subsidies. Indeed, the council faced the possibility of extensive and expensive redundancies if the company did not obtain sufficient work.

"By securing the financial viability of the company for up to 5 years, the council avoided the immediate restructuring costs which local authority bus operators elsewhere were facing. Such assistance, however, should be transparent and direct, rather than through concessions during the tendering process." [735]

"Making The New System Work – In the period prior to 1 July 1991, regional councils designed their passenger transport networks and contracted operators to provide the necessary services. 1 July 1991 marked the day on which the transport systems created by the regional councils began operating. It was their responsibility to ensure that this transition was successful. Furthermore, the councils had to ensure that the transport services they were funding continued to meet the needs of travellers and maximised the value obtained from the public money used to subsidise them.

"There are three key areas where we expected regional councils to participate in the on-going operation of the system:
- Promotion and publicity for public passenger transport;

- Provision of amenities for travellers; and
- Service adjustment and co-ordination.

"While Auckland has recognised a need to promote the use of public transport, it has taken no steps to do so. This leaves only the operators, who can be expected to promote the use of public transport outside their own service areas only where it is in their commercial interests to do so. In Auckland, therefore, there is no agency ensuring that public passenger transport is adequately promoted." [735]

"Overall Conclusions – Transit and regional councils are both supporting public passenger transport out of public funds. This carries with it the obligation to monitor and review how that money is spent. There is only limited scrutiny of how regional councils are using the funds collected and distributed by Transit. All regional councils need to take an ongoing interest in the system and its operation. More generally, they must continually review how services are being used and, where necessary, make changes to accommodate the changing requirements of the travelling public and to maximise value from the subsidy paid." [735]

Land Transport Strategy

That *ongoing interest and review* of public passenger transport by regional authorities, as suggested by the Audit Office report, was subsequently legislated for in the Land Transport Amendment Act 1995 which was passed by Parliament on 29 July 1995.

Sections 29A and 29F of the Act, respectively, required the Minister, on behalf of the Crown, to complete a national land transport strategy and every regional council to prepare a land transport strategy for its region. The latter strategy was required to…

"(2) (a) Identify the future land transport needs of the region concerned;

"(b) Identify the most desirable means of responding to such needs in a safe and cost effective manner, having regard to the effect the transport system is likely to have on the environment; and

"(c) Identify an appropriate role for each land transport mode in the region, including freight traffic, public passenger transport, cycling, and pedestrian traffic; and

"(d) State the best means of achieving the objectives referred to in paragraphs (b) and (c) of this subsection…" [737]

In order to accomplish such a strategy, each council was required to establish a land transport committee "…including (but not limited to) representatives of all or any of the following:

"(a) The [Land Transport Safety] Authority: (b) The [Transfund New Zealand] Board: (c) Transit New Zealand: (d) The Commissioner [of Police]: (e) The regional council: (f) The territorial authorities in the region (if any): (g) Commercial road users: (h) Private road users:

(i) Railway operators: (j) Public transport users: (k) Representatives of cycle users and pedestrians…"

"(3) The functions of each regional land transport committee shall be to prepare for approval by the relevant regional council the regional land transport strategy prepared under section 29F of this Act and the regional programme prepared under section 42F of the Transit New Zealand Act 1989 for its region." [737]

A New Direction

Auckland planners wasted no time formulating a new direction as part of their Land Transport Strategy – as described by the Auckland City Council's Transportation Planning Manager, Ross Rutherford:

"The September 1995 Auckland Regional Land Transport Strategy (RLTS) sets out a new direction for the development and management of the region's transport system. This new direction recognises that short term, reactive planning and investment decisions will not achieve a more sustainable future; that the potential environmental, social and economic costs of attempting to meet the ever increasing demands for travel by car are too high.

"The Auckland RLTS recognises the link between land use form and the transport system; the importance of attitudes and perceptions; and the need to provide a good alternative to travel by car, particularly in the congested peak periods. This last point is very relevant. For many, public transport is simply not perceived to be a realistic or acceptable option.

"The major challenges are to provide realistic alternatives while recognising economic constraints, and the need to change public attitudes to these alternatives and to the car itself. These challenges are great in a region typified by low density sprawl, and where buses are seen as second class form of transport typically used by those with no choice. They are made more difficult by funding, statutory and administrative systems which currently favour the road based status quo…

"Strong emphasis is placed on alternatives to the single occupant private car. A series of measures are proposed including improvements to bus service design; better integration between services and modes; bus priority measures; improvements to suburban rail (higher frequencies, station upgrading, bus/rail integration, park-and-ride facilities, and a new terminal at Britomart, Central Auckland); encouragement of new ferry services; improved public passenger transport marketing; better passenger information; and improved facilities for cyclists and pedestrians. Two major higher capacity public transport infrastructure projects are proposed, namely the Northern Priority Lane and Light Rail in the western and southern rail corridors…

"The main weakness of the 1995 RLTS is that it does not set clear priorities for the implementation of key projects. Part of the explanation for this lies in a funding system which centralises project programming and seeks to maximise national economic benefit through the application of cost benefit analysis…Further work on the development of performance targets is also required and must be given a high priority. It is vital that strong emphasis be given to the achievement or non-achievement of targets and that the community as a whole be involved as much as possible." [734]

Government Funding Required

The establishment of a land transport committee to determine a land transport strategy certainly provided the Auckland region with the incentive to plan for its future transport requirements. However, as Ross Rutherford explained, the question of how those requirements were to be funded remained unanswered.

In her 1995 Metro article, *City Limits*, Nicola Legat examined the same issue:

"…it is crucial that central government becomes actively involved in funding Auckland's transport requirements. At present, 35 cents of every dollar spent on petrol is taken in government tax. Fifteen cents of that is given to Transit New Zealand; the rest goes into the consolidated fund. Transit New Zealand then dispenses its funds back to the regions but imposes a cap of $28 million per year on public transport, *nationally*. Of that, Auckland gets around $12 million towards a system which costs the region $50 million to operate.

"The region's politicians argue that not only is the lower level of Transit New Zealand funding for public transport manifestly unjust, but it also forces the region to continue its reliance on the car as a transport solution…The sum of $50 million is simply inadequate to meet the region's real needs…"

"One fact is abundantly clear: if the government does not provide subsidy assistance and if the new legislation does not provide the funding flexibility to enable solutions other than roading expansion, there will be no LRT [light rail transit] for Auckland. Yet LRT, and appropriate bus feeder routes to it, is clearly pivotal to the region's future health, especially if a full network, running out to Pakuranga/Howick and to the airport, is established. Without it, and with clogged roads, doing business will become less efficient and more costly…" [723]

Transfund New Zealand

The *new legislation* referred to by Nicola Legat is thought to be the Transit New Zealand Amendment Act 1995, the relevant parts of which came into force on 1 July 1996. The legislation established a Board known as Transfund New Zealand – a Crown entity consisting of two employees or members of Transit New Zealand, one member representing local government, one member representing road users, and one member representing an aspect of public interest that is not represented by the other members of the Board. [738]

Unfortunately, the Act did not provide for *the funding flexibility to enable solutions other than roading expansion*. On the contrary, the principal objective of the Transfund Board, as stated by the Act, "…shall be to allocate resources to achieve a safe and efficient roading system." [738]

Alternative Forms of Transport

However, as a concession to what is described as *alternative forms of transport*, the Act did declare that:

"(a) The power of the Board to fund any outputs under this Act authorises the Board to fund outputs that consider or develop efficient alternatives to the provision or maintenance of roading; and

"(b) Any such output may relate to one or more of the following, namely, passenger services, rail transport, and maritime transport; and, for the purposes of this paragraph, the terms 'passenger services', 'rail transport', and 'maritime transport' include the carriage of freight and the carriage of passengers." [738]

Of course, in doing so, the Board had to comply with policy directions:

"In the exercise of its functions, duties, and powers under this Act, the Board shall have regard to the policy of the Government in relation to land transport, and shall comply with any general directions relating to that policy given in writing signed by the Minister…" [738]

Keep Auckland Moving

In other words, central Government remained firmly in charge when it came to the disbursement of funds to its favoured roading projects and its least-favoured public transport options, particularly in Auckland – as described by Andrew Heal in his 1997 Metro article, *Road Rage*:

"Auckland has long been hampered by a lack of autonomy over its own resources. While it is unquestionably New Zealand's economic power base simply by dint of its population, the money its citizens plough into transport expenditure has long been disseminated by central government. The region has arguably done poorly out of this arrangement; road-development funds come from Transfund (previously known as the National Land Transport Fund), the funding for which comes from taxes, road-user charges and vehicle registration. Some 340 million Auckland dollars go into Transfund's coffers each year, $115 million of which is returned to Auckland as transport funding. About $34 million goes to other regions.

"It was this perceived inequity in what Auckland spends and what it receives that led, in part, to the formation of the Keep Auckland Moving lobby group last year. The group, made up of members of the region's seven local authorities and the ARC, wants the money from these road-user charges to be managed by regional authorities in a bulk-funding arrangement. Transport developments and maintenance could be contracted out, devolving transport services from central government…" [717]

Costs of Road Congestion

The Keep Auckland Moving Campaign and regional business interests "…commissioned consultants [Ernst & Young] to estimate the economic costs of regional road congestion. The [1977] report [*Alternative Transport Infrastructure Investments and Economic Development for the Auckland Region*] produced a figure of $755 million annually and advocated public transport improvements as a solution. However, the business lobby ignored this and demanded completion of the motorway network according to the plans of the 1950s and 1960s." [231]

Auckland Transport Study (ATS)

Nevertheless, continuing with the maturing concept of a *Greater Auckland* collaboration as a means to the development of an efficient, region-wide transport system, the planning continued as the Auckland Transport Study:

"The Auckland Transport Study (ATS) was initiated in June 1996 to provide the technical background for and input into the 1997 review of the Auckland Regional Land Transport Strategy. The technical work was undertaken using the Auckland Regional Transport (ART) and Auckland Strategic Planning (ASP) models which were developed by the Auckland Regional Council (ARC) during the early 1990s.

"The purpose of the ATS was to investigate regionally significant transport projects and policies in sufficient depth to establish feasibility, regional significance, approximate timing and approximate benefits and costs. The ATS was controlled by the Auckland Transport Study Steering Group which was responsible for directing the work and ensuring that the outcomes were robust.

"The Steering Group comprised officers from Transit New Zealand, Transfund, Auckland Regional Council, North Shore City, Waitakere City, Auckland City, Manukau City and Rodney District Council and reported to the Regional Land Transport Strategy Technical Advisory Committee. Most of the modelling work was undertaken in-house by ARC officers." [739]

Land Transport Act 1998

In the meantime, the regulation of land transport was consolidated by the Land Transport Act 1998 – the relevant parts of which came into force on 1 March 1999 –

"(a) To promote safe road user behaviour and vehicle safety; and

"(b) To provide for a system of rules governing road user behaviour, the licensing of drivers, and technical aspects of land transport, and to recognise reciprocal obligations of persons involved; and

"(c) To consolidate and amend various enactments relating to road safety and land transport;

"(d) To enable New Zealand to implement international agreements relating to road safety and land transport." [740]

The 1998 Act re-affirmed the requirements of the Land Transport Amendment Act 1995 for the Minister, on behalf of the Crown, to *complete a national land transport strategy* and *every regional council* to *prepare a land transport strategy for its region*. Both Acts required regional councils to establish regional land transport committees to prepare their land transport strategies. [740]

Auckland Regional Policy Statement (RPS)

As required by the Resource Management Act 1991, the Auckland Regional Council prepared its Regional Policy Statement which became operative on 31 August 1999. The Statement's foreword, signed by the Council's Chairman, Philip Warren, and Chief Executive, Jo Brosnahan, stated in part:

"The Auckland Region is New Zealand's largest and fastest growing region. Every five years, we are accommodating the equivalent of a new Dunedin or Hamilton within our boundaries. The region's rich and distinctive natural and physical resources have attracted successive waves of human migration for over 1000 years and now it is home to nearly one in three New Zealanders - and still growing fast...

"The Regional Policy Statement seeks to maintain a quality environment for the Auckland Region and at the same time, maintain and enhance opportunities for the region's future growth. This is a challenge which [the] Regional Policy Statement places before us - it is now up to everyone within the region to realise this goal. We commend this document to you as a sustainable pathway for present and future Aucklanders." [741]

The Major Direction of Transport Policy

Chapter four of the Policy Statement proposed the major direction to be taken towards the establishment of an *effective and efficient transport system* for the region:

"An effective and efficient transport system is critical to the environmental, social, economic and cultural wellbeing of the Auckland Region and its inhabitants. This is achieved by providing a high level of accessibility to the regions residents to enable them to fully participate in society and to enable the movement of goods and services in a manner which supports the continued economic development of the region...

"The major direction of transport policy in Auckland will be set by the RPS. The components of that policy are more fully developed through the Regional Land Transport Strategy (RLTS) which has been prepared pursuant to section 175 of the Land Transport Act 1998 and which provides a further mechanism for delivering sustainable transport outcomes. The RLTS must contribute to the overall aim of achieving an integrated, safe, responsive and sustainable land transport system.

"The RLTS is also required to:

(i) identify the future land transport outcomes sought for the Region;
(ii) identify an appropriate role for each mode of transport;
(iii) include a travel demand management strategy.

"The Land Transport Act 1998 requires that the RLTS must not be inconsistent with the RPS. The RLTS takes effect through a requirement that any project included in the Land Transport Programmes of the region must be aligned with the RLTS.

"The National Land Transport Programme prepared by Land Transport New Zealand must have regard to the RLTS. The Auckland Regional Transport Authority (ARTA) is required to give effect to the RLTS.

"At the same time, efforts need to be made to diminish or mitigate the transport effects of the dispersed residential patterns developed in recent decades. Thoughtful development of the rapid transit and passenger transport networks can improve access throughout the region's urban areas by more sustainable means, linking High Density Centres with attractive and effective passenger services." [741]

Auckland Regional Land Transport Strategy 1999

Following the publication of its September 1995 Auckland Regional Land Transport Strategy (RLTS), the Regional Land Transport Committee, a standing committee of the Auckland Regional Council, published another in November 1999.

As required by the Land Transport Acts of 1995 and 1998, the Auckland Regional Land Transport Committee consisted of persons representing the Auckland Regional Council, the seven city and district councils, the Police, Transit New Zealand, public transport users, commercial road users, the Bus and Coach Association, Transfund, the Land Transport Safety Authority, vulnerable road users, Infrastructure Auckland, Tranz Rail, and private road users.

Chairman's Comment

In the Foreword to the Regional Land Transport Strategy document, the Committee's Chairman, Les Paterson, commented:

"An efficient transport system is an integral part of our lives. The Auckland region is facing major decisions on how to improve and manage our transport system to cope with the pressures of growth. This Auckland Regional Land Transport Strategy 1999 (RLTS) has been produced to respond to these challenges.

"The RLTS recognises that roads, and the vehicles and pedestrians which use the roading network, form the basis of the region's transport system. This base must be protected, and in some locations new roads are required. However, the Strategy clearly indicates that roading can have heavy social, safety, environmental and economic costs and that the Auckland region can no longer rely on increasing roading capacity alone to meet its accessibility needs. Renewed emphasis is required upon more sustainable initiatives, particularly in terms of improving transport alternatives to the private vehicle such as passenger transport, cycling and walking.

"The region's transport issues are closely related to the pattern of growth that the region is experiencing. For this reason, the Regional Land Transport Strategy has been produced in tandem with the Regional Growth Strategy. Together, these documents establish a vision and the means for achieving the region's growth and transport objectives.

"The Strategy was developed after undertaking a thorough technical analysis in partnership with the region's transport stakeholders…The consultation process confirmed that Aucklanders want a much improved passenger transport system and that measures should be implemented to better integrate transport and land use planning.

"As a result, considerable work has been carried out to bring the RLTS and Growth Strategy even closer together. The Passenger Transport Action Plan has been developed as the key tool for implementing high speed, high frequency and high quality passenger transport services as part of an integrated regional system.

"Rapid transit services will be developed in the main northern, southern, eastern and western corridors as a key means for improving our transport system and supporting more intensive types of land use development that is envisioned by the Growth Strategy. These initiatives have proceeded alongside other positive developments including the establishment of Infrastructure Auckland as a potential funding source to help realise our objectives...

"As we are poised to enter the new millennium, the region faces challenging transport issues. The Regional Land Transport Strategy recognises that there are no simple solutions to these issues. By providing for a range of complementary initiatives, however, this Strategy aims to pursue a balanced approach that will help keep Auckland moving." [742]

Passenger Transport Investment

Parts of the 1999 Regional Land Transport Strategy relating to Passenger Transport Investment included:

"Due to the region's dispersed travel patterns, investment in passenger transport alone would address only some of the accessibility issues facing the region and would not avoid extensive and severe congestion, particularly for trips not involving the CBD (Central Business District) or major sub-regional centres. Passenger transport can provide good levels of accessibility in situations where there is heavy demand to a common destination and where separate rights-of-way, or at least priority measures can be provided.

"The CBD is currently such a destination. In the future these same conditions are likely to apply to the growth centres and corridors proposed by the Regional Growth Strategy. Passenger transport also clearly has a role in providing mobility to those without access to a car or who choose not to use a car.

"This is particularly true for north-south accessibility due to the constraints imposed by the need to cross the Waitemata Harbour and to construct new approach roads through built-up urban areas. Lack of north-south accessibility impacts on other travel patterns, including accessibility to the Central Business District...

"In the short term the RLTS addresses north-south accessibility by making best use of the existing transport system. This will involve upgrading the approach roads to the Auckland Harbour Bridge, and investing in significant cross-harbour passenger transport improvements. In the long term, the RLTS preserves the ability to construct another harbour crossing for both passenger transport and general traffic.

"The most significant change proposed by this Strategy is an increase in passenger transport investment which will be dramatically higher than in the past 20 years. Passenger transport investment in the first five years will be concentrated in the corridors serving the CBD.

"Major short term passenger transport projects include:
- Implementation of the North Shore Bus Rapid Transit system

- Implementation of the Passenger Transport Action Plan comprising major infrastructure investment and passenger service improvements in the Northern, Southern, Western and Eastern Corridors
- Further implementation of bus priorities on arterial roads.

"Passenger transport investment is a critical element in the pattern of growth proposed by the Regional Growth Strategy. The passenger transport investments outlined in this Strategy will give a strong start to that process. Additionally, investment in pedestrian and cycling facilities will be essential to maintain and improve levels of accessibility throughout the region." [739]

Allocation of Transport Funding

As per Figure 7 (Appendix 2), the 1999 Regional Land Transport Strategy included a breakdown of allocations by Transfund for the 1998-1999 year and the local authority share to match Transfund's allocation (Road expenditure includes maintenance, minor safety projects, commitments, construction).

"Transfund is the largest contributor to expenditure on transport infrastructure in the Auckland region. Figure 8 (Appendix 3) tracks the level of Transfund's Auckland expenditure over the last eight years and shows the significant increases in expenditure over the last four years. This increase is partly a result of a national increase in transport expenditure, but mainly a result of an increase in the proportion allocated to the Auckland region…

"In the past, expenditure on transport infrastructure in the Auckland region has come predominantly from Transfund supplemented by Local Authorities (including the ARC) and private developers. For a short period, 1992 to 1995, additional passenger transport funding was made available through an additional regional petrol tax which has since been revoked by Central Government." [739]

Central Government's Response

The Central Government's response to the co-operative strategy put forward by the Auckland region was, of course, to vaunt its own, eventual contribution. This was announced by Prime Minister, Jenny Shipley, by way of a press release, on 23 November 1999:

"The Government has offered Jeff Todd as a mediator to help Auckland local bodies and Tranz Rail to identify the best way forward for Auckland's passenger transport problems, Prime Minister Jenny Shipley said today in response to a request from Mayoral Forum Chairman Phil Warren. Mrs Shipley said the Government also expected to increase funding for new transport projects in the Auckland region in the near future.

"She made the comments during the launch of the Auckland Regional Growth Strategy, and related plans for Auckland's infrastructure development. 'The Growth Strategy does not provide all the answers to Auckland's urban sprawl and transport problems but it represents great progress by local authorities in the Auckland region. I think Aucklanders will be happy with the way their local bodies have co-operated in the development of the strategy.'

"Mrs Shipley said the local authorities would now have to engage the people of Auckland to turn the vision into a reality. She said the local authorities would also have to use a range of other tools, not included in the strategy, to solve some of Auckland's transport problems.

"'Might I be so bold to suggest that perhaps the Government's Better Transport, Better Roads document contains some of the tools needed to achieve the full vision. The most significant tool will be the ability for roading authorities to anticipate demand for roads rather than continuing to lag behind. I am also talking about lifting roading issues to a regional level, which is at the heart of the strategies we are looking at today. For the Government's part, we are committed to making decisions on these proposals next year.

"'In the interim, the Auckland Regional Land Transport Strategy lays out a range of transport projects that will focus on key pressure points within the region in the next few years, for which the Government is providing $195 million. The Auckland region will receive 33 per cent of Transfund's total allocated new construction budget and 47 per cent of Transfund's passenger transport funding, this financial year.

"'This pattern of substantial Government support for new regional projects and public transport is expected to increase sharply within the framework established by the Regional Land Transport Strategy.'

"The Prime Minister also announced that the Government had offered Jeff Todd to assist Auckland local bodies and Tranz Rail to find a way forward in solving Auckland's passenger transport problem. Mr Todd, a former managing partner of Price Waterhouse, has extensive experience in many business areas and knowledge of Government policy. 'Mr Todd's appointment should help the parties resolve their differences so that improvements can be made to key parts of Auckland's passenger transport system sooner rather than later,' Mrs Shipley said." [743]

Road Transport

Roads continue to be built in most cities but the reason for building them has long since changed. Where they once opened new land for settlement and industry, new roads are now built to supplement those that can no longer cope with the additional traffic they generate.

More Vehicles

The reasons for New Zealand's dramatic traffic increase during the 1990s were explained by Opus International Consultants', Vince Dravitzki & Tiffany Lester, in their paper, *Economics drove our first sustainable urban transport system and the unsustainable one that followed*:

"The New Zealand economy up until the early 1970s was highly regulated. Slow Reforms had occurred between 1970 and 1984 but in 1984 and the years following, the economy was greatly liberalised. However with respect to transport and cars the main effects occurred in the early 1990s with the removal of tariffs on imports, the closure of all local vehicle assembly, and the effective privatisation of public transport.

"The outcomes are that since 1995 new car prices have decreased by over 30% and simultaneously second-hand cars began to be imported into New Zealand with a dramatic impact on used car prices so that over the same ten-year period used vehicles have decreased in price by about 50%.

"The effects of these lower prices show in several ways…car numbers increased by 550,000 vehicles in the period 1996 to 2005, essentially double the rate of the previous thirty years…also…the number of cars per household has increased so that 50% of the households have two or more vehicles (even though 60% of households have only one or two residents) and only 8% of households have no vehicles." [517]

A National Roading Programme

As previously described, the Transit New Zealand Amendment Act 1995, which amended the Transit New Zealand Act 1989, established Transfund "…to allocate resources to achieve a safe and efficient roading system." [738]

The functions of Transfund, as legislated, included:

"3c. (1) (a) To approve and to purchase a national roading programme…

"(b) To approve capital projects and to purchase outputs…

"(c) To make payments from the National Roads Account as authorised by this Act:

"(d) To review and revise the national roading programme in accordance with its most recent performance agreement:

"(e) To approve competitive pricing procedures…

"(f) To audit the performance of the Authority as compared with its State highways programme:

"(g) To assist and advise local authorities in relation to their functions, duties, and powers under this Act and the Land Transport Act 1993:

"(h) To audit the performance of every local authority as compared with its regional programme or district roading programme, as the case may be:

"(2) For the avoidance of doubt, it is hereby declared that in performing or exercising any functions or powers in relation to-

"(a) The inclusion of outputs and capital projects in the national roading programme; and

"(b) The making of payments from the National Roads Account, – the Board shall act independently of the Minister and the Authority…" [738]

Future Planning

The Transit New Zealand Amendment Act 1995 allowed for the future planning of road construction and the consideration of regional and district needs:

"42A. National roading programme –

"(1) In each year, the [Transfund New Zealand] Board shall approve a national roading programme for the next year, which shall include –

"(a) Those outputs and capital projects recommended in the State highways programme, the regional programmes, and the district roading programmes forwarded to the Board under this Act that the Board considers should be included in the national roading programme; and

"(b) The proposed funding of those outputs and capital projects for that financial year.

"(2) Subject to subsections (3) and (4) of this section, a national roading programme shall be in accordance with the requirements of the performance agreement that is in force at the time of approval of that roading programme.

"(3) The national roading programme shall not be inconsistent with any national land transport strategy that is in force at the time of the preparation of the programme.

"(4) The Board shall ensure that only outputs and capital projects that are not inconsistent with any relevant regional land transport strategy are included in a national roading programme…

"42D. State highways programme –

"(1) In each year, the Authority shall prepare after consultation with the Land Transport Safety Authority, by a date appointed by the Board, a State highways programme for the next year.

"42F. Regional programmes –

"(1) Each financial year, a regional council or a territorial authority that has the functions, duties, and powers of a regional council under this Act may prepare a regional programme for the next year in relation to its region or district and in respect of outputs for which the regional council or territorial authority is responsible…

"42H. District roading programmes –

"(1) Each financial year, every territorial authority shall prepare a district roading programme for the next year in relation to its district." [738]

Geographic and Capacity Constraints

However, no matter how regulated the provision of roading programmes might be, the physical constraints imposed upon transport planning in the Auckland region remained – as described by the Auckland Regional Land Transport Strategy produced in November 1999:

"The Auckland region occupies a unique geographical position, distinguished by two major harbours and dotted with a series of volcanic landforms. These geographic constraints impose restrictions on the transport system so that in key locations transport links are confined to narrow corridors. For many trips these constraints mean few alternative routes are available and providing new routes or additional capacity has unacceptable environmental and community costs…

"The geographical and developed form of the region's urban area is difficult to serve effectively with options such as passenger transport, cycling and walking. This is one of the major difficulties the region's transport system faces. The reality is that in many situations, the private vehicle offers greater convenience and flexibility than other travel options for taking people to where they want to go, particularly for multi-purpose journeys." [739]

Unacceptable Congestion

In his presentation to the Australasian Transport Research Forum at Auckland in 1996, the Auckland City Council's Transportation Planning Manager, Ross Rutherford, described the traffic conditions that then prevailed in Auckland:

"Between 1981 and 1991 the average length of the trip to work increased from 10.8 km to 12.6 km. The proportion of commuters using public transport (bus and rail) was 14% in 1981 and 1986 but fell sharply to 7% in 1991. Over the same period the proportion of commuters driving a car to work increased from 55.3% to 70.9%.

"It has been estimated that the cost of 'unacceptable' congestion (travel speeds less than 46 km/h) on Auckland's motorways is $60M/year based on 1994 traffic counts. Available data suggest that motorway congestion increased tenfold from 1989 to 1994…

"Public concerns over traffic congestion, noise, pollution and safety have been heightened by the possibility of a 40% increase in the region's population over the next 20 years…

"Frustrations at the apparent lack of action by public authorities are adding to pressures to build a Second Harbour Crossing. Delays to weekday morning peak period southbound traffic on the Northern Motorway are substantial with queues extending over several kilometres. The extension of the Northern Motorway north of Greville Road programmed to commence in the 96/97 year for completion three years later will add to these pressures.

"In recognition of the high environmental cost of a Second Harbour Crossing and a capital cost including approach roads estimated at around $1 billion, the RLTS [Auckland Regional Land Transport Strategy] states that no new crossing of the Waitemata Harbour will be constructed prior to 2011…" [734]

Population Explosion Northward

Those *pressures to build a Second Harbour Crossing* were, of course, a replay of the many, many decades of pressure that eventually led to the construction of the first crossing. From the time it opened in 1959, the Harbour Bridge struggled to cope with demand. So did the short piece of Motorway extending northward to Tristram Avenue, finished soon after.

By 1995, the Northern Motorway had reached Constellation Drive (8 km); by 2000, Greville Road (10 km), Oteha Valley Road (12 km), and Silverdale (24 km). [744]

These "…Motorway extensions over 1995–2000 resulted in substantial changes in areas near, and to the north of the new exits. Population and employment increased substantially faster in these areas than occurred across the Auckland region. Relative land values rose for land close to the new exits." [744]

Arthur Grimes and Yun Liang examined the effects of this extension on population, employment and land values in areas to the north of the bridge in their study, *Bridge to Somewhere: Valuing Auckland's Northern Motorway Extensions*, published in 2010 in the *Journal of Transport Economics and Policy*. Some of their findings were again published in 2011 in a working paper by Arthur Grimes, *Building Bridges: Treating a New Transport Link as a Real Option*:

"The population in North Shore City that was within three kilometres of a newly opened motorway exit increased by 57% in the 15 years to 2006, compared with an increase of just 21% for the rest of the North Shore. Similarly, employment within three kilometres of a new exit increased by 67% compared with an increase of 34% in the remainder of the North Shore.

"In each case, the population and employment increases for areas close to a new exit considerably exceeded the increases for Auckland Region as a whole (38% and 55% respectively). Population and employment effects of the motorway extension in Rodney District were even more material. In the area closest to the northern-most exit of the motorway extension, the population rose by 80% and employment rose by 120% in the 15 years to 2006." [720]

North-South Corridor

The 1999 Auckland Regional Land Transport Strategy acknowledged the north-south motorway system as one of the more problematic transport corridors in the region:

"The busiest part of the transport network is the north-south motorway system which passes through the centre of the urban area. This has the effect of concentrating north-south travel in a corridor which is now facing severe capacity constraints and where viable options for expanding road capacity are limited.

"Major structures in this corridor – Newmarket Viaduct, the Khyber Pass Viaduct, the Spaghetti Junction motorway interchange under Karangahape Road, and the Auckland Harbour Bridge itself – are operating close to capacity and in places where expansion would pose major difficulties." [739]

"Development of Options – During the development of this Strategy a study was undertaken to investigate options for constructing an additional North-South route through the region, including a new crossing of the Waitemata Harbour. Options considered included bridges and tunnels, and crossings for passenger transport only (either bus or rail) as well as for general traffic. The study looked at the costs of each option, their transport effectiveness, and their effects on the natural environment and on communities. The study considered 48 options in 14 corridors initially and then investigated 11 of those options in more detail.

"The study showed that:
- A new crossing is likely to form just one link in a new transport corridor through the Auckland region.
- The roading options assessed ranged in cost from $0.42 billion to $1.72 billion.
- The passenger transport options assessed ranged in cost from $0.25 billion to $0.62 billion.
- All crossing options would have major environmental and community effects, although passenger transport options would have fewer adverse effects than roading options.
- Tunnel options would significantly reduce the environmental impacts of an additional crossing but would be approximately double the capital cost of bridge options.
- Highway crossings would have a much greater effect in reducing congestion than passenger transport crossings.
- Construction of new highway crossings would result in an increase in cross harbour traffic, and traffic forecasts for roading options indicate that the additional cross-harbour capacity provided by a four lane crossing is likely to be fully utilised not long after the planning horizon.

"Consideration of Options – The question of whether the accessibility benefits of constructing an additional crossing outweigh the costs of the project, including the community and environmental costs, as well as the capital costs was specifically raised as an issue for public feedback during the consultation phase of preparation of this Strategy.

"By far the largest number of submissions on the draft Strategy were on this issue, and these were dominated by opposition to an additional road crossing. Most submissions were from people or organisations adversely affected by one or other of the crossing options…" [739]

Suburban Rail
Light Rail Transit Evaluation

As road congestion became an increasingly costly problem, only exacerbated by the construction of more roads, planners had no alternative but to consider the viability of existing railway corridors so long discounted and neglected as inferior rights of way. Accordingly, in August 1995, the Auckland Regional Council set up a Steering Group to consider the implementation of a Light Rail Transit (LRT) system on existing railway tracks. The Steering Group reported in May 1996:

"Outline of Previous Evaluations – The proposal for the LRT system arose from the Comprehensive Transportation Study Update…completed in August 1988 by the then

Auckland Regional Authority...Following a review of the recommendations of the study, the Regional Council in September 1989 adopted a set of resolutions which included inter alia:

"That in the Southern and Western Corridors, a Light Rail Transit system on existing rail tracks be constructed subject to agreement being reached with the New Zealand Railways Corporation and Auckland City Council on appropriate operating conditions, and confirmation of the economics of the system.

"Following this, the New Zealand Railways Corporation (NZRC) engaged consultants to further evaluate and develop the LRT proposal. The findings of the NZRC study were presented to the Transportation Planning Committee of the Council on 27 February 1990.

"This committee resolved to form a working party of officers of the Regional Council, Auckland City Council, Manukau City Council, Papakura District Council, Waitakere City Council, New Zealand Railways and Transit New Zealand to review the NZRC Proposal.

"The Working Party was established and its findings reported to the Transportation Planning Committee of the Regional Council on 31 July 1990, wherein it recommended a version of the NZRC proposal. This modified proposal forms the basis of the LRT system assessed in this report.

"In May 1990, the Council appointed a Project Manager to develop the LRT proposal to the implementation stage. The project manager recommended amongst other things that implementation of the LRT proposal should be deferred.

"However, the Council resolved to continue the necessary work towards implementation of the LRT proposal and established the LRT/Busway Implementations Special Committee on 7 December 1990. This Committee undertook investigation into projected patronage estimates, economic evaluation, financial analyses, and ownership and funding options.

"The Committee reported its findings to the Council in June 1991 and then again in December 1991 whereby the Council resolved inter alia:

"That Council pursue a funding contribution towards the LRT project from Central Government as a matter of priority, and that the Council develop a rational case for such funding [...and...] That all necessary steps be taken to ensure the protection of the right of way stations and parking areas."

"The funding contribution sought from Central Government however proved to be difficult to obtain, due to Transit NZ's funding criteria. The Regional Council therefore turned its efforts towards securing the existing diesel unit rail system, thereby raising the profile of rail and providing the base patronage necessary for a step to LRT in the future.

"During this period, New Zealand Rail was sold out of public ownership. This sale impacted significantly on the protection of access to the existing rail infrastructure and the availability of this infrastructure in the future.

"In June 1993, the Council secured a 10 year service contract with the then NZ Rail Limited (later to become Tranz Rail Limited) for the provision of rail services using diesel multiple unit (DMU) rolling stock.

"In July 1994, the base contract with NZ Rail Limited was varied to provide for increased frequencies and a regular 'clockface' schedule on both the southern and western lines. As a result of these initiatives, rail patronage levels have increased significantly, from approximately 1.2 million passengers per annum in 1993 to approximately 2.0 million per annum currently [May 1996].

"Brief For Investigation Into LRT – In early 1995 the issue of LRT for Auckland received heightened prominence due to a number of factors, including:
- Increasing public concern about traffic congestion and the need for an improved passenger transport system in the region.
- Plans by Auckland City Council to develop a major underground transport terminal incorporating the Britomart and CPO sites, with provision for rail and ultimately LRT as a central part of the development.
- A proposal by the private sector *Superlink* consortium to develop an LRT system in Auckland, unveiled in May 1995.
- Public debate over the proposed Eastern Highway in Auckland City which focused attention on the potential for a rail-based alternative in that corridor.
- The America's Cup success which focused attention on the need to upgrade the region's infrastructure.
- The recent increase in rail patronage, placing some pressure on the capacity of the existing system, particularly on the single-track Waitakere line.

"A draft brief for an investigation into LRT was prepared in July 1995 and circulated to interested parties for comment. The brief sought to review the Council's position on LRT, concentrating on what would need to be resolved in order to make firm commitment to LRT.

"In particular the brief outlined that the investigation should include an economic evaluation, consideration of legal and institutional matters and address funding options. Following consideration of a report on the consultation that had been undertaken, the Transport Committee of the Council resolved on 23 August 1995:

"That the draft brief be confirmed and that the consideration of submissions be incorporated into the review programme.

"Following the adoption of the brief a Steering Group was established to oversee the investigation. The group included senior staff from the Auckland Regional Council and the territorial local authorities identified as most affected by the proposal, being Auckland, Manukau, Waitakere and Papakura.

"Directives in Auckland Regional Land Transport Strategy – In September 1995, the Regional Council released the Auckland Regional Land Transport Strategy (RLTS) as a requirement of the Transit New Zealand Act 1989.

"Included in the are RLTS were…policy directives and methods which endorsed the Regional Council's commitment to investigate the matters to be resolved in order for the Council to make a firm commitment to LRT…This report details the findings and recommended outcomes from the investigations referred to in the directives in the RLTS…" [745]

"Although the upgrade of the rail system is predicted to increase annual rail patronage significantly, the ART model indicates that much of this increase (approximately 45%) is expected to come from existing bus users switching mode. The remaining increase in rail usage is expected to come from car drivers driving to park and ride stations and then using rail (approximately 40%); car passengers (approximately 8%); and cyclists and walkers (approximately 7%).

"Effect on traffic congestion – The net effect of the rail system improvements is unlikely to be a dramatic reduction in congestion. For example, volumes on the Southern

Motorway are likely to be around 0% to 2% less than they would otherwise be. While this is a worthwhile reduction, it will soon be overtaken by normal traffic growth.

"Away from the Southern and Western Motorways where the travel time advantages of rail will be less marked, effects will be further diminished as they spread over the road network. In the vicinity of major park and ride stations, there will be a slight net increase in traffic due to park and riders driving to the station.

"Rail upgrading will not solve Auckland's congestion problems. It will however give a long term assurance of good quality access to the areas served by the rail line and the areas connected to it by bus services. Over time, as traffic congestion increases, this advantage should grow.

"Environmental Effects – A principal environmental benefit of upgrading the rail system would be to support the land use and life style changes to enable an urban form to develop which is less reliant on motor vehicles. Such an urban form would produce less motor vehicle emissions and would be more efficient in the way land was used.

"There are also direct environmental benefits to greater use of rail. By inducing car drivers to switch to rail there is a direct saving in fuel use. It is estimated that for the LRT options these savings in the Auckland region would amount to approximately 17.9 million litres of fuel per year…" [745]

Executive Summary

The Steering Group's Light Rail Transit Evaluation Report provided an Executive Summary which stated in its conclusions:

"Auckland is faced with a major challenge with respect to the transportation ramifications of its growth. The low density development, the deregulated transport system, the ownership structure of the existing rail infrastructure and the lack of appropriate legislation to facilitate changes in a number of these issues, make the transport problem a very difficult one.

"The view expressed in this report is that the development of a quality rail system should proceed, but only if there is a total commitment to modifications of land use proposals as envisaged in the PARPS [Proposed Auckland Regional Policy Statement], the RLTS and the Strategic and District Plans now being produced by associated Territorial Local Authorities.

"Another key prerequisite is the commitment to an equitable funding system which recognises the benefits of this investment at both the national and regional levels.

"The challenge to all Aucklanders is to aggressively and constructively attack that task. The danger if we fail is that traffic volumes will continue to grow from the present unsatisfactory situations, with serious environmental, social and economic consequences. The issue is not whether we should throw substantial funds at public transport, but whether we have the will, as a community, to change land use patterns using an expanded rail service as an incentive." [746]

Railway Ownership – A Brief History

The *ownership structure of the existing rail infrastructure* mentioned by the LRT Steering Group referred to the various transformations undergone by the New Zealand Railways Department since it became the Railways Corporation in 1982.

"The same year, the [National] Government began deregulation of the transport industry removing statutory protections for rail against competition by road.

"In 1986, the Labour Government made railways a state-owned enterprise but, by 1990, the Corporation had accumulated a debt of $1.1 billion and it is reformed as a limited liability company.

"In 1993, the Government announced the sale of New Zealand Rail Limited to a consortium of Wisconsin Central Transportation Corporation and Berkshire Partners (60%) and Fay Richwhite (40%) for $328.3 million.

"In 1995, New Zealand Rail Limited is renamed Tranz Rail and 31 million shares are floated to the public at $6.19 per share in 1996.

"The shares peaked at $9 in 1997 but fell to only 30 cents a share by 2003 and details emerged of how the company needed to sell assets to meet lease payments and repayments of debt required by its bankers.

"In 2003, Toll Holdings Limited, an Australian-based transportation and logistics operator, acquired approximately 85 percent of the shares in Tranz Rail. As a result of Toll's offer for shares becoming unconditional, an agreement between Toll and the Crown was triggered, a key feature of which was the buy-back of track and associated infrastructure by the Crown.

"The Crown undertook to invest $200 million in improving rail infrastructure while Toll undertook to invest $100 million in new rolling stock. In September 2004, ownership and management of the network and its assets were vested in the existing Railway Corporation of New Zealand which adopted the trading name, KiwiRail Network (ONTRACK). Under the agreement, Toll retained exclusive rights to the network for freight purposes, subject to meeting minimum tonnage levels annually.

"On July 1 2008, after several months of negotiations, the Government buys back Toll's rail and ferry business for $665 million and ONTRACK and KiwiRail form a single integrated above and below rail business under New Zealand Railways Corporation banner." [747]

Chapter Eight:

2000 - 2009 – Is There an Exit?

Planning and Politics
Infrastructure Auckland
By the end of the 1990s, there had been increased concern for the capacity of Auckland's infrastructure and management to cope with the City's constant population growth. This concern had resulted in the creation of *Infrastructure Auckland* as a funds provider and a *Regional Growth Forum* to develop a *Regional Growth Strategy* that might best meet the needs of the region.

Auckland's many, historically-diverse local bodies had, by then, been distilled to just seven city and district councils, ostensibly overseen by the one Auckland Regional Council. The result was not quite the *Greater Auckland* envisaged by past mayors, Arthur Myers, John Allum, and Dove-Myer Robinson, but the attempt was edging closer to what had been their vision.

Local Government Act 2002
The most recent changes to Auckland's local government had been achieved by means of the Local Government Amendment Act 1998 and further legislation was subsequently introduced in the form of the Local Government Act 2002. This Act defined and consolidated local government activities and responsibilities:

"The purpose of this Act is to provide for democratic and effective local government that recognises the diversity of New Zealand communities; and, to that end, this Act—

(a) states the purpose of local government;

(b) provides a framework and powers for local authorities to decide which activities they undertake and the manner in which they will undertake them; and

(c) promotes the accountability of local authorities to their communities;

(d) provides for local authorities to play a broad role in meeting the current and future needs of their communities for good-quality local infrastructure, local public services, and performance of regulatory functions.

"The purpose of local government is—

(a) to enable democratic local decision-making and action by, and on behalf of, communities;

(b) to meet the current and future needs of communities for good-quality local infrastructure, local public services, and performance of regulatory functions in a way that is most cost-effective for households and businesses." [748]

Local Government Commission
Section 28 of the 2002 Act allowed for the continuation of the Local Government Commission originally created by the Local Government Act 1974. However, its functions and powers were updated:

"The Commission may consider, report on, and make recommendations to the Minister and any relevant local authority on matters relating to a local authority or local government considered appropriate by the Commission…" [748]

Community Boards

The 1974 Act had also established Community Councils and these were also continued by the 2002 Act but renamed *Community Boards*. Their roles were to:

"(a) represent, and act as an advocate for, the interests of its community;

"(b) consider and report on all matters referred to it by the territorial authority, or any matter of interest or concern to the community board;

"(c) maintain an overview of services provided by the territorial authority within the community;

"(d) prepare an annual submission to the territorial authority for expenditure within the community;

"(e) communicate with community organisations and special interest groups within the community;

"(f) undertake any other responsibilities that are delegated to it by the territorial authority." [748]

Land Transport Management Act 2003

Land transport activity was also in need of some legislative reform, and this was a requirement of the Green Party, the support of which the recently re-elected Labour Party needed to govern. The reform began with the Land Transport Management Act 2003, passed in November of that year. The purpose of the Act: "…to contribute to the aim of achieving an integrated, safe, responsive, and sustainable land transport system. To contribute to that purpose, this Act-

"(2)(a) provides an integrated approach to land transport funding and management;

(b) improves social and environmental responsibility in land transport funding, planning, and management;

(c) changes the statutory objectives of Transfund and Transit to broaden the focus of each entity;

(d) improves long-term planning and investment in land transport;

(e) ensures that land transport funding is allocated in an efficient and effective manner;

(f) improves the flexibility of land transport funding, including provisions enabling new roads to be built on a tolled or concession agreement basis or on a basis involving a combination of those methods…" [749]

The broader focus of the responsibilities of Transfund allowed the Crown entity to operate a national land transport account to provide funds for 'approved activities' to Transit New Zealand, regional councils, and to territorial authorities (other than for public transport services activities).

Transit New Zealand continued as a body corporate "(a) to control the State highway system, including planning, design, supervision, construction, and maintenance in accordance with this Act and the Transit New Zealand Act 1989 (b) to prepare a land transport programme for the State highway system…" [749]

Section 27 of the Land Transport Management Act 2003 set the stage for ownership of public transport services by local authorities, something they had been unable to do since the deregulation of public transport in late 1989:

"Any interest that a local authority has in a public transport service to which this section applies must be held in a council controlled trading organisation, whether or not in conjunction with another local authority…A regional council may…hold an interest in, or acquire the ownership of, a public transport service or any public transport infrastructure." [749]

Section 46 of the 2003 Act also provided for the tolling of new roads:

"The Governor-General may, by Order in Council made on the recommendation of the Minister, establish a road tolling scheme to provide funds that may be applied by or on behalf of a public road controlling authority for the purposes of – (a) 1 or more of the following activities, namely, the planning, design, supervision, construction, maintenance, or operation of a new road…" [749]

It would be many years before such a provision would be put to any practical use in Auckland but it nevertheless remained an option.

Joint Officials Group

In July 2003, the Government established a 'Joint Officials Group' (JOG) comprised of central, regional and local government officials.

The objective: "To develop a funding plan for Auckland transport…that enables the timely implementation of an agreed network strategy…to advance a broader range of government policies and initiatives within this context of addressing transport issues in Auckland…"

On 30 October 2003, the Officials Group met with Auckland's Mayors at which time various proposals were discussed and agreed in principal, including:

"fuel taxes be increased by no more than 5 cents per litre excluding GST (fuel excise duty and equivalent road user charges for diesel vehicles), with a proportionate share (up to 35%) being allocated to Auckland;

"the Crown matches this by making a contribution of potentially up to $500m over 10 years;

"tolling be introduced on new roads where practicable, with project specific debt used in relation to those roads;

"the Land Transport Management Act 2003 provides the basis for assessing projects for funding; and

"an in principle decision be made to move towards road pricing of existing roads, but with further work to be done, including around the social and economic impacts." [750]

A discussion document, presented to Cabinet in November 2003, set out various key findings of the Joint Officials Group, including:

"The rate at which infrastructure can be constructed is subject to three main constraints: consents, buildability and funding.

"It should be possible to double the amount of annual investment in civil construction in Auckland transport to $400m p.a. (this figure does not include other types of expenditure such as rail electrification, and operating and maintenance expenditure), provided skills shortages can be addressed…

"Road pricing can deliver significant gains against the NZTS [New Zealand Transport Strategy] objectives and provides a further source of funding for investment in transport.

"Transport demand management (non-pricing initiatives to optimise the network and change behaviour, e.g. walking and cycling investment, school and business travel plans) can provide early and effective gains against the NZTS.

"Increased investment in public transport is essential. Additional public transport investment will be required if significant road pricing is introduced in Auckland and best practice indicates that this needs to be in place before road pricing is operational.

"Accelerated roading does not appear to deliver significant benefits when evaluated at a high level under NZTS objectives. New roads are however likely to be important for community acceptance of road pricing. JOG noted also that increased investment in PT and roading are not mutually exclusive, as buses are an important component of the public transport network…" [750]

Investing for Growth

"In late-2003, the national government announced a further Auckland transport funding package titled *Investing for Growth* to achieve the 'network completion' plan proposed by the JOG. The package provided Auckland with an extra $1.62 billion during 2005-2015 above projected disbursements of the National Land Transport Fund, through increases to petrol excise and road user charges and thus confirmed the accelerated road programme..." [231]

Local Government (Auckland) Amendment Act 2004

However, before much *Investing for Growth* funding could be implemented, some refinement to Auckland's transport management and polices was required. Accordingly, the Local Government (Auckland) Amendment Act 2004 was passed in July 2004, the purpose of which was "(a) to improve the integration of –

"(i) the Auckland regional land transport system; and

"(ii) the management of land transport funding and assets for the   Auckland Region…

"(b) to require Auckland local authorities to change the policy statement
and plans prepared under the Resource Management Act 1991 to   integrate the land transport and land use provisions and make those provisions consistent with the Auckland Regional Growth Strategy." [751]

Business New Zealand

The latter requirement had caused some consternation among business leaders, as illustrated by the submission of Business New Zealand (an affiliation of the NZ Employers and Manufacturers Federations) to the Transport & Industrial Relations Committee during the Local Government (Auckland) Amendment Bill hearings in May 2004:

"…over recent years it has become increasingly apparent that New Zealand's land transport infrastructure constrains rather than facilitates economic growth…While agreeing that there is a great need for change, Business New Zealand has serious concerns about whether this legislation would result in any improvement on the existing Byzantine structure of transport decision-making in Auckland – and could in fact make matters worse.

"Business New Zealand recommends that the Government should:
(b) Take decisive action to resolve the wider issues constraining land   transport infrastructure development, particularly problems with the Resource Management Act and the Land Transport Management Act;

(c) Do more to encourage the regional clustering of roading management; and
(d) Consult and engage more effectively with business and road user groups during the development of transport policy.

"Business New Zealand is concerned that the Local Government (Auckland) Bill is another example of an agreement between local and central government that has had minimal involvement or attempt of buy-in from either road users or the business community. While it is clear that there has been close collaboration between local and central government on this issue...the concept of 'partnership' with those that pay the bills is not at all apparent...

"While Business New Zealand agrees that Auckland's transport governance structures must be improved, the Local Government (Auckland) Bill is flawed and could even make the situation worse, for example by entrenching yet more provisions into legislation that lift the importance of environmental considerations above all others. This would add yet another constraint to infrastructure development causing traffic congestion to worsen and road safety to continue to be compromised, all in the name of the 'environment'." [752]

Auckland Regional Transport Authority

Despite the concerns of some, such as Business New Zealand, Part 2 of the Local Government (Auckland) Amendment Act 2004 assigned the Auckland Regional Council principal responsibility for:

"(i) setting the strategy for the Auckland regional land transport system;

"(ii) integrating the planning, funding, and development of the Auckland regional land transport system..." [751]

The Act also established the *Auckland Regional Transport Authority* (ARTA) and *Auckland Regional Holdings* to assist the Auckland Regional Council to discharge that responsibility;

"8(1) The objective of ARTA is to plan, fund, and develop the Auckland regional land transport system in a way that contributes to an integrated, safe, responsive, and sustainable land transport system for the Auckland Region.

"(2) In meeting its objective, ARTA must exhibit a sense of social and environmental responsibility, which includes-

(a) avoiding, to the extent reasonable in the circumstances,
    adverse effects on the environment; and
(b) ensuring, to the extent practicable, that-
    (i) the views of affected communities are taken into account;
    (ii) land transport options and alternatives are given early and full consideration in a manner that contributes to paragraph (a) and subparagraph (i); and
    (iii) early and full opportunities are provided to the persons and organisations who are required to be consulted in order to contribute to the development of land transport programmes." [751]

Auckland Regional Holdings

The Act dissolved Infrastructure Auckland, and transferred its assets and liabilities to a new entity, *Auckland Regional Holdings* (ARH), on and from 1 July 2004:

Section 20 of the Act recorded the functions of ARH are to –

"(a) own, directly or indirectly, and manage assets (including funds) in the long-term interests of the Auckland Region; and

"(b) provide funds to ARC in accordance with ARH's long term funding plan...;

"(c) make land transport assets available to assist ARTA to achieve ARTA's objective..." [751]

Income from the regional assets held by Auckland Regional Holdings at the time of its establishment was "...used primarily by the Auckland Regional Council to fund transport and water quality projects. It then had more than $1 billion worth of assets, including 80 per cent of the shares in the Ports of Auckland Limited, the America's Cup Village Limited and other investments formerly held by Infrastructure Auckland." [753]

"The aim of the restructuring was to strengthen the regional approach to transport in the Auckland region, and to reduce the fragmentation. It brought two separate sources of funding together at the ARC – regional rates and Infrastructure Auckland's investments.

"It also integrated within ARTA the decisions about passenger transport capital expenditure (formerly made by ARTNL) and decisions about expenditure on services (formerly made by the ARC). The Government also reduced the number of funding flows by making ARTA the primary conduit for Land Transport NZ funding into the Auckland region." [753]

[ARTNL was the *Auckland Regional Transport Network Limited* – a limited liability company of which the Auckland, Manukau and Waitakere City Councils were shareholders. It was incorporated in July 2001 and deregistered with the formation of the Auckland Council in November 2010.]

Land Transport Management Amendment Act 2004

The Labour Government's reform of land transport continued during 2004 with passage of the Land Transport Management Amendment Act 2004 which came into force on 1 December of that year. However, unlike the previous, Auckland-centred legislation, this Act provided for national funding of land transport and other measures.

In particular, the Act replaced Transfund with a new crown entity, Land Transport New Zealand (LTNZ) – "...to allocate resources and to undertake its functions in a way that contributes to an integrated, safe, responsive, and sustainable land transport system..." [754]

Again, the emphasis for change was on commitment to environmental responsibility:

"(2) In meeting its objective, the Authority must exhibit a sense of social and environmental responsibility, which includes-

"(a) avoiding, to the extent reasonable in the circumstances, adverse effects on the environment..." [754]

Land Transport New Zealand

"Land Transport New Zealand...established to promote a safe and sustainable land transport system and to allocate resources from the National Land Transport Account. It works closely with road controlling authorities, regional councils and approved organisations to evaluate and approve funding for planning, maintaining, managing and developing the land transport system. This includes road construction and maintenance as well as funding assistance for passenger transport services, travel demand strategies, education and safety initiatives.

"Land Transport NZ allocates funds to:
- Transit New Zealand to fully fund the planning, maintenance, management and development of the state highway network
- ARTA for the provision of passenger transport services, including rail and travel behaviour change initiatives

- Local authorities and approved organisations for the planning, maintenance, management and development of the local land transport system, including walking and cycling networks, safety activities and programmes
- Other community organisations for the promotion of land transport safety and education." [753]

The Rise and Fall of the Eastern Motorway

While the national land transport initiative appeared from the legislation to favour a mix of both road building and support for public transport, Auckland's local government was not so keen to share its resources equally – as illustrated by Paul Mees and Jago Dodson in their paper, *Backtracking Auckland: Bureaucratic rationality and public preferences in transport planning*:

"John Banks, a former national government Minister and populist Auckland radio host, was elected Mayor of Auckland in 2001, on a platform of relieving Auckland's road 'gridlock'. A pro-road council was elected along with the Mayor, and advocated the completion of the Auckland motorway network. The cornerstone of this campaign was the Eastern Motorway, a project from the 1999 RLTS [Regional Land Transport Strategy] routed through Auckland's affluent inner-eastern suburbs.

"Estimated costs of the Eastern Motorway expanded rapidly between 2002 and 2004, from $495 million...to $2.9 billion...before being scaled back to $1.2 billion...Mayor Banks' schemes drew substantial support from business lobbyists, including the 'Roads Before Rail' Trust which advocated against regional rail improvements in favour of motorways...as well as the *New Zealand Herald* newspaper which argued that the 'absolute need' for the Eastern Motorway required its immediate construction...

"The Eastern Motorway plan generated local opposition in the form of the Stop the Eastern Motorway (STEM) group, which drew substantial support from the affluent population of the inner eastern suburbs. STEM promoted improved public transport, including an upgrading of the rail system, as an alternative to the motorway. Mayor Banks staked his re-election in 2004 on public support for the Eastern Motorway plans and described opponents as "small in number and centred mainly on a few selfish, vested-interest property owners..."

"STEM subsequently endorsed anti-motorway candidates in the 2004 Auckland City Council election. The 2004 local government elections in Auckland thus provided a rare opportunity to test public preferences for transport alternatives in the face of substantial political, media and official promotion of motorways over alternative travel modes...

"Opinion polls taken prior to the 2004 election suggested strong regional public support for investment in public transport projects over new motorways...The election results emphatically validated the opinion polls: Mayor Banks was defeated and the election of anti-motorway candidates gave the Auckland City Council its first centre-left majority for 70 years. A centre-left, pro-public transport grouping also gained a majority on the Auckland Regional Council...

"Interviewed the following day, the outgoing Mayor attributed his defeat to public opposition to the Eastern Motorway. Auckland, it seemed, had experienced a 'freeway revolt' of the type found in other Australian and North American cities during the 1960s and 1970s...

"Even the *New Zealand Herald* reluctantly conceded that the polls and elections had seen the expression of clear public preferences for public transport investment over motorways and that the region's transport officials should take note..." [231]

Regional Transport Strategy 2005

As previously noted, a Regional Growth Strategy was developed in the late 1990s and this was refined in 2005 with particular emphasis on the role expected to be played by public transport – but in a more environmentally-sustainable way than previously planned:

"Regional Growth Strategy was developed to direct and shape the form of growth and development for the next generation and beyond. In an environment where traffic congestion has increased significantly, with associated environmental and economic costs, there is growing awareness that Auckland's transport and land use need to develop in a sustainable and integrated way.

"The growth strategy aims to concentrate a bigger proportion of the region's population and employment in growth centres along the major passenger transport corridors. This will improve the efficiency and convenience of passenger transport and increase opportunities to walk and cycle...

"To realise the potential of the region's public transport opportunities, improvements are needed to bus, rail and ferry services. The Regional Land Transport Strategy sets out the broad policy direction for these improvements...Travel demand management is an essential component of the Auckland Regional Land Transport Strategy...It aims to reduce car trips and to encourage more people to walk, cycle, catch public transport, share car trips, and to work, shop and play locally..." [753]

An Opposite Outcome

However, the 2005 Regional Transport Strategy was not all that it seemed – according to Paul Mees and Jago Dodson in their paper, *Backtracking Auckland: Bureaucratic rationality and public preferences in transport planning*:

"Just as their predecessors in the 1950s and 1970s had succeeded in heading off public pressure for investment in rail rapid transit at the expense of motorways, the ARC staff responsible for the 2005 strategy (in many cases the same people behind the 2003 and 1999 strategies) managed to produce an outcome that was the opposite of that clearly expressed by the public at the elections of 2004. But somehow the transport planners remain convinced that it is the public, not themselves, who need to change. The ARC's 2005 draft RLTS consultation brochure states:

"Transport improvements alone will not be enough. We all need to think about our individual lifestyle and travel behaviour – are we willing to change? Working from home or car sharing would help. So would walking and cycling for local trips, and using buses and trains more.

"During the preparation of and since the 2005 RLTS was released the major transport projects that have begun or have reached the advanced planning stages in Auckland are all motorways: the Victoria Park Tunnel, the State Highway 20 extension and the Upper Harbour Motorway extension.

"Some initial gains for public transport have occurred. In December 2005 the national government agreed to fund modest improvements to Auckland's rail tracks, including double tracking of the Western Line, a short branch track to Manukau city centre and various signalling and junction upgrades...The serious rail upgrade proposed by ARTA, including electrification and the CBD tunnel, remained as far away as ever..." [231]

Rail Will Never Work

That lack of support for Auckland's public transport aspirations, financial or otherwise, continued into 2006 – as reported by The New Zealand Herald's transport reporter, Mathew Dearnaley, on 16 May:

"Finance Minister Michael Cullen has delivered a blunt message to Auckland's political leaders to pick up more of the region's transport tab with heftier rates rises. He expressed irritation at a meeting with the Auckland Mayoral Forum at a proposed 5 per cent annual cap on regional rates rises over 10 years.

"One official at the closed-door Beehive meeting said that Dr Cullen told the mayoral delegation, led by Auckland City Mayor Dick Hubbard and joined by regional council chairman Mike Lee, that 'putting rates up 5 per cent is not enough.'

"Dr Cullen is also understood to have indicated a preference for buses over rail to get Auckland moving. 'He said the future lies with roads and buses – that rail will never work,' said an official. A second source claimed the minister was 'rough' on the Aucklanders.

"…the Government is concerned the regional council may be expecting a bailout similar to the $1.6 billion 10-year package of extra transport funding it promised in 2003, much of which is going on new state highways rather than public transport. Dr Cullen is also known to be irked that Auckland Regional Holdings, a council subsidiary, is holding back revenue from the ports company and other assets for future transport operating needs rather than contributing more to infrastructure development.

"Although the Government has indicated it will contribute $780 million to Auckland's rail upgrade, this compares with a regional council share of $1.1 billion leaving a shortfall of more than $700 million. Dr Cullen has previously listed priorities for Auckland's rail network for the next three years as completing the $200 million western line duplication project, upgrading the Newmarket junction and building a 1.8 km spur line to central Manukau.

"In a letter in December, he and former Transport Minister David Parker said electrifying the network was not an immediate priority, even though that is favoured by the Auckland Regional Transport Authority. Although that agency was set up under the regional council at the Government's behest, Dr Cullen is keen to assert the Beehive's right to dictate terms of the rail upgrade through its own organisation, Ontrack. He is understood to have been unenthusiastic last week about a compromise pitch from the regional council to electrify only the western line in time for the 2011 Rugby World Cup…" [755]

Regional Fuel Tax

Apart from raising rates, there were few alternatives left to Auckland councils to remedy the rail funding shortfall – that is, until after the Government's May 2007 budget when Minister of Transport, Annette King, announced:

"Budget 2007 paves the way for regions to raise funds through a regional fuel tax for specific transport capital projects that would otherwise not attract funding within the timeframe that regions might desire..." [756]

Although it would be some years before that avenue of funding could be exploited by councils, its eventual implementation was facilitated by the Land Transport Management Amendment Act 2008 – Section 65A of which states:

"(1) This subpart enables a region to obtain, by the imposition of a fuel tax for the region (known as a regional fuel tax), the funding that it needs to contribute to capital projects that—
"(a) will result in a net benefit to the region; and
"(b) are a priority for the region; and
"(c) will not reasonably be fully funded from sources other than a regional fuel tax within the time frame desired by the region..." [757]

The New Zealand Transport Agency

The Land Transport Management Amendment Act 2008 also established the New Zealand Transport Agency as of 1 August 2008 – a merger of Transit New Zealand (previously created in 1989) with Land Transport New Zealand (previously Transfund).

The functions of the new Agency:
"(a) to promote an affordable, integrated, safe, responsive, and sustainable land transport system:
"(b) to investigate and review accidents and incidents involving transport on land in its capacity as the responsible safety authority...
"(c) to manage the State highway system, including planning, funding, design, supervision, construction, and maintenance and operations, in accordance with this Act and the Government Roading Powers Act 1989:
"(d) to deliver or manage the delivery of its other activities and combinations of activities, including (but not limited to) those relating to research, education, training, and coastal shipping:
"(e) to manage funding of the land transport system, including (but not limited to) — (i) administration of land transport revenue and regional fuel taxes; and (ii) auditing the performance of approved organisations in relation to activities approved by the Agency and the operation of the land transport disbursement accounts of approved organisations:
"(f) to manage regulatory requirements for transport on land, including (but not limited to) maintaining and preserving records and documents concerning activities within the land transport system, and maintaining registers..." [757]

The Global Financial Crisis

The age-old question of whether central or local government should fund Auckland's transport services, and in what proportion, was soon to be very much influenced by the Global Financial Crisis that swept the world from early 2007. The crisis was still affecting the funding of civic projects in New Zealand as late as February 2009 - as reported by Bernard Orsman of The New Zealand Herald:

"More than $1 billion worth of major Auckland civic developments are under threat from the global recession which has sent returns from the regional council's strategic investments into freefall. Politicians, directors and senior Auckland Regional Council staff held crisis talks on Friday to get to grips with the rapidly deteriorating books of the ARC's business arm, Auckland Regional Holdings...Auckland Regional Holdings is struggling to pay a $155 million grant to the parent body this year. Serious doubts have also been raised over how it will pay $548 million over the next decade to help fund rail electrification, integrated ticketing and development of the Tank Farm.

"ARC chairman Mike Lee said he was concerned, but not surprised by its business arm's performance. He was adamant his council was 'past the point of no return' for the signature projects of rail electrification and integrated ticketing. The council has sought expressions of interest for the $1 billion rail electrification project. Half the bill is being funded by the Government, the other half by the council.

"A regional fuel tax, due to be phased in, starting at 1c a litre in July, will pay for the ARC's capital costs. Money from its holding company and rates will go towards the operational costs for electrified rail. The holding company's income is also expected to contribute to the operational costs of a $170 million integrated ticketing project. A tender process is nearing completion for the project…" [758]

Fix Auckland – One Auckland
While many organisations, businesses, and individuals struggled with the downturn caused by the global financial crisis, some Aucklanders decided that the City was no longer working as it should and that substantial change was urgently needed – as stated by a full-page advertisement published by the Northern Employers and Manufacturers Association in the North Harbour News on 20 July 2007:

"Last year, a group of people from Auckland's eight councils got together to hatch a plan. It was a plan to change Auckland. You might have heard something about it. Chances are you've heard nothing about it. These people have been working away in secret on their plan to change Auckland. They've written a report without consultation and they've given it to the powers that be in Wellington, who, in due course will make their own announcement about how to change Auckland. Or not. As the case may be…

"The facts of the matter are these: the Auckland region, from Warkworth to Waiuku and everywhere in between, is in trouble. More trouble than the early settlers. The public transport system doesn't work. Rates keep going up. And up. And up. Don't even get us started on Metrowater.

"It's a region in crisis and this is largely due to inefficient local government. Get this: we have, for example, eight separate councils, their eight CEOs and seven mayors. In fact, the only thing local government in Auckland seems to be really good at is duplication. Well, we think enough is enough. We've come up with a real plan, not just to change Auckland but to fix Auckland. Once and for all.

"As an overview: Our plan gets rid of all the fat and the excessive overheads that exist in our councils. Then we'd like to put that money back into local communities, and that money should be looked after by the people in - you guessed it - our local communities.

"We've had some people do the numbers and they reckon we could save about $200 million a year, or about $400 per ratepayer. That works. Our plan is called One Auckland. It's bold. It's big and it would be fair to say we quite like it. But what do you reckon? Have a look at it. Tell us what you think. Pull it apart. Come up with something better. But please do something. Let's fix Auckland. Now…" [759]

A Royal Commission of Inquiry
Reference to the plan *hatched* by the City's councils was made in a later New Zealand Herald report:

"Last year, the four city mayors discussed the proposal of a super-council. But the idea was shelved after opposition from the Rodney, Papakura and Franklin districts, the Auckland Regional Council, and many councillors from the four cities, who were all shut out of the discussions…" [760]

However, the *plan* had not been shelved by the Government – as demonstrated by the Minister of Local Government, Mark Burton's announcement, on 31 July 2007, his

Government's decision to establish a Royal Commission of Inquiry to "...examine and report on what local and regional governance arrangements are required for the Auckland region over the foreseeable future..." [761]

Mark Burton announced the Commission's terms of reference and membership on 31 October 2007:

"I am very pleased that Hon Peter Salmon QC has accepted the position of Chair of the Royal Commission, and that Dame Margaret Bazley and David Shand have agreed to be Commissioners. The three Commissioners have a range of expertise and experience, including with the World Bank and the International Monetary Fund, making them ideally suited to carry out the work of the Royal Commission...

"The Royal Commission has wide powers to identify what local and regional governance arrangements will best provide for current and future local, and future regional, interests as well as national interests in respect of the region. The Royal Commission is required to report back to Government by 1 December 2008." [762]

The Commission's terms of reference included:
- "what governance, institutional and ownership structures and funding responsibilities would best help the Auckland region provide key infrastructure services and facilities;
- "what legislative changes would be needed to meet the commission's recommendations;
- "what changes to the boundaries of the Auckland region are necessary;
- "what transition arrangements would need to be put in place in moving to any new structure.

"Mr Burton said a healthy Auckland was crucial to a successful New Zealand economy. 'The issues about Auckland's future governance are complex and the Royal Commission will provide for careful and thorough investigation and consultation to identify the most appropriate long-term governance arrangements for Auckland, to secure its future as an internationally competitive city and region.'" [760]

Submissions to the Commission

During the public submission process, the Commission received more than 3,500 written and 550 verbal submissions. The Commission conducted formal hearings over 27 hearing days in nine locations throughout the region, including Waiheke and Great Barrier Islands.

A selection of submissions containing varying views included:

The Eden Albert Community Board – "Drivers of Change –

"Some in the community have called for change, suggesting that 'nothing is working' – meaning that the infrastructure for Tamaki Auckland is deficient in some manner. Governance is not infrastructure. The Commission should not fall into the trap of conflating issues such as infrastructure problems with governance.

"These are two different things; infrastructure is about agreeing, designing, building and maintaining essential pieces of infrastructure for all citizens to use. Governance is about the welfare of all citizens; it is about dynamically identifying issues of concern both in the short and long term, discussing these with citizens, and making arrangements for the holistic resolution of the issues. These issues are more than simple infrastructure problems; they are cultural, social and environmental issues as well.

"However, we note that these two areas overlap, and it may be more helpful to see infrastructure concerns as subsidiary to overall governance. In this sense, infrastructure meets governance when setting zoning limits around certain areas of the region e.g. industrial uses alongside heavy freight rail with its noise/vibration effects.

"At the junction between governance and infrastructure it becomes a community/planning issue that requires expertise…

"The Board does not see any great desire for change amongst the community; rather the community simply wants their communities of interest to work i.e. that the rubbish gets collected, that the footpaths are of a reasonable standard and that elected representatives are responsive to their wide-ranging concerns about development in their area.

"However, a blank sheet of paper exercise is not the answer as suggested. Any proposed models need to identify and build on the strengths of existing models; such strengths need to be wedded to best practices in governance to build a strong, resilient and durable governance structure. 'Blank sheet' thinking does nothing except waste scarce resources, time, money and energy as people struggle to cope with new systems, then cope with refinements to the system as shortcomings become apparent. Evolution is a more appropriate path to follow for the region." [763]

The Auckland Regional Council and City Council –

"There will be nowhere for politicians and bureaucrats to hide if a super city for Auckland fails to deliver savings for ratepayers, the Royal Commission of Inquiry on Auckland Governance heard yesterday. The Auckland Regional Council has promised big savings from a plan to abolish itself and the seven councils for a 'Greater Auckland Authority'. The ARC is the second council in as many days to propose a super city for Auckland.

"On Tuesday, the Auckland City Council proposed a Greater Auckland Council with 29 councillors, a Greater Auckland mayor elected at large and neighbourhood councils. A super city would be the largest council in Australasia, representing 1.4 million people.

"ARC chairman Mike Lee said he was absolutely confident of major savings from moving to a Greater Auckland Authority, which the council has estimated at $160 million a year…Mr Lee said the ARC model was radical but essential for the persistent Auckland 'disease' of fractiousness, disunity and cost duplication. 'We were struck with a paradox. How to achieve critical mass, regional cohesion, regional unity and how to retain the local in local government,' he said…Mr Lee said the strongest part of the model was the creation of 30 community councils to restore local democracy and revitalise communities…" [764]

North Shore City –

"North Shore city vigorously opposes a single city. It fears its residents will be unfairly rated to fix huge infrastructure problems in other cities that haven't been investing as heavily…They could also be hit the hardest by rates rises under a super-city structure because the Shore has the highest value properties in the region.

"North Shore City Council wants councils and community boards retained and changes only to the regional authority. It seeks changes to representation on the regional authority it believes would give it a genuine mandate to talk to central government.

"Shore mayor Andrew Williams says the suggestion the region could be governed by one super-city council is 'horrifying'…'From the outset it is North Shore city's strong belief that local councils are working very effectively for their communities, and that each part of Auckland has their unique strengths and community identities,' says Mr Williams." [765]

Royal Commission of Inquiry Report

The Royal Commission of Inquiry on Auckland Governance delivered its report to the Governor-General, Hon. Anand Satyanand, on 25 March 2009.

The main parts of that report included:

"The Commission proposes the dissolution of the Auckland Regional Council and all seven territorial authorities existing in Auckland, and the creation of a new single unitary authority called the Auckland Council. The Auckland Council will have all the powers and responsibilities of a regional council and territorial authority across the region. Staff and all assets and liabilities from existing Auckland councils will be transferred to it.

"The Auckland Council will hold all council assets and employ all staff. There will be one long-term council community plan, one spatial plan, one district plan, one rating system, one rates bill, one voice for Auckland.

"The boundaries of the Auckland region will be unchanged to the north and for the Hauraki Gulf. In the south, the boundary between the Auckland and Waikato regions will be changed in two ways:

"The area currently in the Waikato region north of the Waikato River, including Tuakau, Pokeno, and Mercer, is to be included in the Auckland region.

"The area currently in Auckland region and Franklin District, bordering the Firth of Thames from Matingarahi Point to Whakatiwai, is to be included in the Waikato region.

"Adjustments to territorial authority boundaries are proposed to reflect the new regional boundary. The parts of Franklin District that will be outside the new Auckland region, including Onewhero and Kaiaua, will be transferred to Waikato District.

"In addition to the elected governing body of the Auckland Council, local democracy will be maintained through six elected local councils operating within the unitary Auckland Council. Local councils will oversee the delivery of services by Auckland Council staff and will undertake local engagement in four urban and two rural districts.

"The boundaries of the new local councils will be centred (with some important boundary adjustments) on the existing council territories of Rodney District, North Shore, Waitakere, Auckland, and Manukau Cities, and Franklin District, thus enabling new local councils to utilise existing infrastructure and service centres...

"Generally, community boards will no longer be required in the model the Commission proposes. The Commission recommends that an exception be made for the Great Barrier and Waiheke Island Community Boards, which should be retained, with wider delegated powers. It also recommends the establishment of a community board for the central city and waterfront, with powers delegated to it from the Auckland Council. This area will not be within a local council area...

"The Commission's approach to transition is based on the understanding, conveyed to it by Government, that necessary changes should be in place in time for the next local body elections in October 2010..." [766]

Making Auckland Not So Great

Following receipt of the Royal Commission's report, the Government worked quickly to modify the Commission's recommendations to fit more with its preferences. Instead of the six elected local councils suggested by the Commission, the Government opted for the one unitary City Council, as the sole council for the district, overseeing 20 to 30 local boards. This was seen as a betrayal of 'local' government by many - as described by the Editor-in-chief of the North Shore Times, David Kemeys, in his front-page article, "Who stole our voice?" published on 17 April 2009:

"ENOUGH is enough. The government's insistence on forcing change in Auckland's governance is bullying. There is no evidence Aucklanders want it and plenty that they don't...This government's stance strips democracy from residents. The Royal Commission on Auckland Governance's position, reached after months of work, submissions and consultation, has been dumped. It proposed shared governance within the region and Wellington, and outlined how to achieve that...

"But Prime Minister John Key and [Local Government Minister] Mr Hide know better. Despite not doing any research and with limited analysis, they have dumped the recommendations, wiping out the local councils and giving all the power to the Auckland Council, while cutting it from 23 members and an elected mayor to 20 and a mayor. The local councils are replaced by 20 to 30 utterly powerless community boards.

"Mr Key and Mr Hide might as well have set fire to the money the commission cost, though that appears not to matter since neither man can say what cost savings their proposal will bring..." [767]

Making Auckland Greater

Despite the criticism, the Government pressed on with its preferred version of a Greater Auckland – praised by others – such as Kenneth Palmer, Associate Professor, University of Auckland:

"The Government's decisions on Auckland governance - 'Making Auckland Greater' - are bold, decisive and overall radical. Finally we have a workable prescription for Auckland to speak with one voice and act boldly in the regional and national interest. The Government has moved swiftly on this issue, possibly inspired by the urgency of the global financial crisis.

"The report of the Royal Commission on Auckland Governance released in March was itself radical in recommending a unitary Auckland Council...Although innovative in promoting the Super City concept, the report's overall thrust was incremental, basically retaining the existing territorial governance level. The Government's decision on Auckland Governance provided a far more radical blueprint. The Auckland Council, being a unitary authority, is to be the sole council for the area...This is dramatic, ending the historic evolution of the competing councils originating in 1851..." [768]

Legislative Programme

Of course, nothing was for certain until legislation made it so. The first was the Local Government (Tamaki Makaurau Reorganisation) Act 2009, enacted on 23 May 2009 – the purpose of which was:

"7) (b) to dissolve the existing local authorities that govern the Auckland region (being 1 regional and 7 territorial authorities) on 1 November 2010;

(c) to establish an entity to facilitate the transition to the new local government arrangements; and to require the existing local authorities and other local government organisations to support the reorganisation

(d) to require the existing local authorities and other local government organisations to support the reorganisation by both doing specified things and refraining from doing specified things;

(da) to provide for the Governor-General, Ministers, and other public officials and bodies to undertake specified duties to facilitate the reorganisation;

(e) to make any necessary amendments to any other enactments." [769]

Auckland Council

Subsequent legislation included:

The Local Government (Auckland Council) Act 2009, enacted on 22 September 2009 – Section 6 of which established the Auckland Council as a territorial authority, as of 1 November 2010, with the responsibilities, duties and powers of a regional council – defined as...

"7(1)(a) the Auckland Council has a two-tier governance structure comprising the governing body and the local boards;

"8 Governing body of Auckland Council –

(1) The governing body of the Auckland Council must comprise a mayor and 20 members elected in accordance with the Local Electoral Act 2001.

(2) The mayor must be elected by the electors of Auckland as a whole.

"10 Local boards

(a) A local board must be established for each local board area for the purposes of enabling democratic decision making by, and on behalf of, communities within the local board area..." [770]

Auckland Transport

This Act also established Auckland Transport to replace the Auckland Regional Transport Authority:

"38 Establishment of Auckland Transport

(1) This section establishes Auckland Transport.

(2) Auckland Transport is—

(a) a body corporate with perpetual succession; and

(b) a council-controlled organisation of the Auckland Council

"39 Purpose of Auckland Transport

The purpose of Auckland Transport is to contribute to an effective, efficient, and safe Auckland land transport system in the public interest.

"43 Governing body of Auckland Transport

(1) The governing body of Auckland Transport is the board of directors.

(2) The board of directors comprises—

(a) no fewer than 6 and no more than 8 voting directors, of whom 2 may be members of the governing body of the Auckland Council;

(b) 1 non-voting director nominated by the New Zealand Transport Agency...

"45 Functions of Auckland Transport

The functions of Auckland Transport are to—

(a) prepare the regional land transport programme for Auckland in accordance with the Land Transport Management Act 2003; and

(b) manage and control the Auckland transport system in accordance with this Act..." [770]

Spatial Plan Requirement

Part 6 of the Local Government (Auckland Council) Act 2009 set out the requirement for the new Auckland Council to prepare a spatial plan for the region:

"79(1) The Auckland Council must prepare and adopt a spatial plan for Auckland.

(2) The purpose of the spatial plan is to contribute to Auckland's
social, economic, environmental, and cultural well-being through a comprehensive and effective long-term (20- to 30-year) strategy for Auckland's growth and development…" [770]

Public Transport
Not the Right Structure
Following publication of the Auckland Regional Council's Regional Land Transport Strategy (RLTS) in November 1999 and Prime Minister Shipley's assurance, that same month, that the Government "…expected to increase funding for new transport projects in the Auckland region in the near future…", [743] there was some optimism on the part of Aucklanders that an exit from congested motorways could soon be reached.

However, according to J W Lello in an article published in the July 2000 edition of ESR [Engineers for Social Responsibility] News, more than anything, the City lacked effective transport management. In that article, he quoted the (unnamed) chairman of the transportation committee of the Institution of Professional Engineers:

"'*We don't have the right structure. We have a privatised bus system, we have the ARC which has the power to plan, but can't own anything. We are going about the whole thing the wrong way around. If we want good public transport the first thing we do is sort out our organisational and finance structure – then sit down and run a decent bus system*'." [771]

J W Lello then commented:

"Transport planning in Auckland has been a farce for half a century. The problems are increasing more rapidly now…Unfortunately the ARC has been stripped of many functions and no longer has the necessary power to implement its planning. It is time central government took an interest in Auckland's transport problems and helped to establish an Auckland Transport Authority. With an effective Transport Authority the need for Infrastructure Auckland to consider transport applications would cease. The need for a greater Auckland Council also requires attention. Mayors and Councillors are unlikely to move in this direction on their own." [771]

Regional Land Transport Strategy Planning
In a later ESR News article, Derek Pringle commented on what little effect the Regional Land Transport Strategy had on the planning of transport projects:

"By the time the RLTS is approved by the ARC…it represents a consensus of opinion of all the parties involved in providing transport facilities in the region. It takes a balanced approach to the provision of roading and public transport infrastructure and services, and includes policies on parking, walking, cycling, congestion pricing and other related issues. Despite this consensus and balanced approach, the emphasis in implementation is always on roading projects…

"Because funding for transport infrastructure is on the basis of individual projects meeting certain benefit/cost criteria, rather than on the basis of an agreed plan, it is difficult to achieve implementation of that plan. To the extent that nationally raised funds are involved, funding allocations are made on the basis of national priorities rather than regional priorities…

"Since transport was deregulated in 1989, Regional Councils have been the only organisations with the power to plan, fund and call tenders for public transport services. While there are some shortcomings in the system, having the one agency to plan and fund services has resulted in an improvement in services compared with 10 years ago. To some extent, this improvement is the result of a smaller number of larger private operators taking a co-operative approach...

"The situation with respect to the provision of public transport infrastructure is far less satisfactory. At the time of deregulation, the power to construct, own and operate infrastructure facilities was specifically removed from regional councils. It remained with Transit New Zealand, the TLAs and individual operators – a mix of responsibilities which has failed to produce badly needed infrastructural improvements.

"Major expenditure on public transport infrastructure has been acknowledged as an essential alternative to further motorway construction within the urban area by all interested parties for about 10 years now, but nothing has happened. This is because there is no funding system in place, and despite one agency having responsibility for planning and funding the operation of public transport services, there is no single agency with the power to provide the infrastructure for those services..." [772]

A Collective Mindset

In their paper, *Backtracking Auckland: Bureaucratic rationality and public preferences in transport planning*, Paul Mees and Jago Dodson also addressed the issue of why road expansion continued to dominate Auckland's transport planning:

"Since the late 1990s, elected officials in Auckland have attempted to re-balance transport policies, and the ensuing documents have promised a greater role for public transport. This new rhetoric is largely due to strong public support for a new transport policy direction. But the substantive policies pursued have remained dominated by motorways despite the changed rhetoric.

"We argue that the attempts to reverse car dependence in Auckland have failed because the region's transport planners employ policies and processes that promote road capacity expansion over investment in other modes. This bias, which appears to be only partly deliberate, is a result of a strong pro-automobile mindset collectively held over decades by Auckland's transport planners, and in similar national mindsets that are expressed through New Zealand's institutional framework for transport planning and funding.

"Auckland adds an extreme case study to recent international scholarship that has examined the extent to which institutionalised processes and mindsets can distort the articulation of public preferences in strategic transport plans...

"There is a need to ensure that any policy directions or options are publicly deliberated rather than left to obscure technical analysis. In the case of Auckland, we contend that the opposite has occurred. The recent attempts to reconfigure urban transport planning around conceptions of sustainability have simply reproduced the kind of auto-dominated transport plans that have been pursued since the 1950s, albeit with 'greener' rhetoric..." [231]

Britomart Transport Terminal

During the mid-1990s, the Auckland City Council had decided to refurbish its rather run-down bus station at Britomart at a cost of about $17 million. However, a council employee, Peter Cross, managed to convince the Mayor and several councillors to accept a more grandiose plan to develop the site at a substantially increased cost of $1.5 billion.

About December 1996, the Auckland City Council signed a contract with NatWest Markets (Australia), a division of the UK banking group, to develop the Britomart site and

Peter Cross was appointed executive director of developments for Britomart Investments, a subsidiary of NatWest Markets. However, there was substantial public opposition. "...in March, the Auckland Regional Council received 1093 submissions on Britomart, of which 1065 were opposed to the development..." [773]

Expensive Blunder

In his April 2000 ESR News article, J W Lello explained why, what was to become acceptable in a couple of decades, was then *ill-advised*:

"The grandiose Britomart proposal was an expensive blunder – an ill-advised attempt to create an elaborate underground transport centre in advance of transport systems. It was proposed by a Council employee and supported by the past mayor and several councillors. At first they described it as almost cost-free to ratepayers in return for granting approval for eleven large buildings above the centre (these were given resource consent without public notification).

"Pacific Capital Assets Ltd, formed to handle the development, listed 65 million $1.00 shares on the sharemarket...The Council was to contribute $125 million for the underground transport centre and Council also provided an interest-free loan of $56 million. A subsidiary company of Pacific Capital Assets, Britomart Investments Ltd, was set up to manage the project and a subsidiary of Britomart Investments Ltd, Britomart Developments Ltd, was to develop the underground Stage 1. This and the whole centre was described in an impressive well-written prospectus.

"The Council officer who originated Britomart went to work for the developer. There was opposition from citizens, professional groups and some politicians but finally, after Environment Court hearings, resource consents were obtained in 1998 for the underground stage. Despite requests for investigations central government maintained a 'hands-off' policy. The Minister for the Environment would not 'call it in' for full appraisal under the Resource Management Act.

"The 1998 election removed support for Britomart and after delays it was stopped by Council in 1999...

"Because new owners of the old railway land east of Britomart apparently do not want a surface rail line, Council decided to build a tunnel (by open cut construction) to bring rail to an underground station in Britomart. This appears to commit council to an expensive railway station before many issues are resolved (e.g. electrification of railway, cost of station, extent of underground work)." [771]

First Train to Britomart

The Britomart Railway Station was finally completed by 7 July 2003 and, after more than 70 years, received its first train into the CBD on that day – as described by an Auckland City Council press release:

"Aucklanders were able to witness a moment in history today when the first passenger train rolled in to the impressive Britomart Transport Centre early this morning. Britomart railway station is now fully operational and providing a convenient hub for commuters in downtown Auckland. This opening is one of the first event milestones for Auckland City Council: it is the culmination of all the hard construction work started in November 2001...

"The opening of the train station supports Auckland City Council's inspired vision for the Central Business District (CBD). It is a beginning for Auckland and its public transport network. The new Britomart Transport Centre will serve existing bus and rail services and the adjacent ferry to suburban destinations around the harbour.

"'Britomart is a major step in creating a modern, integrated public transport network for Auckland,' says Councillor Greg McKeown. 'Britomart not only gives the CBD a world class transport centre, but it is also a crucial part of an integrated public transport network, that will link many thriving centres within Auckland City and the region.'" [774]

A Central Hub

The Britomart Transport Centre was officially opened by Sir Edmund Hillary, Government Ministers, and civic officials on Friday 25 July 2003. With buses at ground level, trains underground, and its proximity to the Quay Street ferry terminals, Britomart soon became the central hub for public transport in Auckland.

A Funding Crisis

Despite what seemed to be a bright future for public transport in 2003, Auckland continued to suffer from a funding shortfall, particularly for its bus fleet – as reported by The New Zealand Herald on 26 May 2006:

"Auckland's public transport funding crisis threatens to leave fast-growing suburbs such as Flat Bush in Manukau City without buses in their early boom years. This is despite an acknowledgement by transport planners that new home-owners need early access to public transport if they are not to worsen congestion by buying more cheap second-hand cars.

"The Government intends building seven new schools in Flat Bush for about $270 million to cater for population growth from 3000 now to 40,000 in 15 years but Manukau Mayor Sir Barry Curtis yesterday bemoaned a lack of regional funding for bus services to match.

"Waitakere City is also concerned that a potential $1.4 billion shortfall in regional and Government funds for public transport over 10 years will prevent buses being re-routed to connect to trains at its new $40 million-plus civic centre in Henderson.

"The funding shortfall, even after a $1.6 billion commitment from the Auckland Regional Council, means the region's transport authority is giving priority for the next five years to strengthening the spine of a rapid transit network. New bus services to feed the network will generally have to wait until after 2011.

"Rapid transit for Auckland means completing the $290 million Northern Busway by early 2008 and upgrading the rail system south of the Waitemata Harbour. Although the Government is paying for much of the busway, and has set aside $600 million for rail-track development, the Auckland Regional Transport Authority faces a big bill to operate existing and new services. It also wants to buy a fleet of 30 new electric trains, although the Government is dubious about funding rail electrification before seeing a business case which the authority's board is due to start considering today…" [775]

Sylvia Park Chaos

Even the roads were too often unable to cope with demand – as reported by The New Zealand Herald on 9 June 2006:

"Transit NZ says it will not hesitate to close access routes off the Southern Motorway at Mt Wellington again if there is a repeat of yesterday's traffic chaos around the opening of the Sylvia Park mega-shopping centre…

"With traffic banked up past Otahuhu on the Southern Motorway, and local roads clogged for two to three kilometres in other directions, Transit closed both its Mt

Wellington off-ramps for more than two hours after 10am. The worst congestion was from the south, prompting the initial closure of just the northbound exit, but access from the other direction was also blocked after frustrated motorists turned around at Ellerslie to try to get to Sylvia Park that way…" [776]

Many Aucklanders knew exactly why the chaos had ensued – expressed by way of Letters to the Editor published some days later by The New Zealand Herald:

"What a surprise: traffic chaos at Sylvia Park. How could this development be allowed to proceed without significant changes to roading? Why is development permitted without the appropriate infrastructure being put in place first? It should have been a condition that the developers improve the Mt Wellington junction to handle the increased traffic before opening the mall. But that would reduce the developers' profits. While they count their money, I and many others will sit in gridlock on the Southern Motorway…(Steve Lucas, Beachlands)" [777]

"The Sylvia Park shopping centre is next to a rail corridor with the potential to move more than five times as many people as the nearby Mt Wellington Highway. This begs the question as to why successive National and Labour governments have refused to adequately fund Auckland's regional rail upgrade, in spite of more than 50 years of requests from local government.

"Their refusal to finance rail has meant thousands of shoppers have no alternative than to drive on already congested roads. The resulting mayhem has highlighted the folly of the Budget announcement to pour more money into roads. Sylvia Park already lies at the intersection of the Southern Motorway, the southeastern corridor and the Mt Wellington Highway, and additional funding will do nothing to improve flows. Meanwhile, spiralling vehicle emissions and oil prices are damaging our wallets and our health…(S Donovan, Newmarket)" [778]

New Zealand Transport Strategy

As previously referred to, the Land Transport Management Act 2003 reversed much of the deregulation of public transport imposed by 1989 legislation. In particular, the 2003 Act provided the legislative framework to implement the New Zealand Transport Strategy by:

- "enshrining the objectives sought for land transport (to be an integrated, safe, responsive and sustainable land transport system) in law;
- "removing the prohibition on regional councils having an ownership interest in public transport operations;
- "changing the focus of the procurement framework for public transport from competitive processes to obtaining best value for money in contributing to an integrated, safe, responsive and sustainable land transport system, having regard to the desirability of enabling fair competition and encouraging competitive and efficient markets.

"In December 2003, the New Zealand Cabinet agreed that a joint working group of Auckland and central government officials would be established to assess the need for changes to regulatory arrangements governing Auckland public transport, as part of the Sustainable Cities Programme of Action.

"The joint working group was led by the Ministry of Transport, supported by Land Transport New Zealand. The review focused on the provisions of the TSLA [Transport Services Licensing Act 1989] regarding control over commercial bus and ferry services and their relationship with contracted services. The review did not include passenger rail as all passenger rail services are contracted by regional councils." [713]

Auckland Transport Strategic Alignment Project

The joint working group referred to eventually became known as the *Auckland Transport Strategic Alignment Project steering group* which consisted of senior officials from Auckland Regional Council, Auckland City Council, the Ministry of Transport, the Department of Prime Minister and Cabinet, Land Transport New Zealand and the Treasury.

The steering group released its first report on 20 April 2007 – as per a press statement released by the Treasury:

"The Auckland Transport Strategic Alignment Project (ATSAP) arose out of discussion between Auckland's political leaders and Ministers in May 2006 around the funding of Auckland's land transport system. Ministers and Auckland Mayors agreed that the Crown and the region's views of the long term development of Auckland's land transport system may not be aligned. It was also agreed that before decisions could be made on funding issues, a common strategic vision for Auckland transport, including passenger rail, needed to be agreed.

"The project seeks to get agreement by both central government and Auckland local government leaders on a high level strategic plan for the long term development of Auckland's land transport system. The report sets out officials' recommendations on what should be included in a common strategic view.

"The report shows that there is a large degree of alignment between Crown and Auckland officials, including that a substantial shift to public transport is needed, starting immediately…The steering group also agree on the following modifications to Auckland's current strategic view:

"A 30 year view is needed. The Auckland Regional Land Transport Strategy currently only looks 10 years ahead; Auckland's Regional Land Transport Strategy should examine the value of introducing pricing measures to reduce traffic congestion;

"Greater direction on a local roading should be provided in order to: integrate local roading improvements with public transport objectives; integrate with the investment in, and management of, State Highways, and deliver on other objectives, including safety targets, economic development opportunities and regional growth strategy and needs.

"The need for greater emphasis on travel demand management and traffic management techniques to optimise the use of existing capacity.

"The report sets out two possible growth paths for Auckland's public transport system – rapid and steady growth…The rapid growth path is expected to cost in the order of an additional $1 billion over ten years. The steady growth path has not yet been modelled or costed. Implementing the services of this path may require additional funding, but this is likely to be at a lower level than the rapid growth path." [779]

Regional Fuel Tax

One source for that additional funding was, of course, the possible introduction of a regional fuel tax referred to in the Government's May 2007 Budget and explained a day later in a press release:

"Finance Minister Michael Cullen and Transport Minister Annette King said today that the first region to benefit from a regional fuel tax is likely to be Auckland, where a 10 cents a litre regional fuel tax on petrol and diesel could raise about $120 million a year and could support a debt of about $1.5 billion over 30 years.

"'We know there is a great deal of interest in Auckland in the advantages offered by a regional fuel tax,' the Ministers said. 'A regional fuel tax will allow the government to support Auckland's transport priorities, which includes electrification of the Auckland rail network, other public transport initiatives such as additional buses and integrated ticketing, the Western Ring Route and Penlink...'

"In a further move to give certainty to land transport planning, the Ministers have announced that consideration is being given to permanently directing all revenue generated from fuel excise duty towards land transport expenditure, including public transport. 'This would mean that the Crown would no longer retain any revenue from the sale of petrol for general government revenue and would ensure that every cent of excise duty collected from motorists is used for land transport projects...'" [780]

Public-Private Control

However, by 2008, neither the introduction of regional fuel tax nor *public transport initiatives such as additional buses and integrated ticketing* had eventuated, and Auckland struggled on – inviting comment from Brian Rudman, published in The New Zealand Herald on 25 January:

"…I see nothing wrong with returning Auckland public transport system to community control. The bureaucrats…surely can't do a worse job than the existing 'privatised' set-up which was imposed on Aucklanders by the new right ideologues who controlled Parliament 15 years ago.

"Since then this region has experienced the worst bus patronage growth of any city in either Australia or New Zealand, down 34 per cent relative to population. This year, private passenger transport operators will pocket nearly $100 million in public subsidies.

"Over the next decade ratepayers and taxpayers will pay $1.4 billion subsidising bus and ferry services. Add to that the billions of public funds going into upgrading rail infrastructure, the northern busway, and assorted bus and train stations, and you have to ask, why shouldn't those who are funding the system be calling the tune? Since 2004, subsidies to private bus operators have increased 89 per cent but patronage only went up just 1.2 per cent.

"The existing system allows private operators to cherrypick the most popular routes and time slots for themselves, then leaves the community to try to cobble together a service for the 60 per cent of Auckland the privateers consider non-profitable. The private operators then demand a public subsidy to serve these areas, but refuse to allow their books to be inspected to prove they're not gouging the system. Rivalry between operators continues to stymie attempts to introduce an integrated ticketing system – regarded as normal in most civilised cities…" [781]

Dedicated Bus Lanes

Since Auckland's trams and their immediate replacement, trolleybuses, were found to be too inflexible; restricted to the direction of their rails and overhead wiring, petrol and diesel buses reigned supreme. But their dominance was short-lived. Soon those free-ranging buses were hemmed in on all sides by the private motorcar, the delivery van, and the lorry.

Their turnaround times took longer, distorting their timetables; they could no longer maintain a schedule essential to the commuter. The only answer seemed to be to provide buses with their own dedicated right of way; confined to their own part of the road – just as trams and the trolleybuses had once enjoyed…

The Northern Busway

An express bus service, the Northern Express, had been operating between Albany and the CBD "…since November 2005, carrying some 58,000 passengers a month and resulting in 500 fewer cars on the road…" By February 2008, the service was "…operating every five minutes during peak times and every 10 minutes inter-peak and from 8am to 6pm on weekends." [782]

Because of the popularity of the service, it was a logical route for the city's first dedicated busway which opened on 2 February 2008.

A description of the service and the history of its conception was told by Lucy Vickers in a North Shore Times article published on 7 February 2008:

"This week marks a milestone in the history of New Zealand transport. After 20 years of planning and $300 million in the making the North Shore Busway system is now up and running. Thousands of Aucklanders attended the opening of the country's first two-way bus road by Prime Minister Helen Clark and Transit New Zealand acting chairman Bryan Jackson…

"The route, which runs parallel to State Highway 1 from Constellation Drive to the harbour bridge, will mean faster travel for commuters and less congestion. Two hundred and fifty buses an hour are predicted to use it once it is fully operational, taking 2400 cars off the road in peak traffic.

"There are five new stations along the 6.24km road, and for the first time passengers will be able to buy one ticket which they can use to transfer to other buses. The modern busway stations include lifts, electronic signs providing minute by minute updates, audio assistance posts and 24-hour video monitoring…

"The plan was first conceived in the 1980s and an agreement signed in 2001. Endorsed by former North Shore mayor George Wood during his leadership, it was designed, built and managed by Transit New Zealand…The busway's completion is due to the collaboration of North Shore City Council, Auckland Regional Transport Authority, Auckland Regional and Auckland City Councils…

"With Auckland's burgeoning population, central government has recognised the need for improvements to Auckland's public transport system and gave $210 million towards the busway…" [783]

Inexplicable Change

However, reminiscent of Auckland's history of not fully completing a transport project, the new busway lacked integration with connecting services, many of which were inexplicably discontinued or re-routed when the busway opened – as reported on 20 February 2008 by Rebecca Lewis of The Aucklander:

"A new busway has frustrated North Shore commuters who are shredding their bus passes and instead reaching for their car keys…patrons catching buses from Takapuna, Milford and surrounding areas report long delays in their journeys since the busway opened. A number of services from suburban streets have been discontinued or re-routed, leaving just a handful of buses to catch directly to the city. Buses travelling along Esmonde Road to the motorway have been re-directed through the new Akoranga station, a route which turns the buses back on themselves, adding another five to 10 minutes to the entire journey…" [784]

A month after the opening, little had changed, according to The Aucklander's Edward Rooney:

"A full one month after the Northern Busway was launched with great fanfare, the jury remains out on whether it will succeed…The $300 million bus corridor…has yet to sway interested observers such as Will Wilson.

"'The planners have focused on a transit corridor, but there's still the issue of the feeder routes,' he says. 'The congestion is in the feeder areas and there appears to be no solution to that.' Mr Wilson is an advocate of personal rapid transport…He says there is still no solution to North Shore's greatest congestion challenge – the huge number of commuters on the west side of the motorway.

"'Most of the people likely to catch a bus are on the west side of the city and they are still on the same roads and the same routes as before the busway opened,' he says. 'And they still have to get through the choke-point on the bridge.' Mr Wilson says the transit corridor may prove popular but congestion will remain a fact of everyday life for North Shore people until an entire network is devised for feeder routes and major arterials." [785]

Penalised Commuters

Those commuters who could not catch a convenient bus ride to one of the busway stations and decided to drive there instead, were soon disillusioned by the lack of forward planning and penalised accordingly – as reported by the North Shore Times:

"More than 50 vehicles were ticketed and 22 towed from Albany park and ride station in one day as the council clamped down on illegal parking…Building new carparks at the Albany bus station to ease parking problems would be too costly, says North Shore City Council. The council has already extended carparking but it's now filling up again between 7am to 8am on weekdays…" [786]

Record Patronage

Nevertheless, despite some inconvenience, the mass popularity of the new conveyance to and from the North Shore and the CBD soon resembled that experienced with the opening of the Harbour Bridge – as reported by the North Shore Times on 22 July 2008:

"Record patronage is providing icing on the $300 million Northern Busway cake. From February to May, 858,682 passengers were carried on express buses running exclusively on the busway, says North Shore City Council infrastructure and environment committee chairman Ken McKay.

"Mr McKay says this is a 48 per cent increase over the same period last year. In May alone bus patronage was up by 78 per cent compared to the same period in 2007. He says the busway's efficiency and reliability can best be appreciated during morning and evening peak hours when buses speed past the crawling traffic on the northern motorway…" [787]

Onewa Road Interchange

In order to separate the busway lanes from the Northern Motorway's general traffic and allow the express buses unimpeded access south to the Harbour Bridge, some upgrade to the Onewa Road Interchange was essential. This upgrade was officially opened on 21 November 2008:

"Tomorrow's opening of the $40m Onewa Road Interchange upgrade signals the completion of the Northern Busway project. The new Onewa Rd interchange adds 2.5 kilometres of single bus lane from the Exmouth footbridge to the Auckland Harbour Bridge. The completed interchange incorporates two new ramps separating motorway traffic travelling to and from Onewa Rd, to improve safety for motorists. The upgrade – a NZ Transport Agency project – complements work being undertaken by North Shore City Council to widen Onewa Rd and extend the High Occupancy Vehicle lane from Lake Rd." [788]

Central Connector Bus Lane Project

Amid some obvious objection from motorists, dedicated bus lanes began to impinge upon their road space throughout the city:

"Auckland has a slowly growing network of bus lanes: in Auckland City there were 27 km in 2008. The Central Connector bus lane project, which started construction in the middle of 2008, is expected to substantially improve links between Newmarket and the inner city, while bus lanes are also planned on Remuera Road and St Johns Road to connect the city with the Eastern Bays suburbs." [789]

Your Region, Your Future

In April 2008, the Auckland Regional Council launched a draft Annual Plan for 2008/2009. Entitled *Your Region, Your Future*, the draft plan also included amendments to the Council's previously-released ten-year plan.

By way of an introduction, Council chairman, Mike Lee, wrote:

"This is one of the most significant ARC annual plans in a generation. With the support of the public we intend to build an electric rail system for Auckland. It would be part of a region wide network with better bus and ferry services. People will be able to get around on one smartcard ticket. We can achieve this in the next few years if we close the public transport funding gap. With the support of a regional fuel tax we will buy a fleet of new, quieter and faster electric trains, as part of wide-ranging improvements to train, bus and ferry services, in time for the Rugby World Cup in 2011…" [790]

The publication elaborated on the transport aspect of the plan:

"Public Transport – Delivering a fast, efficient and reliable public transport system continues to be a central focus. Our objective is for electric trains to be running within five years, ideally over the core part of the network by 2011. This, along with a stronger network of quality bus and ferry services, supported by smartcard ticketing, will counter congestion and pollution.

"The ever-increasing number of vehicles on our roads frustrates motorists, causes pollution and makes it harder to do business and get to work and home again. The Northern Busway, new motorway links and record numbers of rail passengers have created momentum in the transport sector, and we have now reached the point where replacing our ageing diesel trains with fast, clean, quiet electric units will be cheaper in the longer term.

"The question facing the region is whether the ARC should raise significant loans, to be repaid using a proposed new regional fuel tax, to accelerate train, bus and ferry projects. This would enable public transport patronage to be doubled within a decade. Loan repayments would be spread over 30 years and be covered through a regional fuel tax of five cents a litre. The Government may collect up to a further five cents in Auckland to fund its share of electrification and for roading…" [791]

Promises, Promises

Unfortunately for the Auckland Regional Council and its transport plans, 2008 was another election year – another year when promises of action were just promises and any action taken depended on which political party was eventually elected to govern. The subject of promises was included in a New Zealand Herald article published on 30 April 2008:

"Political doubt emerging over regional fuel taxes will not deprive Aucklanders of electric trains, says National Party transport spokesman Maurice Williamson. The Pakuranga MP and former National transport minister yesterday echoed the reservations of his leader, John Key, about the desirability of new fuel taxes at a time of spiralling living costs – notably of food and petrol.

"But Mr Williamson insisted that if National won this year's election, there would be no shortage of alternative ways to pay for Auckland's $1 billion rail electrification project. These could include raising money through infrastructure bonds, or electrifying the network as a public-private partnership, a device the Government is considering for the $1.9 billion Waterview motorway tunnels…

"Mr Key said…that a possible 25c added to the price of a litre of petrol…would be 'too high for the average consumer to bear.'

"That warning came as the Auckland Regional Council consults ratepayers on a 5c regional fuel tax to cover its half-share of rail electrification, to which the Government could add a further 5c to underwrite the rest of the project while also contributing to the Waterview tunnels and the 'Penlink' toll road to Whangaparaoa Peninsula.

"The council will start hearing submissions on May 19 on its plan to tax motorists from January 1, ready for a core fleet of electric trains to be running for the 2011 Rugby World Cup, as an alternative to raising rates by 17 per cent for each of 10 years to plug a $700 million public transport funding gap…

"Regional council chairman Mike Lee said his organisation shared concerns about the burden of rising fuel prices, but it highlighted the importance of providing a strong public transport system. 'It is absolutely the highest priority to provide a decent public transport alternative.'

"Although he said the Government had done more for Auckland transport than any of its predecessors 'in living memory', he was reasonably confident a National Administration would keep the electrification ball rolling.

"One cannot assume anything, but if a National Government were to allow the electrification of Auckland rail to collapse for the third time in 50 years, I think there would be a major backlash. Especially so while Aucklanders would see a whole brand new fleet of electric trains being purchased in Wellington right now and 90 per cent paid for by the Government…" [792]

The Burden of Deregulation

As well as the uncertainty of relying on the National Party's political undertakings, the Auckland Regional Council and its Transport Authority laboured under the burden of the public transport deregulation imposed in 1989. The effects of this burden were best explained by Paul Mees in his 2010 article, *Transport for Suburbia: Beyond the Automobile Age*:

"It was similar problems in Auckland [as in Britain] that finally led to the repeal of bus deregulation in New Zealand. The Auckland Regional Transport Authority (ARTA) led the charge after receiving a report from its marketing consultants outlining the impossibility of 'selling' uncoordinated public transport. The consultants cut through the ideological rhetoric about choice to explain what competition really means for passengers:

"Jack is waiting for a bus home at the bus stop. He hasn't come to this bus stop before and only catches the bus at odd times, but his car is at the panel beater and he thought he would give it a go. A bus

arrives, but it is yellow and red, and the one he knows is purple. So he waits, but he notices that this bus has the same destination as where he is going but is unsure what route it actually takes. Three more buses arrive, they are different colours, one has Company 1 name but it has green advertising on it, and he knows his bus is purple. He also notices as the bus pulls away that the number corresponds to his normal route. So he asks a fellow traveller what bus he should catch and they suggest…numbers 027, 028, 025, 31, or 37…Very soon after that a nearly empty number 31 arrives, he boards and presents his ticket however the bus driver says they don't accept that ticket – he is an ABB bus and that is a company 1 ticket. Jack despondently gets off and waits another 30 minutes for his purple bus…the next day he collects his car from the panel beater and tells his friends about the nightmare he had trying to get home last night." [205]

Public Transport Management Act 2008

The Public Transport Management Act 2008 which was passed on 25 September 2008 and came into force on 1 January 2009, restored control of public transport to the regional councils:

"(1) The purpose of this Act is to contribute to the aim of achieving an affordable, integrated, safe, responsive, and sustainable land transport system.

"(2) To contribute to this purpose, this Act—

(a) confers powers on regional councils to set standards for commercial public transport services provided in their regions; and

(b) provides for and regulates the registration of commercial public transport services; and

(c) confers powers on regional councils to require all or any public transport services in their regions to be provided under contract with them, and consequently to discontinue any commercial public transport services provided in their regions that are subject to such a requirement; and

(d) helps regional councils and the [NZ Transport] Agency obtain the best value for money in achieving an affordable, integrated, safe, responsive, and sustainable public transport system, having regard to the desirability of encouraging fair competition and a competitive and efficient market for public transport services..." [793]

Regional Public Transport Plan

However, control also required planning and the new Act required any regional council that might:

"(a) enter into any contract for the supply of any public transport service:

"(b) impose any controls on commercial public transport services:

"(c) impose any contracting requirement:

"(d) provide any financial assistance to any operator or user of -

(i) a taxi service:

(ii) a shuttle service.

"…to adopt a regional public transport plan that must describe:

"(i) the public transport services that the regional council proposes to be provided in its region, and may include (but is not limited to) a statement or description of routes, capacity, times, and frequency of services; and

"(ii) any taxi services or shuttle services for which it intends to provide financial assistance; and "(iii) how the public transport services and any services referred to in subparagraph (ii) will assist the transport disadvantaged; and

"(iv) how the plan gives effect to the public transport service components of the regional land transport strategy that applies to the regional council's region…" [793]

Political Doubt

As the November 2008 election drew near, the doubt that the National Party would keep its transport promises increased – with good reason, wrote Brian Rudman in a New Zealand Herald column published 24 October 2008:

"National's intentions on tolling are part of the credibility gap in the party's plans for Auckland transport infrastructure. With only two weeks of the election campaign left, Auckland voters need some detail to go with the rhetoric…A year ago, Mr Key told the Road Transport Forum conference that 'National is not averse to using tolls on occasion to help pay for major roading projects, particularly where there is private sector involvement in financing. But he is yet to spell out details…Aucklanders deserve to know what, if any, further tolling experiments National has up its sleeve for us.

"In the back of many minds is National's poor record of transport funding in Auckland in the 1990s. Between November 1993 and November 1999, when Mr Williamson was Transport Minister for all but one year, only 25 per cent of Transit NZ's money was spent north of Pukekohe, despite just under 40 per cent of the population living here. Urban Auckland was short-changed around $50 million a year over that period, to subsidise extra lanes of tarmac through National's rural voter heartland.

"The other area of fuzziness is public transport, and in particular, the on-going funding of the electrification of the Auckland commuter network and the proposed line to the airport. National has expressed opposition to the 10c-a-litre regional fuel tax being levied on Aucklanders to fund local transport projects, but has come up with no alternative. If they have one, I'd be as keen to see the tax go as anyone. Should we read their silence on this as ominous or not? What also is their attitude to the proposed underground inner-city loop?

"Battlers for electrification recall how Sir Dove-Myer Robinson's earlier rapid rail network got the green light from the Kirk Labour Government in 1975, only to be thrown out in 1976 by the incoming National Government of Robert Muldoon. Mr Key is too young to remember such things, but there are many who do. They worry National will revert to type. As long as Mr Key remains mum on these details, so do I." [794]

Regional Fuel Tax Cancelled

As usual, another election proved a hindrance to the advancement of the best laid plans and, as anticipated by Brian Rudman and others with long memories, the National Government did not disappoint following its win at the polls. The proposed regional fuel tax, intended to fund Auckland's transport priorities, was the first to go – as announced in a press release by the Minister of Transport, Steven Joyce, on 17 March 2009:

"Transport Minister Steven Joyce says the government will not proceed with regional fuel taxes, which are an 'expensive and inefficient' means of collecting revenue. Regional Fuel Taxes will be partially replaced by smaller increases in national fuel taxes.

"The previous Labour-led government approved a regional fuel tax for Auckland, rising from 2 cents per litre in July to 9.5 cents per litre in two years' time. Auckland road users would have been taxed at that rate for 30 years. This was in addition to national increases in fuel taxes scheduled by the previous government of 1.5 cents per litre for the next three years. The total tax increase by 2011 would have been 14 cents per litre for Aucklanders.

"A number of other regions (Canterbury, Bay of Plenty, Waikato and Wellington) were also considering, or beginning to consider, the implementation of regional fuel taxes to provide additional funding for local transport projects. Mr Joyce says the government is opposed to regional taxes of almost 10 cents in Auckland or anywhere else. 'Regional taxes impose significant compliance costs to businesses and road users, and would result in much higher fuel prices for motorists in some regions. Our preference is for a simpler system which delivers benefits to road users across the board.'

"From 1 October this year motorists will pay an increase of 3 cents per litre in fuel excise duty and drivers of diesel vehicles will pay the equivalent in road user charges. A second 3 cents increase will occur at October 1 next year. Each 3 cent per litre increase includes an annual increase of 1.5 cents per litre scheduled by the previous government.

"Mr Joyce says these smaller adjustments to roading excise and road user charges across New Zealand will make more funding available for roading across the country. Projects that were to be funded out of regional fuel taxes will, for the most part, continue as planned – the difference will be in how they will be funded. The electrification of Auckland's trains will proceed." [795]

Disruption Causes Immediate Problems

The best laid plans of the Auckland region were certainly disrupted this time – as reported by The New Zealand Herald on 19 March 2009:

"Auckland's regional nest egg has taken a $50 million hit on investments at a time of deep funding uncertainty for key public transport projects...Positive returns from the organisation's wholly owned port company, other property holdings and short-term cash deposits softened the overall loss on its $1.15 billion of regional assets to $22.4 million in the six months to December.

"But the result could not have come at a worse time for the council, given that a decision to draw $155 million from the holding company this year for public transport and stormwater improvements was made in expectation of raising a regional fuel tax in July to protect its long-term asset base.

"That plan is in disarray with the Government's sudden decision to discard the tax, which was to have risen from 2c to 9.5c a litre by 2011, in favour of a national fuel excise increase of 3c in October and 3c next year.

"Although the Government has promised to foot the full bill for Auckland's $1 billion-plus rail electrification project, instead of leaving the regional council to pay $508 million for new electric trains, it has yet to offer any funding guarantees for $202 million of other public transport infrastructure reliant on the tax...

"Council chief executive Peter Winder yesterday told the Auckland Regional Transport Committee that the most immediate problems 'pushing right in our face' were two big contracts signed in expectation of the fuel tax. These were for the $35 million Newmarket station, for which a payment of $15.4 million falls due on July 1, as does a $32.8 million instalment for refurbished diesel trains needed to cope with booming rail patronage before the arrival of electric units.

"The Government has acknowledged that its intervention may even delay electrification by at least six months, putting in doubt a target of completing that project by 2013 and the regional council's hope of laying on some electric trains in time for the 2011 Rugby World Cup...

"Regional chairman Mike Lee has told Transport Minister Steven Joyce...The loss of the fuel tax left the council in an invidious position, as it would take a 15 per cent additional rates rise to plug the $202 million capital funding cap without substantial Government assistance...

"In a separate meeting yesterday, the Auckland Regional Transport Committee reported an 8.9 per cent rise in public patronage in the six months to December 31 over the same half of last year, to 28.8 million trips.

"That included a 15 per cent rise in rail patronage, a 94 per cent increase in the Northern Express service boosted by the new busway, and 7.8 per cent more trips taken on other buses." [796]

Northern Busway Birthday

The Northern Busway had been operating for one year on 2 February 2009 and its success was praised by the Auckland Regional Transport Authority – as reported by the North Shore Times:

"The $300 million northern busway has created dramatic boosts in commuter bus patronage on the North Shore says the Auckland Regional Transport Authority...Patronage rose by 86 percent in 2008 to 1.3 million passengers...There are 88 buses using the busway in the morning peak between 7.30am and 8.30am. Improvements to the feeder services have also resulted in significantly increased patronage, growing to 322,712, a 46 percent increase, last year...

"It is owned jointly by the New Zealand Transport Agency, the Auckland Regional Transport Authority and the North Shore and Auckland city councils. Bus operators that use the busway include Ritchies Transport, North Star and Birkenhead Transport. The busway partners have recently allowed airport shuttle services run by Super Shuttle and North Shore Shuttles to use the busway..." [797]

National Fuel Tax

Despite the overwhelming success of the public transport initiative represented by the Northern Busway, the Government's emphasis remained firmly focused on roading infrastructure – as demonstrated by the Minister of Transport's confirmation of the national fuel tax and road user charges increase taking effect on 1 October 2009:

"Transport Minister Steven Joyce says increases in fuel excise duty (FED) and Road User Charges (RUC) which come into force tomorrow will bring benefits to all New Zealanders through better roading and public transport networks. The 3 cent per litre increase includes an annual increase of 1.5 cents per litre scheduled by the previous government. The additional 1.5 cents partially replaces previously planned regional fuel taxes.

"Mr Joyce says the increases will flow into the hypothecated National Land Transport Fund and assist investment in transport projects throughout the country. 'The additional revenue from these increases will contribute to the billion dollars that will now be spent on our state highway infrastructure each year. That ongoing investment is crucial in assisting economic growth and will enable greater productivity to be gained from the transport network...'" [798]

New Regional Transport Authority Proposed

When it delivered its report to the Governor-General on 25 March 2009, the Royal Commission of Inquiry on Auckland Governance proposed a number of changes to Auckland's regional transport management – including the establishment of a new transport authority to replace ARTA:

"The perceived deficiencies of governance for roading and public transport in Auckland loomed large in the submissions made to the Commission and in other material supplied to it by a variety of individuals and organisations.

"The primary objective of the Commission's recommendations is to bring all elements of transport, including roading, rail, public transport, and planning for pedestrians and cyclists, under the management of one body, which would be a council-controlled organisation owned by the proposed Auckland Council.

"More than 25% of all submitters mentioned transport issues...The majority of them considered there were problems with transport governance. The main concerns with governance were lack of integration between transport modes, slow decision making for upgrades to the system, and what was seen as the complicated and chaotic nature of current arrangements...A common complaint was that there were too many disparate organisations involved in transport decisions…" [766]

A Situation Analysis

A transport 'Situation Analysis' by Barry Mein of CityScope Consultants included as part of the Commission's report, concluded:

"Many of the governance issues that have been identified in Auckland have related to the lack of an adequate connection between decision-making and funding powers. It is important that this dimension is not overlooked in any future governance arrangements.

"Structural changes are of value only if they are linked to effective implementation and funding tools. For Auckland, this should include consideration of the following:

- the potential to consolidate transport rates into a single charge
- the desirability for future governance arrangements to incorporate new revenue sources, including regional fuel taxes, tolling, and road pricing
- the potential for central government funding arrangements to be delegated to the region in future, possibly through some form of 'bulk funding' for transport." [799]

New Transport Agency Confirmed

On 26 August 2009, the Transport Minister, Steven Joyce, announced:

"The government has confirmed that a new agency will be established to focus on delivering transport projects and services across Auckland. Transport Minister Steven Joyce says the new Auckland Transport Agency will replace the current nine separate Auckland transport entities and will be responsible for all local authority transport delivery functions in Auckland, including local roads and public transport...

"The Auckland Council will set the strategic direction, appoint the transport directors, including up to two Councillors, provide planning guidance and determine the levels of regionally sourced funding.

"The governance structure of the Auckland Transport Agency will be incorporated in the third Auckland Governance Bill to be introduced later this year..." [800]

Deckchair Shuffling

However, more was needed, and quickly, according to the Auckland Regional Council chairman, Mike Lee, who responded:

"...the region didn't need a new agency, it needed the money to get on with providing transport – particularly an electrified rail network...'My message to the transport minister is as simple as this. If you are serious about improving Auckland public transport, provide the money for electrification & electric trains that you promised us by July, after the Government did away with the regional fuel tax in March.

"'The clock is ticking. Increases in public transport use in Auckland cannot be sustained without investment in electrification and electric trains. We do not need more bureaucratic deckchair shuffling. That will achieve nothing. What we need urgently is the Government to invest in electrification and electric trains as promised.

"'There is no logic to the current gameplaying by the Government. If it is not going to honour its commitment to help fund electrification and electric trains, it should let the people of Auckland know now. Auckland commuters need electric trains, not yet another bureaucracy with a fancy name.'" [801]

Increases in Public Transport Use

"Mike Lee's assertion that *increases in public transport use in Auckland cannot be sustained without investment*...was supported by the numbers:

"Aucklanders took 58.6 million trips on public transport in the year to 30 June 2009, a 7.7 per cent increase on the year before, according to annual figures from Auckland Regional Transport Authority...Not only are more people taking public transport, the rate of uptake is increasing. That 7.7 per cent is better than the 4.4 per cent growth in 2008, which improved on the 2 per cent in 2007 and 1 per cent in 2006..." [802]

Petrol Price Rises

Much of the increased patronage of public transport could be explained by sudden increases in petrol prices and/or improved services. Whatever the reason, the additional passengers were often difficult to accommodate – as observed by John McCrystal:

"From 2002 petrol prices began a sharp rise...By April 2006 premium grade petrol had broken through the $1.70 per litre mark, and there was every indication that it could go higher still...It seemed the shadows were growing longer in the day of the private automobile. In ten short years, buses had begun to look less like the urban transit mode of the future as the mode best suited to the nation's present needs. The urban bus industry found itself embarrassed by sharply increased patronage: there were too few buses to cope with the sudden demand. History is as adept at throwing up ironies as it is at running in circles." [144]

Separate Transport Planning

While the Royal Commission and/or Government recommendations were still to be implemented, former North Shore Mayor, George Wood, outlined the various separate transport plans being considered in November 2009:

"Auckland is at the crossroads in relation to transport planning with major plans for change in the melting pot...Three plans are being consulted upon that will result in a blueprint for the future of transport across the region. It is interesting that three different organisations, namely the Auckland Regional Council, Auckland Regional Transport Agency and the New Zealand Transport Agency, are completing these plans.

"The three consultation documents are:

"Auckland Regional Land Transport Strategy (RLTS). This is a revamp on a strategy completed in 2005. It puts far greater emphasis on public transport spending. The preferred strategy includes the CBD rail loop, rail to Auckland airport, extending the Northern Busway to Orewa, better bus connections in the Westgate and Manukau/Botany areas, integrated public transport ticketing and more frequent public transport services…

"New Zealand Transport Agency Draft NZTA farebox recovery policy consultation document. This document looks at ways of capping spending on public transport. The Auckland region spends nearly $100 million a year on subsidising bus, ferry and metro rail services. This study sets out facts and figures on how we may get better value for money from this overlay…

"The Auckland Regional Transport Agency is preparing a draft public transport management plan. This plan will be released by ARTA in the next couple of weeks. It will deal with all aspects of public transport including value for money and changes in how the ratepayers purchase bus, rail and ferry services from the various operators. This is a first time for this document." [803]

Integrated Ticketing

The changes to public transport ticket purchases referred to by George Wood were another element of public transport use to be developed and funded as an integrated ticketing system. As described by Paul Mees et al. in their research report for the NZTA, *Public Transport Network Planning: a guide to best practice in NZ cities*:

"There was a bewildering array of tickets available for travel on public transport in Auckland. Veolia issued one set of tickets solely for train travel, and nine separate sets of bus tickets were offered by the various private operators. Free transfers between services were generally limited to those run by a single operator. Almost all fares were based on distance, with up to eight fare stages, except for the Northern Busway, which offered time-based tickets. Most tickets were paper, although some 'smart' tickets were available – chiefly as means to store value for multiple trips on the services of a single operator." [804]

Funding Approved

A start could be made on streamlining a public transport ticketing system after funding was approved on 2 November 2009:

"The NZ Transport Agency approved funding yesterday to develop an integrated ticketing & fares system for Auckland's train, bus and ferry users. The chairman of ARTA (the Auckland Regional Transport Authority), Rabin Rabindran, said this meant the authority could move to finalise contract negotiations with its preferred tenderer, a consortium made up of French electronics company Thales SA in partnership with the Bank of New Zealand and Transfield Services (NZ) Pty Ltd. He expected that to happen this month." [805]

Contract Signed

Those contract negotiations were soon finalised – as reported by the North Shore Times on 5 January 2010:

"The Auckland Regional Transport Authority, the Auckland Regional Council and the New Zealand Transport Agency have signed a $47 million contract with the Thales group to deliver a 'super transport ticket for Auckland'. The authority's chairman Rabin Rabindran says it will be New Zealand's first integrated smart card system boasting superior, state-of-the-art technology." [806]

Fare Increases

In the meantime, with or without 'super tickets', fare increases were on the way – as reported by The New Zealand Herald on 23 December 2009:

"Auckland rail passengers can expect average fare rises of up to 7 per cent in February, but bus patrons are likely to face more modest increases. The Auckland Regional Transport Authority yesterday confirmed it had resolved to raise rail fares by an average of 5 per cent to 7 per cent, after three years without an increase.

"Chief Executive Fergus Gammie also acknowledges that his board had approved an average increase of 2 per cent to 3 per cent to the maximum fare scheduled for subsidised bus services. That was 'to recognise recent cost movements and to permit the fare differential between bus and rail to be closed'. But although bus passengers pay an average of 14 per cent more than rail users, Mr Gammie said it would take some years to close the gap under a new 'zonal' fare system to be introduced after the arrival of an integrated public transport ticket across Auckland in 2011…

"A maximum schedule for ferries will remain unchanged, as the transport authority says there is still room within that envelope for operators to increase fares should they choose. None of that uncertainty faces rail passengers, as the authority has direct control over fares collected by train operator Veolia Transport.

"Authority chairman Rabin Rabindran said there was 'never a good time to have a fare increase' but stressed that rail or bus fares had not gone up for three years. In that time, bus operating costs had risen 11.7 per cent compared with inflation of 7.8 per cent, and rail running expenses were up 11 per cent…" [807]

Auckland International Airport

As the decade drew to a close and ARTA and other transport agencies completed their planning studies, one of the apparently least-considered transport hubs voiced its concerns:

"Auckland International Airport Limited called on regional transport planners today to accelerate improvements to airport-related public transport services, including the eventual provision of an airport rail link.

"In its submission to the Auckland Regional Council on the draft Auckland regional land transport strategy, the airport company said plans for a rapid transport network link to the airport, whether rail or some other intermediate step, should be accelerated and ideally put in place before 2020. The draft strategy proposes an airport rail connection in the 2031-40 timeframe.

"Auckland Airport said public transport services should be upgraded in the shorter term to quality transit network standards, such as dedicated bus lanes, to provide an appropriate connection to the airport from both the cbd and the North Shore…

"Auckland Airport said public transport connections to the airport were weak by international comparisons and, as a consequence, patronage was low. Although improvements were being made to Airport Express bus services, service quality was hampered by wide variances in travel times due to traffic congestion.

"The airport company's property general manager, Peter Alexander, said: 'We've made this submission as an advocate for the millions of travellers who fly into and out of Auckland Airport each year, the thousands of airport workers who commute on a daily basis, and the hundreds of companies that reside within or rely on the airport business district…'

"Mr Alexander said pleasing progress was being made on better roading infrastructure, such as the State Highway 20 upgrade & the second Manukau Harbour crossing, but more needed to be done in the area of public transport." [808]

Road Transport
New Transport Funding
In their paper, *Backtracking Auckland: Bureaucratic rationality and public preferences in transport planning*, Paul Mees and Jago Dodson outlined part of the transport situation existing at the turn of the new century:

"A Labour national government was elected in 1999 following nine years of conservative National party rule. Labour initially appeared supportive of improvements to Auckland's public transport and funded an $81 million buy-back of Auckland's privatised rail rights-of-way in 2002. But Labour was vulnerable to pressure from the road lobby in the lead-up to the 2002 national elections, especially after the election of John Banks as Mayor in late 2001.

"Roads in New Zealand were historically financed through hypothecation of petrol excise and road user charges into a National Roads Fund, which was disbursed by the National Roads Board and its successors Transit New Zealand (1989-1996) and Transfund (1996-2002). The decisions over which projects to fund are left to un-elected officials to avoid the 'porkbarelling' of transport expenditure by politicians.

"This arrangement is unusual internationally, and the historical disbursement of the excise funds by road agency officials has produced a strong inbuilt incentive for further road construction. However, the cost of Auckland's 1999 RLTS [Regional Land Transport Strategy] motorway and public transport program exceeded petrol excise revenue. Labour responded to business and political pressure with a new funding package that provided an additional $94 million for Auckland's roads with $30 million for public transport, paid from increases to petrol excise..." [231]

National Roading Programmes Continue
As previously noted, the Land Transport Management Act 2003 included a number of environmentally-responsible measures to appease Labour's coalition partners, the Green Party. However, Section 97 of the Act also provided for a continuation of the existing national roading programmes:

"(1) The national roading programme in effect under section *42A* of the Transit New Zealand Act 1989 immediately before the commencement of this section continues to have effect as a national land transport programme under this Act.

"(2) Every State highways programme, regional programme, and district roading programme under Part III of the Transit New Zealand Act 1989 that was in effect immediately before the commencement of this section continues to have effect as a land transport programme under this Act." [749]

The Section 42A of the Transit New Zealand Act 1989 referred to, was included in a 1995 Amendment Act:

"(I) In each year, the Board [Transfund New Zealand] shall approve a national roading programme for the next year, which shall include-

"(a) Those outputs and capital projects recommended in the State highways programme, the regional programmes, and the district roading programmes forwarded to the Board under this Act that the Board considers should be included in the national roading programme; and

"(b) The proposed funding of those outputs and capital projects for that financial year." [738]

Road Tolling

Sections 46 to 55 of the Land Transport Management Act 2003 also provided for a public road controlling authority to establish a road tolling scheme on new roads, or an existing road or part, if it:

"*…is located near, and is physically or operationally integral to, the new road in respect of which the tolling revenue will be applied.*"

No doubt in anticipation of some public opposition, the Act also required that, prior to the introduction of any such tolling scheme:

"…there is a high degree of support from affected communities…there is available to road users a feasible, untolled, alternative route." [749]

Road Tolling Extolled

The tolling of roads was a solution eagerly extolled by then leader of the opposition National Party, Don Brash, during a speech to the Auckland Chamber of Commerce on 21 May 2004:

"Over time, we should move away from heavy dependence on property taxes, excise taxes on petrol & road user charges towards greater use of tolls, which would vary depending on the road and the time of day. Indeed, there should eventually be scope to reduce both rates & excise taxes on petrol as tolls are introduced, so that the net fiscal effect of introducing tolls is neutral.

"Modern toll roads are not like the toll roads of the past. There will be no fossicking for coins or lengthy queues at toll booths. Most new toll roads around the world are already fully electronic, and the user, by way of an identification tag, is billed for using the road. In most cases, the tolls are of the order of $2 or $3, and represent a small fraction of what the motorist currently pays by way of long delays & heavy fuel use.

"Using tolls has, in fact, 3 advantages. First, if well designed, tolls can encourage road users to use roads at times when there is less congestion, or take alternative forms of transport, such as buses and ferries. Secondly, tolls can support borrowing to provide additional funds for road construction. And thirdly, tolls make possible the participation of private capital in road construction, as happens increasingly overseas…" [809]

The Congestion Question

"In March 2004, Cabinet requested that the Ministry investigate the feasibility and desirability of road pricing and parking levies in Auckland. The request resulted in the Auckland Road Pricing Evaluation Study 2006, which explored the economic and social impacts of several alternative schemes.

"A further phase of the work, the Auckland Road Pricing Study 2008, evaluated two specific road pricing schemes and used feedback from a submissions process in Auckland to assess the public response to regionalised road pricing.

"The Ministry of Transport's Auckland Road Pricing Evaluation Study 2006 and Auckland Road Pricing Study 2008 examine road pricing as a means of reducing congestion and raising revenue for investment in land transport. The study examines several alternative schemes. These were developed to provide enough information to help decide if any work on road pricing should be progressed. The study makes no recommendations on whether road pricing should be introduced in Auckland; its function is to present information and data for politicians, members of the public and stakeholders to consider." [810]

Auckland Road Pricing Evaluation Study 2006

The Ministry of Transport published a summary of its first evaluation study on 21 March 2006 – parts of which included:

"The Ministry of Transport's *Auckland Road Pricing Evaluation Study* examines road pricing and parking levies as a means of reducing congestion and raising revenue for investment in land transport. The study examines several alternative schemes. These were developed to provide enough information to help decide if any work on road pricing should be progressed...

"The underlying causes of congestion in Auckland are varied: low density development, regional growth, geographical and capacity constraints, limited public transport and a high reliance on private vehicles all play a part. Auckland's geography, particularly its harbours and waterways, impose constraints on the transport system. This means the main transport links are confined to narrow corridors. For many trips, few alternatives are available and providing new routes or additional capacity has significant financial, environmental and community costs.

"The schemes were developed to provide enough information to help decide if work on road pricing in Auckland should be progressed. They do not represent any firm proposal and there is no recommended scheme resulting from this study. The scheme designs attempt to balance congestion reduction, revenue raising and social, economic and environmental impacts. The charges between schemes therefore vary significantly and this also affects the outcomes.

"Five schemes were tested in this study:

"Single Cordon – This scheme would charge vehicles travelling into Auckland that cross a single, defined cordon: essentially the Auckland isthmus. Vehicles travelling exclusively within the cordon would not be charged. Vehicles would be charged $6 at the Harbour Bridge or $3 at other charging points - the maximum charge would be $6 per day. The cordon would have a total of 15 charging points.

"Double Cordon – This scheme would charge vehicles that cross either of two cordon rings into Auckland. The western section of the outer cordon would fall inside the completed State Highway 20, otherwise it would follow the same boundary as the Single Cordon above. Travel that is entirely within either cordon would not be charged. Drivers would be charged $6 at the Harbour Bridge (where the cordons intersect) or $3 for crossing each of the two cordons. The maximum charge for this scheme is also $6 per day. This scheme would use 50 charging points.

"Area Charge – This scheme would charge all vehicles entering or travelling within a defined area: the Auckland city CBD and inner suburbs. (The Area Charge scheme is similar to the London Congestion Charging Scheme.) Trips would be charged at $5 (this would also be the maximum charge per day).

"Strategic Network – The Strategic Network scheme would charge congested links of the motorways and some limited access arterial roads would be charged. Motorists would be charged per kilometre travelled up to a maximum of $6 per day. Uncongested links would be free of charge.

"Parking Levy – This scheme would charge for parking on both public and private property (e.g. parking buildings or businesses) within the Auckland/Newmarket, Manukau, Henderson and Takapuna CBDs. The charges modelled were $10 per day, in addition to any parking charges already in place. The scheme is similar to Wellington's Coupon Parking scheme, albeit more comprehensive, as private and public car parks would be required to pay the charge." [811]

Road Pricing v Road Tolls

Following publication of the 2006 Road Pricing Evaluation Study, the Ministry of Transport's principal adviser, Chris Money, explained that there was a difference between the two concepts of road pricing and road tolls:

"The very term road pricing is different from tolls, says Money. The concept of tolling is paying for new infrastructure or maintenance but road use imposes more costs than just building and maintenance, e.g. there's congestion and other social costs.

"Road pricing encourages people to think about transport choices. Tolls facilitate building new infrastructure: there are significant differences. Road pricing is just another tool, like car-pooling, he says." [812]

Public Reaction

The public's reaction to the five possible schemes included in the March 2006 Auckland Road Pricing Evaluation Study was just as the 2003 Land Transport Management Act had anticipated. Objection to the suggested $6 bridge toll was particularly swift and prompted a flood of letters from angry readers of the North Harbour News, published 31 March 2006:

"The Transport Ministry must have consulted the Mafia before proposing this $6 tax. To ring-fence an entire city and a major section of State Highway One, knowing that the only way around is by sea or air charter, is equal to a protection racket…(Stanley T Kivell, Torbay)

"I have lived on Auckland's North Shore almost my whole life, and am now in my late 40s. I have put up with many acts of idiocy by government over the years, but never before have I been so offended as I have been recently by the proposal of a $6 harbour bridge toll…(Beth Wilford, Albany)

"I helped to pay for the bridge once, working in the city and commuting from Birkenhead through the 1960s when tolls were two shillings and sixpence per car each way. At the time that was 11 percent of my salary. Why should I pay for it a second time…? (Ian Bogue, Northcote)

"The proposed cordon tolling of Auckland's roads with the imposition of a $6 one-way bridge toll by the Greater Regional Auckland's Burglars (GRAB) is nothing more than the direct result of 40 years or so of little or no action in addressing the region's transport problems while the population over that self-same time grew by about 40 per cent…" (Hugh Nettleton, Castor Bay)" [813]

Road Users Respond

Many road-user organisations also responded to the Road Pricing Evaluation Study – as published by the April 2006 edition of Business to Business:

"The proposed tolling on existing Auckland roads to reduce congestion has the support of cartage firm, Tapper Transport. Director Simon Tapper says the only way to reduce congestion is to charge people travelling at peak hours. His firm, which operates about 45 trucks, will just pass on charges so in the medium to long term, it won't cost his business – rather, it will increase productivity. In the last five years, congestion has led to a 40 per cent loss of productivity, he says. But he acknowledges some companies are frightened to pass on charges, and might not be happy about the pricing options recently released in the Ministry of Transport report.

"National Road Carriers executive director, Bruce Reid, whose organisation is also a member of road lobby group Auckland Business Forum, considers the report a waste of money. Its proposal to toll existing roads for negligible revenue gain will only detract from the programme underway, he says. The priority should be completing State Highway 20 as fast as possible, to reduce volumes on SH 1. A toll won't affect congestion because there is no alternative. Any public transport alternatives are 15, 20 years away. I was so disappointed when I read this report. There was no recognition of commercial vehicles that deliver into the city. We would have to pass the cost on to customers. And in a competitive industry this would be hard to do and stay in business.

"New Zealand Council for Infrastructure Development chief executive, Stephen Selwood, says the best approach is to look at the long-term infrastructure needs of New Zealand first, then decide how best to fund transport services through a combination of tolls and petrol taxes, with tolls eventually replacing taxes. But he says new roads and some strategic existing roads could be tolled.

"The AA [Automobile Association] says tolling administration is expensive at $700-$900 million over 20 years. It doesn't support tolling existing roads and supports funding through infrastructure bonds.

"The NZ Business Council for Sustainable Development supports tolls to change people's behaviour but says money raised must go back into sustainable transport projects or it will be seen as a Government revenue earner." [812]

Initial Survey
The results of an initial Ministry of Transport survey was subsequently published by The New Zealand Herald on 24 April 2006:

"It's the simplest of five charging schemes being considered in the fightback against Auckland's crippling traffic congestion, but a parking levy looks the most unpopular and least effective option. Parking charges are the devil we know, as opposed to more exotic road-pricing schemes, but a Ministry of Transport study indicates high public resistance to a possible $10 surcharge on top of what motorists already pay. That compares with daily limits of $5 or $6 suggested for each of four road-pricing schemes also under consideration, including cordon tolling and charging motorists for driving within an almost 40sq km spread of central Auckland.

"Even without being told how much they may have to pay, 36 per cent of a surveyed 600 Aucklanders nominated a parking levy as their least preferred option. But 26 per cent deemed it their most preferred option, a paradox the ministry says may be because relatively few people would be affected and it was not seen as particularly effective.

"In a separate survey, only 20 per cent of 416 drivers said they would pay a $10 levy, against 22 per cent who would park outside chargeable zones and walk the rest of the way. Only 2 per cent would park outside the zones and catch a bus from there, although 21 per cent would switch to public transport for the entire journey." [814]

Ministry of Transport Survey

As well as those commenting publicly, many also took advantage of the opportunity to submit their opinions to the Ministry of Transport:

"The request for submissions on the discussion document resulted in over 800 replies from individuals and organisations. Approximately 75% of submissions were identified as being against or conditionally against road pricing either in principle or as a means of addressing Auckland traffic congestion.

"Approximately 78% of submissions were received from individuals, with the remainder coming from organisations and pro forma submissions.

"Submitters opposing road pricing pointed to the inadequate state of Auckland's public transport network, the lack of a 'ring road' to allow travel from south to north (and vice versa) without entering heavily congested areas, an aversion to the concept of road pricing on roads that have been fully funded (financially) through existing taxes, and the perceived unfair application of a flat pricing structure across all groups in society." [815]

Auckland Road Pricing Evaluation Study 2008

The Ministry of Transport produced its second Auckland Road Pricing Study in August 2008 – a part of which included:

"This Executive Summary Report summarises a series of analyses undertaken on the positive and negative impacts of the introduction of two hypothetical road-pricing schemes in Auckland. The analyses were undertaken to supplement and enhance the evaluation carried out for the Auckland Road Pricing Evaluation Study (ARPES 2006) in 2005/06.

"The Ministry's aim was to assess two different schemes that represented two very different approaches to pricing in Auckland; one with a clear focus on reducing peak-hour congestion and one focused on collecting revenue, but without any significant social or economic impacts...

"Congestion Scheme – the primary objective of the Congestion Scheme is to reduce congestion in Auckland during the morning peak period, with a particular focus on the Auckland Central area...The Congestion Scheme, as designed for this Report, is what is commonly referred to as an area scheme. This involves a charge when crossing the 'charging area' boundary as well as a charge for movement within the charging area.

"Revenue Scheme – the primary objective behind the design of the Revenue Scheme for this Report was to generate revenue for transport-related projects by charging users directly for using all or part of the transport system, but at the same time try to minimise or avoid negative social or economic impacts...The Revenue Scheme, as designed for this Report, is what is commonly referred to as a cordon scheme. This involves a charge when crossing the charging area boundary in both directions.

"(Overall) Conclusions – This Report does not aim to make recommendations. Nevertheless, in summary, it is clear that the Congestion Scheme, in parallel with other initiatives, would be a strong contributor to the achievement of national and regional transport objectives. It would reduce congestion, encourage the growth of public transport and active modes (walking and cycling) and generate improved environmental outcomes throughout the region.

"The scheme would yield significant net revenues, providing additional funding for road and PT network upgrades in Auckland. The analysis has also shown that in the absence of pricing it will be difficult to continue improving transport outcomes beyond 2016 (i.e. despite significant investment, congestion levels stay about the same)...

"The Revenue Scheme met its objectives. It would yield significant amounts of revenue to be used for improving transport networks in Auckland, and would do so in a way that would have only minimal social impacts.

"Although to a lesser extent than the Congestion Scheme, the Revenue Scheme would also provide a further incentive to use an improved public transport system, and over time would encourage more sustainable land use and travel choices. A Revenue Scheme could also be seen as an enabler of the suite of initiatives required to deliver the desired transport network in Auckland..." [815]

Shrinking Petrol Sales

While the Ministry of Transport evaluated various pricing schemes as a means of reducing Auckland's road congestion, rising fuel prices appeared to be modifying some drivers' habits – as reported by The New Zealand Herald on 20 April 2006:

"There are signs that fuel price rises are starting to affect driving and purchasing attitudes of New Zealand motorists. Police and lobby groups agree change is happening – there is evidence of a general reduction in driving speed on the highways and growing demand for smaller or more fuel-efficient vehicles – but are unsure how far it will go...

"Motor Industry Association chief executive Perry Kerr said that in the last four years the trend was to move away from buying large cars of the Ford Falcon/Holden Commodore class in percentage terms. 'But equally there has been an increase in the number of four-wheel-drives sold.'

"Between 2000 and 2006 there was a 44 per cent rise in the sale of new small cars and a 22 per cent drop in large car sales, offset by a 56 per cent increase in all-terrain vehicles (four-wheel-drive sport utility vehicles) sales." [816]

Funding Boost for Roads

Nevertheless, help was on the way for those hard-pressed drivers in the form of a funding boost for more roads – delivered by the Treasurer, Michael Cullen, in his Budget of 18 May 2006:

"Key roading projects in Auckland and elsewhere have received most of a $1.3 billion funding boost that wipes out a tax shortfall from shrinking petrol sales...The Government has stolen the thunder from it opponents by promising to spend $13.4 billion over five years on land transport – a sum $300 million greater than all it will reap from fuel taxes and vehicle registration fees.

"Finance Minister Michael Cullen's budget has answered the dreams of business and motoring groups such as the Automobile Association, which have long demanded all fuel taxes diverted to the Consolidated Fund be spent on roads and other land transport. 'The taxpayer no longer has a hand in the motorist's pocket,' Dr Cullen said.

"But Auckland Regional Land Transport Committee chairman Joel Cayford slated the document as 'a smokestack Budget – all about world-class roads and third-rate public transport for Auckland.'

"Green Party co-leader Jeanette Fitzsimons rose in Parliament to call it a 'mad, petrol-headed, road-building Budget designed for a flat Earth by ignoring likely limits to oil supplies and the effects of global climate change...'

"It was a reduced tax take from declining fuel sales – raising fears of a $685 million funding deficit – which prompted Transit NZ in February to announce delays of two to three years to many large roading projects. The Government which promised at the time to make up the shortfall, disclosed yesterday that the overall deficit in the National Land Transport Fund had swollen to $862 million…

"The Budget contained little or nothing to fix Auckland's public transport problems, although Dr Cullen said the Government would continue to work with the region on these. 'This will include how best to enable local authorities to meet their contributions to local land transport costs,' he said." [817]

State Highway Plan Extended

More good news for motorists was announced in August 2006 – as reported by the Automobile Association:

"The Government announced today that the guaranteed five-year State Highway Plan announced in the Budget will become a guaranteed six-year plan to give the land transport sector even greater certainty. The plan will be updated at three-yearly intervals meaning there will at all times be three years of funding certainty.

"Finance Minister Michael Cullen and Transport Minister Annette King say the extension will allow better synchronisation between central and local government planning cycles, and ensure the roading construction industry will have enough information to make sure it has the capacity and capability to do the work expected of it." [818]

Ramp Signals

Ironically, work was also underway to regulate the motorists' entry to a highway system that could not be built fast enough to accommodate them:

"Transit New Zealand has been given the green light to extend its ramp signalling system…Land Transport NZ has confirmed funding for the installation of ramp signals on 15 Northern…and 15 Northwestern Motorway on-ramps. Design work will start immediately, with construction planned to begin on the Northwestern Motorway in June and on the Northern Motorway in November next year. Installation will take around 18 months to complete.

"Work to install ramp signals on the Southern Motorway is already underway and the first ramp signals, at Papakura and Takanini followed by ramps within the Central Motorway junction will begin operating later this year…" [819]

New Motorway

Highway construction and its planning continued during 2006 – as reported by The New Zealand Herald on 9 October 2006:

"Construction of the new motorway north of the existing Hobsonville Rd section of SH18, would start late next year after a six to nine-month design phase. Earlier funding uncertainty meant the new motorway faced a three-year delay until it was brought forward again by the Government's announcement in the Budget of an extra $1.3 billion of national highway funding. The road will join the new duplicate Upper Harbour Bridge, which was completed about three months [ago] within its $37 million budget and which will in turn connect to a $100 million-plus motorway link due to open next financial year between Greenhithe and Albany." [820]

Central Motorway Junction

And connections between some motorways were finally complete:

"On Wednesday 6 December [2006] at 5 am and for the first time ever, motorists will be able to drive on the Northern Motorway from the North Shore to the west and to the Port without leaving the motorway…Travelling from the North Shore to Western Springs, for example, motorists will be able to complete their whole journey via the motorway – without having to use local roads to connect between state highways. The link between the North and the Port takes motorists to the eastern end of SH16 towards Quay St and Tamaki Drive...The improvements are the penultimate milestone in Transit New Zealand's upgrade of Auckland's Central Motorway Junction. On 18 and 19 December, the final two motorway-to-motorway links will open – from the Port to the North and the Northwest to the North – and the multi-million-dollar project will be complete." [821]

Wiri Inland Port

Another election loomed, and one more chance to reduce the traffic using the new links to and from the port – as reported by Bob Dey on 7 November 2008:

"Just 3 days before the election, Prime Minister Helen Clark said Cabinet had agreed the Government should invest $6 million in Ports of Auckland's Wiri inland port project...

"The Wiri Inland Port is a 15ha depot off Wiri Station Rd, close to State Highways 1 and 20. It has all the road, yard (including empties), e-commerce, MAF & Customs functions of Auckland's cbd port.

"Ms Clark said the Ports of Auckland link would save an estimated 100,000 truck trips/year, reduce vehicle emissions & accident risk and reduce congestion on Auckland's roads. 'This will enable Ports of Auckland to connect the Wiri inland port complex to the rail network. It benefits Auckland by reducing the number of trucking movements through to the port, speeds up the processing of containers and reduces the need for storage...'" [822]

New Government, More Roads

The National Party became the Government after the November 2008 election but motorists need not have worried that the policy for roads would also change – as announced by Prime Minister, John Key, and Transport Minister, Steven Joyce, on 17 March 2009:

"As part of the government's Jobs and Growth plan, Prime Minister John Key and Transport Minister Steven Joyce have today announced almost a billion dollars of additional investment in the state highway network over the next three years.

"The additional funding over three years will come from three sources:

- $420m reallocation from non-state highway classes (including savings on administration costs).
- $258m in new Crown investment (paying for the NZ Transport Agency's share of Wellington Passenger rail infrastructure).
- $283m increases in fuel taxes (commencing 1 October and replacing regional fuel taxes).

"Mr Joyce says that the new draft Government Policy Statement shows investment in State Highway Infrastructure continuing at around 33-34% of the total fund over the 10 year horizon...This will provide around $10.7 billion over 10 years for investment in the state highway network, and that is a much more appropriate level given the importance of the network to New Zealanders.

"This announcement today is about realigning the land transport programme to reflect the realities of how New Zealanders get around and how we transport our goods.

- Around 70% of all freight in New Zealand goes by road, and about 84% of people go to work by car truck or motorbike, so we need good roads to grow and compete.
- Our state highways represent 11% of our roading network but they cater to around 50% of the traffic..." [823]

Value and Fairness of Highway Funding

While most motorists appreciated the additional highway investment, there was some criticism from local and regional councils:

"Councils throughout the country are challenging the economic value of building more state highways at the expense of other transport needs, including local roads. Local Government NZ – representing the country's 82 local and regional councils – says a significant shift of money to highway construction 'is not justified and may have perverse outcomes'.

"It warns in a submission on a draft three-yearly Government transport policy statement that diverting extra money to new highways will not provide short-term economic stimulus under planning and contracting procedures. 'A better spread of economic stimulus, economic efficiency and productivity gains could be achieved by spreading investment across activities,' the organisation says...

"The Local Government submission says that although it supports the rationale for ditching the [regional fuel] tax, given that it would have been inefficient to administer, it is concerned the principle of regional self-determination underpinning it is not recognised. It says a disproportionate share of funding has gravitated to state highways, given that the Government foots the full bill for these while requiring local and regional councils to share of the costs of other transport infrastructure.

"The Government's draft policy forecasts spending of between $9.1 billion and $12.2 billion on state highway construction over 10 years – more than four times its proposed subsidies for building new local roads. Yet the submission notes that half of vehicle kilometres travelled are on local roads, meaning 50 per cent of fuel taxes paid to the national land transport fund are generated from them. 'The sector has long held the view that this is iniquitous, and further disproportionate investment in state highways is not supported,' it says...

"Although Mr Joyce is basing his reallocation decision on a desire to cater for the large majority who drive to work rather than catch buses or trains, or walk or cycle, both the [Auckland] city and Auckland Regional Council point to a need to provide high quality public transport to encourage them to switch..." [824]

The Waterview Connection

The Government's state highway construction programme included the long-planned Waterview Connection – an extension of State Highway 20 from Mt Roskill to Waterview to complete the Western Ring Route, linking Manukau, Auckland, Waitakere and North Shore Cities.

Described as New Zealand's most expensive road project ever, the original plan was for two two-lane tunnels beneath New North Road and Avondale Heights but the tunnel width was later changed to include three lanes in each direction.

How the chosen option for the Waterview connection would affect the communities through which it was to pass was naturally of concern to those who well remembered the devastation caused by the motorways that had bulldozed their way through Auckland suburbs in the past. While some 60 per cent of the proposed route would be underground, that still left many long-established neighbourhoods to be disrupted and divided by the above-ground portion of the motorway and many residents were unhappy – as described by a New Zealand Herald editorial published 14 May 2009:

"The chairman of Avondale's community board and business association, Duncan McDonald, sounded definite. 'They won't get a motorway,' he said. 'The people will lay down in front of bulldozers.' The Government may have underestimated opposition to a motorway through Waterview to complete Auckland's western ring. Opponents may not be mollified by the partial tunnelling announced yesterday.

"National certainly knows its decision against a fully underground connection has put paid to its prospects of taking the Mt Albert seat in the June 13 by-election…But it now runs the risk that the Waterview decision will damage the Government not just in the affected neighbourhood, but more generally. Motorways have divided many older Auckland communities, obliterating some. In most cases the damage was unavoidable; not this time." [825]

Economic Justification

A summation of the Waterview project and its projected economic justification was reported by The New Zealand Herald on 3 September 2009:

"Opponents of Auckland's Waterview motorway have accused the Government of ignoring a prediction by the Ministry of Transport that delaying it 10 years would boost its economic justification…"A ministry report, since released under the Official Information Act, said investment in smaller targeted transport projects would deliver more dispersed but immediate economic stimulation as well as significant network improvements – and the Waterview link could be postponed for 10 years to allow growing traffic volumes to increase its economic value…

"The project has since been amended to a surface-tunnel proposal for $1.4 billion, which would be wide enough for three motorway lanes in each direction, but would require the demolition of up to 365 homes and destruction of 5ha of parkland…

"The [Transport] agency's board is now weighing up strong support from business groups and the Automobile Association against fierce local community opposition, before deciding in the next fortnight whether to prepare planning applications for a 2011 construction start. AA spokesman Simon Lambourne said at a hearing in Mt Albert last week that 67.4 per cent of 3100 surveyed members wanted the Waterview link opened as soon as possible…

"But Waterview resident Margi Watson of the Tunnel or Nothing group said the agency's economic assessment did not stack up as it relied too heavily on overly-optimistic travel-time savings and did not include hefty social and environmental costs. Other opponents urged the board to heed a warning this month from the International Energy Agency that global oil production was likely to peak in 10 years, far earlier than previously estimated, increasing the need for better public transport." [826]

Community Opposition Ignored

Despite community opposition and environmental concerns, the Waterview Connection was to proceed – as reported by The New Zealand Herald on 12 September 2009:

"Concerns over the impact of a massive road-building project in Auckland are valid, says the head of the Transport Agency, but the Waterview motorway will go ahead anyway. Transport Agency chairman Brian Roche said yesterday that his board had confirmed a combined surface-tunnel option for the 4.5 km route...

"That followed its consideration of a litany of community presentations against the $1.4 billion project at a meeting in Mt Albert a fortnight ago, at which he said, 'they certainly left us in no doubt as to the consequences. There were very strongly held views by the community which we fully understand – they are very valid concerns and we appreciated the fact that people were able to articulate them,' Mr Roche said. But he said the completion of Auckland's 48 km western ring route, of which Waterview remains the final major missing link, was crucial for the national economy as well as the region's transport network..." [827]

The Auckland Harbour Bridge
Waitemata Harbour Crossing Study
In June 2007, the Auckland City Council published interim plans to redevelop the Wynyard Quarter. As the redevelopment could very well conflict with any future, second harbour crossing, a study was undertaken to identify a preferred location and mode for such a crossing.

The Waitemata Harbour Crossing Study, completed in April 2008, was undertaken by Sinclair Knight Merz with the collaboration of the Auckland Regional Council, Transit New Zealand, Auckland Regional Transport Authority, Auckland City Council, and North Shore City Council.

The Study identified some 159 possible crossing options and concluded that a combined road and rail tunnel west of the Wynyard Quarter was:

"The best overall performing option in the evaluation assessment...

"Bridge options were not favoured due to their visual impact on the harbour and surrounding areas...Driven tunnel technology provides several advantages, including flexibility as to when the project is implemented..." [828]

Cross-Harbour Route Protection
Even though any start on a second harbour crossing remained as elusive as it had for the first bridge, for many decades, route protection was underway, reported The New Zealand Herald on 30 May 2009:

"Preparations for road and rail tunnels under the Waitemata do not mean Aucklanders will lose their defining 50-year-old harbour bridge any time soon. The Transport Agency is taking steps to protect a route for tunnels to be dug between Esmonde Road and Spaghetti Junction via the Wynyard Tank Farm for about $4 billion, but possibly not for 30 years.

"Agency regional director Wayne McDonald said a route designation needed to be applied for by year's end to ensure foundations for new buildings from the Tank Farm through to Victoria Park would not obstruct any future tunnels. He was confident the main truss bridge would continue to serve Auckland for at least another 50 years, even if eventually downgraded to a connection for local traffic, pedestrians and cyclists, while losing its State Highway 1 status to the tunnels. He said even the problematic box-girder clip-ons should have another 30 to 40 years left..." [255]

Strategic Vulnerability
How long the Bridge's clip-ons might really last no doubt depended on the success of the two-and-a-half year project to strengthen them started in August 2008. And while the

Bridge as a whole was thought by the Transport Agency to have some 50 years of remaining life, others were not so sure that delaying a second crossing was the best idea:

"The government should speed up work on getting a new harbour crossing, a North Shore business leader says…Saying the 'clock is ticking,' North Harbour Business Association general manager Gary Holmes, adding planning for its construction must be given the highest priority…He says the association is concerned about the 'strategic vulnerability of relying on one ageing and already inadequate transport route. Admittedly the problems associated with financing the construction and the potential social dislocation are daunting, but the prospects of not making a responsible effort to get it underway are more disturbing…'

"Shore MP Wayne Mapp says Mr Joyce's announcement for the corridor for the new crossing is welcome news for Shore commuters…'The news that the harbour bridge has 20 to 40 years of life left certainly requires a full look at all the options…'

"The New Zealand Transport Agency is seeking sub-strata or underground designation for four separate tunnels beneath the bridge – two each for road and rail." [829]

Movable Lane Barriers

In the meantime, the volume of traffic crossing the Bridge required a new movable lane barrier system to replace that first installed in 1990 to prevent head-on collisions and manage traffic flows in the 'tidal' morning and evening peak system. The new system, with two new machines working twice as fast, taking around 20 minutes to change lane configurations, was installed in February 2009. [830]

Victoria Park Tunnel

In order to better accommodate the 160,000 vehicles using the southern Harbour Bridge approaches each day, construction of the Victoria Park tunnel was brought forward – as announced by the Minister of Transport, Steven Joyce, on 3 April 2009:

"Transport Minister Steven Joyce has today announced that construction on the Victoria Park project on State Highway 1 in Auckland will commence almost a year earlier than previously planned, thanks to the government's billion dollar boost for state highways.

"The Victoria Park bottleneck was recently identified as a Road of National Significance, meaning it was ear-marked for priority treatment. 'The NZ Transport Agency has advised that it will this weekend call for expressions of interest in the $430 million project, with construction due to start in January,' says Mr Joyce…

"The project comprises of:

- Increasing the capacity of St Mary's Bay from 4-lanes in each direction to 5-lanes northbound, and 5-lanes southbound with a southbound bus lane.
- Increasing the capacity across Victoria Park from 2-lanes in each direction to 3-lanes northbound (in a new tunnel) and 4-lanes southbound (on the existing Victoria Park Viaduct)." [831]

Contract Announced

On 13 July 2009, Steven Joyce announced that the contract to construct the tunnel had been assigned to Fletcher Construction as part of an alliance alongside the NZ Transport Agency, Beca Higgins, and Parsons Brinkerhoff. The contract was to undertake the construction of a 440m cut and cover tunnel which carries three lanes of northbound traffic metres below Victoria Park and widen the existing motorway through St Mary's Bay. Also, to modify the existing four-lane viaduct to carry southbound traffic. [832]

Suburban Rail
Passenger Rail Negotiations
In his article, *Briefing Paper on Transport in Auckland*, published by ESR [Engineers for Social Responsibility] News in November 2000, Derek Pringle recounted the moves then under way to rejuvenate suburban railway passenger services:

"There have been proposals for upgrading suburban rail services in Auckland for the last 88 years. It is 35 years since 'Robbie's Rapid Rail' was adopted by the then Auckland Regional Authority. It is 12 years since the ARC adopted a plan for light rail in the southern and western corridors. The only investment made in recent years has been to replace the old locomotive-hauled rolling stock with some second-hand diesel multiple units and some minor station upgrades.

"The problem is that the operator of rail services has also been the owner of the infrastructure, so that no public agency has had the power to use the rail corridors in the best interests of the region. Also, despite the ARC decision of 1988 in favour of a light rail system no action has been taken to ensure that any organisation actually has the power to construct such a system.

"Recently, the ARC has been negotiating a deal with Tranzrail whereby for a payment of $65 million, Tranzrail will make the western corridor between Swanson and Newmarket, and the southern corridor between Auckland and Westfield via Newmarket, available solely for passenger service during the day; 'The Region' will take over Tranzrail's rights to the Britomart Station, the Onehunga-Avondale rail corridor designation and the Onehunga branch line; while the TLAs [territorial local authorities] will take over Tranzrail's rights at railway stations.

"It is not clear what is meant by 'The Region', or whether the TLAs will actually want the run-down station facilities. There is no regional organisation with the power to develop public transport services within these corridors, and there are currently no firm plans for their use. The ARC claims there is 'significant commercial interest in developing and operating the region's passenger transport infrastructure', but given the opposition to the previous government's commercial model for roading, will the commercial operation of public transport infrastructure be any more acceptable, and will it be attractive to investors? And more importantly, does this expenditure of $65 million guarantee that anything will happen?" [772]

Auckland Rail Corridor
As outlined in the previous chapter, the national railway track and infrastructure was sold to private owners in 1993 but had been restored to public ownership by 2003.

While the national railway remained in private hands, the Government was able to negotiate the purchase of the Auckland rail corridor. Those negotiations were concluded in early 2002 – as announced by Transport Minister, Mark Gosche, on 13 May:

"The Crown and Tranz Rail have completed the final outstanding details of the Crown's purchase of the Auckland rail corridor. The announcement today by Finance Minister Michael Cullen, Transport Minister Mark Gosche and Tranz Rail Managing Director Michael Beard follows a satisfactory conclusion to negotiations over train control, track maintenance and other interim services.

"At the time of the sale and purchase agreement in December 2001 there were a number of unresolved technical issues. It was therefore agreed that $75 million of the $81 million purchase price would be paid immediately with the balance to be paid on resolution of the outstanding details. As these details have been satisfactorily resolved the final $6 million will now be paid.

"'The Government now looks forward to concluding a lease of the rail corridor and infrastructure assets to Auckland. This will allow Auckland to start developing the rail network to help address traffic congestion,' the Ministers said." [833]

Green Party Transport Policy

Following the November 1999 election, New Zealand was governed by a coalition of Labour, Alliance and Green Parties. As per their *raison d'etre*, the Greens took a particular interest in promoting public transport – as per their press release of 23 July 2002:

"Green MPs Sue Kedgley, Jeanette Fitzsimons and Keith Locke today launched the Green Party's transport policy with a commitment to buying back the national rail track and investing an additional $100 million per year on public transport, and other sustainable solutions.

"Launching the policy at the Newmarket railway station today the Greens called for a rapid rail system along the western, south-western, southern and south-eastern corridors as part of the solution to Auckland's congestion problems, and rapid rail access to Auckland airport with guaranteed connections.

"Today some of New Zealand's major exporters including Fonterra, Carter Holt Harvey and Fletcher Challenge Forests warned that if rail freight services are allowed to collapse there would be thousands of extra trucks on the roads each day and the international competitiveness of New Zealand's key export industries would be at risk.

"'The rail system is literally falling to pieces under private ownership and it is becoming daily more urgent that this strategic asset is returned to public ownership,' said Ms Kedgley." [834]

Audit of Passenger Rail Service

The railways would be returned to public ownership in 2004. In the meantime, the Auckland Regional Council through its suburban rail entity, City Rail Auckland, continued to operate its suburban services as per a contract signed with New Zealand Rail Limited on 3 May 1991 for the provision of passenger services: Waitakere – Auckland (3-year term) and Auckland - Papakura (4-year term).

On 4 November 1992, the contract was extended to a maximum 10-year period and then temporarily extended in 2002 pending the renegotiation of a new contract for which the Council engaged in a tender process.

At the time, "Following receipt of a recent taxpayer enquiry in respect of the current passenger rail service in the Auckland region..." the Auditor General, Kevin Brady, "...conducted a high level review of the contract monitoring protocols..." [835]

His report was released to the Auckland Regional Council (ARC) on 4 November 2003 – parts of which included:

"ARC has acknowledged that there are issues with the current rail passenger service...We requested an extract from the customer complaints registration and examples of performance monitoring reporting.

"Key themes in the complaints registration include:
> Overcrowding

Inconsistent/incorrect fare charges
Delays to service/no service
Children left on station
Maintenance/break down

"We note that both parties have acknowledged that improvement to the rail operator service is required. Tranzrail has agreed to continue to provide the passenger rail service until the new tender round is concluded…

"Conclusion – It is evident that there are issues with the current passenger rail service which cannot be resolved overnight. The availability and reliability of the rolling stock and rail corridor are intrinsically linked to service delivery. Also, the overall train system cannot meet the passenger demand, particularly during peak periods. The position is not assisted by the deficiencies of the current contract.

"We note that ARC is actively engaged in a tender process to select an Operator to provide future passenger rail services. The ARC has included within the draft Passenger Services Agreement (tender document) details of draft operating service management and monitoring protocols. The new contract should be explicit in its requirements. The public needs an assurance now that this will happen and that future services will meet appropriate standards." [835]

Veolia and Transdev

As it happened, Tranz Rail did not bid for the Auckland passenger rail contract which was taken over by Connex Auckland Limited on 23 August 2004. In January 2006, Connex Auckland changed its name to Veolia Transport Auckland Limited and to Transdev Auckland Limited on 1 July 2013. As of 2020, the sole shareholder of Transdev is Transdev Australasia Pty Limited of Melbourne and ultimate owner, Transdev Group SA, France. [836]

"Transdev Auckland…runs Auckland's urban passenger trains under contract from Auckland Transport on infrastructure owned and managed by KiwiRail. Auckland Transport receives funding to subsidise these services from the NZ Transport Agency, which receives funding from road and user taxes and Crown appropriations, and from the Auckland Council through rates…" [837]

Britomart West Rail Link

In January 2003, the Auckland City Council "…revived the idea of a rail link under the central city that would run from the new Britomart terminal to the North Auckland line near Mount Eden. A 3 km long tunnel would have stations near Sky City, the Town Hall, and Karangahape Road. The January report added that a more detailed report from consultants Tonkin and Taylor was to be considered by the City Council in February…" [838]

That report, the *Britomart West Rail Link*, was prepared by Tonkin and Taylor in December 2002 and was followed by a Geotechnical Appraisal in July 2003.

Auckland Passenger Rail Upgrade Project

In May 2003, a consortium of the Auckland Regional Council, Auckland Regional Transport Network Limited (ARTNL) and Infrastructure Auckland (with assistance from international strategic management consultants the Boston Consulting Group) developed the *Auckland Passenger Rail Upgrade Project draft business plan* and presented that plan for public consideration…

As part of the Plan's promotion, Auckland City Councillor, Dr Bruce Hucker, outlined the need for an improved suburban railway system in an article published by The New Zealand Herald on 17 June 2003:

"...the plan dismisses the idea that rail is a panacea for Auckland's traffic woes. It makes a case for an improved, sustainable regional commuter rail system as part of a transport network that includes road and ferry services...

"At present only 700 people take the commuter rail services to the CBD each day. That's not surprising; the rolling stock and stations are dilapidated, uncomfortable, poorly lit and not always safe after dark. Services are infrequent and irregular. That's why the business plan proposes investing $1.5 billion to upgrade the system in the next 20 years.

"Stations will be renovated or replaced. They will have better interchange facilities, retail services and larger and more secure car parks. They will be fitted with security systems and improved lighting. Some of that work has started already.

"The Western Line through Waitakere City will be double-tracked to allow for greater service frequency. A Manukau City link is to be constructed. All lines and the signalling systems will be upgraded. A new fleet of rolling stock will be brought into service.

"The system will do more than just encourage commuters into the CBD. It will help to get the whole region moving, allowing people to travel easily from city to city as well. The business plan is based on a goal of increasing annual passenger rail trips from a present total of 2.5 million to more than 25 million trips by 2015. By 2021, this target rises to more than 30 million a year.

"The goals are bold because without these increases, rail will make little impact on congestion. And it will be difficult to justify the major capital expenditure if we do not lift our sights and gear the whole system to achieving higher patronage levels. The critics say the region's population is not dense enough for a rail system to be economic but, worldwide, the experience has been that efficient, convenient and comfortable urban rail has encouraged population centres to grow around transport hubs...

"The business plan proposes that the metro rail network should eventually be electrified. Although it will initially cost $110 million more than using diesel, electric trains are quieter, faster and cheaper to run. They are also more environmentally friendly. Lowering emissions will become more important as residential development around transport nodes becomes denser and as people become more sensitive to health-related environmental issues.

"There can't be half measures. That's why the draft plan is a big and bold vision, part of a blueprint for an integrated multi-modal transport network that will service the region's growth. Local authorities and other interested parties are vigorously debating the detail, but they all agree on one thing. Doing nothing is no longer an option." [839]

Britomart West Rail Extension Feasibility Study

The Auckland Council also commissioned two additional engineering and environmental consultants, URS New Zealand Limited and GHD to "...confirm the technical and economic feasibility of developing an underground rail extension tunnelled westwards from Britomart Station to connect with the Western Rail Line..." [840]

Their final report, the *Britomart West Rail Extension Feasibility Study*, completed on 19 January 2004, concluded:

"The capacity of Britomart Station can be enhanced to the meet the projected 2021 Rail Business Plan patronage on the Auckland Rail Network by the construction of the

Britomart West Rail Extension. The project could be economically viable between 2019 and 2020, and although this analysis does not conclude that the project should go ahead for 2009 (when the Britomart Station reaches capacity), the analysis also does not rule out this earlier implementation.

"The capital cost of the Britomart West Rail Extension is in the range of $469,000,000 to $515,000,000 with an accuracy of ±30%. There could be potential costs savings in the order of $120,000,000 dependent on when the project is built...

"While the project may be economically viable, it is not financially viable (that is, does not provide an acceptable return on investment). Few public transport projects in New Zealand are financially viable. It is therefore important to ascertain whether funders would be willing to commit to the project, the amount they would be willing to commit and the level of justification they require before confirming that commitment. In essence, if funders are not available, then there is little point in continuing the analyses." [840]

Cost Saving Identified

While funders for the Britomart West Rail Extension remained unavailable, and decades of reports gathered dust, some saw an opportunity to save on the ultimate cost – as reported by The New Zealand Herald on 5 August 2005:

"The Civic Carpark leaky roof crisis could be the ideal time to build a railway station in the Aotea precinct, says Auckland City Mayor Dick Hubbard. Mr Hubbard says it may be cost-effective to use the $73 million leaky roof crisis to make a start on the $1.6 billion rail plan to electrify most of the rail network by 2011 and build a 3.5km rail tunnel from Britomart under the central business district to Mt Eden..." [841]

Onehunga Branch Railway Line

While plans for electrification and tunnelling remained dormant, less expensive improvements to the Auckland suburban line did sometimes eventuate – as announced by Finance Minister, Michael Cullen, in a media release of 14 March 2007:

"Passenger and freight trains will return to Auckland's Onehunga line following a multi-million dollar upgrade, Finance Minister Michael Cullen announced today. 'I have given approval for ONTRACK to invest in the upgrading of the Onehunga Branch railway line and additional work associated with the changes needed at the Newmarket Junction,' said Dr Cullen. 'This is great news for Onehunga as passenger trains ceased 34 years ago and the line stopped carrying freight last year.'

"The upgrade will form part of the current projects being carried out in Auckland by ONTRACK and ARTA and funding will come from the $600 million granted by government in December 2005. Upgrading the line is expected to cost $10 million with platform work and relocation of the old Newmarket station to cost around $5 million." [842]

Budget 2007

Support for the electrification of Auckland's suburban railway network finally came with the Labour Government's budget of May 2007 – albeit as part of a 'national' upgrade and with the aid of a regional fuel tax not yet in place:

"We are supporting the electrification of Auckland's urban passenger network, and will provide funding for the necessary infrastructure assisted by revenue from a regional fuel tax. The whole project will cost more than $1 billion, with the Auckland Regional Council being responsible for funding the electric trains. The council will be able to access funding for the project from the proposed regional fuel tax, and the government will raise infrastructure bonds to pay its share with the fuel tax servicing the interest costs.

"The aim is to have electrification completed by 2013. The government has investigated the possibility of having electric trains up and running for the Rugby World Cup in 2011, but this would be too risky and costly in terms of sourcing material for electrifying the system and buying rolling stock. To ensure there is a well-functioning public transport system in place in 2011, ARTA (Auckland Regional Transport Authority) will need to purchase additional interim carriage trains...

"Budget 2007 provides $600 million over six years for the government's contribution to these urban rail development projects in Auckland and Wellington. It also provides an additional $50 million for general track improvements to the national rail network over 2008 to 2010.

"Dr Cullen said Budget 2004 provided $100 million for national track improvements. 'We are now committing another $25 million in both 2008/09 and 2009/10 to ensure rail remains a major transport option both complementing and competing with roading...'" [843]

Railway Improvements

While there would be no improvements to Auckland's railway network to the extent promised by this Government, some progress was being made to meet demand – as described by Bruce Ringer in his essay, *The Railway Renewed - 150 years of railways in Manukau*:

"The little used Wiri station was closed to passenger traffic in February 2005. However, in October 2005, after a gap of almost forty years, Sunday rail services resumed on the southern line.

"A new Manurewa station and transport interchange was opened in July 2006, the Sylvia Park station in July 2007. Suburban rail was definitely making a comeback.

"The most important symbol of its resurrection may yet prove to be the start of work on the new Wiri railway interchange on 15 June 2009 and the Manukau railway station on 20 September 2009." [844]

Another Election – Another Plan

Following another election in November 2008, the National Party was back with a new Transport Minister, Steven Joyce. The former Government's intention of introducing a regional fuel tax to fund transport initiatives, particularly the electrification of Auckland's railway network, was discounted by the new Government in March 2009.

However, the Minister apparently remained committed to electrification – as per his media release of 17 March 2009:

"Transport Minister Steven Joyce has today confirmed the government's commitment to the electrification of Auckland rail, which was to have been funded through the regional fuel tax. After double tracking, electrification is the important next stage in the development of Auckland's rail network. Rail is an important and growing way for Aucklanders to get to work each day.

"Ontrack's electrification plans will proceed unchanged. The purchase of electric trains was to come out of Auckland's regional fuel tax but will now be supported by crown funding – either via a capital appropriation or additional debt funding, until such time as patronage levels reach the point where regular passenger transport subsidies are sufficient.

"The government has decided in principle that now that KiwiRail has been repurchased by the government, it should be the owner of the new crown-funded passenger rail stock in Auckland and Wellington.

"Mr Joyce says this will save costs over time and ensure the most efficient use of transport funds. We will be working with regional authorities in Auckland and Wellington to achieve that outcome and manage the transition...Other Auckland projects which were to be funded through regional fuel tax, like Penlink, ferry upgrades and integrated ticketing, will be subject to the usual funding processes through the NZ Transport Agency..." [845]

Budget 2009

However, that promised crown funding for the purchase of Auckland's electric trains was not included in the Government's May 2009 budget and that meant yet more uncertainty and delay for transport planners – as reported by The New Zealand Herald on 29 May 2009:

"KiwiRail will be kept ticking over with a $90 million Government operating subsidy, but the Budget has offered Auckland no funding certainty for electric trains...The subsidy will mainly cover freight operations, however, leaving Auckland Regional Council chairman Mike Lee and Labour lamenting a lack of provision for electric trains for urban commuters.

"Although Transport Minister Steven Joyce has repeatedly assured the Herald Auckland's $1 billion rail electrification project is on track for completion in 2013, Mr Lee fears the lack of budgetary provision for new trains means they cannot be ordered for at least another year. He said it scuttled Auckland Regional Transport Authority plans to call tenders this month for 35 four-car electric train sets from a short-list of preferred suppliers.

"He feared it was a case of history repeating, after Auckland was denied rail electrification in the 1950s and the 1970s. He said many other countries were responding to the global recession by boosting their rail networks. Mr Joyce said on Wednesday, in announcing that he was considering whether a public private partnership could be used to buy electric trains, that he saw no reason why such an exercise should cause the project to miss a deadline which was four years away." [846]

National Land Transport Programme

In the meantime, there was more money to come, with the announcement on 28 August 2009, of the Government's National Land Transport Programme:

"An $8.7 billion programme of investment in New Zealand's transport system has been detailed today with the launch of the National Land Transport Programme (NLTP). Transport Minister Steven Joyce says this is the largest ever investment in the system and represents a 17 per cent increase from the previous three-year period.

"This sustained boost to investment reflects the importance of transport to our economic prospects. This targeted investment will deliver real gains both in the short term – as we move out of recession – and in the longer term, by boosting the productivity we need to support prolonged economic growth.

"The $8.7 billion includes investment of:
- $4.6 billion in the state highway network (up 19%)
- $1.9 billion in local roads (up 14%)
- $900 million in key urban public transport networks (up 21%)

"The $900 million in public transport investment is in addition to the $1.85 billion in capital investment currently being made into the Auckland and Wellington commuter rail networks..." [847]

Better Than Expected

The Government's National Land Transport Programme promised to deliver a little more funding to Auckland's public transport network than expected – as reported by The New Zealand Herald on 28 August 2009:

"Mr Lee, who chastised Mr Joyce on Wednesday for failing to produce funds for electric trains, was more conciliatory last night after learning that Auckland would receive $2.8 billion – or 32 per cent – of the national transport budget. Although that is still less than Auckland's 34 per cent share of the national population, the agency's budget does not include the Government's promised $1 billion for the region's electric rail system.

"Mr Lee acknowledged that, apart from uncertainty over $500 million for electric trains, Auckland's public transport capital projects were well supported by the programme. 'The ARC is always ready to call it as we see it and this is better than we thought it might be,' he said.

"He welcomed commitments of cash for seven railway station construction or upgrade projects – at Newmarket, Avondale, New Lynn, Grafton, Manukau, Kingsland and Onehunga – but said a lack of money for another at Parnell was disappointing..." [848]

New Ownership and Operating Model

Possibly because of the uncertainties that a proposed Auckland 'super city' could bring, the Government decided to protect the ownership of its railway infrastructure there and elsewhere – as announced by Steven Joyce on 6 October 2009:

"The Government has today released the new ownership and operating model for metro commuter rail services in Auckland and Wellington. Transport Minister Steven Joyce says the plan provides a strong base for quality commuter services as new government-funded electric rolling stock arrives in both cities.

"The model builds significantly on the best of what we already have in place, and will ensure the operation of commuter rail services is contestable, so that we get the best possible service for commuters at the best possible price. The new rolling stock purchased by Government will be held in special KiwiRail subsidiary companies and leased to train operators who provide the service.

"KiwiRail will be able to bid to operate the services alongside other train operators, but all bidders will face the same price to lease the trains, and to access the track. 'This move will ensure that while KiwiRail owns the trains, it is not necessarily the case that they operate the services. They will have the opportunity to bid, but it is the regional transport authorities alongside NZTA who will determine the successful operators,' says Mr Joyce. That is appropriate as it is the regional organisations and NZTA that provides the public transport subsidies that make the services viable.

"KiwiRail currently operates the commuter rail services in Wellington, while private company Veolia operates them in Auckland.

"Mr Joyce says train operating contracts will be performance-based, utilising some of the best practice internationally to ensure punctual reliable services.' Performance-based contracts ensure the train operator is rewarded for providing reliable services and penalised when they don't. We will ensure that operators have sufficient control over their operations to ensure they can be held accountable for performance.'

"This announcement is one of a number of related decisions being worked on in relation to the provision of metro rail services, and rail services generally. Further announcements will address the procurement of new electric trains for Auckland, and the outcomes of the current official's review of KiwiRail's wider operating and company structure." [849]

Electric Trains at Last

When it finally came, the announcement about the *procurement of new electric trains for Auckland* was the only one that mattered – as reported by The New Zealand Herald on 25 November 2009:

"Auckland's long-awaited $1 billion rail electrification project is back on track, under Government funding approval to buy a fleet of zippy and low-polluting new trains. After keeping rail passengers in suspense for eight months, Transport Minister Steven Joyce yesterday announced the Cabinet had approved $500 million for electric rolling stock to start running in 2013. That is on top of a commitment of $500 million the Government inherited from Labour to electrify Auckland's railway tracks out to Papakura and Swanson, and will include the purchase of up to 114 electric multiple unit (EMU) railcars…

"The minister won strong praise from Auckland Regional Council chairman Mike Lee, a strong critic of the Government's abolition of a regional fuel tax designed to pay for electrification and other public transport spending.

"'This is an historic moment for Auckland,' Mr Lee said. 'Fast, frequent, efficient and modern electric train services can now be a reality…' Mr Lee said that Auckland had been waiting for the announcement for more than 60 years, during which it had twice had its rail electrification hopes dashed. Public transport in the region was now set to take 'a huge leap forward'…" [850]

Leading On

Long before the Government had made up its mind about funding Auckland's suburban railway services, some communities had taken the initiative to invest in the infrastructure needed to sustain the demand:

"Waitakere is investing heavily in its rail network and is building communities around rail hubs. More than 250,000 rail passengers travel the west line every month and patronage is growing. The Henderson Central rail station was opened in 2006. A $300 million transit development with capacity for electric rail is due to open in New Lynn in October 2010. Double-tracking of the western line will be completed as part of the wider upgrade to the Auckland rail network." [851]

Experiment to End

But not all suburban railway services were successful at this time – their success or otherwise very often depending on the resources applied:

"ARTA (the Auckland Regional Transport Authority) will end an experiment guaranteed to fail when it stops the daily Helensville rail service at Christmas. The trial was funded 60:40 by the NZ Transport Agency & Auckland Regional Council. An alternative, running between Britomart & Huapai, will be put to the regional council's finance committee next week. But as this option would be fully funded by the council, it faces an uphill battle to even get to start.

"The Helensville trial on the western line began on 14 July 2008, amid heavy publicity. ARTA offered a 6:32am Helensville departure for the city, 95-minute journey, 5:30pm return and 7:15pm train back to the city. Between the 3 daily trains, just over 8000 passenger trips were taken in 12 months, at a net subsidy/passenger journey of $45.72 & net cost/passenger km of 99c.

"After an average of 72 passengers/day in the first month, the average dwindled to 30-50 and the average number of passengers boarding or alighting at Helensville, Waimuku or Huapai averaged 14/train or 43/day.

"Compared to the $45.72 Helensville subsidy/passenger journey, the subsidy on the Britomart-Waitakere service was $14.34/passenger (84c/passenger km), Pukekohe $4.39/passenger (11c/passenger km) & the whole Auckland region subsidy was $4.64/passenger (29c/passenger km).

"Surveyed passengers heaped criticism on the trial, saying they'd consider using the train more if: the service was regular, more departure times were offered, the journey was quicker – the regular bus service into Britomart took 17 minutes less, and the journey was more reliable…" [852]

Chapter Nine

2010 to 2019 – A Greater Auckland at Last

Planning and Politics

In his book, *Big Bang Localism*, British author and newspaper columnist, Sir Simon Jenkins, described his view of the relationship between central and local government: "*I am a minimalist about all tiers of government. Free citizens need constantly to be on guard against them. But I am particularly sceptical of the upper tier of government because it is the most detached from private citizens and, by experience, the least efficient.*" [853]

A Greater Auckland

The *Auckland governance reforms* that eventuated from the Royal Commission of Inquiry and the Government's modifications and legislation culminated in the creation of the 'Super City'. Envisaged by many civic leaders for decades, the 'Greater Auckland' council was created from the merger of seven councils and the November 2010 election of a single mayor, 20 councillors, and 149 members of 21 local boards.

"Len Brown, the former mayor of Manukau City, was elected Mayor with 49.24 per cent of the vote and John Banks was the runner-up with 35.57 per cent. Councillors elected to the first Auckland City Council included:

"Penny Webster (Rodney), Michael Goudie & Wayne Walker (Albany), George Wood & Ann Hartley (North Shore), Penny Hulse & Sandra Coney (Waitakere), Noelene Mary Raffills (Whau), Christine Fletcher & Cathy Casey (Albert-Eden-Roskill), Mike Lee (Waitemata & Gulf), Cameron Brewer (Orakei), Richard Northey (Maungakiekie-Tamaki), Sharon Stewart & Jami-Lee Ross (Howick), Alf Filipaina & Arthur Anae (Manukau), John Walker & Calum Penrose (Manurewa-Papakura), and Des Morrison (Franklin)." [854]

Council-Controlled Organisations

In order to manage the new city's day-to-day operations, its former authorities were reconstituted as Council-controlled organisations (CCOs).

The Auckland Regional Transport Authority (ARTA) which provided and maintained Auckland's transport services and infrastructure, became Auckland Transport, by means of the Local Government (Auckland Council) Amendment Act 2010.

Auckland Transport

Section 38 of the Local Government (Auckland Council) Amendment Act 2010 established Auckland Transport as a CCO from 1 November 2010.

Some provisions in the Act relating to transport included:

- "Auckland Transport has a Board of up to eight voting members, including up to two Councillors nominated by the Auckland Council. The New Zealand Transport Agency is able to nominate a further non-voting member.
- "Auckland Transport is accountable to the Auckland Council who appoint the board and govern it as a Council Controlled Organisation under the Local Government Act 2002.

- "The Act makes the Auckland Council responsible for setting the strategic direction for the Auckland transport system through the Auckland Regional Land Transport Strategy and in providing funding to Auckland Transport.
- "Auckland Transport is responsible for the management and control of Auckland's local roads and public transport system, including responsibility for preparing the Auckland Regional Land Transport Programme.
- "Auckland Transport controls:
    - Local roads fence-to-fence (although these will be owned by the Council)
    - Public transport services
    - Public transport assets owned by the Council or Auckland Transport
- "The Auckland Council is able to delegate other transport functions to Auckland Transport, including management of off-street parking..." [855]

Transport Planning Powers

Although the Local Government (Auckland Council) Amendment Act 2010 delegated Auckland Transport as a CCO *accountable to the Auckland Council*, there remained the anomaly that the majority of Auckland Transport's Board's members were appointed by the Transport Minister. As such, it was suspected in some quarters that the Minister could influence local transport planning matters to favour the Government's national aspirations – thus negating the whole point of Auckland achieving greater autonomy.

Evidence supporting this suspicion was later revealed in a New Zealand Herald report published on 2 December 2011:

"Transport Minister Steven Joyce rejected advice from three Government departments that the Auckland Council should retain a direct role in transport planning, official papers reveal. He has persuaded the Cabinet to give Auckland Transport – a council subsidiary but with five of seven voting directors appointed by himself – planning powers now the domain of elected councillors.

"Among papers issued under the Official Information Act to Auckland University public health doctor Alex Macmillan is a Ministry of Transport report showing Mr Joyce rejected a ministry proposal to let the council specify planning outcomes and objectives.

"Another paper reported concerns by the Ministry of Economic Development and the Ministry for the Environment about a lack of clarity over transport planning. Officials felt the level of ratepayer funding for transport 'merits a stronger accountability relationship between Auckland Transport and Auckland Council'.

"Dr Macmillan…said the papers showed the minister trying to water down the democratic process in his push for new roads. Auckland Council's transport committee has voted to resist the move. Chairman Mike Lee, a council's appointee to Auckland Transport's board, said Mr Joyce was promoting another form of 'Auckland exceptionalism'. 'It's something that has been imposed on us from Wellington and it would be healthy for democracy in New Zealand and for Auckland that we sent a message to the minister that his absolutist tendencies when it comes to managing transport are to be resisted,' he said. 'After all, a huge amount of our budget – 51 per cent of Auckland Transport's capital expenditure at least – comes from our rates...'" [856]

The Auckland Plan

"Following Auckland's 2010 restructure into a single unitary authority..." and as required by Part 4 of the Local Government (Auckland Transitional Provisions) Act 2010, "...the previously discrete policies of Auckland's various local governments were expanded and consolidated into the Auckland Plan and associated Unitary Plan...

"As described later, the first Auckland Plan was published in 2012, offering a new consolidated vision for Auckland and the city's spatial development that emphasises a 'quality compact urban form'..." [857]

Infrastructure Investment

That *quality compact urban form* that the Auckland Plan and subsequent plans would seek to deliver, would require a good deal of future infrastructure investment to meet the challenges of its rapidly-growing population. In his address to a Spatial Plan Summit at the Aotea Centre in March 2011, Infrastructure New Zealand chairman, John Rae, stated:

"We are not about setting aspirations that cannot be delivered. That's why we talk about outcomes. We say that timely investment in infrastructure provides a tremendous opportunity to lead growth and shape the city of the future. We should positively plan for it and provide support for it in our regional policies and planning documents.

"While this might seem obvious to most people, it is not how the Auckland region (nor New Zealand for that matter) has been planned, regulated, controlled or developed over the last 30 years. Rather, investment in infrastructure has been reactive, not proactive. And as a consequence we are currently backfilling decades of under-investment in our electricity, road and rail, telecommunications & water networks.

"And, to make matters worse, our planning & consenting processes have been far from supportive. In fact, infrastructure development has, in many instances, been seen as something one should avoid. It has been seen as a cost rather than as the investment that it really is. Even today we see pressure on officers within the council to defer capital investment in an effort to contain rates increases. We need to understand that this sort of short-term political gain puts as much (and in many cases more) debt on to future generations as would borrowing to fund the infrastructure today...

"...new ways of raising the necessary revenue will have to be found. Our estimates are that, depending on the transport investment choices that we choose to make, Auckland is facing a transport infrastructure deficit of at least $5 billion..."

"...it's time for a paradigm shift in how we fund our investment in Auckland's transport...In the end, we Aucklanders have a choice. If we want to continue in the slow lane of infrastructure investment and give away our aspiration to be the world's most liveable city, we should just carry on doing what we have always done. But if we want to take the step up and achieve our vision, then it's time for a step change in the way we do things." [858]

National Infrastructure Plan

It was of considerable interest, then, when the Minister for Infrastructure, the Hon. Bill English, announced the release of his Government's 'National Infrastructure Plan' on 2 March 2010. As described, "The plan provides a snapshot of public and private infrastructure, planned investment and the Government's priorities..." [859]

Of particular interest to Auckland:

"Effective alignment and integration between national and local infrastructure investment frameworks, particularly in our large urban areas, is important for getting the right infrastructure built in the right place at the right time, and providing greater long-term certainty for developers, investors, firms and residents.

"It is also important to identify and enable the integration of different types of infrastructure so that they can work together in a complementary manner, e.g. hospitals and transport, or urban growth areas and water services. The Auckland governance reforms – still under way during publication of this document – provide an opportunity for the new Auckland Council to present a comprehensive and agreed vision for the shape of the city and the infrastructure it will need to deliver the vision…" [860]

Government Control

Despite the conciliatory tone of the National Infrastructure Plan, the initial suspicion that the Government wished to retain national control of many of Auckland's local affairs, even after the region had assumed a greater, more unified voice, persisted. The conflict was particularly obvious as the Government continued to seek greater managerial control over Auckland Transport – as reported by The New Zealand Herald on 5 July 2011:

"The Government is undermining Auckland's big rail projects by trying to abolish the 30-year transport strategy prescribing them, says a Super City councillor. Transport chairman Mike Lee says legislation the Government wants to pass within nine months will annul the strategy, which was completed by a large regional committee last year, before the Super City amalgamation. He believed it would erase the rail projects contained in the document, a claim denied by Transport Minister Steven Joyce…

"But Mr Joyce said transport strategy would be contained with land use intentions in a 30-year regional spatial plan, which the Auckland Council expects to sign before Christmas…He said the Government would not stop the Super City from including the three big rail projects championed by Auckland Mayor Len Brown in the new plan. These are the $2.4 billion central city tunnel, trains to the airport and a rail link across Waitemata Harbour to Albany. But the Government would ultimately have to be convinced of the appropriateness of these before it would be willing to help pay for them.

"The proposed legislation will make Auckland Transport take on the responsibilities of a regional transport committee…Mr Lee believed the move would make Auckland Transport and its $1.4 billion annual budget less accountable to ratepayers and more beholden to the Government's transport priorities. 'In effect the minister is de-amalgamating transport as a regional democratic responsibility in Auckland,' said Mr Lee…" [861]

Government Policy Statement on Land Transport Funding

The *Government's transport priorities* were soon made clear when it published its 'Policy Statement on Land Transport Funding' (GPS) 2012/13 -2021/22 on 26 July 2011. Destined to come into force on 1 July 2012, this latest Statement built on one previously launched in 2009.

Parts of the 2012 Statement again accentuated the requirement for national and local co-operation in the planning of land transport services:

"Since 2009, we have embarked on a significant programme of improvement in key land transport infrastructure, with an intention to invest nearly $11 billion in new infrastructure for New Zealand's State highways over the 10 years from 2009 to 2019. The main focus of this funding is the seven Roads of National Significance (RoNS).

"These projects will move people and freight between and within New Zealand's five largest population centres more safely and efficiently. They enable economic growth rather than simply responding to it, providing high quality connections to our major ports and airports from our key export production and urban areas...

"In addition, the government has agreed to allocate more than $2 billion of Crown funding for improvements to metro rail in Auckland and Wellington...

"We recognise the important role local roads have in connecting our communities and businesses to these key routes, and this GPS continues the investment that will allow existing levels of activity to be maintained.

"Similarly, we see the need for public transport to reduce congestion and to help unlock the potential of our cities, particularly in Auckland. This GPS continues to invest in public transport with up to $690 million available for public transport services over the next 3 years...

"In turn, regional land transport strategies must take account of the GPS, and regional land transport programmes must be consistent with the GPS. This means the direction and aims of the GPS have a direct influence on the funding that goes to regions and activities...

"To help ensure that investment in land transport boosts New Zealand's long-term growth prospects, the NZ Transport Agency and local authorities need to continue to consider transport networks from a national perspective. Regional transport committees should consider the national aspect of networks, including the contribution local networks can make to achieving significant impacts at a national level.

"Central and local government are partners in building, maintaining, improving and funding land transport infrastructure and activities. Some activities, like State highway activities, road policing and sector research, are fully funded by central government, while activities that are delivered by local government are co-funded by central and local government, according to the NZ Transport Agency's funding assistance policy..." [862]

Policy Failures

While the Government's Land Transport Funding Policy Statement called for national and local co-operation, the policy in general provided for little in the way of local infrastructure spending, particularly for Auckland – as Council for Infrastructure Development chief executive, Stephen Selwood, commented:

"...the policy statement failed to recognise a number of longer-term issues...several big-ticket items are conspicuously absent. An additional Waitemata harbour crossing, for example, will need allocations from the national land transport fund within the next decade if it is to be delivered before restrictions start affecting the existing Auckland Harbour Bridge. The policy statement provides no assurance that these costs have been recognised and will be met.

"Nor is there mention of Auckland mayor Len Brown's cbd rail link project, reaffirming that the Government has no capacity to contribute to this $2.4 billion project. That's $2000 that every Aucklander is going to have to stump up if the region wants a cbd rail loop.

"The only way centres such as Auckland are going to be able to deliver big-ticket transport projects not included in the policy statement is if there is some adoption of road pricing. The policy statement acknowledges such mechanisms may be required long-term, but doesn't enable or facilitate them. We need these types of funding sources today. Without additional funding, it is clear that the growth plans set out in the new Auckland Plan will not be able to be realised...The policy statement provides good certainty of direction in the short term but signals some significant funding challenges in the near future." [863]

Draft Plans

The new Auckland Council wasted no time in planning its way forward. Four draft planning documents were released on 20 September 2011, including a 30-year spatial plan (the Auckland Plan), an economic development strategy and two area plans – a city centre masterplan and a waterfront plan.

Property reporter, Bob Dey, described the draft plans as:

"The documents are aspirational, but with the detail that will enable the council to implement change. All up, they contain more than 650 pages of proposals that, implemented, would send Auckland on a quantum leap into the future..." [864]

"The mayoral vision is for transformational development around new stations – more intensive residential development accompanied by new office areas. It would be a positive start to the council's affirmation of its predecessors' attempts at the compact city concept, which were beleaguered by low-quality development, construction & urban planning..." [865]

The Auckland Plan

After five weeks of consultation and some rewrites, the final Auckland Plan was launched at the Auckland War Memorial Museum on 29 May 2012. At the time, "Mayor Len Brown said the Auckland Plan would [make] the city a very appealing place to invest in...Two of the key divisions of opinion on the way to producing this plan...have been over constraining urban sprawl and creation of a transport system that will be unclogged...

"On...transport, Mr Brown confirmed the priority for the central rail link – now with a price of $2.86 billion on it – and the Ameti project (Auckland-Manukau eastern transport initiative) and the east-west link...

"Mr Brown said investment wouldn't be confined to the cbd and waterfront: 'There will be investment all around the suburbs, much of it predicated on the plans for the 7 predecessor councils.' Mr Brown said the level of support for the plan impressed him: 'It's surprised me. Aucklanders are in danger of agreeing with each other." [866]

Auckland Plan Analysis

In his analysis of the Auckland Plan, Auckland Barrister, Stuart Ryan, described it as:

"The single most important policy development to date in the life of the 'super city' Auckland Council...As required by section 79 of the Local Government (Auckland Council) Act 2009, the Plan exists to create an effective long-term (20 to 30 year) strategy for Auckland's growth and development. The Plan is supported in this aim by three separate documents: The City Centre Masterplan; A Waterfront Plan; and An Economic Development Strategy.

"The Plan is as a precursor to the proposed Unitary Plan. The proposed Unitary Plan will replace the seven legacy district plans made under the Resource Management Act 1991 and which control land use in the Auckland area. The Unitary Plan is planned for release in the first quarter of 2013.

"The Plan sets out several challenges that must be addressed to accommodate Auckland's planned growth. Firstly, medium to high growth scenarios forecast an additional 700,000 to 1 million new Aucklanders by 2040. These people and their businesses will need to be accommodated alongside nearly 1.5 million current residents.

"Secondly, the plan articulates the competing challenge of preserving the rural and natural elements of Auckland's environment in the face of this growth. New people have to live somewhere, but the city's periphery is vulnerable to urban sprawl.

"The third challenge involves improving the quality of urban living. The plan describes problems of inadequate planning, poor architecture and congested transport infrastructure. Finally, Auckland City may be New Zealand's economic powerhouse, but it is also home to many who suffer from high unemployment, low education and inadequate housing. The plan describes a housing affordability crisis in Auckland. The plan states that remedying these issues are matters of social and economic necessity.

"Nine areas are prioritised for growth during the first three years: The City Centre including the waterfront; The Southern Initiative area; Hobsonville; New Lynn Metropolitan Centre; Onehunga Town Centre and suburban area; Tamaki – Town Centre and suburban area; Takapuna Metropolitan Centre; Warkworth Satellite; and Pukekohe Satellite.

"While the Council considers many parts of the southern area are well served by public transport, a redesign of the bus service is planned during 2012. A new bus service between the airport and Onehunga is expected within the next twelve months." [867]

Government Response

Just in case the new Auckland Council had forgotten who was really in charge, the Government took the opportunity to remind the Mayor and Council of the Plan's responsibility to meet central government objectives.

In a letter to Mayor Len Brown accompanying the Government's formal response to the Plan, the Minister of Local Government, David Carter, congratulated the Council on reaching such a milestone. The Government's response included:

"The Government views the Auckland Plan as a key vehicle for developing an integrated approach to managing Auckland's growth, meeting central government objectives and avoiding duplication of effort across local and central government.

"The Government will continue to engage closely with the Council to seek greater alignment between the Auckland Plan and Government priorities as the Plan transitions to implementation. Greater alignment will help ensure that the Plan works towards both national and Auckland goals.

"Finalisation of the Plan has occurred in a challenging economic environment. The Government has set specific goals and targets to ensure best possible value is achieved from spending on public services and critical infrastructure. Local government has an important role in this. As the Auckland Plan moves towards implementation, the Government is looking to Auckland Council to play its part in achieving this important national objective...

"In our response to the draft Auckland Plan, we signalled our concern that the transport strategy in the Auckland Plan will not effectively address the anticipated growth in demand for travel and associated congestion. The final Auckland Plan continues to emphasise a transformational mode shift to public transport as the primary means of addressing congestion...

"The Auckland Plan proposes an ambitious programme of roading and public transport projects. However, the modelling results show that, even if these projects are implemented, congestion is forecast to increase significantly from 2021, affecting the majority of trips on the Auckland network.

"Average travel speed is forecast to drop by 18 per cent in the peak and 24 per cent in the interpeak periods. Trip reliability is also expected to decrease, with the number of congested vehicle kilometres travelled increasing by 43 per cent in the peak and 100 per cent during the interpeak. Travel conditions during the interpeak period are forecast to deteriorate significantly, becoming similar to the peak period by 2041...

"The Auckland Plan estimates $10 to $15 billion in additional funding will be needed over the next 30 years to deliver the proposed transport programme. The cost of the proposed programme, particularly within the next 10 years, will pose significant affordability challenges for the Government. Consequently, the Government does not support the Plan's assumptions about likely additional funding.

"Given the forecast results, and taking into account the projected growth, the Government also remains to be convinced that the programme as a whole represents the right mix of projects and will provide value for money.

"To improve the prospects for alignment on transport policy, the Government encourages the Council to review the proposed projects to ensure the transport strategy is optimised to address forecast congestion under the likely land use pattern...

"The Government will consider the transport projects proposed in the Auckland Plan on their merits through the National Land Transport Programme and Better Business Case processes. However, the challenging economic environment means that the Government will not be in a position to support programmes or projects which do not deliver benefits to justify the cost.

"This also applies to any new revenue generating tools the Council wishes to utilise which may divert revenue away from more growth enhancing investment in the broader economy. Consequently, the Council needs to undertake further work to ensure the Auckland Plan's transport strategy delivers value for money and to improve effectiveness and affordability before the Government will consider legislative change enabling new funding tools..." [868]

Consensus-Building Group

Before any *funding tools* could be enabled, by means of legislation or otherwise, they had to be first identified. This was attempted by means of a discussion document presented to the Council's strategy and finance committee in February 2012.

That document put forward 12 options, including:

"...general rates, targeted rates, development contributions, regional income tax, regional payroll tax, regional sales tax, tax increment funding, regional fuel tax & road user charge diesel levy, tolling new roads, road pricing on existing roads, additional parking charges, visitor tax, airport departure tax..." [869]

By July 2012, those possible tools to fund a $10-15 billion shortfall on proposed transport projects had been reduced to three:

"...regional fuel taxes, congestion/network charging and higher parking charges..." [870]

A consideration of departure taxes and visitor charges was also added to the list when the Council decided to appoint a consensus-building group to investigate how those options could best be used to generate the needed funds. The group was intended to include representatives of business, the transport industry, the Government, Auckland Council, Auckland Transport, and various individuals representing Maori interests, non-

automobile modes of transport, the Environmental Defence Society, and the Child Poverty Action Group. [870]
Government Objection
The Government was naturally quick to give its opinion of what funding tools should not be considered – as reported by Bernard Orsman of The New Zealand Herald on 20 July 2012:

"There will be no tolls or a regional petrol tax to pay for Auckland's $2.86 billion city rail link, Transport Minister Gerry Brownlee says. Mr Brownlee yesterday made the strongest statement yet by the Government to shoot down plans by Auckland Mayor Len Brown to introduce tolls to raise funds for his pet rail project. This followed a council decision hours earlier to establish a 'consensus building group' costing $1.1 million to focus on tolls and higher parking charges while keeping in mind other options, such as tourism charges…

"But before the group has met to find a consensus to sell to the Government, Mr Brownlee has ruled out two of the main options - tolls and a regional petrol tax. The minister said it was ridiculous for the Auckland Council to think it could use taxpayer-funded roads to raise its own funds. The Government had said 'no' to what was effectively a tax. He also opposed congestion charges at peak hours, saying that internationally, congestion charges were used to deal with congestion, not to raise money…" [871]

Land Transport Management Amendment Act 2013
The Government maintained its supervisory role by means of legislation – the Land Transport Management Amendment Act 2013, passed on 12 June 2013. Section 14 of the Act stipulated that:

"Before a regional transport committee submits a regional land transport plan to a regional council or Auckland Transport (as the case may be) for approval, the regional transport committee must—
"(a) be satisfied that the regional land transport plan—
(i) contributes to the purpose of this Act; and
(ii) is consistent with the GPS [Policy Statement On Land Transport Funding] on land transport;" [872]

The 2013 Act also required a regional council:

"…by resolution on or before 1 July 2015, adopt a regional public transport plan unless it does not intend to—
"(a) enter into any contract for the supply of any public transport service:
"(b) provide any financial assistance to any operator or user of—
(i) a taxi service
(ii) a shuttle service" [872]

Consensus-Building Group Final Report
When the Consensus Building Group released its final report on 15 July 2013, it provided the Auckland Council with three realistic options to address the city's transport funding gap: road tolls, higher rates, and/or fuel taxes. As reported by The New Zealand Herald, the report:

"…gives Auckland Council and the Government a clear timetable for when new revenue sources will be needed to raise an extra $400 million for each of 30 years – $12 billion in total. The money will be for projects such as the City Rail Link and new roads, including another Waitemata Harbour crossing.

"But Transport Minister Gerry Brownlee immediately ruled out two options. 'We say no to regional fuel tax and no to tolls on existing roads,' he told 3 News.

"The report, by the Consensus Building Group (CBG), a 17-member think-tank appointed by Mayor Len Brown, concluded that unless Aucklanders were prepared to accept significantly higher rates increases and heavier congestion, introducing some form of congestion charge by 2021 would be required.

"CBG chairman Stewart Milne said these decisions would need to be made by 2015. 'The group has also strongly recommended that the Government increase its funding for transport in Auckland and establish mechanisms that support an ongoing commitment to increased government funding…'" [873]

The options in the final report were summarised as:

"1. Larger increases to rates & fuel taxes, tolls to fund major roads, further Government contributions and small fare increases for public transport users.

"2. Road pricing, supplemented by smaller increases to rates & fuel taxes, plus the Government & public transport contributions…"

The road pricing mechanism "…was a pricing cordon around the inner city, where the greatest congestion occurs, and possibly a second cordon. The natural line for this would be around Greenlane & Balmoral Rds through St Lukes to Western Springs and through Orakei to Tamaki Drive. You would pay to cross it but there would be concessions for multiple journeys and pricing changes for certain time periods..." [874]

Draft Unitary Plan

Auckland Mayor, Len Brown, launched the Council's draft Unitary Plan for 'informal' feedback on 15 March 2013. Part of his speech at the time included:

"We've been here before. In a 1969 report Sir Dove-Myer Robinson warned the Government of the consequences of ignoring Auckland's challenges. He wrote of the 'accelerated urban sprawl, ruinous decentralisation of the cbd and continuing increase of the cost to the community already resulting from congestion.'

"We did not ignore Aucklanders. The Auckland Plan, which we released last year, reflects the desire & the necessity for a modern, compact city. It reflects the need for an integrated transport system which provides quality public transport alongside the roading network. It reflects the need for a concerted drive to develop an export-focused regional economy. And it reflects the need for the region's development to be achieved in a way which improves – not injures – the environment.

"The next step was to bring together Auckland's array of district and regional plans into a new, single unitary plan. The Auckland Plan sets the vision for 30 years. The unitary plan provides the detailed policy framework for how we implement the Auckland Plan. It will eventually replace Auckland's 14 existing district & regional plans with a simpler set of rules for the management of the built & natural environment. It is through the unitary plan we can begin to deliver on the goals of the Auckland Plan..." [875]

More Infrastructure Investment Needed

Just prior to the close of submissions for feedback on the Auckland Council's draft Unity Plan, the Council for Infrastructure Development submitted a commissioned review of the Plan on 21 February 2014:

"An independent review of Auckland's planning framework by Australian consulting firm SGS Economics & Planning Pty Limited, released today, identifies a lack of city-shaping infrastructure investment as the principal impediment to achieving a quality compact city.

"The report recommends that the productivity benefit from investment, demand management and urban intensification needs to establish the case for expanded co-investment and policy reform by central government.

"The review was commissioned by the Council for Infrastructure Development and has been released one week before the close of submissions to Auckland Council on its proposed unitary plan – the detailed planning framework intended to implement the overarching policy document, the Auckland Plan.

"…SGS found that the Auckland plan objective of a quality compact city was unlikely to be achieved without increased investment in city-shaping infrastructure, identification of the means to fund that investment and policy reform to support road-pricing and value-capture mechanisms.

"On current plans, there simply is not sufficient investment in transport infrastructure to support a transition to an efficient and competitive higher density urban form. To reverse many decades of low-density, motor-vehicle-oriented growth will take much more than the city rail link & other projects prioritised in the Auckland Plan. This finding helps explain why transport modelling of future land use and transport investment completed last year showed Auckland's congestion worsening significantly over the course of the next 30 years, even with all proposed investment committed…" [876]

The Funding Gap

The infrastructure investment needed by the City over the next 30 years was given some monetary value by the Mayor – as reported by The New Zealand Herald on 28 April 2014:

"Mr Brown acknowledged spending by the Government and its Labour-led predecessor accounted for more than 75 per cent of the rail electrification project, and said it would be up to Aucklanders to guide the council on new revenue sources needed to fill a $12 billion funding gap over the next 30 years on top of $56 billion already earmarked for spending on roads and public transport. 'They know there is no easy fix and in the end it's basically back to us - in our hands, in our pockets – dealing with the challenge we have got as a city.'

"He has meanwhile reconvened an advisory 'consensus-building group' which last year left the council with two unpalatable funding options, the first relying on hefty rates and fuel tax rises and the other involving road user fees such as motorway network tolling or 'congestion charging' for peak-time trips on arterial routes.

"The group, slightly reduced to 15 representatives of sector organisations after the withdrawal of the Automobile Association and a parking company, has been asked to construct financial models for each of the options for the council to put to public consultation early next year…" [877]

Land Transport Funding Update

Same Government but, following the November 2014 election, another Transport Minister, who announced the latest version of the Government's Policy Statement on Land Transport Funding on 18 December 2014:

"Transport Minister Simon Bridges confirmed yesterday that the Government would spend $38.7 billion on the land transport system over the next 10 years. He said regional networks, public transport, cycleways and road maintenance would benefit. The investment programme is set out in the Government policy statement on land transport, which went out to public consultation from June to August and was released in its final version yesterday…

"The Minister of Transport updates the policy statement every 3 years. The policy statement doesn't determine which projects will be funded, or how much funding any particular project will receive, but sets ranges of funding the Government will make available for different types of activity. The NZ Transport Agency then determines which projects receive funding – and to what level – within those overall funding ranges…" [878]

Interim Transport Levy

While the Mayor's consensus-building group continued to mull over the means by which the City could fund its needed transport infrastructure, and pending a greater Government contribution, there was no alternative but to utilise standard means:

"Auckland Council's governing body voted today [25 June 2015] for a rates increase that will average 9.9% for residential ratepayers including a flat $99 residential and $159 business (plus gst) interim transport levy.

"Mayor Len Brown introduced the transport levy last month at the final budget committee meeting for debating content of the annual budget and the council's 10-year plan. It replaced 2 options, a fuel tax and motorway tolls, proposed in consultation but rejected by the Government. The interim levy is to be in place for 3 years…" [879]

Terms of Reference

Faced with the increasing pressure of transport chaos and the urgency to find a solution, the Government agreed to seek that solution by means of a collaborative effort with the Auckland Council. There had been many instances of such collaboration in the past, but those instances had included a number of separate, and often parochial, local bodies. This time, the Government had Auckland City, as a unified entity, to deal with – as reported by The New Zealand Herald on 27 August 2015:

"The Government and Auckland Council have today signed off terms of reference setting out how central and local government will work together to develop the city's transport system. Finance Minister Bill English said more than 700,000 additional people were expected to live in Auckland by 2045. 'Long-term solutions for Auckland's transport system are central to ensuring it remains a great place to live and do business, and it is also important for the economy as a whole…'

"Transport Minister Simon Bridges said that together the Government and Council planned to invest $4.2 billion in Auckland's transport system over the next three years. 'While that work will continue as agreed on the roads, public transport, walkways and cycleways, we are now turning our focus to the next three decades and beyond…'

"The terms of reference set out a structure under which officials from the Ministry of Transport, Auckland Council, Auckland Transport, the NZ Transport Agency, Treasury and the State Services Commission would work together to test alternative options for how the transport system could develop. A preferred approach was expected to be presented by officials in about one year.

"'The Government and Council will then consider the preferred approach and how it may be delivered, including whether changes might be needed to legislation and funding arrangements,' Mr Bridges said." [880]

Auckland Transport Alignment Project (ATAP)

As reported by The New Zealand Herald, the Government and Council collaboration produced a 'Foundation' report on 26 February 2016:

"For the first time, central and local government have agreed to work together to find solutions for the city's transport issues and on Friday they released the Auckland Transport Alignment Foundation Report. The report sets out a common local-central government vision of the transport challenges facing the city and the objectives and measures of success that will guide transport decision-making in the coming decades.

"Auckland's population is growing at three per cent a year, or more than 800 new people a week. And over the past two years, the city's economy has been growing at an extra $3 billion a year. Nearly a third of this growth will occur beyond 20km of the city centre. This growing population will put pressure on Auckland's transport networks, the report said.

"One of the key performance indicators of the future framework will be to make jobs accessible by car within 30 minutes and by public transport within 45 minutes during the morning peak. A spokesman said this travel time will be from anywhere in the city and will be a measure of how successful the transport solutions, like the City Rail Link, are.

"The report also explores the impact of future technologies – including how role autonomous cars and ride-sharing will change public transport and whether they will 'blur the distinction between public and private transportation'.

"It found Auckland lags behind Australian cities in travel time reliability, public transport and the overall size of its available labour pool. And the freight industry is projected to grow in size by 78 per cent...

"AA spokesman Barney Irvine said the report was 'exactly the sort of shared thinking that's been missing in the Auckland transport debate in the past'. He said one of the key elements of the report was the focus on achieving more out of Auckland's existing transport plan. 'What it shows is that, under the current plan, the outlook for congestion and public transport performance is really pretty grim, particularly if you live in the South or the West of the city.'" [881]

ATAP – Second Report

The Government and Auckland Council released their second Auckland Transport Alignment Project (ATAP) report on 21 June 2016:

"The Government appears to have softened its stance on road tolls in Auckland, saying that direct charges for road use will be needed to fund the growing city's infrastructure. The Government and Auckland Council today released their second report on the Auckland Transport Alignment Project, which will decide how the city's transport system will be developed over the next 30 years and how it will be funded.

"Transport Minister Simon Bridges said the joint project had found that achieving a 'step change' in Auckland's transport system would require 'a range of interventions'. [The report] concludes that while ongoing investment in new road and public transport projects will clearly be needed, greater use of technology and in the longer term, road pricing – or directly charging for road use, will also be part of the toolkit...

"The report said that directly charging road users, and varying the charges by location or time of day, would have a 'potentially significant positive impact on system performance'. But while the measure had 'major potential' to influence travel patterns, it would require 'substantial further investigation'.

"Auckland Mayor Len Brown said the report's finding that road pricing was part of the solution to Auckland's traffic woes was 'good news'. The policy would need to be considered soon, he said, because an 'interim transport levy' paid by businesses and residents was set to expire in 2018..." [882]

ATAP – Third Report

The Government and Auckland Council released their third Auckland Transport Alignment Project (ATAP) report on 14 September 2016 – as reported by The New Zealand Herald:

"Aucklanders will have to pay to drive at peak times if the city is to overcome its growing traffic problems, says outgoing Auckland mayor Len Brown. A joint transport strategy report released by the council and the Government yesterday said a dedicated project should develop 'smarter transport pricing' for implementation within the next ten years.

"Brown said this meant a specific focus on congestion charges. 'To reduce congestion, Aucklanders need to make different choices about how to travel and at what time of day. Demand management is crucial to achieving this. Road pricing offers Auckland a fairer means of funding transport than over-reliance on property rates. Any revenue raised must go to improvements into the transport system.'

"The report also gave a green light to a busway on the Northwestern Motorway from Westgate to Te Atatu over the next decade. The first phase of the Northwestern Motorway, more electric trains and extending rail electrification to Pukekohe are among an indicative package of projects for priority funding.

"Finance Minister Bill English, Transport Minister Simon Bridges and Auckland Mayor Len Brown today released a joint report which sets out a strategy for the development of Auckland's transport system over the next 30 years. For the past year, the council and the Government have been working together on the strategy through the Auckland Transport Alignment Project (ATAP).

"Other projects on the 10-year horizon are new and upgraded roads for new housing, motorway improvements to address congestion and upgraded access to Auckland Airport from the east…" [883]

Auckland Smarter Transport Pricing Project

Of the numerous recommendations put forward by the September 2016 ATAP report, the *demand management* aspect was, by far, the most controversial.

The report "...recommended the early establishment of a dedicated project to progress *smarter transport pricing* with a primary focus on influencing travel demand to address congestion. The report said that this should be progressed alongside other opportunities to influence demand, such as better integrating land use and transport, and actively encouraging increases in vehicle occupancy." [884]

In December 2016, Government Ministers agreed that "...plans for a multi-agency pricing project be developed to support a decision on whether to implement a form of pricing in Auckland..." [885]

Known as the Auckland Smarter Transport Pricing Project, its purpose was stated to be "...to undertake a thorough investigation sufficient to support a decision on whether or not to proceed with introducing pricing for demand management purposes in Auckland." [885]

The Project's participating agencies included the Ministry of Transport, Auckland Council, the Treasury, State Services Commission, the New Zealand Transport Agency, and Auckland Transport.

The broad scope of the Project was separated into three phases:

"Phase I – The objective of this phase is to develop baseline data and background information, the right analytical tools to be able to evaluate and test pricing options, and a comprehensive communications and engagement plan…

"Phase II – The objective of this phase is to identify options, and analyse these based on the findings from Phase I. A shortlist will be developed, which will form the basis of recommendations on which options to progress to further design and testing in Phase III…

"Phase III – The objective of this phase is to undertake further design, testing and analysis of the shortlist of options, to support a decision on whether to proceed with introducing pricing for demand management purposes in Auckland…" [885]

Greater Discipline Needed

While the *pricing for demand management purposes in Auckland* debate continued, the legacy *cost-benefit* basis of funding transport services remained firmly entrenched in the minds of some less imaginative politicians – as reported by The New Zealand Herald on 7 June 2017:

"Finance Minister Steven Joyce is looking for greater discipline in assessing the benefits of large infrastructure projects in the future. Some projects in Auckland, such as the City Rail Link, did not stack up on a traditional cost-benefit basis, he said, although the Government has committed to funding for it. 'I think there is unfinished business now for all of us to think about what are the true wider benefits of some of these projects and trying to get a bit more discipline to them in the years ahead,' he told the finance and expenditure committee at Parliament in response to questions from Greens co-leader James Shaw.

"'From my perspective, I think it is important that we go through the benefit-cost ratio discussion. However I would signal that some of the projects that we collectively have all committed to, including the CRL, doesn't really stack up on a traditional cost-benefit basis.'

"He said the tendency in New Zealand had been for parties to commit to a project without looking for a way to unlock some of the benefits to help pay for the project, such as a planning change.

"Just about every motorway in Auckland was being expanded or was about to be expanded which would give real benefits for a few years. He could not recall the next year that those benefits started to recede. But that was why the Government was having a discussion with Auckland on demand management 'which might achieve an outcome in the medium term which is better than what we are getting now. That is a conversation which is going to unfold over the next few years.'" [886]

ATAP – Fourth Report

The Government and Auckland Council released their fourth Auckland Transport Alignment Project (ATAP) report in August 2017:

"[Transport Minister] Mr Bridges said the ATAP update report 'identifies faster growth is now expected to occur in North and South Auckland, requiring some transport investment to be brought forward to support the housing development in these areas. We will also need to bring forward transport investment to accommodate additional public transport demand.'

"He said key initiatives from the first-decade package that would be brought forward into the next 3 years with this extra funding included:

"Advancing development of the 'next generation' of state highway projects, including the State Highway 16-State Highway 18 interchange, Southern Motorway widening between Papakura and Drury, improved eastern airport access (State Highway 20B) and the North-western Busway.

"Accelerating Auckland Transport's programme, targeting high priority and well-developed investments, including the Mill Rd, Ameti (Auckland-Manukau eastern transport initiative), Eastern Busway and associated Reeves Rd flyover, the earlier purchase of new electric trains, along with earlier completion of key city centre bus lanes & interchanges.

"Completing approximately $250 million of rail network infrastructure upgrades to cater for ongoing rapid growth in rail use and increasing freight volumes, including an additional track from Westfield to Wiri and a variety of key network resilience and performance upgrades.

"Current and committed investments include $3.4 billion for the City Rail Link, $1.85 billion for the East-West Link, and up to $1 billion in upgrades to the Northern & Southern motorway corridors.'

"One major factor in the review is that Auckland's population is projected to rise by 100,000 more over the next decade than the ATAP projections were based on last year..." [887]

ATAP – Fifth Report

There was another election in November 2017 when the National Government was replaced by Labour – a whole new set of Ministers – a whole new mindset as illustrated by the fifth Auckland Transport Alignment Project (ATAP) report released by the Government and Auckland Council in April 2018 – as described by Bernard Orsman in The New Zealand Herald:

"A $28 billion transport programme has been unveiled for Auckland in what's been described by the Government and Auckland Mayor Phil Goff as the country's largest ever civil construction programme. Its backers say the work will help create a 21st century transport network for the city...

"The investments are made possible by a $4.4 billion funding boost resulting from the Auckland regional fuel tax, increased revenue from the National Land Transport Fund, and a new funding mechanism, Crown Infrastructure Partners...

"Projects in the joint Government-Auckland transport programme, known as Auckland Transport Alignment Project (ATAP), include:

- Committed projects like the City Rail Link and Northern Motorway improvements.

- Light rail, or modern trams.
- Eastern busway (Panmure-Botany).
- Airport-Puhinui State Highway upgrade, including a high quality public transport link to an upgraded Puhinui railway station.
- Bus priority programme, to more rapidly grow Auckland's bus lane network and support faster, more reliable and more efficient bus services.
- Albany-Silverdale bus improvements.
- Lower cost East West Link to address key freight issues in the area.
- Papakura-Drury motorway widening.
- First phase of the Mill Rd corridor.
- Penlink road (motorists will pay a toll to help fund this).
- Walking and cycling programme to expand the network and complete key connections, such as Sky Path...
- Rail network improvements including electrification to Pukekohe, additional trains and other track upgrades...

"'This plan is funded to deliver the projects we are committed to,' Twyford said. 'The previous ATAP report, released by former Transport Minister Simon Bridges in August 2017, had a $5.9 billion funding gap.

"National had no plan to fix that fiscal hole, which would have meant the projects they promised couldn't have been delivered. This $28 billion plan will help ease the awful congestion that has been caused by a decade of under-investment. We will create a congestion-free rapid transit network and boost other alternatives to driving to help free up the roads, enable growth, and improve safety for drivers and others...'" [888]

Regional Fuel Tax (RFT)

The *$4.4 billion funding boost resulting from the Auckland regional fuel tax*, referred to by the April 2018 ATAP report, was legislated for by the Land Transport Management (Regional Fuel Tax) Amendment Act 2018 which was passed on 26 June 2018.

The Act provided for a maximum rate of regional tax of 10 cents a litre and established the rules by which a region could apply the tax:

"A regional council may prepare a proposal to establish or replace an RFT scheme for the region, or a part of the region, if the council, having regard to the views of the regional transport committee, considers that there are one or more capital projects that—

(a) would benefit the region or the part of it to which the proposal relates;
(b) are included in the relevant regional land transport plan (including a draft plan); and
(c) cannot reasonably be fully funded from sources other than a regional fuel tax within the time frame desired by the council." [889]

Regional Land Transport Plan (RLTP)

Now that there were more revenue sources from which to draw the funds needed for Auckland's transport infrastructure, shopping lists were quickly drawn up by Auckland Transport and the Government.

The first to be published was Auckland Transport's Regional Land Transport Plan – described by The New Zealand Herald on 20 June 2018:

"Auckland Transport is expected to sign off a brand-new 10-year budget today, allocating $10 billion in capital expenditure and another $6.5 billion for running costs. It will mean improved roads all over the city, more public transport – especially buses – and the introduction of 'smart systems' to help deal with congestion.

"But it's not all good news. The transport plans don't yet align with housing growth. Only half the proposed cycling and walking projects will be approved, and there's very little money for ferries.

"The Regional Land Transport Plan (RLTP) is AT's 10-year funding plan. An earlier version was rejected in January because it didn't align with the priorities of council and the new Government...

"10 key points in AT's 10-year plan
1. Over 10 years, AT will spend about $10 billion on capital expenditure and $6.5 billion on operating expenditure.
2. The money is widely spread, with most of it going on roads and few projects getting all the money they need.
3. Ferries are the big loser.
4. Almost half the spending requested for cycling and walking has been rejected.
5. New bus interchanges on Quay St and Albert St will just be ready in time for the America's Cup.
6. 'Intelligent transport systems' will be introduced to help ease congestion.
7. Growth spending in fast-growing town centres and Housing NZ developments is not yet funded.
8. The problem of double-decker buses hitting shop verandas is getting a permanent fix.
9. Light rail will be paid for by government, not council.
10. SkyPath and SeaPath, taking cyclists and walkers over the harbour bridge and on to Takapuna, will be paid for by government and finished by 2021." [890]

Government Policy Statement on Land Transport

Not to be outdone, the Minister of Transport, Phil Twyford, launched his Government's 10-year plan for transport on 28 June 2018:

"Cabinet has approved a new 10-year plan for transport which will unlock record investment in the roads, rail and public transport for our growing regions and cities, and save lives on our roads, Minister of Transport Phil Twyford has announced.

"The Government Policy Statement 2018 on Land Transport increases investment from $3.6 billion in 2017/18 to a record $4 billion in 2018/19. It will continue to rise to $4.7 billion a year by 2027/28. Additionally, the Government is also investing $1 billion this year in specific projects, such as the City Rail Link, and councils will invest a further $1 billion a year.

"The Government, through the National Land Transport Fund, will invest more than ever in transport, to boost the economies of our cities and our regions, while making travel safer for everyone, Phil Twyford said. 'Auckland alone loses $1.3 billion a year in productivity to congestion. We will tackle gridlock in Auckland by giving commuters options through major road projects and upgrades such as Mill Road and Penlink.

"Throughout New Zealand more commuters will be able to leave the car at home because of investment in public transport, walking, and cycling. This investment will unleash the potential of our cities. It will complete the expressway projects begun under the previous government and allow for future state highway upgrades, with up to $9.5 billion for state highway improvements...

"The New Zealand Transport Agency will increase their share of costs for certain high and very high priority locally-led projects, meaning councils can get more transport investment without asking more of ratepayers...

"To fund the infrastructure for our cities and regions to thrive, and save lives, there will need to be increases in excises and charges. There will be three increases in Petrol Excise Duty of 3.5 cents a litre from 30 September, and equivalent increases in Road User Charges from 1 October, and further 3.5 cent increases in 2019 and 2020. This will cost the average family 83 cents a week this year, rising to $2.50 a week by 2020. The increased excise will fund $5 billion of investment over the next decade…" [891]

National Land Transport Programme

The New Zealand Transport Agency also produced its shopping list of transport projects going forward. Part of the Agency's National Land Transport Programme (NLTP) Summary for Auckland for 2018 to 2021 included:

"…expanding Auckland's rapid transit network. The Transport Agency's first significant rapid transit project, the Northern Busway, started operating in 2008 on Auckland's North Shore.

"Moving forward, light rail is being investigated for several key routes. The Transport Agency is leading the delivery of the light rail programme. It is working in partnership with Auckland Council, Auckland Transport and HLC [now Kainga Ora], to give people more choice about how they travel and to support the creation of more accessible communities…

"Much of Auckland's strategic road transport network is now complete, but the Transport Agency is working to create targeted improvements at the same time as it prepares for the networks that will be needed to connect growth areas and ensure they are great places to live.

"The walking and cycling programme will be strategically planned and delivered to achieve maximum impact for short trips to the city centre, public transport interchanges, schools, and local and metropolitan centres. A new footpaths regional programme will construct new and widened footpaths.

"The NLTP 2018-21 will continue to invest in Auckland's public transport network, with new electric trains to provide for growth and reduce crowding that would otherwise occur. There will be electrification of the rail line from Papakura to Pukekohe, provision of a third main line between Westfield and Wiri and an upgrade of Westfield rail junction to provide better separation of passenger and freight services.

"A programme of works to improve the performance of the city's rail network includes an upgrade of the Onehunga Line to accommodate higher frequency services and longer trains. The works also include progressive improvement and removal of road/rail level crossings to better manage safety risks, allow for more train services and reduce road congestion.

"The bus network carries the most passengers of any mode in Auckland, and the Transport Agency will invest in city centre improvements. They include bus priority lanes along Wellesley Street and a new Learning Quarter bus interchange. In the downtown area, there will be new bus interchanges on Quay Street East and Lower Albert Street in conjunction with the City Rail Link and Auckland Council's downtown projects…" [892]

New Zealand Transport Agency Failure

However, while the Transport Agency's 2018 programme concentrated a good deal of its resources on Auckland's public transport system, it seems that was not always the case, and it had apparently cut a few corners in the past – as reported by The New Zealand Herald on 9 October 2019:

"The Government will inject the New Zealand Transport Agency with an extra $45 million after an independent report concluded it had failed in one of its major responsibilities. But the Government blames National for the failures in the transport sector that led to Transport Minister Phil Twyford commissioning an independent report investigating NZTA.

"The review, undertaken by agency Martin Jenkins, found that previous transport ministers had directed NZTA to 'focus on building roads' at the expense of keeping people safe. The report also found that NZTA had failed to properly regulate the transport sector under the previous Government.

"In response to the review, the Government has confirmed it will adopt all of its recommendations and plans to implement them as soon as possible.

"The recommendations include:
- Injecting NZTA with an extra $45 million to help bolster its regulatory obligations
- Create a statutory Director of Land Transport who is responsible for carrying out NZTA's regulatory functions and powers
- Getting NZTA's board to develop a new regulatory strategy Instructing the Ministry of Transport to update the NZTA's regulatory objectives

"Twyford said these changes would help to equip NZTA for the massive transformation the agency will undergo in the coming years…The review comes on the back of a number of concerns which emerged around NZTA's regulatory function and a backlog of compliance cases that have not been properly managed..." [893]

Public Transport
Public Transport Network Planning

A New Zealand Transport Agency-commissioned study, *Public Transport Network Planning: a guide to best practice in NZ cities*, was undertaken by Paul Mees, J Stone, M Imran, and G Nielson in 2009 and reported in March 2010. Parts of their report relevant to this chapter include:

"In the 1960s and 1970s it became fashionable to argue that smaller cities, such as those in New Zealand, did not require traditional CBDs, and that retailing, entertainment and much employment should be decentralised to suburban centres.

"However, since the 1990s, urban economists have realised the importance of 'agglomeration benefits' in supporting economic growth in an 'information economy'. This has led to a renewed focus on prosperous CBDs and subcentres, and the effective public transport systems needed to support them...

"To contribute to productivity in this way, public transport needs to move beyond the traditional commuter role, and also serve shoppers, tourists and business visitors…The essential purpose of public transport is to carry people with different trip origins and destinations in the same vehicle…"

"Until recently, public transport in New Zealand has been treated as a 'back-up' mode to the automobile, for the disadvantaged and city-centre commuters."

"Many bus services competed directly with trains for travel into the city centre despite trains holding a significant competitive travel-time advantage – for example, peak-period express buses from New Lynn took 50 minutes to reach Britomart, compared with 33 minutes by train; Papakura to Britomart took 80 minutes by peak express bus, compared with 53 minutes by a stopping-all-stations train and 38 minutes by express train.

"There was also a price penalty for using the slower buses – for example, the three-stage journey by GoWest bus from New Lynn to Britomart was $4.30 for a single trip, while the same journey by train was only $3.80.

"This competition between bus and train could be partly explained by the poor location of the central rail station relative to employment and retail opportunities in the CBD – a situation that was even worse before the opening of the Britomart terminal..." [804]

More Buses

As well as the planned public investment in transport infrastructure, private interests were also preparing to meet the expected demand – as reported by The New Zealand Herald on 12 January 2011:

"Infratil's NZ Bus has awarded its Auckland supply contract to British manufacturer Alexander Dennis, which says it will use the contract as a springboard into local manufacturing. 'Our aim is not simply to supply buses to New Zealand, but to become an active player in the country's manufacturing sector, said Alexander Dennis chief executive Colin Robertson...

"NZ Bus will pay £25 million for 120 of Alexander Dennis's single-deck Enviro 200 midi buses. That's the single-biggest investment since the Wellington-based infrastructure investment company [Infratil] acquired the public transport operator [NZ Bus] in 2005, and could lead to further deals in coming years.

"The first of the 55-seat vehicles will arrive in time for the Rugby World Cup this year, with the remainder progressively introduced over the following 12 months...Alexander Dennis' Robertson said the manufacturer's buses will be shipped in parts to New Zealand, where Tauranga-based Kiwi Bus Builders will assemble the kit sets..." [894]

Rocketing Demand

Those buses were certainly needed, as reported by The New Zealand Herald on 31 March 2011:

"Extra buses are being pressed into service in Auckland to cope with rocketing demand for public transport, driven largely by high fuel prices. Auckland Transport yesterday reported that the number of people boarding buses, trains and ferries was 9.6% higher in February than for the same month of last year. That helped to boost public transport patronage for the 12 months until the end of February by almost 5 million passenger trips, to 64 million...

"Passenger trips 12 months to February 28:
    Buses: 50,189,901 – up 7.9 per cent
    Trains: 9,233,040 – up 13.5 per cent
    Ferries: 4,662,665 – up 3.5 per cent
    Total: 64,085,606 – up 8.3 per cent" [895]

March Madness

Public transport services struggled to meet the demand of commuters leaving their cars at home – as reported by The New Zealand Herald on 6 April 2011:

"Emergency measures are being drawn up to cope with overcrowding on Auckland buses, including more Northern Express buses and expanding the Albany park-and-ride station. With full buses now regularly whizzing past angry commuters on busy routes such as the Northern Busway, the Central Connector and Dominion Rd, Auckland councillors are demanding action from Auckland Transport.

"Rising petrol prices and the 'March madness' caused by the return of tertiary students to classes, has resulted in a 9.6 per cent jump in public transport use in February compared with the same month last year.

"Yesterday, Auckland Council's transport committee issued Auckland Transport with a list of immediate measures, including a temporary expansion of the Albany park-and-ride station, providing more buses and sorting out what Albany councillor Wayne Walker called 'bus congestion at the bottom of town'. The downtown bus terminal is becoming cluttered with buses and queues of commuters are adding to the problem. Congestion and delays at Fanshawe St and Victoria Park have also been handed to Auckland Transport to fix.

"Deputy mayor and Waitakere councillor Penny Hulse said that yesterday at the Avondale station about 30 people were unable to board the train she was on. 'We literally needed one-gloved pushers to get people on the train. We have all had 15 or 20 years of people waving their fingers and saying Aucklanders will simply not get out of their cars. Aucklanders are pouring out of their cars and we need to do everything we can to support people to make those choices,' she said." [896]

Link Bus Network

Improvements to the inner city bus services were underway with an expansion of the network in 2011:

"Auckland transport will expand its Link bus network in August. Auckland Transport's public transport network planning manager, Anthony Cross, told the Auckland Council's transport committee yesterday the changes would simplify the original City Link.

"The Inner Link would serve Britomart, suburbs and hospitals but not the universities, and the Outer Link would serve the universities. Each service would be colour-coded, including the colour of the buses. Every second City Link bus would run through to the Wynyard Quarter.

"Other changes include making the City Link the only bus service up and down Queen St, diverting suburban buses to Albert St. Auckland Transport proposes to introduce the changes on Sunday 21 August. Mr Cross said 40 new buses were being assembled in Tauranga to serve the links and another 70 were under construction in Auckland for NZ Bus Limited." [897]

City Centre Masterplan

By August 2011, the Auckland Council had published its vision for the development of the city centre. In an article published by The New Zealand Herald on 2 September 2011, Brian Rudman commented on the City Centre Masterplan and its possible effects on the interaction between Queen Street buses and pedestrians:

"…(the plan) manages to balance the eternal conflict between Aucklander-the-motorist and Aucklander-the-pedestrian about as well as could be hoped. The proposal to turn

Queen Street into a pedestrian mall has been resisted as unnecessary and overly-expensive but…they then try to have a bob each way by saying 'desired outcomes could be delivered through a shared space approach with buses, service vehicles and local traffic…sharing the street with pedestrians'…

"The report comments on the trouble pedestrians have crossing various main streets and…proposes grand plans to calm traffic. But it ignores the creeping cancer of the ever-expanding central bus terminus, centred on Queen Elizabeth Square, but oozing out into surrounding streets for blocks around.

"When the old Britomart bus station was bowled to make way for redevelopment, it was to be replaced with an underground station linked to the new railway station. Costs, and complaints by bus operators that driving in and out of the station would add time to busy schedules, led to that plan being canned. The third world compromise was to blight Queen Elizabeth Square and streets for blocks in all directions with waiting buses, belching noise and exhaust fumes on all who were forced to venture near." [898]

Integrated Ticketing

As noted in the previous chapter, in January 2010, the Auckland Regional Transport Authority, the Auckland Regional Council and the New Zealand Transport Agency signed a $47 million contract with the Thales group to deliver a 'super transport ticket for Auckland'.

As reported by The New Zealand Herald on 17 December 2010, the super ticket was expected to be operational in early 2011:

"Aucklanders can expect an early version by March [2011] of what will ultimately become a seamless ticket for all modes of public transport. NZ Bus, which operates about 75 per cent of Auckland public bus services, will introduce the ticket for its fleet of more than 600 buses with the aim of completing the task in time for the September kickoff of the Rugby World Cup. Stations and the Downtown and Devonport ferry terminals will also be equipped with 'integrated ticketing' swipe points in time for the rugby tournament.

"That follows an agreement in which NZ Bus and its sister company in the Infratil stable, Snapper Services, have been allowed on board an $87 million integrated ticketing contract signed last year with French electronic giant Thales.

[Initially, there were two ticketing consortiums competing with each other – firstly, ARTA and Thales SA in partnership with the Bank of New Zealand and Transfield Services (NZ) Pty Limited and, secondly, NZ Bus and its sister company in the Infratil stable, Snapper Services…]

"The agreement was announced yesterday by Auckland Transport and the NZ Transport Agency, which is paying $56 million towards the contract – covering 10 years of operations as well as capital spending. It is accepting the lion's share of the contract in anticipation of developing the ticketing system as a platform for schemes in other regions.

"That has left Auckland ratepayers contributing $31 million to the contract plus $11 million on work which Thales expects to start next month to provide cabling to about 40 railway stations and ultimately 11 ferry terminals.

"Although NZ Bus is the only bus operator to have joined the scheme, Auckland Transport chief executive David Warburton said his organisation was at various stages of negotiations with others.

"Bus operators Ritchies Transport and Howick and Eastern said they were still investigating various options for joining the scheme, and were unlikely to sign up in time for the rugby cup.

"Ritchies director Andrew Ritchie said the ticketing machines on his 200 or so Auckland buses were relatively new, and he saw no urgency to join the scheme until restructured fares become available as a sequel to the ticketing project…" [899]

Hop Smart Card

Finally, on 5 April 2011, the 'Hop' smart card for use on New Zealand Bus buses was introduced as the "…first step towards an integrated ticket system…" [896]

However, that first step proved costly when the 'Hop' smart card provided by Snapper Services was found not to be fully compatible with the Thales-provided integrated system – as reported by The New Zealand Herald on 26 June 2012:

"Auckland's $98 million public transport ticketing project is in deep trouble, with an admission that a technology supplier to the Super City's largest bus fleet expects to miss a crucial deadline.

"Concern about delays by Snapper Services, supplier of cards and machine readers to its sister company NZ Bus, in making the technology compliant with the Hop ticketing project on about 650 buses has exploded into a strong ultimatum from Auckland Transport lawyers.

"The council body says it is suffering significant costs because of Snapper's failure to deliver a side deal to an $87 million supply and operations contract with French technology giant Thales, which has completed its major part of the long-awaited project ahead of time.

"Labour's transport spokesman, Phil Twyford, blames the 'shambles'…on Government interference that let the company work on the scheme despite failing to win the main contract. 'It was the National Government that insisted Snapper be allowed to roll out their card in Auckland well before the implementation of the integrated system,' he said yesterday. 'That has led to the delays that are costing the taxpayers hundreds of thousands of dollars every month…'

"The lawyers have put Snapper, a subsidiary of Infratil, on notice of recovering costs of retaining Thales experts to ensure NZ Bus' electronic ticketing is fully inter-operable with trains and ferries by the deadline [of 30 November 2012]." [900]

Some Success

The threat of legal action obviously worked – as reported by The New Zealand Herald on 29 October 2012:

"Auckland rail passengers should allow extra time to get to work this morning, in expectation of delays at new exit-entry barriers at Britomart and Newmarket stations. Extra Veolia rail staff have been assigned there to shepherd passengers through electronically and manually operated gates in the first big test of the new $110 million Hop card ticketing system on trains. Ferries will be added to the system late next month and buses from April…" [901]

Northern Busway Success

There was also a good deal of success to report concerning the Northern Busway:

"A report for the Transport Agency has found the busway largely responsible for a 15 per cent increase in passenger numbers crossing the bridge, which is good news not only for bus patronage but for the revival of the central business district. It estimates that 43 per cent of the 7500 bus passengers on the bridge in morning peak periods in 2010 had previously commuted by car...

"The Northern Motorway still suffers its share of peak-hour congestion but it would be much worse by now without the busway. It takes buses out of general traffic and allows both the buses and the traffic to move faster. A private car might still beat the bus on most journeys door-to-door, but for commuters within easy reach of a busway station there is no contest."
[902]

National Fuel Tax Increase

Despite the increasing need to further expand public transport services, the Government continued to rule out any form of regional fuel tax as a funding source for Auckland's transport infrastructure but did increase the national fuel tax by 3 cents a litre on 1 July 2013.

Accelerated Transport Program (ATP)

In the meantime, Auckland had no choice but to forge ahead – as reported by The New Zealand Herald on 22 May 2015:

"A half-billion dollar bundle of projects to fix Auckland's transport woes was welcomed last night but also described as a quick-fix. Auckland Council has agreed to support the [Government's] Accelerated Transport Program (ATP) of high-priority projects. The interim transport levy will help fund the projects.

"The transport projects include 45km of new bus lanes, intersection upgrades, Te Atatu road corridor improvements, a walkway and cycleway funding boost and new 'park and ride' facilities.

"The council said its budget committee approved $523 million of additional spending over the next three years. Funding from the New Zealand Transport Agency and council debt will also bankroll the projects.

"Transport Minister Simon Bridges said although the Government and council had some disagreements, he was trying to find common ground. 'All the projects look worthy and in due course the Government, through the NZTA, will come out with the National Road Transport Plan.' He said the plan, expected to be unveiled in July, would address some of the city's transport issues.

"Mr Brown said: 'While we continue to work with the Government to secure an alternative funding system to deliver the Auckland Plan Transport Network [as required by the Land Transport Management Amendment Act 2013] and work towards an agreed and funded plan for Auckland's transport future, this interim solution will help us to keep moving.'

"The council is funding $308 million, the New Zealand Transport Agency (NZTA) will chip in $185 million and the Urban Cycleway Fund will contribute around $30 million." [903]

Private Bus Services Success

While the Council struggled to meet demand, the increased patronage and a more collaborative public transport regime meant that private bus services were doing a lot better than they had during the previous decade – as reported by The New Zealand Herald on 2 April 2014:

"Prime Minister John Key has opened a new $18 million depot and maintenance workshops for bus operator Ritchies Transport's west Auckland and inter-city services.

"The family-owned company, which was founded in Timaru in the 1930s and now runs more than 1000 buses throughout the country, employs 300 staff through the new depot which Mr Key opened this morning on 2.15ha of reclaimed swamp land in Swanson...

"The depot replaces a smaller base from which the company has moved across Swanson Rd, and includes a 160,000-litre underground tank for recycling rainwater through a wash for the 200 buses stationed there..." [904]

New Trams for Auckland

While there was obviously less congestion experienced at Ritchies' new depot, the same could not be said for those buses when they plied Auckland's roads. Apart from when darting along the Northern Busway and edging through the few dedicated bus lanes, public transport buses were otherwise entrapped by the City's throng of general traffic.

It's no wonder, then, that the dedicated right of way once enjoyed by Auckland's trams was again aspired to by transport planners.

Since the final City tram ran in December 1956, there have been instances of tram tracks laid – a tramline was laid between Motat 1 [Museum of Transport and Technology] to the Zoo, opened in 1980. A second, 800 metre line from Motat 2 to the Zoo, was officially opened on 29 April 2007.

"Motat supplied the steel tram rails, which had previously been used in Auckland city and had been stored for decades since the passing of the tram era..." [905]

Waterfront Trams

By 2011, trams were about to return to the CBD – as reported by The New Zealand Herald on 7 January 2011:

"Trams are expected to run on Auckland's waterfront by August in an $8 million project which saw the first modest section of tracks laid this week. As well as securing a lease of two heritage trams from a museum in Bendigo, Victoria, the Auckland Waterfront Development Agency also hopes to borrow an electric light-rail car for demonstration purposes during the Rugby World Cup.

"The trams will run clockwise on a 1.5km circuit of Wynyard Quarter – between Jellicoe, Halsey, Gaunt and Daldy Sts – to draw visitors to the developing precinct and to provide them with on-board information about its attractions.

"But development agency chief executive John Dalzell said yesterday that the council-controlled organisation also wanted to use the circuit as a demonstration pilot for a possible light-rail extension across Viaduct Harbour to the Downtown ferry terminal, Queens Wharf, or even further along the waterfront..." [906]

After its official opening on 6 August 2011, the waterfront tram service operated as a unique tourist attraction but was closed intermittently for long periods while the development of the Wynyard Quarter and the improvement of its approach roads continued.

What seemed to be the tram's final run was reported by The New Zealand Herald on 30 July 2018:

"The once popular tram service at Auckland's Wynyard Quarter is being suspended until further notice. The Dockline Tram is due to halt its service from next Monday, August 6, as the area gears up for a busy period of construction work. A statement released today said the 'beloved Dockline' historic tram, which opened for service in 2011, had operated a reduced out-and-back service since late 2015 due to ongoing development within the Quarter area.

"However, the service has not been as hugely popular with members of the public since the Rugby World Cup, in 2011, when fans from around the world took in the sights of Auckland's waterfront from a different perspective. The tram's original loop was a 1.5km trip.

"'Ongoing roadworks and construction in the Quarter mean it is not cost-effective to run a tram service during this time,' the statement said. 'It is unknown how long the tram will be out of operation. We are having ongoing discussions with our development partners to assess future options.'

"In recent months there have been calls for the service to return to its original route and there was an indication that this would not happen until late next year…The suspension coincides with the service's seventh birthday; being celebrated this weekend…" [907]

Tramway Suspended Then Reprieved

"The Tramway was suspended indefinitely on 5 August 2018 due to Panuku selling an area that included part of its tracks to a developer, but was given a reprieve on 22 November 2018 with Auckland Councillors voting to reinstate the full original loop and have the tram running for the 2021 America's Cup." [908]

The anticipated restart of the waterfront trams was reported by The New Zealand Herald on 24 November 2019:

"Auckland's historic trams at Wynyard Quarter are set to resume service this summer. Auckland Council has advertised for an operator to run the service on a 1.5km circular track around the popular Wynyard Quarter. It follows a decision by the council's governing body in November last year to reinstate the route until the America's Cup in 2021 at a cost of $1.8 million, then review its future.

"The tram's operator, Panuku Development Auckland, had wanted to scrap the service, which was introduced in 2011 and struggled to attract passengers. Numbers fell from a peak 52,653 during the Rugby World Cup to a few hundred before the loop was decommissioned in August last year."
[909]

["Panuku Development Auckland is a council-controlled organisation (CCO). It was established in September 2015, the result of merging Auckland Council Property Limited and Waterfront Auckland. Panuku works closely with Auckland Council, other CCOs and local boards to contribute to implementing the Auckland Plan and encourage economic development."] [910]

Trams to Light Rail

While the waterfront service struggled to attract passengers after the tourists had left, the carrying capacity and right-of-way potential of the tram along congested roads remained a salient reminder to transport planners.

Of course, by the twenty-first century, the scruffier term 'tram' had been modernised to the more sleek 'light rail' – as reported by The New Zealand Herald on 30 January 2015:

"In AT's [Auckland Transport] draft Regional Land Transport Plan 2015-2025, it repeats the earlier warning that 'the city centre is already facing access capacity issues across all road entry points which, if not addressed now, will steadily worsen'.

"It says bus routes along 'key arterials such as Dominion Rd and Symonds St' will be significantly over-capacity in the 'near future', even with the CRL and bus improvements. Light rail would be part of the public transport mix, integrated into a network including electric trains and buses. It could carry 12,000 to 18,000 people an hour, compared to the 2500 to 6000 on buses..." [911]

Light Rail Dream

Auckland Transport planners dreamed of a return to the nostalgic days of the trams but with their sleeker version of course:

"Auckland Transport is investigating light rail on six main arterial roads, based on the old tram network, which was ripped up...in the 1950s. The first stage would run from Wynyard Quarter, where an historic tram service already operates, to Britomart, up Queen St and along Dominion Road. The network could then branch off into other major roads which used to have trams - Symonds St, Mt Eden Rd, Manukau Rd and Sandringham Rd.

"[Auckland Transport chairman] Lester Levy says the first stage could cost less than $1 billion but is non-commital about costs after that. He says either light or conventional rail could be extended to the airport and light rail could ultimately run out to Botany and along the Northwestern Motorway...

"...Levy stresses the CRL is still the number one priority for the region but it leaves a 'void' in the suburbs directly south of the city centre, which are not served by rail. Buses are already clogging many of these routes, such as Dominion Rd and Symonds St, in rush hour..." [912]

Light Rail Dream Continued

By the end of 2015, the light rail dream continued – as reported by The New Zealand Herald on 30 December 2015:

"Auckland Transport is considering running trams to the airport via Dominion Rd, one of the Super City's busiest commuter routes. Its consultants have nominated 20 potential tram stops between the airport and Britomart – including eight along Dominion Rd and four on Queen St – but questions are being raised about how the route could serve both long-distance travellers and commuters.

"An estimated journey time of 44 minutes for the 21km trip is seen as optimistic by the Campaign for Better Transport and Auckland Council infrastructure chairman Michael Lee, who heads a steering group of parties including KiwiRail considering 'rapid transit' options for the airport...

"Mr Lee said he had reservations about the effectiveness of a longer-distance rapid transit airport service using Dominion Rd and was sceptical about some of the numbers and assumptions in a report by the consultants. He believed there was 'a major flaw' in business case comparisons estimating the cost of extending trains to the airport at $2.3 billion compared with $1.1 billion for trams. That was because electric rail already ran to Onehunga – just 10km from the airport – yet a tram line via Dominion Rd 'exists only in the imagination at this stage'...

"An Auckland Transport spokeswoman said yesterday a decision was likely by the middle of next year on whether the airport should be served by trains or trams...The transport body is under pressure from the airport company to choose between heavy and light rail by then, to fit in with the company's plans to build a new domestic passenger terminal by 2021 and a second runway a few years later..." [913]

Airport Trains Dropped

As assured by the Auckland Transport spokeswoman, a decision was made on 27 June 2016:

"The Auckland Transport board yesterday opted to drop trains as an option for a rapid and congestion-free network to the airport, backing the earlier decision by the New Zealand Transport Agency.

"The board cited a report saying trains could cost up to $1.3 billion more than trams, though both could reach the airport from downtown Auckland in around 40 minutes. AT members also elected to protect the route for trams and buses, but board chairman Lester Levy said the technology could change from the vehicles in use today…

"Mr Levy said the business case for a heavy rail was so weak it had to be dumped. According to the report, a heavy rail line along SH20A could cost between $2.6 billion and $3 billion while light rail offered similar benefits for $1.2 billion to $1.3 billion…" [914]

Light Rail Dream Route-Protected

By March 2017, a 'separated corridor' for buses was all the dream of a light rail solution from the city to the airport had come to:

"Auckland Council and the Government have agreed to start route protection for a mass transit corridor between Auckland Airport and the city centre. The route will be along Dominion Rd. The NZ Transport Agency and Auckland Transport worked together to develop a joint solution that will progress from bus services to a light rail transit solution. The study found an advanced bus option could provide a credible solution over the next 30 years that could progress from the current bus-based system to a long-term solution.

"Transport Minister Simon Bridges said…by drawing on international expertise, they have identified a range of opportunities for bus travel through a separated corridor, using innovative technology and customer-focused solutions. In the medium to long term, this will make it possible for a staged, integrated transition to light rail along the preferred 'airport-city' route based on future demand and capacity. This work follows the Auckland transport alignment project that identified the future pressure on mass transit corridors and the need for route protection to ensure future economic growth & productivity..." [915]

Trams for 2025

A year later and the dream of light rail to the airport, or anywhere, has at least some real investment set aside – as reported by The New Zealand Herald on 13 April 2018:

"Papers released to the *Herald* under the Official Information Act show Auckland Transport and external professional advisers say the 'best case' timescale to start running trams to Mt Roskill is 2025…The papers are made up of briefing documents to Auckland Mayor Phil Goff, who is a big fan of trams but has not publicly committed any money.

"Last week, the Government put aside $4 billion for trams in Auckland in its draft 10-year transport plan. A briefing paper to Goff last November contained 'broad estimates' of $2.17b to $2.985b for trams from the CBD to the airport. No costs were given for trams from the CBD to West Auckland.

"The Labour-led Government, Auckland Transport and New Zealand Transport Agency are committed to building trams to the airport. Transport Minister and Te Atatu MP Phil Twyford has promised an immediate start on trams from the CBD to Westgate in West Auckland…" [916]

Overseas Funding

As Bernard Orsman of The New Zealand Herald reported on 9 February 2019, there was at least one keen investor eager to start construction of Auckland's proposed light rail projects. However, there was always a reason not to proceed before a *strong examination*:

"Last April [2018], the NZ Super Fund teamed up with a Canadian pension fund, CDPQ, with funds of about $350b worldwide, to submit an unsolicited proposal to the Government to design, build, own and operate light rail in Auckland. Government ministers welcomed the proposal, but said the project would be open to all comers...

"The NZ Transport Agency (NZTA) has been working on a business case and procurement process for light rail since May last year, which a spokesman said is nearing completion...

"A Treasury paper, written last year by national infrastructure manager David Taylor, called for a strong examination of light rail in Auckland given the size of the project, the fiscal risks and the building and operational challenges. 'This is one of the biggest projects New Zealand has seen and extremely complex, given that it is to be built through the middle of some of the busiest streets in Auckland. It entails digging up the streets to a considerable depth, causing major disruptions to traffic and business,' said Taylor, who noted Edinburgh light rail took six years to build and cost more than twice initial estimates." [917]

Light Rail Dream Setback

The light rail dream for Auckland remained just a dream – as reported by the Stuff Limited website on 19 September 2019:

"The Labour-led Government has been forced into another humiliating rail backdown during its 'year of delivery', conceding that most of the $463 million set aside by the NZ Transport Agency to spend on the Auckland light rail project will now be spent on other projects, including roads.

"Transport Minister Phil Twyford admitted on Tuesday that the NZTA was now looking at other ways of spending $313 million of the $463 million it had planned to spend on light rail, after the project hit serious delays. The reversal has come about because construction on the light rail – which will run from Auckland's central business district to Mt Roskill, a distance of 8 kilometres by car – has been delayed until at least 2021.

"In the lead up to the 2017 election, Prime Minister Jacinda Ardern promised that this section of the light rail track, which would later continue out to Auckland airport, would be built in just four years. Now it won't be started until at least 2021, a significant back down for the Government which directed NZTA to start funding light rail for the first time in its history last year…" [918]

Back to Reality

The Greater Auckland website hosted a post written by Auckland Transport's Chief AT Metro Officer, Mark Lambert, on 30 May 2017. That post explained the realities of Auckland's transport situation and the practical steps underway to rectify *decades of underinvestment*:

"Public transport is all about numbers – literally bums on seats…And in Auckland those numbers keep heading skywards, reaching 87 million passenger trips in the year to March, a growth of 6.8 per cent on the previous year. March itself was a record with 9.4 million passenger trips across Auckland's bus, train and ferry services. That's the most trips since 1956, when most Aucklanders weren't even born and the last Auckland tram was decommissioned...

"Trains carried 19 million passenger trips in the year to March, with 2.2 million carried in March alone. And once the City Rail Link is built both the capacity and the convenience of the network will push it even further towards the train system Aucklanders need.

"Buses are the backbone of public transport used by Aucklanders, with 61.9 million passenger trips in the year to March. The huge success of the Northern Busway now means that more than half of the people who travel across the Auckland Harbour Bridge on a weekday do so on a bus...To keep Aucklanders moving AT is in the process of revolutionising the city's entire bus network...

"The New Network will bring a whole new transport philosophy to Auckland. Instead of longer direct routes, there will be shorter, more frequent routes which connect with other bus, train and ferry services at interchanges. This way Aucklanders can take advantage of rapid transit routes such as the Northern Busway, the train network and the ferries which are unencumbered by general traffic...

"New bus stops and shelters are being provided as the new bus routes of the New Network are implemented...Park-and-Ride also has its part to play in proving access to the AT Metro system. More spaces are being provided across the network, particularly at the periphery where good local and feeder bus services are less economical to provide. Enhanced facilities will be provided in the next year at Silverdale, Papakura and Pukekohe with a number of other investigations underway.

"The AT HOP card is used on more than 91 percent of public transport journeys, which is better than most bigger cities in the world. The HOP card also enabled the introduction of Simpler Fares so that customers can tag-on and tag-off for each trip on buses and trains but only pay a single zone-based fare for their entire journey of up to five transfers over four hours...

"With the rollout of the AT Metro New Network, new buses are being introduced and the age of the fleet is reducing with improvements in emissions and air quality. We plan to introduce the first zero emission bus into the AT Metro network in the next year...

"On one hand we are working to catch up to where we should already be because of decades of underinvestment while on the other we are working hard to keep up with the 45,000 people entering Auckland every year. Adding that many people to the city is fantastic for the economy and for building a city we all want to live in but it does provide challenges for the transport system…" [919]

The New Bus Network

The new bus network referred to by Mark Lambert was first proposed in 2013 and completed in September 2019. Auckland Transport published a progress table of bus passenger journeys per district for 2018 in November of that year:

"South – New Network launched 30 October 2016 - September 2017 - up   11%   on previous year - September 2018 - up 6%

"West – New Network launched 11 June 2017 - May 2018 - up 11% on previous year

"East – New Network launched 10 December 2017 - October 2018 - up 17% on previous year

"Central – New Network launched 8 July 2018 - October 2018 - up 7% on previous year

"North – New Network launched 30 September 2018 - October 2018 - up 12% on previous year

"Pre-New Network – buses travelled 44.6 million kilometres every year and Post-New Network - buses travelled 59.1 million kilometres every year." [920]

Park and Ride

While more park and ride spaces were said by Mark Lambert to be on the way, a chronic shortage remained by March 2019, and Auckland Transport sought to prosper from that shortage by charging excessively for nearby parking:

"Auckland Transport is under fire for stinging motorists who miss out on scarce North Shore park-and-ride spots with new parking fees in the town centre. The Automobile Association has hit out at the transport authority, saying the city's park and ride facilities are already 'woefully inadequate' and the move will discourage motorists from ditching cars and using public transport.

"It comes as Auckland motorists are being hit with a regional fuel tax to help solve the city's crippling congestion which is costing the city up to $2 billion a year in lost productivity...Commuters say things have got worse since a $1-an-hour fee was imposed for street parking near the park-and-ride facility. Parking is free at the park-and-ride, if you can find a space...

"All the city's park-and-ride spaces are generally taken by 8.30am, and even at 7.30am only 15 per cent are vacant. Albany's park-and-ride has long been a focus of complaints, with motorists who miss out forced to park on grass verges and berms, risking a $40 fine, or find other nearby spaces.

"Auckland Transport says park-and-rides are an essential component of public transport, but a Herald assessment last year found they were well down the Auckland Council-controlled organisation's pecking order, accounting for around 2 per cent of the 10-year budget..." [921]

More Park and Rides On the Way

Keen to meet the demand, Auckland Transport promised more park and ride spaces – as reported by Bob Dey on 24 July 2019:

"Auckland Transport said yesterday it would open a new 281-space park and ride at Takaanini and add more spaces at Albany & Hibiscus Coast Busway Stations.

"Auckland Transport's integrated networks executive general manager, Mark Lambert, said just over 500 more parking spots would be opened this financial year. Auckland bus stations have almost 6000 park & ride bays and most of them are full by 8am. The largest is at Albany, where another 135 parking spaces have been added to the existing 1100.

"Auckland Transport is also planning another 90 parking spaces at the Hibiscus Coast Busway Station at Silverdale, which would be open by the middle of next year." [922]

Public Transport Milestone

It was no wonder that, by 2019, public transport facilities and infrastructure was stretched to the limit – as reported by Radio New Zealand on 6 June 2019:

"Aucklanders will have a day of free transport later this month to celebrate 100 million public trips taken in the past year. Trains, buses and most ferries will be free on Sunday 23 June to thank Aucklanders and encourage more people to try public transport, Auckland Transport said.

"Mayor Phil Goff said it had been the biggest year of public transport use since 1951 when trams and trolley buses were still used in the city. The milestone had been reached months ahead of schedule, he said.

"Auckland Transport chairman Lester Levy said when he took over in 2012, the number of trips taken was just 70 million a year, and before Britomart opened in 2003, it was as low as 28 million…" [923]

Cycling Milestone

One mode of public transport not heralded by Auckland Transport or the Mayor – probably because it generated no fare revenue – was cycling. Yet, it had also recently reached a milestone and achieved exponential growth as an alternative to commuting by train, bus, or ferry – as reported by The New Zealand Herald on 12 March 2018:

"The Tamaki Drive cycleway has just turned 42. The milestone is significant because it is a reminder that cycling has been part of Auckland's urban landscape for decades, yet its acceptance as part of the transport mix still faces bumps and impediments.

"Hundreds of cyclists turned up when the harbourside cycleway opened on a sunny Saturday in March 1976. The budget for the route from the city to St Heliers was $1000, which included white paint for a separation strip.

"Budgets for contemporary projects, such as along Karangahape Rd, run to millions of dollars and take forever to get signed off. The evidence is clear that cycling will become more, not less, widespread, and the benefits to the city will mount. The problem cycleways have getting into gear lies with their planning.

"The use of cycles is rising steadily. Last year, counters laid across the city recorded 3.67 million cycle trips, up 6.2 per cent on 2016. Since July last year, 5.2km of new cycleways have been added to the network. Auckland Transport aims to complete 10km by June. Growth is certain to increase as the cost of electric bikes fall and bike-sharing expands…

"Cycling appeals to commuters weary of congestion and delays as it is economical and because it is a healthy and green alternative to sitting in a car for a couple of hours a day. It should appeal to city planners because protected bike lanes are far cheaper than road projects.

"The challenge for Auckland, a city designed for vehicles, is to find better ways to accommodate the wave of cycles coming down the path. There needs to be better consultation than has occurred with affected parties along K Rd, in West Lynn, in Mt Albert and across the bridge at Northcote.

"It is easy to assert that residents and businesses get a chance to have a say. They do, but in the long lead time costs rise, doubts creep in and designs change. The other lesson from these projects is the tendency for planners to embrace gold-plated schemes. Two years ago, the K Rd budget was $11.7 million. The latest figure is $17 million.

"Cycle lanes do not always need to be high-end projects. The 3m dedicated lane on Nelson St has 400mm concrete slabs along its road edge, sufficient to keep cyclists safe from heavily-laden trucks. The route was installed quickly and gets plenty of use on week days…" [924]

Ferry Milestone

The number of passengers boarding the ferries had also increased at a steady rate. In December 2016, The New Zealand Herald reported:

"Six million passengers used Auckland's ferries this year, a milestone not reached since 1959 when the harbour bridge opened..." [925]

However, by May 2019, the service provided by the ferries was the focus of a great deal of criticism – particularly that the ferry owner, the Fullers Group, was not operating as a true affiliate of the otherwise-united Auckland public transport network:

"The Government is being urged to step in to resolve issues with the Waiheke ferry service, as irate commuters face being left out in the cold over the winter months. It comes as reduced winter sailings to the island have seen many passengers stranded on the dock, missing appointments and unable to get home.

"Auckland councillor Chris Darby is writing to Minister of Transport Phil Twyford to ask for Fullers to lose a special status which exempts its ferry services from Auckland Transport oversight and competitive tendering rules. That would bring Fullers' Waiheke and Devonport routes under the oversight of Auckland Transport, allowing for integrated fares and giving the organisation a close look at Fullers' operations, he says.

"Currently Auckland Transport can penalise rail and bus companies that fail to deliver on their contracts, but Fullers' Waiheke and Devonport routes have no such rules. 'They can be as late as possible and they only have to answer to their customers,' Darby said.

"The National Government brought in the current public transport model to encourage competition in the sector. But former National Transport Minister Steven Joyce exempted Fullers' services from the model, against Auckland Transport's wishes.

"'Auckland Transport argued way back then to the then-minister that all services were integral to the wider public transport network,' Darby said. 'The then-minister took that all into account and decided with Fullers. That exemption means Auckland Transport can't see into that business - it can't see its revenues, can't see the patronage mix, and they don't have control over the fare structures in the same way...'" [926]

Fullers Petition

By August 2019, Chris Darby's call for change had gathered pace – as reported by The New Zealand Herald:

"Two months ago [North Shore ward councillor Chris] Darby started a petition 'Let's bring Fullers into line' – which has received over 4,200 signatures, and is due to close next week. The petition calls for the Minister of Transport, Phil Twyford, to remove Fullers' special status - which exempts its ferry services from Auckland Transport oversight and competitive tendering rules.

"'They are the only part of the Auckland public transport network exempt from transport regulator oversight, which ensures competitive tendering and prescribed levels of service,' the petition website said. 'We wish to make the Devonport and Waiheke services contracted provisions under the Land Transport Management Act 2003, to ensure fare structure integration and consistent levels of service with Auckland Transport oversight. These mechanisms are otherwise known as the Public Transport Operating Model (PTOM).'

"Despite Fullers meeting with local MPs, board members, local councillors, Auckland Mayor Phil Goff, and Auckland Transport representatives over the past few months – any 'promises have proven to be hollow', Darby said.

"In May [2020], it was announced the PTOM would be reviewed, however, Transport Minister Phil Twyford said this would not be completed until mid-next year..." [927]

Working Toward PTOM

As reported by Stuff.co.nz, the petition had some 5500 signatures when it was handed to the Transport Minister, Phil Twyford, by Chris Darby on 20 September 2019:

"Twyford in accepting the petition repeated that a review of PTOM and any changes to legislation could take a good two years.

"'I'll be convening a meeting with the chief executive officer of AT and Fullers, to begin that journey, and to begin to look at fare integration (discounts) and fleet resilience (reliability),' said Darby...

"Fullers has said it is happy to become part of AT's integrated ticket system, meaning from February connecting journeys by bus or train could be free. But AT has to get them on board via purely commercial negotiations, and one thing we already know is that ferry services are expensive.

"A two-year attempt to launch a new strategy, new ferries, and new contracts across all services, effectively stalled when the cost to AT became apparent. A June report by AT also noted the high level of subsidies for ferry services would continue to be an issue.

"'Funding pressures for added service is likely to restrain growth on ferries so a modest growth path can be expected and is currently projected at 6.3m passengers,' it said. Which means anything which needs significantly more public funding, will become highly political...

"Fullers said it had invested $15 million in two refurbished ferries, each with capacity for 400 passengers to back-up the Waiheke and Devonport runs. 'The new vessels are a demonstration of our commitment to improving our service and developing an integrated network,' said Mike Horne, the chief executive,

"Horne said the company was continuing to work with AT and the council on a more efficient, integrated ferry network. Fullers has commissioned consultants PWC to assess what the cost would be for Auckland Transport, if the service was run on the normal PTOM, subsidised model. That is when the real test of political commitment to a better ferry service for Waiheke Island and Devonport, will come." [928]

However, 2020 brought with it Covid-19 which significantly reduced Fullers' domestic commuter and international tourist business...

Road Transport
Roads, Roads, Roads

"Auckland has been lambasted by an Australian transport expert as one of the world's most car-biased cities. Paul Mees, who for 10 years has portrayed Auckland to his students at Melbourne universities as having worst-practice transport systems, said the city would rank top of a world league table for motorways...

"Dr Mees said he had no doubt Transport Minister Steven Joyce was correct in observing that about 85 per cent of Aucklanders travelled to work each day using road-based transport, compared with only '1.5 per cent or so' taking trains. The minister cited those statistics in defence of a 1.4 billion budget for the Waterview motorway project, for which the Transport Agency has selected a Fletcher Construction-led consortium.

"Dr Mees…said…'For half a century Auckland has pursued the most car-based transport policy of just about any city in the developed world, so it would be amazing if the car didn't dominate the travel patterns of Aucklanders…The question is not what people are doing when they haven't really got a choice – the evidence is that the very modest public transport upgradings that have happened already in Auckland have been flooded by passengers.' He believed the local community and Auckland's elected councillors were more appreciative of the need for better public transport than a decade ago, but the Government still resisted 'that uncomfortable route'." [929]

Planned Road Funding

In keeping with Dr Mees' assessment, the Government did not disappoint – as reported by The New Zealand Herald on 26 July 2011:

"Transport Minister Steven Joyce this morning released the Government Policy Statement on Land Transport Funding 2012 which details plans to invest about $36 billion over the next ten years in state highways, local roads, public transport, road policing and road safety promotion. The plan makes about $2.95 billion available in 2012/13 for investment in the land transport sector, rising to $3.25 billion in 2014/15 and a total of about $36 billion over ten years which is a similar level of spending to that in current policy…

"It lifts the funding available for new and improved state highways by $125 million for the first three years to further support the State Highway improvement programme including progressing the seven Roads of National Significance." [930]

Indeed, the decade, 2010 to 2019, was to be a busy time for road construction which was not all that surprising given that the National Party governed for most of those years. One of the first projects out of the blocks was the Auckland-Manukau Eastern Transport Initiative. That was followed closely by a start on the western ring route, including the Waterview connection.

Auckland-Manukau Eastern Transport Initiative

The Auckland-Manukau Eastern Transport Initiative (AMETI) was first endorsed by the Auckland City Council's Transport and Urban Linkages Committee in July 2007 but any progress on the design of the project was not started until March 2010 – as reported by The new Zealand Herald:

"Auckland's long-awaited, $1.33 billion package of eastern suburban transport projects is about to gather steam under a $15 million design contract [awarded to Opus Transport Consultancy]. A tender for detailed design work needed to start about $200 million worth of projects around Panmure, including a new four-lane road and the abolition or replacement of the suburb's difficult mega-roundabout, was endorsed yesterday by Auckland City Council's transport committee.

"The Ameti package of projects is being developed as a joint venture between the Auckland and Manukau city councils with the Auckland Regional Transport Authority and the Government's Transport Agency, which has required it to be staged over about 20 years.

"Auckland City's share of the package – to be paid for from a combination of government subsidies, development levies, rates and, possibly, road tolls – amounts to $893 million…

"Opus will also design traffic improvements between the highway and Panmure Bridge, with provision for bus priority lanes and a separate structure for cyclists and pedestrians to be attached to the bridge in a project with Manukau City.

"The traffic improvements are likely to include replacing the five-way Panmure roundabout with a radically remodelled intersection, possibly controlled by traffic lights…Auckland City transport policy group manager Don Munro said the target construction start date for the Panmure phase of Ameti was 2012, with completion expected by 2019." [931]

The Western Ring Route

The oft-repeated adage that building more roads will attract more cars was obviously believed by western ring route planners – as reported by The New Zealand Herald on 21 December 2010:

"Both ends of Auckland's western ring route will be widened at a cost of up to $160 million as early as next year, after the Transport Agency admitted underestimating traffic demand. It said yesterday its board had given approval for sections of the Southern and Northern motorways to be widened to ease congestion and improve travel times. That follows serious traffic delays where the ring route was joined to the Southern Motorway at Manukau in September in a $220 million project, which was meant to provide a seamless link.

"Congestion has eased somewhat since the agency restricted flows from the ring route to the main motorway, before installing traffic lights on the connecting ramp last week. But after complaints from commuters about delays of up to 40 minutes reached Transport Minister Stephen Joyce, the agency decided to bring forward the first stage of a previously unfunded plan to widen the Southern Motorway between Manukau and Papakura.

"Its board has also decided to avoid similar congestion problems at the top end of the ring route, by widening the Northern Motorway between Constellation Drive and Greville Rd to cope with the extra traffic expected once the $1.75 billion Waterview connection completes the bypass route in 2016…" [932]

The Southern Gateway

By January 2011, the southern end of the western ring route was complete:

"South Auckland motorists are set to benefit from a more direct route to the airport with the completion of the new $220 million Manukau motorway. The opening of the SH20 Cavendish to Puhinui connecting road and westbound on-ramp in Manukau marks the completion of the final stage of the project, which has opened progressively since August. The Manukau extension motorway connects the southwestern (SH20) and southern motorways (SH1) in Manukau and has taken four years to construct…The project forms the southern gateway to the western ring route…" [933]

The Northern Gateway

Progress was also being made at the northern end of the western ring route – as reported by The New Zealand Herald:

"Yesterday [6 August 2011] the $220 million Hobsonville motorway opened to the public, a milestone in plans to ease pressure on Auckland's State Highway 1…The public were allowed to walk on the new 6km, four-lane motorway yesterday before it opened, connecting the northwestern motorway at Hobsonville Road to Upper Harbour Bridge. The project also includes a 3km, four-lane extension of the northwestern motorway north to Whenuapai…" [934]

The Waterview Connection

The Waterview Connection was described by Transport Minister, Steven Joyce, in May 2009, as: "New Zealand's most expensive roading project ever…essential to the continued growth and economic development in the Auckland region. It will also contribute to better links for business and freight between key industrial hubs in the cities of Manukau, Auckland, Waitakere and North Shore…" [935]

On 1 July 2010, long-awaited funding for the Waterview Connection was granted – as reported by the Automobile Association:

"Drivers in Auckland and local communities will both benefit from the NZ Transport Agency's announcement today of funding for the Waterview Connection, says Auckland AA District Council Chairman Paul Hesseling.

"The Waterview Connection is the final link in a chain of improvements to Auckland's Western Ring Route. If work goes ahead on schedule, it will complete the Western Ring Route in 2015, providing a single motorway between Manukau and the North Shore as an alternative to SH1 and the Auckland Harbour Bridge crossing...

"The AA is pleased with the NZ Transport Agency's design for a tunnel with three lanes in each direction. 'The Government has decided to fund a design which is future proof and one that mitigates impact on the community it goes through as much as possible,' says Mr Hesseling." [936]

Community Impact

As referred to in the previous chapter, the impact of the proposed Waterview tunnels and motorway on the local community was not as readily accepted as the Government and its motor-centric supporters would have liked. One of the main concerns for residents was the siting of a main control building next to the Waterview Primary School and ventilation stacks at each end of the tunnels – as reported by The New Zealand Herald:

"The [Transport] agency also intends building 25-metre ventilation stacks at each end of the tunnels, saying that it will be high enough to disperse vehicle fumes without the need to filter them.

"[North West Community Association chairman Bill] McKay said his community would prepare evidence to show that on a still and foggy day, emissions pollution would fall down on the school. Transport Agency principal project director Clive Fuhr said traffic fumes falling on the school would be a rare occurrence which would not justify spending up to $70 million on filtration equipment." [937]

It wasn't until July 2011 that community concerns were judged to be allayed – as reported by The New Zealand Herald:

"A board of inquiry has given the green light to the Waterview Connection…In September 2010 the Government directed that the Waterview Connection Proposal be considered by an independent Board of Inquiry chaired by Environment Court Judge Laurie Newhook… Construction is expected to begin before Christmas." [938]

First Sod Turned

However, it was not until August 2012 that a real start was made on the Waterview tunnels:

"Work has finally begun on the $1.4 billion Waterview Connection in Auckland, with the first sod turned over. Officials gathered at the site in Owairaka this morning where excavation will begin on the 30m-deep trench. It is the first step for the construction of the twin 2.4km tunnels beneath suburban Auckland, which is on track to begin next year…" [939]

Waterview Tunnel Open to Traffic

The Waterview Tunnel was open to traffic in both directions on 2 July 2017 and that opening day drew thousands of motorists eager to drive through.

One of the principal contractors, Fletcher Construction, described the scale of the project and its connecting roading infrastructure:

"When the Waterview Connection opened in 2017 it was touted as the biggest change to Auckland's roading network since the opening of the Harbour Bridge in 1959. The new tunnel and interchange connects the Southwestern and Northwestern Motorways (State Highways 20 and 16) to complete the Western Ring Route – a 48km motorway alternative easing pressure on SH1.

"More than just a highway, the Waterview Connection is a multi-modal corridor that provides pedestrian and cyclist routes, and public open spaces.

"Half of the new motorway – 2.4km – is underground. A custom built tunnel boring machine (the tenth largest in the world) was used to construct twin, three-lane tunnels up to 40m below ground.

"The other main feature of the project is the Great North Road Interchange that connects the twin tunnels to the existing road network. Four ramps, totalling 1.7km in length carry traffic to and from the tunnels onto the Southwestern and Northwestern motorways." [940]

Additional Harbour Bridge

In 2008, the New Zealand Transport Agency began a study to ascertain the precise positioning of an additional harbour crossing in the form of another bridge or tunnel. This positioning was becoming increasingly important to the redevelopment of the Wynyard Quarter.

Further to that study, the Agency published a progress report on 22 March 2011 in which it indicated a second bridge, operated in conjunction with the first, as a preferred option – as reported by The New Zealand Herald:

"A Transport Agency report issued yesterday estimated the cost of a bridge at up to $3.9 billion, whereas two three-lane tunnels would cost $5.3 billion. A new crossing is needed within about 20 years to cope with the city's growth and to bolster the ageing harbour bridge. A new bridge would run close to the existing 52-year-old structure, diverging from it at Northcote Pt and then forming a triangle to the Auckland isthmus through Westhaven.

"Auckland Council transport chairman Mike Lee said the combination of new and old bridges would make the city look 'pug ugly' and would not increase transport resilience, given how close together they would be. He said the Transport Agency had revived the bridge option, which was ruled out in a 2008 study, at the behest of Transport Minister Steven Joyce...

"But Mr Joyce said there would be a strategic need for another harbour link within 20 years, before the clip-on lanes of the old bridge would need replacing, although he understood a newly completed $86 million strengthening project had 'moderated' the Transport Agency's view about their longevity. 'It's still within a 20-year cycle, but I think they've got a bit less urgent about when.'

"Both a bridge and tunnels would cater for public transport, cycling and walking lanes – but not trains. The agency estimates that a rail tunnel, which the new report indicates would be difficult to justify for 30 years, could add $1.6 billion to the bill..." [941]

Victoria Park Tunnel

Two lanes of the Victoria Park Tunnel were ready for northbound traffic on 14 November 2011 – as reported by The New Zealand Herald:

"Serious traffic delays in Auckland last night were blamed on cautious and curious drivers travelling through the new Victoria Park tunnel after two lanes were opened yesterday...

"Although the northbound-only tunnel has three lanes...the [Transport] agency was unable to open it to full capacity for the 55,000 vehicles travelling through it each day until it could complete motorway works along St Mary's Bay by March...

"The third lane would remain coned off until the bridge's movable lane barrier could be brought to the northern end of the tunnel to manage traffic emerging from the tunnel. That could not be done until work was completed on widening the surface motorway through St Mary's Bay by one lane in each direction – an integral part of the $406 million project." [942]

The four Victoria Park flyover lanes were open to southbound traffic on 9 January 2012 – as per the New Zealand Transport Agency media release of that date:

"One of the most significant changes to Auckland driving conditions for half a century will be made tomorrow morning...when the NZ Transport Agency opens the Victoria Park flyover on State Highway 1 in a new layout to carry four lanes of southbound traffic.

"The fifty year old flyover beside Auckland's CBD carried two-way traffic until last November, when northbound traffic was diverted into the recently completed Victoria Park tunnel..." [943]

The third, northbound lane through the tunnel was open to traffic on 26 March 2012.

"On the same day, the NZTA will open a fifth lane for the extra traffic during the afternoon peak from the Beaumont Street/Fanshawe on-ramp through St Marys Bay to the Auckland Harbour Bridge..." [944]

Newmarket Viaduct Replacement

When the contract to build the Newmarket Viaduct was awarded in September 1963 at a contract price of $1,038,792, it was then the largest contract ever let for a bridge structure in New Zealand.

By 2009, the Viaduct had become the busiest stretch of motorway in the country, carrying 161,490 vehicles a day, of which southbound and northbound sections carried 83,117 and 78,373 vehicles a day respectively...

The concerns about its inability to comply with earthquake standards and to cater to the increasing traffic, the expansion of the viaduct was called for and because it was unable to be widened, a complete deconstruction and replacement of the structure was opted for as a solution. The $244 million, four-stage replacement project began in June 2009.

"Stage one included construction of a four-lane southbound bridge beside the old southbound section. The old southbound viaduct was dismantled in stage two to construct new northbound lanes in stage three. Stage four involved the demolition of the old northbound sections and relocation of the northbound traffic to a new three-lane structure." [945]

All this was done while maintaining normal traffic flows throughout the construction and deconstruction period.

The new southbound side of the viaduct was opened in September 2010 and the whole project was completed and opened by Transport Minister, Gerry Brownlee on 15 March 2013:

"Transport Minister Gerry Brownlee says the formal completion today of the Newmarket Viaduct Replacement Project marks a key milestone in the Government's long-term strategy to improve transport connections in Auckland and grow the region's economy…Today's ceremony also marks the completion of a wider transport milestone for Auckland – the end of more than a decade of staged improvements through the city's Central Motorway Junction, Mr Brownlee says.

"The $244 million Newmarket project marks the southern end of the Central Motorway Junction – the busiest section of motorway in New Zealand. At its northern end is the Victoria Park Tunnel, which opened in late 2011 – the first of the Government's Roads of National Significance to be completed…" [946]

Travel Time Savings

Following the official opening of the Newmarket Viaduct replacement and the recent publication of a New Zealand Transport Agency survey, Gerry Brownlee continued with his positive spin on the benefits of his government's 'roads of national significance' programme.

The survey showed that average travel time savings of up to five minutes per trip were achieved on sections of state highways that are part of the programme designed to target congestion and environmental concerns around the country. For instance, one of the highway sections quoted in the survey, Auckland's Victoria Park tunnel, is said to have "…reduced travel times by between five and 17 minutes." [947]

NZTA Research Report

The survey quoted by the Transport Minister was included in a study undertaken for the Transport Agency by Ian Wallis and David Lupton of Ian Wallis Associates Limited. Their report, *The costs of congestion reappraised*, was published in February 2013.

The New Zealand Herald commented on 24 March 2013:

"Snarled-up Auckland roads are costing the country $1.25 billion a year, new Government-commissioned research reveals. It is commuters and businesses who pick up most of the tab, through wasted petrol, wasted time and delayed shipments.

"Consultants Ian Wallace and David Lupton say getting the city's roads flowing freely is now 'uneconomical, if not impossible', and the Government should instead aim to run the road network at capacity: moving relatively slowly, but still moving.

"The report, commissioned by the New Zealand Transport Agency, indicates the cost of congestion has increased $550 million since the last study in 2004, though the two studies' methodologies differed…" [948]

While that estimated, total cost of congested roads might be somewhat arbitrary and mean little to the average commuter, the report's proposed definition of congestion certainly hit the mark: *"Congestion occurs when the demand for the road exceeds its capacity"* [949] – brazenly obvious to the motorist trapped in his or her metal box, going nowhere fast in a carpark that stretches on, seemingly forever.

Traffic Numbers

In a separate article published on 24 March 2013, The New Zealand Herald quoted NZTA and Auckland Transport traffic statistics for 2011:

"The stretch of State Highway One between Khyber Pass and Gillies Ave is just 900m, but it is the busiest stretch in Auckland's highway network.

"New Zealand Transport Agency figures from 2011 show the road carried more than 196,000 vehicles a day…Auckland Harbour Bridge is next off the rank, at 158,220 vehicles a day, and the Northwestern Motorway between Western Springs and Newton Rd carried an average of 121,542 vehicles a day in 2011.

"Auckland Transport figures show local roads also bear a heavy burden. The South Eastern Highway caters to 56,000 vehicles a day; Great North Rd's load is 50,000. Out west, Lincoln Rd has fewer vehicles each day (48,000) but is still one of the city's most congested..." [950]

Rapid Vehicle Growth

An answer to the obvious question of 'where are all these vehicles coming from?' was provided by Brian Gaynor in The New Zealand Herald, published on 14 February 2015:

"The total number of vehicles in Auckland is growing more rapidly than the rest of the country based on 2000 to 2013 statistics. During this 13-year period Auckland's road vehicle fleet expanded by 35.5 per cent compared with 25.8 per cent for the rest of the country. As a result Auckland's roads are becoming more and more congested as the number of vehicles continues to grow rapidly…" [951]

Dire Congestion

More than a year later and congestion was worse:

"Auckland transport officials are being told to front up and tackle the dire congestion which is driving people out of their own city. The results of an Automobile Association survey of its members found almost half were reaching breaking point and were considering moving house or changing jobs because of traffic.

"Two-thirds said congestion had significantly worsened over the past five years. The morning peak was heavier and lasted longer, while the traffic even during off-peak hours on motorways and arterial roads was deteriorating...Of the 1300 survey respondents, almost 75 per cent considered transport policy either a very high or high priority for the incoming mayor…" [952]

Increasing Traffic Chaos

Another year and more traffic chaos:

"Auckland's rapid population growth is increasing traffic chaos on the city's roads with a dire prediction that one in three main roads will be congested by 2020...

"Every week, 800 new vehicles are registered in Auckland, further challenging the city's geography of a narrow isthmus where all the land available for roads and public transport has been developed, says NZTA Auckland highway manager Brett Gliddon. 'That's forced existing transport corridors to absorb more and more traffic,' he said.

"Bumper-to-bumper traffic, overcrowded buses and trains and long journeys to the airport are a daily nuisance and a reminder of a city under pressure from decades of under-investment in infrastructure...

"National Road Carriers boss David Aitken says truckies are quitting out of sheer frustration at sitting idle in traffic. Aitken said about 10 years ago trucks could do five trips a day across the city. That was now down to two or three trips today. He blamed under-investment in infrastructure going back to the 1960s and Auckland Council's Unitary Plan for increasing housing and industry without a parallel plan for infrastructure…" [953]

Losers and Winners

As the losers – the road-weary commuters and truckies – struggled with the numbers, the winners – the vehicle importers and dealers – kept winning – as observed by Brian Gaynor in The New Zealand Herald of 15 July 2017:

"The New Zealand vehicle market is booming...Motor Industry Association data shows that there were 107,880 new car sales in the year ended June [2017], an 11.8 per cent increase over the previous corresponding period...Commercial vehicle sales have also soared in recent years with 49,048 new sales in the June 2017 year, an 18.9 per cent increase over the June 2016 year...

"These figures clearly demonstrate that car importers and dealers are experiencing unprecedented boom conditions. Consequently, the country's total vehicle imports have increased by 15.8 per cent, in dollar terms, over the past 12 months and are our largest import category by a wide margin.

"These vehicle registration figures explain why our roads have become more and more congested. The total number of registered vehicles has increased by 637,676 over the past five years with around a third of these, around 215,000, in Auckland.

"Neither the Government, nor the Auckland City Council, anticipated this massive growth in vehicle numbers and our roads cannot cope with this volume increase. Another few years of national vehicle registration growth of more than 150,000 per annum will put further pressure on the country's roads..." [954]

Deficient Road Safety

As well as the choking of Auckland's roads, the increasing number of vehicles was also responsible for the increasing number of road-related deaths and injuries – as reported by The New Zealand Herald on 25 May 2018:

"The number of people killed on Auckland roads in the past three years rose by 77.8 per cent. The number seriously injured rose 72.5 per cent. These figures are far higher than those for the rest of the country, which recorded rises of 22.9 and 27.6 respectively...

"The startling evidence for all this comes in a report commissioned last year by the AT board from Australian consultants Whiting Moyne.

"The report is called *Auckland Transport: Road Safety Business Improvement Review*, but behind that unexciting name the conclusions are clear. Road safety performance in Auckland in recent years...reflects a number of deficiencies of public policy at central government and local level. Most of all it reflects an absence of commitment to improving safety on New Zealand and Auckland's roads...

"In Auckland, where the problem is far worse than elsewhere, there's only 15 per cent more traffic on the roads, compared with 2014. As Mayor Phil Goff has noted, the rate of deaths and serious injuries has risen five times faster than the increase in traffic...

"The report is scathing of AT, noting that before this year, it had failed to initiate a single review of safety strategy since it was formed in 2010. Safety was valued so little in the organisation, it was the responsibility of a fourth-tier manager.

"The report recommends remedial training in road safety principles for all AT's senior managers. It also says they should have KPIs set to keep them focused on the importance of safety. They're among 45 recommendations specifically aimed at Auckland Transport...

Auckland Transport chairman, Lester Levy, responded:

"...AT has treated convenience as being more important than safety, and there would now be a 'paradigm shift'. It's going to be unpopular with a lot of people, but it's going to happen. We are determined.

"Levy means many people will not like the safety of the more vulnerable road users – motorcyclists, pedestrians and cyclists – being prioritised. Even though the report makes it clear they are the main victims in our fast-rising death and injury rates. There is a widespread quite negative attitude to vulnerable users. We are expecting resistance, but the board is resolute…" [955]

Road Tolling

By 2017, the Government had not entertained any previously-suggested solutions to solve Auckland's traffic congestion problem. Public transport had long since taken a planning and funding back seat to the Government's preferred option of building more roads.

But it was another election year and too many prospective National Party electors sitting in their cars all day, without hope, was not a good thing. Accordingly, it was time to provide some hope – as reported by The New Zealand Herald on 16 February 2017:

"The Government has confirmed it is now open to the introduction of electronic road tolling in Auckland. Finance Minister Steven Joyce has told a business audience the Government could support road tolling but will not support a regional fuel tax. 'There is no getting away from the fact that central Auckland is built on a narrow isthmus which makes it hard to get around - and the available land transport corridors are rapidly being used,' Joyce said…'So beyond the current building programme we are going to have to look at demand management to reduce the reliance on the road corridors, in favour of better use of buses, trains and ferries.'

"Joyce said the Government is developing a work programme to look at demand management tools including electronic road tolling in the medium to long term. 'But to be clear, we see this as a way to make the roading system work better – not as a revenue raising exercise.' The Government's had an expectation that any road pricing initiative on existing motorways and highways would be as a replacement for petrol taxes and road user charges, and not in addition to them…'I stress that we are not interested in introducing a regional fuel tax,' Joyce said.

"Auckland Mayor Phil Goff has expressed his disappointment at the decision to rule out a regional fuel tax. 'While the Government has the power to rule out a fuel tax, it has a duty to the people of Auckland to come back to council with alternative solutions,' he said…'Aucklanders are fed up with sitting in their cars on the motorway for hours at a time. It's lost time for them and lost productivity for the city...'" [956]

The Nimby Effect

In an editorial published 9 June 2017, The New Zealand Herald also expressed some scepticism about the Government's acceptance of 'congestion pricing':

"Many Auckland motorists will feel sceptical that road tolls are once again being touted as a possible answer to the city's growing transport problems. The reservations come on several fronts.

"It has taken Wellington-based politicians years to come round to the idea, so any action remains several years away while an extra 800 cars clog up Auckland's streets every week.

"There are several practical problems to work through before drivers can have confidence that tolling – euphemistically known as 'congestion pricing' – will be fair and effective. And there is the understandable Nimby effect. Just as many people say they support intensification to make housing more affordable ('but not in my street'), congestion pricing can sound reasonable until the cost forces motorists to leave their warm cars at home and stand at a rainy, windswept bus stop on a cold winter night.

"These are the challenges facing Government and Auckland Council officials who will work together on the Smarter Transport Pricing Project, announced by Transport Minister Simon Bridges and mayor Phil Goff this week.

"The project will investigate whether or not to charge motorists to use certain roads - most likely motorways and main arterial routes – at busy times of the day. Officials will test different options and evaluate whether they would improve traffic flows and how they would affect the city's households and businesses." [957]

The Congestion Question

That collaboration between the Government and Auckland Council officials resulted in a Phase One Report, *The Congestion Question – Could road pricing improve Auckland's traffic?* – completed in November 2017.

Parts of the report included:

"This phase has involved establishing baseline data, background information and our communications and engagement approach to provide a foundation for the rest of the project...

"This investigation builds on the findings of the Auckland Transport Alignment Project (ATAP), which set out a 30-year vision for Auckland's transport system.

"This vision comprised three integrated elements: targeting investment to the most significant challenges, making better use out of the existing network and focusing more on managing travel demand.

"ATAP identified pricing as having significant potential to manage travel demand and reduce congestion, in conjunction with implementing the wider strategic approach. The work we have undertaken in this project to date reaffirms this...

"Our review shows technology is not a constraint to implementation, but we need to be flexible to adapt to future technology changes. Automatic number plate recognition technology is likely to be the best immediate technology solution, but satellite-based technologies could offer a more sophisticated solution in the near future...

"Our analysis in phase one of this project has built a compelling case for continuing the work we have done so far, so we can better understand the social, economic and environmental costs and benefits of congestion pricing for Auckland...

"There are conceptually four types of congestion pricing:

"Area-based – Charging vehicles for crossing a boundary or driving within that boundary at specific times of day

"Cordon-based – Charging vehicles for crossing a ring or line of charge points across a series of roads at specific times of day. Unlike area-based schemes, cordon-based schemes do not charge for traffic movement solely within the cordon

"Corridor-based – Charging vehicles to use one or more of the roads in a specific congested corridor or corridors (main highway and secondary routes)

"Network-based – Charging vehicles for travel on all congested roads in a defined geographical area" [958]

The Congestion Question – Phase Two

November 2017 and came another election with Labour and New Zealand First forming a coalition government. As reported by The New Zealand Herald on 10 February 2018, Government and local collaboration continued, and it was time to look at Phase Two of the Congestion Question:

"Commuters have been warned Auckland's gridlock nightmare is set to dramatically escalate, and the thorny issues of congestion charges is back on the agenda as Auckland Council grapples with solutions. Aucklanders already spend the equivalent of four working weeks, or 160 hours, in traffic...

"The report said severe congestion is expected to increase by 30 per cent at peak hours, and 50 per cent between the morning and evening peaks. And while the Waterview Tunnel has successfully reduced congestion, the report warns that could be short-lived…

"Finance Minister Grant Robertson, Transport Minister Phil Twyford and Auckland Mayor Phil Goff have approved the project to proceed to the second phase…The latest plan for tolls in Auckland comes after the former National Government and Auckland Council decided last June to look at the 'taboo' subject of charging motorists at different times of the day and different locations across the city…

"Building public understanding and acceptance will be critical to successfully introduce congestion pricing, the report said. The project was originally called the 'Auckland Smarter Transport Pricing Project', but has been renamed 'The Congestion Question'." [959]

A Political Twilight Zone

The Congestion Question was obviously not one to be answered in a hurry – as described by Todd Niall in a Stuff.co.nz comment published on 12 October 2020:

"OPINION: The idea of paying a fee for each trip on a road that already exists is one that only a brave politician will enthusiastically champion.

"Which may be why a joint Auckland Council-Government proposal which *Stuff* understands is complete, is sitting in a political twilight zone pending the final step from agencies to politicians…

"The mayor Phil Goff has previously favoured the idea of a congestion charge, but while seeking re-election in 2019, said it would not be in this term – so not before 2022.

"Goff also saw it replacing the regional fuel tax – meeting a political desire for any new impost to be "revenue neutral". In plain English, new charges must replace old ones…

"The political climate for courage on congestion charging, looks worrying. Auckland Council is implementing big spending cuts under its Covid-19-impacted Emergency Budget, and room for new public transport carrots to accompany a congestion charge stick, looks tight. No one said this would be easy, but neither are these decisions that can be put off, awaiting a more favourable time.

"NZTA and Auckland Transport's boards are due to soon receive The Congestion Question report, and then the council and the government need to move quickly to build community backing for it." [960]

Regional Fuel Tax is Back

While the politicians hesitated to introduce any form of congestion charge, the less palatable regional fuel tax was back on the table – as announced by the Minister of Transport, Phil Twyford, on 22 March 2018:

"Legislation to allow regions to apply for a regional fuel tax, initially for Auckland, will be introduced to Parliament today, Transport Minister Phil Twyford has announced. 'The Land Transport Management (Regional Fuel Tax) Amendment Bill will enable Auckland Council to seek funding for specific transport-related projects. It would allow funds raised in Auckland to be spent only in Auckland.'

"Auckland is at a standstill and the Auckland Council understands the frustration of its ratepayers who are spending hours of their day stuck in traffic. Auckland has gone through a massive population growth in recent years and its current infrastructure can no longer support the city.

"Improving infrastructure in Auckland is vital for its businesses and its people for whom just getting to work, school and about their daily activities can be a struggle..." [961]

Regional Fuel Tax Starts

The authority to charge a regional fuel tax was effected by means of Section 65 of the Land Transport Management (Regional Fuel Tax) Amendment Act 2018 which was passed by Parliament on 26 June 2018. The Act allowed for the establishing, replacing or varying of a Regional fuel tax scheme by Order in Council. [889]

"The Auckland regional fuel tax scheme began on 1 July 2018, at a rate of 10 cents per litre (plus GST), on petrol, diesel and their bio-variants." [962]

Tax Spent Where?

As well as the regional fuel tax, the Government also increased its fuel tax take the following year, on 1 July 2019, and some asked where it was all being spent – as reported by The New Zealand Herald:

"Fuel price hikes which come into force today will cost motorists an extra $45 a year, based on a person driving a medium-sized car 14,000km a year, the Automobile Association says.

"The 3 cent per litre tax increase is the second of three annual increases by the Government, and for Aucklanders it comes on top of a 11.5 cent additional increase last year. The price hikes were designed to fund large infrastructure projects in the city, and for some Aucklanders the progress in the last year had not been as fast as hoped.

"Auckland Business Forum chairman Michael Barnett said there had been some progress in growing public transport numbers, but traffic congestion was still worsening and the transport network was not being upgraded at a rate to match Auckland's rapid growth. 'What are we getting for our money?' he said.

"Auckland Mayor Phil Goff defended the rate of progress, saying funding from the regional fuel tax had directly contributed to eight infrastructure projects in the last year. They included arterial roads in South Auckland, the Eastern Busway which links Panmure and Pakuranga and will later be extended to Botany, and upgrades to the Auckland Airport route.

"Other projects which had been given regional fuel tax funding in the last year included the downtown ferry terminal upgrade, road safety improvements, 52km of new walkways and cycleways, and purchases of properties to allow for the construction of the Mill Road corridor.

"'This regional fuel tax is on target to raise $150 million a year, and that is matched by the Government,' Goff said. 'Without that, we would be completing already announced projects and there would be no new projects. Raising the same amount of funding through rates would lead to a 10 per cent hike for each household,' he said." [963]

Harbour Bridge – Time Running Out

As reported by The New Zealand Herald on 9 March 2019, time was running out for decisions to be made about a new harbour crossing:

"A new official report on Auckland Harbour Bridge traffic has taken the road-only option off the table and replaced it with rail-only. It's a big shift in thinking. The report also says we're well behind with the planning. The Auckland Harbour Bridge will be at full capacity for all transport modes by 2030. But a new Waitemata harbour crossing will take at least 10 years to plan and another five to seven to build...

"NZTA expects the Northern Busway to hit capacity by 2030. The paper suggests that because of this, the city will need a new Waitemata harbour crossing by then. It's just 11 years away.

"But as Transport Minister Phil Twyford told the *Weekend Herald*, the planning and approvals process for that crossing will take 'no less than a decade'. And, he said, construction is 'likely to take five to seven years. Let's say it will take at least that. That means there will be a gap of at least five years, perhaps even 10, when on current projections the Auckland Harbour Bridge will simply not be capable of handling demand.

"Adding to the problem, the number of trucks is also rising sharply. There are now 11,000 heavy vehicles on the bridge per day, most of them trucks. By 2046, that number is expected to reach 26,000: an increase of 136 per cent.

"Next surprise: the NZTA paper reveals there has been a big shift in thinking about what a new harbour crossing might be. The options used to be: road, or road and rail. Now, the road-only option has been dropped and a new one – rail only – has been added...

"Despite the NZTA paper, the whole question of a new harbour crossing languishes at the back end of the 30-year joint strategic agreement between the Government and Auckland Council, called the Auckland Transport Alignment Accord (ATAP).

"But on this question at least, the paper implies ATAP is already out of date. There are many decisions to be made. As the paper proposes, we need a business case – which does not yet exist – so we can start making them."
[964]

Suburban Rail
Project DART
As well as the tentative, preliminary advances being made to extend the city end of the suburban railway network, detailed later, real progress had already been made to the network in the outlying suburbs – including a branch line to the new station of Manukau which was opened for passenger services on 15 April 2012.

The inclusion of Manukau station to the suburban railway network represented the culmination of Project DART (Developing Auckland's Rail Transport) – agreed to by the Government in 2005 – "...to upgrade the Auckland rail network to improve its reliability, safety, and service." [965]

"Project DART involved a number of upgrades, the most significant being the redevelopment of the Newmarket Station and junction, the duplication of the Western Line to Swanson and improvements of stations along it, and the construction of the New Lynn Station and trenching the rail line through the New Lynn Township..." [965]

Project DART also included the modernisation of some 41 of the region's railway stations.

"The most significant component of Project DART is the duplication (double tracking) of the Western Rail Line between Avondale and Swanson...Work on this part of the project began in late 2005 with the double-tracking between Titirangi Road and Henderson. This piece of tracking was completed in June 2007 and, subsequently, the section between Henderson and Swanson was completed.

"In late 2007, work began on the sections between Whau Creek and Titirangi Road including the major work being done at the New Lynn station. This section was completed June 2010. The section between Avondale and Whau Creek began double-track construction in late 2008 and was also completed June 2010...

"Ontrack was given permission to begin work on electrifying the Auckland rail network in 2008, with a deadline of 2013 for completion...Electrification of the lines...extend from the CBD to Papakura in the south and to Swanson in the west, and include the Onehunga Branch Line and Manukau Rail Link...

"In total, central Government has contributed a total of $1.6 billion to the upgrades of the Auckland rail network; $600 million on Project DART, $500 million on the electrification and $500 million on the purchase of new electric trains. The Regional Council (ARC and ARTA) has contributed a total of $900 million, and other parties have contributed around $150 million. Thus the total cost associated with the Auckland upgrades is in the vicinity of $2.65 billion..." [965]

Electric Trains for Auckland

As well as the track and station upgrades, Auckland suburban services have gradually replaced its diesel locomotives with electric multiple units (EMUs) starting with a tender process that followed the Government's allocation of funds for their purchase – as reported by the Railway Gazette on 16 July 2010:

"KiwiRail has shortlisted Hitachi, Hyundai Rotem, Bombardier Transportation and a consortium of CAF and Mitsubishi for the contract to supply up to 38 three-car electric multiple-units to operate Auckland suburban services.

"KiwiRail is working with Auckland Regional Transport Authority to procure the 1067 mm gauge trains as part of the 25 kV 50 Hz suburban electrification programme. Last November the government allocated NZ$500 million to fund the new rolling stock.

"The suppliers have been asked to provide feedback on the technical specifications before a full request for proposals is issued in August; final bids are to be submitted by November. The winner will be announced late in the first quarter or early in the second quarter of 2011, and the first trains will be delivered for the Eastern and Western suburban lines in 2013…"
[966]

Tender Integrity Questioned

However, before the tender was awarded, it was alleged that the Government had shifted the goal posts in a move reminiscent of the Muldoon Government involvement in a similar tender process in 1979. That tender process had resulted in the awarding of a contract to the Hungarian firm, Ganz-Mavag, for the supply of electric passenger units for the Wellington commuter services.

This time, a shortlist had been expanded at a crucial time – as reported by The New Zealand Herald on 13 December 2010:

"The Government's tender process for supplying electric trains for Auckland is being criticised by a company that was originally shortlisted for the work, but has since pulled the plug. Three other firms in the expanded shortlist of 10 companies have also withdrawn.

"In July Bombardier Transportation Australia was one of four companies selected to compete for the KiwiRail contract – worth up to an estimated $500 million – to provide

38 three-car trains. But KiwiRail, citing a desire to secure the 'best possible whole-of-life outcome', extended the shortlist to 10 in September.

"In a letter from Bombardier to KiwiRail...managing director Dan Osborne lambasted the process and withdrew altogether...'Your decision raises questions on the level of confidence that Bombardier can have in the tender process.'

"KiwiRail chief executive Jim Quinn said three other companies had also pulled out, but would not say who they were and questioned whether it was over the tender process...

"There are no New Zealand bids, though the company that wins the contract can use local industries to fulfil the contract. Labour's Dunedin South MP Clare Curran hoped the winning bidder would use Dunedin-based industries, creating local jobs and injecting money into the community. She said the decision to extend the original shortlist was 'questionable'...'Is it about local skills and the capacity to create jobs or is it about going for the lowest cost and doing a chummy deal behind the scenes?'

"One of the bidders that benefited from the extended shortlist is LORIC Import and Export Corporation, a subsidiary of China CNR Corporation which has been linked to Sammy Wong, husband of former cabinet minister Pansy Wong. But Mr Quinn said Mr Wong had nothing to do with KiwiRail or the tender process for the Auckland electric trains..." [967]

Supplier Selected

Regardless of what suspicions there may have been as to the integrity of the tender, the final choice of which company was to supply Auckland's electric trains was not to be decided by KiwiRail in any case.

Following the establishment of the Auckland Council, the Government decided that the city should own the trains and so the final choice of provider was eventually decided by Auckland Transport.

By then, the bidders had been reduced to two – CAF of Spain and Hyundai Rotem of South Korea – and the Spanish tender was eventually awarded the contract – as reported by The New Zealand Herald on 6 October 2010:

"Auckland's first generation of electric trains are set to be running in three years under a $500 million deal signed this afternoon with Spanish supplier CAF. The region's transport authority has selected the company, which has been making trains for more than 100 years and has supplied a dozen world capitals, over four other bidders.

"The deal will include $400m for 57 three-car trains between September 2013 and the end of 2014. It will also include 10 years of maintenance cover at a cost of about $100m. CAF, which stands for Construcciones y Auxiliar de Ferrocarriles, has already set up a New Zealand subsidiary company, which will provide an unquantified number of jobs locally at a maintenance depot to be built at Wiri by Auckland Transport. That will add another $100m to the project..." [968]

Network Electrification

Of course, all those trains would need a powered network on which to operate and construction and installation started in late December 2010:

"About 200 rail workers threw themselves into a hectic summer construction programme throughout Auckland yesterday [26 December 2010], including erecting the first of 3500 power supply masts for the $1 billion electrification project.

"Several masts were erected through the Newmarket railway junction and above a new platform being built at the Baldwin Avenue station on the western line, as work began elsewhere around the region demolishing bridges and lowering tracks to create enough head-room for electrification.

"The construction programme, which also includes installing new signals along tracks through the Britomart railway tunnel and the nearby Quay Park junction between the eastern and southern lines, has required a full shutdown by KiwiRail of Auckland's rail network for two weeks until January 10..." [969]

Memorandum of Understanding

As electrification of the network continued and before the first electric trains arrived, it was time to formally establish the ground rules and this was done when the Transport Minister, Steven Joyce, and Council Mayor, Len Brown, signed a memorandum of understanding at Henderson Railway Station – as reported by The New Zealand Herald on 1 September 2011:

"Auckland will gain ownership of 57 new electric trains in return for taking responsibility for repaying a $500 million Government loan over 35 years. But the loan repayments will in turn be subsidised by the Government through the Transport Agency, starting at 60 per cent before reducing over 10 years to a new financial assistance rate of 50 per cent.

"Transport Minister Steven Joyce confirmed the Government will also provide a grant of $90 million to further sweeten a funding and ownership deal…Annual repayment costs of the loan will amount to about $34 million, with Auckland ratepayers paying about half of that.

"Mr Brown expected the new electric fleet, to be introduced by the end of 2014, would lead to a doubling of existing patronage of 10 million passenger trips a year and put Auckland in pole position for further modernisation through a $2.4b central city rail tunnel.

"The agreement, which has been reached before a supply and maintenance contract expected to be announced by the end of this month, means Auckland will own more electric trains than originally planned. It replaces an earlier plan for the provision of just 38 three-car electric multiple unit (EMU) trains, to be supplemented by 12 electric locomotives which would have had to haul existing carriages on Auckland's southern railway line.

"Mr Joyce said the package now agreed to would provide full electrification on all lines 'so we have a single homogeneous electric fleet right through the city and I think that's a very exciting result.' He said ownership of its own fleet with a new maintenance depot, would give the city greater independence 'and it means passengers more importantly can look forward to faster and more reliable service…'

"The Government through KiwiRail is almost half way through electrifying and resignalling the rail network out to Papakura in the south and Swanson in the west for a further $500 million." [970]

Modern Rail Transport

By December 2013, the first electric trains were undergoing trials and almost ready to start on rejuvenated and electrified tracks:

"Ninety years after Auckland's leaders began hankering after electric trains in 1923, the city is poised to join the world of modern rail transport. The first of a 57-strong fleet of electric trains has been undergoing closed-track trials at nights and weekends on the city's southern line, ready to start whisking passengers between Onehunga and Britomart by the end of April, at greater speed and comfort.

"KiwiRail has largely completed its share of the project, which has not only involved erecting 3500 masts to string overhead lines carrying 25,000 volts of electricity across 80km of railway tracks, but has also included a $90 million effort since 2009 to replace all points machines and signals with a computerised system capable of overriding drivers to cut power to any trains heading too fast towards red 'stop' lights.

"Infrastructure and engineering general manager Rick van Barneveld says the first electric unit's high-speed performance under new wires has been completed 'without any issues'. 'This is very encouraging for a new train and new infrastructure being introduced at the same time...'" [971]

Electric Train Services Commence

Indeed, the first electric train service started in April 2014:

"The first revenue service ran on 28 April 2014 on the Onehunga Line, following a public open day the preceding day on which the trains were used to run free shuttle services between Britomart and Newmarket.

"Electric Eastern Line services commenced on 15 September 2014 as far as Manukau; Eastern Line services to Papakura were diverted to terminate at Manukau from 8 December 2014, completing the Eastern Line electrification.

"Electric Southern Line services to Papakura commenced on 15 January 2015, running two return off-peak services on weekdays.

"From 16 May 2015, all weekend services, with the exception of the shuttle service between Papakura and Pukekohe were operated by electric trains, including the Western Line..." [972]

And, as reported by The New Zealand Herald on 20 July 2015:

"Auckland transport has replaced its remaining diesel trains with electric trains on all lines from Papakura and Swanson to Britomart today...

"Timetables have been adjusted to allow daily diesel shuttles between Pukekohe and Papakura from today and buses will replace trains between Waitakere and Swanson." [973]

Preparatory work for the $371 million electrification of the 19km line between Pukekohe and Papakura began in late 2020. The work includes new signalling and track upgrades as well as the redevelopment of Pukekohe station. [974]

The City Rail Link – Another Mayor's Vision

Just days after his election, the mayor of the new Auckland City broadcast his vision for a Greater Auckland transport system:

"Auckland Super City mayor Len Brown swept to power after promising three ambitious rail projects within 15 years. His vision is already putting his new council on a collision course with the Government, and yesterday Prime Minister John Key tried to rein in Aucklanders' expectations. Mr Brown wants the projects completed consecutively, in blocks of roughly five years. The first would see a rail tunnel to service the western side of the central business district, between Britomart and Mt Eden. That would be followed by a link or links to the airport and then a line from central Auckland to Albany through tunnels under the Waitemata Harbour..." [975]

Chequebook Closed
Like many such visions of Auckland suburban rail expansion before them, this latest was again reined in by the Government:

"The Prime Minister yesterday poured cold water on Super City Mayor-elect Len Brown's ambitious plans for rail, indicating the Government was closing its chequebook for extra projects.

"John Key, who with Transport Minister Steven Joyce is prepared to spend an extra $1.6 billion on what has been dubbed the 'holiday highway' from Puhoi to Wellsford, said ratepayers would have to pay for Mr Brown's plans to fast-track rail. The PM said the Government shared the goal of an efficient transport system for Auckland, but 'not all roads, or all rail tracks, can lead to the Government…'

"Last night, Mr Brown played down the Prime Minister's comments, saying discussions on paying for rail projects would take place over years, not three days after an election…Mr Brown said his rail plans were set in the short, medium and long term and had four possible cash sources.

"These were city and Government funding, infrastructure bonds and private-public partnerships. He said the Government wanted Auckland to turn itself into 'much more of an economic powerhouse' than it was now, and transport and fixing congestion were important parts of that…

"Even without the attraction of double-tracking and fast electric trains, rail patronage in Auckland has soared since the construction of the Britomart transport terminal in 2003 – from 2.5 million to 8.5 million passengers a year…" [976]

APB&B Business Case Study
Just prior to the establishment of the Auckland Council, the Auckland Regional Transport Authority and KiwiRail commissioned APB&B (a consultant group comprising AECOM, Parsons Brinckerhoff, Beca and Hassell) to investigate the economic viability of using a tunnel to improve rail linkages into the Auckland CBD.

The resulting study, published on 22 October 2010, commented in part:

"The CBD Rail Link investigated in this Business Case consists of a tunnel through the CBD and three new stations at key locations configured to provide maximum rail coverage that makes most CBD areas accessible to stations within a 500 metre walk.

"The investigations reported here show that the CBD Rail Link as configured is economically viable under standard transport appraisal. Furthermore, the potential urban regeneration and additional growth that can be derived from investment in this infrastructure also makes it transformative for Auckland and New Zealand…The proposed CBD Rail Link is the best high-capacity foundation for meeting the increased transport needs of Auckland CBD until 2041…

"The massive opportunity that exists for Auckland is to unlock the existing capacity within the rail network to meet a significant proportion of the CBD's current and future transport needs. The rail network provides complementary capacity to support the road network and recent investments there, helping to improve journey times and reliability – therefore helping to optimise the region's transport network. There is also the opportunity to capitalise on infrastructure investment as a catalyst for growth in both economic competitiveness and productivity…

"Multi-criteria analysis and cost-effectiveness analysis were used to rank the four main alternatives. These analyses concluded that the CBD Rail Link was ranked highest for cost effectiveness and impact because of the way the project unlocks the unused capacity that exists within the rail network. In this way, the CBD Rail Link aligns with national strategic priorities, as over 50% of transport benefits are decongestion related…

"Auckland's strategic role in the national economy is intertwined with the CBD Rail Link - the City needs the Rail Link to support its current growth but also to stimulate its future growth along the lines described by the Regional Growth Strategy. Therefore the CBD Rail Link Project is not just an essential element in Auckland's transformation into a globally competitive urban centre; it is perhaps the most critical…" [977]

Transport Committee Debate

On 25 November 2010, the Auckland Council Transport Committee debated whether to endorse the [APB&B] business case so the project could advance to the next stage of designating land required for it…

"After the transport committee debate, Cllr Brewer…issued a statement saying: 'We are told that unless we move with speed, the cbd will be gridlocked with commuters within 10 years. That is a huge assumption and goes against the actual trend, where overall we're seeing the decentralisation of our workplaces.

"'Only 13% of Aucklanders currently work in the central city. I believe that percentage is only going to fall, not increase, when you consider the likes of business park growth and the fact that computer technology is enabling more people to work from home and businesses to operate locally.

"'This assumption that by 2021 people will be pushing each other over to get into the cbd every morning seems a little unrealistic. Corporates aren't exactly lining up to get into cbd Auckland, there are no cranes on the skyline and cbd office vacancies are at a generational high…'

"The transport committee was asked to endorse the cbd rail link business case and to direct staff to work with other agencies on the next phase of the project, 'addressing funding consenting & further investigation & design of the cbd rail link…'" [978]

Webs on Steroids

Naturally, the APB&B business case did not attract immediate approval from the Transport Minister:

"…Transport Minister Steven Joyce says a report from a $5 million study commissioned by KiwiRail and the former Auckland Regional Transport Authority raises many questions to be worked through before the Government can consider contributing to such a costly endeavour.

"Despite the funding uncertainty, the consultants believe the investment will be repaid more than three times over, in 'transformational' economic benefits…

"But Mr Joyce last night described the inclusion of transformational benefits to calculate a return of $3.50 for each dollar invested as 'webs [wider economic benefits] on steroids' and said it was the first time he had seen such an approach in a business case. He said an estimated $1.99 billion cost for the tunnel did not include $340 million for extra tracks and trains needed to run through it, making a total of $2.3 billion. 'It would be the biggest thing that would suck up all the money in Auckland for quite some time…'" [979]

Echo of Events

Memories of similar 'profit and loss' arguments put forward by past governments as reasons not to proceed with underground rail schemes were resurrected by Mike Lee – as reported by The New Zealand Herald on 1 December 2010:

"Auckland Council transport chairman Mike Lee has made a caustic attack on the Transport Minister on his blog for refusing to accept the case for a central city rail tunnel...In the blog, Mr Lee compared Mr Joyce to former National Minister of Works Stan Goosman, who cancelled Auckland's rail plans in the 1950s.

"'Not only is there an echo of events, but also of personalities, with Steven Joyce the present-day 'minister for everything' playing the role of the 1950s era National 'minister for everything' Stan Goosman,' he wrote.

"'In the late 1940s, the Ministry of Works formulated a scheme which was accepted by all parties...before being killed off by the National Government of the time. Again in the late 1960s, the ARA and NZ Railways worked up another plan, this was in turn killed off in 1975 by the National Government.'

"Mr Joyce denied the Government was out to kill the project, but said the $2 billion plus price tag was part of the reason the project would not get his blessings for a quick start..." [980]

Government-Ordered Review

In order to prove his point and to keep the constant flow of studies and reports since at least the 1920s flowing, Transport Minister Steven Joyce ordered a Ministry of Transport-led review of the ARTA/KiwiRail business case for the CBD rail link.

As reported by The New Zealand Herald on 31 May 2011, the Ministry's review naturally found that:

"...a council business case overstated the potential economic benefits of an Auckland CBD rail link by nearly $3 billion. Transport Minister Steven Joyce today released a Ministry of Transport-led review of the Auckland Council and Auckland Transport Agency business case for the CBD rail link.

"The review found the estimated construction costs for the project – a total of $2.4 billion – are correct, he said. But he said the transport benefits of the project are estimated at $387 million, rather than the $1.3 billion assessed...Its assessment of $3.3 billion in wider economic benefits from the project was also 'very significantly overstated' and the real figure was 'more like $305 million', he said.

"'In short, the review says more work needs to be done to determine the full future transport needs of central Auckland before proceeding with a project like the CBD rail link,' Mr Joyce said. 'However, the review suggests that in the meantime, it makes strategic sense for Auckland Council to move to protect the route, and I agree with that.'

"The review also said the project would have only a modest impact on traffic volumes. It found the link was likely to remove up to 1400 cars of the estimated 29,000 cars travelling into the CBD during the morning peak in 2041.

"Auckland Mayor Len Brown countered with a claim the project would be transformative for the region. It was vital to start planning the project now to prevent future cost increases and potential overloading in Auckland's public transport network, he said.

"He announced plans to protect the rail link route and to buy property necessary for its construction. The need for the tunnel is now urgent.

"'Within two years most of the usable train paths in and out of Britomart will be in use, providing virtually no room to add future services at a time when public transport patronage is going through the roof. The potential urban redevelopment and additional growth derived from investment in this infrastructure would make the project transformational not just for Auckland, but for New Zealand as a whole...'" [981]

At Loggerheads Again

By August 2011, identifying a method of funding transport infrastructure remained as elusive as ever:

"Auckland Mayor Len Brown and the Government are at loggerheads again over the $2.4 billion inner city rail loop – this time over how it will be funded. Mr Brown yesterday proposed road tolls and congestion charges in the central area as ways to pay for what he called the city's key project for the next 10 years. A regional fuel tax and a 'betterment' levy on properties which benefit from the rail loop are also being considered by a council team that has spent months investigating alternative cash sources for large transport projects.

"Last night, Transport Minister Steven Joyce ruled out a regional fuel tax and said he had 'significant reservations' about tolls and congestion charging, as motorists already contributed about 11 per cent of their fuel taxes to public transport...The minister says an economic case for the 3.5km tunnel has not been made.

"Mr Brown must provide funding for the rail loop in a 10-year budget being prepared under his name, and say where the money is coming from. He said the project would require new funding sources if rates increases were to be held at around the rate of inflation. Details about possible tolls, congestion charges or a regional fuel tax will have to be released shortly if they are to be debated and included in the 10-year budget for approval next June." [982]

Central v Local Government (Again)

By way of an editorial published on 8 August 2011, The New Zealand Herald made its opinion known about the matter:

"Transport Minister Steven Joyce should button his lip if the Auckland Council resolves to finance an inner-city rail tunnel from sources other than taxation. Road tolls and congestion charges are perfectly proper local devices. Having given the city a single voice, national politicians should listen to it...

"New Zealand has long had a highly centralised system of government in which local government has been restricted to roles, powers and rate finance approved by Parliament. The creation of a single council for Auckland, which comprises a quarter of the country's population and more than a quarter of its wealth, poses a challenge to the national apparatus.

"Central government has done much for Auckland's development but its decisions have not always been far-sighted. The Harbour Bridge is the shining model of an Auckland initiative, long delayed and frustrated by the reluctance of governments to provide finance or to allow the city to raise loans for its construction.

"There was no reluctance then to pay for the project with a toll. When eventually the bridge was built, its use was so heavy that the capacity quickly had to be doubled and all capital costs were recovered long before tolls were removed..." [983]

Rugby World Cup Embarrassment

Speaking of the original Harbour Bridge that was unable to cope with demand...

"Auckland Mayor Len Brown is considering compensation to angry and frustrated Rugby World Cup ticket holders left out of pocket after last night's public transport debacle in Auckland. Thousands of commuters had their night disrupted by trains, buses and ferries that were unable to cope with the number of people wanting to join in the festivities…

"At least 2000 people missed last night's opening ceremony at Eden Park as the trains backed up on the tracks to Kingsland station. Last night, huge crowds also built up at Britomart station in the central city as people waited for hours to catch a train home.

"It was still full at 12.30am, so several trains stopped at a re-opened emergency station at the Strand, at the bottom of Parnell Rise. Passengers then had to walk the rest of the way into town.

"Mr Brown said about 200,000 people descended on the city, with 60,000 people trying to use the train network. Ferry services were stopped when the waterfront reached capacity." [984]

Advance Budgeting
Pending the discovery and implementation of any real funding avenues for the city rail link, the Auckland Council borrowed from future revenue to maintain some sort of forward momentum:

"The Auckland Council's strategy & finance committee agreed yesterday [8 March 2012] to advance $8 million of spending on the city rail link project, including $1.7 million for a revised business case which the Government has asked for.

"The decision takes the money out of next year's budget and increases the 2011-12 budget allocation for the rail link to $10 million. The money will come from public transport & travel demand management projects that can't be progressed this year due to external factors such as delays in securing necessary resource consents.

"The other $6.3 million will be spent on work such as geotechnical surveys, utility & building assessments, contaminated site reports and rail operations modelling." [985]

Forward Momentum
With total disregard for the Government's lack of enthusiasm, Auckland Transport used the Council's advance funding to maintain some forward momentum of the city rail link proposal:

"Auckland Transport today [3 July 2012] released its preferred path for the City Rail Link, which is expected to cost up to $2.86 billion. It extends the rail line through Britomart, under Albert, Vincent and Pitt Streets, then beneath Karangahape Road and the Central Motorway Junction to Symonds Street before rising to join the western line.

"Authorities would need to buy property from 210 owners to secure the route…Underground land from 70 interests, including 12 unit title developments with multiple owners, would also need to be purchased for the tunnels and stations…

"Auckland Transport chief executive David Warburton said officials were now informing landowners whose properties would be directly affected by the route. 'Our focus is on protecting a route…We first want to work with landowners to help ensure they are well informed and to help us understand their issues. Property purchase is a second step.'" [986]

City Centre Future Access Study
Following the 2011 Ministry of Transport-led review of the ARTA/KiwiRail business case for the CBD rail link and the Minister's advice to Auckland City that *more work needs to be done* before Government funding would be considered, the Auckland Council and Auckland Transport commissioned Sinclair Knight Merz (SKM) to undertake a City Centre Future Access Study (CCFAS).

The purpose of the study was:

'...to identify the city centre access issues Auckland will face over the next 30 years and how best to address them.' The Study was "...developed in consultation with senior officials and technical specialists from government agencies and Auckland Council." [987]

The principal findings of the Sinclair Knight Merz study, officially released by Auckland Mayor, Len Brown, on 13 December 2012, included:

"The Study says that in 30 years Auckland will have more than 700,000 new residents and need 400,000 extra houses. City centre and city fringe residents and employee numbers will have doubled and student numbers grown by 30%. As a result buses won't be able to meet demands and vehicle speeds in the city centre halve in the morning to walking speed. Private trips to the city centre from some areas will take up to twice as long. Trains will be at capacity.

"Forty six options were identified and evaluated. Three were shortlisted; surface bus, underground bus and underground rail – the City Rail Link (CRL).

"1. Surface bus improvements would provide only 3-5 years of extra capacity beyond current funded works, would significantly lower private vehicle speeds and would require a lot of residential and commercial property purchase for bus priority measures.

"2. An underground bus option provided marginally more capacity than surface bus, required less land, was much more expensive than the surface bus option and had a similar capital cost to the CRL.

"3. Underground rail (CRL) was the only option to deliver increased capacity beyond 2030, had the greatest multi modal capacity to get people into the city centre and provided the highest speeds for private vehicles within the city centre.

"...a multi modal solution of the City Rail Link with integrated surface bus improvements would best meet city centre access needs and suggested implementation by 2021 as delays would limit employment, growth and the ability to capture economic benefits." [987]

Positive and Negative Responses

Responses to the findings of the City Centre Future Access Study were predictably different – as reported by The New Zealand Herald on 14 December 2012:

"While the study "...was hailed by Auckland Mayor Len Brown as providing a strong basis for entering funding negotiations for the rail project...Transport Minister Gerry Brownlee said the study was a useful addition to the debate on long-term transport management in central Auckland but fell 'some way short of convincing the Government it should provide financial support to any fast-tracking of the proposed city rail link'.

"He believed an assumption of central city employment growth of 46 per cent in the next 10 years, compared with an increase of just 18 per cent in the past decade, was too ambitious. And he said the report underplayed the role of highway improvements such as completing the western ring route in 2017, which would draw many thousands of traffic movements away from the city centre." [988]

Benefit/Cost Madness

As the SKM report had been leaked some three weeks earlier, the press had plenty of time to comment on its findings – as did Brian Rudman in an article published by The New Zealand Herald on 23 November 2012:

"The [Sinclair Knight Merz] report highlights the fact that many downtown streets have already reached capacity as far as buses are concerned. So what hope for the CBD in

30 years when Auckland is home to another million residents and still tunnel-less…? This is the nightmarish scenario looming if the nervous Nellies in the government continue to think small and hope more buses is all Auckland needs.

"What the SKM report also highlights is the shortcomings of relying on the economic modelling alchemy of benefit cost ratios. According to the government formula followed by SKM, the proposed rail tunnel will return only 78c in economic benefit for every dollar spent building it. Even extending the life of the benefits to 60 years – twice the time accepted by government rules – takes predicted benefit to just $1.05.

"In the Government's eyes this is an inadequate return – unless, that is, it's a proposed new highway running through National-held electorates. Any sane bystander would say something must be wrong with a formula that suggests it is better for Aucklanders and the nation to stand aside and watch the Auckland central business district slowly die from congestive heart failure, rather than plan for a bypass operation…

"The Auckland Council's chief economist, Geoff Cooper…said that: 'New Zealand policymakers have settled on some of the most short-sighted appraisal methods of the developed world'. He said that if we applied the British framework to the city rail link, the project benefits would be around six times higher and 'the resulting benefit-to-cost ratio would likely stoke a great deal of public confidence. The hurdle for long-lasting infrastructure in New Zealand is far too high, which erodes public confidence [and] means that short-lived, piecemeal projects are usually given priority,' he said.

"He highlights that the reason the second harbour crossing and the rail tunnel are assessed as having such poor economic returns is that the government 'guidelines for appraisal miss many of the economic benefits'.

"He says really big projects such as the existing harbour bridge 'can fundamentally change the drivers of economic growth by creating changes in land use, enticing population inflows and generally increasing the amount of economic activity…yet none of these benefits are considered in the economic appraisal of modern transport projects'.

"As for the exclusion of any economic benefit beyond 30 years, he points to Auckland's 50-year-old bridge and century-old water and rail networks and says it was lucky our forebears didn't use modern day cost benefit guidelines to decide on these projects. How many reports will the Government demand, before the penny drops?" [989]

A Big Step Forward

Although the news was not good that Auckland roading projects would take priority, it was an astounding announcement from a National Government that it would back the City Rail Link, albeit sometime in the future – as reported by The New Zealand Herald on 28 June 2013:

"The Government will push major roading projects in Auckland including a wider southern motorway, upgraded roading to the airport, and a freight corridor in Manukau before it begins work on the City Rail Link and a second Waitemata Harbour Crossing, Prime Minister John Key has revealed this afternoon.

"Mr Key confirmed that Government would back Auckland's three top transport priorities – the City Rail Link, another Waitemata Harbour crossing, and the Auckland Manukau Eastern Transport Initiative (AMETI), which includes the East-West Link.

"'These three projects are all identified as the highest transport priorities in the Council's Auckland Plan,' he said. 'They have a price tag of around $10 billion and they are projects that need to be planned for over a long period of time.'

"Mr Key said construction of the City Rail Link would not begin until 2020 unless employment levels in the central city climbed by 25 per cent and annual rail trips hit 20 million a year. 'We will consider an earlier start date if it becomes clear that Auckland's CBD employment and rail patronage growth hits thresholds faster than current rates of growth suggest.

"'I realise 2020 is not what the Council leadership is wanting, but while we may differ on timeframes, there is clear recognition by the Government that the project will be needed to address access to the Auckland CBD and improve the efficiency of rail...'

"It has not yet been made clear how Government will source its funding for its share of these projects, but the Prime Minister has confirmed that some of the $2.86 billion rail link could be paid for with proceeds from asset sales.

"Auckland Mayor Len Brown welcomed the Government's support for the ambitious projects and said it marked a big step forward for both Auckland and New Zealand...'Backing for the City Rail Link (CRL) in particular, is a major milestone...'" [990]

The Government is Listening

Following the Prime Minister's announcement, Auckland Mayor, Len Brown, commented further:

"...After 2½ years of amalgamation, Auckland is now speaking with one voice, and the Government appears to be listening. Auckland's success is critical to New Zealand's success. We are a third of the population, responsible for around 38% of gdp, and the gateway for 70% of visitors to New Zealand.

"It is not our size that is driving our need for infrastructure but our growth rate. Currently half of New Zealand's population growth is happening in Auckland. By 2030 it will be as much as 70%. It is critical that we make the upfront investments in infrastructure to enable us to meet this challenge...

"Around 70% of the funding for the rail link is now secured and work on options for the remaining funding – which will be around $30 million/year – is underway. My focus will be on securing the best possible deal for Auckland..." [991]

Customer Revolution Required

With the benchmark set at 20 million rail passengers per year before a start on the CRL could be brought forward, all options were being considered by Auckland Transport – as reported by The New Zealand Herald on 30 June 2013:

"Auckland Transport boss Lester Levy won't rule out ditching the rail operator Veolia if it can't shape up. Levy was confident he could get the necessary 20 million rail passengers per year required to bring the start date forward, and was prepared to dump Veolia if necessary....

"Levy said 'customer revolution' was required to get Aucklanders back onto public transport – with improvements needed to park and ride facilities, bus shelters and timetables. 'We need to change almost everything we do, re-frame everything we do to actually deliver on frequency and precision. We need to have a total relook at pricing, which must be attractive and appealing. It's a total change.'

"Veolia's contract to operate Auckland's passenger rail network runs out in June 2016, but Levy called for major improvements in the next 18 to 24 months..." [992]

PWC Report

A study by PricewaterhouseCoopers to analyse the logistics of initiating an early start to the CRL, commissioned by Len Brown, drew the usual response from the Government – as reported by The New Zealand Herald on 27 May 2014:

"Auckland Mayor Len Brown's latest attempt to make an early start to the $2.86 billion City Rail Link in 2016 has been dismissed by Transport Minister Gerry Brownlee.

"A report commissioned for the mayoral office says the Government has set unrealistic rail patronage and downtown-employment targets to start the project before 2020. The report, by PWC (PricewaterhouseCoopers), said the goals should be set on rates of progress towards targets, such as high patronage growth on rail after the full introduction of electric trains in 2016…

"Yesterday, a spokesman for Mr Brownlee said the Government had accelerated the start date by a decade from 2030 to 2020 and the two targets for an earlier start were not unreasonable. The spokesman said Mr Brownlee had seen the PWC report and there was nothing in it that would alter the Government's position…" [993]

A Major Change

The search for ways and means by which the Government could be convinced that an earlier start than 2020 could be made for the CRL continued – this time with a major change to the original plan:

"Auckland Transport lopped about $500 million of the $2.86 billion estimated cost of the city rail link on Friday, with two decisions. In response, mayor Len Brown saw a 2016 construction start as 'even more realistic'.

"First, for a saving of $150 million-plus, was the decision not to build a new station 42m underground at Newton, but instead to redevelop the Mt Eden station and connect it to the city rail link. The second, for $330 million-plus more savings, was the conclusion that more electric trains won't be required for the core city rail link project…

"Meanwhile, patronage rose in June, taking the number of trips to 11.4 million for the June year, up 13.9%..." [994]

New Transport Minister

When Simon Bridges replaced Gerry Brownlee as Transport Minister on 6 October 2014, he received some advice beneficial to Auckland from the New Zealand Transport Agency – as reported by The New Zealand Herald on 13 November 2014:

"Government transport officials are urging their political masters to support an early start to Auckland's $2.4 billion underground rail project. Strong advice from the Transport Agency to new Transport Minister Simon Bridges was welcomed…by Auckland Mayor Len Brown, who wants construction of the 3.5km link from Britomart to Mt Eden to start in 2016.

"…Mr Bridges said he was considering whether to approve Transport Agency involvement in 'enabling works' from 2016 on the understanding those would be funded by Auckland Council. He was referring to plans for 'cut and cover' tunnelling from Britomart to Wyndham Street, under the Downtown shopping centre and Albert St.

"The Transport Agency, in its briefing to Mr Bridges as the incoming minister, points to a risk of the Government not being involved in the ground-floor of the project. It called the council's timetable for enabling works as 'sensible sequencing' to minimise disruption to the CBD.

"The council is budgeting $250 million for the work to coincide with a major redevelopment of the shopping centre and for initial tunnelling to be completed before…April 2017…" [995]

Planning Frustration

As the Auckland Council tried to agree on a long-term plan, it was frustrated first by the usual lack of any Government commitment and then by the oversight of the Auditor-General. Nevertheless, an approximate year for a start on the CRL was decided upon:

"Auckland Council's governing body firmly rejected a 5-year delay in starting construction of the city rail link and accepted a 2018-19 start when the 2 proposals were put to an extraordinary meeting yesterday [9 December 2014].

"The start time has moved about. The Government at one point grudgingly accepted a 2030 start then brought it forward to 2020, with provisos that passenger volume & cbd employment targets be met.

"Mayor Len Brown…told Prime Minister John Key in January he wanted construction brought forward to start in 2016, but Auditor-general Lyn Provost has told the council it needs to be more prudent – the council could [be] up for 100% of funding in initial years for a project brought forward, and it still didn't have funding lines determined.

"Hence an extraordinary meeting of the governing body just 9 days before the meeting where the council will finalise the content of the draft long-term plan to be put out to consultation in the New Year…

[Describing the council debate…] "And so it was about tactics in the old Auckland v Wellington standoff again – on one side those with an ear to the Government, on the other those who want to forge ahead with infrastructure upgrades they see as vital if Auckland is to cope with an extra million residents, and in the middle a group mostly leaning to the forge-ahead view…" [996]

First Steps

Despite the funding uncertainty, those of the Council and Auckland Transport wishing to forge ahead, did so in February 2015 – by initiating the first step of any construction process:

"Auckland Transport has lodged its application for resource consent for the first section of the proposed city rail link…The first stage will take the rail tunnel from Britomart to Wyndham St…" [997]

On 7 April 2015 another important step was taken:

"Auckland transport named 2 consortiums today to start the first phase of downtown city rail link construction. Project director Chris Meale said the 2 joint venture contractors appointed were Downer NZ and Soletanche Bachy JV and Connectus (McConnell Dowell & Hawkins JV) for the first phase of design at a cost of about $3 million. The next phase will provide for a negotiated contract to construct the city rail link.

"Auckland Transport has chosen the Downer-led joint venture to progress the rail link work through & under Britomart Station & Queen St to the Downtown Shopping Centre site, with construction likely to start in early 2016. The contract includes establishing temporary accommodation for Britomart Station's ticketing and customer service operations, underpinning the historic former Chief Post Office building to allow the construction of the rail tunnels beneath and reinstating Britomart Station, and upgrading urban space & surrounding roads.

"The Connectus Consortium will construct the cut-&-cover tunnels under and along Albert St from Customs St to Wyndham St. The work is likely to start in October with the relocation of a major stormwater line in Albert St between Swanson and Wellesley Streets..." [998]

All Clear

"Auckland Transport said on Wednesday [26 August 2015] all appeals to its land designation for the city rail link (CRL) had been resolved by agreement or dismissed. Chief executive David Warburton said 5 of the 6 appeals were settled and the only appeal that went to the Environment Court had been dismissed.

"The designation is now confirmed, subject to finalisation of conditions by the court. The court's decision ends a 2½-year planning process to get the designation for the project.

"Dr Warburton said: 'It's a big step forward for Auckland. A proposal to extend rail through the city centre has been around for almost a hundred years but has never got much beyond an idea. Now we have a designated route...'" [999]

Train Passenger Numbers Increase

By the end of the year to 31 March 2015, train passenger numbers had increased to 13.4 million, an annual increase of 21%. [1000]

On 4 August 2015, The New Zealand Herald reported:

"The annual rail patronage in Auckland has hit a record number with more than 14 million passengers using the service during the past 12 months.

"Auckland Transport's General Manager AT Metro, Mark Lambert says it is the highest ever 12 month total. 'In March we reached 13 million passengers and here we are just five months later adding another million trips.' Mr Lambert says this record comes just days after the introduction of the full fleet of electric trains on 20 July..." [1001]

Reliability and Punctuality

November 2015, and passenger numbers continued to grow:

"4 months after recording 14 million rail trips in a year, Auckland Transport lifted patronage on the regional rail system to 15 million/year yesterday. 10 years ago, the region's passenger trains carried 4 million passengers/year. AT Metro general manager Mark Lambert said yesterday patronage had grown by 22% in the last year..."

"Mr Lambert said reliability and on-time performance had improved markedly since the rail network went all-electric from Papakura to Swanson in July: 'In October 93% of services arrived at their destination within 5 minutes of their scheduled time and the previous month 94.9% of services arrived on time, a new record for Auckland trains...'" [1002]

Early Work Begins

It was still only 2015 and nearly Christmas, but it was time to begin work on the CRL – as reported by The New Zealand Herald on 21 December:

"Early work for the $2.5 billion City Rail Link project started today with a dawn blessing of the work site. About 80 people gathered on the corner of Victoria and Albert streets in central Auckland as kaumatua blessed the site. Mayor Len Brown said it was a day that Aucklanders have been contemplating for almost a century.

"CRL project director Chris Meale said…'Today was a celebration, but for most Aucklanders the first piece of work will be largely invisible. A replacement stormwater pipe will be built under Albert St so that the existing one can be removed when work on the CRL tunnels starts in the middle of next year…" [1003]

Planned Early Start for Main CRL Works

By January 2016, there was a great deal of pressure on the Government to reach some sort of CRL funding agreement with the Auckland Council. With the encouragement of the Council and its Mayor, the project had attained a momentum of its own and now seemed unstoppable.

There were also a number of affected infrastructure projects underway, including the redevelopment of the Downtown Shopping Centre, located across Queen Elizabeth Square from the Britomart Station.

"The first section [of the CRL], from Britomart to Albert St, will be built in conjunction with the start of work on Precinct Properties NZ Ltd's Commercial Bay development which will replace the Downtown shopping centre with an office tower & new retail…" [1004]

As reported by The New Zealand Herald on 27 January 2016, a welcome softening of former conditions was evident from the Prime Minister:

"Prime Minister John Key has today outlined a plan to make an early start on the main works of the $2.5 billion city rail link in 2018. In a state of the nation speech to the Chamber of Commerce in Auckland, Mr Key said the Government will work with Auckland Council to bring forward a business plan and formalise Government funding from 2020. 'It's become clear that we need to provide certainty for other planned CBD developments affected by the rail link,' Mr Key said.

"Mr Key said the council had indicated this would allow construction of the rail link main works to start in 2018 – two years earlier than envisaged. It would also allow the council to get on with negotiating contracts, give investors certainty for other important projects in the CBD and reduce disruption in the central city.

"A number of important and quite complex issues still needed to be worked through with the council, Mr Key said. 'These included how project costs will finally be shared between the Government and the council and how the rail link will be owned and managed. Providing these issues are resolved, and I'm confident they can be, we'll aim to finalise the business plan later this year,' Mr Key said…

"Bringing forward funding from 2020 to 2018 will make financing of the project much easier for council. The council hopes the Government will pay half the $2.5 billion cost, but that remains to be seen. If the Government only pays a half share from 2018, its share will be about $1 billion and the council will pay about $1.5 billion. The completion date remains at 2023." [1005]

Costly Upgrades Needed

However, it wasn't just the CRL construction costs to consider if an efficient and safe suburban railway network was to eventually serve the transport needs of Auckland.

As might be expected, despite the electrification and double-tracking that had been carried out, the existing rail network was in need of an extensive upgrade – as reported by The New Zealand Herald on 20 March 2016:

"Auckland's rail network could require a further $1.4 billion in upgrades – on top of the $2.5b to be spent on the City Rail Link – for it to hit maximum potential.

"State-owned enterprise KiwiRail has told Auckland Council the city's existing rail network needs costly upgrades – some described as urgent some four months ago…

"Minutes from a council infrastructure committee meeting last September…detail a KiwiRail presentation and a diagram that showed about $400m was needed prior to the CRL opening to upgrade the wider rail network. On top of that, between $500m and $1b would be needed 'post-CRL'. "General manager David Gordon said those figures were initial projections…" [1006]

Wiri to Westfield

One section of the southern line in need of an upgrade was that running between Wiri and Westfield. In December 2016, consultants WSP/Parsons Brinckerhoff, in collaboration with KiwiRail, the NZ Transport Agency, and Auckland Transport, produced a report: *Wiri to Westfield - The Case for Investment*. The report described the Wiri to Westfield line as:

"…a key link in the national and regional rail network. It carries a mix of suburban passenger services, inter-regional freight trains and freight shunts between the Ports of Auckland and Wiri. It is a major conduit for the movement of goods across New Zealand and a key public transport artery connecting South Auckland with the CBD and the wider region.

"The current twin track configuration (one up line and one down line) has reached the maximum operational capacity during peak periods as a result of the mixture of freight and passenger traffic.

"…Without improvements to the Wiri to Westfield section…the current mixed use section of rail will continue to adversely affect passenger and freight rail services, with additional delays and reduced reliability for customers and operators…

"Benefits from investment in the Auckland City Rail Link will potentially be diminished, as passenger trains from South Auckland will be restricted to the current level of service (which is already affected by delays imposed to provide access to freight trains)…" [1007]

Historic Agreement

While it had taken Mayor Len Brown some six years to obtain a funding commitment from the Government for the CRL, as this history illustrates, it had taken many decades for the project to be formally considered:

"Today [14 September 2016] Len Brown and Transport Minister Simon Bridges signed an agreement on their contractual relationship between the parties, including procurement structure and a 50/50 funding arrangement of the entire project.

"This will allow the 'main works' tendering process to begin and for specialist constructors to make available the people and machinery needed to build the CRL.

"Features of the Heads of Agreement include:
- A 50/50 funding arrangement where Auckland Council and the Crown each pay half of the total capitalised costs of the project.
- The principals to the agreement, referred to as 'sponsors', are the Government and Auckland Council.
- The establishment of a company (City Rail Link Limited) through which the Government and Council will oversee the delivery of the project. [agreement operational from 1 July 2017]
- Joint share in development opportunities arising from the project.
- The technical and operational aspects of project delivery are to be carried out by Auckland Transport working to the City Rail Link company.

- KiwiRail have a formal role in ensuring the CRL's interoperability with the wider rail network and the services it provides, such as freight.
- Today's signing took place at the Victoria St underground shaft from where tunnel boring machines will start the work.
- The Mayor said the CRL had been his number one priority and today's agreement was the culmination of six years of Auckland negotiating with the government..." [1008]

CRL Tender Process Starts

Eager for a start to be made on the tunnels and underground stations, Auckland Transport released its first tender documents on 1 February 2017:

"The largest component of the City Rail Link (CRL) project – the construction of the tunnels and new stations – took a major step forward today with the release of its first tender documents to the industry. The project is picking up speed with Expressions of Interest sought only a fortnight ago for the design, procurement, installation and commissioning of all tunnel track work and rail systems between Britomart Station and the Western Line at Mt Eden.

"There will be two new stations as part of the build of the underground rail line linking Britomart with the existing western line near Mt Eden. The new stations will be near Aotea Square with entrances at Wellesley and Victoria Streets and a station in Mercury Lane, just off Karangahape Road. The present Mt Eden train station will be extended and redeveloped.

"Tender documents sent out today are for the tunnel and station works that involve:
- Aotea Station: Cut and cover construction of a 15m-deep, 300m-long underground station and plant room box, including platforms, lifts and escalators to street level, plant rooms housing station and tunnel equipment, full station fit-out and entrances at either end at Victoria and Wellesley Streets.
- Karangahape Road Station: Mined construction of a 32m-deep underground station, including platform tubes and 150m-long platforms, lifts and inclined escalator to street level, plant rooms housing station and tunnel equipment within two shafts, full station fit-out, entrance at Mercury Lane and provision for a future entrance at Beresford Square.
- Tunnels: Twin-bored tunnel construction (circa 7m diameter) between the Mt Eden station and the southern end of Aotea Station.
- The provision of maintenance services for the new stations..." [1009]

Tunnel Work Started

By Monday 17 July 2017, work had started "...on bulk excavation for the city rail link cut-&-cover rail tunnels under Albert St in downtown Auckland…" [1010]

Costlier but Far-Sighted

At last, the project's sponsors agreed to fund an infrastructure project beyond the historically-accepted practice of putting frugality before public benefit – as reported by The New Zealand Herald on 17 April 2019:

"The cost of Auckland's City Rail Link project has soared by more than $1 billion. The new cost 'envelope' of $4.419b has been unveiled today along with the announcement of the successful bidder to build the bulk of the 3.4km underground railway, which will run from Britomart Station to Mt Eden Station by 2024.

Gas Pedal to Back-Pedal   Chapter Nine

"The successful bidder is a consortium comprising Sydney-based Downer, two subsidiaries of the Paris-based Vinci Group, the global Los Angeles-based Aecom engineering group and Auckland-based Tonkin and Taylor.

"CRL Ltd's (CRLL) Chief Executive, Dr Sean Sweeney, said that after a rigorous and comprehensive review of project costs, a revised cost envelope had been submitted to the project's sponsors – the Crown and Auckland Council - for approval. 'The $1 billion cost increase on the previous $3.4 billion estimate made in 2014 reflects significant changes impacting the project in the past five years. No-one could have foreseen the competitive pressures that have occurred in the construction industry over the past few years and the impact that has on costs, particularly for a project the scale and complexity of the City Rail Link.'

"A decision was made last year to increase the scope of the project to accommodate longer, nine-car trains at stations. Planning today for a city that would be much bigger in the future reinforced the benefits the City Rail Link City would deliver to the way people travel, work and live in Auckland, Dr Sweeney said. 'Other factors contributing to the revised cost envelope are higher escalation, or construction inflation costs, and an increase in the contingency risk allowance for any future unplanned events.

"Put together, they have all helped add costs to the project overall. Keeping a growing city moving is a serious challenge, but when we complete the City Rail Link it will double the number of Aucklanders within 30 minutes travel of the CBD...'" [1011]

Selling the Silverware

However, the increased, but necessary, costs meant that the Auckland Council might have to sell some silverware:

"Auckland Council is looking to sell or lease its four carpark buildings to help pay its share of the $1 billion blowout in the cost of the city rail loop...

"[Mayor Phil] Goff said the proposal to sell or lease the carparks was part of a five-point plan suggested by council officials after the council was notified of the $1 billion increase in the cost of the city rail link on Friday night. The other four proposals are

• Renegotiating council debt to take advantage of falling interest rates, which could save $120m 'probably for at least a 10-year period'.

• Revaluing under-valued assets and over-valued liabilities, such as future bus contracts, to reduce the council's stated net debt, helping it to keep within a cap set last year of group debt being less than 270 per cent of group revenue.

• Halving the council's cash holdings from about $200m to $100m.

• Asking the Government to pay more of its half-share of the rail loop costs earlier in the construction period, allowing the council to pay more of its share towards the end of the period around 2024, by which time net debt will be falling because of higher depreciation allowances for assets built by then..." [1012]

Stations and Tunnels Contract Signed

Nevertheless, another milestone was reached when the 'stations and tunnels' contract was signed on 19 July 2019:

"Auckland's $5.5 billion City Rail Link project hit another milestone this morning with the signing of the tunnel contract between state officials and the winning Link Alliance bid. The Government/Auckland Council entity, City Rail Link invited guests to the event which it said 'marks an important milestone in the delivery of the project.'

"CRL and the Link Alliance signed the project alliance agreement and that now marks the formal start of construction of the project's substantive stations-and-tunnels contract, by far the largest part of the project…The signing was at the Chief Post Office heritage building in lower Queen St.

"The Link Alliance is six international companies and New Zealand companies with experience delivering big infrastructure projects like CRL.

"Three of the companies will do the design side of CRL and the other three will build the tunnels and stations. Several of the companies already have some involvement with the CRL.

"The Link Alliance is Vinci Construction Grands Projets S.A.S., Downer NZ, Soletanche Bachy International NZ, WSP Opus (NZ), AECOM New Zealand, and Tonkin & Taylor…" [1013]

Chapter Ten

2020 to Infinity – A Public Transport Victory

Planning and Politics
Government Infrastructure Package

Following the launch of its Policy Statement on Land Transport – a 10-year plan produced in June 2018 – the Government subsequently released a $12 billion infrastructure package on 29 January 2020 that included a number of transport-related projects for Auckland – as reported by The New Zealand Herald:

"After a two-year hiatus, the Government has given the green light to several four-lane highways, including State Highway 1 from Whangārei to Port Marsden, Mill Rd in South Auckland, widening SH1 from Papakura to Drury, the Tauranga Northern Link and SH1 from Otaki to north of Levin.

"The package also includes $1.1b for rail, including electrification from Papakura to Pukekohe, a third rail line in South Auckland, two new rail stations in Drury Central and Drury West and upgrades in Wellington and the Wairarapa.

"Work on the SkyPath for Auckland's Harbour Bridge is also confirmed – a walking and cycling link between Westhaven and the North Shore. The project will cost $360m and is due to start next year.

"The 7km Penlink road is consented to run between Auckland's Northern Motorway at Redvale and the heart of the Whangaparaoa Peninsula, reducing by an estimated 50,000 the nearly 130,000 vehicles a day that travel through the heavily congested Silverdale business area...

"Of the $6.8b in transport spending, $1.1 billion will be spent on rail and $2.2 billion on new roads for Auckland. Auckland will receive the most funding in its package with $3.48b being spent on:
- Improvements to State Highway One Papakura to Drury South.
- The Northern Pathway – a new walking a cycling link...
- Penlink- a new transport link between State Highway One and the Whangaparaoa Peninsula
- Mill Road- a new connection from Manukau to Drury South...
- $315 million for improvements to the Wiri to Quay Park Corridor in Auckland including construction of a third rail line to ease the bottleneck between Wiri and Westfield, providing additional capacity around Westfield Junction, and works around Quay Park to improve rail access to the Ports of Auckland
- $371 million to extend electrification from Papakura to Pukekohe of the Auckland metro network by 19km...
- $247 million to develop the Drury railway station, with two new stations at Drury East and Drury West, to increase transport access and amenity value for this fast-growing centre." [1014]

Access for Everyone
While the Government planned for roads and more roads, the Auckland Council provided a bit of contrast by way of a City Centre Masterplan adopted on 5 March 2020. As reported by The Spinoff:

"…various areas of the CBD will be rebuilt to make them more accessible – in some cases exclusively so – for walkers, cyclists, public transport and freight. Cars are definitely not favoured in the plan, as the council wants to achieve its goal of a zero-emission zone in a more green and liveable city centre by 2030.

"While the Masterplan as a whole was conceived in 2012 and encompasses greater Auckland, the city centre part has been refreshed somewhat…

"…the plan's Access for Everyone concept essentially shows Waihorotiu Queen Street valley – the area from the town hall down to the waterfront – as being a 'pedestrian friendly' zone where cars are ostensibly excluded.

"Nine peripheral areas of the CBD including Victoria Park, K Road and the universities have been designated as 'traffic zones' – neighbourhoods which will handle the bulk of the cars while preserving city centre access to emergency, freight and rubbish vehicles. The council has not said how it intends to regulate traffic through the area and whether this will involve construction or a virtual no-drive zone." [1015]

Public Transport
SkyPath
The SkyPath project due to start in 2021 was included in the Government's January infrastructure package. As described by Bernard Orsman of The New Zealand Herald, the SkyPath design now differed greatly from the original first thought of in 2018:

"The SkyPath project over Auckland Harbour Bridge has undergone radical changes to separate it from the existing steel structure. The new design has increased in size to a 5m wide open path connected to the existing concrete piers on the southern side of the bridge.

"The changes to the original plans for a 4m wide enclosed cycling and walking path attached to the bridge's clip-ons help explain the huge cost increase from $67 million in 2018 to about $240m for the latest design.

"'It's just a really complex build,' NZTA senior project delivery manager Andy Thackwray said. He said if the shared path was supported by one of the clip-ons the extra load would reduce the bridge's capacity for traffic in future.

"It is preferable, said Thackwray, for the path to be supported by the fixed concrete piers and not the clip-ons, which move up and down under vehicle loading…

"Two weeks ago, Prime Minister Jacinda Ardern and senior ministers announced the Government would spend $360 million building SkyPath and a 3km extension of the cycleway and walkway to Esmonde Rd at Takapuna, known as SeaPath…

"The Government has promised to start building SkyPath and SeaPath early next year for completion in 2023 or 2024." [1016]

Light Rail
In September 2019, the Government announced that most of the $463 million set aside by the New Zealand Transport Agency for a light rail service to run from the Auckland CBD to Mount Roskill, and ultimately to the airport, was instead to be spent elsewhere. Although no reason for the change, other that it had been *delayed*, was given, commentators

believed at the time that Labour's coalition partner, New Zealand First, had stopped the project from going ahead.

As reported by Stuff on 13 May 2020, the light rail proposal had again been considered but the Government had still to decide who was to build it:

"The Government is currently at the point of deciding who it wants to build the scheme. The two bidders are NZTA[NZ Transport Agency], the Government's infrastructure builder and NZ Infra, a group made up of the NZ Super Fund and CDPQ Infra, a Canadian pension fund.

"After an analysis of the two bids by the Ministry of Transport, which finished in February, the decision had been put before ministers.

"[Transport Minister] Twyford's office could not clarify when a decision will be made on who will build the project, given New Zealand is expected to be fighting the economic effects of Covid-19 for some time. He said the Government remained committed to light rail…" [1017]

An Election Issue

By 24 June, The New Zealand Herald reported that the light rail project had become too hard for the present Government:

"Auckland's light rail project is officially an election issue after the Government gave up on trying to reach an agreement on which plan to back. Transport Minister Phil Twyford announced the Auckland Light Rail process had 'ended' with the Ministry of Transport to consider the issue and come up with a proposal for the next Government to consider…" [1018]

Eastern Busway

The Eastern Busway was first endorsed as part of the Auckland-Manukau Eastern Transport Initiative (AMETI) by the Auckland City Council's Transport and Urban Linkages Committee in July 2007. However, design work did not start until March 2010 and it took until 2018 for work to begin.

"When complete [the busway] will be supported by three new stations at Panmure, Pakuranga, and Botany…

"Stage one of the project between Panmure and Pakuranga is due for completion next year [2021]. When the busway is fully operational in 2025, commuters will be able to travel between Botany and Britomart, by bus and train, in less than 40 minutes." [1019]

Alliance Formed

By October 2020, construction of the busway between Panmure and Pakuranga was underway and Auckland Transport announced the signing of an *alliance* to complete the final stage to Botany:

"Four world-class organisations have been selected to form an Auckland Transport led alliance to design, consent and build the completion stages of the Eastern Busway project.

"'Signing up Fletcher, Acciona, AECOM and Jacobs to form an alliance is a significant milestone for Auckland. This is a game-changing project for Auckland. The formation of an alliance is a major step towards delivering rapid transit and improved travel options for people in our eastern and southern suburbs,' says Mayor Goff.

"Following the enormous success of the Northern Busway, the Eastern Busway is expected to carry more than 30,000 people per day between the rapidly growing south-eastern suburbs and the rail network in Panmure. This project will make journeys faster and more convenient, reducing travel time between Botany and Britomart. It will also help reduce traffic congestion and vehicle emissions.

"'The organisations have entered into an interim project alliance agreement phase to start critical design and consenting work, before progressing towards construction expected to start in 2022,' says Auckland Transport Chief Executive Shane Ellison.

"The remaining stages of the Eastern Busway will extend the rapid transit, high frequency busway currently under construction between Panmure and Pakuranga, through to a new station in Botany Town Centre.

"The project will include new walking and cycling connections, placemaking, urban renewal initiatives and improvements for general traffic. The project is due to be complete in 2025 - subject to consent approvals…" [1020]

Northern Corridor Improvements

North of the Harbour Bridge, the popularity of the Northern Busway and other public transport initiatives continued to require constant improvements:

"A new busway station is to be built at Rosedale on the North Shore providing a major boost to public transport in Auckland. Resource consent for the facility has been granted by Auckland Council, following a decision by two independent commissioners…the new station will tie in with work underway to extend the Northern Busway to Albany…

"The $70 million project includes a new station and split level plaza at Arrenway Drive with a drop off area and a small number of mobility parking spaces. This is similar to Smales Farm and Akoranga stations but does not include a park and ride facility…

"The station will add to an upgrade at Hibiscus Coast Station and recently completed extension of the Albany Station park and ride…The consent application was lodged with the Auckland Council in September 2019. Construction of the station and local road work is expected to begin in 2022 as part of the Northern Corridor Improvements project.

"The Northern Corridor Improvements project will provide a much needed transport upgrade for the whole Albany and North Harbour community. It includes a new motorway connection between SH1 and SH18 and will open up access to the Western Ring Route and travel to the airport. It will extend the Northern Busway to Albany and deliver over 7kms of walking and cycling paths and a wide range of local road and park connections." [1021]

Road Transport
The Congestion Question

As outlined in the previous chapter, *The Congestion Question* (TCQ), previously known as the *Auckland Smarter Transport Pricing Project*, was another of those consigned to the 'too hard' basket by early 2020.

Nevertheless, the groundwork was completed, as explained by the Congestion Question Technical Report, published in July 2020.

That Report explains that the investigation:

"…builds on the findings of the Auckland Transport Alignment Project (ATAP), which set out a 30-year vision for Auckland's transport system. ATAP confirmed that the well-discussed adage, 'you can't build your way out of congestion', is also true in Auckland.

"While there are necessary capacity improvements and new projects required, ATAP identified that a greater focus is required on influencing travel demand through smarter transport pricing. This is in conjunction with implementing a substantial investment programme with an emphasis on public transport and generating more efficient use of our existing networks.

"The ATAP report recommended the early establishment of a dedicated project to progress 'smarter' transport pricing with a primary focus on addressing congestion.

Three Phases

The Technical Report outlined the process of introducing smarter transport pricing, divided into three phases:

"Phase One could entail the implementation of the City Centre Cordon by 2025 to coincide with the opening of the City Rail Link (CRL).

"Phase Two could build on the City Centre Cordon with the addition of the following strategic corridors by 2028:

    Northern Motorway and parallel corridors to Albany
    Southern Motorway inside the Auckland isthmus and key corridors
    Pakuranga Highway and Ti Rakau Drive to Botany

"Phase Three could build on Phase Two through the addition of the following strategic corridors in the period following 2028:

    Outer sections of the Northwest Motorway and key corridors towards Westgate
    Outer sections of the Southern Motorway and key corridors towards Papakura

The Congestion Question Technical Report concluded:

"Based on the technical work undertaken in the TCQ investigation, there is a strong case for implementing congestion pricing in Auckland for demand management purposes. However, prior to a final decision on whether or not to implement congestion pricing, TCQ recommends that a comprehensive stakeholder and public engagement exercise should be undertaken…" [1022]

In other words…wait for the advertising…

Suburban Rail

Papakura to Pukekohe Electrification

As detailed in the previous chapter, Auckland Transport had replaced its remaining diesel trains with electric trains on all lines from Papakura and Swanson to Britomart on 20 July 2015. From that date, the only diesel trains still running on the suburban network were those between Papakura and Pukekohe.

It wasn't until June 2020 that the KiwiRail contract to electrify the 19km line was "…awarded to a joint bid from Chinese-owned firm John Holland and South African-owned McConnell Dowell…" [1023]

The work includes new signalling and track upgrades as well as the redevelopment of Pukekohe station.

Puhinui Station Interchange

The concept of integrated public transport, the ideal so sought after since the 1950s, was gradually becoming a reality – as demonstrated by the bus and train interchange at Puhinui and reported by Rail Express on 24 June 2020:

"A joint venture has been selected to complete the NZ$46.6 million ($43.4m) Puhinui station interchange. McConnell Dowell and Built Environs will construct the bus and rail interchange.

"Auckland Mayor Phil Goff said that the project, estimated for completion in 2021 is responding to the needs of the surrounding area.

"'The Puhinui Station Interchange will guarantee reliable and convenient connections for bus and train commuters and help ease congestion,' he said...

"New Zealand Transport Minister Phil Twyford said that the interchange will enable better access to Auckland airport. 'When the upgrades to SH20B/Puhinui Road and the Interchange are complete, any Aucklander with access to the rail network will have a fast and convenient 10-minute bus connection to the airport.'" [1024]

Widespread Wear

While the modernisation of the suburban rail network continued, there nevertheless remained the legacy of many years of neglect to remedy – as reported by The New Zealand Herald on 13 August 2020:

"Wear on Auckland's metro rail network is more widespread than first thought, triggering urgent work to replace 100km of track in six months.

"From Monday, track speeds will be lowered from 80 to 40 km/h so commuter trains can continue to operate safely in the meantime. Journeys will take longer and fewer services will be able to run during the morning and afternoon weekday peak travel periods.

"It's possible changes will also be made to the frequency of train services at other times of the day, and at weekends...KiwiRail Group Chief Executive Greg Miller said the work was anticipated as part of the $1 billion programme to modernise the network and prepare it for the growth that will come with the City Rail Link..." [1025]

Dame Whina Cooper Arrives

In the meantime, despite the uncertainties of the Covid-19 pandemic, construction of the City Rail Link continued. Following the arrival of the tunnel-boring machine at Auckland on 21 October 2020, what could stop it now?

"New Zealand's biggest transport infrastructure job leapt forward today with the arrival of the $13.5 million tunnel-boring machine for the $4.4 billion City Rail Link.

"The machine, officially named Dame Whina Cooper, is now at the Ports of Auckland after a voyage of more than 9000km from its factory in southern China...Tunnelling is due to start next April (2021)." [1026]

Additional Waitemata Harbour Connections

Just as this saga more or less started with a vision to bridge the Waitemata in April 1860, so it ends with a business case prepared in November 2020 by the New Zealand Transport Agency planning to span the harbour a second time.

That first dream took a century to become a reality and the NZTA does not expect its concept of an *Additional Waitematā Harbour Connection* to eventuate much before the 2030s.

"The business case analyses the current and future issues faced in Auckland's Northern Motorway corridor (including the Auckland Harbour Bridge and the Northern Busway), assesses a number of options for addressing these issues, and recommends a way forward to provide a comprehensive and long-lasting response.

"Mayor Phil Goff says, 'The success of the Northern Busway has helped to reduce immediate pressure on the Harbour Bridge, but with Auckland's population set to hit nearly 2 million by 2030, in the longer-term an additional harbour crossing will be essential...'

"A key finding of the business case has been the urgent need to enhance the highly successful Northern Busway. AT [Auckland Transport] is now progressing that investigation which will examine ways of upgrading the Northern Busway to increase its capacity, reliability and overall service quality into the future.

"The business case recommends a phased approach to developing an additional rapid transit connection for the North Shore (including across the Waitemata Harbour to the city centre) that supplements and integrates with the busway and the wider transport system to provide more public transport options. Road improvements are also required in the future to improve resilience and address growing interpeak congestion.

"The next phase will confirm the mode, form and function of an additional crossing as well as a timeline for it to be in place before the enhanced busway reaches capacity. This will be followed by a phase to route protect land required for the options developed as part of the process.

"This roadmap will take an integrated full network approach including integration with other plans and projects like City Centre to Mangere and North West rapid transit, work to support land use and growth on the North Shore, the construction of a connection for walking and cycling and any plans for road pricing in Auckland.

"The long-term solutions being investigated would likely be New Zealand's biggest transport investments, costing billions of dollars and would be expected to take more than 15 years of design and construction work…

"Apart from the Northern Busway improvements, construction is not anticipated to start until the 2030s…" [1027]

Afterword

If you've read this far (or perhaps skipped a bit), you may be astounded by the countless, costly, transport studies and reports that have been generated over the years. And yet few recommendations from those studies and reports were actually implemented, even in part.

At the same time, so many central and local governments have formulated transport policies, sometimes based on those studies and reports, only to have those policies reversed or binned by a succeeding administration before they could be actioned. (Perhaps an extension of the parliamentary term from three to four years, as recently suggested, could have helped in the past.)

A second source of astonishment revealed by this narrative is that, for a country as small as New Zealand, there has been such a disconnect between central and local governments about planning and funding.

This disconnect has resulted in central government's overall control of funding by means of which it has dictated both the form and size of its preferred infrastructure models (mostly roads), regardless of Auckland's transport needs.

Of course, Auckland's local government has also been its own worst enemy at times. For instance, in 1927, Auckland's ratepayers voted against raising a special loan to fund the needed expansion of the city's extensive tram service. As a result, the trams were eventually lost altogether.

What had been Auckland's most profitable, mass people-mover was never replaced and the whole transportation landscape was left a gaping wound – open to the acceptance of the Road Gang's 1955 'Master Transportation Plan for Metropolitan Auckland' and the infectious motor vehicle that followed.

While this narrative is generally a history of failure to revive public transportation in time to abate the dominance of the motor vehicle, it is also a record of the successes that eventually led to the transformative force that created a unified Auckland – the same force that may finally overcome the private motor vehicle as the predominant mode of urban travel.

Obviously, Auckland's transport adventure continues and does not end with the final page of this narrative. There will be more to record by future historians eager to relate ensuing events, many of which are bound to rival, and probably repeat, those that have gone before.

Gas Pedal to Back-Pedal   Appendices

(Appendix 1) – From Page 92:
Overall Pattern of Proposed System and Table of Distances for existing and proposed city rail routes by J R Lee – July 1949:

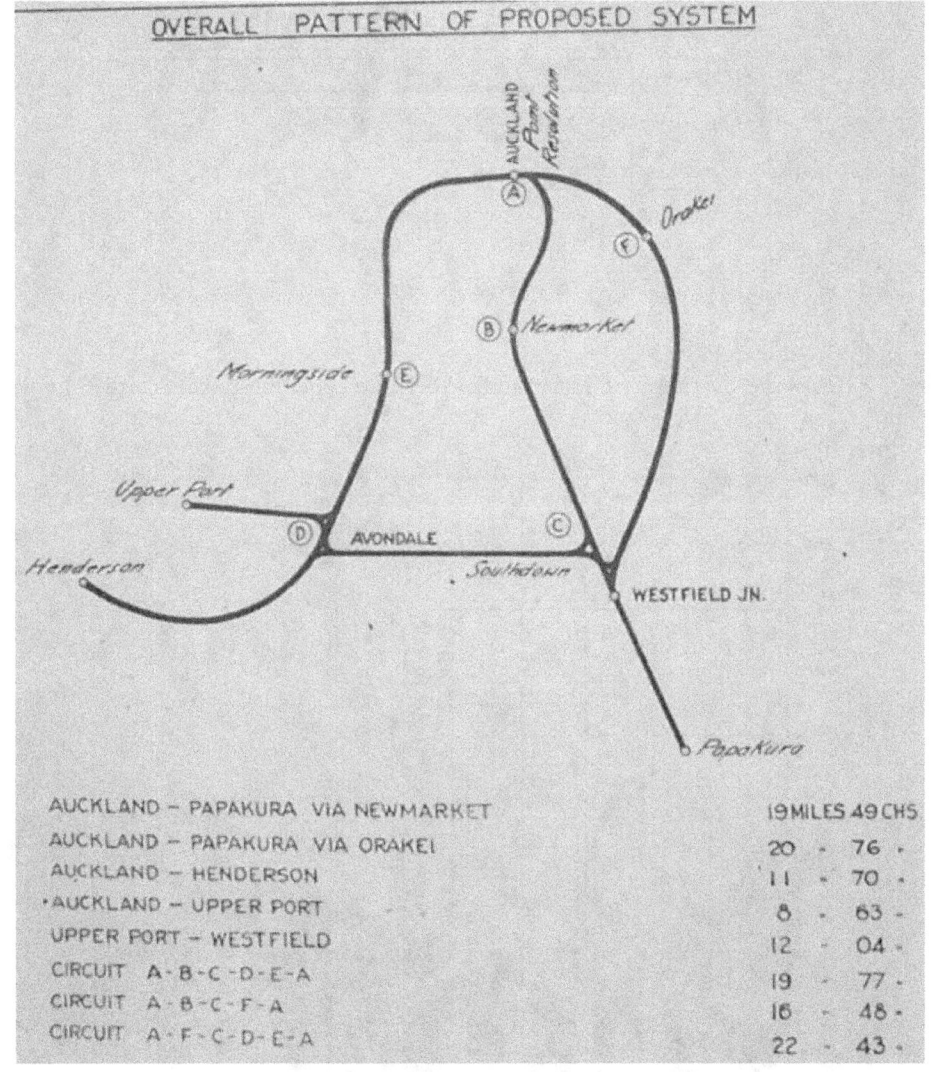

(Appendix 2) – From Page 573:
Allocation of Transport Funding
A breakdown of allocations by Transfund for the 1998-1999 year and the local authority share to match Transfund's allocation (Road expenditure includes maintenance, minor safety projects, commitments, construction).
   Figure 7

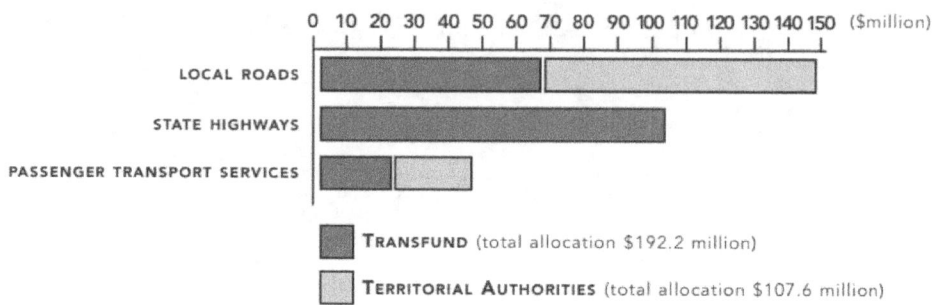

(Appendix 3) – From Page 573:
"Figure 8 tracks the allocation of Transfund's Auckland expenditure between 1991 and 1999:
   Figure 8

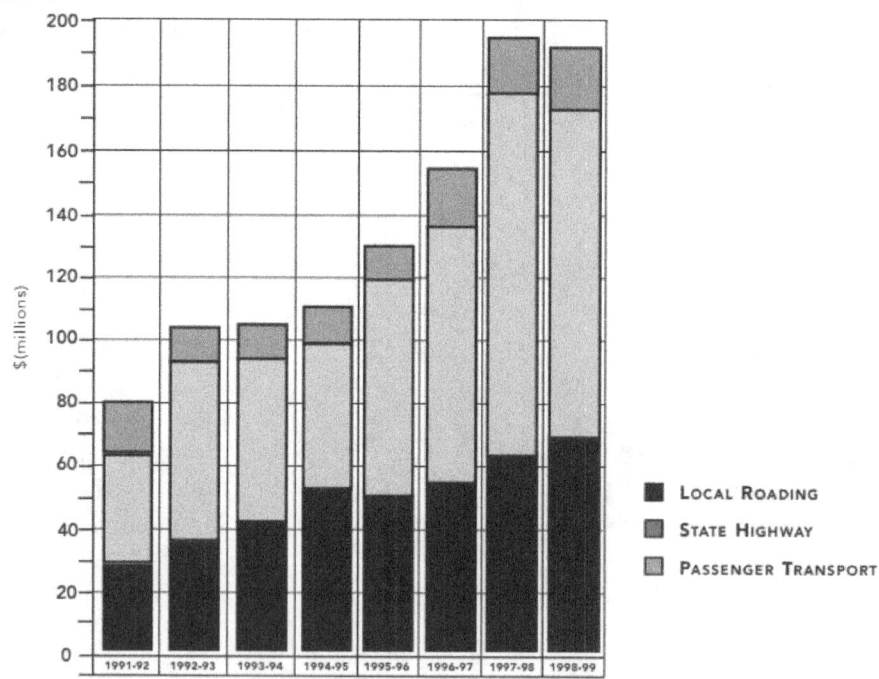

References

1. Wynn, G., *Reflections on the Writing of New Zealand History.* New Zealand Journal of History, 1984. 18(2): p.3, 4, 104-116.
2. *The History of Local Government in New Zealand*, in *Timaru Herald* 1868: Timaru.
3. Green, E.K., *He Believed That He Knew A Better Site For Auckland*, in *Auckland Star.* 1945: Auckland.
4. *Hobson's Bay Proposals Become Bogey For Auckland Town Planners*, in *Comment* 1955, Hobson Publications Limited Auckland.
5. *1840-1940 - Hundredth Birthday - Auckland Nearly Century Old*, in *Auckland Star.* 1930: Auckland.
6. Bloomfield, G.T., *The Growth of Auckland 1840 - 1966*, in *Auckland In Ferment* J.S. Whitelaw, Editor. 1967, New Zealand Geographical Society: Auckland. p.1-21
7. Latham, M.M.B., *Planning Objectives In Local Government.* 1973, Auckland.
8. *The Local Government Commission*, in *Christchurch Press.* 1932: Christchurch.
9. *Local Government Reform*, in *Christchurch Press.* 1935:
10. *Local Body Amalgamation*, in *Evening Post.* 1937: Wellington.
11. *To Cost £25,000 - Newmarket Works Plan*, in *Auckland Star.* 1937:
12. *Olympic Pool*, in *Auckland Star.* 1940: Auckland
13. *Reports Of The Local Government (Amalgamation Schemes) Bill Committee.* 1938, New Zealand Government: Wellington.
14. *Reports Of The Local Government (Amalgamation Schemes) Bill Committee* 1938, New Zealand Government: Wellington.
15. Dahms, Dr. F., *Urban Passenger Transport and Population Distribution in Auckland: 1860 - 1961.* New Zealand Geographer, 1980. 36: p.2-10
16. Bloomfield, G.T., *Urban Tramways in New Zealand 1862-1964*, in *New Zealand Geographer* 1975. p.101, 114
17. Hodgson, T., *The Heart of Colonial Auckland 1865-1910.* 1992, Auckland: Random Century New Zealand Limited.
18. Stewart, G., *The End of the Penny Section - A History of Urban Transport in New Zealand.* 1973, Wellington: A H & A W Reed Limited.
19. Lowe, D., *Auckland 1900 - A Pictorial Entertainment.* The Lodestone Press: Auckland.
20. *City Transport Control*, in *The New Zealand Herald.* 1925:
21. *Motor-omnibus Traffic Act 1926.* 1926.
22. Ford, A. E., *Auckland Transport Board Annual Report For Year Ended 31 March 1929.* 1929, Auckland Transport Board: Auckland.
23. *Auckland Transport Board Act 1928.* 1928: New Zealand.
24. Allum, J. A. C., *Auckland Transport Board Annual Report for the Year Ended 31 March 1930.* 1930, Auckland Transport Board:
25. Allum, J. A. C., *Auckland Transport Board Third Annual Report for the Year Ended March 31st 1931.* 1931, Auckland Transport Board:
26. Allum, J. A. C., *Auckland Transport Board Annual Report for the Year Ended 31 March 1932.* 1932, Auckland Transport Board:

27. Allum, J. A. C., *Auckland Transport Board Annual Report for the Year Ended 31 March 1933*. 1933, Auckland Transport Board: Auckland.
28. Allum, J. A. C., *Auckland Transport Board Annual Report for the Year Ended 31 March 1934*. 1934, Auckland Transport Board: Auckland.
29. *Jubilee Of Ferries*, in *The New Zealand Herald*. 1931: Auckland.
30. *Auckland Transport Board Empowering Act 1934*. 1934: New Zealand.
31. Allum, J. A. C., *Auckland Transport Board Annual Report for the Year Ended 31 March 1935*. 1935, Auckland Transport Board:
32. Mason, H. G. R., *Auckland Transport Board Annual Report for the Year Ended 31 March 1936*. 1936, Auckland Transport Board:
33. Mason, H. G. R., *Auckland Transport Board Annual Report for the Year Ended 31 March 1937*. 1937, Auckland Transport Board:
34. Mason, H. G. R., *Auckland Transport Board Annual Report for the Year Ended 31 March1938*. 1938, Auckland Transport Board:
35. Mason, H. G. R., *Auckland Transport Board Annual Report for the Year Ending 31 March 1939*. 1939, Auckland Transport Board:
36. *Motor-spirits Taxation Act 1927*. 1927.
37. *Town-Planning - New Zealand Conference*, in *The Dominion*. 1919: Wellington.
38. *Roads - Administration*, in *Te Ara - An Encyclopaedia of New Zealand*, A.H. McLintock, Editor. 1966.
39. Arbury, J., *From Urban Sprawl to Compact City - An analysis of urban growth management in Auckland*
40. Taverner, W. B., *Railways Statement for the Year Ending 31 March 1929*, Department of Railways. 1929, New Zealand Government: Wellington.
41. *Waitemata Harbour Transit Facilities (Report of Royal Commission Appointed To Inquire Into)*. 1930: Wellington.
42. *Letters To The Editor - Harbour Traffic*, in *The New Zealand Herald*. 1938: Auckland.
43. *Harbour Transport - Prime Minister's View*, in *The New Zealand Herald*. 1938: Auckland.
44. *Crowded Ferries*, in *Auckland Star*. 1939: Auckland.
45. *Harbour Bridge - Delayed Conference*, in *The New Zealand Herald*. 1939: Auckland.
46. Robinson, D. -M., *Auckland Suburban Railway System - Historical Background*. 1953>: Auckland. p.2-7
47. *The Nelson Examiner*, in *The Nelson Examiner and New Zealand Chronicle*. 1860: Nelson.
48. *New Railway Outlet To North Auckland - Handling Suburban Traffic*, in *Auckland Star*. 1926: Auckland.
49. Hiley, E. H., *Report On New Zealand Government Railways*. 1914: Wellington.
50. *Railway Control - New General Manager*, in *Evening Post*. 1928: Wellington.
51. *Heavy Railway Losses*, in *Auckland Star*. 1929: Auckland.
52. *What Remedy? - Railway Transport Riddle*, in *Evening Post*. 1929: Wellington.
53. Sterling, H. H., *Railways Statement for Year Ended 31 March 1929*, Railways Department. 1929, New Zealand Government: Wellington.
54. *Officially Opened - Auckland Railway Station* in *Auckland Star*. 1930: Auckland.
55. *Fixing The Site - Department's Reasons*, in *Auckland Star*. 1930:
56. *Auckland Of The Future*, in *The New Zealand Herald*. 1943:
57. *Town Planning - Auckland's Future*, in *The New Zealand Herald*. 1943: Auckland.
58. *Auckland Plans - Metropolitan Needs*, in *Auckland Star*. 1944:

59. *Reports Of The Local Government Committee*. 1945, New Zealand Government: Wellington. p.154
60. *Future Planning - Peacetime Projects*, in *The New Zealand Herald*. 1945: Auckland.
61. *Merger Issue*, in *The New Zealand Herald*. 1945: Auckland.
62. *Mt Eden Opposed*, in *Auckland Star*. 1945: Auckland.
63. Green, E.K., *Auckland - With A 400,000 Population – Increasing Transport problems*, in *Auckland Star* 1945: Auckland.
64. Green, E.K., *Town Planners Expect - Engineers Scheme*, in *The Auckland Star*. 1945: Auckland.
65. NZ Institute of Engineers. *Biographies - Arthur James Dickson*. Engineering Heritage New Zealand; from: http://www.ipenz.org.nz/heritage/bio-detail.cfm?id=42
66. Dickson, A.J., *Town Planning - Auckland Lags*, in *Auckland Star*. 1945: Auckland.
67. Baker, J.V.T., *War Economy*, in *The Official History of New Zealand in the Second World War 1939-1945*. 1965, New Zealand Electronic Text Collection: Wellington.
68. *Regional Plans - Functions Over-Lap*, in *Auckland Star*. 1945:
69. *Future Planning*, in *Auckland Star*. 1945: Auckland.
70. *City Control*, in *The New Zealand Herald*. 1945: Auckland.
71. *Local Government Commission Act*. 1946: New Zealand.
72. Harris, C. E., *Slow Train Coming: The New Zealand State Changes its Mind about Auckland Transit, 1949-1956*. Urban Policy and Research, 2005. 23(1): p.5, 6, 9, 12-16, 37-55, 72
73. Semple, H.R., *Public Works Statement*, P.W. Department, Editor. 1946, New Zealand Government: Wellington.
74. McKillop, E.R., *Report of the Commissioner Of Works For The Period Ended 31st March 1946*, M.O. Works, Editor. 1946, New Zealand Government: Wellington. p.32, 33
75. Semple, H.R., *Ministry of Works Statement*, Ministry of Works. 1947, New Zealand Government: Wellington.
76. McKillop, E.R., *Report of the Commissioner of Works*, Ministry of Works. 1947, New Zealand Government: Wellington.
77. McKillop, E.R., *Report of the Commissioner of Works*, Ministry of Works. 1948, New Zealand Government: Wellington.
78. *Town-planning Amendment Act 1948*. 1948: New Zealand.
79. Commission, Local Government, *The History of the Commission*. [cited 2017 9 January 2017]; from: http://www.lgc.govt.nz/the-role-of-the-commission/the-history-of-the-commission/
80. *Report Of The Local Government Commission*, Internal Affairs. 1948, New Zealand Government: Wellington.
81. Dickson, A. J., *Correlation and Integration - A Study in City Building*. New Zealand Engineering, 1949(10 May 1949): p.366-370.
82. Nagle, W. H., *Auckland Transport Board Annual Report for the Year Ended 31 March 1940*. 1940, Auckland Transport Board:
83. Nagle, W. H., *Auckland Transport Board Annual Report for the Year Ended 31 March 1941*. 1941, Auckland Transport Board:
84. *Effect On Traffic - Free Tram Service*, in *Auckland Star*. 1941: Auckland.
85. Sayegh, J. C., *Auckland Transport Board Annual Report for the Year Ended 31 March 1942*. Auckland Transport Board: Auckland. p.4

86. Sayegh, J. C., *Auckland Transport Board Annual Report for the Year Ended 31 March 1943*. 1943, Auckland Transport Board: Auckland.
87. Nagle, W. H., *Auckland Transport Board Annual Report for the Year Ended 31 March 1944*. 1944, Auckland Transport Board:
88. *Purchase Of Bus - New Hospital Service*, in *Auckland Star*. 1945:
89. Anderson, H. A., *Auckland Transport Board Annual Report for the Year Ended 31 March 1950*. 1950, Auckland Transport Board: p.3, 4
90. Transport, Auckland, *Britomart - Chapter 1 - The Historic Land 1600-1959*. Britomart Transport Centre - Where Rail Meets The Road [cited 2010 1 January 2010]; from: www.britomart.co.nz/history1.html. p.10
91. Woolston, A., *Equal to the Task - The City of Auckland Traffic Department 1894-1994*. 1996, Auckland: Auckland City Council & New Zealand Police.
92. Nagle, W. H., *Auckland Transport Board Annual Report for the Year Ended 31 March 1945*. 1945, Auckland Transport Board:
93. Green, E.K., *Auckland - With A 400,000 Population - Increasing Transport Problems*, in *Auckland Star*. 1945: Auckland.
94. *Crowded Trams - Capacity Overtaxed*, in *Auckland Star*. 1945:
95. *News Of The Day - Auckland Trolley Buses*, in *Evening Post*. 1945: Wellington.
96. Nagle, W. H., *Auckland Transport Board Annual Report for the Year ended 31 March 1946*. 1946, Auckland Transport Board:
97. *Engineers' Request - Transport Inquiries*, in *The New Zealand Herald*. 1945: Auckland.
98. Nagle, W. H., *Auckland Transport Board Annual Report for the Year Ended 31 March 1947*. 1947, Auckland Transport Board:
99. *Local Legislation Act 1946*. 1946: New Zealand.
100. *The Tramway Carriage Regulations 1947*. 1947: New Zealand.
101. Semple, H. R., *Ministry of Works Statement 1948*, Ministry of Works. 1948, New Zealand Government: Wellington. p.10
102. Nagle, W. H., *Auckland Transport Board Annual Report for the Year Ended 31 March 1948*. 1948, Auckland Transport Board
103. Anderson, H. A., *Auckland Transport Board Annual Report for the Year Ended 31 March 1949*. 1949, Auckland Transport Board:
104. Neale, D. E. P., *Auckland's Transport Problems*. 1949, Auckland Chamber of Commerce Incorporated: Auckland. p.4
105. *The Transport Act 1949*. 1949: New Zealand.
106. Holcroft, M. H., *Carapace - The Motor Car in New Zealand: A Roadside View*. 1979, Dunedin: John McIndoe Limited. p.60, 61, 82
107. *Huge Project - New Auckland Suburb*, in *Evening Post*. 1943: Wellington.
108. *Road Outlets*, in *The New Zealand Herald*. 1943: Auckland.
109. Green, E. K., *To Meet Problems Relating To Auckland's Traffic Outlet*, in *Auckland Star*. 1945: Auckland.
110. Langbein, F., *Ministry of Works Statement*, Ministry of Works. 1948, New Zealand Government: Wellington. p.33, 76
111. Semple, R., *Ministry of Works Statement*, Ministry of Works. 1949: Wellington. p.3, 4
112. Langbein, F., *Ministry of Works Statement* Ministry of Works. 1949, New Zealand Government: Wellington. p.31
113. *Wharf Or Bridge*, in *Auckland Star*. 1943: Auckland.
114. *Strongly Criticised - Proposed Ferry Terminal*, in *Auckland Star*. 1944: Auckland.

115. *Harbour Bridge Issue*, in *Auckland Star*. 1944: Auckland.
116. *Harbour Link*, in *The New Zealand Herald*. 1944: Auckland.
117. *Waitemata Council's View*, in *Auckland Star*. 1944: Auckland.
118. *Trans-Harbour Transport*, in *Auckland Star*. 1944: Auckland.
119. *The Bridge Project*, in *Auckland Star*. 1945: Auckland.
120. *Inquiry Sought* in *The New Zealand Herald*. 1945: Auckland.
121. *Harbour Bridge - Commission Urged*, in *Auckland Star*. 1945:
122. *Transharbour Traffic*, in *Auckland Star*. 1945: Auckland.
123. *Cost To Community*, in *Auckland Star*. 1945: Auckland.
124. *Inquiry Sought*, in *Auckland Star*. 1945: Auckland.
125. *Trans-Harbour Facilities*, in *Auckland Star*. 1945: Auckland.
126. *City's Traffic*, in *Auckland Star*. 1945: Auckland.
127. *A New Highway*, in *Auckland Star*. 1945: Auckland.
128. *Railways System*, in *Auckland Star*. 1945: Auckland.
129. *Transport Inquiry*, in *The New Zealand Herald*. 1945: Auckland.
130. *Report Of The Royal Commission - Trans-Harbour Facilities*. 1946, House of Representatives: Wellington. p.6, 8, 16, 18, 31, 34, 35
131. Langbein, F., *Supplies of Steel for Maintenance of existing Works*, Public Works Department. 1948: Wellington.
132. *Auckland Harbour Bridge Repeal Act*. 1948.
133. *Suburban Traffic - Suggestion By Mayor*, in *Auckland Star*. 1940:
134. *Railway Problem - Site Of The Station*, in *Auckland Star*. 1940:
135. *Early Planning* in *The Auckland Star*. 1944: Auckland.
136. *Tunnel Scheme - Post-War Proposal*, in *Auckland Star*. 1944:
137. *New Civic Centre Being Planned For City*, in *Auckland Star*. 1945:
138. *Auckland's Access To North*, in *Auckland Star*. 1945: Auckland.
139. Langbein, F., *Ministry of Works Statement*, Ministry of Works. 1947: p.32
140. *The Government Railways Amendment Act*. 1931: New Zealand.
141. *The Transport Licensing Act 1931*. 1931: New Zealand.
142. *The Transport Law Amendment Act 1933*. 1933: New Zealand.
143. *The Transport Licensing Amendment Act 1935*. 1935: New Zealand.
144. McCrystal, J., *On the Buses in New Zealand - From Charabancs to the Coaches of Today*. 2007, Wellington: Grantham House Publishing & Bus and Coach Association. p.10, 11, 86, 87, 162, 163, 168
145. *The Transport Licensing Amendment Act 1936*. 1936: New Zealand.
146. *The Government Railways Amendment Act 1936* 1936: NZ
147. *The Transport Law Amendment Act 1939*. 1939: New Zealand.
148. *The Transport Law Amendment Act 1948*. 1948: New Zealand.
149. *The Transport Licensing Amendment Act 1949*. 1949: New Zealand.
150. *Master Transportation Plan For Metropolitan Auckland - Report And Survey*. 1955, Auckland Regional Planning Authority: Auckland. p.3, 15, 20, 26, 27, 30, 31, 63, 128-132
151. *Report of The Local Government Commission* Internal Affairs. 1950, New Zealand Government: Wellington. p.45
152. *Draft Outline Development Plan for Auckland*. New Zealand Engineering, 1950. 5(5): p.431-434

153. Jones, F.W.O., *Record Of Attendances 6/6/52 to 8/10/54*. 1954, Auckland Regional Planning Authority - Technical Advisory Committee: Auckland.
154. *Town and Country Planning Act 1953*. 1953: New Zealand.
155. Boileau, Dr. I. E., *Town Planning and the Shape of Auckland*, in *Auckland At Full Stretch - Issues Of The Seventies*, Bush, G. & Scott, C., Editors. 1977, Auckland City Council and University of Auckland Board of Urban Studies: p.45, 47, 48
156. Committee, Town and Country Planning Act Review, *Report to Government*, NZ Ministry of Works and Development. 1973, NZ Government Wellington. p.1 & Appendix
157. Stone, R. C. J., *Myers, Arthur Mielziner*, in *Dictionary of New Zealand Biography*. 2012, Encyclopedia of New Zealand.
158. Edgar, J. T., *Urban Legend - Sir Dove-Myer Robinson*. 2012, Auckland Hachette New Zealand Limited p.122-128, 130, 138, 140, 144, 150
159. Bush, G. W. A. (1998) *Bloodworth, Thomas* Dictionary of New Zealand Biography.
160. Luxford, J., *Mayor's Monthly Letter*. Comment Magazine, 1955(August 1955). P.4
161. Bassett, J. (1998) *Luxford, John Hector*. Dictionary of New Zealand Biography.
162. Bush, G. W. A., *Moving Against the Tide*. 1980, Palmerston North: The Dunmore Press Limited. P.159
163. *Citizens! Know your Councillors*, in *Comment Magazine*. 1955. P.21
164. Edgar, J. T., Metropolitan Reform and Decision Making: Dove-Myer Robinson's Challenge To Local Body Morphological Fundamentalism. 1987, University of Waikato: Hamilton. p.ii-v, 192-196, 201-204, 218-220, 223-226, 233-235, 241-250, 257-259, 281-282, 253-254
165. Robinson, D.-M., *Untitled Press Release*. 1956: Auckland.
166. Hercock, F. (1998) *Eady, Lewis Alfred*. Dictionary of New Zealand Biography.
167. Robinson, D.-M., *Untitled*. 1955: Auckland.
168. Bell, N. C., *Regionalism Comes to New Zealand*. NZ Local Government, 1965. 1(8): p.3-9
169. Steel, J., *The Role of Local Government in Expanding Auckland*, in *Auckland In Ferment*, J.S. Whitelaw, Editor. 1967, New Zealand Geographical Society: Auckland. p.112-130
170. *City Faces New Housing Policy*, in *Comment Magazine*. 1955. p. 45, 46
171. Luxford, J. H., *Subdivision of City Land*. Comment Magazine, 1955(September 1955). p.4
172. Heritage, Ministry for Culture and, *Unveiling Parliamentary Centenary Plaque*. [Film Clip] 1956 4 February 2016 21 January 2018]; from: https://nzhistory.govt.nz/media/video/unveiling-plaque-at-parliament
173. Office, Auckland Provincial Public Relations, *Programme for the Visit to Auckland of Members of Parliament*. 1956, Auckland: Whitcombe and Tombs. p.11
174. Robinson, D.-M., *Message To Electors*. United Independent Party Pamphlet, 1956. p.1, 11, 27
175. Robinson, D.-M., *President's Report to Members*. 1956, United Independents Party: Auckland.
176. *Transport Amendment Act 1950*. 1950: New Zealand.
177. Anderson, H.A., *Auckland Transport Board Annual Report for the Year Ended 31 March 1951*. 1951, Auckland Transport Board Auckland. p.1-3
178. Hill, J., *Was Joey Saved by the Taniwha?* 2009: Whangarei.

179. Anderson, H. A., *Auckland Transport Board Annual Report for the Year Ended 31 March 1952*. 1952, Auckland Transport Board: Auckland. p.2, 3
180. Laurenson, G. L., *Annual Report of Transport Department* 1950, Transport Department: Wellington. p.8, 36
181. Laurenson, G. L., *Annual Report of Transport Department*. 1953, Transport Department: Wellington. p.16
182. Anderson, H. A., *Auckland Transport Board Annual Report for the Year Ended 31 March 1953*. 1953, Auckland Transport Board: p.1-3
183. *Report of the Roading Investigation Committee*, Ministry of Works. 1953, New Zealand Government: Wellington. p.3-13, 22-26, 65, 83, 84, 135, 160, 148-156
184. *Transport Amendment Act (No. 2) 1953*. 1953: New Zealand.
185. Anderson, H. A., *Auckland Transport Board Annual Report for the Year Ended 31 March 1954*. 1954, Auckland Transport Board: Auckland. p.3, 4
186. Welch, J. W. F., *Modernization of Municipal Public Transport*. New Zealand Engineering, 1954: p.192-199
187. Anderson, H. A., *Auckland Transport Board Annual Report for the Year Ending 31 March 1955*. 1955, Auckland Transport Board: Auckland. p.3, 4
188. *Sales Tax Act 1932-33*. 1932: New Zealand.
189. *Customs Acts Amendment Act 1934*. 1934: New Zealand.
190. *Official Civic, Commercial and Industrial Year Book for the City of Auckland*. 1955, Auckland: Hobson Publications Limited. p.13, 15
191. *A New Era In Transport*, in *Comment Magazine*. 1955, Auckland City Council: Auckland. p.32
192. *Greater Auckland*, in *Comment Magazine*. 1955, Auckland City Council: Auckland. p.33
193. Spencer, N. B., *Auckland Transport Board Annual Report for the Year Ended 31 March 1956*. 1956, Auckland Transport Board: Auckland. p.3, 4
194. Spencer, N. B., *Auckland Transport Board Annual Report for the Year Ended 31 March 1957*. 1957, Auckland Transport Board: Auckland. p.5
195. *Report By Passenger Transport Committee*. 1956, Auckland Metropolitan Council: Auckland. p.1-5
196. Hanson, F. M., *Removal Of Remaining Tram Tracks, Auckland*, W. Commissioner of Works. 1956: Wellington.
197. Bell, W. L., *Removal of Further Portions of Tram Tracks Auckland Transport Board*, Auckland District Commissioner of Works. 1956:
198. Spencer, N. B., *Auckland Transport Board Annual Report for the Year Ended 31 March 1958*. 1958, Auckland Transport Board: Auckland. p.5
199. Spencer, N. B., *Auckland Transport Board Annual Report for the Year Ended 31 March 1959*. 1959, Auckland Transport Board: Auckland. p.3, 4
200. *Meter Scheme Will Cut Number Of Parking Spaces*, in *The New Zealand Herald*. 1953: Auckland.
201. Te Ara – The Encyclopedia of NZ, *Balance of payments - Arnold Nordmeyer and his 'black budget'*. 1958, Te Ara - The Encylopedia of NZ.
202. *Customs Acts Amendment Act 1958*. 1958: New Zealand.
203. Perry, H. C., *Committee of Enquiry - Change Over From Electric Trams To Trackless Trolley Omnibuses And Motor Omnibuses*. 1958: Wellington.
204. Perry, H. C., *Committee Of Enquiry - Change Over from Electric Trams to Trackless Trolley Omnibuses and Motor Omnibuses* R.D. The Permanent Head. 1958: Wellington.

205. Mees, P., *Transport for Suburbia: Beyond the Automobile Age*, (In Association with the International Institute for Environment and Development). 2010, London: Sterling, VA: Earthscan. p.21-26
206. Goosman, W. S., *Annual Report of Transport Department for the Year Ended 31 March 1950*. 1950, Transport Department: Wellington. p.2, 3
207. *National Roads Act 1953*. 1953: New Zealand.
208. Goosman, W. S., *Roads - Statement of Policy*, Ministry of Works. 1954, Government Printer: Wellington. p.3-11, 20, 21
209. Noonan, R. J., *By Design: A brief history of the Public Works Department, Ministry of Works 1870-1970*. 1975, Wellington: Government Printer. p.231, 235
210. Parsons, R., *Giant roadbuilding programme*, in *Auckland Expanding To Greatness*. 1962, Brekell & Nicholls Limited Auckland. p.202, 203
211. *Dramatic reversal of motorway policy*, in *Auckland Star*. 1954:
212. Robinson, D.-M., *Notes In Moving Motion to Call In Overseas Experts To Prepare Transport And Traffic Plan - Auckland City Council*, Auckland City Council. 1954: Auckland.
213. Robinson, D.-M., *Notice of Motion* in *Auckland City Council Archives*. 1954: Auckland. p.262
214. *Auckland Obeys 'No-Men'* in *The New Zealand Herald*. 1954:
215. Robinson, D.-M., *Letter To The Editor*, The NZ Herald. 1954:
216. *Plan prepared by thirty authorities*, in *Auckland Star*. 1955:
217. *Give Transport to an Auckland Minister*, in *The Auckland Star*. 1954: Auckland.
218. *Minutes, Auckland Regional Planning Authority Technical Advisory Committee*. 1955: Auckland.
219. *Minutes Of Meeting Of The Transport Committee* in *The Technical Advisory Committee*. 1955: Auckland.
220. Dickson, A. J., *Master Transportation Plan for Metropolitan Auckland - Report & Survey*. 1955: Auckland. p.5
221. *Basic Causes Of The Problem*, in *The New Zealand Herald*. 1955:
222. *Dominance Of Cars And Trucks*, in *The New Zealand Herald*. 1955:
223. *£5 Million Bill Yearly For Congestion*, in *The New Zealand Herald*. 1955: Auckland.
224. *Express Services On New Traffic Routes*, in *The New Zealand Herald*. 1955: Auckland.
225. *Two More Bus Terminals, One For Trucks - Urgent Parking Requirements*, in *The New Zealand Herald*. 1955: Auckland.
226. *13,000 Parking Spaces Needed By 1963*, in *The New Zealand Herald*. 1955: Auckland.
227. Luxford, J. H., *Introduction to Master Transportation Plan for Metropolitan Auckland*. 1956: Auckland. p.3
228. *MP's doubts on rail plan challenged*, in *The New Zealand Herald*. 1969: Auckland.
229. Gunder, M., *Auckland's Motorway System: A New Zealand Genealogy of Imposed Automotive Progress, 1945-1966*. 2002.
230. Mees, P. & Dodson, J., *The American Heresy: Half a century of transport planning in Auckland*, in *New Zealand Geographical Society/Australian Institute of Geographers*. 2001: University of Otago, Dunedin. p.4
231. Mees, P. & Dodson, J., *Backtracking Auckland: Bureaucratic rationality and public preferences in transport planning*. 2006, Griffith University: Brisbane. p.3, 4
232. *Outside Finance Sought*, in *The New Zealand Herald ???* 1955:
233. *Transport Plan Discussions In Wellington*, in *The New Zealand Herald*. 1955: Auckland.

234. *Must Remember Other Places As Well - Government View On Auckland Needs*, in *The New Zealand Herald*. 1955: Auckland.
235. *Haste Required With City Transport Plan*, in *The New Zealand Herald*. 1956: Auckland.
236. *Taxicabs*. Comment Magazine, 1955(September 1955).
237. Vosslamber, R., *Tax history and tax policy: New Zealand's "black" budget*. 2010, University of Canterbury: Christchurch. p.21
238. *Auckland's £15M Plan For Roads*, in *The Auckland Star*. 1955:
239. Roughan, J., *Auckland: The bridge builders*, in *The New Zealand Herald*. 2010:
240. Robinson, D.-M., *Speech Notes*. 1956: Auckland.
241. Robinson, D.-M., *Notes*. 1956: Auckland.
242. Robinson, D.-M., *Passenger Transport in Auckland*. 1969, Rapid Transit Committee, Auckland Regional Authority: Auckland. p.3
243. *Auckland Harbour Bridge Act 1950*. 1950: New Zealand. Sections: 4, 25, 28, 68, 69
244. *Waitemata Bridge - Navigation Viewpoint*, in *Auckland Star*. 1929:
245. *Auckland Harbour Bridge Amendment Act 1956*. 1956.
246. *Auckland Harbour Bridge Amendment Act 1957*. 1957: NZ
247. *Auckland Harbour Bridge Amendment Act 1958*. 1958: NZ
248. Office, Auckland Provincial Public Relations, *The Story of the Auckland Harbour Bridge*. 1958, Auckland:
249. Langbein, F., *Annual Report on Public Works - Auckland Harbour Bridge*, Transport Department. 1950: Wellington. p.35
250. Engineers, Institution of Civil, *Discussion On Auckland Harbour Bridge: Design: Oleg Alexander Kerensky & Gilbert Roberts Construction: Hubert Shirley-Smith & John Freeman Pain*. Proceeding of the Institution of Civil Engineers, 1961. 18: para. 198, p.142-144, 155, 423-478
251. Dearnaley, M., *The history of the Auckland Harbour Bridge*, in *The New Zealand Herald*. 2009:
252. Authority, The Auckland Harbour Bridge, *1951-1961 The Auckland Harbour Bridge Authority*. 1961, Auckland: p.53
253. Smith, B. G., *Auckland Harbour Bridge: road across the Waitemata*. 1959, Wellington: A H & A W Reed.
254. Lang, R., *Auckland harbour bridge: 50 years of a city icon*. 2009,
255. Dearnaley, M., *Agency in no hurry to replace bridge with harbour 'tubes'*, in *The New Zealand Herald*. 2009: Auckland.
256. *Bridge father right to trim plans - Readers' Forum Emmerson's View* in *The New Zealand Herald*. 2009: Auckland.
257. Julian, H. L., *Sea in my Blood*. 1999, Auckland: Harry L Julian. p.149, 151
258. Lewis, P., *Auckland's 175th anniversary: The bridge that nearly sailed away*, in *The New Zealand Herald*. 2015, Independent News & Media: Auckland.
259. Agency, NZ Transport, *History: Auckland Harbour Bridge*. 2016 [cited 2016 29 June 2016]; from: https://www.nzta.govt.nz/projects/auckland-harbour-bridge/history/.
260. McKillop, E. R., *Report of the Commissioner Of Works* Ministry of Works. 1950, New Zealand Government: Wellington. p.12
261. *Problems Of N.Z. Railways*, in *Launceston Examiner*. 1952: Launceston.
262. Commission, Royal, *Royal Commission To Inquire Into And Report Upon The New Zealand Government Railways*. 1952: Wellington. p.1, 2, 8-10, 13-15, 36, 38, 69-71, 76

263. *News, Note, And Comment.* The New Zealand Railway Observer, 1953(January - March 1953). p.11
264. *Government Railways Amendment Act 1952.* 1952: New Zealand.
265. *Electrification Of Railways*, in *Auckland Star.* 1930: Auckland.
266. *Suburban Rail Plan Vetoed - Minister Agreed with Report*, in *The New Zealand Herald.* 1955: Auckland.
267. *Mission Abroad*, in *Auckland Star.* 1945: Auckland.
268. *Auckland Transport Board Advertisement*, in *Comment.* 1955, Hobson Publications Limited: Auckland. p.8
269. Goosman, W. S., *Ministry of Works Statement for the year ended 31 March 1950*, Ministry of Works. 1950: Wellington. p.2
270. Goosman, W. S., *Railways Statement for the year ended 31 March 1950*, NZ Railways. 1950: Wellington. p.2
271. McGavin, T., *More On Auckland Suburban Railway Proposals* The New Zealand Railway Observer 2003(April - May 2003): p.10-12
272. *Railways not suited to 'dispersed' city* in *The New Zealand Herald.* 1955: Auckland.
273. *Roading scheme can and must be done*, in *Auckland Star.* 1955:
274. *Motorways Instead Of Railways*, in *The New Zealand Herald.* 1955:
275. Gandell, A. T., *Master Transportation Plan for Metropolitan Auckland*, Railways Chief Civil Engineer. 1955: Wellington.
276. Engineer, Railways District, *Master Transportation Plan for Metropolitan Auckland*, to Chief Civil Engineer. 1956: Auckland.
277. Cooper, A. L., *Passenger Transport*, to District Engineer, NZ Railways. 1956: Auckland.
278. Robinson, D.-M., *Letter To The Editor*, in *The New Zealand Herald.* 1956: Auckland.
279. *Electric Trains For Suburbs*, in *The New Zealand Herald.* 1956:
280. *Bus Tunnel Plan*, in *Comment Magazine.* 1955, Auckland City Council: Auckland. p.33
281. McLeod, R., *Imagine There's No Government*, in *Howick Rotary Club.* 2004: Howick, Auckland. p.2
282. *The New Zealand Official Year-Book*, Statistics New Zealand. 1964: Wellington.
283. Kennedy, R. T., *Urban Renewal in Auckland*, in *Auckland In Ferment*, J.S. Whitelaw, Editor. 1967, New Zealand Geographical Society: Auckland. p.83, 84
284. *Auckland Regional Authority Establishment Act 1960.* 1960: NZ
285. *Two Small Signs Of A Big Move*, in *The Auckland Star.* 1960:
286. *Criticism of ARA Bill*, in *The New Zealand Herald.* 1963: Auckland.
287. *Auckland Regional Authority Act 1963.* 1963: New Zealand. Sections 3, 45, 61
288. *Auckland Regional Planning Authority Act 1963.* 1963: NZ
289. Council, Auckland City, *Auckland Regional Authority.* 6 March 2017]; from: www.aucklandcity.govt.nz
290. Robinson, D.-M., *Chairman's Comments On Transport Clauses Of The Authority's Amending Bill 1964.* 1964, Auckland Regional Authority: Auckland. p.1-3
291. *No holding Auckland*, in *The Auckland Star.* 1967: Auckland.
292. Ling, A., *One hundred days around the world.* The Architects' Journal, 1969: p.489
293. Turner, A. R., *A Summary: Development in the Auckland Region.* 1968, Planning Division, Auckland Regional Authority: Auckland.
294. Planning Division, Auckland Regional Authority, *a summary: Development in the Auckland Region.* 1968: Auckland. p.24, 25, 43-48

295. *Ministry of Transport Act 1968*. 1968: New Zealand.
296. Robinson, D.-M., *The Practical Politics of Achieving Success in Planning and Implementation*, in *Australian Institute of Urban Studies*. 1969: Canberra. p.2-9
297. Robinson, D.-M., *Statement by his Worship the Mayor*. 1969:
298. Robinson, D.-M., *Letter to The Editor, O. S. Hintz, The New Zealand Herald*. 1969: Auckland.
299. Robinson, D.-M., *Local Government Commission Report*, to L.K. Brown. 1969: Auckland. p.2
300. Hart, M. A. C., *Submissions to the Carter Enquiry*. 1969, Civic Action Party Inc.: Auckland.
301. Dodds, D. A. C., *Submission to Carter Enquiry*. 1969: Auckland.
302. Duffield, B. D., *Re: Urban Passenger Transport: Committee of Enquiry*, to the Town Clerk, Auckland City Council. 1969:
303. Robinson, D.-M., *City Concept Best - Costly Satellites No Answer To Basic Transit Need*, in *The New Zealand Herald*. 1969:
304. Salmon, E. P., *Report of Urban Renewal Committee*. 1969, Auckland City Council: Auckland.
305. Spencer, N. B., *Minutes Of A Meeting Of The Passenger Transport Sub-Committee*. 1961, Auckland Regional Authority Establishment Committee: Auckland. Attachment C
306. Spencer, N. B., *Auckland Transport Board Annual Report for the Year Ended 31 March 1960*. 1960, Auckland Transport Board: p.3,4
307. Spencer, N. B., *Auckland Transport Board Annual Report for the Year Ended 31 March 1961*. 1961, Auckland Transport Board: p.5
308. Spencer, N. B., *Auckland Transport Board Annual Report for the Year Ended 31 March 1962*. 1962, Auckland Transport Board:
309. Lyne, J., *Public Transport - Drastic Measures Are Called For To Woo Passengers Back To Travel-By-Bus*, in *Auckland Expanding To Greatness*, F. C. Symes, Editor. 1962, Breckell & Nicholls Auckland. p.152-157
310. Dickson, A. J., *Reports Prepared By De Leuw, Cather & Company*. 1966: Auckland. p.1-8
311. *Transport Act 1962*. 1962: New Zealand.
312. Spencer, N. B., *Auckland Transport Board Annual Report for the Year Ended 31 March 1963*. 1963, Auckland Transport Board:
313. Spencer, N. B., *Auckland Transport Board Annual Report for the Year Ended 31 March 1964*. 1964, Auckland Transport Board:
314. *Auckland Regional Authority Amendment Act 1964*. 1964: NZ Sections 7, 12
315. Robinson, D.-M., *Press Statement*. 1964: Auckland.
316. Robinson, D.-M., *Untitled*, Letter to Minister of Transport Hon. John K McAlpine. 1964.
317. McAlpine, J. K., *Letter to C S Passmore*, Railways Department. 1964: Wellington.
318. Robinson, D.-M., *Auckland Region Half Million Celebrations 1964*. 1964: Auckland. p.14-17
319. Gribble, C. R., *Some Information About The Division*. 1964, Passenger Transport Division, Auckland Regional Authority: p.1, 4, 5
320. De Leuw, C. E., *Summary Report On The Transit Plan For Metropolitan Auckland*. 1965, De Leuw, Cather & Company: Auckland. p.2-4
321. Robinson, D.-M., *Opening Address*, in *Conference On Problems Of Central Business District*. 1964: Auckland.

322. *State Share In Bus-Rail Plan Sought - Region Policy*, in *The New Zealand Herald*. 1965: Auckland. p.1
323. *Reports Could Not Be Ignored*, in *The New Zealand Herald*. 1965:
324. *Opportunity for Railways*, in *The New Zealand Herald*. 1965:
325. *Shape, Economy Of City At Heart Of Matter*, in *The New Zealand Herald*. 1965:
326. *Transit Plan Contribution "Injustice"*, in *Auckland Star*. 1965:
327. *'White Elephant' Fear - Rail-Bus Scheme Too Costly Says Councillor*, in *The New Zealand Herald*. 1965: Auckland.
328. McElroy, R. G., *De Leuw Cather Reports (2) On Transportation*. 1966: Auckland. p.1, 4
329. Council, Auckland City, *Copies of Resolutions Passed At A Meeting Of The Auckland City Council Held On The 6th April 1966:*. 1966, Auckland City Council: Auckland.
330. Unknown, *Summary Of Decisions Relating To Rapid Rail Proposals*. 1972: Auckland.
331. Buchanan, C., *City of Auckland - Planning in the Central Area - An Assessment*. 1966, Colin Buchanan and Partners London. p.1-4, 9-17, 31-32, 37-38, 42-48
332. Committee, Officials, *Urban Transportation Proposals Auckland Region*. 1967: Wellington. p.1-7
333. *Some seasonal resolutions*, in *Auckland Star*. 1967: Auckland.
334. *Cabinet Delay On Discussing Transit Plan*, in *The Auckland Star*. 1967: Auckland.
335. *New Minister Must See Transit Plan*, in *The New Zealand Herald*. 1967: Auckland.
336. *Bus and Rail Plan To Be Submitted*, in *The New Zealand Herald*. 1967: Auckland.
337. *Red Herring Comment On Bus-Rail Plan*, in *The New Zealand Herald*. 1967: Auckland.
338. *Govt Assurance On Auckland Subway Link*, in *The Auckland Star*. 1967: Auckland.
339. *Rail Scheme Move Makes Stir*, in *The New Zealand Herald*. 1967:
340. *Lack Of Co-Operation Delays Progress, Councillor Claims*, in *The Auckland Star*. 1967: Auckland.
341. *Auckland needs common purpose on underground*, in *The Auckland Star*. 1967: Auckland.
342. *Mayor Clarifies Council Views On Rapid Transport System*, in *The New Zealand Herald*. 1967: Auckland.
343. *Mr Lambie is eager for rail plan talks*, in *The Auckland Star*. 1967:
344. *Bus-Rail Plan Hopes*, in *The New Zealand Herald*. 1967: Auckland.
345. *Ex-Mayor anxious on city traffic*, in *The Auckland Star*. 1967:
346. *Authority Wants Meeting On Road-Rail Plan*, in *The New Zealand Herald*. 1967:
347. *ARA insists on need for decision*, in *The Auckland Star*. 1967:
348. Nilsson, K., to Hon. J. B. Gordon. 1967: Auckland.
349. *The Financial Position Of Urban Passenger Transport In New Zealand*. 1966, New Zealand Institute of Economic Research Inc.: Wellington. p.2-8
350. *No Road-Rail Approval For A Year*, in *The Auckland Star*. 1967:
351. *Why wait for a year?*, in *The Auckland Star*. 1967: Auckland.
352. *Mayor gives Big Brother a push in right direction*, in *Central Suburbs Leader*. 1967: Auckland.
353. *City support for rapid rail transport*, in *The Auckland Star*. 1967:
354. *Concern Mounting - Action Awaited On City Transport Plan*, in *The New Zealand Herald*. 1967: Auckland.
355. *Not penny this year for rail plan*, in *The Auckland Star*. 1967:
356. *By slow boat to rapid rail system*, in *The Auckland Star*. 1967:
357. *City Rail Scheme 'Unconvincing' Says Professor*, in *The Auckland Star*. 1967: Auckland.
358. *Bus idea is labelled 'superficial'*, in *The Auckland Star*. 1967:
359. *Auckland traffic chaos predicted*, in *The Auckland Star*. 1967:

360. *Better transport or 'dignity loss'*, in *The Auckland Star.* 1967:
361. *Mr Allen Wants Talks*, in *The Auckland Star.* 1967: Auckland.
362. *Minister's Plan 'Unacceptable'*, in *The Auckland Star.* 1967:
363. *Government Asked For Decision On Rapid Rail Route*, in *The New Zealand Herald.* 1967: Auckland.
364. *Officials Body To Hold Tunnel Talks In City*, in *The New Zealand Herald.* 1967: Auckland.
365. Holyoake, K., *A Copy of the Report of the Officials Committee on the De Leuw Cather Proposals*, to Dr. R. G. McElroy. 1967:
366. *Transport Doubts Need To Be Resolved*, in *The New Zealand Herald.* 1967: Auckland.
367. *So Rome wasn't built in a day...* in *The Auckland Star.* 1967:
368. *Rapid-Rail Report 'Inaccurate'* in *The New Zealand Herald.* 1967:
369. Dickson, A. J., *Urban Transportation Proposals: Auckland Region.* 1967: Auckland. p.1-3, 6
370. *Council Planners In Favour Of All-Bus System - Engineer Sees Rail Link As Costly And Remote*, in *The New Zealand Herald.* 1967:
371. Brunt, A.J., *Bus-Rail Scheme Should Streamline Transport*, in *The New Zealand Herald.* 1967: Auckland.
372. *A hearing*, in *Auckland Star.* 1967: Auckland.
373. *Engineers Report On Transit Plan A Bombshell*, in *Auckland Star.* 1967: Auckland.
374. *Transport Unity Needed*, in *The New Zealand Herald.* 1967:
375. Robinson, D.-M., (probably) *Note.* 1966.
376. *Support For Bus Scheme*, in *Auckland Star.* 1967: Auckland.
377. Wilkinson, E. D., *Untitled.* 1967, Wilkinson, Christmas, Steen & Co.: Auckland.
378. Unknown, *Benefits Of Rapid Transit That Cannot Be Evaluated In Terms Of Cost In Dollars And Cents.*
379. *More fumes but not dangerous*, in *The Auckland Star.* 1967:
380. Bush, G. W. A., *Letter to The Editor - Reliance On Buses Short-sighted*, in *The New Zealand Herald.* 1967: Auckland.
381. *Rapid rail basic to regional plan*, in *The Auckland Star.* 1967:
382. *Mr Robinson: Go Rail Or Decay*, in *Auckland Star.* 1967: Auckland.
383. *Better Service Aim In Bus Study By Government*, in *The Auckland Star.* 1967: Auckland.
384. *Letter to the Editor - Public Transport*, in *The Auckland Star.* 1967:
385. *Letter to the Editor - Transport System*, in *The Auckland Star.* 1967:
386. *Letter to the Editor - Motorways*, in *The Auckland Star.* 1967:
387. *Letter to the Editor - City Transport*, in *The New Zealand Herald.* 1967: Auckland.
388. *Dense Traffic Hindering Buses More*, in *The New Zealand Herald.* 1967: Auckland.
389. *Interim All-Bus System Urged*, in *The Auckland Star.* 1967:
390. Wright, J., *Magnificent Railway Concept Frustrated By City Planners*, in *The New Zealand Herald.* 1967: Auckland.
391. Lambie, H. D., *Facts About The Public Passenger Transport System In Auckland.* 1967, Auckland Regional Authority: Auckland. p.1-4
392. *Big Effort On Bus Rail Plan - Feasibility Study*, in *The new Zealand Herald.* 1967: Auckland.
393. Transit, The Working Party on Rapid, 1969: Auckland. p.5, 7, 13, 24
394. Transport, The Committee of Inquiry into Urban Passenger, *Report of the Committee of Inquiry into Urban Passenger Transport.* 1970: Wellington. p.5, 6

395. Newton, R. H., *Auckland Rapid Transit Working Party Report*. 1969, New Zealand Railways: Auckland.
396. *Adequacy Of Plan Questioned*, in *The New Zealand Herald*. 1969:
397. Robinson, D.-M., *Don't Confuse The Transport Issue*. 1969:
398. *False Transport Economy*, in *The New Zealand Herald*. 1967:
399. *Agreement Over Paying For Tube May Take Years*, in *The New Zealand Herald*. 1969: Auckland.
400. *Talk money on rail plan, Govt urged*, in *The Auckland Star*. 1969:
401. Robinson, D.-M., *Telegram*, to Prime Minister K J Holyoake & Minister of Finance, R D Muldoon. 1969: Auckland.
402. Gordon, J. B., to D.-M. Robinson. 1969: Wellington.
403. Allen, P. B., *Steering Committee*, to D.-M. Robinson. 1969:
404. Robinson, D.-M., *Steering Committee*, to P. B. Allen. 1969:
405. Holyoake, K., to D.-M. Robinson. 1969:
406. Committee, Rapid Transit Steering, *Report of the Steering Committee*. 1972: Auckland.
407. *Rapid Transport Scheme - Government And ARA Agree On Special Study*, in *The New Zealand Herald*. 1969: Auckland.
408. Authority, Auckland Regional, *Submission to Carter Enquiry*. 1969: p.10-12, 27
409. Robinson, D.-M., *Submissions to Committee of Enquiry into Urban Transport* 1969, Auckland City Council: p.18
410. Robinson, D.-M., *Auckland City Council Proposals to Carter Enquiry* 1969: p.1
411. Robinson, D.-M., *Oral Submission to Carter Enquiry*. 1969: p.2
412. *Separate Petrol Tax Sought*, in *The New Zealand Herald*. 1969:
413. Morton, H. J., *Re Petrol Tax*, to D.-M. Robinson. 1969:
414. Robinson, D.-M., *Re Petrol Tax*, to H. J. Morton. 1969:
415. *Precis Of Government Position On Urban Passenger Transport*. 1969, New Zealand Railways Department: Wellington. P.1-7, Appendix II
416. Porter, R., *Submissions to the Carter Enquiry*. 1969, Auckland Transport Holdings Limited: Auckland.
417. Harris, F., *Boilermakers' Union Submissions to the Carter Enquiry*. 1969, Boilermakers' Union: Auckland.
418. *The Municipal Association of New Zealand - Submissions to the Committee of Enquiry Into Urban Passenger Transport*. 1969, The Municipal Association of New Zealand: Auckland. p.11
419. Dart, J. R., *Verbal Submission to the Carter Enquiry*. 1969, Department of Town Planning, Auckland University: Auckland.
420. Robinson, D.-M., *Report to Auckland City Council Finance Committee*. 1969, Auckland City Council: p.3
421. Hart, M., *Passenger Transit Proposals for the Auckland Region*, to J. B. Gordon. 1969: Auckland.
422. Gordon, J. B., *Re: Auckland Passenger Transit Proposals*, to M. Hart. 1969: Wellington.
423. Douglas, R. K., *A General and a suggested economic appraisal of rapid transit in Auckland - 1970*. 1971, University of Waikato: Hamilton.
424. Robinson, D.-M., *Development of Auckland's Transit Plan*, in *Auckland Rapid Rail Symposium*. 1969: Auckland. p.7, 8
425. Robinson, D.-M., *Re: Rapid Transit Scheme*, to J. Hauge. 1969:

426. Carter, D. J., *Interim Report of Committee of Inquiry into Urban Passenger Transport*. 1969: Wellington.
427. Robinson, D.-M., *A F Thomas Article*, in *The New Zealand Herald*, to Takapuna City Council Town Clerk. 1969:
428. Robinson, D.-M., *Improve Public Passenger Transport*, to F T (Trevor) Long, Transport Division, ARA. 1969:
429. Thomas, A. F. F., *Objection to My Statement*, to D.-M. Robinson. 1969:
430. Robinson, D.-M., *Improvement of Bus Services*, to A F F Thomas. 1969: Auckland.
431. Robinson, D.-M., *Suggested Parliamentary Questions*, to H. Watt. 1969:
432. Hintz, O. S., *City Council's Submissions*, to D.-M. Robinson. 1969:
433. Robinson, D.-M., *Re: George Gair Statements*, Press Statement. 1969:
434. Allen, P. B., *Rapid Transit Costs*, to T. Pearce. 1969: Wellington.
435. Reid, A., *USSR Trade Deal*, to D.-M. Robinson. 1969: Auckland.
436. Robinson, D.-M., *Reply to USSR Trade Deal*, to A. Reid. 1969:
437. Marshall, J. R., *Re: Reciprocal Trade*, to A. Reid. 1967: Wellington.
438. *Wool Stocks Reduced By 48 Per Cent*, in *The New Zealand Herald*. 1970: Auckland.
439. Marshall, J. R., *Barter Proposal With USSR*, to A. Reid. 1970:
440. Johnson, C. N., *Application for Subsidy*, to F. W. O. Jones. 1963:
441. Jones, F. W. O., *Comprehensive Transportation Survey*. 1963, Technical Advisory Committee, Auckland Regional Planning Authority Auckland.
442. District Engineer, Ministry of Works, *Auckland Urban Motorways: Newton Gully*, to Ministry of Works Chief Civil Engineer, Auckland. 1964: Auckland.
443. Duder, B., *Transport and the Auckland Metropolitan Form*, in *Auckland In Ferment*, J.S. Whitelaw, Editor. 1967, New Zealand Geographical Society: Auckland. p.69, 71
444. *De Leuw, Cather for Manukau*, in *The Auckland Star*. 1967:
445. *Authority deputation on roads*, in *The Auckland Star*. 1967:
446. *Country Spends One Third Of Income On Transport*, in *The New Zealand Herald*. 1967: Auckland.
447. *City Of Auckland Traffic Department Report*. 1967, Auckland City Council: Auckland.
448. *Can This Miracle Be Repeated?*, in *The Auckland Star*. 1967:
449. Harris, R., *Motorway Giant Forges Ahead*, in *The Auckland Star*. 1967: Auckland.
450. *Motorway Work Delayed*, in *The New Zealand Herald*. 1967:
451. Rankin, K., *New Zealand's Income Tax in the Rollercoaster Muldoon Years: 1967-84*, in *Asia Pacific Economic and Business History Conference*. 2014: Hamilton, New Zealand. p.2, 5
452. *AKLD Motorway Hit By 10% Roading Cut*, in *The Auckland Star*. 1967: Auckland.
453. *Motorway plans set back 2 years*, in *The Auckland Star*. 1967:
454. *Protest at road-fund diversion*, in *The Auckland Star*. 1967:
455. *Roads Board independence under threat*, in *The Auckland Star*. 1967: Auckland.
456. *Minister Defends Cutback In Road Spending*, in *The New Zealand Herald*. 1967: Auckland.
457. *Works warning but...* in *The Auckland Star*. 1967:
458. *Roading 'twists' development*, in *The Auckland Star*. 1967:
459. *Roading problems of N.Z. given light of day*, in *The New Zealand Herald*. 1967: Auckland.
460. Beatty, D. W., *Heavy trucks damaging soft surfaces*, in *The New Zealand Herald*. 1967:
461. Goosman, W. S. *Roading in New Zealand: a brief summary*. in *The Pacific Regional Conference of the International Road Federation*. 1961. Sydney. p.5
462. *Running Risk Of Road Failures*, in *The New Zealand Herald*. 1967:
463. *Motorway decision defended*, in *The Auckland Star*. 1967: Auckland.

464. *Road Funds Warning - Spending On Highways Cut By $1m*, in *The New Zealand Herald*. 1967: Auckland.
465. *Cuts in Roading*, in *The New Zealand Herald*. 1967: Auckland.
466. *No Provision For Extra Lanes*, in *The New Zealand Herald*. 1967:
467. *Preference? Not Really*, in *The Auckland Star*. 1967: Auckland.
468. *The Newmarket Viaduct - Developments Illustrated*. The Journal of the International Roads Federation 1966. p.57
469. *Motorway route still not decided*, in *The Auckland Star*. 1967:
470. *Cemetery Land For Street*, in *The New Zealand Herald*. 1967:
471. *Roads Committee - Regional Road Network - Operational Improvements To Existing Roads*. 1969: Auckland.
472. *Auckland Harbour Bridge opened* in *The New Zealand Herald*. 1959: Auckland.
473. McLauchlan, G., *The Auckland Harbour Bridge*, in *The Illustrated Encyclopedia of New Zealand*, G. McLauchlan, Editor. 1989, David Bateman: Auckland. p.3, 4
474. Robinson, D.-M., *Provision of Additional Harbour Crossing Facilities*. 1964, Auckland Regional Authority: Auckland. p.1-5
475. *Auckland Harbour Bridge Amendment Act 1965*. 1965: NZ
476. Smith, B.G., *Auckland Harbour Bridge extensions*. New Zealand Engineering, 1974. 29(No. 3): p69-75
477. *Cut in Bridge Tolls Approved*, in *The New Zealand Herald*. 1969:
478. *North Motorway Extension Not Fully Used*, in *The New Zealand Herald*. 1969: Auckland.
479. Verran, D., *The History of the Greenhithe Bridge*. 2012: West Auckland Historical Society Inc. – Digital Research File: WAHS-DRF-0153.
480. Robinson, D.-M., *Passenger Transport in Auckland*. New Zealand Railway Tradesmen's Association 1969. 20(No. 5): p.11-14
481. *Rail transport*, in *Auckland Expanding To Greatness*. 1962, Breckell & Nicholls Limited: Auckland. p.144
482. Gandell, A. T., *Auckland Transport Survey*, 1964: Wellington.
483. Bolz, D. T. G., *Auckland Regional Authority Public Transport Survey – Report No. 2*. 1964, New Zealand Railways Department:
484. *New Proposal On Suburban Trains*, in *The Auckland Star*. 1965:
485. Gandell, A. T., *Message from General Manager to Chief Civil Engineer - Auckland Regional Authority Transport Report*, to Chief Civil Engineer, Mr Bridges. 1965: Wellington.
486. *Railway Station Ill Used*, in *The New Zealand Herald*. 1967:
487. Lamb, D. I., *Railway Facilities on the North Shore*, to Minister of Railways Hon. J B Gordon. 1968: Auckland.
488. Newton, R. H., *Rail Connection To North Shore*, to NZ Railways Chief Civil Engineer. 1968: Auckland.
489. Keith, H. H. C., *Rapid Transit System For Auckland An Urgent Priority*. 1969.
490. Holmes, N., *Rapid Rail*, to Neville G Walker, Modern Bags Ltd. 1969: Auckland.
491. Walker, N. G., *Rapid Rail*, to N. Holmes. 1969: Auckland.
492. Robinson, D.-M., *Rapid Transit Scheme*, to N. Holmes. 1969:
493. *What's wrong with our town planning?*, in *The Auckland Star*. 1970:
494. Commission, NZ Productivity, *A history of town planning*. 2015: Wellington. P.8-11
495. Watt, H., *Council's District Scheme*, to Town Clerk, Auckland City Council. 1975: Wellington.
496. Taylor, D. M. J., *Who is blatantly parochial?*, to The Editor, Auckland Star. 1975:

497. Robinson, D.-M., *Statement for the Herald*, to the Editor, New Zealand Herald. 1972:
498. Robinson, Sir D.-M., *The Development And Future Of The City*. Council of the Auckland Institute and Museum, 1971.
499. Dart, J. R., *Planning and Transport*. 1973: Auckland.
500. *'Godfather' offer can't be refused*, in *The Auckland Star*. 1973:
501. Robinson, D.-M., *Notes for Opposing Recommendation of Policy and Finance Committee and Moving Amendment*, Auckland Regional Authority Meeting. 1973:
502. Robinson, S.D.-M., *Letter to Chamber of Commerce*, to President and Members of the Executive, Auckland Chamber of Commerce. 1973:
503. *Local Government Act 1974*. 1974: New Zealand. Sections: 14, 71
504. *Nothing To Hide Says Mayor*, in *The New Zealand Herald*. 1975:
505. Robinson, D.-M., *Property Investment*, to J. Hood. 1963: Auckland.
506. Gardiner, N., *Where is master plan?*, to The Editor, Auckland Star. 1975: Auckland.
507. Authority, Auckland Regional, *The Auckland Comprehensive Transportation Study Review - Final report*. 1976.
508. Authority, Auckland Regional, *The Auckland Comprehensive Transportation Study Review - Interim Report*. 1976. p.4
509. *Buses Are Favoured Over Rapid-Rail*, in *The New Zealand Herald*. 1976: Auckland.
510. *Study finds for $175m cheaper transit scheme*, in *The Auckland Star*. 1976: Auckland.
511. *City's Transport Needs Forecast*, in *The New Zealand Herald*. 1976:
512. Morton, J., *Swelling crazy thrombosis - Auckland Politics and Planning*, in *The City News*. 1976: Auckland.
513. *Motorcar & motorway madness*, in *NZ Tribune*. 1976: Auckland.
514. Robinson, Sir D.-M., *Mayor's Annual Report to Ratepayers 1977-78*. 1977, Auckland City Council:
515. Rankin, D. G., *Auckland Regional Authority 1963-1978*. New Zealand Geographer, 1979(April 1979): p.41-43.
516. Cumberland, K. B., *The Essential Nature of Auckland*, in *Auckland At Full Stretch - Issues Of The Seventies*, Bush, G. and Scott, C. Editors 1977, Auckland City Council and University of Auckland Board of Urban Studies: Auckland. p.20, 21
517. Dravitzki, Vince, & Lester, Tiffany, *Economics drove our first sustainable urban transport system* 2006, Opus International Consultants: Auckland. p.6-8
518. Carter, D. J., *Final Report of Committee of Inquiry into Urban Passenger Transport (Carter Report)* 1970:
519. *Lack Of Precision On Transport*, in *The New Zealand Herald*. 1970:
520. *Regional Control Of Passenger Transport Wanted*, in *The New Zealand Herald*. 1970: Auckland.
521. *No Word On Auckland Rapid Rail Scheme*, in *The New Zealand Herald*. 1970: Auckland.
522. *Not Only The Users*, in *The New Zealand Herald*. 1970: Auckland.
523. *No Certainty Yet On Meeting ARA Bus Losses*, in *The New Zealand Herald*. 1970: Auckland.
524. *Motorists to be Stung Again Says AA Head*, in *The New Zealand Herald*. 1970: Auckland.
525. *Report Pleases Bus Owners*, in *The New Zealand Herald*. 1970:
526. *Road Operators Critical*, in *The New Zealand Herald*. 1970:
527. Association, Sub-Committee of Municipal, *Report on Inquiry Into Urban Passenger Transport*. 1970, Municipal Association:
528. *Ministry of Transport Amendment Act 1971*. 1971: New Zealand.

529. *Parliamentary Debates (Hansard)*. 1972. 381. p.2596, 2598, 2600, 2602-2604, 2608, 2609
530. Smith, W., *New Zealand Transport Policy Study*. 1973: Wellington. p.128-130
531. *Major Projects of the Auckland Regional Authority Which Are Affected by the Rail/Bus Rapid Transit Scheme*. 1970. Auckland Regional Authority Auckland.
532. *Order Paper for Special ARA Meeting*. 1971: Auckland.
533. Coates, R. D., *Report on Investigation of Public Passenger Transport on the North Shore* to S.D.-M. Robinson. 1971:
534. Town Clerk, Takapuna City, *North Shore Transport Holdings Limited*, to Auckland Regional Authority. 1971: Auckland.
535. Gordon, P., *North Shore Passenger Transport*, to Auckland Regional Authority. 1971:
536. Allsopp-Smith, J., *Henderson Borough Council v Auckland Regional Authority & Others*. 1982: Auckland.
537. *City Bus Loss $2734 a Day*, in *The New Zealand Herald*. 1975:
538. Apcon, *An Alternative Rapid Transport System for Auckland*. 1975, The Apcon Group: Auckland.
539. *Mayor Says Bus Plan 'Crack-pot'*, in *The New Zealand Herald*. 1975: Auckland.
540. *All-bus system still the best, says economist*, in *The Auckland Star*. 1975: Auckland.
541. *Robbie wants to lower boom over bus report*, in *The Auckland Star*. 1975: Auckland.
542. *Wellington Rail Conspiracy Charge Rebutted*, in *The New Zealand Herald*. 1975: Auckland.
543. Robinson, D.-M., *Conspiracy Suspicions*, to the Editor, The New Zealand Herald. 1975: Auckland.
544. *Railway Versus Buses*, in *The New Zealand Herald*. 1975:
545. *Red-Herring Alternatives*, in *The Auckland Star*. 1975:
546. *Improved Public Transport*, in *The New Zealand Herald*. 1975:
547. *Rapid Transit Decision Imminent*, in *Transit Magazine*. 1975, Transit Publications Limited: Auckland.
548. Fry, L. J., *Reasons For Phasing Out Trolleybuses*. 1972, Auckland Regional Authority:
549. *Auckland Trolley Buses - Is There a Future?*, in *Transit Magazine*. 1975, Transit Publications Limited: Auckland. p.17, 18
550. *Europe, US 'are rejecting rail'*, in *The Auckland Star*. 1975:
551. *Public Transit Role Urged*, in *The New Zealand Herald*. 1975:
552. Robinson, D.-M., *Government Non-Committal to Rapid Transit*, to The Editor, Auckland Star. 1975:
553. *Robbie on rapid rail: I expect party answers*, in *The Auckland Star*. 1975:
554. Muldoon, R. D., *Response to Questions*, to D.-M. Robinson. 1975:
555. Rowling, W., *Reply re Auckland Rapid Transit*, to D.-M. Robinson. 1975:
556. Robinson, D.-M., *Reply to Rowling*, to W. Rowling. 1975:
557. *Support for rapid transit urged*, in *The Auckland Star*. 1975:
558. *Rapid transit*, in *South Auckland Courier*. 1975: Auckland.
559. *Grant To Buy City Buses Stopgap for Rapid Rail*, in *The New Zealand Herald*. 1976:
560. Robinson, D.-M., *Public Passenger Transport*, in *Public Passenger Transport Association*. 1976: Auckland.
561. Muldoon, R. D., *Financial Statement (Budget)*. 1977: Wellington. p.1514-1516
562. McLachlan, C. C. A., *Urban Transport New Zealand*. Ministry of Transport. 1977: Wellington.
563. Robinson, D.-M., *Governments Take It Out Of Ratepayers Hides*. 1979: Auckland.

564. *New transport plan big fraud, claims Robbie*, in *The Auckland Star*. 1979: Auckland.
565. Allen, P. B., *Roads to Resources*, in *Sixth World Meeting of the International Road Federation*. 1970: Montreal. p.5, 8, 15
566. Flynn, E. A., *Steering Committee Report*. 1972, Auckland Regional Authority Rapid Transit Committee: Auckland. p.1, 2
567. Committee, Rapid Transit, *Integrated Transport Or Chaos?* 1973, Auckland Regional Authority: Auckland. p.1-3, 5, 16
568. Board, National Roads, *Auckland Motorways*. 1973, National Roads Board: Wellington.
569. *Mayor: I fear for 400 homes*, in *The Auckland Star*. 1973: Auckland.
570. Wilson, J., *Cost of Auckland Road Congestion*. 1975, Auckland City Council:
571. *Rapid transit delay could cost city $5m*, in *The Auckland Star*. 1975:
572. Robinson, D.-M., *Notice of Motion From Councillor Anderton*, to J. Allsopp-Smith. 1975: Auckland.
573. *Solution: Put firms on Shore*, in *The Auckland Star*. 1975: Auckland.
574. *Second Big Crossing Not Needed*, in *The New Zealand Herald*. 1975: Auckland.
575. McLachlan, C., *Restriction On Road Transport*. 1977: Wellington. p.1512-1514
576. Robinson, D.-M., *George Gair*. 1971: Auckland.
577. Robinson, D.-M., *Auckland's Rapid Transit Proposals*. 1972:
578. Robinson, D.-M., *Motorway Completion*, to the Editor, Auckland Star. 1972:
579. Bradwell, Paul M., *Superbus, those cars and strangling cities*, in *The Auckland Star*. 1972:
580. Flynn, E. A., *Rapid Transit*. 1972, Auckland Regional Authority Rapid Transit Committee: Auckland. p.1, 2
581. Robinson, D.-M., *Report to ARA Members - Subject: Rapid Transit Steering Committee's Report*. 1972: Auckland. p.16
582. *Finance For Rail Plan*, in *The New Zealand Herald*. 1972:
583. Mortiboy, A. T., *Rapid Transit System: Report from the Secretary*. 1972, The Auckland Chamber of Commerce: Auckland.
584. *Memorandum to Members of the Executive*. 1972, Auckland Chamber of Commerce: Auckland.
585. Picot, B. H., *Government Funding of Rapid Transit Proposals*, to A. T. Mortiboy. 1972: Auckland.
586. Gordon, J., *Rapid Transit Proposals*, to T. H. Pearce. 1972:
587. Robinson, D.-M., *Election Questions*, to Members of All local Bodies in the Auckland Region. 1972:
588. Pearce, T. H., *Politicising of Rapid Transit*, to All Regional Town and County Clerks. 1972: Auckland.
589. Robinson, D.-M., *Rapid Transit – An Election Issue*. 1972:
590. Robinson, D.-M., *Notice of Meeting of the ARA Rapid Transit Committee*. 1972: Auckland.
591. Council, Devonport Borough, *Rapid Transit Report*, to Auckland Regional Authority. 1972:
592. Robinson, D.-M., *Request from Minister of Transport for Views Of Auckland Local Bodies*. 1972, Auckland Regional Authority Rapid Transit Committee:
593. Bell, N. C., *ARA and Local Bodies Meeting*, Auckland Region Town and County Clerks. 1972: Auckland.
594. Pearce, T. H., *Memo re Rapid Transit Scheme*. 1972: Auckland.

595. Ensor, M. C., *Grave Concern*, to Labour Government. 1972: Auckland.
596. Robinson, D.-M., *Events leading up to meeting of Mayors*. 1972, Auckland Regional Authority:
597. *Hope of Rapid Rail Start Next Year Says Mayor*, in *The New Zealand Herald*. 1972:
598. *To Honour Rapid-Rail Aid Promise*, in *The New Zealand Herald*. 1972:
599. Watt, H., *Government Support of Rapid Transit*, to Tom Pearce, Chairman, Auckland Regional Authority. 1972:
600. Authority, Auckland Regional, *Statement on Behalf of the Authority for submission to combined meeting of representatives of local bodies and members of the Authority*, 1973:
601. Coulam, J. H., *Result of Local Body Vote*, to Auckland Regional Authority Chairman & Members. 1973:
602. Thomas, A. F., *Government Policy - Public Passenger Transport for Auckland and New Zealand* 1973: Auckland.
603. Dudson, B. H., *Transport Or Status Symbol*, Auckland District Engineer, NZ Railways. 1973: Auckland.
604. *Mr Watt to study rapid rail systems overseas*, in *The New Zealand Herald*. 1973:
605. *Watt wants rapid rail*, in *The Auckland Star*. 1973:
606. *Watt: Rapid-bus plan is 'not on'*, in *The Auckland Star*. 1973:
607. Robinson, D.-M., *Study Trip To North America*. 1973, Rapid Transit Committee, Auckland Regional Authority: Auckland.
608. Committee, Auckland Public Transport Action, *In the Matter of: Rapid Transit Proposals Auckland Region*, to H. Watt. 1973: Wellington.
609. *Re: A deputation from an Auckland group*, in *The New Zealand Herald*. 1973:
610. *Underground And Narrow Electric Line South*, in *The New Zealand Herald*. 1973:
611. *Sceptical on 'expensive experiment'*, in *The Auckland Star*. 1973:
612. Robinson, D.-M., *Government's Offer to Provide a Suburban Rail Service to Papakura* 1973, Auckland Regional Authority Rapid Transit Committee: Auckland.
613. Robinson, D.-M., *Government Proposals for Electrified Southern Railway Line*. 1973, Auckland City Council Policy and Finance Committee: Auckland.
614. Robinson, Sir D.-M., *Why Urban Rail Proposals Arouse Dismay*, in *The New Zealand Herald*. 1973:
615. Keys, L. G., *Auckland Rapid Transit*, Auckland District Engineer, NZ Railways. 1973: Wellington.
616. *Double Track And Longer Loop For City Subway*, in *The New Zealand Herald*. 1974: Auckland.
617. McLeod, N. C., *Auckland Rapid Transit*, Auckland District Engineer, NZ Railways. 1973: Wellington.
618. Directorate, Auckland Rapid Transit, *Auckland Rapid Transit - A Summary of the Proposal*. 1974.
619. Project Manager, A.R.T., *Expenditure on ART: Stage 1*, Ministry of Works Chief Civil Engineer, Wellington. 1974: Auckland.
620. Director, Finance and Accounts Branch, New Zealand Railways, *Over-Expenditure*, to Ministry of Works and Development, Chief Accountant. 1974: Wellington.
621. Project Manager, Auckland Rapid Transit, *Project Expenditure Year Ending 31.3.76*, to Ministry of Works Chief Civil Engineer. 1974:
622. *Rapid Rail Costs Rise Hushed-up Says Economist*, in *The New Zealand Herald*. 1975: Auckland.

623. *Witten critical of Press and rapid rail*, in *South Auckland Courier*. 1975: Auckland.
624. *Rapid Transit Decision*, in *The New Zealand Herald*. 1975:
625. *Oh so slow on rapid transit*, in *The Auckland Star*. 1975:
626. Robinson, D.-M., *Central Area Plan*, to H. Watt. 1975: Auckland.
627. *Rapid Rail Irks Authority*, in *The New Zealand Herald*. 1975:
628. *Fast trains with feeder bus fleet - the $150m plan?*, in *The Auckland Star*. 1975:
629. *Govt concerned over cost of rapid transit*, in *The Auckland Star*. 1975:
630. *Time for decision*, in *The Auckland Star*. 1975:
631. *Roll On, Rapid Rail*, in *The New Zealand Herald*. 1975:
632. Anderton, J., *Rapid rail: People have not the faintest idea*, in *South Auckland Courier*. 1975:
633. *Pearce: Twice left to ARA*, in *The Auckland Star*. 1975:
634. *Demolition shock - rapid transit will axe 13 buildings*, in *The Auckland Star*. 1975:
635. *Mayor slates the Star*, in *The Auckland Star*. 1975:
636. *No Buildings On Trust List*, in *The New Zealand Herald*. 1975:
637. *Pace slower for rapid rail men*, in *The Auckland Star Weekender*. 1975:
638. *Council defers debate on rapid rail*, in *City News*. 1975: Auckland.
639. *Transit Scheme Hangs On Talks*, in *The New Zealand Herald*. 1975: Auckland.
640. *Re-think denied on rapid-rail payment*, in *The Auckland Star*. 1975:
641. Pearce, T. H., *Meeting Between ARA and Government*, to M. A. Connelly. 1975: Auckland.
642. *Govt Doubts Over Rapid Rail for City*, in *The New Zealand Herald*. 1975:
643. *Robbie says don't delay*, in *Sunday News*. 1975: Auckland.
644. *Rapid Rail Roundabout*, in *The New Zealand Herald*. 1975:
645. *Inflation Hits Rapid Rail*, in *The New Zealand Herald*. 1975:
646. Bennett, P. M. Hoyle, *Rapid Rail System*, to Sir D.-M. Robinson. 1975: Auckland.
647. Robinson, D.-M., *Concern About Rumours*, to Prime Minister W E Rowling. 1975: Auckland.
648. Robinson, D.-M., *Different Situation*, to Prime Minister W E Rowling. 1975: Auckland.
649. Robinson, D.-M., *Response to ARA Proposal*, to Michael Connelly, Minister of Development. 1975: Auckland.
650. *Final Appeal by Mayor on Rapid Rail*, in *The New Zealand Herald*. 1975:
651. *Two experts disagree on urban transport*, in *The Auckland Star*. 1975:
652. Cope, S. W., *The Rapid Rail System*, to D.-M. Robinson. 1975:
653. *Chamber Backs Rapid Rail System for City*, in *The New Zealand Herald*. 1975:
654. Bush, D.G., *Call for 'steel' in transport*, to The Editor, Auckland Star. 1975:
655. Freer, W., *Rapid Transit*, to D.-M. Robinson. 1975: Wellington.
656. Robinson, D.-M., *A Short Note*, to W. Freer. 1975: Auckland.
657. *Transit Issue 'Much Alive'*, in *The New Zealand Herald*. 1976:
658. *Banks Offer City Loans*, in *The New Zealand Herald*. 1976:
659. *Policy, Not Finance To Blame*, in *The New Zealand Herald*. 1976:
660. *Integrated Bus-Rail Link Hopes Fade*, in *The New Zealand Herald*. 1976:
661. *This Year, Next Year...* in *The New Zealand Herald*. 1976:
662. *Suburban Railway Paralysis*, in *The New Zealand Herald*. 1976:
663. *Rail Services Plain Facts*, in *The New Zealand Herald*. 1976:
664. *Rapid-rail put 'on ice' by ARA*, in *The Auckland Star*. 1976:
665. *Rapid Transit Postponed*, in *The New Zealand Herald*. 1976:

666. *State won't pay - Muldoon kills rapid rail - new study*, in *The Auckland Star*. 1976:
667. *Keep On To The Last Gasp*, in *The New Zealand Herald*. 1976:
668. *State 'Won't Ever Pay' For Rapid Transit Plan*, in *The New Zealand Herald*. 1976:
669. *Is Rapid-Rail Idea Dead?*, in *The New Zealand Herald*. 1976:
670. *Pressure mounts to improve rail*, in *NZ Tribune*. 1976: Auckland.
671. Yates, D., *Rapid rail - lost on a branch line?*, in *City News*. 1976:
672. *$40m Sought to Boost Suburban Trains*, in *The New Zealand Herald*. 1976:
673. McLachlan, C., *Extension of the 3:15 Train*, to M.G. Devoy. 1976: Wellington.
674. Robinson, D.-M., *Co-Ordination of Railway and Bus Services in Region*. 1976, Policy and Finance Committee, Auckland City Council: Auckland.
675. *Rail improvement committee states case at Papatoetoe*, in *South Auckland Courier*. 1976: Auckland.
676. Railways, Minister of, *Auckland Regional Authority Resolutions*, to Secretary ARA, J H Coulam. 1977: Wellington.
677. Robinson, D.-M., *Reply re ARA Resolutions*, to Acting Minister of Railways, Allan McCready. 1977: Auckland.
678. Muldoon, R. D., *Award of Contract for Wellington Railway Coaches*. 1979: Wellington.
679. Robinson, D.-M., *Report to Council re Government Decision On Railway Coaches*. 1979, Auckland City Council: Auckland.
680. *PM Says Mayor Insulting*, in *The New Zealand Herald*. 1979:
681. *Still Have Not Made Up*, in *The New Zealand Herald*. 1979:
682. *Time to Bury the Hatchet*, in *The New Zealand Herald*. 1979:
683. *Rail row*, in *The Auckland Star*. 1979:
684. *Rail decision for review*, in *The Auckland Star*. 1979:
685. *PM Dashes Hopes of Govt Rethink On Railways*, in *The New Zealand Herald*. 1979:
686. *Showdown nears as city transport crisis deepens*, in *The Auckland Star*. 1979:
687. Turley, M. J., *Rail Passenger Service - South Auckland area*, to C. McLachlan & T. Hayward. 1979: Auckland.
688. Muldoon, R. D., *Rail Passenger Service - South Auckland area*, to M. J. Turley. 1979: Wellington.
689. *Disastrous For Auckland*, in *The New Zealand Herald*. 1979:
690. Hunt, T. de. V., *Appropriation Bill - Estimates*, in *First Session - 39th Parliament*. 1979, Hansard: Wellington. p.2714
691. *No Stock - No Facelift*, in *The New Zealand Herald*. 1979:
692. *Auckland Down the Track*, in *The New Zealand Herald*. 1979:
693. Robinson, D.-M., *Govt may have gone too far, says Robbie - Auckland Misses Out Again*, in *The Auckland Star*. 1979:
694. *Buses beat rail here, says PM*, in *The Auckland Star*. 1979:
695. *Auckland Rail Fight Starts Rolling*, in *The New Zealand Herald*. 1979:
696. *The Time To Electrify*, in *The New Zealand Herald*. 1979:
697. White, R. H., *Invitation to Meeting*, to R. D. Muldoon. 1979:
698. Muldoon, R. D., *Reply to Invitation*, R. H. White. 1979: Wellington.
699. White, R. H., *Reply to R D Muldoon*, R. D. Muldoon. 1979:
700. Murdoch, L. I., *Let's Put It On The Line - Chairman Murdoch ARA, Auckland*, in *Sunday News*. 1979: Auckland.
701. *Fighting for rail*, in *The Auckland Star*. 1979:
702. *Fight or go, MPs warned*, in *The Auckland Star*. 1979:

703. Bottomley, J. M., *Suburban Railway Services*, to D.-M. Robinson. 1979: Auckland.
704. Robinson, D.-M., *Railway Coaches Tender*, to J.M. Bottomley. 1979:
705. Ember, A., *Enlarged Europe, Shrinking Relations? The Impacts of Hungary's EU Membership On The Development of Bilateral Relations Between New Zealand and Hungary*, in *European Studies*. 2008, University of Canterbury: Christchurch. p.214, 215
706. Hansard, *Appropriations Bill - Estimates (In Committee) - Prime Minister's Department*. 1980: Wellington. p.2681-2685
707. Stewart, M., *Wellington's asbestos-laden trains being scrapped and buried at dump*, in *Dominion Post (Stuff)*. 2018: Wellington.
708. Department, Transportation Planning, *Comprehensive Transportation Study - Stage 1 Report*. 1987, Auckland Regional Authority:
709. Wikipedia. *Auckland Regional Council*. 2017 [cited 2017 13 February 2017]; from: https://en.wikipedia.org/wiki/Auckland_Regional_Council.
710. *Local Government Amendment Act (No. 2) 1989*. 1989: New Zealand.
711. *Urban Transport Act 1980*. 1980: NZ. Sections: 14, 15, 19, 21, 33, 35-36, 46
712. *Robbie says 'curse' has struck again*, in *The Auckland Star*. 1983:
713. Sergejew, A., *Review of Regulation of Commercial Urban Bus and Ferry Services in New Zealand*. 2007, New Zealand Ministry of Transport: Wellington. p.2, 3
714. *Transit New Zealand Act 1989*. 1989: New Zealand. Sections: 5-8, 23-25, 111
715. *Transport Services Licensing Act 1989*. 1989: New Zealand. Section: 4, 48
716. *Local Government Amendment Act (No 4) 1989*. 1989: NZ Section: 594ZR, 594ZU, 594ZZD
717. Heal, A., *Road Rage*, in *Metro Magazine*. 1997: Auckland. p.62, 64, 65, 66
718. Office, Audit, *The Planning of Roads*. 1989, The Audit Office: Wellington.
719. *Auckland Harbour Bridge Authority Dissolution Act 1983*. 1983: NZ
720. Grimes, A., *Building Bridges: Treating a New Transport Link As a Real Option*, in *Government Economics Network Annual Conference*. 2011. p.4, 6
721. Muldoon, R. D., *New Zealand Railways v Irish Railways*, Letter to D.-M. Robinson. 1980: Wellington.
722. Bush, G., *Local Government & Politics in New Zealand*. Second Edition. 1995, Auckland: Auckland University Press. p.68
723. Legat, N., *City Limits*, in *Metro Magazine*. 1995: Auckland. p.54, 55, 58, 59, 63
724. *Resource Management Act 1991*. 1991: NZ. Section: 9, 30
725. Council, Auckland Regional, *A brief history of Auckland's urban form*, Auckland Regional Council. 2019: p.55, 57
726. *Oh Auckland Region! My, how you've grown!*, in *Auckland Today*. 2004: p.26
727. *Local Government Amendment Act 1992*. 1992: NZ. Section: 707z(b), 707zzA
728. Roundtable, NZ Business, *Submission on the Discussion Document - Pathways for Auckland* in *- Concerning the Future of the Auckland Regional Services Trust*. 1997: Auckland. p.2
729. Rankin, K., *Whither the Auckland Regional Services Trust?* 1998:
730. *Local Government Amendment Act 1998*. 1998: NZ. Section: 707ZZK, 375G(4)
731. Council, Auckland Regional, *A Place Sought by Many: a brief history of regional planning for Auckland's growth*, Auckland Regional Council. 1997:
732. *Report of the Auckland Transport Commission*. 1928: Wellington. p.9
733. Davis, D., *Auckland Patronage Plummets*, in *Passenger Transport Magazine*. 1992.
734. Rutherford, R., *Auckland - At The Crossroads*, in *Australasian Transport Research Forum*. 1996: Auckland. p.2, 3, 5-6, 8-9, 11

735. Office, The Audit, *Competitive Pricing of Public Transport*. 1992, The Audit Office: Wellington. p.3, 7-8, 10-28, 38-46, 66
736. *Local Government Amendment Act (No. 2) 1992*. 1992: NZ.
737. *Land Transport Amendment Act 1995*. 1995: NZ. Section: 29F, 29I
738. *Transit New Zealand Amendment Act 1995*. 1995: NZ. Section: 14
739. Council, Auckland Regional, *Auckland Regional Land Transport Strategy* 1999, Auckland Regional Council Auckland. p.13-16, 30, 79, 104-106, 113
740. *Land Transport Act 1998*. 1998: NZ. Section: 170, 175, 178
741. Council, Auckland Regional, *Auckland Regional Policy Statement*. 1999: p.5, Section: 4.1-p.1
742. Paterson, L., *Auckland Regional Land Transport Strategy 1999 - Foreword*. 1999, Auckland Regional Land Transport Strategy: p.7
743. Shipley, J., *Govt Offers Mediator and Promises Funding For Auckland Transport Projects*. 1999, Central Government: Wellington.
744. Grimes, A. & Liang, Y., *Bridge to Somewhere: Valuing Auckland's Northern Motorway Extensions*. Journal of Transport Economics and Policy, 2010. 44:3: p.287-315
745. Group, Steering, *Light Rail Transit Evaluation (Report)*. 1996, Auckland Regional Council: p.2-4, 19, 20
746. Group, Steering, *Light Rail Transit Evaluation (Executive Summary)*. 1996, Auckland Regional Council: p.9
747. Ontrack. *Chronological History*. [cited 2010 2 October]; from: www.ontrack.govt.nz/Aboutus/History/pages/Chronological...
748. *Local Government Act 2002*. 2002: NZ.
749. *Land Transport Management Act 2003*. 2003: NZ.
750. Treasury, Ministry of Transport and, *Auckland Transport Strategy and Funding*. 2003: Wellington.
751. *Local Government (Auckland) Amendment Act 2004*. 2004: NZ.
752. *Submission by Business New Zealand*, in *Transport & Industrial Relations Committee on Local Government (Auckland) Amendment Bill*. 2004: Wellington.
753. Committee, Auckland Regional Land Transport, *Auckland Regional Land Transport Strategy 2005 - "Moving forward"*, 2005. Auckland Regional Council:
754. *Land Transport Management Amendment Act 2004*. 2004: NZ.
755. Dearnaley, M., *Cullen tells Auckland to pay more for roads*, in *The New Zealand Herald*. 2006:
756. King, A., *Funding certainty for transport improvements*. 2007: Wellington.
757. *Land Transport Management Amendment Act 2008*. 2008: NZ.
758. Orsman, B., *Slump hits Auckland's major projects*, in *The New Zealand Herald*. 2009:
759. (Northern), Employers and Manufacturers Association, *Fix Auckland*, in *North Harbour News*. 2007: Auckland. p.8, 9
760. *Auckland commission terms of reference announced*, in *The New Zealand Herald*. 2007:
761. Burton, M., *Auckland governance report is positive first step*. 2007: Wellington.
762. Burton, M., *Royal Commission of Inquiry into Auckland Governance - Terms of Reference and Membership Announced*. 2007: Wellington.
763. *Eden Albert Community Board Submission on Regional Governance in Auckland*, in *Royal Commission of Inquiry into the Governance of Auckland*. 2008:
764. Orsman, B., *Super city challenged to deliver*, in *The New Zealand Herald*. 2008:
765. Willis, L., *Supercity report unhelpful - Salmon*, in *North Shore Times*. 2009:

766. Governance, Royal Commission of Inquiry on Auckland, *Royal Commission of Inquiry on Auckland Governance Volume 1 Report* 2009: Wellington.
767. Kemeys, D., *Who stole our voice?*, in *North Shore Times*. 2009:
768. Palmer, K., *Radical Super City blueprint bold, decisive and workable*, in *The New Zealand Herald*. 2009:
769. *Local Government (Tamaki Makaurau Reorganisation) Act 2009*. 2009: NZ.
770. *Local Government (Auckland Council) Act 2009*. 2009: NZ.
771. Lello, J.W., *Transport Planning in Auckland: A Tactical Exercise Without Troops?* ESR News, 2000(April 2000): p.2, 3
772. Pringle, D., *Briefing Paper on Transport in Auckland*. ESR News, 2000(November 2000): p.1-4
773. Hyde, T., *Cross Purposes II - A Britomart Update*, in *Metro Magazine*. 1997: Auckland.
774. Council, Auckland City, *World class travel for Britomart users*. 2003, Auckland City Council:
775. Dearnaley, M., *New suburb bus links urged*, in *The New Zealand Herald*. 2006:
776. Dearnaley, M. & Orsman, B., *Sylvia Park routes could be closed again*, in *The New Zealand Herald*. 2006:
777. Lucas, S., *Letters to the Editor*, in *The New Zealand Herald*. 2006:
778. Donovan, S., *Letters to the Editor*, in *The New Zealand Herald*. 2006:
779. Treasury, The, *Report on Auckland Transport Released*. 2007, The Treasury: Wellington.
780. Cullen, M. & King, A., *Funding Certainty for transport improvements*. 2007: Wellington.
781. Rudman, B., *Rudman's City - Public cash propping up buses so we need bigger say in system*, in *The New Zealand Herald*. 2008:
782. *Shore commuters big winners*, in *North Shore Times*. 2008:
783. Vickers, L., *On the buses*, in *North Shore Times*. 2008:
784. Lewis, R., *Slow and the furious*, in *The Aucklander*. 2008:
785. Rooney, E., *Driven mad by traffic chaos*, in *The Aucklander*. 2008:
786. Cadacio, J. & Roberts, H., *Park and tow policy hits commuters*, in *North Shore Times*. 2008:
787. Cadacio, J., *Busway popular*, in *North Shore Times*. 2008:
788. City, North Shore, *SH1 Onewa Rd Interchange completes Busway project*. 2008, North Shore Times:
789. Unknown. *Public transport in Auckland*. 2008 [cited 2010 1 January 2010]; from: wikipedia.org/wiki/Public_transport_in_Auckland.
790. Lee, M., *From the Chairman*, in *Your Region, Your Future*. 2008, Auckland Regional Council: Auckland.
791. Council, Auckland Regional, *Region Wide*, in *Your Region, Your Future*. 2008, Auckland Regional Council: Auckland.
792. Dearnaley, M., *Cutting fuel taxes will not halt electric trains: National*, in *The New Zealand Herald*. 2008:
793. *Public Transport Management Act 2008*. 2008: NZ.
794. Rudman, B., *Brian Rudman: Time for National to come clean on tolls*, in *The New Zealand Herald*. 2008:
795. Joyce, S., *Regional fuel taxes replaced*. 2009: Wellington.
796. Dearnaley, M., *Investment loss hits at worst time*, in *The New Zealand Herald*. 2009:
797. Cadacio, J., *Busway a huge success & Free rides to mark busway anniversary*, in *North Shore Times*. 2009:
798. Joyce, S., *Fuel tax changes tomorrow*. 2009: Wellington.

799. Mein, B., *Transport Governance in Auckland - Situation Analysis*. 2008, CityScope Consultants, Auckland:
800. Joyce, S., *New agency to improve Auckland transport*. 2009:
801. Lee, M. (2009) *Joyce confirms Auckland will get new transport agency, Lee says what region needs is rail money*. The Bob Dey Property Report.
802. Council, Auckland Regional, *Public transport popular*, in *Region Wide - News and views from the Auckland Regional Council*. 2009, Auckland Regional Council: p.7
803. Wood, G., *Transport developments reach a crucial turning point*, in *North Shore Times*. 2009:
804. Mees P., Stone, J., Imran, M., & Nielson, G., *Public Transport Network Planning: a guide to best practice in NZ cities*. 2010, New Zealand Transport Agency: Wellington. p.14, 36, 38, 39
805. Dey, B., *Transport agency approves integrated ticketing funding*. 2009, Bob Dey Property:
806. Cadacio, J., *Smart tickets for Auckland transport*, in *North Shore Times*. 2010:
807. Dearnaley, M., *Rail fares to rise by up to 7pc - buses dearer too*, in *The New Zealand Herald*. 2009:
808. Dey, B. *Airport company says work on public transport links must speed up*. 2009 [cited 2009 23 December 2009]; 21 December 2009:[from: www.bdcentral.co.nz/afa.asp?idWebPage=8338&idBobDey....
809. Brash, D., *Roading*. 2004: Bob Dey Property Report.
810. Transport, Ministry of, *Tackling congestion in Auckland*. Previous ministry of transport studies [cited 2020 19 September 2020]; from: https://www.transport.govt.nz/land/auckland/the-congestion-question/previous-ministry-of-transport-studies/.
811. Transport, Ministry of, *Tackling Congestion in Auckland*. 2006, Ministry of Transport: Wellington.
812. *To toll or not to toll is vexing question*, in *Business to Business*. 2006: Auckland.
813. *$6 bridge toll - your angry letters*, in *North Harbour News*. 2006:
814. Dearnaley, M., *Where The $10 Charge Would Hit*, in *The New Zealand Herald*. 2006:
815. Transport, Ministry of, *Auckland Road Pricing Study 2008*. 2008, Ministry of Transport: Wellington.
816. *Fuelling change in our life on the road*, in *The New Zealand Herald*. 2006:
817. Dearnaley, M. & Oliver, P., *Cash boost puts road projects into top gear*, in *The New Zealand Herald*. 2006:
818. Association, Automobile, *Government To Be Congratulated on Six-Year Funding*. 2006: Wellington.
819. Transit, New Zealand, *Ramp Signalling Given Go Ahead On Northern And Northwestern Motorways*. 2006: Wellington.
820. Dearnaley, M., *Hobsonville road changes mark first step towards western ring route link*, in *The New Zealand Herald*. 2006:
821. Transit, New Zealand, *History In The Making For Auckland Motorists*. 2006: Wellington.
822. Dey, B., *Clark confirms $6 million for Wiri inland port*. 2008, Bob Dey Publishing: Auckland.
823. Key, J. & Joyce, S., *$1 billion more for state highways*. 2009: Wellington.
824. Dearnaley, M., *Councils tackle Govt on big roading projects*, in *The New Zealand Herald*. 2009:
825. *Editorial: Waterview route should be scrapped*, in *The New Zealand Herald*. 2009:

826. Dearnaley, M., *Report to postpone motorway ignored*, in *The New Zealand Herald*. 2009:
827. Dearnaley, M., *Motorway to go ahead despite concerns*, in *The New Zealand Herald*. 2009:
828. Merz, Sinclair Knight, *Waitemata Harbour Crossing Study 2008 - Study Summary Report*. 2008: Auckland.
829. Cadacio, J., *Calls to fast-track new crossing*, in *North Shore Times*. 2009:
830. Agency, NZ Transport, *Auckland Harbour Bridge History*. [Website] 2016 [cited 2016 29 June 2016]; from: www.nzta.govt.nz/projects/auckland-harbour-bridge/history/
831. Joyce, S., *Victoria Park project accelerated*, Minister of Transport. 2009: Wellington.
832. Construction, Fletcher, *Victoria Park Tunnel*. [Website] 2020 [cited 2020 23 November 2020]; from: https://www.fletcherconstruction.co.nz/projects/transport/victoria-park-tunnel.
833. Gosche, M., *Auckland rail deal finalised*. 2002: Wellington.
834. Kedgley, S., *Invest in state of the art public transport say Greens*. 2002, Green Party: Auckland.
835. Brady, K., *Auckland Region Passenger Rail Service Report*. 2003, The Audit Office: Wellington.
836. Office, NZ Companies, *Transdev Auckland Limited*. 2020, New Zealand Companies Office.
837. Transdev. *About Transdev*. [cited 2020 22 October 2020]; from: https://transdev.co.nz/about/transdev-auckland/.
838. *Rail Link Revival*, in *The New Zealand Railway Observer*. 2003.
839. Hucker, D. B., *Commuter rail vital cog in efficient transport system*, in *The New Zealand Herald*. 2003: Auckland.
840. URS NZ Ltd and GHD NZ. *Britomart West Rail Extension Feasibility Study - Final Report*. 2004, URS New Zealand Limited & GHD New Zealand: Auckland.
841. Orsman, B., *Rail base in carpark urged*, in *The New Zealand Herald*. 2005:
842. Cullen, M., *Onehunga rail upgrade gets green light*. 2007: Wellington.
843. King, A., *Towards a sustainable rail network*. 2007: Wellington.
844. Ringer, B., *The railway renewed: 150 years of railways in Manukau*, in *Connexions*. 2009. p.5, 6
845. Joyce, S., *Government committed to Auckland rail electrification*. 2009: Wellington.
846. Dearnaley, M., *Budget 09: Electric trains take back seat to freight*, in *The New Zealand Herald*. 2009:
847. Joyce, S., *$8.7 billion plan for transport investment unveiled*. 2009: Wellington.
848. Dearnaley, M., *Big-money plan opens door for $2b motorway*, in *The New Zealand Herald*. 2009:
849. Joyce, S., *New Metro Rail Operating Plan Released*. 2009: Wellington.
850. Dearnaley, M., *$1 b electric rail project gets go-ahead at last*, in *The New Zealand Herald*. 2009:
851. Dey, B. *Government writes cheque for Auckland's electric trains*. 2009 24 November 2009]; from: www.bdcentral.co.nz/afa.asp?idWebPage=8338&idBobDey.
852. Dey, B. *Helensville rail: an experiment guaranteed to fail*. 2009 [cited 2009; 12 November 2009: from: www.bdcentral.co.nz/afa.asp?idWebPage=8338&idBobDey.
853. Jenkins, S. S., *Big Bang Localism*. 2004, London: Policy Exchange.
854. Wikipedia. *Auckland Local Elections 2010*. [Website] 2010 [cited 2020; from: https://en.wikipedia.org/wiki/2010_Auckland_local_elections
855. *Local Government (Auckland Council) Amendment Act 2010*. 2010:

856. Dearnaley, M., *Joyce rejected council control for transport*, in *The New Zealand Herald*. 2011
857. Hoffman, L., *A brief history of Auckland's urban form*. 2019, Auckland Council: Auckland.
858. Rae, J., *Don't set aspirations that can't be delivered*, in *Spatial Plan Summit*. 2011: Aotea Centre, Auckland.
859. English, B., *Infrastructure Plan outlines large programme*. 2010: Wellington.
860. Unit, National Infrastructure, *National Infrastructure Plan*, The Treasury. 2010, National Government: Wellington.
861. Dearnaley, M., *Govt undermining city rail plans - Lee*, in *The New Zealand Herald*. 2011:
862. Joyce, S., *Government Policy Statement on Land Transport Funding* Minister of Transport. 2011: Wellington.
863. Selwood, S. *Government proposes $36 billion land transport spend under new policy, Selwood says rail loop & second harbour crossing are missing*. [Web Page] 2011; 27 July 2011: [from: www.propbd.co.nz/afa.asp?idWebPage=8338&idBobDeyProperty.
864. Dey, B. *4 draft planning documents ready Auckland for quantum leap*. [Website] 2011 [cited 2011 21 September 2011]; from: www.propbd.co.nz/afa.asp?idWebPage=8338idBobDeyProperty.
865. Dey, B. *Head-banging on economics & the Auckland spatial plan - Hide writes his exit monologue and council endorses argument for changing discount rate*. [Website] 2011 [cited 2011 26 October 2011]; from: www.propbd.co.nz/afa.asp?idWebPage=8338idBobDeyProperty_Articles=16855&SID=80.
866. Dey, B. *Auckland Plan launched with a jinky explanatory video*. [Website] 2012 [cited 2012 29 May 2012]; from: www.propbd.co.nz/BobDeyProperty Report
867. Ryan, S., *Auckland's spatial plan for a quality compact city*. 2012, Stuart Ryan, Barrister: Auckland.
868. Carter, D., *Government response to Auckland Spatial Plan (Auckland Plan)*, Local Government Department. 2012: Wellington.
869. Dey, B., *Transport funding discussion document goes to council this week*, in *The Bob Dey Property Report*. 2012, Bob Dey Publishing: Auckland.
870. Dey, B., *Council cuts alternative transport funding options to 3, irritating ones rather than imaginative*, in *The Bob Dey Property Report*. 2012, Bob Dey Publishing: Auckland.
871. Orsman, B., *Govt rejects city's tolls, fuel tax ideas*, in *The New Zealand Herald*. 2012:
872. *Land Transport Management Amendment Act 2013*. 2013: NZ.
873. Theunissen, M., *Auckland's choice: Road tolls or fuel taxes*, in *The New Zealand Herald*. 2013:
874. Dey, B., *Options not related to transport ruled out as reference group argues for fuel tax & road pricing*, in *The Bob Dey Property Report*. 2013, Bob Dey Publishing: Auckland.
875. Dey, B. *Mayor marks out the Auckland position for absent Government MPs*. [Website] 2013 [cited 2013 15 March 2013]; from: The Bob Dey Property Report.
876. Dey, B. *Study finds investment to shape compact city not in plans*. [Website] 2014 [cited 2014 24 February 2014]; from: www.propbd.co.nz/study-finds-investment-shape-compact-city.
877. Dearnaley, M., *Stunning' electric trains launched - but soon face delays*, in *The New Zealand Herald*. 2014:

878. Dey, B. *Minister confirms $39 billion land transport spend over decade, rail still an afterthought.* [Website] 2014 [cited 2014 19 December 2014]; from: www.propbd.co.nz./minister-confirms-$39-billion-land-transport.
879. Dey, B. *Council approves rates, transport levy & long-term plan after 2 close shaves.* [Website] 2015 [cited 2015 26 June 2015]; from: www.bobdeyproperty.
880. *$4.2 billion to be invested in Auckland's transport system*, in The New Zealand Herald. 2015:
881. Wade, A., *Auckland transport goal: 30 minute work commute*, in The New Zealand Herald. 2016:
882. *Government warms up to Auckland road tolls*, in The New Zealand Herald. 2016:
883. *Is this the way to solve Auckland's traffic woes?*, in The New Zealand Herald. 2016:
884. *Auckland Transport Alignment Project - Third Report.* 2016: Wellington.
885. *Auckland Smarter Transport Pricing Project - Terms of Reference.* 2016, Ministry of Transport: Wellington.
886. Young, A., *Finance Minister wants better discipline in assessing benefits of big infrastructure projects*, in The New Zealand Herald. 2017:
887. Dey, B. *Billions astray, but political thinking on Auckland transport infrastructure is positive.* [Website] 2017 [cited 2017 14 August 2017]; from: www.bobdeyproperty.
888. Orsman, B., *$28 billion funding package for Auckland roading and public transport projects unveiled*, in The New Zealand Herald. 2018:
889. *Land Transport Management (Regional Fuel Tax) Amendment Act 2018* 2018: NZ.
890. Wilson, S., *Big new spending plans for transport, roads and buses in Auckland*, in The New Zealand Herald. 2018:
891. Twyford, P., *Record transport investment to grow the economy and improve safety.* 2018, New Zealand Government: Wellington.
892. Agency, NZ Transport, *National Land Transport Programme - Auckland 2018 Summary.* [Website] 2018 [cited 2020 31 October 2020]; from: https://www.nzta.govt.nz/planning-and-investment/national-land-transport-programme/2018-21-nltp/regional-summaries/auckland-region/auckland-2018-summary/.
893. Walls, J., *Government has given NZTA an extra $45m after damning 'wake-up call' report*, in The New Zealand Herald. 2019:
894. *UK bus-maker targets NZ manufacturing base*, in The New Zealand Herald. 2011:
895. Dearnaley, M., *Bus use surges as fuel prices bite commuters*, in The New Zealand Herald. 2011:
896. Orsman, B., *Emergency plan to ease bus overcrowding*, in The New Zealand Herald. 2011:
897. Dey, B. *Link bus expands to 3 services.* [Website] 2011 [cited 2011 6 July 2011]; from: www.propbd.co.nz/afa.asp?idWebPage=8338&idBobDeyProperty…
898. Rudman, B., *A new language...and an old horror story*, in The New Zealand Herald. 2011:
899. Dearnaley, M., *Seamless public transport ticketing gets first outing on buses in March*, in The New Zealand Herald. 2010:
900. Dearnaley, M., *Deep trouble for Auckland transport ticketing*, in The New Zealand Herald. 2012:
901. Dearnaley, M., *Morning rush hour test for new ticket system*, in The New Zealand Herald. 2012:
902. *Editorial: Busway great but let other vehicles use it*, in The New Zealand Herald. 2012:
903. Weekes, J., *Auckland plans transport quick-fix*, in The New Zealand Herald. 2015:
904. Dearnaley, M., *PM opens new $18m bus depot*, in The New Zealand Herald. 2014:

905. *Laying it on time - Motat's new tram tracks*, in *Contractor Magazine*. 2007.
906. Dearnaley, M., *Tram tracks first step in harbour transport project*, in *The New Zealand Herald*. 2011:
907. *Wynyard Quarter tram service's last ride will be next week*, in *The New Zealand Herald*. 2018
908. Wikipedia. *Trams in New Zealand - Wynyard Loop*. [Website] 2020 [cited 2020 9 October 2020]; from: https://en.wikipedia.org/wiki/Trams_in_New_Zealand#Wynyard_loop_tram.
909. Orsman, B., *Wynyard Quarter's historic trams to resume this summer*, in *The New Zealand Herald*. 2019:
910. Council, Auckland, *Panuku Development Auckland*. [Website] 2020 [cited 2020 2 November 2020]; from: https://www.aucklandcouncil.govt.nz/about-auckland-council/how-auckland-council-works/council-controlled-organisations/Pages/panuku-development-auckland.aspx
911. Rudman, B., *Brian Rudman: Get real, Len, and look at the trams*, in *The New Zealand Herald*. 2015:
912. Laxon, A., *Auckland City trams: Back to the future*, in *The New Zealand Herald*. 2015:
913. Dearnaley, M., *Trams proposed for airport route*, in *The New Zealand Herald*. 2015:
914. Wade, A., *Auckland Airport link a distant reality*, in *The New Zealand Herald*. 2016:
915. Dey, B. *Goff raises funding question as airport mass transit corridor agreed*. [Website] 2017 [cited 2017 27 March 2017]; from: www.propbd.co.nz/goff-raises-funding-question-airport-mass-transit....
916. *Trams to Mt Roskill*, in *The New Zealand Herald*. 2018:
917. Orsman, B., *Trams could run under Queen St as part of Auckland's $6 billion light rail project*, in *The New Zealand Herald*. 2019:
918. Coughlan, T. *NZTA backs down from light rail, looks at spending millions elsewhere*. [Website] 2019 [cited 2019 19 September 2019]; from: https://www.stuff.co.nz/national/politics/115885818/nzta-backs-down-from-light-rail-looks-at-spending-millions
919. Lambert, M. *AT on their PT journey*. [Website] 2017 [cited 2017 30 May 2017]; from: www.greaterauckland.org.nz/2017/05/30/at-on-their-pt-journey.
920. Transport, Auckland, *New Public Transport Network Update*, Auckland Transport Metro, Editor. 2018, Auckland Transport:
921. Johnston, M., *Auckland Transport under fire for stinging Albany motorists who miss out on park and ride spaces with new parking charges*, in *The New Zealand Herald*. 2019:
922. Dey, B. *More park & ride spaces at Takaanini, Albany & Silverdale*. [Website] 2019 [cited 2019 24 July 2019]; from: www.propbd.co.nz/.
923. Radio New Zealand, *One day of free train and bus travel for Aucklanders to celebrate milestone*. [Website] 2019 [cited 2019 7 June 2019]; from: https://www.rnz.co.nz/news/national/391360/
924. *Editorial: Cycle lanes can do the job without being gold-plated*, in *The New Zealand Herald*. 2018:
925. *Auckland ferry use at highest level since 1959*, in *The New Zealand Herald*. 2016:
926. *Waiheke ferry woes: Auckland councillor Chris Darby to seek urgent Government intervention as commuters fume*, in *The New Zealand Herald*. 2019:

927. *Fullers ferry service reaches 'peak failure': 'They're operating like a bunch of cowboys'*, in *The New Zealand Herald*. 2019:
928. Niall, T. *Waiheke Island: Thousands sign petition, but politicians hold key to ferry future*. 2019 20 September 2019 [cited 2020 8 December 2020]; from: https://www.stuff.co.nz/auckland/115947513/waiheke-island-thousands-sign-petition-but-politicians-hold-key-to-ferry-future
929. Dearnaley, M., *Auckland one of the most 'car-biased' cities in world*, in *The New Zealand Herald*. 2011:
930. Bennett, A., *Govt pumps billions into road and rail*, in *The New Zealand Herald*. 2011:
931. *Design contract kick-starts $1b road plan*, in *The New Zealand Herald*. 2010:
932. Dearnaley, M., *Unexpected demand brings motorway fix of up to $160m*, in *The New Zealand Herald*. 2010:
933. *New $220 million Manukau motorway opens*, in *The New Zealand Herald*. 2011:
934. Nash, K., *New harbour crossing inches closer as motorway opens*, in *The New Zealand Herald*. 2011:
935. Joyce, S., *Waterview decision well-considered, balanced*. 2009: Wellington.
936. Hesseling, P., *Waterview connection - the keystone in Auckland's Western Ring Route*, Automobile Association. 2010: Auckland.
937. Dearnaley, M., *Residents refused more time to fight motorway*, in *The New Zealand Herald*. 2010:
938. Dearnaley, M., *Waterview motorway link gets approval*, in *The New Zealand Herald*. 2011:
939. *Work finally starts on NZ's 'most complex' road project*, in *The New Zealand Herald*. 2012:
940. Construction, Fletcher, *Waterview Connection*. [Website] 2017 [cited 2020 30 October 2020]; from: https://www.fletcherconstruction.co.nz/projects/transport/waterview-connection.
941. Dearnaley, M., *Auckland tunnel threat: you'll pay*, in *The New Zealand Herald*. 2011:
942. Dearnaley, M., *Auckland tunnel delay blamed on curiosity*, in *The New Zealand Herald*. 2011:
943. Agency, NZ Transport, *NZTA says Vic Park flyover ready for Monday's big change*. 2012, New Zealand Transport Agency: Wellington.
944. Agency, NZ Transport, *Final works to have Vic Park Tunnel at full capacity*. 2012, New Zealand Transport Agency: Wellington.
945. Technology, Road Traffic, *Newmarket Viaduct / Connection Project*. [Website] 2020 [cited 2020 10 December 2020]; from: https://www.roadtraffic-technology.com/projects/newmarket-viaduct/.
946. Brownlee, G., *Newmarket Viaduct Replacement completed*, National Party. 2013:
947. Brownlee, G., *Investments add up to travel time savings*, Transport Minister. 2013: Wellington.
948. Howie, C., *Auckland's $1.25b gridlock bill*, in *The New Zealand Herald*. 2013:
949. Lupton, D. & Wallis, I., *The costs of congestion reappraised*. 2013: Auckland.
950. Howie, C., *Honk if you're stuck in Auckland's traffic*, in *The New Zealand Herald*. 2013:
951. Gaynor, B., *Brian Gaynor: Plenty of cars, shame about the roads*, in *The New Zealand Herald*. 2015:
952. Wade, A., *Abandoning Auckland only way out*, in *The New Zealand Herald*. 2016:
953. Orsman, B., *Traffic chaos: A third of Auckland's main roads will be congested by 2020*, in *The New Zealand Herald*. 2017:

954. Gaynor, B., *Brian Gaynor: Car boom looks like last hurrah for petrol power*, in *The New Zealand Herald*. 2017:
955. Wilson, S., *Failings all round: Auckland's catastrophic road safety record*, in *The New Zealand Herald*. 2018:
956. *Government 'open to introduction of electronic road tolling in Auckland'*, in *The New Zealand Herald*. 2017:
957. *Editorial: No road tolls without improved transport options*, The New Zealand Herald. 2017
958. Government & Auckland Council, *Phase One Report: The Congestion Question – Could road pricing improve Auckland's traffic?* 2017: Auckland.
959. Orsman, B., *Congestion charges on table in fight against Auckland gridlock*, in *The New Zealand Herald*. 2018:
960. Niall, T. *Auckland congestion charge: City's next political potato is already baked*. [Stuff Website] 2020 [cited 2020 31 October 2020]; 12 October 2020:[from: https://www.stuff.co.nz/national/123034921/auckland-congestion-charge-citys-next-political-hot-potato-is-already-baked.
961. Twyford, P., *Regional fuel tax for Auckland a step closer*. 2018: Wellington.
962. Agency, NZ Transport, *Auckland Regional Fuel Tax*. [Website] 2020 [cited 2020 18 August 2020]; from: https://www.nzta.govt.nz/vehicles/regional-fuel-tax/.
963. Davison, I., *Where the fuel taxes have gone: Auckland Mayor Phil Goff says eight projects already started*, in *The New Zealand Herald*. 2019:
964. Wilson, S., *The next harbour crossing: road and rail, or just rail?*, in *The New Zealand Herald*. 2019:
965. Grimes, A. & Young, C., *Anticipatory Effects of Rail Upgrades: Auckland's Western Line*, in *Motu Working Paper 10-11*. 2010, Motu Economic and Public Policy Research Auckland.
966. *KiwiRail announces Auckland electric train shortlist*. Railway Gazette, 2010.
967. Cheng, D., *Electric rail shortlist extension under fire*, in *The New Zealand Herald*. 2010:
968. Dearnaley, M., *Auckland's $500m electric trains signed off*, in *The New Zealand Herald*. 2010:
969. Dearnaley, M., *Rail work under way*, in *The New Zealand Herald* 2010:
970. Dearnaley, M., *Fleet of new electric trains for Auckland on the way*, in *The New Zealand Herald*. 2011:
971. Dearnaley, M., *Electric trains are coming your way*, in *The New Zealand Herald*. 2013:
972. Wikipedia. *First Auckland EMUs running 2014*. 2020 [cited 2020 21 October 2020]; from: https://en.wikipedia.org/wiki/New_Zealand_AM_class_electric_multiple_unit -
973. *Auckland trains go electric*, in *The New Zealand Herald*. 2015:
974. KiwiRail. *Auckland Metro Rail Programme - Papakura to Pukekohe electrification*. 2020 [cited 2020 15 December 2020]; from: https://www.kiwirail.co.nz/what-we-do/projects/amp/papakura-to-pukekohe-electrification/.
975. Dearnaley, M. & Davison, I., *Rail projects - way of future or a train wreck?*, in *The New Zealand Herald*. 2010:
976. Orsman, B. & Trevett, C., *Tight-fisted Key deals blow to Brown's rail plan*, in *The New Zealand Herald*. 2010:
977. APB&B, *Business Case - Auckland CBD Rail Link*. 2010: Auckland
978. Dey, B. *Brewer casts doubt on cbd growth predictions in rail loop case*. [Website] 2010 26 November 2010.

979. Dearnaley, M., *Glowing case for Akl rail tunnel gets cool response*, in *The New Zealand Herald*. 2010:
980. Tan, L., *Lee gets stuck into Joyce over rail tunnel*, in *The New Zealand Herald*. 2010:
981. Donnell, H., *Rail link benefits 'significantly overstated' - review*, in *The New Zealand Herald*. 2011:
982. Orsman, B., *Rail loop toll plan triggers new clash*, in *The New Zealand Herald*. 2011:
983. *Editorial: Mind your own business on rail loop, Mr Joyce*, in *The New Zealand Herald*. 2011:
984. Dearnaley, M. & Others, *Compensation talk after Cup transport debacle*, in *The New Zealand Herald*. 2011:
985. Dey, B. *Council advances $8 million of budget for rail loop work*. [Website] 2012 [cited 2012 9 March 2012].
986. Donnell, H., *Auckland Transport reveals inner city rail link route*, in *The New Zealand Herald*. 2012:
987. Merz, Sinclair Knight, *City Centre Future Access Study*. 2012: Auckland.
988. Dearnaley, M., *Motorists face slow future*, in *The New Zealand Herald*. 2012:
989. Rudman, B., *Enough reports - get on with rail*, in *The New Zealand Herald*. 2012:
990. Davison, I., *Government reveals shape of Auckland's transport future*, in *The New Zealand Herald*. 2013:
991. Dey, B. *Mayor welcomes Government support, says 70% of rail link funding secured*. [Website] 2013 [cited 2013 1 July 2013].
992. Theunissen, M., *Rail operator told to shape up*, in *The New Zealand Herald*. 2013:
993. Orsman, B., *Govt targets for rail link 'unrealistic'* in *The New Zealand Herald*. 2014:
994. Dey, B. *$500 million lopped off rail link cost - and we're told it'll be better*. [Website] 2014 3 August 2014 [cited 2014 4 August 2014]; from: www.propbd.co.nz/500-million-lopped-rail-link-cost-told-itllb
995. Dearnaley, M., *Crown agency backs City Rail Link*, in *The New Zealand Herald*. 2014:
996. Dey, B. *Council majority rejects softer approach to Government on rail link*. [Website] 2014 [cited 2014 10 December 2014]; from: www.propbd.co.nz/council-majority-rejects-softer-approach-g...
997. Dey, B. *Consent application lodged for first rail link section*. [Website] 2015 [cited 2015 5 February 2015]; from: www.propbd.co.nz/consent-application-lodged-first-rail-link-se....
998. Dey, B. *2 downtown rail link contracts let*. [Website] 2015 [cited 2015 8 April 2015].
999. Dey, B. *All city rail link appeals resolved*. [Website] 2015 [cited 2015 28 August 2015].
1000. Transport, Auckland, *Auckland's public transport numbers keep going up*. [Website] 2015 [cited 2015 17 April 2015]; from: https://at.govt.nz/about-us/news-events/aucklands-public-transport-n
1001. *Auckland rail patronage hits record number*, in *The New Zealand Herald*. 2015:
1002. Dey, B. *Rail patronage climbs to 15 million/year*. [Website] 2015 [cited 2015 20 November 2015].
1003. *Blessing for City Rail Link project*, in *The New Zealand Herald*. 2015:
1004. Dey, B. *Thursday groundbreaking for city rail link*. [Website] 2016 31 May 2016 [cited 2016 1 June 2016].
1005. Orsman, B., *John Key to kickstart $2.5b Auckland city rail link*, in *The New Zealand Herald*. 2016:
1006. Plumb, S., *Extra $1.4b needed for rail system*, in *The New Zealand Herald*. 2016:
1007. Brinckerhoff, W. P., *Wiri to Westfield - The Case for Investment*. 2016: Auckland.

1008. Brown, L., *Historic agreement on CRL funding - Media release from the Mayor of Auckland.* 2016: Auckland.
1009. Transport, Auckland, *Largest City Rail Link tender process starts.* 2017, Auckland Transport:
1010. Dey, B. *Tunnel dig starts on Albert St.* [Website] 2017 [cited 2017 19 July 2017].
1011. Collins, S., *Auckland's City Rail Link cost jumps to $4.419 billion*, in *The New Zealand Herald.* 2019:
1012. Collins, S., *Auckland Council looking to sell carpark buildings to pay for City Rail Link blowout*, in *The New Zealand Herald.* 2019:
1013. Gibson, A., *$4.4b City Rail Link milestone: tunnel contract sealed as officials sign up Link Alliance*, in *The New Zealand Herald.* 2019:
1014. Orsman, B., *Auckland motorways, Harbour Bridge Skypath big winners in Government's $12 billion infrastructure spend-up*, in *The New Zealand Herald* 2020:
1015. Andrew, M. *Cheat Sheet: The pedestrian revamp planned for Auckland's CBD.* [The Spinoff News Website] 2020 [cited 2020 9 March 2020].
1016. Orsman, B., *Radical design changes behind cost blowout for Auckland's SkyPath project*, in *The New Zealand Herald.* 2020:
1017. Coughlan, T. *Government puts light rail 'on hold'.* [Stuff News Website] 2020 [cited 2020 13 May 2020].
1018. Rutherford, H., *'Disappointing and frustrating': Auckland's light rail process 'ended'*, in *The New Zealand Herald.* 2020:
1019. Orsman, B., *Auckland's $1.4b Eastern Busway gets giant steel beams for a bridge over Tamaki River*, in *The New Zealand Herald.* 2020:
1020. Transport, Auckland, *Auckland Transport builds momentum on $1.4b Eastern Busway.* 2020, Auckland Transport:
1021. Agency, NZ Transport, *new bus station rosedale.* 2020, New Zealand Transport Agency: Wellington.
1022. Project, Auckland Transport Alignment, *The Congestion Question - Technical Report.* 2020, Auckland Transport Alignment Project:
1023. Dillane, T., *NZ firms Fletchers and Downer 'fuming' as $371m Govt KiwiRail contract goes overseas*, in *The New Zealand Herald.* 2020:
1024. Pearce, C. *Contract awarded for Puhinui station interchange main works.* [Website] 2020 24 June 2020 [cited 2020 31 October 2020]; from: www.railexpress.com.au/contract-awarded-for-puhinui-station-interchange-main-works/
1025. Campbell, G., *Auckland metro rail network in worse condition than first thought*, in *The New Zealand Herald.* 2020:
1026. Gibson, A., *It's here - $13.5m tunnel boring machine for $4.4b City Rail Link arrives in Auckland*, in *The New Zealand Herald.* 2020:
1027. Agency, NZ Transport, *Additional Waitematā Harbour Connections.* [Website] 2020 [cited 2020 17 December 2020]; from: https://www.nzta.govt.nz/media-releases/building-the-case-for-additional-waitemata-harbour-connections/

Abey, F. F., 318, 329, 463
Accelerated Transport Program, 665
Aecom Engineering Group, 707
AECOM New Zealand, 708
Aimer, Hugh, 543
Air, Alisdair
    Automotive Nightmare, 462
Aitken, David
    National Road Carriers, 682
Alexander Dennis, 661
Alexander, Peter, 617
Algie, R. M., 83
Alison, Ewen William, 16
Allan, Dr., 535, 536
Allen, Alfred E., 224
Allen, Percy B., 281, 282, 283, 284, 291, 292, 294, 295, 297, 298, 299, 300, 325, 326, 327, 328, 329, 349, 360, 365, 384, 447, 459
Alliance Party, 554
Allsopp-Smith, John, 226, 267, 269, 346, 391, 422, 423, 424, 431, 432, 455, 459, 510, 512
Allum, John A. C., 14, 15, 16, 17, 18, 33, 34, 35, 39, 40, 51, 54, 89, 90, 93, 189, 193, 194, 195, 202, 218, 219, 369, 374, 556, 583
Anae, Arthur, 641
Anderson and Partners, 420
Anderson, Henry A., 65, 105, 113, 114, 115, 116, 117, 118, 119, 123, 125, 128, 129, 131
Anderson, S. E., 360
Anderton, Jim P., 395, 455, 497, 498, 499, 502, 524
Annual Regional Implementation Programmes, 543

Ansaldo S.p.a., 534
Apcon Group, 425
Ardern, Jacinda, 670, 710
Armishaw, Eric C., 112, 270
Arthur, Sir Basil, 416, 417, 475
Ashby, Thomas W. M., 112
Ashwin, B. C., 193
Auckland Advisory Committee, 48
Auckland Bus Company Ltd, 423
Auckland Chamber of Commerce, 65, 88, 93, 100, 107, 282, 393, 466, 467, 506, 515, 619
Auckland Citizens' & Ratepayers' Association, 104
Auckland City Council, 7, 12, 14, 34, 41, 49, 51, 55, 92, 104, 108, 109, 111, 112, 113, 120, 123, 129, 138, 163, 164, 168, 185, 187, 191, 200, 214, 225, 242, 250, 272, 275, 283, 284, 286, 293, 307, 321, 356, 357, 358, 406, 595, 641, 676
    avoids costly rail option, 273
    centenary, 388
    central area plan 1975, 494
    core city principle, 389
    district scheme 1961, 237
    district scheme 1961-1970, 386
    housing redevelopment, 238
    ratepayers transport levies 1976-78, 406
    submissions by Dove-Myer Robinson, 332
    transport & urban linkages committee, 711
    urban renewal committee, 242
    ways & means committee, 32
Auckland Community Trust, 554

Auckland Comprehensive
   Transportation Study Review,
   397, 539
   final report 1976, 402
   interim report 1976, 398
   interim report response, 400
   'motor car and motorway
      madness', 405
Auckland Council
   Auckland Plan, 643, 646, 647,
      650
   carpark buildings for sale, 707
   city centre masterplan 2011, 662
   draft planning documents 2011,
      646
   draft unitary plan 2013, 650
   infrastructure investment needed,
      651
   interim transport levy 2015, 652
   spatial plan required, 598
Auckland Council Transport
   Committee, 694
Auckland Electric Tramways
   Company, 11
Auckland Governance
   Royal Commission of Inquiry,
      614
      2007, 594
      critics, 596
      report 2009, 596
      submissions, 594
Auckland Harbour Board, 76, 77,
   78, 80, 81, 86, 92, 101, 102, 169,
   189, 191, 197, 224, 226, 270
Auckland Harbour Bridge, 75, 169,
   172, 339, 548, 629, 645
   austerity bridge, 193
   clip-ons, 372, 629
   construction begins, 195
   contract signed, 194
   daily traffic 1970, 372
   design complete, 191
   government approval 1953, 193
   leads to population increase, 372
   new movable lane barrier, 630
   opens 1959, 197
   operation, 369
   proposal 1945, 72
   Royal Commission of Inquiry
      1930, 7
      1946, 83, 85
      petition 1945, 79
      report 1930, 23
   second crossing, 455, 576, 679,
      687, 714
   tenders received 1952, 191
   traffic volumes, 368
   tunnel proposal 1945, 91
   Waitemata Bridge Commission,
      189
   Waitemata Harbour Bridge
      Association, 23
   Waitemata Harbour Crossing
      Study, 629
      committee, 455, 456
Auckland Harbour Bridge Act 1950,
   189, 372
Auckland Harbour Bridge
   Amendment Act 1965, 372
Auckland Harbour Bridge
   Amendment Acts, 190
Auckland Harbour Bridge
   Association, 27, 76, 79, 80
Auckland Harbour Bridge
   Authority, 165, 189, 191, 194,
   224, 226, 369, 370, 371, 390,
   486, 727
   income, 370

lower tolls 1969, 373
Auckland Harbour Bridge Authority Dissolution Act 1983, 548
Auckland Harbour Bridge Company Ltd, 87
Auckland Harbour Bridge Empowering Act, 87, 88, 189
Auckland International Airport, 617
Auckland Metropolitan Co-ordinating Town-planning Scheme, 70
Auckland Metropolitan Council, 105, 133, 134, 142, 244, 353
Auckland Metropolitan Drainage Board, 41, 100, 101, 106, 112, 169, 223, 225
Auckland Metropolitan Local Bodies Association, 105
Auckland Metropolitan Planning Authority, 142
   Outline Development Plan, 101
Auckland Metropolitan Planning Committee, 39, 40, 102, 220
Auckland Metropolitan Planning Organisation
   Technical Advisory Committee, 101, 104, 168
Auckland Provincial Public Relations Office, 110
Auckland Public Transport Action Committee, 389, 390, 483, 486
Auckland Rapid Rail Symposium 1969, 343
Auckland Rapid Transit
   a consolation prize, 485
   a repeat of disunity, 469
   agreement delayed, 504
   an election issue, 469
   another delaying tactic, 470
   another election delay, 508
   another report called for, 484
   apparent consensus, 472
   ARA & local bodies meet, 471
   ARA summary of benefits, 477
   Chamber of Commerce support, 466
   chief supporter leaves, 494
   City Council support, 466
   committee disbanded, 391
   cost sharing blurred, 496
   costs 1974, 492
   costs 1975-76, 492
   costs escalate, 503
   cost-sharing disagreement, 501
   councillors opposed, 479
   decision time, 496
   demolition shock, 498
   Devonport Council support, 471
   Directorate appointed, 489
   Directorate report, 495
   Directorate view, 491
   dissent by telegram, 473
   disunity again, 506
   endorsed by Labour, 475
   escalating costs criticised, 492
   Godfather offer, 488
   Government acceptance of major costs, 476
   Government's offer accepted, 487
   killed, 513
   not just profit & loss, 509
   office, 427
   on ice, 512
   opponents protest, 472
   overseas finance available, 508
   overseas study trips, 482
   political machinations, 459

progress unlikely, 503
railways embarrassment, 509
reaction to Government proposal, 486
reply to critics, 481
Robinson to fight on, 513
scheme improved, 490
spitting against the wind, 395
the fight to continue, 437
who pays?, 465
working party report 1969, 319
Auckland Regional Authority, 108, 136, 142, 165, 188, 220, 222, 223, 224, 225, 226, 227, 229, 230, 231, 238, 239, 241, 242, 244, 252, 254, 260, 262, 268, 269, 274, 275, 284, 286, 289, 293, 298, 304, 306, 307, 313, 315, 316, 321, 326, 335, 346, 349, 370, 376, 387, 444, 470, 501, 539, 541, 551
Establishment Committee, 223
Government usurping its role, 392
inaugural report, 228
regional development plan, 313
regional master plan, 280
Transport Committee, 226, 257
transport upgrades needed 1970, 419
Auckland Regional Authority Act 1963, 225, 254, 255
Auckland Regional Authority Amendment Act 1964, 255
Auckland Regional Authority Empowering Act 1972, 423
Auckland Regional Authority Establishment Act 1960, 222

Auckland Regional Council, 540, 551, 562, 595
1991-92 Annual Plan, 562
draft annual plan 2008-09, 608
funds crisis 2009, 612
Passenger Transport Action Plan, 572
Regional Policy Statement, 570
steering group
light rail transit, 578
Auckland Regional Development, 231
Auckland Regional Growth Forum, 555
Auckland Regional Holdings, 591, 592
established 2004, 587
Auckland Regional Land Transport Committee, 545, 546, 566, 571
Auckland Regional Land Transport Strategy, 567, 569, 571, 576, 577, 580, 590, 599, 616
Auckland Regional Planning Authority, 183, 224, 225, 354
Technical Advisory Committee, 38, 102, 103, 109, 142, 168, 179, 180, 183, 214, 220, 223, 250, 270, 353
Auckland Regional Planning Authority Act 1963, 225
Auckland Regional Planning Council, 39
Auckland Regional Planning Organisation, 39, 40, 103, 220
Auckland Regional Services Trust, 554
Auckland Regional Transport Authority, 571, 587

Auckland Regional Transport
    Network Limited, 588
Auckland Road Pricing Evaluation
    Study 2006, 619, 620
Auckland Road Pricing Evaluation
    Study 2008, 619, 623
Auckland Rotary Club, 38, 47, 143
Auckland Suburban Rail
    Improvement Committee, 515,
    517
Auckland Town-Planning
    Association, 24
Auckland Transport, 641, 690
    consensus-building group, 648,
        649
    funding tools, 648
    Government influence, 642
    Government v local control, 644,
        648
    infrastructure deficit 2011, 643
    Regional Land Transport Plan,
        657
    replaces ARTA, 598
    transport funding terms, 652
Auckland Transport Alignment
    Project, 685, 712
    2nd report, 653
    3rd report, 654
    4th report, 656
    5th report, 656
    foundation report, 653
Auckland Transport Board, 13, 14,
    15, 16, 17, 19, 20, 21, 41, 49, 50,
    51, 55, 56, 57, 58, 59, 60, 61, 62,
    64, 67, 86, 87, 95, 101, 102, 109,
    113, 114, 115, 116, 117, 119,
    121, 123, 126, 128, 129, 130,
    133, 134, 135, 136, 137, 139,
    141, 142, 169, 170, 198, 200,
    211, 223, 224, 225, 226, 244,
    245, 248, 252, 256, 377, 542,
    556
    amendment act, 254
    becomes ARA passenger
        transport committee, 260
    borough council rebellion, 131
    case for survival, 247
    first rates levy, 128
    opposes proposed Regional
        Authority, 252
    rates levy 1957, 133
    replaced by ARA, 254
Auckland Transport Board Act
    1928, 13, 57, 252, 421
Auckland Transport Board Annual
    Report
    1929, 15, 50
    1930, 15
    1931, 15
    1932, 16
    1933, 16
    1934, 16, 17
    1935, 18
    1936, 19
    1937, 19
    1938, 19, 49
    1939, 19
    1940, 49
    1941, 50, 51
    1942, 52, 126
    1943, 53
    1944, 53, 55
    1945, 56
    1946, 59, 60
    1947, 62, 63
    1948, 64
    1949, 64, 65
    1950, 113, 114, 115

1951, 115
1952, 117
1953, 119, 123
1954, 123, 125
1955, 128, 129, 131
1956, 131, 132
1957, 133
1958, 138
1959, 139
1960, 245
1961, 246
1962, 248
1963, 252
1964, 253
final report 1964, 256
Auckland Transport Board Empowering Act 1934, 17
Auckland Transport Commission, 13, 556
Auckland Transport District, 14, 95, 131, 252, 421
area of benefit extended 1972, 423
enlarged 1974, 424
Auckland Transport Holdings, 332, 338, 374, 413, 419
Auckland Transport Strategic Alignment Project, 604
Auckland Transport Study, 569
Auckland-Manukau Eastern Transport Initiative, 646, 676, 677, 699, 711
Audit Office, 547, 559, 562, 566
passenger rail report, 632
Australasian Transport Research Forum, 559
Automobile Association, 24, 76, 79, 80, 412, 622

Bailey, A. S., 40, 51
Bailey, Ron, 439
Baker, Pearl, 479, 483
Bank of New Zealand, 663
Bank of New Zealand Assets Company, 11
Banks, John, 589, 641
Barker, D. W. A., 319
Barnard, W. E., 9
Barnett, Michael
Auckland Business Forum, 687
Barneveld, Rick van, 692
Barton, John S, 13
Bassett, Michael, 540, 553
Bazley, Dame Margaret, 594
Beachen, J. E., 282
Beard, Michael, 631
Beatty, D. W., 363
Beaver, William R., 83
Beca Carter Hollings & Ferner, 375, 415
Beca Higgins, 630
Beechey, H. G., 134
Beeson, T. V. G., 390, 483
Begbie, W. E., 169
Bell, A. T., 479
Bell, Joseph, 17
Bell, Noel C., 108, 223, 472
Bell, W., 309
Bell, W. L., 137, 169, 170, 172
Belloc, Hilaire
The Old Road, 21
Bennett, P. M. Hoyle, 504
Berg, Brian K., 391, 509, 515
Berkshire Partners, 582
Better Transport, Better Roads, 574
Birkenhead Transport, 613
Black Budget, 140, 184
Bland, C., 169, 170

Bloodworth, Hon. Thomas, 100, 104
Bloomfield, G. T.
    Urban Tramways in New Zealand, 11, 67, 221
Bogue, Ian, 621
Boileau, Dr. I. E., 144, 455
Bolz, D. T. G., 377
Bombardier Transportation, 689
Bonnett Bell & Fenton, Messrs., 17
Bonnett, Thomas Henry, 17
Boston Consulting Group, 633
Bottomley, John M., 533, 538
Boyce, L. B., 170
Bradwell, Paul, 461
Brady, Kevin, 632
Brash, Don, 619
Bray, C. H., 208
Brewer, Cameron, 641, 694
Bridges, G. F., 380, 489
Bridges, Simon, 652, 653, 654, 665, 669, 701, 705
British Royal Engineers, 25
Britomart Developments Ltd, 601
Britomart Investments, 601
Britomart Place, 88, 386, 511, 518, 519
    Auckland Municipal Bus Station, 56
    railway station, 601
    transport terminal, 600
Brosnahan, Jo, 570
Brown, H., 134
Brown, John V., 424, 524
Brown, L. K., 238
Brown, Len, 1, 641, 644, 645, 646, 647, 649, 650, 651, 652, 654, 665, 691, 692, 695, 696, 698, 700, 701, 702, 703, 705

Brownlee, Gerry, 649, 650, 680, 681, 698, 701
Buchanan, Colin, 242, 274, 275, 283, 305, 306, 307, 311, 353, 357
    report, 277, 279, 280
Built Environs, 713
Bullen, Prof. A. G. R., 506
Burnett, J. L., 146, 151, 152
Burton, Mark, 594
Bus Proprietors' Association, 56
Bush, Dr. Graham W. A., 311, 507, 549
Business New Zealand, 586
Butler, R. A., 193
Buttle, K. N., 165

CAF of Spain, 690
Cameron, J. W., 559
Carr, Clyde MP, 81
Carter Committee, 319, 326, 329, 349, 350
Carter David J., 319, 345, 353
Carter Inquiry, 238, 353, 440
    ARA Submission, 330
    Auckland Boilermakers' Union submission, 340
    Auckland City Council submission, 331
    Auckland Transport Holdings submission, 338
    Dove-Myer Robinson submission, 332
    final report 1970, 408
    final report response, 411
    interim report 1969, 345
    Internal Affairs submission, 338
    J H Macky submission, 337

J R Dart submission, 341
Ministry of Transport submission, 335
Ministry of Works submission, 336
Municipal Association of NZ submission, 341
National Roads Board submission, 336
NZ railway submission, 334
T F S Johnson submission, 337
Carter, David C., 647
Carter, F. A., 324
Casey, Cathy, 641
Cayford, Joel, 624
Caygill, David F., 536
Charges Appeal Authority, 68, 97, 113, 114, 335
Chelsea Sugar Works, 189
Citizens & Ratepayers Party, 111, 112, 187, 188, 500
Citizens' and Ratepayers' Association, 106
City Centre Future Access Study, 697
responses, 698
City Centre Masterplan 2020, 710
City of Auckland District Scheme 1961, 276
City of Auckland Tramways and Suburban Land Company Limited, 11
Civic Action Party, 238, 239, 342, 729
Civic Carpark, 635
Civic Reform Party, 112
Clark, Helen, 606
Cleveland Bridge-Dorman Long, 191, 193, 194, 196

Coates, Joseph G., 12, 26, 29, 88, 208
Coates, R. D., 420
Cobham, Viscount, 197
Coleman, D. W., 9, 80
Collom, C. C., 170, 172
Commercial Bay Development, 704
Commissioner of Transport Annual Report
1950, 145
Community Councils
renamed community boards 584
Competitive Pricing Special Review Committee, 564
Comprehensive Transportation Study Review, 514
Comprehensive Transportation Study Update, 539
Coney, Sandra, 641
Conference on Problems of Central Business District
1964, 262
Congestion Question, The
phase two, 685
report pending 2020, 686
types of congestion pricing, 685
Connectus (McConnell Dowell & Hawkins JV), 702
Connelly, Michael, 485, 495, 501, 507
Cooper, A. L., 217
Cooper, Dame Whina, 714
Cooper, Geoff, 699
Co-ordination Council, 67, 97, 107, 145
Cope, S. W., 506
Coras Iompair Eireann, 549
Corbett, S. L., 269
Costello, C. G., 413

Coulam, J. H., 478, 518
Council for Infrastructure Development, 651
Coutts Transport Vehicles Ltd., 132
Crofton Staveley, N., 22
   City Streets & Country Roads, 22
Cross, Anthony, 662
Cross, Peter, 600
Cross-Country Bus Service, 114
Crown Infrastructure Partners, 656
Croy, M. W., 319
Cullen, Michael, 591, 604, 624, 625, 631, 635
Cumberland, Kenneth B., 108, 112, 162, 165, 167, 168, 180, 188, 214, 308, 407
Curran, Clare, 690
Curran, Patrick T., 105, 134, 165
Curtis, Sir Barry, 602
Customs Acts Amendment Act 1934, 127, 156
Customs Acts Amendment Act 1958, 140
Cycling milestone, 673

Dahms, Dr. Fred, 10, 202, 376
Dalzell, John, 666
Darby, Chris, 674
Dart, J. R., 341, 389, 483, 486
Davis, Sir Ernest, 78, 80, 88
De Leuw Cather, 188, 230, 233, 234, 240, 242, 258, 267, 268, 269, 270, 271, 272, 273, 274, 275, 278, 282, 283, 284, 286, 292, 293, 294, 297, 298, 300, 303, 306, 313, 344, 353, 355, 357, 358, 366, 370, 376, 378, 379
   ARA support, 266
   benefit analysis for motorway construction, 356
   comprehensive transport report, 477
   engaged by Manukau City, 356
   essential Government support, 267
   motorway plans revised, 356
   rail survey, 377
   railways co-operation, 376
   report non-committal, 303
   reports 1965, 261, 264
   transportation plans 1965, 356
De Leuw, Charles E., 264, 378
Dearnaley, Mathew, 591
Devonport Ferry Company's Employees' Industrial Union of Workers, 190
Devonport Steam Ferry Company, 16, 17, 78, 190
   monopoly 1945, 80
Dey, Bob, 646, 672
Dickson, A. J., 38, 47, 142, 143, 166, 168, 169, 170, 172, 173, 181, 250, 270, 271, 272, 273, 304, 305, 306, 307, 308, 309, 310, 311, 313, 314, 315, 318, 323, 329, 359
Dobson, Ken, 500
Dodds, David A. C., 239, 342, 483
Dodson, Jago, 179, 589, 590, 600, 618
Donovan, Barry, 455
Donovan, S., 603
Douglas, N. V., 304
Downer & Company Ltd., 375, 702, 707, 708
Dravitzki, Vince, 407, 574

Dreaver, A. J. R., 165
Druzhin, Mr., 350
Dryden Construction Company, 375
Duder, B., 356
Dudson, B. H., 480, 482
Duffield, B. D., 240, 318, 329, 463

Eady, Lewis A., 107
Eden Albert Community Board, 594
Edgar, John, 112, 226, 367, 389, 459, 464, 488
Edward, Alfred, 13
Edwards, A. J., 427
Ellison, Shane, 712
Ember, Adrienna, 534
Engineers for Social Responsibility, 599
English, Hon. Bill, 643, 652, 654
Ensor, M. C., 473
Everiss, L. E., 64

Farmers' Trading Company, 20, 51, 64, 178
Farrell, F. G., 76
Faulkner, Mr., 417
Fay Richwhite, 582
Fay, Sir Sam & Raven, Sir Vincent Report 1924, 26
Federation of Labour, 542
Fenton, Rupert Leslie, 17
Filipaina, Alf, 641
Finance Act 1948, 151
Firth, C. W., 169
Fitzgerald, J. E., 170
Fitzsimons, Jeanette, 624, 632
Fletcher Construction, 630
Fletcher, Christine, 641

Fletcher, Sir James, 3
Flynn, E. A., 318, 319, 326, 329, 353, 359, 390, 449, 463, 464, 475
Fooks, Dr. E., 180
Ford, A. E., 51, 55
Forsyth, A. E., 142
Foster, E. B., 60, 61
Foster, J., 401
Fraser, P. E., 170
Fraser, Peter
    Prime Minister, 80
Frater, J. H., 77
Frazer, Sir Francis V., 83
Freeman Fox & Partners, 190, 191, 193, 372
Freer, Warren, 507
Frogatt, K., 172, 173
Fry, L. J., 430
Fuhr, Clive, 678

Gair, George, 348, 459, 460
Gammie, Fergus, 617
Gandell, A. T., 200, 208, 292, 376, 379
Ganz, Messrs., 533
Ganz-Mavag, 519, 689
Gardiner, Noel, 396
Gardiner, W. I., 170, 172
Gaynor, Brian, 682
General Equipment Co. Ltd, 350, 351
GHD Limited, 634
Gibb, Walter O., 202
Gibson, H. T., 77
Glasse, A. O., 299
Glen Eden Progressive Ratepayers' Association, 314

Gliddon, Brett, 682
Global Financial Crisis, 592
Goff, Phil, 656, 673, 683, 686, 714
Goldstine, I. J., 40
Goodman, W G T, 13
Goosman, W. S., 121, 144, 146, 147, 154, 156, 158, 160, 161, 168, 171, 183, 201, 205, 209, 211, 212, 213, 364, 695
Goosman, W. S. and Company Limited, 144
Gordon, David, 705
Gordon, John B. (Peter), 281, 282, 287, 292, 293, 294, 314, 326, 328, 342, 343, 362, 380, 411, 415, 416, 421, 459, 468, 473, 474
Gosche, Mark, 631
Goudie, Michael, 641
Government housing policy, 109
Government Policy Statement on Land Transport Funding 2012, 676
Government Policy Statement on Land Transport Funding 2018, 658
Government Railways Act 1926, 95, 96
Government Railways Amendment Act 1925, 95
Government Railways Amendment Act 1931, 95, 96
Government Railways Amendment Act 1936, 96
Government Railways Amendment Act 1952, 207, 728
Government Railways Board, 95, 96
Government Ten-Year Plan 1944, 63

Grant, Ken, 196
Grayburn, P. W., 374
Great Depression, 16
Greater Auckland, 3, 7, 31, 33, 77, 104, 105, 106, 107, 112, 130, 131, 133, 142, 165, 220, 226, 270, 291, 388, 389, 556, 569, 583, 597, 641, 670
  1945, 34
Greater Auckland blog, 557
Green Party, 584, 618
  transport policy, 632
Green, E. K., 35, 37, 38, 57, 71, 89, 91
Greenhithe Bridge, 374, 625
  opened November 1975, 375
Greensmith, E. L., 352
Gregory, Mr., 217
Greville, R. H., 23, 134
Grey, Sir George, 4, 108
Gribble, C. R., 60, 61, 102, 142, 170, 172, 200, 260, 267, 313, 319, 377
Griffiths, A. T., 170
Grimes, Arthur, 577
Guiniven, J., 25

Halcrow & Thomas, 93, 143, 199, 200, 209, 214, 242, 270, 273, 298, 308
  final report 1950, 99, 198
  interim report 1949, 99
  railways royal commission support, 205
  report 1953, 274
  second inquiry 1953, 208
Halcrow, Sir William, 93, 98, 198, 205, 209, 215, 316

Hall, J., 170
Hansen, P. A., 142
Hanson, F. M., 137
Hanson, F. M. H., 161, 162
Harris, C.
   Slow Train Coming, 49, 166, 168, 179
Harris, F., 340
Harrop, R S, 139
Hart, Michael A. C., 238, 342, 483
Hartley, Ann, 641
Hauge, J., 344
Hay, Keith
   Mt Roskill Mayor, 105
Hayward, Thomas M., 511, 516, 517, 524
Heal, Andrew, 546, 569
Hearn, A. QC, 540
Henderson Borough Ratepayers' and Citizens' Association, 217
Herne Bay Trolley Bus Service, 114
Herne Bay trolleybus service, 114
Hesseling, Paul, 678
Hide, Rodney, 597
Highet, David A., 282, 298, 381, 531
Hiley, Ernest H., 25, 88
Hill, G. A., 479
Hill, John, 116
Hillary, Sir Edmund, 602
Hintz, O. S., 237, 348
Hobson, Captain, 5
Hodges, W. E., 208, 210
Holcroft, Monte H., 69, 456, 458
Holdaway, Mr., 405
Holland, Sidney G., 110, 170, 182, 183, 192, 193
Holmes, Gary

North Harbour Business Association, 630
Holmes, Noel, 382
Holyoake, Keith J., 110, 193, 224, 225, 283, 302, 326, 328
Horne, Mike, 675
Hospital Bus Company Limited, 62
Howick and Eastern Buses, 664
Hubbard, Dick, 591, 635
Hucker, Dr. Bruce, 634
Hulse, Penny, 641, 662
Hunt, T. de V., 526
Hurley, A. E., 146
Hutchison, G., 76
Hyundai Rotem of South Korea, 690

Imran, M., 660
Infrastructure Auckland, 555, 556, 572, 583
   dissolved 2004, 587
Infratil
   NZ Bus
      Snapper Services, 663
Institute of Economic Research, 287, 289, 340, 353, 425, 426, 427, 436, 493
Irvine, Barney, 653
Isbey, Edward E., 415, 525
Ishikawajima-Harima Heavy Industries, 372
Ivanzov, A., 350

Jackson, Bryan, 606
Jenkins, Sir Simon, 641
John Holland Group, 713
Johnson, C. N., 354

Johnson, T. F. S., 337
Joint Officials Group, 585
Jones, Dale, 531
Jones, F. W. O., 169, 170, 227, 267, 313, 354, 376, 380
Joyce, Steven, 611, 613, 626, 630, 636, 637, 638, 639, 642, 644, 655, 674, 675, 676, 684, 691, 693, 694, 695, 696
Julian, Harry, 195, 727
   Sea in my blood, 196

Karangahape Business Men's and Ratepayers' Associations, 88
Kedgley, Sue, 632
Keep Auckland Moving Campaign, 569
Keith, Hamish H. C., 381
Kemeys, David, 597
Kennedy, J. F., 231
Kennedy, R. T., 222, 231, 297
Kerr, Perry
   Motor Industry Association, 624
Key, John, 597, 609, 626, 665, 692, 699, 702, 704
Keys, Dr. O. H., 311
Keys, L. J. Ltd, 56, 114
King, Annette, 591, 604, 625
King, N. J. MP, 352
Kirk Motors Ltd., 130
Kirk, J. N., 390, 483
Kirk, Norman, 130, 390, 475, 495, 611
Kitts, Sir Francis, 413
Kivell, Stanley T., 621
Kiwi Bus Builders, 661
KiwiRail, 638, 689, 704, 713
   OnTrack, 582

Knapp, G. W., 146
Knight, H. J.
   Industrial Transport Assoc. Inc., 146
Knight, Professor Cyril R., 169, 180
Knox, W. W., 413

Laing, P. L., 281, 292, 336
Lamb, Derek I.
   North Shore Chamber of Commerce, 380
Lambert, Mark, 670, 671, 672, 703
Lambie, Hugh D., 227, 241, 242, 266, 267, 268, 270, 281, 282, 285, 286, 292, 295, 298, 299, 306, 308, 316, 318, 393
Lambourne, Simon, 628
Lancaster, Mike, 498, 499
Land Transport Act 1998, 570, 571
Land Transport Amendment Act 1995, 566, 570
Land Transport Funding
   2011, 644
   2014, 651
   2018, 709
Land Transport Management (Regional Fuel Tax) Amendment Act 2018, 657, 687
Land Transport Management Act 2003, 584, 603, 618, 674
Land Transport Management Amendment Act 2004, 588
Land Transport Management Amendment Act 2008, 591
Land Transport Management Amendment Act 2013, 649
Land Transport New Zealand, 571
   replaced Transfund 2004, 588

Land Transport Safety Authority, 576
Lang, J. D., 281
Langbein, F. A., 365, 366, 433
Langbein, Fritz, 73, 75, 86, 92, 161, 190
Lange, David, 533
Latham, Malcolm, 7
Laurenson, G. L., 119, 145
Lee, J. R., 92, 717
Lee, Mike, 195, 591, 592, 595, 608, 609, 613, 615, 637, 638, 639, 641, 642, 644, 668, 679, 694
Legat, Nicola, 551, 553, 567
Lello, J. W., 599, 601
Lester, Tiffany, 407, 574
Levy, Lester, 668, 669, 673, 683, 700
Lewis, Rebecca, 606
Liang, Yun, 577
Light Rail Transit
  proposals 1995, 580
  steering group evaluation report, 581
  working party 1990, 579
Light Rail Transit/Busway
  implementations special committee, 579
Linehan, C. A., 200
Ling, Professor A., 230, 242
Link Alliance, 707
Liskmann, W. H., 178
Local Authorities Loans Board, 237
Local Bills Committee, 80, 81, 220, 224, 226, 252, 253
Local Body Morphological Fundamentalism
  John Edgar, 226, 367, 459

Local Government (Amalgamation Schemes) Bill
  1937, 9
  1938, 31
  1945, 35
Local Government (Auckland Council) Act 2009, 598, 646
Local Government (Auckland Council) Amendment Act 2010, 641
Local Government (Auckland Transitional Provisions) Act 2010, 643
Local Government (Auckland) Amendment Act 2004, 586
Local Government (Parliamentary Select) Committee
  1945 Report, 40
Local Government (Tamaki Makaurau Reorganisation) Act 2009, 597
Local Government Act 1974, 394, 541, 552, 560, 583
Local Government Act 2002, 583
Local Government Amendment Act (No. 2) 1989, 541
Local Government Amendment Act (No. 2) 1992, 561
Local Government Amendment Act 1992, 554
Local Government Amendment Act 1998, 555, 583
Local Government Appeal Authority, 131
Local Government Commission, 7, 42, 46, 47, 100, 131, 142, 220, 225, 226, 229, 238, 348, 541, 583
  new commission established 1974, 394

North Shore inquiry, 100
report 1950, 100
Local Government Commission Act 1946, 42
Local Government Commission Act 1967, 394, 415
Local Government Loans Board, 9, 15, 117, 119, 192, 194
Local Government Select Committee
1944, 33
1945, 59
Local Legislation Act 1946, 61
Locke, Keith, 632
Long, Trevor, 346
LORIC Import and Export Corporation, 690
Lowndes, Hilton, 537, 538
   Public Transport [Systems] Ltd., 533
Lucas, Steve, 603
Lupton, David, 681
Luxford, John H., 105, 106, 109, 110, 111, 112, 130, 133, 167, 168, 173, 178, 182, 183, 185, 187, 193, 220, 244
Lyne, John, 248, 249, 542

Macky, J. H., 291, 337, 364
Macky, W. G., 170
Macmillan, Alex, 642
Mahon, C., 134
Main Highways Act 1922, 22, 148
Main Highways Board, 8, 22, 73, 74, 75, 76, 148, 151, 153, 154, 156, 157, 158, 159, 161, 162, 171
Mair, S. A. R., 22

Manning, L. A., 267
Manukau City Council, 356, 357, 367
Mapp, Wayne, 630
Marshall, John R., 351, 352, 459
Martin Jenkins Agency, 660
Martin, R., 208
Mason, B., 483
Mason, B. N., 512
Mason, Henry G. R., 19
Massey, J. N., 35
Master Transportation Plan for Metropolitan Auckland, 110, 135, 142, 168, 169, 172, 177, 180, 181, 186, 187, 188, 214, 217, 218, 250, 270, 271, 304, 308, 356, 357, 453
forward, 173
Government approved, 187
government non-committal, 182
instances of strategic misrepresentation, 179
introduction, 178
lacks detail, 178
local bodies non-committal, 183
motorways first, 187
parking needed, 177
produced 1955, 173
proposed arterial roads, 184
recommendations & traffic statistics, 176
roads board subsidy, 353
roads first, 215
roads the predominant solution, 179
some doubt expressed, 215
transportation survey, 188, 353, 354
where is it?, 396

who's paying?, 181, 185
Mathew, Felton, 3
Mawson, J. W., 33, 34, 40
McAleese, J., 509
McAlpine, Hon. John K., 171, 257
McBreen Jenkins, 375
McClintock, L. C., 51
McConnell Dowell, 713
McCormick, C. H., 170
McCorquindale, C. J. R., 390
McCready, Allan, 519
McCrystal, John, 96, 556, 615
McCulloch, Alan, 524
McDonald, Duncan, 628
McDonald, T. K., 426, 493, 494
McDonald, Wayne, 629
McElroy, Roy G., 271, 272, 273, 283, 285, 291, 292, 294, 299, 302, 307, 316, 358
McEwen, Malcolm, 362
McIntosh, Daniel T., 25, 88
McKay, Bill, 678
McKay, Ken, 607
McKeen, R., 35
McKeown, Greg, 602
McKewen, T. M.
    NZ Counties Assoc., 146
McKillop, E. R., 43, 82, 199
McKinnon, I. W., 283, 294, 296, 300
McLachlan, Colin, 441, 446, 457, 517, 522, 523, 524
McLean, William, 21
McLeod, E. G., 170, 172
McLeod, N. C., 489
McLeod, Rob, 221
McShane, Owen, 483
Mead, C. B., 456

Mead, Ian A., 427, 437, 499, 503, 526
Meale, Chris, 702, 703
Mees, Paul, 143, 179, 180, 181, 211, 589, 590, 600, 609, 616, 618, 660, 675
Meharry, Hugh, 483
Mein, Barry
    CityScope Consultants, 614
Mercep, Ivan, 483
Merz & McLellan, 94, 209
    report 1926, 26
    report 1954, 208
Metropolitan Association of Mayors and Chairmen of Auckland, 531
Metropolitan Authority, 142, 165
Metropolitan Board of Works, 105, 175
Metropolitan Licensing Authority, 18, 49, 50
Metropolitan Local Bodies Association, 107
Metropolitan Transport Authority, 134, 136, 244
Metropolitan-Vickers Electrical Co. Ltd., 59
Miller, Greg, 714
Mills, Robert C., 453, 479
Mills, Robert J., 35
Milne, F. W. L., 134
Milne, Stewart, 650
Minister of Railways
    Statement 1929, 28
Minister of Works
    Statement of Road Policy 1954, 156
Ministry of Transport Act 1968, 234, 414, 415

Ministry of Transport Act Repeal
  Act 1990, 235, 415
Ministry of Transport Amendment
  Act 1971, 414, 542
Ministry of Works Statement
  1947, 44, 92
  1948, 63, 73, 74, 92
  1949, 75, 93
  1950, 212
Ministry of Works ten-year plan
  1946, 91, 144
Moir, J. I., 170, 172
Money, Chris, 621
Morrison, Des, 641
Mortiboy, A. T., 467
Morton, Henry T., 77, 79
Morton, Honor J., 333
Morton, John, 401
Moss, N. H., 146
Motor Spirits Taxation Act 1927,
  67, 148
Motor Vehicles Act 1924, 67
Motor Vehicles Amendment Act
  1936, 67
Motor-omnibus Traffic Act 1926,
  13, 14, 49, 95
Motor-spirits Taxation Act 1927, 21
Mount Eden Borough, 35
Muldoon, Robert D., 326, 342, 343,
  359, 361, 373, 435, 440, 459,
  508, 512, 513, 514, 515, 519,
  520, 521, 523, 525, 528, 529,
  530, 535, 537, 549, 611, 689,
  740
Municipal Association of New
  Zealand, 9, 21, 31, 146, 154,
  341, 413, 542
Municipal Corporations Act 1954,
  103

Murdoch, Alfred J., 81
Murdoch, Lee I., 439, 517, 524,
  529, 531, 532, 533
Murphy, R., 223
Myers, Arthur, 104, 556, 583

Nagle, W. H., 49, 51, 55, 56, 57, 58,
  59, 60, 61, 62, 63, 64
Nash, Walter, 110
National Infrastructure Plan
  released 2010, 643
National Land Transport Fund, 658
National Land Transport
  Programme, 637
National Roads Act 1953, 123, 154,
  156, 157, 158, 360, 548
National Roads Board, 149, 150,
  152, 154, 156, 157, 160, 161,
  162, 183, 186, 187, 188, 213,
  235, 270, 274, 291, 333, 335,
  336, 354, 355, 357, 358, 360,
  363, 364, 365, 366, 375, 401,
  433, 444, 542
  cuts spending 1967, 360
  independence threatened, 361
  subsidy, 353
National Roads Fund, 123, 149,
  150, 152, 154, 155, 160, 175,
  182, 185, 186, 269, 274, 360,
  361, 363
  revenue sources 1970, 447
Naumov, A. I., 351, 352
Neale, Dr. E. P., 65, 66, 93, 94, 95
Nettleton, Hugh, 621
New Zealand Business Council for
  Sustainable Development, 622
New Zealand Business Roundtable,
  221, 554

New Zealand Council for
  Infrastructure Development, 622
New Zealand Counties Association
  Incorporated, 9, 31, 542
New Zealand First, 711
New Zealand Infra, 711
New Zealand Institution of
  Engineers, 38, 89, 101, 142, 143,
  170, 181, 344, 493
New Zealand Motor Bodies Ltd.,
  118
New Zealand Railway Tradesmen's
  Association, 375
New Zealand Railways
  10-year service contract, 579
  annual report 1929, 27
  concern for image 1965, 379
  crisis point 1976, 435
  mileage restriction relaxed 1977,
    457
  ownership - a brief history, 581
  privatised, 579
  road services, 23
  road transport too competitive
    1931, 456
  Royal Commission of Inquiry
    appointed 1952, 202
      financial report 1952, 203
      management report 1952, 206
      proposed 1952, 201
      report 1952, 202
  statement 1929, 23
  transport riddle 1929, 27
  Tranz Rail, 573, 582
New Zealand Railways Commission,
  154, 163, 207, 208, 209, 210,
  211, 212
  findings 1955, 209

New Zealand Railways Corporation,
  206, 579, 582
New Zealand Road Carriers
  Association, 413
New Zealand Road Federation, 360,
  413
New Zealand Roading Symposium
  1967, 363
New Zealand Town Planning
  Conference and Exhibition, 21
New Zealand Transport Agency,
  652, 711, 714
  established 2008, 592
  national land transport
    programme 2018, 659
  past failures, 660
  survey 2013, 681
New Zealand Transport Policy
  Study, 550
New Zealand Urban Public
  Passenger Transport
  Council, 414
  abolished 1980, 415
New Zealand Wool Board, 352
New Zealand's First Parliament
  102nd anniversary, 110
Newhook, Laurie, 678
Newmarket Borough Council, 8, 9
  olympic pool, 9
Newmarket Viaduct
  completed December 1965, 366
Newton, R. H., 318, 321, 323, 329,
  376, 378, 380, 463
Niall, Todd, 686
Nielson, G., 660
Nilsson, K., 287, 289
Nisbet, L. C., 203
No.2a Licensing Authority, 257
Noonan, Rosslyn J., 161

Nordmeyer, Arnold, 140, 184
North Shore Buses Limited, 422
North Shore City Council, 595
North Shore Transport Co. Ltd, 419
North Shore Transport Holdings Ltd, 421
North Star Transport, 613
Northcote Borough Council, 76, 191, 423
Northern Corridor Improvements Project, 712
Northern Employers and Manufacturers Association, 593
Northern Suburban Railway League, 88
Northey, Richard, 641

O'Brien, Hon. J., 54
O'Dea, P. J., 338
O'Flynn, Francis D., 537
Officials Committee, 242, 280, 281, 287, 302, 304, 305, 306, 310, 343, 353, 468
   report, 300, 302
   report crticised, 303
Omnibus Proprietors' Association, 287
One Auckland, 593
Onehunga Branch railway, 635
Opus Transport Consultancy, 676
Oram, Matthew, 110
Organisation for National Development, 38, 39, 40
Orsman, Bernard, 592, 710
Osborne, Dan, 690
Outline Development Plan, 101, 102, 143, 144, 169, 178

Pacific Capital Assets Ltd, 601
Packwood, Mr., 190
Packwood, Roland H., 83
Palmer, Kenneth, 597
Panuku Development Auckland, 667
Parker, David, 591
Parsons Brinkerhoff, 630
Parsons, R. R., 329, 360, 463
Passenger Transport
   1970s a difficult decade, 408
   a city divided, 307
   a new era, 129
   all bus & bus/rail cost analysis, 342
   another Auckland investigation, 520
   another election delay, 434
   another urban transport study 1976, 513
   ARA losses, 527
   ARA review 1967, 316
   ARC Regional Plan, 562
   Auckland Bus Company, 314
   Auckland Transport overview 2017, 670
   Audit Office Report, 562
   benefit cost ratios, 699
   buses, 52, 114, 116, 120, 121, 129, 132
      cbd accessibility, 572
      central connector lane project, 608
      City Link network, 662
      city routing, 120, 138
      crisis 1971, 422
      cross-country service, 56
      deregulation 1989, 546
      deregulation burden, 609

Eastern Busway, 711
Eastern Busway Alliance
    project, 711
fleet falling apart 1976, 512
fleet shortage 1975, 439
from Hungary 1975, 424
funding shortfall 2006, 602
Government to replace 1977,
    441
hospital service, 55
improved services 1990s, 556
losses 1975, 424
new network from 2013, 671
Northern Busway, 602, 712
    birthday, 613
    opens 2008, 606
    patronage 2008, 607
    success, 664
NZ Bus Ltd (Infratil), 661, 662
operations 1964, 258
park and ride, 672
private operators in trouble
    1971, 419
Queen Street congestion, 246
Queen Street services 1966,
    277
remission of sales tax, 140
replacing trams, 59
road damage, 123
services cost structure, 289
Transport Bus Services
    Limited, 17, 56, 61, 62
urgent grants needed 1969, 345
v trains, 661
Yellow Bus Company, 541,
    554, 564, 565
zonal fares 1975, 430
Carter inquiry, 319
collapsing 1969, 332

commuter survey 1992, 558
Competitive Pricing Procedures,
    560
fare increases 2009, 617
Ferries
    Fullers ferry investment, 675
    Fullers Group, 674
    Fullers Petition, 674
    milestone 2016, 673
    vehicular terminal, 76
financial v social benefits, 310
for profit or a public service, 211
for profit or public service?, 341,
    550
Government study 1967, 314
in crisis March 1979, 524
integrated ticketing, 616, 663
    Hop smart card, 664
land use, 239
levies paid to ARA, 543
light rail
    a dream, 668
    deferred, 710
    postponed 2019, 670
    proposal ended, 711
    proposals, 667
    proposed funding 2019, 670
    suggested 1975, 434
local body disunity, 269
motor-omnibus, 12, 13, 18, 49,
    62, 122
no change needed 1955, 176
options identified 2012, 698
patronage 1955, 129
private motor car competition,
    124
public transport
    ARTA policy 2009, 616
    debacle 2011, 696

dropping patronage 1962, 248
historic usage 1961, 249
integration, 319, 428, 521
NZTA policy 2009, 616
patronage increases 2009, 615
patronage milestone 2019, 672
regional 1956, 134
regional plan, 610
restored to council control 2009, 610
rocketing patronage 2011, 661
slow strangulation, 249
social benefit analysis, 308
regional fuel tax
proposal 2018, 686
starts 2018, 687
regional fuel tax funding
1992, 561
2018, 657
cancelled 2009, 636
proposal 2007, 604
proposal abandoned 2009, 611
proposed 1969, 333
proposed 2007, 591
summary 1963-78, 446
summary of inquiries 1960s, 353
summary of transport undertaking 1964, 260
trams, 10, 50, 57, 58
airport proposal, 668
investment for 2025, 669
passenger record 1944, 54
services 1956, 132
steady replacement, 129
the last tram 1956, 136
track removal, 137, 141
trams or buses?, 57
Tramway Workers' Union, 142

Tramways Carriage Regulations 1947, 63
waterfront tram, 666
trolleybus, 20, 55, 56, 59, 60, 61, 64, 65, 66, 67, 114, 117, 118, 119, 120, 121, 123, 125, 129, 132, 136, 137, 141, 211, 430, 431, 432, 433
final run 1980, 433, 542
phasing out, 430
Ponsonby service, 118
road damage, 122, 123
sales tax & customs duty, 126, 127
Passenger Transport Committee, 134, 136, 240, 244, 353
Passenger Transport Company Ltd, 419, 422
Passmore, C. S., 257, 258, 377
Paterson, Les, 571
Paterson, N., 22
Patterson Brothers, 11
Pearce, T. H., 226, 267, 269, 283, 286, 294, 296, 300, 325, 327, 349, 390, 391, 393, 437, 459, 468, 469, 473, 475, 486, 488, 495, 496, 497, 500, 501, 505, 512, 514
Penlink, 709
Penrose, Calum, 641
Perkins, Harvey C., 552
Perry, H. C., 141
Phelan, E. J., 77
Picot, B. H., 506
Progressive Enterprises, 467
Polaschek, R. J., 281, 291, 426, 427
Population Growth
1945, 35
1954, 105

1961, 222
1966, 230
1975, 386
1990s, 552
Porter, Rolf, 338, 413
Ports of Auckland, 554
Prebble, Richard W., 534, 537
Pringle, Derek, 599, 631
Pringle, W. D., 402
Professional Engineers' Association, 60
Provost, Lyn
  Auditor-general, 702
Prudential Assurance Co., 194
Pt Chevalier Community Committee, 456
Public Passenger Transport Association, 126, 127, 140, 141, 439
Public Passenger Transport Authority's Industrial Union of Employees, 142
Public Passenger Transport Committee
  1958, 122, 126, 135, 141
Public Petitions Committee, 78
Public Transport Management Act 2008, 610
Public Transport Operating Model (PTOM), 674
Public Works Act 1928, 73, 88
Public Works Amendment Act 1947, 73
Public Works Amendment Act 1948, 148
Public Works Annual Report 1950, 190
Public Works Statement 1946, 42, 73
  1949, 92
Putt, C. E. H., 169, 170

Queen Street Business Association, 382
Quinn, Jim, 690

Rabindran, Rabin, 616
Rae, Hon. John, 237
Rae, John
  Infrastructure New Zealand, 643
Raffills, Noelene M., 641
Rait, T. W., 146, 151, 152
Rankin, D. G., 406, 446
Rankin, Keith, 359, 554
Reeves, S. E. K., 483
Regional Growth Forum, 556, 583
Regional Growth Strategy, 555, 583, 586, 590, 694
Regional Planning Councils, 39
Reid, Andrew, 350, 351, 352
Reid, Bruce
  National Road Carriers, 622
Resource Management Act 1991, 551, 570, 646
Resource Management Act 1993, 540
Resource Management Amendment Act 1993, 551
Reynolds, I. B., 305, 309
Reynolds, P. F., 365
Ringer, Bruce, 636
Rippon, Geoffrey, 482
Ritchie, Andrew, 664
Ritchies Transport, 613, 664, 665
Road Management
  a brief history, 158

Road Traffic Safety Research
    Council, 235
Road Transport
  1970s a difficult decade, 407
  car parks
    charges evaluated 2006, 621
    first meters, 139
    first municipal car park, 139
    needed 1975, 454
  congestion, 25, 48, 82, 88, 111,
    132, 135, 153, 160, 162, 165,
    176, 178, 179, 187, 188, 219,
    228, 242, 262, 263, 268, 270,
    286, 288, 297, 301, 303, 313,
    324, 348, 358, 453, 461, 466,
    477, 509, 552, 581
    bottlenecks 1945, 81
    Congestion Question Technical
      Report, 712
    cost 1977, 569
    cost 2013, 681
    cost to 1981, 454
    critical by 2020, 450
    electronic road tolling, 684
    proposed tolling 2004, 619
    road pricing considered 2003,
      585
    road pricing v tolls, 621
    smarter transport pricing 2020,
      713
    Smarter Transport Pricing
      Project, 654, 685
    The Congestion Question, 685
    user pays, 159
    user pays 1922, 148
  cost v quality 1960s, 364
  energy crisis 1975, 429
  fees diverted to Consolidated
    Revenue Account, 360

funding boost 2006, 624
government preference?, 440
heavy traffic licence fees, 123
heavy vehicle distance charge
  introduced 1977, 457
hundreds & road districts, 5
motoring cost, 184
motorways, 73, 74, 153, 154, 161
  Auckland v Wellington
    funding, 366
  before suburban rail 1972, 448
  central junction, 625
  construction needed, 160
  construction slows 1963, 355
  eastern motorway, 589
  expenditure needed 1971, 449
  first section 1953, 213
  inadequate by 2020, 450
  northern gateway, 677
  northern motorway progress,
    577
  northern motorway progress
    1969, 374
  north-south motorway, 577
  Onewa Road interchange, 607
  physical limitations, 461
  planning 1955, 171
  progress delayed 1967, 365
  projects delayed 1967, 359
  ramp signals, 625
  sections opened 1953-71, 450
  south-eastern motorway, 367
  southern gateway, 677
  spaghetti junction contract
    1968, 368
  state highway investment 2009,
    626
  stop the Eastern Motorway
    group, 589

Sylvia Park chaos, 602
Symonds St cemetery, 368
Victoria Park Tunnel, 630, 679
Waterview Connection, 627, 675, 677
   community impact, 678
   construction starts 2012, 678
   opens 2017, 679
Western Ring Route, 677
national fuel price increases 2002-06, 615
national fuel tax
   increase 2013, 665
   increases 2018, 659
   spent where?, 687
national roading programmes, 618
Newmarket Viaduct replacement, 680
poor capital investment 1967, 357
road construction
   2010-19, 676
   cost 1975, 428
   road condition 1989, 548
   southern motorway failure, 364
   surface failure 1960s, 364
   The Planning of Roads, 547
road haulage industry, 160
road safety deficiencies, 683
roads of indirect value, 150
traffic growth
   1940-54, 159
   2015, 682
   chaos 2017, 682
   registered Auckland 1950 & 1952, 119
   registered Auckland 1965-67, 357
   registered Auckland 1972, 450
   registrations increase 2017, 683
   vehicles registered 1952, 149
traffic statistics 2011, 681
Transport Amendment Bill 1967, 361
underground roads proposed 1945, 81
Roading Investigation Committee, 121, 122, 127, 146, 147, 149, 153, 154, 159, 182
   disagreement, 151, 152
Roads Before Rail Trust, 589
Roads of National Significance, 644
Roberts, G., 438
Robertson, Colin, 661
Robertson, Grant, 686
Robertson, H. A., 88
Robinson, Sir Dove-Myer, 106, 107, 111, 112, 113, 162, 163, 164, 165, 167, 168, 185, 186, 187, 199, 201, 213, 214, 218, 220, 222, 223, 224, 227, 228, 237, 240, 254, 256, 257, 262, 269, 270, 286, 297, 298, 300, 306, 307, 310, 313, 326, 327, 332, 333, 334, 341, 344, 346, 348, 349, 350, 351, 355, 370, 375, 377, 382, 387, 391, 393, 425, 426, 460, 465, 466, 469, 472, 475, 482, 486, 487, 488, 492, 494, 498, 499, 500, 502, 504, 505, 507, 508, 512, 513, 514, 517, 519, 521, 527, 528, 529, 533, 543, 549, 556, 583, 611, 650
   accused of insulting Prime Minister, 521
   Orewa Rotary Club remarks, 392
   property interests 1963, 395

property interests 1975, 395
The Practical Politics of Achieving Success in Planning and Implementation, 235
Roche, Brian, 629
Rodger, T. M., 412
Roe, P. S., 118, 169
Rooney, Edward, 607
Rose, J., 218, 219
Ross, Jami-Lee, 641
Roughan, John, 185, 195, 368
Rowling, W. E., 485, 504, 528, 534
Rudman, Brian, 605, 611, 698
Rutherford, Ross, 559, 567, 576
Ryan, Frank, 533
Ryan, Stuart, 646

Sales Tax Act 1932-33, 127
Salmon, E. P., 242, 384, 742
Salmon, Hon. Peter, 594
Sargeant, Captain H. H., 189
Satyanand, Hon. Anand, 596
Saunders-Roe Company, 118
Savage, Michael Joseph, 9, 24, 96
Sayegh, J. C., 52, 53
Schischka, J. F. Y., 489
Scott, William John (Jack), 224
SeaPath, 710
Selwood, Stephen, 622
   Council for Infrastructure Development, 645
Selwyn, Bishop, 3
Semple, Robert, 42, 44, 63, 64, 73, 74, 75, 76, 77, 78, 81, 82, 83, 89, 93, 94, 98
Sergejew, Anatole, 544, 557
SGS Economics & Planning Pty Limited, 651

Shand, David A., 594
Shand, Thomas P., 357
Shaw, James, 655
Sheat, W. A., 146
Shipley, Jenny, 573
Sinclair Knight Merz, 629, 697
SkyPath, 709, 710
Small, T. M., 509
Smith, B. G.
   Freeman Fox & Partners, 372
Smith, Carl V., 202
Smith, H. B., 134, 146, 200
Smith, Mr. MP, 80
Socialist Unity Party, 438
Soletanche Bachy International NZ, 708
Soletanche Bachy JV, 702
Spencer, Norman B., 131, 133, 134, 136, 138, 139, 141, 200, 224, 244, 245, 246, 248, 252, 256, 257
St. Heliers and Northcote Land Company Limited, 11
Stabilisation Commission, 54
Steel, John, 108, 220, 221, 229, 267, 280
Steering Committee
   report reactions, 465
   reported August 1972, 448, 462
Sterling, Herbert H., 26, 28
Stevens, F. S., 296
Stevenson, B. P., 456, 486
Stewart, Sharon, 641
Stirrat, A. G., 489
Stone, J., 660
Stout, Hon. R., 221
Strevens, W. J., 454
Suburban Buses Ltd, 419, 422
Suburban Drainage Board, 7

Suburban Rail
- Auckland Railway Station
  - Beach Road, 26, 92
  - Beach Road opens 1930, 29
  - bleak & forbidding, 379
  - Britomart Place declined 1940, 88
  - proposed at Britomart Place 1976, 510
- Auckland Rapid Transit
  - cost assessment 1968, 321
  - proposal 1965, 264
  - proposals 1972, 460
  - rail scheme, 380
  - spending doubts 1975, 502
  - statements of intent 1975, 434
  - working party 1968, 318
  - working party report, 321
- bus feeder services, 173
- City Rail Auckland, 632
- City Rail Link, 650, 658, 692, 704
  - APB&B study 2010, 693
  - Britomart extension feasibility study, 634
  - City Rail Link Limited, 705
  - contractors chosen, 702
  - criticism, 694
  - funding agreement signed 2016, 705
  - funding dispute 2011, 696
  - funds advance, 697
  - further study needed 1969, 325, 326
  - Government backing 2013, 699
  - Government review, 695
  - Government to share costs 1969, 349
  - mayor's vision reined in, 693
  - new cost envelope, 706
  - no financial committment 1969, 328
  - possible early start, 701
  - preferred route, 697
  - PricewaterhouseCoopers report 2014, 701
  - profit and loss argument, 694
  - proposed 2003, 633
  - proposed 2012, 646
  - resource consent lodged 2015, 702
  - Russian proposal, 350
  - savings, 701
  - scaled-down rapid transit plan, 390
  - start brought forward, 704
  - stations & tunnels contract, 707
  - steering committee proposed 1969, 327
  - steering committee set up 1969, 329
  - tender documents released, 706
  - track gauges, 325, 328
  - tunnel work started 2017, 706
  - tunnel-boring machine arrives, 714
  - work begins, 703
- deterioration of passenger services 1976, 515
- Electrification
  - delay 2009, 612
  - diesel trains replaced 2015, 692
  - electric rolling stock approved 2009, 639

electric train funding
    uncertainty 2009, 637
electric trains tender awarded
    2010, 690
first electric service started
    2014, 692
funding shortfall 2007, 591
government support 2007, 635
memorandum of understanding
    2011, 691
network electrification starts
    2010, 690
overseas study 1949, 93
ownership & operating model
    2009, 638
Papakura to Pukekohe
    electrification contract 2020,
    713
permission to start line
    electrification 2008, 689
priority need 2009, 615
tender process criticised, 689
tenders for electric multiple
    units, 689
extensive network upgrade
    needed, 704, 714
Government to replace carriages,
    441
Helensville rail service ends, 639
improvements needed 1976, 510
last opportunity to save, 532
minister meets Auckland
    representatives 1976, 517
Morningside deviation, 25, 26,
    83, 88, 89, 90, 91, 92, 174,
    186, 198, 199, 200, 205, 208,
    379
    cost, 213
    cost 1954, 163
    cost 1955, 209
    plan & distances 1949, 92, 717
    proposed 1940s, 83
    proposed 1945, 82
    spur line compromise 1955,
        215
    the shape of things to come
        1946, 42
no airport trains, 669
overhead railway suggested, 519
passenger decline 1952, 203
passenger service audit 2003, 632
patronage 1961, 376
patronage 1979, 526
patronage soars, 693
petitions signed 1979, 529
profit & loss 1955, 172
Project DART, 688
proposed extensions 1965, 268
Puhinui Station Interchange, 713
rail infrastructure investment, 639
record number of passengers
    2015, 703
season ticket journeys 1920-40,
    30
season ticket journeys 1920-53,
    201
services to be cut? 1979, 522
suggested line to North Shore
    1968, 380
upgrade business plan 2003, 633
upgrade cancelled 1954, 209
upgrade proposals 2000, 631
Veolia Transport, 617
    contract, 700
Wellington
    conspiracy?, 427
    first Ganz Mavag units run
        1982, 538

779

irregular tender, 533
losses 1979, 526
new coaches for Wellington, 519
Westfield station rebuilt 1979, 526
Wiri to Westfield report 2016, 705
Sussex, T. R., 283, 284, 294
Sustainable Cities Programme of Action, 603
Sutherland, W. A.
Nth & Sth Island Motor Unions, 146
Sweeney, Dr. Sean, 707

Takapuna Borough Council, 25
Tamaki Residential Development, 69
Tappenden Motors Ltd., 59
Tapper, Simon
Tapper Transport, 621
Taverner, Hon. W. B., 23, 28
Taxi Licensing, 49
Taylor Woodrow (Overseas) Ltd, 367
Taylor, David, 670
Taylor, Dr. M. J., 386, 395
Thackwray, Andy, 710
Thales SA, 616, 663
Thomas, Arthur F., 241, 242, 269, 346, 390, 473, 479, 482, 483, 486
Thomas, Ivan, 281, 321, 323
Thomas, J. P., 93, 98, 198, 205, 215, 316
Thomson, H. H., 170
Thorns, David C., 552

Thornton, O. G., 169, 170, 172
Tilly, Horace S. J., 319, 332
Tizard, Kath, 500
Tizard, Robert J., 362, 502, 525
Todd, Jeff, 573, 574
Toll Holdings Limited, 582
Tonkin & Taylor, 707, 708
Tonkin and Taylor
Britomart West Rail Link report 2003, 633
Toogood, H. F., 22
Town and Country Planning Act 1953, 102, 103, 168, 220, 230
Town and Country Planning Act 1977, 385
Town and Country Planning Amendment Act 1957, 385
Town and Country Planning Appeal Board, 102
Town and Country Planning Review Committee
appointed 1970
reported 1973, 384
Town Planning
what's wrong with it? 1969, 384
Town Planning Act 1926, 44
Town Planning Association, 6
Town Planning Board, 32, 36, 38, 43, 44, 46
Town Planning Committee, 109, 214, 243
Town-planning Act 1926, 45, 102
Town-planning Amendment Act 1948, 46
Town-planning Amendment Act, 1929, 44, 45
Transdev Auckland Limited
formerly Connex & Veolia, 633

Transfield Services (NZ) Pty Limited, 663
Transfund New Zealand, 568, 575, 584, 618
   funding allocation 1998-99, 573, 718
   replaced 2004, 588
Transit New Zealand, 544, 568, 584
Transit New Zealand Act 1989, 544, 560, 575, 584, 618
Transit New Zealand Amendment Act 1995, 568, 575
Transport Act 1949, 67, 68, 97, 113, 123, 141, 155, 156, 251
Transport Act 1962, 251
Transport Advisory Council, 235, 415, 416, 417
Transport Amendment Act (No 2) 1953, 123
Transport Amendment Act 1950, 113, 116
Transport Amendment Act 1967, 363
Transport Auckland Ltd
   trading as Yellow Bus Company, 541
Transport Charges Committee, 67, 68, 97, 113
Transport Co-ordination Board, 95, 96
Transport Department Annual Report
   1950, 144
Transport Funding
   Investing for Growth, 586
Transport Investigation Committee, 54
Transport Law Amendment Act 1933, 95, 96
Transport Law Amendment Act 1939, 97
Transport Law Amendment Act 1948, 97, 113, 145
Transport Licensing Act 1931, 18, 67, 95, 96, 97
Transport Licensing Amendment Act 1935, 96
Transport Licensing Amendment Act 1936, 96, 98
Transport Licensing Amendment Act 1939, 50
Transport Licensing Amendment Act 1949, 97
Transport Licensing Authority, 287
Transport Services Licensing Act 1989, 545, 560, 603
Transport Workers' Union, 141
Transportation Auckland Corporation Ltd, 564
Truman, H. A., 170
Turley, M. J., 525
Turner, A. R., 77, 231, 267, 269, 285, 300
Turner, F. G., 293
Turner, H., 77
Turrell, L. E. A., 170, 172
Twyford, Phil, 658, 660, 664, 669, 670, 674, 686, 688, 711, 714
Tyler, James, 32, 33, 69, 70, 71

United Independent Party, 111, 187
United-Reform Coalition, 8
Urban Cycleway Fund, 665
Urban Public Passenger Transport Council, 408, 414, 415, 427, 441, 442, 443, 542

Urban Sprawl, 11, 57, 71, 109, 172, 230, 236, 238, 240, 242, 285, 286, 405, 428, 553
satellite cities, 240
subdivision of city land, 109
Urban Transport
a management problem, 405
budget 1977, 440
Government proposals 1977, 443
Urban Transport Act 1980, 415, 444, 542
Urban Transport Authorities, 443
Urban Transport Bill, 529, 549
gigantic fraud? 1979, 445
Urban Transport Committee, 539
Urban Transport Council, 441, 443
Urban Transport in New Zealand
Colin McLachlan, 441
Urban Transport Policy
threat to local body autonomy 1979, 444
URS New Zealand Limited, 634

Valuation of Land Act, 1925, 14
Vautier, Dr C., 506
Veitch, W. A., 29
Verran, David, 374
Vickerman N. L., 169, 170, 172
Vickers, Lucy, 606
Vinci Construction Grands Projets S.A.S., 707, 708
Vosslamber, Rob, 184
Waitakere & Auckland Isthmus Passenger Transport Strategy, 559
Waitemata County Council, 77, 375, 380, 423
Walding, J. A., 536
Walker, A. Greville, 169

Walker, John, 641
Walker, Neville G., 382
Walker, Wayne, 641, 662
Wallis, Ian, 681
Wallis, Ian & Associates Ltd, 681
Warburton, David, 663, 697, 703
Ward, Sir Joseph, 88
Warren, Philip, 570, 573
Waterfront (Tamaki) Drive, 7
Watson, Margi
Tunnel or Nothing Group, 628
Watson, V., 390, 483
Watt, Hon. Hugh, 304, 347, 362, 365, 385, 391, 459, 474, 475, 476, 480, 482, 483, 485, 490, 493, 494, 495
Webster, Penny, 641
Welch, J. W. F., 132, 432
Modernization of Municipal Public Transport, 125
Wheeler, W. J. and Sons Ltd, 56, 114
White, Robert H., 529, 530
Whiting Moyne
road safety review, 683
Wilbur Smith & Associates, 416, 417, 457, 550
transport policy study published 1973, 418
transport study, 415
Wilford, Beth, 621
Wilkins and Davies Construction Co. Ltd, 367
Wilkinson, D.
Wilkinson, Christmas, Steen & Co., 309
Wilkinson, Peter I., 416
William C. Daldy, 197
Williams, Andrew, 595

Williamson, Maurice, 609, 611
Willmott, David, 483
Wilson, H. S., 64, 315
Wilson, Henry W., 8, 41, 42
Wilson, J., 453
Wilson, W., 506
Wilson, Will, 607
Winder, Peter, 612
Wiri Inland Port, 626
Wisconsin Central Transportation Corporation, 582
Witten, L., 479
Witten, Ralph J., 390, 483, 493, 494, 524

Wong, Sammy & Pansy, 690
Wood, George, 606, 615, 641
World Bank Loan, 416
Worley, R. P., 170
Wright, Joseph, 181, 316, 324
WSP Opus (NZ), 708
WSP/Parsons Brinckerhoff, 705
Wyber, W. L., 208

Yates, Deryk, 515
Young, L. A., 367
Young, W. L., 508

www.ingramcontent.com/pod-product-compliance
Lightning Source LLC
Chambersburg PA
CBHW060526010526
44107CB00059B/2607